# Newsmakers®

# *Newsmakers*®

## *The People Behind Today's Headlines*

**Laura Avery**

Project Editor

# 2009
# Cumulation

Includes Indexes from
1985 through 2009

GALE
CENGAGE Learning

Detroit • New York • San Francisco • New Haven, Conn • Waterville, Maine • London

**Newsmakers 2009, Cumulation**

Project Editor: Laura Avery

Image Research and Acquisitions: Savannah Gignac, Robyn Young, Gwendolen Youngblood-Johnson

Editorial Support Services: Emmanuel T. Barrido

Rights Acquisition and Management: Jackie Jones, Barb McNeil

Imaging: John Watkins

Composition and Electronic Capture: Amy Darga

Manufacturing: Cynde Bishop

R
920
N477

For product information and technology assistance, contact us at
**Gale Customer Support, 1-800-877-4253.**
For permission to use material from this text or product,
submit all requests online at **www.cengage.com/permissions.**
Further permissions questions can be emailed to
**permissionrequest@cengage.com**

*Gale*
27500 Drake Rd.
Farmington Hills, MI 48331-3535

ISBN-13: 978-1-4144-0686-2
ISBN-10: 1-4144-0686-X

ISSN 0899-0417

This title is also available as an e-book.
ISBN-13: 978-1-4144-5334-7
ISBN-10: 1-4144-5334-5
Contact your Gale, Cengage Learning sales representative for ordering information.

Printed in the United States of America
1 2 3 4 5 6 7 13 12 11 10 09

# Contents

**Introduction xiii**

**Cumulative Nationality Index 565**

**Cumulative Occupation Index 597**

**Cumulative Subject Index 641**

**Cumulative Newsmakers Index 681**

Adele 1988- ....................................... 1
*Singer and songwriter*

Jane Aronson 1951- ............................ 4
*Physician and nonprofit foundation director*

Abdullah Ahmad Badawi 1939- .............. 7
*Prime minister of Malaysia*

Simon Baker 1969- ........................... 11
*Actor*

Russell Banks 1940- ......................... 14
*Author*

Pat Barker 1943- .............................. 18
*Author*

Kim Barnouin and Rory Freedman ....... 22
*Authors*

Omar al-Bashir 1944- ........................ 26
*President of Sudan*

Karen Bass 1953- .............................. 30
*Speaker of the California Assembly*

Pamela Baxter 1949- ......................... 33
*Chief Executive Officer of LVMH Moët
Hennessy Louis Vuitton Perfumes & Cosmetics,
North America*

Beyonce 1981- .................................. 35
*Singer and actress*

Jessica Bibliowicz 1959- ..................... 40
*Chief Executive Officer of National Financial
Partners*

Usain Bolt 1986- .............................. 44
*Track and field athlete*

Danny Boyle 1956- ........................... 47
*Director*

Benjamin Bratt 1963- ........................ 51
*Actor*

Carla Bruni 1967- ............................. 55
*Singer*

Gisele Bundchen 1980- ...................... 58
*Model*

Tory Burch 1966- .............................. 61
*Fashion designer*

Carol Ann Cartwright 1941- ............... 63
*President of Bowling Green University*

Debra Martin Chase 1956- .................. 66
*Film producer, television producer, and attorney*

Kate Christensen 1962- ...................... 70
*Author*

Maxine Clark 1949- ........................... 74
*Founder of Build-A-Bear Workshop*

Diablo Cody 1978- ............................ 78
*Author and screenwriter*

Marion Cotillard 1975- ...................... 83
*Actress*

Erica Courtney 1957(?)- ..................... 87
*Jewelry designer*

Daft Punk ....................................... 89
*Dance music duo*

Deanna Dunagan 1940- ............................................. 93
*Actress*

Ann Dunwoody 1953(?)- ......................................... 96
*Four-star general*

Aaron Eckhart 1968- ............................................... 99
*Actor*

David Ellis 1971- .................................................. 103
*Artist*

Tracey Emin 1963- ................................................ 106
*Artist*

Leonel Fernández 1953- ......................................... 109
*President of the Dominican Republic*

Cristina Fernández de Kirchner 1953- ................. 113
*President of Argentina*

Suzanne Finnamore 1959- ..................................... 116
*Author*

Tana French 1973- ................................................ 120
*Author*

Kathy Freston 1965(?)- ......................................... 122
*Author*

Timothy F. Geithner 1961- .................................... 124
*U.S. Secretary of the Treasury*

Paul Giamatti 1967- .............................................. 126
*Actor*

James Gordon 1941- .............................................. 130
*Psychiatrist*

Ron Graves 1967(?)- .............................................. 134
*Chief Executive Officer of Pinkberry*

Josh Groban 1981- ................................................ 136
*Singer*

Abdullah Gul 1950- .............................................. 140
*President of Turkey*

Guo Jingjing 1981- ............................................... 144
*Diver*

Sanjay Gupta 1969- .............................................. 147
*Surgeon and news correspondent*

Maggie Gyllenhaal 1977- ...................................... 150
*Actress*

Cole Hamels 1983- ............................................... 154
*Professional baseball player*

Jon Hamm 1971- .................................................. 157
*Actor*

Chelsea Handler 1975- .......................................... 159
*Comedian, television host, and author*

Sally Hawkins 1976- ............................................. 162
*Actress*

Nikki Hemming 1967- ........................................... 165
*Chief Executive Officer of Sharman Networks*

Susan Hockfield 1951- .......................................... 167
*President of Massachusetts Institute
of Technology*

Eric H. Holder, Jr. 1951- ....................................... 171
*Attorney General of the United States*

Mike Horn 1966- .................................................. 174
*Explorer*

Jeffrey Housenbold 1969(?)- .................................. 177
*Chief Executive Officer of Shutterfly*

Jonathan Ive 1967- ............................................... 179
*Industrial designer*

Nina G. Jablonski 1953- ........................................ 181
*Scientist, professor, and author*

Lisa P. Jackson 1962- ............................................ 184
*Administrator of U.S. Environmental Protection
Agency*

Nina Jacobson 1965- ............................................ 187
*Film executive*

Shawn Johnson 1992- ............................................ 190
*Gymnast*

Costas Karamanlis 1956- ....................................... 193
*Prime minister of Greece*

Jonathan Kellerman 1949- ......................... 197
*Author, pediatric psychologist, and professor*

Jemma Kidd 1974- ..................................... 201
*Founder of Jemma Kidd Make Up*

Kwame Kilpatrick 1970- ........................... 203
*Former mayor of Detroit*

Jimmy Kimmel 1967- ................................ 207
*Television show host and comedian*

Jeff Kinney 1971- ...................................... 211
*Author and cartoonist*

George and Lena Korres ........................... 215
*Founders of Korres Natural Products*

Peter Krause 1965- .................................... 218
*Actor*

Ellen Kullman 1956- .................................. 222
*Chief Executive Officer of DuPont*

Kengo Kuma 1954- .................................... 225
*Architect*

Derek Lam 1966- ....................................... 228
*Fashion designer*

Lee Myung-Bak 1941- ................................ 230
*President of South Korea*

Zachary Levi 1980- .................................... 233
*Actor*

Kenneth D. Lewis 1947- ........................... 236
*Chief Executive Officer of Bank of America*

Nicklas Lidstrom 1970- ............................. 239
*Professional hockey player*

Lil Wayne 1982- ........................................ 243
*Rap musician*

Laura Linney 1964- ................................... 247
*Actress*

Blake Lively 1987- ..................................... 251
*Actress*

Mario Lopez 1973- .................................... 253
*Actor and television show host*

Olivia Lum 1961- ...................................... 257
*Founder of Hyflux*

Patti LuPone 1949- ................................... 260
*Actress and singer*

Heidi Manheimer 1963- ............................ 264
*Chief Executive Officer of Shiseido Americas*

Mary Mary .................................................. 266
*Gospel duo*

Ma Ying-jeou 1950- ................................... 270
*President of Taiwan*

Patrick McDonnell 1956- .......................... 274
*Cartoonist and philanthropist*

Ryan McGinley 1977- ................................ 278
*Photographer*

Scott McNealy 1954- ................................. 281
*Chairman of Sun Microsystems*

Dmitry Medvedev 1965- ........................... 284
*President of Russia*

Stephenie Meyer 1973- ............................. 288
*Author*

Ann Moore 1950- ...................................... 292
*Chief Executive Officer of Time, Inc.*

Tracy Morgan 1968- .................................. 295
*Actor and comedian*

Elsa Murano 1959- .................................... 299
*President of Texas A&M University*

Heidi Murkoff 1958(?)- ............................. 302
*Author*

Kathleen Murphy 1963(?)- ........................ 305
*Executive*

Rafael Nadal 1986- .................................... 308
*Professional tennis player*

Nas 1973- .............. 312
*Rap musician*

Gavin Newsom 1967- .............. 316
*Mayor of San Francisco*

Ne-Yo 1982- .............. 320
*R&B singer and songwriter*

Peggy Northrop 1954- .............. 323
*Editor-in-chief of Reader's Digest*

Alexander Ovechkin 1985- .............. 326
*Professional hockey player*

Wayne Pacelle 1965- .............. 329
*Chief Executive Officer of the Humane Society of the United States*

Sarah Palin 1964- .............. 332
*Governor of Alaska*

Thakoon Panichgul 1974- .............. 336
*Fashion designer*

Anna Paquin 1982- .............. 338
*Actress*

Willie Parker 1980- .............. 342
*Professional football player*

Simon Pegg 1970- .............. 344
*Actor and screenwriter*

Kal Penn 1977- .............. 348
*Actor*

Michael Phelps 1985- .............. 352
*Swimmer*

Renzo Piano 1937- .............. 355
*Architect*

Paul Pierce 1977- .............. 358
*Professional basketball player*

Amy Poehler 1971- .............. 361
*Actress and comedian*

Zac Posen 1980- .............. 364
*Fashion designer*

Paul Potts 1970- .............. 368
*Singer*

Radiohead .............. 371
*Alternative-rock group*

Lisa Randall 1962- .............. 375
*Physicist*

Alex Rigopulos 1970(?)- .............. 378
*Chief Executive Officer of Harmonix Music Systems*

Seth Rogen 1982- .............. 380
*Actor and screenwriter*

Mally Roncal 1972(?)- .............. 384
*Makeup artist*

Kevin Rudd 1957- .............. 386
*Prime minister of Australia*

Paul Rudd 1969- .............. 390
*Actor*

Mary Doria Russell 1950- .............. 394
*Author*

Mark Rylance 1960- .............. 398
*Actor*

Serzh Sargsyan 1954- .............. 401
*President of Armenia*

Betsy Saul 1968(?)- .............. 404
*President and co-founder of Petfinder.com*

Sheri Schmelzer 1965- .............. 406
*Entrepreneur*

Amy Sedaris 1961- .............. 408
*Actress and comedian*

Glen Senk 1956(?)- .............. 412
*Chief Executive Officer of Urban Outfitters*

Richard Serra 1939- .............. 415
*Sculptor*

Amanda Seyfried 1985- .............. 418
*Actress*

Joan Silber 1945- .................................... 420
*Author and educator*

Ashlee Simpson-Wentz 1984- ............................... 423
*Singer and actress*

Lanty Smith 1942- .................................... 427
*Chairman of Wachovia*

Russell P. Smyth 1958(?)- .......................... 430
*Chief Executive Officer and President of H&R Block, Inc.*

Peter Som 1971(?)- ................................ 433
*Fashion designer*

Shreve Stockton 1977(?)- ......................... 437
*Author and photographer*

Elizabeth Strout 1956- ............................ 439
*Author*

Trudie Styler 1954- ............................... 442
*Producer and activist*

Kierán Suckling 1964- ............................ 446
*Executive director for the Center for Biological Diversity*

Sugarland ....................................... 449
*Country music duo*

Taylor Swift 1989- ................................ 453
*Singer and songwriter*

Paulo Szot 1969- ................................. 457
*Actor and opera singer*

Boris Tadic 1958- .................................... 460
*President of Serbia*

John Thain 1955- .................................... 464
*Executive*

Laura Tohe 1953(?)- ................................... 467
*Author*

Dara Torres 1967- .................................... 471
*Swimmer*

Danilo Turk 1952- ................................... 474
*President of Slovenia*

Yulia Tymoshenko 1960- ............................. 478
*Prime minister of Ukraine*

Nora Volkow 1956- .................................. 482
*Research psychiatrist*

Michael Lee West 1953- ............................. 485
*Author*

Brian Williams 1959- ............................... 488
*Broadcaster and journalist*

Andrea Wong 1966- ................................. 492
*Televison executive*

Joe Wright 1972- ................................... 495
*Director*

Robert Wyland 1956- ............................... 498
*Artist*

# Obituaries

Anne Armstrong 1927-2008 .................................... 503
*Diplomat*

Eddy Arnold 1918-2008 .......................................... 504
*Singer*

Maurice Bejart 1927-2007 ....................................... 505
*Ballet director and choreographer*

Bernie Brillstein 1931-2008 .................................... 506
*Producer and talent manager*

Youssef Chahine 1926-2008 .................................... 507
*Filmmaker*

Cyd Charisse 1922-2008 ........................................ 509
*Actress and dancer*

Arthur C. Clarke 1917-2008 .................................. 510
*Author*

Bruce Conner 1933-2008 ....................................... 511
*Artist*

Erik Darling 1933-2008 ............................ 512
*Folk musician*

Mahmud Darwish 1942-2008 ................... 513
*Poet*

Michael DeBakey 1908-2008 .................... 514
*Heart surgeon*

Bo Diddley 1928-2008 .............................. 516
*Musician*

Dith Pran 1942-2008 ................................ 517
*Photojournalist*

Bobby Fischer 1943-2008 ......................... 518
*Chess player*

Dan Fogelberg 1951-2007 ........................ 520
*Musician*

Estelle Getty 1923-2008 ........................... 521
*Actress*

Simon Gray 1936-2008 ............................. 523
*Playwright*

Edmund Hillary 1919-2008 ...................... 524
*Mountaineer*

Patrick Hillery 1923-2008 ........................ 525
*Politician*

L. Rust Hills 1924-2008 ............................ 526
*Editor*

Hua Guofeng 1921-2008 .......................... 527
*Party leader*

Michael Kidd 1915-2007 ........................... 528
*Dancer and choreographer*

Evel Knievel 1938-2007 ............................ 530
*Daredevil*

Harvey Korman 1927-2008 ...................... 532
*Actor and comedian*

Tom Lantos 1928-2008 .............................. 533
*Politician*

Dorian Leigh 1917-2008 ........................... 534
*Model, agency founder, and restaurant owner*

Ira Levin 1929-2007 .................................. 535
*Author*

Bill Melendez 1916-2008 .......................... 537
*Animator*

Lydia Mendoza 1916-2007 ....................... 538
*Singer*

Igor Moiseyev 1906-2007 ......................... 539
*Choreographer*

Randy Pausch 1960-2008 ......................... 540
*Professor*

Oscar Peterson 1925-2007 ........................ 542
*Jazz pianist and composer*

Suzanne Pleshette 1937-2008 ................... 543
*Actress*

Sydney Pollack 1934-2008 ........................ 544
*Filmmaker*

Julius B. Richmond 1916-2008 ................. 545
*Pediatrician*

Tim Russert 1950-2008 ............................. 546
*Journalist*

Yves Saint Laurent 1936-2008 .................. 548
*Fashion designer*

Roy Scheider 1932-2008 ........................... 549
*Actor*

Irena Sendler 1910-2008 ........................... 550
*Social worker*

Ian Smith 1919-2007 ................................. 551
*Politician*

Tony Snow 1955-2008 ............................... 553
*Press secretary and journalist*

Aleksandr Solzhenitsyn 1918-2008 .......... 554
*Author*

Jo Stafford 1917-2008 ............................... 555
  *Singer*

Suharto 1921-2008 ................................... 556
  *Politician*

Germaine Tillion 1907-2008 ................... 558
  *Anthropologist and French Resistance fighter*

Ike Turner 1931-2007 .............................. 559
  *Musician*

Jerry Wexler 1917-2008 .......................... 561
  *Record producer*

Richard Wright 1943-2008 ..................... 562
  *Musician*

# Introduction

*Newsmakers* provides informative profiles of the world's most interesting people in a crisp, concise, contemporary format. Make *Newsmakers* the first place you look for biographical information on the people making today's headlines.

## Important Features

- **Attractive, modern page design** pleases the eye while making it easy to locate the information you need.

- **Coverage of all the newsmakers** you want to know about: people in business, education, technology, law, politics, religion, entertainment, labor, sports, medicine, and other fields.

- **Clearly labeled data sections** allow quick access to vital personal statistics, career information, major awards, and mailing addresses.

- **Informative sidelights essays** include the kind of in-depth analysis you're looking for.

- **Sources for additional information** provide lists of books, magazines, newspapers, and internet sites where you can find out even more about *Newsmakers* listees.

- **Enlightening photographs** are specially selected to further enhance your knowledge of the subject.

- **Separate obituaries section** provides you with concise profiles of recently deceased newsmakers.

- **Publication schedule and price** fit your budget. *Newsmakers* is published in three paperback issues per year, each containing approximately 50 entries, and a hardcover cumulation, containing approximately 200 entries (those from the preceding three paperback issues plus an additional 50 entries), *all at a price you can afford!*

- And much, much more!

## Indexes Provide Easy Access

Familiar and indispensable: The *Newsmakers* indexes! You can easily locate entries in a variety of ways through our four versatile, comprehensive indexes. The Nationality, Occupation, and Subject Indexes list names from the current year's *Newsmakers* issues. These are cumulated in the annual hardbound volume to include all names from the entire *Contemporary Newsmakers* and *Newsmakers* series. The Newsmakers Index is cumulated in all issues as well as the hardbound annuals to provide concise coverage of the entire series.

- **Nationality Index**—Names of newsmakers are arranged alphabetically under their respective nationalities.

- **Occupation Index**—Names are listed alphabetically under broad occupational categories.

- **Subject Index**—Includes key subjects, topical issues, company names, products, organizations, etc., that are discussed in *Newsmakers*. Under each subject heading are listed names of newsmakers associated with that topic. So the unique Subject Index provides access to the information in *Newsmakers* even when readers are unable to connect a name with a particular topic. This index also invites browsing, allowing *Newsmakers* users to discover topics they may wish to explore further.

- **Cumulative Newsmakers Index**—Listee names, along with birth and death dates, when available, are arranged alphabetically followed by the year and issue number in which their entries appear.

## Available in Electronic Formats

**Licensing.** *Newsmakers* is available for licensing. The complete database is provided in a fielded format and is deliverable on such media as disk or CD-ROM. For more information, contact Gale's Business Development Group at 1-800-877-4253, or visit our website at http://www.gale.cengage.com/bizdev.

**Online.** *Newsmakers* is available online as part of the Gale Biographies (GALBIO) database accessible through LexisNexis, P.O. Box 933, Dayton, OH 45401-0933; phone: (937) 865-6800, toll-free: 800-227-4908.

## Suggestions Are Appreciated

The editors welcome your comments and suggestions. In fact, many popular *Newsmakers* features were implemented as a result of readers' suggestions. We will continue to shape the series to best meet the needs of the greatest number of users. Send comments or suggestions to:

The Editor
*Newsmakers*
Gale
27500 Drake Rd.
Farmington Hills, MI 48331-3535

Or, call toll-free at 1-800-877-4253

# Adele

## Singer and songwriter

**B**orn Adele Laurie Blue Adkins, May 5, 1988, in London, England. *Education:* BRIT School for Performing Arts, London, England, 2006.

**Addresses:** *Contact*—XL Recordings, One Codrington Mews, London, England W11 2EH. *Home*—London, England. *Management*—Jonathan Dickins, September Management Ltd., 80 Chiswick High Rd., London, England W4 1SY. *Web site*—http://www.adele.tv.

## Career

**S**igned with XL Recordings, 2006; released debut album, *19,* 2008.

**Awards:** Critics' Choice BRIT (British Record Industry Trust) Award, British Phonographic Industry, 2008; Grammy Award, best new artist, 2009; Grammy Award for best female vocal pop performance, Recording Academy, for "Chasing Pavements," 2009.

## Sidelights

**B**ritish singer-songwriter Adele achieved instant success with the release of her 2008 debut album, *19,* the title of which referenced her age. The album entered the British music charts at No. 1 and went on to garner four Grammy Award nominations. On *19,* Adele sings about love and loss, penetrating a range of emotions with her husky yet gentle voice and singing with a maturity be-

yond her years. She won two Grammy Awards for her work on the album—one for best new artist and one for best female pop vocal performance. "It's really cheesy, but I feel like I'm living the dream," Adele told the *Daily Telegraph*'s Craig McLean shortly after learning of her Grammy nominations. "Even if nothing at all happened for me after 2008, I can say I've done it once and it's been amazing."

When Adele was born on May 5, 1988, her 18-year-old mother named her Adele Laurie Blue Adkins, though she decided to use only her first name once she began performing. Adele spent her early years in the North London working-class neighborhood of Tottenham, living with her mother. Adele's father was not involved in her life. Adele always enjoyed singing. At five she entertained dinner guests by standing on the table and belting out "Dreams," a 1993 U.K. No. 1 single by the British pop singer Gabrielle.

Growing up, Adele listened to a broad range of music as she tried to fit in with peers. This included R&B from Destiny's Child, as well as music from Aerosmith, the Backstreet Boys, Spice Girls, Korn, and Papa Roach. Though she enjoyed exercising her vocal chords, Adele never considered becoming a singer until she heard American soul-blues singer

Etta James. Adele came across an Etta James CD while browsing the bargain bin at a local music store. The CD caught her attention because she liked the picture on the front and wanted to show it to her hairdresser as an idea for a new hairstyle. "Then one day I was clearing out my room and I found it and put it on," Adele told *MX* writer Jacqui Swift. "When I heard the song 'Fool That I Am,' everything changed for me. I never wanted to be a singer until I heard that."

Her interest piqued, Adele began paying closer attention to other song masters. She listened to Ella Fitzgerald to learn about vocal improvisation, or scat singing. She turned to Etta James to study passion and Grammy winner Roberta Flack to master control. As a teen, Adele earned admittance to the famed BRIT School for Performing Arts. Besides Adele, BRIT counts other noted singers among its graduates, including Amy Winehouse, Kate Nash, and The Kooks front man Luke Pritchard. Adele graduated from BRIT in 2006 and within a few months published some of her musical compositions on PlatformsMagazine.com and began lining up small, London-area gigs. One of the first songs she wrote was an ode to London called "Hometown Glory." At the time the song was written, Adele's mother was encouraging her to move to Liverpool, England, to go to school but Adele just wanted to stay home.

In 2006, Adele toured as an opener for Jack Penate and soon signed with XL Recordings. In 2007, she released the singles "Hometown Glory" and "Chasing Pavements," which garnered significant airtime on British radio. "Chasing Pavements" peaked at No. 2 on the U.K. singles chart. Adele was inspired to write "Chasing Pavements" after a nightclub spat with her boyfriend. They fought and she ran out on him but he did not follow. In her Web site biography, she recalled the event. "I was running down these gigantic, wide sidewalks that stretch for miles, thinking to myself, 'Where are you going? What are you doing? You're just chasing pavements … that you're never going to catch.'"

The British press went wild for Adele and called her the next Amy Winehouse, the famously troubled British singer who rocketed to early fame. In 2008, Adele won the Critics' Choice BRIT Award and followed up with a sold-out British tour upon the release of *19,* which hit British music stores in January 2008. Within six months, the album was out in the United States and she began a U.S. tour. Most often, Adele performs with an acoustic guitar, treating audiences to stripped-down sets that leave her voice and emotions raw and exposed. Adele's rise in the United States was slower but she received a boost in the fall of 2008 when she appeared on *Saturday Night Live* on the same show as Republican vice presidential candidate Sarah Palin. Millions of extra viewers tuned in. The album rose to No. 10 on the Billboard 200.

At the 2009 Grammys, Adele was up for four awards—best new artist, best female pop vocal performance, record of the year, and song of the year. She won in the first two categories. Winning the best new artist award placed her in the footsteps of the Beatles, the first British act to win a Grammy in that category. By early 2009, Adele was busy working on songs for a second album. She told Billboard. com's Gary Graff that the new songs have "more depth and subject." She went on to explain that *19* was more of a heavy-hearted breakup album, whereas the new material will be "about a relationship I was quite pleased to get out of rather than feeling a bit deprived of someone's attention. It's more grown up."

Something else that sets Adele apart from other stars is her carefree attitude about her weight. Adele, who wears a size 14 to 16, is not interested in changing her body. As she noted on her Web site profile, "I love food and hate exercise." She went on to say she is comfortable with her body image and does not care what others think. "I don't want to be on the cover of *Playboy* or *Vogue.* I want to be on the cover of *Rolling Stone* or *Q.* I'm not a trend-setter … I'm a singer. I never want to be known for anything else. I'd rather weigh a ton and make an amazing album.…"

## Selected discography

*19,* XL Recordings, 2008.

## Sources

### Periodicals

*Billboard,* May 10, 2008, p. 29.
*Daily Telegraph,* December 11, 2008.
*MX* (Melbourne, Australia), February 14, 2008, p. 21.
*Sun* (London, England), November 6, 2008, p. 52.

### Online

"Adele: Bio," Adele Official Web site, http://adeleus.com/about.html (May 7, 2009).

"Adele Plotting 'Grown Up' Second Album," Billboard.com, http://www.billboard.com/bbcom/news/adele-plotting-grown-up-second-album-10039206.tif64.story (May 7, 2009).

"It's Her Party," *Observer,* http://www.guardian.co.uk/music/2009/mar/15/adele-us-tour-grammy (May 7, 2009).

"Mad About the Girl," *Observer,* http://www.guardian.co.uk/music/2008/jan/27/popandrock.britawards2008 (May 7, 2009).

*—Lisa Frick*

# Jane Aronson

## Physician and nonprofit foundation director

**B**orn November 10, 1951, in New York, NY; daughter of Harold (a grocer) and Selma (a teacher) Aronson; partner of Diana Leo (a law school director of development); children: Ben, Desalegn. *Education:* Hunter College, B.A., 1976; University of Medicine and Dentistry of New Jersey, D.O., 1986.

**Addresses:** *Office*—151 East 62nd St., Ste. 1A, New York, NY 10065.

## Career

**W**orked as a teacher, carpenter, photographer, and bartender, c. 1971-c. 1981; served as pediatrics intern and resident at Monmouth Medical Center, Long Branch, NJ, 1986-87, and Newark Beth Israel Medical Center, Newark, NJ, 1987-89; served as chief pediatric resident at Morristown Memorial Hospital, Morristown, PA, 1989-90; attending doctor in general pediatrics and medical coordinator of the Morris County Child Sexual Abuse Program, 1989-91; worked as fellow and clinical instructor of pediatrics, Columbia Presbyterian/Babies Hospital, New York City, 1990-91; chief of pediatric infectious diseases and later director of international adoption services as well at Winthrop-University Hospital, Mineola, NY, 1992-2000; founded and served as director of Worldwide Orphans Foundation, New York City, 1997—; served as director, physician, and adoption medicine specialist, International Pediatric Health Services, New York City, 2000—.

**Member:** Fellow, American Academy of Pediatrics, 1990-08; American College of Osteopathic Pediatricians, 1993; fellow, Pediatric Infectious Diseases Society, 1994-2000; International Association of Physicians for AIDS Care, 1999; honorary member of board of directors, International Law Center, 2007.

**Awards:** Named Angel of Adoption, Congressional Coalition on Adoption Institute, 2000; Family Building Award, American Infertility Association, 2000; World of Children Humanitarian Award, 2006; Azerbaijan Society of America Humanitarian Award, 2007; Distinguished Alumna Award, University of Medicine and Dentistry of New Jersey, 2007.

## Sidelights

**K**nown as the "Orphan Doctor," Dr. Jane Aronson is an expert in the growing field of international adoption medicine. She uses her medical skills to help evaluate potential international adoptees for American parents and treats such children after they arrive in the United States. Dedicated as well to helping children living in orphanages, she created the nonprofit Worldwide Orphans Foundation to improve conditions for orphans living in various countries, including Russia and Vietnam as well as Eastern European and African nations. Fellow adoption medicine expert Dr. Jerri Jenista told Richard Jerome and Sharon Cotliar of *People*, "It's definitely a calling for her." Aronson herself wrote in her CV (curriculum vitae) on OrphanDoctor.com, "I have always loved the inner spirit of a child. I look to the child in myself and my childhood experiences to guide my work with families.... I am an adoptive parent, visionary, and I am dedicated to changing the world one child at a time."

Born on November 10, 1951, in the borough of Brooklyn in New York City, Aronson is the younger of two children of Harold and Selma Aronson. The children were raised on Long Island in the community of Franklin Square, where her father was a grocer and her mother worked as a teacher. From an early age, Aronson knew she wanted to have children. She told Melissa Faye Greene of the *New Yorker*, "I saw myself in a big brownstone in Manhattan, with lots of kids, being a doctor, and walking my kids to school." Aronson was also deeply impressed by the television show *The Lone Ranger*, wanting to help those in need as the show's hero did. In addition, she was inspired by a great uncle who used his expertise in tuberculosis to treat Native Americans in the 1930s.

Aronson graduated from Valley Stream North High School in Franklin Square, New York, in 1969. Moving to New York City, she attended Hunter College part time and eventually earned her undergraduate degree in biology and psychology in 1976. Aronson then worked primarily as a teacher, as well as a carpenter, photographer, and bartender for a decade. Her dream of becoming a parent became tempered over time, however, as she reached adulthood and came out as a lesbian. Friends did not understand her desire for children, and as she grew older, she had concerns that her own fastidiousness would not make her a good parent.

Though Aronson put aside her parental dreams for a time, she met another long-standing goal. From an early age, she wanted to be a doctor. To achieve her ambition, Aronson applied to medical schools and entered the University of Medicine and Dentistry of New Jersey in the early 1980s. After graduating with her D.O. in 1986, she completed her pediatric residency at Monmouth Medical Center in Long Branch, New Jersey, and Newark Beth Israel Medical Center in Newark, New Jersey. Aronson then was chief pediatric resident at Morristown Memorial Hospital in Morristown, New Jersey, from 1989 to 1990. Aronson later earned a fellowship in Pediatric Infectious Diseases at New York City's Columbia Presbyterian/Babies Hospital.

In 1992, Aronson took a position at Winthrop-University Hospital in Mineola, New York, serving as the chief of Pediatric Infectious Diseases. Her career took a turn toward adoption during this time. Of the experience, she told Greene of the *New Yorker*, "The first time I got involved with an adoptive family, in the early nineties, they struck me as so desperate for information. There was a kind of intimacy and creativity that came into the work. When I'm in the room with these families—all these different personalities, different stories, people feeling abandoned by the forces that be, because of infertility, and now they have a child—I'm singing inside."

Because of such experiences, Aronson founded and served as director of the International Adoption Medical Consultation Services, which was part of Winthrop-University Hospital. As director, she visited orphanages in such countries as Russia, China, and various Eastern European nations several times in the late 1990s on fact-finding missions. During a 1997 visit to Russian orphanages prompted by the ill health of many orphans adopted by Americans, Aronson found that the children were living there in often horrendous conditions. The orphans suffered from malnutrition, poor mental health, and diseases that could be easily prevented or cured. She spoke about the matter publicly hoping to affect change.

As part of her work with International Adoption Medical Consultation Services, Aronson also provided expert adoption medical opinions for potential parents. She annually evaluated hundreds of children who were to be adopted from abroad based on short videotapes of them shot at the orphanages. For potential adoptive parents, Aronson provided her opinion of the child's condition, information which could help the adopters decide whether they should adopt this particular child. The staff, including Aronson, of International Adoption Medical Consultation Services also treated such children after they were adopted.

While holding these posts, Aronson founded an organization that was dedicated to ensuring conditions at orphanages worldwide would improve. The non-profit group Worldwide Orphans Foundation (WWO) began in 1997 using the proceeds from some AT&T stock a relative had given her. The group worked to achieve this goal in part through its Orphan Ranger Program. Using college students and healthcare professionals as "rangers" who sometimes lived and worked in orphanages, the WWO documented the medical and development conditions of children living in orphanages as well as the conditions of orphanages themselves. By identifying needs and helping staff members at the orphanages, the group worked to establish better living conditions for the children who lived there.

Aronson's work with WWO continued after she left Winthrop-University Hospital in 2000 to found New York City's International Pediatric Health Services. Again serving as director of this clinic, she also continued to work as a highly regarded international adoption medicine specialist. Aronson often drew on her background in infectious diseases in this practice. Because of her efforts in the area, adoption medicine was becoming a recognized medical field that focused on the health and development issues of children adopted from abroad. In addition to continuing to provide evaluations for potential adopters, Aronson also continued visiting orphanages. As part of International Pediatric Health Services, Aronson had a private practice in which she treated children adopted from abroad using her expertise to address health issues often related to their institutionalization. By 2003, she had seen at least 2,100 adopted children as patients and, by 2007, had helped more than 6,000 adoptions.

In 2000, Aronson's own life became transformed by adoption. She and her partner Diana Leo adopted two boys, first Ben from Vietnam and then Desalegn from Ethiopia a few years later. When Aronson and Leo adopted Ben in 2000, Aronson admitted to being moved by the experience. She told Jerome and Cotliar of *People*, "I cried. I couldn't believe I was really going to have a little boy."

Throughout the early 2000s, Aronson came to international prominence for her work, a recognized expert who regularly spoke on international adoption to the media. The doctor always emphasized that the issues were difficult and prospective parents had to keep their expectations in check. She also stressed that the adoptive families needed to ensure that their adopted children had connections to their native country and culture as well as role models from the same background. Such ties, she believed, helped them grow into self-assured teens and adults.

Aronson also continued to expand the scope of WWO, dealing with how to improve the lot of HIV-positive orphans in such countries as Vietnam and Ethiopia. In 2005, she set a goal of raising a million dollars for this cause in Ethiopia and, after receiving that government's approval, began medically treating orphans with HIV and AIDS there later that year. In Ethiopia, WWO operated the only nongovernmental freestanding outpatient clinic which educated local healthcare providers about dealing with and treating these children. Aronson also helped actress Angelina Jolie with her adoption of an Ethiopian girl, Zahara, in 2005, by tending to the child's medical needs shortly after her arrival in the United States.

For her work, Aronson received a number of accolades, including winning the World of Children's Humanitarian Award in 2006. That same year, she was named one of twelve "Uncommon Women" in an issue of *Elle Magazine* for her work with international adoption issues. In 2007, Aronson was lauded by the Azerbaijan Society of America with a Humanitarian Award and received a Distinguished Alumna Award from the University of Medicine and Dentistry of New Jersey.

Aronson was not particularly concerned with such honors, only with positively affecting the children living in orphanages abroad. She told Lisa Hendricksson of *Marie Claire*, "That's what my foundation, Worldwide Orphans, is about: trying to do something for kids who are rotting in an orphanage. That'll be my main legacy—trying to help those left behind, because they are the most disenfranchised, the most unentitled, the most victimized. That's what keeps me up at night: trying to make a dent in it."

## Sources

### Periodicals

*Business Wire*, March 9, 2006; April 6, 2006.
*Connecticut Post* (Bridgeport, CT), June 11, 2003.
*Daily News* (NY), August 13, 2007, p. 46.
*Financial Times*, October 21, 2008, p. 12.
*Marie Claire*, January 2007, p. 164.
*Moscow Times*, August 26, 1997.
*New Yorker*, July 17, 2000, p. 38.
*New York Times*, September 4, 2001, p. F7; July 4, 2004, p. 14WC4; July 22, 2004, p. F1.
*People*, November 12, 2001, p. 131; May 2, 2005, p. 89.
*Physician Law Weekly*, December 14, 2005, p. 479.
*USA Today*, April 21, 2006, p. 5E.
*U.S. Newswire*, November 7, 2006.
*Washington Times*, August 1, 2004, p. D01.

### Online

"About Doctor Aronson," OrphanDoctor, http://www.orphandoctor.com (January 24, 2009).
"About Dr. Aronson—CV," OrphanDoctor, http://www.orphandoctor.com/bio.html (January 24, 2009).

*—A. Petruso*

# Abdullah Ahmad Badawi

**Prime minister of Malaysia**

**B**orn November 26, 1939, in Bayan Lepas, Penang, Malaysia; son of Ahmad Badawi (a politician); married Endon Dato Mahmood, 1965 (died 2005); married Jeanne Abdullah, 2007; children: two. *Education:* Graduated from University of Malaya, Kuala Lumpur, Malaysia, 1964.

**Addresses:** *Office*—United Malays National Organization (UMNO), Tingkat 38, Menara Dato Onn, Jalan Tun Ismail, 50840 Kuala Lumpur, Malaysia.

## Career

**J**oined Malaysian civil service, 1964; served on the National Operation Council, 1969-70; elected to Malaysian parliament, 1978; minister of education, 1984-86; minister of defense, 1986-87; minister of foreign affairs, 1991-99; deputy prime minister, 1999-2003; prime minister, 2003-09.

## Sidelights

**W**hen Abdullah Ahmad Badawi became prime minister of Malaysia in 2003, he had a reputation as a clean politician and a reformer. Hopes were high that Abdullah, Malaysia's first new leader in 20 years, would root out corruption, tolerate more criticism of the government, and make the country friendlier to international investment. But his popularity fell in the Southeast Asian nation of 21 million people as ethnic tensions rose, corruption continued to flourish, political rivalries intensified, and economic progress faltered. After leading the nation's longtime ruling party to poor results in a national election in 2008, Abdullah announced he would retire in March of 2009.

Abdullah was born in November of 1939 in Bayan Lepas, a town in Penang, a northern state of Malaysia. His father, Ahmad Badawi, was one of the founders of the United Malays National Organization, or UMNO, the country's ruling party. Abdullah graduated from the University of Malaya in 1964 with an Islamic studies degree and entered the Malaysian civil service. He served on the National Operation Council, a body that governed Malaysia from 1969 to 1970, during a state of emergency after racial riots. When his father died, Abdullah followed him into politics, winning election to the Malaysian parliament in 1978. He served as the nation's minister of education from 1984 to 1986 and minister of defense from 1986 to 1987. His career faltered in 1987 when he supported a group within UMNO that challenged prime minister Mahathir Mohamad, but he remained in the party and regained Mahathir's favor within a few years.

In 1991, Abdullah was named minister of foreign affairs of Malaysia, a position he held for eight years. He stepped into the international spotlight in 1997, at the thirtieth anniversary meeting of the Association of Southeast Asian Nations, or ASEAN. Because he held ASEAN's rotating chair, Abdullah responded to the United States' criticism of the group. American diplomats were upset that ASEAN had admitted Myanmar into the group despite its ruling military junta's record of human rights violations and suppression of democracy. Abdullah defended Myanmar's membership. "The constructive engagement relationship with them will continue," Abdullah said, as quoted by Keith B. Richburg of the *Washington Post*. By including Myanmar in ASEAN, he said, "we have been able to express to them what our concerns are." Abdullah repeated Malaysia's accusation that American financiers were manipulating Southeast Asian countries' currencies to punish them for admitting Myanmar. "The ASEAN economies continue to be bedeviled by currency fluctuations caused by hostile elements bent on such unholy actions," he alleged (according to Steven Erlanger of the *New York Times*). U.S. diplomats called the charge a false conspiracy theory.

Abdullah's next promotion came during a power shift that set the course of Malaysian politics for at least the next decade. He was named deputy prime minister in January of 1999, replacing Anwar Ibrahim, who had criticized the prime minister and been kicked out of the government, then jailed on corruption and sodomy charges. Many Malaysians saw the case against Anwar as politically motivated, and protesters took to the streets, demanding political reforms and Mahathir's resignation.

Malaysians often called Abdullah "Mr. Clean" because they saw him as honest and pious. A devout Muslim, he was considered untainted by the scandals that had tarnished other Malaysian leaders. During his four years as deputy prime minister, Abdullah retained his reputation as a quiet, steady leader. He remained loyal to Mahathir and was considered partially responsible for a government crackdown on dissent in 1999 and 2000, including the arrest of four political opponents and the removal of a newspaper editor. When the mercurial Mahathir suddenly announced in June of 2002 that he would resign, Abdullah was one of several other leaders who rushed to change his mind. Mahathir backed out and declared that he would remain prime minister until October of 2003, when Abdullah would take his place.

Abdullah was sworn in as Malaysia's fifth prime minister on October 31, 2003. He soon took several actions that suggested he would be a different leader than Mahathir. He promised to lift Malaysians out of poverty and to crack down on corruption. He canceled some large public works

projects begun by Mahathir and increased rural development efforts instead. Two major arrests in corruption cases in February, one of a member of Abdullah's own cabinet, seemed to show that the new prime minister was serious about cleaning up government. He also aimed to attract new international investment by insisting on more transparency and discipline in financial matters. "Fairness and justice are key to the substance that we are trying to deliver," Abdullah told Assif Shameen of *Institutional Investor*. Observers also expected Abdullah to be more sedate in his public speeches than Mahathir, who would often lash out angrily at Western nations for perceived misdeeds, sometimes throwing in anti-Semitic comments.

In March of 2004, after only four months in office, Abdullah quickly called new parliamentary elections. The ruling coalition won a landslide victory in the vote. "People voted for [Abdullah] because he represents change," Malaysian author Chandra Muzaffar told Shameen of *Institutional Investor*. "He has started talking about corruption, inefficiency, justice and fairness, and that has struck a chord with ordinary people, some of whom felt left out under Mahathir." However, when Abdullah named his cabinet after the election, critics noted that it included several veterans of the Mahathir government who had been tainted by scandal.

Abroad, Abdullah sought to improve relations with Singapore, Malaysia's small but economically powerful neighbor. In 2004, he asserted that Southeast Asia should form a stronger economic community, more links with its trading partners, and more initiatives to help develop the region's poorer countries, such as Vietnam and Cambodia. Abdullah also argued Western and Muslim nations needed to mend their relationships, which were hurt by the 2003 U.S. invasion of Iraq. "If this feeling of mistrust and animosity becomes worse, it will have an impact on security for all of us," he told Nora Boustany of the *Washington Post*. "The best way is to have a dialogue." He also said Muslim nations needed to fight terrorism in the long term by modernizing religious education. "It should be taught not to condone terrorism but to emphasize that seeking knowledge is compulsory," he said.

By 2006, Abdullah appeared to be doing well in his term as prime minister. He had not only made Malaysia more attractive to foreign businesses, he also took credit for an increase in political freedoms. "People tell me Malaysia is now a more open, free, and inclusive society," Abdullah told Assif Shameen, writing for *Business Week Online*. "The media is now [a] lot freer than before. Even the parliamentary debates have changed a lot because we encourage people to participate and express themselves." Abdullah also said he was working to develop Malaysia's economy so it was less dependent on manufacturing, which China was beginning to dominate because of its low labor costs. "In my first two and half years, we have tried to change the mindset and stress things like education, developing human capital, and preparing the country as we move toward developed status," he told Shameen.

However, by late 2007, Abdullah and his ruling coalition saw their popularity plummet. Anwar Ibrahim, released from jail by the country's supreme court in 2004, organized the country's opposition and led mass protests in the capital, Kuala Lumpur, to demand electoral reforms. Police broke up the protests with water cannons and tear gas. Abdullah declared that the government would not tolerate street demonstrators. "They are challenging the patience of the people who want the country to be peaceful and stable," he said, according to the *New York Times*.

By early 2008, the opposition was accusing Abdullah of slow, listless leadership. To make the point, activists came to the prime minister's office and delivered a pillow for him. "He has a reputation for liking to sleep," Rahmat Haron, a poet and critic of the government, told Thomas Fuller of the *New York Times*. "He sleeps in cabinet meetings, he sleeps in Parliament," Haron added. "So we thought, why not make him more comfortable?"

Abdullah reacted defensively to the criticism. "We are not deaf, for we hear what the people say," he said, according to Fuller. "We are not asleep, for we are working." However, scandals and controversies in Abdullah's cabinet also harmed his reputation. Many Malaysians had come to consider his former nickname, "Mr. Clean," an ironic joke. The biggest scandal surrounded deputy prime minister Najib Razak. Two of his longtime assistants and two Malaysian commandoes were facing a murder trial, charged with killing a Mongolian woman, Altantuya Shaariibuu, and destroying her body with grenades. Razak denied persistent rumors that linked him romantically to the woman.

Abdullah and his party suffered a major setback in the March 2008 elections. Though the coalition held onto a majority in parliament, it won only 51 percent of the vote and 140 seats out of 222, losing its two-thirds supermajority that had allowed it to amend the constitution. The opposition surged from 19 seats in parliament to 82. It was the governing coalition's worst performance since Malaysia's independence in 1957. Voters blamed the government for rising crime and inflation, a failure to fight poverty and corruption, deteriorating race relations, and continued discrimination against ethnic Indians and Chinese. After five decades of rule by the same party, Malaysia was on the brink of developing a true two-party system.

In the wake of the vote, Abdullah replaced half of the ministers in his cabinet, promising his government would perform better. However, criticisms of his leadership grew. Party delegates from Penang, his home state, called on him to step down, stung by the opposition's victory in local elections there. In June of 2008, after rising fuel prices sparked protests, Abdullah announced he would hand over power to Najib, but he did not say when. Meanwhile, Anwar spent much of 2008 trying to woo enough defectors away from the governing coalition to win a vote of no confidence in parliament and unseat Abdullah as prime minister. (A new sodomy charge was filed against Anwar in July of 2008, alleging sexual misconduct with a young former campaign volunteer. But it did not hurt Anwar's popularity; polls showed a large majority of Malaysians considered the new charge, like the old one, politically motivated.)

In October, after months of sustained pressure on him to leave office, Abdullah announced that he would resign in the spring of 2009. Though he had taken the job promising stability and clean government, at the end of his time as prime minister, Malaysian politics were as unstable and full of plots and scheming as ever. Abdullah's departure set up a titanic battle for power in Malaysia between two scandal-plagued politicians, Najib and Anwar.

In late March of 2009, Abdullah gave a farewell address to the ruling party congress. "I wish to retire with a feeling of peace," he said, according to the *New York Times*. "I want to carry no negative emotions with me." He said he would remain a member of Parliament but would not hold any leadership role in his successor's cabinet. In a final interview with Malaysian journalists (quoted by the *Times* of London), Abdullah acknowledged that "missed opportunities" had marked his time as leader. He said the party's losses in the 2008 elections were his biggest regret. Abdullah submitted his resignation to the king of Malaysia on April 2, 2009.

## Sources

### Periodicals

*Business Week Online*, August 16, 2006.
*Institutional Investor*, September 2004, p. 11.
*International Herald Tribune*, March 10, 2008.

*New York Times,* July 29, 1997; November 17, 1998; January 26, 2000; June 26, 2002; October 31, 2003; March 19, 2004; November 29, 2004; November 11, 2007; April 14, 2008; March 7, 2008; March 9, 2008; June 14, 2008; August 4, 2008; September 14, 2008; October 9, 2008; March 29, 2009.

*Washington Post,* July 26, 1997; January 9, 1999; January 14, 2001; June 23, 2002; June 26, 2002; November 1, 2003; March 4, 2004; March 22, 2004; July 21, 2004; March 9, 2008; March 19, 2008.

## Online

"A Lifetime's Opportunity," AsiaWeek, http://www-cgi.cnn.com/ASIANOW/asiaweek/99/0122/cs2.html (February 6, 2009).

"Badawi, Datuk Seri Abdullah Ahmad" Encyclopedia Britannica Online, http://www.britannica.com/EBchecked/topic/1001273/Datuk-Seri-Abdullah-Ahmad-Badawi (February 6, 2009).

"Biography" Prime Minister's Office of Malaysia, http://www.pmo.gov.my/?menu=page&page=1880 (February 6, 2009).

"Prime Minister of Malaysia, Abdullah Ahmad Badawi, resigns to the king," *Times* Online, http://www.timesonline.co.uk/tol/news/world/asia/article6019822.ece (April 2, 2009).

"Profile: Abdullah Ahmad Badawi," BBC News, http://news.bbc.co.uk/1/low/world/asia-pacific/2064535.stm (February 6, 2009).

*—Erick Trickey*

# Simon Baker

## Actor

**B**orn July 30, 1969, in Launceston, Tasmania, Australia; immigrated to the United States, 1995; son of Barry Baker (a mechanic and groundskeeper) and Elizabeth Labberton (a high school English teacher); married Rebecca Rigg (an actress), 1998; children: Stella Breeze, Claude Blue, Harry Friday. *Education:* Attended nursing school in Sydney, Australia, c. 1987-88.

**Addresses:** *Agent*—Greg Siegel, Endeavor Talent Agency, 9701 Wilshire Blvd., 10th Fl., Beverly Hills, CA 90210. *Home*—Malibu, CA.

## Career

**W**orked as a model and appeared in television commercials in Australia, c. 1988-91; actor in films, including: *L.A. Confidential*, 1997; *Most Wanted*, 1997; *Love from Ground Zero*, 1998; *Restaurant*, 1998; *Ride with the Devil*, 1999; *Red Planet*, 2000; *Sunset Strip*, 2000; *The Affair of the Necklace*, 2001; *Book of Love*, 2004; *Land of the Dead*, 2005; *The Ring Two*, 2005; *The Devil Wears Prada*, 2006; *Something New*, 2006; *The Key to Reserva*, 2007; *Sex and Death 101*, 2007; *The Lodger*, 2009; *Not Forgotten*, 2009; *Women in Trouble*, 2009. Has also appeared in the television series *E Street* (as Simon Baker-Denny), 10 Network (Australia), 1991-92; *Home and Away*, 7 Network (Australia), 1994; *The Guardian*, CBS, 2001-04; *The Mentalist*, CBS, 2008—.

**Awards:** Logie Award for most popular new talent, *TV Week*, 1992.

## Sidelights

**S**imon Baker's raffish good looks have won him romantic-comedy film roles and helped make his two television series for CBS surefire hits. The Australian actor first gained notice for the network in 2001 in the *The Guardian*, in which he played an attorney trying to redeem his past errors of judgment. In 2008, he took on the title role in what became the top-rated new series of the fall season, *The Mentalist*. Though he never wanted to star in a police procedural, Baker was intrigued by the premise of a television psychic whose career ended in tragedy, and now works with the police to help solve crimes using his wits. "It's a tough character, being the character who always knows better than other people," the show's creator, Bruno Heller, told Kelley L. Carter of *USA Today*. "And he manipulates other people and gets in other people's faces. So it needs to be someone that you really want to spend time with. That's clearly what Simon brings."

Baker was born in 1969 in Launceston on Tasmania, an island state located off Australia's southeast coast. His parents separated when he was a toddler, and he had no contact with his father for many years. Baker and his older sister lived in several different places along the mainland Australian coast and eventually settled in the town of Lennox Head when their mother remarried. Like many coastal-living Australians, he began surfing at a young age—in his case, at age seven—and was also a skilled water polo player in his teens. "I didn't grow up with money, but I grew up with a lot of space," he told writer Mark Morrison, who profiled him for *In Style* magazine in 2003. "All I did was surf. I was committed to the ocean."

Baker's experiences at home and in school presented certain challenges, however. He and his stepfather did not get along, and sometimes he stayed out all night and slept on the beach in order to catch the morning's first waves. He did poorly in school, he admitted in an interview with David A. Keeps for the *Sydney Morning Herald.* "I couldn't pay attention in class," he recalled. "All I thought about was sports." After graduating from Ballina High School in 1987, he moved to Sydney, Australia's largest city, to attend nursing school, but dropped out to pursue a career as a model. He segued from print ads to television commercials, and even appeared in a few Australian music videos as a dancer.

In 1991, Baker met his future wife Rebecca Rigg, who was already a well-known television and film actor in Australia dating back to her childhood years. Her connections helped him land an audition for a role in a popular Australian soap opera called *E Street* that marked his television debut. Baker played a police constable in the gritty urban drama, and Rigg also appeared as his on-screen girlfriend. The job won him Australia's Logie Award, sponsored by *TV Week* magazine, for best new male talent of 1992. He later went on to appear on another top-rated series, *Home and Away,* which was set at a family-run beach resort. During this period of his career he was known as Simon Baker-Denny, a hyphenated surname that combined his father's and stepfather's last names.

Baker continued to use this name during his first few years in Hollywood. He and Rigg decided to move to the United States in 1995 as relatively new parents. "We had a young daughter, Stella, and enough money to eat for about two months," he told Keeps in the *Sydney Morning Herald* interview. He made his feature film debut in the 1997 *noir* hit *L.A. Confidential* as a struggling young actor/ doomed male prostitute. He gained further notice for a supporting role in the Ang Lee-directed *Ride with the Devil,* a 1999 drama set during the U.S. Civil War that starred Tobey Maguire and Skeet Ulrich as members of a band of pro-Confederacy guerrillas.

In 2000, Baker appeared in a big-budget science-fiction thriller that starred Val Kilmer, *Red Planet,* which added to his growing list of film credits. His fortunes improved considerably when he landed a starring role in a new CBS drama series, *The Guardian,* that debuted in the fall of 2001. Baker was cast in the title role as Nick Fallin, an attorney in a Pittsburgh family firm run by his formidable father, played by Dabney Coleman. When Fallin's substance abuse puts him on the wrong side of the law, the judge sentences him to 1,500 hours of community service as a child advocate with the city's department of Children's Legal Services. The new series, noted *Entertainment Weekly*'s Ken Tucker, "could be—indeed, by many critics, has been—dismissed as an excuse for a large segment of America to spend 60 minutes a week gazing at the battered good looks of star Simon Baker." Yet Tucker also praised the show's creator, David Hollander, for churning out scripts with compelling storylines and dialogue. Hollander, Tucker asserted, "never passes up an opportunity to render … Fallin, as a selfish heel. In weekly television, this is nearly unheard of; it's commonly believed that your central character must be likable."

Several months later, when CBS was re-running the first season in the moribund summer prime-time line-up to pick up new viewers, Tucker gave *The Guardian* a more solid review that emended his initial assessment of its handsome blond star. "Baker's look of perpetual woundedness is actually very effective," the *Entertainment Weekly* critic wrote. "Watched week after week, his inner suffering becomes compelling—you root for this complex screwup, who's obviously locked in a fierce psychological battle with his father-who's-also-his-boss." Baker also earned notice for effectively submerging his distinctive Australian accent. Asked by Bergen County *Record* staff writer Virginia Rohan why so few American actors could master the Down Under accent, Baker explained that "A lot of Americans don't get exposed to it. We get American television. We get American films, but you guys get like a handful of Australian films."

Baker was nominated for a Golden Globe award by the Hollywood Foreign Press Association for his *Guardian* role, but the show ended after three seasons. This allowed him to return to feature films full-time, and in 2005 he appeared in *The Ring Two,* the sequel to the original horror film starring fellow Australian Naomi Watts, a friend of Baker's and his wife. That same year, he also appeared in *Land of the Dead,* the much-anticipated new entrant in the successful George A. Romero franchise. Critics sharpened their knives in anticipation of the film that would mark his debut as a romantic-comedy lead, *Something New,* partly because of its somewhat formulaic interracial romance set-up. Yet Baker and his co-star, Sanaa Lathan—playing the affluent financial-services executive who falls for the gardener despite her intentions and the objections of family and friends—earned high marks and was even a *New York Times* Critics' Pick of 2006. "The chemistry between the leads is as unmistakable as the setup is contrived," noted the *New York Times'* Manohla Dargis, who also wrote that "'Something New' isn't especially new, which is actually part of its low-key charm. There's something reliably agreeable about watching two pretty people go through the usual romantic motions, especially since Big Hollywood seems to have more or less given up on love, perhaps because it's also more or less given up on women."

Baker also appeared in another 2006 release, *The Devil Wears Prada,* as a Manhattan magazine writer pursuing Anne Hathaway's character during her indentured-servant job as assistant to the editor of a top fashion magazine. He returned to television that same fall in a short-lived CBS series about a criminal gang, *Smith,* that also starred Ray Liotta and Virginia Madsen. He then finished work in a couple of feature films before taking a break from acting in order to spend time at the Malibu home he and Rigg shared with their three children. He was lured back to work after reading the script for a planned CBS series called *The Mentalist.*

Baker agreed to take the title role of Patrick Jane, a former television psychic whose seemingly miraculous "gifts" were merely the product of an observant mind and bag of standard-issue stage tricks. One of his victims extracted revenge by killing Jane's wife and child, and the crime is still unsolved when, five years later, Jane agrees to come out of hiding and work as an investigative consultant with the California Bureau of Investigation. Baker's character, wrote Adam Sternbergh in *New York* magazine, "is part con artist, part lethal charmer, and part snake-oil salesman—and this is the guy we're supposed to be rooting for." The crime-case storylines were bolstered by continuing subplots involving Jane and the other members of the CBI team.

Baker's new series brought in an average of 16.2 million viewers a week on its Tuesday-night slot, and the audience grew weekly; one week it even beat ABC's ratings colossus *Dancing with the Stars.* It also earned enthusiastic reviews from critics. "*The Mentalist* is smart enough to know how silly its premise is," wrote *Entertainment Weekly*'s Gillian Flynn, who commended both Baker's performance and the chemistry between his character and the boss, played by Robin Tunney. "Like any good grifter, he gets a genuine thrill out of entertaining, manipulating, or confusing people," Flynn remarked. Other critics conceded defeat as well when faced with Baker's on-screen charisma. "Baker turns on the charm and insouciance," noted *New York Times* television critic Alessandra Stanley. "He glides in to people's houses and riffles through their secrets with a con man's ease and rascally assurance." The *Mentalist* star was even cited in an article about television actors' hairstyles in *Maclean's* magazine in which Jaime J. Weinman explained that "Baker plays a crime-solving genius with a tragic past, but wears his mop of curly blond hair in what looks like a hand-knitted pattern. The look establishes Baker as a charming rogue with no regard for police procedure, even before the scripts do."

In 2009 Baker appeared in another title role, this time in the film *The Lodger.* The creepy psychological thriller was a remake of a 1926 British silent movie of the same name that was one of Alfred Hitchcock's first films. He made another appearance that year in an ensemble piece that followed the stories of several women in varying degrees of distress, *Women in Trouble. Not Forgotten,* another film from 2009, featured Baker as a former cult member whose daughter goes missing. Returning to work on the top-rated *Mentalist* remained his primary focus, however. "I used to want to move people and let people identify with me as an actor, you know? But with this show, I just want to entertain people," he explained to Carter in the *USA Today* interview. "I just want to have a good time."

## Sources

*Entertainment Weekly,* December 7, 2001, p. 81; August 2, 2002, p. 56; September 26, 2008, p. 78.
*In Style,* June 1, 2003, p. 310.
*Maclean's,* January 26, 2009, p. 50.
*New York,* September 8, 2008, p. 82; October 13, 2008, p. 70.
*New York Times,* February 3, 2006; September 23, 2008; November 30, 2008.
*Record* (Bergen County, NJ), May 21, 2002, p. F1.
*Sydney Morning Herald,* March 18, 2009.
*USA Today,* November 11, 2008, p. 1D.

—*Carol Brennan*

# Russell Banks

## Author

**B**orn March 28, 1940, in Newton, MA; son of Earl (a plumber) and Florence (a bookkeeper) Banks; married Darlene Bennett, June 1960 (divorced, February 1962); married Mary Gunst (a poet), October 29, 1962 (divorced, 1977); married Kathy Walton (an editor), 1982 (divorced, 1988); married Chase Twitchell (a poet), 1989; children: Leona Stamm (from first marriage), Caerthan, Maia, Danis (from second marriage). *Education:* Attended Colgate University, 1958; University of North Carolina, A.B., 1967.

**Addresses:** *Agent*—Steven Barclay Agency, 12 Western Ave., Petaluma, CA 94952. *E-mail*—rusbanks@princeton.edu.

## Career

**M**annequin dresser, Montgomery Ward, Lakeland, FL, 1960-61; plumber in New Hampshire, 1962-64; Lillabulero Press, Inc., Chapel Hill, NC, publisher and editor, c. 1964-66; Northwood Narrows, NH, publisher and editor, 1966-75; Emerson College, Boston, MA, instructor, 1968, 1971; University of New Hampshire, Dunham, NH, instructor, 1968-75; New England College, Henniker, NH, instructor, 1975, 1977-82; writer, 1975—; Princeton University, instructor, 1981—.

**Member:** International PEN, Coordinating Council of Literary Magazines, American Academy of Arts and Sciences, Phi Beta Kappa.

**Awards:** St. Lawrence award for fiction, St. Lawrence University and *Fiction International*, 1975; O. Henry Award, for "With Che at Kitty Hawk,"

1975; American Book Award, Before Columbus Foundation, for *The Book of Jamaica*, 1982; American Academy and Institute of Arts and Letters Award, for work of distinction, 1986; John Dos Passos Award, 1986; New York State Author, 2004-08.

## Sidelights

**A** novelist, short story writer, poet, and educator, Russell Banks is perhaps best known for such novels as *Continental Drift, Affliction,* and *The Sweet Hereafter.* Many of his novels focus on the theme of children, especially broken ones, and how adult American society has used and corrupted them. This focus, among others, reveals much about a nation that deeply troubles him for its obsessions. As Cynthia Joyce wrote in Salon.com, "Infusing his novels with a brutal honesty and moral rectitude that his characters struggle to live up to, Banks writes in beautiful and often tragic tones about the drama of daily life.... No modern author writes more perceptively about ordinary men's stumbling quest for the American grail of material comfort and self-respect."

Born on March 28, 1940, in Newton, Massachusetts, he is the son of Earl and Florence Banks. His plumber father was a violent alcoholic who left the family when Banks was 12 years old. His mother was a bookkeeper who used her meager salary to support Banks and his three siblings; she was also a heavy drinker. As a child, Banks was raised in poverty and was wild, though he had to work to help out his family. He shoplifted and used marijuana, and both activities caught the attention of police. At 16, Banks ran away from home and stole a car. Yet he was also a gifted student and had talent as an artist, which he demonstrated from an early age. In childhood, Banks believed he was going to be a visual artist, though by his late teens he became more fascinated by reading and soon became interested in writing.

Banks tried to go to college at 18—the first in his family to do so—but dropped out of Colgate University in 1958, though he had a scholarship. He intended to join the Revolution in Cuba, but only made it to Florida. Of this time in his life, Banks told Hillel Italie in the Lakeland, Florida *Ledger,* "(When) I left college I felt … I had almost trapped myself in a life that I did not want and I had not chosen. I felt well, 'If I go somewhere else, far away and drop myself in that world, as if a newborn person, I could reinvent my life whole.' And it turned out I couldn't. You take that person with you."

Banks married his first wife, Darlene Bennett, at 19 and had a child. He found blue-collar jobs to support himself and his family. From 1960 to 1961, he worked at a Montgomery Ward in Lakeland, Florida, as a mannequin dresser, for example. By 1962, Banks was obsessed with writing and living in New Hampshire, where he worked as a plumber for two years. He first became inspired by Jack Kerouac, a writer with a similarly working-class background. Banks began writing his own pieces, beginning with poetry and short stories. Looking back, Banks acknowledged that writing changed the course of his life. He told Salon.com's Joyce, "I think writing saved my life. I was so self-destructive, so angry and turbulent, that I don't think I could have become a useful citizen in any other way. So I don't think it worked as exorcism, or therapy, but I think it saved my life."

In 1964, Banks moved to Chapel Hill, North Carolina, where he worked at Lillabulero Press, Inc., as an editor and publisher. Banks also worked on his undergraduate degree, earning his A.B. in English from the University of North Carolina in 1967. While an undergraduate, he helped organize a chapter of the Students for a Democratic Society on campus and was active in the civil rights movement. By the time Banks earned his degree, he was back in New Hampshire, working as a publisher and editor

beginning in 1966. While his home base remained New Hampshire until 1975, he also taught at various schools. Banks was an instructor at Emerson College in 1968 and 1971. He also was an instructor at the University of New Hampshire from 1968 to 1975. During this time period, Banks published several collections of poetry, though he soon turned to short stories and novels.

In 1975, Banks began focusing more of his attention on writing, publishing his first collection of short stories, *Searching for Survivors* as well as his first novel, *Family Life.* While he was a part-time instructor at New England College in 1975 and 1977 to 1982, much of his time was spent on his writing, including several more short story collections and novels published in this time period. By 1981, Banks took on a new teaching position, serving as a part-time instructor at Princeton University while living elsewhere. (After 1987, he resided in upstate New York. He lived there with his fourth wife, Chase Twitchell, whom he married in 1989.)

Banks' novels soon gained him a reputation as an author. He touched on American imperialism and international politics in 1980's *The Book of Jamaica*—about a professor who is a white American and travels to Jamaica to finish his novel—as well as 1985's *Continental Drift.* Banks first gained fame with *Drift,* which was primarily set in Florida. The novel focuses on the story of a working class man, Bob DuBois, from New Hampshire, who looks for a better life in the South. At the same time, an impoverished mother from Haiti seeks the same thing in Florida. Though he is a racist, they eventually fall in love. Both of their lives have tragedy, including the loss of the woman's son, Claude.

Banks continued to receive acclaim with the release of his next novel, *Affliction,* published in 1990. The novel focused on a cop, Wade Whitehouse, whose life takes unexpected dark turns. Set in a small town in New Hampshire similar to his father's hometown, Whitehouse must deal with his alcoholic father, a divorce, and a daughter who no longer respects him. Wade also becomes fixated on a deer-hunting accident which he believes is being used as a cover-up to a real murder. Many critics consider this novel Banks' most autobiographical work. It was adapted into a popular film in 1997 which was well-received by critics.

In 1991, Banks published *The Sweet Hereafter,* a novel which brought him much praise. The novel focuses on a tragic incident which affects many impoverished residents of Sam Dent, a small town in upstate New York. A school bus plummets into a pond causing the drowning death of 14 children and life-changing injuries to at least one other. In the aftermath, a lawsuit ensues which reveals many sentiments in the community about the accident as well as the American legal system.

Many critics praised the novel, including Philip Marchand of the *Toronto Star*: "*The Sweet Hereafter* is a gripping tale from beginning to end, enriched by the author's acute sense of social nuances in towns like Sam Dent. These nuances will be unfamiliar to many readers of the novel—the symbolic resolution of the story involves a demolition derby, for example, which is not a favorite spectator sport for literate people. But his recreation of these nuances is utterly convincing, and helps to make the novel unforgettable." *The Sweet Hereafter* was adapted for a well-received film in 1997.

Banks' next novel, 1995's *Rule of the Bone,* also focuses on lost children. A modern retelling of Mark Twain's classic novel *The Adventures of Huckleberry Finn,* Banks explores the life of 14-year-old Bone, a teenager whose family does not care about him and who is trying to find his place in the world after getting into trouble. He finds a mentor in I-Man, a Jamaican Rastafarian. Bone was inspired in part by Banks' own misspent youth. Praising the novel, Allan Hepburn of the Toronto *Financial Post* wrote, "As *Rule of the Bone* shows, it is possible to find truth outside of conventions and family outside of homes. This is a beautifully crafted novel that stretches the imagination and rethinks those family values that are too often taken for granted and too often wrong."

After *Rule of the Bone,* Banks wrote a lauded historical novel about abolitionist John Brown entitled *Cloudsplitter.* Published in 1998 and a bestseller, the novel is narrated by Brown's son Owen, and depicts Brown as a fascinating, though abusive, man. As Marchand wrote in the *Toronto Star,* "The central irony of *Cloudsplitter* is that Brown is unaware he is oppressing his own children at the same time as he is passionately devoted to liberating his surrogate children. It is an irony that loses none of its bitterness for being such a familiar story." *Cloudsplitter* was a finalist for the Pulitzer Prize in 1998.

In 2000, Banks published his first short story collection in more than a decade, *The Angel on the Roof: The Stories of Russell Banks.* The collection included stories from his previous collections, periodicals, and other sources, from the beginning of his career to the date of publication. Touching on many of the themes of his novels, this collection was praised by critics such as Janet Maslin of the *New York Times* who called it a "beautifully lucid, frequently wrenching collection." She also noted that "Among Mr. Banks' extraordinary skills, the technical prowess and storytelling grace that hook a reader so seemingly easily should not be overlooked."

Continuing to look to the past for inspiration, Banks' next novel was set in Africa and the United States during the 1960s. Entitled *The Darling* and published in 2004, the novel focuses on the life of Hannah Musgrave, who pushes aside her privileged upbringing during the Vietnam War and becomes a political activist. After participating in radical bombings in the 1960s, she becomes a fugitive and goes to Liberia. There, she marries, becomes involved in animal rights by working to save the chimpanzee population, and later becomes part of the destructive civil war that breaks out in Liberia. Banks was inspired to write the novel in part because of his interest in Liberian history, from its creation to the present, as well as the radical student movement of the 1960s and 1970s. As he told Paul Grondahl of the Albany *Times Union,* "I wanted to revisit the role of women in the radical movement, because they always get the short shrift. They're always treated as thwarted, neurotic, comic or simply as followers. They're never treated as having the same complexity as men were allowed."

Similarly, Banks' 2008 novel *The Reserve* is also set in the past, in this case the Adirondacks during the Great Depression of the 1930s. The hero of the novel is a seemingly happily married left-wing artist, adventurer, and father named Jordan Graves who becomes involved with Vanessa, the twice-divorced, troubled daughter of a well-to-do acquaintance. With characters based on real people (Graves is based on artist-adventurer Rockwell Kent), the novel received only mixed reviews from critics, some of whom compared it to *Gone with the Wind.* As Mark Shechner wrote in the *Buffalo News,* "*The Reserve* strikes me as a cross between a period romance, with the flames of encroaching war flickering in the background, and a lesson in prudence...." Shechner concludes, "He places disposable characters doing disposable things that feel so terribly insubstantial amid the rugged, durable wilderness that overshadows them."

In addition to his novels, Banks has also written several screenplays based on his works, including *The Book of Jamaica* and *The Darling.* The author appreciated his success considering his background, mistakes, and struggles. He told Italie in the Lakeland, Florida *Ledger* interview, "I never expected my life to turn out like this. It's a source of constant amazement to me, a source of considerable anxiety. I get very superstitious. It feels so fragile. I look around me, and say, Jesus, how did this happen? I have no idea what I did to end up here."

## Selected writings

### Poetry

*30/6,* Quest (New York City), 1969.
*Waiting to Freeze,* Lillabulero Press (Northwood Narrows, NH), 1969.
*Snow: Meditations of a Cautious Man in Winter,* Granite Press (Hanover, NH), 1974.

### Short stories

*Searching for Survivors,* Fiction Collective (New York City), 1975.
*The New World,* University of Illinois Press (Urbana, IL), 1978.
*Trailerpark,* Houghton (Boston, MA), 1981.
*Success Stories,* Harper & Row (New York City), 1986.
*The Angel on the Roof: The Stories of Russell Banks,* HarperCollins (New York City), 2000.

### Novels

*Family Life,* Avon (New York City), 1975, rev. ed., Sun & Moon (Los Angles, CA), 1988.
*Hamilton Stark,* Houghton, 1978, new ed., Harper-Collins, 1996.
*The Book of Jamaica,* Houghton, 1980.
*The Relation of My Imprisonment,* Sun & Moon (College Park, MD), 1984.
*Continental Drift,* Harper & Row, 1985.

*Affliction,* HarperCollins, 1990.
*The Sweet Hereafter,* HarperCollins, 1991.
*Rule of the Bone,* HarperCollins, 1995.
*Cloudsplitter,* HarperCollins, 1998.
*The Darling,* Ecco/HarperCollins (New York City), 2004.
*The Reserve,* HarperCollins, 2008.

## Sources

### Books

*Contemporary Authors,* Gale (Detroit, MI), 2008.

### Periodicals

*The Age* (Melbourne, Australia), April 5, 2008, sec. A2, p. 27.
*Atlanta Journal and Constitution,* February 14, 1999, p. 1L.
*Buffalo News* (NY), March 30, 2008, p. F6.
*Financial Post* (Toronto, Canada), January 17, 1995, sec. 2, p. 28.
*Ledger* (Lakeland, FL), May 28, 1995, p. 4G.
*New York Times,* November 30, 1997, sec. 2, p. 17; June 1, 2000, p. E10.
*Observer* (England), May 4, 2008, p. 25.
*Pittsburgh Post-Gazette* (PA), April 29, 2008, p. C3.
*South Bend Tribune* (IN), May 12, 2002, p. F5.
*Times Union* (Albany, NY), October 17, 2004, p. J1.
*Toronto Star,* September 14, 1991, p. K14; March 14, 1998, p. M14.
*USA Today,* May 18, 1995, p. 5D.

### Online

"Russell Banks," Salon.com (October 10, 2008).

*—A. Petruso*

# Pat Barker

## Author

**B**orn May 8, 1943, in Thornaby-on-Tees, England; daughter of a Royal Air Force officer and Moyra; married David Barker (a professor of zoology), January 29, 1978; children: John, Annabel. *Education:* London School of Economics and Political Science, B.Sc., 1965.

**Addresses:** *Agent*—Aitken Alexander Associates, 18-21 Cavaye Place, London SW10 9PT, England. *Home*—Durham, England.

## Career

**A**uthor. Worked as a teacher in England, 1965-70. Published first book, *Union Street,* 1982.

**Awards:** Fawcett Prize, Fawcett Society, for *Union Street,* 1982; *Guardian* Fiction Prize, for *The Eye in the Door,* 1993; Booker Prize for fiction, for *The Ghost Road,* 1995; decorated Commander of the British Empire, 2000.

## Sidelights

**B**ritish novelist Pat Barker portrays life in the gritty, industrial cities in the north of England where she grew up, and habitually revisits an event that shaped her childhood a full generation before she was born—England's involvement in World War I. In 2006 Barker's eleventh novel, *Life Class,* kicked off what would become her second World War I-themed trilogy. In an interview with *Publishers Weekly*'s Tim Peters, the novelist offered an explana-

tion of why this particular conflict and its emotional carnage fascinated her so. "The Great War was the first time most people were made aware of the terrible effects of modern weapons on fragile human bodies," Barker said. "The shock of this still lingers."

Barker was born in 1943, when England was in the midst of World War II, its epic battle against Nazi Germany. Her place of birth, Thornaby-on-Tees, is a North Yorkshire town situated on the River Tees in the northeast region of England. Barker never knew her father; she was told that he had died in the war, but on another occasion her mother, Moyra, claimed she had been the victim of a sexual assault.

Prior to Barker's birth, Moyra was a member of the Women's Royal Naval Service, a wartime auxiliary outfit whose members were called "Wrens." As Barker explained to *New Yorker* writer Kennedy Fraser, her mother "really adored the war. She was one of those women whose lives were expanded by the experience of it. She was on this huge mixed-service base, and there were lots and lots of young men." Barker later uncovered the truth about her parentage: Her mother had indeed been in love, but when the Royal Navy recruit died in battle, Moyra's Wren roommate took her out drinking to console her, and a one-night stand resulted in an unplanned pregnancy.

Barker and her mother lived with Moyra's mother and stepfather, and she was sometimes hidden upstairs when distant relatives came to visit. When she was seven, her mother married, but Barker remained with her grandparents, who ran a chips shop. Her step-grandfather—who had served in World War I and had a gruesome scar from a German bayonet wound as a daily reminder— died when she was 15, and Barker's grandmother was forced to apply for public assistance. Barker's future prospects appeared bleak, but she worked as a nursery school teacher for a time and then entered the prestigious London School of Economics and Political Science in 1962. Three years later, she graduated with a degree in international history and began a teaching career at the junior-college level. In 1970 she met her future husband, a professor of zoology named David Barker, and they wed eight years later.

Barker began writing when her two children were small, encouraged by her husband. She completed three novels, none of which interested the publishers or literary agents to whom she sent the manuscripts, but a writers' workshop taught by Angela Carter—an English novelist whose works have a strong feminist and mystical undercurrent—helped her find her own voice as a writer. Carter put her in touch with someone at Virago Press, a pioneering publishing house founded in 1973 as exclusively devoted to works by female writers. Virago issued Barker's debut novel, *Union Street*, in 1982.

*Union Street* was loosely adapted into a 1990 Hollywood film starring Robert De Niro and Jane Fonda in the title roles of *Stanley and Iris*. In Barker's novel, the focus is less on one working-class woman than a group of seven, all of whom are interconnected to one another. They live in an ailing northern industrial factory town and, if employed, work at the local cake factory; most of the other companies have since shut down. "In this first novel Barker stakes out a distinctive territory for herself: the lives of working women," wrote Merritt Moseley in *Dictionary of Literary Biography: British and Irish Novelists Since 1960*. "There is little about these lives to admire or envy: chaotic, endlessly disappointed, limited, they seem bound to an endless cycle of modest hope followed by major disappointment; too few resources; bad housing, bad employment, bad education."

Barker's second novel was *Blow Your House Down*, published in 1984. Its plot drew upon an actual series of murders in the late 1970s in Manchester and Leeds known as the Yorkshire Ripper slayings. Several women, most of them prostitutes, were brutally attacked, and the case terrorized northern English cities during an already bleak time when massive unemployment was causing widespread hardship in most of England's once-powerful industrial cities. After a midway point in the novel, Barker devotes her story to a pair of the victims, including one who survived her attack. Writing in the *Times Literary Supplement,* Jane Rogers preferred the first half of the novel, calling it "compulsively readable, engulfing us in a bleak world of limited choices, squalid sex, and flashes of gutsy female warmth and humour."

Barker's next novel, *The Century's Daughter*, was later published as *Liza's England*. Its titular heroine is Liza, who is 84 years old in the mid-1980s as the novel opens. A social worker visits regularly in an attempt to lure her out of her home, where her only company is a parrot, and into a care facility. The decrepit block is scheduled for demolition, and Liza, who has lived there since 1922, is the last holdout. Her life's hardships are recounted in flashback, while the story's conclusion was viewed by some critics as a scathing indictment of Britain's Conservative (Tory) government at the time.

In her 1989 novel *The Man Who Wasn't There*, Barker experimented with a male narrative viewpoint for the first time. Its protagonist is a 12-year-old boy named Colin, neglected by his mother and pining for a father he has never known. Her next novel, *Regeneration*, also featured a male point of view in its tale of the emotional trauma inflicted on the men who served in World War I. Barker's inspiration was her step-grandfather, who seemed to have never fully recovered from the psychic and physical wounds, and also her stepfather, who was drafted into the British Army at age 15 and served at the front. He married Barker's mother when he was a widower with a young son whom he abused terribly; the boy wound up becoming a career criminal despite her mother's efforts to help him.

Published in 1991, *Regeneration* is the first in a trilogy of novels from Barker. It centers around a real-life psychiatrist from that era, Dr. William Rivers, who counseled shell-shocked veterans of World War I at a Scottish military hospital. The novel imagines the interplay between Rivers and a pair of British poets who were well-known conscientious objectors, Siegfried Sassoon and Wilfred Owen. Both served at the front and were profoundly demoralized by it. Rivers' task was to counsel the men with the goal of returning them to active duty, but he, too, becomes disillusioned with the system.

The response from *Regeneration*'s readers that Barker received was immensely gratifying, she told Fraser in the *New Yorker* profile. The letters she received expressed gratitude for helping them to learn about their own families' legacy of dysfunction in households dominated by mute or angry fathers and grandfathers. As Barker noted in the interview, "the overwhelming burden of caring for someone who will never be the same again falls on women."

Barker followed *Regeneration* with two more novels with the same characters—Rivers, Sassoon, and Owen. The next installment, *The Eye in the Door,* begins in 1918 in the final months of the war and won the 1993 *Guardian* Fiction Prize. Two years later, Barker's third in the series, *The Ghost Road,* won the prestigious Booker Prize for Fiction. Its story focuses less on Sassoon and Owen, instead delving into the trials of a officer named Billy Prior, whom Fraser described as "a complex, amoral, seductive, and knowing antihero: a man defiant of boundaries of class or sex. Once he recovers from his mutism (he lost the power of speech around the time when he came to in a trench holding a dead man's eyeball), he is by far the trickiest of Rivers' patients."

In 1998's *Another World,* Barker sets the story in the present day, but one important element is the 101-year-old grandfather of Nick, who is expecting a second child with his second wife; their two older children are Nick's unhappy 13-year-old daughter and her equally dispirited eleven-year-old stepbrother. As the family renovates their old house in Newcastle, they uncover a disturbing portrait of the previous owners that has been covered up by wallpaper. The father was an arms manufacturer during the First World War, and one of his younger children was found dead; the likely culprit was a family member. In the middle of Nick's own family dysfunction, he keeps watch at his dying grandfather's bedside. Writing in the *Los Angeles Times,* Michael Frank asserted that in this as well as in the *Regeneration* trilogy, Barker "succeeds in thus humbling her readers. Her remarkable visits to the past help replenish the emptying containers of memory by substituting storytelling for forgetting. With her novels, she adds dignity to this century's often bleak and undignified human record."

Barker's next novel, *Border Crossing,* appeared in 2001. Its contemporary plot centered around a young man named Danny, who killed an elderly woman when he was ten years old and has recently been released from custody. The other significant character is the psychologist whose testimony helped convince the court of Danny's guilt, and who now agrees to work with him again to help him come to terms with his past.

*Double Vision* was Barker's tenth novel. Published in 2003, its plot centers on several characters dealing with the aftermath of the U.S. terrorist attacks of September 11, 2001, including a newly widowed artist, a journalist who once covered war zones, and a young man with a suspicious past who comes to work as Kate's assistant at her art studio near Newcastle. Nearby is Stephen, the war correspondent who knew Kate's photojournalist husband and whose own marriage has recently ended. "No matter what the privilege of their position, the creative and financial possibility in their lives," wrote Neil Gordon in the *New York Times,* "the members of the small cast of Barker's book quickly show themselves to be entrapped within a highly restricted constellation of relationships, as if frozen in a crystal—at the center of which is the sinister Peter."

Artistic endeavors also play a role in Barker's next novel, *Life Class.* The 2006 work imagines the events in the life of a real-life art professor named Henry Tonks, who taught at the Slade School of Fine Arts in London before his 1937 death. Returning again to World War I as her theme, here Barker follows the intersecting lives of three of Tonks' students on the eve of the conflict. The novel was part of another trilogy, with the next, as-yet-untitled book finding Tonks working with plastic surgeons to repair the war's carnage.

Barker still lives in the north of England in the city of Durham, which also lies on the River Tees. In an interview with the *Guardian*'s Maya Jaggi, she quoted from the nineteenth-century German philosopher Friedrich Nietzsche: "Whoever fights monsters should see to it that in the process he does not become a monster. And when you look long into an abyss, the abyss also looks into you." Barker explained to Jaggi that her goal in writing about such emotionally difficult terrain was to "enable people to think clearly and feel deeply simultaneously.... I hope they're not cast into the abyss, but given guide ropes and a way out."

## Selected writings

*Union Street,* Virago Press (London, England), 1982; Putnam (New York City), 1983.
*Blow Your House Down,* Putnam, 1984.
*The Century's Daughter,* Putnam, 1986; also published as *Liza's England,* Picador (London, England), 1996.
*The Man Who Wasn't There,* Virago Press, 1989; Ballantine (New York City), 1990.
*Regeneration,* Viking (London, England), 1991; Dutton (New York City), 1993.
*The Eye in the Door,* Viking, 1993; Dutton, 1994.
*The Ghost Road,* Viking, 1995; Dutton, 1996.
*The Regeneration Trilogy,* Viking, 1996.
*Another World,* Viking, 1998.

*Border Crossing,* Farrar, Straus (New York City), 2001.
*Double Vision,* Farrar, Straus, 2003.
*Life Class,* Penguin (London, England), 2006.

## Sources

### Books

Moseley, Merritt, "Pat(ricia) Barker," *Dictionary of Literary Biography,* Volume 271: *British and Irish Novelists Since 1960,* edited by Moseley, Gale, 2003.

### Periodicals

*Guardian* (London, England), August 16, 2003, p. 16.
*Los Angeles Times,* June 6, 1999, p. 3.
*New Yorker,* March 17, 2008, p. 41.
*New York Times,* April 15, 1992; March 18, 2001; December 14, 2003.
*Publishers Weekly,* November 12, 2007, p. 34.
*Times Literary Supplement,* July 13, 1984, p. 790.

—*Carol Brennan*

# Kim Barnouin and Rory Freedman

## Authors

**B**arnouin: born c. 1971; married Stephane (a chef); children: Jackson. Freedman: born c. 1975. *Education:* Barnouin: Clayton College of Natural Health, Birmingham, AL, M.S.

**Addresses:** *Publisher*—Running Press, 2300 Chestnut St., Ste. 200, Philadelphia, PA 19103. *Web site*—http://www.skinnybitch.net.

## Career

**B**arnouin: Worked as model, through 1999. Freedman: Worked as a booker and agent, Ford modeling agency and other agencies, through 2002; kindergarten enrichment program teacher in Wyckoff, New Jersey; animal rights activist. Together: became friends in 1996 through modeling agency; published *Skinny Bitch: A No-Nonsense Tough-Love Guide for Savvy Girls Who Want to Stop Eating Crap and Starting Looking Fabulous!*, 2005; *Skinny Bitch* became best-seller, 2007; signed two-book deal with Running Press, 2007; published *Skinny Bitch in the Kitch: Kick-Ass Recipes for Hungry Girls Who Want to Stop Eating Crap (and Start Looking Hot!)*, 2007; signed additional two-book deal with Running Press, 2008; published *Skinny Bitch Bun in the Oven: A Gutsy Guide to Becoming One Hot and Healthy Mother!*, 2008; appeared in workout DVD, *Skinny Bitch Fitness Boot Camp*, 2009; published *Skinny Bastard*, 2009.

## Sidelights

**T**he authors of the popular *Skinny Bitch* guide to improving one's diet, Kim Barnouin and Rory Freedman used a brazen attitude, uncompromising ethics, and a cheeky tone to promote a vegan lifestyle packaged for mass consumption. Both authors worked in the modeling industry before becoming passionate about animal rights and perfect bodies through a diet free of meat, dairy, caffeine, alcohol, and simple carbohydrates. The irreverent authors even questioned the findings of such government entities as the World Health Organization. *Skinny Bitch* turned into a series of books and other lifestyle products. As stated on their Web site, www. skinnybitch.net, "*Skinny Bitch* is the lifestyle we live, and rest assured, we would never maintain it if we felt deprived.... We devised the *Skinny Bitch* plan so we could have our cake and eat it!"

The authors came from similar professional backgrounds. Born around 1975, Freedman worked as a booker and agent at the famous Ford modeling agency, among other agencies. She left her last modeling agency in 2002. Freedman then worked as a kindergarten enrichment program teacher in Wyckoff, New Jersey, as well as an animal rights activist. Born around 1971, Barnouin was a model for Ford as well as other agencies for a number of years. She ended her modeling career in 1999 and later earned a master's degree in holistic nutrition from an alternative health school. Freedman called her qualification to write a diet book as being a self-educated know-it-all.

Barnouin and Freedman became friends in 1996 when they met at a modeling agency. Barnouin was signed as a model at the agency where Freedman worked, and Freedman would book her jobs. The pair found they shared an interest in animal rights and healthy eating. Within a few years, they began laying plans to write a diet book, coming up with the *Skinny Bitch* title early on.

The pair then wrote a 20-page proposal that included an in-your-face tone and the use of profanity. Many publishers were unwilling to take a chance on unknown authors, but they eventually signed with Running Press for a low five-figure advance. Barnouin conducted much of the research for the book using her nutrition class textbooks and the Internet. Ultimately, the authors had a nutrition scientist, Amy Joy Lanou, review the final text and incorporated a few of her suggestions.

In December of 2005, Barnouin and Freedman published *Skinny Bitch: A No-Nonsense Tough-Love Guide for Savvy Girls Who Want to Stop Eating Crap and Starting Looking Fabulous!*, their guide for women to gaining the perfect body. In the bold book, they said for women to achieve this goal they must stop eating meat as well as drinking milk. The pair also provided a list of foods to avoid (including alcohol, sugar, fat, caffeine, refined carbohydrates, junk foods like soda, and many chemicals and additives, such as aspartame), listed substitute food products, and offered meal plans. The authors underscore their point with sassy and strong, if not harsh, language.

To encourage readers to make these radical changes, Barnouin and Freedman went into detail about their problems with meat and dairy products. The duo especially focused on the conditions under which chickens and cows live, and provide photographic evidence. They blasted the Atkins diet in particular for promoting the consumption of more meat products and the elimination of nearly all carbohydrates. In addition, Barnouin and Freedman detailed their lack of faith in the findings of government agencies. Though a group overseen by the World Health Organization declared aspartame safe, for example, the authors state their belief that the government officials who approved the use of aspartame had conflicts of interest. The duo believed the decision was about business, not health or consumers' best interests.

Initially, critics responded somewhat positively. In the *St. Louis Post-Dispatch,* Theresa Tighe commented "This book's title is outrageous and compelling." She concluded, "*Skinny Bitch* fulfills its title's sensational come-on."

It was not until the spring of 2007 that the book took off, however. At that time, Victoria Beckham was seen in Los Angeles reading *Skinny Bitch.* The rail-thin native of Great Britain is a member of the once-popular all-female singing group, the Spice Girls—she was Posh Spice—and is married to one of the most popular soccer players in the world, David Beckham.

Because of her implied endorsement, the sales of Barnouin and Freedman's book vastly increased in both the United States and the United Kingdom. By August of 2007, *Skinny Bitch* had reached number three on the *New York Times* paperback advice, how-to, and miscellaneous book list. Seen in a new light, critics spent more time questioning the book as well as the authors' qualifications to write it.

A few reviewers were quite harsh. Writing in the London *Daily Mail,* Ursula Hirshkorn commented on their lack of credentials. Hirshkorn then offered, "This is perhaps how they came to their laughably simplistic theory, that the secret of weight loss is just to eat healthy food. Oh if it were that easy, we'd all be size eight and they'd never have been published, killing two birds—and I don't mean them—with one stone."

Hirschkorn, like other critics, noted that in essence, *Skinny Bitch* promoted veganism. Nutrition experts also believed that the book's program was unrealistic for most people. One such dietary expert, Amanda Ursell, told the *Belfast Telegraph*'s Caitriona Palmer "As with any diet, if you follow it to the letter then you will lose weight, but for your average woman it's not particularly easy to follow and you would have to be incredibly dedicated."

Despite such detractors, the book sold more than a million copies and Running Press signed Barnouin and Freedman to a six-figure deal for two more books. In December of 2007, they published their second book, *Skinny Bitch in the Kitch: Kick-Ass Recipes for Hungry Girls Who Want to Stop Eating Crap (and Start Looking Hot!)*. It was a vegan cookbook based on the principles of their *Skinny Bitch* book.

Though the pair had limited knowledge of cooking themselves before their first book was published, readers wanted recipes and menus. Barnouin and Freedman used a vegan cookbook expert to write the actual recipes in *Skinny Bitch in the Kitch* (though half of them were dishes they would make but did not have exact measurements for). The pair contributed the commentary and irreverent titles to the recipes.

Barnouin and Freedman's intended audience for the cookbook included those inspired to change to a vegan diet by *Skinny Bitch*. When asked about the heavy emphasis on processed meat substitutes, Freedman told Siri Agrell of the *Globe and Mail*, "I think this cookbook is more for people who are just transitioning or who are curious and want to try vegetarian cooking than for die-hard vegans. I don't eat as many fake meat products as I did when I first transitioned 14 years ago. But I would not have survived; I would still be eating meat right now if not for all the fake meats."

However, Lynn Weaver, a registered dietician, took issue with their emphasis on such processed vegan food. She told Megan Ogilvie of the *Toronto Star*, "In this food revolution, where people are getting back to basics and looking to eat simpler meals made with locally grown, natural foods, I can't see why people are so intrigued by this book. So much of the authors' suggestions are based on processed foods." Weaver concluded, "Even if you choose a vegan lifestyle, you can choose not to eat all the processed foods."

Like *Skinny Bitch, Skinny Bitch in the Kitch* was also a best seller. However, critics again had a divided response to the book. *Publishers Weekly Reviews* commented, "Perhaps not a great gift book for grandma (unless she happens to be a foul-mouthed vegan), this will be embraced by readers seeking healthful recipes with an entertaining twist." In contrast, Ogilvie of the *Toronto Star* concluded, "If you are a skinny vegan bitch (or want to be one), you might like this book. For anyone else, it will only make you bitch about how such vacuity and vulgarity could make it to the top of the *New York Times* best-seller list."

Because of the continued success of the *Skinny Bitch* series, Running Press signed Barnouin and Freedman to an additional two-book deal in January of 2008. Making the announcement of the signing, the publisher of Running Press, Jon Anderson, commented to Kimberly Maul of thebookstandard.com, "*Skinny Bitch* has been nothing less than a phenomenon. With two books now perched atop the *New York Times* best-seller list, and a third on its way later this year, it's apparent that Kim and Rory have tapped into the desire of people all over the world to eat—and think—for themselves, all in a voice that is utterly original."

Published later in 2008, Barnouin and Freedman's next book was a guide to eating during pregnancy, *Skinny Bitch Bun in the Oven: A Gutsy Guide to Be-coming One Hot and Healthy Mother!* Barnouin conducted some of the research for this book on herself. She is married to a French chef named Stephane, and had an infant son. Under a doctor's supervision, Barnouin maintained a vegan diet during her pregnancy. Much of the information in the book focused on how what a pregnant woman eats affects the baby or babies she is carrying. The authors especially emphasized the negative effects of hormones, antibiotics, and pesticides on meat and other food products on a woman and her progeny.

Critics were divided on *Skinny Bitch Bun in the Oven*. *Publishers Weekly Review* commented positively, "Passionately questioning the status quo, Freedman and Barnouin make a compelling case for a vegan pregnancy." The book did not attract an audience, however, with only 26,000 copies sold by the spring of 2009.

In 2009, Barnouin and Freedman moved into a new medium with one of at least three workout videos they produced, *Skinny Bitch Fitness Boot Camp*. The pair actually did the workouts themselves, though critics found their presentation and attitudes lacking. Reviewing the DVD in the *Houston Chronicle*, Mary Flood concluded, "Like, OMG, this video generally sucks. It's not just bad direction, it's often no direction, yet there is plenty of obnoxious chatter.... These smart Skinny Bitches would have done much better having a trainer do the video and following along so we could too."

The pair also published a new entry in the *Skinny Bitch* series in 2009. Titled *Skinny Bastard*, Freedman and Barnouin adapted the original ideas in *Skinny Bitch* for a male audience and an appeal to the male psyche. They emphasized that eating vegan will help men prevent such illnesses as heart disease, diabetes, and prostate cancer.

With the publishing deals they have in place, Barnouin and Freedman planned further entries in the *Skinny Bitch* series as well as a *Skinny Bitch* journal. More workout DVDs and other related products were in the works as well. While the pair were happy with their success, Freedman told Grist.org that readers should not take the authors' word on everything.

When asked about readers trusting them, Freedman said to grist.org, "They shouldn't. One of the things we talk about is 'trust no one.' Don't believe us and put us on a pedestal because you like our book or you saw us on the *Today* show, or because we're on the *New York Times* best-seller list. We have to question everything we learn. We have to find ways to validate our own ideas, our own beliefs, or beliefs that other people are presenting to us—or we have to invalidate them—but to just trust anything that anyone says is naïve and irresponsible."

## Selected writings

### Nonfiction

*Skinny Bitch: A No-Nonsense Tough-Love Guide for Savvy Girls Who Want to Stop Eating Crap and Starting Looking Fabulous!*, Running Press (Philadelphia, PA), 2005.

*Skinny Bitch in the Kitch: Kick-Ass Recipes for Hungry Girls Who Want to Stop Eating Crap (and Start Looking Hot!)*, Running Press, 2007.

*Skinny Bitch Bun in the Oven: A Gutsy Guide to Becoming One Hot and Healthy Mother!*, Running Press, 2008.

*Skinny Bastard: A Kick-in-the-Ass for Real Men Who Want to Stop Being Fat and Start Getting Buff*, Running Press, 2009.

## Sources

### Periodicals

*Belfast Telegraph* (Ireland), June 11, 2007.
*Daily Mail* (London, England), May 24, 2007, p. 57.
*The Express* (England), May 30, 2007, p. 20.
*Globe and Mail* (Canada), January 9, 2008, p. L1.
*Houston Chronicle*, January 19, 2009, p. 3.
*New York Times*, August 1, 2007, p. E1; January 2, 2008, p. F1; April 23, 2009, p. C1.
*Publishers Weekly Reviews*, November 19, 2007, p. 53; July 21, 2008, p. 156.
*St. Louis Post-Dispatch*, July 31, 2006, p. H3.
*Sunday Mirror* (London, England), May 27, 2007, p. 34.
*Toronto Star*, January 17, 2009, p. L9.
*USA Today*, December 12, 2007, p. 9B.

### Online

"About the Authors: Rory Freedman & Kim Barnouin," Skinny Bitch, http://www.skinnybitch.net/authors.html (April 25, 2009).

"Hey, skinny bitch!," Salon.com, http://www.salon.com/mwt/feature/2008/02/11/skinny_bitch/ (April 8, 2009).

"An interview with Rory Freedman, coauthor of vegan manifesto *Skinny Bitch*," Grist.com, http://www.grist.org/article/freedman/ (April 25, 2009).

"*Skinny Bitches* Sign Additional Two-Book Deal," The Book Standard, www.thebookstandard.com (April 8, 2009).

—*A. Petruso*

# Omar al-Bashir

## President of Sudan

**B**orn Omar Hassan Ahmed Bashir, January of 1944, in Sudan; married to two wives, Fatma Khalid and Widad Babaker. *Education:* Graduated from the Sudan Military Academy, 1966.

**Addresses:** *Office*—General Revolutionary Command Council, Khartoum, Sudan.

## Career

**J**oined Sudanese military, 1960; fought in war with Israel, 1973; military attaché to the United Arab Emirates, 1975-79; garrison commander, 1979-81; commanded armored parachute brigade in Khartoum, Sudan, 1981-87; general in Sudanese army, late 1980s; chairman of Revolutionary Command Council for National Salvation, 1989-93; president of Sudan, 1993—.

## Sidelights

**O**mar al-Bashir, the president of Sudan, took power in a 1989 coup with the goal of replacing feuding political parties with Islamic law. But history will almost certainly remember him for his roles in two murderous civil wars. Bashir led his nation through 15 years of bloody civil war between the central government and rebels in southern Sudan. A peace agreement in 2005 ended that conflict. But starting in 2003, Bashir responded to a new rebellion in Sudan's western region of Darfur with such vicious force, many world leaders called it genocide.

Writing in *Time* in 2007, humanitarian activists Don Cheadle and John Prendergast called Bashir one of the world's five worst dictators since World War II. They charged that his war strategies resulted in the deaths of 2.5 million people in Darfur and southern Sudan and the destruction of 1,500 villages, leaving seven million people homeless. According to *New York Times* journalists Marlise Simons, Lydia Polgreen, and Jeffrey Gettleman, a war-crimes prosecutor agreed. In 2008, he asked judges in the International Criminal Court to indict Bashir on charges of genocide and crimes against humanity.

Omar Hassan Ahmed Bashir was born in January of 1944 to a farming couple in a village in the Nile Valley in northern Sudan. He joined the military at age 16 and graduated from Sudan's military academy in 1966. He fought alongside Egyptian forces in the 1973 war with Israel and was Sudan's military liaison to the United Arab Emirates from 1975 to 1979, a garrison commander from 1979 to 1981, and head of the armored parachute brigade in Khartoum from 1981 to 1987.

Bashir served a tour of duty in the fight against rebels in the southern part of the country. Since gaining its independence in 1956, Sudan, Africa's largest country, has been ruled by the Arabs in northern Sudan, around Khartoum, the capital, while Christian and animist tribes in southern Sudan have resisted Arab rule. The conflict grew into an open civil war in 1983, after the central government instituted rule by Islamic sharia law. An uprising led to the suspension of sharia law in 1986, but the civil war continued.

On June 30, 1989, Bashir seized power in Sudan, leading a military coup that overthrew Prime Minister Sadiq al-Mahdi and his democratically elected government. In a televised address, Bashir declared he had mounted the coup "to save the country from rotten political parties," according to the BBC News. He quickly banned political parties and dissolved the country's parliament. To run the country, he set up the 15-member Revolutionary Command Council for National Salvation, which he chaired. Bashir also announced he was abandoning a peace agreement in southern Sudan. In April of 1990, the regime executed 31 army and police officers, allegedly for plotting a coup, though journalists and diplomats reported that was a pretext for eliminating people the regime did not trust.

For years, Bashir ruled Sudan in partnership with his strongest ally, Hassan al-Turabi, head of the National Islamic Front. Turabi, a militant Muslim cleric, was likely behind the reintroduction of Islamic sharia law in northern Sudan in March of 1991. Bashir gained more power in 1993 when the Revolutionary Command Council dissolved itself and named him president. Bashir and Turabi allowed for a new constitution to be drawn up in the mid-1990s, and began to allow some opposition to their government; however, political parties were still banned. Elections were held in 1996, with the stated goal of moving from a military government to an "Islamic democracy," but major opposition parties, which were not allowed to operate openly, boycotted the elections. Bashir defeated more than 40 little-known candidates to win election. Turabi became speaker of the parliament. "We have fully returned power in full to the people," Bashir claimed in a victory address (as quoted by the *New York Times*). He promised the country would be run by "Islamic law and dignity," not party politics.

Some observers saw Turabi as holding the real power in Sudan, with Bashir as his top ally. However, when the two men clashed in 1999, Bashir came out on top. Turabi introduced a bill in November of 1999 that would have restored the post of prime minister and given parliament the power to remove the president. Bashir responded by dissolving parliament and declaring a state of emergency, which allowed him to order indefinite detentions and appoint officials the public would otherwise elect. In May of 2000, Bashir accused Turabi of plotting a coup and froze his post as secretary general of the ruling party. "The secretary general has always been in that habit of defying me," Bashir said in a national broadcast (as quoted by the *New York Times*). In 2001, after Turabi's party signed an agreement with southern rebels, Bashir had Turabi arrested on charges of treason. He was imprisoned until 2003 but never brought to trial.

Elections were held in December of 2000, but the opposition, including Turabi's party, boycotted them, charging that Bashir was rigging the vote. Bashir was reelected president with 87 percent of the vote, and members of his National Congress Party took most of the seats in parliament. When Bashir was sworn in for a second presidential term in February of 2001, he offered some conciliatory gestures toward the south, including naming southerners to important positions. Bashir called for an end to the civil war. "There should be a fair relationship between the north and the south," he told the parliament (as quoted by the *New York Times*).

For most of Bashir's time as Sudan's leader, his country has had strained relations with foreign countries, especially the West. Reasons include Bashir's autocratic rule, the Sudanese military's poor human-rights record in the civil war, and Sudan's ties to terrorists. Osama bin Laden, the leader of al-Qaeda, the terrorist group that attacked the United States on September 11, 2001, lived in Khartoum for part of the 1990s. In 1998, the United States launched a missile attack against a factory in Khartoum that it believed was making ingredients for chemical weapons; Sudan said it was merely a pharmaceutical plant.

After the September 11 attacks, Sudan changed course and cooperated with the United States in its efforts against al-Qaeda. By 2002, the U.S. Secretary of State, Colin Powell, said Sudan had made progress toward peace in the south and in counter-terrorism cooperation. Under Bashir, Sudan also developed a reputation as a good manager of its own economy. It followed International Monetary Fund reform guidelines, cutting government spending, selling off state-owned businesses, and building new infrastructure.

In 2003, a second conflict exploded in Sudan, this time in its western region, Darfur. A rebel group there began an armed revolt, demanding that the central government distribute more power and wealth to the region. Bashir's government unleashed a vicious counterattack that did not distinguish between rebel forces and civilians. Sudanese air forces often attacked villages from the air, a war-crimes prosecutor later reported, while the *janjaweed*, Arab militias backed by Bashir's government, attacked on the ground, destroying the villages and murdering and raping their residents. Investigators later said the *janjaweed* had called Bashir directly for instructions before the attacks. By 2008, the United Nations estimated, 300,000 people had died in the Darfur conflict, and 2.7 million others had been driven from their homes.

In January of 2005, Bashir's government signed a historic peace agreement with the rebels in southern Sudan. The agreement ended the 21-year civil war, Africa's longest, which had cost the lives of 1.5 million people. It created a government of national unity, with some former rebels serving in a cabinet headed by Bashir. It also allowed some autonomy in the south and promised a referendum on independence for the south after six years. However, the peace accord remained fragile. The main party in southern Sudan walked out of the government in 2007, saying Bashir was not living up to his side of the bargain. Three months later, the rebels returned, and Bashir swore in a new government that again gave several posts to southerners.

Nontheless, Bashir often refused to cooperate with international efforts to send peacekeepers and humanitarian aid to Darfur. The United States maintained a long-running embargo of the country. But thanks to increased oil production, Sudan's economy boomed despite the embargo, emboldening Bashir. In an attempt to win over Sudanese rebelling against his rule, he also spent hundreds of millions of dollars on new hospitals, schools, roads, and bridges.

In July of 2008, the top prosecutor of the International Criminal Court asked its judges to indict Bashir on charges of genocide, crimes against humanity, and war crimes related to the Darfur conflict. The prosecutor, Luis Moreno-Ocampo, charged that Bashir had "masterminded and implemented" a plan that "purposefully targeted civilians" in three ethnic groups there, the Fur, the Masalit and the Zaghawa. He said Bashir had used soldiers and Arab militias to kill 35,000 people and create a reign of terror meant to completely wipe out the three ethnic groups. "Bashir organized the destitution, insecurity and harassment of the survivors," Moreno-Ocampo said (as quoted by Simons, Polgreen and Gettleman of the *New York Times*). "He did not need bullets. He used other weapons: rapes, hunger and fear." The prosecutor rejected Bashir's

argument that his actions were simply a military reaction to a rebellion. "His motives were largely political," the prosecutor said. "His alibi was a 'counterinsurgency.' His intent was genocide."

Bashir was the first sitting head of state to face charges before the International Criminal Court. (Other international war-crimes courts had indicted two other heads of state, Slobodan Milosevic of the former Yugoslavia and Charles Taylor of Liberia.) The case set off intense international debate. Many African and Arab leaders argued that it imperiled humanitarian and peacekeeping efforts in and near Sudan. Other diplomats felt it created new leverage on Sudan to end the conflict in Darfur.

The possible indictment strengthened Bashir's hold on power. Sudanese political figures united behind him, even many of Bashir's former enemies, including Mahdi, the prime minister he deposed in 1989. Some did so for reasons of national loyalty, others because they feared the country would disintegrate into chaos if he were removed as leader. Despite Bashir's genocidal reputation abroad, many Sudanese saw him as a moderate figure holding Sudan together through the peace deal with the southern rebels. However, some Sudanese leaders also considered whether the country should make a concession to international pressure by arresting and prosecuting two men already indicted on war-crimes charges, a former interior minister and a former militia leader accused of directing the attacks on civilians in Darfur.

Tensions between Bashir's government and the international community increased as the end of 2008 neared. Bashir declared a unilateral cease-fire in Darfur in November, but rebel groups dismissed it as meaningless, noting that a similar declaration of Bashir's a year earlier had come to nothing. Meanwhile, some observers expected the International Criminal Court to indict Bashir and issue a warrant for his arrest around the beginning of 2009.

## Sources

### Periodicals

*Christian Science Monitor*, November 24, 2008.
*New York Times*, July 5, 1989; July 8, 1989; March 16, 1996; March 24, 1996; January 25, 2000; May 7, 2000; December 14, 2000; February 13, 2001; July 3, 2002; December 18, 2002; October 24, 2006; December 4, 2007; December 28, 2007; July 15, 2008; July 24, 2008; July 28, 2008; August 26, 2008; September 30, 2008.

*Scotsman* (Edinburgh, Scotland), July 15, 2008.
*Time*, April 25, 2007.
*Times* (London, England), November 13, 2008.

**Online**

"Country Profile: Sudan," BBC News, http://news.bbc.co.uk/1/hi/world/middle_east/country_profiles/820864.stm (November 9, 2008).

"Factbox: Sudan's President Omar Hassan al-Bashir," Reuters, http://www.reuters.com/article/topNews/idUSL10655271.tif20080511.tif (November 23, 2008).

"Profile: Sudan's President Bashir," BBC News, http://news.bbc.co.uk/2/hi/africa/3273569.stm (November 24, 2008).

*—Erick Trickey*

# Karen Bass

**Speaker of the California Assembly**

*Kevin Winter/Getty Images*

**B**orn on October 3, 1953, in Los Angeles, CA; daughter of DeWitt (a postal worker) and Wilhelmina (a hair salon owner) Bass; divorced; children: Emilia Wright (died 2006), four stepchildren. *Education:* California State University-Dominguez Hills, BS; University of Southern California School of Medicine, physician assistant certificate.

**Addresses:** *Home*—Los Angeles, CA. *Office*—California Assembly District 47, 5750 Wilshire Blvd., Ste. 565, Los Angeles, CA 90036.

## Career

**L**os Angeles County/University of Southern California Medical Center, physician assistant practitioner and clinical instructor, 1980s; Community Coalition, founder, early 1990s; elected to the California State Assembly from the 47th District, 2004, elected Speaker of the Assembly, 2008.

**Member:** African American Leadership Council for the Obama Campaign; chair, California African Americans for Obama.

## Sidelights

**A**ctivist and politician Karen Bass made history in 2008 when she became the first African-American woman in U.S. history to serve as the speaker of a state legislature. Elected through a unanimous voice vote to be the 67th speaker of the California Assembly, the Democrat is known for her

work ethic and for her efforts to work with both Democrats and Republicans. Given the economic crisis in the United States and particularly in California, Bass was anticipated to face many challenges during her three-year tenure as Speaker, but she accepted the position with graciousness and hope. "Thank you so much for your vote of faith and confidence in me as your next speaker," she said in response to the vote, recorded in an article in *Jet* magazine. "I am deeply honored and deeply humbled by the trust you have placed in me. I will work to be worthy of that trust every day I am speaker."

The daughter of a postal worker and a hair salon owner, Bass was born in 1953 in Los Angeles, where she grew up in the Venice/Fairfax neighborhood. Early on, she was encouraged to care about political activism. Unable to sign up on her own to be a precinct captain for Robert F. Kennedy's presidential campaign, she signed her mother up for the position then took on all the work herself. "When Kennedy and Martin Luther King were assassinated it was devastating in my life," she recalled in *State Legislatures.* Her father also shaped her early political views. "He was the one who introduced me to politics, watching the civil rights movement on the nightly news and trying to help me understand the concept of legal segregation in the South where he was from—he instilled in me the passion to fight for justice and equality," she recalled in her first speech as California Speaker of the House.

She studied health sciences at California State University, where she was also active in the anti-war movement. After completing her physician-assistant training at the University of Southern California School of Medicine, she practiced and was a clinical instructor at one of the busiest trauma centers in the United States. There, she saw how drug use was tearing apart inner-city black communities. The emergency room staff treated many cases of drug overdoses and wounded victims of drug-related violent crime. "Back then, the prevailing view was to throw the book at anyone having to do with drug trafficking," Bass said in *Los Angeles Business Journal*. But Bass was convinced that the issue was not drugs, but public health. "I wanted to see if I could shift the policy agenda away from law enforcement toward a public health and economic response," she is quoted as saying in *State Legislatures*. "I thought it was a health and economic issue."

Proclaiming the goals of creating job opportunities and offering better education to inner-city residents who, without other options, would turn to drug dealing, Bass formed Community Coalition, a non-profit group that involved middle school students in community based projects. The Coalition also tried to improve police-community relations and fought for better zoning laws, so that abandoned homes, lots, and other havens for drug dealers would be carefully monitored. Because liquor stores were a large part of the problem, the Coalition tried to limit the number that could be opened in an area, and after the 1992 Los Angeles riots, Bass fought to keep many of the damaged liquor stores from reopening.

The focus on liquor stores brought other problems: Most of the liquor stores were owned and operated by Korean-Americans, and tensions between the Korean-American and African-American communities in Los Angeles were high. According to Bong-Hwan Kim, who became the manager of Neighborhood Empowerment for the city of Los Angeles and who worked with Bass in the early 1990s, Bass did everything she could to keep the peace and work with leaders from both communities. "We tried to work to redirect the racial divide and demonstrate to people that it was not so much about race as it was an economic issue," Kim is quoted as saying in *State Legislatures*. "I found Karen to be very committed, smart, a good listener, very hardworking." During the riots, more than 200 liquor stores were burned down, and due to the Coalition's efforts,

only 50 of those reopened. Forty-four other businesses moved into those areas to replace them. The efforts were reflected by a downturn in crime in the areas where the liquor stores did not rebuild.

Bass and the Community Coalition also took on legislation that changed the Aid to Families with Dependent Children program, changing it to Temporary Assistance for Needy Families (TANF). A program that had previously provided unlimited care to families now had restrictions: Recipients either had to find a job or be enrolled in a job-training program to be enrolled for benefits. In addition, a time limit was placed on the program: Families on TANF could only receive benefits for five years. Bass and other community activists protested these changes, noting that many families depended on the meager aid checks and food stamps, particularly in urban communities such as Los Angeles. Because the federal bill for TANF allowed individual states to revise the five-year limit, Bass and others launched a campaign to allow extensions on that limit to recipients who showed a good faith effort to get a job during their five-year period.

One of Bass's other passions evolved as she fought against illegal narcotics in the city of Los Angeles. Because the crack epidemic affected both men and women, who became addicted equally, families were fragmented, and the need for foster families increased dramatically. Bass worked to ensure that grandparents who took in their grandchildren received the same compensation that foster families would receive, helping more extended families to stay together. Bass also tried to improve the transition that 18 year olds went through in leaving their foster families, hoping to decrease the number of those former foster children who end up homeless or in prison.

Foster care was still on her mind when she made the decision to run for political office. Originally intending to run for Los Angeles city council, Bass was convinced to run for State Assembly by Antonio Villaraigosa, a Los Angeles city councilman who went on to become mayor. Though she wanted to continue to work at a local level, Villaraigosa and Assemblyman Mark Ridley-Thomas pointed out to Bass that there were no African-American women in the legislature at that time. It made her realize her "voice was really needed up there," she was quoted as saying in the *Los Angeles Business Journal*. Bass defeated a former city council member in the 2004 primaries, and when she was elected in 2005, she became the state's only female African-American legislator. She took her causes to Sacramento, where she represented approximately 423,000 residents in a district that includes Culver City, West Los Angeles, Westwood, Cheviot Hills, Leimert Park, Baldwin Hills, Windsor Hills, Ladera Heights, the Crenshaw District, Little Ethiopia, and portions of Korea Town and South Los Angeles. She was quickly chosen by Assembly Speaker Fabian Núñez to serve as majority whip, the task of which was to ensure that Democrats held a unified front on priority issues. But while making sure that Democrats agreed, Bass reached across the aisle to Republicans, teaming up with Assemblyman Bill Maze, a conservative from the Central Valley of California. Maze agreed with Bass's focus on the foster care system and endorsed her efforts to find $300 to $500 million in additional funding.

Bass, who also supported an initiative by Maze to bring California State University professors into community colleges to teach, was surprised at the lack of partisan rancor she found in the California Assembly. "I've been surprised and excited at some of the legislation from Republican lawmakers and have found myself working with some of them much more than I expected," Bass was quoted as saying in the *Los Angeles Business Journal* interview.

During the 2007-2008 legislative season, Núñez named Bass the majority floor leader. Because of her former position as majority whip and her inclusion in the team of ten assembly members surrounding the Speaker, she was a front runner in the competition to become the next Speaker when Núñez's term ended. In California, the Speaker of the Assembly is second only to the governor in political importance and influence. Núñez nominated Bass to succeed him, and the Assembly voted her into the position in February of 2008. From February through May, she worked closely with Núñez to prepare for her new position, which would include guiding bills through the legislative process and assigning assembly members to committees. In one of her earliest appointments, she showed her continued commitment to building a team that would work together despite political rivalry or party conflicts: She appointed Assemblyman Alberto Torrico, one of her chief rivals, as the majority floor leader.

Despite her lofty position, Bass continued to believe that people can have a huge impact on the local level. "Change is best defined by the people who are most impacted," she was quoted as having said in *Essence*. She has made it clear that she hopes to work with grassroots activists throughout her term. Bass also plans to work closely with Governor Arnold Schwarzenegger to end the state's budget deficits. Her goals for her three-year term also include continuing her efforts to gain further funding

for foster care and initiating conversation about tax reform and pushing for a tax increase. She acknowledged in *State Legislatures* that the budget issues facing the state would make her job difficult. "In the best of all worlds, it would be wonderful to be speaker back in the days when we had tons of money and could build colleges and roads and do all of that. But I am very motivated in a crisis. I'm motivated to step up. I'm motivated to attempt to build the type of coalitions that I've been building pretty much all my life. If ever there was a place that needed a coalition, it is this place."

Many Assembly members celebrated Bass's appointment, including Republican Maze. "She's developed some pretty good relationships with members across the aisle," he told *State Legislatures*. "She just has a whole different style of addressing people, how she treats individuals. She's respectful. She listens. When you are in a conversation she pays attention to what individuals are saying." Others who have followed Bass's career over the years noted that her leadership style is one of delegating and empowering others, bringing people together to work on a common goal.

On the Karen Bass, Speaker of the Assembly Web site, Bass presented her vision for the Assembly's future. Painting an image of working together and focusing on helping people who most need it, Bass offered her mission for leadership in a "just, responsible, and prosperous state that its people deserve." She expressed her faith in the Assembly's potential in her first speech as Speaker: "If we could only harness the power of our common humanity, I don't think there's anything we couldn't do for the people of this state."

## Sources

### Periodicals

*Essence*, August 2008, p. 92.
*Jet*, March 24, 2008, p. 16; June 2, 2008, p. 30.
*Los Angeles Business Journal*, April 18, 2005, p. 24.
*State Legislatures*, July-August 2008, p. 24.

### Online

California State Assembly, http://www.assembly.ca.gov/acs/makebio.asp?district=47 (February 13, 2009).
Karen Bass, Speaker of the Assembly, http://democrats.assembly.ca.gov/speaker/ (February 13, 2009).

—*Alana Joli Abbott*

# Pamela Baxter

**Chief Executive Officer of LVMH Moët Hennessy Louis Vuitton Perfumes & Cosmetics, North America**

---

**B**orn Pamela Kathryn Lohman, February 14, 1949, in Pawhuska, OK; daughter of William Desmond and Gloria Mae (maiden name, Young) Lohman; married Barry Richard Baxter, August 17, 1968 (divorced, 1971); married John; children: Shannon Richard (son). *Education:* Attended the University of South Dakota; University of California—Los Angeles, B.A.

**Addresses:** *Office*—LVMH Moët Hennessy Louis Vuitton Perfumes & Cosmetics—North America, 19 E. 57th St., New York, NY 10022.

## Career

**S**pecial representative, Charles of the Ritz, 1973-77; account executive, Princess Marcella Borghese, 1977-80; regional marketing director, Aramis, Inc., 1980; vice president and West Coast regional marketing director, Aramis U.S.A., 1984-94, then vice president and national sales manager, 1994-97; vice president for marketing at Estée Lauder Companies, 1992; general manager, Aramis and Tommy Hilfiger, 1997-2001; president, Estée Lauder Specialty Brands Group, May 2001-September 2003; president and chief executive officer, LVMH Moët Hennessy Louis Vuitton Perfumes & Cosmetics, North America, January 2004—.

**Awards:** Beautiful Apple Award, March of Dimes, 2007.

## Sidelights

**P**amela Baxter runs the North American operations of LVMH Moët Hennessy Louis Vuitton Perfumes and Cosmetics, which includes some of the oldest and most prestigious French fragrance brands as well as makeup lines like BeneFit and Dior. Baxter became president and chief executive officer of this division of the luxury conglomerate in 2003 after 22 years with Estée Lauder, the skin-care, cosmetics, and fragrance giant.

Baxter was born in 1949 in Pawhuska, a small town in Oklahoma's Osage County. She attended the University of South Dakota and married in 1968. Three years later, her marriage ended, and she went on to earn an undergraduate degree in business administration from the University of California at Los Angeles. She began her career in the fragrance and cosmetics industry in 1973 as a special representative at Charles of the Ritz, the maker of the namesake scent as well as lines like Jean Naté and Enjoli. In 1977 she moved on to a job as account executive with Princess Marcella Borghese, a division of cosmetics giant Revlon that at the time was one of the most prestigious cosmetics and skin-care lines sold at U.S. department-store counters.

Borghese was created to compete with the Estée Lauder brands, a New York-based company whose top-selling products included the Re-Nutriv, a skin moisturizer, and Youth Dew, a bath oil that evolved into an entire line of women's fragrances. The Lauder company expanded into men's scents and grooming products in 1964 with their new brand Aramis, and in 1980 Baxter went to work for Aramis as a regional marketing director. She became its West Coast regional marketing director in 1984 as well as a company vice president. After moving to New York City, she was made a vice president and national sales manager at Estée Lauder in 1992, and oversaw the launch of the fragrance Tuscany per Donna in 1994.

A year later, Baxter was put in charge of Crème de la Mer, a fantastically expensive skin potion made from seaweed extract acquired by the Lauder Companies. By this point Baxter was becoming an expert on licensing deals, and was given the task of working with American sportswear designer Tommy Hilfiger to launch a fragrance line. The result was "Tommy," introduced in 1995, which proved such a success that the line was expanded into several different scents. One of the decisions that Baxter made at this juncture of her career was expensive but precedent-setting: Tommy Girl was launched in 1996 with a "z-fold" magazine cover, or a foldout front cover that has become commonplace in magazines like *Vogue* and *Vanity Fair.*

In 2001, Baxter was promoted to president of Estée Lauder Specialty Brands Group, which included the cosmetics company Prescriptives, the Jo Malone fragrance line, and Kate Spade fragrances. She spent two years on the job before moving over to a major competitor, LVMH Moët Hennessy Louis Vuitton, the French luxury-goods conglomerate, which created the post of president and chief executive officer of LVMH Moët Hennessy Louis Vuitton Perfumes & Cosmetics for North America just for her.

The creation of French dealmaker Bernard Arnault, LVMH is a vast company that dominates the luxury-goods and designer-fashion markets. LVMH is either a licensee, or manufacturer plus marketer, of such venerable products as Moët et Chandon champagne, Hennessy cognac, namesake leather-goods maker Louis Vuitton, watchmaker TAG Heuer, and designer-clothing lines ranging from Marc Jacobs to Fendi. It also owns the cosmetics retailer Sephora and several fragrance brands, including Givenchy, Guerlain, and Parfums Christian Dior.

Baxter oversees those three fragrance and cosmetics lines as well as dozens of others, such as BeneFit and Acqua di Parma. The marketing campaigns for such classics as Dior's Poison, Very Irrésistable Givenchy, and Guerlain Homme are all run under her supervision, including the recruiting of celebrity spokespersons for the brands. These include film stars Charlize Theron, Sharon Stone, Liv Tyler, and Hilary Swank.

One of the most significant events under Baxter's tenure at LVMH was the phasing out of the "gift with purchase" sales strategy at Dior. First pioneered by Estée Lauder herself, the incentive had become commonplace in the department-store cosmetics industry for brands like Clinique and Lancôme. "It took us 24 months to achieve that, but it has been well worth it, and we've had no resistance from stores," Baxter told *WWD*'s Julie Naughton. "A gift-with-purchase customer isn't loyal to a brand. She buys the minimum she needs to get her gift, and lives for the next brand's gift-with-purchase. We decided to spend those dollars on a national makeup artist team and events. With a team, you build a customer base that comes back."

Remarried and a grandmother, Baxter is active in fund-raising efforts for the American Cancer Society and the March of Dimes. The latter charity honored her with its Beautiful Apple Award in 2007 for her efforts on behalf of the organization, which works to prevent birth defects. Baxter said at the event that when she was a little girl in the 1950s, she had a younger brother who died after being born prematurely. "After that," *WWD*'s Naughton quoted her as saying, "any time my mother and I would pass a March of Dimes fund-raising can, she would give me extra change to put in it."

# Sources

### Periodicals

*New York Times*, January 22, 2006.
*WWD*, February 27, 2007, p. 32B; March 9, 2007, p. 10.

### Online

"Pamela Baxter," March of Dimes—New York Chapter, http://www.marchofdimes.com/newyork/6649_22652.asp (April 22, 2009).

—*Carol Brennan*

# Beyonce

## Singer and actress

**B**orn Beyonce Giselle Knowles, September 4, 1981, in Houston, TX; daughter of Mathew (a salesman and music manager) and Tina (a hair dresser, salon owner, stylist, and designer) Knowles; married Sean Corey Carter (known professionally as Jay-Z, a rap artist), April 4, 2008.

**Addresses:** *Office*—c/o 1505 Hadley, Houston, TX 77002. *Web site*—http://www.beyonceonline.com.

## Career

**M**ember of Girls Tyme (a dancing and singing group), c. 1989-c. early 1990s; member of Destiny's Child (an R&B singing group), 1997-2005; released first album, *Destiny's Child,* 1998; became spokesperson for L'Oreal cosmetics, 2001, and for Pepsi, 2002; launched solo singing career, 2003; launched (with Tina Knowles) the House of Deréon (a fashion line), 2005; toured in support of album *B'Day,* 2007. Actress in films, including: *Austin Powers in Goldmember,* 2002; *I Know,* 2003; *The Fighting Temptations,* 2003; *The Pink Panther,* 2006; *Dreamgirls,* 2006; *The Beyonce Experience,* 2007; *Cadillac Records,* 2008. Executive producer of films, including: *Cadillac Records,* 2008. Television appearances include: *Smart Guy,* 1998; *The Famous Jett Jackson,* Disney, 2000; *Destiny's Child Live* (special), 2001; *Intimate Portrait: Destiny's Child* (special), Lifetime, 2001; *Carmen: A Hip Hopera* (movie), MTV, 2001; *Saturday Night Live,* NBC, 2001, 2002, 2003, 2004, 2008; *The Beyonce Experience Live* (special), 2007. Worked as television producer on *The Beyonce Experience Live* (special), 2007.

**Awards:** Grammy Award (with others), for best R&B song, Recording Academy, for "Say My Name," 2000; Grammy Award (with Destiny's Child) for best R&B performance by a duo or group with vocal, Recording Academy, for "Say My Name," 2000; Grammy Award (with Destiny's Child) for best R&B performance by a duo or group with vocal, for "Survivor," 2001; Sammy Davis, Jr. Award for entertainer of the year (with Destiny's Child), Soul Train Music Awards, 2000; named pop songwriter of the year, ASCAP (American Society of Composers, Authors, and Publishers), 2001; ASCAP Film and Television Music Award (with Samuel J. Barnes) for most performed songs from motion pictures, for "Independent Woman Part 1" from *Charlie's Angels,* 2002; Grammy Award for best female R&B vocal performance, for "Dangerously in Love," 2003; Grammy Award (with Luther Vandross) for best R&B performance by a duo or group with vocals, for "The Closer I Get to You," 2003; Grammy Award (with Jay-Z and Rich Harrison) for best R&B song, for "Crazy in Love," 2003; Grammy Award (with Jay-Z) for best rap/sung collaboration, for "Crazy in Love," 2003; Grammy Award (with Tony Maserati) for best contemporary R&B album, for *Dangerously in Love,* 2003; MTV Video Music Award for best female video, for *Naughty Girl,* 2004; American Music Award (with Destiny's Child) for favorite R&B album, for *Destiny Fulfilled,* 2004; Sammy Davis, Jr. Award for entertainer of the year, Soul Train Music Awards, 2004; BET (Black Entertainment Television) Award, best female R&B artist, 2004; Black Reel

Award (with Walter Williams, Sr.) for film: best song, for "He Still Moves Me," from *The Fighting Temptations*, 2004; NRJ Radio Award for best international female artist, 2004; Brit Award for best international female solo artist, British Phonographic Industry, 2004; Grammy Award (with Stevie Wonder) for best R&B performance by a duo or group with vocals, for "So Amazing," 2005; American Music Award (with Destiny's Child) for favorite R&B album, *Destiny's Child*, 2005; Grammy Award (with Jason Goldstein and Jim Caruana) for best contemporary R&B album, for *B'Day*, 2006; World Music Award for best-selling R&B artist, 2006; MTV Video Music Award (with Slim Thug and Bun B) for best R&B video, for *Check On It*, 2006; Star on Hollywood Hall of Fame (with Destiny's Child), 2006; BET Award for video of the year, for *Irreplaceable*, 2007; MTV Video Music Award (with Shakira) for best collaboration, for "Beautiful Liar," 2007; BET (Black Entertainment Television) Award, best female R&B artist, 2007; Gold Media Prize, BRAVO Supershow, 2007; Critics Choice Award for best song, Broadcast Film Critics Association, for "Listen" from *Dreamgirls*, 2007; Black Reel Award (with others) for best ensemble, for *Cadillac Records*, 2008.

## Sidelights

A singer, songwriter, producer, and actress, Beyonce found fame first as a member of the popular R&B singing group Destiny's Child before launching her own successful solo career with a R&B pop sound. In the early 2000s, she took on new challenges when she began acting regularly on television and in films, most notably in 2002's *Austin Powers in Gold Member* and 2006's *Dreamgirls*. Of Beyonce, singer Tamia told Keith Spera of the New Orleans *Times-Picayune*, "She is one of the hardest-working women in the business. I'm sure she's sacrificed a lot to get to where she is and put in a lot of hard work. It isn't a fluke that she is where she is."

Born on September 4, 1981, in Houston, Texas, Beyonce is the daughter of Mathew Knowles and his wife, Tina. Her father was a successful salesman who sold life insurance, telephone equipment, postage meters, Xerox machines, and expensive hospital equipment over the years. Her mother was a hairdresser who owned her own hair salon, Headliners. Both her parents had been singers in groups in their youth. While Beyonce was a shy child, she enjoyed dancing and took dance classes. She soon showed talent as a singer, winning her school's talent show in 1989 then a city-wide talent show soon after. Entering and winning more contests, Beyonce was determined to have a singing career.

When she was still in elementary school, Beyonce was asked to be the lead singer of Girls Tyme, an all-girls dancing and singing act, which included girls who would later become members of Destiny's Child. Girls Tyme did both dancing and singing of pop and R&B numbers at schools and talent shows. By 1990, Girls Tyme was being managed by Andretta Tillman, who further trained the girls, both by educating them with tapes of the Jackson 5 and the Supremes as well as having them extensively critique their own performances. In 1992, the group made it all the way to the finals of *Star Search* before losing. By this time, Mathew Knowles took control of the group, first as co-manager and eventually replacing Tillman.

Inspired by the way Berry Gordy ran Motown, Mathew Knowles educated himself about artist management and trained the girls about how to sing, dance, create harmonies, present themselves, model, and do interviews. Eventually the seven members of Girls Tyme was trimmed down to the four original members of what soon became known as Destiny's Child: Beyonce, Kelly Rowland, LaTavia Roberson, and LeToya Luckett. Beyonce explained that her father helped them prepare for the demands of live performance in unusual ways. In 2004, she told the *Times-Picayune*'s Spera, "I don't use backing tapes. I've been dancing and singing (simultaneously) since I was 9. When we were younger, my dad would have us jogging and singing in harmony. We were able to do cartwheels and sing. Back then, I hated him for that and I thought it was really mean; it was pretty harsh. But now I'm very happy. It's definitely come in handy."

Mathew Knowles eventually quit his sales job to devote himself to managing the group full time through his Music World Management Company. In the mid-1990s, he was attracting interest from record labels for the act, but a 1995 deal with Elektra Records fell through. Despite such setbacks, he believed in the group and his ability to sell them. In 1997, the group finally landed a record deal with Columbia. With his guidance, Girls Tyme went through several name changes, including Somethin' Fresh and Cliché, before settling on Destiny's Child soon after signing with Columbia.

The newly named Destiny's Child released its self-titled debut album in 1998. Beyonce herself contributed songs to the record, both as a writer or co-writer and as a co-producer, as she would continue to do throughout her singing career. The group had a hit with "No, No, No Part 2," featuring Wyclef Jean, and the album sold more than a half million copies. The foursome released another smash album, *The Writing's On the Wall*, in July 1999 to which Beyonce contributed more songs. Destiny's Child had a hit single off the album with "Bills, Bills, Bills," released in June of 1999.

With the video of the second single from *The Writing's On the Wall*—"Say My Name"—a line-up change was announced. Roberson and Luckett were out, replaced by Michelle Williams and Farrah Franklin. Destiny's Child made the official announcement a short time later, citing creative differences but rumored to be related to the way that Beyonce was often put in the spotlight. (Roberson and Luckett eventually sued Mathew Knowles over the issue.) It was not the only line-up change. Five months later, Franklin was let go, leaving Destiny's Child as a trio. Despite the chaos, *The Writing's On the Wall* sold more than ten million copies and won the group a number of awards, including several Grammy Awards.

Because of the line-up changes, Beyonce and her parents were accused of management misdeeds and favoring the interests of Beyonce over the group's other members. Williams disagreed, telling Margena A. Christian of *Jet*, "The group is not what people think it is. Beyonce and Kelly are not what people think. They say Kelly is just riding the coattail of Beyonce and Beyonce is hogging everything. Beyonce has a God-given talent. It's just plain. It's not about her father managing the group. She's a great writer and producer. Kelly has a wonderful spirit and a beautiful voice. We're just ordinary people. We have feelings too, and it hurts when people say things about us. Why don't they step in our shoes?"

While Destiny's Child stirred up such controversies, it was a trendsetter for other female groups. In the same *Jet* interview, Williams claimed that they were the first to "do that fast, 'rapping singing'" with their single "No, No, No" and that other groups were copying the fast singing style. Destiny's Child also began affecting culture in other ways by both appearing in commercials and by modeling. In addition, as Diane Caldwell noted in the *New York Times,* they had a powerful created persona. Caldwell wrote, "The mythology of Destiny's Child is that they are strong, independent women in control of their lives, and it is saturated with a kind of sisters-doing-it-for-each-other positivity. They are partners, and their wealth and attention are shared equally."

As Destiny's Child was at a peak of fame, the trio insisted that despite such line-up changes the group was not breaking up any time soon. However, each member, including Beyonce, was also negotiating solo recording deals during this time. It was also acknowledged that Beyonce attracted the most attention of any member of the group, with some believing the group was intended to be little more than a launching pad for Beyonce's solo career. Beyonce also began taking her acting career more seriously, first with a role in the 2001 MTV movie *Carmen: A Hip Hopera,* an updated version of the film *Carmen Jones,* which was itself based on the opera *Carmen.* Destiny's Child released one more album—2001's *Survivor,* which sold almost four million copies and featured songs primarily written and produced by Beyonce, and then the group members stated they would focus on their solo careers for a time.

Over the next few years, Beyonce worked on a number of projects outside Destiny's Child. In addition to signing on as the spokesperson for Pepsi and L'Oreal cosmetics, she made her film debut in the comedy *Austin Powers in Goldmember* in 2002. Talking about the film in the *St. Petersburg Times,* Gina Vivinetto commented, "In *Austin Powers in Goldmember,* Beyonce was a highlight as Foxxy Cleopatra, a spoof on female blaxplotation characters from the 1970s. Did it help that she broke into song? You bet."

Beyonce went on to appear in two more films in 2003, *I Know* and *The Fighting Temptations.* The latter depicted a church choir about to enter a competition. Beyonce played Lilly, a church outcast with a beautiful voice who is convinced to come back and give the choir a chance to win. Beyonce enjoyed playing the role, especially its many non-singing moments. She told Marion Ross of the Sydney, Australia *Daily Telegraph,* "The overall theme and the feeling of it was really pure and uplifting and I was able to show a little more of my range."

In early 2003, Beyonce also released her first solo album, *Dangerously in Love.* She co-wrote 15 of the 16 songs on the album and co-produced it with her father. The album showed the depth of her artistry, including R&B, party tracks, rock-influenced guitars, soul and jazz-influenced slow songs, and '80s-sounding ballads. The London *Times* critic, Lisa Verrico, especially praised "Crazy in Love" as "a fabulous, funky R&B number with daring production of the Missy/Timbaland type and a slinky vocal from Beyonce." Verrico also lauded "Hip Hop Star," calling it "[t]he highlight by a mile."

*Dangerously in Love* produced at least three hit singles, including "Crazy in Love," which was number one for eight weeks in the United States alone and helped define Beyonce as a solo artist. The album also won five Grammy Awards and sold at least seven million copies. Of her success in 2003, Beyonce told Cameron Adams of the *Advertiser,* "It's crazy. I definitely feel like I've gone to another level, personally and also as an entertainer, a vocalist and songwriter, and my celebrity has gone up. That's something I didn't think about and didn't expect to happen."

After touring in support of *Dangerously in Love* on the Ladies First tour with Alicia Keys and Missy Elliott, Beyonce went back to Destiny's Child. The fact is Williams, Rowland, and Beyonce were not done with the group yet. Beyonce told the *Times-Picayune*'s Spera, "Everyone's been successful individually. We'll be one of the first female group to come back together after all that.... We've all grown so much. I've learned a lot over the past years, and so has Michelle and so has Kelly. We're all stronger, so it will make the group stronger." Destiny's Child reunited in 2004 to record what would be their last original record, *Destiny Fulfilled.* The album received mixed reviews with "Lose My Breath" becoming a minor hit single.

Though Destiny's Child officially disbanded on friendly terms after a tour in 2005, Beyonce did not slow down. She recorded a fierce, more mature second solo album released in 2006, *B'day*, which went double platinum. Beyonce also had featured roles in two films, *The Pink Panther* and *Dreamgirls*. In the former, she plays a jewel thief suspect/pop star named Xania, and she contributed several songs to the soundtrack. In the latter, she plays a singer named Deena who grows into a Diana Ross-like diva. Beyonce also continued to grow her fashion line, House of Deréon, which she and her mother started in 2005.

After marrying long-time boyfriend, rapper Jay-Z, in 2008, Beyonce released her next solo album, *I Am … Sasha Fierce*. The first single, "Irreplaceable," was well-received, with Ann Powers in the *Los Angeles Times* commenting, "It's a powerful and complex view of sexual politics from an artist who's truly come into her own." Beyonce also had a lauded turn as Etta James in *Cadillac Records*, a film for which she also served as executive producer. James herself endorsed Beyonce's depiction of her in the film, which focuses on the evolution of artists linked to the influential Chess Records label.

While Beyonce continued her singing career as a solo artist, many of her ambitions focused on acting. She hoped to do a musical like *Chicago*, appear on Broadway, take a role in one film per year minimum, and win an Academy Award. In 2009 alone, Beyonce had at least one film lined up for release, the thriller *Obsessed*. Through it all, she had many admirers, including *Dreamgirls* co-star Jamie Foxx, who told Cindy Pearlman of the *Chicago Sun Times*, "What can I say about Beyonce? Hey, we know she has one of the most gifted voices in the world. She's gorgeous. She's nice. Now, you'll see her act and the whole package will come together. I just can't say enough about the girl. She's a superstar."

## Selected discography

(With Destiny's Child) *Destiny's Child*, Columbia, 1998.
(With Destiny's Child) *The Writing's On the Wall*, Columbia, 1999.
(With Destiny's Child) *8 Days of Christmas*, Columbia, 2001.
(With Destiny's Child) *Survivor*, Columbia, 2001.
*Dangerously in Love*, Columbia, 2003.
(With Destiny's Child) *Destiny Fulfilled*, Columbia, 2004.
(With Destiny's Child) *#1's*, Columbia, 2005.
*B'day*, Columbia, 2006.
*I Am … Sasha Fierce*, Columbia, 2008.

## Sources

### Books

*Complete Marquis Who's Who Biographies*, Marquis Who's Who, 2008.

### Periodicals

*Advertiser* (Australia), December 13, 2003, p. W03.
Associated Press, December 18, 2002.
*Boston Globe*, August 5, 2007, p. N1.
*Chicago Sun Times*, February 5, 2006, p. D4.
*Daily Telegraph* (Sydney, Australia), March 4, 2004, p. T09.
*Jet*, May 14, 2001, p. 56; February 13, 2006, p. 60.
*Los Angeles Times*, October 10, 2008, p. E17; November 13, 2008, p. E1; November 16, 2008, p. F1.
*New York Times*, September 9, 2001, sec. 6, p. 110; November 14, 2004, sec. 2, p. 35.
*Press Enterprise* (Riverside, CA), December 4, 2008, p. D1.
*St. Petersburg Times* (FL), October 2, 2003, p. 1D.
*Sunday Telegram* (MA), September 17, 2006, p. G4.
*Texas Monthly*, April 2004, p. 112.
*Times* (London), June 20, 2003, p. 18.
*Times-Picayune* (New Orleans, LA), March 12, 2004, p. 23.
*Vanity Fair*, November 2005, p. 336.
*Washington Post*, September 9, 2006, p. C1.

**Online**

"Beyonce Knowles," Internet Movie Database, http://www.imdb.com/name/nm0461498/ (January 20, 2009).

"Grammy Award Winners," Grammy.com, http://www.grammy.com/GRAMMY_Awards/Winners/Results.aspx (January 20, 2009).

*—A. Petruso*

# Jessica Bibliowicz

## Chief Executive Officer of National Financial Partners

**B**orn in 1959, in New York; daughter of Sanford I. (a financial-services executive) and Joan (Mosher) Weill; married Natan Bibliowicz (an architect), 1982; children: two sons. *Education:* Cornell University, A.B., 1981.

**Addresses:** *Home*—Westchester, NY. *Office*—National Financial Partners, 340 Madison Ave., 19th Fl., New York, NY 10173.

## Career

**A**ssociate in credit-card division, American Express, Inc., 1981-82; first vice president, Shearson Lehman Brothers, Inc., 1982-1990; director of asset management, Salomon Brothers, 1990-91; director of sales and marketing, Prudential Mutual Funds, Inc., 1991-94; executive vice president for mutual fund sales and marketing, Smith Barney Shearson, Inc., 1994-97; president and chief operating officer, John A. Levin & Company, 1997-99; president and chief executive officer, National Financial Partners, 1999—, chairman of the board of directors, 2003—.

## Sidelights

**J**essica Bibliowicz is the daughter of Sanford "Sandy" I. Weill, a Wall Street titan who rose from cold-calling at a brokerage house to running Citigroup, Inc., one of the world's largest consumer-banking and wealth-management companies. Bibliowicz once worked for her father, but through the late 1990s and into the early 2000s, she prospered on her own merit as head of National Financial Partners, a financial-services firm that she took public in an impressively short period of time. She admits that she does sometimes seek out her father's advice, telling *Crain's New York Business* writer Anna Robaton, "You always learn from a guy like that."

The second child and only daughter in the family, Bibliowicz was born in 1959 to Sandy and Joan Weill, who had been married four years by then and were living in an apartment in East Rockaway, New York. At the time, her father was a broker with Burnham & Company, persuading clients with assets to invest to sign on with the firm and its brokerage services. Weill was a native of Bensonhurst, in the New York City borough of Brooklyn, and came from rather humble circumstances, which was an early source of conflict with his wife's more affluent family.

In 1960 Weill became one of the founding partners of Carter, Berlind, Potoma & Weill, a securities brokerage firm that underwent various name changes over the years; by 1968 it was known as Cogan, Berlind, Weill & Levitt, and Weill was chairman of the company and earning a handsome salary. In 1970, he moved his family into an affluent Manhattan apartment building, but as Weill admitted in *The Real Deal: My Life in Business and Philanthropy*, his 2006 autobiography, "life became exceptionally stressful … my temper flared regularly both at home and at work. I asked my family to make plenty of sacrifices even if I refused to acknowledge these at the time." A few years later, Weill was forced to sell the family's luxury apartment during one of Wall Street's periodic downturns, and the family lived in a hotel for a time before settling into more modest quarters on 79th Street. They also bought a second home in Greenwich, Connecticut.

The Weill fortune increased considerably after Bibliowicz's father put together a lucrative deal with Shearson Hamill, another brokerage firm, and by the early 1980s his firm was called Shearson Loeb Rhoades and was just behind Merrill Lynch in size in the securities brokerage field. Intrigued by the business, Bibliowicz worked summers during her teens as a file clerk at her father's company, though women in non-clerical positions anywhere on Wall Street were few and far between at the time. "I had a fourth-grade teacher who said to me, 'You're not very good at math but don't worry about it. You won't need it,'" Bibliowicz recalled in an *Executive Female* roundtable discussion.

Bibliowicz went on to her father's alma mater, Cornell University in Ithaca, New York, and earned her degree in government—the same major as his—in 1981. Her first job out of school was with American Express, which had bought her father's company in 1981 in a deal that enriched the Weill fortune significantly. She quit the credit-card company a year later when she wed Natan Bibliowicz, a former classmate from Cornell and now an architect, but she returned to work at Shearson Lehman Brothers, Inc., in its asset management division, where she spent nearly a decade. Her father's career, meanwhile, had slumped after the sale to American Express: He had been given an office, but had no real duties. "For the first time in their lives," Weill wrote in his autobiography about Bibliowicz and her brother Marc, "they could see my vulnerable side and felt a measure of equality, which allowed us to relate to one another on a new level. For instance, Jessica joked, 'I guess I'm going to have to buy your cigars now since I have a job and you don't!'"

In 1990, Shearson Lehman's asset management department was sold to Salomon Brothers, and Bibliowicz remained with her title of first vice president but felt increasing pressure to resign because of internal politics. She went on to Prudential Mutual Funds, Inc., as director of sales and marketing in 1991, but for much of this period of her career, she

was known more as Sandy Weill's daughter—and, with that, the rich roster of job leads and investment clients that her family connections yielded—than for her own achievements. In the interim, her father had regained his reputation on Wall Street after brokering several notable deals, even buying back Shearson Lehman from American Express in 1993. A year later, he offered Bibliowicz a job at the newly created Smith Barney Shearson as an executive vice president. "I was in agony over the decision," she recalled in an interview with Jacqueline S. Gold in *American Banker*. "There are so many politics in an organization to begin with, then you throw in being the CEO's daughter on top of it."

Bibliowicz proved herself, however, in running Smith Barney Shearson's mutual funds sales and marketing divisions, plus the marketing efforts for its line of insurance and annuity products. Her father tried to remain out of her way as much as possible, and both avoided discussing internal corporate drama in their private time together. He remained unabashedly proud of her, however, and once took to the podium after she gave a speech at a major brokers' meeting to praise her presentation and point out to the audience that she had given it "without the benefit of any notes," he said, according to the *Wall Street Journal*. "I slid under the table" in embarrassment, Bibliowicz recalled in the same article.

Some predicted Bibliowicz was on the fast track to the president's office, but her abrupt resignation in 1997 caused a bit of a stir on Wall Street. Insiders, wrote Tunku Varadarajan in the *Times* of London were "gripped by a family saga of soap-opera proportions. Why, everyone is asking, did Jessica Bibliowicz leave her father's broking house to work for someone else?" Some believed there was a long rivalry with James "Jamie" Dimon, to whom her father had served as a mentor for many years. The Dimons lived near the Weills in Greenwich, and the two families had spent a great deal of time together when Bibliowicz and Jamie were growing up, even taking joint family vacations. Dimon—described by Varadarajan as "just as clever and ambitious as Ms. Bibliowicz"—was also thought to be a top contender for the president's office at Smith Barney. The mystery of her departure would be revealed a few years later. At the time, for a front-page *Wall Street Journal* story about her departure that appeared in July 1997, Bibliowicz would say only, "One of the things that's trickiest of being someone's daughter is the trust factor. And something that will make you uptight is if someone doesn't trust you."

After leaving Smith Barney, Bibliowicz took job with much smaller firm, John A. Levin & Company, as president and chief operating officer. She spent nearly two years at the money-management and investment-advice company before joining National Financial Partners (NFP) in the spring of 1999 as president and chief executive officer. NFP was also a financial services company and was on a steady growth curve through its acquisition of smaller money-management firms across the United States. NFP, explained Robert Julavits in *American Banker*, was "betting on a strategy of acquiring boutique financial firms but requiring them to operate independently, in brand and management."

Bibliowicz's role was to persuade as many owners of those 2,000 or so small estate-planning, investment, and insurance-service entities to join the NFP stable. "Bibliowicz courts firms by making an offer of cash and NFP stock up front," wrote Gold in *American Banker*. "She also pitches prospective sellers an economy of scale for accessing insurance and investment products, obtaining expansion capital, and plugging into back-office services without their independence being sacrificed. In return, companies that sell out give up a percentage of their income—typically as much as half."

Upon taking the NFP job, Bibliowicz announced a goal of five acquisitions per month on the path to an eventual initial public offering (IPO) of NFP stock. On that day, the holders of that stock would then become rich overnight once NFP became a publicly traded company. In a four-year period, she signed up more than a hundred new companies, and NFP's income grew immensely as the stock market also went through another boom period. NFP became a publicly traded company on the New York Stock Exchange on September 18, 2003, and Bibliowicz rang the opening bell with her father at her side that morning. On its first day of trading, the stock reached a high of $23 per share, and the IPO raised $239 million in new capital.

In the meantime, Bibliowicz's father had presided over the merger in early 1998 of the Travelers Group, which he ran, with Citicorp, the financial services giant, to form the newly named Citigroup. Dimon, Bibliowicz's onetime rival at Smith Barney, was made president but was forced out several months later, causing some to speculate that Weill was still rankled over how Dimon had treated Bibliowicz when they clashed over Smith Barney's mutual-funds marketing strategy a year or two earlier. Weill wrote about the rift between his two protégés in his autobiography, *The Real Deal*, noting that once he involved himself in the debate, "I adopted a point of view that turned out to resemble Jessica's position.... the incident probably hurt my daughter politically as she faced off against Jamie and his cohorts.... [Dimon] openly criticized her financial analyses. The repeated criticisms soon became humiliating ... Jessica increasingly felt trapped in a situation in which she couldn't possibly succeed."

Bibliowicz's triumph in leading NFP to be a successful, publicly traded company proved to be the ultimate rebuke to her detractors. Though she had benefited over the years from her father's name and influence, "I realized that I needed to build something of my own," she told Gold in the *American Banker* interview. "Something that has lasting value in the industry, something that is good for the clients of our firm, something that brings value to the businesses we acquire and I can make people believe in me, believe in the vision of the company."

Between 1982 when Bibliowicz began her career on Wall Street and the early 2000s, some notable progress was made in gender equity. Many women like her rose to senior-executive ranks, and barriers to entry-level investment-analysis and trading positions no longer existed. Bibliowicz felt that Wall Street and the competitive world of high-stakes finance was ideally suited to her gender, telling Virginia Citrano, a journalist with *Crain's New York Business*, "Women like to see how they are doing, and Wall Street is very performance-driven." She said, "And look at who the clients are: The clients are women. They're inheriting wealth; they're making the money. I think Wall Street is a great place for women."

Bibliowicz lives in Westchester, New York, with her husband and their two sons. With the 2003 IPO of her company, Bibliowicz became a millionaire several times over, with *Barron's* estimating her holdings of NFP stock to be worth about $12 million the same month of the New York Stock Exchange debut. Perhaps her wealth was affected by the recession a few years later, but there is no denying she was very successful.

## Sources

### Books

Weill, Sandy, with Judah S. Kraushaar, *The Real Deal: My Life in Business and Philanthropy*, Warner Business Books, 2006.

### Periodicals

*American Banker*, February 23, 2001, p. 1; December 4, 2003, p. 10A.
*Barron's*, September 23, 2003, p. 40
*BusinessWeek*, July 21, 2003, p. 64..

*Crain's New York Business*, June 15, 1998, p. 17; September 27, 1999, p. 28.

*Executive Female*, January-February 1997, p. 53.

*New York Times*, November 3, 1998; September 19, 2003.

*Times* (London, England), June 18, 1997, p. 11.

*Wall Street Journal*, July 3, 1997, p. A1.

—*Carol Brennan*

# Usain Bolt

## Track and field athlete

**B**orn August 21, 1986, in Montego Bay, Jamaica. Son of Wellesley and Jennifer Bolt (grocery store owners).

**Addresses:** *Contact*—Jamaica Olympic Association, 9 Cunningham Ave., Kingston 6, Jamaica. *Home*—Kingston, Jamaica.

## Career

**B**egan running at William Knibb Memorial High School, Trelawny parish, Jamaica, c. 2000; captured his first world title in the 200 meters at the IAAF World Junior Championships, Kingston, Jamaica, 2002; eliminated in his first heat run at the Athens Olympics, 2004; earned three gold medals and set three world records at the Beijing Olympics, 2008.

**Awards:** First place, 200 meters, IAAF World Junior Championships, Kingston, Jamaica, 2002; first place, 200 meters, IAAF World Youth Championships, Sherbrooke, Quebec, Canada, 2003; first place, 200 meters, Carifta Games, Hamilton, Bermuda, 2004; first place, 200 meters, Central American and Caribbean Championships, Nassau, Bahamas, 2005; first place, 100 meters, Reebok Grand Prix, New York City, 2008; Olympic Games, gold medal, 100 meters, 200 meters and 4x100-meter relay, Beijing, China, 2008.

*Reuters/Michael Buholzer/Landov*

## Sidelights

**J**amaican sprinter Usain Bolt won three gold medals and set three world records at the 2008 Beijing Summer Olympics, emerging from the Games as the fastest man on earth. His sensational performance in the 100-meter dash left spectators both bewildered and awe-inspired. During the race, Bolt caused a stir with his on-field antics. Coming down the stretch with about 10 meters to go, Bolt was so far ahead of the other runners that he stopped racing, threw up his arms and smacked his chest in celebration as he glided across the finish line. Even though he did not race full-out, Bolt won gold and set a new world record of 9.69 seconds. He went on to win another gold in the 200-meter dash and a third as part of Jamaica's 4X100-meter relay team.

Running coach Stephen Francis, who works with Bolt's Jamaican rival Asafa Powell, told Lynn Zinser of the *New York Times* that Bolt is one of those rare humans with an extraordinary talent. "You have people who are exceptions. You have Einstein. You have Isaac Newton. You have Beethoven. You have Usain Bolt. It's not explainable how and what they do."

Bolt was born on August 21, 1986, in Montego Bay, Jamaica, to Wellesley and Jennifer Bolt, owners of a local grocery store. He grew up in rural Trelawny parish, which is located in the northwestern portion of Jamaica. The area is known for its yams and green bananas. Bolt's father has said these foods helped Bolt grow into a strong sprinter. A naturally gifted athlete, Bolt took up cricket as a child. However, after he entered William Knibb Memorial High School, the athletic coaches took note of Bolt's talent and steered him toward running. Speaking to the *Observer*'s Anna Kessel, Bolt's physical education teacher, Dwight Barnett, recalled his early fascination with Bolt's speed. "Sometimes I'd look at that stop-watch and think, 'There's something wrong with this watch. No kid can run that quickly.'"

Once Bolt started running, his coaches had trouble figuring out which race best suited his abilities. He ran the 200 meters, the 400 meters, and the 800 meters and was competitive in each. In fact, Bolt fared well in pretty much any track and field event he tried. "I remember one time he came to the long-jump pit and said, 'Can I have a try?' And without training or technique, he jumped over seven meters," Barnett told the *Times*' Owen Slot. Seven meters is a respectable jump—in Beijing, the women's gold medal winner jumped 7.04 meters.

While Bolt was blessed with athletic ability, he lacked discipline and often shirked training. Staff members at his school were reduced to tears at times trying to get him to train. Speaking to the *Observer*, former Olympic sprinter Pablo McNeil recalled working with the adolescent Bolt. "The first time I saw Usain bowling I knew he was a born sprinter, he was so fast. But he was so cricket-mad that he took a bit of persuading. Initially he was quite hard to work with, he needed to be kept in line ... nothing malicious, just pranks that got a bit out of hand, he certainly kept you on your toes."

Nonetheless, Bolt kept running. At age 15, he captured his first world title, winning the 200 meters at the IAAF (International Association of Athletics Federations) World Junior Championships with a time of 20.61 seconds. He was the youngest runner to hold the title. The next year, Bolt snapped up another world junior title, winning the 200 meters in 20.40 seconds.

After winning his second world title Bolt relocated to Kingston, Jamaica, to train with national coaches, but was often distracted by city life. He frequented nightclubs, ate fast food, and spent his time playing basketball. Eventually, Bolt matured and took his training more seriously. He appeared at the 2004 Olympics in Athens but, hindered by a leg injury, did not make it through the first round.

As the 2008 Olympics approached, Bolt was in fine form. He easily won the 100-meter dash, breaking the world record while showboating across the finish line. The win was remarkable given that Bolt had only begun competing in the 100-meter dash some 13 months before. A few days after that race, Bolt won another gold, finishing the 200-meter dash in 19.3 seconds and smashing another world record. During the 200 meters, Bolt averaged 23.3 miles per hour. After the race, Bolt took off his spikes and danced around the track, energizing the crowd with his personality and charm. Bolt is the first runner to win both the 100 meters and the 200 meters at the same Olympics since U.S.-sprinter Carl Lewis did it in 1984. Bolt won his third gold a few days later in the 4x100-meter relay, helping Jamaica set a world record time of 37.10 seconds.

Bolt's current coach, Glen Mills, believes Bolt has yet to peak and will continue to get better as he develops his technique and improves his upper-body physique. "He is not as strong as he should be," Mills told the *Daily Telegraph*'s Garry Linnell. "If he gets stronger, his stride frequency will improve and when we achieve that in perhaps the next two years, he is going to run even faster." Bolt also amazes coaches for his size—at 6-foot-5, 198 pounds, he is the tallest man to hold a sprinting world record. Most sprinters are short and stocky.

Bolt's performance at the Olympics has inspired an entire generation of Jamaican children. Speaking to Cam Cole of the Montreal *Gazette*, Olympic gold medal sprinter and Jamaican team coach Don Quarrie put it this way: "Now that Usain has done this, it might take us another 20 years to produce another athlete as outstanding as him, but we will. Because the seed has been sown now. There are kids running around Jamaica right now wanting to be Usain Bolt, and it's something we're going to have to channel in the right manner, so that we can maintain our position in the world in sprinting."

## Sources

### Periodicals

*Daily Telegraph* (Australia), August 22, 2008, sec. Sport, p. 6.

*Gazette* (Montreal, Canada), August 22, 2008, p. C2.

*New York Times*, August 21, 2008, p. D1.

*Observer* (England), August 24, 2008, sec. Sports, p. 8.

*Times* (London, England), September 11, 2008, sec. Sport, p. 76.

**Online**

"Just How Fast Will Bolt Go When He Really Puts His Mind to It?," *Guardian,* http://www.guardian .co.uk/sport/2008/aug/18/olympics2008. usainbolt (September 30, 2008).

"2008 Beijing Summer Olympics: Usain Bolt Profile," NBC, http://www.nbcolympics.com/ athletes/athlete=271/bio/ (September 30, 2008).

—*Lisa Frick*

# Danny Boyle

**Director**

**B**orn October 20, 1956, in Manchester, England; son of Frank (a power station employee) and Annie (a food-service worker) Boyle; children (by Gail Stevens, a casting director) Grace, Gabriel, Caitlin. *Education:* Attended the University of Wales-Bangor, mid-1970s.

**Addresses:** *Home*—London, England. *Office*—c/o Fox Searchlight Pictures, 10201 W. Pico Blvd., Bldg. 38, Los Angeles, CA 90035.

## Career

**D**rama producer, British Broadcasting Corporation (BBC)—Northern Ireland, after 1980; director, Joint Stock Company, c. 1981; director, Royal Court Theatre, 1982, then deputy director, 1985; directed first television project, *Scout*, 1987. Executive producer of film *28 Weeks Later*, 2007. Director of films, including: *Shallow Grave*, 1994; *Trainspotting*, 1996; *A Life Less Ordinary*, 1997; *The Beach*, 2000; *28 Days Later*, 2002; *Alien Love Triangle* (short), 2002; *Millions*, 2004; *Sunshine*, 2007; *Slumdog Millionaire*, 2008.

**Awards:** Alexander Korda Award for best British film, BAFTA, for *Shallow Grave*, 1995; Golden Globe Award for best director, Hollywood Foreign Press Association, BAFTA Award for best director, British Academy of Film and Television Arts, and Academy Award for best achievement in directing, Academy of Motion Picture Arts and Sciences, all for *Slumdog Millionaire*, 2009.

*Mike Marsland/WireImage/Getty Images*

## Sidelights

**B**ritish director Danny Boyle caused a sensation on both sides of the Atlantic in the summer of 1996 with *Trainspotting*, his gritty, gallows-humor adaptation of the Irvine Welsh novel of the same name about heroin addicts in contemporary Scotland. Since then, Boyle has gone on to bust through several film genres as a director, making a romantic comedy, a feel-good family tale, and a gory zombie flick. In 2009, he won multiple awards for *Slumdog Millionaire*, his Mumbai-set underdog tale that not only won the Academy Award for Best Picture of the Year but gave Boyle his first Oscar for directing.

A twin to his sister Grace, Boyle was born in 1956 and grew up in Radcliffe, a town near the industrial urban center of Manchester, in a Roman Catholic household with two more siblings. His father, who worked at a power station, was born in England to Irish immigrants, whereas his cafeteria-worker mother came from County Galway, Ireland. She hoped her son would enter the priesthood—a vocation of immense honor for Roman Catholic parents of the era—and at age 13 Boyle agreed to enter a seminary school in preparation, but one of the men of the cloth he knew from his altar-boy duties convinced him that he was not cut out for religious life. Instead he attended Thornleigh Salesian College, a Roman Catholic preparatory school for boys in Bolton, Lancashire.

It was at Thornleigh that Boyle became captivated by theater and film. One of his English classes involved a trip to see noted British actor Ian Richardson in *Richard II,* considered one of the best interpretations of the Shakespearean tragedy in the history of the Royal Shakespeare Company. Boyle was also fascinated by Stanley Kubrick's *A Clockwork Orange* when he and some friends sneaked into a cinema to see the film adaptation of Anthony Burgess' novel of a dystopian future society; the movie was so unreservedly violent that it was quickly pulled from theaters and went on to become a rarely shown cult masterpiece.

Boyle studied English and drama at the University of Wales, Bangor, where he met Frances Barber, a future stage and screen star in Britain, with whom he eventually moved to London. His first job after college, however, was as a drama producer with the British Broadcasting Corporation (BBC) in Belfast, Northern Ireland, during the height of sectarian troubles in that city. When he and Barber moved to London, he became involved with the Joint Stock Company, a theater company co-founded by noted playwright David Hare. He also joined the prestigious Royal Court Theatre in the early 1980s, where he served as director for such works as *Cinders,* a youth-theater production set in a Polish reform school, and *Saved,* a once-banned play by Edward Bond that includes an infanticide scene.

Around 1985 Boyle was promoted from artistic director to deputy director at the Royal Court, and eventually began directing for television, too. Between 1987 and 1991 he directed six television movies, which led to episodic work on the popular detective series *Inspector Morse* on ITV, and then the acclaimed three-part drama for BBC Television, *Mr. Wroe's Virgins,* in 1993. Based on the novel about a real-life nineteenth-century British evangelist, the project starred a young Australian actress, Kerry Fox, whom Boyle would cast as one of the three leads in his first feature film, *Shallow Grave.*

Released in early 1995, *Shallow Grave* was a darkly comic tale of three roommates in Edinburgh who advertise for a fourth to share their spectacular vintage flat. The snarky, close-knit trio are Ewan McGregor's "insolent Alex, a wisecracking journalist; blithe Juliet, a doctor," wrote Janet Maslin in the

*New York Times* of Fox's character, and "tightly wound David, a prim, withdrawn accountant," played by Christopher Eccleston. When Hugo, the new roommate they finally agree upon, is found dead in his bedroom shortly after his arrival, the room is empty save for a suitcase full of money, and the three decide to keep the cash and get rid of the body. *Shallow Grave* garnered some excellent press in Britain, where the *Guardian*'s Derek Malcolm called it "a latterday parable about greed and ambition that is also highly entertaining—a commentary on [British prime minister Margaret] Thatcher's era that never once mentions her name." In the *Observer,* film critic Philip French commended Boyle's directorial debut as "a good piece of storytelling, admirably acted, thoughtfully designed, skilfully photographed, and sensibly modest in its ambitions. Hitchcock would have admired its ruthlessness and cruel humour."

Boyle cast McGregor to star in his next project, *Trainspotting.* Welsh's novel of the same name had already gained a certain infamy in the British Isles for its relentlessly ruthless and disjointed portrayal of the lives of a passel of young heroin addicts in Edinburgh. McGregor played Renton, the breezy narrator who tries valiantly to kick his habit, and eventually betrays his best friends, who include the vicious Begbie (Robert Carlyle), Sick Boy (Jonny Lee Miller), and Spud (Ewen Bremner), for a large sum of cash.

*Trainspotting* was a massive hit on both sides of the Atlantic, despite the fact that some pundits faulted it for glamorizing drug use and it was even mentioned by U.S. Senator Bob Dole, a Republican, in his presidential campaign. "From the first image—Renton jumps over the camera and hurtles down the street as store detectives chase after him," wrote *Time*'s Richard Corliss, "the film is a nonstop visual and aural assault. Slo-mo, fast-mo, a hallucinogenic editing pace and the thick music of Scottish accents mean that you'll have to cram for *Trainspotting.* Attention must be paid, and will be rewarded with the scabrous savor of the movie's lightning intelligence." Writing in the *New Statesman & Society,* Lizzie Francke called it "one of the most ferocious indictments of the sordid state we're in. It's funny, but in that way that gets to the gut and hurts hard." A critic for *Rolling Stone* commended it as "a singular sensation, a visionary knockout spiked with insight, wild invention, and outrageous wit."

Despite the impressive box-office numbers for *Trainspotting*—it was made for $2.5 million and earned more than $72 million worldwide for producer Andrew Macdonald, who had also found financing for

*Shallow Grave* and would work with Boyle on a number of subsequent projects—the suddenly famous director made some admittedly poor decisions that nearly jettisoned his film career entirely. He made a bona-fide Hollywood movie called *A Life Less Ordinary* that starred McGregor and Cameron Diaz, but the ghostly romantic comedy baffled critics and audiences alike. Boyle followed this with *The Beach,* another screen adaptation by John Hodge, the third member of the film-production troika with Andrew Macdonald. McGregor had been promised the lead in the Thailand-set tale of hippie backpackers who stumble across a sinister cult community, but the role went instead to Leonardo DiCaprio, one of Hollywood's youngest, most-sought after names at the time. Most critics deemed *The Beach* a failure, and initial box-office tallies were also disappointing. It was made for an astonishing $50 million, but took in only $39 million in U.S. theaters.

Boyle later said that working on films like *The Beach* and *A Life Less Ordinary* proved to be the opposite of challenging for him as a director. "Once you've had anything like a hit in the movie business it's easy to get lost," he explained in an interview with *Sunday Times* journalist Cosmo Landesman. "All these people are scuttling around trying to get you to make things and offering deals. The pressure of what to do next is horrible." Returning to his roots, he made two BBC television films using a new format, digital video (DV). *Strumpet* featured Christopher Eccleston from *Shallow Grave,* and *Vacuuming Completely Nude in Paradise* starred Timothy Spall. Both were written by playwright Jim Cartwright, whom Boyle knew from their days together at the Royal Court Theatre. "The entire budget for these two films would barely have covered the catering on *The Beach,*" Boyle told Rupert Smith in the *Guardian.* "The great thing about working cheaply and quickly is that you don't spend time agonising over every decision." He also discussed his decision to use DV, as digital video is known in industry parlance. "DV is very liberating for actors as well: the cameras are so unobtrusive that they don't feel they're being watched so much," he told Smith. "And you don't have to treat them with the same technical exactness. You don't have to hit your mark in the same way."

Boyle also used DV for his next work, which returned him to the big-budget, heavily marketed side of filmmaking. *28 Days Later* cost $10 million to make, but earned $80 million after its 2002 release, thanks in part to its gripping tale of a post-apocalyptic world terrorized by zombies. "The ominous grainy mood of docu-realism makes every detail—a wall of 'Missing' posters, a car alarm—part of a specifically contemporary dreamscape of fear,"

wrote Owen Gleiberman in *Entertainment Weekly,* who summarized Boyle's latest as "a swankily austere piece of jeepers-creepers sci-fi."

Boyle did not direct that movie's sequel, *28 Weeks Later,* but did serve as executive producer. His next work marked a drastic departure for him: *Millions* was a heartfelt, family-oriented movie about two brothers, age seven and nine, grieving over the loss of their mother. One of them discovers a bag filled with pound notes, in an echo of *Shallow Grave*'s plot. Asked once by a journalist why so many of his films have that duffel-bag-full-of-cash element, Boyle said it seemed a reflection of his early years in the entertainment industry. "When you start off making films, you think the pressure is that you're never gonna be able to raise money. And you realize as soon as you start making films that the pressure is to resist people giving you money," he told Jeff Gordinier in *Entertainment Weekly.*

Currency had absolutely no role in 2007's *Sunshine,* Boyle's epic science fiction thriller about a manned mission to the sun that starred *28 Days Later*'s Cillian Murphy and was written by Alex Garland, who wrote both that zombie-filled film and *The Beach.* Few expected Boyle's next movie, *Slumdog Millionaire,* to earn anything at the box office, and one studio interested in a distribution deal even considered releasing it straight to DVD. Instead the story of 18-year-old Jamal (Dev Patel), an orphan from the streets of Mumbai who goes on to win millions of rupees on the Indian version of the hit television quiz show *Who Wants to be a Millionaire?* became the surprise hit of the 2008 holiday season.

*Slumdog Millionaire* earned Boyle Director of the Year honors from the British Academy of Film and Television Arts (BAFTA), the Hollywood Foreign Press Association, and the Academy of Motion Picture Arts and Sciences. It also won the Academy Award for Best Picture of the Year, and swept that year's Oscars by winning six other categories, including those for cinematography and music. It marked the best performance by a British production in the history of the Academy Awards, and was also the first film ever to win the Best Picture Oscar without a major Hollywood player in its cast.

Boyle used six different actors to play Jamal, his brother, and the childhood pal whom Jamal later romances at varying stages of their young lives, and shot the film in Mumbai, which presented a host of new challenges for the director. "The style in this film felt dictated by what it felt like to move to Mumbai and live there for eight months. In this case, the style is that there is very little control that you can have in Mumbai," he told Andrew O'Hehir in an interview that appeared on Salon.com. "You have to be honest about some of the ... suffering that goes on. But I think it's got a happy ending, if not a Hollywood happy ending. The spirit of the city is overwhelming in the end, and it is a positive spirit."

## Sources

### Periodicals

*Entertainment Weekly,* August 2, 1996, p. 30; June 27, 2003, p. 115; March 18, 2005, p. 43.
*Guardian* (London, England), January 5, 1995, p. 10; August 10, 2001, p. 6.
*Independent on Sunday* (London, England), January 4, 2009, p. 8.

*New Statesman & Society,* February 16, 1996, p. 35.
*Newsweek,* February 9, 2009, p. 42.
*New York Times,* February 10, 1995; July 8, 2007.
*Observer* (London, England), January 8, 1995, p. 9.
*Rolling Stone,* August 8, 1996.
*Sun* (London, England), January 14, 2009, p. 32.
*Sunday Times* (London, England), April 8, 2007, p. 19.
*Time,* July 15, 1996, p. 64; March 2, 2009, p. 4.

### Online

"Thrill Ride Through a 'Maximum City,'" Salon.com, http://www.salon.com/ent/movies/btm/feature/2008/11/12/slumdog/print.html (April 14, 2009).

—*Carol Brennan*

# Benjamin Bratt

## Actor

**B**orn December 16, 1963, in San Francisco, CA; son of Peter (a sheet-metal worker) and Eldy Bratt (a nurse and Native American activist); married Talisa Soto (an actress), April 13, 2002; children: Sophia Rosalinda, Mateo Bravery. *Education:* University of California, Santa Barbara, B.F.A., 1986; also attended the American Conservatory Theater, San Francisco, CA.

**Addresses:** *Contact*—c/o N2N Entertainment, 120 Montana Ave. #203, Santa Monica, CA 90403.

## Career

**A**ctor in films, including: *Lovers, Partners & Spies,* 1988; *One Good Cop,* 1991; *Bright Angel,* 1991; *Bound by Honor,* 1993; *Demolition Man,* 1993; *Clear and Present Danger,* 1994; *The River Wild,* 1994; *Follow Me Home,* 1996; *The Next Best Thing,* 2000; *The Last Producer,* 2000; *Red Planet,* 2000; *Miss Congeniality,* 2000; *Traffic,* 2000; *Piñero,* 2001; *Abandon,* 2002; *The Woodsman,* 2004; *Catwoman,* 2004; *Thumbsucker,* 2005; *The Great Raid,* 2005; *Love in the Time of Cholera,* 2007; *Trucker,* 2008; *La Mission,* 2009. Television appearances include: *Juarez* (pilot), 1987; *Police Story: Gladiator School* (movie), 1987; *Knight Watch,* 1988-89; *Nasty Boys* (pilot), 1989; *Capital News* (movie), 1989; *Chains of Gold* (movie), 1991; *Shadowhunter* (movie), 1993; *Texas* (miniseries), 1994; *Law & Order,* NBC, 1995-99; *Woman Undone* (movie), 1996; *Homicide: Life on the Street,* NBC, 1996, 1997, 1999; *Exiled* (movie), 1998; *After the Storm* (movie), 2001; *Frasier,* 2001; *E-Ring,* 2005-06; *The Andromeda Strain* (miniseries), 2008; *The Cleaner,* A&E, 2008—; *We Shall Remain,* 2009. Stage appearances include: *Richard III,* Utah Shakespeare Festival, 1987. Worked as film producer, including: *Follow Me Home,* 1996; *Mission,* 2009.

*Ethan Miller/Getty Images for CineVegas*

**Awards:** ALMA Award for outstanding actor in a drama series, National Council of La Raza, for *Law & Order,* 1998; ALMA Award for outstanding actor in a made-for-television movie or miniseries, National Council of La Raza, for *Exiled,* 1999; ALMA Award for outstanding actor in a drama series, National Council of La Raza, for *Law & Order,* 1999; Blockbuster Entertainment Award for favorite supporting actor—comedy for *Miss Congeniality,* 2001; Screen Actors Guild Award (with others) for outstanding performance by the cast of a theatrical motion picture for *Traffic,* 2001; ALMA Award for outstanding actor in a motion picture, National Council of La Raza, for *Piñero,* 2002.

## Sidelights

**A**merican television and film actor Benjamin Bratt attracted attention for his exotic looks, diverse roles, and confident talent. He is perhaps best known for his four-year stint on the long-running television series *Law & Order* as well as prominent roles in such films as *Miss Congeniality* and *Love in the Time of Cholera.* In 2008, Bratt took on the starring role in the popular cable series *The Cleaner.* In an interview with Liz Braun of the *Toronto Sun,* Bratt stated that he got interested in acting as a teenager. He said, "There's something about inhabiting the skin of someone else that frees you up, allows you to explore emotional and physical boundaries—break those boundaries. You don't become an actor. You just never find anything else that makes you feel as alive, and that was certainly the case for me."

Bratt was born on December 16, 1963, in San Francisco, California. His father, Peter, was a German-American sheet-metal worker, and his mother, Eldy, was a Quechua native from Peru, who emigrated to the United States at the age of 14. She was a nurse who became a Native American activist after she and her husband divorced when Bratt was five. Raising her five children on her own, Bratt's mother would bring them to protest events, including the 1970 takeover of Alcatraz. Bratt's family was incredibly close, and his mother insisted that her children stay off the streets and get a college education.

As a child, Bratt focused on athletics, not acting, and planned on a career as a physical education teacher or a dentist. However, as he neared the end of his high school education, his interests turned toward acting in part because of his father's encouragement. Bratt's paternal grandfather, George Bratt, had been an actor in New York City, and his father encouraged Bratt to try out for a high school play. Though Bratt was initially reluctant, he was cast in a part and then became interested in acting.

After he entered the University of California at Santa Barbara in the early 1980s, Bratt was being cast in plays on campus on a regular basis. In 1986, Bratt graduated with his B.F.A in theater with honors. He then continued his acting training at the American Conservatory Theater in San Francisco, where he focused on classical drama and comedy while working on his master's degree. To support himself, he was a waiter, drove an airport shuttle bus on weekends, and worked at a photo engraving store.

While Bratt was studying at the conservatory, his talent was noticed by a casting director from Los Angeles. This connection led to his first role on television; he appeared on the pilot and one episode of the 1987 show *Juarez*. Though only the pilot actually aired, he was paid for six episodes and used the money as well as the experience to launch his acting career in Hollywood. However, Bratt did not abandon the stage entirely despite this first taste of television. He spent the summer of 1987 at the Utah Shakespeare Festival, appearing in such plays as *Richard III*.

When Bratt returned to Los Angeles, he continued to build his career but sometimes found his striking appearance—the product of his mixed ethnic background—affected his ability to land roles. He told Jae-Ha Kim of the *Chicago Sun-Times*, "On some level, industry standards of how people of color are perceived and therefore hired reflect a microcosm of what exists in society. Unfortunately, that's limiting. My early experience in Hollywood was disappointing and sometimes shocking."

In 1988, Bratt had his first leading role in a television series. He starred in *Knightwatch*, which was cancelled shortly thereafter. This drama focused on a Guardian Angels-type group, with Bratt playing leader Tony Maldonado. Two years later, Bratt had his second role in a regular series. He was a lead in the short-lived hour-long crime drama *Nasty Boys*, about undercover vice cops working in Las Vegas. The executive producer of this series, Dick Wolf, had a bigger hit with *Law & Order*, which also began airing in 1990.

After the failure of *Nasty Boys*, Bratt focused his attention primarily on feature films. The actor had supporting roles in such films as *The River Wild*, *Clear and Present Danger*, and *Demolition Man*. Bratt also appeared in several highly regarded television productions, including the 1994 miniseries *Texas*.

In 1995, Bratt returned to series television with a role on the Emmy Award-winning *Law & Order*. He played Detective Reynaldo "Rey" Curtis, a character that changed the energy of the show. Of the role, Bratt told Harriet Winslow of the *Washington Post*, "When Dick Wolf told me about the job he said, 'Don't worry about it, you won't draw your gun or chase anybody.' But I did within the first four days."

Bratt's portrayal of Curtis drew many positive reviews, and his appearance one of the top-rated shows on television was highly regarded especially by other minorities. Bratt told Andrea Higbie of the *New York Times*, "As a person of color, there's no getting around the reality of its responsibility." He added about being recognized on the street, "most of the time it's by other Latinos or Native Americans or African Americans. The feeling I receive from them is pride, and that's the feeling I have, too."

While appearing on *Law & Order*, Bratt continued to work on other projects, including a film he made with his brother, filmmaker Peter. Bratt both served as a producer and played Abel in *Follow Me Home*. The film is an allegory about four urban muralists who want to paint the White House in the colors of their various cultures. Bratt's character is a racist Latino painter who has a hidden addiction to cocaine.

Bratt left *Law & Order* in 1999, after four seasons. Several reasons prompted his departure. In 2000, Bratt told Dennis Hunt of the *San Diego Union-Tribune,* "On that show, the story is the most important thing. They concentrate on the story almost exclusively. That's the draw for audiences. They never really deal with the personal lives of the characters. From a creative standpoint, it's very restrictive. The work, the money, the people, the exposure on that show are all great. But I got to a point where, creatively, I just had to have more. I had to go."

Though the actor liked living and working in New York City—where *Law & Order* is set and shot—he also missed the West Coast and his family. He was also dating high-profile film actress Julia Roberts, a relationship that began in 1997. Bratt went back to Hollywood, where his professional focus returned to films. He appeared in such films as 2000's relationship comedy *The Next Best Thing,* in which he played the love interest of a character played by Madonna.

In 2000, Bratt had major roles in other major motion pictures. He played Lieutenant Ted Santen in *Red Planet,* a science-fiction film about an American mission to Mars. Like *The Next Best Thing, Red Planet* was a box-office failure. Fortunately, Bratt found greater success with the comedy *Miss Congeniality,* which co-starred Sandra Bullock and Michael Caine. Bratt plays the boss of an FBI agent, played by Bullock, who forces her to enter a beauty pageant to help catch a serial killer.

Bratt's fourth film of 2000, the ensemble drama *Traffic,* directed by acclaimed director Steven Soderbergh, was both a critical and a box-office success. In December of 2000, Bratt told Louis B. Hobson of the *Toronto Sun,* "I begged big-time for that part. I'm like everyone else in Hollywood these days who'll make any concession to work with Soderbergh."

In 2000, Bratt also filmed *Piñero*—an indie biopic about the short life of Latino playwright, poet, and actor Miguel Piñero—which was released in 2001. Critics praised Bratt's work in the role, seemingly the opposite of most of his Hollywood-related work to date, and there was talk of an Academy Award nomination. Reviewing the film in the New Jersey *Record,* Virginia Rohan wrote, "In *Piñero,* Bratt delivers poetry readings that are inspired. In an ever-present haze of cigarette smoke, he is almost unrecognizably scruffy, frenetic, and passionate. His eyes are everything from flaming, suggesting the fire in his character's soul, to so heavy with heroin they are almost dead."

Bratt's co-star in *Piñero* was actress Talisa Soto, with whom he became involved after his relationship with Roberts ended in 2001. Bratt and Soto married in April of 2002, and had their first child, Sophia Rosalinda, later that year. The couple had a son, Mateo Bravery, in 2005. After an initial rush of film roles, Bratt's acting career slowed as his family was growing. In addition to his role in *Piñero,* Bratt also appeared in the television movie *After the Storm* in 2001. This movie is based on the Ernest Hemingway short story of the same name.

Over the next few years, Bratt's film roles were primarily in independent films such as 2004's *The Woodsman,* which starred Kevin Bacon as an allegedly reformed pedophile. Bratt also appeared in a few Hollywood films, such as the 2004 box-office bomb *Catwoman,* starring Halle Barry in the titular role. While 2005's *The Great Raid* was better received, the World War II military drama about perhaps the greatest rescue mission in U.S. military history was also a box-office failure.

Bratt also began moving back into television roles. He was impressed by the quality of work being done on television, telling Marisa Guthrie of the New York *Daily News,* "Most of us just want to do good work, and it's become very clear lately that the level of quality to be found on television is equal to, if not greater than, the quality of a lot of the films that are being produced in Hollywood. And that line that was every distinctly drawn that separated film actors from television actors has all but disappeared at this point."

In 2005, Bratt returned to a regular starring role in a television series with the short-lived drama *E-Ring.* Produced by Jerry Bruckheimer, the series focused on Bratt's James Patrick Tisnewski who is an altruistic Special Ops Green Beret forced to leave the war in Afghanistan to take a staff position in the Pentagon. Bratt returned to series television in part because of his wife and children as well as the more regular hours and pay. In August of 2005, he told Hobson of the *Toronto Sun,* "Family is the reason I took the *E-Ring.* I want to be able to go home after a day's work and be with my wife and children."

After *E-Ring* was cancelled in 2006, Bratt had a role in the highly regarded 2007 film *Love in the Time of Cholera,* based on the novel by the Gabriel García Márquez. He then had a featured part in the independent film *Trucker* as well as a starring role the television miniseries adaptation of the science fiction classic *The Andromeda Strain.*

When Bratt returned to series television in 2008, it was on the challenging cable series *The Cleaner.* On the A&E show, Bratt plays a former heroin addict,

William Banks, who teams with two other ex-drug users to stage hardcore interventions to save needy junkies of any variety by any means necessary. Bratt's Banks sees his rescue missions as the fulfillment of a promise made to God and neglects the family he loves to complete them. While the show received mixed reviews from critics, Robert Lloyd of the *Los Angeles Times* praised the actor's performance, noting: "Bratt is good, even when required to spout expository dialogue while saving the life of an overdose victim."

During its first season of 13 episodes, *The Cleaner* attracted an average of 4.2 million viewers per episode. A&E regarded these numbers as high enough to greenlight the show for a second season in 2009. Bratt also had a film scheduled for release that year, *La Mission*. Bratt evaluated his success on both the big and small screens, telling Hobson of the *Toronto Sun* in 2000, "I can honestly say when I started out to be an actor I never dreamed of anything beyond being employed. I would never have allowed myself to dream of being a star. I'm just a working actor who's had a couple of incredibly lucky breaks."

## Sources

### Books

*Complete Marquis Who's Who Biographies,* Marquis Who's Who, 2008.

### Periodicals

Associated Press, June 28, 2001.
Associated Press Worldstream, July 10, 2008.
*Chicago Sun-Times*, January 20, 2002, p. 1.
*Daily News* (New York), September 8, 2005, p. 86.
*Edmonton Journal* (Alberta, Canada), January 6, 2001, p. C1.
*Edmonton Sun* (Alberta, Canada), February 29, 2000, p. 3.
*Los Angeles Times*, July 15, 2008, p. E11.
*New York Magazine*, July 21, 2008.
*New York Times*, November 26, 1995, sec. 2, p. 38.
*Record* (Bergen Country, NJ), December 17, 2001, p. F6.
*San Diego Union-Tribune,* December 17, 2000, p. F1.
*San Jose Mercury News* (CA), November 6, 2004, p. 3E.
*Star Tribune* (Minneapolis, MN), February 18, 1998, p. 8E.
*Toronto Star,* December 17, 1995, p. B3.
*Toronto Sun,* December 18, 2000 p. 46; August 10, 2005, p. 46; November 14, 2007, p. 64.
*Vancouver Sun* (British Columbia, Canada), May 1, 1999, p. E22.
*Washington Post*, November 5, 1995, p. Y8.

### Online

"Benjamin Bratt," Internet Movie Database, http://www.imdb.com/name/nm0000973/ (January 1, 2009).

—*A. Petruso*

# Carla Bruni

**Singer**

**B**orn Carla Gilberta Bruni Tedeschi, December 23, 1967, in Turin, Italy; naturalized French citizen, 2008; daughter of Maurizio Remmert (a grocery-store chain owner) and Marisa Borini (a concert pianist); married Nicolas Sarkozy (a politician), February 2, 2008; children: son Aurélien (with Raphaël Enthoven, a philosophy professor). *Education:* Studied art and architecture at the Sorbonne, mid-1980s.

**Addresses:** *Home*—Paris, France. *Office*—c/o Palais de l'Elysée, 55, rue du Faubourg Saint-Honoré, 75008 Paris, France.

## Career

**M**odel, c. 1987-97, and signed to City Models of Paris; released first album, *Quelqu'un M'a Dit*, 2002.

## Sidelights

**C**arla Bruni was one of France's most famous women long before she wed French president Nicolas Sarkozy in early 2008 after a whirlwind romance that stirred international media attention. An Italian industrial-fortune heiress who had segued from a lucrative career as a top fashion model in the early 1990s to bestselling pop chanteuse within a decade's time, Bruni had been linked to a number of prominent men before she met the French president, but her star rose even higher when she began dating Sarkozy, who is also head of France's center-right party, the Union pour un Mouvement Populaire (UMP). France's newest First Lady was de-scribed by the *New York Observer* as "a new icon of fashion, sex and sensibility—a 21st-century amalgam of Jackie O, Lady Di and J-Lo." The *New Yorker*'s correspondent from Paris, Adam Gopnik, remarked that "the American press has portrayed the bizarre story of this courtship ... as typically French." Gopnik wrote, "The French press, by contrast, has seen in the story something so obviously second-rate and vulgar that it must be in some way American."

One of three children, Bruni was born Carla Tedeschi two days before Christmas of 1967 in Turin, Italy. As a young woman, she used her father's middle name, Bruni, as her professional moniker, and this was also the middle name of her grandfather, an Italian industrialist. The family's fortunes came from CEAT, which stood for *Cavi Electrici Affini Torino* (Electrical Cables and Allied Products) of Turin, which was sold to Italian tire manufacturer Pirelli in the 1970s. Bruni-Sarkozy's legal father was Alberto Bruni Tedeschi, a composer and director at Turin's main concert hall; her mother, Marisa, was a concert pianist.

When Bruni's father was dying in 1996, he revealed that he was not actually her biological father and that she was actually the result of her mother's six-year liaison with Maurizio Remmert, an Italian guitarist who later moved to Brazil and founded a chain of grocery stores. "It was not a shock, and that is how I knew it was true, because I felt calm when he told me that," Bruni recalled of her father's deathbed revelation in an interview with *Vanity Fair*'s Maureen Orth. "I think lies are toxic for children, much more than a bad truth. Sometimes lies, when you are growing up, make you walk in a funny way to adapt."

Whatever her parentage, Bruni grew up in a wealthy and well-connected family whose members led an idyllic, jet-set lifestyle. The sole hint of trouble was a spate of high-profile kidnappings in the mid-1970s carried out by a radical leftist group in Italy called the Red Brigades, and fear prompted her parents to move the family to France around 1975. At about this same time, Bruni first picked up a guitar and taught herself how to play. She was educated at a Swiss boarding school and returned to Paris to study art and architecture at the Sorbonne, or University of Paris. Her brother's model-girlfriend suggested she give modeling a try, too. So Bruni decided to try. "I just brought my underground Metro pass to an agency," Bruni recalled in an interview with *Sunday Times*' journalist John Follain. "It was the only photograph I had. They took me."

Bruni spent more than a decade as one of Europe's top models. Both runway and magazine-editorial work quickly came her way, and in the end she appeared on more than 200 magazine covers. For a time, she was the Guess? jeans model and was a runway and print-ad favorite for such designers or couture houses as Yves Saint-Laurent, Chanel, Christian Dior, Givenchy, John Galliano, and Versace. "Modeling meant I did not have to rely on my parents or a man," she told Orth in the *Vanity Fair* interview, adding that she also relished the opportunity to travel and discover other parts of the world. "Modeling has a reputation for emptiness, but it's not. It is certainly not German philosophy, but it was very instructive, because it was made up of real life. You travel, you are always alone, and you better be well grounded, because it's easy to lose yourself."

Along the way, Bruni also dallied with some important figures from outside the world of fashion. She was briefly linked to musician Eric Clapton and real-estate mogul Donald Trump, but it was her reported affair with rocker Mick Jagger that was the entire focus of a 1992 article by Karen S. Schneider in *People*, in which unnamed sources claimed that their romance had began when Jagger's longtime partner model Jerry Hall was pregnant with their

third child. "I hardly know this man," Schneider quoted Bruni as telling reporters. "I'm fed up with these rumors." Whenever the onset, the romance with the legendary Rolling Stones frontman apparently lasted six years, much of it while Jagger was still with Hall and fathered a fourth child.

Bruni-Sarkozy's romance with a handsome French philosophy professor, Raphaël Enthoven, was also the target of scurrilous gossip. Some sources claimed that she had actually been dating Enthoven's father, a well-known publisher, before becoming involved with the younger man, who was married to Justine Lévy, a novelist and daughter of one of France's most prominent intellectuals, Bernard-Henri Lévy. Justine Lévy's 2004 novel *Rien de Grave*—published in English translation in 2005 as *Nothing Serious*—features a thinly disguised version of Bruni as Paula, the model who poaches the main character's husband.

By that point, Bruni had already embarked on her second career as a pop singer after retiring from modeling in 1998. Her debut album *Quelqu'un M'a Dit* ("Someone Told Me") was released in October 2002 and became a massive hit in France, selling more than a million copies and receiving credit for single-handedly reviving the French pop-music industry. "With its simple melodies and poetic lyrics rooted in the tradition of chanson francaise, the wonderfully lo-fi album … stunned those expecting just another embarrassing misfire from a vapid ex-supermodel," noted Missy Schwartz in *Entertainment Weekly*. The *New York Observer* described the record as "a collection of simple ballads and plucky tunes all sung in a husky half-whisper, the words spilling out on the infectious title track as fast as she can form them. (And yes, Ms. Bruni wrote her own songs—lost love, end of the affair, etc.—and plays the guitar charmingly.)"

Of the unexpected transition from modeling to music, Bruni reflected in another interview. "Most records aren't really a collection of songs, they're just a product," she told Alix Sharkey in the London *Observer*. "And the artist is a product. And I'm used to that—that's what modelling is all about. So when I did the record I wrote my own songs. Of course, I'm not Björk. I wrote the songs I could write." Bruni-Sarkozy's second album was *No Promises,* released in 2007. A collection of original music set to some well-known poems by William Butler Yeats, Emily Dickinson, and others, this first record for her in English failed to repeat the success of the debut.

Bruni was already the subject of lengthy press profiles thanks to the combination of her recording career, intriguing personal life, and sometimes scandalous pronouncements. Right around the time her relationship with Enthoven—which had produced a son, Aurélien, in 2001—was ending, she famously told an interviewer for *L'Express,* a widely read French newsweekly, "I'm monogamous occasionally, but I prefer polygamy and polyandry," the *Sunday Times* quoted her as saying. "Love lasts a long time, but burning desire, two to three weeks."

Bruni met her future husband at a dinner party in November of 2007. Nicolas Sarkozy had been elected president of France six months earlier, but his rather messy personal life had provided fodder for serious political pundits and tabloid journalists alike. For example, that October, his second marriage to Cécilia Ciganer-Albéniz had ended after infidelities reportedly occurred on both sides. When he and Bruni met, "It was pretty much love at first sight," the singer told Follain in the *Sunday Times.* The pair were photographed together frequently, and rumors swirled that they had secretly wed. The actual marriage took place on February 2, 2008, after Bruni renounced her Italian citizenship. Just four days later, the newspaper *Le Nouvel Observateur* ran a story claiming that Sarkozy had sent his ex-wife a text message in December hinting that he would abandon Bruni if Cécilia agreed to return to him. The president went as far as filing a criminal complaint against the newspaper, which could have resulted in a jail term for the newspaper's editor if convicted, but the complaint was dropped in March when the editor was said to have written a note apologizing to Bruni-Sarkozy.

Bruni made her first official visit abroad as France's First Lady in March of 2008, when the couple visited Great Britain. Just before the trip—on which Bruni and her husband were scheduled to meet with Queen Elizabeth II and other members of the royal family— the auction house Christie's sold a nude photograph of Bruni dating back to 1993, when she appeared in an anti-AIDS public service campaign. The photograph fetched $91,000 at the final gavel, six times more than the Christie's catalog estimate. The attendant publicity did little to dampen the British media's enthusiasm for Bruni-Sarkozy, which chronicled her every move and outfit during the brief visit. When Sarkozy was asked about all the attention given to his wife, he told one journalist, "I have been deeply moved by what has been said over the last two days," the *Independent* quoted him as saying. "I think she has been an honour to our country, not simply because of the way she looks, but beyond that everyone understands that this is a woman who has belief, sensitivity, and humanity," Sarkozy asserted.

Just after marrying the French president, Bruni spent nearly a month recording several already-written songs that would appear on her third album, *Comme Si de Rien N'Était* ("As If Nothing Happened"). Released in July of 2008, the record was not be accompanied by any concert tour, and its royalties were to be donated to charity, but Bruni also noted that becoming First Lady of France did not automatically spell the end of her music career. "It's not that I want to use my husband's power to sell my songs," she told Schwartz, the *Entertainment Weekly* writer. "I just don't believe that women should drop everything."

Two months after *Comme Si de Rien N'Était*'s release, the couple made their first joint visit to New York City, which also coincided with Bruni-Sarkozy's appearance on the cover of the September issue of *Vanity Fair.* She was the target of criticism for the photo shoot for the magazine, which took place at the official residence of France's president, the Élysée Palace, for it was viewed as a promotional effort for her latest record. Bruni admitted that her new role as the spouse of one of the world's most powerful political figures presented an entirely new set of challenges. "When you are a songwriter and you say, 'I like polyandry, ha, ha, ha,' it is written down and it doesn't matter," she told Orth in *Vanity Fair.* "But if you're a First Lady and you say, 'I like Coca-Cola Light,' it's a drama. I have to pay attention to every detail, and that is very new for me."

## Selected discography

*Quelqu'un M'a Dit,* Naïve, 2002.
*No Promises,* Naïve, 2007.
*Comme Si de Rien N'Était,* Naïve, 2008.

## Sources

*Entertainment Weekly,* August 15, 2008, p. 38.
*Guardian* (London, England), August 7, 2008, p. 30.
*Independent* (London, England), March 29, 2008, p. 10.
*New Yorker,* January 28, 2008, p. 23.
*New York Observer,* April 15, 2008.
*Observer* (London, England), April 4, 2004, p. 14.
*People,* August 17, 1992, p. 50.
*Sunday Times* (London, England), July 13, 2008, p. 14.
*Vanity Fair,* September 2008, p. 338.

—*Carol Brennan*

# Gisele Bundchen

## Model

**B**orn July 20, 1980, in Três de Maio, Rio Grande do Sul, Brazil; daughter of Valdir (a construction company owner) and Vania (a bank clerk; maiden name, Nonnenmacher) Bundchen.

**Addresses:** *Home*—New York, NY. *Office*—IMG Models, 304 Park Ave. South, 12th Flr., New York, NY 10010.

## Career

**B**egan modeling career in São Paulo, Brazil, as a catalog model, c. 1994; moved to New York City; represented by Elite Models, Inc., until 2001; signed with IMG Models, 2001; under exclusive contract with Victoria's Secret, 2001-07; launched line of sandals, Ipanema Gisele Bundchen, with Brazilian footwear maker Grendene, 2001; appeared in ads for the Swiss watchmaker Ebel, 2006; model for cosmetics brand MAX Factor, 2008—.

**Awards:** Model of the Year, VH1/Vogue Fashion Awards, 1999.

## Sidelights

**I**n just a few short years Brazilian-born Gisele Bundchen became one of the world's highest-paid models. A decade after starting her career, Bund-

chen was ranked at No. 66 on *Forbes* magazine's 2008 rankings of the Top 100 highest-paid celebrities in the world, squeezed in between singer-actress Alicia Keys and actress Gwyneth Paltrow with her annual earnings estimated at $35 million, much of it from lucrative endorsement contracts. "Some people start modeling because they want to be models and they want the parties and the recognition," she once reflected in an interview with *Vanity Fair* writer Suzanna Andrews, "and then there are people like me. I come from a simple family, and for me getting into modeling was a chance to make money and create a business."

Born on July 20, 1980, Bundchen is from Brazil's southernmost state, Rio Grande do Sul, and grew up in a small town of just 10,000 called Horizontina. She is one of six sisters in her family, which includes her fraternal twin, Patrícia, and though they grew up speaking Brazilian Portuguese, the Bundchen daughters were of German heritage thanks to great-great-grandparents who emigrated to Brazil earlier in the century. Bundchen's mother Vania worked as a bank clerk and her father had a small construction business; they were not poor, but neither were they wealthy. "We shared everything. I never had new clothes," she told Andrews in *Vanity Fair*.

In her early teens Bundchen was devoted to horses and volleyball, and had reached her full height of five feet, eleven inches by age 14. Concerned about her daughter's poor posture, Bundchen's mother enrolled her and Patrícia in a class at a modeling school that had recently opened in Horizontina. Bundchen agreed to it because the course finished with a trip to São Paulo, Brazil's largest city, which was a 25-hour bus ride away. On that first trip to a real city, Bundchen was eating at a McDonald's restaurant inside a mall when she was approached by an executive with a São Paulo modeling agency.

Not long afterward, the agent suggested she watch a modeling contest that was being held in the same town where Bundchen was scheduled to play in a volleyball tournament. To her surprise, the agent had actually signed her up for the contest and brought a dress for her to wear, and a once-reluctant Bundchen walked away with one of the five winning slots for a modeling contract in São Paulo. When she arrived back in São Paulo in January of 1995, she was almost immediately robbed of all the cash she had brought with her. A passerby took pity on the weeping teen and loaned her money to telephone her parents for help.

Bundchen did mostly catalog work for the next two years, and primarily for Japanese companies. At the time, she was considered too athletic for high-end fashion work, and it was also suggested that a nose job would be in order. "People said I would never make it because my eyes were too small, I had weird angles, and an androgynous face," she recounted to Deanna Kizis in *Allure.*

Bundchen left school at the age of 16 and moved to New York City with her mother. Signed to Elite Models, she searched for work, took a crash English-language course, and began to land a few runway jobs. Soon, some of the major photographers in the business were noticing her and championing her to magazine editors and creative directors in the advertising industry. At the time, an emaciated "waif" look dominated the fashion magazines and runways, and Bundchen's strapping athleticism looked out of place. One of the leading photographers used by *Vogue* and other fashion magazines, Patrick Demarchelier, was among the first to take notice of the Brazilian teen. "She was so different, so healthy," Demarchelier told Andrews, the *Vanity Fair* writer. "At the time the models were all edgy, with the look like drug addicts."

Bundchen made her first real splash during London Fashion Week when she appeared on the runway for designer Alexander McQueen. In Milan, Italy's fashion capital, she modeled the latest designs from Versace and Dolce & Gabbana during its twice-yearly presentation of next season's designer collections. Her first magazine cover was French *Vogue,* and her appearance in the July 1999 issue of the U.S. edition of the same magazine, under the headline "The Return of the Curve," caused a minor sensation. She went on to appear five times on the cover of American *Vogue* in less than a year, and soon netted a lucrative five-year deal with lingerie-maker Victoria's Secret estimated at $24 million.

In 2001 Bundchen retired from runway work, though she still appeared in print ads for top designers. That same year she also launched her first business venture, a line of sandals manufactured by a Brazilian footwear company and sold under the label Ipanema Gisele Bundchen. In 2004, she made her feature-film debut as a bank robber in *Taxi,* which co-starred Jimmy Fallon and Queen Latifah. She also appeared briefly in *The Devil Wears Prada* in 2006 as an employee at a *Vogue*-like fashion magazine.

Bundchen reportedly donates five percent of her earnings to various charities, which have included organizations that work with Brazilian street children, raise awareness for Acquired Immune Deficiency Syndrome, or are active in reclaiming Brazil's Amazon rainforest. In 2008, *Forbes'* annual issue ranking the world's highest-paid celebrities cited her previous year's earnings at $35 million, making her the world's highest-paid model. Though her contract with Victoria's Secret expired in 2007, Bundchen still appeared in ads for Pantene hair-care products and for Ebel, the Swiss watchmaker. In October of 2008, she became the new face for MAX Factor cosmetics.

Bundchen has been linked with a number of high-profile men, including actor Leonardo DiCaprio and Tom Brady, quarterback for the New England Patriots. In July of 2008, she appeared on the cover of the men's fashion magazine *GQ,* and good-naturedly fielded a slew of questions about Brady, wearing angel wings in the Victoria's Secret catwalk shows, and the modeling industry in general. "I think there is danger obviously when you're really young and they make you all glamorous and you start thinking you are that," she told staff writer Nate Penn. "The important thing for me that helped save me is that I never believed.... I get there, I put on the clothes, I leave it on the hanger, and I go home. And that's what I do."

## Sources

### Periodicals

*Allure*, May 1, 2007, p. 262.
*GQ*, July 2008.
*Sunday Times* (London, England), September 23, 2007, p. 18.

*Vanity Fair*, October 2004, p. 324.
*WWD*, August 29, 2000, p. 4.

### Online

"No. 66: Gisele Bundchen," *Forbes*, http://www.forbes.com/lists/2008/53/celebrities08_Gisele-Bundchen_2VPP.htm l (August 27, 2008).

—*Carol Brennan*

# Tory Burch

## Fashion designer

**B**orn Tory Ann Robinson, June 15, 1966, in Valley Forge, PA; daughter of Buddy (an investor) and Reva (an actress and event planner) Robinson; married William Macklowe (an investment and development consultant), 1993 (divorced, c. 1993); married Christopher Burch (a venture capitalist), 1996 (divorced, c. 2006); children: twins Henry and Nicholas, son Sawyer. *Education:* University of Pennsylvania, B.A., 1988.

**Addresses:** *Home*—New York, NY. *Office*—Tory Burch, 11 W. 19th St., 7th Fl., New York, NY 10011.

## Career

**A**ssistant at the fashion house of Zoran, after 1988; worked for *Harper's Bazaar* and in advertising, public relations, and special events for Polo Ralph Lauren, Vera Wang, Narciso Rodriguez, and Loewe; Tory Burch, Inc., founder, 2004, and creative director and co-chair, 2004—.

**Awards:** Accessories Designer of the Year, Council of Fashion Designers of America, 2008.

## Sidelights

**T**ory Burch's eponymous clothing line became one of the most surprising success stories in American fashion in the first decade of the twenty-first century. Burch was a Manhattan socialite with no design experience when she launched her label in 2004, and her apparel quickly captured an elu-

sive dual market—that of mainstream consumers and the women who decide what is seen in high-end fashion magazines like *Vogue*. The press often refers to her as a socialite-turned-designer, but Burch takes issue with the first descriptor. "I don't know the definition of that word," she told *New York Times'* journalist Josh Patner. "It's a term that has become commonplace. Maybe back in the day. But does it mean someone who goes to charity events? Who doesn't work?"

Born in 1966, Burch grew up in a 250-year-old farmhouse in Valley Forge, Pennsylvania, near Philadelphia. Her father, Buddy, came from a family whose fortune had been made in the paper-cup business, while her mother, Reva, was a style icon who had dated actors such as Steve McQueen and Yul Brynner before her marriage. Burch and her two brothers—and the son of their housekeeper, whom they also considered part of the family—grew up in a home with horses, dogs, and even a macaw that was nearly as old as their mother. The family's roots were Jewish, but they celebrated the traditional Christian holidays.

Burch went to a private school, Agnes Irwin, where she was captain of the varsity tennis team. At the University of Pennsylvania, she majored in art history and moved to New York City after graduating. Through the connections of her fashionable mother, she was able to land a job at Zoran, the cult Yugoslavian-émigré designer, and later went to work for *Harper's Bazaar*. For most of the 1990s, Burch worked in advertising and public relations for Polo Ralph Lauren, Vera Wang, and Loewe, the Spanish luxury brand. She was married briefly, at

26, to William Macklowe, son of the real estate mogul Harry Macklowe, a well-known developer or owner of several Manhattan skyscrapers.

In 1996, Burch married Christopher Burch, a venture capitalist 14 years her senior. Her husband was also a Pennsylvania native, and his father owned a mining supply business that capitalized his two sons' clothing import business, Eagle's Eye, that helped launch the fad for holiday-themed sweaters back in the late 1980s. Burch became mother to three stepdaughters upon her marriage to Burch and was soon pregnant with twins. A third son, Sawyer, arrived as their union neared the five-year mark.

Burch's husband made his second fortune during the dot-com rush of the late 1990s, and that wealth eased their way into the Manhattan charity circuit. After she quit working full-time, Burch was active in two major institutions: the Society of Memorial Sloan-Kettering Cancer Center and the Junior Chair Committee at the American Ballet Theater. She also collaborated with an interior designer to redecorate the family home, a palatial spread inside the Pierre Hotel.

Burch still felt the pull of the fashion industry, however, and considered her options. She did some research into "reviving Jax, the classic sixties American sportswear brand," wrote Hamish Bowles in *Vogue*, "famed for their cigarette pants and slash-neck tops, beloved by her mother and such style icons as Jacqueline Kennedy." Deciding that was unfeasible, Burch decided to launch her own line, inspired in part by her mother and a floral-printed vintage tunic she had picked up at a Paris flea market. Her husband's manufacturing contacts in Asia from Eagle's Eye played a crucial role in the birth of "TRB by Tory Burch," as did the $2 million he invested. Some of that money was used to open a 1,900-square-foot space in New York's NoLita neighborhood, while another expenditure was the manufacture of 50 units in 15 different categories, beginning with the iconic tunic and including a line of accessories and home items.

On the night before her store opened in February of 2004, Burch worked through the entire night with the help of her stepdaughters readying the merchandise, and by the end of the day almost every item in the store had sold out. Over the few months and into the spring of 2005, Burch's apparel line caught on with New York City women, especially the tunics, which came in an array of colors and vintage-inspired prints. Writing for *Town & Country*, Carrie Karasyov described them as "the uniform for everyone from the Upper East Side lady who lunches to women across America who wanted to look like an Upper East Side lady who lunches—or, more correctly, her modern-day version: younger, hipper and on a tighter schedule." In April of 2005, sales for Burch's year-old company went through the roof when she appeared on *Oprah* after talk-show host Oprah Winfrey discovered the label and began touting the tunics.

Burch opened boutiques in selected U.S. cities throughout 2005 and 2006 and rebranded the actual company name as "Tory Burch" in the spring of 2006. She and her husband were co-chairs of the privately held company, which was run by a president with fashion-industry experience, but rumors of a marital rift began to float in certain Manhattan-socialite circles, and in January of 2006 Burch's husband moved out of their Pierre Hotel home. Two months later, the couple formally announced their divorce. "He is still a very important part of the company," Burch told journalist Meenal Mistry in a profile that appeared in *W* later that year, adding, "I don't work with him day to day, and that was probably something that wasn't great for us."

Burch kept the 9,000 square-foot Pierre apartment with views of Central Park, where she has been known to take her sons for early-morning skateboard runs before school. By 2009, there were 16 Tory Burch boutiques and the privately held company was believed to do about $115 million in sales annually. The gloomy economic forecast in 2008 had put some future plans on hold, including a fragrance and a full line of home goods. Burch was often asked why she started a fashion label—a notoriously fickle business with high overhead costs and reliant almost entirely upon either buzz or major advertising expenditures to succeed—when she was already wealthy and could afford to buy any designer she liked. "I knew I loved working," she told Mistry in *W*. "It's important to be challenged. I want to teach my children to have a work ethic."

## Sources

*New York Times*, October 3, 2004.
*Town & Country*, January 2008, p. 118.
*Vanity Fair*, February 2007, p. 174.
*Vogue*, October 2004, p. 350.
*W*, September 2006, p. 264.
*WWD*, November 10, 2005, p. 10.

—*Carol Brennan*

# Carol Ann Cartwright

*AP Images*

## President of Bowling Green University

**B**orn June 19, 1941; daughter of Carl (a railroad worker) Anton and Kathryn Marie (a homemaker; maiden name, Weishapple) Becker; married G. Phillip Cartwright, June 11, 1966; children: Catherine E., Stephen R., Susan D. *Education:* University of Wisconsin—Whitewater, B.S., 1962; University of Pittsburgh, M.Ed., 1965, Ph.D., 1968.

**Addresses:** *Office*—Bowling Green State University, Office of the President, 220 McFall Center, Bowling Green, OH 43403.

## Career

**W**orked as instructor then associate professor at Pennsylvania State University's College of Education, 1968-72; associate professor, then assistant professor, professor, Pennsylvania State University, 1972-79; dean of academic affairs, Pennsylvania State University, 1981-84, then dean of the undergraduate program and vice provost, 1984-88; served on the editorial boards of *Topics in Early Childhood Special Education* and *Exceptional Education Quarterly,* 1982-88; vice chancellor of academic affairs and professor of human development at the University of California—Davis, 1988-91; president of Kent State University, 1991-2006; member of the Knight Commission on Intercollegiate Athletics, 2000—; chairman of the NCAA Executive Committee, 2002-05; interim president of Bowling Green State University, 2008-09, then president, 2009—.

**Member:** American Association for Higher Education; American Association of University Women; American Council on Education; American Educa-

tional Research Association; Cleveland Tomorrow; Council for Exceptional Children; board of directors, Davey Tree Expert Company; board of directors, First Energy Corp.; Greater Akron Chamber of Commerce; board of directors, KeyCorp.; National Association of State Universities and Land-Grant Colleges; board of directors, PolyOne Corp; Commission on Women in Higher Education, 2003—; board of directors, National Public Radio, 2004—; board of directors, American Association of Colleges and Universities, 2005—.

**Awards:** Distinguished alumni award, University of Wisconsin—Whitewater; distinguished alumni award, Clairol Mentor award; Women of Achievement award, YWCA of Greater Cleveland; Franklin Delano Roosevelt humanitarian award for excellence, March of Dimes; University of Pittsburgh School of Education, 1994; inductee of the Ohio Women's Hall of Fame, Ohio Department of Job and Family Services, 1996; inductee of the Athletics Hall of Fame, Kent State University, 2008.

## Sidelights

**I**n 2009, Carol Ann Cartwright became the eleventh president of Bowling Green State University, located in Bowling Green, Ohio. She had previously spent 15 years as the president of Kent State University, also in Ohio, making her the first woman to serve as the president of a public college or university in that state. A former professor at Pennsylvania State University and the University of California—Davis, Cartwright also held administrative posts at both schools. She is known as an innovative administrator who wants to make her schools greatly affect the lives of both students and the public at large.

Cartwright was born on June 19, 1941, in Sioux City, Iowa, the daughter of Carl and Kathryn Becker. Her father worked for a railroad, whereas her mother was a homemaker. Because of her father's job, Cartwright and her family moved every few years. She lived in Kansas City and St. Louis, Missouri, in Oklahoma, and in Wisconsin. Though she attended high school in three different states, Cartwright proved to be an excellent student.

Because of her great grades, Cartwright became the first person in her family to go to college. While attending the University of Wisconsin—Whitewater, however, she had to work to pay for school. She held a number of part-time jobs during her school years, including waitress, typist, and statistician. Cartwright also encountered discrimination as a female student in the late 1950s and early 1960s. Women were expected to become teachers or nurses, and her interest in science was actively discouraged. While she was interested in science, Cartwright chose to major in early education, focusing on special education which was then more science-oriented.

Cartwright graduated from Wisconsin—Whitewater with her bachelor of science degree in 1962. Continuing her education, Cartwright entered the University of Pittsburgh, where she was granted her master of education degree in 1965 and her Ph.D. in 1968. Both of her advanced degrees were in special education and educational research. After completing her education, Cartwright began a college teaching career. The year she earned her Ph.D., she joined the faculty of Pennsylvania State University's School of Education as an instructor. Cartwright then became an associate professor in the education school, a post she held until 1972. Remaining at Penn, she moved through the ranks from associate to assistant to full professor by 1979.

Two years later, Cartwright moved from her professorship to administration posts. In 1981, she became the dean of academic affairs at Penn. By taking the position, she was the first female dean at Penn State.

Cartwright was later promoted to vice provost and the dean of undergraduate programs in 1984. While working in these positions, she served as a member of the editorial boards of two academic journals, *Topics in Early Childhood Special Education* and *Exceptional Education Quarterly.*

In 1988, Cartwright left Penn for the University of California—Davis where she served as both a professor of human development and the vice chancellor of academic affairs. She again broke new ground, serving as the first female vice chancellor at the school. In 1991, Cartwright reached new heights in her academic administrative career when she became the tenth president of Kent State University. As the first woman to lead a public institution of higher learning in Ohio, Cartwright faced intense media scrutiny in the state.

While she understood the interest, Cartwright told Jennifer Haliburton and Felix Winternitz of *Ohio* that it was secondary to her job performance. She said, "It wasn't earth shattering, as far as I was concerned ... I've gone through this thing of being 'the first.' But I also know that what really matters is results. People very quickly start focusing on what your plans are, what you're getting done, and the whole issue of being 'first woman' takes a backstage postion—which is fine." She also faced personal challenges as she was diagnosed with breast cancer in 1992. Sharing the information with faculty, staff, and students, Cartwright underwent successful treatment and missed little time in her then-new position.

Kent State had eight campuses, 34,000 students, and an annual budget in excess of $385 million, as of 2003. During her 15 years in charge of the second-largest university in Ohio, Cartwright demonstrated her spirit of innovation by emphasizing university and corporate partnerships in both the United States and abroad to improve neighborhoods, the environment, and people's lives in general. Cartwright was instrumental in creating several international projects with the country of Turkey such as a water resources and human sustainability project and improvements to schools.

Of her philosophy as president of Kent, Cartwright told Abby Cymerman of *Smart Business Akron/Canton,* "I'm committed to making a difference, and Kent makes a difference in people's lives. It's the reason I'm here and the reason I stay. I'm the symbol of that, and that's what excites me. It happens in thousands of ways, in so many lives." Later in the interview, Cartwright added, "You have to encourage creativity, then try to align resources with the innovation of the staff. The fundamental role is to empower others in the organization." Cartwright and her husband G. Phillip Cartwright did this in another way, by contributing more than $310,000 to the school over the course of her tenure, including the establishment of two Founders Scholarships worth $35,000 each.

During her time at Kent State, Cartwright also played key roles in U.S. college athletics. She served as both the chairman of the NCAA (National Collegiate Athletic Association) Executive Committee from 2002 to 2005 and was a member of the Knight Commission on Intercollegiate Athletics beginning in 2000. In the former post, she played a pivotal role in creating the NCAA's policies on academic, ethical, and financial issues for student athletes. The latter group had no power to create policies but was a group external to the NCAA intended to oversee and affect change through leadership about issues such as graduation rates, the effect of midweek football games on athletes and campuses, and the question of payment for student athletes.

While holding these prestigious positions, Cartwright had to deal with problems with Kent State's own athletic programs including the arrest of the football team's quarterback, Joshua Cribbs, on felony charges of domestic violence and drug trafficking. There were also complaints and problems within the women's basketball team about their practice regime and some of the actions of the head coach, Bob Lindsay. Both of these incidents came to a head in early 2004, and were dealt with swiftly by her office.

Cartwright formally retired from Kent State in 2006, remained at the school through the summer of 2007 to help with the transition, and then spent nearly a year away from academia. In June of 2008, she returned to an academic administrative position when she agreed to become the interim president of Bowling Green State University (BGSU) for one year after Sidney Ribeau left to become the president of Howard University. The school continued to pursue her as president though she was initially firm in her decision. After the economic downturn hit the United States, BGSU's enrollment dropped for a second straight year, and a provost, Shirley Baugher, resigned, Cartwright saw the need for leadership to address these issues and agreed to take the post. She became BGSU's first female president, telling Meghan Gilbert of the Toledo, Ohio *Blade,* "I know through experience what it means to have stable leadership."

Cartwright signed a contract to be president through June 2011 worth $375,000 per year. She intended to address the university's enrollment woes as well as funding problems in the face of wide-spread economic problems in the United States, which greatly affected funding for institutions like BGSU. One of her first moves was to lay off a significant number of administrative staff members. Within two months, however, she faced another challenge as it came to light that the university had invested $15 million with Westridge Capital Management, which had been run fraudulently by Paul Greenwood and Stephen Walsh. Cartwright vowed to get the school's money back.

No matter what happened, Cartwright looked at her position as BGSU as a chance to make the school better. She told the *Blade*'s Gilbert, "This is also an opportunity to think about the kind of institution Bowling Green State University is, how we want to protect our strengths and priorities, and how we want to make the right investments so that we are even better going forward."

## Sources

### Books

*Complete Marquis Who's Who Biographies,* Marquis Who's Who LLC, 2009.

### Periodicals

*Akron Beacon Journal* (Akron, OH), January 7, 2009.
*Blade* (Toledo, OH), January 7, 2009; March 17, 2009.
*Ohio,* April 1, 2004, p. 90.
*Plain Dealer* (Cleveland, OH), February 9, 2004, pp. C1, C10; January 7, 2009, p. B2.
*Smart Business Akron/Canton,* September 1, 2003, p. S8.
University Wire, November 22, 2004; January 13, 2009.

—A. Petruso

# Debra Martin Chase

## Film producer, television producer, and attorney

Born Debra Martin, October 11, 1956, in Great Lakes, IL; daughter of Douglas (a police officer) and Beverly B. (a teacher; maiden name, Barber) Martin; married Anthony B. Chase (divorced, 1987). *Education:* Mount Holyoke College, B.A., 1977; Harvard Law School, J.D., 1981.

**Addresses:** *Office*—c/o Martin Chase Productions, 500 South Buena Vista St., Animation 2E-6, MC1757, Burbank, CA 91521-1757.

## Career

Attorney, Mearday, Day, and Caldwell (law firm), Houston, TX, c. 1981-83; freelance writer, *Houston City,* c. early 1980s; attorney, Tenneco, Houston, TX, c. 1983-85; attorney, Stroock, Stroock, and Lavan (law firm), New York City, 1985; legal counsel, Avon Products, New York City, c. mid-1980s; worked on political campaigns for Michael Dukakis and David Dinkins, 1988; moved to Los Angeles, c. 1988; joined Columbia Pictures' legal department, c. 1988, then executive assistant to Frank Price, 1989-91; head of production, Mundy Lane Entertainment (a production company), CA, 1992-95; executive vice president, Brown House Productions (also known as Houston Productions), 1995-2000; co-produced *The Preacher's Wife,* 1996; produced *The Princess Diaries,* 2000; formed production company, Martin Chase Productions, 2000; signed first-look deal with Disney, c. 2001; produced television movie *The Cheetah Girls,* 2003; produced film *Sisterhood of the Traveling Pants,* 2005; produced film *Sisterhood of the Traveling Pants 2,* 2008.

## Sidelights

One of the few female African-American film and television producers, Debra Martin Chase primarily produces films and television movies intended for a female audience. She is responsible for such hits as *The Princess Diaries, The Sisterhood of the Traveling Pants,* and *The Cheetah Girls.* Her films, she believed, shared a common theme as she told Carol A. Sliwa of *Mount Holyoke Alumnae Quarterly:* "For me, there's usually some variation of: 'We all have the power within ourselves to be anything that we want to be.'" Before starting her own production company, Chase worked at the production companies of Denzel Washington and Whitney Houston.

Born on October 11, 1956, in Great Lakes, Illinois, Chase is the daughter of Douglas Martin and his wife, Beverly. Her father was a police officer while her mother was a teacher. Her father was a big fan of films and passed down this love to his daughter. Chase told Audrey Edwards of *Essence,* "I'm the kid who was in the movie theater every Saturday. I've been a movie fanatic since I was a child, and my images of the world were shaped by what I saw on the screen."

Raised in Chicago until the age of six, Chase and her family then moved to California, and later to

Massachusetts. She graduated from Amherst High School in 1973, then remained in the east to further her education. Chase entered Mount Holyoke College, where she earned her B.A. magna cum laude in political science in 1977. Deciding on a legal career, she went to Harvard Law School where she met her future husband, Anthony Chase. (The couple later divorced.) Chase was granted her J.D. in 1981.

For much of the next decade, Chase focused on her legal career. She began by joining a law firm in Houston, Texas, called Mearday, Day, and Caldwell, where she concentrated on corporate securities and municipal finance. Even then Chase wondered if she had done the right thing. She told Dinah Eng in *USA Today*, "I was in a corporate skyscraper thinking, 'How did I end up here? This wasn't where I was supposed to be.'" Chase also wrote on a freelance basis for the magazine *Houston City.*

In 1983, Chase began a two-year stint as a lawyer for Tenneco, a multi-national corporation which focused on oil and gas. Moving to New York City in 1985, Chase joined the firm of Stroock, Stroock, and Lavan. She then became the in-house counsel for Avon Products, the beauty company. Chase was already thinking about a career in film, reading related books and periodicals, attending seminars, and talking with people working in the industry.

By the late 1980s, Chase was working outside of the legal profession. In 1988, she worked for the presidential campaign for Democratic nominee Michael Dukakis. Chase also helped David Dinkins get elected as New York City's mayor. Her focus then turned towards the film industry. Though she realized that she did not enjoy practicing law, she launched her film career by working in the legal department of Columbia Pictures. There, Chase learned how the film business operated and how the related deals came together.

In 1989, Chase became the executive assistant to Frank Price, then the chairman of Columbia. She spent a year-and-a-half in the post, impressing Price and gaining even more inside information on how the Hollywood system works. Price praised her, telling Crystal Nix Hines of *Essence*, "She is not a shrinking violet. This is a business in which you've got to aggressively pursue opportunities and fight for them, and Debra is good at that."

While working for Price, Chase took a chance which took her career to the next level. Walking to a commissary for lunch, she introduced herself to actor Denzel Washington, who, unbeknownst to her, was on the hunt for a new producing partner. In 1992, she became the head of Mundy Lane Entertainment, Washington's production company.

Chase worked on a number of projects for Mundy Lane, including the 1995 documentary *Hank Aaron: Chasing the Dream.* That year, she was nominated for an Emmy Award for her work on the special. Chase also served as an executive producer on the 1996 film *Courage Under Fire* and co-producer of the 1996 film *The Preacher's Wife.* During her time with Washington, Chase also learned much about how to read scripts for what attracts an actor, the significance of character, and the importance of emotions and motivations to films.

Leaving Mundy Lane in 1995, Chase became the executive vice president of Brown House Productions (also known as Houston Productions), the production company owned by singer/actress Whitney Houston. During her stint at Brown House, Chase worked on such films as the remake of the 1947 film *The Bishop's Wife.* Chase served as the co-producer of 1996's *The Preacher's Wife,* which starred Houston.

At Brown House, Chase also served as executive producer of a television movie version of *Cinderella.* Based on the musical by Rodgers & Hammerstein, this version of *Cinderella* aired on ABC. Houston had a major role in the production, which featured R&B singer Brandy in the title role. In 1998, Chase was nominated for her second Emmy Award for outstanding variety, music, or comedy special for *Cinderella.* Of this movie, Chase told *Mount Holyoke Alumnae Quarterly*'s Sliwa, "This is the fantasy stuff that I love. When I'm successful, I'm able to take that fantasy, that wish fulfillment, and imbue it with values and messages that I believe are valuable to everybody, but particularly to young people."

In 2000, Chase moved on from Brown House and formed her own production company, Martin Chase Productions. Through this company, she produced primarily family friendly, girl-oriented films as well as various television series and movies. Chase's first film as producer was 2001's G-rated *The Princess Diaries,* a modern day fairy tale about an awkward teenage American girl who finds out she is European royalty. Based on the novel of the same name by Meg Cabot, the film was a smash hit with box office receipts of more than $109 million. Chase told Eng in *USA Today*, "It's been amazing and gratifying to see how *Princess Diaries* spoke to girls everywhere. When the first film came out in 2001, the conventional wisdom was that if you made movies for boys, the girls would come, but there was no market for girl movies."

The success of *The Princess Diaries* also landed Chase a first look deal at Disney for Martin Chase Productions, and led to her being named one of ten producers to watch by *Variety*. Chase thus became the first African-American female producer to be given a solo producing deal with a major studio. Disney paid overhead for her company while gaining first refusal rights for her productions. Under the deal, Chase went on to produce *The Princess Diaries*'s 2004 follow-up, *The Princess Diaries 2: Royal Engagement*, which follows the main character as her life as a college student at Princeton University and princess in training changes dramatically when she learns she must marry within 30 days or lose the throne.

For the Disney Channel in 2003, Chase produced *The Cheetah Girls.* Based on the novels by Deborah Gregory, this television movie emphasized the importance of female friendships through the experiences of four young, multi-talented friends who aspire to music stardom through their singing group. One of the actresses was Disney star Raven. *The Cheetah Girls* was a ratings smash, and led to follow-ups. Chase also served as executive producer on the subsequent Cheetah Girls movies: 2006's *The Cheetah Girls 2* and 2008's *The Cheetah Girls: One World.* Both were as popular as the first, with *The Cheetah Girls 2* attracting 7.8 million viewers.

Another television project for which Chase served as executive producer was the 2004-06 Lifetime series *1-800-MISSING*. This series was based on the novel *1-800-Where-R-U* by Meg Cabot and focused on an FBI agent, Brooke Haslett (played by Vivica A. Fox), who locates the missing with the help of a psychic, Jess Mastriani. Of the series, Chase told Eng in an article for the Gannett News Service, "It's really about female empowerment.... They're both women who are smart and savvy. They're vulnerable and have needs and desires, but they believe in themselves."

Another popular film franchise that Chase produced was based on the best-selling novels for teen readers by Ann Brashares called *The Sisterhood of the Traveling Pants*. Chase spent four years to get the project from its conception to the release of the film. Like the novels, *The Sisterhood of the Traveling Pants* was about four teenage girls who became friends for life, but are spending their first summer apart. The 2005 film was not a hit in theaters but gained a huge following through its DVD release. The 2008 follow-up, *The Sisterhood of the Traveling Pants 2*, also attracted a loyal audience.

For all her projects, Chase was very hands on. She read her many scripts, and was present for many of the shoots. Chase also constantly looked for new actors, writers, and directors with which to work. After *The Sisterhood of the Traveling Pants 2*, she had many producing projects lined up including *The Dirty Girls Social Club*, expected to be released in 2008, and *Little Scarlet*, scheduled for 2010. Nina Jacobsen, the president of Disney's Buena Vista Motion Pictures Group, told Eng in *USA Today*, "Debra represents a new generation of black filmmakers. She's smart and has great taste for material. Her taste is color-blind, which is one of the things I respect about her."

In addition to running her production company and its projects, Chase served as a producing mentor for the University of Southern California and was a member of the board of Columbia College, located in Chicago, Illinois, which had a large number of African-American film students. She also volunteered for the Heartland Film Festival and the Community Resource Advisory Committee of the Los Angeles County Museum.

Assisting others, particularly other African Americans in the film industry, was important to Chase. She told Aldore Collier of *Ebony*, "I'm proud of the work I've done, and along the way I've been able to help a lot of African Americans get their feet in the door and move up the ladder. That's very important. It's a responsibility that we as blacks have. Whitney and Denzel helped me ... and I'm obligated to help others."

Chase also realized any position in the film industry was tenuous, but had no plans to give up no matter how difficult her position might become. She told Hines of *Essence*, "I've been very fortunate. Every now and then I look down and realize there's no safety net. But I remind myself to keep looking up and have the strength to move forward."

## Sources

### Periodicals

*Black Enterprise,* March 2007, p. 99.
*Daily Variety,* May 1, 2006, p. 10.
*Ebony,* January 1998, p. 52; May 2002, p. 150.
*Essence,* September 1997, p. 108; April 2003, p. 138.
Gannett News Service, September 16, 2003.
*Jet,* August 21, 2006, p. 48.
*Newsweek,* July 24, 2006, p. 42.
*New York Times,* August 6, 2008, p. E7.

*USA Today,* August 12, 2004, p. 3D.
*Variety,* May 7-13, 2001, p. C21.

**Online**

"Debra Martin Chase Biography," Entertainment-Makers, http://www.thehistorymakers.com/biography/biography.asp?bioindex=1005&category=entertainmentMakers (August 16, 2008).

"Debra Martin Chase," Internet Movie Database, http://www.imdb.com/name/nm0153744/ (August 16, 2008).

"Debra Martin Chase '77: Chasing Hollywood: One Producer's Search for 'Material with a Message,'" *Mount Holyoke Alumnae Quarterly,* http://www.alumnae.mtholyoke.edu/quarterly/sum05/chase_feature.pdf (August 16, 2008).

—*A. Petruso*

# Kate Christensen

**Author**

---

**B**orn in 1962 in Berkeley, CA; married Jon Lewis (a photographer and painter), c. 1996. *Education:* Reed College, Portland, OR, B.A., 1986; University of Iowa Writers' Workshop, M.F.A., 1989.

**Addresses:** *Contact*—Todd Doughty, director of publicity, Doubleday, 1745 Broadway, New York, NY 10019. *Home*—Brooklyn, NY. *Web site*— http://www.randomhouse.com/features/katechristensen.

## Career

**W**orked various positions, including secretary, waitress and editorial assistant, New York City, 1989-mid-1990s; fulltime writer, mid-1990s—.

**Awards:** First prize, *Mademoiselle* Fiction Contest, 1989; PEN/Faulkner award for fiction, PEN/Faulkner Foundation, for *The Great Man*, 2008.

## Sidelights

**K**ate Christensen's first novel, 1999's *In the Drink*, arrived on the heels of the *Bridget Jones' Diary* craze. Christensen's book—about a single, overly self-observant young woman trying to find her way—was eagerly embraced by the emerging "chick-lit" set, prompting a quick dismissal from literary critics. One decade and three books later, Christensen scored a literary coup d'état when she won the coveted PEN/Faulkner Award for Fiction in 2008 with her fourth novel, *The Great Man*.

The oldest of three girls, Christensen was born in Berkeley, California, in 1962, to parents involved with 1960s political activism. Her mother was a Juilliard-trained cellist, unable to make her way in the music world because of stage fright. She ended up in Berkeley, where she met Christensen's father, a Marxist-loving lawyer whose passion included defending those who stirred the political pot. Tensions ran high in the 1960s with the Vietnam War raging and the civil rights movement in full swing. Christensen's attorney father spent his time representing members of the Black Panthers, as well as draft dodgers and conscientious objectors, on a pro bono basis.

As a child, Christensen possessed an extraordinary imagination and created her own fictional country called Zenobia. By age six, she was putting pencil to paper. An early story, called "My Magic Carpet Ride," dealt with sisters who traveled the globe on a magic carpet but were sure to return home in time for tea. Speaking to the *Washington Post*'s Bob Thompson, Christensen said she knew all along that she would become a writer. "I'm no good at anything else," she quipped. "There were a lot of eggs in that basket."

In 1968, Christensen's parents separated and within two years her mother moved her and her sisters to Tempe, Arizona, so she could begin graduate work at the university there. Christensen has fond memories of her mother from that time. She and her sisters piled into their mother's room to watch *The Carol Burnett Show* and *Sonny and Cher* and snuggle on Saturday mornings. In a personal narrative printed in a collection called *The Bitch in the House*,

Christensen referred to her mother as "an invincible Wonder Woman who hosted raucous poker games but also enforced a comforting schedule, practiced her cello, made us dinner, and took us shoe shopping." With their father long out of the picture, the family scraped by, living on a graduate stipend Christensen's mother received. "We were poor, but so was everyone else we knew, and we didn't feel our poverty because my mother didn't let us," Christensen wrote in the essay.

When Christensen was eleven, her mother remarried and they relocated to the Phoenix suburbs. By her teen years, they were living in Jerome, Arizona. During her last two years of high school, Christensen attended a Waldorf School and thrived in the interdisciplinary environment of the school, which encouraged imagination and creativity. Christensen studied the writing of Wordsworth and Thoreau, sang Mozart's "Requiem" and immersed herself in her creative writing classes. Next, Christensen headed to Reed College, a private, liberal-arts school in Portland, Oregon. She graduated in 1986, then honed her writing craft at the University of Iowa Writers' Workshop, graduating in 1989.

Christensen moved to New York to pursue her writing career but struggled to find her voice. To support herself, she took jobs as a waitress, secretary, and editorial assistant. Along the way, she met an aspiring photographer and painter named Jon Lewis. Christensen gave him some early pages of *In the Drink* and knew instantly she was on to something. "When I heard him laugh on the first page, and then keep laughing, it was a real turning point," she told the *Oregonian*'s Jeff Baker. "As corny as it sounds, I felt like I had found my reader."

Christensen married Lewis around 1996. Working as a building contractor, Lewis was able to support both of them, allowing Christensen to quit her secretarial job and write fulltime. Lewis read every draft she presented him and offered her reassurances that it was going well. Published in 1999, *In the Drink* was a semi-autobiographical novel, following the life of New York City singleton—and cynic—Claudia Steiner. Having given up on her dreams of becoming a successful writer in her own right, Claudia takes a job as a secretarial assistant and ghostwriter. As she struggles to find her way, Claudia fills her life with cocktails, meaningless sex, and takeout food. Reviews were fairly positive, though many critics dubbed Claudia as New York City's version of Bridget Jones—the fictional London singleton who appeared in two novels in the 1990s and was made famous onscreen in a portrayal by Renee Zellweger.

Try as she might, Christensen could not shake off the comparisons. *Entertainment Weekly* called *In the Drink* "one of the sassy new *Bridget Jones* look-alikes." The book sold well but failed to generate any long-lasting interest in Christensen. In an interview with *Bold Type*, Christensen shrugged off the comparison and said Claudia had more in common with other literary characters than with Bridget Jones. "I trace Claudia's lineage through an august tradition of hard-drinking, self-destructive, hilarious anti-heroes beginning with Dostoevsky's *Underground Man*."

Undaunted, Christensen started another novel. She began with the idea of writing a book about a woman trying to save her sister from a cult. Christensen struggled through 125 pages but felt the book was lacking. In an interview posted on the Anchor Books website, Christensen described the epiphany she had that pushed her through her next novel. "Then, one night as I was lying awake worrying about how the hell I was going to send a jolt of electricity through this moribund thing, a character came to me—from where I have no idea. It was the image of a gay man with his arms outstretched standing in a loft high above Manhattan, looking down at the lights of the city."

In that moment, a new character and an entirely new book emerged. *Jeremy Thrane* was published in 2001. It follows the life of a gay, 30-something, unemployed struggling writer who is secretly provided for by his closeted—and married—celebrity lover. When Jeremy is dumped, he must make his way on his own for the first time in his life. The book follows the snobbish and immature Jeremy as he wanders the streets of Manhattan in search of himself. *Jeremy Thrane* was released a few weeks before 9/11 and quickly faded into the background.

For her third novel—*The Epicure's Lament* (2004)—Christensen chose to stay with a male protagonist. The book revolves around Hugo, a middle-aged hermit struggling with Buerger's disease, an autoimmune disorder that causes inflammation and gangrene of the limbs. The disease is associated with the use of tobacco products, and Hugo could overcome it if he would stop smoking. As an arrogant, aging, and failed writer, Hugo is not interested in saving himself. Besides smoking, his gluttony involves eating fat-rich foods and indulging in self-loathing as he writes in his journal, which is how the story is told. For years, Hugo has been living alone in a family-owned estate along the Hudson River. His solitude comes to a quick end when his brother—who is going through a divorce—shows up, followed by his ex-wife, toting a child she claims is his.

Speaking to the *Star-Ledger*'s Dylan Foley, Christensen said the dark novel was written in response to 9/11. "I needed to write about someone my own age, someone who felt it was all over. I was pretty angry and so was Hugo. I was enraged, but I couldn't get revenge. I couldn't write directly about somebody living in New York and seeing all the smoke at Ground Zero." Writing the book proved so intense that Christensen took four months off right in the middle to train for the New York Marathon. "I'd never run before," she told Cassandra Braun of the *Contra Costa Times.* "I just needed to reconnect with New York in a positive way, and I needed to do something to counteract the effect of Hugo and all his smoking and negativity and his death-affirming philosophy." Whereas reviews were encouraging, sales were low.

After the book was published, Christensen suffered a long period of writer's block. Finally, she decided to try writing in third person instead of first person, as she had done in her previous novels. In an essay posted on *Critical Mass,* the Web site of the National Book Critics Circle, Christensen wrote about her struggle with writer's block and her third-person epiphany. "To buck myself up, I decided I needed to write something in the third person, as a bracing technical challenge. For me, writing in the first person is a zenlike floating along, breathing, organic, letting another persona take over my brain and keyboard, whereas third person is like wrestling with a big, greasy, mean, cheating bear."

Feeling invigorated with a new challenge, Christensen began writing again, creating what would become her award-winning fourth novel, *The Great Man* (2007). The title character is Oscar Feldman, a deceased New York painter who made his mark in the art world creating portraits of nude women. Five years after he dies, two biographers show up and begin questioning the elderly women who played prominent roles in his life. Readers learn about Abigail, his wife of four decades and mother of his autistic son. There is also his longtime bohemian mistress, Teddy, with whom he fathered a set of twins, and his lesbian sister, Maxine, also an artist. Once the biographers show up and begin asking questions, long-kept secrets bubble to the surface.

Speaking to Dennis Lythgoe of the *Deseret Morning News,* Christensen said her aging agile mother inspired her to write about strong, older women. Christensen went on to say that her intent was "to stick up for older women in literature, women who are usually portrayed as an annoying old neighbor or a needy grandmother. I look for real people who have bad moods, ego, wit and veracity. I want to get away from stereotype. These people are not old in their minds."

The book hit a nerve and went on to win the 2008 PEN/Faulkner Award for Fiction—a prestigious literary award that has been won by writers such as John Updike and Philip Roth. Christensen was only the fifth woman in 28 years to win the award, which came with a $15,000 prize. Judges read some 350 submissions before selecting her novel as the winner. Judge Victor LaValle told the *Washington Post* that Christensen's book was the one he "kept coming back to again and again," despite there being plenty of books from more noted authors, including Annie Dillard, who ended up a finalist.

When she is not busy writing, Christensen enjoys reading English novels and mysteries, drinking tea, playing Solitaire, and listening to NPR. Her fifth book—*Trouble,* about a Manhattan psychotherapist who leaves her passionless marriage—was set for publication in 2009. In a commentary posted on *Critical Mass,* Christensen discussed how she never really knows which books will be hits and which will not. She called writing an "exciting and challenging and somewhat surreal job" because authors often pour their hearts out only to be completely ignored for their work, or misunderstood. "I've always identified with underdogs and losers and malcontents; being a winner has caused a bit of a psychic seismic shift," she wrote. "I'll probably never lose my innate sense of being an outsider, but it sure is nice to win a prize."

## Novels

*In the Drink,* Doubleday (New York, NY), 1999.
*Jeremy Thrane,* Broadway Books (New York, NY), 2001.
*The Epicure's Lament,* Doubleday, 2004.
*The Great Man,* Doubleday, 2007.
*Trouble,* Doubleday, 2009.

## Sources

### Books

Hanauer, Cathi, ed. *The Bitch in the House,* William Morrow, 2002.

### Periodicals

*Contra Costa Times,* March 14, 2004, p. C14.
*Deseret Morning News* (Salt Lake City, UT), September 16, 2007.

*Oregonian* (Portland, OR), September 21, 2007, p. 46.
*Star-Ledger* (Newark, NJ), February 15, 2004, p. 4.
*Washington Post,* March 13, 2008, p. C1.

## Online

"An Interview with Kate Christensen," *Bold Type,* http://www.randomhouse.com/boldtype/0699/christensen/interview.html (April 27, 2009).
"Guest Post: Kate Christensen on Winning the PEN/Faulkner Award," *Critical Mass,* http://bookcriticscircle.blogspot.com/2008/04/guest-post-kate-christensen-on-winning.html (April 27, 2009).

"In the Drink," *Entertainment Weekly,* http://www.ew.com/ew/article/0,,273760,00.html (April 27, 2009).
"Jeremy Thrane," Anchor Books, http://www.randomhouse.com/anchor/catalog/display.pperl?isbn=97803857.tif20342&view=qa (April 27, 2009).
"PEN/Faulkner Award Winner: Kate Christensen," Why Waldorf Works, http://www.whywaldorfworks.org/03_NewsEvents/documents/Kate%20Christensen. pdf (April 27, 2009).

*—Lisa Frick*

# Maxine Clark

## Founder of Build-A-Bear Workshop

**B**orn Maxine Sandra Clark, March 6, 1949, in Miami, FL; daughter of Kenneth and Anne (Lerch) Kassleman; married Robert Fox (a business executive), September 1984. *Education:* University of Georgia, B.A., 1971.

**Addresses:** *Office*—Build-A-Bear Workshop, Inc., 1954 Innerbelt Business Center Drive, St. Louis, MO 63114. *Contact*—12 Greenbriar, St. Louis, MO 63124.

## Career

**J**oined Hecht Company as an executive trainee, 1971, then hosiery buyer, 1971-72, misses sportswear buyer, 1972-76; manager of merchandise planning and research, May Department Stores Company, 1976-78, then director of merchandise development, 1978-80; vice president of marketing and sales promotion, Venture Stores division, 1980-81, then senior vice president of marketing and sales promotion, 1981-83, executive vice president of marketing and softlines, 1983-85; vice president of merchandising, Lerner Shops division of the Limited, Inc., 1986-88; executive vice president, Venture Stores, 1988-92; president of Payless ShoeSource, 1992-96; founder and chief executive officer, Smart Stuff, Inc., 1996—; founded Build-A-Bear Workshop, 1997; chief executive bear of Build-A-Bear Workshop, 1997—; president of Build-A-Bear Workshop, 1997-2004; chairman of board of directors of Build-A-Bear Workshop, 2000—.

**Member:** Lafayette Square Restoration Committee, 1978-79; national advisory council, Girl Scouts, U.S.A., 1995-97; trustee, University of Georgia Foundation, 1995—; Committee of 200; chair, Teach for America, St. Louis. Board of directors for Earthgrains Company, Girl Scout Council of Greater St. Louis, J.C. Penney Company, Inc., KETC Channel 9 PBS, Simon Youth Foundation, Tandy Brands Accessories Company, Teach for America, and Wave Technologies, Inc.

**Awards:** Entrepreneur of the year in the Emerging Business Category, Ernst & Young, 1999; retail innovator of the year, National Retail Federation, 2001; Customers First award for customer-centered leader, *Fast Company,* 2005; inductee, Junior Achievement National Business Hall of Fame, 2006; luminary award for Entrepreneurial Achievement, Committee of 200, 2006; one of 25 most influential people in retailing, *Chain Store Age,* 2008.

## Sidelights

**T**he founder of Build-A-Bear Workshop, Maxine Clark has had a long career in retail business. Before Build-A-Bear, she was the president of Payless ShoeSource, Inc., in the mid-1990s. She also spent 19 years working in divisions of the May Department Stores Company. Clark was well-known and highly regarded for her imaginative ideas and creative approach to retailing. Also lauded for valuing her employees, Clark told Christine Imbs of the *St. Louis Commerce Magazine,* "I do believe it takes a village to raise a bear. In order for anything to be successful it takes the work of many people."

Maxine Sandra Clark was born on March 6, 1949, in Miami, Florida. The daughter of Kenneth and Anne Kassleman, she was raised in Coral Gables, Florida. Because of her mother's firm belief that people were meant to help others and her own extensive charitable activities, Clark once worked at a home for the mentally challenged as a manager and fundraiser. She even made sure the residents had their own Boys Scout and Girl Scout troops. Clark also became interested in retail because of her mother, favorably remembering bus trips to Miami with her mother and sister to shop at Burdine's department store.

While her mother wanted her to have a career in social work, Clark earned her B.A. in journalism from the University of Georgia in 1971. After completing her education, she began her career with the Hecht Company in Washington as an executive trainee at Hecht's department stores. (Hecht was a division of the May Department Stores Company.) Later in 1971, Clark began a short stint as a hosiery buyer for the company then spent four years as a misses sportswear buyer. In the latter post, she focused on budget sportswear.

After impressing the chairman and president of May when they visited Hecht's, Clark was brought to the parent company in St. Louis in 1976. She worked as the manager of merchandise planning and research for May. Two years later, she became the director of merchandise development, a post she held until 1980. During this time period, she was charged with creating a shop for kids, and, in what became her trademark inventive way, came up with a concept that incorporated play and shopping.

After May bought the discount chain Venture Stores, Clark was named the vice president of marketing and sales promotion for Venture in 1981. She then had two-year stint as the executive vice president of marketing and softlines for Venture from 1983 to 1985. By this time, Clark was also being recognized for her ability to anticipate consumer trends. For example, she saw that Cabbage Patch dolls had potential in 1982 and ordered more for Venture than other retailers had ordered for themselves. When the dolls became a craze, Venture, like most other stores, still quickly ran out. However, Clark lured customers in by devising adoption ceremonies in the stores for customers whose dolls were yet to come.

Still remaining within the May family, Clark then briefly worked for St. Louis' Famous-Barr as the executive vice president of apparel, then moved to New York City to work as the vice president of merchandising for the Lerner Shops division of the Limited, Inc., from 1986 to 1988. Returning to St. Louis and the Venture Stores, Clark worked as the executive vice president of the company for four years through 1992.

In 1992, Clark took on new challenges when she moved to Topeka, Kansas, to become the president of Payless ShoeSource, the massive discount shoe retailer. Footwear had been traditionally male-dominated, making her appointment a high point in both the industry and her career. During her four years at the helm of the May-owned company, Payless had $2 billion in sales annually in its more than 4,000 stores.

However, Clark did not enjoy the experience since many of her ideas were dismissed by the company's male executives. Price was the most important aspect at Payless, with innovation and fun very secondary. Clark quit Payless in part because of the corporate atmosphere there, and trend toward poorly made, cheap, non-trendy shoes. She told Richard H. Weiss of *St. Louis Post-Dispatch,* "It can't JUST be about money. This is about learning and living and having fun with people and making memories." With the shoe industry in disrepair, sales slumping at Payless, and her own lack of enthusiasm about the company, Clark resigned in 1996.

Clark had accumulated a nest egg from her nearly two decades at May and was doing some consulting for retail businesses, but she was not done with retail yet. She decided to open her own business a short time after leaving Payless. First came Smart Stuff, Inc., a children's retail concept development firm. Better known to the general public was her other company, Build-A-Bear Workshop, founded in 1997. At its inception, she served as both president and chief executive bear, as Build-A-Bear called its chief executive officer.

Clark was inspired to found the company after looking at various businesses to buy and coming up with her own concept for a children's entertainment company. She also found wisdom in a ten-year-old friend who once mentioned, while shopping in vain for then-popular Beanie Babies, that they could make their own. Clark's experience at May also played a role in devising Build-A-Bear. She told Adelia Cellini Linecker of *Investor's Business Daily,*

"Early in my career, Stanley Goodman, then CEO of the May Department Stories, said 'Retailing is entertainment, and the store is a stage, and when the customer has fun they spend more money.' This has been a guiding principal throughout my retail career."

At Build-A-Bear, customers literally created their own stuffed animal. The store primarily focused on teddy bears, though it also sold frogs, pigs, bunnies, puppies, and cows. Customers picked out their animal's plush skin, noise, heart, clothing, and accessories. After the animal was completed, customers took their creations home in a special box. Each animal was sewn and fluffed in the store while the customer gives their creation a personalized name and story. Clark explained the logic behind the experience to Brett Wilcoxson of the *St. Louis Post-Dispatch*, "What is considered entertainment in retail sales really isn't. I felt I had the opportunity to create something unique, interactive, and most important, fun."

After financing Build-A-Bear herself, Clark and her company faced challenges. In October of 1997, a roof collapse at the company's warehouse resulted in the destruction of $130,000 worth of inventory, approximately two-thirds of their stock. Because of the loss, Clark and the employees at her first store at the St. Louis Galleria suffered much worry before the all-important holiday retail season. Stock was sent from China, allowing the store to have its first successful Christmas.

Over the next few years, Clark continued to shape Build-A-Bear with the help of investors like St. Louis venture capitalist Barney Ebsworth. More stores opened throughout the late 1990s, first in Kansas City and Chicago. She tried to double the number of stores opened each year with the goal of having 200 stores open in the United States by 2005 and eventually open stores internationally as well. Clark was successful in reaching her goal, with sales growing exponentially throughout this time period. In 1999, sales reached $19 million, whereas sales in 2000 were $57 million. In 2001, sales nearly doubled again to more than $107 million.

By this time, Clark had reorganized Build-A-Bear. In 2000, Build-A-Bear Workshop was converted to a corporation and Clark began serving as chairman of the board as well as chief executive bear. Four years later, Build-A-Bear went public and had a successful initial public offering. That same year, 2004, Clark stepped down as president, though she retained her chief executive bear and chairman of the board titles.

During and after this reorganization period, Clark continued to grow Build-A-Bear in innovative ways. In 2003, she opened her first stores outside the United States. The first international stores were in Canada, followed by franchises in Japan, Denmark, and Great Britain. Korean, French, and Australian outlets were added in 2004. In addition to opening more Build-A-Bear Workshops in the United States and abroad, Clark made deals for Build-A-Bear videos and publishing related books for children, greeting cards, and scrapbooking. Videogames around the Build-a-Bear concept were also developed for the Nintendo game system. Of this aspect of her venture, Clark told Peter Brieger of the *National Post's Financial Post & FP Investing*, "There are many opportunities for expanding Build-A-Bear beyond just retail stores. When I started, I had a pretty aggressive plan and I wanted this to be a global company."

Sales continued to grow in the early 2000s, reaching $280 million in 2004 alone. Clark continued to be innovative in the ways she expanded her company. In 2005, mobile stores were introduced so that Build-A-Bear Workshops could find new customers with whom to build retail relationships at sporting events and various family entertainment venues. By 2008, Clark's company had permanent stores in a number of Major League Baseball stadiums, with plans to add more. She told Juston Jones of the *New York Times*, "The ballparks have been a successful venue. We want to be wherever the family goes to have fun, whether it's a ballgame or the mall. It's the simple pleasures in life, you know. It's something as simple as the hug of a stuffed bear that makes a kid smile. Our first ballpark store was in Philadelphia. Opening it was driven by the owner. It was incredibly successful from the get-go."

Clark's goal was ultimately to reach about 400 stores in North America, 90 in the United Kingdom, and hundreds of franchises in other countries. To that end, Build-A-Bear reached the Persian Gulf in 2009. Yet Clark continued to face challenges as the company's stock price lost 60 percent of its value in late 2007 and 2008. Retailers nationwide suffered in the economic downturn of 2008 and 2009, but Clark believed her company would survive elimination of certain jobs, services, and space. When Build-A-Bear opened, a customer could make a bear for $10. She continued to offer $10 bears in 2009.

While some naysayers had doubts about the longevity of Build-A-Bear, Clark believed her company would be around 100 years from now. Responding to a query by *St. Louis Post-Dispatch* reporter Linda Tucci in 2004 about how long her company would last as most "concepts and brands don't last forever," Clark stated "They can last forever. It is how you make it fresh and new. These jeans (for a teddy bear)—you know the kids these days wear these baggy jeans. This is it, and they wear the chains on them. We wouldn't have done this three years ago. We're almost seven years old, so I don't think we're a fad anymore."

## Sources

### Books

*Complete Marquis Who's Who Biographies,* Marquis Who's Who, 2008.
*ICC Directors,* ICC Information Group, Ltd., 2009.

### Periodicals

*The Australian,* March 11, 2004, p. 23.
Business Wire, September 30, 2003.
*Investor's Business Daily* December 21, 2004, p. A6.
Middle East Company News Wire, April 8, 2009.
*National Post's Financial Post & FP Investing,* August 11, 2003, p. FP1.
*New York Times,* August 30, 2008, p. C2.
*Ottawa Citizen,* June 16, 2006, p. E1.
*Pittsburgh Post-Gazette,* November 30, 2008, p. J1.
PR Newswire, February 26, 1997.
*St. Louis Business Journal,* November 30, 1992, sec. 1, p. 19.
*St. Louis Commerce Magazine,* July 1, 2004, p. 24.
*St. Louis Post-Dispatch,* January 26, 1988, p. 12; January 17, 1999, p. D1; May 14, 2001, p. 2; November 26, 2002, p. C1; April 2, 2004, p. C5.
*Topeka Capital-Journal,* January 6, 1996, p. A1.

—A. Petruso

# Diablo Cody

## Author and screenwriter

**B**orn Brook Joan Busey, June 14, 1978, in Chicago, Illinois; daughter of Greg (an Illinois state tollworker) and Pam (a secretary) Busey; married Jon Hunt (a musician), October 2004 (divorced, 2007). *Education:* University of Iowa, 2000.

**Addresses:** *Home*—Los Angeles, CA. *Management*—Mason Novick, Benderspink Management, 110 S. Fairfax Ave., Ste. 350, Los Angeles, CA 90036. *Publisher*—Gotham c/o Penguin Group, 375 Hudson St., New York, NY 10014-3657. *Web site*—http://www.myspace.com/diablocody.

## Career

**A**uthor, blogger, columnist, and screenwriter. Secretary for Minnesota ad agency where she first began blogging about her experiences and reactions regularly under the fictitious name Diablo Cody, 2001; full-time stripper, pole-dancer, and phone sex operator chronicled in her blog *Pussy Ranch*, 2003; published articles in *City Pages, Village Voice,* and *Jane,* 2003; memoir *Candy Girl: A Year in the Life of an Unlikely Stripper,* 2005; appeared on *The Late Show with David Letterman,* 2006; wrote the screenplay for *Juno,* 2007; recurring columnist for *Entertainment Weekly,* 2007—; teamed with producer Steven Speilberg to executive produce and write the Showtime television series *The United States of Tara,* 2008.

**Awards:** CFCA Award for best original screenplay, Chicago Film Critics Association Awards; DFWFCA Award for best screenplay, Dallas-Fort Worth Film Critics Association Awards; FFCC Award for best screenplay, Florida Film Critics Circle Awards; Hollywood Breakthrough Award for breakthrough screenwriter of the year, Hollywood Film Festival; NBR Award for best original screenplay, National Board of Review, USA; PFCS Award for best screenplay written directly for the screen, Phoenix Film Critics Society Awards; SDFCS Award for best original screenplay, Sandiegi Film Critics Society Awards; Sierra Award for best screenplay, Las Vegas Film Critics Society Awards; Satellite Award for best original screenplay, Satellite Awards; SEFCA Award for best original screenplay, Southeastern Film Critics Association Awards, all for *Juno,* all 2007. Academy Award for best writing and screenplay written directly for the screen, Academy of Motion Picture Arts and Sciences; BAFTA Film Award for best original screenplay, British Academy of Film and Television Arts; Critics Choice Award for best writer, Broadcast Film Critics Association Awards; COFCA Award for best original screenplay, Central Ohio Film Critics Association; Christopher Award for a feature film (shared with various producers and directors), Christopher Awards; Independent Spirit Award for best first screenplay, Film Independent; KCFCC Award for best original screenplay, Kansas City Film Critics Circle Awards; OFCS Award for best original screenplay, Online Film Critics Society Awards; WGA Award for best original screenplay, Writers Guild of America, all for *Juno*, all 2008.

## Sidelights

**B**est known as the Academy Award-winning screenwriter of the surprise 2007 hit *Juno*, Diablo Cody is the pen name and alter ego of an Illinois native named Brook Busey. Utilizing her sparkling gift for wry observations and deadpan irony, she has become the first writer of note to parlay an Internet web log (or blog) into a serious Hollywood career.

Nearly as interesting as her work—which incorporates smart, zany dollops of pop culture youthspeak into every written exchange—is how Cody made the transition from a blogger with a bite to a multiple award-winning screenwriter. Initially a burned out secretary hoping to become a copywriter, she decided to quit her day job, become a full-time stripper, and then write about it. Subsequently, she blogged about her trials and travails as a pole dancer and phone sex worker, which in turn became the basis of her book *Candy Girl: A Year in the Life of an Unlikely Stripper.* Just a few years later, the eccentrically attired scribe had an awardwinning film under her belt and was working with famed producer Steven Spielberg on a hot new television series.

Born on June 12, 1978, in Chicago, Illinois, Cody was raised in the Chicago suburb of Lemont in a normal Catholic family. The Buseys ran a Germanthemed supper club called the Matterhorn for a time but, after the restaurant closed, her father, Greg, went to work for the Illinois state tollway commission and her mother, Pam, worked as a secretary for a construction firm. In an interview with Desson Thomson for the *Washington Post,* Cody claimed she was overshadowed by her "high-maintenance" older brother Marc. That said, nothing about the Buseys' homelife would suggest they would spawn a child as media savvy and filled with comedic attitude as daughter Brook. Neither of Cody's middle class parents wrote nor cared about movies and she described herself as the family wild card. "I've always been different," she told Steve Marsh of *MSPMag.com.* "I think I have one member of my extended family that people frequently compare me to: this sort of eccentric aunt in San Francisco. But that's about it. I couldn't really relate to anybody else in the family."

Cody attended the Benet Academy, a strict college preparatory Catholic high school in nearby Lisle. In an interview with Prairie Miller for *NewsBlaze* she

recalled being something like the lead character in *Juno*. "You know, not popular, not unpopular. I bounced from one group to another. And I had a core of boys that followed me around, that I could bully.... And I played in a band [called Yak Spackle]. I was kind of rebellious, but in a safe way. I never landed in jail, but the cops would drive me home for tossing toilet paper around the neighborhood, stuff like that."

Today, the writer seems confident and self-assured, but that wasn't always the case. "I was very socially awkward and not very attractive," she confided to Thomson of the *Washington Post.* "Severely nearsighted. Coke bottle glasses. Weird body. Teeth really messed up. Weirdly shaped—I still am. Stringy hair. I dated geeks exclusively. And even when I blossomed—to use a nauseating term—it was so ingrained in me that I was a nerd, it didn't matter."

Upon graduation, Cody enrolled at the University of Iowa, hoping to take advantage of their highly regarded writing program. "I mainly focused on poetry," she told *Written By*'s Matt Hoey. "I laugh about that now. I actually think it wound up being helpful because as a poet you develop a certain efficiency with language that I think you use as a screenwriter." Averse to competition, Cody also wrote short stories that she never attempted to sell.

Cody seldom mentions her college years, but according to the University of Iowa Web site, the future author worked in the University Libraries and as an administrative director for the student-run radio station KRUI where she hosted a late-night show. After her Oscar win, the Libraries newsletter indulged in a bit of comic understatement as they summed up her post-college life. "After her work in the Libraries, she went on to make several other interesting career choices before becoming a screenwriter."

After graduation, Cody took a job as a secretary at a Chicago bankruptcy law firm, which proved tedious and unrewarding. To alleviate her boredom, she took a night class to learn HTML so she could hand-code a blog presenting entries from a fake diary called *The Red Secretary.* "It was this proto-Borat character," she told Rachel Abramowitz of the *Los Angeles Times.* "I would write about my ancient computer, this flat with no hot water. All I wanted for X-Mas was an American Frisbee." Still quite shy, Busy blogged because it was a way for her to write and have her words be seen by others without subjecting her entries to the criticism of editors or publishers; however, the only people who read these deadpan postings were her family.

Cody met her future husband, Jon Hunt, through his Minnesota-based Beach Boys tribute site *Girls, Cars and Surfing,* which has since closed. Hunt, who fronted several local bands including an aggregation known as Landing Gear, encouraged her talent from the start. After exchanging funny and romantic e-mails, they began to shuttle back and forth from Chicago and Minnesota until Cody moved to Minneapolis in 2003. "Romantic ruin is probably the best way to describe our emotional history," she told the *Star Tribune*'s Colin Covert. "But when we met, there was no sense of maturity or sobriety. It was like, 'Let's get married!'" Eventually, the two participated in a marriage ceremony on the *Star Trek* ship at the Las Vegas Hilton.

Hoping to become a copywriter, Cody took a secretarial position at Fallon, a local advertising agency. When opportunities to advance did not materialize, she began a new blog about her married life called the *Darling Girl,* which did not attract many readers. With boredom setting in, she found that she didn't have anything fresh to contribute to her blog and began casting about for things she could experience that would feed her writing. One night she walked past the Skyway Lounge and noticed they had an amateur night for strippers. Figuring it would be a fun, one-time only experience, she participated, lost the contest, and wrote about it on her blog. Readers responded immediately and Cody knew she was on to something. "You know what's funny," she told *NewsBlaze,* "I was the world's worst stripper. But I think I danced for two hours that night, and came home with one hundred bucks!"

Cody began stripping periodically to supplement both her blog and her income. Eventually she left her day job and began stripping and writing about it full-time. Cagey and clever, she knew that a pseudonym would help protect her from the more unseemly elements of the seedy bar scene in Minneapolis. At first she billed herself as Bonbon, Roxanne, and Cherish, but while driving through Cody, Wyoming the couple heard a song by Arcadia called "El Diablo." Instantly, Cody was inspired to take on the exotic stripper/pen name Diablo Cody.

The change in persona allowed the writer to cast aside her shy Catholic school girl self-image and publicly embrace the kitsch fashion choices that became her trademark. After she rechristened her blog as the adult-oriented *Pussy Ranch,* interest in Cody's writing resulted in 10,000 readers regularly tracking her salacious exploits. Looking for fresh avenues to cover, Cody also worked as a peep show girl at a place called Sex World and became a phone sex operator, adding a hilarious twist to her clients' requests to her blog. As her popularity grew, she landed a regular spot writing for a weekly Minneapolis publication called the *City Pages,* which led to some freelance pieces for the *Village Voice* and *Jane.*

Claiming that she was propositioned more as a secretary than she was as a stripper, Cody initially believed that working in the sex industry was an empowering experience that allowed for decent pay, reasonable hours, and opportunities for female camaraderie. As time wore on, the reality of the situation proved quite different. "I thought strippers would be these off-the-wall feminist chicks who were best friends and drank gin," she recalled for Keri Carlson of the *Minnesota Daily,* "But that is not the case. Everyone hates each other." Gradually, she stopped stripping and concentrated on her duties as TV critic for the *City Pages.*

One of Cody's readers was Mason Novick, a manager of the Hollywood management/production company Benderspink. "She was distinctively funny, and her tone was so great, and she's so current," Novick told *Entertainment Weekly*'s Karen Vilby. However, Cody was unaware of Novick's legitimacy and quickly dismissed him. Undeterred, Novick kept in touch, and eight months later he was able to direct her to a New York literary agent who secured a six-figure advance from Gotham for Cody's book *Candy Girl: A Year in the Life of an Unlikely Stripper.* The deal proved to be a learning experience and a turning point in her career. "Writing the memoir might not have helped in terms of mechanics," she told Chad Gervich of *Writer's Digest,* "but it helped me in terms of discipline, because I knew that I could sit down and complete something, and I had never done that prior to the book."

Based on her blogs, *Candy Girl* provides a unique perspective that is both honest and amusing, much like Cody herself. Now bandying about a fully formed persona, Cody made an impression when she promoted the book—which she jokingly called an anthropological study—on *The Late Show with David Letterman.* Her book had so impressed the ironic talk-show host that he made it the only inductee into "Dave's Book Club," a comedic response to Oprah Winfrey's far more legitimate enterprise. As reported by David Carr for the *New York Times,* she described herself to Letterman as the "naked Margaret Mead" and cynically claimed "Everything is prostitution in a way," which instigated a minor controversy. "I actually think everything is prostitution. We're kind of constantly bartering with our dignity in life," she explained to Carr. "Same goes for people's ideas, talents, emotions, etc. There's a price on everything."

As Cody promoted *Candy Girl*, Novick worked to get a film adaptation made and he wanted Cody to write the screenplay. Having never even seen a film script before, she went to her local bookstore and bought printed screenplays for the films *Ghost World* and *American Beauty*. The movie *Superbad* inspired her to do a teen comedy from the female perspective and, while sitting in a coffee shop, she began to write *Juno*. One of the freshest characters in recent movie history, Juno McGuff has much in common with her creator; intelligent and pop-culture savvy, she employs a vernacular that crackles when she speaks. "I made most of it up," Cody told Hoey of *Written By*. "I didn't research 'Teen Speak' or anything. It's all totally manufactured. I'm pretty immature. I didn't have to dig real deep."

Cody recalls only being asked for one serious revision from director Jason Reitman—an additional scene for Michael Cera who played Paulie Bleeker—and says that actress Ellen Page as Juno McGuff brought in many of the music-related touches. However, the sparkling dialogue, the surprising uplift of the tale, and the odd little touches, like the hamburger phone, were all part of Cody's 90-minute apology to a teenage boy she hurt long ago. This story of a cynical but sweet pregnant teenage girl looking to hook her baby up with a nice loving couple proved a winner with audiences. Budgeted at $6.5 million—a low figure for a Hollywood film—the finished project made back more than 20 times its cost. More importantly, Cody won an Academy Award, about which she characteristically quipped, "I have this Oscar in my house, and it looks like some novelty that your friend picked up for you on Bourbon Street," she joked with *Bust* magazine's Jenna Wortham, "'World's Best Supporting Friend' or something."

Multiple awards for *Juno* raised her profile considerably, but also instigated a backlash. Several journalists and critics attacked her stylized dialogue, campy fashion choices, and decried her work as a stripper, seeing it more as exploitation than anthropology. "The world is so keen on dredging women through the mud, and saying, 'Stripper past!'" she exclaimed to Wortham. "I've chosen to own all of my actions. I've never denied or hidden anything along the way." Indeed, when nude pictures of the writer were leaked to the internet, it was Cody who took credit for releasing them.

For a time Cody commuted back and forth to Los Angeles, but after moving there full-time, she and Hunt quietly divorced in 2007. Despite her carefully crafted reputation as a hard-partier, Cody has worked constantly since her Academy Award win.

*Entertainment Weekly* hired her to write a recurring column, which features the same breezy quality as her blogs. Moreover, by her count, she has written nine scripts, some of which were already in production, including the horror comedy *Jennifer's Body* and the teen comedy *Girly Style*. In June of 2008, the Showtime cable network announced that the Cody-created, Spielberg-produced comedy series *United States of Tara* had been picked up for 12 episodes. At this stage, Cody seems happy with her unprecedented success and new living situation. "I've been fired from so many jobs," she told *MSPMag.com*'s Marsh. "I've been told that I'm incompetent, socially retarded, maladjusted. I still know that I couldn't function in reality. Los Angeles is a good place for me." What if her post-*Juno* projects all flop and she is no longer welcome in Hollywood? Cody gave David Letterman the perfect tongue-in-cheek response (according to the *New York Times*' Carr): "If this writing stuff doesn't pan out, I'm getting right back on the pole.'"

## Selected writings

### Novels

*Candy Girl: A Year in the Life of an Unlikely Stripper*, Gotham (New York, NY), 2005.

## Sources

### Periodicals

*Bust*, June/July 2008, pp. 67-71.
*Chicago Tribune*, December 9, 2007.
*Los Angeles Times*, December 6, 2007, p. E1.
*Minnesota Daily*, January 19, 2006.
*Mpls.St.Paul Magazine*, December 2007.
*New York Times*, December 2, 2007.
*Star Tribune* (Minneapolis, MN), December 7, 2007.
*Washington Post*, December 9, 2007, p. M10.
*Written By*, January 2008.

### Online

"Diablo Cody: Biography," *All Movie Guide*, http://www.allmusic.com (August 11, 2008).
"Diablo Cody: Biography," *Ask Men*, http://www.askmen.com/celebs/women/actress/diablo-cody/index.htm#bio (August 9, 2008).
"Diablo Cody: Biography," *Variety Profiles*, http://www.variety.com/profiles/people/Biography/2164682/Diablo+Cody.html?dataSet+1 (August 9, 2008).

"Diablo Cody for Juno," *SuicideGirls,* http://suicide girls.com/interviews/Diablo+Cody+for+JUNO/ print/ (August 17, 2008).

"Diablo Cody: From Ex-Stripper to A-Lister," *Entertainment Weekly,* http://www.ew.com/ew/arti cle/0,,20155516.tif_20155530.tif_20157948.tif,00. html (August 9, 2008).

"Diablo Cody inks out her husband," *Los Angeles Times,* http://theenvelope.latimes.com/env-diablo-cody-tatoo4dec04,0,171480,print.story (August 9, 2008).

"Diablo Cody," *Internet Movie Database,* http:// www.imdb.com (August 9, 2008).

"Diablo Cody Interview: From Strip Clubs and Phone Sex to the Big Screen," *NewsBlaze,* http:// newsblaze.com/story/20071205.tif142309tsop. nb/topstory.html (August 17, 2008).

"Diablo Cody's Tips for Blogging Your Way to Hollywood Success," *Wired,* http://www.wired. com/print/entertainment/hollywood/news/ 2007/11/cody (August 9, 2008).

"Former Student Assistant Wins Oscar," *University of Iowa Libraries,* http://at-lamp.its.uiowa.edu/ virtualwu/index.php/main/entry/ui_graduat e_di ablo_cody_wins_oscar/ (August 17, 2008).

"Juno Writer Diablo Cody: I Leaked My Own Topless Pics," *US Magazine,* http://www.usmagazine .com/juno_writer_diablo_cody_i_leaked_my_ own_topless_pics (August 17, 2008).

"Showtime Picks Up Cody's 'Tara,'" *Entertainment Weekly,* http://www.ew.com/ew/article/0,,2020 4459.tif,00.html (August 9, 2008).

"The WD Interview: Diablo Cody," *Writer's Digest. com,* http://www.writersdigest.com/article/ diablo-cody (August 9, 2008).

*—Ken Burke*

# Marion Cotillard

## Actress

**B**orn September 30, 1975, in Paris, France; daughter of Jean-Claude Cotillard (an actor and director) and Niseema Theillaud (an actress and teacher).

**Addresses:** *Agent*—Bastien Duval, ArtMedia, 20 Avenue Rapp, 75007 Paris, France.

## Career

**A**ctress in films, including: *L'Histoire du garçon qui voulait qu'on l'embrasse*, 1994; *Snuff Movie*, 1995; *Comment je me suis disputé (ma vie sexuelle)*, 1996; *Taxi*, 1998; *Du Bleu jusqu'en Amérique*, 1999; *Furia*, 1999; *La Guerre dans le Haut Pays*, 1999; *Taxi 2*, 2000; *Les Jolies choses*, 2001; *Lisa*, 2001; *Une affaire privée*, 2002; *Big Fish*, 2003; *Jeux d'enfants*, 2003; *Taxi 3*, 2003; *Innocence*, 2004; *Un long dimanche de fiançailles* (A Very Long Engagement), 2004; *La Boîte noire*, 2005; *Cavalcade*, 2005; *Edy*, 2005; *Mary*, 2005; *Sauf le respect que je vous dois*, 2005; *Dikkenek*, 2006; *Fair Play*, 2006; *A Good Year*, 2006; *Toi et Moi*, 2006; *La môme* (also *La Vie en Rose*), 2007. Made television debut in a 1993 episode of *Highlander*.

**Awards:** César Award for best supporting actress, Académie des Arts et Techniques du Cinema, for *A Very Long Engagement*, 2005, and for best actress, for *La Vie en Rose*, 2008; Academy Award for best performance by an actress in a leading role, Academy of Motion Picture Arts and Sciences; BAFTA Award for best leading actress, British Academy of Film and Television Arts; Golden Globe Award for best performance by an actress in a motion picture—musical or comedy, Hollywood Foreign Press Association, all for *La Vie en Rose*, all 2008.

## Sidelights

**M**arion Cotillard had just a few leading roles to her credit when she was cast in *La Vie en Rose*, the 2007 biopic of celebrated singer Édith Piaf. A pop-culture icon in France, Piaf led a storied, somewhat tragic life and rose to become one of France's most esteemed performers before her death in 1963. Cotillard's performance as "The Little Sparrow," as the beloved Piaf was called, earned her several top industry honors, including an Academy Award for Best Actress. Writing in *Back Stage West*, Sarah Kuhn described it as "a ferocious performance that doesn't merely mimic Piaf; Cotillard inhabits the role so fully, it almost seems she's channeling the legendary singer."

Cotillard was born on September 30, 1975, in Paris, France, but grew up near Orléans in north-central France. Her parents were both involved in theater and the performing arts: her father, Jean-Claude Cotillard, once worked as a mime and later ran a children's drama ensemble before becoming a theater director; Niseema Theillaud, her mother, was also a veteran of the stage and an acting teacher. Despite her genetic inheritance, Cotillard was an introverted child. "I was shy, not at ease with myself," she told *Sunday Times* journalist Demetrios Matheou."I did not speak much. So my imagination was big. Then, one day, I started to act, and I realised it was my way of sharing things with people, to talk with them."

Cotillard made her television debut in the series *Highlander* in 1993, the year she turned 18. Over the next few years she appeared in French television projects and in a handful of theatrical releases. Her break came when famed French filmmaker Luc Besson offered her a role in a new movie he was producing from a script he had written. Besson—who made the original *La Femme Nikita* in 1990 and the 1997 Hollywood sci-fi confection *The Fifth Element*—cast Cotillard in *Taxi,* the story of a pizza delivery man on the trail of German bank robbers in Marseilles. The movie was a hit and Cotillard was so memorable in her portrayal of Lili Bertineau that her screen time and storylines were considerably more significant in the two *Taxi* sequels that were made in 2000 and 2003.

*Taxi* and Cotillard's other projects usually did well in France, but failed to find an international audience. That changed with the dark comedy *Jeux d'enfants* in 2003, whose title, roughly translated, means "childish games" but was changed to *Love Me If You Dare* for wider release. She played Sophie, one-half of a pair of childhood sweethearts who challenge one another to increasingly outlandish pranks as they grow older though not at all wiser. It was the first of her movies to be distributed widely outside of France, but favorable reviews were scarce. "Whether you find its dual resolution hopelessly pretentious or profound depends on your tolerance for a certain strain of Gallic sentimentality that takes itself more seriously than it lets on," asserted Stephen Holden in his *New York Times* critique.

Shortly following *Love Me If You Dare*'s worldwide release Cotillard appeared in her first Hollywood project, Tim Burton's *Big Fish,* which was shot mostly in Alabama and France. She played the daughter-in-law of Albert Finney's character, Ed Bloom, a man known for his lifelong exaggerated tales. Her on-screen husband, played by Billy Crudup, is a Paris-based journalist whose career has been devoted to seeking out the truth. Upon learning his father has taken ill, Will Bloom reluctantly returns to his family's Alabama home.

In 2004, Cotillard's breakthrough role arrived when she appeared in *Un long dimanche de fiançailles,* which was released in the United States as *A Very*

*Long Engagement.* The film starred French cinema's most recognizable export of recent years, Audrey Tautou (*Amélie*), as a woman determined to uncover the truth about the shameful death her fiancé allegedly suffered after he and several other soldiers were accused of self-mutilation during World War I. Cotillard played Tina Lombardi, a Corsican woman of equal determination who finds a deadly outlet for her anger. Though she had a small role, Cotillard's performance was cited by several critics as noteworthy. In citing the movie's supporting cast, Salon.com writer Charles Taylor ended his list with the words, "and spectacularly—Marion Cotillard as the tale's dark avenging Corsican angel. Her appearances are so startling that they very nearly derail the film."

Cotillard's portrayal of Tina won her a César Award for Best Supporting Actress from the Académie des Arts et Techniques du Cinema, the French equivalent of an Academy Award. The next few years would bring a flurry of work culminating in another César for her Edith Piaf role. In the dark fairy tale *Innocence* in 2004, she played the dance instructor at a mysterious boarding school for girls located in a remote forest. In 2005, she appeared in several projects, including an Abel Ferrara film, *Mary,* which featured Juliette Binoche as a woman who becomes obsessed with the biblical figure Mary Magdalene, and *Sauf le respect que je vous dois,* also known as *Burnt Out,* about a fed-up white-collar worker who embarks upon a crime spree.

In 2006, Cotillard appeared in four films, two of which gave her much more screen time. In *Toi et Moi,* she was the cellist sister to a writer who imagines how their lives might have turned out had they made different choices, and in the English-language romance *A Good Year* she was paired with major box-office star Russell Crowe. He was cast as a London banker who inherits a vineyard in the south of France and Cotillard was his foil: an American who advances her own claim on the property.

In mid-2005, Cotillard won the highly coveted role of Piaf, the legendary French chanteuse. Famed for her magnetic stage presence and emotive vocal style, the diminutive Piaf endured a dreadful childhood and was discovered singing on the street for money; her storied life went on to include immense fame as well as morphine addiction, alcoholism, a crippling automobile accident, and even being implicated in the death of her manager. Some of the executives involved in the project—released in France as *La Môme* or "Street Urchin," another of Piaf's nicknames—were unimpressed with Cotillard's résumé to date and wanted a more famous French film star instead. Director Olivier Dahan was adamant that Cotillard was ideal for the part, though it was decided that a more experienced cabaret singer would serve as a voice double for the actual Piaf songs.

Cotillard spent several months preparing for the role, reading every book about Piaf and working with a voice coach to learn how to make her lip-synching less obvious. She also made a radical transformation from twenty-something, twenty-first-century siren to an old woman, for Piaf's hard life and substance abuse aged her considerably in her final years. "I only knew three or four of her songs," Cotillard admitted in an interview with *Sunday Times* writer Ryan Gilbey. "For me, she was an amazing voice with a little black dress. I knew nothing of her tragic life."

Released in the United States with the title of one of Piaf's signature tunes, *La Vie en Rose* (roughly translated, "A Rosy Life") the biopic earned some mixed reviews. The *New York Times'* movie critic, A. O. Scott, found fault with the meandering narrative, explaining that the film "has an intricate structure, which is a polite way of saying that it's a complete mess," but conceded that "it is true that Ms. Cotillard is a dynamic, quick-witted performer, one whose sheer force of will goes some way toward showing how a funny-looking, abrasive street urchin could become the idol of postwar France." Writing in *Vanity Fair,* Graham Fuller asserted that Cotillard "has perfected Piaf's coat-hanger posture, shuffling gait, and toothy grin. And she elicits empathy as she makes the turbulent journey of a sickly, brothel-raised waif [to] icon." Other critics immediately hailed Cotillard's performance as Oscar-caliber, with *Entertainment Weekly*'s Owen Gleiberman hailing it as "less a performance than a possession" and extolling "the mad intensity of Cotillard's acting. She fills the diminutive, firebrand Piaf with life force at every age."

*La Vie en Rose* premiered at the Berlin International Film Festival in February of 2007, and was released worldwide a few months later. A year after that Berlin premiere, Cotillard began collecting a slew of honors for her role: On February 10, she became the first French actress to win the Best Actress in a Leading Role from the British Academy of Film and Television Arts (BAFTA) since the category was created in 1969, and 12 days later picked up the César for Best Actress. Two days later, Cotillard delivered a heartfelt, halting thank-you in English when she took the stage at the 2008 Academy Awards to accept the Oscar for Best Performance by an Actress in a Leading Role. Her recognition by the Holly-

wood establishment was a relative rarity, for seldom has the honor been awarded for a foreign-language performance; moreover, Cotillard was the first French woman ever to win that Oscar.

Cotillard's brief but charming speech was one of the most frequently shown Oscar-telecast recaps the next day, but a few days later she became the target of a media takedown when remarks she had made a year earlier on a French talk show surfaced in which she seemed to voice support for conspiracy theorists who claim that 9/11 was actually the work of sinister forces inside the U.S. government. "There was a tower—I believe it was in Spain—which burned for 24 hours," she said, according a translation that appeared in the London *Observer.* "It never collapsed. None of these towers collapsed. And there in a few minutes, the whole thing collapsed!" In response, her lawyer commented that her remarks had been taken out of context.

Cotillard's Oscar win immediately raised the price she could command per picture, from about one million Euros to tenfold that, as one French newspaper estimated. Her next movie was *Public Enemies*, Michael Mann's dramatization of the last days of John Dillinger, with Johnny Depp in the role of the 1930s outlaw, scheduled to be released in 2009. She was also cast in *Nine*, a film adaptation of the hit Broadway musical that won a Tony Award in 1982 that was, in turn, a stage version of Federico Fellini's semi-autobiographical 1963 classic *8 1/2.* She was also signed to portray Jessie "Chubbie" Miller in a project tentatively titled *The Last Flight of the Lancaster.* Miller was a pioneering Australian aviator who was involved in a sensational Miami murder trial in 1932 over the murder of her alleged lover by Bill Lancaster, a British pilot with whom she was also romantically involved. Lancaster was acquitted, and then set out to break the England-to-Cape Town speed record as a way to revive his flagging fortunes. He disappeared somewhere over the North African Sahara in April of 1933, but the wreckage was not found until 29 years later, though Miller flew her own fruitless mission over the African desert in search of him.

Cotillard has been romantically linked with Guillaume Canet, her co-star in *Love Me If You Dare.* She is a spokesperson for Greenpeace who once allowed her Paris apartment to be tested in the environmental-activism group's home-toxicity campaign. "I will quit Greenpeace when we don't need Greenpeace any more," she told Matheou, the *Sunday Times* journalist. "I hope it will be before I die, but I'm not optimistic."

## Sources

### Periodicals

*Back Stage West,* June 7, 2007, p. 19.
*Entertainment Weekly,* June 15, 2007, p. 61.
*Interview,* July 2007, p. 64.
*New York Times,* May 21, 2004; May 6, 2007; June 8, 2007.
*Observer* (London, England), March 2, 2008, p. 30.

*Sunday Times* (London, England), September 18, 2005, p. 4; May 13, 2007, p. 4.
*Vanity Fair,* May 2007, p. 92.

### Online

"War, Wizardry and Love," Salon.com, November 26, 2004, http://dir.salon.com/story/ent/movies/review/2004/11/26/engagement/index.html (June 23, 2008).

—*Carol Brennan*

# Erica Courtney

**Jewelry designer**

**B**orn Tasha Ingram, c. 1957, in Lafayette, LA; daughter of Helyn Ingram (a homemaker); stepdaughter of W. C. Lamb (a business owner); married Ron Cappo (a cabinetmaker), 1977 (divorced, 1982); married Michael Fonseca (a furrier; divorced); married Vince Flores (a musician), June 1999 (divorced); children: (with Cappo) Joshua Ryan. *Education:* Attended Louisiana State University, Baton Rouge, mid-1970s.

**Addresses:** *Office*—Erica Courtney, 7465 Beverly Blvd., Los Angeles, CA 90036.

## Career

**J**ewelry designer, 1985—; opened first eponymous store, Erica Courtney, in Los Angeles in 1998.

## Sidelights

**L**os Angeles-based jewelry designer Erica Courtney creates vintage-inspired pieces that have earned her a devoted celebrity clientele who favor her unique designs for red-carpet galas. Her clients include Jessica Alba, Uma Thurman, Sandra Bullock, Jennifer Aniston, and even Madonna, but Courtney's own life story rivals that of any character those stars have played on screen.

"Erica Courtney" is actually the name that the jewelry designer adopted when she went into hiding after an abusive marriage and bitter divorce. Born around 1957, Courtney grew up in a family in which

*Amanda Edwards/Getty Images*

creativity was encouraged by her mother, Helyn, and her stepfather, who owned a successful equipment-rental business near the oilfields of Lafayette, Louisiana. She made her first piece of jewelry at age nine, when a neighbor gave her some costume-jewelry crystals and she created a necklace for her cat. After high school, Courtney enrolled at the Baton Rouge campus of Louisiana State University but soon dropped out to marry a local boy, Ron Cappo, when she was just 20 years old. The couple struggled financially and soon had a son, Joshua, but the marriage quickly disintegrated over personality clashes and money woes. They were divorced by 1982, and Cappo began fighting Courtney for custody of their son.

The court battles intensified after Courtney moved to New Orleans with Josh and into an apartment with her boyfriend, Michael Fonseca, who had a successful fur business. After learning the art of making stained glass, she planned to open her own shop in the French Quarter. When she realized that judges and social workers took a dim view of single mothers who cohabitated with their boyfriends, she married Fonseca; her ex-husband, meanwhile, had become a born-again Christian and was still pushing to rescind her parental rights. Fearing she would lose custody altogether when their next round in court was slated to be heard by a judge who was a friend of the Cappo family, on Labor Day weekend of 1983 Courtney put a pair of jeans and her son's teddy bear into a bag and told her new husband she was going out to buy a pie. She never returned and instead went underground with Josh.

With the help of her mother, Courtney was able to settle in a small Florida town called Mexico Beach, but investigators hired by Cappo tracked her down there, and she narrowly escaped. She wound up in Dallas and began using the name Erica Courtney, based in part on a character from the long-running ABC daytime drama *All My Children.* Searching for a way to make money on the side, she began embellishing sunglasses with rhinestones, which were a hit in Texas, and she soon wound up with a successful small business at the Dallas Apparel Mart. When she used some rhinestones to create a glamorous new watch, her jewelry-design business took off in earnest. "People would chase me down to see this watch," she told *Los Angeles Times'* journalist Booth Moore. "I couldn't believe it!"

Courtney sold more than 500 of those watches and used the income to start making crosses, hearts, and jewelry items of her own design using the soft-wax casting method. She began to garner favorable attention in the fashion press, which put her in legal peril, because her ex-husband was still trying to locate Josh with the help of private investigators. In 1989, Courtney and Josh moved to Los Angeles when she became romantically involved with the musician Vince Flores, and the new location brought with it a significant upswing in her business. Within a few years her gold, silver, and diamond pieces were sold in top retailers, such as Fred Segal and Bergdorf Goodman, and found their way into magazine editorial spreads. However, her past life as Tasha Ingram caught up with her in February of 1992, when she was arrested at her New York City hotel room while on a business trip by agents of the Federal Bureau of Investigation (FBI). Her son, by then in his early teens, was sent to live with Cappo and his second wife in Louisiana. The court handed down a sentence of a few years' probation, and Josh eventually returned to Los Angeles and began working with Courtney as a jewelry designer.

Courtney opened her eponymous first store in Los Angeles in 1998 on Beverly Boulevard. Its exuberant interior design, in hues of red, orange, and lime green, was a marked contrast from the cool, mono-chrome formality found in most jewelry stores. *WWD's* writer Kristi Ellis asserted, "What sets Courtney apart from the cookie-cutter designs of some well-known jewelry retail chains is her attention to uncommon detail. This season, for example, she constructed dainty butterflies and flowers on pearls and precious stones. She even adds unique twists to her simple sterling silver or gold charms, which include hearts, crowns and crosses."

Two more Erica Courtney stores debuted in the Los Angeles area, each with a different look. The one on Robertson Avenue, which opened in 2005, featured an all-pink interior palette. "Everything is the same color, so the jewelry is the star of the show," Courtney told *National Jeweler's* Glenn Law. "There is so much work in the detail but it is understated, so all you see is the jewelry, and you have to look to see how the details all work together." The stores served as the Southern California center for Courtney's line, but she also had accounts with jewelry retailers across the United States.

In a telling detail of just how far Courtney had traveled from her Louisiana roots, the 2008 wedding of her son Josh was featured in *In Style* magazine, which noted that both he and his mother worked on the design of his bride's one-of-a-kind engagement ring cut from a two-carat diamond. In the *Los Angeles Times* interview with Moore from a few years earlier, she reflected back on her nearly two decades on the run and the ensuing legal battles, saying, "I realized everything that happened to me I let happen to me. It's easy to sit back and say, 'He did this to me and that to me, and he was so mean.' Blah, blah, blah, who cares, cry me a river. But I had a part in that, and when you find out you are in control of your own life ... it's so cool."

## Sources

*InStyle,* December 1, 2005, p. 210.
*Jewelers Circular Keystone,* June 1, 2007, p. 97.
*Los Angeles Magazine,* December 1993, p. 96.
*Los Angeles Times,* August 27, 1999, p. E1.
*National Jeweler,* September 1, 2005, p. 1.
*People,* May 5, 2003, p. 105.
*WWD,* October 22, 1998, p. 42S; March 26, 2001, p. 30.

—*Carol Brennan*

# Daft Punk

## Dance music duo

Group formed in Paris, c. early 1990s; members include Thomas Bangalter (born January 3, 1975, in Paris, France; son of Daniel Vangarde, a musician; married Élodie Bouchez [an actress]; children: Tara-Jay [son], Roxan [son]), DJ; Guy-Manuel de Homem-Christo (born February 8, 1974, Paris, France), DJ.

**Addresses:** *Record company*—Virgin Records, 150 Fifth St., New York, NY 10011. *Web site*—http:// www.daftpunk.com/.

## Career

Bangalter composed film scores, including *Irré-versible* (2002); records under his name and Stardust; operates Roulé (a record label). De Homem-Christo created short films and produced albums, including Sebastian Tellier's *Sexuality*, 2008. Bangalter and de Homem-Christo met in 1987; formed indie cover band Darlin' (also known as Darling), c. early 1990s; pair formed Daft Punk, c. early 1990s; released first single "The New Wave," 1993; signed with Virgin Records, 1996; released first album, *Homework,* 1997; worked as producer on and appeared in music video compilation *D.A.F.T.,* 1999; worked as writers and producers on animated film *Interstella 5555: The 5tory of the 5ecret 5tar 5ystem,* 2003; released album *Human After All,* 2005; Bangalter worked as a director, writer, and cinematographer, and de Homem-Christo worked as director and writer on film *Electroma,* 2006; released album *Alive 2007,* 2007; released album *Leftovers,* 2008; signed deal to compose and record score for remake of film *Tron,* 2009.

**Awards:** Grammy Award for best electronic/dance album, Recording Academy, for *Alive 2007,* 2008; Grammy Award for best dance recording, Recording Academy, for "Harder Better Faster Stronger," 2008.

## Sidelights

Widely considered a major step forward in the evolution of dance music, the Grammy Award-winning Daft Punk is a French techno/ progressive dance duo who combined acid house and techno with pop, indie rock, funk, electro, and hip-hop beats. Consisting of Thomas Bangalter and Guy-Manuel de Homem-Christo, the pair is often compared to the Chemical Brothers and Money Mafia for crafting a disco dance sound that clearly illustrated a variety of influences but most obviously from 1970s funk and disco and 1980s Chicago house music scene. Humor is also an important part of their music, and is often quite sly. Explaining a primary tenant of their musical philosophy, Bangalter told Lorraine Ali of *Newsweek,* "What we have learned from the independent electronic scene is to constantly reinvent: question yourself, innovate, experiment. If you have a minimum of success, you become the establishment very fast. The only good thing about that is that you have more control to innovate and then destroy it at your own will."

The pair behind Daft Punk had a relatively long history together, and one member had an enviable background in the kind of music they made together. Born on January 3, 1975, in Paris, Bangalter is the son of Daniel Vangarde, a composer of disco hits such as the Gibson Brothers' "Cuba" and Ottawan's "D.I.S.C.O." He had weekly piano lessons as a child, but did not appreciate them until he started making music himself as a teenager. Bangalter met de Homem-Christo, who was born on February 8, 1974, in Paris, while attending the same school in 1987. The pair tried to fulfill early film ambitions by going to film school, and they soon formed their own musical group.

Bangalter and de Homem-Christo's first collaboration was an indie guitar cover band known as Darlin'. The group's music featured no vocals, but complex instrumentation. Songs by Darlin' (an original and a cover) were included on a compilation album that was reviewed by *Melody Maker*, the popular music weekly published in the United Kingdom. The negative review dismissed Darlin's cover of a Beach Boys song as "daft punk." Bangalter and de Homem-Christo adopted the moniker for their new project, one which moved from rock to dance. Daft Punk was formed after a brief hiatus following the demise of Darlin'.

In 1993, the newly named Daft Punk released their first single, "The New Wave." It was released on the highly regarded dance label, Soma. "The New Wave" was widely reviewed as an innovative kind of house (a form of dance music). Soon after, the pair released their first true hit, "Da Funk." It sold 30,000 copies and became an influential work among other dance artists and listeners. In 1996, Daft Punk released another single, the limited edition "Musique." They also remixed songs by other artists, including the Chemical Brothers' "Life Is Sweet."

The year "Musique" was released, record labels began bidding for the right to sign the band to a recording contract. The pair ultimately signed with Virgin. In 1997, Daft Punk released their first full-length album *Homework*. Like the singles before it, *Homework* used a variety of samples and sound influences from across musical genres in its dance-oriented sound. It was recorded in the duo's bedrooms.

Reviewing the album in the *San Diego Union-Tribune*, Jeff Niesel wrote "Because Daft Punk's groove-laden bass beats and pulsating drum machines often coalesce into noisy, dance-inducing melodies, the group's debut represents one of the better electronica releases to find domestic distribution." While *Homework* reached #150 on the *Billboard* top 200 album charts, it was a bigger hit in Britain and the rest of Europe, with smash hit single "Da Funk" talked about as single of the year. *Homework* eventually sold at least 2.5 million copies worldwide.

The duo behind Daft Punk were publicity-shy, and worked to keep their physical identities hidden by covering their faces. Bangalter and de Homem-Christo did put on a highly regarded live show, but still kept themselves, as DJs, relatively anonymous. Reviewing a show at the London Astoria in November of 1997, Nick Hasted commented in the *Independent*, "where the Chemical Brothers make some attempt to replicate the diversity of their records on stage, Daft Punk have stripped their sound to its essentials. It's the beat, the same beat, over and over. It's all the crowd want.... What the crowd really roar for, what Daft Punk toys with, is the return, never refused, to the most basic, chest-thudding techno heartbeat."

Because of the power of the album, there were high expectations and media hype surrounding Daft Punk and their next release. Both Bangalter and de Homem-Christo were not particularly enamored with the music industry nor the entertainment media, and shrugged off pressure to put out another record right away. Instead, Bangalter released an album, *Music Sounds Better with You*, under the name Stardust, then spent more than two years working on the next Daft Punk record.

In 2001, Daft Punk finally released their eagerly awaited second full-length album, *Discovery*. It reached number 44 on the *Billboard* top 200 album charts, and was number three on the top electronic albums. Again, the album was a bigger hit in Europe and elsewhere than it was in the United States, reaching at least double platinum status internationally on the basis of the smash hit singles "Around the World" and "One More Time."

Reviewing *Discovery* in the Melbourne, Australia *Herald Sun*, Cyclone Wehner lauded "The neo-disco celebration "One More Time" ... is hardly typical of an album that traverses progressive jazz, synth-rock, disco, New Wave, electro and tech-house yet flows like a continuous mix-CD. It's more out there than *Homework*, but Daft Punk have too much warped humour to let self-indulgence get the better of them." Wehner concludes, "Yes, it has been too long, but the wait was worth it."

Stateside, critics especially praised the production of *Discovery*. Michael Endelman of the *Boston Globe* wrote, "*Discovery* is pop to the nth degree. Polished almost to the point of glistening, the disc is laden with huge emotive hooks, actual songwriting, and a production style that's clean enough to cook on." In the *New York Times*, Neil Strauss lauded Daft Punk as a leader in the French electronic music movement.

He declared, "One of the best instruments the new French electronic wave bands have is their ears. They have an almost preternatural understanding of arrangement and instrumentation, of timbre and tone, of producing each sound to deliver the greatest visceral impact. As a result, rather than being a niche album, an ironic experiment or a statement of obsessiveness by two record collectors, *Discovery* is an immediately likeable album...."

Bangalter and de Homem-Christo remained vigilant about hiding their identities with the release of *Discovery.* Instead of hiding behind face paint, masks, and costumes as they previously had done, the pair created a story about their re-invention as robots. They told the media that a computer virus erased the original tapes of *Discovery* and the album was then recreated by the robots. Robots were then said to make up the band. To fully create the effect, the pair hired Hollywood costume designers to make two robotic costumes that cost nearly a quarter million dollars. The robot costumes had LCD displays and were worn by the duo during photo shoots and some of music videos created in support of the album. Bangalter told Cameron Adams of the *Townsville Bulletin/Townsville Sun,* "It's nice we can make more than the music, and we can work with animators and also special effects companies in Hollywood with the robots. These are our childhood dreams."

By this time, Bangalter and de Homem-Christo also owned their own studio, a production company called Daft Life, and the rights to their own publishing. The pair had their own label within Virgin, through which they continued to release their albums. Continuing to expand Daft Punk's influence beyond music, the pair moved into film in 2003 when they produced the animated *Interstella 5555: The 5tory of the 5ecret 5tar 5ystem.* Created by Japanese anime legend Leiji Matsumoto, Bangalter and de Homem-Christo also wrote the story for the film which focuses on an Earth-based evil record producer who kidnaps some alien musicians and makes them into stars. The pair had been fans of Matsumoto since childhood, primarily through his 1980s cartoon *Albator.* The music from *Discovery* acts as the film's soundtrack, and music videos for singles from the album were culled from the film.

Two years later, in 2005, Daft Punk released its third studio album, *Human After All.* It reached number one on *Billboard*'s top electronic albums in the United States and had a hit single with "Aerodynamic," but was less of a critical success. Fiona Shepherd of the *Scotsman* wrote, "this album breaks no new ground for Daft Punk. But at least, unlike the equally laurel-resting Chemical Brothers, their formula is not quite as stagnant." She added, "*Human After All* is a tease of an album, offering up hopeful snatches of the signature Daft Punk sound— the vocoder vocals, the robotic rhythms, the casual synth hooks—but ultimately delivering very little." Another critic, Joshua Klein of the *Washington Post,* asked "Is Daft Punk trying to send a message that emotion is repetitive? ... Surely the human side of the band understands that pile-driver arrangements wear the listener down to the point where what once seemed fun suddenly feels like a chore to sit through, let alone dance to. Then again, maybe the title is misdirection. Maybe the Daft Punk guys are actually robots after all...."

Daft Punk's stage show as the duo toured stadiums in 2006 and 2007 in support of *Human After All* was an elaborate crowd pleaser. Music and live performance continued to be only part of Daft Punk's focus, however. They returned to film in 2006 with *Electroma.* Bangalter and de Homem-Christo wrote and directed the art-house film, and Bangaltar also served as cinematographer. Set in the Southwest, the story focuses on robots who go on a journey of self-discovery by seeking to become more like people by, for example, having their robotic heads become human with liquid latex. The soundtrack featured no Daft Punk music, but continued to work in the spirit of the band. Bangalter told Alex Rayner of the London *Guardian,* "the film is experimental and inaccessible; however, it's a movie that does not require your brain to function." Rayner found the film fascinating, writing "Daft Punk's widescreen debut is a beautiful, sun-blushed nugget of cinema."

Soon after *Electroma* hit theaters, Daft Punk's second live album, *Alive 2007,* was released in 2007. It reached number one on *Billboard*'s top electronic albums chart, and was highly praised by critics for capturing what had become a must-see live show. The album won a Grammy as did a track from it, "Harder, Better, Faster, Stronger." The following year, Daft Punk released another album *Leftovers.* In 2009, the duo continued to make unexpected choices when they signed a deal with Walt Disney Pictures to provide an original score and record the soundtrack for a remake of the 1982 science fiction classic *Tron.* The film was scheduled for release in 2011.

As Daft Punk moves forward, both Bangalter and de Homem-Christo promised to continue to make unexpected music and choices outside the mainstream. Bangalter said to David O'Mahony of the *Irish Times,* "Since we started Daft Punk, both the music and visual elements, we have tried to never do the same thing twice. We are always happy when people follow us on a different path." He added to *Newsweek*'s Ali, "Being in a safe situation is the least exciting thing in life. You take challenges when you start, and you should not stop taking challenges when you get some success."

## Selected discography

*Homework*, Virgin, 1997.
*Discovery*, Virgin, 2001.
*Alive 1997*, Virgin, 2001.
*Human After All*, Virgin, 2005.
*Musique, Vol. 1: 1993-2005* (compilation), Virgin, 2007.
*Alive 2007*, Virgin, 2007.
*Leftovers*, Virgin, 2008.

## Sources

### Periodicals

*Billboard*, September 1, 2007.
*Boston Globe*, April 8, 2001, p. M12.
*Daily Record*, June 15, 2007, p. 50.
*Guardian* (London, England), October 17, 2003, p. 15; July 14, 2007, p. 4.
*Herald Sun* (Melbourne, Australia), March 15, 2001, p. 52.
*Hollywood Reporter*, March 5, 2009.
*Independent* (London, England), January 31, 1997, p. 8; November 11, 1997, p. 4.

*Irish Times*, August 3, 2007, p. 9.
*Music Week*, March 21, 2009, p. 12.
*Newsweek*, April 19, 2001.
*New York Sun*, December 4, 2007, p. 18.
*New York Times*, April 13, 2001, p. E25; August 11, 2007, p. B9; August 1, 2008, p. E17.
*Observer* (London, England), July 15, 2007, p. 71; October 12, 2008, p. 26.
*San Diego Union-Tribune*, April 3, 1997, sec. Entertainment, p. Night & Day-21.
*Scotsman*, February 25, 2005, p. 44.
*Sunday Herald*, March 18, 2001, p. 6.
*Townsville Bulletin/Townsville Sun* (Australia), April 6, 2001, p. 28.
*Washington Post*, March 27, 2005, p. N9.

### Online

"Daft Punk—Biography," allmusic, http://www. allmusic.com/cg/amg.dll?p=amg&sql=11:dvfox quglddde~T1 (April 22, 2009).
"Grammy Award Winners," Grammy.com, http:// www.grammy.com/GRAMMY_Awards/ Winners/ (April 22, 2009).
"Guy-Manuel De Homem-Christo," Internet Movie Database, http://www.imdb.com/name/ nm0208878/ (April 22, 2009).
"Thomas Bangalter," Internet Movie Database, http://www.imdb.com/name/nm0051939/ (April 22, 2009).

—*A. Petruso*

# Deanna Dunagan

## Actress

**B**orn May 25, 1940, in Monahans, TX; daughter of J. Conrad (a businessman) and Kathlyn Dunagan; married and divorced; children: one. *Education:* University of Texas, Austin, B.A., 1963; Trinity University, M.A., 1970.

**Addresses:** *Agent*—Stewart Talent Chicago, 58 W. Huron, Chicago, IL 60654. *Home*—Chicago,IL.

## Career

**A**ctress in films, including: *The Naked Face,* 1984; *Running Scared,* 1986; *Men Don't Leave,* 1990; *Losing Isaiah,* 1995; *Dimension,* 2007. Television appearances include: *Any Friend of Nicholas Nickleby is a Friend of Mine,* 1982; *Will: The Autobiography of G. Gordon Liddy,* 1982; *Two Fathers' Justice,* 1985; *Amerika,* 1987; *Missing Persons,* 1993; *Two Fathers: Justice for the Innocent,* 1994; *A Will of their Own,* 1998; *What About Joan,* 2001; *Prison Break,* 2005. Stage appearances include: *Bleacher Bums,* The Organic, Chicago; *Sunday in the Park with George,* Goodman Theatre, Chicago; *Man and Superman,* Circle in the Square Theatre, Broadway, New York City, 1979; *Children of a Lesser God,* first national tour, 1981; *Quilters,* Northlight Theatre, Chicago, 1985-86; *Hamlet,* Wisdom Bridge Theatre, Chicago, 1986; *The Oresteia,* Court Theatre, Chicago, 1986-87; *Stepping Out,* Steppenwolf Theatre Company, Chicago, 1988; *A Chorus of Disapproval,* Court Theatre, Chicago, 1989-90; *The Caucasian Chalk Circle,* Court Theatre, Chicago, 1990-91; *Coriolanus,* The Next Theatre, Chicago, 1991; *Six Degrees of Separation,* Madison Repertory, Madison, WI, 1994-95; *A Touch of the Poet,* Goodman Theatre, Chicago, 1995-96; *The Merry Wives of Windsor,* Shakespeare Dallas Theatre, Dallas, TX, 1999; *The Glamour House,* Victory Gardens, Chicago, 2001-02; *Bounce,* Goodman Theatre, Chicago, and Kennedy Center, Washington, D.C., 2003; *James Joyce's The Dead,* Court Theatre, Chicago, 2003; *A Delicate Balance,* Remy Bumppo Theatre Company, Chicago, 2004-05; *The Chalk Garden,* Northlight Theatre, Chicago, 2005-06; *I Never Sang to My Father,* Steppenwolf Theatre Company, Chicago, 2006; *August: Osage County,* Steppenwolf Theatre Company, Chicago, 2007; *August: Osage County,* Imperial Theatre, Broadway, New York City, 2007-08.

**Awards:** After Dark Award, *Gay Chicago Magazine,* for *The Glamour House,* 2002; Joseph Jefferson Award, best actress in a supporting role, for *James Joyce's The Dead,* 2003; After Dark Award, *Gay Chicago Magazine,* for *A Delicate Balance,* 2005; Joseph Jefferson Award, best actress in a supporting role, for *I Never Sang for My Father,* 2005; Joseph Jefferson Award, best actress in a principal role, for *August: Osage County,* 2007; Theatre World Award, for *August: Osage County,* 2008; Drama Desk Award, outstanding actress in a play, for *August: Osage County,* 2008; Antoinette Perry Award for Excellence in Theatre, best leading actress, *August: Osage County,* 2008.

## Sidelights

Deanna Dunagan spent more than two decades on stage in Chicago, enjoying a successful career in relative obscurity. But she needed only six months on Broadway to secure a Tony Award for best leading actress in 2008. Dunagan won the coveted stage award for her raging, cutting performance as an acid-tongued matriarch in Tracy Letts' *August: Osage County,* a comic melodrama about a dysfunctional family. Having spent her career on stage in the Midwest, winning a Tony Award was the furthest thing from Dunagan's mind.

"When we started rehearsals in Chicago … none of us dreamed we would be here," Dunagan said in her acceptance speech from Radio City Music Hall, according to the *Philadelphia Inquirer.* "After 34 years in regional theatre, I never even thought about it. I watched it on TV like everybody else."

Dunagan grew up in Monahans, Texas, the daughter of Kitty and J. Conrad Dunagan. Her father managed the family's Coca-Cola bottling operation. Dunagan dabbled with acting as a child. "She would get her cousins together and organize them and put on plays for the family," her mother told the *Odessa American*'s John Corrales. "She was always the director and the villain—never the sweet one."

Dunagan married at 17, had a child at 18, and earned a music education degree from the University of Texas, Austin, in 1963. She taught in Midland, Texas, and performed at the Midland Community Theatre. Her marriage fell apart and Dunagan enrolled in graduate school at the Dallas Theater Center, which offered a degree program in conjunction with Trinity University in San Antonio. While completing her degree, Dunagan spent time in San Miguel de Allende, Mexico, working on a thesis in costume design.

In 1979 Dunagan landed a role as an understudy in a Broadway production of *Man and Superman* at the Circle in the Square Theatre in New York City. One night, she arrived at the theater less than 30 minutes before the show and was told the principal actress was ill and she needed to go on. Dunagan nailed her performance and International Creative Management signed her the next day.

For the next several years, Dunagan worked at regional theaters across the United States. She ended up in Chicago in 1981 as part of a touring produc-

tion of *Children of a Lesser God.* Dunagan fell in love with Chicago and decided to make the Windy City her home. She has lived there ever since and has performed a variety of roles at more than 30 Chicago-area theaters. In the ensuing years, Dunagan played the queen of Denmark in *Hamlet,* the mother in Shakespeare's *Coriolanus,* Mistress Page in the Shakespeare comedy *The Merry Wives of Windsor,* an alcoholic in *A Delicate Balance,* and a polished 1950s-era wife in *I Never Sang for my Father.* "I enjoy being able to work on a show for three months and then go on to the next project," she told Broadway.com's Kathy Henderson. "I get to do twice, if not three or four times, the number of plays I could do in New York." She has also made television and film appearances.

In the mid-2000s, Dunagan was approached to play the lead in Pulitzer Prize-winning playwright Tracy Letts' new work, *August: Osage County,* set to premier at Chicago's Steppenwolf Theatre. After reading through the script, Dunagan wanted to turn down the role. "[The story] was so devastating to me, I was so disturbed. I was literally shaking as a result of the reading," Dunagan told the *Telegraph.* "Then I re-read the script and knew that I had an affinity for the part, perhaps because I'm from that part of the country. The language was indigenous to my mouth."

Set in Pawhuska, Osage County, Oklahoma, the play—both wickedly funny and severely dark—follows the unraveling of the Weston family. Dunagan plays the disheveled Violet Weston, a pill-popping, cancer-stricken aging mom who spews venom at her grown daughters and anyone else who visits. Playing the role proved grueling. The play runs three and a half hours, with Violet appearing on stage throughout most of the show, constantly making her way up and down the stairs on the three-tiered set and often screaming. At the end of each performance, Dunagan found her voice worn, her back and knees aching.

Speaking to the *Chicago Tribune*'s Stevenson Swanson, fellow cast member Amy Morton discussed the demands of the stage. "Your body doesn't know you're lying. Your body thinks you're in trauma all the time. People think actors are hypochondriacal, but what we traffic in, human emotion and psychology—your body doesn't know you haven't lost your love." When producers decided to take the show to Broadway after its successful Chicago run, Dunagan began working with physical therapists and voice coaches and had acupuncture and spinal injections to get in shape. Once on Broadway, she had to perform eight shows a week.

Despite the hardships, Dunagan enjoyed the role, particularly because she got to showcase many moods. Speaking to Georgia Temple of the *Midland Reporter-Telegram*, Dunagan described her character's varying personalities. "When she's relatively sober or when she's all drugged up, she acts differently. And she's very vocal and extroverted. She takes charge a lot and creates a lot of scenes. She demands attention so the actress playing it also demands attention. It's a flashy role and very demanding physically as well as emotionally and vocally."

The play opened in Chicago to rave reviews in July of 2007. Within months, it had created such a splash that producers decided to take it to Broadway. The show opened in December of 2007 at the Imperial Theatre, the former home to the Broadway sensation *Les Miserables*. On opening day, Dunagan woke with a sore throat and spent the day inhaling steam, bent over a pot of boiling water.

After the Broadway debut, papers were filled with glowing reviews and within 48 hours, ticket sales topped $1 million. *New York Times* critic Charles Isherwood had this to say (according to the *Chicago Tribune*): "It is, flat out, no asterisks and without qualifications, the most exciting new American play Broadway has seen in years." Isherwood described the play as "fiercely funny and bitingly sad."

Dunagan stayed on Broadway through June of 2008 before handing the role off to Estelle Parsons. She had been at it more than a year and wanted to rest. Following her Tony win, Dunagan became a media darling and was interviewed by countless publications. Every time a reporter asked her age, she refused to answer. "I don't tell," Dunagan told Broadway.com. "And the reason I don't is that nobody can divorce that [number] from who you are. It starts getting that way in your 40s." In November of 2008, the Steppenwolf Theatre took the production to London and played to a sold-out crowd at the National Theatre on opening night.

## Sources

### Periodicals

*Chicago Sun Times*, July 27, 2007, p. NC11.
*Chicago Tribune*, February 24, 2008, sec. Magazine, p. 10; June 15, 2008, sec. Arts & Entertainment, p. 3.
*Midland Reporter-Telegram* (TX), June 20, 2008.
*Odessa American* (TX), June 17, 2008.
*Philadelphia Inquirer*, June 17, 2008, p. E01.
*Staten Island Advance* (NY), December 20, 2007, p. W44.

### Online

"Deanna Dunagan," Stewart Talent Chicago, http://www.stewarttalent.com/media/806-resume. (November 20, 2008).
"Fresh Face: Deanna Dunagan," Broadway.com, http://www.broadway.com/buzz/buzz_story_print.aspx?id=557687 (November 25, 2008).
"How *August: Osage County* Launched Reluctant Star Deanna Dunagan," *Daily Telegraph*, http://www.telegraph.co.uk/arts/main.jhtml?xml=/arts/2008/11/13/btaugust213.xml (November 25, 2008).

—Lisa Frick

# Ann Dunwoody

## Four-star general

**B**orn Ann E. Dunwoody, c. 1953, at Fort Belvoir, VA; daughter of Harold (a one-star general) and Elizabeth Dunwoody; married Craig Brotchie (an Air Force colonel), c. 1990. *Education:* State University of New York, B.A., 1975; Florida Institute of Technology, M.S., 1988; Industrial College of the Armed Forces, Fort McNair, Washington, D.C., M.S., 1995.

**Addresses:** *Office*—U.S. Army Materiel Command, 9301 Chapek Rd., Fort Belvoir, VA 22060-5527.

## Career

**C**ommissioned as second lieutenant, U.S. Army, 1975; supply platoon leader, Fort Sill, OK, 1976; attended U.S. Army Quartermaster Center & School, 1980; division parachute officer, 82nd Airborne Division, Fort Bragg, N.C., c. 1990; battalion commander, 82nd Airborne Division, Fort Bragg, N.C., 1992; promoted to general, 2000; head of 1st Corps Support Command, Fort Bragg, N.C., 2000; commanding general, Surface Deployment and Distribution Command, 2002-04; promoted to three-star general, 2005; promoted to four-star general, 2008; commanding general, U.S. Army Materiel Command, Fort Belvoir, VA, 2008—.

**Awards:** Distinguished Alumni Award, State University of New York, Cortland, 2001; DoD Distinguished Service Award, National Defense Transportation Association, 2004; Distinguished Service Award, Military Order of the World Wars, 2007; promoted to four-star general, 2008. Other awards include the Distinguished Service Medal with Oak Leaf Cluster, Defense Superior Service Medal, Legion of Merit with two Oak Leaf Clusters, Defense Meritorious Service Medal, Meritorious Service Medal with Silver Oak Leaf Cluster, Army Commendation Medal, Army Achievement Medal, National Defense Service Medal with Bronze Star, Southwest Asia Service Medal (with two campaign stars), Kuwait Liberation Medal.

## Sidelights

**I**n 2008, Ann Dunwoody became the first female four-star general in military history. During a press conference after her promotion ceremony at the Pentagon, Dunwoody downplayed her extraordinary rise through the ranks of the male-dominated military and credited her family with teaching her that through hard work, anything is possible. "I never ... even heard of the word 'glass ceilings,'" Dunwoody said, according to the *Washington Post.* "It was always ... the glass was always half-full. You could always be anything you wanted to be."

In earning that fourth star, Dunwoody surpassed the rank her father attained during his military career—Harold Dunwoody retired as a one-star general. According to the *Army Times*, Harold Dunwoody was not surprised by his daughter's achievement. "I have followed her career for 33 years," he said. "Every assignment she has ever had, she's done in an outstanding manner. So it really doesn't surprise me she was the first woman selected for four stars."

It is no surprise, either, that Dunwoody ended up dedicating her life to the military. Her ancestors have served the United States in nearly every conflict from the Revolutionary War onward, including the Civil War and the Spanish-American War. Her brother, father, grandfather and great-grandfather are all West Point graduates. Dunwoody, herself, was born at Fort Belvoir, Virginia, around 1953. Her father served in World War II, the Korean War, and Vietnam and was blown out of a tank during combat in Europe.

Initially, Dunwoody conceived of a different path. She dreamed of becoming a physical education teacher and joined the army for what she thought would be a two-year commitment before getting on with her life. Dunwoody attended the State University of New York at Cortland, competing in gymnastics and tennis. She enrolled in the army to help pay for school. After graduating in 1975, she was commissioned as a second lieutenant and sent to airborne school, where she learned to pack parachutes and jump out of planes.

In 1976, the army sent Dunwoody to Fort Sill, Oklahoma, where she became a supply platoon leader. In 1980, she headed to Fort Lee, Virginia, enrolling at the U.S. Army Quartermaster Center & School. At the Quartermaster school, she learned about troop provisioning. Dunwoody's military career has focused on logistics and support services. In 1992, while stationed at Fort Bragg, North Carolina, she became the 82nd Airborne Division's first female battalion commander. Prior to becoming battalion commander, she served the 82nd Airborne as a division parachute officer and was deployed to Saudi Arabia for Operation Desert Shield, a precursor to the Persian Gulf War.

In 2000, Dunwoody became Fort Bragg's first female general and took over as head of the 1st Corps Support Command, a unit that conducts large-scale logistical operations. From 2002 to 2004, Dunwoody served as commanding general of the military's Surface Deployment and Distribution Command (SDDC). One of her biggest endeavors during this time was to support the troops in the run-up to Operation Iraqi Freedom. From December of 2002 to March of 2003, the SDDC transported 12 million square feet of cargo aboard 163 vessels, which docked at 26 seaports. For this work, she received the National Defense Transportation Association's DoD Distinguished Service Award in 2004. In 2005, Dunwoody earned a promotion to three-star general.

In June of 2008, U.S. President George W. Bush nominated Dunwoody to become the military's first female four-star general and to take over as head of the army unit that is responsible for supplying the troops with their equipment. After senate confirmation, Dunwoody was promoted in November of 2008. The first female one-star general was appointed in 1970, yet women continue to lag behind their male counterparts in rank, making Dunwoody's promotion all the more remarkable. As of June of 2008, women made up 14 percent of the army's active duty personnel yet accounted for only five percent of its generals.

Dunwoody's promotion was a cause for celebration among female soldiers, including those in active duty and those already retired. "I was twirling and throwing my hat in the air," retired Lt. Gen. Claudia Kennedy told Rachel L. Swarns of the *New York Times*. "It shows people that the leaders in the Army think it's important to pick the best qualified, not just the men."

Along the way, Dunwoody married Craig Brotchie, now a retired colonel with 26 years of experience in the Air Force. She and her husband have a dog, Barney. In her spare time, Dunwoody enjoys sailing, playing tennis, and running. She is not the first woman in her family to break barriers in the military: Dunwoody's older sister, Susan Schoeck, achieved notoriety by becoming the army's third female helicopter pilot.

After receiving her fourth star, Dunwoody was installed as the 17th commander, and first female leader, of the U.S. Army Materiel Command (AMC), which is located at Fort Belvoir, her birthplace. As commanding general of the AMC, Dunwoody's job entails providing soldiers—stationed at 149 locations worldwide—with everything they need, including food, water, bullets, bombs, and vehicles. The Army Materiel Command Web site explains its mission this way: "If a Soldier shoots it, drives it, flies it, wears it, communicates with it, or eats it— AMC provides it." Dunwoody's first order of business was to focus on supporting operations in Iraq and Afghanistan.

## Sources

### Periodicals

*Defense Transportation Journal,* September 2004, p. 31.
*Los Angeles Times,* June 24, 2008, p. A10.
*New York Times,* June 30, 2008, p. A17.
*Washington Post,* June 24, 2008, p. A2; November 15, 2008, p. A7.

### Online

"About the U.S. Army Materiel Command," U.S. Army, http://www.amc.army.mil/pa/about.asp (September 30, 2008).
"Dad Proud of Daughter in Line to Be 4-Star," *Army Times,* http://www.armytimes.com/news/2008/07/ap_dunwoody_dad_071908/ (September 30, 2008).
"Dunwoody Becomes First Female Four-Star General," Associated Press, http://www.google.com/hostednews/ap/article/ALeqM5gOVHjD7DCtQVV0A7O5I_abqTr3owD94ETDU80 (November 16, 2008).
"First Female Four-Star U.S. Army General Nominated," CNN.com, http://www.cnn.com/2008/US/06/23/woman.general (September 30, 2008).
"Lt. Gen. Ann E. Dunwoody, U.S. Army Materiel Command Deputy Commanding General," U.S. Army, http://www.army.mil/-news/2008/06/30/10506-gen-ann-e-dunwoody-us-army-materiel-command-commanding-general/index.html (September 30, 2008).

*—Lisa Frick*

# Aaron Eckhart

## Actor

**B**orn March 12, 1968, in Cupertino, CA; son of James C. (a computer company executive) and Mary Lawrence (a children's book author) Eckhart. *Education:* Brigham Young University, B.A., 1994.

**Addresses:** *Agent*—Creative Artists Agency, 2000 Avenue of the Stars, Los Angeles, CA 90067.

## Career

**A**ctor in films, including: *Slaughter of the Innocents*, 1994; *In the Company of Men*, 1997; *Thursday*, 1998; *Your Friends and Neighbors*, 1998; *Any Given Sunday*, 1999; *Molly*, 1999; *Erin Brockovich*, 2000; *Nurse Betty*, 2000; *The Pledge*, 2001; *Possession*, 2002; *The Core*, 2003; *The Missing*, 2003; *Paycheck*, 2003; *Suspect Zero*, 2004; *Conversations with Other Women*, 2005; *Neverwas* (also co-producer), 2005; *Thank You for Smoking*, 2005; *The Black Dahlia*, 2006; *The Wicker Man*, 2006; *Bill* (also executive producer), 2007; *No Reservations*, 2007; *The Dark Knight*, 2008; *Towelhead*, 2008; *Traveling*, 2008. Television appearances include: *Double Jeopardy* (movie) 1992; *Aliens in the Family*, 1996. Stage appearances include: *The Mercy Seat*, Acorn Theater, New York City, 2002-03; *Oleanna*, Garrick Theatre, London, 2004.

## Sidelights

**A**ctor Aaron Eckhart has carefully chosen his roles to avoid typecasting as the handsome cad, but his best-known parts have been exuberantly villainous ones. He first garnered notice in writer/director Neil LaBute's 1997 debut *In the Company of Men* as a loathsome seducer, then won over female audiences as the appealing biker-boyfriend of Julia Roberts' *Erin Brockovich* in 2000. Eckhart's "distinctive qualities of malevolent charm," as *New Yorker* film critic David Denby put it, returned in 2005's dark comedy *Thank You for Smoking*, and some hinted that his performance as Harvey Dent in the 2008 Batman saga *The Dark Knight* was possibly an Oscar-worthy one. "Although his blond good looks suggest that he could find steady employment as a B-list romantic lead," asserted *New York Times* film critic Manohla Dargis about Eckhart's career, "there is something overly hard about the cut of his jaw, something too intense in his gaze, which may explain why he routinely shows up as the heavy."

Eckhart was born in 1968 in Cupertino, California, the future headquarters of the Apple computer company, as the youngest of three boys. His father was an executive in the computer industry based in the area that would later become known as Silicon Valley, and his mother has written poetry and children's books. The family belonged to the Church of Jesus Christ of Latter-Day Saints, more commonly known as the Mormon faith. In 1981, when Eckhart was 13 years old, the family moved to England because of his father's job. They lived in the town of Cobham, about 20 miles from London, and Eckhart attended the American Community School (ACS). Though his classmates were fellow expatriates, he recalled being traumatized by the move from sunny California to overcast England. "It was raining, we lived in a small flat, I had to take the bus," he told *Observer*'s Geraldine Bedell.

Eckhart's first acting experience came when he was cast as Charlie Brown in the school play. He formally finished high school by correspondence course because the family had relocated once more by then, this time to the paradisiacal, laid-back city of Sydney, Australia. There Eckhart was able to return to his first passion—surfing—and subsequently spent a few years roaming other famous vacation spots as a surf and ski bum. Finally, he entered Brigham Young University, the renowned Mormon institution in Utah, where he majored in film. There he met playwright Neil LaBute, who was working on a doctorate in drama and cast Eckhart in some of his early plays that were produced at the school.

Eckhart graduated in 1994, two years after making his television debut in a bit part in a joint CBS/Showtime movie *Double Jeopardy*, a marital murder mystery. He made his feature-film debut in *Slaughter of the Innocents*, a serial-killer thriller that appears to have followed the "straight-to-video" release route. Settling in New York City, Eckhart looked for stage and television work, but found a way to get to Fort Wayne, Indiana, when LaBute began shooting what would be his debut as a screenwriter and director. *In the Company of Men* premiered at the 1997 Sundance Film Festival and caused a stir at the annual independent-film showcase event for its controversial plot.

The movie won LaBute a Filmmaker's Trophy for Best Dramatic Feature at Sundance, but distributors were nervous about buying it because of its distasteful subject matter and the rampantly misogynistic dialogue. In the movie, Eckhart plays Chad, a junior corporate executive who, while on a business trip with co-worker Howie (Matt Malloy), schemes to deliberately seduce a woman and then break up with her. The calculating Chad picks a vulnerable target—in this case, a young hearing-impaired woman they meet in the course of their unnamed line of work—but then their plan begins to go awry when one of the pair begins to develop actual feelings for the woman.

LaBute finally found a distributor for *In the Company of Men*, and it went on to immense success at the box office while igniting rancorous debate about its misogynstic subject matter. Moreover, Eckhart was immediately hailed as a future star. "In a career-

making performance, Eckhart, who physically is a cross between William Hurt and Michael York, aptly embodies a 1990s yuppie: nastily cocky and ruthlessly ambitious," noted Emanuel Levy in *Variety*. Reviewing it for the *San Francisco Chronicle*, Ruthe Stein maintained that "Eckhart is especially strong. He has Chad's swagger down cold. It's a difficult role because it requires two layers of acting. Around the guys, he's coolly manipulative. But around Christine, he has to act loving, which is truly an act because he doesn't mean it."

Eckhart appeared in another LaBute project a year later, titled *Your Friends and Neighbors*, alongside Ben Stiller, Catherine Keener, Jason Patric, and Nastassja Kinski. He gained nearly 50 pounds for the role, and some reviewers claimed he was nearly unrecognizable from his portrayal of the blandly handsome and malevolent Chad. Eckhart's character in this film is trapped in a lackluster marriage to Amy Brenneman's character, who cheats on him with the siren played by Kinski. Reviewing it for the *New York Times*, Janet Maslin commended the ensemble cast. "Stiller, who can bring so much sneaky allure to playing unappealing characters, embodies many of the filmmaker's most misanthropic notions, sharing with Mr. Patric and Mr. Eckhart a physical brutishness that turns sexual swagger into something monstrous. In the end, these characters are devastatingly true to Mr. LaBute's idea of self-annihilating manhood. They're hard to watch and even harder to forget."

Eckhart later said he was so unnerved by the critical attention he garnered in LaBute's debut film that it scared him away from Hollywood for a time and the fast track to stardom that some were predicting for him. Instead he chose to work with directors he respected who were willing to hire him, even if it was for smaller roles. This included Oliver Stone's 1999 football movie *Any Given Sunday* and Steven Soderbergh's *Erin Brockovich*. The latter film, which won Julia Roberts an Academy Award, was based on a true story about a secretary at a Los Angeles law firm who does a little research on her own into mysterious deaths that are possibly the result of a utility company's use of a toxic chemical. Eckhart was cast as George, Erin's biker boyfriend. After commenting on the often-inappropriate officewear that Roberts sports in some scenes, *Newsweek* David Ansen wrote that "George, like Erin, belies his outer appearance. Great with kids, he becomes Erin's ... full-time babysitter, a role he begins to resent when she becomes too obsessed with her cause to notice him. Eckhart should have no trouble getting leading-man parts after this: he's sexy and tender and funny, endowing this scruffy Harley dude with a delicate mix of yin and yang."

*Erin Brockovich* was released in 2000, the same year as LaBute's *Nurse Betty*, which featured Eckhart as Renee Zellweger's loutish husband who meets an appropriately gruesome end that sets in motion the rest of the plot. In 2001's *The Pledge*, he worked with Sean Penn, who directed the drama, and Jack Nicholson. *Possession*, released in 2002, reunited him with LaBute and gave him what would be his first heroic leading-man role. He co-starred with Gwyneth Paltrow in a dual-plotline story involving a pair of literary scholars intrigued by a possible romance between two long-dead writers.

In 2003, Eckhart appeared in three movies, two of them action thrillers in which he played the male lead. *The Core* was a sci-fi romp with Hilary Swank, and *Paycheck* was his first chance to work with Ben Affleck. He also had a supporting role in the *The Missing,* a historical drama featuring Cate Blanchett. What many critics considered his truly breakout role came in the 2005 dark comedy *Thank You for Smoking,* in which he starred as a distressingly cheerful government lobbyist for the tobacco industry. The character, Nick Naylor, "is the intellectual equivalent of the golden-maned bruisers in professional wrestling—he's magnetically villainous," wrote David Denby, film critic for the *New Yorker.* "In the person of Aaron Eckhart, he makes lying a lot sexier than telling the truth." In Dargis' *New York Times* review of the film that earned Eckhart a nomination for a Golden Globe in the Best Performance category, the critic declared it to be "the first role that has given him the room to play both ends of his usual character types, to turn his ingratiating smile into a leer, to charm even as he repels."

Eckhart also appeared in two other films released in 2005: the British-made drama *Neverwas* and *Conversations with Other Women,* a unique split-screen project that pitted him against Helena Bonham Carter. A year later, he appeared in *The Black Dahlia,* a film by Brian DePalma based on a notorious Hollywood murder, and briefly in a LaBute remake of the 1973 thriller *The Wicker Man* that earned terrible reviews.

The decade-long prediction that Eckhart was an ideal Hollywood leading man finally came to fruition in *No Reservations* in 2007. A remake of a German feel-good romance, the movie co-starred him with Catherine Zeta-Jones. A pair of drastically different restaurant chefs, Zeta-Jones's Kate is a frosty perfectionist, but her regimented, somewhat lonely life is disrupted by sudden parenthood when she becomes guardian to her young niece Zoe (Abigail Breslin) and is forced to share her Manhattan eatery duties with hot-shot chef Nick. "Zeta-Jones is in her element as a formidable woman one messes with, professionally and personally, only at one's peril," wrote *Variety*'s Todd McCarthy, who noted further that "the lanky, exuberant Eckhart might seem an odd match for his costar's cool, dark beauty, but this mostly works to the film's benefit; [he] makes Nick's quirkiness winning rather than grating as he stealthily charms Zoe while restraining himself with Kate."

Eckhart also took a starring role as the hapless *Bill* in 2007, which also featured Jessica Alba and Elizabeth Banks, for which Eckhart was executive producer. Some amount of controversy surrounded his next project, which was originally titled *Towelhead* but was also released under the title *Nothing Is Private.* Its debut at the 2007 Toronto Film Festival prompted some critics to question the original title—a slur against people of Arab descent—as well as the subject matter in which its teenage protagonist, played by Summer Bishil, is lured into an inappropriate relationship with her new neighbor in Texas, a repellant Army reservist played by Eckhart.

Some of the criticism surrounding *Towelhead*'s release was lessened by the good reviews Eckhart earned for his portrayal of New York District Attorney Harvey Dent in *The Dark Knight,* the highly anticipated but ill-fated entrant in the Batman saga that turned out to be Heath Ledger's final performance. Eckhart's Dent is a public paragon of virtue, but is mutilated in an accident and becomes the villainous Two-Face. NYMag.com, the Web site of *New York* magazine, wondered if the role might not earn Eckhart his first nomination for an Academy Award. "He's vivid, specific, and energetic in a way we haven't seen before," the article asserted, "and the performance is the first in his career that perfectly taps into Eckhart's weird mix of handsomeness and creepiness."

Eckhart has done some stage work over the course of his career. In 2002, he appeared in LaBute's 9/11-centered drama *The Mercy Seat* at the Acorn Theater, an off-Broadway venue, and had a starring role in a revival of David Mamet's *Oleanna* at London's Garrick Theatre in 2004. That role—a college professor who becomes entangled in a sexual harassment case—was yet another one in which he played a widely reviled character, but he was by then comfortable with such challenges. "Anything that's been inspiring or that I've been proud of has been in controversial territory," he told Bedell, the *Observer* journalist. "I've done things that have been more entertaining and crowd-pleasing, and I've not been happy with those."

## Sources

### Periodicals

*Advocate,* August 14, 2007, p. 26.
*Best Life,* October-November 2005, p. 76.
*Entertainment Weekly,* March 24, 2006, p. 28.
*Newsweek,* March 13, 2000, p. 60.
*New Yorker,* April 3, 2006, p. 88.
*New York Times,* March 28, 1997; August 19, 1998; March 17, 2006.
*Observer* (London, England), April 4, 2004, p. 8.
*People,* September 9, 2002, p. 81.

*San Francisco Chronicle,* August 8, 1997, p. D1.
*Variety,* January 27, 1997, p. 73; July 23, 2007, p. 36.

### Online

"Aaron Eckhart, the Forgotten Great Performance of 'The Dark Knight,'" NYMag.com, http://nymag.com/daily/entertainment/2008/07/aaron_eckhart_the_forgotten_ma.html (September 15, 2008).

—Carol Brennan

# David Ellis

**Artist**

Born in 1971, in Raleigh, NC. *Education:* The Cooper Union, New York, B.F.A., 1994.

**Addresses:** *Gallery*—Roebling Hall, 606 West 26th St., New York, NY 10001. *Home*—Brooklyn, NY.

## Career

Artist. Has exhibited work in several countries, including the United States, the United Kingdom, France, and Japan. Artist in residence, Smack Mellon gallery, Brooklyn, NY, 2004; Metal gallery, Liverpool, England, 2008; Mattress Factory, Pittsburgh, PA, 2008; Theory Icon Project, New York, NY, 2008.

## Sidelights

Artist David Ellis grew up among musicians, and the ideas of music and motion form key components to his sculptural and painted installments. From using drums and player pianos to making videos of his artwork, then speeding up the recordings as performance art, Ellis has rejected the notion of art as something static and has applied movement to all his pieces. In an effort to make his art seem more like jazz music, Ellis also practices improvisational painting, working in public, open spaces where passers-by can watch his ongoing process.

Ellis has exhibited his moving painting and installations in several countries, including the United States, the United Kingdom, France, and Japan. With a group called the Barnstormers, Ellis brings together rural imagery with an urban sentiment, painting graffiti-style, collaborative paintings on barns and farm equipment in his home town of Cameron, North Carolina.

Born in Raleigh, North Carolina, Ellis grew up in the tobacco-growing town of Cameron. Because his entire family played music, Ellis was encouraged to pursue music as well. He had little patience for practicing piano or reading sheet music, but he loved the late-night radio program of hip-hop music broadcast from Fort Bragg military base. "I tuned into that like nothing I've ever tuned into in my life," Ellis said in the brochure *David Ellis: Conversation.* He also explained the difficulties in getting the program, "Super Mix," to come in clearly, without his mother discovering he was up late, listening. "It was just far enough away that reception required one hand on the pause button and the other on an elaborate assembly of coat hangers, duct tape, and tin foil jammed into the hole that was once an antenna on my boom box," he recalled.

Ellis was also captivated by the 1983 PBS documentary, *Style Wars,* which introduced him to graffiti art. With permission, he painted his family's barns in his own graffiti style. Along with working in tobacco fields, he painted murals on music clubs in nearby towns to earn money. He studied art at North Carolina School of the Arts before moving to New York, where he earned his B.F.A. from the Cooper Union. He pursued work designing sets for hip-hop music videos, but by the mid 1990s, he became frustrated with hip-hop culture, which he felt had lost its soul.

In 1999, Ellis invited a group of urban artists from New York and Japan to travel to Cameron to paint barns as a collaborative experiment. The process had a huge impact on Ellis. He was finally able to reconcile his rural heritage with his urban career. "Looking back on the first trip, it was overwhelming. I don't know what I thought would happen, but what did was an awakening," he explained in *David Ellis: Conversation*. "The two communities in my life, which in my head had nothing to do with one another, sat down at the table together, held hands, and became one."

The artists who made that first trip to Cameron formed a collective called the Barnstormers. The group features 25 New York and Tokyo-based artists, often revolving as some artists leave and others take their places. The Barnstormers return yearly to Cameron as an artistic pilgrimage, painting barns and farm equipment. They also integrate their experiences from the trips to North Carolina into the art they create and perform in urban environments. The artists also work together in "jam sessions," much like musicians do, filming their work as they paint collaboratively, creating layers of paintings. Their first project was a studio floor in New York, where they worked, tag-team style, while a mounted camera filmed their work. This became one of the early "motion paintings" that Ellis has continued to work into his exhibitions throughout his career.

Along with motion, Ellis has worked music into many of his pieces, allowing music to help create the artwork. Using technology based on player piano reels, he has created moving pieces of sculpture. He has also installed a series of "drum paintings," pieces that use ordinary objects, such as oil drums, with skins Ellis has designed stretched over their heads. A player piano style reel, or an electronic program, manipulates beaters, which create a series of rhythms and moving parts.

Ellis uses several motifs that appear in his installations. His signature cloud was inspired by a visit to an active volcano, where he saw lava cooling in the water of the ocean. The patterns he saw there are repeated in his cloud form. He also created a character called the *grouse*, a combination of several rural animals into one almost alien-looking form. The idea of the *grouse* came from a stain that Ellis created from boiled tobacco leaves, which he had received from a Cameron farmer. As he painted, he saw several patterns that reminded him of the animals of the wild places where he grew up. He has depicted the *grouse* as a Trickster figure, similar to those that appear in North American or African lore, and the creature has appeared not only in his painted work, but as sculpture.

Ellis and the Barnstormers have adapted their style of art to appeal to a commercial audience as well. In 2003, Ellis worked with two other artists in an advertisement campaign for Nike Presto, performing graffiti on film in several locations in Los Angeles. The campaign was set to music spun by a Japanese DJ. Ellis also worked with several Barnstormers in the 2004 Absolut Vodka campaign. Each artist painted a design on an Absolut bottle. Again, the artists were filmed, and their eight-hour painting jobs were sped up to show in 30-second commercials. The kinetic quality of even the commercial versions of his art shows his distance from formal artistic communities. "Art is so institutionalized, it can make people feel not invited," he told Karin Nelson of the *New York Times*. Instead, Ellis continues to think of his artwork as music. "Music has movement," he explained. "It can cross borders."

## Selected exhibitions

*Mural*, Village Vanguard, New York, 1996.
*Mural and Gourd-Speaker Installation*, GSSA, Osaka, Japan, 2000.
*The Number Nine, the Letter O, and Zero*, Mother Mural, London, 2002.
*Roots, Branches, and Leaves*, Gas/Dyezu Experiment, Tokyo, 2002.
*Paint on Trucks in a World in Need of Love*, Tidal, Osaka, Japan, 2002.
*David Ellis*, Korn Gallery, Madison, NJ, 2002.
*Like the Motion of Water*, Jessica Murray Projects, Brooklyn, NY, 2002.
*Request Line*, Agnes B. Homme, New York, 2003.
*Beat Box/A Painting Is a Drum*, 222 Gallery, Philadelphia, PA, 2004.
*Boars Head/Wars Head*, Lump Gallery, Raleigh, NC, 2004.
*Bound*, Savannah College of Art and Design, Savannah, GA, 2005.
*Orchestrion*, Jessica Murray Projects, Brooklyn, NY, 2005.
*Su*, Atlantic Artwalk, Brooklyn, NY, 2006.
*It's Yours*, Deitch Projects Art Parade, New York, 2006.
*Hive Mind Sound System*, Miss Rockaway Armada, Mississippi River, 2006.
*We People*, Bridge Progressive Arts Initiative, Charlottesville, VA, 2006.
*Conversation*, Rice University Gallery, Houston, TX, 2006.
*Motion Paintings*, Zoller Gallery, Philadelphia, PA, 2006.
*Dawn's Early Light*, Red Gallery, Savannah, GA, 2006.
*Dozens*, Roebling Hall, New York, 2008.
*Uh-oh*, Country Club, Cincinnati, OH, 2008.

## Selected group exhibitions

*Cirk and Watching Paint Dry,* Downtown Arts Festival, New York, 2000.
*Vox,* Kent Gallery, New York, 2001.
*Clocktower Show,* P.S. 1, New York, 2001.
*San Francisco, California, Rappers Delight,* Yerba Buena Center for the Arts, San Francisco, CA, 2001.
*No Condition Is Permanent,* Smack Mellon, Brooklyn, NY, 2001.
*One Planet Under a Groove,* Bronx Museum, Bronx, NY, 2001.
*Painting Is Dead ... Or Is It?* Lance Fung, New York, 2002.
*Final Modification 001,* Ex'Realm, Tokyo, 2002.
*Grotto,* Jessica Murray Projects, Brooklyn, NY, 2002.
*Streetwise One,* Apart, London, 2002.
*Art Nights,* Museo de Arte de Puerto Rico, San Juan, Puerto Rico, 2002.
*Live Painting with John Ellis Quintet,* Contemporary Arts Center, New Orleans, LA, 2002.
*Apostrophe,* Mori Museum, Tokyo, 2003.
*Letter to the President,* Res Fest, International Film Festival, 2003, 2006.
*Coast to Coast,* Punch Gallery, San Francisco, CA, 2003.
*Bazaar,* Cuchifritos, New York, 2003.
*NYC Now,* Galerie du Jour, Paris, 2003.
*Smudge Good,* CWC Gallery, Tokyo, 2003.
*Hive Mind Sound System,* Lump Gallery/Projects, Raleigh, NC, 2003.
*Unseen Messages,* Transport Gallery, Los Angeles, 2003.
*Compost: Doze Green and David Ellis,* Studio Number 1, Los Angeles, 2004.
*Grotto 2,* Jessica Murray Projects, New York, 2004.
*Beautiful Losers,* Contemporary Art Center, Cincinnati, OH, 2004.
*Ill Communication,* Urbis Museum, Manchester, England, 2004.
*Motion Paintings,* South Eastern Center for Contemporary Art, Winston Salem, NC, 2004.
*Psych-Opus and B-Stormers Mural,* Contemporary Museum, Honolulu, HI, 2004.
*2004 Studio Artists: 9X,* Smack Mellon, Brooklyn, NY, 2004.
*Barnstormers Selected Films,* AIGA Move Conference, New York, 2004.
*Paint on Trucks in a World in Need of Love,* Museum of Modern Art, Queens, NY, 2004.
*360,* Atlantic Artwalk, Brooklyn, NY, 2005.
*Urban Edge,* Spazio P4, Milan, Italy, 2005.
*Digital Cotton,* Savannah Gallery, Atlanta, GA, 2005.
*GADGET: Mechanics and Motion in Contemporary Art,* Contemporary Art Center, Cincinnati, OH, 2005.
*Greater New York 2005,* P.S. 1/Museum of Modern Art, Long Island, NY, 2005.

*Casita,* Museo de Arte de Puerto Rico, San Juan, Puerto Rico, 2006.
*Motion Barn,* South Eastern Center for Contemporary Art, Winston Salem, NC, 2006.
*Live Scores,* Monkeytown, Brooklyn, NY, 2006.
*Salvage + Assemble,* Space Gallery, Portland, ME, 2006.
*Good & Thuggy,* Lump Gallery, Raleigh, NC, 2006.
*Music Show,* Publico, Cincinnati, OH, 2006.
*50,000 Beds,* Aldrich Contemporary Art Museum, Ridgefield, CT, 2007.
*Elevator Mural Project,* New York, 2007.
*Graffiti Stories,* Musée des Arts Modestes, Séte, France, 2007.
*Music Show II,* Publico, Cincinnati, OH, 2007.
*Doodle Crush,* Lump Gallery, Raleigh, NC, 2007.
*10 Curators,* Colette, Paris, 2007.
*Burning House,* New Image Art, Los Angeles, 2007.
*BMG Artists' Annual '07,* Black Market Gallery, Los Angeles, 2007.
*Brodeo,* New Image Art, Los Angeles, 2007.
*Animated Painting,* San Diego Museum of Art, San Diego, CA, 2007.
*Ensemble,* Institute of Contemporary Art, Philadelphia, PA, 2007.
*Heap,* Black Rat Press Gallery, London, 2007.
*Rubicon Sun: David Ellis and Doze Green,* Fifty24 SF Gallery, San Francisco, CA, 2007.
*2003-2008,* Publico, Cincinnati, OH, 2008.
*Transformers,* Corridor Gallery, Brooklyn, NY, 2008.
*Inner/Outer Space,* Mattress Factory, Pittsburgh, PA, 2008.

## Sources

### Periodicals

*ADWEEK Online,* September 3, 2004.
*Creative Review,* May 2003, p. 74.
*Fashion Rocks* (supplement to *Glamour*), Fall 2008.
*New York Times,* March 23, 2008, p. 3.
*W,* September 2008.

### Online

"Artists: Who Are the Barnstormers?" Barnstormers Web site, http://www.b-stormers.com/artists/ (April 25, 2009).
"Biography," David Ellis' Home Page, http://www.freshwatercatfish.org/bio/ (April 25, 2009).
"David Ellis: Conversation," Rice Gallery Online, http://ricegallery.org/images/PDF/ELLIS_brochure.pdf (April 25, 2009).

*—Alana Joli Abbott*

# Tracey Emin

## Artist

**B**orn July 3, 1963, in Croydon, England; daughter of Envar Emin (a hotel owner) and Pamela Cashin (a hotel manager). *Education:* Attended Medway College of Design, 1980-82; Maidstone College of Art, B.A., 1986; studied at the Royal College of Art, London, and at Birkbeck College of the University of London.

**Addresses:** *Gallery*—White Cube, 25-26 Mason's Yard, London, SW1Y 6BU, England; Lehmann Maupin Gallery, 540 W. 26th St., New York, NY 10001. *Home*—London, England.

## Career

**A**rtist in various media, including painting, printmaking, film, neon, and needlework. Works are in the permanent collections of the British Museum (London), Saatchi Collection (London), Tate Gallery (London), National Portrait Gallery (London), Pompidou Centre (Paris), Guggenheim Museum of New York, and the Stedelijk Museum (Amsterdam).

**Awards:** Inducted into British Royal Academy of Arts, 2007.

## Sidelights

**T**racey Emin belongs to a new generation of visual artists who emerged in the late 1990s to energize Britain's contemporary art scene. Among those collectively known as Young British Artists, or YBAs, Emin stirred up her own particular controversy with a pair of installation works that were shocking for their level of personal revelation, *Everyone I Have Ever Slept With 1963-1995* and *My Bed.* In 2007, she was chosen to represent British art at the 2007 Venice Biennale, one of the top career honors an artist can achieve.

Emin and her twin brother, Paul, were born in 1963 in Croydon, near London, but grew up in Margate, a seaside resort town on southeast England's Kent coast. There, her mother managed a hotel that was owned by Emin's father, an immigrant from the Turkish part of Cyprus, who had a family elsewhere with his legal wife. When he lost the hotel, the family struggled financially, and Emin's distress was compounded by a sexual assault that occurred when she was 13. That incident initiated several years of problems at home and at school, and by the age of 15 she had run away from both places, which left her free to indulge in drinking heavily and engaging in a series of sexual liaisons.

In the early 1980s, Emin studied fashion design at Medway College, also in Kent, where she became involved with a group of young poets. She gravitated toward visual art, however, and went on to earn her undergraduate degree from the Maidstone Art College in Kent before moving to London around 1987. There, she entered the graduate program at the prestigious Royal College of Art, but her personal life continued to intrude upon her productivity, and she wound up destroying all of her paintings and prints in a fit of despair.

In 1993, Emin and another young artist, Sarah Lucas, opened "The Shop" in the vibrant East London area of Bethnal Green, an area that had long attracted waves of new immigrants to Britain but was beginning to become known as a cheap-rent haven for young artists, musicians, and other creative types. The Shop sold their handmade T-shirts, prints, and various *objets d'art*. In a 2001 interview with *W*'s Christopher Bagley, Emin recounted how she found her first artistic patron, gallery owner Jay Jopling. "I was doing this thing where I invited people to invest in my Creative Potential," she said. "They'd pay me £10, and I'd write them personal letters about my life. I used to write hundreds of letters to people, including Jay, and he loved them."

Jopling's White Cube Gallery hosted Emin's first solo show in 1994, which she cheekily titled *My Major Retrospective.* It included photographs of the paintings she had destroyed along with various personal memorabilia she had held onto over the years, such as the cigarette pack her uncle was holding when he was decapitated in an automobile accident. After that, she opened a South London storefront she called the Tracey Emin Museum, where she would sit and entertain visitors with tales about her life and art. A comment made by a boyfriend at the time prompted her first noteworthy installation piece. *Everyone I Have Ever Slept With 1963-1995,* which was a tent embroidered with 102 names of every person with whom she had ever shared a bed with. On the floor of the hexagonal tent were letters that spelled out the words, "with myself, always myself, never forgetting."

Emin's piece caused a stir when it was first shown at *Minky Manky,* a group exhibition at the South London Gallery in 1995. Not all of the appliquéd names reflected sexual relationships, however: there was also her grandmother's name, and two panels for two abortions Emin had undergone. "What was important about it to me was that when I wrote out the names and sewed them it was like carving out tombstones, having to deal with my past," she told the artist Julian Schnabel in *Interview* magazine in 2006. "That was pretty cathartic actually."

Emin's infamy rose to new heights in 1997 when she appeared to be under the influence of alcohol on a live British television program as part of a panel discussion about contemporary art. "After hilariously upbraiding her fellow panelists—a group of straitlaced philosophers and art critics, all of them men—she stumbled off the set, declaring that she was going to go ring her mum," wrote Bagley in *W*. In a somewhat ironic twist, Emin had been booked to discuss the current Turner Prize nominations, an annual art event recognizing Britain's top visual artists under the age of 50. Two years later, she made it onto the Turner Prize shortlist, which provoked another spate of sometimes-derisive articles about her in the British press. Some critics characterized her as less an artist than a savvy public-relations expert, but most agreed that her Turner Prize entry at the Tate Museum, *My Bed*, was the most malodorous piece in the exhibition.

*My Bed* was a 1998 work that was an exact re-creation of Emin's sleeping quarters. "The sheets are discoloured by murky spillages, while the torn pillows ooze feathers," wrote Richard Cork in the *Times* of London. "As for the heap of belongings dumped on the floor alongside, they are frankly repellent.... The entire deposit seems to be festering." Emin explained *My Bed*'s genesis to Schnabel in *Interview* magazine, linking it to a bout of depression that kept her in bed for four days. Finally struck by thirst, she made her way to the kitchen sink. "My flat was in a real mess—everything everywhere, dirty washing, filthy cabinets, the bathroom really dirty, everything in a really bad state. I crawled across the floor, pulled myself up on the sink to get some water, and made my way back to my bedroom, and as I did I looked at my bedroom and thought, 'Oh, my God. What if I'd died and they found me here?'"

Since then Emin has moved on to various other art projects from a spacious home and studio near East London's Brick Lane area where she works and lives. A memoir she titled *Strangeland* was published in 2005, which Schnabel asserted "ought to be required reading for young artists" in *Interview* magazine. Of her financial success, she told *Sunday Times* journalist John-Paul Flintoff that "it's not about possessions. It's freedom. When you have been really, really poor, earning money is such a liberating thing. If I'm ill, I have a private doctor, and if I miss a flight I can catch another. And being able to eat the food I want to eat is brilliant."

## Selected works

### Solo exhibitions

(With Sarah Lucas) The Shop, 103 Bethnal Green Road, London, 1993.

*My Major Retrospective*, White Cube Gallery, London, 1994.

*Tracey Emin Museum*, 221 Waterloo Road, London, 1995-98.

*I Need Art Like I Need God*, South London Gallery, 1997.

*Every Part of Me is Bleeding*, Lehmann Maupin Gallery, New York, 1999.

*You Forgot to Kiss My Soul*, White Cube, 2001.

*I Think It's in My Head*, Lehmann Maupin Gallery, 2002.

*Ten Years: Tracey Emin*, Stedelijk Museum, Amsterdam, 2002.

*Menphis*, Counter Gallery, London, 2003.

*Can't See Past My Own Eyes*, Sketch Gallery, London, 2004.

*Tracey Emin*, Tate Britain, 2004.

*When I Think About Sex...*, White Cube Gallery, 2005.

*I Can Feel Your Smile*, Lehmann Maupin Gallery, 2005.

### Group exhibitions

*Minky Manky*, South London Gallery, 1995.

*Sensation*, Royal Academy of Arts, London, 1997.

*Turner Prize*, Tate Gallery, London, 1999.

*For the Love of Dog*, Pump House Gallery, London, 2001.

*Independence*, South London Gallery, 2003.

*Kiss the Frog! The Art of Transformation*, National Museum of Art, Oslo, 2005.

*52nd Annual Venice Biennale*, Venice, 2007.

*Summer Exhibition*, Royal Academy of Arts, 2008.

### Writings

*Strangeland* (memoir), Scepter (London), 2005.

## Sources

*Harper's Bazaar*, November 2001, p. 195.

*Interview*, June 2006, p. 102.

*Sunday Times* (London, England), September 17, 2006, p. 56.

*Times* (London, England), October 20, 1999, p. 45.

*W*, April 2001, p. 318.

—*Carol Brennan*

# Leonel Fernández

## President of the Dominican Republic

**B**orn December 26, 1953, in Santo Domingo, Dominican Republic; son of José Antonio Fernández-Collado and Yolanda Reyna-Romero; married Margarita Cedeño; children: Nicole, Omar, Yolanda. *Education:* Autonomous University of Santo Domingo, J.D., 1978.

**Addresses:** *Office*—Oficina del Presidente Santo Domingo, Distrito Nacional, Dominican Republic. *Web site*—http://www.presidencia.gob.do.

## Career

**C**ontributed articles to newspapers at home and abroad, 1980s; editor-in-chief, *Política, Teoría y Acción,* 1980s; professor, Autonomous University of Santo Domingo and Latin-American Faculty of Social Sciences, 1980s; named to the Dominican Liberation Party's central committee, 1985; named to the Dominican Liberation Party's political committee, 1990; unsuccessful candidate for vice-president of the Dominican Republic, 1994; president of Global Foundation for Democracy and Development, c. 2000—; president of the Dominican Republic, 1996-2000 and 2004—.

## Sidelights

**L**eonel Fernández, president of the Dominican Republic, has played a major role in modernizing his nation's politics and economy. An early follower of the leftist political leader Juan Bosch, Fernández took Bosch's place at the head of his political party in the mid-1990s. Taking office at the end of an era when aging strongmen had dominated the country's politics, Fernández promised to provide more energetic leadership and to open the nation to the rest of the world. After a four-year hiatus imposed by the country's laws, Fernández returned to the presidency in 2004. His attempts to lift Dominicans out of poverty by funding development and encouraging foreign investment achieved mixed results amid economic and energy crises, but Fernández won a third term in office in 2008.

Fernández was born in Santo Domingo, the capital of the Dominican Republic, in 1953. His parents, José Antonio Fernández-Collado and Yolanda Reyna-Romero, moved the family to New York City when he was seven, and he attended elementary, middle, and high school there. He returned to his home country to enroll in the Autonomous University of Santo Domingo, where he was elected to a top position in the student government. Swept up by the progressive wing of his country's politics, he became a supporter of university professor Juan Bosch, the leading figure of the Dominican political opposition, and the political party Bosch founded in 1973, the Dominican Liberation Party.

Fernández earned a law degree in 1978 and established himself as a prominent figure in Dominican intellectual life, contributing articles about law, history, and culture to newspapers at home and abroad. He was named to the Dominican Liberation Party's central committee in 1985 and its political committee in 1990. He also served as editor-in-chief of the party magazine *Política, Teoría y Acción*.

In 1994, when Bosch ran to unseat longtime Dominican president Joaquín Balaguer, the party chose Fernández as Bosch's vice-presidential running mate. Balaguer officially won reelection to his seventh term as president, but international observers charged that his party had employed severe fraud and intimidation, and that a third candidate, José Francisco Peña Gómez of the Dominican Revolutionary Party, would likely have won a free and fair vote. Civil unrest resulted, and to keep the peace, Balaguer agreed to shorten his presidential term to two years and hold new elections in 1996. Dominicans changed their constitution to require presidents to serve only one term, preventing Balaguer from running again.

That shifted political power in the Dominican Republic to a new generation. By 1996, Bosch was 89 and unable to run for president again because of illness and age. So the Dominican Liberation Party chose Fernández as its presidential candidate. Fernández, who was 42 in 1996, played up the differences between himself and the 89-year-old Balaguer. To emphasize Fernández's youthfulness, some of his television ads showed him playing basketball. Fernández had never been elected to office before, but that became a point in his favor with voters. He referred to himself as "the new road," sensing correctly that, after decades of Balaguer as president, voters were looking to see which candidate would change the country's politics the most. Voters had so soured on Balaguer that his party's candidate, vice-president Jacinto Peynado, attracted little support in polls. Fernández's main rival in the election was Peña Gómez, a former mayor of Santo Domingo. Fernández finished second in the first round of voting, with 39 percent of the vote, behind Peña Gómez, who won 46 percent. After making a controversial deal with Balaguer for his support, Fernández won the presidency with 51 percent of the vote in the June runoff. Election observers called the vote free and fair.

"We are beginning a new era," Fernández said at a news conference (according to Larry Rohter of the *New York Times*). "A new generation of politicians has taken office with the desire to do things for the good of the nation." Sworn in as president in August of 1996, Fernández promised to fight poverty and root out corruption in government bureaucracy. He also promised to forsake Balaguer's authoritarian ways.

Once in office, Fernández governed with a new style that excited Dominicans. Because his party held few seats in the country's congress, the president held friendly lunches with opposition politicians to try to build support for his policies. Often, after working 12-hour days in his office, Fernández would visit markets, hospitals, and poor neighborhoods unannounced. "It is the best way for me to maintain some level of contact with people and to resolve some of their smaller problems," Fernández explained to Rohter of the *New York Times*. "Besides, I was raised in neighborhoods like those, so I feel comfortable and interested and protected in them."

In his first month in office, activist groups staged a protest outside the presidential palace, trying to reverse Balaguer's policies that pressured residents to move out of a poor neighborhood in the capital city. Fernández invited the protesters into the palace, heard them out, and immediately issued a decree reversing the old policies. He also promised to pave the neighborhood's main street and build a new school there. Later, he visited the neighborhood alone to check on its progress. "There are little things that can be done that in budgetary terms cost almost nothing, which people see as positive and which let them know that I am their President and am interested in them and their barrios," Fernández told Rohter.

Fernández implemented new social spending on health and education, working toward installing computers in every high school in the country. He appointed several new heads of government agencies, many of whom soon discovered and revealed financial irregularities. Instead of filling the government with his supporters, Fernández retained several public officials he felt were qualified and honest. He moved swiftly to reform the military, pushing 24 of its 76 generals into retirement.

In foreign policy, the new president moved the Dominican Republic from Balaguer's isolationist stance, distrustful of foreigners, toward open markets and globalization. His 1999 visit to France and Italy made him the first Dominican president to travel to Europe. His 2000 visit to Haiti, the Dominican Republic's neighbor, was the first by a Dominican president in years. Fernández sold off much of the country's electricity industry to American investors. He also created programs to encourage foreign investment and helped create a free-trade agreement with Central American nations and other Caribbean nations. The country's economy boomed during his term in office, averaging eight percent growth.

By the end of Fernández's first term, political analysts praised the country's economic progress and the end of its isolationism. However, many also said the president had not made enough progress fighting patronage and corruption in government, or in alleviating poverty, which still affected more than half of the population. Fernández's alliance with Balaguer's party, formed to help him win the presidential runoff and gain support in the Congress, also prevented him from making some changes. He engaged in controversial power plays meant to limit the success of Peña Gómez's Dominican Revolutionary Party.

When Fernández's term expired in 2000, he could not run for re-election because of a law prohibiting presidents from serving more than one term. The country's economy was starting to falter, and voters rejected the candidate from Fernández's party, instead choosing Hipólito Mejía, a businessman with a populist appeal, to succeed him. However, in 2002, the law about presidential terms was repealed, clearing the way for Fernández to run again. Meanwhile, the Dominican Liberation Party elected him its president in 2002. Fernández also served as president of a nonprofit group he founded, the Global Foundation for Democracy and Development.

As Fernández prepared to run for the presidency again, the Dominican Republic plunged into an economic crisis. Several major banks failed in 2003, some because of fraud. The government reimbursed depositors for their lost funds at an immense cost, about one-fifth of the country's annual domestic product. Electricity shortages followed because the government could no longer afford to subsidize electricity for poor residents, and it fell behind on its payments to energy companies in the United States. The International Monetary Fund suspended its aid program to the Dominican Republic, criticizing the government's handling of the problem. The bank failures also helped lay bare the political corruption and massive government bureaucracy sapping the country. Prices for food doubled and gas shortages kept people from driving. Many Dominicans, unable to cope in the shrinking economy, tried to leave the country by rowing flimsy boats to Puerto Rico; some died on the journey.

Seizing on the economic meltdown, Fernández challenged Mejía in the May 16, 2004 presidential election. Mejía blamed Fernández's 1990s privatization of the electricity industry for the power shortage. But Dominican voters sided with Fernández, returning him to the presidency with 57 percent of the vote. The country's crisis continued between Fernández's election and inauguration, with foreign energy companies continuing to cut off electricity, complaining the government was not paying its bills, and citizens protesting. The government

came very close to defaulting on its foreign debt. When Fernández was sworn in as president that August, he warned the country to brace itself for tough measures meant to relieve the crisis. He said he would restrict government spending, and argued that Dominican Republic needed to convince the International Monetary Fund to resume lending to it.

True to his internationalist instincts, Fernández traveled to Venezuela to seek an oil-importing agreement with that country's president, Hugo Chávez. That December, Fernández also visited his other hometown, New York City. He spoke at a seminar at the City College of New York, discussing ways Dominican Americans could help the country, including a possible Dominican Peace Corps.

The biggest legacy of Fernández's second term, however, ended up being a massive public works project he championed: a subway for Santo Domingo. It was inspired by the New York City Metro, which Fernández rode in his youth. The subway was only the second in the Caribbean (the first is in San Juan, Puerto Rico). Some Dominicans thought the $700 million project wasteful, given the country's dire poverty, health care, education, and energy needs. Others saw it as an important solution to Santo Domingo's severe traffic congestion. Fernández himself saw it as a way to modernize the country and convince Dominicans not to move to the United States. "Leonel [Fernández] spent an important part of his life in New York, and he understands the benefits of a Metro," the subway project's assistant director, Leonel Carrasco, told Marc Lacey of the *New York Times*.

In May of 2008, Fernández won re-election with about 53 percent of the vote, enough to avoid a runoff election. "No time will be lost in the continuation of our work and progress," he told supporters in his victory speech (according to BBC News). Miguel Vargas Maldonado, his main opponent, refused to congratulate him, claiming that Fernández had misused government resources to aid his re-election campaign. However, the Organization of American States called the vote a clear victory for Fernández and said the election had mostly gone smoothly.

Many of the problems Fernández had hoped to address remained challenges in his third term, the president admitted at an appearance in Coral Gables, Florida, in October of 2008. Speaking at the annual Americas Conference, Fernández named several crises the Dominican Republic was facing: recovery from hurricanes that had hit the Caribbean in the summer of 2008, the international effects of the crisis in the United States' financial markets that autumn, rising food prices, and the continued energy crisis. The country's energy bill had increased from $1.8 billion in 2004, when he returned to office, to $6.5 billion in 2008, he reported.

Fernández lamented the slow pace of social progress in all of Latin America and said it had shaken people's faith in representative government. "Thirty years ago there was a lot of joy in Latin America about the coming of democracy," Fernández said, according to Jane Bussey of the Miami Herald. "Lately, there is some sort of disappointment." However, he also reported that his country's economy was projected to end 2008 with inflation of less than ten percent and with seven percent economic growth. "That would be a miracle for the Dominican economy," he said.

## Sources

### Periodicals

*Miami Herald,* October 3, 2008.

*New York Times,* May 17, 1996; July 2, 1996; August 17, 1996; December 1, 1996; January 7, 1997; April 25, 1999; August 6, 2004; August 14, 2004; August 17, 2004; December 5, 2004; September 3, 2007.

### Online

"Biography of the president of the Dominican Republic," Consulat Général de la République Dominicaine, http://www.la-republique-dominicaine.org/Dominican-Republic-Leonel-Fernandez-President-of-the-Republic.html (November 9, 2008).

"Dominican leader wins third term," BBC News, http://news.bbc.co.uk/go/rss/-/2/hi/americas/7406030.stm (November 9, 2008).

"President Leonel Fernández" Consulado General de la Republica Domincana, http://www.consuladord-ny.org/Staff/profileOresidente.htm (November 9, 2008).

*—Erick Trickey*

# Cristina Fernández de Kirchner

Marlene Awaad/IP3/drr.net

## President of Argentina

**B**orn Cristina Elisabet Fernández, February 19, 1953, in La Plata, Buenos Aires, Argentina; daughter of Eduardo Fernández and Ofelia Esther Wilhelm; married Néstor Carlos Kirchner Ostoić (an attorney and politician), March 9, 1975; children: Máximo, Florencia. *Education:* National University of La Plata, law degree, 1979.

**Addresses:** *Office*—Casa Rosada, Hipólito Yrigoyen 211, Buenos Aires, Distrito Federal 1086, Argentina.

## Career

**A**ttorney in private practice in Río Gallegos, Santa Cruz province, after 1979; elected to the provincial legislature of Santa Cruz province, 1989, 1993; elected to the Senate of Argentina, 1995, 2001, 2005, and to the Chamber of Deputies, 1997; First Lady of Argentina, 2003-07; elected president of Argentina, 2007.

## Sidelights

**I**n 2007, Cristina Fernández de Kirchner became the first woman ever to win election to the presidency of Argentina. A former attorney whose political résumé includes stints in both houses of Argentina's Congress, she is sometimes called the South American version of Hillary Clinton. Both women married their law-school boyfriends, who went on to become governors of southern states and then president, and both women were elected to a Senate seat from one of the largest and most influential districts in their nations before entering a hotly contested and historic race for the top job. "Hillary really acquired her national standing because her husband was president," Fernández noted in a television interview, according to *Maclean's* writer Isabel Vincent. "She didn't have a political career beforehand, and that really isn't my case."

Fernández was born in 1953 in La Plata, the city that serves as the center of government for the province of Buenos Aires. The respective backgrounds of her parents are illustrative of Argentina's history as a haven for European immigrants—her father was from a Spanish family and her mother of German heritage. Two years after Fernández was born, a right-wing coup ousted President Juan Perón from power, and set in motion a three-decade battle for control between leftists, the military, and right-wing forces in the nation.

Perón was the founder of Argentina's dominant political party, the *Partido Justicialista*, or Justicialist Party (PJ), which derived its name from a combination of the words for "socialist" and "justice." Fernández joined its youth group in the early 1970s when Perón returned to power and was elected president in 1973. Though years later she would make Argentine history as the first woman ever elected to the presidency, Fernández was not actually the first woman to hold that office—Perón's third wife was his vice president, and when he died in office a year later Isabel Perón succeeded him. She was the first female, non-royal head of state in the Western hemisphere, but as Argentina's economy faltered, her grip on power diminished, and she was ousted in a 1976 military coup.

Fernández was by then a law student at the National University of La Plata, and married to fellow law student Néstor Kirchner. Three years her senior, Kirchner was of mixed Swiss and Croatian heritage and came from one of Argentina's southernmost provinces, Patagonia. They were wed in March of 1975 at a time when political violence in Buenos Aires, the capital, appeared to be escalating—that same month, a kidnapped U.S. State Department official was found dead with a bullet to his head, and eight members of the extreme left wing of the PJ were killed by one of the new death squads loyal to the conservative political and military elite. Finally, a cadre of top military officials took over in March of 1976, arresting Isabel Perón, dissolving the legislature, and severely restricting freedom of the press and freedom of speech. The junta called this the "National Reorganization Process" and asserted harsh tactics were necessary to end the domestic terrorist activities of both the right and the left.

The junta granted sweeping powers to Argentina's military and internal police apparatus with the goal of rooting out left-wing dissent. Middle-class university students like Fernández and her husband were the most frequent targets, and thousands of young people began to vanish. The number of *desaparecidos* ("one who has disappeared") rose steadily in the late 1970s, and as many as 30,000 were killed, often after being tortured. Fernández, who graduated with her law degree in 1979, and her husband retreated from the turmoil to Santa Cruz, far removed from the capital Buenos Aires. They settled in the town of Río Gallegos and opened a private practice specializing in property law. Finally, the 1982 Falklands War helped bring an end to what Argentines called *La Dictadura,* or the "the Dictatorship." A small group of islands about 500 miles east of Río Gallegos, the Falklands were inhabited by descendants of British immigrants and the cluster of islands had remained an overseas territory of Britain, though Argentina laid claim to them. In the ten-week conflict, Argentina's navy was crushed by British air and sea forces, and the junta suffered a humiliating defeat.

With the end of *La Dictadura* and the restoration of the democratic process in 1983, Fernández and her husband became more active in the PJ. In 1989, she ran for a seat in the provincial legislature of Santa Cruz and won; reelected four years later, she gave up her seat in 1995 when she won a seat in the Argentina's Senate as one of three senators from the province. In 1997 she was elected to the other house, the Chamber of Deputies. Four years later, she returned to her Senate seat from Santa Cruz. In both houses she became known as a vocal critic of Argentina's president, Carlos Saul Menem, even though they belonged to the same party. At one point, her PJ colleagues in the Senate barred her from their caucus meetings.

Fernández's husband Néstor Kirchner was also elected to public office, first as mayor of Río Gallegos in 1987 and then as governor of Santa Cruz for three four-year terms beginning in 1991. His 2003 bid for the presidency came in the wake of a massive financial crisis in Argentina that began two years earlier; the collapse of the nation's banking system affected the middle class and Argentina's reputation in international financial circles, and had devastating effects on the poorest citizens. Kirchner won the election and was inaugurated on May 25; during the ceremony Fernández chose to sit in her Senate seat rather than stand alongside her husband.

Kirchner enacted several economic reforms that brought a measure of stability then steady growth to Argentina. His administration's management of the economy resonated with Argentina's poor, whose numbers actually began to diminish, but were unpopular with the International Monetary Fund (IMF) and the so-called Paris Club of wealthy nations that had loaned the country's treasury some significant sums. His critics claimed that some economic indicators were manipulated by the government, such as the rate of inflation, which some argued was probably double what official statistics claimed.

In 2005, Fernández was elected to Argentina's Senate once again, but this time from the province of Buenos Aires. That October election pitted her against another female candidate who was half of the country's other political power couple, Eduardo and Hilda (Chiche) Duhalde. Eduardo Duhalde had been Néstor Kirchner's predecessor in the president's office, and put his wife in charge of the government's numerous social welfare programs. Both women were vying for a Senate seat from the province that is home to more than a third of the nation's entire population, and though Duhalde was the official PJ candidate, Fernández won a searing victory, besting Duhalde by a margin of two to one at the polls. "Though neither Mr. Kirchner nor his wife has talked about their plans, the press is convinced that they are trying to build a dynasty to exceed the Peróns'," noted *New York Times* correspondent Larry Rohter. "According to such speculation, Mr. Kirchner is certain to run for a second term in 2007 and then make way for his wife, who if elected twice, would leave office only at the end of the next decade."

In July of 2007, Néstor Kirchner announced that he would not run for a second term later that year, but instead would support his wife's candidacy for the top job. "Why not finally a woman to be the one to deepen change and transformation?" he enthused at a press conference, according to Rohter in the *New York Times,* and further asserted that "all of us profoundly believe in the capacity to excel that Cristina is going to offer."

There were more than a dozen candidates for the presidency, but Fernández's most formidable opponents were Elisa Carrió—like her, a lawyer and former legislator—and Roberto Lavagna, the one-time Minister for the Economy Kirchner had sacked in 2005. Fernández was the candidate of *Frente Para La Victoria,* or Front for Victory, the wing of the PJ created to elect her husband four years earlier. Eschewing newspaper and television interviews, she appeared instead at political rallies under a banner that carried her campaign's official slogan, "Change Is Just Beginning." She also made a few international appearances designed to showcase her interest in foreign policy, which had not been her husband's strong suit as president.

Fernández won the October 28 balloting with a record 45 percent of the vote, and was sworn into office on December 10. This time, her husband was at her side, because it was his duty to formally hand over the blue-and-white presidential sash. It was a first for Argentina, declared another *New York Times* correspondent, Alexei Barrionuevo, who also pointed out that "no modern-day couple in a democracy has carried out a comparable transfer of power." In her inauguration speech, Fernández mentioned the *Madres de la Plaza de Mayo,* or Mothers of the Plaza de Mayo, a famous group of women who began gathering on the main government square in the capital of Buenos Aires in April of 1977. They came every week, ostensibly to ask the junta what had happened to their teenagers and young-adult children who appeared to have simply vanished into thin air, and grew into a formidable human-rights organization that was instrumental in prosecuting members of the junta for crimes after democracy was restored. The Plaza de Mayo Mothers wore trademark white scarves, and a delegation of them were present at Fernández's swearing-in ceremony. She hailed them as "mothers and grandmothers of the homeland," reported Barrionuevo in the *New York Times,* and her voice cracked when she commended them because "they dared to go where nobody else did."

Fernández inherited some problems from her husband's administration that quickly became evident in the first months of 2008. Fears that the official inflation rate was a sham continued, and Kirchner's economic revitalization plan had included generous energy subsidies, which meant that the rates that consumers paid were artificially low; by the time his wife took office there were worries that the system was overburdened and heading for crisis once the cold season—in June, July, and August—arrived. In early 2008, her government enacted its second increase in five months on agricultural export taxes, which prompted widespread demonstrations from farmers in the countryside. She made a rare televised appearance on June 17 in response to the anti-government protests, declaring that "the country cannot be governed by casserole dishes, bullhorns and roadblocks" according to Barrionuevo for the *New York Times.*

Fernández and her husband have two children: a son, Máximo, and daughter Florencia, whose Web site postings on the fotolog.com site caused a stir in the weeks following the inauguration but were eventually taken off-line. The unusual transfer of power meant that the family remained in the official presidential palace, the Casa Rosada (Pink House). Some pundits speculated that Fernández and her husband's first terms would be the start of a long stay at the official residence. She might run for re-election in 2011, or step aside for her husband, who was again eligible under the terms of Argentina's constitution to serve two consecutive terms. For the time being, however, Fernández was busy building her own legacy as her nation's first elected female leader. "Women bring a different face to politics," she told *Time'*s Tim Padgett shortly before her win. "We see the big geopolitical picture but also the smaller, daily details of citizens' lives. We're wrapped up as much in what our daughter's school principal says as we are in what the newspapers are saying."

## Sources

*Christian Science Monitor,* October 30, 2007, p. 6.
*Economist* October 20, 2007, p. 52.
*Independent* (London, England), October 17, 2007, p. 32.
*Maclean's,* October 22, 2007, p. 30.
*Newsweek International,* August 22, 2005, p. 32, p. 35.
*New York Times,* October 23, 2005; July 3, 2007; October 28, 2007; December 11, 2007; June 18, 2008.
*Time,* October 8, 2007, p. 48.

—*Carol Brennan*

# Suzanne Finnamore

## Author

**B**orn in 1959; married Mark, September 21, 1996 (divorced, 2000); children: Pablo. *Education:* University of California—Berkeley, B.A., c. 1980.

**Addresses:** *Agent*—Kim Witherspoon, InkWell Management, 521 Fifth Ave., 26th Fl., New York, NY 10175. *Home*—Marin County, CA. *Office*—Foote Cone & Belding, 1160 Battery St. #250, San Francisco, CA 94111.

## Career

**C**opywriter, Ketchum, Inc., early 1990s; copywriter then senior copywriter, Hal Riney & Partners, after 1993; vice president and creative director, Foote Cone & Belding, 1994-98; author, 1996—; copywriter, Foote Cone & Belding, October 2005.

## Sidelights

**S**uzanne Finnamore's trio of published works serve as quasi-autobiographical accounts of three important stages in her life—marriage, motherhood, and divorce. Her first two books, *Otherwise Engaged* and *The Zygote Chronicles,* were works of fiction, and while her 2008 book *Split: A Memoir of Divorce* marked Finnamore's first foray into nonfiction, it retained the same wry, humorous tone of her previous titles. She admitted to a certain amount of unease in writing *Split* because of its intensely personal and painful nature. "I think I still felt married, in some soul sense, as though loyalty were owed," she told Salon.com writer Katharine Mieszkowski. "But once I did it, it became a lot less frightening."

Born in 1959, Finnamore earned a degree in English literature from the University of California—Berkeley and worked in advertising before writing her first novel. She was a copywriter at the San Francisco office of Ketchum, Inc., in the early 1990s before joining Hal Riney & Partners, which she departed as a senior copywriter to take a job with Foote Cone & Belding's San Francisco branch. Finnamore advanced to the rank of vice president and creative director at the agency, which handled such accounts as Levi's Jeans and Keds in the late 1990s. With the type of college degree she held, Finnamore said the advertising industry was actually a good match, describing it as "sort of a salon mentality," to Celeste Ward, a writer for *AdWeek.* "You can talk about ancient Greek literature in the middle of a Doubletree meeting, and no one yells at you."

Finnamore married in 1996, and quit her job two years later when motherhood loomed and she decided to try her hand at a novel. The manuscript that became *Otherwise Engaged* was sent to several publishing houses, and finally an editor picked it out of the "slush pile"—the collection of unsolicited manuscripts sent to publishers who usually assign the junior-most employee to read—at Alfred A. Knopf. Finnamore's dual post-corporate goals dovetailed nicely: she inked a deal with Knopf on the same day she delivered her son, Pablo.

*Otherwise Engaged* was published in the spring of 1999 and rode in on a wave of post-*Bridget Jones* books that publishers in both Britain and the United States were issuing at a steady pace at the time.

Bridget Jones was the titular heroine first of a fictional newspaper column by London journalist Helen Fielding and then a best-selling novel that was made into a 2002 film starring Renee Zellweger. The success of Fielding's creation spawned a series of imitators instantly dubbed "chick lit" and generally centered around a hapless, semi-comic heroine and her romantic troubles. In Finnamore's case, however, the story was essentially her own. Her literary debut featured Eve, a San Francisco advertising executive who issues an ultimatum to Michael, her boyfriend of four years, who complies and proposes marriage. The course of the novel deals with Eve's suddenly conflicted feelings about her long-hoped-for nuptials. To her surprise, she realizes she harbors some unease regarding the permanence of marriage now that it looms before her. Take her fiancé's "sock on the floor," Finnamore writes as Eve, as quoted by Evelyn Theiss in the *Plain Dealer*. It "isn't just a sock on the floor. It's a sock on the floor for the rest of my life."

Finnamore spoke of the real-life similarities between Eve's dilemma—which ends happily, as chick-lit requires—in an interview with David Templeton, a columnist for the *Sonoma County Independent*. The interview included a movie-theater excursion to see *Runaway Bride*, the Julia Roberts-Richard Gere romantic comedy. Finnamore mentioned the part where Roberts' character is "visibly hyperventilating as she was walking down the aisle. That's *exactly* how I felt when I got married. I was a wreck. I didn't expect to be, but I was." Admitting to Templeton that her own parents' failed marriage was some of the reason for her unease—"I always feel the specter of divorce hanging over my head"—she reflected that "I don't think you really get married on the day of the wedding. You have an opportunity to start working toward a marriage at that point, but I don't think the marriage actually occurs until later."

Reviews for Finnamore's debut novel were favorable. Many of them noted the similarity to the Bridget Jones genre, but found that Finnamore effortlessly surpassed it. Critiquing it in *Time* along with two similar titles, Ginia Bellafante asserted that the books each "feature heroines who might enjoy Bridget's company but eventually tire of her ninny-ness." In *Booklist*, reviewer Brad Hooper made a richer comparison, referring to two famous female humorists of a previous generation. "Finnamore has a touch of Erma Bombeck and a pinch of Nora Ephron, but her voice is sharply original," Hooper asserted.

Finnamore's candid remarks in press rounds seemed to show that she and her fictional heroine share a sense of humor. Interviewed by Kathleen Jacobs of *Redbook* for the May 1999 issue, Finnamore was asked what was the best thing about being married. "Not having to worry about whether you're going to get married," she claimed. Jacobs also asked her thoughts on how men and women view the milestone event. "I think men know what marriage represents, and that's why they fear it," Finnamore said. "They see marriage as the whole 50 years, the whole lifetime together. Women romanticize marriage much more—we're dazzled by the idea of being a bride and being validated in that social sense."

Finnamore's second novel was *The Zygote Chronicles*, published by Grove Press in 2002. Again, its plot shared a basic similarity to Finnamore's own life: its narrator mom-to-be is an executive with an advertising agency who confesses her fears about how motherhood will affect her prestigious, well-paying job in passages addressed directly to her as-yet-unborn child. Finnamore, quoted by Katherine Dieckmann for the *New York Times*, writes, "I sometimes feel a sense of unease. For not being the perfect, young, spry mother, the unblemished canvas you deserve. I have been fired three times, have been to jail once in New Jersey for four hours and have had 22 lovers.... I should not be telling you any of this.... Pregnancy strips off the veneer, the protective casing. It husks the soul." At other times, the narrator commiserates with her best friend, who is also expecting, and recounts minor, hormone-and-anxiety-fueled skirmishes with her husband.

Again, Finnamore's work won mostly positive reviews. Writing in the *New York Times* Dieckmann liked one passage in which Finnamore writes, "in the end, I will split open and you will emerge. I have heard tell that this is the way of birth." Dieckmann noted that "it's moments like this that elevate a birthing story beyond the merely autobiographical, by suggesting, even to those who might not seem interested at first, just how powerfully, mysteriously transformative the experience can be." A reviewer for *Publishers Weekly* remarked that "for all her neurotic complaints, there is a sincere sweetness to the heroine's complaints," and noted that the child who arrives at the end of the story shares the same first initial, "P.," as Finnamore's own son, Pablo—"perhaps the reason that this witty and poignant chronicle rings true."

By the time *The Zygote Chronicles* appeared in print, however, Finnamore's personal life had undergone a dramatic upheaval. In 2000, her husband left her, and she eventually discovered that the reason for the sundering was indeed another woman. As

Finnamore wrote in an article for Salon.com, "I became a single mother overnight, which is nothing like becoming famous overnight: I believe it is the emotional equivalent of having a stroke.... Life as I knew it was over, my bills were doubled and my fear and loneliness and sense of complete failure rose like bone dust into the night air."

Finnamore chronicled the trauma in 2008's *Split: A Memoir of Divorce,* her first work of nonfiction. It begins on the day that her husband announces he is leaving, and in subsequent chapters she comes to realize the signs pointing to the eventual dooming of their union, and how correct her initial suspicions had been that the situation was heading toward a crisis point. She is, nevertheless, devastated, and her divorced mother arrives to help out, and dispenses wisdom to her daughter over cocktails. Everyone tells Finnamore that it takes about two years to feel normal again after a divorce, and she wonders how she will endure in the meantime. In the Salon.com article, she recounts the sadness she feels in just leaving the house. "When I looked at other people," she wrote, "I automatically formed thought bubbles over their heads. Happy Couple With Stroller. Innocent Teenage Girl With Her Whole Life Ahead of Her. Content Grandmother and Grandfather Visiting Town Where Their Grandchildren Live With Intact Parents." Any divorce is difficult, but couples with young children have a incessantly fresh wound to deal with at every encounter should they try to share custody. On a practical level, Finnamore admitted she "coped with it by not wearing my glasses," she told Mieszkowski in the Salon.com interview. "I can't see without my glasses—I am extremely nearsighted. In my eyes, my ex became a blob; anyone can deal with a blob."

*Split* also details Finnamore's sudden fascination with self-help books and insights gleaned from sessions with a therapist. In the Salon.com article, she admitted that others were right—that time does heal the wound, and brings with it the necessary life lessons. "You learn that you can love someone and be divorced from them at the same time, in the same way that you loved them before you were married—except now you know they are capable of ripping your heart out." Committing her thoughts to paper—or a word-processing program—also proved beneficial, and led to this third book for Finnamore, which earned the most glowing reviews of all. "This is familiar domestic territory," noted *USA Today's* Deirdre Donahue. "What makes Finnamore's story original is her willingness to expose herself and her efforts to get her husband back." Writing for *Entertainment Weekly,* Jennifer Reese called *Split* "funny, furious, and elegantly crafted.... Finnamore takes

brutally precise inventory of the toxic fallout of a failed marriage: the murderous rage, inappropriate lust, and general wretchedness. Anyone who has been through a shattering divorce, or even just watched one, will appreciate the candor and wit."

In 2005, Finnamore returned to advertising full time at the San Francisco offices of her former employer, Foote Cone & Belding. She was uninterested in returning to her previous executive title, however, and was content to be merely a copywriter, albeit a well-compensated one. "I don't prance around and ... have teams under me," she told Ward in the *AdWeek* profile. She gave no hint if she had any further stories in her for a fourth book, but in an essay she penned for *Redbook* in 1999, she mused on the unexpected bonuses that came after her 40th birthday. "I am able to sing in front of people, something I could not do at 30," she wrote. "I don't feel the need to run five miles a day in the heat.... A feeling of community flavors my life; I talk to waiters and women in supermarket lines and strange dogs. I am no longer so firmly locked into my own suspense-filled mini-drama. I extend myself to others in ways I would not have dreamed of at 30, when protecting my privacy seemed crucial, when people loomed frightening and better than me. No one is better than me, I know now. Or everyone is. I'm not sure which."

## Selected writings

*Otherwise Engaged* (novel), Alfred A. Knopf (New York City), 1999.
*The Zygote Chronicles* (novel), Grove Press (New York City), 2002.
*Split: A Memoir of Divorce,* Dutton (New York City), 2008.

## Sources

### Periodicals

*AdWeek,* November 14, 2005, p. 37.
*Booklist,* March 1, 1999, p. 1104.
*Entertainment Weekly,* April 18, 2008, p. 66.
*New York Times,* April 7, 2002; April 6, 2008.
*Plain Dealer* (Cleveland, OH), June 13, 1999, p. 11.
*Publishers Weekly,* December 24, 2001, p. 38.
*Redbook,* May 1999, p. G1; November 1999, p. 122.
*Sonoma County Independent,* August 12, 1999.
*Time,* April 19, 1999, p. 78.
*USA Today,* May 1, 2008, p. 5D.

## Online

"Aspirin for a Severed Head," Salon.com, October 15, 2002, http://dir.salon.com/story/mwt/feature/2002/10/15/divorce/index.html (June 19, 2008).

"Broadsheet: Burning the Keepsake Wedding Invitations," Salon.com, April 25, 2008, http://www.salon.com/mwt/broadsheet/2008/04/25/divorce/index.html (June 19, 2008).

*—Carol Brennan*

# Tana French

*Photograph by Anthony Breatnach*

## Author

**B**orn in 1973 in Vermont; daughter of an economist. *Education:* Diploma in theatre studies at Trinity College (Dublin), 1995.

**Addresses:** *Agent*—Darley Anderson Agency, Estelle House, 11 Eustace Rd., London SW6 1JB, England. *Home*—Dublin, Ireland.

## Career

**A**uthor. Began career as a stage actor; signed with Hodder Headline, 2006; published *In the Woods,* 2007.

**Awards:** Edgar Award, Best First Novel by an American Author, Mystery Writers of America, 2008, for *In the Woods.*

## Sidelights

**N**ovelist Tana French won an Edgar Award in 2008 from the Mystery Writers of America for her sensational debut thriller, *In the Woods,* which made it onto best-seller lists in both Britain and the United States. French's novel is set in the Dublin, Ireland, area and links two missing-children incidents 24 years apart. French lives in the Irish capital, where she acted in theater productions for several years before turning to crime fiction. "I'm almost glad that I went into this with so little clue, because if I had enough sense to be scared, I would've been terrified," she told Anna Richardson in *Bookseller* about the publishing business.

French was named after Lake Tana in Ethiopia, a land where her aristocratic Russian great-grandparents eventually settled after fleeing the 1917 Bolshevik Revolution. Born in 1973 in Vermont, French lived in several exotic locales during her youth thanks to her father's work as an economist with the United Nations. There were stints in Italy and Washington, D.C., before the family moved to the southeast African nation of Malawi when French was seven. "It was incredible," she told Pavel Barter in an interview for the *Sunday Times.* "At that age, you're in your own world anyway, so if you and your friends have four acres of bushland in which to play, it becomes a magical experience."

French lived in Malawi until the age of eleven, when the family returned to Italy and settled in Rome. Summers were spent in Ireland, and she chose Trinity College in Dublin when it came time to enroll at a university in 1990. Five years later, she graduated with a diploma in theatre studies, and she spent several years as a stage actor in Dublin. French struggled financially, however, and took side jobs whenever she could, including working on archeological digs. One of these was in 2003 near a public-housing estate that bordered a forest and served as the inspiration for the plot of her acclaimed debut novel.

In early 2006, French signed with British publishing giant Hodder Headline for a substantial sum, and her debut novel was published exactly a year later.

*In the Woods* centers on a pair of police detectives in Ireland, Rob Ryan and Cassie Maddox, and their investigation into the murder of a 12-year-old girl near a housing project. As the mystery unfolds, Rob's own traumatic experience near that same spot more than two decades earlier comes to light: At age 12, he had ventured into the woods with two friends, and was the only one who returned. "When I had the basic idea for *In the Woods* the character of the narrator came with it," French explained to Alyson Rudd in the *Times* of London, citing Ryan as "intelligent, proud, secretive, too badly damaged to be honest either with himself or with his readers."

French's novel won terrific reviews. The *Times* of London called it "startlingly accomplished...." The reviewer explained further, "Many detective stories are described as 'superior' to differentiate them from the many lazy and predictable thrillers out there—but this really is." Writing in the *New York Times Book Review*, Marilyn Stasio found some fault with the relationship between Ryan and Maddox, but noted that French "sets a vivid scene for her complex characters, who seem entirely capable of doing the unexpected ... even smart people who should know better will be able to lose themselves in these dark woods."

In French's first novel, only Cassie Maddox knows about Rob Ryan's past. In the follow-up to *In the Woods*, French brings one part of that plot to the fore and uses it as the basis for a new story. To help Ryan solve the mystery of 12-year-old Katy Devlin's disappearance in *In the Woods*, Maddox goes undercover and poses as a young woman named Lexie Madison. In *The Likeness*, French's 2008 novel, there really is a Lexie Madison, and Cassie is her doppelgänger, it turns out, when Lexie turns up dead. The victim is found near her residence, a mysterious, once-grand manor home now inhabited by a group of anti-social young intellectuals. Cassie and her boss, Frank Mackey, decide she will assume Lexie's identity in order to help solve the case.

French's second story earned laudatory reviews. Janet Maslin of the *New York Times* found that the book "teases considerable suspense from this tricky arrangement. Before Cassie goes anywhere, she must be drilled in every known aspect of Lexie's behavior, even though some identifying traits will be impossible for her to learn.... Cassie's masquerade is so perilous that at one point she nearly blows her cover by eating onions at a communal meal." Writing in *Entertainment Weekly*, Kate Ward summed up *The Likeness* as "*The Parent Trap* meets *The Departed*," commenting further that "It's an ambitious concept that would be wholly unbelievable in the hands of a less capable writer. Thankfully, French takes her time developing her story."

French has admitted she essentially flies blind when writing her stories. "I don't know what I'm doing when I start a book," she told Richardson in the *Bookseller* interview. "I can't have a plot summary, because I don't know the characters well enough at that point to know what they would or wouldn't do." In another interview, this one with *Publishers Weekly*'s writer Jordan Foster, French said of her second novel, "I didn't have a clue who killed Lexie until halfway through." The scruffy cast of characters living in *The Likeness*'s Whitethorn House offer similar back stories to explore on the page, as French did when writing Rob Ryan's tale. "I'm interested in huge turning points in people's lives, in that moment where you know that whichever way you decide, there are two divergent lives ahead of you," she told Foster.

For her third novel, French expected to use Frank Mackey, Cassie's boss, as the protagonist. As of 2009, she was no longer appearing on the Dublin stage, having started to turn down roles when she was immersed in writing *In the Woods*. "In acting you're dependent on other people who decide whether you're allowed to work. If a director doesn't cast you you're not in the show," she told the London *Daily Mail* journalist Miriam Fitzpatrick. "The great thing about writing is, I've got a notebook, I've got a Biro [brand of ballpoint pen], nobody can stop me. The liberation when you realise that you can write whenever you want, as much as you want."

## Selected writings

### Novels

*In the Woods*, Viking, 2007.
*The Likeness*, Viking, 2008.

## Sources

*Bookseller*, March 24, 2006, p. 7; May 16, 2008, p. 29.
*Daily Mail* (London, England), July 11, 2008, p. 43.
*Entertainment Weekly*, July 25, 2008, p. 74.
*New York Times*, July 17, 2008.
*New York Times Book Review*, May 20, 2007.
*Publishers Weekly*, May 26, 2008, p. 36.
*Sunday Times* (London, England), July 20, 2008, p. 8.
*Times* (London, England), December 15, 2007, p. 16; January 12, 2008, p. 16.

—*Carol Brennan*

# Kathy Freston

## Author

**B**orn c. 1965; married Tom Freston (a philanthropist), c. 1999.

**Addresses:** *Home*—New York, NY, and Los Angeles, CA. *Office*—c/o Weinstein Books, 99 Hudson St., 5th Fl., New York, NY 10013.

## Career

**W**orked as a catalog model in the United States and Europe, after c. 1981; became life coach, visualization therapist, and spiritual counselor in Los Angeles.

## Sidelights

**K**athy Freston is a self-help expert and spiritual counselor whose 2008 book *Quantum Wellness: A Practical and Spiritual Guide to Health and Happiness* became a *New York Times* bestseller thanks to a boost from television talk-show host Oprah Winfrey. Freston earned much positive press for her self-help guide, which touts veganism and a daily meditation practice as the keys to happiness and well-being. A former model, Freston married media titan-turned-philanthropist Tom Freston, the former head of cable channel MTV. "Had I been successful in modeling, I wouldn't be doing what I'm doing now," Freston said of her unlikely transformation from a model to a mogul's wife and healthy-lifestyles guru, in an interview with Emily Holt of *W*. "They always say, do what you love and the money will follow."

Freston was born in the mid-1960s and grew up in the Atlanta, Georgia, area. At the age of 16, she embarked upon a career as model, and she moved to Paris following her high school graduation. She was not cut out for the competitive nature of the business, she later recalled. In an interview with Megan Othersen Gorman for *Prevention*, Freston described herself as "a nerdy girl from Atlanta with mall hair, zits, and an intense desire to please." She confessed, "I just never felt like I fit in. The successful models were so cool. They would walk into a room and own it. I was less sure of myself and went through a lot of rejection—which, of course, made me feel even less confident."

Adrift, Freston sought solace in self-help books she borrowed from English-language libraries in the city or bought for herself when she settled in the Los Angeles area. It took years, however, before she was able to free herself from one particularly damaging relationship with a serial cheater. Toward the end, she was so obsessed with keeping track of her boyfriend's whereabouts that she lost friends and modeling jobs, too. She was finally able to end the relationship and move forward, beginning a new career as a life coach and visualization therapist with an emphasis on meditation. "My work in meditation, both as a counselor and a practitioner, is rooted in the belief that we create our own reality, that healthy relationships can occur only when we are healthy inside," she told Gorman in *Prevention*. "We tend to give our energy to what we fear instead of what we hope for. When you meditate, you do the opposite, strengthening your focus even as you direct it on what's affirming, what's positive. And as a result, you become more positive, you become healthier—and you start to draw people who are healthful for you to you."

By the time Freston met her future husband in 1996, she had transformed herself and her life. At that time, Tom Freston was chief executive officer of MTV, having been with the revolutionary music channel even before its official launch. They were fixed up by mutual friends and were married a little more than three years later. "He's as positive as my other relationships were negative—the yin to their yang," Freston enthused to Gorman in the *Prevention* interview. "Yet I honestly think that if I'd met him several years earlier, he wouldn't have been interested in me nor would I have been able to see him."

Freston continued to hone her practice as a meditation therapist, and in 2002 released *Transformational Meditations*, a three-CD set of 20-minute guided meditations. She also began working on her first book, *Expect a Miracle: Seven Spiritual Steps to Finding the Right Relationship*, which was published by St. Martin's Press in 2003. The next step on her journey was to think more about the food she ate and how it arrived on her plate. In *Quantum Wellness*, she cites several documentary films about the meat and dairy industry that had a profound impact on her state of mind. These films along with books on the subject brought her to the point at which, she writes, "I fell into a deep depression and wondered what I was supposed to do.... It is a rude awakening, realizing that our diet is based in cruelty."

Freston was a practicing vegan by the time her second book, *The One: Finding Soul Mate Love and Making It Last*, was published in 2006. It became a bestseller, as did her next title, 2008's *Quantum Wellness*, which Oprah Winfrey invited her to discuss on the daytime-television star's widely watched show. Winfrey announced she would be trying the book's suggested 21-day cleanse—abstaining from meat, alcohol, dairy, gluten, sugar, and caffeine—which prompted sales of *Quantum Wellness* to skyrocket to a place on the *New York Times* best-seller list. Winfrey wrote about her experience on Freston's diet plan in the October issue of her magazine, *O*. "For three weeks, I—a person who seldom eats eggs—obsessed over not being able to have an omelet," Winfrey confessed, and when it was over, she found herself "more mindful of my choices. I'm eating a

far more plant-based diet. Less processed food." She also cited Freston's advice, "'Lean into it.' Don't try to break a lifetime of bad habits overnight."

Freston and her husband live on the Upper East Side of Manhattan in a noted residence that was once home to the artist Andy Warhol. Her husband ended his long run at MTV in 2006, when he was ousted from the parent company, Viacom, in an internal battle. Some of his estimated $85 million severance package has been used for philanthropic ventures such as ONE: The Campaign to Make Poverty History, an international humanitarian project touted by Bono, the lead singer for the Irish band U2. "What looks like a disaster can turn out to be a blessing," Freston told Holt in *W* about her husband's midlife change of career. "Since then he has done so many incredible things."

## Selected writings

### Books

*Expect a Miracle: Seven Spiritual Steps to Finding the Right Relationship*, St. Martin's Press, 2003.
*The One: Finding Soul Mate Love and Making It Last*, Miramax Books, 2006.
*Quantum Wellness: A Practical and Spiritual Guide to Health and Happiness*, Weinstein Books, 2008.

### Other

*Transformational Meditations*, Lime Tree Productions, 2002.

## Sources

### Books

Freston, Kathy, *Quantum Wellness: A Practical and Spiritual Guide to Health and Happiness*, Weinstein Books, 2008.

### Periodicals

*Forbes*, May 8, 2006.
*New Yorker*, May 15, 2006, p. 32.
*O: The Oprah Magazine*, October 2008, p. 310.
*Prevention*, January 2004, p. 134.
*W*, May 2008, p. 146.

—*Carol Brennan*

# Timothy F. Geithner

## U.S. Secretary of the Treasury

**B**orn Timothy Franz Geithner, August 18, 1961, in New York, NY; son of Peter (a foundation executive) and Deborah (a piano teacher) Geithner; married Carole Marie Sonnenfeld (a social worker), June 8, 1985; children: Elise, Ben. *Education:* Dartmouth College, B.A., 1983; Johns Hopkins School for Advanced International Studies, M.A., 1985.

**Addresses:** *Home*—Larchmont, NY. *Office*—Department of the Treasury, 1500 Pennsylvania Ave. NW, Washington, DC 20220.

## Career

**R**esearch associate, Kissinger Associates, 1985-88; analyst, International Affairs department, U.S. Treasury, then deputy financial attaché to the U.S. Embassy in Tokyo, Japan; assistant secretary of the Treasury for International Affairs, U.S. Treasury, 1997, then undersecretary, 1998; director of policy development and review department, International Monetary Fund (IMF), 2001-03; president and chief executive, Federal Reserve Bank of New York, 2003-09; U.S. Secretary of the Treasury, 2009—.

## Sidelights

**L**ess than a week after U.S. President Barack Obama took office in January of 2009, Timothy Geithner was sworn in as the 75th U.S. Secretary of the Treasury. Prior to taking the job, Geithner had served as president of the New York branch of the Federal Reserve for the past five years, and in the weeks prior to the November election had played a crucial role in working to resolve Wall Street's fiscal crisis. "No Treasury Secretary has ever entered office with as much responsibility as Geithner will have," asserted James Surowiecki, finance columnist at the *New Yorker*. "For better or worse, we now live in a world in which the Treasury Secretary controls hundreds of billions of dollars in spending and shapes the fate of some of the nation's biggest companies. That's quite a job to ask someone to do. If anyone is up to the task, Geithner seems to be."

Geithner is a native of the New York City borough of Brooklyn, where he was born in 1961. His parents were graduates of two elite East Coast colleges, Dartmouth and Smith, and his father went on to work for the prestigious Ford Foundation as its program officer for developing countries. Because of his father's job, Geithner and his siblings lived all around the world, including the African nations of Zambia and Zimbabwe and then India and Thailand. He and Barack Obama actually met at one point as teenagers at a Ford Foundation event—Obama's mother had ties to the Foundation through her anthropological field work in Javanese handicrafts, while Geithner and his family were in Jakarta, Indonesia, when his father was administering a microfinance program.

After graduating from the International School in Bangkok, Thailand, Geithner followed his father into Dartmouth College, where he majored in government and Asian studies. This rigorous degree course required fluency in Japanese and Chinese, and he spent time in Beijing to further hone his skills in the latter language. After graduating in 1983, he went on to the Johns Hopkins School for Advanced International Studies to earn a master's degree in international economics and East Asian studies. He finished in 1985, the same year he married a fellow Dartmouth graduate, Carole Sonnenfeld, and began working at Kissinger Associates, the New York City-based consulting firm headed by former U.S. Secretary of State Henry Kissinger. During his time there, Geithner conducted research for one of Kissinger's books.

In 1988, Geithner was hired at the U.S. Treasury Department in its International Affairs department. He was eventually posted to the U.S. Embassy in Tokyo, Japan, as a deputy financial attaché, where he was involved in negotiating the details of an historic agreement that allowed foreign companies to enter the Japanese financial-services market for the first time. He eventually became special assistant to Lawrence Summers, who was Undersecretary for International Affairs at the Treasury Department during the first Clinton Administration and then became Treasury Secretary in 1999. Geithner is considered a protégé of both Summers and Robert Rubin, who served as Treasury Secretary from 1995 to 1999. Geithner succeeded Summers as Undersecretary for International Affairs in 1998, and both before and after this promotion he worked with top Treasury Department officials to minimize the impact of the Asian financial crisis on international markets.

The Clinton era ended in 2001 and Geithner went to work at the International Monetary Fund (IMF) as director of its policy development and review department. In October of 2003, he was named president and chief executive of the Federal Reserve Bank of New York. Though it was just one of the 12 banks in the Federal Reserve system, the New York office bore the greatest responsibility for regulating the financial markets and overseeing monetary policy in conjunction with the Federal Reserve chairperson in Washington. Over the next five years, Geithner periodically sounded alarms about the long-term effects of the banking deregulation that began under a Republican-led administration in the 1980s. "The present fiscal trajectory entails an uncomfortable scale of borrowing and little insurance against possible adverse outcomes in an uncertain world," he told a group of financial professionals about the growing federal budget deficit and a worrisome climate of speculative investments on Wall Street in early 2005, according to a *New York Times* report by Edmund L. Andrews.

In 2008, some of those warnings came to fruition. The first major Wall Street firm to fail was Bear Stearns, followed by Lehman Brothers. Geithner worked with Treasury Department officials in the outgoing Bush administration to provide emergency help via the Troubled Assets Relief Program, or TARP. This provided cash to struggling banks and securities-insurance companies on the verge of failure in exchange for stock or some form of equity in the company.

Obama was elected president on November 4, 2008, and two days later Geithner's name surfaced as a potential Treasury Secretary in the new administration. Summers' name was also put forth, but he was considered a riskier candidate for a cabinet appointee because of his problematic tenure as president of Harvard University. On November 24, the president-elect announced that Geithner was indeed the Treasury Secretary-designate, but this news had already leaked out two days earlier, which caused the Dow Jones Average to rise six percentage points in one day's trading.

During his Senate confirmation hearings, Geithner faced scrutiny over his failure to pay Social Security and Medicare taxes for the 2001-2004 tax years when he worked for the IMF, which does not withhold those taxes for employees who are U.S. residents. He blamed the oversight on a commonly available software program he had used to do his taxes. He was confirmed by a Senate vote of 60-34 and sworn in on January 26, 2009. He lives in Larchmont, New York, with his wife and two teenage children, who attend local public schools.

Geithner's first few months in office were difficult ones. He unveiled a preliminary bank rescue plan on February 10, and global financial markets nosedived. "The torrent of abuse that rained down on Geithner was withering and ceaseless," noted John Heilemann in *New York* magazine, who also noted that President Obama voiced enthusiastic support for his Treasury Secretary. "Nobody's working harder than this guy," the president said, according to Heilemann. "You know, he is making all the right moves in terms of playing a bad hand."

## Sources

### Periodicals

America's Intelligence Wire, January 26, 2009.
*New York*, March 22, 2009.
*New Yorker*, December 8, 2008, p. 40.
*New York Times*, January 23, 2005; January 4, 2009.

### Online

"Geithner Facing Own Stress Test Amid Economic Woes," Salon.com, http://www.salon.com/wires/ap/2009/03/28/D9770PSO1_geithner_profile/print.html (April 16, 2009).

—*Carol Brennan*

# Paul Giamatti

*Joe Kohen/Getty Images*

## Actor

**B**orn Paul Edward Valentine Giamatti, June 6, 1967, in New Haven, CT; son of A. Bartlett (a professor, university president, and Commissioner of Major League Baseball) and Toni (an actress and teacher; maiden name, Smith) Giamatti; married Elizabeth Cohen, October 13, 1997; children: Samuel. *Education:* Yale University, B.A., 1989; M.F.A., 1994.

**Addresses:** *Home*—Brooklyn, NY. *Management*—Kipperman Management, 243 W. 72nd St., New York, NY 10023.

## Career

**A**ctor in films, including: *Past Midnight*, 1991; *Singles*, 1991; *Mighty Aphrodite*, 1995; *Sabrina*, 1995; *Breathing Room*, 1996; *Arresting Gena*, 1997; *Donnie Brasco*, 1997; *A Further Gesture*, 1997; *My Best Friend's Wedding*, 1997; *Private Parts*, 1997; *Cradle Will Rock*, 1998; *Doctor Doolittle*, 1998; *The Negotiator*, 1998; *Safe Men*, 1998; *Saving Private Ryan*, 1998; *The Truman Show*, 1998; *Man on the Moon*, 1999; *Big Momma's House*, 2000; *Duets*, 2000; *Planet of the Apes*, 2001; *Storytelling*, 2001; *Big Fat Liar*, 2002; *Thunderpants*, 2002; *American Splendor*, 2003; *Confidence*, 2003; *Paycheck*, 2003; *Sideways*, 2004; *Cinderella Man*, 2005; *Robots*, 2005; *The Ant Bully*, 2006; *The Hawk Is Dying*, 2006; *The Illusionist*, 2006; *Lady in the Water*, 2006; *Fred Claus*, 2007; *The Nanny Diaries*, 2007; *Shoot 'Em Up*, 2007; *Too Loud a Solitude*, 2007; *Pretty Bird*, 2008; *Cold Souls*, 2009; *Duplicity*, 2009. Television appearances include: *She'll Take Romance* (movie), 1990; *NYPD Blue*, ABC, 1994; *The Show* (pilot), 1996; *Homicide: Life on the Street*, NBC, 1998; *The Tourist Trap* (movie), 1998; *Winchell* (movie), 1998; *If These Walls Could Talk 2*, HBO, 2000; *King of the Hill* (voice) FOX, 2001; *The Pentagon Papers* (movie), 2003; *John Adams* (miniseries), HBO, 2008. Stage appearances include: *Racing Demon*, Lincoln Center, New York City, c. early 1990s; *Arcadia*, New York City, c. early 1990s; *Three Sisters*, Roundabout Theatre Company, New York City, 1997. Producer of films, including: *Pretty Bird*, 2008; *The Owl in Daylight*, 2009.

**Awards:** National Board of Review Award for best breakthrough performance by an actor, for *American Splendor*, 2003; Boston Society of Film Critics Award for best ensemble cast (with others), for *Sideways*, 2004; Chicago Film Critics Association Award for best actor, for *Sideways*, 2004; New York Film Critics Circle Award for best actor, for *Sideways*, 2004; Phoenix Film Critics Society Award (with others) for best ensemble acting, for *Sideways*, 2004; San Francisco Film Critics Circle Award for best actor, for *Sideways*, 2004; Critics Choice Award for best acting ensemble (with others), Broadcast Film Critics Association, for *Sideways*, 2005; Comedy Film Honor for best actor, U.S. Comedy Arts Festival, for *Sideways*, 2005; Dallas-Fort Worth Film Critics Association Award for best actor, for *Sideways*, 2005; Florida Film Critics Circle Award for best supporting actor, for *Cinderella Man*, 2005; Independent Spirit Award for best male lead, Film Independent, for *Sideways*, 2005; Online Film Critics Society Award for best actor, for *Sideways*, 2005; Screen Actors Guild Award (with others) for outstanding performance by a cast in a motion picture, for *Sideways*, 2005; Boston Society of Film Critics Award for best supporting actor, for *Cinderella Man*, 2005; Southeastern Film Critics Association Award for best supporting actor, for *Cinderella Man*, 2005; Toronto Film Critics Association Award for best supporting performance—male, for *Cinderella Man*, 2005; Washington D.C. Area Film Critics Association for best supporting actor, for *Cinderella Man*, 2005; Critics Choice Award for best supporting actor, Broadcast Film Critics Association, for *Cinderella Man*, 2006; Kansas City Film Critics Circle Award for best supporting actor, for *Cinderella Man*, 2006; Screen Actors Guild Award for outstanding performance by a male actor in a supporting role, for *Cinderella Man*, 2006; Sant Jordi Award for best foreign actor, for *Cinderella Man*, *Sideways*, and *American Splendor*, 2006; Emmy Award for outstanding lead actor in a miniseries or movie, Academy of Television Arts and Sciences, for *John Adams*, 2008; Golden Nymph Award for best performance by an actor—miniseries, Monte-Carlo TV Festival, for *John Adams*, 2008; Satellite Award for best actor in a miniseries or a motion picture made for television, International Press Academy, for *John Adams*, 2008; Television Critics Association Award for individual achievement in drama, for *John Adams*, 2008; Golden Globe Award for best performance by an actor in a miniseries or a motion picture made for television, for *John Adams*, 2009; Screen Actors Guild Award for outstanding performance by a male actor in a television movie or miniseries, for *John Adams*, 2009.

## Sidelights

**B**est known for his work in such films as *Sideways*, *Cinderella Man*, and *American Splendor*, actor Paul Giamatti had an award-winning turn as President John Adams in the HBO miniseries *John Adams* in 2008. After beginning his career in the theater and doing work in other media only to support himself as he sought stage work, Giamatti became identified as a memorable supporting actor who often stole films away from their stars. As Jenelle Riley wrote in the *National Post*, "Giamatti has steadily been building up a dossier of quirky, offbeat, and just plain grouchy character roles that have earned the Yale-educated actor a devoted following. Giamatti has specialized in creating individuals you might not necessarily want to know in real life but can't get enough of on the screen." With *American Splendor*, Giamatti began taking on starring roles in films and, on occasion, television, which were often just as unforgettable. He has continued to move between starring and supporting roles in film, television, and the theater, becoming a widely respected actor among his peers, critics, and audiences.

Born on June 6, 1967, in New Haven, Connecticut, he was the son of A. Bartlett and Toni Giamatti. His father was a professor of Renaissance literature at Yale University, who later become the president of Yale. A. Bartlett Giamatti briefly served as the Commissioner of Major League Baseball until he unexpectedly died in September of 1989. Toni Giamatti was an actress before her marriage and later became a prep school English teacher. Like Giamatti, his elder brother Marcus also became an actor.

Somewhat directionless as a youth growing up in New Haven, Giamatti received his education at Choate Rosemary Hall prep school, then entered Yale University. He majored in English and earned his bachelor's degree in the subject. While an undergraduate, Giamatti discovered acting. He told Ed Caesar of the London *Independent*, "I was in college, and a friend persuaded me to do a play. I wasn't a drama major or anything—it was all very extracurricular. Then I moved to Seattle intending to do something in the animation business, but I knew a guy who ran a theatre out there. I started making a living out of acting. I thought, Well I'm making money and I'm enjoying it, so I better keep doing it. Anyway, this isn't such a bad second career." Giamatti also said that he found himself drawn to acting in part because he was unsure of what he wanted to do with his life and the craft afforded him the ability to be many different people.

Giamatti also attended the Yale School of Drama from which he earned his master of fine arts degree in 1994. As an actor, his first love was the theater, beginning with his years at Yale. After completing his education, Giamatti appeared on the stage in San Diego and Williamstown, Massachusetts, as well as in Broadway productions. In New York, he appeared in productions of both *Racing Demon* and *Arcadia*. Giamatti also had a few film and television roles in the early 1990s. While a few of his early credits were on stage and television—such as his debut in a small role in the 1990 television movie *She'll Take Romance*, guest spots on such shows as *NYPD Blue*, and the 1996 pilot *The Show*—he primarily appeared in films.

Many of Giamatti's film roles in the 1990s and into the early 2000s were small or supporting turns. He made his living as a character actor, enhancing every genre of film with his acting skills. His first films came in the early 1990s: 1991's *Past Midnight* and 1992's *Singles*. By the mid-1990s, the number of small film roles greatly increased with Giamatti taking parts in such productions as the 1995 Woody Allen comedy *Mighty Aphrodite* and as an FBI technician in the 1997 reality-based undercover FBI agent drama *Donnie Brasco*. Giamatti often played characters who were based on real-life people.

By the late 1990s, Giamatti was becoming more recognized by audiences and critics alike for his memorable supporting roles. In 1997, for example, he played Kenny (also known as Pig Vomit), a put-upon radio executive who tries and fails to control radio shock jock Howard Stern in the film *Private Parts.* Kenny ends up losing his job. The film was based on the memoir by Stern of the same name. At the time of the release, Giamatti showed his depth as an actor by also appearing on Broadway in an adaptation of Anton Chekhov's *Three Sisters* as Andrei Prozorov. While the play was not well-received, Giamatti was lauded for his work as the cowardly brother who has his life ruined by an unfaithful wife.

Giamatti admitted he loved both roles, which typified his career at that point. He told Jean Nathan of the *New York Times,* "I play abused people all the time. The guy in *Three Sisters* is just horribly abused, too, but the *Private Parts* character is also abusive in a way that I hadn't gotten to play that much. It was fun to play a guy who was a real psychotic lunatic, who depends so much on pathetic hysteria, who was releasing that much rage all the time."

In the late 1990s and early 2000s, Giamatti's film and television roles vacillated between low-brow comedies, quality dramas, Hollywood blockbusters, and unexpected hits. For example, he appeared in another Woody Allen film in 1997, *Deconstructing Harry,* then had small roles in the 1998 hit Hollywood comedies *The Truman Show* and *Doctor Doolittle.* Yet Giamatti also appeared in the 1998 Steven Spielberg-directed World War II drama *Saving Private Ryan,* the 1999 Andy Kaufman biopic *Man on the Moon,* the 2000 indie comedy *Duets,* and played an orangutan in the 2001 remake of the science fiction classic *The Planet of the Apes.*

Continuing to show the breadth of his talent and scope of his film roles, Giamatti had a larger supporting role in the teen comedy *Big Fat Liar.* In the 2002 film, he played Marty Wolf, a Hollywood film producer who steals a 14-year-old's essay and tries to turn it into a film. While critics panned *Big Fat Liar,* Giamatti's work in the role was praised by such critics as Mark Burger of the *Winston-Salem Journal.* Burger commented, "*Big Fat Liar* has a few funny moments—most of them belonging to Giamatti, who infuses Wolf with a kind of malevolently manic glee reminiscent of Danny DeVito."

While Giamatti occasionally appeared in this quality and type of film after 2003, his career began a trajectory toward bigger parts in better films beginning with that year's *American Splendor.* In his first leading role, he played Harvey Pekar, a real-life hospital clerk and author of a comic-book series with a cult following. The film, which combined live action, animation, and documentary, won the top prize at the 2003 Sundance Film Festival. Giamatti's ability to capture the everyday genius of Pekar and his world won him many critical kudos, talk of an Academy Award nomination, and led to opportunities to take on more leading roles.

Such roles included a co-starring turn in the 2003 futuristic film *Paycheck,* which was directed by John Woo, and another career-defining part as Miles Raymond in the 2004 indie film *Sideways.* While the former was essentially a box-office bomb, Giamatti's work in *Sideways* brought him an even bigger audience. Directed by Alexander Payne, Giamatti's Miles is a wanna-be writer who knows a lot about wine but is a neurotic loser in life. He goes on a bachelor road trip to Napa Valley with an old friend, a failing actor (played by Thomas Haden Church) who is about to get married, and finds their friendship falling apart.

Critics lauded the film, and often picked out Giamatti for special praise. For example, Eleanor Ringel Gillespie of the *Atlanta Journal-Constitution* wrote that "The acting is superb.... The standout is Giamatti.... He's created a Giamatti type: someone tortured by his own oversensitivity but too tired—afraid?—to do anything about it." While there were again calls for an Academy Award nomination which never came, Giamatti was rewarded with numerous honors for his work in *Sideways,* including a Screen Actors Guild Award and an Independent Spirit Award.

After *Sideways,* Giamatti provided the voice of Tim the Gate Guard in the 2005 animated feature *Robots.* His next major release was 2005's *Cinderella Man,* for which he finally received an Academy Award nomination. The film was a biopic about Jim Braddock, a real-life Depression era boxer who captured the American imagination. Braddock was played by controversial Australian actor Russell Crowe, and Giamatti played his manager/trainer Joe Gould. Giamatti followed the success of *Cinderella Man* with a leading role in a small indie film, 2006's *The Hawk Is Dying,* in which he played a Southerner who teaches a red-tailed hawk to fly. He received some negative publicity for his starring role as Cleveland Heep in M. Night Shyamalan's adult fairy tale, 2006's *Lady in the Water.* The film was his first leading role in a big-budget film, and both the film and his performance in what was considered a poorly written script were panned.

Though *Lady in the Lake* was not a hit, Giamatti continued to move between starring and supporting roles in films both big and small. In the 2006 art house melodrama *The Illusionist*, he played a conflicted inspector general investigating a magician in 1900 Vienna who is trying to court an upper class woman. Giamatti also lent his voice to another animated film, *The Ant Bully*, played the distant father Mr. X in the failed 2007 adaptation of the hit novel *The Nanny Diaries*, and appeared as Hertz in the violent action film *Shoot 'Em Up* with Clive Owen. Giamatti did not neglect comedies, playing the supporting role of Santa Claus in the 2007 Vince Vaughn vehicle *Fred Claus*.

As Giamatti's film career went on the rise, he did not work as often in television. That situation changed in 2008 when he was tapped to play President John Adams in the HBO miniseries about the Founding Father's life, based on the Pulitzer Prize-winning biography *John Adams* by David McCullough. Critics widely praised the miniseries for its depth, breadth, and accessibility. Giamatti was highly regarded as a primary reason for the success of the miniseries, with Matthew Gilbert of the *Boston Globe* noting, "As Adams, Giamatti is riveting. He has the time to let Adams' principled nobility emerge slowly, alongside his vanities and egotism…. Giamatti also elevates his portrayal of Adams with a phenomenal magnetism." For his work in the role, the actor won both an Emmy and a Golden Globe Award.

After *John Adams*, Giamatti again appeared with Owen in the romantic caper *Duplicity*. He had several others films scheduled for release in 2009, including *The Last Station* and *The Owl in Daylight*. In the latter film, a biopic, he played acclaimed science fiction writer Philip K. Dick. While Giamatti's talent ensured he would have a steady career as an actor, he was not entirely convinced that he would continue to land leading roles. He told the *Independent*'s Caesar, "People in the industry and people like yourselves are saying that actors like me can flourish in this 'new' environment, but I'm not convinced I believe them. I guess I'm just more cynical than that. There's no great paradigm shift in my opinion, and neither should there be. I just think I got really lucky."

Outside of acting, Giamatti is a voracious reader, with thousands of books packed into the Manhattan apartment where he lives with his wife, Elizabeth Cohen, and their son, Samuel. Giamatti admits to buying an average of one book per day. He reads both fiction and nonfiction with no particular pattern to his choices, though he admits to a love of science fiction. He told the *New York Times'* Nathan, "My reading is really out of control. I buy way too many books. I read anything."

## Sources

### Books

*Complete Marquis Who's Who Biographies,* Marquis Who's Who LLC, 2009.

### Periodicals

*Atlanta Journal-Constitution,* November 5, 2004, p. 1H.
*Boston Globe,* March 14, 2008, p. D1.
*Chicago Sun-Times,* August 17, 2003, p. 6.
*Daily Variety,* January 4, 2005, p. 16.
*Gazette* (Montreal, Canada), November 1, 2004, p. D5.
*Hartford Courant* (CT), March 15, 2009. P. G1.
*Houston Chronicle,* November 26, 2004, p. 9; August 18, 2006, p. 1.
*Independent* (London, England), February 2, 2005, pp. 14-15.
*National Post,* December 22, 2004, p. AL14; July 21, 2006, p. PM1.
*Newsweek,* August 11, 2003, p. 52.
*New York Magazine,* July 24, 2006; March 10, 2008.
*New York Times,* March 9, 1997, sec. 2, p. 25.
*Philadelphia Inquirer,* August 17, 2003, p. H1.
*Plain Dealer* (Cleveland, OH), September 1, 2006, p. T4.
*Seattle Post-Intelligencer,* July 21, 2006, p. 5.
*Washington Post,* March 15, 2008, p. C1.
*Winston-Salem Journal* (Winston-Salem, NC), February 8, 2002, p. E1.

### Online

"Paul Giamatti," Internet Movie Database, http://www.imdb.com/name/nm0316079/ (April 14, 2009).

—*A. Petruso*

# James Gordon

## Psychiatrist

**B**orn James Samuel Gordon, October 12, 1941, in New York, NY; son of Jules David and Cynthia (maiden name, Hymanson) Gordon. *Education:* Harvard University, A.B., 1962, M.D., 1967.

**Addresses:** *Office*—Center for Mind-Body Medicine, 5225 Connecticut Ave., NW, Ste. 414, Washington, DC 20015-1845.

## Career

**W**orked as teaching fellow in general education at Harvard University, 1963-67; National Institute of Health research fellow and teaching assistant in the department of pathology, Cornell Medical School, 1964-65; intern at Mt. Zion Hospital, San Francisco, California, 1967-68; resident in psychiatry at Albert Einstein College of Medicine, 1968-70, then chief resident and clinical instructor in psychiatry, 1970-71; research psychiatrist at the National Institute of Mental Health (NIMH), Rockville, Maryland, 1971-82; served as a commander in the United States Public Health Service, 1971-82; directed a special study for the President's Commission on Mental Health at NIHM, 1977-78; chief of adolescent services at St. Elizabeth Hospital, Washington, D.C., 1980-82; clinical professor at Georgetown School of Medicine, 1980—; published *Mind, Body and Health: Toward an Integrative Medicine,* 1984; founder and director of Center for Mind-Body Medicine, Washington, D.C., 1991—; worked with Office of Alternative Medicine at the National Institute of Health (NIH), 1994-97; member of the cancer advisory panel at the NIH, 1998—; chairman of the White House Commission on Complementary and Alternative Medicine Policy, 2000-02; published *Unstuck: Your Guide to the Seven-Stage Journey Out of Depression,* 2008.

**Member:** Fellow, American Association of Social Psychiatry; American Psychiatric Association; advisory board, Cleveland Clinic, Cleveland, OH; advisory board, Integrative Healthcare Symposium; founding member, American Holistic Medical Association, 1980, then trustee, 1980-86; executive committee, Physicians for Social Responsibility, 1984-86; founding member, American Association of Medical Acupuncture, 1987; editorial board, *Alternative and Complementary Therapies,* 1994—; editorial board, *Alternative Therapies in Health and Medicine,* 1994—; advisory board, *Natural Health,* 1994—.

**Awards:** Ford Foundation Award, 1982; O. Spurgeon English Humanitarian Award, Temple University, 2002.

## Sidelights

**T**he founder and director of the Center for Mind-Body Medicine, Dr. James Gordon emphasizes a holistic, whole body approach to health and wellness. A Harvard-trained medical doctor, he believes that conventional medicine should work with alternative therapies like acupuncture, herbs, adjustments, nutrition, and emotional support to better people and their lives. Gordon studied the effectiveness of these treatments, promoting their use in scientific studies as well as in a number of popular books. As Gordon told Diane Guernesy of *Town & Country*, "Alternative medicine is exciting; it is truly a frontier. If you're interested in something really new in medicine, this is one area. It's a new field, it's growing, it's useful to people—and it's wide-open."

Born on October 12, 1941, in New York City, Gordon was the son of Jules and Cynthia Gordon. He was born into a family of doctors. A grandfather was a pediatrician, while his father was a surgeon and team physician for the New York Yankees. Gordon knew he would be a doctor from an early age, telling Suzanne Gerber of the *Vegetarian Times*, "When I was eight, I told my father I wanted to be either a rabbi or a farmer. His response was, 'Why don't you be a doctor because if you're a doctor, you can do anything.' Those words stuck in my mind, even though I had no idea what being a doctor meant."

While his father provided inspiration for his career in terms of his passion, he was not an ideal father figure since he was prone to anger and distance. Still, Gordon decided to follow in his professional footsteps. He received his education at Riverdale Country Day School, an elite school in New York, where he found another role model. As a 12 year old, Gordon came into contact with the ideas of Greek philosopher Socrates. Gordon explained to the *Vegetarian Times*' Gerber, "He stood up against the establishment, helped people find the truth, and sat around talking and somehow made a living. I wanted to be like that, and I thought the way to do that was to become a psychiatrist." Reading the lectures of Sigmund Freud, the father of modern psychology, only confirmed his career path.

To that end, Gordon attended and graduated from Harvard University, earning his A.B. in English literature in 1962, then his M.D. in 1967. While a medical student, he served as a teaching fellow in general education for Harvard. During these years, Gordon also worked as a National Institute of Health fellow and teaching assistant in the department of pathology at Cornell Medical School from 1964 to 1965. After completing his medical degree, Gordon continued his training as an intern at Mt. Zion Hospital in San Francisco, California, from 1967 to 1968. During this time period, the height of the hippie movement and the summer of love, he also volunteered at the famous Haight-Ashbury Free Clinic.

Talking about the experience, Gordon told Gerber of the *Vegetarian Times*, "It was the first time I'd worked with runaways, with homeless teen-agers. I

felt connected to them. They were like my younger brothers and sisters. We were all searching for a new better world. Working with the kids who'd taken too much LSD, I saw the difference between treating them in a medical setting, where their trips would get worse and they'd need medication to come down, and at the clinic, where we helped them see even the bad part of a drug trip as a journey toward understanding." Gordon also participated in anti-war protests that were common in San Francisco in the time period.

Going back east in 1968, Gordon spent two years as a resident in psychiatry at Albert Einstein College of Medicine in the Bronx, New York. In 1970, Gordon began a stint as a chief resident of the affiliated Bronx State Hospital and clinical instructor in psychiatry there. At the hospital, he operated a more open ward which allowed freedom of movement and favored yoga, meditation, music, and arts therapy as treatments over medication.

With his education complete, Gordon began working as a research psychiatrist at the National Institute of Mental Health (NIMH) in Rockville, Maryland in 1971. He remained in the post and also served as a commander in the United States Public Health Service through 1982. For the NIMH, he again often worked with runaway and homeless teenagers, and continued to emphasize treatments that focused on improving their bodies and their minds rather than treatment through medication.

While working at the NIMH, Gordon held other posts, many prestigious. For example, he directed a special study for the President's Commission on Mental Health at the NIHM from 1977 to 1978. From 1980 to 1982, Gordon served as the chief of adolescent services at St. Elizabeth Hospital in Washington, D.C. He joined the Georgetown School of Medicine as a clinical professor in psychiatry and community and family medicine in 1980.

Thus from the time he launched his professional career, Gordon was interested in alternative medical treatments for both his patients and himself. He experimented with acupuncture, yoga, and nutrition, including an emphasis on fresh foods and herbs. This appeal reached new heights when, in 1974, he suffered a lower back injury while doing yoga incorrectly. Orthopedic doctors and other specialists could not help him nor could bed rest. He was in such agony for several months that he took medication, including muscle relaxants, but it negatively affected his work and his ability to complete scientific papers. Surgery seemed to be the only option to relieve the pain.

It was not until Gordon saw an acupuncturist and naturopath, Shyam Singha, that he found relief. Though Singha's advice—taking hot baths with Epsom salts and eating pineapple with honey three times a day for a week—was completely contradictory to what he had learned at Harvard. Yet the malic acid in the pineapple contributed to loss of nearly 90 percent of his pain within a week. The rest was helped by an adjustment from an osteopath. Gordon also cured his allergies and other conditions based on Singha's advice.

Of the experience, Gordon told Eric Patterson and Luise Light of *Vegetarian Times*, "From then on, I had a whole new perspective on health care." Gordon soon explored spirituality as well, spending two months in India in 1979 as part of a research team working for the administration of U.S. President Jimmy Carter. Gordon lead the team as the director of the Special Study on Alternative Services for President Carter's Commission on Mental Health. Gordon spent three weeks of the trip with an infamous spiritual leader, Bhagwan Shree Rajneesh, who combined Eastern mediation and Western psychotherapy.

These experiences contributed to Gordon's exploration of and belief in alternative medical therapies as valid. While Gordon promulgated alternative treatments to his patients, he did not dismiss conventional medicine as it was practiced in the United States and Europe. He told Mat Edelson of the *Washingtonian*, "Say you have a nagging belly pain and disturbed bowel movements and difficulty eating. Somewhere along the line, you need a Western diagnosis as well. Western medicine is very good at uncovering serious problems." He firmly believed that patients should work with both a conventional and alternative practitioner.

Gordon then dedicated his professional career, both as a researcher and as a practitioner, to exploring alternative medical treatments. What this meant evolved throughout the rest of his career. In the 1980s, Gordon began publishing books on such subjects, including 1987's *The Golden Guru* (about Rajneesh, in part), 1988's *Holistic Medicine,* and 1989's *Stress Management.* By 1991, Gordon had founded and began serving as director of his own alternative/complementary medical clinic, the Center for Mind-Body Medicine in Washington, D.C. The clinic's staff also taught relaxation and stress reduction techniques to interested parties.

At his clinic and in his private practice, Gordon used both conventional medicine and alternative medical treatments like acupuncture, meditation, osteopathic adjustments, and herbs to treat psychological and psychiatric disorders like panic attacks. Such treatments were also given to patients with chronic pain or to the boost the immune systems of AIDS and cancer patients. In addition, Gordon emphasized the importance of the mind-body connection by beginning sessions with about 20 minutes of talk, discussing their lives and their health problems. Gordon believed that support—both psychological and emotional—helps boost the immune system.

Gordon shared his ever-growing knowledge about alternative medical treatments with other experts by working with the Office of Alternative Medicine at the NIH. Founded in 1991, the mission of the Office was to research alternative therapies. Gordon worked with the group as the chairman of its advisory council from 1994 to 1997. He completed clinical studies which were published in respected medical journals, conducted informative clinics on how to incorporate mind-body practices for conventional medical professionals, and gave related lectures to both professional and lay groups. Many of Gordon's vacations even turned into experiences to teach or learn. A trip to South Africa in the 1990s led to him meeting with native healers, whom he brought to Washington, D.C. to help young African-American students bond with a part of their heritage.

Gordon continued to publish significant literature on various alternative medicine topics in the 1990s and early 2000s. In 1996, for example, he put out *Manifesto for a New Medicine: Your Guide to Healing Partnerships and the Wise Use of Alternative Therapies.* This tome, his fourth book, offered his ideas about how to effectively combine alternative and conventional medical treatments. Gordon published *Comprehensive Cancer Care* in 2000. He had begun focusing on cancer in the late 1990s, as a member of the NIH's cancer advisory panel.

While Gordon's take on medicine was not always considered mainstream by his colleagues, he shared his insights with them in other ways as well. In 2000, for example, he presented the keynote address at the 50th anniversary national convention of the American Medical Student Association. That same year, Gordon was named the chairman of the White House Commission on Complementary and Alternative Medicine Policy by U.S. President Bill Clinton.

In the early 2000s, Gordon's work emphasized the health crisis of depression. He believed that positive words and actions helped lift moods and stave off this debilitating disease. The proliferation of depression compelled him to publish *Unstuck: Your Guide to the Seven-Stage Journey Out of Depression* in 2008. In the book, Gordon outlined his belief that antidepressants are generally ineffective, if not dangerous, for most people suffering from the condition. He believed depression would be better served by treating it as a whole body condition, including working with guided imagery, addressing dietary issues, and often taking supplements.

Gordon remained humble in his take on depression, telling Donna Caruso of *Life Extension*, "I don't know if my approach can help everybody. I'm not saying that. But I would say that 80 to 90 percent of people with depression will do significantly better if they adopt this approach. We need to look at our troubles and difficulties as an opportunity and not simply as a disaster."

Summarizing his career, Gordon said to Patterson and Light of the *Vegetarian Times*, "I give people the tools to take care of themselves in ways similar to those I learned to help myself." He hoped to further what he considered the necessary revolution in medicine throughout his life. Gordon told Gerber of the *Vegetarian Times*, "Things are becoming more important now. There are more things to do, more people who need advice. What I'm interested in doing is helping to transform the planet so that people treat each other with more kindness and that we celebrate our lives more, so that we learn more about how to heal ourselves and one another—and have a good time while we're here."

## Selected writings

### Nonfiction

(Editor with Dennis T. Jaffe and David E. Bresler) *Mind, Body and Health: Toward an Integrative Medicine*, Human Sciences Press (New York), 1984.

*The Golden Guru*, Stephen Greene/Viking (New York), 1987.
*Holistic Medicine*, Chelsea House (New York), 1988; reprinted, 2000.
*Stress Management*, Chelsea House, 1989; reprinted, 2000.
*Manifesto for a New Medicine: Your Guide to Healing Partnerships and the Wise Use of Alternative Therapies*, Addison-Wesley (Reading, MA), 1996.
(With Sharon Curtin) *Comprehensive Cancer Care: Integrating Alternative, Complementary, and Conventional Therapies*, Perseus Publishing (Cambridge, MA), 2000.
*Unstuck: Your Guide to the Seven-Stage Journey Out of Depression*, Penguin Press (New York), 2008.

## Sources

### Books

*Complete Marquis Who's Who Biographies*, Marquis Who's Who LLC, 2008.

### Periodicals

*Daily News* (New York City), August 3, 1998, p. 27.
*Financial Post* (Toronto, Canada), December 14, 1996, sec. 2, p. 65.
*Life Extension*, December 1, 2008.
PR Newswire, July 13, 2000.
*Town & Country*, January 1, 1997, p. 97.
U.S. Newswire, March 13, 2000.
*Vegetarian Times*, February 1, 1997, p. 60; February 1, 1998, p. 60.
*Washingtonian*, February 1996, p. 68.
*Washington Times*, December 25, 2001, p. B1.

—*A. Petruso*

# Ron Graves

## Chief Executive Officer of Pinkberry

**B**orn c. 1967. *Education:* United States Air Force Academy, B.S., 1985; J. L. Kellogg School of Management, Northwestern University, M.B.A.

**Addresses:** *Office*—c/o 6310 San Vicente Blvd., Ste. 100, Los Angeles, CA 90048.

## Career

**S**erved as instructor pilot and F-16 fighter pilot, United States Air Force, 1985-95; general partner, Maveron Equity Partners, 1999—; member of board of directors, Auctionpay; interim chief executive, Pinkberry, October 2007-August 2008, chief executive officer, Pinkberry, August 2008—.

## Sidelights

**I**n 2008 Ron Graves was named the permanent chief executive officer of Pinkberry, the immensely successful frozen-yogurt chain launched in the Los Angeles area less than three years earlier. Graves came on board as part of Pinkberry's financing deal with Maveron Equity Partners, the venture-capital firm started by Starbucks founder Howard Schultz. Pinkberry's novel frozen treat ignited a craze in Southern California when it was first launched in 2006, with customers spending up to an hour in line to wait for its appealingly tart taste. Even celebrities such as Lindsay Lohan were spotted carrying Pinkberry paper cups and plastic spoons. "We're not out there trying to get people to endorse Pinkberry," Graves told *Seattle Times* journalist Joe Bel

Bruno. "It has been a natural phenomenon. We're focused on building the right infrastructure, growing in other regions, and building a fantastic company."

Graves graduated from the United States Air Force Academy in 1985 and went on to spend the next ten years as a U.S. Air Force officer. He was an instructor pilot and flew F-16 fighters before returning to civilian life. After earning his graduate business degree at Northwestern University's Kellogg School of Management, he joined Maveron Equity Partners in Seattle. Maveron was the brainchild of Schultz, who earned a fortune with his Starbucks coffee-to-go concept in the 1990s, to fund new businesses with similarly promising concepts.

At Maveron, Graves spent some time working with Auctionpay, a Portland, Oregon, company that made fund-raising software, before becoming involved with Pinkberry. Founded in Southern California in 2005, Pinkberry was the brainchild of Hyekyung "Shelly" Hwang, who had left South Korea more than a decade earlier to study business at the University of Southern California. She had already opened two food-service businesses, both of which failed, before teaming with Young Lee, also of Korean heritage and a graduate of the Parsons School of Design in New York City. They originally sought to open a tea parlor at the West Hollywood address they had leased, but their liquor license application was rejected by local zoning authorities. Instead they opened Pinkberry, which served frozen yogurt in just two flavors—plain and green tea—and billed itself as an all-natural healthy frozen treat.

Pinkberry's first store opened on Huntley Drive in a residential part of West Hollywood during a rainy January and endured some slow first weeks, but by the time Southern California's early summer weather arrived the location was buzzing with customers. The store became so popular, in fact, that nearby residents complained of parking issues and litter on their lawns from discarded Pinkberry paper containers. "The store was ordered to shorten its evening hours and place guards in front to help control the crowds," wrote Jennifer Steinhauer in the *New York Times*, adding that "Employees began to pick up litter."

Soon paparazzi photographers were following celebrities carrying the distinctive chartreuse and pink Pinkberry containers, and Hwang and Lee opened three more stores in Los Angeles and three in New York City between the fall of 2006 and the spring of 2007. They also entered into talks with Maveron, and a deal was struck in October of 2007 in which Maveron invested $27.5 million in the company for its expansion plans and Graves came on board as its Pinkberry's interim chief executive officer.

There were a few legal issues for Graves to sort out before Pinkberry reached its full brand potential. One was a class-action suit claiming that the company practiced deceptive advertising for touting its frozen yogurt as all-natural and nonfat. When pressed, Pinkberry revealed that its concoction contained 22 different ingredients besides yogurt; those ingredients include corn-syrup derivatives and others could be considered fillers, which are used to give the yogurt its shape. "In the company's early days some of its point-of-sale material contained the words 'all natural'—which was an honest mistake by the founders," Graves explained to *New*

*York Times* journalist Julia Moskin. "The yogurt used was 'all natural,' which was the source of confusion." There was also an issue with the level of active yogurt cultures in its product, which the California Department of Food and Agriculture required before it could be sold as yogurt; the company stopped using the word "yogurt" in its marketing materials for a time but was re-certified by the state's food bureau in the spring of 2008.

Graves became Pinkberry's permanent CEO in August of 2008, just before some of the chain's California stores rolled out Granita, a new yogurt-shake product. By the end of that year there were 72 Pinkberry stores across the United States. Scores of imitators had cropped up by then, including Kiwiberry, Fiore, Snowberry, and BerriGood, but most of the competition was confined to the Southern California area. Celebrities such as Paris Hilton and Jerry Seinfeld were known to be Pinkberry fans, and Graves told *Los Angeles Business Journal* writer Daniel Miller that he, too, eats it daily. He likened the pace of growing a company to flying fighter jets, telling Miller, "There is a lot of adrenaline with the early stages of a startup."

## Sources

*Financial Times*, August 1, 2007, p. 12.
*Fortune*, May 28, 2007, p. 20.
*Los Angeles Business Journal*, June 19, 2006, p. 16; May 19, 2008, p. 3.
*New York Times*, February 21, 2007; April 23, 2008.
*New York Times Magazine*, September 5, 2008, p. 32.
*Seattle Times*, August 20, 2008, p. C1.

—*Carol Brennan*

# Josh Groban

## Singer

**B**orn February 27, 1981, in Los Angeles, CA; son of Jack (an executive headhunter and corporate recruiter) and Lindy (an art teacher) Groban. *Education:* Attended Carnegie Mellon University

**Addresses:** *Agent*—Special Artists Agency, 9465 Wilshire Blvd., Ste. 890, Beverly Hills, CA 90212. *Contact*—c/o Studio Fan Mail, 1122 S. Robertson #15, Los Angeles, CA 90035.

## Career

**P**erformer at the inauguration ceremonies of Governor Gray Davis, 1999; released first album, *Josh Groban*, 2001; appeared on the television series, *Ally McBeal*, FOX, 2001; appeared on television special, *A Home for the Holidays with Mariah Carey*, 2001; performer at closing ceremonies of the Winter Olympics, Salt Lake City, UT, 2002; appeared in episode of *Great Performances*, PBS, 2003; released number-one album *Closer*, 2003; headlined first tour beginning in 2004; released record-breaking Christmas album, *Noel*, 2007.

## Sidelights

**S**inger Josh Groban performs a popular pop sound greatly influenced by classical and opera music. On number-one albums like 2001's *Josh Groban*, he sang power ballads with an operatic touch. A baritone, Groban is the protégé of well-known producer David Foster and is often compared to Italian opera/pop singer and tenor Andrea Bocelli. Though Groban receives limited airplay on

the radio, his music attracts legions of loyal fans, many of them female, who have dubbed themselves "Grobanites." Of his passionate music which attracts such fans, Groban told Kimberly Cutter of *W*, "I definitely wear my heart on my sleeve."

Born on February 27, 1981, in Los Angeles, California, he is the son of Jack and Lindy Groban. His father was an executive headhunter and corporate recruiter, while his mother was an art teacher who loved the theater and shared her interest with her son. Attracted to music from an early age, Groban was first fascinated by show tunes. He particularly liked show tunes by Stephen Sondheim. Desiring to make music as well, Groban first tried piano and drums.

When Groban was in seventh grade, he tried singing for the first time when a teacher asked if someone could demonstrate scat. Groban went on to perform a scat number at the school's talent show. His parents encouraged but did not push his interests, and he soon began taking voice lessons. To gain the education needed to have his desired career in musical theater, Groban attended the High School for the Arts in Los Angeles. He also studied at the famed Interlochen Arts Academy at least one summer, making his stage debut in a production of *Sweeney Todd*.

After earning his high school diploma, Groban entered Carnegie Mellon University where he studied musical theater. He dropped out after a semester when well-known producer David Foster—who worked with the likes of Celine Dion, Chicago, and Earth Wind & Fire—learned about Groban through his vocal coach, Seth Riggs, as he looked for performers for the inauguration ceremonies for California governor Gray Davis in 1999. Groban stunned the audience with his performance there of "All I Ask of You" from *Phantom of the Opera*. Groban told Renee Fleming of *Interview* that he "ended up performing for 20,000 people in a basketball arena with a full orchestra. It was an experience unlike any I'd ever had before. I was walking on air."

Also in 1999, Foster asked Groban to sub for tenor Andrea Bocelli at Grammy rehearsals. The host of Grammys, Rosie O'Donnell, heard Groban and invited him to appear on her talk show. She dubbed him "Opera Boy," a label which caused Groban to cringe. He told the *Irish Times*, "Oh God! When I heard that I thought, that's gonna stick. That's gonna leave a mark."

While Groban evaded being stuck with the label, this appearance led to further opportunities for him, including a role on two episodes of the hit television series *Ally McBeal* in 2001. He played an agoraphobic high school student with an extraordinary voice which is shown off in a climatic prom scene in his first appearance and in an afterlife anthem in the second. The show's executive producer, Bill D'Elia, told *Entertainment Weekly*'s Chris Willman, "We expanded his part once we realized he could act. I don't think even Josh realized he could act."

Foster also had signed Groban to his label, 143 Records, early on, but it took several years to figure out how to best package Groban's greatest gift: his voice. Groban released his self-titled first album in 2001. *Josh Groban* sold more than 5.3 million copies, in part because of his affiliation with *Ally McBeal* and other television appearances. His album featured power ballads as well as several songs in Italian, and included a duet with Charlotte Church, "The Prayer." It also produced the hit single "To Where You Are."

Building on the success of *Josh Groban*, he released a live version of the album packaged with a DVD of a concert in 2002, *Josh Groban in Concert*, which sold more than a half million copies. That same year, Groban was a performer in the closing ceremonies of the Winter Olympics in Salt Lake City, Utah, again stunning an audience estimated at one billion worldwide with his performance of "The Prayer" with Church. Soon after his fanatical devotees, the "Grobanites," created a fantasy world, dubbed Grobania, with its own theme song and flag, which featured the curly haired singer in front of a fairy-tale type castle. The zealous Grobanites followed his every move.

Groban released his third album in 2003, *Closer*, the first to feature songs co-written by the artist. The album reached number one on the *Billboard* album charts, sold at least 4.1 million copies, and was certified multiplatinum. He told Tom Nawrocki of *Rolling Stone*, "Number One is not something I thought I'd ever see. I was happy at Number Ten. I was happy the day my dad walked into my room and said, 'You're at Number 149. Congratulations.'"

Still covering both pop and classical territories, the album was musically more ambitious but with a deeper sense of artistry. *Closer*'s first single, "You Raise Me Up," reached the top ten on *Billboard*'s Adult Contemporary chart. Groban himself favored a cover of Don McLean's "Vincent (Starry Starry Night)." Among the album's classical pieces is Bach's "Jesu, Joy of Man's Desiring," done with Lili Haydn. Other tracks were sung in French (a cover of Edith Piaf's "Hymne A L'amour"), Italian, and Spanish. Critics praised the album, with Susanne Ault of *Billboard* commenting, "His majestic bald eagle of a voice flies at incredible speeds, across a variety of challenging terrain.... Still, these songs roll out more as glowing epic film scores than simple tracks on a disc."

Groban's then-voice teacher, opera singer David Romano, greatly influenced how he trained his voice and the musical choices he made. Groban told the *New York Times*' Matthew Gurewitsch, "He's very good at teaching all kinds of vocal styles. He knows voices. Deep down, his specialty is classical. I wanted to work with him, to have that training, to develop a legit classical technique. I know when I wake up in the morning and sing that my voice isn't suited for rock 'n' roll.... But I also love writing music, experimenting with different genres."

In 2004, as *Closer* reached the top of the *Billboard* album charts, Groban headlined his first solo tour and performed his first full-length concerts ever. Many of the shows in the United States sold out in minutes, with scalpers charging more than double the face value for tickets. The shows on this international tour included songs which did not make his albums, such as his lauded take on hard-rock band Linkin Park's "My December."

Groban was impressed by the range of his fans showing up on tour, not just the hardcore, female Grobanites. He told Jon Bream of Minneapolis *Star Tribune,* "It's so diverse; it really makes me happy. One my goals was to reach my own peers as well." Groban ultimately spent about two years on the road in support of *Closer.*

Groban followed *Closer* with another live album, 2004's *Live at the Greek,* and a studio album, 2005's *Awake.* For the latter, Groban wanted to do something different while still melding pop and classical. He told Chuck Taylor of the *Grand Rapids Press,* "I realized at the start of this album that I had a blank canvas. And I found my mission: This was not about being anything that I'm not—it's about not being afraid to be everything that I am."

On *Awake,* Groban collaborated with such artists as Ladysmith Black Mambazo, Herbie Hancock, Dave Matthews, and Five for Fighting's John Ondrasik for more challenging tracks. Groban also co-wrote four songs on *Closer,* including the sad "February Song." He continued to sing in Italian on songs like the critically praised "Un Giorno Per Noi (Romeo & Guilietta)." *Billboard*'s Taylor wrote "this collection proves that the momentous talent is just finding his footing."

Groban spent another two years touring in support of *Awake.* In 2007, he recorded and released his first Christmas album, *Noel.* The album sold at least 6.6 million copies in the United States alone, and was number one on the *Billboard* Adult Contemporary Charts for at least a month. By topping the *Billboard* album charts for more than five weeks, it set a record, surpassing Elvis Presley's *Elvis Christmas,* which had been number one for three weeks in 1957. *Noel* ultimately became the best-selling album of 2007.

In the spring of 2008, Groban released his second live compact disc/DVD *Awake Live.* He also was named of the "most beautiful" people in *People* magazine. Groban told Nekesa Mumbi Moody of the *Grand Rapids Press,* "For me, the whole beauty and the whole idea of people saying you're beautiful or you're not is not something I generally paid attention to. But I was very, very honored that they included me in their issue."

In addition, Groban broke out of his squeaky clean public image and showed his humorous side by appearing in a spoof video featuring Jimmy Kimmel and Ben Affleck which was a hit on YouTube. In the piece, Groban plays piano and sings in his usual broad voice, but with more explicit lyrics. Of the bit, he told Moody in the *Grand Rapids Press,* "It's definitely my kind of humor, and I thought it would be really fun…. I hope soon to do something like that in the future." He did just that when he performed at the 2008 Emmy Awards, singing a medley of more than 25 television theme songs in little more than four minutes.

Despite all his success as a singer, Groban also hoped to have career perhaps singing legitimate opera, but more definitely musical theater on Broadway. He longed for roles in such classics as *Sweeney Todd* and *Sunday in the Park with George,* but was open to any possibilities. Groban told the *Irish Times,* "The combining of a great lyric with an amazing melody, a great book, amazing acting and storytelling can touch an audience like nothing else." While he made his Broadway debut in 2003 with a one-night benefit performance in a production of *Chess,* Groban still hoped to have a longer stint in a role.

No matter what happens with his singing career, Groban and his voice are highly regarded. Broadway legend Barbara Cook told Gurewitsch in the *New York Times,* "Some people just have a natural connection with their voice, with their emotional barrel. Rosemary Clooney had that. Josh Groban has it, too, in spades. It's amazing to me that someone of that age can communicate so well, with so much emotion and such wonderful musical instinct. And he has that ability to sustain the line, which so many young people don't have. … There's great intelligence there, an ability not to overdo things, just to be there."

## Selected discography

*Josh Groban,* 143/Reprise, 2001.
*Josh Groban in Concert,* Warner Bros., 2002.
*Closer,* Reprise, 2003.
*Live at the Greek,* Reprise, 2004.
*Awake,* Reprise, 2005.
*Noel,* Reprise, 2007.
*Awake Live,* Reprise, 2008.

## Sources

### Books

*Complete Marquis Who's Who Biographies,* Marquis Who's Who, 2008.

## Periodicals

*Billboard,* December 6, 2003, pp. 1, 35; January 24, 2004, p. 53; November 18, 2006, p. 55; July 12, 2008, p. 15.

Business Wire, October 21, 2003; November 6, 2003.

*Daily Variety,* April 25, 2003, p. 4.

*Entertainment Weekly,* March 8, 2002, p. 32; May 16, 2008, p. 16.

*Grand Rapids Press* (Grand Rapids, MI), November 21, 2006, p. E4; May 8, 2008, p. B9.

Internet Wire, December 19, 2007.

*Interview,* March 2004, p. 140.

*Irish Times* (Dublin, Ireland), April 12, 2003, p. 56.

*New York Times,* July 28, 2002, p. AR25.

*People,* June 17, 2002, p. 116; December 30, 2002, p. 134; June 21, 2004, p. 117.

*Record* (Bergen County, NJ), July 22, 2007, p. F1.

*San Francisco Chronicle,* January 17, 2002, p. D1.

*Seattle Post-Intelligencer* (Seattle, WA), January 23, 2004. p. 3.

*Star Tribune* (Minneapolis, MN), February 6, 2004, p. 1E.

UPI NewsTrack, December 27, 2007.

*W,* October 2003, p. 238.

## Online

"Josh Groban: Discography," *Rolling Stone,* http://www.rollingstone.com/artists/joshgroban/discography (August 14, 2008).

"Opera Boy," *Rolling Stone,* http://www.rollingstone.com/artists/joshgroban/articles/story/5940000/opera_boy (August 14, 2008).

—*A. Petruso*

# Abdullah Gul

## President of Turkey

**B**orn October 29, 1950, in Kayseri, Kayseri province, Turkey; son of Ahmet Hamdi (an aviation mechanic) and Adviye (maiden name, Satoglu) Gul; married Hayrünissa Özyurt, August 20, 1980; children: Ahmet Münir (son), Kübra (daughter), Mehmet Emre (son). *Education:* Earned degree in economics from Istanbul University, 1971; postgraduate work at London University; Istanbul University, Ph. D., 1983.

**Addresses:** *Office*—Cumhurbaşkanliği Genel Sekreterliği Yürütume ve Koordinasyon Başkanligi, 06689 Çankaya, Ankara, Turkey.

## Career

**I**nstructor in management, Istanbul Technical University—Sakarya University, 1980-83; economist, Islamic Development Bank, 1983-91; associate professor of international economics, Instanbul University, 1991—; elected to the Grand National Assembly of Turkey on Welfare Party ticket, 1991; reelected 1995, 1999 (Virtue Party), 2003 (AK Party), and 2007 (AK Party); co-founder, AK Party, 2001; prime minister of Turkey, November 2002-March 2003; minister of foreign affairs, March 2003-August 2007; elected president of Turkey by the Grand National Assembly, August 2007.

## Sidelights

**A**bdullah Gul became president of Turkey in August of 2007 following a period of intense debate about his suitability for the office. Turkey's con-

stitution expressly forbids any form of religious influence on the public sphere as a strategy to prevent the state from being overtaken by a strict, Islamic-centered code of law, and gives the army broad powers to intervene. Yet Gul is a supporter of secularist values as well as a strong champion of Turkey's bid to join the European Union. Writing of the new president and his longtime political associate, prime minister Recep Tayyip Erdoğan, the *Guardian*'s Stephen Kinzer asserted that the pair "have led a political revolution that has brought Turkey closer to democracy than any regime in the modern state's 85-year history."

The son of an aircraft mechanic, Gul was born in 1950 in Kayseri, a city in the Central Anatolian region of Turkey whose name reflects its Roman and Byzantine roots as the Turkish version of "caesar." Kayseri was once the intersection of ancient trade routes, and during Gul's youth the city became home to several thriving manufacturing enterprises, along with other Anatolian urban areas, that brought substantial growth to the region.

At Istanbul University, Gul became active in the National Turkish Students' Union, a conservative group with an Islamist outlook. Taken from the term "Islamism," Islamist refers to the promotion of Muslim values as a political ideology. Gul was also drawn to the writings of Necip Fazil Kisakürek, a well-known Turkish poet who objected to the rapid modernization that the country had undertaken since the end of the Ottoman Empire at the close of World War I. Kisakürek asserted that adopting European political systems and cultural standards was ruining Turkey's national character and compromising its deep-rooted Muslim values.

After graduating from Istanbul University with a degree in economics in 1971, Gul spent two years studying at the universities of London and Exeter, and returned to Istanbul University to earn a doctorate in his field. He also taught for a time at a new campus of Istanbul Technical University that eventually became Sakarya University in the city of the same name in northwestern Turkey. Upon earning his Ph.D. in 1983, he took a job as an economist with the Islamic Development Bank at its headquarters in Jeddah, Saudi Arabia, and spent the next several years working on various projects undertaken by the bank, which funds major infrastructure and entrepreneurial ventures throughout the Middle East.

Returning to Turkey, Gul became a professor of international economics and joined the Refah Partisi (RP), or the Welfare Party, an Islamist organization that sought increased ties to Turkey's Muslim neighbors in the Middle East and North Africa. In 1991 he stood for and won election to the country's parliament, the 550-member Grand National Assembly of Turkey, on the RP ticket. He became the RP's deputy chair for foreign affairs in 1993 and held various committee assignments within the Assembly and the Council of Europe. In 1995, he and his fellow RP candidates were favored by a strong surge of voter support for the party and its leader, Necmettin Erbakan. The RP formed a coalition government with another party in 1996 amidst intense political turmoil, and Gul was appointed to the posts of government spokesperson and minister of state.

Gul's party was the first Islamist organization to form a government in Turkey's modern era, but was ousted by a military coup after just a year in office. Turkey's constitution features strong wording concerning secularism, or the principle that religion has no role in political or civic affairs. This was the belief of Mustafa Kemal Atatürk, the man considered the founder of modern Turkey, who asserted that centuries of Muslim-anchored Ottoman Empire rule had effectively kept the nation a backward, impoverished land at the edge of a prosperous, industrialized Europe. Atatürk looked to the West for inspiration, and carried out a drastic reform program upon taking office as president in 1923.

Turkey's constitution allows the military broad powers to intervene in the event that the country's secular principles are deemed to be under threat, or those of its democratic core are threatened by extremists on the far left or far right. The military has intervened on four occasions, the last of which was in 1997 when Erbakan and the RP were ousted. A year later, Turkey's constitutional court outlawed the RP altogether. In 1999, Gul stood for and won reelection to parliament as a candidate of the Fazilet Partisi (FP), or the Virtue Party. It, too, was outlawed by Turkey's constitutional court and forced to disband in 2001.

In August of 2001, Gul and Recep Tayyip Erdoğan, along with other former FP members, founded the Adalet ve Kalkinma (Justice and Development) Party. The party is also known by its acronym AK, which is the Turkish word for white, or pure. Erdoğan was a former mayor of Istanbul who had once famously asserted that to be both secular and Muslim was impossible. These ideas had been gaining ground since the 1980s in Turkey and were a reflection of a shift in the country's center of economic power. Beginning in the Atatürk era, Turkey's political and economic spheres had been dominated by a cultural elite who, while Muslim, considered themselves more European in outlook than their less-progressive counterparts outside of Istanbul. This began to change in the 1980s and '90s, when Gul's hometown and other cities in the broad swath of provinces in the country's center, Anatolia, began to experience impressive economic growth. The prosperity created a new middle class voter who supported the Islamist principles of parties like the RP, FP and, finally, the AK.

The AK picked up several new National Assembly seats in the November of 2002 elections, but because Erdoğan had been convicted on charges of stirring religious hatred in 1998, he was barred from political office and thus from assuming the post of prime minister. Gul was appointed instead, and served until March of 2003, when the Assembly permitted Erdoğan to run for a seat in a by-election and assume the office of prime minister. Erdoğan then made Gul foreign minister and also deputy prime minister.

Gul became foreign minister at a dramatic time in international relations, when the United States sought and received permission to use Turkish air bases as a staging ground for the invasion of Iraq. Public opinion in Turkey was sharply divided on the issue, with some believing it was inappropriate to allow a superpower to use Turkish resources to attack a Muslim population. Turkey was also angling to join the European Union (EU), and Gul was instrumental in setting up the formal membership negotiation talks that began in 2005. Though these alliances with the West seemed at odds with an Islamist party, a still-vocal secularist movement in the country viewed Erdoğan's AK Party as having "a hidden agenda which, once revealed, will show the AK Party in its true colour: an intense Islamic green," explained the *Economist*. The secular opponents of the AK, the article continued, "sincerely believe that it is merely using the prospect of EU membership to reduce the power of the armed forces before turning the country into an Islamic state, something akin to Iran."

In Turkey, the prime minister serves as head of government while the president is considered the head of state. The president, elected by a minimum of a two-thirds majority of the National Assembly, must give up his party allegiance and seat in the Assembly upon taking office for a five-year term. In April of 2007, Erdoğan announced Gul's candidacy in the coming presidential election. This prompted vociferous protests from the main opposition party, the Cumhuriyet Halk Partisi (CHP), or Republican People's Party, a center-left party founded by Atatürk. The CHP asserted it would boycott the presidential election in the National Assembly, and Gul withdrew his candidacy for a few days. As a compromise, Erdoğan announced new parliamentary elections to be held in July, and the AK lost a few seats, but so did the CHP. In August, Gul stood as the AK's presidential candidate, and won the balloting on the third round.

Gul's candidacy stirred intense debate in Turkey for two reasons. The first concerned his Islamist background, which seemed to some to place him at odds with the role of the president to safeguard the principles of the constitution. The other issue was the fact that his wife wore a traditional headscarf, or hijab, that has long been the common practice in more devout Muslim countries and in some cases even decreed compulsory by genuine Islamist regimes. Turkish law, by contrast, prohibits the wearing of religious attire in public and government buildings. Women wearing the hijab are barred from entering schools and universities, courts of law, and other government properties. This extends to the National Assembly and even the presidential palace, and women are not even allowed to have their passport or other identification photos taken while wearing the hijab.

Gul wed Hayrünissa, his wife, in 1980, when he was 30 and she was 15. In 2002, the mother of three filed a legal motion attempting to have the ban on wearing the hijab at the university level overturned when she wanted to return to school. She petitioned the European Court of Human Rights, but was forced to abandon her cause when her husband became foreign minister and was thus responsible for arguing Turkey's case for the defense.

When the AK announced Gul's candidacy for president, top military officials in Turkey reacted with strongly worded statements that international observers considered a harbinger of another military coup. A day before the August election, Army chief of staff Yaşar Büyükanit issued a statement claiming that "our nation has been watching the behaviour of centres of evil who systematically try to corrode the secular nature of the Turkish Republic," according to Donald Macintyre, Ankara correspondent for the London *Independent*. "Nefarious plans to ruin Turkey's secular and democratic nature emerge in different forms every day. The military will, just as it has so far, keep its determination to guard social, democratic, and secular Turkey."

While top military officials remained conspicuously absent at Gul's swearing-in ceremony as president on August 28, 2007—as did his wife, who is not permitted to enter the National Assembly building—the powerful cadre of top army brass did seem to back down from their threats. Gul, meanwhile, asserted his commitment to secularist principles. "We have been going through a period in which we have been able to show the world just how mature Turkey's democracy has become," he said in his first speech before the National Assembly, according to *Times* of London journalist Suna Erdem. "I will embrace all my citizens without discrimination and carefully guard my impartiality."

Gul, Erdoğan, and the AK still faced strong opposition from the CHP and other political groups. There was an attempt to outlaw the AK and ban its founders from political office, but this was rejected by Turkey's constitutional court as Gul's one-year anniversary as president neared. Both this and the backing off of the army were deemed milestones in the history of modern Turkey, the *New York Times* declared in an editorial describing this as the triumph of democracy in the nation of 71 million. "Had it gone the other way, Turkey's chances of joining the European Union would have been demolished and the clearly expressed will of Turkish voters outrageously thwarted," the paper asserted.

One of Gul's other main duties as president was to represent Turkey on the international stage. In interviews with the Western media, he has voiced his hope that Turkey will serve as a beacon to the rest of the Muslim world as a place where democracy and Islam can indeed flourish concurrently. "I wish to see Turkey as an island where the European standard of democracy is being fulfilled and the free market economy is functioning very well," he told Kinzer in the *Guardian* interview. "This will be a real gift to the region, to the world, for peace. And this Turkey will be a source of inspiration for so many."

## Sources

*Economist*, March 19, 2005, p. 7; May 12, 2007, p. 64.
*Guardian* (London, England), August 16, 2008, p. 26.
*Independent* (London, England), August 28, 2007.
*Newsweek International*, September 3, 2007.
*New York Times*, August 3, 2008.
*Time International*, September 10, 2007, p. 9.
*Times* (London, England), August 29, 2007, p. 25; July 18, 2008, p. 4.

*—Carol Brennan*

# Guo Jingjing

**Diver**

**B**orn October 15, 1981, in Baoding, Hebei, China. *Education:* Attended Beijing University.

**Addresses:** *Contact*—Chinese Olympic Committee, Beijing, China.

## Career

**B**egan diving at the age of seven; made the Chinese national team, c. 1992; won synchronized platform diving event at the World Cup, 1995; Olympic debut, Summer Games in Atlanta, GA, 1996; silver medal, 3 meter springboard competition, World Championships, 1998; won 3 meter springboard competition, Asian Games, 1999; won 3 meter springboard competition, FINA Grand Prix Superfinal, 1999; silver medals, 3 meter springboard and synchro springboard diving events, Summer Olympics in Sydney, Australia, 2000; won the 3 meter springboard event, FINA Grand Prix Superfinals, 2000, 2001; won gold medals in 3 meter springboard and 3 meter synchro springboard, World Championships, 2000, 2001, 2005, 2007; won gold medals in 3 meter springboard and 3 meter synchro springboard events, 2004 Summer Olympic Games, Athens, Greece; briefly removed from China's national team, 2004; won gold medals in 3 meter springboard and 3 meter synchro springboard events, Summer Olympic Games, Beijing, China, 2008.

## Sidelights

**A** multiple medal-winning member of three Chinese women's Olympic diving teams, Guo Jingjing was nearly undefeated in every major world competition after the 2000 summer games in Sydney, Australia. Competing in 3 meter springboard and 3 meter synchro springboard, she was praised for her diving technique. Guo was one of the most famous athletes in China, had a number of endorsements, and earned more money than any Chinese female athlete. However, she also sometimes suffered from unwanted attention. As her former coach Yu Fen told Martin Zhou of the *South China Morning Post* before the 2008 Summer Olympics, "On the one hand, the fact that Guo remains the star attraction puts her under extraordinary media scrutiny. On the other hand, people think she is a princess—spoiled by pampering coaches and team officials. It seems she is a bit disoriented by being sandwiched in between."

Guo was born on October 15, 1981, in Baoding, Hebei, China. When she was seven years old, she began diving. She was selected to train by her first coach, Yu Fen—who had made his reputation by coaching diving phenom Fu Mingxia—while he toured elementary schools to find potential athletes. Guo spent up to nine hours a day training at a national sports school, and made the national team at the age of eleven.

By 1995, Guo was competing internationally. That year, she won the synchronized platform event at the World Cup. She made her Olympic debut in the 1996 Atlanta Games, and competed fifth in the 10 meter platform competition. Guo also made a coaching change in this time period. Yu retired after the Atlanta Games, and Guo's new coach became Zhou Jihong, who had won the first diving gold for China in 1984.

As she reached maturity and gained weight, it was harder for Guo to dive with the same grace off the 10 meter platform. She switched to springboard and took a silver medal in the 1998 World Championships in the 3 meter springboard competition. Guo also won the 3 meter springboard at the Asian Games that year, and the FINA Grand Prix Superfinal in 1999.

In the 2000 Summer Olympic Games in Sydney, Australia, Guo won two silvers in springboard and synchro springboard diving events. She competed in synchro with Fu, who retired later that year. (Guo then took on Wu Minxia as her partner.) After the games ended, Guo was forced to spend a few months not training because she had to have surgery to fix a detached retina. This condition was common among divers because of the impact of repeatedly hitting the water.

Guo then became ascendant in international events. In the 2000 and 2001 FINA Grand Prix Superfinals, she won the 3 meter springboard event. At the 2001 and 2003 World Championships, Guo started dominating, winning golds in both 3 meter springboard and 3 meter synchro springboard with Wu. At the 2004 Summer Olympic Games in Athens, Greece, Guo won gold medals in both springboard and synchro springboard diving events. After winning the gold, Guo was quoted by Meredith May in the *San Francisco Chronicle* as saying, "It's what I expected." May added that on Guo's last dive for the 3 meter springboard competition, "Her domination was so complete, it didn't even matter that she over-rotated and washed out slightly...."

Because of such victories, Guo became a celebrity in China and her every move was scrutinized. She appeared in numerous television commercials for a glucose drink, McDonald's, and Budweiser. Guo was also a brand ambassador for McDonald's. Guo

was criticized for focusing on sponsors and commercial-related interests because it was believed that she was not spending enough time practicing diving.

For her part, Guo was not particularly interested in fame and was sometimes uncomfortable with the attention she received. She was more concerned with her studies at Beijing University's school of physical education and with her training. Some of the celebrity also came from Guo's relationship with fellow Olympic diver Tian Liang, whom she began dating before the 2004 Olympic Games. Like Guo, Tian won gold at Athens, and the pair was seen as a diving super couple until the relationship ended later that year. While Tian eventually married someone else, Guo was later linked to Kenneth Fok, the grandson of a Hong Kong-based business mogul.

At the end of 2004, Guo was removed from the team because of her many activities outside of diving. She disappeared from the spotlight for a few months and took a break at home. After apologizing to authorities and being reinstated on the team, she told *South China Morning Post*, "Earlier on, I attended public functions and starred in advertisements. These are even more tiring than going through training and competitions. Adding to my fatigue is the load of fabricated stuff that has been imposed upon me. Now that I am back in training, I am sure things will get better."

Such concerns proved unwarranted as Guo continued to overshadow her competition, winning golds in both of her events at the 2005 and 2007 World Championships; however, at the 2008 Worlds, she finished second in the 3 meter springboard event, and there were concerns about her ability to compete in that summer's Olympic Games. As China prepared to host the 2008 Summer Games in Beijing where Guo was expected to dominate, it was rumored that Guo was pregnant and unable to compete. The rumor proved false and Guo repeated as champion at the Summer Olympic Games held in her home country. At the Beijing games, Guo won gold medals in both of her events.

After the Beijing games, there were many rumors that Guo was going to retire. There was also talk that she might move to Hong Kong with her longtime boyfriend Fok. For her part, Guo was happy to just take a break before resuming training again. Tom Weir of *USA Today* quoted her as saying after her gold medal-winning performances, "I suffered a lot of frustrations. I have given a lot, and I have suffered a lot." Guo dispelled the retirement rumors in September of 2008, telling Chinadaily.com.cn, "I am not calling it quits. I have not thought about retirement. I still have many things to do as a member of the Chinese diving team."

# Sources

## Books

Commire, Anne, and Deborah Klezmer, eds., *Dictionary of Women Worldwide: 25,000 Women Through the Ages,* Vol. 1, Yorkin Publications (Detroit, MI), 2007.

## Periodicals

*Guardian Unlimited,* August 10, 2008.
*San Francisco Chronicle,* August 27, 2004, p. D11.
*South China Morning Post,* August 9, 2004, p. 10; September 30, 2004, p. 1; December 2, 2004, p. 5; July 31, 2008, p. 21.

*Straits Times* (Singapore), September 5, 2004; August 2, 2008.
*Sydney Morning Herald* (Australia), August 18, 2008, p. 7.
*Times* (London, England), August 9, 2008, p. 74.
*USA Today,* August 18, 2008, p. 8D.
*Windsor Star* (Ontario, Canada), August 8, 2007, p. B1.

## Online

"Guo Jingjing Profile & Bio, Photos & Videos," NBC Olympics, http://www.nbcolympics.com/athletes/athlete=694/bio/ (October 26, 2008).
"Guo Not Done Making a Big Splash," Chinadaily. com.cn (September 19, 2008).
"In the Spotlight: Guo Jingjing, China," *WashingtonPost.com,* http://www.washingtonpost .com/wp-dyn/content/article/2008/08/04/ AR20080804.tif 02620.html (October 26, 2008).

*—A. Petruso*

# Sanjay Gupta

*AP Images*

## Surgeon and news correspondent

**B**orn October 23, 1969, in Novi, Michigan; son of Subhash and Damyanti Gupta (both engineers); married Rebecca Olson (an attorney), May 15, 2004; children: Sage, Sky, Soleil. *Education:* University of Michigan, B.S., 1990; University of Michigan Medical School, M.D., 1993.

**Addresses:** *Office*—Emory University School of Medicine, Neurological Surgery, 80 Jesse Hill Dr. SE, Faculty Office Bldg. #339, Atlanta, GA 30303. *Office*—Cable News Network, One CNN Ctr. NW, Atlanta, GA 30303.

## Career

**W**hite House Fellow, 1997; private practice physician, Great Lakes Brain and Spine Institute, Michigan, 2000-01; news correspondent, Cable News Network (CNN), Atlanta, 2001—; chief medical correspondent, health and medical unit, CNN, 2001—; assistant professor, department of neurological surgery, Emory University School of Medicine, Atlanta, 2001—; associate chief of neurosurgery services, Grady Memorial Hospital, Atlanta, 2001—; published *Chasing Life: New Discoveries in the Search for Immortality to Help You Age Less Today,* Wellness Center, 2007.

**Member:** American Association of Neurological Surgeons; Congress of Neurological Surgeons; Council of Foreign Relations; board member, Lance Armstrong LiveStrong Foundation.

**Awards:** "Sexiest Men Alive," *People* magazine, 2003; "Pop Culture Icon," *USA Today,* 2003; Humanitarian Award, National Press Photographers Association, 2003; journalist of the year, Atlanta Press Club, 2004; Emmy Award, Academy of Television Arts and Sciences, for "Charity Hospital," 2006; National Headliner Award, first place—health reporting, Press Club of Atlantic City, for "Killer Flu," 2006; GOLD Award, National Health Care Communicators.

## Sidelights

**I**n 2001, CNN hired Sanjay Gupta to report medical stories for the cable news network. Since then, the highly telegenic neurosurgeon has become a popular television personality whose roles as journalist and doctor often overlap. In 2003, Gupta gained notoriety for performing emergency brain surgery on an Iraqi boy while reporting on military medical doctors working the front lines in Iraq. Gupta's 2005 coverage of Hurricane Katrina's aftermath at a local New Orleans hospital earned him an Emmy Award. Along the way, Gupta began writing a medical column for *Time* magazine, making him one of the most widely read and seen U.S. journalists. In 2008, the Obama administration approached Gupta and asked him to become the nation's surgeon general, a position Gupta turned down so he could spend more time with his family and in the operating room.

Those who know Gupta are not surprised by his dual success as a doctor and journalist. "We all know smart doctors, but they're not compassionate and empathetic," Emory Hospital doctor Daniel L. Barrow told Jill Vejnoska of the *Atlanta Journal-Constitution.* "He possesses all those qualities that make a physician truly outstanding. And frankly, those are the necessary qualities to make a good reporter."

Gupta is of Indian descent. The oldest of two boys, he was born on October 23, 1969, in the Detroit suburb of Novi. His parents, Subhash and Damyanti Gupta, were born and raised in India. Both worked as engineers at the Ford Motor Co. Gupta's mother was the first female engineer hired by the automaker. Growing up, Gupta was interested in medicine and acting. After graduating from Novi High School in 1986, Gupta attended the University of Michigan. He earned his undergraduate degree in 1990 and his medical degree in 1993, then stayed on to complete his residency at the university's hospital.

In 1997, Gupta was selected to serve as a White House Fellow, allowing him the opportunity to develop his leadership skills while working alongside high-ranking government officials. As a fellow, Gupta assisted then-First Lady Hillary Rodham Clinton, who was busy promoting the president's health-care reform package. Gupta helped the First Lady write healthcare speeches. As a result, he left the White House with a deep-rooted interest in health-care policy and continued writing about the topic.

Gupta moved to Atlanta in 2001 to work as a part-time CNN medical correspondent, a part-time neurosurgeon at Grady Memorial Hospital, and a part-time professor at the Emory University School of Medicine. When he was not in surgery or teaching, Gupta covered breaking news that dealt with medical situations. Soon, he became a regular on CNN's *American Morning* and began hosting a weekend medical program called *House Call With Dr. Sanjay Gupta.*

In 2003, Gupta traveled to the Middle East to report on the U.S. Navy's mobile surgical unit called the "Devil Docs." He caused a stir when he added himself into the storyline, performing brain surgery on an Iraqi boy, age 2. The boy, who later died, was injured when he was shot by Marines after the taxi he was riding in failed to stop at a U.S. checkpoint. Some industry insiders felt he overstepped his bounds. Gupta filed two live reports for CNN concerning the surgery.

According to the *Globe and Mail,* the Poynter Institute's Bob Steele was concerned about Gupta's dual role-playing. "I think it's problematic if this is a role that he's going to be playing on any kind of frequent basis," Steele said. "I don't think he should be reporting on it if he's also a participant. He can't bring appropriate journalistic independence and detachment to a story." Gupta, however, maintained that he was "medically and morally obligated" to help, according to Julie Hinds of the *Detroit Free Press.* Gupta also saved the life of an injured U.S. Marine by removing a bullet from his brain.

In December of 2004, Gupta traveled to Sri Lanka to report on the tsunami that caused more than 155,000 deaths. In 2005, he covered Hurricane Katrina. Traveling by boat to New Orleans' Charity Hospital five days after the hurricane struck, Gupta arrived to discover more than 200 patients and staff members trapped in the flooded hospital, though reports indicated the site had been evacuated. On the air, Gupta offered jarring details of the situation, noting the facility was without electricity or water and that because the basement morgue had flooded, bodies sat in the stairwells. Gupta earned a 2006 Emmy Award for his report, which also contributed to CNN winning a Peabody Award for its hurricane coverage.

During his tenure with CNN, Gupta has produced several medical documentaries, including 2006's "Quake Zone," which dealt with a Pakistani earthquake; 2006's "Killer Flu," which discussed avian flu; 2007's "Sleep," an exploration of sleep; and "Blood Spilled," which documented the challenges faced by wounded Iraqi veterans. In 2008, he launched into the presidential campaign with "First Patient" and "Fit to Lead," which examined the toll of being president and the health of the presidential candidates.

Gupta also published a book, *Chasing Life: New Discoveries in the Search for Immortality to Help You Age Less Today* (2007). "I've always been fascinated with the idea of immortality," he told Emiliana Sandoval of the *Detroit Free Press.* "I think science is moving at breakneck speed, and I think we'll be able to create practical immortality." Gupta wrote the book after interviewing experts in the field. He advised readers to exercise, stop smoking, eats lots of fruits and vegetables, reduce stress levels, be social and have an optimistic outlook. In other advice, Gupta wrote that people should eat seven different colors of foods a day.

Following the November 2008 election, Gupta was offered the post of U.S. surgeon general. The surgeon general serves as the United States' chief health educator. Gupta turned down the opportunity, preferring to concentrate on his family and career. If Gupta took the position, he knew he would not have time to perform surgery anymore. Gupta likes surgery; while in the operating room, he listens to Frank Sinatra and the Gipsy Kings.

In his free time, Gupta enjoys running with his wife, bike-riding, and being a father to three young girls. While it may seem like Gupta has a lot of obligations in his life, he told *Television Week*'s Elizabeth Jensen that he is able to maintain his busy schedule because he is focused. "I don't waste a lot of time. When I come in to work, whether for CNN or the magazine, I really come to work. I show up, work hard, and go home to my family."

## Sources

### Periodicals

*Atlanta Journal-Constitution,* September 30, 2004, p. 1E; January 7, 2009, p. A1; January 11, 2009, p. A11.

*Detroit Free Press,* April 4, 2003, p. 1H; April 8, 2007, p. 2A.

*Globe and Mail* (Canada), April 5, 2003, p. A8.

*Nation* (Thailand), April 4, 2004.

*Television Week,* March 12, 2007, p. 11.

*Washington Post,* March 6, 2009, p. A2.

### Online

"10 Things You Didn't Know About Sanjay Gupta," *U.S. News & World Report,* http://www.usnews.com/articles/news/obama/2009/01/09/10-things-you-didnt-know-about-sanjay-gupta.html (April 9, 2009).

"Anchors & Reporters: Sanjay Gupta," CNN.com, http://www.cnn.com/CNN/anchors_reporters/gupta.sanjay.html (April 9, 2009).

*—Lisa Frick*

# Maggie Gyllenhaal

## Actress

**B**orn November 16, 1977, in New York, NY; daughter of Stephen Gyllenhaal (a filmmaker) and Naomi Foner (a screenwriter); children: Ramona (with Peter Sarsgaard, an actor and filmmaker). *Education:* Columbia University, B.A., 1999; also attended the Royal Academy of Dramatic Arts, London, England.

**Addresses:** *Agent*—Creative Artists Agency, 2000 Avenue of the Stars, Los Angeles, CA 90067.

## Career

**A**ctress in films, including: *Waterland*, 1992; *A Dangerous Woman*, 1993; *Homegrown*, 1998; *Cecil B. Demented*, 2000; *The Photographer*, 2000; *Donnie Darko*, 2001; *Riding in Cars with Boys*, 2001; *40 Days and 40 Nights*, 2002; *Adaptation*, 2002; *Confessions of a Dangerous Mind*, 2002; *Secretary*, 2002; *Casa de los Babys*, 2003; *Mona Lisa Smile*, 2003; *Criminal*, 2004; *Pornographer: A Love Story*, 2004; *The Great New Wonderful*, 2005; *Happy Endings*, 2005; *Monster House*, 2006; *Paris, je t'aime*, 2006; *SherryBaby*, 2006; *Stranger Than Fiction*, 2006; *Trust the Man*, 2006; *World Trade Center*, 2006; *High Falls*, 2007; *The Dark Knight*, 2008. Television movie appearances include: *The Shattered Mind*, 1996; *The Patron Saint of Liars*, 1998; *Shake, Rattle and Roll: An American Love Story*, 1999; *Resurrection*, 1999; *Strip Search*, 2004. Stage appearances include: *Homebody/Kabul*, Mark Taper Forum, Los Angeles, CA, 2003.

**Awards:** Boston Society of Film Critics Award for best actress, for *Secretary*, 2002; Breakthrough Award, Gotham Awards, for *Secretary*, 2002; National Board of Review Award for best breakthrough performance by an actress, for *Secretary*, 2002; Central Ohio Film Critics Association Award for best actress, for *Secretary*, 2003; Chicago Film Critics Association Award for most promising performer, for *Adaptation, Confessions of a Dangerous Mind,* and *Secretary*, 2003; Directors' Week Award for best actress, Fantasporto, for *Secretary*, 2003; Pauline Kael Breakout Award, Florida Film Critics Circle, for *Secretary*, 2003; best actress award, Paris Film Festival, for *Secretary*, 2003; best actress award, Karlovy Vary International Film Festival, for *SherryBaby*, 2006; best actress award, Stockholm Film Festival, for *SherryBaby*, 2006; best actress award, Milan International Film Festival, for *SherryBaby*, 2007; Prism Award for performance in a feature film, for *SherryBaby*, 2007.

## Sidelights

**A**fter a breakout role in *Secretary*, American actress Maggie Gyllenhaal became a high-profile actress appearing in a number of independent films of note, including *Adaptation* and *SherryBaby*. While Gyllenhaal did not avoid Hollywood films—she had significant roles in *World Trade Center* and *The Dark Knight*—she always sought roles which were daring. As she told Tiffany Rose of London's *Independent on Sunday*, "if you make choices as an artist which inspire you, and do things you think are important, then even if your level of fame wanes, you continue growing as an artist."

Born on November 16, 1977, in New York City, Gyllenhaal is the daughter of Stephen Gyllenhaal and Naomi Foner. Both of her parents worked in the entertainment industry, but were as idealistic as possible in their vision. Her father was a film and television director, who directed such films as *Losing Isaiah* and episodes of *Everwood* and *The Shield*. He was also a poet. Her mother was a screenwriter responsible for such scripts as *Running on Empty*, which was nominated for an Academy Award. She has a younger brother, Jake, who also became an actor. (Jake Gyllenhaal is perhaps best known for his Academy Award-nominated role in 2005's *Brokeback Mountain*.)

The family moved to Los Angeles when Gyllenhaal was a toddler; she spent the rest of her childhood in the city. Gyllenhaal and her brother did plays together at home for fun when they were small, but she was not particularly attracted to acting early on. She described herself as an intense child, a daydreamer. Gyllenhaal received her education at Harvard-Westlake prep school.

After taking an acting class at the age of eleven, Gyllenhaal became more interested in acting. She made her screen debut while in her teens, appearing in her father's film *Waterland* in 1992. The following year, she appeared with her brother in another film directed by her father, *Dangerous Woman*. The pair also appeared in Stephen Gyllenhaal's 1998 film, *Homegrown*.

By the time *Homegrown* was released, Gyllenhaal was attending college. She studied English at Columbia University. During her time at Columbia, she also gained stage experience. Gyllenhaal earned her B.A. from the university in 1999. She then studied briefly at the Royal Academy of Dramatic Arts in London, England.

Focusing on an acting career in earnest in the early 2000s, Gyllenhaal appeared in a series of films, often in supporting roles. In 2001's *Donnie Darko*, Gyllenhaal played the sister of her real-life brother in a small role. Additional supporting roles of note include 2000's *Cecil B. Demented*, directed by John Waters, 2001's *Riding in Cars with Boys*, directed by Penny Marshall, and 2002's *40 Days and 40 Nights*.

In 2002, Gyllenhaal had her first starring role, playing the lead in the dark comedy *Secretary*, based on the short story by Mary Gaitskill. Her character, Lee Holloway, cuts herself and is masochistic. She has a stress-filled job at an office with a new boss, the sadistic Edward Grey, played by James Spader. Lee ultimately pursues an S&M-type affair with Grey, an attorney. The film won a special prize at the 2001 Sundance Film Festival, was one of the most talked about small films of the fall of 2002, and launched Gyllenhaal to stardom as the indie it girl of the moment.

Yet because of the nature of *Secretary*, Gyllenhaal knew the film had the potential to fail. She told Colin Covert of the Minneapolis *Star Tribune* that she knew she and the filmmakers were "walking such a fine line we could fall off any minute. That's much more interesting than being safe and acceptable. In the wrong hands, this could have been an antifeminist, reactionary movie. I chose it because it's challenging and transgressive about things in the world that seem immovable and set.... I like the possibility of shaking that up and making people question what they believe."

After *Secretary*, Gyllenhaal continued to appear in a number of smaller, but high profile, films. Later in 2002, she appeared in two films scripted by Charlie Kaufman, *Adaptation* and *Confessions of a Dangerous Mind*. Her film roles continued to be varied in 2003 as she appeared in an ensemble film about international adoption directed by John Sayles, *Casa de los Babys*. Gyllenhaal played Jennifer, a rich woman from New England who desperately wants to adopt a baby and save her failing marriage. Later that year, Gyllenhaal appeared in another ensemble film, *Mona Lisa Smile*. A drama set at a women's college in the 1950s, the film co-starred Julia Roberts and Kirsten Dunst.

Also in 2003, Gyllenhaal appeared in what she labeled her ideal role. She played Priscilla Ceiling in *Homebody/Kabul*, a stage play written by Tony Kushner. She played the role at the Mark Taper Forum in Los Angeles that fall. Gyllenhaal's Priscilla goes to Afghanistan with her father to claim the body of her mother, who was allegedly murdered there. When there is no body, Priscilla begins looking for her mother on the streets of Kabul.

Because of the success of *Secretary* and her burgeoning film career, Gyllenhaal remained committed to *Homebody/Kabul*, even though Kushner's rewrites after earlier productions took a year. She told Evan Henerson of the *Daily News of Los Angeles*, "It was so clear from the very beginning that this would be my first priority no matter what happened. I feel like I have a very specific clear connection to this character. I don't know where exactly that comes from. It's something I'm trying to figure out. The line between what's me and what's this character is a hazy one at the moment, and I love that."

After appearing in two films in 2004, *Criminal* and *Pornography: A Love Story,* Gyllenhaal was in two more films in 2005: *Happy Endings* and *The Great New Wonderful.* Her role in *Happy Endings,* directed by Don Roos, was particularly challenging. She played the manipulative Jude, an aspiring singer who is temporarily homeless and manipulates people to achieve her goal. Among her victims is her band's drummer, played by Jason Ritter, who is struggling over his sexuality, and his father, played by Tom Arnold, who is a rich widower. Her Jude seduces them both in an attempt to get what she wants. Though Gyllenhaal had no real experience or professional training, she did her own singing during filming, an experience she called scary.

Gyllenhaal gained unwanted media attention during a red carpet appearance related to *The Great New Wonderful.* The film consists of stories about New Yorkers who must deal with the outfall from the September 11, 2001, terrorist attacks on their city. During the New York premiere of *The Great New Wonderful,* the actress stated that she thought the United States had been in some way responsible for the attacks.

Because of the comments, Gyllenhaal suffered a media backlash. The incident taught her, as she told Nancy Mills of the New York *Daily News,* "that neither the red carpet nor an interview about a movie is the right place to talk about my politics. I realize I have to be careful, because it's very easy to misunderstand a complicated thought in a complicated world. I was so surprised by the way it was misunderstood, and the disdain that came back at me was a real shock. I regret what I said, but I think my intentions were good."

The backlash also affected her career in other ways. Gyllenhaal had already signed on to appear in Oliver Stone's *World Trade Center,* which focused on the actual terrorist attacks. She was set to play Allison Jimeno, whose husband was a Port Authority officer who became trapped during rescue operations at the World Trade Center. After the hullabaloo around Gyllenhaal's 9/11 comments, the actress met with the Jimenos, explained what she was trying to say, and would have dropped out if Allison Jimeno was uncomfortable with the actress. The meeting smoothed over any concerns the Jimenos might have had, and Gyllenhaal depicted Allison in the moving film.

*World Trade Center* was not Gyllenhaal's only film released in 2006. She also provided the voice of a babysitter for three rambunctious children for the animated children's film *Monster House* and played a woman whose long-term relationship with her boyfriend falls apart because he will not commit in the dramedy *Trust the Man.* In addition, Gyllenhaal appeared in the indies *Paris, je t'aime* and *Stranger Than Fiction.*

Gyllenhaal's best received work of 2006 came in the low-budget film *SherryBaby,* for which she received numerous awards and was nominated for a Golden Globe. In the film, the actress plays Sherry, a former convict trying to establish a relationship with her young daughter, Alexis, who lives with Sherry's brother and his wife. Sherry must also tackle the outfall from her old life as well as her years of drug abuse. Playing the role was draining for Gyllenhaal, as she told Christy Lemire of the Associated Press. Gyllenhaal explained, "I have no idea how I did it when I look at it now. It was almost like I was hypnotized when I was doing it. I didn't actually feel horrible until after I finished shooting it, and then I felt awful. But while I was shooting it I was kind of like, 'I'm fine, I'm totally fine. Yeah, I did just take off all my clothes in a nasty, disgusting basement in New Jersey, but I'm cool, it's totally cool.'"

Also in 2006, Gyllenhaal gave birth to a daughter, Ramona, whom she had with her fiancé, actor Peter Sarsgaard. After the birth, Gyllenhaal cut back on the number of films she made. She only appeared in one film released in 2007—*High Falls*—and one in 2008—*The Dark Knight.* In *High Falls,* she co-starred with Sarsgaard, playing a self-obsessed wife to his mean-spirited husband. The couple spends a weekend in the country where they reveal their secrets to a mutual friend. *The Dark Knight,* the sequel to *Batman Begins,* was a rare appearance in a Hollywood blockbuster for Gyllenhaal. She played Rachel Dawes, the former love interest of Bruce Wayne/Batman and current interest of Harvey Dent/Two Face, replacing Katie Holmes, who played the role in the first Batman film. The film was a box-office smash in the summer of 2008.

Gyllenhaal had two films scheduled for release in 2009, *Crazy Heart* and *Away We Go.* In choosing her roles, the actress always sought challenges. She told David Germain of the Associated Press, "It has to be about humans. A lot of scripts pretend they're about humans, but they're about androids. I want my scripts to be about humans, and I want them to be provocative in some way, challenging something in the world. I want the world to be exposed as moveable and changeable and malleable, as it actually is. I like scripts that kind of show something that's true and asks, now how do you feel?"

## Sources

### Books

*Complete Marquis Who's Who Biographies,* Marquis Who's Who, 2008.

### Periodicals

Associated Press, May 8, 2006; July 21, 2006; November 27, 2006; January 12, 2007.
Associated Press Online, July 29, 2005.
Associated Press Worldstream, September 19, 2002.
*Austin American-Statesman* (Austin, TX), July 29, 2005, p. E1.
*Buffalo News* (NY), October 15, 2002, p. C1.
*Daily News* (NY), July 10, 2005, p. 15.
*Daily News of Los Angeles,* September 30, 2003, p. U4.

*Independent* (London, England), May 9, 2003, pp. 10-11.
*Independent on Sunday* (London, England), February 29, 2004, p. 3.
*Inside Bay Area* (CA), January 26, 2007.
*Los Angeles Times,* July 17, 2008, p. E3.
*Marie Claire,* August 1, 2008, p. 94.
*Star Tribune* (Minneapolis, MN), October 4, 2002, p. 1E.
*Toronto Sun,* August 17, 2006, p. 76; July 18, 2008, p. E3.

### Online

"Maggie Gyllenhaal," Internet Movie Database, http://www.imdb.com/name/nm0350454/ (October 20, 2008).

—*A. Petruso*

# Cole Hamels

*Jeff Fusco/Getty Images*

## Professional baseball player

**B**orn Colbert Michael Hamels, December 27, 1983, in San Diego, CA; son of Gary (a principal) and Amanda (a teacher) Hamels; married Heidi Strobel (a reality television star), December 31, 2006.

**Addresses:** *Office*—Philadelphia Phillies, One Citizens Bank Way, Citizens Bank Park, Philadelphia, PA 19148. *Web site*—http://www.colehamels.com/.

## Career

**D**rafted by the Philadelphia Phillies, 2002; pitcher in the minor league system, 2003-06; pitcher in the major league, 2006—.

**Awards:** National League All-Star, 2007; Most Valuable Player, National League Championship Series, 2008; Most Valuable Player, World Series, 2008.

## Sidelights

**M**VP Philadelphia Phillies pitching phenom Cole Hamels is a master of the changeup, a pitch that looks almost exactly like his fastball when thrown. That pitch, and Hamels' ease at throwing a variety of pitches, helped win the Phillies their first World Series in 28 years.

"[Hamels is] the type of pitcher that when he takes the mound, everybody expects him to win," said Reggie Jackson to Stephen Borelli and Bob Nighten-

gale of *USA Today* during the 2008 World Series between Philadelphia and Tampa Bay. "His teammates. Philly fans. Even the Tampa Bay fans."

Born in 1983, the same year that the Philadelphia 76ers won the NBA Finals, the last time a Philadelphia professional sports team had won a championship before 2008, Hamels grew up idolizing baseball stars Tony Gwynn and Ken Griffey, Jr. He played both baseball and soccer as a child, and at age ten, he experienced his first travel competition on a youth soccer league. He also joined an AAU baseball team and traveled to local tournaments, playing centerfield and pitching. At home, he played Griffey's Nintendo game, imagining himself in the major leagues.

It was at the age of 14 that Hamels realized the power of the changeup pitch. He watched the San Diego Padres regularly, and he saw how, in the ninth inning, pitcher Trevor Hoffman dominated the game with his changeup. "The Padres got to the World Series that year because of that pitch. I'd think to myself, I need that pitch," he recalled in *Sports Illustrated* to reporter Albert Chen. As a high school freshman, his fastball was unintimidating; early into the season, Rancho Bernardo High School coach Mark Furtak offered to teach Hamels to throw the changeup. Furtak showed him the grip and trained him on how to use it, and when Hamels started throwing it, the change was obvious: Hamels was a force to be reckoned with on the mound.

During his sophomore season, Hamels experienced a setback so big it was thought he might never pitch again. While playing street football, he lowered his shoulder into a parked car. On the mound, his humerus snapped, and he was out of the game for six months. That break was one that only two other professional baseball players had suffered, and no one had ever come back from that injury. Hamels sought out the doctor who treated the San Diego Padres, hoping that treatment would save his pitch. The doctor recommended that Hamels seek out other sports, or at least another position in baseball. "I can't," Hamels recalled protesting to Bob Nightengale of *USA Today*. "Pitching is the only thing I'm good at."

With therapy and hard work, Hamels returned to the mound the summer before his senior year, throwing his changeup and his 94 mph fastball. Scouts watched his season eagerly, and after he graduated in 2002, he was drafted by the Phillies, making him the 17th pick of that season's draft. Pitching in the minors from 2003 to 2006, Hamels continued to be plagued by injuries. Despite the setbacks, he had a minor league total of 14-4 with 273 strikeouts in 35 games pitched. He made the majors in 2006, and in his debut, he pitched five scoreless innings, allowing only one hit. His performance throughout the season helped restore the Phillies' optimism, putting the World Series in their sights. That season was also the first in which he faced idol Griffey over the plate, rather than through a video game. In April of 2007, he pitched his first complete game, striking out 15 Cincinnati Reds. That season he was the first National League pitcher to win nine games, a feat that brought him to the All Star Team, where he played beside Griffey and other major league veterans.

Though Hamels did not make the All Star Team in 2008 with a more modest pitching record, the Philadelphia Phillies overtook their competitors, the New York Mets, to make the playoffs for the National League. The Phillies defeated the Brewers, in part due to a game in which Hamels pitched eight shutout innings. Against the Los Angeles Dodgers, Hamels had a shaky start, but in the fifth game of the series, he held the Dodgers to five hits and one run, leading the Phillies to their first National League championship since 1993 and earning the most valuable player award.

In the 2008 World Series, the Phillies faced the Tampa Bay Rays, who were making their first World Series appearance after losing for ten straight seasons. By Game 5, the Phillies were up three to one; a win would mean winning the Series. But the game was interrupted by a downpour, which made Hamels' famous changeup far less effective, and during a tie in the sixth inning, the game was suspended. Two nights later, the game picked up with Brad Lidge pitching, and the Phillies won the game, and the World Series.

Hamels spent the off-season after the 2008 World Series training in Philadelphia, and spending time in San Diego with his family and Springfield, Missouri, where his wife, *Survivor: Amazon* star Heidi Strobel grew up, and near where Hamels and Strobel have a 100-acre farm. During the pre-season training, Hamels found his pitches were much less confident. "In my last start, I could hit the glove on a dime at 90 mph. Today I threw 70 and my pitches were all over the place," he told Mel Antonen for *USA Today*. "It's a wake-up call." The 2009 season began with a rough start, for which Hamels himself took the blame. Due to a delay in his spring training because of television appearances and other distractions in January, Hamels worked his arm too hard, too fast, making his left elbow painful and swollen. In his first two starts of the season, Hamels allowed 19 hits and 12 earned runs; the Phillies lost both games. Hamels took his responsibility to get back into shape seriously. "If it comes down to the end of the year and we lose the division by one game, I can easily raise my hand and say I [messed] up," Hamels said to Jim Salisbury for the *Philadelphia Inquirer*. "I should be ready, and by not being ready I'm jeopardizing the team."

Despite Hamels' serious attitude toward competing, the media often focus on his laid back, Southern California personality and his celebrity good looks. His teammates have given him the nickname "Hollywood." Hamels embraces nutritional supplements, and, for an energy drink, he has green tea before games. He persuaded the Phillies to bring on a team chiropractor and massage therapist full time. Hamels practices yoga and hangs upside-down on an inversion table to stretch. Once, he slept so well in a hotel the team stayed at, he bought the bed. Also an avid fantasy football player, Hamel has taken breaks from team celebrations to check the scores. "I can't even tell the difference on the day he's pitching and when he isn't," his wife told *USA Today*'s Nightengale "He's just always so relaxed." Hamels explained his philosophy in the same article. "I know everything can end in a flash, so you better enjoy it as long as you can. And that's what I'm doing. I'm focusing on the moment." He told something similar to *Sports Illustrated* reporter Chen: "I just go out there and do my thing, and the results follow.... I've always believed I could do this."

# Sources

## Periodicals

*New York Times,* April 27, 2008, p. 2; October 2, 2008, p. D4; October 16, 2008, p. B16; January 19, 2009, p. D7.

*Sports Illustrated,* May 22, 2006, p. 68; June 5, 2006, p. 24; November 5, 2008, p. 58; January 26, 2009, p. 15.

*USA Today,* July 11, 2007, p. 5C; October 9, 2008, p. 1C; October 28, 2008, p. 5C; October 31, 2008, p. 4C; February 16, 2009, p. 7C.

## Online

*Biography Resource Center Online,* Gale (Detroit, MI), 2009.

"Cole Hamels," Major League Baseball Web site, http://mlb.mlb.com/team/player.jsp?player_id=430935 (April 21, 2009).

"Cole Hamels Takes the Blame," *Philadelphia Inquirer* Online, http://www.philly.com/inquirer/front_page/20090421.tif_Cole_Hamels_takes_the_blame.html (April 21, 2009).

Cole Hamels Web site, http://www.colehamels.com/ (April 21, 2009).

*—Alana Joli Abbott*

# Jon Hamm

## Actor

**B**orn Jonathan Daniel Hamm, March 10, 1971, in St. Louis, MO; partner of Jennifer Westfeldt (an actress and screenwriter). *Education:* Attended University of Texas; University of Missouri, B.A., 1993.

**Addresses:** *Home*—Los Angeles, CA. *Office*—c/o AMC Viewer Services, 200 Jericho Quadrangle, Jericho, NY 11753.

## Career

**A**ctor in films, including: *Space Cowboys,* 2000; *Early Bird Special,* 2001; *Kissing Jessica Stein,* 2001; *We Were Soldiers,* 2002; *Ira and Abby,* 2006; *The Ten,* 2007; *The Day the Earth Stood Still,* 2008; *The Boy in the Box,* 2008. Television appearances include: *The Hughleys,* 2000; *The Trouble With Normal,* 2000; *Providence,* NBC, 2000-01; *The Division,* Lifetime, 2002-04; *CSI: Miami,* 2005; *What About Brian,* ABC, 2006-07; *The Unit,* CBS, 2006-07; *Mad Men,* AMC, 2007—. Stage appearances include: *Lipschtick.* Worked as a daycare assistant and high school and early elementary teacher, 1990s.

**Awards:** Golden Globe Award for best performance by an actor in a television series (drama), Hollywood Foreign Press Association, for *Mad Men,* 2008.

## Sidelights

**J**on Hamm was a relatively unknown Hollywood actor when his lead role in the cable television drama *Mad Men* catapulted him to fame in the summer of 2007. Hamm plays Don Draper, the "embodiment of the midcentury American Dream," asserted Paul Rudd in *Interview.* "He looks the way movie stars used to look, smokes the way people used to smoke, contemplates life the way men used to contemplate it, and feels like nothing else on TV."

Hamm was born in 1971 in St. Louis, Missouri, and first appeared on stage in his first-grade class production of *Winnie the Pooh.* His adolescence was a difficult one, however: Hamm lost his mother when he was ten, and his father died when he was a sophomore at the University of Texas. "I suddenly had no parents," he said in an interview with Gabriel Snyder for *W.* "It was like I had no mooring." He dropped out of school, admitting in the same interview that his grades were abysmal because of an overindulgent undergraduate lifestyle.

Hamm returned to the St. Louis area and entered the University of Missouri as an English major. By this point he had already set his sights on an acting career thanks to the encouragement he received at his private high school, the elite Burroughs School, and sought a part-time job that would allow him to appear in stage productions at "Mizzou," as the University of Missouri is known locally. He wound up at a daycare center called Kids Depot, telling

Pete Bland, a journalist with the *Columbia Daily Tribune,* the newspaper for the Missouri city located roughly between St. Louis and Kansas City where Hamm lived during his college years, "I basically went out and pitched myself saying, 'Here's the deal. I was always a latchkey kid, so I was coming home or going to day care, and there were never any guys around.'" Hamm was immediately hired, and after earning his degree in 1993 went on to teach drama at his alma mater, the Burroughs School, before moving to Hollywood in 1995.

Hamm worked for a time as a teacher in the Los Angeles area while he auditioned for roles. He made his television debut in an episode of *The Hughleys* in 2000, and his film debut that same year in a bit role in the Clint Eastwood drama *Space Cowboys.* He was in the pilot episode of a one-season ABC sitcom, *The Trouble with Normal,* and was struggling to make ends meet when a woman cast him as the male lead in a play called *Lipschtick.* He reprised the Los Angeles stage role when the project was adapted for film as *Kissing Jessica Stein,* which became a minor hit on the independent-film circuit in 2001 and 2002.

Hamm won a recurring role on the NBC drama *Providence,* and went on to the well-received Lifetime cable series *The Division,* playing Inspector Nate Basso from 2002 to 2004. He also had a minor role in the 2002 Mel Gibson Vietnam War drama *We Were Soldiers,* but his roles before *Mad Men* debuted in 2007 were confined mostly to episodes of *CSI: Miami, What About Brian,* and *The Unit* and little-seen movies like the Ten Commandments-based comedy *The Ten.*

The script for *Mad Men,* an hour-long drama created by former *Sopranos* writer Matthew Weiner, came to Hamm via his agent, and he was wary about signing on for a recurring television series role, which would limit the time he would be available for film projects. Once he read it, however, he told his partner—Jennifer Westfeldt, the *Kissing Jessica Stein* playwright and screenwriter—"this is the best script I've ever read," he recalled in the interview with Snyder for *W,* and added, "I'll never get it."

After seven auditions, Hamm did indeed land the role of Don Draper, the self-assured creative director at Sterling Cooper, the top Madison Avenue advertising agency that serves as the backdrop for *Mad Men.* The series debuted on AMC in the summer of 2007 to enthusiastic reviews and developed a cult following. Audiences were entranced by the pitch-perfect look of America at the height of its postwar economic boom, just before the Vietnam War, political assassinations, and the women's rights

movement forever altered the social fabric of the nation. As Draper, Hamm embodies a middle-class ideal of that era—the breadwinner who considers himself the boss both at the office and at home to his wife Betty, played by January Jones.

As *Mad Men's* first season ended, viewers were treated to a shocking revelation about Don's real identity that had been hinted at in a few brief flashbacks. "*Mad Men* makes the '60s fresh again with delicious details and a timeless story of self-reinvention," wrote James Poniewozik in *Time,* who also noted that "the subtle, deliberately paced drama has a wider sense of history. Don is not defined by his time. He's an American archetype of self-reinvention: a Gatsby or a Huck Finn, who lights out for the territory but cannot escape from himself."

*Mad Men* proved such a success on AMC—the basic cable channel whose acronym once stood for American Movie Classics—that it became the first basic-cable series ever nominated for an Emmy Award in the Best Drama category, along with *Damages* on the FX Channel. Hamm's portrayal earned him an Emmy nomination as well as the Golden Globe Award for Best Actor in a Television Series—Drama. Not surprisingly, his newfound fame boosted his appeal in Hollywood, and in between the first and second seasons of *Mad Men* he filmed a significant role in the big-budget science fiction thriller *The Day the Earth Stood Still,* which starred Keanu Reeves.

Hamm lives with Westfeldt in the Los Feliz area of Los Angeles. Of his role as the calculating, aloof Don Draper, the actor admitted it was a switch. "Don, in a lot of ways, can be kind of mean, and that's not my go-to thing," Hamm told *Daily Variety's* Jon Weisman. "He's kind of mean to a purpose, but it was a little tough." Hamm noted that Weiner, the show's creator, "was kind of constantly on top of me to be meaner," including in one scene with Elisabeth Moss, who plays his secretary-turned-copywriter Peggy. Moss, he said. "looks about nine years old. It's like kicking a puppy."

## Sources

*Columbia Daily Tribune* (Columbia, MO), July 27, 2008.
*Daily Variety,* June 6, 2008, p. A4.
*Interview,* August 2008, p. 40.
*New York Times,* September 30, 2007; October 5, 2008.
*People,* September 10, 2007, p. 87.
*Time,* August 4, 2008, p. 73.
*W,* July 2008, p. 58.

—*Carol Brennan*

# Chelsea Handler

**Comedian, television host, and author**

**B**orn Chelsea Joy Handler, February 25, 1975, in Livingston, NJ.

**Addresses:** *Agent*—Jim Wiatt, William Morris Agency, 1 William Morris Pl., Beverly Hills, CA 90212.

## Career

**S**tand-up comic in Los Angeles after 1996; made television debut on *Spy TV,* 2001; appeared in the feature films *Cattle Call,* 2006, and *Steam,* 2007; series regular on *Girls Behaving Badly,* Oxygen Network, after 2003; host of the *The Chelsea Handler Show,* E! Entertainment Network, 2006, and *Chelsea Lately,* 2007—; series regular on *In the Motherhood,* 2008—.

## Sidelights

**C**omedian Chelsea Handler was nearly a complete unknown outside the Los Angeles comedy-club circuit when she landed her own late-night talk show on the E! Network in 2007. The half-hour *Chelsea Lately* turned the New Jersey native into an overnight star, and a few pop-culture pundits predicted she might eventually step up to a more serious late-night talk show on a major network. "So far the show has been almost embarrassingly watchable. She's just good," declared *New York Times'* television critic Virginia Heffernan. "She's also genuinely good looking, and has a way of saying withering things through a smile that works. She makes late-night look pretty easy."

Handler was born in 1975 and grew up in the relatively affluent town of Livingston, New Jersey, the youngest of six children. She recounted tales from

her childhood in her memoir, *Are You There, Vodka? It's Me, Chelsea,* noting that her father's financial shortcomings did not afford them the same luxuries as her classmates enjoyed and that all her siblings were in college by the time she was 12. "I would lie awake night after night, praying that none of them would enter into a serious enough relationship that could lead to an expensive wedding," Handler wrote.

Handler moved to Los Angeles at age 19 to try her luck in Hollywood. Working as a waitress to support herself—a job she admitted to being fired from, usually for sassing patrons or management, on several occasions—she auditioned for various roles, but quickly realized she did not possess the requisite appearance-maintenance discipline. "I got out here and realized how many beautiful people there are, and they're skinny and perfect," she told Jessica Young in an interview that appeared the *Daily Herald* of Arlington Heights, Illinois.

A drunk-driving arrest at the age of 21 proved to be the turning point for Handler's career. She was pulled over after a night out with a friend, spent the night in the drunk tank, and was then informed she was being handed over to the county jail because of an outstanding warrant for her arrest for fraud. This was the result of Handler's appropriating her older sister's I.D. a few years earlier in order to get into bars. She spent two long nights in the Sybil Brand Correctional Facility, where her only friend was a seemingly harmless-looking blonde who had killed her sister with a hammer. The fraud and driving-while-impaired charges netted Handler a community-service sentence, but she was also required to attend a class about the dangers of drunk driving. Everyone was required to share the details of their arrest, and Handler's recounting of her experience had her classmates convulsing in laughter.

Hoping to get a slot at a comedy club, Handler filmed her own audition tape. She told *Back Stage West* writer Jamie Painter Young, "I made a tape of me doing standup in my … living room—which if it ever resurfaces I will kill myself—and I was telling waitressing jokes to a VHS camcorder, and I sent it to The Improv. The owner of The Improv called me and was, like, 'I think you're great. Come on down.'" She was admittedly terrified before she went on stage for the first time, but quickly learned important tricks of timing and how to deal with hecklers in the audience, who can be especially rude to female comics. Asked to describe her worst experience on the circuit by *New York Times*' writer Edward Lewine, Handler said that it was early on in her new career, and she had invited family members. "Everybody was screaming, 'Take your top off!'" she told Lewine. "My father was just staring at me. It was one of the most humiliating experiences of my life."

Handler's first real break came after nearly four years on the circuit, when she appeared at the Montreal Comedy Festival and was signed by an agent in attendance. Her second stroke of good fortune occurred at a comedy festival in Aspen, Colorado, when one of the bookers for *The Tonight Show with Jay Leno* was in the audience, which led to a deal to do occasional street-interview features for the long-running NBC late-night show. In 2001, she appeared on a *Punk'd*-style ABC series called *Spy TV,* and over the next few years seemed on the verge of genuine stardom. She signed a few contract-development contracts, but as she explained to Young in the *Back Stage West* interview, none of them amounted to anything serious. "They want to give you a deal because of that edge—because of my point of view and my persona—and then they end up softening it up for the network to make it sweeter and saccharine it out, which is not what I want to do."

Handler found her niche in another hidden-camera prank series for the Oxygen Network, *Girls Behaving Badly,* that began attracting viewers in 2003 and 2004. Handler's strong improvisational skills made her a natural fit for the show, while she continued to hone her storytelling skills in a new medium: the printed word. After regaling her friends for years with her tales of dating mishaps, Handler finally heeded the advice to write a few of them down. "I wrote ten short stories that I sent to my manager," she told *Entertainment Weekly*'s Ari Karpel. "I had three [publishing] offers in two days. And I thought, 'Oh my gosh, I just wrote a book!'"

*My Horizontal Life: A Collection of One-Night Stands* was published by Bloomsbury in 2005, and earned some good reviews. Writing in the *San Francisco Chronicle,* Jane Ganahl described its author as "a female Don Juan, careening from one alcohol-fueled mishap to another. Far from glorifying the urban sex-spree lifestyle typified by Samantha on *Sex and the City,* Handler's stories are usually groan inducing. That she can laugh at herself draws our sympathy rather than our scorn."

Handler finally earned some film credits with small roles in *Cattle Call,* a 2006 entrant into the National Lampoon movie franchise, and in a few television and feature films that never saw the light of day, including 2007's *Steam,* which starred Ally Sheedy and Ruby Dee and appears to be set in a sauna. Handler was friends with another attractive blond comic who had once been the breakout star of 1994, Jenny McCarthy, and appeared in episodes of McCarthy's newest project, a Web television show called *In the Motherhood,* which moved to primetime television late in 2008.

Another breakthrough for Handler came when the E! Entertainment Network signed her to do a sketch comedy series, *The Chelsea Handler Show,* that aired in the spring of 2006. It fizzled, but producers wanted to find a new format for Handler's humor and offered her another role as host of an entertainment-news type of show. Appalled, Handler made a counteroffer, recounting in the interview with *Entertainment Weekly*'s Karpel that she told them she would agree only on the condition that "'I could make fun of everything that E! reports.'" They accepted her challenge, and *Chelsea Lately* debuted on the cable channel in July of 2007.

Handler's nightly show begins with riffs on the day's tawdriest gossip headlines, usually involving Paris Hilton, Lindsay Lohan, or various other celebrities whose antics provide the tabloids with daily fodder. This is done in a roundtable-type discussion with regular commentators—usually comedians or those familiar with the public-relations merry-go-round in Hollywood—and ends with a quasi-celebrity guest star who drops in for a chat. Few are actual bona-fide stars, and the bookers for Handler's show rely heavily on reality-television regulars such as Kim Kardashian or the female wrestler once known as Chyna Doll.

The first reviews for *Chelsea Lately* were not promising and included a scathing one that appeared on the Web site for Hollywood trade journal *Variety* by

Brian Lowry, who claimed the show "has high-lighted the by-now obvious point that not everyone can host a talkshow" and described Handler as "a poor woman's Kathy Griffin with a grating voice that could curve the spine." A *New York Times* critic was more charitable while also comparing Handler to the red-headed Griffin and veteran comedienne Joan Rivers. "Handler specializes in biting the hand that feeds," noted Brian Stelter, "tearing down celebrities on a channel devoted to building them up. Her weapon of choice is a voice of sugary sarcasm."

Despite the rocky start, Handler's half-hour late-night show began attracting new viewers and posted steady increases in ratings. It aired in the 11:30 p.m. time slot, which put her up against NBC's Jay Leno and another major player in late-night, David Letterman on CBS, but it was moved to 11:00 p.m. in early 2009. Her core audience seemed to be women in the 18 to 34 age group—a highly coveted demographic among advertisers—and the series proved to be a boon for both E! and Handler. The show saw a spike in viewership in the fall of 2007 during the Hollywood writers' strike, with *Broadcasting & Cable*'s Ben Grossman noting that the contract dispute by the Writers Guild of America and the corresponding dearth of new network programming "has made Hollywood look even more self-important to many, if that's possible. So the timing couldn't be better for someone like Handler to get a little traction by tearing it back down to size."

In December of 2008, E! renewed Handler's contract for the series for another year. That coup came after her second book, *Are You There, Vodka? It's Me, Chelsea,* had spent much of the year on the *New York Times* best-seller list. Like her previous memoir, *Are You There, Vodka* relies heavily on tawdry anecdotes from her personal life. Handler's dating prospects improved considerably when her involvement with E! introduced her to Ted Harbert, president of the Comcast Entertainment Group, which owns the cable network. Harbert is a television veteran who spent several years as head of programming for ABC, and instead of attempting to keep their relationship quiet, Handler and Harbert decided that he would instead recuse himself from any involvement in her show. Her comic attacks on the roster of celebrities who provide E! with its raison d'etre have not prevented the two from occasionally sparring over content, however. "Have Chelsea and I had loud arguments about whether or not she could say something?" Harbert rhetorically asked in the *Entertainment Weekly* interview with Karpel. "Yes. Is it personal? No." Adding that he is a veteran of net-work comedy and thus experienced in working with comics such as Roseanne Barr who sometimes crossed the line, Harbert pointed out, "I've been fighting with talent for a long time."

Handler's contract with E! expires at the end of 2010. Conceding that poking fun of Tom Cruise and other major Hollywood names likely restricts bookers at *Chelsea Lately* from luring the truly top-tier guests, she told Stelter in the *New York Times,* "I'm sure in a couple years I'm going to want to move up and do something a little more highbrow. There's only so much you can say about celebrity, obviously."

## Selected writings

*My Horizontal Life: A Collection of One-Night Stands,* Bloomsbury, 2005.
*Are You There, Vodka? It's Me, Chelsea,* Simon & Schuster, 2008.

## Sources

### Books

*Are You There, Vodka? It's Me, Chelsea,* Simon & Schuster, 2008, p. 19.

### Periodicals

*Back Stage West,* March 18, 2004, p. 4.
*Broadcasting & Cable,* November 26, 2007, p. 6.
*Daily Herald* (Arlington Heights, IL), May 5, 2006, p. 9.
*Entertainment Weekly,* July 18, 2008, p. 32.
*New York Times,* September 6, 2007; December 16, 2007; January 18, 2009.
*San Francisco Chronicle,* August 1, 2005, p. C1.
*Star-Ledger* (Newark, NJ), August 28, 2008, p. 61.
*W,* December 2008, p. 220.

### Online

"Chelsea Handler," Internet Movie Database, http://www.imdb.com/name/nm1314546/bio (February 9, 2009).
"Chelsea Lately," Variety, http://www.variety.com/review/VE11179342.tif29.html?categoryid=32&cs=1&p=0 (February 13, 2009).

—*Carol Brennan*

# Sally Hawkins

## Actress

**B**orn April 27, 1976, in England; daughter of Colin and Jacqui Hawkins (children's book authors). *Education:* Royal Academy of Dramatic Arts, London, 1998.

**Addresses:** *Agent*—John Grant, c/o Conway Van Gelder Grant Ltd., 8-12 Broadwick Street, London, W1F 8HW. *Home*—Richmond, England.

## Career

**A**ctress in films, including: *All or Nothing,* 2002; *Layer Cake,* 2004; *Vera Drake,* 2004; *The Painted Veil,* 2006; *Cassandra's Dream,* 2007; *Waz,* 2007; *Happy-Go-Lucky,* 2008; *Happy Ever Afters,* 2009. Television appearances include: *Tipping the Velvet,* 2002; *Byron,* 2003; *Little Britain,* 2003-05; *Promoted to Glory,* 2003; *The Young Visiters,* 2003; *Fingersmith,* 2005; *Twenty Thousand Streets Under the Sky,* 2005; *H.G. Wells: War With The World,* 2006; *Shiny Shiny Bright New Hole in My Heart,* 2006; *Persuasion,* 2007. Stage appearances include: *Accidental Death of an Anarchist,* Battersea Arts Centre, London, 1998; *Romeo and Juliet,* York Theatre Royal, York, England, 1998; *The Cherry Orchard,* York Theatre Royal, 1999; *The Dybbuk,* Battersea Arts Centre, 1999; *A Midsummer Night's Dream,* Regent's Park, London, 2000; *Much Ado About Nothing,* Regent's Park, 2000; *Misconceptions,* Octagon, Somerset, England, 2001; *Country Music,* Royal Court Theatre, London, 2004; *House of Bernarda Alba,* Royal National Theatre, London, 2005; *The Winterling,* Royal Court Theatre, 2006.

**Awards:** Golden Nymph Award for best actress, Monte-Carlo Television Festival, for *Persuasion,* 2007; Silver Berlin Bear for best actress, Berlin Interna-

tional Film Festival, for *Happy-Go-Lucky,* 2008; best actress award, Boston Society of Film Critics, for *Happy-Go-Lucky,* 2008; Peter Sellers Award for comedy, *Evening Standard,* for *Happy-Go-Lucky,* 2009; Hollywood Breakthrough Award for actress of the year, Hollywood Film Festival, for *Happy-Go-Lucky,* 2008; Satellite Award for best actress, International Press Academy, for *Happy-Go-Lucky,* 2008; best actress award, Los Angeles Film Critics Association, for *Happy-Go-Lucky,* 2008; best actress award, New York Film Critics Circle, for *Happy-Go-Lucky,* 2008; Television Award for best actress, Royal Television Society, for *Persuasion,* 2008; best actress award, San Francisco Film Critics Circle, for *Happy-Go-Lucky,* 2008; Golden Globe for best actress, Hollywood Foreign Press Association, for *Happy-Go-Lucky,* 2009; best actress award, National Society of Film Critics, for *Happy-Go-Lucky,* 2009.

## Sidelights

**B**ritish actress Sally Hawkins spent a decade appearing on the London stage, on BBC television, and in full-length features before landing—and nailing—a breakout, lead role in the 2008 romantic comedy *Happy-Go-Lucky.* Playing an eternally optimistic teacher named Poppy Cross, Hawkins dazzled moviegoers with her bubbly, infectious character and went on to earn a coveted Golden Globe for her performance. In a *Rolling Stone* movie review, film critic Peter Travers called *Happy-Go-Lucky* "heartfelt and hilarious." He warned moviegoers to "get ready for Sally Hawkins, a dynamo of an actress who will have her way with you … leaving you enchanted, enraged to the point of madness, and utterly dazzled."

Hawkins was born on April 27, 1976, to noted British children's picture-book authors Colin and Jacqui Hawkins. Hawkins grew up in Dulwich, an area of southeast London, alongside her older brother in a household where artistic expression was encouraged. "They were always drawing," Hawkins said of her parents, "and it was incredibly creative to be around that," she told the *Guardian*'s Maddy Costa. "I was encouraged to draw and paint and express myself and create things."

For a time, Hawkins thought she might trail behind her parents and go into visual arts, but as she got older she felt a tug toward acting, particularly after she learned the joys of making others laugh. "At primary school I was always creating little theatre pieces to show the rest of the school … whether they wanted to be shown or not," Hawkins told the *Independent*'s Cathy Pryor. "I loved comedy from very early on and that's what I wanted to do, make people laugh. And then as I got older I realized that you could not only make people laugh but move them in other ways that were equally rewarding."

Hawkins attended the private James Allen Girls' School, located in Dulwich. She was part of the drama troupe, which put on productions in conjunction with a local boys' school. Hawkins graduated in 1994 and went on to develop her acting skills at London's Royal Academy of Dramatic Arts. After graduating in 1998, she earned roles onstage, appearing in *Romeo and Juliet* (1998) and *The Cherry Orchard* (1999) at England's York Theatre Royal. Hawkins also performed at London's outdoor theater in Regent's Park, appearing in *Much Ado About Nothing* and *A Midsummer Night's Dream*, both in 2000. In 2002, Hawkins made her feature-length debut playing a sex-crazed teen in British director Mike Leigh's *All or Nothing*.

Over the next few years, Hawkins honed her craft on television. She appeared in 2002's *Tipping the Velvet*, a BBC adaptation of British author Sarah Waters' bestseller about Victorian-era lesbians. In the 2003 television biopic *Byron*, Hawkins portrayed *Frankenstein* author Mary Shelley. Between 2003-05, Hawkins made guest appearances on the British sketch

comedy *Little Britain*. In 2005, Hawkins dazzled British television viewers with her role in the BBC miniseries *Fingersmith*, also based on a Waters novel. Hawkins played the protagonist—Sue Trinder—an orphan, pickpocket, and swindler who gets involved in an elaborate scam, only to fall in love with the female victim.

Hawkins also earned supporting roles on the big screen and appeared in Leigh's melodrama *Vera Drake* (2004), portraying a rape victim in need of an abortion in 1950s London. That same year, Hawkins turned up in the British gangster film *Layer Cake*, playing a machete-wielding maniac. New York director Woody Allen made use of Hawkins in his 2007 drama *Cassandra's Dream*, casting Hawkins as Colin Farrell's girlfriend. That same year Hawkins appeared on British television in an adaptation of Jane Austen's novel *Persuasion*, playing the lead role of Anne Elliot.

In time, Leigh called Hawkins back to work on another project, which he dubbed *Untitled '06* and which turned out to be *Happy-Go-Lucky*. Besides having no title, the film had no script, plot, or specific characters when work began. That is how Leigh works—he usually starts a new project with a vague idea or feeling, then gathers actors so they can improvise and create the characters and plot. Speaking to *The Stranger*'s Sean Nelson, Leigh described his process. "Now, to talk about *Happy-Go-Lucky*, the first decision on the journey of deciding what film to make and how to make it was to get Sally Hawkins at the center of things. I mean, I had a sense of a kind of character, but it wasn't until we started to work together that Poppy began to be born. I knew that with Sally's intelligence and extraordinary capacity to play characters, and her humor and her ebullience and energy, that we could create a remarkable but real woman."

Through weeks of unscripted rehearsals, Hawkins, Leigh, and the other actors developed the characters and plotted out scenarios, mostly working off-the-cuff. The character that emerged was Poppy—an upbeat schoolteacher whose optimism could not be squelched. When Poppy's bike gets stolen, she simply laments that she did not get to say goodbye. Bikeless, Poppy begins taking driving lessons and her instructor turns out to be a sour introvert—the opposite of Poppy. After the film's release, critics went wild and Hawkins won a Silver Berlin Bear award for best actress at the Berlin International Film Festival, then followed with many more awards, including a Golden Globe.

On the heels of her success, Hawkins found herself in demand. She was cast in several films set for release in 2009 and 2010, including the Irish wedding comedy *Happy Ever Afters.* Production was slow because during filming, Hawkins snapped her collarbone doing a stunt. She was also cast to play the lead in *The Roaring Girl,* a biography of Irish civil rights leader Bernadette Devlin.

Hawkins was looking forward to her upcoming projects but hoped to work with Leigh again. She was fond of his lengthy movie-making process, which allowed her to figure out her character before filming began. Speaking to the *Guardian,* Hawkins put it this way: "On other jobs, you tend not to get that luxury: you just get the script and have to almost step into the character's shoes. With Mike, you can create the shoes around your character. If I could work like that for the rest of my life, it would be brilliant."

## Sources

### Periodicals

*Daily Telegraph* (London, England), March 3, 2007, sec. Art, p. 10.

*Guardian* (London, England), April 11, 2008, sec. Film and music, p. 8.
*Philadelphia Inquirer,* October 23, 2008.
*Sunday Times* (London, England), January 11, 2009, sec. Style, p. 5.

### Online

"Cathy Pryor: Shiny Future," *Independent,* http://www.independent.co.uk/news/people/profiles/cathy-pryor-shiny-future-409024.html (April 24, 2009).
"Getting On With It: An Interview with Mike Leigh," *The Stranger,* http://www.thestranger.com/seattle/getting-on-with-it/Content?oid=703640 (April 26, 2009).
"Happy-Go-Lucky," *Rolling Stone,* http://www.rollingstone.com/reviews/movie/18298108.tif/review/23356406.tif/happygolucky (April 25, 2009).
"Sally Hawkins," *W* magazine, http://www.wmagazine.com/celebrities/2008/10/sally_hawkins (April 24, 2009.

*—Lisa Frick*

# Nikki Hemming

## Chief Executive Officer of Sharman Networks

**B**orn Nicola Anne Hemming in 1967 in Northampton, England.

**Addresses:** *Home*—Sydney, Australia. *Web site*—http://www.sharmannetworks.com.

## Career

**W**ith Grand Slam Entertainment until 1992; head of international sales, Virgin Interactive, 1992-c. 1997; emigrated to Australia, 1995; general manager, Sega World, Sydney, Australia, c. 1997-2000; with Viacom after 2000; founder, Sharman Networks, 2002, and chief executive officer, 2002—.

## Sidelights

**N**ikki Hemming stepped into the public spotlight in 2002 as the chief executive officer of Sharman Networks, the company that held the rights to the file-sharing software used by the Kazaa Media Desktop. Available as a free download, Kazaa allowed Internet users access to a vast peer-to-peer file-sharing network where they could download songs, computer games, and even movies for free. Like its predecessors, Kazaa was the target of copyright infringement lawsuits filed by a consortium of record labels and movie studios. Hemming was widely thought to be merely the frontperson for the investors behind Sharman, but collected a generous salary and share of the profits for her role.

Born in 1967, Hemming is a native of Northampton, a town in England's East Midlands. Little background information is available about her, but it is known she once worked for a British company called Grand Slam Entertainment that, back in the early 1990s, was one of the sponsors of England's Football Association, the professional soccer league. She joined Virgin Interactive in 1992, then known as Virgin Games Ltd. This was a division of the immensely successful media empire built by Sir Richard Branson from a small record store in Notting Hill; Virgin's assets included a record label, a mobile telephone service, an airline, and even a space-travel division. Hemming joined the company just as Virgin Interactive was making a concerted effort to capture a segment of the market in games for computers and stand-alone systems. She rose to become head of international sales, and set up Virgin Interactive's German, Spanish, and South African operations.

Hemming moved to Australia in 1995 to establish a Virgin Interactive office there. She eventually left the company to take a job as the general manager of Sega World in Sydney, a much-ballyhooed new theme park that was hyped as the Disneyland of Australia. With rides based on popular Sega console games like Sonic the Hedgehog, the park opened to great fanfare in 1997 but failed to attract a sufficient number of visitors, even during the Sydney Olympics in 2000, and shut down shortly afterward. Hemming went to work for Viacom before becoming involved in Kazaa.

Kazaa was founded in 2001 by Sweden's Niklas Zennström along with Janus Friis, a Dane. "At its simplest, Kazaa is a freely downloadable software system that allows users (or 'peers') to swap digital files—any files—of music, video, photos and words," explained Paul Ham in London's *Sunday Times* newspaper. Kazaa used a peer-to-peer (p2p) protocol called FastTrack that Zennström and Friis had developed along with a team of programmers based in Estonia. The Kazaa site allowed Internet users to download its file-sharing software free of charge, and Kazaa quickly became the music-sharing network of choice following the shutdown of Napster after copyright infringement lawsuits filed in the courts were judged to have legal merit. Napster had indexed all of its songs on its own servers, which enabled record companies to easily sue for copyright infringement. Kazaa, by contrast, relied on a model in which users themselves became proxy servers.

When the Recording Industry Association of America (RIAA) turned its focus on Kazaa in late 2001, Zennström reportedly wanted to exit the company, and a technology investor named Kevin Bermeister whom Hemming knew from her stint at Virgin arranged the sale and the establishment of a complicated corporate structure. At the head of this was Sharman Networks, which Hemming founded in early 2002. Though its offices were in Sydney, Sharman Networks was registered in the tiny South Pacific island nation of Vanuatu, which had become a haven for businesses looking to maintain some secrecy about their corporate officers and operations. Then, the Kazaa interface was sold to Sharman Networks. Another company called LEF Interactive Pty. Ltd. was also set up—its name an acronym for "Liberté, Égalité, et Fraternité," the slogan of the 1789 French Revolution. Sharman employees were contracted through LEF.

Kazaa first attempted to evade legal trouble by offering legal downloads at a fixed price, but few music labels were interested in participating. The Kazaa site, meanwhile, was raking in millions of dollars thanks to advertising sales for banner and pop-up ads on its network, which by early 2003 had an estimated 60 million members. It was among the top ten most-visited Internet sites, ranked near Google, eBay, and Amazon.

Hemming emerged as the public face of Kazaa in the spring of 2002 after keeping a deliberately low profile for a few months. She began granting press interviews to defend the company against the charges that Kazaa was violating copyright infringe-

ment laws recognized by U.S., Australian, and other legal jurisdictions by allowing users to download songs, games, and movies for free. Kazaa even launched a public-relations effort with well-placed ads that urged users to rally around the issue. As Hemming explained to an interviewer for *The Age*, a Melbourne, Australia magazine, the record labels and other media companies were pursuing a misguided legal strategy because peer-to-peer networks were the next frontier. "The VCR was initially seen by the movie industry as a frightening prospect," she pointed out. "It became a mechanism for delivering content to the home, but it also became a mechanism to deliver more income from most of the movie titles coming out of Hollywood."

In 2003, a Los Angeles court agreed with the suit filed on behalf of the RIAA, that Kazaa was indeed subject to U.S. copyright law along with Grokster, Morpheus, and similar file-sharing networks. That suit wound through the courts as *MGM Studios, Inc. v. Grokster, Ltd.* and the U.S. Supreme Court ruled against the file-sharing sites in June of 2005. Kazaa also lost a separate case that was filed in Australian Federal Court, and a few months later Sharman's assets were frozen. Hemming's house was also raided by authorities for evidence as part of that case.

At Kazaa's peak it had some 60 million users and an estimated 300 million songs had been downloaded. The suits filed by the RIAA and its counterpart, the Australian Record Industry Association (ARIA), requested financial damages, with the RIAA demanding $150,000 per song. Legal teams from both sides reached a settlement in July of 2006 in which Sharman paid $110 million to a group of record labels and film studios. Hemming remains CEO of Sharman Networks, which bills itself as a developer of Internet applications. Kazaa is still a downloadable file-sharing program.

## Sources

*The Age* (Melbourne, Australia), March 5, 2003.
*Billboard*, August 26, 2006, p. 23.
*New York Times*, May 12, 2002.
*Sunday Times* (London, England), September 11, 2005, p. 8.
*USA Today*, November 17, 2003, p. 3B.
*Wired*, February 2003.

—Carol Brennan

# Susan Hockfield

© Rick Friedman/Corbis

**President of Massachusetts Institute of Technology**

**B**orn Susan Joan Hockfield, March 24, 1951, in Chicago, IL; married Thomas Byrne (a neuro-oncologist), March 2, 1991; children: Elizabeth. *Education:* University of Rochester, B.A., 1973; Georgetown University, Ph.D., 1979; Yale University, M.A., 1994.

**Addresses:** *Office*—Massachusetts Institute of Technology, 77 Massachusetts Ave., Rm. 3-208, Cambridge, MA 02139.

## Career

**P**ostdoctoral fellow, Department of Anatomy and Neuroscience Program, University of California San Francisco, National Institute of Health, 1979-80; junior staff investigator, Cold Spring Harbor Laboratory, Cold Spring Harbor, NY, 1980-82, then senior staff investigator, 1982-85; assistant professor, Department of Neurobiology, School of Medicine, Yale University, New Haven, CT, 1985-89, then associate professor, 1989-94, then professor, 1994-2004; dean of Graduate School of Arts and Sciences, Yale University, 1998-2002; provost, Yale University, 2003-04; president and professor of neuroscience, Massachusetts Institute of Technology, Cambridge, MA, 2004—. Also holds at least three patents in the field of neuroscience; contributed opinion pieces to periodicals such as the *Boston Globe*; contributed to professional journals.

**Awards:** Public Health Service (PHS) Post-doctoral Research Award, National Institutes of Health, 1980; Grass Traveling Science Award, Society for Neuro-

science, 1987; Charles Judson Herrick Award, American Association Anatomists, 1987; Wilbur Lucius Cross medal, 2004; Golden Plate Award, 2005; Meliors Citation for Sheffield Medal, University of Rochester, 2004; Amelia Earhart Award, Women's Union, 2005; Cold Spring Harbor Labor Honors, 2006; honorary degree, Brown University, 2006.

## Sidelights

**I**n 2004, Susan Hockfield became the first woman to serve as the president of the Massachusetts Institute of Technology (MIT). The scientist had previously served as the provost of Yale. Long associated with Yale as a professor as well, Hockfield was a neurobiology expert who focused specifically on neuroanatomy. Her research was on the development of the mammalian brain. Of her position as the first female president at MIT, Hockfield told Marcella Bombardieri and Jenna Russell of the *Boston Globe*, "People should know it doesn't make any difference what you look like. What makes a difference is what's in your brain and how you want to use it to make the most out of MIT."

Born on March 24, 1951, in Chicago, Illinois, Hockfield's father was a patent attorney for General Electric (GE). Because of his job, the family moved often as he took positions of increasing responsibility within GE. By third grade, Hockfield was living in Danbury, Connecticut, where she first became interested in how things worked by taking apart a watch and having its inner mechanisms explode all over the place. She told Charles P. Pierce of the *Boston Globe Magazine*, "I remember my overwhelming sensation being one of surprise and not guilt. So [the watch] must have been mine. But I was always fascinated by how living things work. I would pull apart leaves and flowers and things, to try and understand how they were put together."

The family eventually settled in New York. Hockfield graduated from a high school in Chappaqua, then stayed in-state for college, entering the University of Rochester. From her early childhood, her family believed that she would become a doctor, and to that end she studied biology at Rochester. While a student there, she realized that the medical profession did not seem like a good fit. A summer program helped her understand that medical research, not treatment, was her life's calling.

While a biology senior at the University of Rochester, a professor also changed Hockfield's life by supporting her concept for an experiment. Hockfield told *Newsweek*'s Barbara Kantrowitz, "I said, 'What? Me? People like me don't do this thing.' And he said, 'No, you do it.'" The professor's encouragement led Hockfield, who earned her B.A. in biology from the University of Rochester in 1973, to continue her education at the Georgetown University School of Medicine where she was a graduate student in anatomy and neuroscience. Focusing on neuroscience in her dissertation, she did her related research at the National Institutes of Health. Hockfield earned her Ph.D. in 1979, then moved to the west coast. She was a National Institutes of Health postdoctoral fellow at the University of California San Francisco for a year.

Returning east in 1980, Hockfield joined the staff of the Cold Spring Harbor Laboratory in Cold Spring, New York. She began as a junior staff investigator, then was promoted to a senior staff investigator in 1982. During her tenure at Cold Spring, she worked under the Nobel laureate James D. Watson, who was given the honor for his role in the discovery of DNA's double helix. Hockfield told *BusinessWeek*'s William C. Symonds, "I was analyzing data late into the night and never went home before midnight."

While the hours were long, Hockfield was exposed to early work in the then-emerging field of neuroscience, including the use of new tools like mono-

clonal antibodies to detect brain proteins. She told Cornelia Dean of the *New York Times*, "I had a visceral feeling of just profound curiosity and interest." When Hockfield moved on from Cold Spring to a professional position at Yale in 1985, she also began a stint as the director of the laboratory's prestigious Summer Neurobiology Program, which lasted until 1987. She later became a trustee of Cold Spring Harbor Laboratory.

In 1985, Hockfield joined the faculty at Yale University, becoming an assistant professor in the section of neurobiology in the school of medicine. She was promoted to associate professor in 1989, then professor in 1994. In 2001, Hockfield was named to an endowed chair when she became the William Edward Gilbert Professor of Neurobiology. During her tenure as professor, Hockfield's research on the mammalian brain and its development led to interesting developments. She worked on how the brain's visual system worked. She and her research team also were able to identify a family of cell surface proteins, one of which might play a role in how brain tumors progress, using monoclonal antibody technology. Hockfield was especially interested in studying gliomas, an often fatal type of brain tumor. Her research also led to the discovery of a gene and proteins that might be relevant to stopping certain types of brain cancers.

While holding her professorship, Hockfield earned an M.A. from Yale in 1994 and moved into a university administration position. She was named the dean of the Graduate School of Arts and Sciences in 1998. When Hockfield took the post, she was the first member of the faculty of the Medical School to helm this school. As the head of one of Yale's most significant graduate schools, her leadership was highly regarded. She took charge of the academic and administrative policies for the Graduate School, and was considered a successful recruiter of senior scholars. In particular, Hockfield was lauded for creating a sense of community within the school and implemented a number of policies which improved students' quality of life, including an increase in stipend for certain students as well as free health care for Ph.D. students.

In the fall of 2002, Hockfield was appointed to a second term as dean, but soon a new position came her way. Hockfield was named Yale's provost in December of 2002, beginning her term in early 2003. She replaced Alison Richard, who left for a position at Cambridge University. In this position, Hockfield was the chief academic officer as well as the chief administrative officer for the university. She was also responsible for supervising the educational policies and plans of each sector of the school. Operating budgets, capital budgets, and long-range planning also fell under her domain.

Hockfield's tenure as Yale's provost was short lived. She left her position as provost and her professorship behind in 2004 when she was offered the presidency of MIT, a prestigious school of 20,000 student and staff members with a $5.1 billion endowment known for its engineering and hard sciences department. Her predecessor, Charles Vest, retired after 14 years in the post. The chairman of MIT's presidential search committee, James Champy, told Andrew Lawler of *Science,* that Hockfield had "a rare combination of scientific achievement, outstanding managerial talent, and an extremely engaging personal style."

MIT was predominantly male in both its faculty and student bodies, but since a 1999 acknowledgment of past discrimination against women, including in the pay of female faculty, changes had been made. The school worked to increase opportunities for women, both as faculty members and as students. Though Hockfield's appointment as the first female president of MIT was significant because of her gender, it was also noteworthy because she was the first life scientist to head the school in its history as well.

Commenting on the significance of her appointment as a both a woman and a life scientist, Hockfield told Justin Pope of the Associated Press, "These are both very remarkable things. The thing I would wish is that my being president of MIT, a woman being president of MIT, will give kids and people around the world the confidence that for them, too, there will be opportunities that no one imagined they would have." Hockfield's future colleagues at MIT were also enthusiastic. Nancy Hopkins, a biology professor at MIT who filed a discrimination report in 1994, told the *New York Times'* Katie Zezima, "It could not have been imaginable to any of us that this could have happened. It's a milestone for sure. It's something you really have to take the day off and sit back and say, 'This is what social change looks like.'"

Hockfield also praised MIT's commitment to life sciences. She told Mark Jewell of the Associated Press, "My being a life scientist does not mark a departure from where MIT has been. It's a logical extension of where MIT has been for a long, long time. As a life scientist myself, I have known about MIT for decades as really a wellspring of incredible achievements in the life sciences."

When she took the post, Hockfield hoped to implement more innovative policies and initiatives at MIT. She wanted to encourage more collaboration between schools at MIT, especially biology and engineering. On a national stage, Hockfield hoped to add to the school's practice of advocating various national technology, education (including science and math education in all grades), and science policies. She also planned on continuing to lobby for more money for scientific research, especially in the physical sciences. Hockfield told Symonds of *BusinessWeek,* "In the second half of the 20th century, we led the world in innovation, but now we're not keeping up with other countries in our investments in science and engineering."

Within the first year of her tenure, Hockfield faced challenges. In January of 2005, Lawrence Summers, the president of Harvard, said during a speech that he wondered if a study should be done to determine if there is something inside women that makes them less attracted to science careers. The audience included a number of female scientists. Hockfield deftly dealt with the situation by publishing an piece in the *Boston Globe,* co-authored with John Hennessy, the president of Stanford University, and Shirley Tilghman, the president of Princeton. In the piece, the authors only gently reproached Summers but focused on their belief that there should be more programs to encourage women in science.

It was not the only controversy Hockfield would be forced to face. As soon as she took office, she had to deal with the long-running feud professor Ted Postol had with the school. Postal, a critic of the national missile defense program, regularly accused MIT of complicity with the federal government and believed he was being forced off campus. Hockfield also had to deal with questions about MIT's commitment to women, especially in early 2008 when only one woman was granted tenure. Hockfield hired Dr. Barbara Liskov as an associate provost who focused her attention on the subject.

Hockfield is married to Dr. Thomas Bryne, a neurooncologist, and they have a daughter, Elizabeth. As she took on administrative roles, Hockfield made time for her family but had little time for the lab. After becoming president of MIT, she told Pierce of the *Boston Globe Magazine,* "I was very active in my lab while I was dean of the graduate school. As provost, it would be just a few hours every other week. Obviously, I didn't move my lab up here, because I think balance for me is impossible, and partly because the research environment here is so rich with fabulous discoveries and fabulous science going on, why do I need to do my own? People ask me if I miss it. And I love being a scientist.... I love being part of academic administration. I find it enormously important."

## Selected writings

(With S. Carlson, P. Levitt, E. Evans, L. Silberstein and J. Pintar) *Molecular Probes of the Nervous System: Selected Methods for Antibodies and Nucleai Acid Probes,* Cold Spring Harbor Laboratory Press (Woodbury, NY), 1993.

## Sources

### Books

*Complete Marquis Who's Who Biographies,* Marquis Who's Who, 2008.

### Periodicals

Associated Press, August 26, 2004; December 7, 2004.
*Boston Globe,* August 27, 2004, p. B1; February 12, 2005, p. A13.
*Boston Globe Magazine,* May 1, 2005, p. 18.
*BusinessWeek,* October 4, 2004, p. 98.
*Newsweek,* December 27, 2004, p. 97.
*New York Times,* August 27, 2004, p. A15; May 3, 2005, p. F3.
M2 Presswire, December 16, 2002.
*Science,* September 3, 2004, p. 1389.
*Women in Higher Education,* January 1, 2008, p. 5.

### Online

"Biography: Susan Hockfield," Massachusetts Institute of Technlogy, http://web.mit.edu/hockfield/biography.html (October 14, 2008).

—*A. Petruso*

# Eric H. Holder, Jr.

*Scott J. Ferrell/Congressional Quarterly/Getty Images*

## Attorney General of the United States

**B**orn January 21, 1951, in New York, NY; son of Eric H. Holder, Sr. (a real estate broker), and Miriam R. Yearwood Holder; married Sharon Malone (an obstetrician); children: Maya, Brooke, Eric. *Education:* Columbia University, B.A., 1973; Columbia School of Law, J.D., 1976.

**Addresses:** *Office*—U.S. Department of Justice, 950 Pennsylvania Avenue, NW, Washington, DC 20530-0001. *E-mail*—AskDOJ@usdoj.gov.

## Career

**T**rial attorney, Department of Justice, Public Integrity Section, Washington, DC, 1977-88; associate justice, Superior Court of the District of Columbia, 1988-93; U.S. attorney for Washington, D.C., Department of Justice, 1993-2008; deputy attorney general of the United States, 1997-2001; attorney general of the United States, 2008—.

**Awards:** The Best Lawyers in America, Woodward/White, 2007.

## Sidelights

**I**n 1997, Eric H. Holder, Jr., became the highest-ranking African-American law enforcement official in U.S. history, a journey that has continued as he has been appointed to higher positions. Holder was named U.S. Attorney for the District of Columbia in 1993, making him the first American-American to hold that post. In 1997, he was con-

firmed by the Senate as deputy attorney general of the United States, and in 2009, he was confirmed as the U.S. attorney general.

Holder has a reputation for his strong desire for justice, regardless of the position and clout of those who may be guilty. His lack of patience for the political maneuverings inside of the Department of Justice has made him determined to restore public confidence in the federal judiciary branch. "The attorney general has sent an unequivocal message that prosecutions of any kind, whether against Republicans, Democrats, independents or others, must be done right," Patrick Leahy, Vermont Democrat and Senate Judiciary Committee Chairman, said as quoted in *USA Today*.

Born in the borough of Queens in New York City, Holder is the son of emigrants from Barbados. His father, Eric H. Holder, Sr., joined the U.S. Army and served during World War II before becoming a real estate broker. Holder attended high school in Manhattan at the prestigious Stuyvesant High School. He was a good student and earned a Regents scholarship, and was a member of the basketball team. Early on, Holder hoped he would become a basketball star, and later, he thought he might be a history teacher. He earned a degree in

American history from Columbia College before deciding to continue on at Columbia Law.

While attending Columbia, Holder attended Harlem's Apollo Theater, one of the landmark theaters for introducing African American and Latino talents to the entertainment industry. He was a regular parishioner at Adam Clayton Powell's sermons at the Abyssinian Baptist Church. His involvement in these communities and his concern that young African Americans from the inner city did not have enough good role models led him to become one of the founding members of the Harlem branch of Concerned Black Men, a national organization dedicated to helping minority youth. Holder spent his Saturday mornings at a Harlem youth center, and took young people on tours around New York.

Holder had worked as a clerk at the National Association for the Advancement of Colored People (NAACP) Legal Defense Fund and at the Department of Justice's Criminal Division as a student. After graduating from Columbia Law in 1976 and passing the New York Bar in 1977, Holder was recruited into the Department of Justice as part of the attorney general's Honors Program. Assigned to the new Public Integrity Section in 1976—a division formed to investigate and prosecute official corruption—he began his career as a trial lawyer. In that position, he helped to prosecute high-level cases of noted public officials, including FBI agents, organized crime figures, and politicians. In 1988, Holder was appointed associate justice of the Superior Court of the District of Columbia by President Ronald Reagan. The position, which meant presiding over cases from violent crime to school truancy, was a difficult one for Holder, due in part to the large number of defendants who were young black males. "Conceptually, yeah, I knew that's what it was going to be because it's a city that's 70 percent black, and black males are disproportionately represented in the criminal justice system," Holder told the *Washington Post.* "I guess the reality of it struck me after a while. I mean, it's not an easy thing to deal with, if you are a person who's concerned about the black community, to see what ought to be the future standing before you charged with some sort of criminal offense."

In 1989 at a fund-raiser for Concerned Black Men, Holder met Dr. Sharon Malone, an obstetrician-gynecologist involved in the sister cause Coalition of 100 Black Women. They were married, and in 1993, the couple had their first daughter, Maya. That same year, Holder was selected by President Bill Clinton as the U.S. attorney for Washington, D.C. The job paid substantially less than Holder had earned as a Superior Court judge, but offered many opportunities for upward mobility. Local area leaders supported the decision, in part because Holder had shown so much dedication to Washington, D.C. Politicians in the district also thought it would help to have an African-American U.S. attorney; Holder was the first African American to fill that position. "In some ways, I came in as prepared as I could have been because of my 12 years in Public Integrity," Holder said in an interview with the *Washington Post.* "I think potentially I'm a better U.S. attorney now than I was then, from being on the bench for five years." Given how many high profile cases he had handled, Holder was aware that there would be public scrutiny on his decisions in his new position. "I guess the reality is [that] there is something personally at stake for me. You have to do the investigating and just call it."

As U.S. attorney of Washington, D.C., Holder continued to fight government corruption, indicting Illinois Congressman Dan Rostenkowski, chair of the House Ways and Means Committee, on charges of misusing official House funds. He also fought discrimination in lending in a D.C. area bank, which was accused of limiting its marketing to white areas. The bank declared black areas off-limits to advertising, a process called "redlining." The bank's neglect had a tremendous negative impact on the community, and the Justice Department ruled that the institution had violated the Fair Housing Act.

Holder also called on the African-American community to work to better its situation. In a speech given on Martin Luther King Jr. Day, 1994, and quoted by the *Washington Post,* he said, "There has been for too long a conspiracy of silence in the black community—a reluctance to discuss our manifest problems, a desire to avoid painful truths. The defenders of the silence say we are not the ones who import or manufacture guns. This logic has been used to shield us from the ugly truth that we are the ones who pull the triggers, and we are the ones who sell and use drugs. We must talk about these things and confront these truths." Holder worked to increase communication between Asian and African-American communities, praising Asian-American business owners for staying in the inner city while many others fled to the suburbs, fearing crime.

In 1997, Clinton nominated Holder to fill the position of deputy attorney general of the United States, the position immediately under Attorney General Janet Reno. At the time, a stumbling block to his appointment was his position against the death penalty. However, he stated his willingness to place aside his personal beliefs to uphold the Constitution and the laws determined by Congress. Holder was sworn in with an unanimous confirmation by the Senate.

Involved with some controversial pardons under the Clinton administration, Holder left the Justice Department for some years during the Bush administration. As a citizen and litigation partner at the private firm Covington & Burling LLP in Washington, D.C., Holder grew increasingly frustrated with the Justice Department under President George W. Bush. The use of waterboarding—which Holder believed to be torture—by the CIA at Guantanamo Bay, on terrorists during interrogations made many citizens lose faith in federal law enforcement. In 2009, he was offered the opportunity to give the Justice Department a new reputation when he was nominated to the position of U.S. attorney general by President Barack Obama. Holder stated that if confirmed, he would seek to prosecute terrorists being held at Guantanamo Bay in American courts, offering them full trials. He also pledged that fighting terrorists would be his top priority.

The controversial pardons issued by Clinton, apparently at Holder's recommendation, were a stumbling block in the hearings before his appointment. In 1999, Holder had supported clemency for 16 Puerto Rican militants; an FBI agent who had worked on that investigation stated in the *New York Times* that he was "outraged" by the clemency decision. Holder, however, held to his decision, defending it as "reasonable"; none of the people granted clemency, who had been sentenced 16 to 20 years, had been accused of crimes that resulted in death.

The other pardon, however, was a source of greater contention. Marc Rich was a financier who fled to Switzerland rather than being prosecuted for tax related charges. Rich's wife had made a large donation to Clinton's library. Holder stated that his advice on the case, given before he had gained all the facts, had been "neutral, leaning toward favorable," a statement used as support by the Clinton administration and now regretted by Holder. Louis J. Freeh, who had been head of the FBI from 1993 to 2001, spoke in support of Holder, recognizing that the pardon of Rich was corrupt, but that the guilt lay with former president Clinton rather than Holder. Freeh believed that Holder had learned from the mistake, and would never allow himself to be put in that situation again.

Despite these controversies, Holder was confirmed to the position of attorney general in a Senate vote of 75 to 21. Upon his appointment, Holder immedi-ately began working to separate the Justice Department under his leadership from the work of the department under the Bush administration. He was made one of the leaders in the initiative to close the Guantanamo Bay detention center. He also sought to investigate corruption inside the Justice Department, particularly surrounding a scandal in which nine U.S. attorneys were abruptly dismissed. Holder also dismissed charges of corruption against former Alaska senator Ted Stevens due to a failure by the prosecution to provide critical information to the defense lawyers. The dismissal of the case of Stevens, a Republican, served not only as a symbolic statement against political alliances in the Justice Department, but also as a precedent for fixing bad cases that did not follow proper procedures.

Holder has also promised to revitalize the Department of Justice's Civil Rights Division. There were internal reports that 63 attorneys were hired into that division based on their political affiliations. Holder pledged to look into the case against former senior civil rights lawyer Bradley Scholzman over accusations of making false statements to Congress, which the department refused to investigate. Leahy praised Holder's appointment as attorney general in the *New York Times*, feeling that the appointment was "a statement that we all want to restore the integrity and competence of the Justice Department and to restore another critical component—the American people's confidence in federal law enforcement."

## Sources

### Books

*Contemporary Black Biography*, vol. 9, Gale (Detroit, MI), 1995.
*Notable Black American Men*, Gale (Detroit, MI), 1998.
*Who's Who Among African Americans*, 22nd ed., Gale (Detroit, MI), 2008.

### Periodicals

*Jet*, June 20, 1994, p. 10; March 31, 1997, p. 4.
*New York Times*, January 16, 2009, p. A1; January 17, 2009, p. A12; February 3, 2009, p. A17.
*USA Today*, April 6, 2009, p. 10A.
*U.S. News & World Report*, November 19, 2008.
*Washington Post*, July 30, 1993, p. B1; August 5, 1993, p. J1; September 21, 1993, p. B1; January 17, 1994, p. D1; April 29, 1994, p. A25; May 6, 1994, p. A1.

—*Alana Joli Abbott*

# Mike Horn

AP Images

## Explorer

Born July 16, 1966, in Johannesburg, South Africa; married Cathy; children: Annika, Jessica. *Education:* Attended the University of Stellenbosch, South Africa.

**Addresses:** *Home*—Chateau-d'Oex, Switzerland.

## Career

Writer, traveler, explorer, athlete, public speaker, and adventurer. Worked as a ski instructor and a river and canyon guide. founder and owner, "No Limits" Outdoor Activity Sports Center, Switzerland, 1995. Works as a motivational conference speaker and lecturer. Worked as a seller of fruits and vegetables in South Africa.

**Awards:** Multicocques Grand Prix winner; Laureus Award for Best Alternative Sportsman of the Year; Adventurer of the Year, *Out There* magazine; Toison d'Or, Dijon Film Festival; elected a member of the Laureus World Sports Academy, 2007.

## Sidelights

Explorer Mike Horn has swum the Amazon, circled the globe at the Equator, circumnavigated the Arctic Circle, and reached the North Pole, one of an unsupported team of two, starting the trek in total darkness. He has paraglided in the Peruvian Andes, taken a body-board down a glacier, and has written three books about his expeditions. His exploits have made him "one of the most revered explorers in Europe," according to Brad Wieners of *National Geographic Adventure.*

Born in Johannesburg, South Africa, in 1966, Horn studied human movement science at the University of Stellenbosch. He was drafted by the South African Army and fought in Angola against a communist insurgent group backed by Cuba, an experience that led him to prefer the honest brutality of nature over the treachery of men. As an athlete, Horn aspired to compete in the Olympics, but South Africa was banned from the games, due to apartheid. Horn moved to Europe, settling in Switzerland in 1990, where he was so poor he had to make a living sweeping the floor of a youth hostel. There, he met his wife, Cathy, who later served as a vital supporter of his expeditions, the voice on the other end of the radio who can send supplies to agreed upon destinations.

Horn became a ski instructor, a rafting guide, and a paraglider. He worked for No Limits, a company in Les Marécottes, Valais, where he added rock climbing, hydrospeed, rap jumping, and canyoning to his resume. He joined a 1991 paragliding and rafting expedition in the Peruvian Andes, completing a descent by delta plane from the summit of Huascaran and crashing near Machu Picchu, a stunt which earned him an invitation to join the "Sector No Limits" extreme sports team.

In 1994 and 1995, Horn focused on breaking hydrospeed records, descending the Mont Blanc glacier to the French Riviera; the Colca Canyon, the deepest canyon in the world; and the Pacuare River in Costa Rica, which earned him a world record for highest descent of a waterfall on a hydrospeed. He drew more public attention when he crossed South America on foot and went down the Amazon River by hydrospeed. The six-month journey, during which he swam long portions of the river, took him the entire length of the Amazon, finishing at the Pacific Ocean.

Horn began his Latitude Zero expedition in 1999, circling the globe along the Equator, using no motorized vehicles to help him. The trip lasted 17 months, during which he at least once was positive he was going to die. He was bitten on the finger by a venomous snake and went blind; for two days, his condition worsened, and he was not only ill, but began to lose feeling in his body. On the third day, certain he was not going to recover, he sent an electronic beacon to Cathy to say goodbye. On the fourth day, he regained some sensation, though he was still seriously ill; on the fifth day, his vision returned, and he was able to walk. At another point in his journey, he was dragged before a firing squad in the Democratic Republic of the Congo. In the end, the journey was a success, and Horn became the first man ever to complete such an expedition. He received several awards and accolades from sportsmen and explorers alike. Horn recounted the journey in his first book, *Latitude Zero.*

In 2002, Horn attempted his first journey to the North Pole. A month into his trek, he made a dangerous mistake: He removed his mitts to fix a broken shoestring. His fingers developed frostbite, and Horn had to choose between giving up the expedition and losing his fingers. "That was a big, big lesson for me and one of the hardest decisions I've ever made," he told Wieners. "Here I was 10 or 15 days from my goal, and such stupidity cost me the Pole. I was humbled." Horn called for evacuation and only lost the tips of his fingers and part of his thumb bone. After his recovery, Horn returned to the Arctic with a new expedition planned: He would complete the first solo circumnavigation of the Arctic Circle. The journey took two years and three months to complete and earned him greater international renown. His book *Conquering the Impossible: My 12,000-Mile Journey around the Arctic Circle* became a best-seller in Europe.

In 2006, Horn received a unique offer: Borge Ousland, one of the most experienced polar explorers, asked him to join a team to trek to the North Pole. The catch to this expedition was that it would start in January, 2006, during complete darkness in the polar region. The trek was planned as unsupported, meaning Ousland and Horn would drag all their own gear with them and then would be picked up by helicopter at the North Pole. They began each dragging 330 pounds of food and equipment, covering 620 miles from Cape Arkticheskiy to the Pole itself. On this trip, not only did nature provide challenges, but personality conflicts early on made the journey dangerous. "A simple misunderstanding, after a bone-tiring day fighting to stay alive, could escalate unpredictably and require energy neither could afford," noted Marguerite Del Giudice of *National Geographic,* noting that the pair had to overcome not only different styles of exploration, but also cultural miscommunications. Near the end of the trip, Horn suffered from an infection throughout his body, and their progress slowed. They reached the North Pole days after they had planned, and spring crested before they finished, beating them to their goal of reaching the Pole during the winter. Despite that, Horn was still cheerful about their success; he told Melissa Block of *All Things Considered,* "living through the conditions that we were living in, this has been one of the real great stories ever accomplished in the Arctic. To ever think of making a winter crossing to the North Pole from Russia was really ambitious."

Horn planned an educational expedition beginning in 2008 and running through 2012. With funding from various sources and the help of experts, Horn was able to build the polar exploration sailboat *Pangaea* that would allow him to circumnavigate the world around the Poles. But not only would this expedition be a trip of adventure for Horn: The explorer planned to share his travels via his Home Page, where young adults could follow his route and learn more about the natural world. According to the *Pangaea* mission statement on Horn's Home Page, "This dream has taken Mike Horn years to realize, but it is now becoming a reality from which Mike can do his part to instill his passion and wonderment for the natural world in today's youth."

The expeditions often bring in sponsorship money to fund exploration, but much of Horn's income while not exploring comes from taking pictures, making films, serving as a specialized guide, giving motivational lectures, along with the sale of his books. Horn's Home Page bears his inspirational motto: "The impossible exists only until we find a way to make it possible."

## Selected writings

### Travelogues

*Latitude Zero,* XO, 2001.
*Breitengrad Null,* Piper Verlag GmbH, 2004.
(With Jean-Philippe Chatrier) *Conquering the Impossible: My 12,000-Mile Journey around the Arctic Circle,* translated by Antony Shugaar, St. Martin's Press, 2007.

## Sources

### Periodicals

*Men's Fitness,* October 2005, p. 37.
*National Geographic,* January 2007, p. 130.
*National Geographic Adventure,* February 2006, p. 50.

### Online

*All Things Considered,* NPR, http://www.npr.org/templates/story/story.php?storyId=5300099 (February 11, 2009).
Bid the Dream: The Laureus Collection, http://www.bidthedream.com/Biography.aspx?bioId=horn (February 11, 2009).
Biographies: Special South Africans, http://zar.co.za/horn.htm (February 11, 2009).
Celebrities in Switzerland, http://www.switzerland.isyours.com/E/celebrities/bios/204.html (February 11, 2009).
Mike Horn's Home Page, http://www.mikehorn.com/ (February 11, 2009).

*—Alana Joli Abbott*

# Jeffrey Housenbold

*Courtesy of Shutterfly, Inc.*

## Chief Executive Officer of Shutterfly

**B**orn c. 1969; married Ruth (a business consultant); children: three sons. *Education:* Carnegie Mellon University, B.S.B.A., 1991; Harvard Business School, M.B.A., 1996.

**Addresses:** *Office*—Shutterfly, Inc., 2800 Bridge Pkwy., Redwood City, CA 94065.

## Career

**W**orked as a business consultant, c. 1991-94; founding manager of Media & Entertainment Strategy Group, Accenture, late 1990s; vice president of corporate development, WinStar Communications, late 1990s; chief operating officer, Raging Bull (a community finance portal), c. 2000; vice president and general manager, AltaVista, 2000-01; vice president of mergers and acquisitions, eBay, March 2001-June 2001; then vice president and general manager of business-to-consumer group, June 2001-January 2002; then vice president of business development and Internet marketing, January 2002-January 2005; president and chief executive officer, Shutterfly, Inc., 2005—.

## Sidelights

**J**effrey Housenbold is president and chief executive officer of Shutterfly, Inc., the Web-based photo-sharing site that retooled itself into an innovative personal publishing venture. The company's two high-tech printing plants enable anyone to create a bound book of their photography or even a custom calendar, which helped it post revenues of $187 million in 2007. Shutterfly also stores more than a billion images from its core of devoted users on its servers. "Your hard drive might crash, your house might catch fire, and if something like that happened your memories are safe with us," he told business journalist Sramana Mitra in a 2008 interview.

Housenbold grew up in Brooklyn and New Jersey in the 1970s and '80s. His parents struggled financially for many years, and for a time relied on a government program known as Aid to Families with Dependent Children and the food-stamp program. "Although there were times of self-pity, I quickly decided the only way to change my situation was to dream big," he wrote in *Newsweek* in 2007. "When my high-school guidance counselor told me not to waste $35 on a college application, I was all the more motivated." Housenbold applied to one of the top undergraduate business programs in the United States, at Pittsburgh's Carnegie Mellon University, and even won a scholarship. He graduated in 1991 with a dual degree in economics and business administration after having earned 4.0 grade-point averages for most of the semesters, despite the fact that he also worked two jobs at times to pay his living expenses.

Housenbold worked for a time as a strategy consultant before entering Harvard Business School for his master's in business administration. He went on to create the media and entertainment strategy group for Accenture, the consulting division spin-off of accounting firm Arthur Andersen, before joining WinStar Communications, a telecom giant, as vice president of corporate development. A technology venture-capital firm called CMGI (formerly College Marketing Group Information and later to become ModusLink Global Solutions) hired him to serve as chief operating officer at one of their newly launched companies, an online investment community called Raging Bull.

In 2000, Raging Bull was sold to AltaVista, one of the hot Internet portal sites of the era, and AltaVista made Housenbold vice president and general manager. He joined online-auction pioneer eBay in March of 2001 as vice president for mergers and acquisitions, and then took on responsibilities for its business-to-consumer group, "which was all about getting large companies to sell on eBay, versus Mom and Pops," he explained to Mitra. "I signed up Dell, Wal-Mart, Lexmark, Kitchen Aide, and Home Depot." In January of 2002 he became vice president of business development and Internet marketing at eBay, and in that post, he told Mitra, "I did the first deal with Google—I was Google's very first AdWords customer in the world."

Housenbold was not looking for a new job in late 2004, but was tempted when an offer came through to run Shutterfly, Inc. Some of the allure was that he was a devoted user of the photo-sharing and printing Web site. "My wife and I spent $1,900 on Shutterfly the year before," he admitted in the interview with Mitra. "I was a big customer and had been using it for five years." Shutterfly was founded in 1999 by Jim Clark—whose other successes included Netscape and Silicon Graphics—after two Silicon Graphics employees asked Clark to fund their idea. At the time, digital cameras were a new—and expensive—consumer item and Shutterfly was launched with the goal of making it easy to upload picture files into a computer and then share or print them.

Shutterfly exploded so quickly after its launch that it grew to more than 300 employees and batted away rumors that it was about to buy Kodak. Like other highly touted ventures of the Web 1.0 era, the company barely survived the dotcom bust of 2000—when the six-year speculative bubble of investment in new-technology ventures began to burst—and had to lay off three-quarters of its workforce. Shutterfly survived only because Clark kept it afloat financially, but it also had a core base of devoted users who remained loyal and even increased. By 2003 Shutterfly was profitable again, and in 2004 there was talk of a long-awaited initial public offering of stock, or IPO.

Housenbold was brought on board to help Shutterfly move forward with the IPO plan, but in the *Newsweek* article he wrote that he quickly discovered that "we were not forward-looking—we hadn't even updated our home page in four years. At my first board meeting, I announced we weren't ready to go public." Housenbold came up with ways Shutterfly could position itself apart from its main competitors—Snapfish, owned by Hewlett-Packard since 2005, and Kodak Gallery, formerly Ofoto—by adding new services. "It was all about ... prints and price," he told Mitra. "We were not helping people do more with their images and memories, we were much more along the old paradigm which was drop off a roll of film, develop prints and place them in clear sleeves for users to put in a binder on a bookshelf."

Shutterfly added a unique scrapbook creation tool to its Web site, and also began offering a range of custom products, including photo books, greeting cards, and calendars, all of which are printed at two production facilities in Hayward, California, and Charlotte, North Carolina. The company finally went public September of 2006 with a $87 million IPO, and is traded on the NASDAQ under the ticker symbol SFLY. In 2007, it posted revenues of $187 million.

Housenbold has often described his family—his business-consultant wife, Ruth, and their three sons—as the ideal Shutterfly household. An avid "shutterbug" since his teens, when he served as yearbook photographer at Cedar Ridge High in Old Bridge, New Jersey, Housenbold stores more than 100,000 images on his own Shutterfly account. "I've always had an interest in human connections and an interest in building a great brand," he told *Chain Store Age.* "I've been very fortunate to work in businesses that I'm very passionate about."

## Sources

### Periodicals

*Chain Store Age,* December 2006, p. 54.
*Newsweek,* October 1, 2007, p. E4; June 2, 2008, p. E8.
*New York Times,* October 30, 2006.

### Online

"Shutterfly's Strategy: A Conversation with CEO Jeff Housenbold," http://www.sramanamitra.com (October 22, 2008).
"A Picture of Success," Carnegie Mellon Tepper School of Business, http://www.tepper.cmu.edu/news-multimedia/tepper-multimedia/tepper-stories/a-picture-of-success/index.aspx (October 22, 2008).

—*Carol Brennan*

# Jonathan Ive

Duffy-Marie Arnoult/WireImage/Getty Images

## Industrial designer

**B**orn Jonathan Paul Ive in February of 1967 in London, England; married to Heather (a writer and historian); children: twin sons. *Education:* Newcastle Polytechnic University, art and design degree, then doctorate, c. 1990.

**Addresses:** *Home*—San Francisco, CA. *Office*—Apple, Inc., One Infinite Loop, Cupertino, CA 95014.

## Career

**C**o-founder and consultant to Tangerine, a London industrial design firm, 1990-92; designer, Apple, Inc., 1992-96, then director of design, 1996-98, then vice president of industrial design, 1998-2002, then senior vice president for design, 2005—.

**Awards:** Designer of the Year, British Design Museum, 2002, 2003; Commander of the Most Excellent Order of the British Empire (CBE), 2005; National Design Award in Product Design, Cooper-Hewitt Museum, for iPhone, 2007; MDA Personal Achievement Award, Mobile Data Association, for iPhone, 2008; recipient of four Black Pencil Awards from Design & Art Direction (D&AD).

## Sidelights

**I**ndustrial designer Jonathan Ive may not be a household name, but his products certainly are to most of the Western world. As senior vice president for design at Apple, Inc., Ive is responsible for the iPod, iPhone, and iMac, a trio of top-selling, award-

winning personal-technology items that are widely credited with rescuing the company from financial failure. Writing in London's *Independent,* Claire Beale called him "perhaps the world's most revered product designer.... For everyone who loves Macs and iPods and iPhones for their intuition, for their clean aesthetics, for their leading edge, elegant functionality, Ive is the man who made technology both beautiful and accessible."

Ive, called "Jony" by family, friends, and coworkers, was born in 1967 in London and grew up in Chingford, a town that belongs to the Greater London metropolitan area. His father was a silversmith. At Newcastle Polytechnic in the northeast English city of Newcastle-upon-Tyne, he studied industrial design and eventually earned a doctorate in the subject from the school, which later became Northumbria University. Perhaps somewhat fittingly, Ive was utterly uninterested in the burgeoning new field of information technology as a young adult. "I went through college having a real problem with computers," he once told an interviewer, according to *Times* of London correspondent Chris Ayres. "I was convinced that I was technically inept. Right at the end of my time at college, I discovered the Mac. I remember being astounded at just how much better it was than anything else I had tried to use."

After finishing his degree, Ive moved to London and co-founded the renowned design firm called Tangerine with three other designers. One of its clients was Apple, Inc., the Cupertino, California-based firm that had revolutionized the personal-computer market in 1977 with the Apple II model and the Macintosh seven years later. By the early 1990s, however, Apple's share of the personal-computer market had shrunk and the company's executive leadership had made a number of near-fatal missteps. "Apple does really badly when it plays to other people's criteria," Ive reflected in a rare *New York Times* interview a few years after joining the company. Referring to some of its earlier products that hit the market prior to his tenure, he characterized some as "splendidly banal," according to the newspaper's John Markoff.

Ive moved to California in 1992 when he was hired by Apple. In 1996, when a new chief executive officer named Gil Amelio took over, Ive was made director of design. Amelio's tenure was brief, and when one of the original two founders of Apple, Steve Jobs, replaced Amelio, the company's turnaround began in earnest. In 1998, Jobs made Ive vice president for industrial design at Apple, and Ive's first major product, the iMac, was unveiled that same year. Both Apple devotees and design aficionados hailed the iMac's translucent white plastic casing and bulging forms, accented with plastic that came in a range of candy-colored choices, as a significant step forward in computer design. The novel all-in-one integrated unit was smaller than other personal computers on the market, had no floppy disk drive, and used universal serial bus (USB) ports that later became standard across the industry.

The iMac made Ive a celebrity in the world of design, and a star at Apple; the company sold two million units of the computer in the first year alone. Back at the drawing board, Ive took Apple products in a more minimalist direction with the dawn of the new millennium, epitomized by the Powerbook G4, introduced in 2001 and the first of the company's new designs to become a genuine status symbol. A fast laptop model made of sleek titanium casing, the Powerbook G4 had a wider screen but was both lighter than other laptops and had a longer-life battery.

Later in 2001 Apple introduced the iPod, the most successful product in company history. A portable digital audio player that could store up to 1,000 songs, the first-generation iPod featured a novel, easy-to-use click-wheel that made it much easier to navigate than previous digital-music players. That first iPod and its successors—all designed by Ive and his team—sold 150 million units over the next six years.

Ive's most stunning achievement, however, came in the form of Apple's first mobile telephone/personal communication device, the iPhone. Launched in June of 2007 and featuring a novel touchscreen that the company reportedly spent a small fortune on engineering to perfection, the iPhone was hailed as revolutionary and secured Ive's place as the most important living industrial designer of his age.

Ive has won scores of prestigious design awards for his work. Twice he has been named Designer of the Year by the British Design Museum, and he holds four highly coveted Black Pencil Awards from Design & Art Direction (D&AD), an education charity that seeks out the best global examples in design and other creative endeavors. On New Year's Eve of 2005, his name appeared on the annual New Year's Honors issued by Queen Elizabeth II of England, who is an iPod owner. With that, Ive was permitted to append "CBE" after his name, which is the shortened form for Commander of the Most Excellent Order of the British Empire.

Ive habitually avoids publicity, and in the rare interviews he gives prefers instead to credit his team of about a dozen highly paid designers who work out of a top-secret studio somewhere near Cupertino. Married to a writer and historian, he is the father of twins, and in 2008 bought a ten-bedroom manor in Somerset, England, reportedly because he wanted his two sons to be educated there. The family will likely divide their time between that home and their first in the Twin Peaks neighborhood of San Francisco. Ive's annual salary is thought to be in the $2 million range, and his one known luxury habit is an Aston Martin, the British-made roadster made famous in the James Bond movies. "I'm not driven by making a cultural impact," he told Beale, the journalist with the *Independent*. "That's just a consequence of taking a remarkably powerful technology and making it relevant. My goal is simply to try to make products that really are meaningful to people."

## Sources

*BusinessWeek*, September 25, 2006, p. 26.
*Independent* (London, England), May 19, 2008, p. 14.
*Macworld*, August 2008, p. 22.
*New York Times*, February 5, 1998.
*Times* (London, England), December 8, 2007, p. 26.

—*Carol Brennan*

# Nina G. Jablonski

## Scientist, professor, and author

**B**orn Nina Grace Jablonski in 1953 in New York; married George Chaplin. *Education:* Bryn Mawr, B.A., 1975; University of Washington, Ph.C., 1978, Ph.D., 1981.

**Addresses:** *E-mail*—ngj2psu.edu. *Office*—c/o Department of Anthropology, Pennsylvania State University, 409 Carpenter Bldg., University Park, PA 16802.

## Career

**U**niversity of Hong Kong, lecturer in Department of Anatomy, 1981-90; University of Western Australia, senior lecturer in Department of Anatomy and Human Biology, 1990-94; California Academy of Sciences, San Francisco, CA, Irvine chair of anthropology, associate curator of anthropology, and chair of anthropology department, 1995-98, then Irvine chair of anthropology, curator of anthropology, and head of the Department of Anthropology, 1998-2006; Penn State University, University Park, PA, professor and head of Department of Anthropology, 2006—; found the oldest known chimpanzee fossil, 2004; published *Skin: A Natural History,* 2007.

**Awards:** J. William Fulbright Senior Scholarship, 1998; Alphonse Fletcher Senior Fellowship, 2005; W. W. Howells Award for best book in biological anthropology, American Anthropological Association, for *Skin: A Natural History,* 2007.

## Sidelights

**T**he head of the Department of Anthropology at Pennsylvania State University, Nina G. Jablonski is a scientist and professor with a wide range of interests. In addition to working as an anthropologist, she is a primatologist, evolutionary biologist, and paleontologist. In her research, Jablonski is especially interested in primate evolution and human evolution, including the evolution of human skin and skin coloration as well as evolutionary theories of bipedalism. She has conducted fieldwork in China, Kenya, and Nepal and published regularly on these subjects. In 2006, Jablonski came to national prominence with the publication of her book, *Skin: A Natural History.*

Born in 1953 in New York, Jablonski focused her college studies on biology and anthropology. In 1975, she graduated with her B.A. in biology from Bryn Mawr College. Entering graduate school at the University of Washington, she earned a Ph.C. in 1978 and the Ph.D. in 1981. Both of her graduate degrees are in anthropology. After completing her education, Jablonski taught in the University of Hong Kong's Department of Anatomy, from 1981 until 1990. Along with other courses, she taught gross anatomy for medical school students.

While teaching this course, Jablonski had an epiphany. In 2007, she told Claudia Dreifus of the *New York Times,* "The students had been presented with a cadaver to dissect, and they were tremendously frightened of it. However, their attitude changed the very moment they cut through the skin. With the skin gone, they began seeing it as a mere body devoid of a personal history, and they could get on with their work. That moment showed me how much of what we consider our humanity is imbued in our skin. It stayed with me for a long time."

In 1990, Jablonski left Hong Kong and moved to Australia to teach at the University of Western Australia, where she was a senior lecturer in the Department of Anatomy and Human Biology. Jablonski focused some of her research during this time on primate evolution, especially bipedalism. She and her husband, George Chaplin, worked together to devise an evolutionary theory about why human ancestors moved from walking on four legs to walking upright on two legs. They asserted that such early humans had to have a reason related to survival or evolutionary advantage for standing. Jablonski and Chaplin concluded that standing made them look more threatening.

Jay Ingram of the *Toronto Star,* in summarizing the theory, wrote, "as groups of our ancestors roamed far and wide on the African plains looking for food they came to rely more and more heavily on these two-legged threats. Much better to stand up, make a few threats and then go on foraging than to have a bloody and sometimes fatal battle every time two groups met." While chimps and apes employ this behavior during conflicts or when order needs to be maintain, they have not needed to do it full time. Jablonski continued to refine her bipedalism theory as additional evidence was discovered related to where bipedal ancestors lived. Because these ancestors were known to live in both wooded forests and open savannas, she admitted that bipedalism could have had its origins in forests.

Returning to the United States in 1995, Jablonski took a position at the California Academy of Sciences, a museum in Golden Gate Park, San Francisco. She first served as the Irvine chair of anthropology, associate curator of anthropology, and chair of the museum's anthropology department. In 1998, she retained her post as Irvine chair of anthropology and was promoted to curator of anthropology and head of the anthropology department.

During her time at the California Academy of Sciences, Jablonski began studying human skin in terms of biology, evolution, and social function. Much of her initial research focused on skin color. With Chaplin, she began by studying the data from the Total Ozone Mapping Spectrometer, a NASA (National Aeronautics and Space Administration) project that measured the amount of ultraviolet radiation (UVR) reaching the surface of the Earth. Offering the first wide-ranging theory on the subject, she came to the conclusion that skin color is primarily an evolutionary adaptation related to migration patterns and adaptations for UVR levels. The fact that different amounts of ultraviolet light hit the Earth at different locations seems to explain adaptive variations in skin color among populations in different places.

Jablonski told the *Bryn Mawr Alumnae Bulletin,* "There is a broad range of human skin tones because humans live in a broad range of environments, from those that receive a lot of sun and UV radiation, mostly near the equator, to those that receive very little, near the poles. Some have a lot of melanin because it protected their ancestors from the harmful effects of UV radiation; other people have less melanin because they live where there is less UV radiation, and their skin must be lighter in other to permit the available UVR to be used in vitamin D production." In other words, the less UVR, the more fair the inhabitants' skin, and women are usually fairer than men because of reproductive-related concerns. In 2000, she and Chaplin published some of their findings in the *Journal of Human Evolution.*

Also in while working at the California Academy of Sciences, Jablonski made significant fossil discoveries. Beginning in 1998, she led a research team in Nepal that found 2,000 new fossil specimens of various mammals, reptiles, fishes, and amphibians. These fossils included such animals as ancient horses and hippos that lived in Nepal more than eight million years ago. In 2004, Jablonski attracted media attention when she inadvertently found the oldest-known chimpanzee fossil. While doing research at the National Museum of Kenya, she found a bag labeled "fossil monkeys," which she realized were really chimp fossils. Jablonski's finding turned out to be chimp teeth that were a half million years old, much older than chimps previously in the fossil record and proving that chimpanzees have been in their form for longer than what had been previously suspected. Her findings on this fossil and its significance were published in *Nature* in 2005.

Jablonski left the California Academy of Sciences in 2006 and accepted a position at Pennsylvania State University as both a professor and head of the Department of Anthropology. Along with administrative responsibilities, she taught classes such as primatology. Shortly after moving from California to Pennsylvania, Jablonski also published the book she had been working on for several years, *Skin: A Natural History*. The product of much research but written for a general audience, *Skin* offers extensive biological, evolutionary, and cultural information about the largest organ in the human body.

Jablonski explains the three attributes of skin and how these evolved: its hairlessness and sweatiness; its range of colors, and its various decorations. Reviews of *Skin* were generally positive, with Natalie Angier of *American Scholar* calling it, "fascinating, nuanced, often exhilarating, and for the most part crisply written." *Publishers Weekly* commented, "Jablonski nimbly interprets scientific data for a lay audience, and her geeky love for her discipline is often infectious." *Skin* won the American Anthropological Association's W. W. Howells Award for best book in biological anthropology.

While *Skin* brought Jablonski much media attention—including an appearance on the popular Comedy Central series *The Colbert Report*—this particular work was also extremely personal for the anthropologist. When *New York Times'* Dreifus asked Jablonski about her feelings about her own skin, Jablonski replied, "I like it. It is my unwritten biography. My skin reminds me that I'm a 53-year-old woman who has smiled and furrowed her brow and, on occasion, worked in the desert sun too long. I enjoy watching my skin change because it's one of the few parts of my body I can watch. We can't view our livers or heart, but this we can."

## Selected writings

### Nonfiction

(Editor) *Theropithecus: The Rise and Fall of a Primate Genus*, Cambridge University Press, 1993.
(Editor) *The Natural History of the Doucs and Snub-nosed Monkeys*, World Scientific, 1998.
(Editor, with F. Anapol and R. Z. German) *Shaping Primate Evolution: Form, Function, and Behavior*, Cambridge University Press, 1998.

(With George Chaplin) "The Evolution of Skin Coloration," *Journal of Human Evolution*, 2000.
(With S. McBrearty) "First Fossil Chimpanzee," *Nature*, 2005.
*Skin: A Natural History*, University of California Press, 2006.

## Sources

### Books

*Contemporary Authors Online*, Thomson Gale, 2007.

### Periodicals

*American Scholar*, September 22, 2006, p. 127.
AScribe Newswire, July 31, 2000.
Associated Press State & Local Wire, August 26, 2000.
*Discover*, July 1, 1996, p. 116.
*New York Times*, January 9, 2007, p. F2.
*Publishers Weekly*, August 7, 2006, p. 45.
*San Jose Mercury News*, August 31, 2005.
*Toronto Star*, September 5, 1993, p. B6.
University Wire, March 1, 2007.
Xinhua General News Service, November 8, 2000.

### Online

"Abridged curriculum vitae: Nina Grace Jablonski," Pennsylvania State University, http://www.anthro.psu.edu/faculty_staff/docs/NINA%20CV.pdf (January 22, 2009).
"Department of Anthropology at Penn State," Pennsylvania State University, http://www.anthro.psu.edu/faculty_staff/jablonski.shtml (January 22, 2009).
"Nina G. Jablonski," California Academy of Sciences, http://www.anthro.psu.edu/jablonskiLab/Jablonski/index.html (January 22, 2009).
"The Verdict on Skin Is In," *Bryn Mawr Alumnae Bulletin*, http://www.brynmawr.edu/alumnae/bulletin/jablonski.htm (January 22, 2009).

—*A. Petruso*

# Lisa P. Jackson

## Administrator of U.S. Environmental Protection Agency

**B**orn February 8, 1962, in Philadelphia, PA; married Kenny Jackson; children: Marcus, Brian. *Education:* Tulane University, B.S., 1983; Princeton University, M.Sc., 1986.

**Addresses:** *Office*—Environmental Protection Agency, Ariel Rios Building, 1200 Pennsylvania Ave., NW, Washington, DC 20460. *Web site*—http://www.epa.gov/administrator.

## Career

**W**orked for U.S. Environmental Protection Agency, c. 1986-2002; assistant commissioner, New Jersey Department of Environmental Protection, 2002-06; commissioner, NJDEP, 2006-08; named chief of staff for New Jersey Gov. Jon Corzine, 2008; nominated as administrator of U.S. EPA, 2008; confirmed as administrator, 2009.

**Awards:** Cabinet Member of the Year, New Jersey Conference of Mayors, 2007.

## Sidelights

**L**isa P. Jackson, who took over the U.S. Environmental Protection Agency in January of 2009, wasted no time in addressing what may prove to be the biggest environmental issue of the 21st century. Following up on campaign promises by her boss, President Barack Obama, Jackson quickly moved the U.S. government toward fighting global warm-

ing more aggressively. Within three months of taking her job, Jackson had already changed regulations and testified before Congress to move the country closer to creating mandatory restrictions on greenhouse gas emissions. A strong regulator of industry, dedicated to attaining environmental justice for the poor, Jackson is the first African-American head of the nation's environmental agency.

Jackson was born in Philadelphia, Pennsylvania, on February 8, 1962. Adopted a few weeks later, she grew up in New Orleans, Louisiana, in the Lower Ninth Ward neighborhood. She graduated first in her high school class and later graduated summa cum laude from the School of Chemical Engineering at Tulane University in New Orleans. She obtained a master's degree from Princeton University.

For 16 years, Jackson worked for the U.S. Environmental Protection Agency, or EPA. She helped direct multimillion-dollar hazardous waste cleanup projects and worked in the enforcement division at the New York City regional office. In 2002, Jackson joined the New Jersey Department of Environmental Protection as assistant commissioner for compliance and enforcement. In that job, she led more than 200 environmental inspectors in thorough sweeps through businesses in the cities of Paterson and

Camden, where many residents live in poverty, very close to industrial sites. Later, Jackson moved to another assistant commissioner position, in land use management. During her time in that job, her division drew up new rules to implement a state law limiting development in the Highlands region in northwest New Jersey.

In 2006, New Jersey Governor Jon Corzine promoted Jackson to commissioner of the Department of Environmental Protection. As New Jersey's top environmental regulator, Jackson took an aggressive stance toward regulating polluters and making sure environmental laws protected poorer communities. She also ended the state's controversial bear hunt.

Jackson favored reducing greenhouse gas emissions, which contribute to climate change. She released a plan to cut the state's carbon emissions by 20 percent by 2020 and 80 percent by 2050. In December of 2007, she joined the environmental directors of several other states in a lawsuit against the EPA, challenging its ruling that states could not enact stricter fuel efficiency standards for cars than federal standards. Jackson called the ruling "a horrendous change of course" (according to David Kocieniewski of the *New York Times*). "When it comes to the auto industry, the EPA apparently is the Emissions Permissions Agency," she added.

In New Jersey, Jackson was praised for her leadership and diplomatic skills. But she also attracted some criticism from environmentalists and the EPA. The federal agency felt New Jersey had not moved quickly enough to clean up some hazardous waste sites. Some environmentalists felt Jackson had given in to pressure from industry and developers when she supported a plan to privatize some aspects of hazardous waste cleanup and when her agency decided to make new groundwater quality standards less strict than originally planned. However, after her tenure was over, Dave Pringle, a lobbyist for the New Jersey Environmental Federation, vouched for her to Dunstan McNichol of the *New York Times*. "I think she is an environmentalist at heart," Pringle said. "And she is effective at getting as much as her boss will let her get."

In late October of 2008, Corzine named Jackson his chief of staff. However, she did not serve very long in the position. In mid-November, U.S. President-Elect Barack Obama asked her to join his environmental and energy transition team, and on December 15, Obama nominated Jackson to be the new administrator of the EPA.

During her U.S. Senate confirmation hearings in January of 2009, Jackson pledged to make scientific expertise the basis of the EPA's decisions. "Science must be the backbone of what EPA does," she told the Senate committee (as quoted by John M. Broder in the *New York Times*). "If I am confirmed, political appointees will not compromise the integrity of EPA's technical experts to advance particular regulatory outcomes." This position was important because the outgoing Bush Administration had often been accused of overruling its agencies' scientific experts for political reasons. Jackson also told the Senate committee that environmental protection and economic growth should co-exist. The Senate confirmed her appointment on January 23, 2009.

Jackson moved quickly to address greenhouse gases and global warming. She and Obama quickly reversed or reviewed three Bush Administration policies that had resulted in a slow approach to combating climate change. Obama announced the EPA planned to reconsider its decision not to allow California to regulate greenhouse gas emissions. Jackson said she would reconsider an earlier decision that the EPA could not regulate carbon dioxide emissions from coal plants.

Next, in April of 2009, the EPA complied with a U.S. Supreme Court decision from two years earlier that required it to determine whether to regulate greenhouse gas emissions, including carbon dioxide, as pollutants. In response, the EPA officially declared that greenhouse gases pose a threat to the public's health and welfare. The decision may lead to new regulations of several types of polluters, including cars and coal plants. Global warming is "a serious problem now and for future generations," Jackson said in a statement (quoted by Juliet Eilperin of the *Washington Post*). "This pollution problem has a solution—one that will create millions of green jobs and end our country's dependence on foreign oil."

Later that month, on Earth Day, Jackson was one of three Obama Administration cabinet members to testify before a House of Representatives committee about a bill that would establish the nation's first limits on greenhouse gas emissions. The bill would set up a cap and trade system: a national limit on carbon emissions and pollution allowances that carbon emitters could buy and sell. Opponents argued that the bill would hurt the economy, but Jackson argued that it would create new jobs in the clean energy industry.

Jackson maintains homes in Washington, D.C., and East Windsor, New Jersey. She is married to Kenny Jackson and has two sons, Marcus and Brian. Though she has lived on the East Coast for decades, she still embraces New Orleans culture. A talented cook, her favorite dish is Louisiana gumbo. For years, she was known for her annual Mardi Gras party, a celebration of New Orleans' greatest holiday, though she has not held the party since Hurricane Katrina flooded most of the city in 2005.

## Sources

### Periodicals

*New York Times,* December 11, 2008; January 15, 2009; January 25, 2009; February 23, 2009.
*Washington Post,* April 18, 2009, p. A1; April 23, 2009, p. A3.

### Online

"About Commissioner Lisa P. Jackson's New Jersey Department of Environmental Protection (archived on The Internet Archive), http://web.archive.org/web/20070927.tif183737/www.state.nj.us/dep/commissioner/bio.ht ml (April 22, 2009).
"Biography: Administrator Lisa P. Jackson," U.S. Environmental Protection Agency, http://www.epa.gov/administrator/biography.htm (April 22, 2009).

—*Erick Trickey*

# Nina Jacobson

**Film executive**

*Ryan Miller/Getty Images*

**B**orn Nina J. Jacobson in 1965; life partner of Jen Bleakley (a graduate student in clinical psychology); children: Noah, Josephine, William. *Education:* Brown University, A.B., 1987.

**Addresses:** *Office*—DreamWorks Studios, 1000 Flower St., Glendale, CA, 91201.

## Career

**B**egan career as a documentary researcher for Arnold Shapiro Productions; story analyst, Disney Sunday Movie, 1987; director of development, Silver Pictures, 1987; head of development, McDonald/Parkes Productions, 1987; director of development, Universal Pictures, 1990-92, then vice president of production, 1992-95, then senior vice president of production, 1994-95; senior film executive, DreamWorks SKG, 1995-98; executive vice president of production, Walt Disney Pictures/ Hollywood Pictures, 1998; co-president, Buena Vista Motion Pictures Group (a division of The Walt Disney Co.), 1999-2000, then president, 2000-06; producer, DreamWorks Studios, 2006—.

**Awards:** One of 50 Power Women in Entertainment, *Hollywood Reporter,* 2000; Crystal Award, Women in Film, 2003; one of 100 most powerful women in entertainment, *Hollywood Reporter,* 2004, 2005; one of 50 most powerful people in Hollywood, *Premier,* 2004-06; one of 100 most powerful women in the world, *Forbes,* 2005.

## Sidelights

**R**egularly considered one of the most powerful people in Hollywood, film producer and studio executive Nina Jacobson has held influential positions at leading film studios including Universal, Disney, and DreamWorks. In the early 2000s, she was the head of Disney's Buena Vista Motion Pictures Group. Groundbreaking in her activities, Jacobson is also a lesbian who co-founded Out There, a collection of gay and lesbian activists in the entertainment industry.

Of her approach to films, Jacobson told Richard Duckett of the Massachusetts *Telegram & Gazette,* "There is so much cynicism, so much jaded, so much cool for the sake of being cool out there, and you see that so much in the movies. And I think that in my job I absolutely have to keep my childish enthusiasm. I have to love the movie and get as excited—and sit there with my popcorn and candy— just as I did as a kid. If you don't have that you should not be making movies because you're just cranking out sort of a cynical waste product."

Born in 1965, Jacobson was raised in Los Angeles. As a child, the first film she saw was the 3-D version of *House of Wax.* While seeing the film traumatized her, she came to embrace such films as *National Velvet*, *The Sound of Music*, *Star Wars*, and *Raiders of the Lost Ark*.

Jacobson received her education on the East Coast, attending Brown University. She earned her A.B. from Brown in 1987, then planned on a career working in documentary filmmaking. She began her career as a documentary researcher for Arnold Shapiro Productions. When Jacobson landed a job as a story analyst for the Disney Sunday Movie in 1987, her plans changed. She told the *Lowell Sun*, "From the first time I read a script, I knew that this was my calling. And really, that's still the core of my job—to fall in love with a great script."

Also in 1987, Jacobson served the director of development in Silver Pictures, and then as the head of development for McDonald/Parkes Productions. In 1990, she joined Universal Pictures as a director of development. Jacobson was involved in the development and production of such films as *Beethoven* and *Looters*. Universal promoted Jacobson to the vice president of production in 1992, where she supervised such films as *Sudden Death* and *Tales from the Crypt: Demon Knight*.

Jacobson came out as a lesbian in 1990. While she did not know of anyone else who shared her sexual orientation in Hollywood's executive ranks, over the years she became more active in Hollywood's expanding lesbian community. She was a co-founder of Out There, for example. This gay and lesbian activist group draws its membership from the entertainment community. Jacobson later became involved with graduate student Jen Bleakley, who became her long-term partner. The couple eventually had at least three children together.

In 1994, Jacobson became the senior vice president of production at Universal Pictures. There, she helped develop such films as *Dazed and Confused*, but became increasingly unhappy with her position at company. She left the post in 1995 to become the senior film executive at DreamWorks SKG. Once arriving at DreamWorks, Jacobson was much happier, telling Chris Geitz of the *Daily Variety*, "I approach each day operating with a sense of hope, rather than fear." She added, to the *Hollywood Reporter Women in Entertainment Supplement*, that "[DreamWorks co-founder] Steven Spielberg restored my hope in the movie business. I found [him] to be devoid of cynicism."

Early in her tenure, Jacobson came up with an idea for an animated film, *Antz*, which became one of the first animated features put out by DreamWorks.

When it was made, the film featured the voice of Woody Allen as a main character. Primarily, however, Jacobson played a role in the development and production of such films as *What Lies Beneath*. After three years, Jacobson left DreamWorks for a position at Disney.

When Jacobson returned to Disney in 1998, she became the executive vice president of production for Walt Disney Pictures/Hollywood Pictures. In this position, she oversaw such films as *The Sixth Sense* and *Mission to Mars*. A year later, Jacobson moved within the Walt Disney Company to become the co-president with Todd Garner of Buena Vista Motion Pictures Group. In this position, the pair oversaw all aspects of development and production for films produced under the company's banners, including Walt Disney, Touchstone, and Hollywood Pictures.

In 2000, Jacobson became the president outright after Garner left the company. The beginning of her tenure was turbulent as long-time studio chief Joe Roth was replaced by Peter Schneider during her first year, and she soon became pregnant with her first biological child. Then, the production on several films was negatively affected by striking Hollywood unions, yet the company put out a number of significant films during her tenure including *Pearl Harbor* and *The Royal Tannenbaums*. The latter was written and directed by Wes Anderson, and Jacobson admitted that she particularly favored the work of writer-directors like Anderson, the Coen Brothers, and M. Night Shyamalan. With Shyamalan, Disney released the hits *The Sixth Sense* and *Signs*.

In the summer of 2003, Jacobson led Disney to box-office gold. Under her guidance, the company had a hand in some of the biggest hits of the peak box-office season, including *Finding Nemo*, *Pirates of the Caribbean: The Curse of the Black Pearl*, the remake of *Freaky Friday*, and the Kevin Costner western *Open Range*. Jacobson told the *Lowell Sun*, "Low expectations were really our friend this year. We were able to sneak up on people with these movies, and that's been much more gratifying." In the fall of 2003, Jacobson was proud of the minor hit *Under the Tuscan Sun*, which focused on a writer, played by Diane Lane, who finds herself in Italy after a painful divorce. Other hits during her tenure included *The Princess Diaries* and *The Chronicles of Narnia*.

During her years as the head of Buena Vista, Jacobson was regularly recognized for her significant position of power. She was named to the Women in Entertainment Power 50 list for 2000 and one of the 100 most powerful women in entertainment by the

*Hollywood Reporter* in 2004 and 2005. Jacobson was also lauded one of the 50 most powerful people in Hollywood by *Premiere* magazine in 2004, 2005, and 2006. In addition, *Forbes* recognized her as one of the 100 most powerful women in the world in 2005.

While Disney did not match the blockbuster success of 2003 in subsequent years, Jacobson continued to oversee hit after hit as well as a few misses—*Hidalgo* was one significant failure. In 2005, her contract was renewed with lucrative terms. Yet Jacobson was fired from her position at Buena Vista in July of 2006 while in the maternity ward after her partner gave birth to their third child. Jacobson's firing was seen as unexpected, but believed to be part of the corporate restructuring Disney was undergoing under its new chief Robert Igor. At the time of her firing, Jacobson accepted the change. Kevin West of *W* quoted her as saying "There simply isn't room for everyone in the new structure."

By the end of the 2006, Jacobson signed an overall producing deal with DreamWorks Studios. According to the terms of the contract, DreamWorks had a first look at all her projects at least through 2010. Upon her return to DreamWorks, Jacobson was quoted by the *Hollywood Reporter's* Borys Kit as saying "When I left DreamWorks for Disney in 1998, Steven [Spielberg] encouraged me to look at my time away as 'study abroad.' I feel very lucky to be able to bring all that I have learned over the past eight years back to DreamWorks as a producer…. They have created a culture at DreamWorks that values talent and candor, and I am honored to be able to contribute to their slate."

Soon after signing the DreamWorks deal, the company acquired the film rights to the popular children's book series "Children of the Lamp" by P. B. Kerr. Jacobson signed on as the producer of the project. She had already started on another project for DreamWorks, the science fiction thriller *Dominion*. Jacobson remained with DreamWorks after the company divorced itself from its deal with Paramount in September of 2008. DreamWorks immediately launched a new financing partnership with the Indian-based Reliance Anil Dhirubhai Ambani Group, then signed a distribution deal with Universal the following month.

Being a woman in the male-dominated film industry was a challenge for Jacobson, but she believed she did have an advantage. She told Duckett of *Telegram & Gazette*, "In some ways I think it's easier for me, because I think that for men a lot of times in a hierarchical environment there's a natural kind of innate desire to lock horns and to be the alpha and to take down the reigning alpha and become the alpha yourself…. And as a woman it's more important to me to put my kids to bed at night than it is to be the queen of the universe…. And so you can actually just sort of focus on the work and you don't necessarily get into these big power struggles."

## Sources

### Books

*Complete Marquis Who's Who Biographies*, Marquis Who's Who, 2008.

### Periodicals

*Business Wire*, May 3, 1999.
*Daily Variety*, November 7, 1997, p. 41; November 29, 2000, p. A18; December 6, 2006, p. 1.
*Hollywood Reporter*, December 6, 2006; June 22, 2007, p. 2.
*Hollywood Reporter Women in Entertainment Supplement*, December 2000, p. 40.
*LA Weekly*, September 25, 2008.
*Los Angeles Magazine*, July 1, 2000, p. 105.
*Los Angeles Times*, September 20, 2008, p. C1.
*Lowell Sun* (MA), August 22, 2003.
*Newsweek*, April 14, 1997, p. 68.
*New York Times*, April 24, 2005, sec. 2, p. 1.
PR Newswire, February 7, 1992; October 21, 1994; December 5, 2006.
*Telegram & Gazette* (MA), September 4, 2003, p. C1.
*W*, October 1, 2007, p. 272.

### Online

"Fired in the Maternity Ward," Salon.com, http://www.salon.com/mwt/broadsheet/2006/07/21/fired/ (October 9, 2008).
"Jacobson Out Atop Disney Film Division," THR.com, http://www.hollywoodreporter.com/hr/search/article_display.jsp?vnu_content_id=1002841491 (October 14, 2008).
"Meeting the Gay Parents," *USA Today*, http://www.usatoday.com/news/health/2001-08-23-gay-parents-usat.htm (October 13, 2008).
"Universal to Distribute DreamWorks," *New York Times*, http://www.nytimes.com/2008/10/14/business/media/14studio.html?hp (October 13, 2008).

—*A. Petruso*

# Shawn Johnson

## Gymnast

**B**orn January 19, 1992, in Des Moines, Iowa; daughter of Doug (a carpenter) and Teri (an accounting clerk) Johnson.

**Addresses:** *Agent*—Shade Global, 10 E. 40th St., 48th Flr., New York, NY 10016. *Home*—Des Moines, Iowa. *Web site*—http://www.shawnjohnson.net.

## Career

**B**egan gymnastics at the age of six; earned a spot on the junior national gymnastics team, 2005; made U.S. Olympic gymnastics team, 2008.

**Awards:** First place, balance beam, USA Gymnastics Junior Olympics Western National Championships, 2003; first place, all-around, vault, balance beam, and floor exercise, second place, uneven bars, VISA National Championships (junior division), St. Paul, MN, 2006; first place, all-around, balance beam, second place, vault, United States vs. Great Britain International Competition, Lisburn, Ireland, 2007; first place, all-around, balance beam, and uneven bars, second place, floor exercise, Pan American Championships, 2007; first place, all-around, Tyson American Cup, Jacksonville, FL, 2007; first place, all-around, balance beam, and floor exercise, third place, uneven bars, Visa National Championships, San Jose, CA, 2007; first place, all-around and floor exercise, World Championships, Stuttgart, Germany, 2007; first place, floor exercise, balance beam, and vault, second place, all-around and uneven bars, American Cup, New York, NY, 2008; first place, all-around, Italy-Spain-Poland-USA Competition, Jesolo, Italy, 2008; silver medals, team competition, all-around, and vault, Olympics, Beijing, China, 2008; gold medal, balance beam, Olympics, Beijing, China, 2008.

## Sidelights

**U**.S. gymnast Shawn Johnson left the 2008 Beijing Summer Olympics with a handful of medals—three silver, one gold—and a heart filled with disappointment. After winning the 2007 all-around world title and dominating the event at nearly every competition thereafter, Johnson—a petite but explosive gymnast known for her potency and precision—was a favorite to win the coveted Olympic all-around gold. In the end, that gold went to her teammate and friend Nastia Liukin.

Heading into the final day of women's gymnastics competition, Johnson had three silver medals, but the gold remained elusive. The U.S. women's gymnastics team had taken second, giving her a silver. She earned another in the floor exercise finals and a third in the all-around. Luckily, Johnson had one more event, the individual balance beam competition. During her routine, Johnson tumbled atop the four-inch-wide elevated beam with unmatched passion and poise. Earning a score of 16. 225, Johnson pulled off a gold-medal victory, besting Liukin, the reigning beam world champion, who scored 16.025. "I never felt so proud and so relieved," Johnson told Juliet Macur of the *New York Times*. "To finish off this whole Olympics by finally getting the gold medal, it's the best feeling in the world."

Johnson was born on January 19, 1992, in Des Moines, Iowa. She is the only child of Doug and Teri Johnson, teen sweethearts who met at the roller rink. Teri Johnson is a public schools accounting clerk, while Doug Johnson makes his living as a carpenter. Johnson displayed athletic prowess early on. As a baby, she bypassed crawling and went straight to walking at nine months. Before she was a year old, Johnson could climb out of her baby bed.

When Johnson was a toddler, her parents signed her up for ballet and tumbling, hoping to find a channel for her excessive energy. At six, they tried gymnastics after stumbling upon Chow's Gymnastics, a new facility that had just opened a few blocks from their home. The gym's owner, an immigrant named Liang Chow (or Qiao), had been a member of China's national men's team. He moved to the United States in 1991 to attend the University of Iowa and help coach its gymnastics team.

Speaking to the *New York Times*, Chow recalled his first encounter with a young and toothless Johnson, saying she showed no restraint and jumped right onto the uneven bars "like it was her home." Under Chow's guidance, Johnson flourished. His wife, Li-wen Zhuang (Li), also worked with Johnson. Like Chow, Li had grown up a gymnast in China.

At eleven, Johnson began to stand out, winning the balance beam title at the USA Gymnastics Junior Olympics Western National Championships. Two years later, Chow decided it was time to reveal Johnson's talents to the world. Training and competing in Iowa, Johnson lived a relatively obscure existence. Chow changed that by sending a tape of Johnson's routines to the U.S. national team coordinator, who in turn invited Johnson to join a training session. In 2005, Johnson made the junior national team.

In 2006, Johnson competed at the U.S. Nationals, or Visa Championships, in the junior division, earning first places in the all-around, vault, balance beam, and floor exercise competitions. She placed second on the uneven bars. To honor her coaches, Johnson competed at Nationals with her name written on her leotard in Chinese. In 2007, Johnson placed first in the all-around at several competitions, including the Pan American Championships, the Tyson American Cup, and the World Championships.

Training with Chow allowed Johnson to maintain somewhat of a normal life. Chosen by state officials to become a gymnast, Chow left home at the age of ten to live and train at a special Chinese school that groomed future gymnasts. Having lost his childhood, Chow wanted Johnson to have a more normal life. Unlike most elite gymnasts who spend their days training and studying with tutors, Johnson has been able to attend public school. Chow had her train about 25 hours a week instead of the 40 typical of most top-notch gymnasts. Skipping study hall, physical education and lunch, Johnson was able to attend school and get to the gym by 2:30 every afternoon. Speaking to *People*'s Nicole Weisensee Egan, Chow summed up his philosophy this way: "I tell them, 'Education is number one. Gymnastics is number two.'"

Johnson shined at the Olympic trials in June of 2008 and easily made the team. She was favored for the all-around gold. In the run-up to the Olympics, newspapers around the globe compared Johnson to Mary Lou Retton. Retton won the all-around gold at the 1984 Olympics, becoming the first gymnast from outside Eastern Europe to capture the all-around title. Retton was gunning for her to win. "She's got the whole package," Retton told *People*. "She's powerful. She's graceful. She's fun to watch."

With the explosive 4-foot-9, 90-pound Johnson in the lineup, the United States was favored to win the team competition. China, however, took gold following some missteps by U.S. team captain Alicia Sacramone. Having lost out on that gold, Johnson was hopeful when the all-around began. After the first rotation of that competition, which began with the vault, Johnson stood in the lead but fell to fifth place after the uneven bars. Next came the balance beam and with a solid performance, Johnson stood in third place with 47.20 points going into the final rotation—the floor exercise.

Liukin had 47.80 points and Chinese gymnast Yang Yilin had 47.65. The scores were so close, all three stood in contention for the gold. It all came down to the floor competition. Liukin nailed the performance of a lifetime. Confident, athletic and artistic in her execution, Liukin notched a 15.525. Johnson figured she could not beat it. With pressure for the gold off her chest, Johnson was able to relax and focus on her routine. "I'd felt pressure and nerves the whole meet, and at that point it was just about the gymnastics," she told *Sports Illustrated*'s E. M. Swift. "I just wanted to show everyone I left it all out there and that I'd never give up, no matter what." Johnson received a 15.525, the same as Liukin and enough to surpass Yang for the silver by .075 of a point. With Liukin capturing gold and Johnson taking silver, it was the first time in Olympic history the United States had a one-two finish in the event. Finally, on the last day of competition, Johnson got her gold with a stellar performance on the balance beam.

As for the future, Johnson has kept everyone guessing. "It's hard to think about four more years," Johnson told the *Los Angeles Times*'s Diane Pucin. "After not winning the all-around, it hit me pretty hard, not that I got the silver, but just all my emotions came out. I was training to win gold. I'm just proud of myself that I kept my head up."

## Sources

### Periodicals

*Los Angeles Times*, August 21, 2008, p. S2.
*New York Times*, August 4, 2008, p. H4; August 20, 2008, p. D5.
*People*, August 18, 2008, p. 119.
*Sports Illustrated*, May 5, 2008, p. 44; August 25, 2008, p. 78.

### Online

"Shawn Johnson Bio," The Official Website of Shawn Johnson, http://www.shawnjohnson.net/get_to_know/bio.aspx (November 20, 2008).
"Shawn Johnson Q & A," The Official Website of Shawn Johnson, http://www.shawnjohnson.net/get_to_know/q-a.aspx (November 20, 2008).
"2008 Beijing Summer Olympics: Shawn Johnson Profile," NBC Olympics, http://www.nbcolympics.com/athletes/athlete=619/bio/ (November 20, 2008).

*—Lisa Frick*

# Costas Karamanlis

**Prime minister of Greece**

**B**orn Konstantínos Alexandrou Karamanlís, September 14, 1956, in Athens, Greece; married Natasa Pazaïti, 1998; children: Aliki, Alexandos. *Education:* Studied at the American College of Greece; University of Athens, law degree; Tufts University, Fletcher School of Law and Diplomacy, M.A., Ph.D.

**Addresses:** *Home*—Presidential Mansion, 2 Vassileos Georgiou B' St., Athens 100 28, Greece.

## Career

**E**xecutive with the youth group of the New Democracy Party, 1974-79 and 1984-89; attorney, author, and journalist; elected to parliament on the New Democracy ticket, 1989; elected party chief of New Democracy, 1997; became prime minister, 2004.

## Sidelights

**C**ostas Karamanlis became prime minister of Greece in 2004 after an election that brought an end to two decades of socialist rule. He leads the center-right political party New Democracy, which was founded by his uncle, Constantine Karamanlis, the former prime minister and president of Greece. A relative latecomer to electoral politics, Karamanlis was an attorney, longtime party functionary, and member of parliament before becoming party leader in 1997, and his ascension to prime minister marked his first genuine government post. "Being a leader of the opposition party for eight years is experience enough to run the country," a report from the *Guardian*'s correspondent in Athens, Helena Smith, quoted him as saying.

*Louisa Gouliamaki/AFP/Getty Images*

The Karamanlis name is a famous one in Greece, and the family's roots are in a village called Proti in the northern part of Greece known as Macedonia. Constantine Karamanlis, the uncle, began his storied political career two decades before his nephew was born in 1956. A lawyer by training, the elder Karamanlis was first elected to parliament in 1936, but the country's democratic governance was suspended during World War II when Greece was occupied by Nazi troops. Liberated from the Germans in October of 1944, Greece descended into a bitter civil war over the next five years. The nation known as the birthplace of democracy veered dangerously close to a Communist revolution in this internal conflict that pitted government forces—with British and American aid—against a Soviet-funded Communist insurgency. The pro-democracy side won, but the civil war left the country deeply polarized between right and left—a legacy that remained even when the younger Karamanlis became prime minister several years later.

The elder Karamanlis held several cabinet posts in the first postwar government, and formed his first government as prime minister in 1955 upon request from the Greek monarch. He formed a new political party, the National Radical Union, which won elections in 1956, 1958, and 1961. The party was defeated in 1963 elections by an organization led by the elder Karamanlis' archrival for power, George Papandreou I, whose son Andreas would also become one of Greece's leading political figures. Both of the Papandreous were jailed when a military coup overthrew the elected government in 1967.

Karamanlis was a few months shy of his eleventh birthday when a junta of top military brass seized power that year. On July 23, 1974, his uncle returned from exile when the junta agreed to restore democracy and invited him to head a government of national unity in preparation for elections. Karamanlis' uncle was welcomed by large evening crowds in Athens bearing lit candles and cheering the motorcade that brought him from the airport to the seat of government. By this point the younger Karamanlis had begun his studies, which included stops at the American College of Greece, the law school of the University of Athens, and Tufts University in the Boston, Massachusetts, area, where he earned a doctorate in political science, international relations, and diplomatic history from its Fletcher School of Law and Diplomacy. He went on to author the 1986 work *Eleftherios Venizelos and Foreign Relations of Greece, 1928-32* about the second term of a Greek prime minister considered the founder of the modern Greek state.

In October of 1974 Karamanlis' uncle founded the New Democracy party, and Karamanlis became a key figure in its youth wing. During the 1980s he practiced law and wrote newspaper articles for the *Oikonomikos Tachydromos* (Financial Courier) newspaper. In 1989 he won his first election as a member of parliament from Thessaloniki, Greece's second largest city. Over the next decade he rose within the party's ranks to serve on both its parliamentary board and political planning committee. In 1997, after a disastrous outcome for New Democracy in the previous year's general election, he was elected party chair.

Karamanlis' uncle spent the final years of his six-decade political career as president of Greece, serving from 1980 to 1985 and again from 1990 to 1995. It was a largely ceremonial post, however, and usually placed the elder Karamanlis at odds with the ruling party, the center-left Panhellenic Socialist Movement (PASOK). Founded by Andreas Papandreou back in 1974, PASOK won the 1981 general election and remained in power for the next 23 years, save for a brief New Democracy interlude between 1989 and 1990.

As the leader of New Democracy, Karamanlis was determined to reform the party and make it a more attractive choice at the ballot box. His predecessors had tried before him, but Peter Stothard of the *Times* of London described Karamanlis as "a more cautious moderniser.... He has abandoned his party's more Thatcherite economic rhetoric of the 1990s and aimed for a coalition of the dissatisfied, carefully crafting positions to appeal across Right and Left to those who feel that 20 years of PASOK have not brought the benefits they deserve."

In the April 2000 general election, Karamanlis' party was defeated once again by PASOK, but this time by just a slim margin. Four years later, the next election pitted Karamanlis against another scion of the Papandreou family, George Papandreou II, son of Andreas, who was elected head of PASOK in early 2004. On elections on March 7, 2004, Greek voters ousted PASOK, whose corruption and graft had reached epidemic proportions, and chose New Democracy by a margin of five full percentage points. Rising unemployment and fears that Athens would not be ready to host the 2004 Summer Olympics that August were credited with giving New Democracy that substantial lead at the polls. "There are no winners and losers, only Greece is the winner," Karamanlis was quoted as saying in his victory speech, according to Smith's *Guardian* report.

Karamanlis was sworn in as prime minister on March 10, a rare European leader who had never even served a stint as a cabinet minister before taking office. He was also the first prime minister of Greece born after the country's calamitous World War II-civil war years, and at age 47 was also the youngest ever to lead modern Greece. In his first cabinet, he made himself Culture Minister in order to supervise the fevered preparations for the Olympics. Construction delays and cost overruns had plagued planners in Athens, and several important venues were behind schedule.

Like nearly everything in Greek life, the Olympic preparations were fraught with political overtones. Prior to the election, there were fears that the construction and trades unions—mostly loyal to PASOK—would go on strike if PASOK was ousted, and there were also worries that several thousand civil servants loyal to PASOK would lose their jobs and thereby delay preparation for the Games even further. In a rare interview, Karamanlis was asked by *Time International* journalist Anthee Carassava if he found the enormity of the situation better or worse once he took over as prime minister. "We've been following the course of Olympic preparations very closely from the start, so I didn't confront any surprises," he responded. "There have been delays. However, at this point there is no time for additional criticism.... We have only one goal and responsibility: to make sure that all of us, not just the government, but all Greeks, contribute in order to make good Games and secure Games."

The 2004 Summer Olympics kicked off on time, and were judged a success for Athens and for Greece, where the ancient sporting contest had originated. It was a symbolic victory for Karamanlis' first term as prime minister, and he also made an effort to resolve yet another problematic issue that had bedeviled Greece's foreign policy since 1974: Cyprus. Two groups, Greek Cypriots and Turkish Cypriots, cohabitated somewhat uneasily after Cyprus gained its independence from Britain in 1960, but in the early 1970s violence erupted on the island between the two sides. In 1974, the Turkish intelligence service uncovered a plot by the military junta in Athens to oust Cyprus' democratically elected president and back the island's Greek nationalist group, whose ultimate goal was unification with Greece. In response, Turkey invaded on July 20, and the international incident helped bring a swift end to the junta and the return of Karamanlis' uncle from exile just a few days later.

Since then, however, the situation on Cyprus had reached a stalemate. A month after Karamanlis took office in 2004, Cyprus held a referendum vote on unification between its Turkish and Greek halves, and though the new Greek prime minister urged Greek Cypriots to vote in favor of it, the referendum failed to pass. The inability to resolve the issue had long complicated Turkey's entrance into the European Union (EU): the northern one-third of the island, known as the Turkish Republic of Northern Cyprus, demanded recognition as a sovereign nation, but Turkey was the sole nation to affirm its right to independence. The rest of the island, called the Republic of Cyprus, was an independent nation and laid claim to the Turkish third.

With Karamanlis in office, both Turkey and Greece were now governed by relatively youthful center-right politicians, and the diplomatic ties between Karamanlis and Turkey's prime minister, Recep Tayyip Erdogan, appeared to blossom into genuine friendship. In July of 2004, Karamanlis attended the Istanbul wedding of Erdogan's daughter, and a month later Erdogan was the guest of Karamanlis for the official opening ceremonies of the Athens Summer Olympics. Plans for an official visit, however, were postponed three times, but in the interim Karamanlis was a vocal supporter of Turkey's bid to join the European Union, for which negotiations opened in 2005. "A European Turkey is in everyone's best interests," Karamanlis said, according to Owen Matthews in *Newsweek International*. Fi-

nally, in January of 2008 Karamanlis made his historic visit to Turkey, the first by a Greek leader since 1959, when his uncle made the same journey as prime minister. "Greek people have very good feelings toward Turkish people. I believe they are looking for a new page in relations," two writers for the *New York Times*, Carassava and Sabrina Tavernise, quoted Karamanlis as saying.

Karamanlis is a staunch supporter of the European Union, following the lead of his uncle, who went against tremendous opposition in the 1970s to bring Greece into what was then known as the European Economic Community. Back in 1981, when PASOK ousted New Democracy, PASOK leader Andreas Papandreou had warned that Greece's entry would prove disastrous for the country. Instead Greece prospered, and its strategic position as a conduit between the oil- and natural-gas-rich nations of Russia and Central Asia boosted its fortunes even further in the twenty-first century.

In August of 2007, forest fires erupted in several parts of Greece, but the worst occurred in the western Peloponnesian peninsula and on the island of Euboea. The fires consumed thousands of acres of pine forests—which, with their high resin content, proved disastrously flammable—left 84 dead and destroyed olive crops, livestock, and entire villages. Karamanlis's government was criticized for what was perceived as its slow response to the crisis, and his administration was chastised for one official's remarks that the fires may have been the work of arsonists. The human toll and the ecological disaster was said to have cost New Democracy some votes in the September 16, 2007, general election in which Karamanlis' party beat PASOK but lost some seats in parliament.

Karamanlis is married to a physician, Natasa Pazaïti, with whom he has a son and daughter who are twins. Given the dynastic character of Greek politics, one of them may eventually follow his or her father into elected office, and Karamanlis is likely aware that his own tenure may not prove a long one. In 1980, his uncle sat for an interview with writer Joan Gage that was published in the *New York Times Magazine* and reflected on the ups and downs of his career. "Throughout the centuries," his uncle mused, "almost without exception, Greeks have turned against their greatest leaders."

## Sources

*Global Agenda*, August 30, 2007.
*Guardian* (London, England), March 8, 2004, p. 13.
*Independent* (London, England), March 6, 2004, p. 31.

*Newsweek International,* August 30, 2004, p. 28.
*New York Times,* August 29, 2007; January 24, 2008.
*New York Times Magazine,* September 28, 1980.
*Time International* (Europe Edition), March 22, 2004, p. 6.

*Times* (London, England), April 24, 1998, p. 25; March 9, 2004, p. 6.

—*Carol Brennan*

# Jonathan Kellerman

**Author, pediatric psychologist, and professor**

**B**orn Jonathan Seth Kellerman, August 9, 1949, in New York, NY; son of David Kellerman (an engineer and inventor) and Sylvia Fiacre; married Faye Marilyn Marder (a dentist and author), July 23, 1972; children: Jesse (an author), Rachel, Ilana, Aliza. *Education:* University of California Los Angeles, B.A., 1972; University of Southern California, M.A., 1973, Ph.D., 1974.

**Addresses:** *Agent*—Karpfinger Agency, 357 West 20th St., New York, NY 10011.

## Career

**I**ntern in psychology, Children's Hospital of Los Angeles, Los Angeles, CA, 1973-74, then postdoctoral fellow, 1974-75; postdoctoral fellow, University of Southern California School of Medicine, Los Angeles, CA, 1974-75, then staff psychologist, 1975-78, assistant clinical professor of pediatrics, 1978-79, clinical associate professor of pediatrics, 1979-98, clinical professor of pediatrics, 1998—; director, Psychosocial Program Children's Hospital, Los Angeles, CA, 1977-81; fiction writer, 1985—; child psychologist in private practice, Sherman Oaks, CA, and Glendale, CA, through 1994.

**Member:** American Psychological Association, Mystery Writers of America.

**Awards:** Samuel Goldwyn Creative Writing Award, University of California—Los Angeles, 1972; Edgar Allan Poe Award, Mystery Writers of America, for *When the Bough Breaks*, 1985; Anthony Boucher Award, Bouchercon World Mystery Convention, for *When the Bough Breaks*, 1986; Media Award, American Psychological Association, 1994; Distinguished Alumnus Award, Department of Psychology at University of California Los Angeles, 1997; Presidential Award, American Psychological Association, 1998.

## Sidelights

**A** licensed psychologist who teaches at the University of Southern California, Jonathan Kellerman is better known as the author of a series of mystery novels featuring Alex Delaware. Beginning in 1985 with *When the Bough Breaks*, Kellerman's novels were popular with both critics and readers, though the series had its highs and lows over the years. The author was happy writing books for a living. He told Pat Bell of the *Ottawa Citizen*, "Writing novels is so much fun. As a psychologist, there are so many rules. But as a novelist, you can make up people."

Born on August 9, 1949, in New York City, Kellerman was the son of David Kellerman and Sylvia Fiacre. His father was an engineer and inventor who held 18 patents. David Kellerman also worked for RCA in the 1940s and was involved in the development of television. A talented writer and artist from an early age, writing was the younger Kellerman's passion by the age of nine. Kellerman graduated early from a small private high school and entered the University of California at Los Angeles (UCLA) at the age of 16. During his time at UCLA, Kellerman worked at the college paper as an editor, writer, critic, and staff cartoonist. While still an undergraduate, he co-wrote a comic novel which was never published but won him the Samuel Goldwyn Creative Writing Award from UCLA in 1972.

That same year, Kellerman earned his B.A. from the University of California at Los Angeles. He then entered the University of Southern California to pursue graduate studies in psychology. He earned his M.A. in 1973 and his Ph.D. in 1974. During this time period, Kellerman was an intern and then a postdoctoral fellow at Children's Hospital of Los Angeles. While he focused on oncology, he learned much about sexual abuse and incest, subjects which were then little talked about in child psychology. His experiences at the hospital molded him as a writer. Kellerman told Kate Seago of the *Vancouver Sun*, "I was exposed more than the average psychologist to the dark side of life—first of all, working at a hospital which was not inner city, but drew on a very wide range of people. At a major medical centre you see everything."

In 1974, Kellerman began another year as a postdoctoral fellow at the University of Southern California (USC) School of Medicine. The following year, he became a staff psychologist at the institution, and in 1977, was the founding director of the Psychosocial Program at Children's Hospital. In 1978, Kellerman began a teaching career at the USC School of Medicine, moving from an assistant clinical professor of pediatrics to a full professor in 1998. Kellerman also wrote two nonfiction books about his professional specialty, 1980's *Psychological Aspects of Childhood Cancer* and 1981's *Helping the Fearful Child*.

Summing up his life as a psychologist, Kellerman wrote in the *New York Times*, "By day I treated thousands of children afflicted by tragedy, deformity, disease. Rather than finding all of this depressing, I got hooked on adrenaline and was buoyed by what I learned about the resilience of the human spirit."

While Kellerman had a satisfying professional and family life with his wife, Faye, and their children, he wrote novels in his free time for 13 years before being published. He produced eight unpublished novels in this time period, but later admitted to Carol Kreck of the *Denver Post*, "I didn't have enough to say." By the early 1980s, Kellerman had improved his craft as a writer and focused on writing crime fiction set in Los Angeles after reading the Lew Archer novels by Ross Macdonald. Macdonald's books inspired him to find his own voice and write about what he knew: child psychology.

Kellerman completed what would become his first published book, *When the Bough Breaks*, in 1981, but did not get it published until 1985. As he told Adam Dunn of *Publishers Weekly*, "Nobody wanted to buy it—the subject matter was seen as too difficult—then it became a word-of-mouth bestseller." This mystery novel about the effects of child molestation became the first in a series featuring Alex Delaware, who had much in common with the author. Both were child psychologists who lived in Los Angeles, owned a French bulldog, and had a koi pond in the backyard. But Delaware was also wealthy, single, solved mysteries—at least the ones that interested him and then usually reluctantly—using psychological clues, and sometimes attacked villains.

Kellerman used his experiences as a child psychologist and related knowledge in the characters and novels, but declared he could never use a specific patient as a model for any character in his books. He explained to Dunn of *Publishers Weekly*, "I never write about reality. Because I was trained as a psychologist, I was always bound by confidentiality. So I could never write about patients. I didn't want to. I think it made me a better writer because I was forced to invent.... What my psychological training and contacts do is hopefully to give [my writing] a feeling of authenticity."

Addressing other issues of realism, he told Seago in the *Vancouver Sun*, "The novels themselves are in a sense realistic, and in a sense they're not. There's a major suspension of disbelief that this guy is going to get into this situation. Once we accept this premise, the stories are realistic." Thematically, Kellerman's novels were also often similar. In the *Ottawa Citizen*, Jamie Portman explained, "Kellerman's novels deal with dark, often shocking subject matter, much of it involving inhumanity toward children."

With the success of *Bough*, Kellerman continued his private practice as a psychologist and teaching at the University of Southern California School of Medicine. But he focused much of his time on writing his novels and doing related publicity as well. He generally wrote for three or four hours every morning in this time period. Writing from the point of view of each character, Kellerman averaged about four or five pages of a finished novel a day.

In some ways, writing the novels proved cathartic. With 1986's *Blood Test*, Kellerman excised the stress he sometimes felt working with children suffering from cancer. He told the *Ottawa Citizen*'s Bell of his time treating such patients, "When I was doing it, it didn't seem so hard. The book was my way of working through those feelings, I guess."

Over the years, Kellerman used the Delaware series to explore extremes in psychology and behavior while imparting positive messages. For example, 1986's *Blood Test* focused on the kidnapping of a child with cancer, while 1993's *Devil's Waltz* looked at Munchausen by Proxy syndrome. *Private Eyes*, published in 1992, was full of dark events, but the two of the main characters, Melissa Dickinson and Noel Drucker, survived difficult childhood circumstances to become psychologically healthy teens.

By 1994, Kellerman had published at least eight novels in the Delaware series and sold 14 million copies of them in numerous languages. He then decided to end his private practice as a psychologist. While he still taught on a limited basis at the University of Southern California School of Medicine, his novels, now written in a new home office, took up much of his time. Kellerman also did not limit himself to writing crime novels featuring Delaware. In 1994, he published a children's book of poetry, *Daddy, Daddy Can You Touch the Sky?*, which featured both his words and illustrations. The 1999 novel *Billy Straight* only features a brief appearance by Delaware. Instead the novel focuses on Billy Straight, a 12-year-old street kid living in Hollywood's Griffith Park who steals library books and is a witness to a murder. Another central character is Dr. Petra Connor, who first appeared in the 1997 Delaware novel, *Survival of the Fittest.*

Throughout the 1990s, Kellerman's novels featuring Delaware were usually challenging. In one novel published in 1994, *Bad Love*, Delaware explored a case involving troubled teens and a series of brutal slayings. He discovers that the root cause is a warped psychiatrist who has meddled with their minds. The twelfth Delaware novel, *Survival of the Fittest*, focused on a serial killer ring which targeted the young and disabled. Because of the success of such novels, *Booklist* magazine called him the hottest author in crime fiction.

While some critics believed that the Delaware novels had gone stale by the late 1990s, Kellerman's sixteenth entry into the series was praised as the best in years. Some critics noted that he displayed his strengths—deft plotting and strong character development—in *The Murder Book*, published in 2002. Reviewing the book, Andrea Henry of the London *Mirror* wrote, "Broad in scope but tightly plotted, *The Murder Book* is a spectacular return to form." Kellerman followed this novel with another lauded entry into the series, 2003's *A Cold Heart*. In this book, the author explores Delaware's own past as he starts a new dating relationship and solves the mystery behind the murders of young artists. *A Cold Heart* even includes appearances by characters from *Billy Straight*, Dr. Petra Connor and Billy Straight.

Also in the early 2000s, Kellerman began experimenting with new characters in the same mystery/thriller genre. In 2003's *The Conspiracy Club*, a state hospital psychiatrist Dr. Jeremy Carrier is dealing with the brutal murder of his girlfriend when he is accused of being a "Jack the Ripper"-type killer of prostitutes. Both the call girls and his girlfriend died in similar ways. After meeting the hospital's pathologist Arthur Chess and his friends, Carrier begins investigating who is committing these murders before the killer can strike again. As Carol Deegan wrote in the Associated Press, "*The Conspiracy Club* grabs the reader's attention and never lets go." The novel hit number one on the *New York Times* bestseller list.

In another non-Delaware project, Kellerman and his wife collaborated on a novel in 2004, *Double Homicide*. Faye Kellerman had a fiction-writing career of her own, publishing a series of police procedurals featuring a pair of observant Jews who live in Los Angeles beginning in 1986. She drew on the experiences of herself and her family as practicing Orthodox Jews to give an insider's view of religion. Their book together, *Double Homicide*, was a flip book in which each author wrote half of the text. After *Double Homicide*, Kellerman returned to the best-selling Delaware series with two highly praised, best-selling novels in 2007's *Obsession* and 2008's *Compulsion*.

In his free time, Kellerman enjoyed painting, playing and collecting guitars, as well as collecting books and art. Yet he appreciated the position he was in as he survived thyroid cancer and was able to live his life as he so chose. After being asked how he was handling his success, Kellerman told Jamie Portman of the *Ottawa Citizen*, "Every day I'm astonished. Especially when it took me so long to get published. I'm talking about a 13-year struggle." Later in the same interview, he added, "I can honestly say I never cared about the money…. I just wanted to write and publish books…. So because I had no expectations, anything that happened would have been wonderful."

## Selected writings

*Psychological Aspects of Childhood Cancer*, C. C. Thomas (Springfield, IL), 1980.

*Helping the Fearful Child: A Parent's Guide to Everyday and Problem Anxieties*, W. W. Norton (New York City), 1981.

*When the Bough Breaks* (first in the "Alex Delaware" series), Atheneum (New York City), 1985.

*Blood Test* (second in the "Alex Delaware" series), Atheneum, 1986.

*Over the Edge* (third in the "Alex Delaware" series), Atheneum, 1987.

*The Butcher's Theater*, Bantam (New York City), 1988.

*Silent Partner* (fourth in the "Alex Delaware" series), Bantam, 1989.

*Time Bomb* (fifth in the "Alex Delaware" series), Bantam, 1990.

*Private Eyes* (sixth in the "Alex Delaware" series), Bantam, 1992.

*Devil's Waltz* (seventh in the "Alex Delaware" series), Bantam, 1993.

*Bad Love* (eighth in the "Alex Delaware" series), Bantam, 1994.

*Daddy, Daddy Can You Touch the Sky?* (poems), Bantam, 1994.

*Jonathan Kellerman's ABC of Weird Creatures*, Airtight Seels Allied Production (Royal Oak, MI), 1995.

*Self-Defense* (ninth in the "Alex Delaware" series), Bantam, 1995.

*The Web* (tenth in the "Alex Delaware" series), Bantam, 1996.

*The Clinic* (eleventh in the "Alex Delaware" series), Bantam, 1997.

*Survival of the Fittest* (twelfth in the "Alex Delaware" series), Bantam, 1997.

*Billy Straight*, Ballantine (New York City), 1999.

*Monster* (thirteenth in the "Alex Delaware" series), Ballantine, 1999.

*Savage Spawn: Reflections on Violent Children*, Ballantine, 1999.

*Dr. Death* (fourteenth in the "Alex Delaware" series), Random House, 2000.

*Flesh and Blood* (fifteenth in the "Alex Delaware" series), Random House, 2001.

*The Murder Book* (sixteenth in the "Alex Delaware" series), Ballantine, 2002.

*A Cold Heart* (seventeenth in the "Alex Delaware" series), Ballantine, 2003.

*The Conspiracy Club*, Ballantine, 2003.

*Therapy* (eighteenth in the "Alex Delaware" series), Ballantine, 2004.

(With Faye Kellerman) *Double Homicide*, Warner (New York City), 2004.

*Twisted*, Ballantine, 2004.

*Rage* (nineteenth in the "Alex Delaware" series), Ballantine, 2005.

*Capital Crimes*, Ballantine, 2006.

*Gone* (twentieth in the "Alex Delaware" series), Ballantine, 2006.

*Obsession* (twenty-first in the "Alex Delaware" series), Ballantine, 2007.

(With Thomas H. Cook and Otto Penzler) *The Best American Crime Reporting 2008*, Harper Perennial (New York City), 2008.

*Compulsion* (twenty-second in the "Alex Delaware" series), Ballantine, 2008.

## Sources

### Books

*Complete Marquis Who's Who, Biographies*, Marquis Who's Who, 2008.

### Periodicals

Associated Press, January 12, 2004.

*Daily News of Los Angeles*, April 6, 2008, p. L1.

*Denver Post*, January 17, 1999, p. F3.

*Grand Rapids Press*, April 4, 2004, p. J5.

*Mirror* (London, England), November 23, 2002, p. 50.

*National Post* (Canada), May 17, 2008, p. WP15.

*New York Times*, March 31, 2003, p. E1.

*Ottawa Citizen*, February 15, 1992, p. J1; November 17, 1997, p. B8; June 1, 2003, p. C11.

*Palm Beach Post* (FL), July 27, 2003, p. 5J.

*Publishers Weekly*, October 21, 2002, p. 20; April 14, 2003, p. 50.

*USA Today*, February 7, 1994, p. 3D.

*Vancouver Sun* (British Columbia, Canada), January 12, 1994, p. C7; January 12, 2002, p. D19.

*Windsor Star* (Ontario, Canada), January 10, 2004, p. F7.

—*A. Petruso*

# Jemma Kidd

## Founder of Jemma Kidd Make Up

Born Jemma Madeleine Kidd, September 20, 1974, in Guildford, England; daughter of John Edward Aitken (a businessman and professional equestrian) and Wendy Hodge Kidd; married Arthur Wellesley, June 4, 2005. *Education:* Studied at le Cordon Bleu; trained as an apprentice makeup artist.

**Addresses:** *Office*—Jemma Kidd Make Up, 1 Farnham Rd., Guildford, Surrey GU2 4RG, England.

## Career

Worked as a fashion model, c. 1995-99; professional makeup artist; signed deal with Max Factor, 2001; opened makeup-artist training school, Jemma Kidd Make Up, 2002; started makeup line, Jemma Kidd Make Up, 2005.

## Sidelights

British socialite Jemma Kidd is a former model who launched her own eponymous makeup line in 2005 after starting a professional training school for makeup artists. Based in London, Kidd hails from a prominent English press dynasty and is the older sister of model Jodie Kidd. It was her own unease in front of the camera that inspired Kidd's choice of career, she told Judith Woods in an interview for the *Daily Telegraph.* "I grew into my looks late," she admitted. "When I was younger I was plump and the joke at home was: 'Who can take a good picture of Jemma?' because I always looked dreadful."

Patrick Riviere/Getty Images Entertainment/Getty Images

Born on September 20, 1974, in Guildford, a town in Sussex, England, Kidd is the second child of John Edward Aitken Kidd, known as Johnny, and Wendy Hodge Kidd. Her father is well-known in the equestrian world as a competitive show jumper and polo player. His maternal grandfather was William Maxwell Aitken, better known as Lord Beaverbrook, founder of the *Daily Express* newspaper. Her mother's Hodge family was also titled relatively recently, with Wendy's grandfather having earned his baronetcy in the 1920s after making a fortune in shipbuilding.

Kidd grew up in England and Barbados with her younger sister and an older brother. Their famed estate on the Caribbean island, called Holders House, dates back to the 1600s and was formerly a plantation. As a youngster, Kidd had difficulties in school because of her dyslexia, and her confidence was already shaky after an incident that occurred at age seven when she was bitten by a neighbor's Alsatian. "The dog basically ripped my whole face apart," she recalled in an interview with London's *Mirror* newspaper in 1999. "He was in the back of a car which I climbed into to be taken to school—and, BANG! I don't know what happened next." Skin grafts and other corrective surgeries restored her face by the time she reached adulthood, but internal scars took longer to heal. "I had absolutely no confidence for years," Kidd said in an interview with *Mail on Sunday* writer Jane Gordon, and though she underwent the last of the skin-graft surgeries to correct the damage while still in her teens, "I was terribly self-conscious about the small scar I was left with. If anyone looked at me I thought they were looking at this mark on my face and I began to wear a lot of makeup to cover it up. I now realise that was the worst thing I could do ... it just drew attention to it."

The Kidd children, with their father's life dominated by horses and polo playing, were raised in a sporty, competitive atmosphere. As Kidd told Gordon, the *Mail on Sunday* journalist, she and her sister "couldn't play games when we were children because we would have huge fights over who won." She trained for years as a show jumper herself while at a girls' boarding school, St. Michael's of West Sussex, and even harbored hopes for the Olympics. "I came out of juniors winning everything. I went into the next stage, young riders, and bought a horse that was good but not brilliant," she told the *Daily Mail*'s Alice Fowler. "Suddenly I wasn't winning and it all became a struggle. I thought, 'All my life I've been committed to riding; I've missed family holidays. I want a bit of a break.'"

Kidd went on to a finishing school in London called Lucie Clayton College, and dated a series of prominent young men, including an heir to the Rothschild banking fortune. She took courses at the acclaimed school of French cooking, Le Cordon Bleu, and drifted into modeling not long after her sister became a top model in London in the mid-1990s. "I found it soul-destroying," she confessed to Fowler in the *Daily Mail*. "I was never really good at it, either, which I didn't like." Her brief career did help her find her calling, for she realized she was far more fascinated by the process of readying the models' faces for the runway or camera. She began training as a makeup artist, which she said was "humbling: you're an apprentice, cleaning people's brushes, carrying their bags," she told Fowler, noting that the most stubborn obstacle to her success was the fact that she was "so impatient—I want to be the best as quickly as I can."

By 2002, Kidd had landed a deal with Max Factor as their official makeup artist and took a break from the heavy traveling schedule her work demanded

on the Spanish resort island of Ibiza. At a nightclub there she met Arthur Wellesley, also known as the Earl of Mornington, and the two began dating. Wellesley is a descendant of Queen Victoria and also heir to another title, the Duke of Wellington, bestowed on his ancestor in 1814 for defeating the troops of French emperor Napoleon Bonaparte at the famous Battle of Waterloo. She and Wellesley lived together in New York City while he earned a graduate business degree from Columbia University.

Back in London, Kidd opened her first school for makeup artists in basement of her London home in 2002. She offered two six-week sessions each year with a tuition fee of nearly $15,000. In 2005, she opened a new facility in London and also launched her own cosmetics line. In June of that same year she and Wellesley were wed at St. James' Church in Barbados, the oldest Anglican church on the island. She wore a dress designed by Christian Lacroix with a ten-foot train, and the event was one of the most coveted social invitations of the season.

Kidd's makeup line and brushes are sold in the United States at Bergdorf Goodman, Neiman Marcus, and Target. While she notes her market is a crowded one with many well-established brands, such as Lancôome, Estée Lauder, and Revlon, a once-customary rite of passage for young women has vanished, and her focus is to educate women on proper techniques, not just sell them product. "There used to be a lot of education about cosmetics," she told Samantha Conti in *WWD*. "Women were actually taught how to apply makeup."

## Sources

*Daily Mail* (London, England), November 5, 2005, p. 12.
*Daily Telegraph* (London, England), October 22, 2001.
*Mail on Sunday* (London, England), February 26, 2006, p. 47.
*Mirror* (London, England), February 11, 1999, p. 31.
*WWD*, December 29, 2005, p. 3.

—*Carol Brennan*

# Kwame Kilpatrick

## Former mayor of Detroit

**B**orn Kwame Malik Kilpatrick, June 8, 1970, in Detroit, MI; son of Bernard and Carolyn Cheeks Kilpatrick; married Carlita Poles; children: Jalil and Jonas (twins), Jelani. *Education:* Florida A&M University, B.S., 1992; Detroit College of Law, J.D., 1999.

**Addresses:** *Contact*—Chrysler District Probation Office, 426 Clinton St., 2nd Flr., Detroit, MI 48226.

## Career

**B**egan career as a middle school teacher; state representative for District 9, Michigan House of Representatives, 1996-2001; designer, Clean Michigan Initiative, 1998; mayor of the city of Detroit, MI, 2002-08.

**Member:** Mount Paven Lodge, National Association for the Advancement of Colored People, Wolverine State Bar Association.

## Sidelights

**W**hen Kwame Kilpatrick was elected mayor of the city of Detroit in 2002, it was with great expectation that he would clean up the troubled city. He was expected to approach the city's problems with enthusiasm as the youngest elected mayor of any major U.S. city. However, after several major scandals which cost the city millions in payouts and legal fees, it came to light through a series of text messages on a city-owned pager that Kilpatrick had an affair with Christine Beatty, his chief

*AP Images*

of staff. After denying the affair for months, Kilpatrick faced numerous legal charges and was compelled to resign his post in September of 2008. Kilpatrick began his career as a middle school teacher before serving as a state representative to the Michigan legislature.

Born on June 8, 1970, in Detroit, Michigan, Kilpatrick is the son of Bernard and Carolyn Cheeks Kilpatrick. Both his parents were public servants who held significant offices. His father served as the chief of staff in Wayne County's executive office and was a Wayne County commissioner, while his mother was elected first as a state representative then to the federal House of Representatives. His parents divorced when he was eleven years old, and he then split his time between their homes.

Raised in Detroit, Kilpatrick attended local public schools. By the time he was in fifth grade, Kilpatrick was already aspiring to become the mayor of the city of Detroit. While he was a gifted student from an early age, Kilpatrick was rambunctious. He told Kevin Chappell of *Ebony,* "I got a lot of whippings. My mother had to come to school a lot for me. I was talking, running my mouth, playing. But I always made good grades."

Leaving Michigan behind for college, Kilpatrick attended Florida A&M University, where he studied political science. There, he was an honors student as well as a football player and captain of the football team. Kilpatrick also developed a reputation for a partying and having a good time. He earned his B.S. and became a certified teacher. Kilpatrick began his professional career working as a middle school teacher.

After returning to Michigan with his wife, Carlita, whom he met while in college, Kilpatrick began studying law at the Detroit College of Law. The couple had twin sons before he graduated in 1999. By this time, Kilpatrick had already begun his political career. In 1996, Kilpatrick was elected to the Michigan House of Representatives for District 9. A Democrat, he eventually served as the vice chairman of the Transportation Committee in the state house.

A leader in the Democratic caucus as well, Kilpatrick spent the summer and fall of 2000 traveling the state to make appearances and speeches. By November of 2000, Kilpatrick had been selected as the House's minority leader. At the age of 30, he was the youngest person as well as the first African American to lead a political party in the state legislature. Kilpatrick was later elected the leader of the entire state house. During his time as the head of the Democrats, he gained a reputation as being able to work both sides of the aisle.

While serving in the state legislature, Kilpatrick was the designer of the Clean Michigan Initiative in 1998. In 2000, knowing that he had two more years in office as a state representative, Kilpatrick was looking forward to his next political step. He considered running for his mother's seat—if she chose to step aside—or for mayor of Detroit. Kilpatrick had much support running for such offices. For example, Bill Rustem, the head of a nonpartisan think tank in Lansing, Michigan, told Amy Lane of Crain's Detroit Business, "I think he would be a formidable candidate, with a lot of support. He's articulate, bright, affable. He's a good politician, in the best sense of the word."

Carolyn Cheeks Kilpatrick chose to remain in office, and her son decided to run for mayor in May of 2001 when then-mayor Dennis Archer decided not to seek a third term in office. Facing Detroit City Council president Gil Hill in the nonpartisan primary, Kilpatrick was considered an underdog who could not match Hill in fund-raising; however, Kilpatrick had name recognition on his side both from his own political career and that of his mother's. He also won key endorsements from the Detroit Regional Chamber as well as business and union leadership for promising to reorganize city departments and improve city management. Kilpatrick first won the September of 2001 primary over Hill with more than 50 percent of the vote, then again in the general election in November of 2001. Kilpatrick won 54 percent of the vote to Hill's 46 percent, in part because of his ability to attract both young voters and senior citizens.

Kilpatrick faced many challenges as he took office in 2002. The city's balance was operating at a deficit, and he had to find a way to better balance the budget. He also had to address the city's high crime rate, stifling bureaucracy with little accountability, a failing infrastructure, and numerous expired contracts with unions. Kilpatrick had to engineer the turn-around that he promised would happen during his campaign. One of his first appointees, Detroit Police Chief Jerry A. Oliver, Sr., believed in him. Oliver told Chappell of Ebony, "People can see themselves in the mayor's vision for the city. This is not some abstract vision that you can't really get a hold on, that you can't get your mind around. He can make a vision real in his comments to people. He can energize them to want to accomplish it. That's his strength."

For Kilpatrick, it was very important to modify how Detroit was perceived by the world. He told Ebony's Chappell, "We have to change our national and international image. There are lots of things going on here that people don't know about. We're still trapped on what was happening here in the 1980s. We need to make sure that we erase all that. We need a lot of things to happen, and they are happening. But we need to tell the world about it." He approached this task with enthusiasm and an open, hip-hop-influenced attitude.

In his first few years in office, Kilpatrick was able to make some progress. He balanced the city's budget, initiated a city clean-up project, brokered a permanent casino development deal that netted the city millions of dollars, implemented a profitable tax amnesty program, and began an after-school program to benefit the city's youth.

Yet by 2003, Kilpatrick was facing controversy. In May of that year, he came under fire for dismissing a deputy police chief who was investigating several situations involving Kilpatrick. The deputy police chief, Gary Brown, was the head of the Internal Affairs division of the Detroit Police. He was looking into numerous wrongdoings by the mayor's security detail, including alleged drunk-driving accidents and faked overtime reports, as well as allegations of an out-of-control orgy-type party at the Manoogian Mansion, the mayor's home.

Kilpatrick initially denied the reports. Patricia Montemurri, Alejandro Bodipo-Memba, and Chris Christoff in the *Philadelphia Inquirer* quoted the mayor as saying, "I think the reason that it comes out is that we are sexy. I think this is sexy administration because of the youth. People tell me it is because of the earring [Kilpatrick sported a diamond stud], the way I dress. Having grown up here in the city of Detroit, people know me. They know me very well. So they knew me when I did go to parties, when I did go to a club, and that's where it stems from."

These controversies dogged Kilpatrick for the rest of his term and more were to come. He also replaced Detroit Police Commissioner Nathaniel Head in a controversial manner. Head was removed after complaining that Kilpatrick had two staff members of the police commission fired (Brown and police officer Harold Nelthorpe) and after Head stated that Kilpatrick practiced cronyism. While the initial probe conducted by the Michigan attorney general's office did not result in charges, a related scandal would occur later in his term.

By 2005, Kilpatrick was dealing with other challenges as well, though the city's crime rate was going down and it successfully put on two major sporting events (the Super Bowl and Major League Baseball's All-Star Game). The gap for the city's budget continued to grow, reaching several hundred million by the beginning of the year. To combat the gap, Kilpatrick cut 700 jobs and tried to make other deals, like a pension bond deal that would help save the city millions of dollars and ensure other jobs would be saved. Still, a thousand more workers lost their jobs, 24-hour bus service ended, and the city's roads and stoplights continued to lack needed repairs. While Detroit had such budgetary problems, Kilpatrick admitted that the city paid thousands of dollars to rent a cherry-red Lincoln Navigator for his wife. He also faced scrutiny over his use of a city credit card. Such choices led *Time* magazine to name Kilpatrick one of the three worst mayors in the United States.

Despite these problems, Kilpatrick was re-elected to a second term in November of 2005. Though he trailed opponent Freman Hendrix in the polls shortly before the primaries, Kilpatrick pulled out a

victory on election day winning 53 percent of the votes to Hendrix's 47 percent. Within two years, however, Kilpatrick became mired in a scandal which would bring down his administration. In August of 2007, Kilpatrick and his chief of staff, Beatty, had to testify at several whistleblower civil lawsuits against the mayor related to the 2003 firings of Brown and Nelthorpe. On the stand, both Kilpatrick and Beatty denied they were involved in a romantic relationship. Beatty also denied that she sent any steamy text messages to the mayor.

In January of 2008, however, the *Detroit Free Press* obtained thousands of Beatty's text messages from her city-issued pager through open-records law requests. The text messages revealed that Beatty and Kilpatrick had conducted an affair in 2002 and 2003, and thus had perjured themselves on the stand. The text messages also revealed that the pair had lied on the stand about their intention to fire Brown. As an investigation into the messages and potential perjury charges was being conducted by Wayne County prosecutor Kym Worthy, Beatty resigned. Kilpatrick initially refused to step down, though he did apologize to his wife, family, and city.

Worthy's investigation led to felony charges for Kilpatrick and Beatty, including perjury, misconduct, and obstruction of justice. Kilpatrick was briefly jailed in August of 2008 while awaiting trial after he defied a condition of his bond—not to leave metro Detroit without permission from a judge—when he traveled across the Ambassador bridge to Windsor, Ontario, Canada, for a business meeting. After his release from jail, Kilpatrick faced two more felony charges related to an incident in July of 2008 when he pushed an investigator from the sheriff's department who was trying to serve a subpoena related to Kilpatrick's perjury and obstruction of justice case. Kilpatrick denied these charges.

Despite the mounting legal troubles, Kilpatrick refused to resign as mayor. Indeed, he filed a lawsuit to prevent a hearing helmed by Michigan Governor Jennifer Granholm that could lead to his removal from office. Under the Michigan Constitution, a governor can remove such officials from office for misconduct. Before the hearing could take place, however, Kilpatrick made a deal in September of 2008 with prosecutors in which he would plead guilty to two counts of obstruction of justice and serve four months in jail as well as five years probation. He was to pay a million dollars in restitution to the city, and allow his law license to be revoked. In addition, he pled no contest to the assault cases. Finally, Kilpatrick resigned as mayor, replaced on an interim basis by Kenneth Cockrel, Jr., the president of the Detroit City Council. In October of 2008, Kilpatrick was formally sentenced and began his jail term on October 28.

Kilpatrick was not allowed to hold public office during his probation as well as practice law, leaving his future unclear. The former mayor remained optimistic. Margena A. Christian of *Jet* quoted him as saying, "I truly know who I am. I truly know where I came from. In Detroit I know who I am. And I know because of that, there's another day for me. I want to tell you, Detroit, that you done set me up for a comeback."

# Sources

### Books

*Complete Marquis Who's Who Biographies,* Marquis Who's Who, 2008.
*Who's Who in American Politics,* Marquis Who's Who, 2007.

### Periodicals

Associated Press, January 30, 2008.
Associated Press State & Local Wire, May 19, 2003.
*Crain's Detroit Business,* November 20, 2000, p. 3; November 12, 2001, p. 1; January 7, 2002, p. 11.
*Detroit Free Press,* February 3, 2005.
*Ebony,* December 2002, p. 61.
*Jet,* November 28, 2005, p. 10; February 18, 2008, p. 14; September 22-29, 2008, p. 8.
*Los Angeles Times,* August 8, 2008, p. A8; August 9, 2008, p. A9; August 16, 2008, p. A16; August 29, 2008, p. A26; September 5, 2008, p. A21.
*New York Times,* October 29, 2008, p. A15.
*Ottawa Citizen,* August 8, 2008, p. A10.
*Philadelphia Inquirer,* May 18, 2003, p. A3.
*Windsor Star* (Ontario, Canada), May 16, 2003, p. D11; June 25, 2003, p. A11; April 19, 2005, p. A1; July 16, 2005, p. A1; January 26, 2008, p. A1; January 31, 2008, p. A1.

—A. Petruso

# Jimmy Kimmel

## Television show host and comedian

**B**orn James Christian Kimmel, November 13, 1967, in New York, NY; married Gina, June 25, 1988 (divorced, June 16, 2003); children: Katie, Kevin. *Education:* Attended the University of Nevada—Las Vegas and Arizona State University.

**Addresses:** *Office*—c/o Jimmy Kimmel Live!, 6834 Hollywood Blvd., Los Angeles, CA 90028.

## Career

**B**egan career in radio, working at such stations as KCMJ-FM, Palm Springs, CA, and KROQ-FM, Los Angeles, CA; co-founder, Jackhole Industries (a production company), CA. Television appearances include: *Win Ben Stein's Money,* Comedy Central, 1997-2000, 2002; *The Man Show,* Comedy Central, 1999-2003; *FOX NFL Sunday,* FOX, c. late 1990s-2003; *Donner* (movie), 2001; *American Music Awards,* 2003-08; *Crank Yankers,* 2002-07; *Jimmy Kimmel Live!,* ABC, 2003—; *Robot Chicken,* Cartoon Network, 2006; *Drawn Together,* Comedy Central, 2006; *The Sarah Silverman Program,* Comedy Central, 2008. Writer for television series, including: *The Man Show,* 1999-2003; *Crank Yankers,* 2002; *Jimmy Kimmel Live!,* 2003—. Executive producer for television series including: *Crank Yankers,* 2002-07; *Windy City Heat* (movie), 2003; *Gerhard Reinke's Wanderlust,* 2003; *Jimmy Kimmel Live!,* 2003—; *The Adam Carolla Project,* 2005; *The Andy Milonakis Show,* 2005-06; *Big Night of Stars* (special), 2008. Film appearances include: *Down to You,* 2000; *Road Trip,* 2000; *Like, Mike,* 2002; *Garfield,* 2004; *Danny Roane: First Time Director,* 2006; *Hellboy II: The Golden Army,* 2008.

**Awards:** Daytime Emmy Award for outstanding game show host (with Ben Stein), for *Win Ben Stein's Money,* 1999.

## Sidelights

**T**he self-dubbed "champion of the common man," Jimmy Kimmel is the host of the popular late-night talk show, ABC's *Jimmy Kimmel Live!* He came to prominence on Comedy Central, first as the co-host of the game show *Win Ben Stein's Money,* then the co-host of the extremely popular *The Man Show.* Because of the relatively crude nature of his previous work, some were surprised that Kimmel evolved into a respected talk show host with wide appeal. Yet in 2008, Kimmel reached his 1,000th episode of *Jimmy Kimmel Live!* Upon reaching the mark, he told Bill Brioux of Alberta, Canada's *Fort Mc-Murray Today,* "There were a lot of people who didn't think we'd get to this milestone. In fact, there are still some people who don't think we'll make it to Thursday."

Kimmel was born in 1967 in the borough of Brooklyn in New York City. He was raised in Las Vegas, and by his teens, was an enthusiastic fan of popular late night talk show host David Letterman. He planned on an art career until college when a stint working at a college radio station changed his focus. Kimmel attended the University of Nevada for one year, then Arizona State University for two years.

Kimmel began his professional career working in radio, though he had trouble staying employed. He was fired from at least four radio jobs over the course of his time in radio. He told Alan Sepinwall of the Newark *Star-Ledger*, "I would make it my job to make fun of the program directors at these radio stations and they generally didn't appreciate it." He eventually had a morning show in Palm Springs, California, and worked at KROQ-FM in Los Angeles in the 1990s. By the late 1990s, he was known as "Jimmy the Sports Guy."

While still working in radio, Kimmel moved into television by serving as the co-host of a game show on Comedy Central, *Win Ben Stein's Money*. Beginning in 1997, he and his titular co-host challenged viewers with trivia questions for a chance to win thousands of dollars. The show soon gained a loyal following. As Terry Morrow of the Cleveland *Plain Dealer* explained, "Much of the game show's success has been attributed to the on-screen chemistry between the deadpan Stein and the wiseacre Kimmel...." Because of their work together, Kimmel and Stein won a Daytime Emmy Award for outstanding game show host in 1999. The pair were nominated for the same award in 2001.

Building on the buzz created by *Win Ben Stein's Money*, Kimmel was given his own show on Comedy Central and left radio entirely behind in 1999. Entitled *The Man Show*, Kimmel co-created and co-hosted the program with close friend Adam Carolla, who had himself gained public recognition as a personality on the popular call-in radio and television show *Loveline*. On *The Man Show*, Kimmel and Carolla offered an uninhibited perspective on male interests with crude humor in both talk show and sketch comedy segments.

Explaining the show's take on man's place in society, Preston Turegano of the *San Diego Union-Tribune* quoted Kimmel as saying to a *Man Show* audience, "Millions and millions of women are under Oprah's spell.... We're the ones who are supposed to be telling them what to do.... The Oprahization of America must be stopped."

Critics had a mixed reaction to *The Man Show*, with some embracing the humor and others decrying its lack of any substance. In *Variety* for example, Ray Richmond commented, "The divertingly smug Kimmel and Carolla preside over the live studio audience festivities like cheerleaders at a pep rally for the intimacy-challenged." He concluded, "With *The Man Show*, Comedy Central illustrates that men's bladders have evolved significantly more quickly

than our intellect." Despite such reviews, *The Man Show* was the highest-rated debut of any show in Comedy Central's history.

With the success of *Win Ben Stein's Money* and *The Man Show*, Kimmel added more television appearances to his schedule. In the late 1990s, he began appearing on *Fox NFL Sunday*, offering his picks for football games and making fun of the show's cast, including former NFL players Terry Bradshaw and Howie Long, in his weekly segment. Some critics believed that Kimmel added little to nothing to *Fox NFL Sunday* and wanted him off the show.

Bradshaw took offense to Kimmel's comedy as well. Kimmel told Kevin D. Thompson in the Albany *Times Union*, "He thinks it's funny now, because he knows I mean him no harm. But sports and comedy are completely different worlds. When they get together, it causes some fiction. In sports, when they're going to rip someone, they call the team and tell 'em beforehand. It's weird. There's a real courtesy involved. So, to him, when I just showed up wearing a 'Terry is Bald' hat, and I didn't call to OK it with him, it was such a breach of his ethics. It was shocking, but I think they've gotten used to it."

In the fall of 2000, as *The Man Show* and other projects took up more of his time, Kimmel left *Win Ben Stein's Money*. Among these projects was *Crank Yankers*, which aired on various networks between 2002 and 2007. In addition to executive producing the show, Kimmel provided voices for some of the crank-calling puppets that formed the heart of the program.

Kimmel's career reached new heights in 2003 when he began hosting his own late-night talk show on ABC, *Jimmy Kimmel Live!* With the advent of *Jimmy Kimmel Live!*, Kimmel left *The Man Show* and *NFL Sunday Live* behind, though some pre-taped new episodes of *The Man Show* continued to air in early 2003. Kimmel's deal with ABC was lucrative—a reported seven year deal with the first year at $1.75 million guaranteed—though many late-night talk shows fail within weeks of their introduction.

Kimmel's show was shot at Hollywood's El Capitan Theatre and began airing in January of 2003. His show's debut came after ABC's airing of the Super Bowl, and featured rotating guest co-hosts and sidekicks. At the ABC upfront (an event where networks introduce new shows to the press and advertisers) in May of 2002, *Broadcasting & Cable* quoted Kimmel as introducing himself by saying, "My name is Jimmy Kimmel, and I'm the new king of late night. I know that may sound presumptuous, but I really feel, with the right support and promotion, I could be the best thing to happen to this network since Michael Ovitz."

There were some initial concerns over Kimmel's ability to attract an audience and guests—diehard *Man Show* fans were expected to be disappointed by his more tame show, and those who disliked *The Man Show* might not give him a chance. Former co-host Stein believed in Kimmel as a late-night host from the first, telling Sepinwall of the Newark *Star-Ledger*, "Jimmy is so lively and quick-witted and is so original. It won't really depend on his guests or his musical acts. It's going to depend on his own personality. He is a stand-up, pleasant, nice guy who can be counted on to empathize with his viewers. He is basically a big kid at heart, he's going to appeal to the big kids in the college dorms who are the audience for this kind of show."

Kimmel quickly found a loyal, if rowdy, audience as he slowly developed into a respected talk show host who attracted many high-profile guests. Though he tried to limit the amount of imitation of Letterman, critics noticed that early on at least, Kimmel clearly displayed his reverence for Letterman and his sense of humor. He also was praised for doing his show live, which allowed him to comment on the latest news and information unlike his competitors who tape their shows in the late afternoon. From the first, Kimmel was also able to attract the audience ABC desired (adults, especially men, ages 18 to 34), and improved his ratings during his first years on the air. The show's quality also improved, thanks to him having time to really become knowledgeable and comfortable about his job. Kimmel told the *New York Times'* Bill Carter, "It's confidence. Not just me learning what I'm doing. Most of the people working here had no experience."

Over the next few years, Kimmel did have ups and downs related to his talk show. In 2005, he was nominated for a People's Choice Award for favorite late-night talk show host for his work on *Jimmy Kimmel Live!* However, Kimmel faced controversy for making negative comments about Detroit during the Detroit Pistons' appearance in the NBA finals in 2004. The Associated Press State & Local Wire quoted him as saying that "They're going to burn the city of Detroit down if the Pistons win, and it's not worth it." After the comments were made, Kimmel's show was temporarily pulled off the air by the ABC affiliate there. Kimmel later apologized, and later hosted a series of shows in Detroit. His contract with ABC was also extended to keep him on the air well beyond the 2009 season.

*Jimmy Kimmel Live!* was not his only project. In 2003, Kimmel began an annual gig serving as the emcee of the American Music Awards. That same year, he saw the premiere of his reality-inspired movie on Comedy Central, *Windy City Heat.* The prank at the heart of *Windy City* involves an aspiring actor who is desperate to start a career. The actor is deceived into believing he earned a starring role in a major motion picture. In 2007, Kimmel showed his workaholic side by serving as a fill-in host on *Live with Regis and Kelly* for a week. That show was taped in the morning in New York City, and Kimmel flew back each day to host his own show that night in Los Angeles. Over the years, Kimmel also had small roles in films such as *Danny Roane: First Time Director* and *Garfield.*

No matter what happens with other projects, Kimmel is committed to *Jimmy Kimmel Live!* He told Alex Strachan in the *Calgary Herald,* "It's ruined my life. It's a brutal schedule. It's weird. You look at Jay Leno in his first year, and you see that his hair was black. I see now, I can see the white hairs appearing on my head. But what are you going to do? I mean, you have to keep doing it until you get cancelled. It's the law."

# Sources

### Books

*Complete Marquis Who's Who Biographies,* Marquis Who's Who, 2006.

### Periodicals

*Advertising Age,* January 19, 2004, p. S4.
Associated Press, September 20, 2007; October 14, 2007; October 6, 2008.
Associated Press State & Local Wire, June 17, 2003; September 21, 2005.
*Broadcasting & Cable,* May 20, 2002, p. 20; February 24, 2003, p. 14.
*Calgary Herald* (Alberta, Canada), January 22, 2004, p. F6.
*Daily News* (NY), January 17, 2003, p. 127.
*Daily Variety,* May 14, 2002.
*Ford McMurray Today* (Alberta, Canada), April 3, 2008, p. C1.
*Houston Chronicle,* November 13, 2006, p. 6.
*National Post* (Canada), January 29, 2003, p. AL1.
*New York Times,* September 7, 2006, p. E1.
*Plain Dealer* (Cleveland, OH), September 9, 2000, p. 9E
*Saint Paul Pioneer Press* (MN), February 25, 2007, p. 15A.
*San Diego Union-Tribune,* June 13, 1999, sec. TV WEEK, p. 6..

*Star-Ledger* (Newark, NJ), January 26, 2003, p. 1.

*Television Week*, September 22, 2003, p. 4.

*Times Union* (Albany, NY), November 4, 1999, p. P21.

*Toronto Sun*, January 17, 2003, p. E9.

*Vancouver Province* (British Columbia), January 26, 2003, p. E3.

*Variety*, June 14-20, 1999, p. 24.

**Online**

"Jimmy Kimmel," Internet Movie Database, http://www.imdb.com/name/nm0453994/ (October 20, 2008).

*—A. Petruso*

# Jeff Kinney

**Author and cartoonist**

Born in 1971 in Maryland; married Julie (a newspaper reporter); children: Will, Grant. *Education:* Graduated from the University of Maryland, 1993.

**Addresses:** *E-mail*—jeffkinney@comcast.net. *Office*—c/o Harry N. Abrams, Inc., 115 West 18th St., New York, NY 10011.

## Career

Drew *Igdoof,* for Villanova University newspaper, c. 1989-90, then the University of Maryland's *Diamondback,* c. 1991-93; worked for *Newburyport Daily News,* and a medical software company, c. mid-1990s; design director and game manager, Family Education Network, c. mid-1990s—; began working on what would become *Diary of a Wimpy Boy,* 1998; published daily installments of *Diary of a Wimpy Boy* on www.funbrain. com, 2004; signed publishing deal with Harry N. Abrams, 2006; published *Diary of a Wimpy Kid,* 2007; signed movie deal with Fox 2000 for *Diary of a Wimpy Kid,* 2008; published third *Wimpy Kid* book, *Diary of a Wimpy Kid: The Last Straw,* 2009.

## Sidelights

The mastermind by the extremely popular kids' book series *Diary of a Wimpy Kid,* failed strip cartoonist Jeff Kinney found his voice and outlet for his sense of humor in the day-to-day struggles of middle-schooler Greg Heffley. While the three books in the *Diary of a Wimpy Kid* series were extremely popular—all hit number one on at least one best-

*Will and Grant Kinney*

seller's list, eleven million copies were in print by early 2009, and they had been translated into 28 languages—they only represented Kinney's secondary career. He continued to hold a full-time job managing online games for a children's Web site run by an educational publisher. Through it all, Kinney appreciated the *Diary of a Wimpy Kid* phenomenon and remained humble. Kinney told David Mehegan of the *Boston Globe* in 2008, "I'm still stuck at the starting point. I'm absolutely shocked that the book even got published."

Kinney was born in 1971 in Maryland and grew up in Port Washington, Maryland. Throughout his childhood, Kinney admitted to being a typical kid who had a few odd experiences—like mummifying himself in toilet paper in the bathroom—which ended up in his *Diary of a Wimpy Kid* books. He also wanted to be a cartoonist from an early age, creating his first cartoon when he was in first grade. Kinney's hero was Bill Watterson, who drew and wrote *Calvin and Hobbes.*

As a child, Kinney admitted to being an excellent observer. He told Jan Hoffman of the *New York Times,* "I had a detached viewpoint, even as a kid." Talking about his school years, he added, "I was wimpy and I still don't shave too often. I served a purpose:

to make the star athlete look good. I was the orange cone for other kids to dribble around."

By the time Kinney reached college, he was able to create his own strip. He launched his comic strip writing career while a freshman at Villanova University, which he attended on an Air Force scholarship. *Igdoof* was published in the campus newspaper, but its creator left Villanova after one year and the strip went on temporary hiatus. Kinney then entered the University of Maryland, where he studied computer science. As soon as he started going to Maryland, he tried to get *Igdoof* published in the campus newspaper, the *Diamondback,* but it was rejected by editors during his first two years.

During Kinney's junior and senior years, however, *Igdoof* appeared in the paper and developed a loyal following. In the *Washington Post,* Lisa Leff described the strip's main character as "a jug-eared, big-nosed, bug-eyed freshman with a fondness for booger jokes, miserable study habits and an unfailing sense of how to offend women." Igdoof was also a cartoon character who tried his best not to do any homework. Because of *Igdoof*'s popularity, it was put in several other East Coast campus newspapers and was merchandised on the University of Maryland's campus as well. Kinney had found his calling.

After earning his undergraduate degree in criminal justice (he switched majors to facilitate writing the strip) in 1993, Kinney hoped to turn *Igdoof* into a nationally syndicated comic strip. He told Leff of the *Washington Post,* "The response on campus has been absolutely great. This could possibly be the biggest thing ever to happen to me. But I want Igdoof to live. I don't want to look back at Maryland as when I had a great life." However, despite changes to the strip, which had its hero and his friends live in an apartment, have jobs, and go to night school, Kinney could not get the strip syndicated, and he put his goal of being a professional cartoonist aside for a time. Kinney later admitted that he believed he did not have the technical style needed to be a successful strip cartoonist.

In 1995, Kinney moved to New England, first living in Boston and working as a layout artist at the *Newburyport Daily News.* He was later employed by a medical software company. Kinney eventually settled in Plainville, Massachusetts, got married, had two sons, and found a position as a design director for the Family Education Network, the Internet arm of educational publisher Pearson. In 1998, Kinney began jotting down ideas for what would

become *Diary of a Wimpy Boy.* Instead of just writing and drawing a strip, he combined cartoons with the text of a middle-schooler's journal and a novel-like storyline. Kinney's story focused on Greg Heffley, who has a high opinion of himself but is very imperfect. He struggles to improve his social status through schemes that rarely work and must deal with the daily challenges of school and family life. Greg's journal entries are illustrated with his own cartoons, which add to the story's humor.

Kinney told Powells.com, "I write for kids because I think the most interesting (and most humorous) stories come from people's childhoods. When I was writing *Diary of a Wimpy Kid,* I had a blast talking on the phone to my younger brother, Patrick, remembering all of the things that happened to our family when we were growing up. I think if everyone would write down the funny stories from their own childhoods, the world would be a better place." In another interview, Kinney admitted the book was a blend of fact and fiction. He told Mehegan of the *Boston Globe,* "I did a lot of remembering, and a lot of inventing, about what it was like to be a kid at that age, with a sort of amoral moralism. There are a lot of instances in the book where Greg thinks he has learned his lesson or done the right thing, when it's clear to the reader that he hasn't."

Kinney spent the next six years working on the idea but could not find a publisher for his comic/fiction hybrid. In 2004, he began publishing it online in daily installments on Funbrain.com. The online version of *Diary of a Wimpy Boy* became instantly popular, attracting thousands of visitors every day. The success of the Web site caught the attention of publishers. In 2006, Kinney was able to turn *Diary of a Wimpy Boy* into a printed series after signing a book deal with New York publisher Harry N Abrams.

In 2007, *Diary of a Wimpy Boy,* was published in book form. After 33 weeks on the *New York Times* children's chapter book best-seller list, it reached number one. Talking about being included on the list so quickly after publication, Kinney told Amber Miles of the Albany, New York *Times Union,* "I was shocked and surprised and little dumbfounded. I've been doubting and thinking it was a clerical error. I naively wrote this book for adults, but I had no idea that it would work so well for kids—I didn't see that coming."

*Diary of a Wimpy Boy* was also well-received by critics, with Liz Rosenberg of the *Boston Globe* commenting, "*Diary of a Wimpy Kid* is charming and hi larious from the get-go. It's full of small cartoony black-and-white illustrations, irreverent humor, and an uncanny eye for the depredations and triumphs of middle-school life." Other critics noted that Kinney's novel was helpful to its readers. The *San Diego Union-Tribune*'s Jane Clifford noted, "Kinney has done a wonderful service for preteens by talking about all those awful, embarrassing, and good moments to, if nothing else, let them know they're not alone in feeling really mixed up about everything." More than a million copies of *Diary of a Wimpy Kid* were eventually put in print, and the book was translated into 20 languages.

As the *Diary of a Wimpy Boy* became popular, Kinney kept his position at Family Education Network and worked on more books featuring Greg. In 2008, Kinney published his second book in the series, *Diary of a Wimpy Boy: Rodrick Rules*. This volume focused on Greg's problematic life at school as well as the castigations of his older brother, Rodrick. Like *Diary of a Wimpy Boy*, *Diary of a Wimpy Boy: Rodrick Rules* was instantly popular and a number-one *New York Times* best seller. Reviews were again positive, with Thom Barthelmess of *Booklist* stating, "the real and deeper appeal of Greg's story is the unapologetic honesty of his adolescence; he comes across as a real kid, and his story is one that will appeal to all those real kids who feel just like him."

The *Diary of a Wimpy Boy* books were officially a phenomenon by the end of 2008, with readers anticipating the third in the series. As Kinney prepared the third volume, he put out *Diary of a Wimpy Kid Do-It-Yourself Book*, which gave readers the chance to create their own journal with spaces for illustrations just like Greg's. In early 2009, Kinney published his third official title, *Diary of a Wimpy Boy: The Last Straw*. This book focused on Greg's attempts to improve himself as well his complex relationship with his father, who has wearied of his son's antics. His father seriously considers sending Greg to military school to shape him up.

*The Last Straw* was also extremely popular from the first. The night of its release, Kinney did a book signing in Carle Park, New York, where more than 3,000 people showed up. He told Bob Minzesheimer and Craig Wilson of *USA Today,* "It was overwhelming and exciting but I also felt guilty. Some kids didn't get their books signed until 11:30 p.m. I told their parents, 'Nothing is worth waiting that long for.'" *The Last Straw* shot to number one on *USA Today*'s Best-Selling Books list within two weeks of its publication.

Like other books in the series, *The Last Straw* was well-liked by so-called reluctant readers. Reluctant readers are children, often boys, who do not like to sit still and read. Parents and teachers raved over Kinney's ability to reach these readers and hold their attention long enough to read a book and seek out other titles. Kinney told Minzesheimer of *USA Today*, "I didn't start out by trying to turn non-readers into readers. It was sort of a lark. I'm not a strong writer of narrative fiction, but I can string jokes together. And I'm happy the books have become a gateway to legitimate reading."

Despite his success with the *Diary of a Wimpy Boy* series, Kinney kept his position with the Family Education Network where he managed two game sites and continued to aspire to being a daily newspaper strip cartoonist. He admitted on more than one occasion that he would jump at the chance and had offers to that end in 2008. While deciding what to do about this goal, Kinney reached another milestone for his book series. He had held onto the rights for his books, and in 2008, he signed a deal with Fox 2000 to turn the first *Diary of a Wimpy Boy* book into a feature film. It was scheduled for release in 2009.

Yet Kinney knew that his *Wimpy Boy* book series would have its limits, one reason he kept his day job. He told Jan Hoffman of the *New York Times*, "Five books is my immediate goal, seven is my dream. Every good cartoonist knows when to turn the lights off. There's something creepy about a 60-year-old man writing books from the perspective of a 12-year-old."

## Selected writings

*Diary of a Wimpy Kid*, Amulet, 2007.
*Diary of a Wimpy Kid: Rodrick Rules*, Amulet, 2008.
*Diary of a Wimpy Kid Do-It-Yourself Book*, Amulet, 2008.
*Diary of a Wimpy Kid: The Last Straw*, Amulet, 2009.

## Sources

### Periodicals

*Booklist*, February 1, 2008, p. 46.
*Boston Globe*, May 20, 2007, p. D7; April 8, 2008, p. E1.
*Chicago Tribune*, January 13, 2009.
*Entertainment Weekly*, May 9, 2008, p. 67.
*Los Angeles Times*, November 5, 2008, p. E1.
*New York Times*, December 13, 2007, p. E1; January 11, 2009.

*Philadelphia Inquirer,* April 9, 2008, p. E1.

*Providence Journal* (RI), March 30, 2008, p. J1.

*San Diego Union-Tribune,* May 27, 2007, p. BOOKS-5.

*School Library Journal,* October 2008, p. 15.

*Times-Union* (Albany, NY), June 6, 2007, p. E1.

*USA Today,* January 28, 2008, p. 1D; January 13, 2009, p. 1D; January 22, 2009, p. 7D.

*Washington Post,* February 3, 1994, p. M1.

**Online**

"About the Author," Diary of a Wimpy Kid by Jeff Kinney, http://www.wimpykid.com/ (January 25, 2009).

"Kids' Q&A: Jeff Kinney," Powells.com, http://www.powells.com/kidsqa/kinney.html (January 25, 2009).

*—Carol Brennan*

# George and Lena Korres

## Founders of Korres Natural Products

*Brian Ach/WireImage/Getty Images*

**B**orn George Korres in Greece; married Lena Korres; children: two. Born Lena Korres in 1971 in Greece; married George Korres; children: two.

**Addresses:** *Office*—Korres S.A. Natural Products, 20-26 K. Manou St., 116 33 Athens, Greece.

## Career

**G**eorge Korres worked as a pharmacist, 1989—. Lena Korres worked as a chemical engineer. Together, formed Korres Natural Products, 1996.

**Awards:** George Korres: Entrepreneur of the Year award, *Status* magazine, 2005 and 2007. Together: National Award for innovation and manufacturing procedures, Ministry of Development, Greece, 1998; National Award for entrepreneurship, small and medium enterprises association, Greece, 2000; first packaging award & merit for corporate identity, graphic design and illustration awards, Greece, 2002; development and innovation award, Entrepreneurship Association, Greece, 2003; Golden Star in packaging design, Association of Packaging Materials Production Industries, Greece, 2003 and 2006; Prix de Beaute Award in hair care products, for masiha oil and wheat proteins shampoo, 2004; first prize in packaging and corporate brochure & Merit, Graphic Design and Illustration Awards, Greece, for corporate identity and corporate site (www.korres. com), 2004; Ermis Gold and Ermis Bronze prizes in packaging, Greek Association of Communication and Advertising, for liquid hand soaps and face care line, respectively, 2004; first prize for Korres

Books logo, Graphic Design and Illustration Awards, Greece, 2005; Prix de Beaute Award, for Korres Color Pencils, 2005; retail manager and rising star of the year awards, *RetailBusiness* magazine, 2005; company of the year, *Votre Beaute* magazine, for company development and creativity, 2006; Ermis Gold for product identity and packaging, and for promotional material, 2006; star in packaging design for Krokos Kozanis, World Packaging Organisation, 2006; Prix de Beaute Award, for Korres Color Concealer & Compact Powders, 2007; Ermis Silver for product identity and packaging, for the Korres Bag, 2007; best eye cream, *Sunday Mirror* Beauty Awards, 2007; distinction for international business development, the Leading Companies Greece Awards, 2007; best hand launch award, Pure Beauty Awards, UK, for the Thyme Honey hand cream, 2007; best investor relations by a small cap company, Greek Investor Relations Awards, 2007; best natural eyeshadow, Natural Health Beauty Awards, for Korres in olive green, 2008; best mask, *SELF* Magazine Healthy Beauty Awards, for Korres cinnamon and clay mask, 2008; best body product award, *She* Magazine Beauty Awards, for Korres basil lemon body scrub, 2008; two packaging honors, a store graphics honor, a graphic design honor, and an honor for the Korres U.S. Flagship store, Hellenic Illustration and Graphic Design Awards, 2008; third grooming products award, Beauty Innovation

Awards by *Schaufenster* (*Die Presse* newspaper supplement), Austria, for ruscus & chestnut eye cream, 2008. Korres has been ranked 247 amongst the 500 highest developing companies in Europe, by the 500 Growth Entrepreneurs for Growth Association, 2006; ranked first out of 101 best (product/brand or phenomenon) by *Kotivinkki* magazine, Finland, 2007; ranked 460 amongst the 500 highest-developing companies in Europe, by the 500 Growth Entrepreneurs for Growth Association, 2007; ranked 67th amongst 2,500 Greek companies in the annual *Industry Diamonds* survey by Stat-Bank (Greece), 2007; ranked fourth, Best Listed Companies Greece, by Thomson Extel Survey, 2008.

## Sidelights

Brought together by a shared vision, George and Lena Korres have become internationally known for their Korres Natural Products. The line of skin care and makeup created from all natural and homeopathic ingredients has won many awards, particularly in the Korres' home country of Greece, and their growing dominance in the market has led them to be named two of the world's 40 most influential people under 40 by *Wallpaper* magazine. The line includes more than 500 products and there are nine stand-alone stores devoted to Korres Natural Products. Along with the stand-alone stores, the line is featured in department stores and can be purchased in 30 countries worldwide.

During his college years, George Korres, who was studying to become a physicist, began becoming interested in homeopathic remedies. "He started mixing natural pharmacy ingredients to create herbal preparations, natural remedies, and eventually cosmetic products," Lena Korres explained on the Beauty and the Dirt Web site. Pursuing his interest after graduation, in 1989, George Korres bought the oldest homeopathic pharmacy in Athens, which sold only imported products. Korres had a much wider vision: He hoped to develop and market a line of Greek homeopathic remedies, using traditional Greek ingredients.

Lena Korres was the first staff member brought on board. Trained as a chemical engineer, Lena eagerly embraced George's vision. "There was a passion for natural ingredients and a small but inspired team of people working in the Korres pharmacy that drew me instantly," she explained on the Beauty and the Dirt Web site. The pair "fell in love over chemical engineering and botanical tinctures," wrote a contributor to *Vanity Fair*. Soon working together as a married couple, the Korreses used their organic approach to develop lines of healing products that made the Korres pharmacy the center of homeopathic medicine in Greece.

The Korreses made efforts to listen closely to their customers, and it was soon evident that people wanted a series of herb-based skin care products. With their team, the Korreses began developing such a line, and in 1996, they launched Korres Natural Products. Their vision for the skin care line remained the same as their plans for homeopathic medicine: They would not use mineral oils or silicone common to many beauty products, instead using vegetable oils, natural amino acids, and natural moisturizers. Their first product combined honey and aniseed in an herbal syrup, the idea for which came from George Korres' grandfather. A variation on the mixture was common in his home on the island of Naxos.

On the company Web site, the Korreses explain that they "aim to utilize ... extensive scientific resources for the creation of beneficial and safe products." Still based out of the Korres Pharmacy in Athens, they keep a traditional laboratory for herbal preparations, making tinctures, oils, creams, capsules, and teas. In addition to the traditional side, scientists use state-of-the-art equipment to manufacture the remedies for wider consumption. Lena Korres explained how difficult it was to develop a way to package a traditional recipe that involved yogurt on the Beauty and the Dirt Web site. Describing a Greek tradition of using yogurt as a soothing sun-burn cream, she said, "Yoghurt contains thousands of live cultures and therefore does not take well to mixing in the lab. It was a real challenge for our R&D team to create a stable cosmetic formula preserving all the benefits of live yoghurt." The result of those successes became Korres' Yoghurt Cooling Gel.

In the twelve years since Korres Natural Products launched, the company has produced more than 500 products, from mascara and concealer to shampoo and sun protection. In 2008, they launched a line of men's products and a line of beauty and fashion products inspired by royalty called Kings & Queens. The company draws on more than 3,000 homeopathic remedies to develop their products. In addition to their own research, the Korreses have partnered with the Pharmaceutics department of the University of Athens, participating in industrial research programs and focusing on the unique properties of Greek herbs. In 2008, they developed and patented an anti-aging ingredient to be used in future products once the patent is approved.

In 2007, the Korreses took the company public, allowing them to invest more aggressively in promoting their products internationally, as well as continuing to develop further lines. When asked if they considered buying another company or selling their company to a larger one, the pair replied that they did not intend to do either. They summed up the company's growth from 1996 to 2007 in *Cosmetics International*: "It has been an amazing eleven years and it is great that what started as a three-product range from Athens' first homeopathic pharmacy, is today a company with a 300+ product line and a strong presence in more than 30 countries with a significant global following.... Our ever growing global presence and store opening activity will help us evolve further." Korres Natural Products has standalone stores in cities including New York, Athens, London, Barcelona, Glasgow, and Beijing. They have mentioned plans to open an additional store in Brooklyn, New York, and La Chaux-de-Fonds, Switzerland. While focusing on their international presence, they continue to promote their products in Greece. In the first half of 2008, Korres Natural Products Group sales were enhanced by 49.4 percent, largely due to the presence in foreign markets.

George Korres serves as the lead pharmacist of the company, while Lena Korres is in charge of new product development and international marketing. Both also make public appearances to promote their products. Of their work together as a team, George said, "I've never lived another way. You can't say, 'This is my life and this is my job.'" Answering the same question on the Beauty and the Dirt Web site, Lena said, "I enjoy sharing a vision and the same reality with my husband. I also enjoy working on different parts of the business and sometimes spend-

ing whole days when we do not see each other at all at the office!" The Korreses keep their home in Athens, Greece.

## Sources

### Periodicals

*Cosmetics International* July 6, 2007, p. 15.
*New York Times*, Nobember 4, 2007, p. 3.
*PR Newswire*, August 8, 2008.
*PR Week* (UK), January 19, 2007, p. 5.
*Vanity Fair*, March 2008, p. 252.

### Online

"Korres: Behind the Brand," Sephora, http://www.sephora.com/browse/brand_hierarchy.jhtml?brandId=Korres&contentId= C11259 (August 21, 2008).
Korres Home Page, http://www.korres.com/ (August 21, 2008).
"Korres Opens Glasgow Store," Wallpaper, http://www.wallpaper.com/beauty/korres-opens-glasgow-store/1 536 (August 21, 2008).
"Mimi Talks to Lena Korres," Beauty and the Dirt, http://www.beautyandthedirt.co.uk/show.asp?ID=3471 (August 21, 2008).

*—Alana Joli Abbott*

# Peter Krause

*AP Images*

## Actor

**B**orn Peter William Krause, August 12, 1965, in Alexandria, MN; son of two teachers; children: Roman (with Christine King, a producer and manager). *Education:* Earned degree from Gustavus Adolphus College, 1987; New York University, Tisch School of the Arts, M.F.A., 1990.

**Addresses:** *Agent*—Creative Artists Agency, 9830 Wilshire Blvd., Beverly Hills, CA, 90212-1825.

## Career

**A**ctor in films, including: *Blood Harvest,* 1987; *Lovelife,* 1997; *Melting Pot,* 1997; *My Engagement Party,* 1998; *The Truman Show,* 1998; *It's a Shame About Ray,* 2000; *We Don't Live Here Anymore,* 2004; *Civic Duty* (also producer), 2006; *Jack and Addie* (also executive producer), 2009. Television appearances include: *Carol & Company,* CBS, 1990; *Seinfeld,* NBC, 1992; *Cybill,* CBS, 1995-97; *Sports Night,* ABC, 1998-2000; *Six Feet Under,* HBO, 2001-05; *The Lost Room* (miniseries), SciFi Channel, 2006; *Dirty Sexy Money,* ABC, 2007—. Stage appearances include: *After the Fall,* American Airlines Theater, New York City, 2004.

**Awards:** Screen Actors Guild Award for outstanding performance by an ensemble in a drama series, Screen Actors Guild, for *Six Feet Under,* 2003, 2004.

## Sidelights

**A**ctor Peter Krause (pronounced KROW-zuh) is best known for his starring role on the acclaimed HBO drama *Six Feet Under* from 2001 to 2005. As the deeply flawed yet persistently appealing Nate Fisher, Krause became indelibly associated with that character, but finally seemed to break free of it with his lead in a new hour-long ABC series in the fall of 2007. In *Dirty Sexy Money,* Krause's character was a marked departure from previous roles in which he evinced "a special aptitude for playing rakes, rogues, and cads," declared *New York* magazine writer Adam Sternbergh. In *Dirty Sexy Money,* however, Krause "plays the moral center of the show," Sternbergh continued. "He's the one sane man in an insane world."

Krause was born in Alexandria, Minnesota, located in the scenic Alexandria Lakes region of the state. He is descended from farming families on both sides, and his father was a high school English teacher. The middle of three children, Krause was a talented track athlete at his high school, but suffered an injury while pole vaulting; off for the season, he decided to try out for the school play because he had a crush on one of his classmates who was a drama-club veteran. He won the role in *Charley's Aunt*, took his co-star to the prom, and went on to appear in a number of productions at Gustavus Adolphus College in St. Peter, Minnesota, especially after switching his major to English literature from pre-med. Following his graduation in 1987 he moved to New York City to enter the prestigious graduate theater program at New York University's Tisch School of the Arts.

Krause's parents had been nervous about his choice of career, but not long after earning his M.F.A. in 1990 he landed a steady job on a new CBS television sketch-comedy show, *Carol & Company*, that marked veteran comedian Carol Burnett's return to the screen after an immensely successful run on Saturday nights from 1967 to 1978. The job offer thrilled his parents, Krause recalled in an interview with Neal Justin in the Minneapolis *Star Tribune*. "There's no better stamp of approval than Carol Burnett," he joked. "It was wholesome. It wasn't like I was going off to do some quasi-porno movie in eastern Europe." Certainly, his parents may have had their qualms back in 1987 when Krause made his feature-film debut in a schlocky B-horror movie called *Blood Harvest* that featured eccentric entertainer Tiny Tim.

Krause struggled for a few years in New York City after his *Carol & Company* run ended. He bartended at the Palace Theatre, a Broadway venue that hosted popular musicals like *Beauty and the Beast*, where he came to know another young actor named Aaron Sorkin, who was the bar manager at the time and wrote plays in his spare time. Krause landed the occasional television job—like a 1992 episode of *Seinfeld* in which he played a white supremacist limousine passenger—and between 1995 and 1997, he had a recurring role on the CBS comedy series *Cybill*. He made his major-motion picture debut in 1997's *Lovelife*, a college-set romance that also featured a young Carla Gugino. A year later, he won a supporting role in the Jim Carrey hit *The Truman Show*.

The year 1998 proved Krause's breakout one. His old friend Sorkin—who had since gone on to an impressive Hollywood career—cast him in a new series he created for ABC called *Sports Night*. Krause played Casey McCall, one of the anchors on a fictitious cable-sports network's flagship daily news show, widely thought to be a stand-in for *SportsCenter* on ESPN. Reviewing it for *Sports Illustrated*, MSNBC television anchor Keith Olbermann—who actually spent five years on the real ESPN show—commended the onscreen camaraderie apparent between Krause's character and his co-anchor and best friend, played by Josh Charles, who "evince a bond of genuine affection and cooperation.... Dan Patrick

and I used to call it our foxhole mentality. It's not only the best part of *Sports Night*, it was also the best part of working on *SportsCenter*."

More mainstream media critics adored the show, too. *Entertainment Weekly* called it "a home run, a hole in one, a touchdown—at once the most consistently funny, intelligent, and emotional of any new-season series." Unfortunately, *Sports Night* lasted just two seasons on ABC before it was cancelled. This time, however, Krause was not out of work for long. He was cast in one of the lead roles in an hour-long series for HBO called *Six Feet Under*, which debuted in June of 2001. The dark comedy was created for the cable channel by Alan Ball, who had won an Academy Award for his 1999 movie *American Beauty* but had also done a stint as a writer for *Cybill*.

*Six Feet Under* exposed the private lives of a family running a Los Angeles-area funeral home. Krause was cast as Nate Fisher, who moved to Seattle years ago but is on his way home for a visit when his mortician-father suddenly dies. Nate decides to stay and join the family firm, despite his long-unresolved issues with his chilly brother David, played by Michael C. Hall, who is struggling to fully accept his sexual orientation. There is also the timid, newly widowed mother Ruth (Frances Conroy) and a teen-aged sister Claire (Lauren Ambrose), who appears to be the fiercest of the bunch.

Though the personal relationships of all the Fishers was central to *Six Feet Under*'s storylines over its five-season run, Nate's romantic travails offered some of the juiciest plot twists. He marries twice—first to a friend from his Seattle days played by Lili Taylor and then to his on-again, off-again girlfriend Brenda (Rachel Griffiths). Various self-inflicted troubles, including infidelity and dalliances with the mentally ill, plague each of these three characters. "The brilliance of his Nate Fisher," wrote *Back Stage East* writer Jenelle Riley about Krause, "was that an ostensibly good guy often made poor choices and was sometimes downright unlikable."

Each episode of *Six Feet Under* began with the actual final moments of a person who would become the Fisher Funeral Home's next client. "Despite the fun it has with undertakers and the mildly soapy plot lines, *Six Feet Under* is not really about dying at all, but about how we choose to live," asserted Salon.com reviewer Carina Chocano. "Its big (and obvious, but easily forgotten) idea is that you can't start to live until you come to terms with your own eventual stoppage." The show won several Emmy

Awards, and Krause was nominated three times for an Emmy for Outstanding Lead Actor in a Drama Series. With his cast mates, he shared two Screen Actors Guild awards for Outstanding Performance by an Ensemble in a Drama Series.

*Six Feet Under* ended its acclaimed run on HBO in 2005. By that point Krause had already made his first foray back into a film career with *We Don't Live Here Anymore*, a 2004 drama that also starred Mark Ruffalo, Naomi Watts, and Laura Dern. Its plot was based on two short stories by Andre Dubus that center around a pair of married couples who are all close friends but whose extramarital dalliances threaten their respective households. A. O. Scott, a *New York Times* film critic, described it as "a kind of marital film noir. Emotional violence rarely seems so menacing, or so close to the real thing, and the murk and mystery of marriage, adultery, and friendship have seldom been illuminated with such harsh precision." Writing about Krause's character, a college writing professor named Hank whose habitual philandering has driven his wife (Watts) into an affair with Ruffalo's Jack, Scott noted that "compared with Jack, whose air of unease and self-doubt are part of his attraction, Hank has the smirk of a man who has it all figured out. Even at his moments of torment, when his writing is going badly, he exudes a smooth, knowing self-confidence."

Krause earned his first producing credit after working with both the writer and director on a little-seen thriller from 2006 titled *Civic Duty.* He starred in the film as an unemployed accountant who becomes convinced that his neighbor, a Middle Eastern graduate student played by Egyptian cinema star Khaled Abol Naga, is actually a terrorist. Critics panned the movie, but Krause fared better later in 2006 with the SciFi Channel miniseries *The Lost Room.* In it, he played a Pittsburgh detective searching for his vanished young daughter; the title refers to a mysterious New Mexico motel room that seems to be a portal to another universe. *New York Times* television critic Virginia Heffernan wrote that here Krause "looks too cute for the noir role. Soon enough, however, his weirdness returns ... and his sweet face takes on a cast of something like beatitude." Heffernan also noted that "*Six Feet Under* ultimately stiffed his character for its own purposes," but found a redeeming postscript in *The Lost Room*, where "Krause still comes across as a holy figure who submerges his suffering in the suffering of others."

In the fall of 2007, Krause landed a starring role in a new hour-long comedy series for ABC on which the network lavished a generous heap of marketing dollars in the weeks leading up to its premiere. *Dirty*

*Sexy Money* was the work of a former writer from *Six Feet Under*, Craig Wright, and featured Krause as a do-gooder attorney named Nick George with a lifelong and conflicted relationship with a spectacularly rich Manhattan family. The Darling clan is headed by Donald Sutherland's billionaire tycoon-patriarch, and in the pilot episode, Nick's father has just died, and Sutherland convinces him to take over his father's longtime role as the Darlings' family lawyer. Nick, who rarely saw his father growing up, finds it difficult to resist the lure of a $10 million annual paycheck.

Nick's efforts to keep the Darlings out of the press and out of jail due to their multiple levels of dysfunction made up the bulk of *Dirty Sexy Money*'s story arcs in its first season, and the series was renewed for 2008—no easy feat in a year when serial-plot television shows were gored by a Hollywood writers' strike and struggled to woo back viewers. Sternberg, writing in *New York* magazine likened it to a hybrid of *Dynasty* and *Arrested Development*, while *Variety*'s Brian Lowry asserted the series "benefits from drawing upon Krause's strengths—playing a character that's resourceful but a little overwhelmed—with its brew of dark comedy and salacious drama." An *Entertainment Weekly* critic, Gillian Flynn, described it as "stylized, soapy, silly, it's one of the most interesting new shows this fall." Flynn found that "Krause plays Nick with the perfect blend of affection, annoyance, and righteousness. With just a look, he conjures up each Darling's role in his childhood."

Krause's next film project was *Jack and Addie*, which starred him opposite *Sex and the City*'s Kristen Davis. Never married, he has a son named Roman who was born in 2001 to his former partner, Christine King, a producer and manager. In an interview a few years later he gave to *Best Life* magazine, Krause told writer Oliver Jones that he had recently acquired some rural property, partly in order to give his son the same outdoor-adventure experiences he had enjoyed growing up in semi-rural Minnesota. His new parcel of land was also a retreat for himself, away from the pressures of Hollywood. "I like spending time being me," he told Jones. "Spending a lot of time being other people is a nice exercise, but the greatest joy of life is creating your own character, creating your own self, and doing what you want to do."

# Sources

## Periodicals

*Back Stage East*, April 26, 2007, p. 1.
*Best Life*, May-June 2005, p. 50.
*Entertainment Weekly*, December 4, 1998, p. 71; October 12, 2007, p. 64.
*New York*, October 1, 2007, p. 73.

*New York Times,* July 30, 2004; August 13, 2004; December 11, 2006.

*Sports Illustrated,* October 5, 1998, p. 32.

*Star Tribune* (Minneapolis, MN), September 29, 1998, p. 1E.

*Time,* August 16, 2004, p. 76.

*Variety,* June 12, 2006, p. 31; September 24, 2007, p. 79.

*Vogue,* July 2004, p. 85.

**Online**

"The Naked and the Dead," Salon.com, http://www.salon.com/ent/tv/diary/2002/03/09/six_feet/print.html (September 16, 2008).

—*Carol Brennan*

# Ellen Kullman

## Chief Executive Officer of DuPont

**B**orn Ellen Jamison, January 22, 1956, in Wilmington, DE; daughter of Joseph and Margaret Jamison; married Michael Kullman (a marketing executive); children: Maggie, Stephen, David. *Education:* Tufts University, B.S., 1978; Northwestern University, M.B.A., 1983.

**Addresses:** *Office—* E. I. du Pont de Nemours and Company, 1007 Market St., Wilmington, DE 19898.

## Career

**I**n marketing and sales at Westinghouse Electric, late 1970s; marketing and sales, General Electric, after 1983; marketing manager of the medical imaging division, E. I. du Pont de Nemours and Company, 1988-92, then worldwide business director for electronic imaging, 1992-95, vice president of titanium technologies unit, 1995-2002, group vice president for DuPont Safety and Protection, 2002-06, executive vice president, 2006-08, president and company director, October 2008—; chief executive officer, January 2009—.

**Member:** Board of directors, General Motors, 2004-08; board of trustees, Tufts University, 2006—.

## Sidelights

**I**n 2008 Delaware native Ellen Kullman was named president and chief executive officer of U.S.

chemical giant DuPont. She not only became the first woman in that job in the 206-year history of the company, but also was the first female head of a large publicly traded chemical company anywhere in the world. "I'm not sure being a woman adds or detracts from it," she told Robert Westervelt in *Chemical Week.* "My management style is my own. I'm looking forward to continuing to drive our company's strategy."

Kullman was born in January of 1956 in Wilmington, Delaware's largest city, to Joseph and Margaret Jamison. Her father had been the city of Wilmington's chief forester, but started a landscaping business that eventually grew into Brandywine Nurseries, a well-known local landmark and family-run operation. Kullman seems to have inherited some of her business acumen from her mother, who handled the company's office and bookkeeping tasks and also possessed a college degree in business, which was somewhat rare for a woman of her era.

Like her siblings, Kullman attended St. Mary Magdalen School and then Tower Hill School in

Wilmington, a private academy where she played basketball and lacrosse. She went on to Tufts University in the Boston area, graduating in 1978 with a degree in mechanical engineering, and took a job with the Westinghouse Corporation. Within a few years she re-entered academia when she enrolled at Northwestern University's Kellogg School of Management, which granted her an M.B.A. in 1983. She worked for General Electric for a few years before she was hired by DuPont as a marketing manager in its medical imaging division.

Formally known as E. I. du Pont de Nemours and Company, Kullman's new workplace was one of the United States' oldest companies. Founded in Wilmington in 1802, DuPont rose to prominence as a manufacturer of gunpowder, and branched out into dynamite production and the newly emerging chemicals field later in the century. In the twentieth century, its scientists developed the world's first synthetic rubber, were granted the patent for nylon, and created both Tyvek, the high-density polyethylene fiber used as insulation, and Kevlar, a fabric that resists bullets.

In the spring of 1992 Kullman was made worldwide business director for DuPont's electronic imaging business. Three years later, she moved over to its titanium technologies unit, which mined titanium dioxide and processed it into an array of products for consumer and industrial uses, from sunscreens to plastics. That division was an important part of DuPont's revenue stream, bringing in about $2 billion in sales annually, but in 1998 Kullman's bosses thought she was up for challenge of a different kind and asked her to create a safety products division at DuPont. It would include some of DuPont's trademark products, like Kevlar, but in order to succeed would rely on Kullman's management and marketing skills.

Within a decade Kullman had grown DuPont's Safety and Protection division into a $5.5 billion business by promoting its various products for other uses. These include Corian and Zodiaq, best known for their use as kitchen countertops but which also have versatile applications in the workplace, and Sontara, a synthetic fiber. In 2002, she was made group vice president for DuPont Safety and Protection, the same year she gave an interview to Stephen G. Minter in *Occupational Hazards* in which she explained her division's marketing focus. "If you look at the statistics that show there is $170 billion spent in the United States on industrial injuries, think how positive it would be for our economy if that money was freed up to invest in research or other programs," she told Minter. In that same interview,

she also said that "when I was running chemical plants and we were running injury-free, we had higher uptimes, yields, higher productivity, and certainly happier workers and communities. It was such a positive all the way around."

Kullman was named an executive vice president at DuPont in June of 2006, which put her in charge of three other areas in addition to Safety and Protection. These were DuPont's Coatings and Color Technologies, Electronic and Communication Technologies, and Performance Materials. The move was widely viewed as a stepping stone to succeeding chief executive officer Charles "Chad" O. Holliday. Another top company performer, Thomas Connelly, ran DuPont's Agriculture and Nutrition and Applied BioSciences divisions.

In September of 2008, DuPont's board voted to make Kullman president and company director effective October 1, 2008, and chief executive officer effective January 1, 2009. She succeeded Holliday, who had been with the company since 1970 and remained involved as board chair. Holliday told Toronto *Globe & Mail* that Kullman was the right person to lead DuPont into its third century. "I just believe very strongly that it is important to rotate and give the next series of managers an opportunity to make improvements to what we have in place," Holliday said. "This is the right time to make this transition, and I feel great about it."

Kullman's elevation to DuPont CEO put her at No. 15 on *Fortune* magazine's ranking of the 50 Most Powerful Women in the world in 2009. With the global economic downturn worsening during her first months on the job, Kullman faced immense challenges in attempting to keep the company in the black—and its stock performing well on Wall Street for investors. Its Coatings and Color Technologies division was particularly hard-hit by the decline in U.S. domestic auto production, and the abysmal number of new-housing starts in 2008 had caused revenues from Tyvek and other DuPont products used in the construction industry to plummet.

Kullman is married to a DuPont executive with whom she has three children who have all attended Tower Hill, her alma mater. Her brothers still run the family nursery business, and her 91-year-old father was said to have been pleased with the news of her latest promotion. As a CEO of a multibillion-dollar corporation, Kullman joins just a handful of other women, among them Indra Nooyi at PepsiCo Inc. and the Xerox Corporation's Anne Mulcahy.

## Sources

### Periodicals

*Chemical Week,* September 29, 2008, p. 8.
*Globe & Mail* (Toronto, Canada), September 24, 2008, p. B13.
*Occupational Hazards,* June 2002, p. 27.

*USA Today,* January 2, 2009, p. 6B.

### Online

"Ellen Kullman, TH Alum & Parent Will Succeed Charles Holliday at DuPont Co.," TowerHill.org, http://www.towerhill.org/podium/default.aspx?t=204&id=478909 (April 14, 2009).

*—Carol Brennan*

# Kengo Kuma

## Architect

**B**orn in 1954 in Kanagawa Prefecture, Japan. *Education:* University of Tokyo, Graduate School of Engineering, M.Arch., 1979.

**Addresses:** *Office*—Kengo Kuma and Associates, 2-24-8 BY Cube 2F, Minamiaoyama Minato-ku, Tokyo, 107 0062, Japan.

## Career

**A**rchitect, Japan, early 1980s; visiting scholar, Columbia University, 1985-86; founder, Spatial Design Studio, 1987, and principal, 1987-90; founder, Kengo Kuma and Associates, 1990, and principal, 1990—; professor of environmental information, Keio University, 1998-99, professor of science and technology, 2001; Plym Distinguished Professor, University of Illinois—Urbana-Champaign, 2007-08.

**Awards:** Architectural Institute of Japan award, 1997; Spirit of Nature Wood Architecture Award, Finnish Forest Foundation, 2002.

## Sidelights

**K**engo Kuma advanced into the ranks of internationally known architects with sleek, minimalist buildings that use exquisite all-natural materials. Because he works primarily in stone and wood—and, more recently, in discarded shipping containers for a project in China—skyscrapers are not

Kuma's forte, but he is often cited as the next big "star-chitect," or high-profile celebrity architects who win the showpiece urban projects. Kuma, noted Michael Webb, a writer for the journal *Architecture*, "mingles the ethereal and the earthy, the enduring and the evanescent, to thrilling effect."

Kuma was born in 1954 in Kanagawa Prefecture on Japan's south-central coast, the district that encompasses the city of Yokohama and is also part of the greater Tokyo metropolitan area. As a youngster, he dreamed of becoming a veterinarian, but the build-up to the 1964 Tokyo Olympics and the accompanying construction boom had a profound influence on his ultimate choice of career. Ten years old at the time, Kuma was captivated by the work of one of Japan's most prominent modernist architects, Kenzo Tange. Tange's Yoyogi National Gymnasium, built in time for those 1964 Summer Games, is often cited as one of the twentieth century's most groundbreaking and influential large-scale public structures, in part because of its innovative suspension roof, which would be copied by a generation of arena and stadium architects to come. "Tange explained his buildings and ideas on TV, talking about the relationship between Japanese tradition and his architecture," Kuma told the writer Jeremy Melvin, who profiled him for an article that appeared on the

Web site for Britain's Royal Academy of Arts. "Then I knew that an individual can design the environment; one person can influence the people who use space."

Kuma was also influenced by his father, who collected the paintings of Bruno Taut, a visionary German architect who designed scores of public housing works across Europe before his death in 1938. Following high school, Kuma entered the University of Tokyo, and completed his master's degree in architecture from its Graduate School of Engineering in 1979. He spent a few years working in Japan before moving to New York City in 1985 for a year-long appointment as a visiting scholar at Columbia University. Back in Tokyo in 1987, he founded his own firm, which he called Spatial Design Studio.

Kuma's practice thrived for the next decade as the Japanese economy boomed and new corporate offices and private residences were being commissioned at a heady pace. That era ended in 1997 with the onset of the Asian economic crisis, and the commissions for new buildings grew scarce. Kuma turned to teaching for a time, holding a post on the faculty of Keio University in Tokyo. He also began seeking out smaller jobs in the countryside for his practice, which he had renamed eponymously. He attracted his first serious international attention for a trio of museums in the Tochigi Prefecture about 100 or so miles north of Tokyo. The first of these was Museum of Ando Hiroshige, which honored one of nineteenth-century Japan's most renowned *ukiyo-e*, or woodblock artists. Writing about it in *Architecture*, Webb found "an affinity between the artist's sharp, expressive line and Kuma's precise, meticulously detailed complex. The Hiroshige Museum's restrained palette of wood, paper, dark stone, and silvery aluminum complements the colors of the prints, which glow as brightly as when they were new."

The second of these projects in Tochigi Prefecture was the Stone Museum in Nasu, which was commissioned by a local stonecutting firm and designed to showcase the company's achievements but also serve an educational purpose to show how stone has been excavated and used throughout the centuries. Both this and the third building, the Nasu History Museum, took their inspiration from *kura*, the traditional rice warehouses that have dotted the Japanese countryside for centuries and are as symbolic of rural Japan as grain silos are in the American Midwest. "My aim is 'to recover the place,'" Kuma explained an interview with the Web site DesignBoom. "The place is a result of nature and time, this is the most important aspect. I think my architecture is some kind of frame of nature. With it we can experience nature more deeply and more intimately."

Kuma moved into the hospitality sector of building design when he updated a traditional Japanese inn called a *ryokan* located in Ginzan, a popular tourist destination for hundreds of years because of its restorative hot springs. Kuma and his team actually disassembled the 350-year-old wooden ryokan and used its planks to construct an entirely new one—one much more amenable to modern visitors. "During the 20th century, ryokans introduced baths as large as swimming pools, which didn't serve the human body well," Kuma told *Interior Design* writer Edie Cohen. "The relationship between the dimensions of the bathtub and the body is important."

In the first years of the twenty-first century, Kuma began to win more international commissions, a few of them high-profile. Among them are a spa at Dellis Cay, formerly a privately owned island in the Turks and Caicos chain in the Caribbean. The site underwent a luxurious transformation by the Mandarin Oriental Hotel Group, which hired well-known architect Zaha Hadid to oversee the project. Kuma also worked with LO-TEK (pronounced "low-tech"), the innovative design firm in New York City whose reputation was built on renovating shipping containers. He and the Italian pair who own LO-TEK joined forces for a mixed-use, commercial and residential development in Sanlitun North, located near the embassy district in Beijing, China. Kuma also worked on a luxury hotel in the same area of Beijing that opened in time for the 2008 Olympic Games held in that city.

Kuma's talents have been honored by the Architectural Institute of Japan and the Finnish Forest Foundation, which bestowed its Spirit of Nature Wood Architecture Award on him in 2002. The Scandinavian accolade served as a symbol of the bridge between two cultures that seemed vastly separate—but Kuma had long been inspired by influences from outside of Asia. Asked who his inspirations were by the DesignBoom interviewer, he cited the aforementioned Taut, plus Frank Lloyd Wright and "European architects and the designers from Finland and the north of Europe. Especially the work of furniture and industrial designers, it's very important because they are always thinking of the relationship between the human body and tools. Sometimes architects forget that."

## Sources

### Periodicals

*Architectural Review,* September 2005, p. 82.
*Architecture,* March 2003, p. 66.
*Interior Design,* April 1, 2007, p. 281.

**Online**

"Kengo Kuma's Craft," Royal Academy of Arts, http://www.royalacademy.org.uk/architecture/interviews/kengo-kumas-craft,213,AR.html (July 13, 2008).

"Kengo Kuma," DesignBoom, http://www.designboom.com/eng/interview/kuma.html (July 5, 2008).

—*Carol Brennan*

# Derek Lam

## Fashion designer

**B**orn in March of 1966, in San Francisco, CA; son of antique- and apparel-business owners. *Education:* Attended Connecticut College; earned degree from Parsons School of Design, 1990.

**Addresses:** *Office*—Derek Lam Co. LLC, 601 W. 26th St., Ste. 1730, New York, NY 10001-1103.

## Career

**B**egan career as a design assistant, Michael Kors, 1990-c. 1993; worked briefly for Geoffrey Beene, c. 1994; designer, G2000, a Hong Kong-based retailer, c. 1995-98; vice president for design, Michael Kors, c. 1998; launched eponymous label, 2003; creative director, J. P. Tod, 2006—.

**Awards:** Perry Ellis Swarovski Award, Council of Fashion Designers of America (CFDA), 2005.

## Sidelights

**A**merican fashion designer Derek Lam launched his own label in 2003 with a line of women's ready-to-wear that was an immediate hit with its intended audience of youngish, fashion-conscious women. Lam's feminine yet crisply defined looks have been hailed as both simultaneously retro and modern, and found an epitome of both qualities in First Daughter Barbara Bush, who sported a much-photographed Lam ensemble for her father's 2005 inauguration ceremony. In 2006, Lam was made creative director for J. P. Tod's, the Italian luxury leather goods house.

Born in 1967, Lam was the last of three children in a family that had deep roots in the Chinatown section of San Francisco. His great-grandparents were Chinese immigrants who operated a grocery store in Chinatown, and his grandparents entered the apparel business as a manufacturer of bridal gowns. Lam's parents followed the family's entrepreneurial tradition by running an apparel-importing venture, a custom tailoring business, and then in the early 1970s opening a linen store called Imperial Fashion. They also own Relin, a Chinese antiques and decorative-arts store at the intersection of Grant and California streets.

Lam first learned to sew at his grandparents' garment factory, and has also noted that his early interest in fashion was shaped in part by the glamorous parties and other nightlife scenes he attended as a child with his parents, who had married quite young and often brought their three well-dressed children along with them for an evening out. For college, Lam chose Connecticut College, but eventually transferred to the Parsons School of Design in New York City, from which he graduated in 1990. In 2004, he and fashion designer Isaac Mizrahi sat down for a joint interview conducted by Bridget Foley of *WWD*, and Lam reminded Mizrahi that Mizrahi had been his senior advisor. The older designer asked Lam what he had made for his senior project, and Lam replied, "I think it was a jersey jumpsuit with a big coat you could step into."

Out of Parsons, Lam was hired by noted sportswear designer Michael Kors, and worked as a design assistant at Kors' studio for the next four years. Around 1994, he took a job with legendary American designer Geoffrey Beene, then in the final years of what had been a groundbreaking career. Lam contrasted the experience with his time at Kors, where Kors had "immediately wanted me to participate with design," Lam told Marc Karimzadeh in a *W* interview. "Working with Geoffrey Beene was different. He was a master, with all that that implies. We were never allowed to speak above a whisper, so it was a little stultifying."

Leaving Beene, Lam moved to Hong Kong for a time to take a job with G2000, a leading mass-market retailer, which he described in the *WWD* interview with Foley as "kind of their version of Banana, J. Crew, the Gap. I did men's, women's, a jeans line. At that time, they were trying to import a lot of expatriates from the States and the U.K. to revamp their line. It was fun, and a totally different point of view, coming from Michael Kors and working on a collection."

Lam came back to New York City in the late 1990s and contemplated his next move. He considered leaving fashion altogether, perhaps returning to school with the aim of becoming an instructor at Parsons or another fashion training ground. By chance, he ran into Michael Kors, who asked him about his future plans. When Lam listed his ideas, Kors "looked at me and said, 'You are so not leaving fashion. It's in you. You're just going to come back to work for me,'" Lam recalled in the *W* interview with Karimzadeh.

Lam eventually rose to vice president of design at Kors before leaving to start his own label. His first runway collection took place during New York Fashion Week in September of 2003, when American designers show their upcoming Spring/Summer lines to a select audience of store buyers and fashion journalists. The latter group wrote effusively of the appealing, ultra-feminine designs Lam created, especially a strapless cocktail dress printed in a red-and white carnation-print that appeared in editorial spreads in several fashion magazines. Asked by *San Francisco Chronicle* writer Sylvia Rubin about his inspiration for it, Lam explained that "I found this

vintage scarf in a crumpled-up mess at the bottom of a bin in a New York thrift shop. I loved the carnation print—it was just a little bit vulgar.... But it was also kind of whimsical and sophisticated."

*Harper's Bazaar* profiled Lam for its June 2004 issue, with writer Jenny Rubinfeld commending his "refined, elegant and very wearable pieces." Several months later, Lam became the designer of choice for First Daughter Barbara Bush, one of the twin daughters of President George W. Bush, who wore Lam's belted blue cashmere trench coat and white skirt for Inauguration Day. The outfit garnered Lam an onslaught of favorable press attention in what was the day's most widely published photograph around the world. Later that year, Lam won the Perry Ellis Swarovski Award from the Council of Fashion Designers of America (CFDA), also known as the Emerging Talent Award for Ready-to-Wear.

In June of 2006, Lam signed on with J. P. Tod's, an Italian leather goods maker and family-run business since its founding in the 1920s. In the 1970s, Tod's launched a line of high-fashion footwear, and its signature driving shoe became a must-have for the fashion-conscious on both sides of the Atlantic. Tod's chief executive, Diego Della Valle, hired Lam to design a line of limited-edition sportswear plus accessories like handbags and shoes. There was also a separate licensing deal with Modo for a line of Lam-license eyewear.

Lam still designs under his own name and shows at the twice-yearly New York Fashion Week. The added responsibility of serving as creative director for Tod's forced him to double his creative output, and he admitted in the interview with Karimzadeh for *W* that this was sometimes a challenge. "At the end of the day, I can't satisfy everybody," he reflected. "I can only do what I feel is right from my point of view about luxury. The minute you try to be everything to everybody, you become scared, and you start to second-guess yourself."

## Sources

*Harper's Bazaar,* June 2004, p. 130.
*San Francisco Chronicle,* May 2, 2004, p. F14; February 18, 2007, p. F1.
*W,* April 2007, p. 114.
*Washington Post,* February 13, 2005, p. D1.
*WWD,* June 1, 2004, p. 40S; November 30, 2006, p. 1.

—*Carol Brennan*

# Lee Myung-bak

**President of South Korea**

**B**orn December 19, 1941, in Osaka, Japan; son of Cheung-u (a farm worker) and Taewon Chae (a housewife) Lee; married Kim Yun-ok; children: three daughters, one son (Joo Yeon, Seung Yeon, Soo Yeon, Si Hyong). *Education:* Korea University, B.B.A., 1965.

**Addresses:** *Office*—Office of the President, 1 Jongno-gu, Seoul, Republic of Korea.

## Career

**B**egan as a project manager at Hyundai Engineering and Construction Company, Ltd., 1965, became a company director, 1970, executive director, 1975, executive vice president, 1977-87, and president and chief executive officer, 1978-81; president and chief executive officer, Inchon Iron & Steel Company, Ltd., 1982-87; president and chief executive officer, Hyundai Engineering Company, Ltd., 1987-91; chair, Hyundai Wood Industries, 1990-91; elected to National Assembly, 1992 and 1996 (resigned from office, 1998); published autobiography, 1995; elected mayor of Seoul, 2002; elected president of South Korea as the candidate of the Grand National Party ticket, 2007.

## Sidelights

**L**ee Myung-bak was elected president of South Korea in 2007 on what appeared to be a wave of popular support for the former executive with the Hyundai Group. Long known as "the Bulldozer"

for his tenacity and determination, Lee is the first South Korean president with extensive corporate experience, but his rise had already captivated South Koreans. "Lee's life story is a mirror of the remarkable transformation of South Korea from poverty to the world's eleventh-largest economy," noted a writer for the *Economist*. "The inspiration for two television soap operas, he ... suffered malnutrition and hauled rubbish in a handcart to pay for his university studies."

Lee was born in December of 1941, when the Korean peninsula was under Japanese occupation. His father moved the family to the Japanese city of Osaka to take a job on a farm, and Lee's first years of life were spent in the Korean quarter of the city. The two countries harbored a longstanding historical animosity toward each other as competing powers in the region, and Koreans suffered immense hardships under Japanese rule. When World War II brought an end to Japan's might, the Lee family was able to return to the town of Pohang in the southeastern part of the peninsula. In 1950, however, lingering tensions—between a Communist-allied northern half and the U.S.-backed south—erupted once again into the three-year Korean War.

The war disrupted the economy and the food supply, and for a time Lee's family lived in an abandoned temple. The youngster and his six siblings all worked to help feed the family, and Lee completed high school by taking night classes while working as a popcorn vendor, among other jobs. He went on to Korea University in Seoul, where he majored in business and was elected student president of his department. During his years there in the early 1960s, the school became a focal point for anti-government demonstrations against the normalization of diplomatic ties with Japan under South Korean President Park Chung-hee, and Lee was one of the ringleaders. Arrested, he was charged with insurrection and served three months of a three-year sentence. The highly publicized trial and conviction, combined with an official hiring blacklist, should have ended Lee's career prospects forever, but he wrote a letter to Park pleading his case. As a result, his name was removed from the blacklist and he got a job with the Hyundai Construction Company.

Hyundai would grow into one of South Korea's largest *chaebols*, or conglomerates, but was a small company when Lee began there in 1965. He spent the first three years as a manager on a highway construction project in Thailand, then was given oversight of Hyundai's heavy machinery plant in Seoul. He was made a company director in 1970 and president and chief executive officer (CEO) of Hyundai Engineering and Construction Company in 1978, making him one of the youngest CEOs in South Korean history. Hyundai was by then a powerful entity, deploying thousands of workers every month to large-scale construction projects throughout the Middle East and launching its own automotive nameplate.

Lee held several other executive posts with various Hyundai properties before retiring in 1992 to enter politics and write his 1995 autobiography, *There Is No Myth*. He was elected to the National Assembly in 1992 and again in 1996, but was forced to resign two years later after a court found him in violation of South Korean campaign spending laws. In 2002, he ran successfully for mayor of Seoul, a city of ten million and showcase for South Korea's emergence as a world economic power during Lee's generation.

As mayor, Lee was able to repair a blunder that Hyundai had made in the 1970s, when it paved over a four-mile stream and attendant riverbanks for an elevated highway during Seoul's heady expansion era. Lee reversed the error with a project that re-routed the highway and restored the stream; the

new park, called Cheonggyecheon, became a popular gathering spot, as did Seoul Forest, the city's lush version of New York City's Central Park, which opened in 2005.

Lee's four-year mayoral term ended in 2006, and in the spring of 2007 he announced his bid for the nomination of the Grand National Party on the coming presidential ticket. The Grand National Party is South Korea's center-right, firmly pro-business political party, and Lee won the August primary and December balloting with assured margins despite an attempt by political rivals to implicate him in a bank bankruptcy and stock-manipulation scandal.

Lee was sworn in as South Korea's tenth president on February 25, 2008. Several weeks later, on the eve of his first official visit to the United States, his government announced a plan to resume U.S. beef imports, which had been banned in 2003 after worries about mad-cow disease. Protests erupted in early May in Seoul and dragged on, becoming larger and more vociferous each week. On June 10, Lee's entire cabinet offered to resign in the wake of the largest anti-government demonstrations since 1987.

The crowds and pamphlets derided Lee as a traitor for bowing to foreign pressure, though U.S. beef imports are actually cheaper than Korean beef. As Leo Lewis, a correspondent for the *Times* of London, noted, "the oratory was much farther to the political left than anyone has heard for decades. The list of grievances—from the privatisation of state utilities to the minimum wage and a proposed 'grand canal' across the country—revealed a society profoundly ill at ease with the Government it recently elected."

Lee publicly apologized for the beef issue and replaced three key cabinet ministers. He was also forced to scrap the canal project, which would have connected Seoul and the major port city of Busan. Instead his government announced a new initiative to re-engage with North Korea's isolationist and authoritarian regime. Lee proposed to triple North Korea's gross national income to $3,000 per person through investment and aid if North Korea followed a concise program to dismantle its nuclear arsenal. Kim Jong Il's government responded that Lee was merely following U.S. orders to put pressure on North Korea, but in an interview with *Time International*, Lee explained that South Koreans had little choice with such an unstable neighbor. "Korea will continue to strengthen our traditional close alliance with the U.S.," he said, "because this will not only ensure the peaceful stability of Northeast Asia but also will deter war on the Korean peninsula."

## Sources

*Economist*, August 25, 2007, p. 39.
*Newsweek International*, March 3, 2008.
*New York Times*, December 20, 2007; June 12, 2008.
*Time International* (Asia Edition), April 21, 2008, p. 30; June 16, 2008, p. 33.
*Times* (London, England), June 11, 2008, p. 29.

—*Carol Brennan*

# Zachary Levi

**Actor**

**B**orn Zachary Levi Pugh, September 29, 1980, in Lake Charles, LA.

**Addresses:** *Agent*—Endeavor, 9601 Wilshire Blvd., 3rd Flr., Beverly Hills, CA 90210. *Management*—Joan Hyler Management, 20 Ocean Park Blvd., Santa Monica, CA 90405. *Web site*—http://www.zacharylevi.com/.

## Career

**A**ctor in films, including: *Reel Guerillas* (short), 2005; *Big Momma's House 2*, 2006; *Spiral*, 2006; *Ctrl Z* (short), 2007; *An American Carol*, 2008; *Shades of Ray*, 2008; *The Tiffany Problem* (short), 2008; *Wieners*, 2008; *Alvin and the Chipmunks: The Squeakquel*, 2009; *Stuntmen*, 2009. Also worked as executive producer on *Spiral*, 2006. Television appearances include: *Big Shot: Confessions of a Campus Bookie* (movie) 2002; *Less than Perfect*, 2002-06; *A Mickey Mouse Celebration* (special), 2003; *Curb Your Enthusiasm*, 2004; *The Division*, 2004; *Three*, 2005; *The Worst Week of My Life* (pilot), 2006; *Chuck*, 2007—; *Imperfect Union* (movie), 2007; *Anytime with Bob Kushell*, 2008.

## Sidelights

**S**ome actors might say they are not real geeks, they just play them on TV. While Zachary Levi, whose portrayal of a nerd-turned-super-spy NBC's *Chuck* has turned him into a star, does in fact play a nerd on TV, he freely admits that he shares his character's love of geeky hobbies. Levi and co-star Joshua Gomez "are not actors that are playing gam-

*Jesse Grant/WireImage/Getty Images*

ers," but are gamers off set as well, Levi explained on the Daemon's TV Web site. In fact, Levi once had to get 14 stitches due to an accident during a game of tennis on his Nintendo Wii.

Whether it's that real-life connection to fans or just a charm he grants to his character, *Chuck* has attracted a devoted following. When the program was not immediately picked up for a third season as the second season came to a close, fans banded together on a campaign to let show sponsor Subway know that they were watching. Naming the campaign in the convention of the program's episodes, "Chuck vs. the Footlong" urged fans to visit their local Subway and purchase a five dollar footlong in support of the show. "If you do have a loyal fan base, that really can make a difference," *Chuck* producer Josh Schwartz told the *New York Times*. "Now, more than ever, that kind of fan support can really have an impact."

Born Zachary Levi Pugh in Lake Charles, Louisiana, Levi moved with his family several times while he was growing up before the family settled in Ventura County, California. Levi was interested in acting at an early age, hitting the stage at six years old and performing in various school and community theater productions. After graduating from high school, Levi went to Los Angeles to pursue his career, finding roles in stage productions. His portrayal of Jesus in *Godspell* and his depiction of Hank in *Marvin's Room* brought him the attention he needed to begin earning roles on screen.

Levi's earliest role on television was a part in television movie *Big Shot: Confessions of a Campus Bookie,* alongside David Krumholtz, Jennifer Morrison, and Nicholas Turturro. He was also picked up to perform in the pilot of *Less than Perfect* in the role of scheming Kipp Steadman, who became one of the show's primary antagonists. The show was on the air for four seasons, but it never really found its audience domestically. Overseas, the program was quite popular. Levi performed in all 81 episodes of *Less than Perfect*'s run.

While filming *Less than Perfect,* Levi appeared in several guest roles on other television series, including *Curb Your Enthusiasm, The Division,* and *Three.* Levi also worked on the short film *Reel Guerillas,* and played a potential boyfriend for Charisma Carpenter's character on the television movie, *See Jane Date.* After *Less than Perfect* wrapped in 2006, Levi worked with writer Adam Green on the movie *Spiral,* both as an actor and as the executive producer. He has since appeared in one of Green's short internet films, *The Tiffany Problem.*

In 2007, Levi had two competing opportunities. He took the role of the title character for the pilot of *Chuck,* playing a computer tech leader of the "Nerd Herd," the tech help division of the local "Buy More" electronics store, whose life is upended when a former friend sends him a computer file full of government secrets that wire themselves into his brain. Levi was also invited to audition on Broadway for the run of *Young Frankenstein.* "At that point we hadn't even shot *Chuck* yet," Levi said on the Daemon's TV Web site. He auditioned for *Young Frankenstein* and was offered the part on the condition that *Chuck* was not picked up. NBC pushed *Chuck* through and began filming, which took Levi out of the running for the Broadway role.

Not only was *Chuck* picked up for its first season, NBC placed the new show immediately before the 2006 hit show *Heroes,* hoping that some of the superhero fans who had made *Heroes* successful would start watching early and provide a built-in fan base for *Chuck.* The strategy was a success, and *Chuck* was one of the break-out shows of the 2007 season. The geek-meets-spy theme was popular with viewers, and much of the show's success was attributed to Levi's performance. "What *Chuck* has going for it

... is an incredibly winning performance by Levi," Robert Bianco wrote in a review for *USA Today,* declaring *Chuck* one of his top ten hits of 2007. Noting the high-paced, explosive-filled spy intrigue, Gillian Flynn of *Entertainment Weekly* wrote, "All the action is balanced by the loose-limbed Levi, who has a grin that makes you want to give him all your pudding, immediately." Despite playing the normal guy of the cast, Levi has also gotten a chance to do his own action scenes—a type of acting he's reported to love. The *Daily News* named Levi one of its five actors to watch in 2007, and Levi appeared with *Reaper* star Bret Harrison in a photo shoot for *USA Weekend*'s "Most Likely to Be Breakout Stars." Levi was nominated as the TV Breakout Star in the men's category of the Teen Choice Awards and the Best Actor in a Series, Comedy, or Musical award in the Satellite Awards; he was also ranked 22nd in *Entertainment Weekly*'s "30 under 30" actors list in 2008.

While the Writers' Strike of 2008 interrupted the second half of *Chuck*'s first season, it was renewed and given another chance in the fall of 2008. While many shows struggled to regain their footing after half a season's break, *Chuck* "returns like an old friend back from a year abroad: still likable, still funny, but with an added note of intrigue," wrote James Poniewozik of *Time.* The show continued where it left off: Chuck is still working with CIA Agent and romantic interest Sarah and NSA operative John Casey, played by Yvonne Strahovski and Adam Baldwin respectively, trying to make the best of having all of the government's secrets in his head while also holding down his regular job at the Buy More. The season also begins with a new hope: If the government can get its secret computer database restored, Chuck can have his old life back. The season built as Chuck learned of the potential to get the government secrets that upended his life out of his brain permanently.

*Chuck* does not fit easily into any of the usual categories, combining action, romance, comedy, and drama. "It's a tough show to act, perform, write and shoot," Levi told a reporter for *USA Today.* "It's an ambitious show. Fortunately, there aren't other action/comedy/dramas in [our time slot]. That's definitely one of the strongest things going for us—we're different. And different is so integral in this business." Despite the show's critical reception, ratings did not guarantee a third season, leading fans and critics alike to plead with the network to keep the show. In addition to the "Chuck vs. the Footlong" campaign, critic Alan Sepinwall of the Newark, New Jersey-based *Star-Ledger* released an open letter to network execs, making a case for the show's continued contract. "All due respect to some other fine series," Sepinwall wrote, "[*Chuck*'s] been more consistent than *30 Rock* and *Friday Night Lights*, funnier than *The Office*, and more purely entertaining than them and everything else on your airwaves." Producer Schwartz warned in the *New York Times*, "If, in two weeks, that is the last episode of the show to ever air, it will be one of the least satisfying finales of all time. Chris Fedak, the guy who created the show, said people will set their living rooms on fire."

In addition to his work on *Chuck*, Levi performed in several film projects in 2008 and 2009, including *Wieners*, *Shades of Ray*, *Stuntmen*, and the half-animated *Alvin and the Chipmunks: The Squeakquel*.

# Sources

## Books

*Contemporary Theatre, Film, and Television*, vol. 74, Gale (Detroit, MI), 2007.

## Periodicals

*Entertainment Weekly*, September 28, 2007, p. 93.
*Hollywood Reporter*, February 11, 2009, p. 4.
*People*, November 26, 2007, p. 151.
*Time*, September 29, 2008, p. 61.
*USA Today*, September 7, 2007, p. 2E; September 24, 2007, p. 1D; August 26, 2008, p. 7D.
*Variety*, September 24, 2007, p. 78.

## Online

*Biography Resource Center Online*, Gale (Detroit, MI), 2008.
"Can Chuck Be Saved?" *New York Times* Arts Beat Blog, http://artsbeat.blogs.nytimes.com/2009/04/20/can-chuck-be-saved-even-josh-schwartz-isnt-sure/?hp (April 20, 2009).
"Chuck," NBC Online, http://www.nbc.com/Chuck/ (April 26, 2009).
"Chuck: An Open Letter to NBC to Save It," *Star-Ledger* (Newark, NJ) Online, http://www.nj.com/entertainment/tv/index.ssf/2009/04/chuck_an_open_letter_to_nbc_ to.html (April 26, 2009).
"The Ramblings of Zachary Levi," Daemons TV Web site, http://www.daemonstv.com/2007/12/28/the-ramblings-of-zachary-levi/ (April 26, 2009).
"Zachary Levi," Internet Movie Database, http://www.imdb.com/name/nm1157048/ (April 26, 2009).

—*Alana Joli Abbott*

# Kenneth D. Lewis

*Munshi Ahmed/Bloomberg News/Landov*

## Chief Executive Officer of Bank of America

**B**orn April 9, 1947, in Meridian, MS; son of Brydine Lewis (a nurse); married (divorced, 1978); married Donna, 1980; children: one (from first marriage), stepson (from second marriage). *Education:* Georgia State University, B.A., 1969; Stanford University, graduate of the executive program.

**Addresses:** *Office*—Bank of America Corporation, Bank of America Corporation Center, 100 North Tryon St., Charlotte, NC 28202.

## Career

**C**redit analyst, North Carolina National Bank (NCNB), 1969-77; manager, NCNB International Banking Corporation, 1977-79; senior vice president, NCNB U.S. Department, 1979-83; president of various divisions, NCNB and NationsBank, 1983-90; president of Consumer and Commercial Banking, 1990-93; president, NationsBank, 1993-99; chief operating officer, Bank of America, 1999-2001; chief executive officer, 2001—.

**Member:** Committee to Encourage Corporate Philanthropy; Fifth District representative, Federal Advisory Committee; Financial Services Forum; Financial Services Roundtable; director, Homeownership Education and Counseling Institute; vice chairman of the corporate fund board, The John F. Kennedy Center for the Performing Arts; past chairman, National Urban League; member of the board and executive committee (former president), United Way of Central Carolinas.

**Awards:** Banker of the year, *American Banker* newspaper, 2002; top chief executive officer, *U.S. Banker* magazine, 2002; one of the top 100 influential people in the world, *Time* magazine, 2007; banker of the year award, *American Banker* newspaper, 2008.

## Sidelights

**B**ank of America CEO Kenneth D. Lewis was named Banker of the Year in 2008 for the second time in less than a decade. An employee of the company since 1969, Lewis has climbed the rungs of the organization that would eventually become Bank of America, from credit analyst to top executive. His position led him to be selected for the "Time 100 List" of influential people around the world in 2007.

Born in Meridian, Mississippi, and growing up in Columbus, Georgia, Lewis was raised by his mother Brydine Lewis after his parents divorced when he was seven. Though his mother was a nurse, Lewis helped bring extra income into the household by delivering newspapers, bagging groceries, working at a filling station and a steel mill, and selling Christmas cards. During high school, he worked for a time as a shoe salesman. Lewis graduated from

Georgia State University with a degree in finance and was offered jobs at Wachovia, a well-established banking institution, and at a small local bank, North Carolina National Bank (NCNB). "He chose the latter because they were the underdogs, which appealed to Lewis because he viewed himself in the same manner," wrote a contributor to *International Directory of Business Biographies*.

Lewis' long career with Bank of America began in 1969, when he took a job as a credit analyst with NCNB in Charlotte, North Carolina. Though originally a resident of Georgia, Lewis worked in several southern states representing NCNB; he became the president of NCNB's Florida bank in 1986, and held the same position in 1998 at NCNB Texas. Lewis also worked in New York, managing the international department of NCNB. In all of his positions, he demonstrated leadership skills and innovation; he developed and introduced several programs in Texas that solidified his reputation in banking. In Florida, he acquired Barnett Banks, and despite the challenge critics of the decision expected the merger to be, Lewis successfully kept the operation running while cutting costs and creating a standard for banking operations.

In 1991, NCNB became NationsBank, and later NationsBank Corporation. In 1993, Lewis became the president of NationsBank's retail division, and applied many of his innovative ideas. Called Vision '95, Lewis used the program as a platform to standardize the many companies that had merged together to create NationsBank. Lewis' mission was often repeated in the press: He hoped to make NationsBank the best consumer bank in the United States. One of the changes he made was increasing the proportion of part-time employees at the banks. This cut spending for the company, as a greater percentage of employees did not qualify for benefits, but also increased the amount of time tellers had available to help customers. "We're very pleased to show it's not necessarily a contradiction to be both more efficient and more effective," Lewis told Kenneth Cline in *American Banker*.

Lewis remained in leadership roles throughout those changes, becoming the president and chief operating officer of the newly organized Bank of America Corporation in 1999. As the bank grew, Lewis continued to institute his standardization policies, trying to keep up with the mergers and make overall company policies that would maintain a customer focus. Lewis predicted a shift to increased ATM usage and tried to put a plan into action to increase the number of terminals available to customers; however, Lewis had his hands full managing the acquisitions being made by CEO Hugh L. McColl, Jr. Lewis continued to balance customer-oriented innovation, such as developing Internet banking options, with making sure that the merging companies were smoothly integrated into Bank of America.

There was much speculation that Lewis would take over the helm of the organization when McColl retired, and the predictions proved true in 2001, when Lewis was named CEO. "We're finally running on all cylinders. Hugh McColl was a visionary, but Ken Lewis is an operations guy, which is what we need now," one Bank of America insider was quoted as having said in *Fortune* magazine. McColl himself commented in *USA Today*, "We're different animals. I've always said that Ken is a much better businessman." Lewis spread his customer-centric message across the company, making customer service his main priority. While McColl based his management style on gaining acquisitions to increase the business, Lewis emphasized internal growth. Lewis also hired people from outside the company to fill important positions, making an effort to diversify thought in the organization. Despite bringing in outsiders, Lewis was careful not to decrease morale with his internal employees, and he spent much time in his early years in the position meeting with employees to help them solve problems. Lewis was named Banker of the Year in 2002.

Lewis's transition to the CEO position was not all positive. In 2003, many employees began to feel resentment toward Lewis' rigorous money management. Clients felt that they were losing money in Bank of America investments. Some employees were fired. But as these crises occurred, Lewis followed the model of McColl, purchasing FleetBoston and MBNA, the largest credit issuer in the United States. He also announced plans to expand overseas.

Between 2006 and 2008, Lewis kept a sharp eye on his competitors and was able to take advantage of their mistakes. "In the process [he] expanded his company's reach in two key financial services businesses," a writer for *Internet Wire* described. The writer also noted that, since Lewis became the head of the company, customer satisfaction rates had improved, annual revenue and annual profit doubled, and assets increased enormously. For those accomplishments, Lewis was named Banker of the Year again in 2008.

Despite what Lewis considers a global recession, he has remained optimistic about the economy, believing the 2008 downturn will reverse itself by mid-

2009. Lewis has been critical of the regulatory structure imposed by the United States federal government on banking institutions. He has recommended changing more toward a European system, where private institutions work as intermediaries between mortgage companies and the investors. "What started last year [2007] as a crisis in the subprime-mortgage markets became a global credit crisis, and now has become a global recession," Lewis said, according to CNN Money. He also noted, "It wouldn't hurt to remind ourselves that we play a supporting role in the economy—not a lead role."

In addition to his work at Bank of America, Lewis is a member of the Financial Services Roundtable and the Financial Services Forum, and is the director of the Homeownership Education and Counseling Institute. Lewis serves on the Federal Advisory Committee as the Fifth District's representative. Actively involved with charitable organizations, Lewis is a member of the board and a past president of the United Way of Central Carolinas, Inc., and is a member of the Committee to Encourage Philanthropy. Lewis is the vice chairman of the Corporate Fund Board of the John F. Kennedy Center for the Performing Arts, and a past chairman of the National Urban League.

# Sources

### Books

*International Directory of Business Biographies,* St. James Press (Detroit, MI), 2005.

### Periodicals

*American Banker,* February 9, 1993.

*Fortune,* September 3, 2001, pp. 153-155.

*Internet Wire,* October 27, 2008.

*New York Times,* June 24, 2006, p. C3; November 3, 2008, p. B10.

*USA Today,* September 18, 2008, p. 03B.

### Online

"Bank of America's Lewis: Crisis Has Become 'Global Recession,'" CNN Money, http://money.cnn.com/news/newsfeeds/articles/djf500/20081120.tif1424DOWJONESDJONLINE000815_FORTUNE5.htm (November 20, 2008).

"Kenneth D. Lewis," *Biography Resource Center Online,* Gale Group, 2003.

"Kenneth D. Lewis Biography," Bank of America, http://newsroom.bankofamerica.com/index.php?s=company_bios&item=7 (November 24, 2008).

"Kenneth D. Lewis Profile," *Forbes,* http://people.forbes.com/profile/kenneth-d-lewis/10037 (November 24, 2008).

"The Time 100: Builders & Titans: Ken Lewis," *Time,* http://www.time.com/time/specials/2007/time100/article/0,28804,1595326_1615737_1615533,00.html (December 30, 2008).

—*Alana Joli Abbott*

# Nicklas Lidstrom

## Professional hockey player

**B**orn Nicklas Erik Lidström, April 28, 1970, in Vasteras, Sweden; son of Jan-Eric Lidstrom (a chief with the Swedish highway system); married Annika; children: Kevin, Adam, Samuel, Lukas.

**Addresses:** *Office*—Detroit Red Wings, Joe Louis Arena, 600 Civic Center Dr., Detroit, MI 48226.

## Career

**P**layed for Vasteras IK, 1988-91 and 1994-95; drafted by the Detroit Red Wings, 1989; played on Swedish national teams in World Junior Championships, 1990; World Cup, 1994 and 1997; and the Olympics, 1998, 2002, and 2006; defenseman for the Detroit Red Wings, 1991—; captain of the Detroit Red Wings, 2006—.

**Awards:** Named to National Hockey League all-rookie team, 1992; Norris Trophy for best defenseman, NHL, 2001, 2002, 2003, 2006, 2007, 2008; Stanley Cup (NHL championship), as member of the Detroit Red Wings, 1997, 1998, 2002, 2008; Conn Smythe Trophy for most valuable player in playoffs, NHL, 2002; Olympic gold medal, as member of Swedish national team, 2006.

## Sidelights

**T**hough Nicklas Lidstrom is one of the greatest defensemen ever to play hockey, he spent much of his career under-recognized. In 1991, Lidstrom left his hometown team in the Swedish Elite League to join the Detroit Red Wings, a team full of flashy, speedy players with charming and rowdy personalities. Lidstrom, by contrast, is reserved, almost shy, and his talent is built on stamina, sharp instincts, intelligence, and the subtle skills of passing and positioning. "Like the elements of modern Swedish design, Lidstrom's game is all clean lines and efficiency," wrote Michael Farber and Sarah Kwak in *Sports Illustrated*, praising his "mastery of the blue line geometry, deceiving pass-shot option from the left point on the power play, [and] surgical passes that effectively enhance team speed." Eventually, after 15 years in the National Hockey League, Lidstrom gained recognition as an elite star. In 2006, he was named captain of the Red Wings, and in 2008, he became the first European-born captain to lead a team to win the Stanley Cup, hockey's greatest trophy.

Lidstrom was born in Vasteras, Sweden, on April 28, 1970. "When he was a boy he was a little warrior, always joking and doing little things to get into trouble," his father, Jan-Eric, told L. Jon Wertheim of *Sports Illustrated*. Lidstrom played soccer as well as hockey when he was young, and his soccer footwork helped him hone one of his less-noticed skills as a hockey defenseman: using his skates to keep the puck inside the offensive zone. He spent three years playing for Vasteras IK in the Swedish Elite

League and was a member of the Swedish national team that won the world championship in Finland in 1991. The Detroit Red Wings drafted Lidstrom in 1989, and he left Sweden to join the team in the fall of 1991.

In his first season with the Red Wings, Lidstrom scored eleven goals, had 49 assists, and was named to the National Hockey's League's all-rookie team. At first, his quiet skills attracted little attention compared to the Red Wings' tougher and more experienced defensemen. "Nick was paired with Paul Coffey and then Vladimir Konstantinov, so teams weren't focusing on him," Red Wings right wing Darren McCarty told Wertheim of *Sports Illustrated.* "He always seemed to be the forgotten guy." But his teammates and Detroit fans noticed Lidstrom's talent. "We were perfectly happy to keep him a sleeper," McCarty said. "He's always been the most underrated player in the league—our little secret."

In 1997, during Lidstrom's fourth season in the league, the Red Wings advanced to the Stanley Cup finals. Their opponents were the Philadelphia Flyers, whose top scorers were so large and imposing, they were nicknamed the Legion of Doom. Most teams deployed their toughest, biggest defensemen against the Legion, but Red Wings coach Scotty Bowman assigned the task to Lidstrom, who was 6-foot-2 and 190 pounds, relatively small for a hockey player. Lidstrom helped shut down the Flyer offense, holding star Eric Lindros to one goal in the series. The Red Wings swept the Flyers in four games to win the Stanley Cup for the first time in decades.

Lidstrom faced new pressure and challenges the following season. The Red Wings had lost Konstantinov, their most aggressive defenseman, to severe injuries in a car accident. Lidstrom stepped up, playing a more prominent role for the team. During the regular season, he led the league's defensemen in scoring with 59 points (17 goals plus 42 assists). Meanwhile, in January of 1998, he was named to the World All-Star team, and in February, he played for Sweden's national hockey team in the winter Olympics. In 22 games in the 1998 NHL playoffs, he scored six goals, helping the Red Wings win another Stanley Cup championship.

Wertheim of *Sports Illustrated* described Lidstrom sitting almost unnoticed in the back of the Red Wings' noisy locker room that year. "I'm pretty calm and quiet," Lidstrom told Wertheim. "I don't really avoid attention, but I don't look for it either, in the locker room or on the ice."

Between 1995 and 2003, Lidstrom assisted in at least 40 goals per season. He was rarely penalized; though he played in at least 78 games each season, he typically logged less than 20 minutes in the penalty box per year. Lidstrom hinted that he might leave Detroit and the NHL after his contract expired in 1999 to return to the Swedish Elite League because he missed his home country and wanted his sons to be educated in Sweden. Instead, he decided to stay with the Red Wings, signing a three-year contract that paid him more than $7 million a year. In 2001, he won the Norris Trophy, awarded to the league's best defenseman, for the first time.

When the Red Wings returned to the Stanley Cup Finals in 2002, taking on the Carolina Hurricanes, Lidstrom played a major role. Late in Game 2, Lidstrom broke a 1-1 tie with a goal, and celebrated by shouting, pumping his arms in the air, and kicking out his leg—normal behavior for most hockey players, unusual for him. "I guess my teammates were surprised I showed emotion," Lidstrom told Daniel Habib of *Sports Illustrated.* "It's the old Swedish stereotype: I don't get excited, don't show it as much as others." In Game 3, Lidstrom assisted on a goal with a minute left in the third period to force overtime; the Wings went on to win. Bowman, the coach, praised Lidstrom's stamina and his ability to dominate defensively and also help the Wings attack. The Red Wings took the series, winning their third Stanley Cup in six years. Lidstrom won a second Norris Trophy, as well as the Conn Smythe Trophy for most valuable player in the playoffs.

Lidstrom's teammates call him The Perfect Human for his disciplined mind and physical strength. He is known for missing very few games and staying on the ice for up to half of a game, a feat of endurance in a sport played at intense speed. Unlike many defensemen, his style is based on more on precision than physicality. "Year after year, he stymies them all—not with an overpowering slam into the walls, but with a short stick flick here, a tiny poke steal there, perfect body position, the perfect defensive stance, a seemingly unfailing internal GPS unit that tells him where to go to block a pass or close a shooting lane," wrote Mitch Albom in the *Detroit Free Press.*

In 2006, Lidstrom played on the Swedish national team in the Olympics, along with fellow NHL stars Peter Forsberg and Mats Sundin. All three were part of a wave of ultra-talented Swedish hockey players sometimes known as the Golden Generation, and fittingly, the team won the gold medal. Lidstrom scored the final goal in the medal-winning game against Finland.

Later that year, longtime Red Wings captain Steve Yzerman retired, and Lidstrom was named to succeed him as team leader. The transition was hard for many Red Wings fans, because Yzerman had led the team from perennial loserdom to three championships, and his dazzling scoring skills, good looks, and tenacious recovery from threatening injuries had earned him intense loyalty from Detroiters. But when Yzerman was once told he was the best player on the Red Wings, he insisted Lidstrom was better. While the fans took a while to adjust to Lidstrom's quieter leadership, the team had no problem following his example. "All we say is, 'Watch Nick, how he carries himself and what he does on the ice,'" forward Kirk Maltby once explained (as quoted by Albom in the *Detroit Free Press*).

The team took on some of Lidstrom's character. The 2007-08 Red Wings were less flashy on the ice, and less outgoing off of it, than the Detroit teams of a few years earlier. "This 2008 group, with arguably four Swedes in the top-five skaters on the team, is like a well-functioning watch," wrote Albom in the *Detroit Free Press*. "When it's doing its job, everything is clean, crisp, efficient—sometimes even unappreciated."

Lidstrom was at last getting his due. In December of 2007, the *Hockey News* named him the greatest European-born NHL player of all time and the league's second-best defenseman ever. That same month, he signed a contract extension that would pay him $14.9 million over two years and keep him in Detroit into 2010. "Nick has been the best defenseman in the world for several years," Red Wings general manager Ken Holland explained (according to the Canadian Press). "He's a great captain and role model who does everything right both on and off the ice."

The Red Wings finished the 2007-08 season with a 54-21-7 record, the best in the NHL. Lidstrom had 70 points, the most of any defenseman in the league. During the playoffs, Lidstrom excelled at a less dramatic task: keeping the top scorers of Detroit's opponents from scoring. In the first three rounds, he limited Jason Arnott and J. P. Dumont of Nashville, Paul Stastny of Colorado and Mike Ribeiro of Dallas to three points or less each.

In the Stanley Cup finals in June of 2008, the Red Wings beat the Pittsburgh Penguins in six games. Lidstrom became the first European captain to win the trophy. "It felt great to be the first guy to touch the Cup on our team," Lidstrom said, according to the Associated Press. "I'm very proud of being the first European and of being the captain of the Red Wings." That week, Lidstrom carried the Cup in the Red Wings' victory parade in downtown Detroit. "You are a hardworking city and hardworking state," he told the crowd at a rally afterward (as quoted by Shawn Windsor on the *Detroit Free Press* Web site). "And that's the way we try to be as a team."

That June, Lidstrom was awarded his sixth Norris trophy as best defenseman. Only two players, Bobby Orr and Doug Harvey, won it more times. Lidstrom and Red Wings goalie Chris Osgood also appeared with the Stanley Cup on the *Tonight Show with Jay Leno* to mark their victory. In July, Lidstrom took the Cup with him to Sweden and celebrated in his hometown.

"His biggest asset is probably his brain," Henrik Lundqvist, goalie for the New York Rangers, told Helene St. James in the *Detroit Free Press*. "He's just so smart out there, and he's at the right place at the right time, and that's why he can play almost 30 minutes a game. He's not running around. He just knows where to be all the time. That's probably why he can keep playing another ten years."

## Sources

### Periodicals

Associated Press, June 5, 2008.

Canadian Press, October 5, 2006; December 26, 2007; June 11, 2008; June 12, 2008.

*Detroit Free Press*, June 2, 2008; June 13, 2008.

*Sports Illustrated*, June 24, 1998, p. 54; October 4, 1999, p. 80; June 27, 2002, p. 74; March 6, 2006, p. 46; June 13, 2008, p. 52.

### Online

"Enjoying the Stanley Cup from Afar," *Red Wings Parade Blog*, Freep.com, http://www.freep.com/apps/pbcs.dll/article?AID=/20080606.tif/SPORTS05/80606059.tif (June 6, 2008).

"Lidstrom: No. 1 Euro; No. 2 blueliner of all time," *The Hockey News*, http://www.thehockeynews.com/articles/11520-THNcom-Blog-Lids trom-No-1-Euro-No-2-blueliner-of-all-time.html (August 2, 2008).

"Nicklas E. Lidstrom," Legends of Hockey, http://www.legendsofhockey.net:8080/LegendsOfHockey/jsp/SearchPlayer.jsp?player=10944 (August 23, 2008).

"Nicklas Lidstrom #5 D," ESPN.com, http://sports.espn.go.com/nhl/players/profile?playerId=539 (August 2, 2008).

"Stanley Cup Journals: 24," Hockey Hall of Fame, http://www.hhof.com/html/exSCJ08_23.shtml (August 12, 2008).

*—Erick Trickey*

# Lil Wayne

*Frank Micelotta/Getty Images for MTV*

## Rap musician

**B**orn Dwayne Michael Carter, September 27, 1982, in New Orleans, LA; son of Cynthia Carter; divorced; children: daughter Reginae, Dwayne Michael Carter III.

**Addresses:** *Record company*—Cash Money Records, 2220 Colorado Ave., Santa Monica, CA 90404.

## Career

**B**egan performing at age eight; signed to Cash Money Records; member of group Hot Boys, 1997-2003; began a solo music career, 1999—; president of Cash Money Records, 2005—.

**Awards:** Black Entertainment Television (BET), Viewers' Choice Award (with Birdman), 2007; BET, Viewers' Choice Award, for *Lollipop*, 2008; MTV Video Award for best hip-hop video for *Lollipop*, 2008; won Grammys for best rap solo performance for "A Milli," best rap song for "Lollipop," and best rap duo for "Swagga Like Us," and best rap album for *Tha Carter III*, Recording Academy, 2009.

## Sidelights

**A**s a member of the Hot Boys and as a solo artist, Lil Wayne has made a significant impact on rap music. At the 2009 Grammy Awards, Lil Wayne was the most nominated artist, and he took home four awards. Despite his young age when he began in the industry, Lil Wayne has always been taken seriously as an artist and a rapper. As of 2005 he was the president of Cash Money Records, the label that gave him his start in the music industry.

The five-foot-five, tattoo-covered rapper has long carried himself with a swagger, but many critics have felt his arrogance is firmly supported by his talent. Sasha Frere-Jones of the *New Yorker* called Lil Wayne "indisputably the rapper of the year" in 2007, and she considered him "an artist who may actually deserve the bragging rights to 'best rapper alive,' his current motto." In *XXL* magazine, Lil Wayne likened himself to Martin Luther King, Jr., and Malcolm X. "You're not about to ask him about what he think about what somebody said about him," he said to the reporter. "You ... ask him about his greatness, and his greatness only." Josh Tyrangiel of *Time* also commented on Lil Wayne's growth from his early albums to his solo career: "Over four years, he morphed from a mediocre rapper with a thuggish point of view into a savant who merges sex, drugs, and politics with a sneaky intellect, a freakish knowledge of pop culture, and a voice out of the Delta."

Lil Wayne was born Dwayne Michael Carter in New Orleans, Louisiana. The dates reported for his birth vary. Often given as September 27, 1982, his birth date came into question when a police report of a 2006 incident gave his birth year as 1979. Though this age would have given him more years of experience—perhaps taking away from some of his reputation as a prodigy—his career started early enough either way for his accomplishments to remain remarkable.

When he was very young, Lil Wayne's mother separated from his father and later married Reginald "Rabbit" McDonald. The family lived in the Hollygrove neighborhood of the Uptown section of New Orleans, where McDonald was employed in a lawn-care service. Lil Wayne began rapping early, composing his first tunes by the time he was eight years old. He also had a gift for sampling music and making it his own: He changed the lyrics to the hip-hop number "You Gotta Be Real" into "You Gotta Be Lil," emphasizing his own small stature. With his playground hit, Lil Wayne knew that he wanted to pursue a career in music.

He also knew exactly what label he wanted to represent him. Lil Wayne was mostly interested in southern hip-hop, and he only listened to the music coming out of Cash Money Studios. He was a fan of Cash Money rapper Lil Slim, also from New Orleans, and he cultivated a friendship with the older artist. Lil Slim introduced Lil Wayne to the producers and CEOs at Cash Money, and Lil Wayne did not waste the opportunity: He performed for them to show them how well he could rap at the young age of eleven. "I did a rap where I spelled out my hood, Hollygrove, and they gave me a card. You know, you give a child a card, he ain't never stop callin' that number," he recalled in XXL. Despite his young age, Lil Wayne quickly became part of the inner clique at Cash Money, and he made his first appearance on the B. G.'z (Baby Gangstaz) album True Story under the name Baby D.

The album did well, but Lil Wayne's mother disapproved of the group and pulled him out. Lil Wayne ran away from home in protest, carrying a gun that belonged to his stepfather, McDonald. While on his own, he accidentally shot himself, and when he was questioned by police in the hospital, he acknowledged that the gun was McDonald's. Lil Wayne's stepfather was subsequently arrested and charged with possessing an unregistered handgun.

In 1997, Lil Wayne appeared on his first album under the name that made him famous. Joining other Cash Money rappers Juvenile, Turk, and B. G., he became a member of the group the Hot Boys. Their debut album Get It How U Live sold 400,000 copies.

But that success came alongside tragedy in Lil Wayne's personal life: McDonald, who had been released from prison, was abducted and murdered, killed by a gunshot. To memorialize his stepfather, Lil Wayne got the chest tattoo with the words "Big Bang." The year contained further complications when Lil Wayne married his high school girlfriend, Toya, and they had a daughter, Reginae, together before divorcing.

Based on the success of Get It How U Live, Cash Money planned for a second Hot Boys album, as well as solo albums for each of the group members. Several of the Hot Boys also appeared on each other's solo albums. The group's second release, Guerrilla Warfare, came out in 1999, as did Lil Wayne's solo debut, Tha Block Is Hot, which was produced by Mannie Fresh. Lil Wayne also performed on Juvenile's "Back That Azz Up," which was a major hip-hop hit of the year.

Tha Block Is Hot sold 229,000 copies in the first week of its release, soaring to number three on Billboard's Top 200 chart. The prominence of Lil Wayne's album and several other successes marked a change for Cash Money as a label. The company was now challenging hip-hop labels in New York, Los Angeles, and Atlanta. The album's title single became a staple at Lil Wayne's live performances, and a whisper of "the block is hot" brought crowds under his spell.

Lil Wayne continued to create albums produced by Mannie Fresh, and his successes with Lights Out and 500 Degreez indicated that their relationship was positive. But Cash Money's prominence was beginning to slip; many rappers had left for major labels, weakening Cash Money's team of artists. To bring more attention to both his own music and to Cash Money, Lil Wayne released an underground "mixtape" CD, Da Drought, distributing the release online. Though the album would make no profit, the promise of free distribution meant that Lil Wayne's audience had the possibility of increasing dramatically. As the music industry continued its shift from CDs, which were losing money, to a digital medium, Lil Wayne was in a prime spot to take advantage of distribution channels such as iTunes and other streaming media, keeping himself at the top of his audience's playlists.

Though several of the Hot Boys had already left Cash Money, a new album, Let 'Em Burn, was put out under the group's name. Lil Wayne remained devoted to Cash Money and continued his underground strategy to build a wider network for his music. His next album, *Tha Carter*, included the single "Go DJ," which drew Lil Wayne into the national spotlight. Given that it was produced by Mannie Fresh, the album was thought by critics to have been heavily influenced by the producer. In order to distinguish his own style, Lil Wayne made his next album, *Tha Carter II*, without Fresh. It sold 244,000 copies in its first week, making it the highest earning Cash Money debut to date. The album featured a wide variety of songs, contrasting a more soulful sound in one number with a melodic tune in the next. Lil Wayne explained in *Village Voice* that the diversity in the songs was intentional: "I'm trying to open up a new door for Cash Money itself, and myself alone also. That's what I had to do. People go used to the same sound. Of course, 'Go DJ' was great, but it was done by Mannie Fresh. I've done Mannie Fresh music all my career, so this album here was my new beginning." The success of *Tha Carter II* earned Lil Wayne an appointment to president of Cash Money Records in 2005, then owned by Universal.

Problematically, though mixtapes and underground releases had worked in Lil Wayne's favor before, the artist began having his music leaked. He began creating new music, but it took him four years to put out an album, because so many of the songs he recorded were leaked before they could be released. As desire for *Tha Carter III* continued to grow and his fans became more and more anxious for a release, Universal released a digital-only EP called "The Leak." The EP's single "I'm Me" made number 1 on *Billboard*'s Bubbling Under Hot 100 chart and spent three weeks on the Pop 100. How did Lil Wayne practically give away his songs and, in the words of Josh Tyrangiel of *Time*, get "paid back a million times over?" Tyrangiel offered the following: "Hint: he's good." The release of *Tha Carter III* was no disappointment: It stayed at the top of the *Billboard* album charts and sold more than one million copies in its first week. Not only was the album a huge commercial success, Lil Wayne was nominated for eight Grammy Awards, making him the most nominated artist in 2009.

Although Lil Wayne has mostly made news due to his career, he has also been in headlines that followed his personal life. The rapper first became a father at 15 and welcomed his son Dwayne Michael Carter III into the world in 2008, without revealing the identity of the child's mother. Lil Wayne remains involved in raising both of his children. The artist has also had trouble with the law and has been arrested on drug and weapons charges. In addition, videos of him yelling at members of his band have circulated on the Internet. "Wayne renders himself a larger-than-life creature—a gangster rapper, a drug user, a womanizer, a Martian, and a beast all in one, among other things," wrote Mariel Concepcion in *Billboard*. To dominate the same viral media that spread his burst of temper, Lil Wayne began creating "webisodes" on YouTube and MySpace. He has also attempted to balance his career with getting more education, studying with a tutor for courses at University of Phoenix online.

Lil Wayne continues to perform in guest-features with other artists. "I've found out that I love doing music for others. You're making history when you're making music with somebody else, for somebody else," he was quoted by Concepcion as saying in *Billboard*. Noting that some artists had told him not to do so many guest-features, he explained, "I don't listen to anybody, I'm different, and you'll understand that by the time I'm finished. I breathe nothing else, I smell nothing else, I care about nothing else but music, my family and God. It's like my child."

## Selected discography

(With Hot Boys) *Get It How U Live,* Cash Money Records, 1997.
(With Hot Boys) *Guerrilla Warfare,* Cash Money Records, 1999.
*Tha Block Is Hot,* Cash Money Records, 1999.
*Lights Out,* Cash Money Records, 2000.
*500 Degreez,* Cash Money Records, 2002.
*Da Drought* (underground "mixtape"), Cash Money Records, 2003.
(With Hot Boys) *Let 'Em Burn,* Cash Money Records, 2003.
*Tha Carter,* Cash Money Records, 2004.
*Tha Carter II,* Cash Money Records, 2005.
(With Birdman) *Like Father, Like Son,* Cash Money Records, 2006.
*Tha Carter III,* Cash Money Records, 2008.

## Sources

### Periodicals

*Billboard,* November 20, 1999; February 9, 2008, p. 38.
*New Yorker,* August 13, 2007, p. 72.
*New York Times,* June 19, 2008, p. E2; July 17, 2008, p. E2; December 5, 2008, p. C2.
*People,* February 9, 2009, p. 92.
*Time,* July 14, 2008, p. 69.
*Village Voice,* January 19, 2006.
*XXL,* November 1, 2005; December 2007.
*Washington Post,* February 9, 2009, p. C02.

## Online

All Music Guide, http://www.allmusic.com/ (February 11, 2009).

Grammy Awards, http://www.grammy.com/ (February 11, 2009).

Lil Wayne's Home Page, http://lilwayne-online.com/ (February 11, 2009).

MTV Online, http://www.mtv.com/music/artist/lil_wayne/ (February 11, 2009).

MSNBC.com, http://www.msnbc.msn.com/id/12992671.tif/ (February 11, 2009).

*—Alana Joli Abbott*

# Laura Linney

## Actress

**B**orn February 5, 1964, in New York, NY; daughter of Romulus Linney (a playwright) and Ann Leggett Perse (a nurse); married David Adkins, September, 1995 (divorced, 2000). *Education:* Attended Northwestern University, early 1980s; Brown University, B.F.A., 1986; graduated from Juilliard School, 1989; also attended Arts Theatre School (Moscow, U.S.S.R.).

**Addresses:** *Agent*—Creative Artists Agency, 9830 Wilshire Blvd., Beverly Hills, CA 90212-1804.

## Career

**A**ctress in films, including: *Lorenzo's Oil*, 1992; *Dave*, 1993; *Searching for Bobby Fischer*, 1993; *A Simple Twist of Fate*, 1994; *Congo*, 1995; *Primal Fear*, 1996; *Absolute Power*, 1997; *The Truman Show*, 1998; *Lush*, 1999; *The House of Mirth*, 2000; *Maze*, 2000; *You Can Count on Me*, 2000; *The Laramie Project*, 2002; *The Mothman Prophecies*, 2002; *The Life of David Gale*, 2003; *Love Actually*, 2003; *Mystic River*, 2003; *Kinsey*, 2004; *P.S.*, 2004; *The Squid and the Whale*, 2004; *The Exorcism of Emily Rose*, 2005; *Driving Lessons*, 2006; *The Hottest State*, 2006; *Jindabyne*, 2006; *Man of the Year*, 2006; *The City of Your Final Destination*, 2007; *The Nanny Diaries*, 2007; *The Savages*, 2007; *The Other Man*, 2008. Television appearances include: *Blind Spot*, 1993; *Class of '61*, 1993; *Tales of the City* (miniseries), PBS, 1993; *Law & Order*, 1994; *More Tales of the City* (miniseries), PBS, 1998; *Love Letters* (movie), 1999; *Running Mates* (movie), 2000; *American Masters*, PBS, 2001; *Further Tales of the City* (miniseries), 2001; *Wild Iris* (movie), 2001; *King of the Hill* (voice), FOX, 2002; *Frasier*, NBC, 2003-04; *The*

*American Experience*, PBS, 2005-06; *American Dad* (voice), FOX, 2006; *John Adams* (miniseries), HBO, 2008; *Masterpiece Classic*, PBS, 2009—. Stage appearances include: *Six Degrees of Separation*, Broadway production, 1990; *Beggars in the House of Plenty*, Manhattan Theater Club, New York City, 1991; *The Seagull*, Broadway production, 1992; *Sight Unseen*, Manhattan Theater Club Stage II, New York City, 1992; *Hedda Gabler*, Broadway production, 1994; *Holiday*, Broadway production, 1995; *Honour*, Broadway production, 1998; *Uncle Vanya*, Broadway production, 2000; *The Crucible*, Broadway production, 2002; *Sight Unseen*, Broadway production, 2004; *Les Liaisons Dangereuses*, Broadway production, 2008. Also worked as a waitress at The Manhattan, New York City.

**Awards:** Joe A. Callaway Award for best performance in a classic drama, Actors' Equity Association, for *Hedda Gabler*, 1994; New York Film Critics Circle Award for best actress, for *You Can Count on Me*, 2000; San Diego Film Critics Society Award for best actress, for *You Can Count on Me*, 2000; Toronto Film Critics Association Award for best performance—female, for *You Can Count on Me*, 2000; Dallas-Fort Worth Film Critics Association Award for best actress, for *You Can Count on Me*, 2001; Emmy Award for outstanding lead actress in a miniseries or movie, Academy of Television Arts and

Sciences, for *Wild Iris*, 2001; National Society of Film Critics Award for best actress, for *You Can Count on Me*, 2001; Vancouver Film Critics Circle Award for best actress, for *You Can Count on Me*, 2001; Boston Society of Film Critics Award (with others) for best ensemble cast, for *Mystic River*, 2003; Emmy Award for outstanding guest actress in a comedy series, Academy of Television Arts and Sciences, for *Frasier*, 2004; Florida Film Critics Circle Award for best supporting actress, for *Kinsey*, 2004; National Board of Review Award for best supporting actress, for *Kinsey*, 2004; Phoenix Film Critics Society Award for best performance by an actress in a supporting role, for *Kinsey*, 2004; Desert Palm Achievement Award, Palm Springs International Film Festival, 2005; Glitter Award for best actress, for *Kinsey*, 2005; Gotham Award (with others) for best ensemble cast, for *The Squid and the Whale*, 2005; Mar del Plata Film Festival Award for best actress, for *P.S.*, 2005; Satellite Award for outstanding actress in a supporting role—drama, International Press Academy, for *The Squid and the Whale*, 2005; *Theatre World* Award for *Sight Unseen*, c. 2005; Toronto Film Critics Association Award for best performance—female, for *The Squid and the Whale*, 2005; Austin Film Critics Award for best supporting actress, for *The Squid and the Whale*, 2006; Las Palmas Film Festival Award for best actress, for *The Squid and the Whale*, 2006; Valladolid International Film Festival Award for best actress, for *Jindabyne*, 2006; Dartmouth Film Award, Dartmouth Film Society, 2008; Emmy Award for outstanding lead actress in a miniseries or a movie, Academy of Television Arts and Sciences, for *John Adams*, 2008; Golden Globe Award for best performance by an actress in a miniseries or motion picture made for television, for *John Adams*, 2009; Gracie Allen Award for outstanding female lead—drama special, American Women in Radio & Television, for *John Adams*, 2009; Ken Burns Lifetime Achievement Award, 2009; Screen Actors Guild Award for outstanding performance by a female actor in a television movie or miniseries, for *John Adams*, 2009.

## Sidelights

Nominated for three Academy Awards and a Tony Award, actress Laura Linney has depicted complex women in film, stage, and screen roles. Perhaps best known for her exceptional work in the independent films *You Can Count on Me* and *The Squid and the Whale*, Linney won an Emmy and a Golden Globe for her depiction of Abigail Adams in the highly regarded HBO biographical miniseries *John Adams*. While the actress favored dramas and dramatic thrillers, she also dabbled in comedies such as *The Truman Show* and *Love, Actually*. Linney was open to any type of role, telling Nancy Mills of the New York *Daily News*, "I think of myself as someone who's game. I'm willing to try something different or do something silly." Linney added, "Acting is a difficult life, but hopefully it's a long life."

Born on February 5, 1964, in New York City, Linney is the daughter of Romulus Linney and Ann Leggett Perse. Her father was a respected Off-Broadway playwright who wrote such plays as *A Woman Without a Name*. Her mother worked as a nurse. A grandmother was also an actress. Her parents were divorced when she was an infant, and she lived with her mother on New York City's Upper East Side. Linney knew she wanted to act by the age of six, and spent time with her father during rehearsals of plays, an experience which only increased her desire. She soon became involved with acting and the theater herself. When she was 14 years old, she spent the summer working at a summer stock theater, the New London Barn Playhouse in New London, New Hampshire. Linney eventually graduated from the Massachusetts-based boarding school Northfield Mount Hermon School in 1982, where she said she was last in her class in writing and reading.

Linney then attended Northwestern University for a year, before transferring to Brown University. She earned her bachelor of fine arts degree in theater history from Brown University in 1986. Throughout college, she appeared in plays and pursued further education in the craft. Linney then trained as an actress at the Juilliard School, graduating in 1989, with additional training at Moscow's Arts Theatre School. Linney appreciated what her acting education taught her. She told David Germain in the *Windsor Star*, "I was in school for so long. I was in school forever. Training that long is not for everybody. But what it gave me was a sense of, when I was in trouble, how to help myself out. Maybe when the writing was a little weak or the director is maybe not as astute or I was having my own trouble with getting somewhere. It gave me experiences to help myself out in those situations."

Linney began her acting career primarily on the stage in regional productions as well as in Broadway and Off-Broadway productions, working as a waitress to help support herself between jobs. Among the highlights of her early acting career were the Broadway productions *Six Degrees of Separation* in 1990, *The Seagull* in 1992, and *Hedda Gabbler* in 1994. In *Six Degrees*, she played the daughter Tess as an understudy. This was her first experience on Broadway and an educational one. She told Alison Jones of the *Birmingham Post*, "For me it was the perfect job because I was able to watch the show come together and explode in the way it did. To be part of that straight out of school was fantastic."

Off Broadway, Linney played the daughter in *Beggars in the House of Plenty* in 1991 and Grete in the 1992 Off-Broadway debut of *Sight Unseen* by Donald Margulies. Grete is a German journalist interrogating the main character, a Jewish artist named Jonathan. Of the character, Linney told Andrea Stevens of the *New York Times*, "I love the mysterious aspect of this character. Grete is like a roller coaster in the dark. She goes into scary territory, where you don't know what is going on."

While working on the stage, Linney began appearing in film and a few television roles in the early 1990s. Her first parts were small roles in such films as 1992's *Lorenzo's Oil* and 1993's *Dave*. In 1993, Linney also was cast as Mary Ann Singleton in the television adaptation of *Tales of the City* by Armistead Maupin. Linney's Singleton was a native of the Midwest who moves to San Francisco in the 1970s. Linney repeated the role in the sequels, 1998's *More Tales of the City* and 2001's *Further Tales of the City*. Watching Mary Ann Singleton grow over these years appealed to Linney. She told Peter Johnson of *USA Today*, "It's a great thing to be able to stay with one character for such a long period of time, to see the changes that happen. It's not the same thing over and over again."

Continuing to move between stage, film, and television, Linney appeared in Broadway productions, including 1994's *Hedda Gabler* and 1995's *Holiday*. After a small role in the hit jungle thriller *Congo* (based on a novel by Michael Crichton), Linney's film roles became more substantive with the 1996 legal drama *Primal Fear*. She co-starred as Janet Venable, the prosecutor and feisty ex-girlfriend of the primary character, Martin Vail, played by Richard Gere. With the film's success came heightened media scrutiny for Linney, who expressed a bit of inner disagreement. Because of her family' background in theater, she told Jim Slotek of the *Toronto Sun*, "I can remember when I was kid hearing a lot disparaging remarks about 'going Hollywood.' You used to be looked upon as a traitor [for taking work in Hollywood movies]. But now things are so hard they kiss you goodbye and throw you a party."

Because of her work in the role, Clint Eastwood cast her as his character's daughter in the 1997 political thriller, *Absolute Power*. Linney then had a major role in another high-profile Hollywood film, 1998's *The Truman Show*. She played a bubbly actress playing the wife of the main character, played by Jim Carrey, a man who does not know his life is a reality show. This film brought her the most attention of her acting career to date—in part because of the superstardom of then-megastar comedian Carrey—with premieres world-wide. Keeping her professional life balanced, Linney also appeared in a Broadway production of *Honour* in 1998.

In 2000, Linney became even more high profile following two important films as well as a play. She was nominated for her first Academy Award and won numerous critics' awards for her depiction of Sammy in the small budget independent *You Can Count on Me*. In this, her first leading role, she played a single mother with a young son (played by Rory Culkin) who must deal with challenges such as the re-appearance of her directionless brother (played by Mark Ruffalo) as well as a difficult new boss at the bank where she works as a loan officer. The subtle comedic drama focused on issues of sibling rivalry and identity.

Talking about the film to Dave Kehr of the *New York Times*, Linney explained, "What I responded to is that here are two adults who are still really struggling to grow up, dealing with amusing and frustrating issues about themselves and their lives. They're extremely close siblings who lost their parents at a very early age. I think between the two of them they make one whole human being." The delicate balance of comedy and drama as well as the nuanced performances earned critical raves for Linney and her castmates.

Also in 2000, Linney played Bertha Dorset in the adaptation of Edith Wharton's *The House of Mirth*. Set in New York City at the turn of the twentieth century, the stories focuses on issues of social class class and conflict. Linney's dubious Dorset is an adulterous wife who befriends a financially distressed woman, played by Gillian Anderson, and takes advantage of her. *Mirth* was directed by Terence Davies, who praised her work in the role. Linney also had another film released in 2000, *Maze*, in which she played a pregnant woman who works as a model for the best friend of her lover. In addition, Linney appeared in a number of television productions, including the 2000 television movie *Running Mates*. Another television movie, *Wild Iris*, for which she received an Emmy Award, aired in 2001. Linney played the unhappy daughter of a character played by Gena Rowland.

Returning to Broadway occasionally in the early 2000s, Linney appeared in a production of *Uncle Vanya* in 2000 followed by a 2002 production of

Arthur Miller's drama about the Salem witch hunts, *The Crucible*, which co-starred Liam Neeson. Linney was nominated for a Tony Award for her work in *The Crucible*. Doing such stage work allowed her to return to New York City, where she made her home when she was not shooting films or television productions.

With such award-winning work on film, television, and stage, Linney continued to be cast in challenging roles, including more starring roles in films. In 2002, for example, she again starred with Gere in *Mothman Prophecies*, a science fiction-tinged drama about odd events in a small town in West Virginia. She played a sheriff in the community. The following year, Linney played Annabeth Markum in Boston-set drama *Mystic River*, directed by Eastwood as well as the murder victim/anti-death penalty advocate Constance Harraway in *The Life of David Gale*. In a completely different kind of film, Linney played Sarah in the British romantic comedy *Love Actually* set at Christmas time, also released in 2003.

Returning to the theater in 2004, Linney's stage work continued to be award-winning. She appeared in the Broadway revival of Margulies' *Sight Unseen* that year in the role of Patricia, for which she was nominated for a Tony Award for her work the following year. Also in 2004, she played Clara McMillen in the biopic *Kinsey* about the infamous sex researcher, Alfred Kinsey. Linney was nominated for a second Academy Award for her depiction of McMillan, who was Kinsey's plain wife. In addition, Linney's work as Joan Berckman opposite Jeff Daniels in 2005's dysfunctional family drama *The Squid and the Whale* was also well-received.

After several years of interesting film and television roles, Linney was again nominated for an Academy Award for her work as the bitter, self-obsessed Wendy in the difficult family drama, *The Savages*, released in 2007. She made a return to Broadway after a four-year absence by appearing a production of *Les Liaisons Dangereuses* in 2008. Linney was perhaps even more acclaimed for her portrayal of Abigail Adams in the HBO miniseries *John Adams*, based on the Pulitzer Prize-winning biography by David McCullough. She won several awards for the role, including an Emmy.

Continuing to show the depth of her talent and the diversity of her interest, Linney had several films scheduled for release in 2009, including *Sympathy for Delicious* and *Morning*. She also became the new host of PBS' *Masterpiece Classic* and planned to continue to take on television and stage roles, telling Kehr of the *New York Times*, "I still have the acting bug, pretty strongly. I work in television, I still do stage, I work all over the place, and I find that gratifying because I never take any of it for granted, not for one second."

## Sources

### Books

*Complete Marquis Who's Who Biographies*, Marquis Who's Who LLC, 2009.

### Periodicals

*Birmingham Post*, March 22, 2001, p. 14; March 14, 2003, p. 13.
*Chicago Sun-Times*, November 9, 2003, p. 10.
*Daily News* (NY), January 14, 2002, p. 35; November 8, 2004, p. 37.
*Daily Telegraph* (London, England), December 6, 2008, sec. ART, p. 16.
*Dartmouth* (Hanover, NH), October 9, 2008.
*Lab Business Week*, December 7, 2008, p. 871.
*New York Times*, February 9, 1992, sec. 2, p. 5; September 20, 1998, sec. 9, p. 1; November 3, 2000, p. E20; May 16, 2004, sec. 2, p. 1.
*Patriot Ledger* (Quincy, MA), March 29, 2008, p. ONE59.
*Providence Journal-Bulletin* (RI), March 28, 2009, p. 1 .
*San Francisco Chronicle*, November 19, 2000, p. 54.
*Sunday Times* (Perth, Australia), January 4, 2004.
*Times* (London, England), October 6, 2007, p. 15.
*Toronto Sun*, April 1, 1996, p. 34; September 14, 2000, p. 67; November 29, 2000, p. 51.
*USA Today*, May 4, 2001, p. 11E.
*Vancouver Sun* (British Columbia, Canada), October 21, 2005, p. D1.
*Windsor Star* (Ontario, Canada), November 14, 2000, p. B9.

### Online

"Laura Linney," Internet Movie Database, http://www.imdb.com/name/nm0001473/ (April 14, 2009).

—A. Petruso

# Blake Lively

## Actress

**B**orn Blake Christina Lively, August 25, 1987, in Tarzana, CA; daughter of Ernie (an actor) and Elaine (a talent manager) Lively.

**Addresses:** *Agent*—Alex Yarosh, Gersh Agency, 232 North Canon Dr., Beverly Hills, CA 90210.

## Career

**A**ctress in films, including: *Sandman*, 1998; *The Sisterhood of the Traveling Pants*, 2005; *Accepted*, 2006; *Simon Says*, 2006; *Elvis and Anabelle*, 2007; *The Sisterhood of the Traveling Pants 2*, 2008; *New York, I Love You*, 2008. Also appears in the CW Network series *Gossip Girl*, 2007—.

## Sidelights

**T**hough screen star Blake Lively was known to legions of teenaged moviegoers thanks to her role in 2005's *Sisterhood of the Traveling Pants*, it was her debut in the new CW Network series *Gossip Girl* in 2007 that vaulted her to stardom. The teen soap, set in the rarified world of Manhattan private schools, features Lively as Serena van der Woodsen, a leggy blonde heiress with a recently subdued wild streak. The cult-favorite series, noted Alice Jones in London's *Independent* newspaper, "turned Lively from an appealing, if aspiring, starlet into a Carrie Bradshaw-esque fashion plate and paparazzi-stalked headline-maker."

Lively celebrated her 21st birthday just days before *Gossip Girl* returned for its second season in 2008. Born on August 25, 1987, in Tarzana, California,

*Robert Pitts/Landov*

Lively grew up in a show-business family. Her father, Ernie, is a veteran actor whose credits stretch back to episodes of *Fantasy Island* and *The Dukes of Hazzard*. Lively's mother, Elaine, is a talent manager for child actors, and her brothers Eric and Jason and sisters Lori and Robyn all have film and television experience.

Lively's film debut came in a 1998 project titled *Sandman* that was directed by her father; she was cast as Trixie the tooth fairy. Unlike her siblings, however, she had little interest in acting, and led a fairly normal—if overachieving—teen life. At Burbank High School she was a cheerleader, member of the choir, and even class president. But when one of her brothers passed her photo along to his agent, Lively was cajoled into showing up for a few auditions. Two months later, she landed the part of Bridget in an upcoming screen version of *The Sisterhood of the Traveling Pants*, the best-selling young-adult novel from 2001.

In the first *Sisterhood* movie, Lively played Bridget "Bee" Vreeland, a talented soccer star whose mother died tragically a few years earlier. Bee still has difficulties dealing with that loss, and sometimes finds herself in unhealthy relationships. At the core of the story is the friendship Bee enjoys with her three best friends, each of whom face their own personal challenges, and their alliance is symbolized by the titular pair of magical jeans that mysteriously fits all of them despite their different shapes. Lively's co-stars were Amber Tamblyn, Alexis Bledel, and America Ferrera, and the movie was a hit with its intended audience and critics alike.

Lively easily won subsequent film roles, such as *Accepted* and *Simon Says*, both from 2006, and was even cast in the lead for *Elvis and Anabelle*, released in the spring of 2007. Her co-star in this project was Max Minghella, who played the son of a mortician who manages to bring the local beauty queen back to life after her untimely death. Later that year, Lively debuted in another hotly anticipated screen adaptation of a bestselling young-adult series. This time it was for television, and fans of the racy teen novels in the *Gossip Girl* series by Cecily von Ziegesar had actually clamored for Lively to be cast as the reformed vixen Serena van der Woodsen. Series creator Josh Schwartz—who had an earlier television hit with the teen drama *The O.C.*—called Lively in for a reading and she won the role.

*Gossip Girl* debuted on the CW Network in the fall of 2007 with Lively and Leighton Meester as the longtime best friends whose relationship is continually tested by their respective romantic hijinks. Both are students at an elite private school on Manhattan's Upper East Side, and the show's pilot episode opened with Lively's character returning from a mysterious self-imposed exile at a New England boarding school. Prior to her disappearance, Serena was known for her hard-partying ways but begins the school year with a renewed focus on her schoolwork and family relationships while avoiding the drama on which her scheming best friend Blair Waldorf (Meester) seems to thrive. Serena's off-again, on-again romance with Dan (Penn Badgley), a classmate from Brooklyn, formed the basis of much of the first season's storylines.

*Gossip Girl* featured much more sex and substance abuse than previous teen dramas like *Beverly Hills 90210* and even the *The O.C.*, and the hour-long drama quickly gained a devoted following. That first 2007-08 season was interrupted by the Writers' Guild strike, but when *Gossip Girl* returned to the CW Network in April with all-new episodes, *New York* magazine devoted 5,000 words to the series

and its peculiar appeal. The article was written by two of the show's most ardent fans, journalists Jessica Pressler and Chris Rovzar, who asserted that "*Gossip Girl* is the ultimate teen Frankendrama, with archetypal characters and classic story lines. But it's also a thoroughly modern take on the genre … where teenagers are stalked by camera phones, the parents are as screwed up as the kids, and there are absolutely no consequences for anyone's actions."

The Serena-Blair axis was central to *Gossip Girl*'s constantly shifting storylines, which Pressler and Rovzar discussed. "Theirs is a dynamic that dates back to the dawn of entertainment: the blonde bombshell versus the sassy brunette," they asserted in the *New York* article. "There are fans of *Gossip Girl* who prefer Blake's ethereal Serena, who is all light and earnestness and a little bit foolish. Then there are the viewers who favor Leighton's Blair, the dark princess, fiercely loyal and cruel to the point of farce." Even *Vogue* magazine ran a feature about Lively and Meester and their on-screen wardrobes. Writer Eve MacSweeney called the show "a drama that gives as much weight to its characters' fashion choices as to their dialogue—and, for once, actually gets it right."

Before *Gossip Girl* returned for season two, Lively appeared in a second *Sisterhood of the Traveling Pants* movie, and once again her real-life dad played her on-screen parent. In another odd twist, Lively became involved with her *Gossip Girl* co-star Badgley, though she steadfastly refused to discuss it in interviews. "I try not to talk about my dating life," she explained to Eva Chen of *Teen Vogue*. "I want to, but once you start, it's all downhill from there. And besides, it really isn't that exciting. It's not like I have a ton of time to go out anyway!"

## Sources

*CosmoGirl*, November 2007, p. 85.
*Entertainment Weekly*, November 23, 2007, p. 24.
*Independent* (London, England), August 22, 2008, p. 2.
*New York*, April 28, 2008, p. 30.
*Teen Vogue*, March 2008, p. 218.
*Variety*, April 9, 2007, p. 25.
*Vogue*, March 2008, p. 594.

—Carol Brennan

# Mario Lopez

**Actor and television show host**

**B**orn Mario Lopez, Jr., on October 10, 1973, in San Diego, CA; son of Mario Sr. (a landscaping business co-owner) and Elvira (a telephone clerk and manager) Lopez; married Ali Landry (an actress and model), April 24, 2004 (marriage annulled, May 12, 2004).

**Addresses:** *Agent*—Agency for the Performing Arts, 9200 Sunset Blvd., Ste. 900, Los Angeles, CA 90069. *Management*—3 Arts Entertainment, 9460 Wilshire Blvd., 7th fl., Beverly Hills, CA 90212.

## Career

**A**ctor on television, including: *a.k.a. Pablo*, 1984; *Kids Incorporated*, 1984-86; *The Deacon Street Deer* (movie), 1986; *The Last Fling* (movie), 1987; *Saved by the Bell*, 1989-94; *Circus of the Stars*, CBS, 1989; *Saved by the Bell: Hawaiian Style*, 1992; *Name Your Adventure*, NBC, 1993-94; "Big Boys Don't Cry," *CBS Schoolbreak Special*, CBS, 1993; *Saved by the Bell: The College Years*, NBC, 1993-94; *Saved by the Bell: Wedding in Las Vegas* (movie), 1994; *Killing Mr. Griffin* (movie), 1997; *Breaking the Surface: The Greg Louganis Story* (movie), USA, 1997; *USA High*, 1998; *Pacific Blue*, USA, 1998-2000; *Resurrection Blvd.*, 2000; *Cover Me: Based on the True Life of an FBI Family*, 2001; *Popular*, 2001; *The Other Half*, NBC, 2001-03; *Pet Star*, Animal Planet, 2002-05; *Eve*, 2003; *Will You Marry Me?* (special), 2003; *Search for the Most Talented Kid in America*, NBC, 2003; *50 Greatest TV Animals* (special), 2003; *Miss Teen USA* (special), 2003; *Pyramid*, 2003-04; *Hollywood Squares*, 2003-04; *The Soluna Project* (movie), 2004; *50 Greatest TV Animals* (special), 2004; *You Win Live* (special), 2004; *The Bad Girl's Guide*,

2005; *Extreme Dodgeball*, 2005; *Dating Factory*, 2006; *Dancing with the Stars*, ABC, 2006; *Mind of Mencia*, Comedy Central, 2006; *The Bold and the Beautiful*, 2006; *Nip/Tuck*, FX, 2006, 2009; *Miss America* (special), 2007; *Miss Teen USA* (special), 2007; *Eight Days a Week*, 2007; *George Lopez*, ABC, 2007; *Holiday in Handcuffs* (movie), ABC Family, 2007; *Extra*, syndicated, 2008—; *Husband for Hire* (movie), Oxygen, 2008; *Randy Jackson Presents America's Best Dance Crew*, MTV, 2008—; *Robot Chicken*, Cartoon Network, 2008. Film appearances include: *Colors*, 1988; *Depraved*, 1996; *Fever Lake*, 1996; *The Journey: Absolution*, 1997; *Eastside*, 1999; *A Crack in the Floor*, 2000; *Big Brother Trouble*, 2000; *Outta Time*, 2002; *King Rikki*, 2002; *Pauly Shore Is Dead*, 2003; *Aloha, Scooby-Doo*, 2005. Stage appearances include: *A Chorus Line*, Gerald Schoenfeld Theater, New York City, 2008. Also worked as a morning disc jockey for KHHT, Los Angeles, CA, 2004.

**Awards:** Young Artist Award for best young actor in an off-primetime series, Young Artist Foundation, for *Saved by the Bell*, 1993; Young Artist Award for outstanding host for a youth magazine, news or game show, Young Artist Foundation, for *Name Your Adventure*, 1993; Young Artist Award for outstanding host for a youth magazine, news or game show, Young Artist Foundation, for *Name Your Adventure*, 1994.

## Sidelights

Perhaps best known for work on the long-running teen-oriented comedy *Saved by the Bell*, Mario Lopez has had a varied career in television and film. While he worked primarily as an actor from the age of ten, he also acquired an extensive experience hosting beauty pageants and other television specials and series such as *Extra*. A lifelong passionate dancer, Lopez finished second on the 2006 edition of the hit ABC reality series *Dancing with the Stars* and danced and sang in a Broadway musical, *A Chorus Line* in 2008.

Born Mario Lopez, Jr., on October 10, 1973, he is the son of Mario, Sr., and his wife, Elvira. His parents were immigrants from Mexico. His father co-owned a landscaping business, while his mother was employed as a telephone clerk and later helped manage her son's career. Dance was a passion from a young age, and Lopez began taking classes when he was three years old. While Lopez was taking these classes, an agent noticed him and got him an audition for a new situation comedy. He beat out 800 other children to launch his acting career with a regular role on the short-lived series *a.k.a. Pablo* in 1984. He played the title character's nephew, Tomas Del Gato, on the situation comedy, which was cancelled after one season due to low ratings.

Demonstrating the diversity which would become the hallmark of his career, Lopez then became a regular performer on *Kids, Inc.*, a children's musical show. He learned how to play drums on the popular Saturday morning program. After three years, Lopez was forced to leave *Kids, Inc.* because he had grown too tall to appear on the show. Lopez left the show in 1986 and then appeared in two television movies: 1986's *The Deacon Street Deer* and 1987's *The Last Fling*. He also made his feature film debut by playing a gang member in 1988's *Colors*.

In 1989, Lopez was cast in the role of his career as A. C. Slater on the NBC Saturday morning situation comedy *Saved by the Bell*. His character was the captain of the school's wrestling and football teams, as well as a chauvinist with an emotional, heart-felt side. By 1991, *Saved by the Bell* was the top-rated Saturday morning show for American teens. Though the show made him a star, Lopez could not explain its success. He told Judith Newmark of the *St. Louis Post-Dispatch*, "I don't know why *Saved by the Bell* became so popular. I just think the chemistry in the group was right."

Playing Slater made Lopez a high-profile Latino actor. Even at this young age, he was aware that he could be stereotyped in certain roles. Lopez was more surprised to find himself an inspiration to other Hispanics. He told Greg Joseph of the *San Diego Union-Tribune*, "My people write to me and compliment me to say that I make them proud. I feel I have to carry their banner, in some way ... I feel the weight of wanting to represent the good things about our people."

While appearing on the show, Lopez attended Chula Vista High School for the Creative and Performing Arts in San Diego. When he was unable to attend class there because of work, he worked with a tutor on the set and followed his school's lesson plans. Like his *Saved by the Bell* character Slater, Lopez was an athlete. He was active on his school's wrestling team. He placed seventh in the California State High School tournament during his senior year and was named San Diego County wrestler of the year for 1991. Lopez graduated with his diploma from Chula Vista High in 1991. Though he earned a wrestling scholarship to college, he put his education on hold to continue acting and never put the scholarship to use.

*Saved by the Bell* was cancelled in 1993, but the show remained popular in reruns for years. Lopez's career did not lose steam, however, as he had a leading role in a spin-off from the series, *Saved by the Bell: The College Years*, which aired in prime time on NBC. This spin-off focused on the primary characters from *Saved by the Bell* as they began attending college. The three primary male characters, including Lopez's Slater, shared a dorm room suite with three female students.

Lopez remained on Saturday morning television as well, serving as co-host of *Name Your Adventure* in 1993. On this educational reality program, viewers wrote in about their own adventure dreams. Those who were selected came on the show and experienced their unique adventures such as swimming with dolphins, training animals, and dancing with the Joffrey Ballet. Lopez said that he preferred *Name Your Adventure* to *Saved by the Bell: The College Years*. He told Thomas D. Elias in the Albany *Times Union*, "I get to be Mario and he's a lot more fun than Slater. Not that it's hard work being Slater.... That's cool, but being me is better. I get to do more physical stuff and I get to be outside all the time. I love hosting a show, too, and this gives me more and more experience at being comfortable in front of the camera."

Both *Saved by the Bell: The College Years* and *Name Your Adventure* were cancelled in 1994 after one season. After these shows ended their run, Lopez focused on television movies and series for the rest of the 1990s. In 1994, he appeared in the last *Saved by the Bell* program, the movie *Saved by the Bell: Wedding in Las Vegas*. Three years later, Lopez played the champion Olympic diver Greg Louganis in the USA network movie *Breaking the Surface: The Greg Louganis Story*. His performance received mixed reviews with Caryn James of the *New York Times* noting, "Mario Lopez, who plays Mr. Louganis as an adult, is a fair enough look-alike, but captures little feeling."

In 1998, Lopez returned to series television with a starring role on the USA series *Pacific Blue*. For two seasons, he played Bobby Cruz, a bike cop who patrols the beaches of California. After *Pacific Blue*, Lopez appeared occasionally in guest spots on shows such as *Resurrection Blvd.* and *Popular*. He also had starring roles in such films as 2002's *Outta Time*. In this thriller, Lopez played David Morales, a good-natured San Diego university student who becomes involved in smuggling packages across the Mexican border and must deal with criminals to save his kidnapped mother. *Outta Time* was poorly received by critics, though Lopez received some praise. For example, Glenn Abel of the *Hollywood Reporter* commented, "Lopez … at least possesses a certain affability…." Of similar quality was the 2000 horror film *A Crack in the Floor*.

As his acting roles lessened in the early 2000s, Lopez spent much of his time hosting various talk shows, reality programs, and beauty pageants. From 2001 to 2003, Lopez served as the co-host with Dick Clark and television actor/personality Danny Bonaduce on the NBC talk show *The Other Half*, the male version of the hit ABC women-oriented talk show *The View*. *The Other Half* focused on the male perspective and on how men see women. From 2002 to 2005, Lopez was also the host of the popular Animal Planet series *Pet Star*, an *American Idol*-type show for pets. In 2003, Lopez hosted both the NBC reality series *Search for the Most Talented Kid in America* and the *Miss Teen USA* pageant. He also appeared regularly on such game shows as *Pyramid* and *Hollywood Squares*.

In 2004, Lopez took on a new challenge when he became a radio DJ. He joined KHHT in Los Angeles as a member of its morning show, "Hot 92 Morning Jamz Session." Working with Michelle Visage and Danielle Steele, Lopez explored such morning radio staples as men versus women and odd comedy moments. He enjoyed the spontaneity of live radio after years of working on scripted film and television programming. Lopez had lobbied Roy Laughlin, the vice president for Clear Channel/Los Angeles, for the post to expand his media reach. Lopez told Chuck Taylor of *Billboard Radio Monitor*, "I'm a huge music lover, and I've always been a big fan of radio. It's my goal to attack all forms of entertainment—to be an actor in sitcoms and episodic TV, and I love hosting shows. I've watched my buddies Ryan Seacrest and Danny Bonaduce being able to juggle everything and thought that I would love to do something like that."

Continuing to vary his career choices, Lopez demonstrated his ability to shine in a number of genres in 2006. That year, he had a short-lived stint on his first soap opera. He played Dr. Christian Ramirez on *The Bold and the Beautiful*. Lopez looked at the role as another chance to serve as a Latino role model as the soap had a large Spanish following. He told Seli Groves of the *Tulsa World*, "[A]s someone who is part of the Latin community, I am very proud to play a character like Christian Ramirez because he's more than a role; he's a positive role model for people to look up to. He's a good man who wants to do good things. And he's strong. He proved that you can overcome anything to be the person you want to be." Lopez also had a several episode arc on the hit FX show *Nip/Tuck* as a plastic surgeon and showed off his dance skills on *Dancing with the Stars*, a ballroom dancing competition which paired celebrities with professional dancers. Though he finished second to former Dallas Cowboys running back Emmitt Smith, Lopez was noticed as he showed off his dancing talent with Karina Smirnoff, with whom he later became involved.

In the next two years, Lopez focused more on hosting duties than acting jobs. He had roles in two television movies—2007's *Holiday in Handcuffs* and 2008's *Husband for Hire*—and guest spots on such shows as *George Lopez* and *Nip/Tuck*. Lopez attracted more attention, however, for hosting both the 2007 *Miss America* and *Miss Teen USA* pageants as well as the reality series *Randy Jackson Presents America's Best Dance Crew* on MTV. Lopez also landed a longer-term hosting job when he was named host of the long-running entertainment-oriented news and information show *Extra*, beginning in 2008. He told Matt Ehlers of the Raleigh, North Carolina *News & Observer*, "I love hosting. I think hosting is my niche."

While Lopez was better known for his hosting than his acting by 2008, he again showed his ability to defy expectations by taking on Broadway that year. He made his Broadway debut playing Zach the choreographer in a revival of *A Chorus Line*. Lopez embraced the role, the show, and all it meant, telling Joe Dziemianowicz of the New York *Daily News*, "I love that the show is so iconic and such a strong ensemble piece and that it's got so many great messages. You don't have to be in show business to relate to the idea of striving for a dream."

One reason for Lopez's success is his appearance. His heartthrob looks—including hair, smile, dimples, and sculpted abdominal muscles—attract much attention, especially from female fans. His talent is also noticed. The senior executive producer of *Extra*, Lisa Gregorisch-Dempsey, told Mary Murphy of the *Hollywood Reporter* that she believed "He's the future of the [entertainment news show] genre." Explaining his appeal, Gregorisch-Dempsey noted, "He is relatable on every level. He has a huge following in the Hispanic community. He is on the cover of every single magazine out there. He is a risk taker. He is disciplined. He has the Midas touch."

## Selected writings

(With Jeff O'Connell) *Mario Lopez's Knockout Fitness*, Rodale Books, 2008.

## Sources

### Books

*Contemporary Theatre, Film and Television*, vol. 71, Gale, 2007, pp. 147-49.

### Periodicals

*Atlanta Journal-Constitution*, November 14, 2006, p. 1E.
*Billboard Radio Monitor*, May 28, 2004.
*Chicago Sun Times*, December 31, 2006, p. 9.
*Daily News* (New York City), March 5, 2008, p. 15; April 15, 2008, p. 29.
*Hollywood Reporter*, April 12, 2002; September 15, 2008, p. 9, p. 11.
*Houston Chronicle*, October 17, 2001, p. 8; December 20, 2004, p. 1; May 29, 2008, p. 2.
*News & Observer* (Raleigh, NC), April 27, 2007, p. WUP29.
*New York Times*, March 19, 1997, p. C18.
*San Diego Union-Tribune*, November 21, 1989, p. C1.
*St. Louis Post-Dispatch*, February 3, 1994, p. 1G.
*Times Union* (Albany, NY), February 3, 1994, p. 8.
*Tulsa World* (OK), March 19, 2006, p. TV47.
*Vancouver Sun* (British Columbia, Canada), October 27, 1992, p. C6.
*Video Business*, March 19, 2001, p. 17.
*Virginian-Pilot* (Norfolk, VA), June 2, 2008, p. E5.
*Washington Post*, May 16, 1993, p. Y48.
*Zaptoit*, June 5, 2008.

### Online

"Biography," MarioLopez.net, http://www.mariolopez.net/bio_NEW.php (January 12, 2009).
"Mario Lopez," Internet Movie Database, http://www.imdb.com/name/nm0530249/ (January 12, 2009).

—A. Petruso

# Olivia Lum

Jonathan Drake/Bloomberg News/Landov

**Founder of Hyflux**

**B**orn in 1961 in Perak State, Malaysia. *Education:* National University of Singapore, B.S. (honors), 1986.

**Addresses:** *Office*—Hyflux Ltd., Hyflux Bldg., 202 Kallang Bahru, Singapore, 339339, Singapore.

## Career

**C**hemist, Glaxo Pharmaceutical, 1986-89; founded Hydrochem, 1989; company name changed to Hyflux; president, chief executive officer, and managing director, Hyflux, 1990s—; appointed member of the parliament of Singapore, 2002-05.

**Member:** Indepedent director, Singapore Exchange, early 2000s-08; board member, SPRING Singapore, 2002-06; president, Singapore Water Association, 2004—; trustee, National University of Singapore; member, UNESCAP Business Advisory Council; member of coordinating committee, Singapore Green Plan 2012.

**Awards:** International Management Action Award, 2003; businessman of the year, Singapore Business Awards, 2004; Global Female Invent and Innovate Award, 2004; corporate executive of the year, *Asiamoney,* 2005; Nikkei Asia Prize for Regional Growth, 2006.

## Sidelights

**O**livia Lum is the founder of Hyflux, an innovative company that develops water-treatment systems to meet the growing global demand. Based in Singapore, Hyflux has become a leader in recycling both wastewater and saltwater in parts of the world where population growth and new industries have taxed conventional water supplies. Lum is regularly hailed as an entrepreneurial visionary for her efforts, but dismisses such accolades. "I had no business plan," she told Justin Doebele in an interview that appeared in *Forbes Global.* "I just knew water was a good business."

Born in 1961 in Malaysia, Lum was abandoned as an infant at a hospital but taken in by an older woman whom she called grandmother. The woman already had four other adopted children at her home in the mining town of Kampar, but lost her house because of gambling debts when Lum was three years old. In an article Lum wrote for the *Electric New Paper,* she recalled that she and her siblings then moved with the woman "into a hut that had bare earth for a floor and zinc sheets above for a roof," and it would regularly flood during Malaysia's rainy season. "The only toilet we had was a common squat pan that was shared by all the villagers; the pan was emptied only once a day."

Lum's grandmother became too frail to hold a job, and Lum was forced to work as a child to help support the family. At her school she sold kaya toast—a local treat made with coconut egg jam—and later in her teens earned such impressive grades that her teachers suggested she move to Singapore, which had a much better educational system than Malaysia's. Heeding their advice, the 15-year-old Lum arrived in the city-state, which is located on the tip of Southeast Asia's Malay peninsula, and entered Singapore's Tiong Bahru Secondary School. She supported herself by working as a tutor and salesperson, and moved on to the prestigious Hwa Chong Junior College. In 1986, she earned her degree, with honors, in chemistry from the National University of Singapore.

Lum's first job after graduation was with Glaxo Pharmaceutical, where she worked as a chemist for three years. In the *Electric New Paper* article, she recounted how the idea to start Hyflux came about, writing that "at Glaxo, I could see how many companies were having difficulties treating their waste water, and how much Glaxo spent to treat the waste water from its plant." In what many of her peers considered an unusual move, Lum quit her job to start her own company. Though Singapore is home to many multinational corporations, or MNCs, the country is not known for its entrepreneurial spirit. "The MNCs crowded out entrepreneurs," Lum explained to *Financial Times* journalist John Burton. "Everybody wanted to join the MNCs because the pay was good and they offered lots of perks. Singaporeans became very spoiled."

Hyflux was originally known as Hydrochem when Lum founded it with start-up funds of $12,000 from the sale of her condominium and car. Her company was originally just a distributor of water filters and treatment chemicals made by other companies, and she was its primary salesperson. Eventually she was able to launch a small research-and-development division that used a relatively new form of membrane technology to design and manufacture proprietary water-treatment systems. Lum even took a class in welding so she could save on some costs. "If you go see the plumbing of the early projects, that's all mine," she told Doebele in the *Forbes Global* profile.

The first major account that Lum landed was for Singapore's bird zoo. She soon renamed her company Hyflux, derived from "a technical term meaning the higher the 'flux' of the membrane, the better its cleaning ability," explained Doebele. Seeing the potential in Asia's rising economic powerhouse, Lum began traveling to China to forge the necessary *guanxi*, or connections, with local officials and business leaders to establish a foothold there, where demand for water-treatment systems was immense. Her fluency in Mandarin Chinese proved a strong advantage for her fledgling company.

Lum took Hyflux public in January of 2001 with an initial public offering of stock on SESDAQ, the Singapore stock exchange. It quickly emerged as a solid performer, and its share price rose further after Lum won a major contract for the first desalination water-treatment plant in Singapore. The $200 million project, which filters sea water for human consumption, was finished in 2005 and is the largest desalination plant in Asia. That same year Hyflux opened an office in Dubai, the Persian Gulf city that is part of the United Arab Emirates. This served as Hyflux's base of operations for two major desalination plants in Algeria it was building, along with a water-treatment facility for Dubai's Palm and World artificial islands, which will be the largest manmade islands in the world.

Lum's company both builds and operates their water-treatment plants. Its competitors include some major global names, such as Suez of France, Siemens, and General Electric (GE), but as Lum explained to Burton in the *Financial Times* article, hers is "a company that focuses on filtration technology, while water treatment is just one part of bigger conglomerates like GE. We are small enough to be nimble and flexible and since we are in Asia, we understand Asian culture."

In 2005, the success of Hyflux gave Lum an estimated personal net worth of $240 million, which made her the only woman to appear on *Forbes* magazine's Southeast Asia Rich List. She serves as chief executive officer, president, and managing director of the 800-employee company, whose 2007 revenues were $139 million, with a majority of that income coming from the 39 plants it operated in China.

Lum's name has been mentioned as a possible future candidate to become the first female prime minister of Singapore. She entered politics in 2002 when she was appointed to serve in the parliament of Singapore for a three-year term. She has noted that since she launched Hyflux, Singapore's business climate had entered a new era. "When I started the business, people would say that I did it because perhaps I didn't do well in school or nobody wanted to hire me," she told Burton in the *Financial Times* interview. "The whole culture discouraged entrepreneurship. But attitudes are changing."

# Sources

## Periodicals

*Financial Times,* November 23, 2005, p. 9.
*Forbes Global,* September 19, 2005, p. 30.
*Time,* April 5, 2004, p. 60.

## Online

"My Humble Story," *Electric New Paper,* http://newpaper.asia1.com.sg/printfriendly/0,4139,132153,00.html (July 6, 2008).

—Carol Brennan

# Patti LuPone

## Actress and singer

**B**orn Patti Ann LuPone, April 21, 1949, in North-port, NY; daughter of Orlando Joseph (a school administrator) and Angela Louise (librarian and library administrator; maiden name, Patti) LuPone; married Matthew Johnston (a cameraman), December 12, 1988; children: Joshua Luke. *Education:* The Juilliard School, B.F.A., 1972.

**Addresses:** *Agent*—International Creative Management, 825 Eighth Ave., New York, NY 10019. *Home*—Litchfield County, Connecticut.

## Career

**A**ctress on stage, including: *The Three Sisters,* Broadway production, 1973, 1975; *The Beggars Opera,* Broadway production, 1973; *Measure for Measure,* Broadway production, 1973; *Scapin,* Broadway production, 1973; *Next Time I'll Sing to You,* Broadway production, 1974; *The Robber Bridegroom,* Broadway production, 1975; *Edward II,* Broadway production, 1975; *The Time of Your Life,* Broadway production, 1975; *The Water Engine,* Broadway production, 1978; *Evita,* Broadway production, 1980; *Oliver!,* Broadway production, 1984; *Les Misérables,* London production, 1985; *The Cradle Will Rock,* London production, c. 1985; *Anything Goes,* Broadway production, 1987; *Company,* Broadway production, 1993; *Sunset Boulevard,* London production, 1993; *Master Class,* Broadway production, 1995; *The Old Neighborhood,* Broadway production, 1997; *Noises Off,* Broadway production, 2001; *Anything Goes,* Broadway production, 2002; *Children & Art,* Broadway production, 2005; *Sweeney Todd,* Broadway production, 2005; *Gypsy,* Encore! Summer Stars Series

production, New York City, 2007, then Broadway production, 2008—. Film appearances include: *King of the Gypsies,* 1978; *1941,* 1979; *Fighting Back,* 1982; *Witness,* 1985; *Wise Guys,* 1986; *Driving Miss Daisy,* 1989; *Family Prayers,* 1993; *The 24 Hour Woman,* 1999; *Bad Faith,* 1999; *Just Looking,* 1999; *Summer of Sam,* 1999; *State and Main,* 2000; *The Victim,* 2001; *Heist,* 2001; *City by the Sea,* 2002. Television appearances include: *LBJ* (miniseries), 1987; *Life Goes On,* 1989-93; *Frasier,* NBC, 1993, 1998; *The Song Spinner* (special), 1995; *Falcone,* 2000; *Sweeney Todd* (special), PBS, 2001; *Oz,* HBO, 2003; *Ugly Betty,* ABC, 2007.

**Awards:** Antoinette Perry Award for best actress (musical), for *Evita,* 1980; Drama Desk Award for outstanding actress in a musical, for *Evita,* 1980; Laurence Olivier Award for best actress in a musical, for *Les Misérables* and *The Cradle Will Rock,* 1985; Drama Desk Award for outstanding actress in a musical, for *Anything Goes,* 1987; Outer Critics Circle Award for outstanding solo performance, for *Patti LuPone on Broadway,* 1995-96; National Board of Review Award for best acting by an ensemble (with others), for *State and Main,* 2000; Florida Film Critics Circle Award for best ensemble cast (with others), *State and Main,* 2001; Online Film Critics Society Award for best ensemble cast performance (with others), for *State and Main,* 2001; John Houseman Award, 2006; named to the Theatre Hall of Fame,

2007; Antoinette Perry Award for best actress in a musical, for *Gypsy*, 2008; Drama Desk Award for outstanding actress in a musical, for *Gypsy*, 2008.

## Sidelights

While Patti LuPone is best known as a stage actress who won Tony Awards for her work in *Evita* and *Gypsy* as well as creating the role of Norma Desmond in the London production of *Sunset Boulevard*, the American actress has had a varied career which includes roles in stage dramas, films, and television. An accomplished singer with a strong soprano voice, she has also released a number of albums featuring a variety of sounds, including 2001's *Matter of the Heart*. As David Sacks of the *New York Times* wrote of LuPone, "she is a born performer, extroverted, impetuous. And mischievous— you sense in her a wayward enthusiasm that can hardly be contained."

Born in 1949 in Northport, New York, she is the daughter of Orlando and Angela LuPone. Her father was a school administrator, while her mother was a librarian and college library administrator. As a young child, LuPone was disobedient, but found a calling in the dance training she received. As a four-year-old in her first tap recital, she became hooked on performing. After her parents divorced in the early 1960s, LuPone took various music lessons as well. During that decade LuPone was part of a family singing group, The LuPone Trio. In addition to LuPone, the group consisted of her older twin brothers William and Robert. (Robert LuPone later became an acclaimed stage actor in his own right.) Of her early attitude, Robert LuPone told Sacks of the *New York Times*, "She was rebellious. She would be climbing out the window at 3 A.M. to sing and dance down the middle of Main Street."

After graduating from Northport High School, LuPone entered the drama division of Juilliard in 1968. She was a member of the very first class of the division with such classmates as Kevin Kline and Mandy Patinkin. All were taught by legendary teacher and actor John Houseman. As a student, LuPone was known for one particular skill. She later told Leslie Bennetts of the *New York Times*, "I used to be called 'Melancholy Baby' at Juilliard, because I could cry really easily; if they needed somebody who could emote, I got cast in the part." Upon graduation in 1972, Houseman formed The Acting Company with members of the class. LuPone performed with the group between 1972 and 1975. They put on classic plays by Anton Chekhov and William Shakespeare and toured the country. In 1976, LuPone was nominated for her first Tony Award as best actress in a featured role in a musical for the 1975 production of the musical comedy *The Robber Bridegroom*.

While LuPone was gaining a reputation as a strong singer and actress on stage, it was not until 1979 that she became a star. That year, she landed the lead, Eva Perone, in the Andrew Lloyd Weber musical, *Evita*. In 1980, LuPone won a Tony Award for her performance. After *Evita*, LuPone's major roles were in regional theater productions around the United States, Off Broadway jobs, and the occasional film like 1982's box-office bomb *Fighting Back*. She felt she had no choice, telling Bennetts of the *New York Times*, "Nothing happened after that [*Evita*]. So I went back to my roots, right back into regional and Off Broadway theater. I was in many ways rapped for doing that. 'What's Evita doing here? Why is she taking Off Broadway jobs?' You're supposed to top yourself, to go into an even bigger Broadway musical. But I chose to go to places where I wasn't in the New York eye, and I continued to work."

LuPone also went abroad, performing in London in the mid-1980s. In addition to working with the Royal Shakespeare Company, LuPone played Fantine in the London production of *Les Misérables*. Her performances in the London productions of *Les Misérables* and the leftist musical *The Cradle Will Rock* earned her an Olivier Award as best actress in a musical in 1985. LuPone was the first American actress to win this award. A year later, she was appearing on television, playing Lady Bird Johnson in the movie *LBJ: The Early Years*. She met her future husband, cameraman Matthew Johnston, on the production. LuPone also appeared in two films in this time period, playing small roles in 1985's *Witness* and 1986's *Wise Guys*.

By 1987, LuPone was back on Broadway. She had a Tony Award-nominated turn that year for best actress in a musical for the revival of the musical comedy, *Anything Goes*. LuPone played Reno Sweeney, a nightclub singer in the 1930s, to rave reviews. In addition to tap dancing and performing the tango, she showed off her vocal skills by singing Cole Porter songs. Within a few years, LuPone's career took a new direction.

An economic recession in the late 1980s and early 1990s, which negatively affected the amount of productions being put on in New York City, as well as the birth of her son in 1990, made a steady job on television appealing. She told Hilary De Vries of the *New York Times*, "Today you look at a good script no matter where it comes from. And there are more roles for women in television than there are in film." She and her family moved to Los Angeles to pursue such roles.

In 1989, LuPone landed a part on a television drama, *Life Goes On*. She played Libby Thacher, a middle class mother of three, including a son with

Down syndrome. The show aired for several seasons. LuPone found the experience challenging, telling the *New York Times'* De Vries, "The only difference I can discern is energy. Once the curtain goes up on stage, it is relentless. Doing episodic television without a studio audience is very similar to a long technical dress rehearsal. It's a lot of stop and go."

While appearing on *Life Goes On* into the early 1990s, LuPone performed only occasionally on stage. Most of her stage performances in this time period were concerts and cabaret acts in which she showed off her vocal prowess primarily with songs from her stage hits. In 1993, LuPone returned to the stage by nabbing the role of Norma Desmond in Andrew Lloyd Webber's new musical adaptation *Sunset Boulevard.* She created the role in the London production to much acclaim. Later that year, LuPone also released her first solo album, *Patti LuPone Live.*

After the critical kudos LuPone received for the London version of *Sunset Boulevard,* Lloyd Webber's production company, Really Useful Group, promised her the role when the show moved to Broadway. However, actress Glenn Close was given the role and she received raves for her version of Desmond in the Los Angeles production. When it was announced that Close would take the role, LuPone left the London production in March of 1994 and threatened a lawsuit. Though the case never made its way to court, Lloyd Webber's company and LuPone reached a settlement which was believed to involve a substantial amount of money. Later that year, LuPone faced further challenges when she had to have surgery to remove nodes from her vocal cords.

In the mid- to late 1990s, LuPone worked sporadically in stage, television, and film roles. Moving away from musical theater, she was lauded for her work as Callas in the Terrence McNally drama *Master Class* at New York City's Golden Theatre in 1996. That same year, LuPone was nominated for a Daytime Emmy Award for outstanding performer in a children's special for the 1995 special *The Song Spinner.* In 1998, she was nominated for an Emmy Award for her guest turn on *Frasier,* playing Aunt Zora in the episode "Beware of Greeks." LuPone also won multiple awards for her work in the 2000 film *State and Main.* In addition, she appeared in four other films, including *Summer of Sam* and *Bad Faith.*

Returning to the stage in the early 2000s, LuPone toured the United States in her one-woman shows *Matters of the Heart* and *Coulda, Woulda, Shoulda.* The

former was a scripted solo concert, while the latter was a one-woman musical theater revue of roles she wished she could play. In 2000, LuPone appeared in a staged concert version of *Sweeney Todd* with the New York Philharmonic, which was critically acclaimed and taped for a popular PBS special.

After a well-received turn in the Broadway revival of *Noises Off* in 2001, LuPone appeared in several opera productions, including *Regina* at the Kennedy Center in 2005. That same year, she began playing Mrs. Lovett in the Broadway revival of *Sweeney Todd, the Demon Barber of Fleet Street* to similar critical acclaim. By now well known for her intense work ethic as well as an outsized, if not demanding, personality, Michael Cerveris, her *Sweeney Todd* co-star, told Jesse Green of the *New York Times,* "She's more than capable of living up to every story you hear about her, outrageous as well as courageous. A night out with her is not for the faint-hearted. Neither is squaring off with her onstage, and I mean that as a compliment."

While LuPone's work in *Sweeney Todd* was well received and led to talk of Tonys, she had an even better critical response to her award-winning turn as Mama Rose in the Broadway revival of *Gypsy* in 2008. The show began as part the Summer Stars series at Encores! in 2007 before moving to Broadway the next year. Reviewing the production as well as LuPone's work in the role of Gypsy Rose Lee, Christopher Rawson of the *Pittsburgh Post-Gazette* commented, "It's a breathtaking performance, especially admirable in LuPone's willingness to embrace Rose's mendacity, manipulation and obsession." In the *Los Angeles Times,* Charles McNulty concurred, noting "a Broadway tour de force that will go down as one of the great incarnations of that greatest of musical theater roles." LuPone won several major awards for her performance as Rose, including a Tony Award.

In addition to turning in award-winning turns on Broadway, LuPone continued to tour in her own solo shows and put in guest appearances on such hit television shows as HBO's *Oz* and ABC's *Ugly Betty.* No matter what happened in LuPone's career, she was ready to take on nearly any role that came her way. LuPone told Elysa Gardner of *USA Today,* "I think every actor is capable of developing all aspects of themselves. What happened to me is that, when I studied at Juilliard, they tried to throw me out of school by throwing every conceivable role in my direction, so that I would fail. What they did, unintentionally, was to train one versatile actor. I came out with an understanding of and ability to play a variety of parts—and I've never looked back."

## Selected discography

(With others) *Evita* (original Broadway cast recording), MCA, 1979.

(With others) *Les Misérables,* First Night Records, 1985.

(With others) *Anything Goes,* RCA, 1988.

*Patti LuPone Live,* RCA, 1993.

*Heatwave: Patti LuPone Sings Irving Berlin,* Philips, 1995.

*Matters of the Heart,* LayZLay, 1999.

*The Lady with the Torch,* Sh-K-Boom Records, 2006.

(With others) *Gypsy* (2008 original cast recording), Time Life, 2008.

*Patti LuPone at Les Mouches,* Ghostlight Records, 2008.

## Sources

### Periodicals

Associated Press, August 18, 2008.

*Buffalo News* (NY), February 15, 2002, p. G20.

*Chicago Sun-Times,* August 29, 2001, p. 43; August 6, 2006, p. D15.

*Columbus Dispatch* (Columbus, OH), May 17, 1992, p. 1C.

*Daily Mail* (London, England), May 17, 1994, p. 15.

*Daily News* (NY), July 26, 1996, p. 53; June 16, 2008, p. 3.

*Evening Standard* (London, England), May 7, 1993, pp. 26-27.

*Los Angeles Times,* June 15, 2008, p. F1.

*New York Magazine,* May 26, 2008.

*New York Times,* October 22, 1987, p. C21; January 24, 1988, sec. 6, p. 22; January 19, 1992, sec. 2, p. 31; July 8, 2007, p. AR1.

*Pittsburgh Post-Gazette* (PA), May 4, 2008, p. E3.

*USA Today,* July 7, 1993, p. 8D; November 13, 2001, p. 2D.

*Washington Post,* June 28, 1992, p. Y5.

### Online

"Patti LuPone," Internet Movie Database, http://www.imdb.com/name/nm0526985/ (October 27, 2008).

—*A. Petruso*

# Heidi Manheimer

## Chief Executive Officer of Shiseido Americas

**B**orn July 7, 1963, in New Jersey. *Education:* Ithaca College, Ithaca, New York, 1985.

**Addresses:** *Office*—Shiseido Americas Corp., 900 Third Avenue, 15th Fl., New York, NY 10022. *Web site*—http://www.sca.shiseido.com/.

## Career

**V**arious management positions, including buyer, Bloomingdale's, mid-1980s-early 1990s; manager, Barneys New York, early 1990s; vice president and divisional merchandise manager of Cosmetics, Fragrances and Apothecary, Barneys New York, 1999; vice president of strategy, bluemercury inc., 1999; general manager and vice president, Beauty.com, 2000; executive vice president/general manager, Prestige Cosmetics division, Shiseido Cosmetics (America) Ltd., 2000-02; president, U.S. Operations, Shiseido Cosmetics (America) Ltd., 2002-06; CEO, Shiseido Cosmetics (America) Ltd., 2006-09; CEO, Shiseido Americas Corp., 2009—.

## Sidelights

**W**hen Heidi Manheimer was named chief executive officer of Shiseido Cosmetics (America) Ltd. in 2006, she became the first female and first non-Asian CEO in the Japanese company's 133-year history. Apothecary executive Ian Ginsberg of C.O. Bigelow told *Crain's New York Business* that hiring Manheimer to lead Shiseido's U.S. division was a good choice. "Foreign companies sometimes think

they understand this marketplace when they don't. To take somebody like Heidi, a brilliant merchant—that's a smart move for Shiseido." Turns out, Ginsberg was correct. Since joining Shiseido, Manheimer has successfully increased the company's prominence in the U.S. beauty market. Shiseido's 2008 annual report noted that stateside sales increased 7.7 percent compared to the previous fiscal year.

Manheimer was born on July 7, 1963, in New Jersey. Her mother was a stay-at-home mom who devoted her energy to caring for Manheimer and her two sisters. Manheimer's father worked in retail management. She grew up in West Orange, New Jersey. During high school, Manheimer took a part-time weekend job at the Bloomingdale's department store in Short Hills, New Jersey. She worked as a "floater," meaning she traveled from department to department. She sold sweaters, shoes, and food but asked her boss if she could avoid the cosmetics counter because it made her anxious.

In 1985, Manheimer graduated from Ithaca College in Upstate New York with a degree in business management and was soon accepted into Bloomingdale's executive training program. Right off, she was sent to cosmetics and requested a transfer. Manheimer was told to give it a few weeks and soon found she loved it. Speaking to *womensbiz.us,* Manheimer said that early experience behind the cosmetics counter paved the way for her future success. "You learn everything there—product development, selling skills, people skills, and how to relate to the customer. Your job is to come up with solutions that satisfy both the customer and your company."

Eventually, Manheimer became a buyer for Bloomingdale's, and in the early 1990s she moved to the high-fashion chain Barneys New York. She moved up the ladder quickly and became vice president and divisional merchandise manager of the company's Cosmetics, Fragrances and Apothecary department. During her time with Barneys, Manheimer launched new cosmetics departments at the retailer's flagship stores in New York City and Beverly Hills. She also developed the company's first beauty catalog, called the "How Do I Look Book."

In 1999, Manheimer left the department store world to work at a Web-based cosmetics startup called bluemercury inc. Though bluemercury had two retail outlets to test products, it was primarily an E-tailer that sold lotions, soaps, cosmetics, and other beauty supplies. At bluemercury, Manheimer was charged with locating new product lines. The venture was short-lived, and in 2000, Manheimer joined Beauty.com as a vice president and general manager.

By the end of 2000, Manheimer had joined Shiseido as executive vice president and general manager of the company's Prestige Cosmetics division. Shiseido executives courted Manheimer for nine months trying to get her to accept the position. Initially, Manheimer was skeptical that she could be successful at a company where she did not speak the language or grasp the cultural customs. Speaking to the *New York Times,* Manheimer said she was "nervous about the culture and language barrier."

Founded in 1872, Shiseido (pronounced she-SAY-doe) is recognized as the world's oldest cosmetics company. By early 2000, Shiseido products were sold in 70 countries. By 2005, its product lines could be found in some 850 department and specialty stores across the United States. Shiseido sold product lines under several names, including Pureness, Benefiance, White Lucent, and Bio-Performance. Besides running the Prestige Cosmetics division, Manheimer was placed in charge of sales, marketing and advertising for the company's Shiseido, Qiora, and Clé de Peau brands. In 2002, Shiseido named Manheimer president of U.S. Operations.

In 2006, the Shiseido board of directors promoted Manheimer to CEO of Shiseido Cosmetics (America) Ltd. Shiseido executive Shinzo Maeda told the *WWD*'s Matthew W. Evans that Manheimer's promotion was made "in recognition of her contributions to the company's growth over the past five years in the competitive U.S. marketplace." The numbers tell an amazing story. In 2000, when Manheimer joined Shiseido, U.S. sales sat at $150 million. In 2005, they hit $200 million.

Manheimer's success came with a steep learning curve because the Asian-based business operated differently from the U.S. corporations with which she was familiar. For example, Manheimer discovered that decisions were not made during meetings. At Shiseido, managers held meetings to dispense information. Real decisions were made in the hallway, over coffee, at dinners, or during karaoke outings. "In the beginning, I skipped dinner and karaoke often because I was so exhausted, but not after I learned that's where things get done," she told the *New York Times.*

Under Manheimer's direction, Shiseido's U.S. market share continued to grow through the 2000s. By 2007, Shiseido's skin-care products had captured the number-four spot in the market. In 2008, Shiseido began consolidating several divisions, including Nars Cosmetics Inc., the ZIC Corp., and Shiseido Cosmetics (America) Ltd., which was Manheimer's division. The three divisions merged and were renamed the Shiseido Americas Corp. Manheimer was named CEO of the new consolidated division.

Never married, Manheimer has been able to focus her life on her career. Her goal for the future is to continue growing Shiseido's U.S. customer base. "Our vision is to be in the top three in skin care," Manheimer is quoted as saying by Jenny B. Fine for *WWD.* "My hope overall is to really raise the brand awareness for Shiseido. [When] you go to Tokyo, everyone knows the word Shiseido, and everyone understands that it's high quality, high image, high service. Everyone knows the deep heritage and culture of Shiseido, and I'd love for that to happen in the U.S."

## Sources

### Periodicals

*Brandweek,* October 23, 2000.
Business Wire, September 24, 1999.
*Crain's New York Business,* January 9, 2006, p. 25.
*New York Times,* March 2, 2008, p. BU15.
*WWD,* November 22, 2005, p. 2; May 18, 2007, p. 50.

### Online

"Profiles: Heidi Manheimer Puts On a Shiseido Face," *womensbiz.us,* http://womensbiz.us/archives/profiles0605.asp (February 24, 2009).
"Shiseido Annual Report 2008," Shiseido Co. Ltd., http://www.shiseido.co.jp/e/ir/annual/e0806anu/img/anu00001.pdf (February 16, 2009).

*—Lisa Frick*

# Mary Mary

## Gospel duo

Group formed c. 1998, in Inglewood, CA; members include Erica Campbell (born Erica Monique Atkins, April 29, 1972; daughter of Eddie (a postal worker and youth minister) and Thomasina (a choir director and homemaker) Atkins; married Warryn Campbell, a music producer, May 26, 2001; children: Krista Nicole), singer; Tina Campbell (born Trecina Evette Atkins, May 1, 1974; daughter of Eddie (a postal worker and youth minister) and Thomasina (a choir director and homemaker) Atkins; married Teddy Campbell, a drummer, August 2000; children: Laiah Simone, Meela Jane), singer.

**Addresses:** *Record company*—Columbia, 550 Madison Ave., 6th Fl., New York, NY 10022. *Web site*—http://www.mary-mary.com/.

## Career

Erica and Tina Campbell began singing in church choirs as children; duo and other siblings appeared on BET's *Bobby Jones Gospel Show*; each sister worked as a back-up singer for R&B artists as early adults: Erica sang up back-up for Brian McKnight, Brandy, and Terry Ellis, and Tina sang back up for Kenny Lattimore and Eric Bent; the duo toured in musicals, *Mama I'm Sorry*, 1995, and *Sneaky*; the duo signed a publishing deal and wrote songs for other artists; formed Mary Mary, c. 1998; signed a recording deal with Columbia/C2, 1999; released debut album, *Thankful*, 2000; released second album, *Incredible*, 2002; released Christmas album, *A Mary Mary Christmas*, 2006; served as executive producers of *Sunday Best*, BET, c. 2008; announced plans for BE U product line, 2008; released album *The Sound*, 2008; BE U products appeared in Wal-Mart stores, 2009.

**Awards:** Grammy Award for best contemporary soul gospel album, Recording Academy, for *Thankful*, 2000; Stellar Gospel Music Award for new artist of the year, Gospel Music Channel, 2001; Stellar Gospel Music Award for contemporary CD of the year, Gospel Music Channel, for *Thankful*, 2001; Stellar Gospel Music Award for group/duo of the year, Gospel Music Channel, 2001; Stellar Gospel Music Award for contemporary group/duo, Gospel Music Channel, 2001; American Music Award for contemporary inspirational music, American Broadcasting Company, 2005; Grammy Award for best gospel performance, Recording Academy, for "Get Up," 2008.

## Sidelights

Comprised of sisters Erica and Tina Campbell, the award-winning gospel duo Mary Mary has become the vanguard of the contemporary popular gospel movement and perhaps the most popular gospel act in the world in the early 2000s. They have had great commercial success with their ability to crossover to R&B, urban, and pop audiences because their songs are both uplifting and accessible and their look hip and current. Named after the two prominent Marys in the Bible (Mary, mother of Jesus, and Mary Magdalene), the sisters were greatly influenced by other gospel stars, including the Clark Sisters, the Winans, and Shirley Caesar.

Some journalists called Mary Mary "a more spiritual Destiny's Child" as Anastasia Pantsios wrote in the Cleveland *Plain Dealer Friday Magazine*. The duo hoped to greatly influence their audience as well. Erica Campbell told *Ebony*, "We want people to know that it's okay to listen to gospel music. It's OK to say, 'I love God and I have faith, and I try to let that lead and guide my life and still be young, still look funky, still be just as regular as everyone else in life.'"

The sisters were born into a Pentecostal family where music was important. They were the daughters of Eddie and Thomasina Atkins, who also had five more daughters and a son, whom they raised in Inglewood, California. Her father was a postal worker and youth minister at the Evangelistic Church of God in Christ, while her mother was a homemaker and choir director at the church. Both parents also enjoyed singing, especially gospel, and music was often found throughout the house.

However, the family struggled financially. Tina Campbell told John Aizlewood of the London *Guardian*, "We lived on faith. Looking back, it's hard to see how we didn't become homeless. Each year our parents were $7,000 short of what was needed and just had to trust God. We ate noodles every day, so we never went hungry. We didn't know we were poor because we had so much love and faith. We had a lot of fun, too. The church was our recreational center."

All seven sisters soon began singing in their church in Inglewood (their brother lacked vocal skills) and were not allowed to listen to secular music, but came into contact with hip-hop, rap, and such artists as Michael Jackson and Whitney Houston elsewhere. Erica Campbell told Virginia Norton of the *Augusta Chronicle*, "We heard secular artists at school, but that music had a lot of sexual content that my mind wasn't ready to process. Sex music makes you curious, and before you know it, it makes you want to try it."

As youths, Erica and Tina appeared with other members of their family on BET's *Bobby Jones Gospel Show*. As they reached adulthood, the sisters began working separately as back-up singers to primarily R&B artists. Erica Campbell backed up Brian McKnight, Brandy, and Terry Ellis, while her sister performed with Kenny Lattimore and Eric Bent. By 1995, the sisters were touring in traveling gospel musicals put together by Michael Matthews. The first, titled *Mama I'm Sorry*, was so successful that the siblings appeared in another Matthews tour, *Sneaky*.

While appearing in up to eight performances per week on the Matthews musicals and learning how to be professionals, they were writing gospel songs on the side. Their career was helped along by music producer Warryn "Baby Dubb" Campbell, whom they met during their tour with *Mama I'm Sorry*. Campbell eventually got them signed to a song publishing deal. Erica also became romantically involved with Campbell, and married him in 2000.

The sisters had their first major break in 1998 when they wrote and performed a song with Robin S., "Dance," which was used on the *Dr. Doolittle* soundtrack. Also in 1998, another of their songs, "Let Go, Let God," appeared on the *The Prince of Egypt—Inspiration* soundtrack which accompanied the animated film. These two tracks were produced by Campbell. Other songs written by the sisters were recorded by artists such as Yolanda Adams ("Time to Change" and "Yeah") and 702 ("What More Can He Do").

Forming their own group under the moniker Mary Mary, the sisters signed a recording contract with Columbia/C2 Records in 1999 and were, at the time, the only gospel group on the label. Early in their career the sisters felt like outcasts. Tina Campbell told the *Guardian*'s Aizlewood, "We were shunned initially because we weren't doing drugs. Any time a young girl says, 'I love my life, I love myself, but I'm not going to party and sleep around, I'm going to let God lead my life and try to live morally right,' she's an outcast. If she drinks, smokes and sleeps around, if she doesn't wear any clothes, disrespects her parents, doesn't go to school and rebels, she's on the front page of everything. It's so weird."

Despite such sentiments, Mary Mary soon had a hit single with "Shackles (Praise You)," which was both an R&B and a mainstream pop hit in both Britain and the United States. The duo released their first album in 2000, *Thankful*, which was produced by Campbell and featured "Shackles." The sisters co-wrote all the songs on the album save two: the traditional "Wade in the Water" and another track, "Be Happy." *Thankful* was a smash among Christian audiences, particularly those who were looking for a hipper gospel sound that appealed to their sensibilities. It reached number one on the *Billboard* top contemporary Christian and top gospel album charts.

Reaching beyond the traditional gospel audience was the goal, according to Erica Campbell. She told David Nathan in *Billboard*, "Our music is so hip-hop and has an urban feel. But the songs we write tell the message of Christ specifically. We're coming up behind a lot of great artists like Kirk Franklin and Yolanda Adams. We want to reinforce what they've already delivered and take it one step further." She added, "Our music is for everybody. It's especially for the people who may not come to church. That's who we want to reach."

Critics responded positively to Mary Mary's pop/R&B sound and Christian-centered lyrics. In the *Seattle Times,* J. D. Considine wrote "Mary Mary's *Thankful* (Columbia/C2) sounds like an R&B album that just happens to mention Jesus a lot." Considine concluded, "No doubt, there are some in the sacred music world who will sniff that Mary Mary is too worldly to be praised as a bona-fide gospel group. But judging from the sound of *Thankful,* this duo isn't interested in preaching to the converted, and that makes the album a revelation, indeed." The album won Mary Mary numerous award nominations and several awards, including four Stellar Gospel Music Awards.

As Mary Mary gained popularity, the sisters hoped to affect real change to modern gospel, if not people's lives, with their music. Erica Campbell told *Ebony,* "I hope that we will change the face of gospel music, change the misconceptions that gospel music has to be sad and boring. Hopefully, ten years from now everyone will be listening to positive music, and giving God praise." Mary Mary worked toward this goal with every album and found each became more popular than the last.

For example, in 2002, Mary Mary released *Incredible,* which was another smash crossover hit. The album again featured songs primarily written by the sisters themselves. Like *Thankful, Incredible* also reached number one on the *Billboard* top contemporary Christian and top gospel album charts. The single "In the Morning" was also a hit.

Like many listeners, critics embraced *Incredible* as well as the sisters' talents as vocalists. In the *New York Times,* Ben Ratliff claimed the duo "has the perfect name" because it invokes "old school, new school, and Sunday school." He also praised, "They're gifted singers, divebombing around one another's voices in intuitive patterns." Another critic, *Billboard* gospel columnist Lisa Collins, told the *Grand Rapids Press,* "It's got people dancing, and it kind of enveloped the youth spirit that has taken form in gospel over the last decade. Gospel is kind of a hip thing now."

After the release of *Incredible,* the sisters took several years off to start families. Tina married Teddy Campbell in 2000, and gave birth to Laiah Simone

in 2003. Erica Campbell had a daughter as well Krista. In 2005, the duo returned to recording an released *Mary Mary,* their third album. More popu lar than the first two albums, the album not onl reached number one on the *Billboard* top contempo rary Christian and top gospel album charts but als went as high as eighth on the *Billboard* top 200 al bum charts and number four among the top R&B Hip-Hop albums. The singles "Heaven" and "Yes terday" were also hits.

The duo then released a Christmas album in 200 *A Mary Mary Christmas.* The record featured classic such as "(Have Yourself A) Merry Little Christmas and "Hark the Herald Angels Sing" done with har monies and an R&B style. The popular albun reached number two on the top gospel albums char in *Billboard* magazine.

By 2008, Mary Mary had also expanded into othe business ventures. They served as executive pro ducers of the BET show *Sunday Best,* which was a *American Idol*-style competition for aspiring gospe artists. The pair also announced plans for launchin a line of bath, body, and candle products titled B U (which went on sale at Wal-Mart in 2009) as we as children's books and an album of children' music. In addition, they founded the Paint A Smil Foundation.

Also in 2008, Mary Mary released another ful length album, *The Sound,* which was able to cross over from gospel and Christian audiences to a mair stream pop audience. While reaching the expecte number one on the top Christian and top gospel a bum charts in *Billboard,* it also was number two o the top R&B/Hip-Hop album charts as well as num ber seven on the *Billboard* top 200. The album als won a Grammy award for the single "Get Up." Thi crossover smash had appeal for gospel, urban adu contemporary, R&B, and hip-hop audiences as we as club goers.

No matter how successful Mary Mary become, th sisters were determined to keep their feet on th ground. Erica Campbell told Aizlewood of th *Guardian,* "I still pick up my own bags and was my clothes. Our music isn't a gimmick, and it isn just for me and my kind. It's for anyone who want to be uplifted and motivated. It reflects the area i which we grew up and our faith. Any talent is gift from God. So if I ever start to believe the hyp I'll leave the business."

## Selected discography

*Thankful,* Columbia, 2000.
*Incredible,* Columbia, 2002.
*Mary Mary,* Sony Urban Music/Columbia, 2005.

*A Mary Mary Christmas*, Sony, 2006.
*The Sound*, Columbia, 2008.

# Sources

## Periodicals

*Augusta Chronicle* (GA), September 9, 2000, p. C1.
*Billboard,* March 11, 2000; January 27, 2001; July 16, 2005; October 18, 2008.
*Ebony,* September 2000, p. 100; December 2006, p. 50; Ebony, August 2008, p. 122.
*Grand Rapids Press* (MI), September 11, 2002, p. B9; April 27, 2006, p. 5.
*Guardian* (London, England), July 29, 2002, sec. G2, p. 10.
*Jet,* September 23, 2002, p. 19.
*New York Times,* July 21, 2002, sec. 2, p. 23.
*Plain Dealer Friday Magazine* (Cleveland, OH), October 12, 2001, p. 23.
PR Newswire, November 1, 2008.

*Seattle Times,* May 11, 2000, p. G3.
*Today's Christian Woman,* March-April 2009, p. 22.
*USA Today,* January 12, 2001, p. 8E.
*Women's Health Weekly,* April 9, 2009, p. 410.

## Online

"Erica Atkins," Internet Movie Database, http://www.imdb.com/name/nm0040590/ (April 22, 2009).
"Grammy Award Winners," Grammy.com http://www.grammy.com/GRAMMY_Awards/Winners/ (April 22, 2009).
"Mary Mary: Biography," allmusic, http://www.allmusic.com/cg/amg.dll?p=amg&sql=11:3cftxqygldhe~T1 (April 22, 2009).
"Tina Atkins," Internet Movie Database, http://www.imdb.com/name/nm1921100/ (April 22, 2009).

—*A. Petruso*

# Ma Ying-jeou

*AP Images*

## President of Taiwan

**B**orn July 13, 1950, in Hong Kong, China; son of Ma Ho-ling (a government official and Kuomintang party member) and Chin Hou-hsiu (a civil servant); married Chow Mei-ching, 1977; children: Ma Wei-chung, Ma Yuan-chung (both daughters). *Education:* National Taiwan University, L.L.B., 1972; New York University, L.L.M., 1976; Harvard Law School, S.J.D., 1981.

**Addresses:** *Office*—122, Chongcing S. Rd., Sec. 1, Taipei, Taiwan, R.O.C. *Web site*—http://www.president.gov.tw/en.

## Career

**L**egal consultant, First National Bank of Boston, 1980-81; research consultant, University of Maryland School of Law, 1981; associate lawyer, Cole and Delts, 1981; deputy director-general, first bureau, office of the president of Taiwan, 1981-88; named deputy secretary-general of the central committee of the Kuomintang, 1984; Taiwanese minister of the Research, Development and Evaluation Commission, 1988-91; deputy minister of Mainland Affairs Council, 1991-93; minister of justice, 1993-96; minister without portfolio, 1996-97; associate professor of law, National Chengchi University, 1998; mayor of Taipei, 1998-2006; chairman of Kuomintang, 2005-07; president of Taiwan, 2008—.

## Sidelights

**M**a Ying-jeou, the president of Taiwan, was elected in 2008 on the strength of a potentially historic promise: After 60 years of conflict, he wants Taiwan to forge closer ties with its estranged neighbor, communist China. The charismatic and highly educated Ma played a role in transforming Taiwan's longtime ruling Nationalist party from an authoritarian institution to a more open and moderate one. His eight years as mayor of Taipei, Taiwan's capital city, gave him a reputation as a skilled leader with fresh ideas. Successfully fighting off a corruption charge, Ma ran for president, promising to increase Taiwan's economic prosperity by pursuing trade and an eventual peace accord with China.

Ma's approach was once unthinkable in Taiwan, which has been locked in an ambiguous conflict with mainland China since the 1949 Communist revolution. The Nationalists fled to Taiwan, an island of about 20 million people off the Chinese coast, after losing the civil war to the Communists. China's government, based in Beijing, considers Taiwan a breakaway province. But the Taiwan government, officially known as the Republic of China, insists it is a sovereign country and the legal continuation of the government that ruled most of China from 1912 to 1949. Many countries do not give Taiwan diplomatic recognition, seeing the Beijing government as China's official leaders. Even Taiwan is careful not to officially declare independence from China.

The story of Ma's life and family history mirrors Taiwan's in many ways, from the exodus after the revolution to decades of one-party rule to the contemporary tumultuous modern democracy. Ma was born on July 13, 1950, in Hong Kong. His parents, who had fled mainland China in the wake of the Communist revolution, settled in Taiwan a year after Ma was born. His father, Ma Ho-ling, had fought in China's war with Japan (which started in 1937 and became part of World War II). After the wars, he served in various positions in the government in Taiwan and in the ruling party. Ma's mother, Chin Hou-hsiu, worked for the government as a civil servant.

The elder Ma was a taskmaster, instilling discipline in his son by insisting that he study classic Chinese literature and master the art of Chinese calligraphy. In 1972, Ma Ying-jeou graduated from National Taiwan University, Taiwan's premier college, with a bachelor's degree in law. He moved to the United States to study and received a master of law degree from New York University in 1976 and a doctor of judicial science degree from Harvard Law School in 1981. He worked for a short time in legal jobs in the United States, then returned home to work for the president of Taiwan, Chiang Ching-Kuo.

Ma's job was prestigious: he served as the president's English interpreter and secretary. Following his father's lead, Ma also became involved in the Kuomintang party, also known as the Nationalists, serving as deputy secretary-general of its central committee starting in 1984. At the time, Taiwan was essentially a one-party state under military rule. But in 1986, the president gave Ma a momentous assignment: He asked him to research the possibility of ending martial law, reforming the parliament, and allowing Taiwanese to visit relatives in mainland China. In October of 1986, with Ma translating, Chiang told Katherine Graham of the *Washington Post* that he would lift martial law and end a ban on forming new political parties. It was a major step in Taiwan's road to democracy. When Chiang died in 1988, Ma spoke to reporters from Western nations, reaffirming that reforms would continue. "We believe the time has come for us to move to high gear, to move toward a more advanced stage of constitutional democracy," he said, according to Clyde Haberman of the *New York Times.*

During the 1980s and early 1990s, Ma served on several government and party boards and committees. In 1993, Ma was appointed Taiwan's minister of justice. He launched several reforms, including crackdowns on corruption, vote-buying, drugs, and organized crime. He became minister without portfolio in 1996, then resigned from the government in 1997. Accounts differ as to why. His own official biography suggests that his reputation as a tough law-enforcer was wounded in 1997 by a series of terrible crimes, including the kidnapping and murder of the daughter of a well-known Taiwanese entertainer, and that Ma resigned to take responsibility for failures of justice in the cases. However, a profile in the *New York Times* suggests that Ma lost his job because his staff aggressively investigated members of his own political party, which had a long history of corruption and wielding unchallenged power.

After a year teaching law, Ma ran for mayor of Taipei, Taiwan's capital, pitching himself as a talented government administrator and promising a fresh approach to governing. Ma won the 1998 election with 51 percent of the vote, unseating the incumbent mayor, Chen Shui-ban. The two men would become archrivals. Chen, a prominent figure in the main opposition party, the Democratic Progressives, ran for president two years later and won in an upset, unseating the Nationalist Party from power for the first time in Taiwan's history.

In 2001, Ma visited Hong Kong to met with its chief executive, Tung Chee-hwa. Though he officially went to exchange ideas about city services such as trash disposal and subway tickets, the symbolism of the visit excited people in Hong Kong and Taiwan. Ma was the highest-ranking Taiwanese official invited to visit Hong Kong since the former British colony had gone back to Chinese control in 1997. Excited crowds greeted him, and he gave a keynote address at an event attended by representatives of China's government. Ma's Nationalist party, which had historically opposed compromise with China, had moderated its position, while the Democratic Progressives, led by the new president, Chen, leaned toward more independence from China. So Ma's invitation to Hong Kong was seen as a sign that the Chinese government wanted to strengthen relations with the Nationalists.

When Ma ran for re-election as mayor of Taipei in 2002, the debate over Taiwan's relationship with China became part of the campaign. Ma wanted to convince airlines to start 80-minute plane flights between Taipei's downtown airport and Shanghai, China, an idea the Democratic Progressives opposed. His challenger, Lee Ying-yuan, wanted to tear down the airport and replace it with a giant park modeled after New York City's Central Park. But a freeway and river ran next to the airport, making it less suitable as parkland, Ma pointed out. "I know Central Park quite well, and I know this would not be a Central Park," the New York-educated Ma told Keith Bradsher of the *New York Times*. Ma won reelection with 64 percent of the vote.

In 2005, Ma became chairman of the Nationalists, promising reform of the party's organization and image. That positioned him to be the party's next candidate for president three years later, just as Taiwanese voters were souring on Chen's combative stance toward China. "Ma, the mayor of Taipei, has the movie-star looks and sleaze-free appeal to capitalize on the new political winds," predicted Edward Cody of the *Washington Post*.

By 2006, Ma was already stating his platform, arguing that opening up trade with the mainland would benefit Taiwan's economy. He expressed optimism that China's president, Hu Jintao, would also pursue friendlier relations. "Many in Taiwan believe that Hu Jintao is much more sophisticated than his predecessors in understanding Taiwan," he told Zoher Abdoolcarim and Natalie Tso of *Time*. "He represents a different generation of leaders, more pragmatic, less ideological."

Scandal soon upended Taiwan's politics. Prosecutors began indicting political figures for the once-widespread practice of treating their expense budgets as part of their compensation. In November of 2006, corruption charges were filed against Wu Shu-chen, wife of President Chen, and some of Chen's aides. They were accused of skimming money for personal use from a presidential fund. Ma called for Chen to step down as president.

However, in February of 2007, Ma was indicted on a similar corruption charge. Prosecutors alleged he had misused 11.2 million Taiwanese dollars (about $340,000 in U.S. dollars) from a special allowance fund he controlled as Taipei's mayor. Ma said the money had been misused because of an accidental error, and that he had not benefited personally. Ma resigned as mayor and party chairman to fight the charges. However, he announced that he would still run for president, and the Nationalists confirmed him as the party's candidate. Ma spent much of 2007 in court, fighting the case. In August, a district court acquitted Ma of the charge. That December, an appeals court upheld the ruling.

During his presidential campaign, Ma toured Taiwan by bicycle. He promised to restore the strong economic growth Taiwan had experienced in the 1980s and 1990s by making it easier to conduct business with China, which was already Taiwan's largest trading partner. Chen, the departing president, had become deeply unpopular for his long, unproductive war of words with the Beijing government. Voters were ready for a change. Ma won Taiwan's presidency in March of 2008 with 58 percent of the vote, beating Frank Hsieh of the Democratic Progressive Party. According to Cody of the *Washington Post*, Ma declared that his victory "says that Taiwan should be very open, very pragmatic, that it should not isolate itself." A month later, Taiwan's Supreme Court upheld the dismissal of the charge against Ma. He was inaugurated president in May.

Ma announced he wanted to remove several trade barriers between Taiwan and China and establish direct plane flights between them. (Plane travel to the mainland usually took six to seven hours because travelers had to fly through Hong Kong or other countries.) Ma wanted to retain Taiwan's status under the administration of China, rejecting both unification with China and independence from it. He demanded that China remove the more than 1,000 missiles that it aims at Taiwan to deter it from declaring independence. In the long term, Ma said, he hoped to force a peace accord with China. "I think if we could continue the current talks with them to achieve economic normalization, I'm sure the feeling of a peaceful environment will continue to grow," he told Keith Bradsher and Edward Wong of the *New York Times*.

Ma spent his first year in office pursuing his goals with China. In November of 2008, he hosted Chinese envoy Chen Yunlin for one of the highest-level meetings between representatives of China and Taiwan since 1949. Opponents of détente with China held street protests and criticized the fact that the envoy did not address Ma as "zongtong," or "president." But the two sides signed four agreements that increased plane flights, sea trade, mail shipments, and cooperation on food safety. By December, Ma bragged, daily charter flights were connecting Taiwan with 26 cities in China. Polls showed the agreements were popular in Taiwan.

By late 2008, Taiwan's economy was shrinking as a result of the global financial crisis, giving Ma even more incentive to negotiate with China. In February of 2009, Taiwan and China began negotiating a broad free trade agreement that would allow goods, services, and money to flow freely between them. However, when Chinese premier Wen Jiabao told his parliament that the Beijing government was ready to talk about a peace agreement with Taiwan, Ma responded that it was too early to do so, and that they should focus on trade and economics. In April of 2009, negotiators for both governments met in Nanjing, on the mainland. They were expected to reach a new economic agreement to allow Taiwanese banks to operate in China, expand direct flights, provide for more cooperation in fighting crime, and possibly allow more Chinese investment in Taiwan.

Ma, who is expected to run for reelection in 2012, seemed confident that Taiwanese voters and other nations, such as the United States, would welcome the results of his strategy. "Improvement of relations with the mainland has brought to Taiwan very tangible benefits," he told Bradsher of the *New York Times* and Jeanne Moore of the *International Herald Tribune*: "cost reductions, time savings, freer movement of people, goods, services, capital and information, lower political risks, better investment environment." He said he had also succeeded in taking Taiwan-China relations off the list of tense international issues. "Ever since we came to power we have effectively reduced tensions across the Taiwan Strait [which separates Taiwan from China], so that Taiwan is no longer a problem in relations between the United States and Beijing," he said.

## Sources

### Periodicals

*New York Times,* January 16, 1988; February 14, 2001; November 14, 2002; February 14, 2007; May 3, 2007; August 14, 2007; December 29, 2007; March 23, 2008; March 24, 2008; May 21, 2008; June 19, 2008; November 7, 2008; February 22, 2009.

*Time,* July 10, 2006.

*Washington Post,* January 11, 2005, p. A11; March 19, 2006, p. A19; March 23, 2008, p. A12; November 7, 2008, p. A13; December 10, 2008, p. A20; February 21, 2009, p. A9; March 6, 2009, p. A9; April 24, 2009, p. A12.

### Online

"Biography of President Ma Ying-jeou," Office of the President, Republic of China, http://www.president.gov.tw/en/prog/news_release/print.php?id=11054997.tif69 (April 25, 2009).

"President, Republic of China," Office of the President, Republic of China, http://www.president.gov.tw/en/prog/news_release/print.php?id=11054996.tif88 (April 25, 2009).

"Profile: Ma Ying-jeou," BBC News, http://news.bbc.co.uk/2/hi/asia-pacific/7294938.stm (April 25, 2009).

*—Erick Trickey*

# Patrick McDonnell

*Kim Levin*

**Cartoonist and philanthropist**

**B**orn March 17, 1956, in Elizabeth, NJ; married Karen O'Connell (a yoga teacher), early 1980s. *Education:* School of Visual Arts, New York City, B.F. A., 1978.

**Addresses:** *Contact*—King Features Syndicate, 300 W. 57th St., 15th Fl., New York, NY 10019. *E-mail*—patrickmuttscomics.com. *Home*—Edison, NJ. *Web site*—http://muttscomics.com/.

## Career

**F**reelance illustrator for *Forbes, Parents, Reader's Digest, Sports Illustrated, Time,* and the *New York Times'* Sunday magazine, 1978-1994; creator, writer and illustrator of "Mutts," 1994—.

**Awards:** Greeting Card Award, National Cartoonists Society, 1991; best international comic strip, Max & Moritz Prize, 1996; Adamson Statuette, Swedish Academy of Comic Art, 1997; Genesis Award for outstanding contribution to animal rights by a cartoonist, Ark Trust, 1997, 1999; Harvey Award for best comic strip, Harvey Awards Executive Committee, 1998, 2001, 2002, 2003, 2005; Reuben Award for outstanding comic strip of the year, National Cartoonists Society, 1997; Reuben Award for outstanding cartoonist of the year, National Cartoonists Society, 1999; Humanitarian Award, People for the Ethical Treatment of Animals, 2001; Hollywood Genesis Award, Humane Society of the United States, 2002, 2005.

## Sidelights

**P**atrick McDonnell was 15 years into a successful career as an illustrator—garnering steady and lucrative work from magazines such as *Reader's Digest* and *Time*—when he felt a tug to do something new. He ended up creating a comic strip called "Mutts," which slipped into syndication in 1994 and quickly made its way into the comic sections of countless newspapers across the United States. Within two years, 400 newspapers were carrying "Mutts" on a daily basis and by 2009, some 700 newspapers in 20 countries carried the award-winning strip.

Written from an animals' perspective, "Mutts" revolves around canine and feline pals Earl and Mooch. Unlike many cartoonists who set up storylines over several days, McDonnell attempts to treat his readers to gag-a-day humor. "I feel blessed that I get to make a living doing something I love so much," McDonnell told the *Portland Press Herald's* Melanie Creamer. "I get to draw these little characters and do this creative work that I love." He went on to explain that "dogs and cats are our link to nature and keep us sane. I hope that I can spread some of the joy that my dog gave me to others."

McDonnell was born on March 17, 1956, in Elizabeth, New Jersey. As a child, he was encouraged to develop his artistic side. "I was really lucky, both my mom and dad went to art school," McDonnell told Newsday.com's "Kidsday" reporters. "They were very encouraging, we had a lot of paper and pens and so as soon as I could hold the pencil my mom had me scribbling, I just loved to doodle all the time." One frequent doodle involved a small white dog with black accents. Growing up, McDonnell developed a soft spot for dogs from reading the comics. He was especially taken with Charles Schulz's Snoopy, the beagle from the long-running *Peanuts* strip. When McDonnell was seven, he wrote to Schulz, suggesting the renowned cartoonist add a new character to his strip—a cat friend for Snoopy. Schulz did not comply, but later, as an adult, McDonnell took the cat and dog idea and made it his own.

While attending Edison High, located in Edison, New Jersey, McDonnell dabbled with cartoons and also played music in a group called the Bangone Ensemble. He graduated in 1974 and headed to New York City to attend the School of Visual Arts, earning his bachelor of fine arts degree in 1978. One of his instructors at the school was Will Eisner, creator of the popular 1940s crime-fighter comic series *The Spirit*. During his twenties, McDonnell struggled to balance his dual passions for art and music. In the late 1970s, he spent his days as a freelance illustrator and his nights as a drummer for Steel Tips, a Jersey punk band that opened for Blondie and the Ramones. His wife, Karen O'Connell, sang in the band. "We had three singles and a bit of a cult following," McDonnell told *Sports Illustrated*. "I was definitely torn between the art thing and the band thing. I guess I always have been." Steel Tips, however, broke up in 1981, prompting McDonnell to focus on his artwork.

Early in his fine arts career, McDonnell snagged high-profile jobs. In 1979, he began drawing illustrations for the *New York Times'* Sunday magazine to accompany commentary by Pulitzer Prize-winning columnist Russell Baker. McDonnell illustrated Baker's famed "Observer" column for more than a decade. McDonnell also picked up jobs drawing illustrations for *Parade, Reader's Digest, Time,* and *Forbes*. Along the way, he created the monthly "Bad Baby" strip that appeared in *Parents* magazine. By the late 1980s, he was drawing illustrations for *Sports Illustrated*'s "Scorecard" section.

Always interested in cartoons and inspired by animal characters, McDonnell spent several years working on a book called *Krazy Kat: The Comic Art of George Herriman.* Published in 1986, the book contained a collection of Herriman's strips, as well as other illustrations from his life's work and a biography. Launched in 1913, the humorous yet surreal strip ran for three decades and followed the lives of three central characters—Ignatz Mouse, Officer Pup, and Krazy Kat.

McDonnell enjoyed success as an illustrator but by the early 1990s, he felt something was missing from his life. Speaking to *Editor & Publisher*'s David Astor, McDonnell said he liked his work—"but in the back of my heart and mind, I thought I wasn't doing what I should be doing." McDonnell decided it was time to fulfill his childhood dream of creating his own cartoon strip. For years, McDonnell had been sketching into his illustrations a little white dog with a dark patch around its eye. Initially, McDonnell thought the dog was a generic everyday dog, but an art director told him it resembled a Jack Russell terrier—a breed McDonnell was unfamiliar with at the time. Intrigued, McDonnell acquired his own Jack Russell terrier in 1989 and named him Earl. When McDonnell decided to try his own strip, he turned to Earl for inspiration.

"I knew from the beginning that I wanted to do a strip about a dog from a dog's point of view," McDonnell told the *Pet Press'* Lori Golden. "I wanted to be a cartoonist since I was 5 years old, so I imagine I've been working on versions of it since then. Originally it was just going to be about a dog named Earl and his owner. Before I knew it, the strip had Mooch the cat."

Distributed by King Features Syndicate, McDonnell's strip appeared in 1994. Speaking to "Kidsday," McDonnell described how he settled on the name "Mutts." "I kept on writing a million different names for the comic and that was the one I kept on going back to. I thought it had a nice sound to it and I liked it because you know we are all Mutts. Everybody's got a little mixture of something ... also one of the first comic strips was called 'Mutt and Jeff.'"

From the start, "Mutts" was well-received—even by McDonnell's inspiration, Charles Schulz. In the foreword to McDonnell's first *Mutts* anthology—published in 1996—Schulz wrote, according to *The Pet Press*: "To me, 'Mutts' is exactly what a comic strip should be. It is always fun to look at, and the two main characters are wonderfully innocent. Patrick has created a little world that exists within itself." Schulz went on to say, "It's hard to believe that after 100 years of comics, Patrick could come up with a new and perfect little dog."

McDonnell strives to keep the strip upbeat and steers away from taking a satirical negative look at the world. Earl the pooch and Mooch the cat worry about simple things that affect their everyday lives—like food, sleep, and the weather. McDonnell also works to write from an animals' point of view. "I haven't gotten them up on two legs, walking around doing human things," McDonnell told the *Pet Press*. "I try my hardest to keep them doing things animals would do." The characters in the strip do, however, have well-developed and slightly quirky animal personalities, which drives the strip's humor.

McDonnell does include humans, including Earl's owner Ozzie and Mooch's owners Millie and Frank. Over the years, McDonnell has also introduced several peripheral characters, including Sid the Fish, who is weary of his too-small bowl; Noodles the tomcat; and two unruly squirrels named Bip and Bop. Another frequent character is Shtinky Puddin, an orange striped cat who is an animal-rights activist. Shtinky Puddin pushes animal-shelter adoptions and works to save tigers and other endangered animals.

McDonnell told the *Star-Ledger*'s Peggy O'Crowley that he starts each day with meditation before settling in at his drawing desk. "We live in such a cluttered world ... that to find that stillness is a real gift." While McDonnell works, he often listens to music, preferring a mix of classical, jazz, and Brazilian. His studio overlooks a wooded area filled with raccoons, red foxes, and deer, allowing him a crisp view of many of nature's furry friends. McDonnell often works on a week's worth of cartoons at a time. His first step involves writing the strips, then penciling the drawings and finally adding the ink. Typically, he works on the entire set simultaneously.

Most days, McDonnell's cat MeeMow can be found sitting on his drawing table and for a number of years, his real-life Earl sat at his feet. Earl died in 2007 just before his 19th birthday. In 2009, McDonnell adopted another Jack Russell terrier—an 18-month-old pup named Amelie—to serve as further inspiration for his work. Amelie was a rescue dog, having ended up at New York City Animal Care and Control. When McDonnell started the strip, he did not have MeeMow but drew his inspiration from the pet cats his family owned as a child. Then along came MeeMow, a feral calico his wife found abandoned at a Jersey City parking garage.

McDonnell has tackled many issues facing pets and pet owners. He has drawn strips that included a sad, chained-up dog, hoping pet owners would take notice of how the animal in the cartoon felt. He has also used his strip to promote Spay Day USA and designed an "Animal Friendly" vanity license plate for New Jersey motorists featuring his characters. Proceeds from the plates benefit the state's Animal Population Control Fund. In addition, McDonnell donates a portion of his earnings to support charities like Toys for Tots and the Wildlife Land Trust. McDonnell has earned numerous awards for his work on behalf of animals. He has also been a member of the board of directors of the Humane Society of the United States and the Fund for Animals.

Over the years, McDonnell's strips have been made into countless hardcover and paperback compilations. He switched gears in 2005, publishing his first children's book, *The Gift of Nothing*, which featured Mooch and Earl and ended up on the *New York Times*' best-seller list. McDonnell based the book on a storyline that had appeared in "Mutts." In the book, Mooch frets about choosing a gift for Earl because Earl has everything he needs. Speaking to the *New York Times*' George Gene Gustines, McDonnell elaborated on the plot. "He decides to get him nothing. But he's also giving everything of himself." The lesson of the book is that sometimes, the best gift is nothing—and the really touching gifts are the ones that come from the heart. In 2006, McDonnell published another children's book, *Just Like Heaven*, which was about the joy of simple blessings.

In 2008, McDonnell published *Mutts Shelter Stories: Love. Guaranteed.* Since 1998, McDonnell had been including in his comic periodic storylines about homeless pets. This book included a compilation of those strips interspersed with real photos and stories of pets who found loving homes through shelters and other pet adoption agencies. McDonnell requested adoption stories and photos through his Mutts Web site, then compiled them into his book. Twice a year, McDonnell creates his "Shelter Stories" strips, usually in May and November. The feedback he receives keeps him going. "That's the thing that's made me the most happy," he told the *Record*—"getting letters from people who were inspired by the strip to go out and get a best friend. I think people who work for shelters are some of the unsung heroes of America."

In 2010, McDonnell expected to publish another collection of "Mutts" strips into a volume titled *Wag*. The book's focus was on things that make Earl's tail wag. Like all "Mutts" books, it was to be printed on recycled paper. In keeping with his nature-friendly viewpoint, McDonnell and his wife are vegetarians. In addition, McDonnell uses his Web site to promote animal-rights activism and earth-friendly policies.

## Selected works

(With Karen O'Connell and Georgia Riley de Havenon) *Krazy Kat: The Comic Art of George Herriman*, Harry N. Abrams (New York City), 1986.

*Mutts*, Andrews McMeel Publishing (Kansas City, MO), 1996.

*Cats and Dogs: Mutts II*, Andrews McMeel Publishing, 1997.

*More Shtuff*, Andrews McMeel Publishing, 1998.

*Yesh!*, Andrews McMeel Publishing, 1999.

*Mutts Sundays*, Andrews McMeel Publishing, 1999.

*Our Mutts*, Andrews McMeel Publishing, 2000.

*A Little Look-See*, Andrews McMeel Publishing, 2001.

*Sunday Mornings*, Andrews McMeel Publishing, 2001.

*Mutts: What Now?*, Andrews McMeel Publishing, 2002.

*I Want to Be the Kitty!*, Andrews McMeel Publishing, 2003.

*Sunday Afternoons*, Andrews McMeel Publishing, 2004.

*Dog-eared*, Andrews McMeel Publishing, 2004.

*Mutts: The Comic Art of Patrick McDonnell*, Harry N. Abrams, 2003.

*The Gift of Nothing* (children's book), Little, Brown Young Readers (Boston, MA), 2005.

*Who Let the Cat Out?*, Andrews McMeel Publishing, 2005.

*Mutts: Sunday Evenings*, Andrews McMeel Publishing, 2005.

*Art* (children's book), Little, Brown Young Readers, 2006.

*Everyday Mutts: A Comic Strip Treasury*, Andrews McMeel Publishing, 2006.

*Just Like Heaven* (children's book), Little, Brown Young Readers, 2006.

*Animal Friendly*, Andrews McMeel Publishing, 2007.

*The Best of Mutts, 1994-2004*, Andrews McMeel Publishing, 2007.

*Hug Time* (children's book), Little, Brown Young Readers, 2007.

*Mutts Shelter Stories: Love. Guaranteed*, Andrews McMeel Publishing, 2008.

*South* (children's book), Little, Brown Young Readers, 2008.

*Call of the Wild: A Mutts Treasury*, Andrews McMeel Publishing, 2008.

## Sources

### Periodicals

*Editor & Publisher*, November 16, 1996, p. 40.

*Home News Tribune* (East Brunswick, NJ), July 21, 2003, p. B8.

*New York Times*, September 25, 2005, p. NJ1.

*Portland Press Herald* (Maine), July 31, 2008, p. E1.

*Record* (Hackensack, NJ), July 5, 2008, p. F4.

*Star-Ledger* (Newark, NJ), November 27, 2005, sec. Accent, p. 4; February 18, 2007, sec. Accent, p. 2.

### Online

"Kidsday Talks with 'Mutts' Creator Patrick McDonnell," *Newsday.com,* http://www.exploreli.com/entertainment/localguide/kids/ny-kdmutts0405,0,67 62058.story (April 27, 2009).

"Patrick McDonnell," Mutts Official Web Site, http://muttscomics.com/bio.aspx (April 26, 2009).

"Patrick McDonnell: The Cartoonist Who is King of the 'Mutts,'" *The Pet Press,* http://www.thepetpress-la.com/articles/patrickmcdonnell.htm (April 27, 2009).

"SI Vault: From the Publisher," *Sports Illustrated,* http://vault.sportsillustrated.cnn.com/vault/article/magazine/MAG1066489/index.htm (April 27, 2009).

—Lisa Frick

# Ryan McGinley

## Photographer

**B**orn October 17, 1977, in Ramsey, NJ. *Education:* Parsons School of Design, B.F.A., 2000.

**Addresses:** *Office*—Team (gallery, inc.), 83 Grand St., New York, NY 10013.

## Career

**L**aunched photography career, c. 1998; put together first solo show at 420 W. Broadway, New York City, 2000; *The Kids Are Alright* displayed at the Whitney Museum of American Art, New York City, 2003; showed *New Photographs* at P.S. 1 Contemporary Art Center, 2004; contributed photographs to *New York Times Magazine*, 2006, *Esquire*, 2007; had solo show *I Know Where the Summer Goes*, Team Gallery, New York City, 2008.

**Awards:** Photographer of the Year Award, *American Photo Magazine*, 2003; Young Photographer of the Year Award, International Center of Photography, 2007.

## Sidelights

**C**ontroversial photographer Ryan McGinley focused his lens on the in-crowd in New York City in the early 2000s before moving on to similarly beautiful young people in other settings. Many of his arresting, large-scale picture portraits often feature nudes and have sexual overtones, as do the thousands of Polaroids he has taken over the years. Calling him "the real new deal," Peter Goddard of the *Toronto Star* believed, "Like (reformed) roughhouse photographer Nan Goldin, ... McGinley photographs the life he lives in New York's East Village gay/graffiti/punk art scene."

Born on October 17, 1977, in Ramsey, New Jersey, McGinley was the youngest of eight children of a devout church-going mother. His father, an employee of Owens Corning, wanted him to play professional tennis. Though interested in athletic pursuits, McGinley skateboarded instead. As a teenaged skateboarder hanging out in Manhattan, he met filmmaker and photographer Larry Clark in 1991. Clark, the auteur behind *Kids* (1995), influenced the creative path McGinley would eventually take.

While attending Parsons School of Design and studying graphic design, McGinley began taking pictures after a graphics assignment frustrated him so much that he took a picture intending to trace it for credit. Instead, he found a new medium to work in and began using a camera to take pictures of every aspect of his life. Beginning in 1998, he took Polaroids of anyone who visited his home in Greenwich Village. He then put the pictures up on the wall, covering nearly the whole of his apartment with Polaroids by the time he ended the practice in 2003.

McGinley earned his B.F.A. in graphic design from the Parsons School of Design in 2000. Even before he graduated, he had a successful photography career in hand. McGinley began by publishing his photographs in hip magazines like *Vice* and *Index*, while being mentored by Clark and Bruce LaBruce, among others. Many of the pictures in *Vice*, for example, were shot at beer and cocaine parties. In these pictures, McGinley said that he was not trying to be startling. He told the *New York Times'* Carl Swanson, "It's about the happy effects of the drug, as opposed to Nan Goldin, which is about the dramatic effect. They shouldn't make you sad. It's not about the art of drugs; it's about how the drugs induce your performance for the camera." McGinley included such photos in a self-published book, *The Kids Are Alright.*

McGinley's first solo show came in 2000 at 420 W. Broadway, New York City, was do-it-yourself, and included pictures from that book. Also titled *The Kids Are Alright*, the show was re-mounted at the Whitney in 2003. (When *The Kids Are Alright* was shown at the Whitney, he was the youngest artist ever to have a solo show there.) The images were primarily of friends, lovers, and artists in the social circles that McGinley inhabited in Manhattan. Many of the pictures featured male nudes taken in intimate settings, often involving drug use though some, like "Wading" (2001), combined a figure with a nature-scape. In the *New York Times*, Holland Cotter praised "the apparently carefree spirit of Mr. McGinley's pictures."

As McGinley continued to attract attention, his work appeared in more magazines, like *BUTT, Dazed and Confused*, and *I.D.*, and he had more shows in the United States and abroad. Taking his art more seriously, he also began to cut down on his legendary partying and focus more on the business side of his artistic enterprise. Yet McGinley did not shy away from controversy. In the Spring 2003 issue of *BUTT*, he included nude photographs of himself and his boyfriend having sex, but was determined not to conform to any gay stereotypes anyone wanted to impose on him.

McGinley continued to display his challenging work in high-profile venues. In 2004, for example, he showed *New Photographs* at P.S. 1 Contemporary Art Center, an affiliate of the Museum of Modern Art. All the pictures were less than nine months old. While he continued to shoot young people playing in the nude, the settings were nature and the water, and pictures were more reticent and reflective. The photos were shot in a week when he rented a house in Vermont and invited a group of friends from the New York party scene to accompany him. "Through Branches," for example, showed a group of naked boys and girls in a pine tree. Critics noted a surreal element to some of the more blurry in the show, and that while he still emphasized freedom, he depicted his subjects' exuberance without passion.

While McGinley's profile continued to rise, he was commissioned to take photographs for such mainstream publications as the *New York Times Magazine.* In 2006, he shot pictures of his friends who were modeling swimsuits on Mexican beaches for that publication. A year later, he took pictures of the photographer Robert Frank for *Esquire,* and in 2008, worked with Icelandic art rock band Sigur Ros on a digital video for their single "Gobbledigook," which was inspired by his photographs. McGinley also continued to be more disciplined both personally, by drinking very little and following a strict diet, and professionally. In addition, he came up with new ways of capturing his subjects. In the summers of 2005, 2006, and 2007, for example, he paid friends and models to accompany him on three-month long cross-country trips by van and shot them at cinematic settings along the way. McGinley displayed these photographs at shows like 2008's *I Know Where the Summer Goes* at the Team Gallery in New York City.

While critics were divided over McGinley and his photographs, many fellow photographers disdained him for his lack of technical knowledge about the darkroom, seemingly a prerequisite for any serious photographer. He had no understanding of color printing, but scanned his negatives into his computer and edited them there. Photographer Philip-Lorca diCorcia told Swanson in the *New York Times,* "There's always going to be carping from photographers because there's such a large contingent of them who base their identity on some sort of technical aspect of it. And then somebody comes along and makes it seem easy."

Such cynicism did not affect McGinley, nor did all the media attention over his playful yet voyeuristic photographs even as he accepted the 2007 Young Photographer of the Year Award from the International Center of Photography. He told Philip Gefter of the *New York Times*, "I'm just a photographer, not a movie star. I've worked really hard. I've devoted my life to this. I'm not feeling any expectation from anybody else. I'm doing it for myself. I'm making the art for me first. I'm making it because these are the pictures I want to see. I'm making pictures that don't yet exist." McGinley added, "My photographs are a celebration of life, fun, and the beautiful. They are a world that doesn't exist. A fantasy. Freedom is real. There are no rules. The life I wish I was living."

## Selected exhibitions

### Solo shows

*The Kids Are Alright,* 420 W. Broadway, New York City, 2000; The Whitney Museum of American Art, New York City, 2003.

MC Magma, Milan, Italy, 2002.

*Ryan McGinley: Photographien,* Galerie Giti Nourbakhsch, Berlin, Germany, 2002.

Baily Fine Arts, Toronto, Canada, 2003.

The Red Eye Gallery, Rhode Island School of Design, 2003.

University of the Arts, Philadelphia, PA, 2004.

*New Photographs,* P.S. 1 Contemporary Art Center/ The Museum of Modern Art, Long Island City, NY, 2004.

Rencontres Internationales de la Photographie, Arles France, 2005.

*Laboratorio 987: Entre Nosotros,* Museo de Arte Contemporáneo de Castilla y León, Lóeon, Spain, 2005.

Frieze Art Fair, London, England, 2006.

*Sun and Health,* agnès b. galerie du jour, Paris, France, 2006.

*Project Space,* Kunsthalle Vienna, Vienna, Austria, 2006.

*Irregular Regulars,* Team Gallery, New York City, 2007.

*Ryan McGinley,* FOAM Fotagrafiemusuem Amsterdam, Amsterdam, The Netherlands, 2007.

*I Know Where the Summer Goes,* Team Gallery, New York City, 2008.

*Spring and by Summer Fall,* Ratio 3, San Francisco, 2008.

### Group shows

*You're just a summer love, but I'll remember you when winter comes,* Priska C. Juschka Fine Art, Brooklyn, NY, 2002.

*K48 Teenage Rebel: The Bedroom Show,* John Connelly Presents, New York City, 2002.

*A NEW SCENE: WHAT ABOUT NEW YORK?,* agnes b. galerie du jour, Paris, Franc, 2003.

*Fresh: Youth Culture in Contemporary Photographs* The Center for Photography, Woodstock, NY 2004.

*with us against reality, or against us!,* galerie S.E. Oslo, Norway, 2005.

*The Name of This Show is Not Gay ART NOW,* Paul Kasmin Gallery, New York City, 2006.

*Picturing Modernity: The Photography Collection,* San Francisco Museum of Modern Art, San Francisco CA, 2007.

### Selected writings

*The Kids Are Alright,* self-published, 1999; reprinted by *Index* magazine, 2000.

*Ryan McGinley,* Index Books (Bradenton, FL), 2002.

(With others) *The Photograph As Contemporary Art,* Thames & Hudson (London), 2004.

*Thumbsucker,* Iconoclast USA, 2005.

(With others) *Vitamin Ph: New Perspectives in Photography,* Phaidon Press (London), 2006.

*Sun and Health,* Galerie du Jour Agnès B. (Paris, France), 2006.

(With others) *Interviews 2, Kunsthalle Wien,* Walter Konig, 2008.

## Sources

### Periodicals

*C: International Contemporary Art,* June 22, 2003, p. 27.

*Interview,* July 1, 2004, p. 24.

*New York Magazine,* January 15, 2007; June 18, 2007.

*New York Sun,* July 1, 2004, p. 18.

*New York Times,* February 14, 2003, p. E45; February 23, 2003, sec. 9, p. 1; May 6, 2007, sec. 2, p. 20; May 2, 2008, p. E23; June 25, 2008, p. E1.

*Toronto Star,* February 6, 2003, p. G9.

*W,* February 1, 2006, p. 222.

### Online

"Ryan McGinley: CV," Ryan McGinley.com, http:// www.ryanmcginley.com/cv.php (October 13, 2008).

—A. Petruso

# Scott McNealy

*AP Images*

## Chairman of Sun Microsystems

**B**orn November 13, 1954, in Columbus, Indiana; son of Raymond William (a business executive) and Marmaline (a homemaker) McNealy; married Susan Ingemanson, 1994; children: four. *Education:* Harvard University, BA, 1976; Stanford University, MBA, 1980.

**Addresses:** *Home*—901 San Antonio Rd., Palo Alto, CA 94303. *Office*—Sun Microsystems, 4150 Network Cir., Santa Clara, CA 95054.

## Career

**C**o-founded Sun Microsystems, 1982; vice president, manufacturing and operations, 1982-84; president and chief executive officer, 1984-2006; chairman and chief executive officer, 2002-2004; chairman, president, and chief executive officer, 2004-2006; chairman, 1984—.

## Sidelights

**A**s cofounder, chairman, and former chief executive officer of Sun Microsystems, Scott McNealy is known as an untraditional executive, a maverick, and one of the early leaders in technology to take advantage of the rise of the Internet in the early-1990s. Despite his not having a background in technology, McNealy helped to build Sun into one of the world's foremost computer companies. He has been considered one of the important figures in the development of e-commerce and has been credited with pushing technology as a whole toward greater development.

Founded in 1982, Sun Microsystems focuses on sales of server computers, rather than personal computers. This emphasis positioned the company to become an industry leader in the mid-1990s, when the need for global network servers to support the World Wide Web required the type of powerful machines Sun had made its specialty. In addition, Sun programmers developed Java, which became a dominant programming language, used on more than 3.5 billion devices by 2007, that allows programmers to create better graphics, animation, and sound features for display on the Internet. During the late 1990s, however, Sun failed to recognize the threat posed by Linux, an open-source operating system, and the company began losing ground in the early 2000s as companies settled for less powerful, and less expensive, servers than the ones Sun provided. A change in focus from hardware to services after 2007 put Sun back in the market as a major industry competitor, although it suffered in the 2008 economic climate. The company pinned its hopes on a combination of open-source software and a technology called "webtone" or "cloud computing," which features a grid-like infrastructure where companies could write software and be provided storage online.

McNealy was born on November 13, 1954, in Columbus, Indiana, the son of manufacturing business executive Raymond McNealy. He grew up in Bloomfield Hills, Michigan, a town northwest of Detroit, where he attended the prestigious Cranbrook Kingswood preparatory school. While he was still a young person, it was already clear that he had a competitive nature, and early on, he developed an interest in business. He and his father discussed his father's work at the American Motors Corporation, and he listened to conversations with auto industry heads. But rather than following in his father's footsteps, McNealy set modest goals: He hoped to own a machine shop, retire early, and play golf.

Though he struggled with grades, McNealy did well enough during his senior year to be accepted into Harvard University, where he received a degree in economics in 1976. He was not initially accepted into graduate school and spent some time working as a factory foreman before being admitted into the MBA program at Stanford University. He remained in California after receiving his degree and began to find work in the computer industry. In 1982, he was approached by former Stanford classmates about joining them in starting up a computer firm. That company, called Sun as an acronym for Stanford University Network, became the center of McNealy's career. Focusing on high-speed networks, the company made an early mark with people in technical fields, and the profits increased dramatically from $9 million in 1983 to $39 million in 1984.

McNealy expanded his position with the company from focusing on manufacturing to sales and fundraising. He gained an investment from Eastman Kodak, a customer, on the condition that he be named president of the company. McNealy was given the title at the same time one of his cofounders, who had served as the company's chief executive officer (CEO), left to begin a new startup. Within the year, McNealy was offered the additional position of interim chairman and CEO. No candidate rose to take the position permanently, and McNealy remained at the top spot.

McNealy took Sun public in 1986, and within two years, the company had annual sales reaching $1 billion. The growth was difficult to keep up with, and McNealy restructured the manufacturing systems and selectively culled the product line, focus-

ing on products built around Sun's high-powered processor, the Sparc chip and its operating system, Solaris. The reorganization was a success, and the company climbed to $3 billion by 1992. Despite these gains, however, competition was fierce, particularly from Microsoft and Intel. McNealy declared Microsoft the enemy and began what was to become a long campaign against Microsoft, including appearances testifying in court over the possibility of Microsoft being a monopoly. As part of its anti-Microsoft strategy, Sun developed the slogan, "The network is the computer," putting the emphasis on quality servers.

In 1995, Sun released Java, a software language that can run on any operating system. The idea of the language was so innovative that it was quickly licensed by a number of Sun's competitors, including Microsoft. Java was pivotal because it allowed programmers to create programs once that would work on any number of platforms, rather than tailoring the program to work with each type of computer and operating system. The success with Java, which was used by many of the dominant Internet companies during the late 1990s, allowed McNealy to declare Sun to be "the dot in .com."

When *Wired* magazine introduced its list of the top 40 forward-looking companies in 1998, Sun was one of the obvious inclusions. In 1999, Sun introduced the StarOffice software suite, and in 2000, the company was valued at $210 billion. But as the dot-com bubble burst in the early 2000s, Sun ran into trouble. In 2003, *Wired* dropped it from its list, citing the company's reticence in embracing Linux's opensource ideology as one of the reasons. With companies scaling down on the power required to run their servers, Sun was forced to slash prices on its low-end servers to keep up with the competition. In 2006, McNealy stepped down as CEO of the company, remaining the chair and attempting to drum up excitement from customers about Sun's new market plan: webtone and cloud computing technology.

As the company focused on the telecommunications market, McNealy's new position as chair meant spending time flying around the world to meet with key customers to establish a firmer foothold. "The clever way to describe it is I'm Jonathan's airplane crash dummy," McNealy joked with Alan Burkitt-Gray in *Global Telecoms Business* in 2006. "I've got a fun job.... Someone described it as being a grandparent rather than a parent." McNealy remains positive about the company's future—a "quintessential" trait, according to Gary Rivlin of *Wired*, who in 2003 noted that while "the tech industry is ready to write off the computer maker, ... McNealy and company are smugly imagining future glory." Investors, however, have not placed as much faith in the company as McNealy. A writer for the *Economist* noted that Sun's shares fell from just under $24 in October of 2007 to less than $5 in November of 2008. The reporter did acknowledge that Sun's focus on open-source technology seemed to be a step in the right direction.

In addition to his role as chair for Sun, McNealy has also founded the nonprofit Curriki, a wiki site aimed at saving schools money in textbook replacement by putting much of the curriculum content online. McNealy stated his goal of having lesson plans available for every subject at every grade level, kindergarten through twelfth grade. He told Gregory Mone of *Popular Science* that even if the site did not become a source for every classroom, he hoped the idea would create change in the textbook industry. "We're just trying to irritate the publishers into updating content and moving some of it online," he said, "which absolutely makes a lot of sense."

## Sources

### Periodicals

*Economist,* November 8, 2008, p. 69EU.
*Fortune,* February 4, 2008, p. 52.
*Global Telecoms Business,* November-December 2006.
*Popular Science,* February 2007, p. 36.
*Washington Technology,* January 15, 2007, p. 36.
*Wired,* July 2003, pp. 126-32.

### Online

Sun, http://www.sun.com/aboutsun/executives/mcnealy/bio.jsp (February 11, 2009).

—*Alana Joli Abbott*

# Dmitry Medvedev

*Dmitry Astakhov/AFP/Getty Images*

## President of Russia

**B**orn Dmitry Anatolyevich Medvedev, September 14, 1965, in St. Petersburg, Russia; son of Anatoly Afanasevich Medvedev (a professor) and Yulia Veniaminovna Shaposhnikova Medvedeva (a teacher); married Svetlana Vladimirova Linnik (a financial analyst), 1989; children: Ilya (son). *Education:* Leningrad State University, law degree, 1987, Ph.D., 1990.

**Addresses:** *Office*—Presidential Executive Office, Ilinka St. No 23, 103132 Moscow, Russia. *Web site*—http://www.kremlin.ru/eng/.

## Career

**A**ssistant professor of law, Leningrad State University, 1990-99; advisor to chair of the Leningrad City Council, 1990-91, and to the St. Petersburg mayor's Committee on International Relations, 1991-95; deputy government chief of staff under President Vladimir Putin, 1999; deputy chief of staff of the presidential executive office, 1999-2000; Putin for President campaign director, 2000; board chair, OAO Gazprom, 2000-01 and 2002-08, deputy chair, 2001-02; first deputy chief of staff of the presidential executive office, 2000-03; chief of staff of the presidential executive office, October 2003-November 2005; first deputy prime minister and first deputy chairperson of the Council for Implementation of Priority National Projects, November 2005-08; elected president of Russia on the United Russia Party ticket, 2008.

## Sidelights

**I**n May of 2008, a former law professor named Dmitry Medvedev was sworn in as president of Russia and became one of the youngest leaders in his country's modern age. His political career has been firmly allied with that of Vladmir Putin, his immediate predecessor as president—and the man whom Medvedev made prime minister in one of his first official acts as president—yet Russia's third president is also the first without ties to the country's once-powerful Communist Party, nor its state security service apparatus, the KGB, out of which Putin rose. "We will be able to preserve the course of President Putin," Medvedev proclaimed in his victory speech, according to a BBC News profile, but also affirmed his commitment to democratic principles. "We are well aware that no non-democratic state has ever become truly prosperous."

Born in 1965, Medvedev grew up in St. Petersburg, Russia's westernmost major city and a relatively liberal place during the seven-plus decades of its Soviet era, when the city was known as Leningrad. During the Soviet period, the Communist Party rigidly controlled nearly all facets of life in Russia and the other republics of the Soviet Union. Medvedev's father, Anatoly, was a professor at the Leningrad Technical Institute, and his mother was a teacher. He was their only child, and the family lived in a 430-square-foot apartment in Leningrad's Kupchino district, a rather bleak stretch of modernist high-rise apartments.

Medvedev entered Leningrad State University and earned his first degree in law in 1987. Three years later, he received a doctorate in the same subject. In the interim years, he began teaching courses at the school and also became politically active. This was a dramatic period in Russian and Soviet history, coming just a few short years after the rise of a reformer, Mikhail Gorbachev, as Soviet leader. Gorbachev launched several new economic, social, and political initiatives, one of which was the creation of a new national legislative body, the Congress of People's Deputies, in 1989. One of Medvedev's professors at Leningrad State University was Anatoly Sobchak, who won election to the new Congress and went on to play a leading role in writing the first post-Soviet constitution for Russia.

Medvedev worked Sobchak's campaigns to win a seat on the Congress of People's Deputies and then the Leningrad City Council. In 1991, the city initiated its first direct mayoral elections, and Medvedev was the unofficial campaign manager for Sobchak's run, which was a success. In that same election, voters also approved a dramatically symbolic measure to restore the city's original name of St. Petersburg.

For most of the 1990s Medvedev served as an assistant professor of law at the newly renamed St. Petersburg State University while holding other positions with the municipal government and in the emerging private sector. He was an advisor to Sobchak when the latter was chair of the City Council, and then served on the mayor's Committee on International Relations. He proved particularly adept at finding loopholes to the city government's involvement in various revenue-producing ventures, such as casino gaming. He also worked closely with Putin, who during this period served as chair of Sobchak's Committee on International Relations. In 1992, a scandal loomed that threatened to sink Putin: two City Council members accused him of financial improprieties related to his office. According to *Financial Times* writer Catherine Belton, the rivals claimed that "Putin had handed out export quotas for more than [$100 million] in oil and rare metals, in food barter deals that benefited crony companies while little of the produce ever appeared." Medvedev was part of a team of legal advisors who looked into the matter and declared the charges to be baseless.

Accusations of corruption are customarily used as political tools in post-Soviet Russia—and indeed have an even longer history dating back to the Soviet era—and few elected officials ever escape attempts to smear their name and force them from office. As Sobchak's political career declined when he was linked to personal real estate misdeeds, Putin's rose, and he was summoned to a post in Moscow overseeing property belonging to the office of Russia's newly elected president, Boris Yeltsin.

Medvedev, meanwhile, became involved in his own entrepreneurial ventures, mostly related to the privatization of state-owned paper mills and timber concerns that provided the raw pulp for the mills. He, too, was accused of wrongdoing in 1999, and was forced to step down from one of the companies he chaired. That same year, however, an ailing Yeltsin appointed Putin to serve as prime minister, and then acting president a few months later. Putin, in turn, invited Medvedev to come to Moscow to serve as his deputy chief of staff and campaign manager for the coming election.

In March of 2000, Putin was elected Russia's second president with 52.9 percent of the vote. After this point, Medvedev served as the president's de facto representative on the board of Gazprom, the successor to the Soviet Ministry of the Oil and Gas Industry. Gazprom is a state-owned natural-gas extractor, crude-oil driller and refiner, and pipeline owner and manager, and Medvedev was charged with overseeing it during a rather dramatic period of privatization, scandal, then return of government control.

In 2003 Putin promoted Medvedev to serve as his chief of staff, and two years later named him deputy prime minister. By this point Putin had been elected to a second term as president, this time by a landslide of 71 percent. In his new role as deputy prime minister, Medvedev was handed responsibility for the state's Council for Implementation of Priority National Projects, which oversaw major infrastructure improvement initiatives and efforts to boost a flagging birth rate. Putin was a popular president at home, but raised some alarms in the West for his domestic and foreign policies, which included securing control of the remaining independently owned media outlets and pressuring neighboring states like Ukraine to comply with Moscow by temporarily slowing the flow of natural gas via Gazprom-controlled pipelines. Putin "has been accused of creating a Soviet Union Lite or, alternatively, a new imperial Russia, with himself as a 21st-century czar," noted in an article for the *New York Times Magazine* by Moscow bureau chief Steven Lee

Myers, who went on to write that "there is no question that he has consolidated virtually all political and, increasingly, economic power into his hands, or at least into the hands of the small cadre of aides whom he has entrusted as stewards of the country's natural resources and strategic enterprises." Medvedev belonged to that circle of associates.

Russia's constitution—the one that Sobchak played a vital role in crafting—permitted the direct election of presidents but limited them to two consecutive terms. Therefore, Putin was slated to step down in 2008, though support for him was so strong that a few hardliners suggested he remain in office anyway. A compromise emerged, with Putin appearing to elevate both Medvedev and the country's minister of defense, Sergei B. Ivanov, to prominence in the final years of his second term. A quiet public relations campaign by senior officials in the Kremlin, the seat of government in Moscow, touted Medvedev's liberal credentials and legal background over Ivanov's career in the dreaded KGB of the Soviet period.

Medvedev had never formally joined either the Communist Party or one of the many political parties that sprang up in the post-Soviet era, but in December of 2007 the United Russia Party announced that he would be their candidate in the coming presidential elections in March. He also won the endorsement of several other parties that hold seats in the Duma, as the lower house of Russia's national assembly is called. Shortly afterward, he gave a speech in which he affirmed that if elected, he would appoint Putin as prime minister. Citing a long list of pressing issues for Russia—among them rural poverty, education, and internal stability—he asserted that it was vital that the country "continue the course which was formed at the end of the 1990s," he said, according to a *New York Times* transcript translated from the original Russian. "In order to stay on this path, it is not enough to elect a new president who shares this ideology. It is not less important to maintain the efficiency of the team formed by the incumbent president."

In the run-up to the electoral season, which lasts just one month by Russian law, a few other candidates attempted to win a spot on the ballot, including Putin's first prime minister, Mikhail M. Kasyanov, but state-controlled media outlets launched assaults on their integrity, which were twinned with ominous official inquiries into the suspected wrongdoing. In the March 2, 2008, elections, Medvedev won with 70 percent of the vote, besting his nearest challenger Gennadi Zyuganov, the Communist Party candidate, who won 18 percent of the vote, followed by nationalist Vladimir Zhirinovsky,

who took just under ten percent. "The result was so predictable in an election tightly controlled by the Kremlin that many of Russia's leading newspapers did not make Mr. Medvedev's victory their main story," noted the *Times* of London's Moscow correspondent, Tony Halpin.

In addition to the unusual power-sharing arrangement with Putin as his prime minister, the 42-year-old Medvedev also made history as the youngest person to lead Russia in 114 years, since the coronation of Tsar Nicholas II in 1894. He was sworn in on May 7, 2008, and duly appointed Putin as prime minister as one of his first official acts. Three months later, hopes that Medvedev would break with his predecessor's hardline policies were dashed when there was a renewal of hostilities in Georgia, the Caucasus republic that was once a part of the Soviet Union but now is an entirely separate nation. Georgia is also home, however, to a pair of pro-Russian enclaves, South Ossetia and Abkhazia. When Georgian president Mikheil Saakashvili tried to retake South Ossetia, Russian troops invaded Georgia that summer. After a deadly show of Russian military might, the beleaguered Saakashvili was forced to concede defeat. Not long afterward, Medvedev announced a major military spending package that would include new nuclear submarines and an air and space defense system.

A day after the U.S. presidential election in November of 2008, Medvedev made the surprising pronouncement that Russian missiles would be deployed near Kaliningrad, a city close to Russia's border with Poland, a staunch U.S. ally and long-time Russian foe. A few weeks later he was interviewed by a journalist from the French newspaper *Le Figaro,* who asked him to comment on the matter. Medvedev explained that the decision about the Kaliningrad site was merely in response to plan for a U.S. missile defense system in Europe. "We always asked our American partners one and the same question: why do you need this system, how effective will it be, and who is it directed against?," he told *Le Figaro*'s Etienne Mougeotte. "But we have not received a clear answer to any of these questions."

Medvedev is married to an elementary-school classmate whom he began dating in his teens. They have one son, Ilya. Much has been made in the Western media about the new Russian president's taste in music, which runs to such British heavy-metal stalwarts as Deep Purple, Led Zeppelin, and Black Sabbath. Just before the March elections, Gazprom held a 15th anniversary fete at the State Kremlin Palace, and Deep Purple played a seven-song set in the same hall once used for Communist Party congresses. The *Times* of London's Halpin quoted Medvedev as enthusing that he could not have imagined such a moment when he was a teenager paying dearly for illegal bootleg copies of their records, and remarked how enthusiastic Medvedev was to see his longtime favorites on stage finally. "Such images might seem corny in Britain," Halpin conceded, "but they resonate with a generation of voters that has made the same journey from Communist stagnation through post-Soviet humiliations to modern Russia's economic boom."

## Sources

### Periodicals

*Financial Times*, February 29, 2008, p. 7.

*Guardian* (London, England), May 7, 2008, p. 32; August 13, 2008, p. 1.
*Le Figaro* (France), November 13, 2008.
*New York Times*, December 11, 2007.
*New York Times Magazine*, February 25, 2007.
*Times* (London, England), February 13, 2008, p. 33; March 1, 2008, p. 50; March 1, 2008, p. 51; March 4, 2008, p. 36; May 7, 2008, p. 18; May 7, 2008, p. 38.
*Washington Post*, December 11, 2007, p. A21.

### Online

"Profile: Dmitry Medvedev," BBC News, http://news.bbc.co.uk/2/hi/europe/7136556.stm (March 27, 2009).

—*Carol Brennan*

# Stephenie Meyer

## Author

**B**orn Stephenie Morgan, December 24, 1973, in Hartford, CT; daughter of Stephen (a financial manager) and Candy Morgan; married Christiaan "Pancho" Meyer (an accountant); children: Gabe, Seth, Eli. *Education:* Brigham Young University, B.A., 1997.

**Addresses:** *Home*—Cave Creek, AZ. *Publisher*—Little, Brown and Company, Hachette Book Group USA, 237 Park Avenue, New York, NY 10017. *Web site*—http://www.stepheniemeyer.com/.

## Career

**P**ublished first novel, *Twilight,* 2005; released second novel, *New Moon,* and sold the movie rights for *Twilight* to MTV Films, 2006; released third novel, *Eclipse,* and, along with Meg Cabot, Kim Harrison, Lauren Myracle, and Michael Jaffe, contributed to the HarperTeen book *Prom Night From Hell,* 2007; released first adult novel, *The Host,* and fourth vampire novel, *Breaking Dawn,* 2008; appeared on national television programs such as *Good Morning America* and *Larry King Live!*

**Awards:** Best book of the year and "one of the most promising new authors of 2005," *Publisher's Weekly,* for *Twilight,* 2005; a top-ten best book for young adults and a top-ten book for reluctant readers, American Library Association, for *Twilight,* 2005; editor's choice, *New York Times,* for *Twilight,* 2005.

## Sidelights

**I**nspired by her dream about a human girl falling in love with a vampire, Stephenie Meyer redefined the teen horror genre with her best-selling books *Twilight, New Moon, Eclipse,* and *Breaking Dawn.* Initially enjoyed by teenaged girls, her works are sold in 28 countries, have been translated into 20 different languages and have caught on with adults who savor the author's ability to conjure romance with a supernatural slant almost as much as their kids. The enormous popularity of her work has also resulted in the adaptation of her first novel into a major motion picture due out in December of 2008.

Meyers, whose commercial impact has been compared to *Harry Potter* author J. K. Rowling's, has also changed the way writers connect with their readers. Using various Internet-based social sites like MySpace.com, she has kept her various projects uppermost in the minds of fans by delivering regular updates, live interviews, and answering e-mails. In an era when book sales are dwindling overall, hers have gained strength and have made an indelible impact on popular culture.

Born on December 24, 1973, in Hartford, Connecticut, the unusual spelling of young Stephenie Morgan's first name was a "gift" from her father Stephen, who simply added the letters i and e to his own name. Often described as a typical Mormon family, the Morgans moved to Arizona when Stephenie was four years old. The second oldest of six children—three girls, three boys—she shared a lot of familial responsibility. She babysat, changed diapers and worried about her younger brothers. In the process, she began to hone her insights into human nature. "I think that coming from such a large family has given me a lot of insight into different personality types," she told Cynthia Leiteich Smith of *Cynsations*, "my siblings sometimes crop up as characters in my stories."

A life-long avid reader, she often immersed herself in classic adult literature, her particular favorites being Jane Austen's *Pride and Prejudice*, Margaret Mitchell's *Gone With the Wind*, Charlotte Brontë's *Jane Eyre*, and Daphne du Maurier's *Rebecca*. Others favorites of hers include science fiction author Orson Scott Card, a fellow Mormon, and fantasy author Terry Brooks.

During her teen years, Meyer attended Chaparral High School. In her author profile for *Teenreads.com* she described the experience this way, "I went to high school in Scottsdale, Arizona, the kind of place where every fall a few girls would come back to school with new noses and there were Porsches in the student lot (for the record, I have my original nose, and never had a car until I was in my twenties)."

Courtesy of a National Merit Scholarship, she went to Brigham Young University (BYU) where her personal life changed dramatically. "See, beauty is a lot more subjective than you might think," she explained in the FAQ section of her Web site. "In Scottsdale, surrounded by barbies, I was about a five. In Provo, surrounded by normal people, I was more like an eight. I had dates every weekend with lots of really pretty and intelligent boys (some of whose names end up in my books). It was quite confusing at first, because I knew there was nothing different about me."

At BYU, the future author majored in English, but focused more on reading literature than her own creative writing. "She's always been very creative, but she didn't write a lot," her father told *Arizona Business Woman*. "We always thought she was going to be a painter." For her part, Meyer was happy to have a major that allowed her to read as much as she liked and made vague plans to attend law school.

However, during the summer break before her senior year at BYU, she began dating the man who would eventually become her husband, Christiaan Meyer. Nicknamed Pancho, he had known Stephenie since the age of four but had not befriended her until the summer of 1996. Having shared many of the same experiences from church and various social functions, the young couple instantly developed a strong bond. "On our second official date was when he proposed," she told the *Phoenix New Times*. "He proposed a lot. Over 40 times. He would propose every night and I would tell him no every night. It was kind of our end-of-date thing. Mormons get married a lot faster. The no-sex thing does speed up relationships." Later she would joke that nine months after their first "hello," she and Meyer were married.

Meyer attempted writing a few stories that she never finished before giving birth to her first son. Subsequently, she lived the life of an Arizona stay-at-home mom with a growing family, who worried about the overdue credit card bill and a broken down minivan. Meyer fixes the day that she became a writer as June 2, 2003. That morning she awoke from a powerful dream about a two people having an intense conversation in a meadow. One was a normal girl, the other a handsome vampire. The particulars of their relationship were spelled out by Meyer's dream. The characters were falling in love with one another but it was all the vampire could do to keep from killing her and feeding upon her blood.

In the *Twilight* section of her Web site, Meyer explains that the dream was so intriguing that—despite pending household chores and diaper duty—she stayed in bed savoring the dream and locking in her mental image of the vampire so she would not forget. Eventually, she got out of bed, did what needed to be done around the house, and then sat down at her computer and began writing the ten pages that ended up as chapter 13 of her debut novel *Twilight*. "From that point on," she says on her Web site, "not one day passed that I did not write *something*."

Writing at night after her sons had gone to bed and the house was quiet, Meyer began to flesh out the details of the *Twilight* world. Taking a cue from Brontë's Mr. Rochester and Austen's Mr. Ferrars, she named the vampire Edward. She gave her main female character the name she had been saving for a potential daughter: Isabella, or Bella for short. A Google search helped her choose the rainiest area in the United States—Forks, Washington—as her location and soon the story became an around-the-clock obsession. Writing in-between household chores and at night, she cut herself off from most of her friends. The only person outside her home who knew what she was attempting was elder sister Emily Rasmussen, who encouraged Meyer to publish the finished manuscript.

Admittedly naive about the publishing world, Meyer subscribed to WritersMarket.com, sent out queries to agents and small publishers, and recalls getting six or seven rejections, which she kept. Subsequently, Meyer's younger sister directed her attention to the Q & A section of author Janet Evanovich's website, where Evanovich advised budding authors to check out Writers House, a literary agency. A month after she had been asked to send in her entire manuscript, she received a call from Jodi Reamer, a New York literary agent. Reamer helped Meyer get the book ready to show to publishers by polishing up some rough spots and changing the title from *Forks* to *Twilight*. After shopping the project around to nine different publishing houses, she received an offer from Megan Tingley at Little, Brown and Company with a $300,000 advance, which her agent turned down before asking for $1 million. "I almost threw up," Meyers recalled for the *Phoenix New Times*.

Little, Brown and Company countered with a three-book deal worth $750,000. As a result, six months after she awoke from the most compelling dream of her life, Meyer was on track to be a major American author. Even she could not believe her own good fortune. "For a very long time," she humbly jokes on her Web site, "I was convinced it was a really cruel practical joke, but I couldn't imagine who would go to these wild extremes to play a hoax on such an insignificant little hausfrau."

Backed solidly by Little, Brown and Company—a major publisher of young adult fiction—Meyer's debut novel built upon a staggered market release, eventually hitting number five on the *New York Times* best-seller list. Her keen understanding of the hopes and fears of teenaged girls made the books a word-of-mouth favorite, but when she began making herself accessible to her fans on the Internet, her popularity exploded. Enthralled by the books, teen readers passed them on to their parents, and many of them became fans, establishing fan fiction sites, appreciation pages, and dressing up as characters in the books to attend Internet proms and book signings. Adults and teens alike appreciate both her ready wit and the serious consideration she gives to each inquiry about her characters. Grateful for her phenomenal success, Meyer feels immense affection for her core audience. "I've developed this hu-

mongous love for 12-year-old girls," she joked appreciatively with *Entertainment Weekly*'s Gregory Kirschling. "They have the best questions, and they're so into the stories. You really can't write for a better audience. I say to all other authors: If you're not writing for teenage girls, you're missing out on a lot of love."

Meyer kept building upon that love by staying disciplined and creating fresh material on a regular basis. Unwilling to let go of the characters she had grown fond of, Meyer wrote a series of epilogues that were an intended follow-up to *Twilight*, titled *Forever Dawn*, which she scrapped and used as an outline for *New Moon* and the rest of the Edward and Bella saga. The first two books sold more than 1.6 million copies combined, but it was not until her third book in the series, *Eclipse*, was released that the mainstream press began to compare her success to that of Rowling's.

"It looks like Harry needs to make room for Edward and Bella," announced Jeffrey Trachtenberg of the *Wall Street Journal* before noting that sales of Meyer's *Eclipse* had relegated Rowling's *Harry Potter and the Deathly Hallows* to the number-two spot at Barnes and Noble bookstores, and spent 29 weeks atop the *New York Times*' best-seller lists. *Time* writer Lev Grossman also likened Meyer's rise to Rowling's, observing, "But as artists, they couldn't be more different. Rowling pieces her books together meticulously, detail by detail. Meyer floods the page like a severed artery. She never uses a sentence when she can use a whole paragraph. Her books are big (500-plus pages) but not dense—they have a pillowy quality distinctly reminiscent of Internet fan fiction. (Which she'll readily grant: 'I don't think I'm a writer; I think I'm a storyteller. The words aren't always perfect.')"

Remarkably prolific, Meyer wrote her first science fiction novel aimed at the adult market, *The Host*, while editing *Eclipse* and planning *Breaking Dawn*. According to her interview with *Teenread.com*, *The Host* was a story she told herself to break up the monotony of driving from Phoenix to Salt Lake City. "I have no idea what sparked the strange foundation of a body-snatching alien in love with the host body's boyfriend over the host body's protest. I was halfway into the story before I realized it." Described as a "grittier read" by *Time*, it is also employs the same type of romantic conflicts that fuel her stories of Edward Cullen and Bella Swan.

According to Karen Valby of *Entertainment Weekly*, Meyer's publisher's did not want a fourth book in the *Twilight* series, but the author felt she could not complete her character's storylines in only three volumes. The result was *Breaking Dawn*, the biggest-selling novel of 2008. Although intended as closure, the book will not necessarily be the last word on the star-crossed lovers.

In addition to consulting on the movie debut of her first novel, due out late in 2008, the never idle Meyer has two sequels to *The Host* worked out in her head, is planning a ghost story called *Summer House*, and shows no sign of slowing down anytime soon. Indeed, Meyer told Valby in another *Entertainment Weekly* article that she is currently writing a version of her first novel called *Midnight Sun* but, tired of publishing politics and the occasional negativity towards her works, she is quoted as saying "I haven't sold *Midnight Sun* yet. It's for me still. I'll probably sell it when I'm done, for one reason: I want to have it bound up with the others."

## Selected writings

### Novels

*Twilight,* Little, Brown and Company (New York City), 2005.
*New Moon,* Little, Brown and Company, 2006.
*Eclipse,* Little, Brown and Company, 2007.
(With Meg Cabot, Kim Harrison, Michele Jaffe, and Lauren Myracle) *Prom Nights From Hell,* Harper-Teen (New York City), 2007.
*The Host,* Little, Brown and Company, 2008.
*Breaking Dawn,* Little, Brown and Company, 2008.

## Sources

### Periodicals

*Arizona Business Woman,* July 2007, p. 16.
*Business Week,* July 31, 2008.
*BYU Magazine,* Winter 2007.
*Entertainment Weekly,* August 10, 2007; July 18, 2008.
*Observer,* July 20, 2008.
*Phoenix New Times,* July 12, 2007.
*Time,* April 24, 2008.
*Wall Street Journal,* August 10, 2007.

### Online

"Author Interview: Stephenie Meyer on *Twilight,*" *Cynsations,* http://www.cynthialeitichsmith. blogspot.com/2006/03/author-interview-stephenie-meyer-on.html (August 9, 2008).
"Biography for Stephenie Meyer," Internet Movie Database, http://www.imdb.com (August 9, 2008).
"Exclusive! Stephenie Meyer Reveals a Spoiler," EW. com, http://www.ew.com/article/0,,20215228. tif,00.html?print (August 1, 2008).
"Frequently Asked Questions: *Twilight,*" StephenieMeyer.com (August 9, 2008).
"Stephenie Meyer: Bio," Teenreads.com, http:// www.teenreads.com/authors/au-meyer-stephenie.asp (August 9, 2008).
"The Story Behind Twilight," StephenieMeyer.com, http://www.stepheniemeyer.com/twilight.html (August 9, 2008).

—*Ken Burke*

# Ann Moore

Evan Agostini/Getty Images Entertainment/Getty Images

## Chief Executive Officer of Time, Inc.

**B**orn Ann Sommovigo in 1950, in McLean, VA; daughter of Monty and Bea Sommovigo; married Donovan Moore (a management consultant and screenwriter), c. 1974; children: Brendan. *Education:* Vanderbilt University, B.A., 1971; Harvard University, M.B.A., 1978.

**Addresses:** *Office*—c/o Time, Inc., 1271 Avenue of the Americas, New York, NY 10020.

## Career

**C**orporate financial analyst, Time, Inc., New York City, c. 1978, then media manager, c. 1979; worked for other Time publications, including stints as assistant circulation director for *Fortune* and circulation director of *Discover,* 1980-83; general manager, *Sports Illustrated,* 1983-89, then associate publisher, 1989-91; founding publisher, *Sports Illustrated for Kids,* 1989-91; publisher, *People,* 1991-93, then president, 1993-98; president, *People* Magazine Group (later known as *People/InStyle* Magazine Group), 1998-2001; executive vice president, Time, Inc., 2001-02, then chair and chief executive officer, 2002—.

**Member:** Board member, Avon Products, 1993—; board member, Wallace Foundation, 2004—.

**Awards:** One of the 50 most powerful women in American business, *Fortune,* 1998-2008; publishing executive of the year, *Adweek,* 1998; Civic Leadership Award, AOL Time Warner, 2003; one of the 100 most powerful women, *Forbes,* 2005-08; Alumni Achievement Award, Harvard Business School, 2006.

## Sidelights

**N**amed the chair and chief executive officer (CEO) of Time, Inc. in 2002, Ann Moore was the first woman to serve as the head of the number-one magazine company in the world. She had spent her entire career working for Time, Inc. and its magazines, primarily in publishing positions. Among her accomplishments was the launch of successful spin-offs from already thriving properties, including *Sports Illustrated for Kids, Teen People, In-Style,* and *People en Español. Teen People* publisher Anne Zehren told Valerie Block of *Crain's New York Business,* "It makes us all feel a little better knowing that a woman was rewarded for her excellent results."

Born in 1950 in McLean, Virginia (some sources say Biloxi, Mississippi), Moore is the daughter of Monty and Bea Sommovigo. She was raised in McLean, where she was a sports fan from an early age. After initially majoring in math, she earned her B.A. in political science from Vanderbilt University in 1971. Moore briefly worked in the publishing industry while intending to enter law school. She decided to go to business school instead, and continued her education at Harvard University, earning her M.B.A. in 1978.

After graduation, Moore then joined Time, Inc., taking the post because she liked magazines. Moore was first a corporate financial analyst, then became a media manager for *Sports Illustrated* within a year. Next, Moore worked at three other Time, Inc. publications from 1980 to 1983, including stints as assistant circulation director of *Fortune* and circulation director of *Discover*. She also worked at *Money* in this time period.

In 1983, Moore was named the general manager of *Sports Illustrated.* She held the post until 1989 when she became associate publisher. In 1989, Moore became the founding publisher of *Sports Illustrated for Kids*, a spin-off *Sports Illustrated*. Moore spent 18 months of her tenure at *Sports Illustrated* developing and launching the magazine. After becoming the founding publisher of *Sports Illustrated for Kids*, she remained associate publisher of *Sports Illustrated* as well.

Targeted at children eight to 13 years old and older, the monthly *Sports Illustrated for Kids* featured the kind of stories found in *Sports Illustrated* but its content was original, reflecting the interests and tastes of a younger audience. Moore also hoped that the magazine would encourage young readers and help increase literacy as well as groom future readers of *Sports Illustrated*. She was quoted by Business Wire as saying, "Primary research with children, their parents, and teachers gives us great confidence that we have found a void in the market, that our product concept is exciting, and that the need for fun, inspirational teaching materials in our public schools is real. Everyone wins with this product. Children will love reading it."

Moore remained at her position at *Sports Illustrated for Kids* until 1991, when she joined another Time, Inc. publication, *People*, as its publisher. In 1993, she was promoted to president of *People*, beginning a five-year stint. Also in 1993, Moore was elected to the board of Avon Products, the direct-marketed beauty company. During her period in charge of *People*, Moore launched innovative programs. In 1994, for example, *People* gave several million dollars of advertising space to charities and eliminated perks given to advertisers in favor of charity and volunteer-type experiences. The effort also included helping charities with marketing, printing, creative needs, and even office space, as needed.

By 1998, *Advertising Age* had named Moore one of its "Marketing 100." One reason for the nod was her launching of several successful spin-off titles. The first was *InStyle*, a celebrity-oriented lifestyle magazine, launched in 1994. She followed this success with *Teen People* and *People en Español*. The former was flourishing within a few issues, with its fourth issue, featuring cover boy Leonardo DiCaprio, selling so well that they had to print more copies. Moore later added an international edition of *InStyle* and *Real Simple*, a women's lifestyle magazine which focused on solutions to make life easier. She told *Advertising Age*'s Ann Marie Kerwin, "We're not constrained by a lack of good ideas. There are so many fabulous opportunities. If you've got the courage to do different, innovative projects, you can really score big even in seemingly crowded business."

Moore was promoted again in 1998 to become the president of the group which oversaw *People* and its spin-off titles. This newly created position helped streamline the management structure in the still growing *People* Magazine Group (later known as the *People/InStyle* Magazine Group). Beginning in 1998, Moore was also named one of the 50 most powerful women in business by *Fortune* magazine. She has received this accolade annually through 2008. By the end of her tenure at *People*, the magazine had been the top earner in terms of advertising revenue within Time, Inc. for eleven straight years.

In 2001, Moore moved up to the parent company of *People* and *Sports Illustrated*, Time Warner, Inc. She was named executive vice president and was believed to be under consideration to replace Time, Inc.'s chair and CEO, Don Logan, when he chose to leave the posts. She spent a year as executive vice president, then was given this promotion when Logan was named the head of the media division at AOL Time Warner, Time, Inc.'s parent company. In 2002, Moore became chair and chief executive officer of Time, Inc. It marked the first time that a woman had overseen the number-one magazine company in the world. It was also the first time a female executive served as the head of a unit at AOL Time Warner. Moore was expected to do well. Jack Haire, the executive vice president of Time, Inc., told David Carr of the *New York Times*, "Ann succeeded in a performance-oriented culture that Don has fostered. She has a record of product development and innovation that is second to none."

Moore faced many challenges in her new post. While Time, Inc. had about a quarter of all advertising revenue among American consumer magazines and at least 41 consecutive quarters of growth, the industry was being challenged by the growth of the Internet and difficult economic times, both of which cut into advertising revenue. She also had to manage the integration of the many acquisitions Time,

Inc. had made between 2000 and 2002, including IPC Media, the largest publisher of British consumer magazines, and Times Mirror group of magazines, such as *Transworld Skateboarding* and *Field & Stream,* and Synapse, a company which helped generate subscriptions. Moore did not plan on launching any titles early in her tenure, but to focus on keeping the profitability going. She told Block of *Crain's New York Business,* "Somehow, I've managed to keep *People* growing. I've just added another zero."

Among the choices Moore made as chair and CEO was the folding of *Sports Illustrated Women* in 2002. Two years later, she announced the launch of a new title, *All You,* a quality, but low-priced lifestyle magazine for the American homemaker. Facing continued advertising losses and a vast decrease in stock price, Moore began making more radical changes. Beginning in 2005, she streamlined the management structure of Time, Inc. to speed up decision making while reducing costs and simplifying communications. In the process, she laid off hundreds of employees, including high-ranking executives, sold at least 18 titles, shut down others like *Teen People* and *Life,* and instituted cost-saving measures. Because Web sites such as Time.com and People.com were becoming quite popular, Moore shifted more focus and investment on Time, Inc.'s Web sites and away from its print properties in 2006 and 2007. Hundreds more Time, Inc. employees also lost their jobs, and more titles were sold. As she made these moves, several Time, Inc. Web sites won industry accolades. Moore continued to make changes to evolve Time, Inc. and ensure continued profitability for the company. Despite her triumphs and influence, she planned on stepping down when her contract expired with Time, Inc. in 2010.

Because of her position and success, Moore was regularly recognized as a powerful businesswoman. From 2005 to 2008, she was named one of the 100 most powerful women in *Forbes* magazine. In 2007, she was also named one of the 50 most powerful women in New York City by the *New York Post.* Moore has received these honors because of her business savvy. She told the *New York Times'* Carr, "I worry about being nimble. If you sit back and think that you can just take it to the bank, that's where the trouble starts. If I pull a magazine up out of the archives from ten years ago, I want it to look completely different than the one we are doing now. If it looks the same, that means we aren't staying current with the audience."

## Sources

### Books

*Complete Marquis Who's Who,* Marquis Who's Who, 2008.

### Periodicals

*Advertising Age,* September 26, 1988, p. 78; June 29, 1998, p. S39; October 9, 2006, p. 10; November 6, 2006, p. 69; March 5, 2007, p. 30.
Associated Press, February 11, 1989; December 13, 2005.
Business Wire, August 4, 1988; July 18, 2002.
*Crain's New York Business,* July 23, 2001, p. 27; July 22, 2002, p. 4.
*MIN Media Industry Newsletter,* June 16, 2008.
*New York Post,* July 19, 2002, p. 35; August 31, 2007, p. 39; September 30, 2007, p. 39.
*New York Times,* August 4, 1988, p. D17; September 20, 1993, p. D7; February 14, 1994, p. D6; July 22, 2002, p. C1; April 6, 2003, sec. 3, p. 13; March 30, 2004, p. C4; December 14, 2005, p. C3; January 19, 2007, p. C4.
PR Newswire, July 1, 1991; May 6, 1993; November 3, 1998; September 30, 2007.
*San Diego Union-Tribune,* October 17, 2002, p. D10.

—*A. Petruso*

# Tracy Morgan

## Actor and comedian

**B**orn November 10, 1968, in New York, NY; son of James Morgan II (a musician); married Sabina, 1985 (filed for divorce, 2007); children: Tracy, Malcolm, Gitrid. *Education:*

**Addresses:** *Contact*—c/o David Becky, 3 Arts Entertainment, 9460 Wilshire Blvd., 7th Fl., Beverly Hills, CA 90212.

## Career

**A**ctor and comedian. Television appearances include: *Uptown Comedy Club*, 1993-94; *Martin*, 1994-96; *Def Comedy Jam*, 1995; *Saturday Night Live*, NBC, 1996-2006; *The Chris Rock Show*, 1997; *The Jim Breuer Show*, 1998; *Third Rock from the Sun*, NBC, 2000; *Tracy Morgan: One Mic* (special), Comedy Central, 2002; *Crank Yankers*, 2002; *Comic Groove*, 2002; *Driven*, 2002; *Hollywood Squares*, 2002; *Punk'd*, MTV, 2003; *Saturday Night Live Weekend Update Halftime Special*, NBC, 2003; *The Tracy Morgan Show*, NBC, 2003-04; *The Sharon Osborne Show*, syndicated, 2003, 2004; *ESPY Awards* (special), ESPN, 2004; *Richard Pryor: The Funniest Man Dead or Alive*, 2005; *Jimmy Kimmel Live!*, ABC, 2004-08; *Mind of Mencia*, Comedy Central, 2006; *Where My Dogs At?*, 2006; *Darnell* (movie), 2006; *30 Rock*, NBC, 2006—; *Guys Choice Awards*, Spike TV, 2007; *Hip Hop Honors*, VH1, 2007; *Scare Tactics*, Sci Fi, 2008; *Laffapalooza!* (special), 2008; *Human Giant*, 2008. Film appearances include: *A Thin Line Between Love and Hate*, 1996; *Half Baked*, 1998; *30 Years to Life*, 2001; *Jay and Silent Bob Strike Back*, 2001; *Frank McKlusky, C.I.*, 2002; *Head of State*, 2003; *Are We There Yet?*, 2005; *The Longest Yard*, 2005; *Farce of the Penguins*, 2006; *Little Man*, 2006; *Deep in the Valley*, 2008; *First Sunday*, 2008; *Superhero Movie*, 2008; *Nailed*, 2009; *G-Force*, 2009. Worked as television writer and producer, including: *Tracy Morgan: One Mic* (special), 2002; *The Tracy Morgan Show*, 2003-04.

## Sidelights

**A**fter finding fame as a featured performer on *Saturday Night Live*, comedian Tracy Morgan showed the depth of his acting ability on the highly regarded, award-winning situation comedy *30 Rock*. Morgan began his career as a stand-up comedian and had his own short-lived situation comedy, *The Tracy Morgan Show*. While Morgan also took on film roles—most notably in *The Longest Yard* and *First Sunday*—doing stand-up comedy and making an audience laugh provided the most satisfaction for Morgan. He told Ed Condran of the Bergen County, New Jersey, *Record*, "Being able to make people laugh saved me from some beatings and in ways saved my life, personally and professionally."

Morgan was born on November 10, 1968, in the Bronx borough of New York City, the son of James Morgan II. His father was a musician and a veteran of the Vietnam War. His parents ended their relationship when he was a child, and he was raised by his mother in a housing project in Brooklyn as well as tough sections of the Bronx. As a child, Morgan had athletic aspirations to play in the National Football League as a tailback. Morgan later admitted that he made some poor decisions while living in rough neighborhoods, including dealing drugs. The executive producer of *The Tracy Morgan Show,* David M. Israel, told Bruce Betts of *Entertainment Weekly,* "He could've wound up like a lot of other people—in jail or dead. Comedy was his saving grace."

Morgan married his high school sweetheart, Sabina, in 1985. The couple soon had three sons: Tracy, Malcolm, and Gitrid. He told Condran of the Bergen County, New Jersey *Record,* "That makes you grow up in a hurry. I was in a tough spot. Being a kid from the projects with a son doesn't put the odds in your favor, when you're talking about making it." By the early 1990s, Morgan found a career when he began doing stand-up comedy in clubs in Manhattan and at the Apollo, while his wife worked tirelessly to support him and their family.

As a young comedian, he was greatly influenced by his father's sense of humor as well as Andrew "Dice" Clay, Richard Pryor, Eddie Murphy, Dean Martin, and Lucille Ball. Within a few years, Morgan was appearing on television, first on *Uptown Comedy Club* from 1993 to 1994. He later had roles on shows such as *Martin* (on which he played the recurring character Hustleman) and *Def Comedy Jam.* These shows brought Morgan and his talent to the attention of *Saturday Night Live* (*SNL*) producer Lorne Michaels.

In 1996, Morgan received the break of his career when Michaels asked him to join the cast of the long-running sketch comedy show *SNL.* He told Marijke Rowland of the Raleigh, North Carolina *News & Observer,* "My career fell in my lap. It's on-the-job training. I'm still learning." When Morgan was cast on *SNL,* life changed for him and his family. The Associated Press Online quoted him as saying "My whole life became a series of calming everyone down. They were on my front door. It was like hitting Lotto. I had to really get my family up out of the 'hood first. With the second check, we were gone.... Some people tripped, but they're all right now."

While Morgan had limited screen time during his first years on *SNL,* he soon became one of the fan favorites. He became known for his spot-on impressions of such celebrities as Mike Tyson, Star Jones,

Marion Barry, Oprah Winfrey, and Mr. T. He was also lauded for his extreme original creations such as Astronaut Jones, Dominican Lou, Woodrow, and Brian Fellow.

During his time on *SNL,* Morgan expanded his acting career in other ways. In 2002, he had his own stand-up special on Comedy Central, *Tracy Morgan. One Mic.* Morgan also appeared in a number of films, mostly in small roles. His films included 1996's *A Thin Line Between Love and Hate,* the 1998 stoner comedy *Half Baked,* and the 2001 comedy *Jay and Silent Bob Strike Back.*

Morgan ended his run on *SNL* in May of 2003, though he appeared on at least an episode per year for several years afterward. Though he was arguably at the height of his popularity when he left, Morgan told *Entertainment Weekly*'s Betts, "I didn't want to stay too long. I wanted to leave on top." He and his family then moved to Los Angeles where he began taping his own situation comedy, *The Tracy Morgan Show,* for NBC.

On the show, Morgan played Tracy Mitchell, the owner/operator of an automotive repair shop who was also a family man facing the challenges of everyday life. For Morgan, it was also a chance to see what life might have been like had his parents stayed together when he was young. He told Jae-Ha Kim of the *Chicago Sun-Times,* "It's looking fantastic and I'm just excited to be doing it. It's basically just good old-fashioned television."

*The Tracy Morgan Show* did not catch on, however. Critics like Brian Lowry of *Variety* thought the show underutilized Morgan's comedic abilities. Lowry wrote, "Tracy Morgan has proved he can be a funny guy in sketches on *Saturday Night Live,* but playing another dad-who's-really-just-a-big-kid-himself capitalizes only sparingly on those skills." The *New York Times*' Anita Gates concluded, "Mr. Morgan plays clueless sublimely, but the spell is broken the minute his own natural intelligence comes into his eyes." Other critics found the premise of the show lacking. Matthew Gilbert in the *Boston Globe* noted, "The show ... is familiar, harmless, and loud. It represents yet another mediocre American family comedy with predictable gags and cute kids...."

The series was cancelled after one season, and Morgan returned to touring as a stand-up comedian as he had done when he had time while starring on both *SNL* and *The Tracy Morgan Show.* He told Rowland in the *News & Observer* interview, "Every chance I get, I love to do stand-up. Stand-up is my foundation; that is what I built my career with. If I wasn't able to do that, I'd walk away from all of it." Morgan's stand-up was not intended for the same audience as his sitcom. He told Mark Mcguire of the Albany, New York *Times Union*, "My stand-up is adult-rated.... I'm an adult, I'm 35 years old, I've lived some life and I just want to talk about it. It's not always politically correct, but it is going to show the adult side of me."

Morgan also capitalized on his fame by signing a promotional deal with ESPN to promote a series of sports-themed video games, among other commercial endorsements. In addition to stand up and such promotional interests, Morgan continued to act in films, including comedies such as 2003's *Head of State* and 2005's *Are We There Yet?* Also in 2005, Morgan had a featured role in the remake of the hit Burt Reynolds' film, *The Longest Yard*. In this film, Morgan played Ms. Tucker, a convict who is also a transvestite and cheerleader for the prison football team. Morgan told Bob Thompson of the *National Post*, "I admit I took the role reluctantly. At first I thought, 'Hmm, father of three, doing this?' Then I decided I could do something a little far out and show some range."

Morgan had not given up on television or the situation comedy format, however. In 2006, he was cast in a role on *30 Rock*. Created by former *SNL* performer/head writer Tina Fey and produced by Michaels, the show was a critical smash from its debut. *30 Rock* rotated around a fictional network sketch comedy show, *The Girlie Show*. While *30 Rock* focused on Fey as the show's head writer and Alec Baldwin as the pompous network head, Morgan's Tracy Jordan was a comic juggernaut. His Jordan was an unpredictable black film star who had his own entourage and seemed mentally unstable. His character joins the fictional show to help boost ratings but often presents challenges to Fey's Liz Lemon and other characters. As Emma Rosenblum of *New York Magazine* described it, Morgan's character's "manic antics and well-fed ego suggest a combination of Eddie Murphy, Martin Lawrence, and, well, Tracy Morgan."

Morgan was quite appreciative of the opportunity that *30 Rock* and the Jordan character provided him. He told the *Record*'s Condran, "It's a great role. What makes it great is Tina Fey. She's a comic genius, right up there with Lucille Ball and Carol Burnett. Tina knows my voice. I'm so lucky to be on a show with her and Alec Baldwin, who has the most incredible sense of timing. I couldn't be more fortunate." Morgan added to Andy Smith of the *Providence Journal*, "People do love him. And he's a

likeable guy. But he's crazy, and I'm not. I get to go to work every day and play crazy, which is fun. And I love the way Tina writes for this guy. Tina definitely has a grip on this character."

While Morgan was riding the crest of this success, however, his personal life proved challenging. From late 2005 to 2006, he was arrested three times on drunk or impaired driving charges in California and New York. After these arrests, Morgan admitted he made mistakes and vowed not to repeat them. As part of related court orders, he went to a medically supervised alcohol program, wore an alcohol monitoring device, and performed community service. In 2005 Morgan's problems with alcohol nearly tore his marriage and family apart as well. The couple separated at that time and later reconciled. However, in 2007 Sabina Morgan filed for divorce because of his alcoholism.

Though *30 Rock* struggled in the ratings from the first, NBC kept renewing the show, and it was nominated for several awards. The show nabbed Screen Actors Guild Award nominations in 2008 and 2008 for outstanding performance by an ensemble in a comedy series, and Morgan himself was nominated for an Image Award from the NAACP for outstanding supporting actor in a comedy series in 2008. In 2009, *30 Rock* had a breakthrough as it won the Golden Globe for best comedy. At the ceremony, Morgan accepted the award for the show telling the audience he had a won a bet with Fey. Brooks Barnes and Michael Cieply of the *New York Times* quoted Morgan as quipping "If Barack Obama won, I would speak for the show from now on."

During the run of *30 Rock*, Morgan continued to do stand-up and expand his acting career. He had a starring role in the 2008 film *First Sunday*—in which he played LeeJohn, a criminal who tries to rob a church to pay a debt—and hosted a number of award shows and specials. They included Spike TV's *Guys Choice Awards* and VH1's *Hip Hop Honors*, both in 2007, as well as the Sci Fi series *Scare Tactics*, in 2008. Morgan hoped his career would turn toward more family friendly fare in the future. He told Reed Tucker of the *New York Post*, "I'm a family man first. Children inspire me. I wan to go that route, PG, PG-13. Eddie Murphy, Bill Cosby—these are guys who came before me and set the blueprint for me."

## Sources

### Books

*Complete Marquis Who's Who*, Marquis Who's Who, 2008.

## Periodicals

*Akron Beacon Journal* (OH), June 4, 2006.
*Anchorage Daily News* (AK), April 29, 2005, p. H5.
Associated Press, May 31, 2007.
Associated Press Online, July 29, 2003; November 28, 2006; February 14, 2007.
*Atlanta Journal-Constitution,* December 2, 2003, p. 3E.
*Boston Globe,* December 2, 2003, p. E8.
*Chicago Sun-Times,* November 7, 2003, p. 3.
*El Paso Times,* February 18, 2005, p. 3T.
*Entertainment Weekly,* December 5, 2003, pp. 57-58.
*National Post* (Canada), May 26, 2005, p. AL1.
*News & Observer* (Raleigh, NC), December 2, 2003, p. E5.
*New York Magazine,* October 16, 2006; November 3, 2008.
*New York Post,* January 6, 2008, p. 44.

*New York Times,* December 2, 2003, p. E5; January 6, 2008, sec. 9, p. 4; January 12, 2009, p. C1.
*Pittsburgh Tribune-Review,* April 26, 2007.
*Providence Journal* (RI), September 28, 2005, p. G7; January 17, 2007, p. G6.
*Record* (Bergen County, NJ), November 24, 2006, p. G23.
*San Francisco Chronicle,* January 11, 2008, p. E4.
*St. Petersburg Times* (FL), January 25, 2008, p. 2B.
*Times Union* (Albany, NY), March 25, 2004, p. P20.
*Variety,* December 1, 2003–December 7, 2003, p. 57.

## Online

"Tracy Morgan," Internet Movie Database, http://www.imdb.com/name/nm0605079/ (January 13, 2009).

*—A. Petrusa*

# Elsa Murano

### President of Texas A&M University

Born Elisa Alina Casales, August 14, 1959, in Havana, Cuba; married Peter Murano (a professor), . 1987. *Education:* Attended Miami Dade College, . 1977-79; Florida International University, B.S., 981; Virginia Technological University, M.S., 1987; PhD, 1990.

**Addresses:** *Home*—Bryan, TX. *Office*—Texas A&M University, Rudder Tower, 1246 TAMU, College Station, TX 77843-1246.

### Career

Began career as a research laboratory technician at Florida International University, 1981-83; researcher and teaching assistant, Virginia Technological University, 1984-90; assistant professor, Dept. of Microbiology, Immunology and Preventive Medicine, Iowa State University, 1990-95; associate professor, Dept. of Animal Science, Texas A&M University; associate director then director, Center for Food Safety, Texas A&M University, 1995-2001; undersecretary for food safety and inspection service, U.S. Dept. of Agriculture, 2001-04; vice chancellor, then dean, Agriculture and Life Sciences, Texas A&M University, 2005-08; president, Texas A&M University, 2008—.

**Awards:** One of 100 Most Influential Hispanics, *Hispanic Business* magazine, 2002; Alumni Hall of Fame, Hispanic Scholarship Fund, 2005; American By Choice Award, U.S. State Department, 2008.

*Courtesy of Texas A&M University*

### Sidelights

For more than a decade, college president Elsa Murano has experienced a series of firsts that has made both the Hispanic community and the United States take notice. Fleeing Cuba at a young age with her family, Murano moved to Miami at age 14, where she first learned to speak English. Choosing to pursue a career in research, Murano began her collegiate career at Iowa State University before taking a professorship at Texas A&M (Agricultural & Mechanical) University. U.S. President George W. Bush then tapped her to become the undersecretary of food safety and inspection service of the U.S. Department of Agriculture (USDA). Murano became the first Hispanic woman to hold this post. She returned to Texas A&M as vice chancellor and dean of Agriculture and Life Sciences. She was also the first Hispanic and the first woman to hold these positions. After serving in this position for four years, Murano became the 23rd president of Texas A&M University. Once again she was the first Hispanic, the first woman, and the youngest person to hold the position.

Murano was born Elisa Alina Casales in Havana, Cuba, on August 14, 1959. Two years after Fidel Castro took office, Murano, her parents and siblings left the country. They settled in Curacao but her father found work with IBM, and the family moved to Columbia. They also lived in Peru, El Salvador, and Puerto Rico, before her mother moved the children to Miami, Florida, after divorcing her husband. Murano was 14 years old and a ninth grader enrolled at Coral Park Sr. High School. She enrolled in regular classes taught in English by mistake. At this age she began her tenacity to overcome obstacles by mastering the English language in four months rather than transfer to classes for English language learners. She told Ralph K. M. Haurwitz of the *Austin American-Statesman*, "It was one of those very uncomfortable sink-or-swim situations. It was really hard, but frankly, I think it worked out well."

Murano's mother worked three jobs to support her family and encouraged her children to get an education in order to have a better life. After high school, she took her mother's advice and enrolled at Miami Dade College for two years before transferring to Florida International University to complete her undergraduate education. She majored in microbiology and planned to attend medical school before changing to a career in research after learning marijuana derivatives injected into mice prevented cancer. Murano supported herself through loans, scholarships, and by working as a research laboratory technician at the university.

Murano also met her future husband, Peter, while attending Florida International. After receiving her degree, the two of them enrolled at Virginia Technological University. She majored in anaerobic microbiology and worked as a researcher and teaching assistant at Virginia Tech. Once she obtained her masters degree, Murano married Peter and both secured employment at Iowa State University. She worked as an assistant professor in the department of Microbiology, Immunology and Preventive Medicine. Murano later earned her doctorate in food science and technology from Virginia Tech.

Murano was asked to join Texas A&M, but she declined. One year passed and she was approached again, this time with an offer for her husband as well. When the two arrived in College Station, Texas, they fell in love with the area and the Aggie atmosphere. She began her career with Texas A&M as an associate professor in the department of Animal Sciences. She was also the associate director of the Center for Food Safety, but then was promoted to director.

After six years in Texas, Murano was asked by Bush to serve as the undersecretary for food safety in the U.S. Department of Agriculture. Her appointment was met with criticism from several consumer groups who were concerned about her affiliation with a company named SureBeam that sold irradiation equipment. Irradiation is a process to kill microbes in meat. This process is highly controversial due to safety concerns, and Murano's placement on the board raised issues with the groups, who believed she would push for the process to be instituted in public school systems during her tenure. The confirmation hearing for her appointment went without a hitch and Murano was appointed as the undersecretary She was the first Hispanic woman to hold the position. About her connection with SureBeam, Murano told Holly Hacker and Brian Davis of the *Dallas Morning News*, "she always recused herself from any dealings involving [Texas] A&M" and that "she ... behaved ethically."

Murano's tenure as the undersecretary was not without conflict. Under her leadership, her department dealt with the first bout of mad cow disease. She worked hard to bring the number of food recalls down and by the end of her term, the number had been reduced from 113 in 2002 to less than 50 in 2004.

Murano learned that working in a collegiate atmosphere was very different than working in the Washington political scene. She told Cesar Arredondo of *Latino Leaders*, "I was a proverbial 'Mr. Smith Goes to Washington'. [I was] wide-eyed and thinking I was going to go in there and change Washington D.C." Instead, for example, Murano found herself in a heated discussion with members of Congress who questioned her decision to make recalling food mandatory. The system in place is voluntary.

After three and a half years, the call to return to Texas A&M came, and the Muranos returned south. Both accepted new positions, and Murano became vice chancellor and dean of the College of Agriculture and Life Sciences. Her husband was an associate professor in the Department of Nutrition and Food Science and the director of the Center for Obesity Research and Program Evaluation. She continued to add to her growing list of firsts, this time as the first Hispanic and first woman to hold these positions. As she began her new role, she faced a decline in student enrollment in her department as well as a high turnover rate among faculty. Murano, taking a page from then-president Robert Gates, listened to the concerns of both students and teachers and began to turn the department around. She took steps to address problems with the term "agriculture" and chose to change the name from College of Agriculture and Life Services to the College of AgriLife Services. Murano also opted to change the names of two other divisions in her department: the Texas Cooperative Extension and the Texas Agricultural Extension. They became the Texas AgriLife Extension and Texas AgriLife Research, respectively. The name changes were met with dissension all over the university, from the board of regents to the students. Murano defended her position and won over some of the dissenters. She compromised by allowing the college to keep its name. She told Holly Huffman of the *Eagle*, "They felt I was walking away from [agriculture], which is absolutely not true. My intention was to elevate [agriculture], to bring it to the consciousness of people and develop a really good definition of what it truly does. It's life-changing work."

When Gates left his position to become secretary of defense, a year-long search began to find his replacement. A total of 140 candidates were found, including Murano; however, she did not make the cut when the list was shortened to ten names. A committee consisting of faculty, students, and former students cut the list again to three and presented those names to the regents. The regents rejected those names and located other candidates, including Murano. In December of 2007, Murano found herself the lone candidate waiting for final approval by the regents. According to Texas state law, public institutions had to enact a 21-day waiting period before voting. Murano, as the next president, was met with criticism. This time it was mostly how the selection was done and the timing of the announcement. Murano took the time to listen to the concerns of the students and staff and in January of 2008, she entered the office running. Once again Murano's new position was also a number of firsts. Again, she was the first Hispanic, the first woman, and the youngest person to preside over Texas A&M. She told Cesar Arredondo of *Latino Leaders*, "Here I am, president of Texas A&M University. The possibilities and opportunities [in the U.S.] are limitless. It doesn't mean it's easy; there are obstacles.... You just have to persevere." Murano's first tasks were to allay the fears of those who felt manipulated by the selection process. She also continued to upgrade facilities and technology and increase enrollment, particularly by minority students as well as attracting top-notch faculty to make Texas A&M one of the top ten public institutions in the United States.

Murano, an avid sports fan, also plays the conga drums in the praise band at her church. She has won grants for various research projects totaling $8.7 million. She is also a member of several organi-

zations and was appointed by Bush to the Board for International Food and Agricultural Development. Her term on that board will end in 2012. She was also honored by the U.S. State Department with the "American By Choice" award in 2008. Murano has taken the academic world by storm with her resolve to improve food safety, whether through research or as the undersecretary or by shaping the minds of students to search for solutions. Her journey from Cuban immigrant to college president is truly inspiring.

## Sources

### Periodicals

*Austin American-Statesman* (Austin, TX), December 8, 2007, p. A1; December 16, 2007, p. A1; August 15, 2008, p. B2.
*Dallas Morning News,* December 8, 2007; January 3, 2008.
*Eagle* (Bryan, TX), December 8, 2007; December 9, 2007; January 4, 2008; January 10, 2008; February 3, 2008.
*Food Chemical News,* October 21, 2002, p. 25; March 25, 2002, p. 1.
*Fort Worth Star-Telegram* (Fort Worth, TX), December 8, 2007.
*Latino Leaders,* April 2008, pp. 40-41.
*Miami Herald* (Miami, FL), January 9, 2008.
*Southwest Farm Press,* November 22, 2004; December 11, 2007.

### Online

"A&M President Honored By State Department," KBTX, http://www.kbtx.com/home/headlines/16097952.tif.html (August 18, 2008).
"Aggies Insider: Murano crosses fingers for 'Wrecking Crew Part II,'" *San Antonio Express-News,* http://www.mysanantonio.com/sports/big_12/Aggies_Insider_Murano_Wrecking_Crew_Part_II.html (August 18, 2008).
"Dr. Elsa A. Murano," Office of the President, Texas A&M University, http://www.tamu.edu/president/ (August 18, 2008).
"Self-made immigrant is poised to take the lead at university," *Houston Chronicle,* http://www.chron.com/disp/story.mpl/front/5383486.html (August 18, 2008).

*—Ashyia N. Henderson*

# Heidi Murkoff

## Author

Born Heidi Eisenberg, c. 1958; daughter of Howard and Arlene Eisenberg (both freelance journalists); married Erik Murkoff, April 4, 1982; children: Emma, Wyatt. *Education:* Attended Brandeis University, Waltham, MA.

**Addresses:** *Contact*—What to Expect Foundation, 211 W. 80th St., lower level, New York, NY 10024. *Home*—Los Angeles, CA. *Web site*—What to Expect Foundation, http://www.whattoexpect.org.

## Career

Copywriter, Leber Katz Partners, New York City, c. 1980; published first book, *What to Expect When You're Expecting,* 1984; founder, What to Expect Foundation, 2000; introduced the *What to Expect Kids* series, 2000; launched www.WhatToExpect.com, 2005.

## Sidelights

Working alongside her sister and mother, Heidi Murkoff wrote the groundbreaking pregnancy tome *What to Expect When You're Expecting.* Published in 1984, the book appealed immediately to expectant women and went on to become the pregnancy authority for many U.S. women. Twenty-five years later, the book was still in circulation with some 15 million copies sold. In 2008, Murkoff released a fourth edition with a complete cover-to-cover rewrite.

The youngest of three children, Murkoff was born in the late 1950s. Her parents, Howard and Arlene Eisenberg, were freelance journalists whose co-authored articles appeared in *Ladies' Home Journal* and *Sports Illustrated.* Murkoff spent her childhood in Garden City and Spring Valley, both in New York. She also lived overseas, spending two years in Europe and Israel with her parents as they traveled around conducting interviews. In an article by Hilary MacGregor of the *Los Angeles Times,* Murkoff praised her parents for encouraging her creativity and inspiring her way with words. Murkoff also noted that her parents were undemanding and easygoing. She said her family was "disorganized, clutter-embracing, always late, [and] schedule-phobic."

Murkoff attended Brandeis University, then worked as a copywriter for Leber Katz Partners in New York City. In 1982, she married Erik Murkoff and was soon pregnant. Eager and anxious, Murkoff went to the bookstore to find a pregnancy book that would answer her questions. The few books Murkoff discovered were written by doctors, and she found them patronizing. In addition, they offered little information to women about what was happening to their bodies.

Murkoff had a lot of questions. She worried about the wine she had sipped before realizing she was pregnant; she worried about how much coffee she should drink and how much protein she should eat; she wondered about fetal movements and how often she should feel them. The books "didn't answer my questions and of course I had thousands of questions and worries because it was my first pregnancy," Murkoff told *Total Health* editor Lyle Hurd in an interview for Americanwellnessnetwork.com. "When I found there wasn't a book that provided both of those valuable commodities, answers and reassurance ... it dawned on me that I would have to write it. The first book was a personal crusade to make sure that other expectant parents slept better at night than I did during my pregnancy."

Murkoff finished her book proposal just hours before giving birth to her daughter, Emma. Once the book idea was clear, Murkoff called upon her mother and sister for help. Murkoff's mother had become an expert on medical issues after writing a college textbook on health. Murkoff's older sister, Sandee Hathaway, had trained as an obstetrical nurse. Working together, the three women created the book, the first book of its type written by mothers for mothers. Writing in a breezy tone, the trio composed answers to questions they thought pregnant women would want to ask their obstetricians but might hesitate to pose during a checkup. Written in a question-and-answer format, the book offers a thorough discussion of topics, addressing weight gain, hemorrhoids, abdominal pains, heartburn, and sex. *What to Expect When You're Expecting* was also the first book to cover pregnancy on a month-to-month basis.

Sales started slow but picked up each year as word of the book spread. Five years after its release, *What to Expect When You're Expecting* landed on the *New York Times* best-seller list and has spent more than 355 weeks on the list in the past two decades. A 1998 survey by *USA Today* reported that 93 percent of the pregnant women polled who read a pregnancy book had chosen *What to Expect When You're Expecting*. The threesome followed with 1986's *What to Eat When You're Expecting*, 1989's *What to Expect the First Year*, and 1994's *What to Expect the Toddler Years*.

In 2000, Murkoff launched the What to Expect Foundation, which provides low-income and low-literacy adults with prenatal educational materials. The foundation published *Baby Basics: Your Month by Month Guide to a Healthy Pregnancy*, written at a third-grade reading level and also available in Spanish. The foundation has donated more than 300,000 copies to clinics across the United States.

Capitalizing on the success of her What to Expect franchise, Murkoff launched a picture book series called *What to Expect Kids* in 2000. The books, aimed at preschoolers, feature a floppy-eared dog named Angus. Titles in the series include *What to Expect When Mommy's Having a Baby* and *What to Expect When You Use the Potty*. Murkoff wrote these books on her own.

In 2005, Murkoff launched a Web site—www. WhatToExpect.com. The interactive site includes week-by-week pregnancy calendars, a searchable reference guide, and message boards. Murkoff visits the site frequently to chat with women and find out what is on their minds. The site was popular, with some 1.7 million users a month in 2008, making it the second-most-popular parenting site on the Web.

Murkoff has continually updated *What to Expect* since it rolled off the press in 1984. In 2008, she completely rewrote the book, working with co-author Sharon Mazel. The 2008 edition has been updated for the 21st century. The book's cover no longer features a plain, pregnant woman resting in a rocker. This mom is standing and wearing fashionable maternity jeans that accentuate her baby bump.

The new edition answers questions that were not relevant two decades before. It touches on topics such as getting through pregnancy with an eating disorder and nursing with a nipple ring. There are also chapters on multiple births. In another change, this edition analyzes pregnancy developments on a week-to-week basis, "so you can keep track of your baby's amazing and achingly adorable growth from poppy-seed-sized to fully equipped-for-cuddling newborn," Murkoff told Delia O'Hara of the *Chicago Sun Times*.

While the book has been popular, there have also been critics who think sections of it exaggerate risks, making women anxious. For example, in early editions, Murkoff warned that fetal hiccups—which are common in pregnancy—might be a sign of distress—such as an umbilical cord problem. She downplayed this warning in later editions. Because each chapter contains a section titled "What You May Be Concerned About," some critics, such as users of Urbanbaby.com, refer to the book as *What to Freak Out About When You're Expecting*. Other readers credited the book with helping them detect problems their doctors missed.

Despite the criticism, *Parenting* magazine editor-in-chief Susan Kane swears by the book. "There's nothing else like this book," she told Jocelyn Noveck in an article for the *Mobile Register*. "What I love about it is that so many things can happen during a pregnancy, and Heidi covers them all."

## Selected writings

### Reference guides

(With Arlene Eisenberg and Sandee Hathaway) *What to Expect When You're Expecting*, Workman Publishing, 1984.

(With Eisenberg and Hathaway) *What to Eat When You're Expecting*, Workman Publishing, 1986.

(With Eisenberg and Hathaway) *What to Expect the First Year*, Workman Publishing, 1989.

(With Eisenberg and Hathaway) *What to Expect the Toddler Years*, Workman Publishing, 1994.

(With Sharon Mazel) *What to Expect When You're Expecting*, Workman Publishing, 2008.

## Sources

### Periodicals

*Chicago Sun Times*, May 16, 2008, p. 34.
*Los Angeles Times*, July 29, 2007, p. I46.
*Mobile Register* (Alabama), May 4, 2008, p. Z13.

*New York Times*, March 14, 1982; January 5, 1995; February 10, 2001, p. 13; September 15, 2005.

### Online

"About the Author," WhatToExpect.com, http://www.whattoexpect.com/home/about-the-author.aspx (February 2, 2009).

"Interview with Heidi Murkoff: Meeting the Expectations of Others," AmericanWellnessNetwork.com, http://www.americanwellnessnetwork.com/index.php/20070520.tif415/Interview-with-Heidi-Murkoff.html (February 2, 2009).

*—Lisa Frick*

# Kathleen Murphy

**Executive**

**B**orn c. 1963; daughter of Charles Murphy and Christine Connor; married George Hornyak; children: Jack. *Education:* Fairfield University, B.A.; University of Connecticut Law, J.D.

**Addresses:** *Office*—Fidelity Investments, 82 Devonshire St., Boston, MA 02109-3605.

## Career

**B**egan career at Aetna Financial Services, 1985, held legal and compliance posts, 1988-97, General Counsel and Chief Compliance Officer, 1997-2000; senior adviser, general counsel and Chief Administrative Officer of U. S. Financial Services, ING, 2000-03, Group President, Worksite and Institutional Financial Services, 2004-06, Chief Executive Officer, U.S. Wealth Management, 2006-08; president of personal investing, Fidelity Investments, 2009—.

**Member:** Board, American Benefits Council; chairperson, America's Promise Alliance; national trustee, Boys & Girls Club of America; board of directors, Connecticut Business and Industry Association; chairperson, Connecticut Children's Trust Fund; board, Governor's Prevention Partnership Program; board of directors, Metro Hartford Alliance; board of directors, National Conference for Civil Justice in the Northeast; board, Wheeler Clinic.

**Awards:** Named one of the 50 Most Powerful Women, *Fortune* magazine, 2007, 2008.

## Sidelights

**O**ne of the most powerful women in business, Kathleen Murphy, former CEO of ING's U.S. Wealth Management division, debuted on *Fortune* magazine's "50 Most Powerful Women" list in 2007 at number 40. She remained on the list the following year at number 41, and was noted for her acquisition of CitiStreet, which expanded ING's retirement services offerings.

Murphy grew up in an Irish-American household in Wallingford, Connecticut, very aware of her heritage. One of the rules of her household, which she still keeps posted on her desk, was "Thou Shalt Not Whine." Murphy told Patricia Harty of *Irish America* magazine, "Even if you did whine, it had no impact." Murphy's family was a large one, and she was one of six children in a very child-focused environment. She was encouraged to play sports to learn how to work in a team environment. Murphy also went to state championships with her high school swim team, and took advanced placement classes at the urging of her high school history teacher.

A graduate of Fairfield University, Murphy not only graduated summa cum laude, double-majoring in economics and political science, but she earned her B.A. in only three years. A Roman Catholic herself, Murphy stated in an interview with the *Fairfield Mirror* that she appreciated the atmosphere there. "The environment at Fairfield is very helpful. It's a Jesuit school, so it emphasizes that every person has a contribution to make," she said. After participating in on-campus interviews, Murphy decided she did not want to be the manager of a small store, one of the positions for which she interviewed, and instead chose to pursue a career in law. Murphy attended University of Connecticut Law School, where she earned her J.D. with honors.

After getting a job in a large firm on Wall Street, Murphy became bored with doing low-level work and decided to move to the corporate world, where she could do interesting work even at the lower levels. She took a job with Aetna in 1985 and worked for that company for 15 years in a variety of positions, finally earning the position of General Counsel and Chief Compliance Officer. In 2000, ING acquired Aetna, and Murphy moved from the legal side of the company into the business arena.

The merger of ING, Aetna, and ReliaStar Financial Group was not a smooth one. But as the companies integrated, opportunities opened, and Murphy held several positions on the business side of ING before she became Group President of ING Worksite and Institutional Financial Services in 2004. Murphy held that position for two years before she was made CEO of ING's U.S. Wealth Management. Murphy's legal peers noted her success without surprise. "Kathy handles complicated issues in an effortless way," attorney Michael Kantor, who served as secretary of commerce under U.S. President Bill Clinton, said in *Investment News*. Under Murphy's leadership, the company's assets grew 12 percent to 158 billion dollars, and after-tax profits increased 28 percent.

Murphy's successful leadership was noted in *Fortune* magazine, which declared her number 40 on their list of the 50 most powerful business women. "We are proud of Kathy for this recognition, and we are equally proud of ING for establishing a global work environment that embraces and encourages diverse leadership," Tom McInerney, chairman and CEO of ING Insurance Americas said in a press release acknowledging the award. He continued, "Kathy is an outstanding leader and has an exceptional vision for ING's Wealth Management operations, but more importantly, Kathy is a role model for other future leaders within ING to emulate."

As the CEO of ING's U.S. Wealth Management, Murphy is constantly thinking about ways to make sure the company is offering what their customers need. "Are we offering the best solutions out there, as an industry?" she mused in *Pensions and Investments*. "That keeps me up at night." Noting

the volatility of the economy in a 2008 interview in *On Wall Street*, Murphy said she most worried about the reactions investors have to the market's uncertainty, noting that common reactions are to sell off stock or to stop investing. "Either scenario does not provide a winning strategy for living the life you dream of in retirement," she said.

The position was a particular challenge during the 2008 economic downturn. Murphy's business unit was identified as key to ING's global growth. Under Murphy's reorganization, the group has experienced growth when much of the rest of the market has fallen. Keeping a close eye on Baby Boomer investors, Murphy headed ING's Center for Strategic Innovation, with the goal of developing new business models to accommodate the changing needs of investors. "You've got to be agile in response to customers," she said in *Banking Wire*. "Product preferences change quickly."

Murphy noted in *Irish America* that many managers in ING's business areas are women. "One of the things that I'm conscious of, particularly in the insurance industry, is diversity in the sales organizations," she explained. "You've got to have a workforce that reflects your customer base," she continued, noting that women make up more than 60 percent of ING's customers. "It's not just politically correct. It's business."

Along with her work life, Murphy is an active volunteer. She is a National Trustee of the Boys & Girls Club of America, on the Board of Directors of the National Conference for Civil Justice in the Northeast, on the Board of Directors of the Connecticut Business and Industry Association, and on the Metro Hartford Alliance Board of Directors. In addition, she serves as a chairperson for both America's Promise Alliance and Connecticut Children's Trust Fund, as well as a board member of the Governor's Prevention Partnership Program, the Wheeler Clinic, and the American Benefits Council. Murphy participates in an international women's mentoring program and supported ING's participation in both mentoring and programs to enhance children's education. She also determinedly balances her work life, travel, and her family. "I will tell you, fitting it all in is tough," Murphy told *Irish America* magazine. "I travel a good deal during the week and I try not to do a lot of social or business events on the weekend. If I have to go to a black-tie I will, but I don't seek them out. I just really try to carve out time [for the family]."

On December 4, 2008, Murphy announced she was leaving ING by the end of the year to head up the Personal Investing division at Fidelity, reporting to Abby Johnson, president of Personal and Workplace Investing.

# Sources

## Periodicals

*Banking Wire,* November 6, 2008, p. 40.
*Investment News,* April 9, 2007, p. 46.
*On Wall Street,* April 1, 2008.
*Pensions and Investments,* February 5, 2007, p. 26.
*PR Newswire,* October 1, 2007.

## Online

"Alumna Ranked Among the Most Powerful Women in Business," *Fairfield Mirror* Online, http://www.fairfieldmirror.com/news/1.474834 (November 24, 2008).
"Fidelity Lassos an ING Top Honcho," MutualFundWire.com, http://www.mfwire. com/article.asp?template=article&storyID= 20068&sectionID=1&wire=MFWire&wireID= 2&bhcp=1 (December 30, 2008).

"40. Kathleen Murphy," CNN Money Online, http://money.cnn.com/galleries/2007/fortune/ 0709/gallery.women_mostpowerful.fortu ne/40. html (November 24, 2008).
"41. Kathleen Murphy," CNN Money Online, http://money.cnn.com/galleries/2008/fortune/ 0809/gallery.women_mostpowerful.fortune/41. html (November 24, 2008).
"Kathleen Murphy Board Member Biography," America's Promise Alliance Web site, http:// www.americaspromise.org/APAPage.aspx?id= 6472 (November 24, 2008).
"Management Bios: Kathleen Murphy," ING Web site, http://www.ing-usa.com/us/aboutING/ Newsroom/managementbios/kathleenamurphy /index.htm (November 24, 2008).
"Murphy's Making History," *Irish America* maga- zine online, http://www.irishabroad.com/ irishworld/irishamericamag/decjan08/business 100/Business100Page12.asp (November 24, 2008).

*—Alana Joli Abbott*

# Rafael Nadal

**Professional tennis player**

**B**orn June 3, 1986, in Manacor, Mallorca, Spain; son of Sebastiá (a restaurant and glass company owner) and Ana María (a homemaker) Nadal.

**Addresses:** *Contact*—Carlos Costa IMG Tennis, Augusta 200 4 planta, 08021, Barcelona, Spain.

## Career

**L**aunched professional tennis career by joining ATP (Association of Tennis Professionals) Tour, 2001; won four Futures titles, 2002; won men's doubles title at Umag, 2003; member of Spanish tennis team which won the Davis Cup, 2004; won men's singles titles at Sopot, 2004; won men's double titles at Chennai, 2004; won men's singles titles at the French Open, Salvador, Acapulco, Monte Carlo, Barcelona, ATP Masters Series Rome, Swedish Open, Stuttgart Outdoor, ATP Masters Series Canada, Beijing, Rogers Cup, and Madrid, 2005; won men's doubles title at Doha, 2005; won men's singles titles at the French Open, the Dubai Tennis Championships, ATP Masters Series Monte Carlo, Open SEAT, ATP Masters Series Rome, 2006; won men's singles titles at the French Open, ATP Masters Series Monte Carlo, Open SEAT, Pacific Life Open, Mercedes Cup, ATP Masters Series Rome, Stuttgart Outdoor, 2007; won men's singles titles at the French Open, Wimbledon, Masters Series Monte Carlo, ATP Masters Series Hamburg, Rogers Cup, Barcelona, Queen's Club (London), ATP Masters Series Canada, 2008; won men's double title at ATP Masters Series Monte Carlo; won gold medal in men's singles at Summer Olympics, Beijing, China, 2008; ranked number one on ATP Tour, 2008.

**Awards:** Laureus World Sports Award for newcomer of the year, 2006; ESPY Award for best male international athlete, ESPN, 2008; Prince of Asturias sports award, 2008.

## Sidelights

**S**panish tennis player Rafael Nadal won four straight French Opens and one Wimbledon before the age of 23. The expressive left-handed player was the first true tennis star produced by Spain, and was highly regarded for his charisma, showmanship, and gentlemanly play. A clay court expert with a strong mental game, Nadal once held the record for consecutive men's wins on clay court. Clay best suited his aggressive play as well as his speed, endurance, and creativity as a player. Not content to be limited to success on clay, Nadal worked on other aspects of his game, including his serve, to give himself a chance to win in grass and hard court tournaments. His hard work paid off and in August of 2008, Nadal became the number-one ranked men's player in the world. As Peter Nichols wrote in the London *Guardian,* "No athlete is fitter, no player expends more in a match and no audience gets better value than when the Spaniard is playing."

Born on June 3, 1986, in Manacor, Spain, he is the son of Sebastiá and Ana María Nadal. His father owned and managed a restaurant as well as a glass and window company, while his mother was a homemaker who focused her energies on Nadal and his younger sister, Maria Isabel. The close-knit, wealthy Nadal family had some athletes. One of Nadal's uncles, Miguel Ángel Nadal, was a soccer star for FC Barcelona and the Spanish national team.

Nadal started playing tennis at the age of three when he was introduced to the sport by another uncle, Toni Nadal, who was a competitive tennis player and tennis coach. By the time Nadal was eight, his uncle realized that his nephew was talented enough to win a Grand Slam someday. Though only eight, Nadal won Majorca's under-12 title. At 12, Nadal was still playing both soccer and tennis. He was a talented striker on his soccer team, but when he won the European under-12 tennis title he saw his future. Nadal focused on tennis as a career after that point.

While their son showed his skill from an early age, his parents wanted to instill their values into their son. They turned down financial assistance from the Spanish tennis federation, which would have allowed their son to move to the national training center near Barcelona where most promising junior players trained. Instead, Nadal remained at home, where he was coached by his uncle and attended a local secondary school. Toni Nadal told Christopher Clary of the *New York Times,* "Education was very important to our family. His parents wanted him to grow up in an environment where he did not lose perspective."

In 2001, when he was 15 years old, Nadal turned pro as a tennis player. He reached the second round of the Seville Challenger that year. Nadal ended the year ranked 818 in men's singles by the ATP (Association of Tennis Professionals). In 2002, when Nadal was still 15 years old, he won his first ATP match. It took place at his hometown of Mallorca defeating Roman Delgado. With this victory, Nadal became only the ninth player in the Open Era to win an ATP match before turning 16. While this victory was important, Nadal spent most of his tennis playing time competing in Future tournaments, where he won four titles and had a 20-match winning streak. He did, however, reach the semifinals of the Barcelona Challenger. By the end of 2002, Nadal reached the rank of 235 in the ATP men's singles standings.

Nadal continued to improve as a player in 2003, spending much of the year on the Challenger circuit. He was unable to play in his first French Open that

year because of an elbow injury which occurred while training at Roland Garros, but did win his first two rounds at Wimbledon. Nadal ended the year ranked 47. In 2004, Nadal won an ATP men's singles title at Sopot and an ATP men's doubles title at Chennai, but had to withdraw from the French Open because of a stress fracture in his left ankle. He was also a member of Spain's Davis Cup team. He won a singles match during the tournament finals against the United States, becoming the youngest player to register a singles win for the victorious nation in a Cup final. Nadal defeated Andy Roddick in four sets on the way to Spain's winning the Davis Cup in December of 2004. With the win, he became the youngest man to compete on a winning David Cup team as well. Nadal ended the year ranked 51.

After improving his serve and two-handed backhand, Nadal had a breakout year in 2005 when he showed the depth of his clay court prowess. He won three clay court events in row in Monaco, Barcelona, and Rome, before grabbing his first Grand Slam. Seeded fourth for his first French Open, Nadal impressed observers like Clarey of the *New York Times,* who wrote after Nadal's third round match that "Nadal ... already looks remarkably at home, filling the stage with his energy and self-assurance, and filling the stands with curiosity seekers." Nadal went on to defeat the number-one ranked player in the world in the semifinals, Roger Federer, on Nadal's 19th birthday. Nadal won the men's singles title at the French Open by defeating Argentinean Mariano Puerta in a dramatic four-set victory.

While Nadal was happy with his victory, he wanted to be more than just an expert clay court player. After his French Open semi-final victory, he told *New York Times'* Clarey, "There's a lot that I still need to improve. I'm trying to improve on a daily basis. On clay this year, I've had good results. But I'm going to play on other types of courts, as well." Nadal remained philosophical after winning his first Grand Slam, telling Clarey, "I hope this all won't change me. I would like to stay the same as I've always been. I hope that I will pull it off, and I believe I will be able to pull it off. I want to continue being a 19-year-old youngster and play my tennis." At the end of 2005, after posting more victories in ATP tournaments, including his hard-court victory in the Rogers Cup final in Montreal, Nadal reached the rank of number two, behind Federer. Nadal would remain in this position for the next three years.

Nadal continued to impress in 2006. While he did not match the number of men's singles titles he won in 2005 (12), Nadal repeated as French Open champion in impressive fashion and had victories in four other ATP men's singles tournaments. Nadal continued to add to his record-setting winning streak on clay with 60 straight victories by defeating Federer, denying him his fourth straight Grand Slam title and first French Open victory. While Nadal continued to work on his game—including his serve and transition game—he could not win other Grand Slam tournaments. In 2006, he was not able to compete in the Australian Open because of a small crack in his left foot. Nadal then lost in the Wimbledon finals and the U.S. Open quarterfinals. At the U.S. Open, Nadal lost in five sets to the unseeded Russian player Mikhail Youzhy. Despite the losses, Nadal persevered.

In 2007, Nadal won a total of nine ATP men's singles titles, and improved in all the Grand Slams. His only slam victory came in the French Open, where he again defeated Federer in four sets. Nadal's third straight victory in the finals of the French Open made him only the second man since 1914 to accomplish this feat. Nadal believed the 2007 win at the French Open was magnificent. He told Steve Douglas of the Montreal *Gazette,* "I think I have just played my best Roland Garros. You can't really compare them, they are not the same. But the first year was emotional because it was my first win here, the second was emotional because I was coming back from injury, and the third is good because I played my best tennis. I am a more complete player. I can go to the net, I can be more aggressive with my forehand and I have improved a bit with my backhand. I feel better this year than last year."

In the other 2007 Grand Slams, Nadal reached the quarterfinals of the Australian Open and the round of 16 at the U.S. Open. He also was the runner-up at Wimbledon again. Because of Federer's continued dominance in non-French Open tournaments—including a defeat of Nadal in the final of the Hamburg Masters—Nadal became the first and only player to finish the year ranked number two for three consecutive years.

In the previous few years, Nadal had started the ATP Tour season slowly, and 2008 proved to be no exception. He lost in the semi-finals of the Australian Open to Jo-Wilfried Tsonga, who dominated the Spaniard in the hard-court tournament. Nadal got his revenge by defeating Tsonga in the fourth round of the Pacific Life Open a few weeks later. While Nadal did not win the tournament, he won a number of other ATP titles. For example, he became the second player ever to win both singles and double titles at the same ATP Masters Series event when he won both titles at ATP Masters Series Hamburg. Nadal continued his domination at the French Open, and also broke through on grass to win both the Queen's Club and Wimbledon men's singles titles.

At Wimbledon, Nadal defeated his rival Federer in impressive fashion. Their match went to five sets and lasted four hours and 48 minutes. It was the longest singles final in Wimbledon's history. After the victory, Nadal told the *New York Times'* Clarey, "The most important thing is to win the title. After that, you think about winning against the No. 1, probably the best player in history or close, and the fact that it was so dramatic. But it's one of the most powerful feelings I've had in my life." Many observers believed it was a match for the ages. In the Montreal *Gazette,* Stephanie Myles wrote, "The epic match will go down as one of the best Grand Slam finals in history because of the two combatants, because of the rain delays, because of the darkness, because the tennis was so gripping and because of all that was at stake."

Nadal's 2008 season continued to be triumphant with a win in the finals of the Rogers Cup in July. In mid-August, Nadal finally reached the number-one ranking on the ATP Tour for the first time, replacing Federer. Around the same time, Nadal won the gold medal in tennis for Spain at the Summer Olympics in Beijing, China. He defeated Chile's Fernando Gonzalez in three sets to take the gold. While Nadal was happy to reach number one and win an Olympic medal, he was not content to rest on his laurels, though he lost in the semi-finals of the U.S. Open to Andy Murray in four sets. He still believed he had work to do as he hoped to continue to be the best men's tennis player in the world on all surfaces. He told the *Denver Post's* Anthony Cotton, "Always you can improve, no? If Federer can improve, me for sure. For sure, I can improve the slice. I can improve the serve 100 percent. I have to improve a little bit more the volley, too." But Nadal also admitted, "I have to be happy for everything, no?"

## Sources

### Books

*Complete Marquis Who's Who Biographies,* Marquis Who's Who, 2008.

## Periodicals

*Daily News* (New York, NY), September 7, 2006, p. 72.

*Denver Post* (Denver, CO), August 18, 2008, p. B-02.

*Gazette* (Montreal, Canada), June 11, 2007, p. C1; July 7, 2008, p. C1.

*Globe and Mail* (Canada), June 6, 2005, p. S3.

*Guardian* (London, England), August 18, 2008, p. 8.

*New York Times*, May 28, 2005, p. D6; June 5, 2005, sec. 8, p. 9; June 6, 2005, p. A1; June 13, 2006, p. D6; August 26, 2006, p. D1; July 7, 2008, p. A1; September 8, 2008, p. D5.

*Press Enterprise* (Riverside, CA), March 20, 2008, p. C1.

*San Francisco Chronicle*, June 22, 2005, p. D1.

*Vogue*, September 2005, p. 572.

*Welland Tribune* (Ontario, Canada), July 28, 2008, p. B8.

## Online

"No Clay Specialist," SI.com, http://sportsillus trated.cnn.com/2005/more/08/14/nadal.agassi. ap/index.html (August 15, 2005).

"Player Biography: Nadal, Rafael," ITF Tennis—Men's Circuit, http://www.itftennis.com/mens/ players/player.asp?player=10000793.tif5 (August 20, 2008).

"Rafael Nadal (ESP): Career Highlights & Biography," ATPtennis.com, http://www.atptennis. com/5/en/players/playerprofiles/highlights. asp?playernumber= N409 (August 20, 2008).

"Rafael Nadal (ESP): Player Profile," ATPtennis. com, http://www.atptennis.com/5/en/players/ playerprofiles/?playernumber=N409 (August 20, 2008).

*—A. Petruso*

# Nas

## Rap musician

**B**orn Nasir bin Olu Dara Jones, September 14, 1973, in New York, NY; son of Olu Dara (a jazz trumpeter) and Fannie Ann Jones; married Kelis (a musician), 2005; children: Destiny (with Carmen Bryan).

**Addresses:** *Office*—c/o Sony Music Entertainment, 550 Madison Ave., New York, NY 10022.

## Career

**H**is music has appeared on soundtracks for several movies and television shows, including: *Big Momma's House, Antwone Fisher, Charlie's Angels: Full Throttle, Entourage, Rush Hour 3,* and *The X Factor.* Writer for films *Belly,* 1998, and *Sacred Is the Flesh,* 2001. Director of television documentary *This Is the N,* 2007.

**Awards:** Youth Summit Award, Hip-Hop Youth Summit, 2002.

## Sidelights

**S**elf-proclaimed "King of New York," rapper Nas, who has also called himself Nasty Nas, Nastradamus, and God's Son, is a platinum hip-hop artist as well as one of the East Coast's leading rap voices. Often at the center of media attention, whether through his rivalry with other rappers, his provocative lyrics, or his controversial album titles, Nas has released nine successful albums and has worked on a number of films that incorporate his music.

Born and raised in the borough of Queens in New York City, Nas writes and raps about issues he feels are relevant to the world that shaped him. "I really grew up in the Queensbridge projects. I really grew up around drugs. I've seen my brothers go on trial," Nas told Chris Riemenschneider of the Minneapolis *Star Tribune.* "My whole family was in a struggle, 24/7, 365 days a year. It's all real ladies and gentlemen. It's not makeup I'm wearing, I'm really black. I'm really talking about what I should be talking about as a 30-year-old African-American husband and father."

Born Nasir Jones in 1973, Nas is the son of Olu Dara, a jazz and blues trumpeter, and Fannie Ann Jones. Dara chose the name Nasir for its Arabic meaning: "helper" or "protector." Growing up in the Queensbridge projects was difficult, and Nas dropped out of school in eighth grade, trading education for life on the streets. Despite his lack of formal education, Nas is an extremely literate writer, forming rhymes for his rap verses that depict a rhetoric and imagery that did not glamorize his life, but show it through a clear lens. He established himself in 1991 as a premiere rapper with his song "Live at the Barbeque." In 1992, Nas's brother Jungle and his best friend were shot on the same night. "That was a wake-up call for me," Nas told *Time.*

Nas signed a contract with Columbia, and in 1994 his debut album, the highly celebrated *Illmatic*, was released. *Illmatic* was noted for the same lyricism that had gained Nas attention, as well as his gritty depiction of urban life. Unlike gangsta rappers, Nas refrained from glorifying the violence of his world, instead allowing his songs to inspire feelings of sadness or outrage from his audience. The album had been highly anticipated, and it lived up to the expectations set for it, featuring several hit songs. Nas' "witty lyrics and gruffly gratifying beats draw listeners into [his neighborhood's] lifestyle with poetic efficiency," wrote a critic from *Entertainment Weekly*. Christopher John Farley, writing for *Time*, felt the record "captures the ailing community he was raised in—the random gunplay, the whir of police helicopters, the homeboys hanging out on the corner sipping bottles of Hennessey."

Nas' next album, *It Was Written*, was released two years later and sold more than a million copies. He used a style closer to pop for many of his songs, a creative choice criticized by many of his hardcore hip-hop fans, and his lyrics contained harsh language and gritty violence. Two of the singles from the album, "If I Ruled the World (Imagine That)" and "Street Dreams," both of which sampled pop songs, brought Nas to the MTV crowd, broadening his fan base. Nas responded to criticisms of *It Was Written* in his song "Hate Me Now," which appeared on his third album, *I Am...*. The song, as well as three other tracks, hit the charts, guaranteeing *I Am...*'s status as a popular album.

In 1998, before the release of *I Am...*, Nas made his first feature film, *Belly*, which he wrote and starred in. Fellow rapper DMX played opposite Nas, depicting a criminal out for fame and glory while Nas' character only wants to provide for his girlfriend and child. Though the film received mixed reviews—the director's originality was praised, but the same aspect was found lacking in the plot—Nas continued to work on films, writing *Sacred Is the Flesh* in 2001 and directing the television documentary *This Is The N.*

*Nastradamus,* Nas's fourth album, marked a decline in the quality that listeners had come to expect from Nas, due to its quick recording to meet the sales deadline. Unlike previous Nas albums, *Nastradamus* did not debut at the number-one spot on the Billboard chart, and only ever reached as high as number seven. Fellow rapper Jay-Z was one of the album's critics; in his album *The Blueprint*, Jay-Z openly referred to Nas as "garbage" in his song "Takeover." The two began a feud of words, vying for the position of top rapper in New York. Nas faded from the scene, dealing with more personal matters: he and his daughter's mother were having relationship problems, and his mother was dying of cancer.

Unwilling to go down without a fight, Nas formed his own label at Columbia, Ill Will, and released the album *Stillmatic*, a reference to his first hit album. His song "Ether" was a direct response to Jay-Z, and Nas continued to support his comeback with a number of guest appearances, singing with Brandy in "What about Us?" and J-Lo in "I'm Gonna Be All Right." He also hit the headlines with a controversial no-show to the Hot 97 Summer Jam. Headlines continued when he was rumored to be dating rapper Kelis of Harlem, and when he was charged with assault in 2003. His album *God's Son* featured some introspective titles, notably "Dance," which served as a memorial for his mother, and an instrumental piece featuring his father. Though the albums were not as popular as his early titles, they showed that Nas was still developing as an artist. According to a contributor to *Contemporary Musicians*, "In the early 2000s, Nas accomplished something that had eluded many other hip-hop figures—he continued to develop as an artist and found ongoing popularity."

In 2004, Nas released *Street's Disciple*, a double album that featured songs relating directly to his relationship to his then-fiancée, Kelis. In one song, Nas described the Cinderella-type wedding he felt Kelis deserved; in reality, the couple married in a small ceremony in Atlanta, Georgia. His song "Bridging the Gap" was a collaboration between Nas and his father, featuring elements of both jazz and hip-hop tropes. The album also included several spiritually and politically themed songs, introducing Nas' positions on some issues, which would come further into play during the 2008 presidential elections. Though the record struggled after tremendous opening sales that marked his fastest selling record, it opened the door to reconciliation between Nas and his one-time rival Jay-Z. The pair performed together at one of Jay-Z's concerts, and Jay-Z subsequently invited Nas to record through his new studio, Def Jam.

Nas' first album with Def Jam, *Hip Hop Is Dead*, caused a stir with only its title. Even before the album was released, it began a conversation about the state of hip-hop. Nas refused to cast blame on why he felt hip-hop was failing, but many young rappers went on the defensive, considering Nas a grumpy veteran longing for days gone by. Nas made accusations through his lyrics that modern rap was more about the money than the lyricism of rap in days gone by. Younger rappers countered that hip-hop was no longer a craft, but instead had become a culture. "But here's the thing about Nas' old-fashioned approach to hip-hop: It still works," wrote *New York Times* critic Kelefa Sanneh. "Especially if you've got a smoky voice, a knack for packing syllables into tight rhyme schemes and access to sturdy backbeats by Kanye West, Dr. Dre, Scott Storch, will.i.am and others. Fifteen years on, there's still nothing like hearing Nas assemble an intricate stanza." Though the album did not sell as well as hoped, it sparked conversation about the state of the genre and featured a collaboration with Jay-Z, "Black Republican."

Like *Hip Hop Is Dead*, controversy surrounded Nas' next album, which came out untitled. The rapper wanted to name the album "N*****," and had won support from peers including Alicia Keys and Jay-Z in giving the album the highly sensitive name. The NAACP, in tandem with Al Sharpton and Jesse Jackson, challenged Nas' use of the word, however, and Def Jam chairman Antonio Reid was forced to acquiesce to their requests. When the untitled album hit the charts, Geoff Mayfield of *Billboard* commented, "That sort of scrutiny wouldn't exist were it not for his ongoing relevance, proved this issue by his fifth No. 1 on the Billboard 200."

Nas told Evan Serpick of *Rolling Stone* that he was not sure what to expect releasing an album under that name, but was focused on his mission, exploring his relationship to the word. "'N*****' is from the African-American holocaust—and you can't play around with that. It's probably going to make people uncomfortable. It's definitely no disrespect to my people, or to the people who fought for my rights in this country, and died for us." A few months after the release, however, Nas told Riemenschneider in the *Star Tribune* interview that the name change was for the best. "The title was just offending everybody, and they forgot that this is music, and music is a great outlet for people. [Changing] the title helped them get past it, and they've moved on to what I'm talking about," he said.

The album also featured the song "Black President," which sampled parts of a speech by Barack Obama. The October before the 2008 presidential election, Nas traveled to Hampton University in Virginia to encourage students to register to vote—particularly if they could register in Virginia, which was expected to be a swing state. Noting Nas' reputation for writing politically conscious lyrics, Austin Bogues reported in the Newport, Virginia *Daily News* that Nas "told the audience of 900 that this was the first time he had registered and intends to vote in a presidential election in his life." Though

Nas was touring in Norway at the time of the election, he recorded "Election Night" on the road to mark the election of the first African-American president of the United States. In addition to Nas' political activism in the United States, he has also traveled to Nigeria for Star Mega Jam, performing with Grammy-winner Nelly and a number of Nigerian musicians.

## Selected discography

*Illmatic*, Columbia, 1994.
*It Was Written*, Columbia, 1996.
*I Am...*, Columbia, 1999.
*Nastradamus*, Columbia, 1999.
*Stillmatic*, Ill Will, 2001.
*God's Son*, Ill Will, 2002.
*Street's Disciple*, Columbia, 2004.
*Hip Hop Is Dead*, Def Jam Recordings, 2006.
*Untitled*, Def Jam Recordings, 2008.

## Sources

### Books

*Contemporary Black Biography*, vol. 33, Gale Group (Detroit, MI), 2002.
*Contemporary Musicians*, vol. 49, Gale Group (Detroit, MI), 2004.

### Periodicals

Africa News Service, November 15, 2008.
*Billboard*, August 2, 2008, p. 37.
*Daily Press* (Newport, VA), October 6, 2008.
*Entertainment Weekly*, April 22, 1994, p. 58; July 26, 1996, p. 56; November 22, 2002, p. L2T6.
*Europe Intelligence Wire*, March 10, 2005.
*New York Times*, December 14, 2006, p. E1.
*Rolling Stone*, July 10, 2008, p. 26.
*Star Tribune* (Minneapolis, MN), September 5, 2008, p. 1E.
*Time*, June 20, 1994, p. 62; July 29, 1996, p. 79.
*World Entertainment News Network*, November 5, 2008.

### Online

"Nas," Internet Movie Database, http://www.imdb.com/name/nm0621576/bio (November 24, 2008).
"Nas," MySpace.com, http://www.myspace.com/nas (November 24, 2008).

"Nas Official Web site," Def Jam Recordings, http://www.defjam.com/site/artist_home.php?artist_id=608 (November 24, 2008).

*—Alana Joli Abbott*

# Gavin Newsom

*John M. Heller/Getty Images*

## Mayor of San Francisco

**B**orn Gavin Christopher Newsom, October 10, 1967, in San Francisco, CA; son of Bill (an appellate court judge) and Tessa Menzies (a waitress, saleswoman, and Realtor) Newsom; married Kimberly Guilfoyle (a TV anchorwoman), December 8, 2001 (divorced, 2006); married Jennifer Siebel (an actress), July 26, 2008. *Education:* Santa Clara University, B.S., 1989.

**Addresses:** *E- mail*—gavin.newsom@sfgov.org. *Office*—San Francisco City Hall, 400 S. Van Ness Ave., San Francisco, CA 94103.

## Career

**S**old orthotics and worked in a real estate office, early 1990s; founded PlumpJack Inc., 1992; appointed to the San Francisco Parking and Traffic Commission, 1996; appointed to the San Francisco Board of Supervisors, 1997; elected to the San Francisco Board of Supervisors, 1998, 2000, 2002; mayor of the city and county of San Francisco, 2004—.

**Awards:** Special Recognition Award, Gay & Lesbian Alliance Against Defamation (GLAAD), 2004; named to *Time* magazine's list of "17 People Who Matter," 2004; Distinguished Service Award, *Wine Spectator*, 2006.

## Sidelights

**S**an Francisco's Gavin Newsom is one of the best-known mayors in the United States. Newsom gained national attention in 2004 when, just days after taking office, he ordered city hall to issue marriage licenses to same-sex couples, though the marriages were later annulled by the courts. During his first term as mayor, Newsom tackled homelessness and universal healthcare. He also divorced his wife, admitted to a drinking problem, and confessed to having an affair with his campaign manager's wife. Newsom, however, remained highly popular, capturing 73 percent of the vote when he ran for re-election as mayor in 2007.

Born and raised in the San Francisco Bay Area, Newsom was born on October 10, 1967. His Irish father, Bill, was a justice with the state's appellate court system. His Scottish mother, Tessa, chose the name Gavin for her only son. In Gaelic, "gavin" means "hawk." Newsom's parents divorced after only five years of marriage, leaving Newsom and his little sister, Hilary, to be raised mostly by their mother. Growing up, Newsom straddled two vastly different socioeconomic worlds. He watched his mother take many jobs to support the family. She worked as a saleswoman at I. Magnin & Company, a department store. She also waited tables at a Mexican restaurant and secured jobs for Newsom and his sister to work there as they got older. Later, Tessa Newsom sold real estate. Frequently, she took in foster children.

By contrast, Bill Newsom made a good living but frequently gave his money away, which frustrated Newsom as he watched his mother struggle economically. "We loved and hated my father's extraordinary selflessness," Newsom is quoted as saying by Mike Weiss of the *San Francisco Chronicle*. "That guy helped more people financially, people in need, to a degree that is unimaginable to me. Always giving money away and never expecting it back. And the burden was tremendous financial stress when we were growing up. Our most terrible family moments were always around money. I hated it."

In another contrast from his childhood family life, Newsom spent time with one of San Francisco's richest families. Newsom's father had befriended billionaire oil heir Gordon Getty during high school and the two remained friends. At times, Newsom vacationed with the Getty family, who had boys about his age. The Getty family took Newsom to Spain and on a safari to see lions in the wild. They also went to Canada's Hudson Bay to watch polar bears. Newsom vacationed on their yacht and rode their private jet. These experiences helped Newsom learn firsthand the differences between those who have plenty and those who do not have enough. He realized early on how a name or money confer status and privilege. In his political career he has sought to equalize that gap.

Newsom, who struggled with dyslexia, graduated from Marin County's Redwood High School in 1985 and earned a baseball scholarship to Santa Clara University. After earning a political science degree in 1989, he sold orthotics and worked in a real estate office. In 1992, he joined forces with childhood friend Billy Getty to launch PlumpJack Wines on Fillmore, a San Francisco-based wine shop. Over the next few years, Newsom used his entrepreneurial skills to grow PlumpJack from a simple wine store into a parent company that, by 2005, included a restaurant, a century-old Napa Valley winery, and a resort in California's Sierra Nevada Mountains.

In 1995, Newsom agreed to use PlumpJack for a fund-raiser for San Francisco mayoral candidate Willie Brown, a democrat. Brown won the election and in 1996 appointed Newsom to the San Francisco Parking and Traffic Commission. In 1997, Brown appointed Newsom to the city's board of supervisors to fill a vacancy. The San Francisco Board of Supervisors works like a city council: It makes laws for both the city and county of San Francisco. To keep his seat, Newsom ran for re-election in 1998 and won, repeating in 2000 and 2002.

As one of eleven members on the board of supervisors, Newsom took on homelessness. In 2002, Newsom sponsored the Care Not Cash initiative. Known as Proposition N, the initiative aimed to cut the city's welfare payments to the homeless. Newsom proposed investing the savings in services, such as expanding shelters, developing more affordable housing, and adding more mental health and substance abuse treatment programs. Instead of cash, the homeless were to get vouchers for services. The controversial ballot measure was passed by voters in November of 2002. Contested in the court system, the initiative was never implemented. In 2003, Newsom sponsored Proposition M, an initiative to limit panhandling. The measure passed.

That same year, Newsom decided to run for mayor. Newsom was one of nine candidates whose names appeared on the November 2003 ballot. Newsom came out on top, followed by Green Party candidate Matt Gonzalez, who was president of the board of supervisors. However, because no candidate received at least 50 percent of the vote, Newsom and Gonzalez had to face off in a run-off election a few weeks later. Newsom won that contest and was sworn into office on January 8, 2004. Just 36 years old, he was the youngest mayor of San Francisco since 1897.

In January of 2004, Newsom attended U.S. President George W. Bush's State of the Union address. During the speech, Bush discussed the sanctity of marriage and the need to uphold moral traditions in light of activist judges who would seek to redefine marriage. As the mayor of gay-friendly San Francisco, Newsom was bothered by Bush's remarks and asked his own staff to look into the issue.

Speaking to Sue Rochman of the *Advocate*, Newsom recalled his conversations with friends and advisors who urged him to drop the issue. "They told me, 'This is the end of your political life. This is crazy.' Everyone was feeling good, a tough election was behind us, and now I was going to screw it up." Newsom went on to tell Rochman that yes, he was nervous about pushing the issue, but in the end, he decided, "So what? We talk about principles. And if you can't stand for what you believe in, what's the point?"

Under Newsom's orders, San Francisco issued a marriage license to local gay-rights activists Del Martin and Phyllis Lyon on February 12, 2004. Newsom believed the longtime couple would provide the perfect face for a court challenge. Newsom told the *Advocate* he wanted to "force people to deal with marriage equality in the face of [Martin and Lyon's] 50-year relationship. We wanted to stick it to them, so to speak, to force them to look these two human beings with an incredible history in the face and say, 'No, you're not good enough, you're not the same.'" Some political pundits have said they believe Newsom took up the issue to advance his own political career, knowing full well that he would make national headlines. Whatever the case, the move came with a price. Newsom told the *Advocate* that friends gave him the cold shoulder and an invitation to speak at the Democratic National Convention was rescinded.

Once the word was out, same-sex couples flocked to city hall seeking marriage licenses. For 29 days, San Francisco processed licenses for same-sex couples, marrying some 4,000 couples before the California Supreme Court shuttered the operation. The court said it was unsure if the city had the authority to ignore state marriage laws and said it would look into the matter. In August of 2004, the California Supreme Court annulled the marriages, citing inconsistencies with state law. When Democratic presidential nominee John Kerry lost the November 2004 election to Bush, the incumbent, many Democrats blamed Newsom. Party leaders told Newsom it was not the right time to push the issue.

Speaking to Weiss of the *Chronicle*, Newsom discussed his philosophy on political and social change and said Democrats needed to follow his lead. Newsom mentioned Dr. Martin Luther King Jr.'s famed "Letter from a Birmingham Jail." King wrote the letter in 1963 from the confines of the Birmingham jail in response to some clergymen who condemned his actions. As Newsom explained to Weiss, "Eight of his fellow clergymen wrote to Dr. Martin Luther King Jr., asking him why he broke the law, and King replied that there are just laws and unjust laws. Very powerful.... I really believe people will support you if they believe you're doing what you think is right. If you show real conviction. There's a physiological construct that comes with it."

During his first term, Newsom continued working on the issue of homelessness. In 2004, he launched Project Homeless Connect, sending 250 city employees and volunteers to speak with the homeless and inquire about their needs. Some 300 of those interviewed agreed to visit intake centers to meet with representatives from city agencies and learn about the types of assistance available. The project later spread to other cities. In 2006, Newsom created the Universal Healthcare Council to explore the issue of the uninsured. The council's efforts resulted in the creation of Healthy San Francisco, an initiative that provides care to San Francisco's uninsured. Though the program was put in place, it remained controversial.

Besides attending to issues connected to healthcare and homelessness, Newsom also worked to reduce gang violence and promote green development. These proved to be popular public-policy initiatives and helped boost his approval rating during his first term. But not everything went smoothly. Newsom owned up to a drinking problem and vowed to seek help. In addition, Newsom's marriage collapsed. Partway through his term, his wife, Kimberly Guilfoyle, moved to New York to concentrate on a broadcasting career, and they ended up divorcing. Newsom also admitted to having an affair with his campaign manager's wife.

For many politicians, these missteps could have ended a career, but not for the hardworking and famously charismatic mayor with the Hollywood good looks and devotion to public policy. When it came time for re-election in November of 2007, Newsom snagged 73 percent of the vote. While Newsom had been controversial at times, he had also proven himself as a cutting-edge politician who was willing to look for new solutions to old problems. Because of his innovations, many constituents responded positively. Speaking to Mark Z. Barabak of the *Los Angeles Times,* political science professor Corey Cook summed up the Newsom enigma this way: "He's used the role of San Francisco mayor not just in the traditional way, making sure Muni buses arrive on time, but to pursue innovative policies on a number of national issues."

During his second term in office, Newsom focused his attention on cleaning up the city's housing projects and on making San Francisco a model for green living. In 2009, Newsom announced a pilot program to recycle "brown grease" from restaurants into biodiesel to fuel city vehicles. He also hired a global warming expert to look for ways in which San Francisco could reduce its carbon footprint.

As mayor of San Francisco, Newsom has long work days. A typical day begins at 7 a.m., when Newsom is picked up by a driver in a highly secured, city-issued Lincoln Town Car. Breakfast is usually a cup of coffee—half decaf. His schedule includes some 20 meetings a day. For lunch Newsom likes to eat a turkey sandwich on pita bread and take a break by listening to his iPod. On weekends, Newsom frequently hangs out at the city's housing projects. He picks up carloads of children and takes them to Burger King. He also takes young people to see the 49ers play football. Newsom credits his relationships with his foster siblings with helping him connect with the kids who live in the housing projects. In San Francisco, Newsom is a well-known figure. When he walks down the street, people shout at him; some remarks are positive, while others are downright hateful.

In 2009, political pundits expected Newsom to enter the 2010 race for governor. While highly popular in San Francisco, Newsom acknowledged that he might have trouble winning over voters in rural areas of the state. Nonetheless, he remained optimistic about his chances for higher office. "I'd like to be known as fiscally conservative and socially progressive," Newsom told the *Los Angeles Times* in May 2008. "But I will also be known as the gay-marriage mayor. I'm not naïve about that."

# Sources

### Periodicals

*Advocate,* April 8, 2008, pp. 40-45.
*Los Angeles Times,* May 17, 2008, p. A23; July 2, 2008, p. B1.
*Newsweek,* January 26, 2009.
*San Francisco Chronicle,* February 3, 1997, p. 11A; November 5, 2003, p. A1.
*USA Today,* November 6, 2007.

### Online

"Gavin Newsom, 42nd Mayor of the City and County of San Francisco," Mayor's Home Page, http://www.sfgov.org/site/mayor_index.asp?id=22014 (February 10, 2009).
"Newsom in Four Acts," *San Francisco Chronicle,* http://www.sfgate.com/cgi-bin/article.cgi?f=/c/a/2005/01/23/CMGD9AHK721.DTL (February 10, 2009).

—*Lisa Frick*

# Ne-Yo

**R&B singer and songwriter**

Born Shaffer Chimere Smith, October 18, 1982, in Camden, AR; divorced; children: Chimere (son).

**Addresses:** *Home*—Atlanta, GA. *Office*—Compound Entertainment, PO Box 93303, Atlanta, GA 30277. *Record company*—Def Jam Recordings, 825 Eighth Ave., New York, NY 10019. *Web site*—http://www.neyoworld.com/. *Web site*—http://www.yearofthegentleman.com/.

## Career

Made name as a songwriter under his birth name, Shaffer Smith, for other artists, including Lindsay Lohan, New Kids on the Block, Beyonce, Rihanna, and Enrique Iglesias, c. late 1990s; wrote hit songs sung by Marques Houston and Mario, c. 2003; signed solo recording deal with Columbia Records, but dropped in 2003; signed to Def Jam Recordings, released solo debut *In My Own Words*, 2006; second album *Because of You* appeared in the film *Stomp the Yard*, 2007. Has acted in films, including *Save the Last Dance 2*, 2006, and *Stomp the Yard*, 2007.

**Awards:** Best R&B male artist, Black Entertainment Television Awards, 2007; best song, Music of Black Origin Awards, for "Because of You," 2007; best R&B artist, Music of Black Origin Awards, 2007; best R&B/soul or rap new artist, Soul Train Music Awards, 2007; Grammy Award for best contemporary R&B album, Recording Academy, for *Because of You*, 2008; Grammy Awards for best male R&B vocal performance and for best song, Recording Academy, for "Miss Independent," 2009.

*Beck Starr/FilmMagic/Getty Images*

## Sidelights

Grammy-winning performer and hit songwriter Ne-Yo has been making news since his 2004 song, performed by Mario, "Let Me Love You," topped the charts. Not only has he written songs for such famous performers as varied as Beyonce, Whitney Houston, and Celine Dion, Ne-Yo has met with both popular and critical acclaim for his three albums, for which he was both songwriter and performer. His 2008 album, *Year of the Gentleman*, not only features his Grammy-winning single "Miss Independent," but shares some of Ne-Yo's philosophy on life.

"I always refer back to the days of the Rat Pack, because that's when I should have been around," Ne-Yo told Elysa Gardner of *USA Today*. Though his clothing does not hearken back to Frank Sinatra and Sammy Davis, Jr., Ne-Yo told the interviewer, "being a gentleman isn't about what you wear; it's about how you wear it." The album honors "men who have class and style, charm and charisma, things that have been few and far between" among modern popular music performers, according to Ne-Yo. Not only does his outlook and ideal of the gentleman look back to an earlier era, Ne-Yo's music incorporates inspirations from the Beatles and the Rat Pack to Marvin Gaye and Billy Joel.

Born Shaffer Chimere Smith in the town of Camden, Arkansas, Ne-Yo was brought up surrounded by music. His father left the family while Ne-Yo was young, so his mother moved the family to Las Vegas to try to find a better living. Ne-Yo grew up surrounded by independent women: His mother and his sisters all had strong personalities that impacted his own view on life. He has credited them with giving him a more sensitive outlook, and as a boy, he was more interested in poetry and art than cars or sports.

As a high-school student, Ne-Yo performed with and wrote songs for the group Envy, working under the stage name Gogo. The group was mildly successful, opening for groups like Mya and Destiny's Child. When the band members graduated, they decided to try their luck in Los Angeles. Determined to make it, they pledged to play outside of the offices of Capitol Records until the label signed them. While the label took notice, it was not in a way that brought them fame: The executives threatened to call the police if the members of Envy did not leave their property. Deterred, Envy broke up in 2000, and the members went their own ways.

For Ne-Yo, that meant staying in Los Angeles. He had made some contacts in the music industry while attempting to break in, hoping to make a living as a songwriter. He began to fulfill that plan when a boy band called Youngstown bought several of his tunes. Writing songs under his own name, he also developed his stage persona, calling himself Ne-Yo after a friend compared his knack for music to *The Matrix* character Neo's ability to manipulate reality. Ne-Yo was a fan of the 1999 science-fiction film, and adopted a version of the name for himself. He also went about building a persona for Ne-Yo to distinguish his writing, or real, identity from the performer he planned to become. One part of distinguishing the two identities was to make Ne-Yo three years younger than birth identity Shaffer Smith.

After earning a record contract with Columbia Records, Ne-Yo began to realize that what the company was looking for was different from the type of music he wanted to perform. "I decided I would let them create me, and in the process I figured out I wasn't the person they wanted me to be," he explained in *USA Today*. The album was shelved, and in 2003, the contract was dropped. Though he had continued writing during that period, the loss of the contract was discouraging. His career began looking up, however, when "That Girl," a track Ne-Yo had written and recorded at Columbia, was re-recorded by Marques Houston. The song was a smash hit. "That was the song that made me go

OK, if people are digging this song, I guess songwriting is what I'm supposed to be doing," Ne-Yo told Melody K. Hoffman of *Jet* magazine. "That was my cue that God wants me to be a songwriter."

His confidence was confirmed with the 2004 hit "Let Me Love You," performed by Mario, and Ne-Yo expanded his career beyond songwriting. With Reynell Hay, he founded the production company Compound Entertainment in Atlanta, GA, where he also began learning technical record production skills. When he was approached by Def Jam's Antonio Reid to record an album of his own music, Ne-Yo hesitated. He was happy with the career he had and the money he had made through songwriting and was no longer willing to compromise. Reid was willing to bring Ne-Yo to the label on his own terms, however, and the musician began recording his first full album.

Released in 2006, the multi-platinum album *In My Own Words* features songs either written or co-written by Ne-Yo. His singles "Stay" and "So Sick" launched him to the top of the charts and won him a tremendous amount of radio play. Like the songs he wrote for other artists, the tracks on *In My Own Words* drew on Ne-Yo's personal experiences, including his brief marriage at the age of 18. The story, told in "So Sick," resonated with fans, and the track held a top three spot in *Billboard*'s Hot 100 for six consecutive weeks.

Interested in expanding his career into other areas of entertainment, Ne-Yo performed a cameo part in the 2006 movie *Save the Last Dance 2* and showed his acting chops in the blockbuster film *Stomp the Yard*, which was released in 2007. He continued to write and prepared to release his second album, *Because of You*. But while much of the music industry seemed to be looking for repeat hits of the same style, Ne-Yo did not want to be trapped in a single box. "Success kind of becomes a double-edged sword," he said to Leanne Shear of the *New York Times*. "And I say: 'But wait. I can do this well, and this, and this.' They say: 'We don't want those. We want that [same thing you did before].' But I personally can't do it. If I get bored with the music, it's a wrap."

*Because of You* was a sexier, more up-tempo album, and it debuted at number one on the Billboard 200. His singles "Do You" and "Because of You" continued to woo his audience, and the title song received the Music of Black Origin Award for best song in 2007. The success of the album continued to build his reputation not only as a singer, but as a songwriter. R&B stars Rhianna, Beyonce, and Mary J. Blige sought out his work; his "Irreplaceable" became a top ten hit for Beyonce. Artists outside of the R&B scene also hoped to put Ne-Yo's writing skills to work. Pop icons Celine Dion and Whitney Houston both asked Ne-Yo for songs.

Balancing his life between his public persona and his private writer took some getting used to. But while the fame came in droves, Ne-Yo did not let his popularity get to his head. "Knowing that there's some eleven-year-old at home right now in his mirror dancing and practicing, coming for my spot," he told Aaron Parsley of *Teen People*, "I'll never, ever let it go to my head." Ne-Yo also began to grow increasingly frustrated with the hip-hop scene. He was encouraged to be sexier, removing his shirt during performances to entice his audience. "But if I can get the same amount of screams with my shirt on as another guy does shirtless, who's winning?" Ne-Yo quipped (as quoted by *USA Today*).

That frustration with the modern music scene gave him inspiration for his third album, *Year of the Gentleman*. Focusing on older values held during an era when artists did not wear their pants and shirts many sizes too big, the album praises what Ne-Yo sees as a higher level of class. "Years ago, if you weren't wearing the right suit or have a correct crease in your pants, you couldn't even get in the door—let alone on stage to perform," Ne-Yo noted on his Web site. "For me, the sharpness of Sammy and Sinatra is the kind of style I strive for in clothes and music. *Year of the Gentleman* is named in honor of those guys."

*Year of the Gentleman* once again resonated with fans, despite its stylistic differences from earlier albums. Where *In My Own Words* fit in well with the R&B scene and *Because of You* drew inspiration from Michael Jackson's earlier works, *Year of the Gentleman* was inspired by the crooners of an earlier era. Critic Steve Jones of *USA Today* was impressed that despite the number of songs Ne-Yo has written for other artists, "it's a testament to his attention to storytelling detail that he has so much good material for himself." Ne-Yo's own goal for the album was to encourage both men and women to do something better—whether that meant not waiting for a man to buy the drinks or wearing pants that fit. Whether or not it accomplished that goal, it brought in several Grammy nominations, including Best Album, Best Male Pop Vocal Performance, Best Contemporary R&B Album, and two categories won by the track "Miss Independent": Best Male R&B Vocal Performance and Best R&B Song.

Ne-Yo is not one to bask in his own glory, however, and has made plans to continue breaking out into other creative areas. He has written short stories, poems, and scripts. He has a pitch for an adult animated series in development. Along with a script for a musical he is writing, with the intent of starring in it, Ne-Yo has also arranged the Hennessy Artistry concert series, a private series featuring music acts.

In order to keep some space for himself, and for his writing, Ne-Yo bought a split-level condo in Atlanta, where he feels he can be himself. Some of the elements of his fame are still hard for Ne-Yo to comprehend. "I'm sitting shoulder-to-shoulder with all the people I grew up listening to," he said in *People*, noting that he has collaborated with Michael Jackson on some songs, and that he has written tunes for Michael Bolton. "I'm not a lowly songwriter saying, 'Please take my song' anymore."

## Selected discography

*In My Own Words*, Def Jam, 2006.
*Because of You*, Def Jam, 2007.
*Year of the Gentleman*, Def Jam, 2008.

## Sources

### Books

*Contemporary Black Biography*, vol. 65, Gale (Detroit, MI), 2008.
*Contemporary Musicians*, vol. 62, Gale (Detroit, MI), 2008.

### Periodicals

*Billboard*, March 24, 2007.
*Essence*, August 2008, p. 62.
*Jet*, June 4, 2007.
*Marie Claire*, May 2007.
*New York Times*, November 30, 2008, p. 4.
*People*, January 19, 2009, p. 91.
*Teen People*, July 21, 2005.
*USA Today*, September 15, 2008, p. 1D; September 15, 2008, p. 2D.

### Online

*Biography Resource Center Online*, Gale (Detroit, MI), 2006, 2009.
Ne-Yo Official Web site, http://www.yearofthe gentleman.com/ (April 21, 2009).

*—Alana Joli Abbott*

# Peggy Northrop

## Editor-in-chief of Reader's Digest

*Mark Mainz/Getty Images*

**B**orn in 1954; daughter of John L. S. (a publisher) and Rose Northrop; married and divorced twice; married Sean Elder, c. 1988; children: Franny. *Education:* University of California at Berkeley, B.A., mid-1970s.

**Addresses:** *Contact*—Reader's Digest Association Inc. Headquarters, Reader's Digest Rd., Pleasantville, NY 10570. *Home*—Brooklyn, NY.

## Career

**R**eporter/editor, *San Francisco Examiner*'s Sunday magazine; editor, *Berkeley Monthly*; worked in various editorial positions with *Health, Vogue, Glamour, Redbook,* and *Real Simple*; editor-in-chief, *Organic Style*, 2002-04; editor-in-chief, *More* magazine, 2004-07; editor-in-chief, *Reader's Digest*, 2007—.

**Awards:** Media Industry Newsletter's "21 Most Intriguing People," 2003; Gold Prize for Redesign, *Folio* magazine, 2005; *Advertising Age*'s "A List" of Top 10 Magazines, for *More* magazine, 2005, 2007; Women Who Get it Right Award, National Breast Cancer Coalition, 2006; *Advertising Age*'s Magazine of the Year Award, for *More,* 2006.

## Sidelights

**P**eggy Northrop is a heavyweight in the world of publishing, having held high-ranking editorial positions at some of the most popular mass-circulation magazines, including *Vogue, Glamour,* *Redbook,* and *Real Simple.* In 2007, Northrop became editor-in-chief of *Reader's Digest,* one of the best-known magazine brands in the United States. Northrop was appointed to oversee a redesign at the pocket-sized monthly general interest family magazine. With ten million paid subscriptions, *Reader's Digest* is among the most widely distributed U.S. publications, second only to AARP publications, which are sent to all members.

"This is an iconic brand with the largest circulation of any magazine in the world, with 51 editions reaching nearly 80 million readers," *Reader's Digest* president and CEO Mary Berner said in a corporate press release announcing the appointment. "As one of the premier editors in our industry, Peggy has a remarkable track record of editorial successes and circulation growth ... and she is ideally suited to take on this role as we work to strengthen and grow our flagship."

Northrop, the daughter of John L.S. and Rose Northrop, was born in 1954 and grew up in Washington, Pennsylvania. Her father served as co-publisher of the *Observer-Reporter,* a local daily paper. As a child, Northrop took an interest in the family business and produced her own tabloid, called the *Redstone Weekly,* which she distributed in her neighborhood.

After high school, Northrop earned an undergraduate degree in anthropology from the University of California at Berkeley. Afterward, she stayed on the West Coast and was instrumental in helping launch *Health* magazine. She also worked as a reporter and editor at the *San Francisco Examiner*'s weekly Sunday magazine and edited the *Berkeley Monthly*. In time, Northrop relocated to Brooklyn, New York, and over the next several years worked for *Vogue, Glamour, Redbook,* and *Real Simple.*

In 2002, Northrop was named editor-in-chief of *Organic Style,* a bi-monthly magazine aimed at environmentally minded readers. Published by Rodale Inc., *Organic Style* first appeared on newsstands in 2001. In 2004, Northrop became the editor-in-chief of *More* magazine, a publication with a circulation of more than one million. Published by the Meredith Corp., *More* targeted educated, professional women ages 40 to 60.

It was during her tenure at *More* that Northrop caught the attention of the publishing world. After taking over, Northrop revamped the magazine's style and content to appeal to more women in the 40 to 60 age bracket. At the time, most magazines and advertisers were largely ignoring that demographic, despite the fact that these women increasingly wielded more power and money than ever before.

During that time period, most women's magazines aimed at the post-20 crowd featured stories that offered women tips on how to stay young, look younger, and lose weight. Northrop decided to try a different approach—along with a shift in attitude. It all happened in the July 2005 edition. As Northrop recalled to *Advertising Age*'s Nat Ives: "We put Jessica Lange on the cover, and instead of doing what had sold well ... which were cover lines like 'Age Less,' all of a sudden I decided I was bored with ... anti-aging, and I came up with an idea." Instead, Northrop plastered the cover with the words "Energy, Confidence, Attitude: The New Look of 40+."

Over the next several issues, Northrop worked to redefine the 40s as a time of power, creativity, sexuality, and style for women. "Meredith and Peggy Northrop saw that 40 is the new 30," advertising analyst Brenda White told *Advertising Age*. "*More*, in my opinion, really got that buzz going." Under Northrop's leadership, the magazine's dominance in the world of women's magazines increased. Northrop was able to tap into her demographic and increase newsstand sales, which helped increase advertising.

Besides changing the content, Northrop redesigned the magazine's look. Once implemented, her redesign earned *Folio*'s Gold Prize for Redesign in 2005. Along the way, Northrop stepped out from behind the scenes and in front of the camera to co-host a series of ongoing segments for the CBS News's *Early Show*. Often, the segments focused on a topic Northrop had covered in the magazine.

Northrop enjoyed her time at *More* because she got to edit a magazine aimed at her own demographic. As Northrop told MoneyPants.com, "I've worked at so many magazines where you come across a fascinating story but the subject is a woman in her 40s or 50s, and the editor says, 'Well, we did one of those this year already so let's skip it.'

The changes Northrop implemented, and the increased sales created a buzz in the publishing world. In 2006, *Advertising Age* named *More* the Magazine of the Year. In both 2005 and 2007, the magazine made *Advertising Age*'s "A List" of top ten magazines.

In 2007, *Reader's Digest* lured Northrop away from *More*, giving her the editor-in-chief position. At the time, *Reader's Digest* was on the cusp of a redesign. Northrop was brought in to finish the redesign—to modernize the look and feel. Northrop instituted a new regular feature called "4 Ways of Looking." This feature explores everyday practices from across the globe. "We need to realize how much we are part of a global community," Northrop told Media Week. She also planned to run an international story in every edition and feature articles from *Reader's Digest*'s overseas editions.

Northrop has received inspiration in her career from Elizabeth Crow, who oversaw several successful magazines and mentored young editors. "She had an inspiring sense of mission," Northrop told MoneyPants.com. "Plus she gave herself a year off to play the violin and draw and to have fun. She's one of the few people I've ever desperately wanted to impress."

In her free time, Northrop enjoys gardening, traveling to warm places, and chasing her West Highland terrier around the house. She frequently accepts invitations to speak to women's groups, offering advice and inspiration. Speaking to the *Observer-Reporter*'s Christie Campbell, Northrop shared a few of her tips. "Follow the butterflies in your stomach," she said, noting they often signify that one is on the right track. Northrop also urged women to find their purpose in life and go for it. "If not now, when? What are you waiting for?"

# Sources

## Periodicals

*Advertising Age,* October 23, 2006, p. S4.

*Daily Variety,* December 15, 2004, p. 13.

*Media Industry Newsletter,* November 19, 2007.

*Media Week,* November 9, 2007; May 5, 2008, p. 8.

*New York Times,* November 12, 2007, p. C11.

*Observer-Reporter* (Washington, PA), October 26, 2002; October 8, 2005, p B1.

## Online

"Peggy Northrop: *More* Magazine," MoneyPants. com, http://www.moneypants.com/moneypants /potw/item.php?id=55 (October 6, 2008).

"Peggy Northrop Named Editor-in-Chief of *Reader's Digest* Magazine," Reader's Digest Association, http://phx.corporate-ir.net/phoenix.zhtml?c= 71092&p=irol-newsArticle&ID=1075687&high light= (October 6, 2008).

"Peggy Northrop: U.S. Editor-in-Chief, *Reader's Digest,* http://www.rd.com/images/mediakit/ pdfs/028M_PeggyNorthrop_ss.pdf (October 6, 2008).

—*Lisa Frick*

# Alexander Ovechkin

## Professional hockey player

**B**orn Alexander Mikhaylovich Ovechkin, September 17, 1985, in Moscow, Russia; son of Mikhail (a cabdriver) and Tatiana Kabayeya (a professional basketball player) Ovechkin.

**Addresses:** *Contact*—Washington Capitals, MCI Center, 601 F St. NW, Washington, D.C. 20004. *Home*—Arlington, Virginia; Moscow, Russia. *Office*—Washington Capitals, 627 N. Glebe Rd., Ste. 850, Arlington, VA 22203.

## Career

**B**egan professional hockey career at age 16, joining Dynamo Moscow of the Russian Super League, 2001-05; made World Junior Championship debut leading Russia to the World Under-18 Junior Ice Hockey Championship, 2001-02; first-round, first pick in the NHL entry draft, 2004; left-winger, Washington Capitals, 2005—.

**Awards:** Named top forward, World Junior Championships, 2005; named the NHL's best rookie by several media outlets, including *The Hockey News, The Sporting News, Sports Illustrated*, TSN, and XM Radio, 2006; Calder Memorial Trophy, for NHL Rookie of the Year, 2006; NHL First All-Star Team, 2006, 2007, 2008; Kharlamov Trophy, for top Russian player in the NHL, 2006, 2007, 2008; D.C. Sportsman of the Year Award, Greater Washington Sports Alliance, 2007-08; Hart Memorial Trophy, for NHL MVP, 2008; Lester B. Pearson Award, for most outstanding player as voted by peers, 2008; Art Ross Trophy, for being the NHL's top point-scorer, 2008;

Maurice "Rocket" Richard Trophy, as NHL top goal-scorer, 2008; gold medal for representing Russia at the World Ice Hockey Championships, 2008.

## Sidelights

**S**ince arriving in the United States to play hockey for the Washington Capitals, Russian-born left-winger Alexander Ovechkin has been an incessant scoring machine. Ovechkin is an athletic showman and virtual sniper, able to dart down the rink and slap in goals with both his forehand and backhand. During his inaugural 2005-06 season, Ovechkin earned National Hockey League (NHL) rookie-of-the-year honors by notching 52 goals and 106 points. In 2007-08, he scored 65 goals and won the league's most valuable player award after delivering his team to its first playoff berth in five years. In 2008, the Washington Capitals rewarded Ovechkin with the NHL's first $100 million contract, pinning their hopes on the Russian dynamo to lead the team to a Stanley Cup victory—a feat that has eluded the club since its 1974 inception.

When the *Sporting News* asked former NHL MVP Brett Hull to name the best player in the game, he replied, "That's a no-brainer. Ovechkin. It's not even close, not even close. You know why? Because he loves to do it. You're never going to be a great sniper unless you love to score goals. I love his passion about scoring goals, how he bangs the glass and all that. It's great."

Ovechkin—or Ovie as his teammates call him—was born in 1985 in Moscow, Russia, to Mikhail and Tatiana Ovechkin (pronounced oh-VEHCH-kihn). Both of his parents were athletes. Mikhail Ovechkin played soccer until an injury drove him from the sport and forced him to become a cabdriver. Tatiana Ovechkin overcame a childhood leg injury to play professional basketball. As point guard, she led the former Soviet Union to Olympic gold medals in 1976 and 1980.

Raised alongside two older brothers, Ovechkin developed an early interest in hockey. As a youngster, he took cardboard boxes and fashioned them into hockey goals so he could pretend to play. At the age of eight, Ovechkin suited up for his first official hockey practice and found he already lagged behind the other kids; many of them had been skating together for years. While his peers executed backward figure-eights, Ovechkin struggled to simply skate backward.

Undaunted, Ovechkin decided to work harder. He started getting up at 6 a.m. so he could skate before elementary school. After school, he worked out with a hockey team then practiced his skating on the crude neighborhood rink that stood behind his apartment building. "He'd come home every evening just completely exhausted," Mikhail Ovechkin recalled during an interview with the *Washington Post*'s April Witt. "He would drop in the hallway, and we'd pick him up and just carry him to his room." In addition, Ovechkin collected tapes of Canadian hockey superstar Wayne Gretzky. Together with his father, he watched the tapes over and over, analyzing each play.

Despite Ovechkin's love for the game, there was a brief period in his childhood when he quit playing because his parents were unable to get him to practice. His older brother, Sergei, eventually picked up the slack and got his brother back into the game. Sergei Ovechkin died of injuries sustained in a car crash and never got to see his brother play in the NHL. According to the *Toronto Sun*, Ovechkin has said that he thinks of his brother before every game and is grateful he pushed him to play hockey.

As a child, Ovechkin remained focused on his goal of becoming a hockey player and practiced up to five hours a day. The hard work paid off in 2001 when Ovechkin, just 16, joined Dynamo Moscow, a professional ice hockey club. During the 2001-02 season, he made his debut on the international stage, notching 14 goals and four assists in eight games to lead Russia to the World Under-18 Junior Ice Hockey Championship.

By the time Ovechkin turned 17, NHL scouts were all over him, though he would not be eligible for the draft until he turned 18. During the 2004 NHL entry draft, the Washington Capitals picked Ovechkin as the first-round, first pick. At the time, the Capitals ranked 28 out of 30 NHL teams. Due to an NHL lockout, Ovechkin did not suit up with the Capitals until the start of the 2005-06 season. The 6-foot-2-inch, 220-pounder took the rink wearing jersey No. 8, the same number his mother wore on the basketball court. On his opening game against the Columbus Blue Jackets, Ovechkin scored twice, leading his team to a 3-2 victory. He keeps the game puck from that match on display at his home in Russia, where he spends the off-season.

During his NHL rookie season, Ovechkin lived up to expectations. He amassed 52 goals and 54 assists for a total of 106 points, becoming only the second rookie in NHL history to score more than 50 goals and 100 points. That season, Ovechkin took 425 shots on goal, a rookie record. During an interview, ESPN's David Amber asked Ovechkin if his teammates ever accused him of hogging the puck. "No. Nobody ever tells me to give them a pass or anything," Ovechkin responded. "My job is to score goals, and if I don't shoot the puck, I can't score goals."

He followed the next season with 46 goals and 92 points. In 2007-08, Ovechkin scored 65 goals, a record for a left-winger. No other NHL player had topped the 60-goal mark since Mario Lemieux hit it in 1995-96. With Ovechkin's help, the Capitals made their first playoff appearance since 2002-03. For his performance, Ovechkin earned the Hart Memorial Trophy, given to the NHL's most valuable player, and the Lester B. Pearson Award, given to the best player as voted by peers. After the season, the Capitals gave Ovechkin a 13-year, $124 million contract extension, making him the NHL's first hundred-million-dollar man.

Besides being a great player, Ovechkin has become an ambassador for the sport, which has seen its fan base dwindle in recent years. "This guy is becoming a folk hero in hockey," Capitals team owner Ted Leonsis told the *Washington Post*'s Witt. "No one has seen in a long, long time this rare combination of speed, strength, skill and absolute passion for the game. And, he's a nice kid.... That's where we really hit the jackpot. The new NHL has to be very fan-centric. This young man loves everything about the game. He loves the fans. You can't script that."

## Sources

### Periodicals

*National Post* (Canada), June 13, 2008, p. S1.
*Sporting News,* September 29, 2008, p. 50.
*Toronto Sun,* January 2, 2004, p. S83.
*Washington Post,* November 26, 2006, p. W14.

### Online

"Ovie Speaks Out on Crosby, Caps' Cup Hopes and That $124M Deal," ESPN.com, http://sports.espn.go.com/nhl/columns/story?columnist=amber_david&id=3234192 (November 3, 2008).
"Team: Alex Ovechkin #8," WashingtonCaps.com, http://capitals.nhl.com/team/app?page=PlayerDetail&playerId=8471214&service=page (September 30, 2008).

—*Lisa Fric.*

# Wayne Pacelle

*Robert Pitts/Landov*

## Chief Executive Officer of the Humane Society of the United States

**B**orn August 4, 1965; son of Dick (a physical education teacher) and Patricia (a secretary) Pacelle; married Kirsten Rosenberg (an animal-rights activist; divorced). *Education:* Yale University, B.A., 1987.

**Addresses:** *Home*—Washington, DC. *Office*—Humane Society of the United States, 2100 L St. NW, Washington, DC 20037.

## Career

**W**riter, *The Animals' Agenda,* 1987; national director, Fund for Animals, 1991-94; vice president of communications and government affairs, Humane Society of the United States, 1994-2004, president and CEO, 2004—.

**Awards:** Named to the *Los Angeles Times'* list of the United States' most important animal-rights activists, 1997; executive of the year, *NonProfit Times,* 2005; special achievement for humanitarian service, National Italian American Foundation, 2008.

## Sidelights

**A**s president and CEO of the Humane Society of the United States, Wayne Pacelle oversees one of the largest, strongest, and richest non-profit animal-advocacy groups. Pacelle (pronounced Pah-ell-ee) joined the Humane Society in 1994, serving a decade as its chief lobbyist and spokesman before being promoted to the top spot. During his tenure,

Pacelle has helped the organization increase its membership and assets. In addition, he has overseen the passage of some 20 statewide animal-related ballot initiatives, as well as countless federal statutes aimed at protecting animals.

Upon its founding in the 1950s, the Humane Society made its mark as a quintessential defender of cats and dogs. When Pacelle took over in 2004, he stepped up the organization's mission to include a focus on factory farm animals. Under Pacelle, the Humane Society has become more aggressive and proactive—a change that has drawn criticism. "His game plan is the same as that of the larger animal-rights movement," consumer analyst David Martosko told the *Washington Post*'s Don Oldenburg, "demonize meat and dairy, throw up legal obstacles to farms, increase artificially the price of animal protein and try to convince Americans they would do better without it."

Pacelle, a devout vegan, denies such radicalism in his agenda. "We're simply asking people to expand their sensitivity and to exhibit greater mercy and kindness to the less powerful," Pacelle told the *Hartford Courant*'s Bridget Kelly. "If you're concerned about the well-being of animals, then you inevitably should think about your food choices, your clothing choices, your recreational pursuits."

The youngest of four children, Pacelle was born on August 4, 1965, to Dick and Patricia Pacelle. His Italian father taught physical education and coached football. His mother, who hailed from a large Greek family, worked as a secretary. Pacelle grew up in New Haven, Connecticut, and developed an early fascination with animals. "Ever since I was a kid I've been focused on animals," Pacelle told the *New York Times'* Patricia R. Olsen. "I dog-eared the pages with the animal entries in our encyclopedia and memorized everything about them, from a polar bear to a pronghorn antelope." As a youngster, Pacelle tuned his television to *Wild Kingdom* and fantasized about meeting host Marlin Perkins, who introduced viewers to wild animals in their natural habitats.

During high school, Pacelle worked for his uncle's construction company and also as a country club tennis pro. He attended Yale University, pursuing degrees in history and environmental studies. As Pacelle learned about the history of different species, he became concerned with stories such as that of the American bison, which was hunted to near extinction, and the passenger pigeon, which was hunted to extinction after pigeon meat was commercialized as a cheap form of meat. "I saw that a destructive attitude toward animals in the natural world, along with innovations in technology, could produce colossal damage to animals and ecosystems," he told the *New York Times.* "I thought we should impose some limits on our dealings with animals."

Pacelle read Australian philosopher Peter Singer's book *Animal Liberation,* which prompted him to become a vegan, meaning he gave up eating meat, dairy, and eggs, as well as using or wearing animal products such as leather. Soon, Pacelle persuaded Yale's food services department to add vegan options in the dining halls. He founded the Student Animal Rights Coalition. The group's first political acts included demonstrations against stores that sold furs and condemning the use of research animals at Yale's medical school.

Another defining moment in Pacelle's consciousness occurred during the summer between his sophomore and junior years when he worked as a ranger at the Isle Royale National Park in Northern Michigan. "You're in this pristine environment," he told Carla Hall of the *Los Angeles Times.* "Inside this area, the animals could be protected. It just spoke to me. I could be part of the larger process of protecting animals and the environment."

After graduating from Yale in 1987, Pacelle wrote articles for a magazine called *The Animals' Agenda.* He was soon swept up by the animal-advocacy group Fund for Animals, which hired Pacelle as its national director. He left in 1994 to become the Humane Society's vice president of communications and government affairs. In 2004, Pacelle was promoted to president and CEO, ushering in a new era of animal-protection advocacy at the agency.

Since joining the Humane Society, Pacelle has accomplished a great deal. The organization has placed countless ballot measures in numerous states. In 1996, he helped usher through passage of Initiative 655 in Washington state, which banned hunters from bear-baiting and using dogs to hunt bears, cougars, bobcats, and lynx. Previously, hunters placed heaps of cow parts or doughnuts in piles to attract bears, then shot them as they ate. The Humane Society helped pass similar measures in other states. Other successful initiatives include bans on cockfighting in Arizona (1998), Missouri (1998), and Oklahoma (2002), and a ban on shooting mourning doves in Michigan (2006). Pacelle has also worked to enact legislation at the federal level.

In November of 2008, the Humane Society achieved a big victory in California when it helped gain approval of Proposition 2—known as the Prevention of Farm Animal Cruelty Act. This landmark measure set space requirements for animals, forbidding egg-laying hens, veal calves, and pregnant pigs to be penned up in crates or cages so small they cannot stand up, turn around, or fully extend their limbs or wings. Under Pacelle, the Humane Society has become more proactive. In 2008, the Humane Society used footage from its own hidden camera investigation to get a Southern California meatpacking plant shut down for animal cruelty. The video showed workers dragging cows with chains and using forklifts to get them to the slaughter chute because they were too injured or sick to walk. Because downed cattle may pose a higher contamination risk for E. coli, mad cow disease, or salmonella, federal regulations forbid meat from such cows to enter the food supply. The video's release touched off the largest beef recall in U.S. history.

Some critics argue that Pacelle is determined to get all animal use outlawed. Pacelle contends that is not so. As he explained to the *Washington Post,* his goals are simple. He hopes that one day, every state will prosecute animal cruelty and animal fighting as felonies. He hopes to see fewer shelter cats and dogs put to sleep and he hopes the marketplace will evolve to offer consumers a wide variety of humanely produced products.

# Sources

## Periodicals

*Hartford Courant*, August 30, 2004, p. B1.
*Los Angeles Times*, July 24, 2008.
*New York Times*, December 24, 2006, sec. 3, p. 9.
*Washington Post*, August 9, 2004, p. C1.

## Online

"Executive Staff: Wayne Pacelle, President & CEO," Humane Society of the United States, http://www.hsus.org/about_us/board_and_staff/experts/experts/wayne_pacelle/ (April 20, 2009).
"His Fine Feathered Friends, And Ours," *Newsweek*, http://www.newsweek.com/id/69533 (April 20, 2009).

—*Lisa Frick*

# Sarah Palin

## Governor of Alaska

**B**orn Sarah Louise Heath, February 11, 1964, in Sandpoint, ID; daughter of Chuck (a teacher and coach) and Sally (a school secretary) Heath; married Todd Palin (an oil production operator), 1988; children: Track, Bristol, Willow, Piper, Trig. *Education:* University of Idaho, B.S., 1987.

**Addresses:** *Home*—Wasilla, AK. *Office*—Alaska State Capitol Bldg. Third Fl., P.O. Box 110001, Juneau, AK 99811-0001.

## Career

**S**portscaster, KTUU-TV (Anchorage, AK), c. 1988; sports reporter, *Mat-Su Valley Frontiersman* (AK), c. 1988; worked for a utility company, c. 1988; elected to the Wasilla (AK) city council, 1992; elected mayor of Wasilla, 1996; elected governor of Alaska, 2006; named vice-presidential running mate by Senator John McCain, 2008.

**Member:** Alaska Oil and Gas Conservation Commission, chair, 2003-04.

## Sidelights

**I**n 2006, 42-year-old Sarah Palin became the first female governor of Alaska and the youngest person ever elected to lead the state. Palin bested opponents with far more political experience, but her victory at the polls was viewed as a sign of deep voter dissatisfaction with Alaska's longtime power elite in the wake of an embarrassing ethics scandal.

The Anchorage-area "soccer mom" had long challenged an entrenched political establishment, dating back to her first win at the polls in the early 1990s. "I recognized that if we had the same good old boys serving, nothing would change," she explained to *Vogue*'s Rebecca Johnson about what drew her to politics back then. "We needed some new blood. I also recognized that you had to be the top dog to make those changes."

Palin was born in 1964 in Idaho as the third of four children in a competitive, sports-mad family. A few months later, her parents moved to the town of Skagway, on Alaska's Panhandle, when her father took a teaching job there. Later they relocated to the Matanuska-Susitna Valley, a collection of suburbs surrounding Anchorage known by locals as Mat-Su Valley or simply "the Valley." Like many Alaska teens, Palin grew up to become an avid sport fisher and hunter.

Palin spent her formative years in the town of Wasilla, where her father, Chuck, served as a science teacher and cross-country coach at Wasilla High School. She proved to be an exceptional athlete, and was the point guard and co-captain of the Wasilla Warriors women's basketball team that won the 1982 state championship title. Her teen years also included a stint as Miss Wasilla 1984 after entering the pageant to win college scholarship money. Though she did not win the Miss Alaska crown, she did walk away with the Miss Congeniality title.

The scholarship funds helped finance Palin's journalism studies at the University of Idaho, and she earned her degree in 1987. A year later, she eloped with her high-school boyfriend, Todd Palin, and soon began a family. Her husband is part Alaska Native, and as such had inherited a valuable commercial fishing license passed down from his Yupik grandparents. During the summers, Palin, her husband, and their growing brood decamped to a site on the Nushagak River in Bristol Bay to collect the annual sockeye run. Todd Palin was also an oil-field worker on Alaska's North Slope, and prior to entering politics Palin worked as a sportscaster on Anchorage television stations and for the local utility company.

Palin first ran for a seat on the Wasilla city council in 1992 on a pro-business, anti-sales tax ticket, and won. The next few years saw immense growth in Wasilla and throughout the rest of the Valley, and the area's political allegiances shifted accordingly from Democratic to Republican. In 1996, Palin was elected mayor of Wasilla, beating out several more experienced candidates for the full-time job leading the city of 6,000. Her first term was marked by some hard feelings and even a brief recall movement that failed to gather steam after she fired the police chief, who had been a supporter of the previous mayor. In an interview with *Anchorage Daily News* writer Tom Kizzia, she conceded there were some difficulties during that transition phase. "It was rough with a staff who didn't want to be there working with a new boss," she said. "I learned you've got to be very discerning early on and decide if you can win them over or not. If you can't, you replace them early on."

Palin entered the Republican primary for lieutenant governor in 2002 but lost to Loren Leman, the first person of Alaska Native ancestry to be elected to statewide office. The winner of the gubernatorial contest was Republican Frank Murkowski, a former U.S. senator, who then appointed Palin to serve on the Alaska Oil and Gas Conservation Commission. The Commission serves as the regulatory body for the state's immense oil and natural-gas fields, and the only other member was another new appointee, Randy Ruedrich, who was also chair of Alaska's Republican Party. Early on, Palin was troubled by the ties that Ruedrich maintained with executives of the oil and gas companies that the Commission was charged with regulating; she also raised questions about Ruedrich conducting Republican Party business during work hours.

Palin alerted Murkowski of possible ethics violations and filed a complaint with the state attorney general's office. She took her concerns to the press after becoming convinced that neither Murkowski's office nor the attorney general were interested in fully pursuing the matter, and the resulting coverage incited a firestorm of controversy and a more formal investigation. In the end, Ruedrich resigned, pled guilty, and was fined $12,000, and the state attorney general also resigned. By this time Palin had stepped down from her seat on the Commission after less than a year on the job. "A good friend told me that in politics either you eat well or you sleep well," Kizzia quoted her as saying. "I wasn't sleeping well."

In speaking out against Ruedrich's misdeeds, Palin had made some powerful enemies among the state's longtime Republican elite, and her political career was considered to be all but over. The corruption charges she voiced were not new, however, and the U.S. Department of Justice launched an investigation into payoffs made to legislators serving in the state house by lobbyists for the oil and commercial fishing industries. The probe and subsequent indictments would end the careers of several prominent figures in Alaska politics, among them Murkowski and the senior member of Alaska's Republicans, U.S. Senator Ted Stevens, who had led the push toward statehood back in the late 1950s. Among those charged were Stevens' son Ben, president of Alaska's senate, and Murkowski's chief of staff; several more lawmakers were indicted on charges of accepting bribes in exchange for their vote not to increase Alaska's tax on oil profits.

Palin announced her run for Alaska governor in 2006 in the midst of this federal probe. Few gave her a legitimate chance of winning, but as the investigation widened, she beat Murkowski in the Republican primary; days later, Federal Bureau of Investigation agents raided the offices of several lawmakers, Ted Stevens among them—a dramatic setback for Alaska's Republican leadership. Palin's main opponent in the gubernatorial race was Democrat Tony Knowles, a former Alaska governor who had already served two consecutive terms, but she beat him by a margin of 17,000 votes.

Palin was inaugurated as Alaska's first female governor and its youngest, too, in early December of 2006. During her first year in office, she followed through on a campaign promise to revive a controversial natural gas pipeline scheme. Her predecessor, Murkowski, had invited the three major oil companies—Exxon, BP, and ConocoPhillips—to build it, but because they also owned the natural-gas reserves, the state legislature feared that it would prove another conflict of interest. While the state is rich in oil, particularly on the valuable North Slope, fears of declining reserves made Alaskans nervous about the state's economic future, which is heavily dependent on revenues from corporate oil taxes. The proposed pipeline would tap the rich natural gas reserves underneath the North Slope for sale to energy companies that supply the American Midwest. In March of 2007, Palin introduced the Alaska Gasline Inducement Act (AGIA), which invited proposals from several different companies under stricter guidelines that had been hammered out by lawmakers, and it was approved by the legislature almost unanimously. Transcanada Corporation won the job, which would cost an estimated $26 billion and run a pipeline from the North Slope to Calgary, Alberta, that would be fully operational by 2018.

Palin also fulfilled a pledge to reduce waste and spending in Juneau, the state capital. She sold Murkowski's much-derided private jet on eBay and cancelled Ted Stevens' famous "Bridge to Nowhere" project, which allocated $330 million in federal funds to connect an island airport to the town of Ketchikan on the Alaska Panhandle. Public-opinion polls give her consistently high marks, with 90 percent or more in approval ratings.

Palin's second year in office was marked by the birth of her fifth child, a son named Trig who was born with Down syndrome. Her oldest son, Track, was by then serving in the U.S. Army, which made his mother one of a rare number of elected officials with sons or daughters on active military duty. He completed infantry training at Fort Benning, Georgia, in January of 2008 and was likely to see combat duty in either Iraq or Afghanistan. Palin has voiced support for the Bush Administration's proposal to open up a long-protected federal area, the Arctic National Wildlife Refuge, to developers, but it was Track's decision to enlist "that made it personal for me," she told Johnson in Vogue. "This kid is doing everything he can to protect the safety of the United States. Are we? Are we producing a domestic, secure form of energy instead of relying on foreign sources? We need to be doing more."

Palin and her husband also have three daughters: Bristol, Willow, and Piper. The first was named after Bristol Bay, where the family still operates their commercial fishing site every summer. They live near Lake Lucille in Wasilla, and Palin still hunts and fishes in her spare time; asked her favorite dish, she is apt to reply moose stew or moose burgers. She is a lifelong member of the National Rifle Asso-

ciation and also belongs to the pro-life group Feminists for Life. A conservative on wildlife and conservation issues, in 2008 she penned an editorial piece for the New York Times in which she argued against a proposal to add the polar bear to the list of endangered species, which would have given it added protections under the federal Endangered Species Act. Environmental activists warn that greenhouse gases have caused polar ice to melt at a troublesome new pace, which has imperiled the bears. Palin pointed out that Alaska's 5,000 polar bears already benefit from careful monitoring and protection efforts. "Polar bears are magnificent animals, not cartoon characters," she wrote. "They are worthy of our utmost efforts to protect them and their Arctic habitat. But adding polar bears to the nation's list of endangered species, as some are now proposing, should not be part of those efforts."

In the summer of 2008, as the presidential election campaigns of both Democratic and Republican parties intensified, Palin's name was sometimes mentioned as a possible running mate for Arizona Senator John McCain, the Republican nominee. A journalist with the Seattle Times, Erika Bolstad, noted the "undeniable national buzz surrounding [Palin], seen by many Republicans both within Alaska and outside the state as a fresh, new face to represent the party's future." She was even the subject of a Web site launched by a Colorado college student, "Draft Sarah Palin for Vice President." To the surprise of many, on August 29, 2008, McCain announced that Palin would be his running mate in the upcoming presidential election.

Media coverage of Palin rarely fails to note that she was once a beauty pageant contestant, and usually includes some mention that her fans have dubbed her America's most attractive governor. "I wish they'd stick with the issues instead of discussing my black go-go boots," she joked with Johnson, the Vogue writer. "A reporter once asked me about it during the campaign, and I assured him I was trying to be as frumpy as I could by wearing my hair on top of my head and these schoolmarm glasses, but he said, 'No, that's not what I mean.' I guess I was naive, but when I hear people talk about it I just want to escort them back to the Neanderthal cave while we get down to business."

## Sources

Anchorage Daily News, October 23, 2006; October 24, 2006.

National Fisherman, April 2007, p. 36.

*Newsweek,* October 15, 2007, p. 66.

*New York Times,* October 29, 2006; January 5, 2008; July 31, 2008.

*Seattle Times,* March 13, 2008, p. B2.

*Vogue,* February 2008, p. 244.

*Weekly Standard,* July 16, 2007.

*—Carol Brennan*

# Thakoon Panichgul

## Fashion designer

**B**orn in 1974 in Chiang Rai Province, Thailand; son of Preeyakorn. *Education:* Boston University, business degree, 1997; Parsons The New School for Design, 2001-03.

**Addresses:** *Home*—New York, NY. *Office*—270 Lafayette St., Ste. 810, New York, NY 10012. *Web site*—http://www.thakoon.com/.

## Career

**M**erchandising associate, J. Crew, c. 1997-99; member of public relations staff, Yeohlee Teng, c. 2000; staff writer, *Harper's Bazaar*, 2000-04; launched label, Thakoon, 2004.

## Sidelights

**F**ashion designer Thakoon Panichgul launched his women's line "Thakoon" in 2004 and quickly began to garner accolades for his modern yet feminine classics. In 2008, he became one of several up-and-coming American designers whose fortunes were boosted immensely when future First Lady Michelle Obama began to be photographed at high-profile campaign events in their frocks. Panichgul's reputation even expanded overseas in the spring of 2009 when the First Lady wore two of his designs on the first overseas trip her husband made as U.S. president. "For so long, there was a celebrity culture that kind of took ... fashion into something that was light and frivolous," Panichgul mused in an interview with the *New York Observer*. "Now I hope that fashion will not be looked at in that way. Because I think it's such an important part of culture and living."

Panichgul's rise to the pages of *Vogue, Harper's Bazaar*, and other leading magazines is an achievement on its own, but even more impressive given the fact that he arrived in the United States as a fifth-grader who could not speak or write in English. Born in Thailand's Chiang Rai province in 1974, he came to the United States with his mother, Preeyakorn, and settled in Omaha, Nebraska, where they already had family. Over the summer, he prepared for his first day of school by watching the American television game shows his grandmother liked. At school, he made many new friends thanks to his drawing skills, but as a teenager the art classes at Bellevue West High School failed to interest him. The marketing classes did, however, and he worked with a team creating a public-service campaign that won a state award.

After graduating from Bellevue West in 1993, Panichgul went on to Boston University to study business, and remained on the East Coast during his summers off in order to take internships in the fashion and public relations industries in New York City. That led to a job as a merchandiser with J. Crew after he graduated in 1997, and then he joined the public relations staff for Malaysian-born designer Yeohlee Teng. Though he had always been uneasy with his writing skills—because English was not his first language—friends and colleagues encouraged him, and he wound up on staff at *Harper's Bazaar.* "I never wanted to be a writer, I never wanted to be a reporter," he revealed in the *New York Observer* interview. "I took the job because I knew it was going to give me knowledge in fashion."

During his stint at the Hearst Corporation-owned title from 2000 to 2004, Panichgul began taking night classes at Parsons The New School for Design in tailoring and other fashion-design subjects. On the weekends, he learned the business further with an internship at a small young label called Bruce run by two women, Nicole Noselli and Daphne Gutierrez. He launched his own label in September of 2004 with just ten pieces he unveiled in a Seventh Avenue showroom during the hoopla of Fashion Week. One of the visitors from Ikram, a high-fashion Chicago boutique, put in an order for all ten pieces. "I knew the woman who selected items to be sold at the store so I knew her taste," Panichgul recalled in an interview with the *Bangkok Post* that ran in Asia Africa Intelligence Wire. "But I didn't know she would buy the whole thing!"

The up-front money paid by Ikram permitted Panichgul to formally launch his company and make arrangements with clothing manufacturers. He also landed accounts with a top New York City boutique, Kirna Zabête, and the highly influential retailer Barneys New York. Soon, more mainstream stores began carrying the Thakoon line, among them Saks Fifth Avenue, Nordstrom, and online retailer Net-a-Porter. Another breakthrough came in 2006, when he was shortlisted for a Council of Fashion Designers of America (CFDA) Swarovski/Perry Ellis Award for emerging new talent.

Though he received regular coverage for his spring/summer and fall/winter collections, which by 2006 were debuting in the traditional runway presentation format during the biannual New York Fashion Week, it was not until the morning of August 29, 2008, that Panichgul's name appeared in news stories across the United States. The night before, Michelle Obama joined her husband Barack onstage when he formally accepted the Democratic Party's nomination for the November presidential ticket. She was wearing a floral-print dress in hues of pink, red, purple, and black from the latest Thakoon col-

lection, and its designer was stunned to see it on the front page of *USA Today,* the *New York Times,* and scores of other media outlets. Four weeks later, she wore another of his dresses for the first presidential debate in Mississippi. He was thrilled to have such a fan of his work, he told *Boston Herald* writer Jill Radsken, saying that Michelle Obama "has a sense of confidence in fashion. If you have a certain sense of confidence, you will look good. It sort of exudes: Here is a great woman who exemplifies that it's the confidence from within."

The media attention could not have come at a better time for Panichgul, who was readying both a lower-priced line called Thakoon Addition and a capsule collection for Target's Go! International collection that fall. His fortunes rose so far by the time of New York Fashion Week in February of 2009 that no less than *Vogue* editor Anna Wintour was seated next to White House Social Secretary Desiree Rogers in the front row at the Thakoon runway show.

In interviews, Panichgul has sometimes stressed how grateful he was that he chose business as his undergraduate major, for it gave him the required number-crunching mindset and decision-making abilities vital for survival in a highly competitive industry. He recalled how during his first year, he had to buy boxes from the Container Store just to be able to ship orders, telling *W's* Meenal Mistry. "The bigger you grow, the more of a challenge it becomes. People don't understand the process that young designers have to go through. It's easy for people to make judgments. There are decisions you have to make with limited resources."

## Sources

*Asia Africa Intelligence Wire,* September 5, 2005.
*Boston Herald,* December 18, 2008, p. 42.
*Harper's Bazaar,* September 2008, p. 228.
*New York Observer,* February 23, 2009.
*New York Times,* September 21, 2004.
*Omaha World-Herald* (NE), June 9, 2007.
*Time,* September 27, 2004, p. 64.
*Vogue,* November 2006, p. 364.
*W,* November 2006, p. 96; November 2008, p. 104.

—*Carol Brennan*

# Anna Paquin

## Actress

**B**orn Anna Helene Paquin, July 24, 1982, in Winnipeg, Manitoba, Canada; raised in New Zealand; daughter of Brian (a high school physical education teacher) and Mary (an English teacher) Paquin. *Education:* Attended Columbia University.

**Addresses:** *Agent*—William Morris Agency, One William Morris Place, Beverly Hills, CA 90212. *Home*—Los Angeles, CA. *Management*—Julie Silverman-Yorn, Firm Films, 9465 Wilshire Blvd., Ste. 212, Beverly Hills, CA 90212. *Publicist*—Ina Treciokas, I/D Public Relations, 155 Spring St., 6th Fl., New York, NY 10012.

## Career

**A**ctress in films, including: *The Piano*, 1993; *Charlotte Bronte's Jane Eyre*, 1996; *Fly Away Home*, 1996; *Amistad*, 1997; *Hurly Burly*, 1998; *She's All That*, 1999; *A Walk on the Moon*, 1999; *Finding Forrester*, 2000; *X-Men*, 2000; *Almost Famous*, 2001; *Buffalo Soldiers*, 2001; *Tart*, 2001; *25th Hour*, 2002; *Darkness*, 2002; *X2*, 2003; *The Squid and the Whale*, 2005; *X-Men: The Last Stand*, 2006; *Blue State* (also executive producer), 2007. Television appearances include: *The Member of the Wedding* (movie), 1997; *All the Rage* (movie), 2000; *Joan of Arc* (movie), 2005; *Bury My Heart at Wounded Knee* (movie), 2007; *The Courageous Heart of Irena Sendler* (movie), 2009; *True Blood*, 2009—. Stage appearances include: *The Glory of Living*, MCC Theater Co., New York City, 2001; *This Is Our Youth*, Garrick Theatre, London, 2002; *Roulette*, Ensemble Studio Theatre, New York City, 2004; *The Distance from Here*, MCC Theater Co., 2004; *The 24 Hour Plays*, MCC Theater Co., 2004, 2006; *After Ashley*, Vinyard Theatre, New York City, 2005.

**Awards:** Best supporting actress, Los Angeles Film Critics Association, for *The Piano*, 1993; Academy Award for best supporting actress, American Academy of Motion Picture Arts and Sciences, for *The Piano*, 1993; (with others) best ensemble cast performance, Online Film Critics Society, for *Almost Famous*, 2001; Theater World Award for outstanding actress, for *The Glory of Living*, 2002; Satellite Award for best actress in a series, International Press Academy, for *True Blood*, 2008; Golden Globe Award for best actress in a television drama series, Hollywood Foreign Press Association, for *True Blood*, 2009.

## Sidelights

**C**anadian-born, New Zealand-raised actress Anna Paquin has been making the news since she was a child. At the age of nine, she played the daughter of actress Holly Hunter's character in the film *The Piano*, a role that landed her an Oscar win after the film was released. Her critical reception has continued to earn her international acclaim, as evidenced by her win of the Golden Globe Award for best actress in a series for her performance in the television program *True Blood*.

Paquin received several awards and nominations for her early work before coming to pop-cultural prominence in the film *X-Men* and its two sequels.

But Paquin cares as much about small, independent films as she does about blockbusters: she and her brother have formed their own small film company, Paquin Films. Paquin's work has varied from big screen to small screen, with additional performances on stage, in both New York and the West End, London.

Born in 1982, Paquin had no formal theater training when she decided to audition for *The Piano* on a lark. Paquin saw the advertisement for an open call to cast a young actor in the film. Her father, a high school teacher, told her if she was interested, she would have to call for information herself. She did, and with her older sister and a friend, she auditioned with 5,000 other girls for the role. Director Jane Campion was impressed with Paquin's monologue and cast the girl in the film, which was expected, as an independent feature, to have a relatively small audience. Instead, it was critically acclaimed, and Paquin went from a complete unknown to being the second-youngest Oscar winner in the history of the awards.

In an interview on the AV Club Web site, Paquin explained her feelings about winning the award for her very first acting role. "The work I did when I was, what, *nine*, in *The Piano*? I mean, truthfully, I would say it was more a case of really good handling by an extraordinarily talented director, Jane Campion, and the fact that Holly Hunter and I had a really great connection, and really clicked as far as this sort of mother-daughter relationship," she said. "I didn't know how to *create* something, or think about creating a character, I just showed up and did what it felt like I was supposed to do, and just watched everyone else. It's not really a conscious performance."

Despite her early success, Paquin did not immediately continue as an actor. She was offered several roles immediately after her Oscar win, but her parents wanted to allow her to just be a child, rather than having to work. In a 2001 interview for *Interview* magazine, Paquin explained, "I think I'm still a little kid in a lot of ways, and I was definitely a kid for as long as it was appropriate for me to be one. I think if I had been any more conscious of my career and having some plan and that kind of thing, it would take away something." The family hired an agent, mostly to keep the movie offers from coming to them at their home, and Paquin took only a role in a television commercial over the next several years.

At 13, Paquin made the decision to take on two roles: one as the young Jane Eyre in *Jane Eyre*, the other as the daughter of a troubled widower who raises a flock of geese in *Fly Away Home*. After wrapping the filming of the first, which was shot in England, Paquin traveled to Canada to film the second. During *Fly Away Home*, her parents were in the process of getting a divorce, something that weighed on her. Her parents took turns staying with her during the filming process, and eventually, Paquin moved to Los Angeles with her mother.

Along with the sadness of her parents' divorce, Paquin learned that people had different expectations of her than they had before her Oscar win. She described in an interview on the AV Club Web site how she'd felt about the process: "Okay, so I did it *once*, and everyone made this big fuss, but now I have no idea what I'm doing, and apparently people seem to think I should.... It's like, 'Give me a break! I'm 13!'" Despite those expectations, Paquin kept the process that had made her successful early on. "I still don't really think about acting that much," she said in a *People* interview when she was 13. "I just do it."

At the time, Paquin still had not decided on a career in acting. She had some thoughts about becoming a lawyer so she could be paid to argue with people all day. Continuing to take roles when the parts appealed to her, Paquin grew from a child actor into teen roles with films such as *Hurlyburly* and *A Walk on the Moon*, working alongside well-known actors including Meg Ryan, Viggo Mortensen, Sean Penn, and Kevin Spacey. Her performance in those roles showed that she could play a troubled teen who connected with audiences, making her an excellent fit for the loner mutant, Rogue, in the first movie in what would become a franchise.

Based on the Marvel comic series of the same title, *X-Men* introduced the characters Rogue and Wolverine, as well as the rest of the X-Men heroes, to a movie-going audience, taking them from drawings to live action. Paquin played opposite Hugh Jackman as a teen whose ability to drain the life—and mutant ability—out of anyone she touches has her on the run. The film, with its large ensemble cast, was a blockbuster hit, which paved the way not only for two sequels, but video games and action figures as well. "We had all the *Star Wars* [action figures] when we were kids, and now there's one of me," she said in *Interview*.

The X-Men films also opened a new audience for Paquin: her peers. Previously, the films in which Paquin starred had appealed primarily to adult audiences. Now, however, many of the people who watched her on screen were close to Paquin's own age. In *Interview,* she described, "I feel like I've done some work that my peers or people who I would potentially be friends with can relate to,"

The same year that *X-Men* came out, Paquin appeared in *Almost Famous* and *Finding Forrester,* two more movies that would appeal to a younger audience. In the first, Paquin played one of several groupies who follow a band on tour. In the second, she played a teen from a privileged background who gets into a relationship with an African-American teen against her father's wishes. *Almost Famous* won Paquin her first award since *The Piano*: the Online Film Critics Society Award for Best Ensemble Cast Performance.

In addition to the movies, Paquin began college at Columbia University, hoping to continue to gain real-life experience rather than focusing all her efforts on work. While in New York, she had the opportunity to act on stage, something that became a greater education for her than her classes. She acted in several Off-Broadway productions, for which she won stage awards, and performed in *This Is Our Youth* on the West End in London.

Over the next several years, Paquin balanced small, independent projects, such as *The Squid and the Whale* and the television movie *Bury My Heart at Wounded Knee,* with the blockbusters *X2* and *X-Men: The Last Stand.* Given her love of independent projects, Paquin sought out a way to be able to do the projects she felt passionate about, regardless of who else wanted to make those films. As a result, she and her brother, Andrew, founded Paquin Films, a small independent film studio. Paquin served as executive producer and star of their first film, *Blue State.* When asked about founding the studio in her AV Club interview, Paquin said, "If I find a piece of material that I'm really passionate about, I can get it made. I don't have to wait for somebody else who maybe doesn't feel as strongly as I do about it. I think that those are the best films. Those are the projects that I love being a part of the most, is where whoever's behind it is really, really, really passionate about it. Those are the people that I want to work with, when you walk into a room and a person is just so committed to what they've discovered that they have to make the film."

Taking place after the 2004 election, *Blue State* is the story of a young man who is determined to move to Canada after John Kerry loses to incumbent President George W. Bush. Paquin's character, a brash young woman, tries to get the young man to see that moving out of the country may be a grand stand, but it is only symbolic: creating change at home is the more important decision. Despite the film's message, Paquin has declared herself to be relatively non-political, particularly about U.S. politics, because she is not an American citizen and cannot vote in the United States.

By 2008, the only type of acting work Paquin had not done was act as a regular in a television series. Her chance to expand her career came through *True Blood,* an HBO series based on the "Southern Vampire" series of novels by Charlaine Harris. Produced by Alan Ball, the creator of HBO series *Six Feet Under,* with whom Paquin worked on *Bury My Heart at Wounded Knee, True Blood* is a series about the lives of vampires who live under the radar, existing among humans in southern Louisiana. Paquin plays Sookie Stackhouse, a human woman with psychic abilities who works as a waitress, flaunting her curves and navigating the tricky divide between humans and vampires. Her relationship with the vampire Bill, played by Paquin's real-life boyfriend Stephen Moyer, drags Sookie deeper into the supernatural world. Paquin's performance earned her both a Satellite Award and a Golden Globe for best actress, and the network picked up the show for a second season.

When asked about her decision to move to television in *Interview,* Paquin explained, "You get to actually develop the characters past an hour and a half. You get episode after episode of really interesting writing that makes you go to more and more complex places and you really get deep into a part." Along with continuing her work as Sookie Stackhouse, allowing her to focus on one role for an extended period of time, which she stated in *Interview* was part of the appeal, Paquin has starred in several films and television movies slated for release in 2009. She also addressed her desire to work in different formats in *Interview.* "I love everything. You gain and lose different things in different mediums or different sectors of different mediums."

## Sources

### Books

*Contemporary Theatre, Film, and Television,* vol. 58, Gale (Detroit, MI), 2004.

## Periodicals

*Allure,* June 1, 2007, p. 58.
*Daily Variety,* January 12, 2009, p. 22.
*Interview,* January–April 2001, p. 55; October 2008, p. 84.
*Maclean's,* January 26, 2009, p. 9.
*People,* April 15, 1996, p. 156.
*Spin,* September 2008, p. 54.
*Time,* April 4, 1994, p. 80.
*USA Today,* April 3, 2009, p. 9D.

## Online

"Anna Paquin," AV Club Web site, http://www.avclub.com/articles/anna-paquin,14223/ (April 26, 2009).
"Anna Paquin," Internet Movie Database, http://www.imdb.com/name/nm0001593/ (April 26, 2009).

*—Alana Joli Abbott*

# Willie Parker

## Professional football player

**B**orn Willie Everett Parker, Jr., November 11, 1980, in Clinton, NC. *Education:* University of North Carolina, B.A., 2004.

**Addresses:** *Office*—Pittsburgh Steelers, P. O. Box 6763, Pittsburgh, PA 15212.

## Career

**P**ittsburgh Steelers, 2004—.

**Awards:** Received "Super Ram" status, University of North Carolina, 2003; four-time winner of the NFL Player of the Week, 2005; longest touch down run in Super Bowl history, 2006; selected for the Pro Bowl, 2006 and 2007; Most Valuable Player, Pittsburgh Steelers, 2006; Super Bowl Champion, 2006, 2009.

## Sidelights

**P**rofessional football player Willie Parker was the running back for the 2009 Super Bowl champions, the Pittsburgh Steelers. Due to his exceptional speed, Parker is known by the nickname "Fast Willie." He holds the record for longest run in Super Bowl history, a 75-yard burst of speed during Super Bowl XL in 2006. As of 2009, Parker was third on the Steelers all-time rushing list, and he had been selected twice to participate in the the Pro Bowl, an NFL All-Star game.

Born Willie Everett Parker, Jr., in Clinton, North Carolina, Parker was always fast. As a child, he would race pit bulls, nearly keeping up with their speed. "You should have seen it," his father told the Pittsburgh *Tribune Review.* "I don't know where the idea came from, but they'd have a guy on the far end calling for the dog when the race started. You'd see those two at full gallop, running to the finish line. Willie didn't win, but it was amazing to see so much speed." As a child he would race everyone in the neighborhood, finally beating his only remaining childhood competitor when he was a freshman in college. When his father would drive into the neighborhood, Parker would race the car home. He explained to the *Tribune Review* that he began racing when he was about 12 or 13, and kept working at it because there was one girl who was faster than all the boys. Unwilling to be outraced by a girl, Parker continued building his speed until he was the fastest in the neighborhood.

He was noticed as a fast runner on the field as early as his pee-wee football league. Parker ran 1,801 yards during his high school career, earning the North Carolina state title his junior year for his 11.8 yards-per-carry average. His senior year, he led his team to state playoffs. With a scholarship to the University of North Carolina, Parker expected to continue his football career, but when the coach who recruited him was replaced, he was asked to change his style from being a running back to being a power back. The coaching staff wanted to change the philosophy of football at University of North Carolina, putting more focus on power and less on the finesse that the previous coach had stressed. In addition to his trouble on the team, Parker had trouble at home: his best friend from Clinton was murdered during Parker's sophomore year.

Given Parker's somewhat lack-luster performance during college, mostly from being underused on the field, he went undrafted after he graduated. But as a free agent, he was noticed by the Pittsburgh Steelers, who made him the final player in the 53-man roster. He led the team in rushing during the pre-season and in November made his first NFL regular-season appearance. When the running back was out for a second week, Parker continued on the field and earned play time three more times that season, making a pivotal performance in a December game that led to the Steelers winning, and he rushed 100 yards in a game in early January, marking the longest run for the Steelers since 1997.

Early into his second season, Parker became a starter for the Steelers, starting eight games in a row. Both the team and Parker himself had an incredibly successful season: Parker made an 80-yard touchdown, rushed for 135 yards in a single game, and finished the season with 1,202 rushing yards. In February of 2006, the Pittsburgh Steelers won their fifth Super Bowl, tying the record held by the San Francisco 49ers and the Dallas Cowboys. During that same game, Parker set his own record: His 75-yard touchdown run was the longest in Super Bowl history. In the following season, Parker broke two Steelers records by scoring 16 total touchdowns, 13 of them rushing, and by achieving the single-game rushing record of 223 yards. Declared the team's Most Valuable Player (MVP) and an NFL player of the week, Parker also earned his first Pro Bowl due to his career-high 1,494 rushing yards. In 2007, Parker started the first 15 games before he was sidelined after breaking his leg. Before his injury, he became the eleventh Steelers running back to rush for 3,000 yards over the course of his career.

During the 2008 season, Parker suffered several injuries that limited the number of games he was able to play. He began the season with three consecutive 1,000-yard seasons, but in the third week, Parker injured his knee and found himself sidelined. "It was tough just to see them out there playing and practicing. I wished I could have been out there with them," Parker told Adam Adkins of the *Tampa Tribune*. Friendly teasing from his teammates and his own desire to be back out on the field hurried him back into the game, and he underperformed, still healing over his next seven games. A disagreement with the coach on strategy also made for a rough several games. But as the regular season ended, Parker made a 113-yard rush and a touchdown on 23 carries, solidifying his return to the field. The Steelers again made it to the Super Bowl, where they defeated the Arizona Cardinals, 27 to 23, with Parker holding the lead in rushing yards for the game. His career rushing record is 4,989 yards.

## Sources

### Books

*World Almanac and Book of Facts*, World Almanac Education Group, 2007.

### Periodicals

*St. Petersburg Times* (St. Petersburg, FL), January 15, 2009, p. 1C.
*Tampa Tribune* (Tampa, FL), January 31, 2009, p. 4.
*Tribune-Review* (Pittsburgh, PA), August 31, 2005; January 26, 2009.
*USA Today*, January 12, 2009, p. 4C.

### Online

NFL, http://www.nfl.com/ (February 13, 2009).
Pittsburgh Steelers, http://news.steelers.com/team/player/49229/ (February 13, 2009).
Sports Illustrated Online, http://sportsillustrated.cnn.com/football/nfl/players/7073/ (February 13, 2009).
Willie Parker's Home Page, http://www.fastwillie39.com/ (February 13, 2009).

*—Alana Joli Abbott*

# Simon Pegg

**Actor and screenwriter**

**B**orn Simon John Beckingham, February 14, 1970, in Gloucester, England; son of John Henry (a jazz musician and musical instrument salesman) and Gillian Rosemary (a civil servant; maiden name, Smith) Beckingham; married Maureen McCann, July 23, 2005. *Education:* Bristol University, B.A., 1991.

**Addresses:** *Management*—Dawn Sedgwick Management, 3 Goodwins Ct., Covent Garden, London WC2N 4LL, United Kingdom. *Production company*—Big Talk Productions, 26 Nassau St., London W1W 7AQ, United Kingdom. *Web site*—http://www. peggster.net.

## Career

**P**erformed in comedy troupe David Icke and the Jesus Apostles, c. 1990; standup comedian, mid-1990s. Actor on television, including: *Six Pairs of Pants*, 1995; *Faith in the Future*, 1996-98; *Hippies*, 1999; *Spaced*, 1999-2001; *Band of Brothers*, 2001; *Look Around You*, 2002-05; *Final Demand*, 2003; *I Am Not An Animal*, 2004; *Doctor Who*, 2005. Film appearances include: *The Parole Officer*, 2001; *24 Hour Party People*, 2002; *Shaun of the Dead*, 2004; *Big Nothing*, 2006; *Mission: Impossible III*, 2006; *Hot Fuzz*, 2007; *Run, Fat Boy, Run*, 2007; *How to Lose Friends and Alienate People*, 2008. Voice actor in *Free Jimmy*, 2006. Screenwriter, including: *Spaced*, 1999-2001; *Shaun of the Dead*, 2004; *Hot Fuzz*, 2007; *Run, Fat Boy, Run*, 2007.

**Awards:** British Independent Film Award for best screenplay, for *Shaun of the Dead*, 2004.

## Sidelights

**F**irst in Great Britain, then in the United States, critics have compared British comic actor Simon Pegg to John Cleese, the beloved star of the 1970s comedy troupe Monty Python. Like Cleese, Pegg has developed an original satirical persona that is distinctly British, yet also popular across the Atlantic. In the hit British TV show *Spaced*, zombie movie *Shaun of the Dead*, and British action film *Hot Fuzz*, Pegg has rearranged nerdy pop culture knowledge into affectionate humor. Like a grown-up kid, the science-fiction fanboy has acted in remakes of classic sci-fi series from his childhood, guesting on *Doctor Who* and joining the cast of *Star Trek XI*, in which he will play a young version of the character Scotty. "My whole life is a geek wish-fulfillment trip," Pegg told Erin Biba of Wired.com.

Pegg, who was born in the English city of Gloucester, attended Bristol University, where he set up a comedy club and performed in the comedy troupe David Icke and the Jesus Apostles. During the mid-1990s, he worked as a standup comedian. He befriended Nick Frost, his future collaborator on many shows and films, when Frost was a waiter making very little money. Pegg let him share his apartment, and since there was only one bed in the place, they slept in it next to each other for months—an odd fact that profilers often bring up with raised eyebrows, comparing it with the buddy-film relationships the two men depict on film.

In 1995, Pegg debuted on British television in the comedy series *Six Pairs of Pants*. He performed in several other British television shows, including the sitcom *Faith in the Future* and the lead role in *Hippies*. He also took small roles in the films *The Parole Officer* and *24 Hour Party People*.

Pegg's big breakthrough came with *Spaced*, a peculiar comedy series written by and starring Pegg and his friend Jessica Hynes and directed by another friend, Edgar Wright. The series, shot with a single camera, followed two geeky slackers, Tim and Daisy, who pretend to be a couple to get an apartment. Pegg played Tim, an unemployed cartoonist—the ultimate slacker, geeky job. Frost, naturally, played Tim's best friend, who had a terrifying love of guns. *Spaced* celebrated nerdy pop culture such as the *Star Wars* films. It became a huge hit in Britain.

"When we wrote it, me and Jess were looking at television in the late '90s, and there wasn't a sitcom that was aimed at twenty-somethings," Pegg told Biba of Wired.com. "Everything was really off the mark. It was brightly lit sets with attractive people talking about sex. It was inaccurate."

Meanwhile, Pegg began taking serious roles. In 2001, he had a minor part in the World War II miniseries *Band of Brothers*. He also took on a dramatic role in 2003 in the British series *Final Demand*. At the same time, he and Wright began collaborating on a film.

Their project, entitled *Shaun of the Dead*, was a funny but reverential homage to *Dawn of the Dead*, the George Romero movie that founded the zombie-film genre. Pegg played Shaun, a worker at a London electronics store who finds himself in the midst of a zombie attack. The film's running joke is that, at first, the two main characters are too out of it to notice that undead creatures are stalking them. "It's a toss-up who's deader," wrote Lisa Schwarzbaum of *Entertainment Weekly*. "Shaun, oblivious on his bleary morning round to buy a junky breakfast at the convenience store across the road, or the flesh-hungry ghouls who trail him." Eventually, Shaun gets his act together and saves his mother, friend (Frost), and ex-girlfriend from the zombie hordes.

Pegg often referred to the film as a romantic zombie comedy, or "rom zom com" for short, while *Entertainment Weekly* dubbed it a "zomedy." Britain buzzed about it, and it became a modest success in the United States after its September of 2004 release there. Jason Buchanan of allmovie.com praised its "witty writing and cleverly constructed chills." Made for $6 million, *Shaun of the Dead* grossed $14 million. It also won the ultimate praise for a zombie movie: George Romero himself loved it, and invited Pegg and Wright to play zombies in his next movie, *Land of the Dead*.

After *Shaun*, Pegg acted in more British TV series: *Look Around You*, a spoof of a long-running BBC series on science; *I Am Not An Animal*, a comedy about genetically modified animals who can talk; and one episode of *Doctor Who*, the remake of the British sci-fi series Pegg loved as a child. He lent his voice to a character in *Free Jimmy*, a computer-animated comedy, and had a major role in *Big Nothing*, a film released only on DVD in the United States.

A British interviewer, figuring the success of *Shaun* had given Pegg some international popularity, asked if he would leave Britain for Hollywood. No, Pegg replied (according to Clark Collis of *Entertainment Weekly*): he wasn't about to "go off and do *Mission: Impossible III*." A year later, Pegg had to eat his words. Director J. J. Abrams, casting the third film in the *Mission: Impossible* series, was a Pegg fan, and invited him to join the cast. "J. J. Abrams had seen *Shaun* and really liked it," Pegg told Collis. "He called me at the office and said, 'Do you want to be in *M:I-3*?' It was that simple. Then I was suddenly in L.A. acting alongside Tom Cruise and Ving Rhames. It was very odd. The size of the production was shocking. So much food.... That was the biggest thing I took away from it. Unlimited smoothies!"

Wright and Pegg teamed up again to create another movie, *Hot Fuzz*, a comedic take on police action films. "We started thinking about the cop genre," Pegg told Carole Cadwalladr of the *Observer* of London, "and the whole notion of investing the British police service with some sort of cool because it just seems that the British cops are up against it in some ways—they wear jumpers, they don't have guns." To research the concept, Pegg and Wright spent time with police in London and in England's West Country. They also watched several cop films, buddy movies, and films about small towns, taking notes about recurring clichés and dramatic devices.

In *Hot Fuzz*, Pegg plays a successful London cop transferred to a quiet English village, where he partners with a local detective, played by Frost, who is obsessed with action movies. Timothy Dalton, who played James Bond in several films, co-stars as a shady grocery store owner and murder suspect. Much gunplay, many car chases, and several comedic murders ensue. Collis of *Entertainment Weekly* called the movie "a kinetic mix that fuses the plot and quaint setting of an Agatha Christie mystery with the machismo-drenched tropes of the buddy-cop blockbuster." Cadwalladr of the *Observer* pronounced it "that rarest of very rare things: a British film that's actually funny."

*Hot Fuzz*, like *Shaun of the Dead*, was often described as a parody, but Pegg disagreed. "We're always adamant that they're not spoofs," Pegg told Collis of *Entertainment Weekly*. "They lack the sneer that a lot of parodies have that look down on their source material. Because we're looking up to it."

In April of 2008, Pegg starred in *Run, Fat Boy, Run*, the directing debut of David Schwimmer of the sitcom *Friends*. Though the screenplay was co-written by Pegg and Michael Ian Black, another accomplished culture-junkie comedian, critics savaged it. Pegg plays a guy, inept at romance, who leaves his fiancée at the altar and, five years later, competes against her new boyfriend in a marathon to try to win her back. Katey Rich of *Film Journal International* called its jokes "uniformly predictable," its characters "barely sketched-out," and its ending "entirely forgettable."

That same year, Pegg denounced the forthcoming American remake of *Spaced*, being filmed by Fox, because its creators had not consulted him, Hynes, or Wright. Pegg called the snub "an effective vote of no confidence in the very people who created the show," and an act of "selling out and appropriating our ideas without even letting us know," according to Vanessa Thorpe and Ben Walters of the *Observer*. The idea of a Hollywood remake likely galled Pegg and his friends because it undermined the spirit of the original show: Much of its humor came from its use of bombastic Hollywood clichés to portray the gray, slow-paced life in a North London apartment.

Pegg must have felt some satisfaction a few months later when the original *Spaced* was released on DVD for the first time in the United States. The set featured commentary by accomplished film directors Quentin Tarantino and Kevin Smith. Pegg went on a promotional tour in the States. "It would be entertaining for the American audience to see there are geeks like them in far-off lands," Pegg told Biba of Wired.com.

By mid-2008, Pegg had filmed two more Hollywood roles. He co-starred with Kirsten Dunst in *How to Lose Friends and Alienate People*, the adaptation of a memoir by Toby Young. Presumably more thrilling for the sci-fi-loving actor, he was also cast in *Star Trek XI* as Scotty, the Scottish chief engineer from the original *Star Trek* television series. Pegg took a serious but fun approach to the role, he told Biba of Wired.com. "In some respects he's a racial stereotype," he conceded. "But, I know plenty of Scottish people who like a bit of a drink and have the surname Scott." He said he played the role straight, not as a parody. "I approached the part like James [Doohan, the original Scotty] did when he got the part. To look at who he is. He's an accomplished engineer, a bit cheeky, likes a drink and a brawl."

Pegg is said to be extremely private about his personal life, which includes a number of celebrity friendships. When he married Maureen McCann at a 2005 wedding in Glasgow, Scotland, the guest list included most members of the British rock bands Travis and Coldplay. Pegg had become friends with Coldplay frontman Chris Martin after meeting him at a concert around 2000, and he is also friends with his wife, actress Gwyneth Paltrow, and is the godfather of the couple's daughter, Apple.

Cadwalladr, the *Observer* interviewer, asked Pegg in 2007 if he had started his career with any inkling that he would be so successful and befriend creative icons such as Tarantino. "None," he replied. "It's all amazing. But luckily it happened quite gradually. The idea of doing some of the things that I've been lucky enough to do … if I could have known that before, it would have been too much. I would probably have wet myself. And then cried."

## Sources

### Periodicals

*Entertainment Weekly*, October 1, 2004, p. 52; April 20, 2007, p. 36; November 30, 2007, p. 69; April 4, 2008, p. 45.
*Evening Standard* (London, England), April 8, 2004, p. 6.
*Evening Times* (Glasgow, Scotland), April 21, 2003, p. 19.
*Film Journal International,* April 2008, p. 149.
*Interview,* May 2007, p. 82.
*Mail on Sunday* (London, England), March 14, 2004, p. 29.
*Observer* (London, England), February 4, 2007, p. 10; March 23, 2008, p. 3.
*Telegraph* (London, England), June 2, 2007.

### Online

"Simon Pegg: Biography," All Movie Guide, http://www.allmovie.com/cg/avg.dll?p=avg&sql=2:307202~T1 (August 2, 2008).

"Simon Pegg: Biography," Internet Movie Database, http://www.imdb.com/name/nm0670408/bio (August 3, 2008).

"Simon Pegg's Geek Roots Show in *Spaced*," Wired. com, http://blog.wired.com/underwire/2008/07/simon-peggs-gee.html (August 3, 2008).

"Simon Pegg: Profile," BBC Comedy, http://www.bbc.co.uk/comedy/profiles/simon_pegg.shtml (August 2, 2008).

*—Erick Trickey*

# Kal Penn

## Actor

**B**orn Kalpen Suresh Modi, April 23, 1977, in Montclair, New Jersey; son of an engineer and a fragrance evaluator. *Education:* University of California—Los Angeles, B.A., c. 2000; graduate studies in international security at Stanford University, 2008.

**Addresses:** *Agent*—Gold/Liedtke Agency, 3500 W. Olive Ave., Ste. 1400, Burbank, CA 91505. *Home*— Los Angeles, CA.

## Career

**A**ctor in films, including: *Express: Aisle to Glory,* 1998; *Freshman,* 1999; *American Desi,* 2001; *Badger,* 2002; *Hector,* 2002; *Van Wilder,* 2002; *Love Don't Cost a Thing,* 2003; *Malibu's Most Wanted,* 2003; *Where's the Party?,* 2003; *Ball & Chain,* 2004; *Harold & Kumar Go to White Castle,* 2004; *Dancing in Twilight,* 2005; *A Lot Like Love,* 2005; *Son of the Mask,* 2005; *Sueño,* 2005; *Bachelor Party Vegas,* 2006; *Deck the Halls,* 2006; *Man About Town,* 2006; *Superman Returns,* 2006; *Van Wilder 2: The Rise of Taj,* 2006; *Epic Movie,* 2007; *The Namesake,* 2007; *Harold & Kumar Escape from Guantanamo Bay,* 2008; *Under New Management,* 2008. Executive producer of films, including: *Van Wilder 2: The Rise of Taj,* 2008; *Under New Management,* 2008. Television appearances include: *Brookfield* (pilot), 1999; *Buffy the Vampire Slayer,* 1999; *Sabrina, the Teenage Witch,* 2000; *Spin City,* 2000; *Angel,* 2001; *ER,* 2001; *NYPD Blue,* 2001; *That's Life,* 2001; *All About the Andersons,* 2003; *Cosmopolitan* (movie), 2003; *Tru Calling,* 2003; *Homeland Security* (movie), 2004; *Awesometown* (movie), 2005; *The Danny Comden Project* (movie), 2006; *24,* 2007; *Law & Order: Special Victims Unit,* 2007; *House,* 2007-08; *Two Sisters* (movie), 2008. Also taught at the University of Pennsylvania, 2008.

*Jason LaVeris/FilmMagic/Getty Images*

## Sidelights

**T**he breakout star of such films as 2004's *Harold and Kumar Go to White Castle* and 2007's *The Namesake,* Kal Penn is one of the first actors of Indian descent to have a successful mainstream acting career in the United States. Primarily known for his film work, especially in comedies, he has also appeared in film dramas and a number of television projects. For example, Penn had a regular role on the popular medical show, *House, M.D.,* beginning in 2007.

Penn was born Kalpen Suresh Modi on April 23, 1977, in Montclair, New Jersey, (Penn changed his name to further his acting career, believing he would have more success without a foreign sounding name.) His father was an engineer while his mother was a fragrance evaluator who had a master's degree in chemistry. Living in Freehold, New Jersey, by his early teens, Penn became interested in acting by the time he was in eighth grade. That year, he appeared as the Tin Man in a production of *The Wiz.*

The role changed his life. Penn told Neil Amdur of the *New York Times,* "Here I am 13 years old, suddenly met with this reality, in a very basic way, that acting can change people's thinking." His parents, however, wanted him to be an engineer or doctor. Penn told *BackStage*'s Pamela Bock, "My parents were a little freaked out at first. They just though I would have such a hard life. But as I started really getting into it and studying it they realized that it really did make me happy, and since then they have been really supportive."

For high school, Penn was enrolled in the Fine and Performing Arts Center at Howell High School. The fine arts program gave him training in acting, dance, movement, and voice. Penn later transferred to Freehold Township High School, from which he graduated in 1995. He then moved to California to attend college. Educated at the University of California—Los Angeles, he earned his undergraduate degree in sociology with a specialization in theater, film, and television. Penn also studied acting with Reynold Forman.

Penn faced challenges as he began his professional acting career. He told Bock of *BackStage*, "When I first started out, getting roles as a minority actor was extremely difficult.... I realized really early on the kind of racism that exists, even in very small independent and student films. People just seem to have no desire to tell a realistic story." Despite such obstacles, Penn was cast in roles, and spent his first years primarily working in television. After making his film debut in 1998's *Express Aisle to Glory*, Penn spent several years doing guest spots on shows such as *Buffy the Vampire Slayer*, *Sabrina, the Teenage Witch*, *Angel*, *ER*, and *NYPD Blue*. He also appeared in a failed pilot, 1999's *Brookfield*.

After appearances in films such as 1999's *Freshman*, 2001's *American Desi*, and 2002's *Hector*, Penn gained more attention for his key supporting role in the raunchy college comedy *Van Wilder*. Penn's Taj Mahal Badalandabad is a geeky exchange student and the earnest assistant of the titular Wilder, a popular college student on the seven-year plan. Wilder has no inclination to graduate until his father cuts off his financial support, an event which serves as the catalyst for the film. While the Cleveland, Ohio, *Plain Dealer*'s Julie E. Washington dismissed the film, she praised Penn's take on Taj, writing that "Penn makes this role soar with his double-takes, bumbling eagerness to please, and ill-fated attempts to follow Van's advice on women."

Penn admitted to working hard to make Taj more than a one-note character. When asked by the *Boston Globe*'s Lauren Smiley if the role bothered him, he told her, "Absolutely. And most of those roles I have no problem saying I took because I needed the credit on my resume to compete with the white guys for bigger roles.... Nobody was twisting my arm; I want to make that clear. It was my decision to take all the roles because there was something in each one that could be creative even though it was a limited creativity."

Penn continued to play supporting roles in film and television over the next year. For example, in 2003, he appeared in the comedy films *Where's the Party?* and *Malibu's Most Wanted*. He also had a role playing George in the short-lived series *All About the Andersons*. Penn continued his episodic work in such series as *Tru Calling*. In addition, Penn had roles in television movies, including *Homeland Security* and *Awesometown*.

In 2004, Penn had his first leading role in the groundbreaking stoner comedy *Harold & Kumar Go to White Castle*. The film had at its center two minorities, Penn's Kumar, an Indian-American pot smoking slacker whose father wants him to apply to medical school, and John Cho's Korean-American investment banker/fellow stoner. *Harold & Kumar Go to White Castle* follows the pair during one long night as they drive around New Jersey in search of White Castle hamburgers, partying and getting involved in hijinks along the way.

Penn was impressed by the vision of the film's screenwriters, Jon Hurwitz and Hayden Schlossberg. Penn told Pamela Bock of *BackStage*, "The writers were sick of seeing the same old faces in movies, and they wanted to finally see a film in which the characters looked more like their friends. So they ended up writing *White Castle*.... I happened to meet the writers at a party, and they encouraged me to go out for it." Critics lauded the filmmakers' vision, with the *Atlanta Journal-Constitution*'s Bob Townsend noting, Harold and Kumar are "smart, subversively funny characters who carry the movie as heroes we root for rather than stereotypical minor characters we laugh at."

*Harold & Kumar Go to White Castle* received many positive reviews for the way it broke down racial stereotypes and other biases, though some critics questioned the comedy. In the Montreal *Gazette*, Katherine Monk commented, "Taking over where Sean Penn left Spicoli in *Fast Times at Ridgemont High*, Penn and Cho re-create the classic pothead for a new generations. Gone are the senseless Cheech and Chong exchanges, replaced by surprisingly cerebral dialogue about ambition, race, the career wheel, and self-realization."

Reviewing the film for the *New York Times*, Stephen Holden noted, "The stoner, gross-out comedy *Harold and Kumar Go to White Castle* has one foot here and one foot there. The here is a politically savvy universe where the title characters, 22-year-old New Jersey roommates who are Korean-American and Indian-American, puncture ethnic stereotypes. But the other foot is rutted knee deep in the muck of perpetual puerility according to Hollywood."

After the success of *Harold & Kumar*, Penn focused on films, primarily comedies. He had supporting roles in 2005's *Son of the Mask*, opposite Jamie Kennedy, and *Sueño*, opposite John Leguizamo. Also in 2005, Penn had roles in the romantic comedy *A Lot Like Love* and the romantic drama *Dancing in Twilight*.

In 2006, Penn branched out from acting in comic films. He starred and was the executive producer of *Van Wilder 2: The Rise of Taj*. The spin-off sequel of *Van Wilder* featured Penn reprising his role as Taj, but this time, playing the film's lead. Here, Taj applies what he learned from Van Wilder about attracting female attention and acting smooth at a new school, Camford University in England. There, Taj turns a group of geeky social outsiders into the cool kids at school.

Penn embraced the role and its possibilities, telling Lisa Heyamoto of the *Sacramento Bee*, "That was a wonderful opportunity as an actor to take a character that was stereotypical and a sidekick and [flesh him out]. I didn't want to make this some lame knockoff sequel." Critics appreciated his work, with Katherine Monk writing in the *Calgary Herald*, "Despite the built-in misogyny of the National Lampoon shtick, with its bimbo-riddled landscapes and gratuitous boob shots, the film even manages to find a quiet charm. Don't get me wrong, this is far from a good movie. But thanks to lead actor Kal Penn (star of *Harold and Kumar Go to White Castle*), *The Rise of Taj* escapes a head-on collision with good taste and intelligence."

In addition to *Van Wilder 2*, Penn appeared in several films in 2006 such as *Man About Town* and *Deck the Halls*. He also had a supporting role in the Hollywood summer blockbuster *Superman Returns*. Penn played Stanford, the tech-savvy right-hand man of evil Lex Luthor, played by Kevin Spacey.

While Penn continued to appear in comedies like the spoof-filled *Epic Movie* in 2007, he branched out further that year with *The Namesake*. The film was based on the novel by Jhumpa Lahiri which Penn considered one of his favorite books. When Penn learned that filmmaker Mira Nair was making a film version, he approached her about playing the lead role, Gogol Ganguli. Though Nair had already cast someone, Penn convinced her to put him in the role instead. Gogol is the son of Indian immigrants who settle in the suburbs of New York, and the film explores the divide between him and his parents as he dismisses his parents' more traditional values. Gogol's perspective changes by the end of the film when his parents take him and his sister on a trip back to India.

Reviewing *The Namesake*, Paula Nechak of the *Seattle Post-Intelligencer* commented on Gogol, "he's played with impatience and grace by Kal Penn." Eleanor Ringel of the *Atlanta Journal-Constitution* also praised him, stating that "Penn gives a striking performance as both a restless, self-absorbed teen and a conflicted adult having difficulty reconciling the contradictory aspects of his life."

Also in 2007, Penn returned to television, first with a four-episode arc as a terrorist on the hit drama *24*, then landing a regular role on the hit television series, *House*. He played Dr. Lawrence Kutner, one of a number of fellowship candidates working to gain a spot on the medical team of the titular Dr. House, who is both brilliant and troubled. In 2008, Penn returned to his role as Kumar in *Harold & Kumar Escape from Guantanamo Bay*. The film takes place only hours after *Harold & Kumar Go to White Castle* ends. In this film, the pair are suspected of being terrorists because they try to sneak a bong onboard a passenger plane. It was not as well received as the first movie, though Penn's performance was generally praised.

In 2008, Penn also spent time focusing on education, both of others and his own, while continuing his acting career. He was hired as an instructor at the University of Pennsylvania for a semester. There, he taught two courses, "Images of Asian Americans in the Media" and "Contemporary American Teen Films." Penn also pursued graduate studies in international security at Stanford University. In addition, he served as executive producer and had a featured role in the film *Under New Management*, scheduled for release in late 2008.

Penn knows that he has had to sacrifice to reach his level of success as an actor and do films with meaning like *The Namesake*. He told Raakhee Mirchandani of the *New York Post*, "The original *Van Wilder* is not something I enjoyed working on. I felt stereotypical. The reason I did it was because I was told it would help me get more work. But if I hadn't done that, I wouldn't have been able to do *Harold and Kumar*. And, if I hadn't done *Harold & Kumar*.... I wouldn't have been able to make *The Namesake*."

## Sources

### Periodicals

*Associated Press State & Local Wire*, March 26, 2007.
*Atlanta Journal-Constitution*, July 31, 2004, p. 1C; March 30, 2007, p. 3H.
*Backstage*, July 8, 2004.
*Boston Globe*, July 28, 2004, p. F1; February 13, 2005, p. N13.
*Calgary Herald* (Alberta, Canada), December 2, 2006, p. C5; April 25, 2008, p. C3.
*Edmonton Journal* (Alberta, Canada), January 27, 2007, p. C4.
*Gazette* (Montreal, Quebec, Canada), August 1, 2004, p. B1.
*Houston Chronicle*, August 4, 2004, p. 1.
*Newsday* (New York, NY), April 20, 2008, p. C14.

*New York Post*, March 4, 2007, p. 42.
*New York Times*, July 30, 2004, p. E16; March 18, 2007, sec. 14NJ, p. 6.
*Ottawa Sun*, July 28, 2004, p. 21.
*Plain Dealer* (Cleveland, OH), April 5, 2002, p. 51.
*Record* (Bergen County, NJ), November 27, 2007, p. F3.
*Sacramento Bee* (CA), December 1, 2006, p. TK20.
*San Francisco Chronicle*, April 25, 2008, p. E5.
*Seattle Post-Intelligencer*, March 16, 2007, p. 4.
*Times Union* (Albany, NY), March 30, 2007, p. D5.
*Toronto Star*, April 10, 2007, p. E1.
*Vancouver Province* (British Columbia, Canada), November 28, 2006, p. B11.
*Washington Post*, April 25, 2008, p. C1.

### Online

"Kal Penn," Internet Movie Database, http://www.imdb.com/name/nm0671980/ (August 17, 2008).

—*A. Petruso*

# Michael Phelps

© *Mike Blake/Reuters/Corbis*

**Swimmer**

Born June 30, 1985, in Baltimore, Maryland; son of Frank and Debbie Phelps. *Education:* Attending University of Michigan.

**Addresses:** *Office*—P.O. Box 1734, Olney, MD 20830-1734.

## Career

Professional swimmer, 2001—.

**Awards:** Sullivan Award for best amateur athlete in United States, Amateur Athletic Union, 2003; American-International Athlete Trophy, International Amateur Athletic Association, 2003; six gold medals, two bronze medals, Olympics, Athens, Greece, 2004; eight gold medals, Olympics, Beijing, China, 2008.

## Sidelights

Michael Phelps, the youngest man to break a swimming world record, knew by 2001 that, as part of his career, he wanted to change the way that people looked at the sport of swimming. Over the course of two Olympics—Athens in 2004 and Beijing in 2008—Phelps broke a series of records that brought him an enormous amount of media attention. That spotlight has allowed Phelps to bring swimming into greater prominence in the American sports world.

At the 2008 Beijing Olympics, Phelps broke the record for most gold medals won at a single Olympics, winning a total of eight, one more than his predecessor, swimmer Mark Spitz, received in the 1972 Munich Olympics. Phelps has won a total of 16 Olympic medals: eight gold at the Beijing Olympics, and six gold and two bronze at the Athens Olympics of 2004. In 2000, Phelps placed fifth in his single event in the Sydney Olympics, a rank that he strove to improve. Only five months after the 2000 Olympics, Phelps broke the world record for the 200 meter butterfly event, beginning a trend for record breaking that has marked his entire career.

Born in Baltimore, Maryland, Phelps joined the North Baltimore Aquatic Club when he was seven years old. Phelps took to swimming, finding that some of his normal awkwardness, caused by being hyperflexible, vanished in the water. Phelps was not the first swimmer in his family; his sister Whitney tried out for the Olympics, and his other sister Hillary was a member of the swimming team at the University of Richmond. Though learning to swim was a big moment for his young life, the same year was a difficult one at home. Phelps was diagnosed with attention deficit hyperactivity disorder, and his family life changed shape as his parents divorced.

The three Phelps children moved to Baltimore, with their mother, from their country home, making it easier for them to get to swim training.

At eleven, Phelps began training with Bob Bowman, who saw immediately that Phelps had Olympic potential. "You saw a kid who couldn't wait to get in the water. A kid who pushed himself beyond where you tried to push him," Bowman explained to Brian Cazeneuve of *Sports Illustrated for Kids*. Bowman said that he tried "not to get too excited, even as I wondered how good he could be." Bowman began discussing long-term plans with Phelps's mother, Debbie. "I'm thinking, This man is crazy," Debbie told Alice Park in *Time*. "This is my eleven-year-old baby, and you're projecting 2012?"

Phelps' competitive streak was easy for Bowman to pick out. "What I noticed about him was that he was fiercely competitive in everything he did, whether it was swimming a race or playing a game at the pool," Bowman told Park. In the same article, Phelps admitted, "I hate to lose. I absolutely hate to lose. I can't stand it." Bowman encouraged Phelps to train to a degree where he could watch the 2000 Olympics, but Phelps pushed himself harder. At 15, Phelps placed in the Olympic trials and became the youngest member of the American team for the Sydney Olympics.

Despite achieving a place on the team at such a young age, and placing fifth in his only event, Phelps was frustrated with his performance. "I was disappointed walking away from Sydney with nothing," he told Park in the same *Time* article. "People were saying [fifth is] good, and I was saying, 'No, it's not. I want more.' It's something that's been with me ever since." Phelps continued to push himself, setting his first word record five months after the Sydney Olympics, and winning his first world championship four months later. At 16, Phelps became the youngest American male swimmer to become a professional. In the 2003 World Championships, Phelps won six medals, broke five world records, one of them the one he set in 2001, and was named the Swimmer of the Meet due to his performance.

In the 2004 Olympic trials, Phelps became the first swimmer to qualify in six individual Olympic events. "He is really redefining our expectations of swimming excellence," two-time Olympian Pablo Morales told Alice Park of *Time* as the Athens Olympics approached. "He is blazing his own trail now, and there is probably a whole global army of young swimmers who are looking up to him." Given the intensity of the scheduling, Phelps chose to participate in only five events, racing 17 different times, creating the opportunity for him to challenge Mark Spitz's record of seven gold medals in one Olympics. As a professional swimmer, Phelps had already received a number of endorsements from companies including Visa, AT&T, and Speedo, who offered Phelps a million dollar bonus if he broke Spitz's record. At his first event, the results were promising: Phelps won the 400 meter individual medley by a full three-and-a-half seconds, setting a world record.

But breaking the gold-medal record at the 2004 Olympics was not to be. The American team placed third in the 4x100 freestyle relay, and Phelps took a bronze in the 200 meter freestyle, losing to Australian Ian Thorpe, who had beaten him in the 100 meter butterfly at the 2003 World Championships. Thorpe had belittled Phelps's goal of breaking Spitz's record, saying it couldn't be done. Phelps responded, in *Time* magazine, "He's saying he doesn't think it's possible for him to do that. I don't think I would say it's impossible." Even after his close run, with six gold and two bronze medals in Athens, Phelps continued to nurture his goal, determined to make another go at it in 2008.

When Bowman took the head coach position for the University of Michigan's swimming team after the 2004 Olympics, Phelps went with him, enrolling for classes and continuing to train with him in Ann Arbor. Due to his status as a professional, he was unable to race for the university, and instead served as a volunteer assistant coach under Bowman. Phelps won six medals—five gold and one silver—at the 2005 World Championships, where he broke one championship record. At the 2007 World Championships in Melbourne, Phelps met the seven gold medal goal, matching but not breaking Spitz's record for gold medals in an international meet. This made him the most successful swimmer ever at the World Championships; he might have made the attempt for eight gold medals at that meet, but he missed the opportunity when he and his teammates were disqualified in the 400 meter medley relay. Phelps continued to train all 365 days of the year—including Christmas morning—typically swimming between 7 and 12 miles per day. In July of 2008, just one month before the Olympics, Phelps placed second in the 100 meter breaststroke, long his worst event. Beaten by less than four tenths of a second, Phelps showed that he had gotten over having a weak stroke. "That's one of the most impressive things I've ever seen him do," Bowman told Susan Casey of *Sports Illustrated*.

As in 2004, at the Games in Beijing, Phelps raced 17 times in nine days, taking the gold medal in all eight of the events he raced and succeeding in his goal of breaking Spitz's record as well as tying the record of gymnast Aleksander Dityatin for eight medals at a single Olympics. He competed in five individual events and three team events, allowing him to tie the record for individual gold medals won at a single Olympics, which had been set by Eric Heiden in the 1980 Winter Olympics. The American team also set a world record in the 4x100 meter medley relay. The games brought Phelps' career totals of world records to four individual world records and two team world records.

The record winning streak at the Beijing Olympics marked the sports world. "Michael is the biggest thing that sport has ever seen," Phelps' teammate Brian Hansen told *New York Times* reporter Karen Crouse. "Not swimming, but sport in general. He just made the pressure putt to win the U.S. Open. He just won the Tour of France. He just knocked out Muhammad Ali. And he did it in one week." But despite his fame—and the 4,000 text messages he received during the 24 hours after he won his eight golds—Phelps expressed hope to have his life return to normal. "I'm going to live my life the way I always have," he told Crouse, admitting that the one exception he'd make would be meeting two of his inspirations: Tiger Woods and Michael Jordan. He expressed hopes to have as big an impact on swimming as Woods and Jordan had on golf and basketball, respectively.

In addition to his record-breaking career, Phelps has won many successful sponsorships. Before the 2008 Olympics, Phelps had endorsements worth about five million dollars. After Beijing, not only did Phelps win the million dollar bonus from Speedo for breaking Spitz's record, but analysts put his potential value at 700 million dollars over his lifetime. Phelps' agent, Peter Carlisle, was aware of Phelps' desire to make swimming a sport that merited greater attention, and cultivated sponsorships that would not only increase Phelps' image, but also the image of swimming. "Every sponsor I've had has been something that fit my lifestyle, fit my personality," Phelps told Mike Beirne in *Brandweek*. "The big thing is, is it something I'm comfortable with, something I use and something I like to use? So I think if it meets all that, then it fits my personality." In addition to sponsorships, Phelps' celebrity garnered him guest spots on the *Oprah Winfrey Show*, the MTV Video Music Awards, and *Saturday Night Live*.

To enhance the visibility of swimming, Phelps founded a social networking site, SwimRoom.com. The site offers "an opportunity for swimmers from all over the world to have a special bond with one another," he told Cynthia Wang of *People*. "I think swimmers are a different breed, and I think just being able to interact with people and kids from all over the world is something that the sport has never seen." Phelps is also the founder of the Michael Phelps Foundation, which he funded with the million dollar bonus he received from Speedo upon winning his eighth gold medal at the Beijing Olympics. The foundation promotes health and activity, primarily for children, through the sport of swimming. "I just want people to get involved," Phelps told Karen Crouse in an interview for the *New York Times*. "My whole goal is to change the sport of swimming in a positive way. I think it can go even farther. That's where I hope to take it." Phelps intends to continue staying active in the sport, and hopes to compete in the 2012 Olympics in London, England. Asked in *Time* what he would do once he was no longer competing as a swimmer, Phelps replied, "I definitely want to stay in sports, but I'm not sure what field I want to go into. And no, I'm not dreading it. There is going to be a time when I'm ready to retire. But definitely not yet."

## Sources

### Periodicals

*Brandweek*, September 8, 2008, p. 14.
*New York Times*, August 18, 2008, p. D1; August 19, 2008, p. D4.
*People*, July 21, 2008, p. 101.
*Sports Illustrated*, July 28, 2008, p. 68.
*Sports Illustrated for Kids*, August 1, 2004, p. 26.
*Time*, August 9, 2004, p. 72; April 30, 2007, p. 6.

### Online

*Biography Resource Center Online*, Gale Group (Detroit, MI), 2004, 2008.
"Michael Phelps: Eight Swimming Medals in One Olympics," International Olympic Committee Web site, http://www.olympic.org/uk/athletes/profiles/bio_uk.asp?PAR_I_ID=136177 (November 21, 2008).
"Michael Phelps's Charity Work," Look to the Stars Web site, http://www.looktothestars.org/celebrity/1483-michael-phelps (November 21, 2008).
Michael Phelps's Home Page, http://www.michaelphelps.com/2004/ (November 21, 2008).

—*Alana Joli Abbott*

# Renzo Piano

## Architect

**B**orn September 14, 1937, in Genoa, Italy; son of a contractor; married Magda Arduino, 1962 divorced); married Emilia Rossato, 1992; children: Carlo, Matteo, Lia, Giorgio Anthony. *Education:* Polytechnic University of Milan, diploma in architecture, 1964; Pratt Institute, Ph.D., 2002.

**Addresses:** *Home*—Genoa, Italy. *Office*—Studio Renzo Piano, Via Rubens 29, 16158, Genoa, Italy.

## Career

**A**ffiliated with Franco Albini, Milan, 1962-64; affiliated with engineering firm of Z. S. Makowsky, London, and Louis I. Kahn office in Philadelphia, 1965-70; partner, Piano and Rogers Architects, London, Paris, and Genoa, 1970; partner, Piano and Rice, Genoa, Paris and London, 1977-93; partner, Renzo Piano Building Workshop, Genoa, Paris, and London, 1994—. Major projects include Italian Industry Pavilion, Expo '70, Japan, 1970; Centre Georges Pompidou (with Richard Rogers), Paris, France, 1977; Menil Collection, Houston, TX, 1987; renovation of Potsdamer Platz, Berlin, Germany, 1992-2000; Kansai International Airport, Osaka, Japan, 1994; Padre Pio Pilgrimage Church, San Giovanni Rotondo, Italy, 2004; J. P. Morgan Library expansion, New York City, 2006; New York Times Building, New York City, 2007; California Academy of Sciences, San Francisco, 2008; Art Institute of Chicago (new wing), 2009.

**Awards:** Arnold W. Brunner Memorial Prize in Architecture, American Academy of Arts and Letters, 1994; Pritzker Architecture Prize, 1998; National Or-

© *James Leynse/Corbis*

der, Legion of Honor (France), 2000; Médaille D'Or, International Union of Architects, Berlin, 2002; gold medal, American Institute of Architects, 2008.

## Sidelights

**I**talian architect Renzo Piano is the creator of several well-known landmarks in Europe and the United States, and in his early seventies was still jetting around the world to supervise several ongoing projects. One of them was the new California Academy of Sciences in San Francisco's Golden Gate Park, which won effusive praise from architecture critics when it opened in the fall of 2008. "The entire building serves as a sort of specimen case, a framework for pondering the natural world while straining to disturb it as little as possible," declared *New York Times* architecture critic Nicolai Ouroussoff of Piano's innovative, green-roofed design.

Piano comes from a family of builders in the seaport city of Genoa, Italy, where he was born in 1937. It was expected that he, too, would become a contractor like his father, grandfather, four uncles, and brother, and he recalled his father as being less than thrilled when Piano announced his intention to study architecture at the Polytechnic University of

Milan. "In his opinion, being an architect was a good deal less worthy," Piano told *Smithsonian* writer Richard Covington.

After earning his degree in architecture in 1964, Piano apprenticed under a Milanese architect and also worked for a time for his father's company. In the late 1960s, he trained at an engineering firm in London and in the Philadelphia office of the late architect Louis I. Kahn. In London he met another young architect, Richard Rogers, and they opened their own practice in 1970. A year later, the two unknown upstarts won a major commission for a new cultural center in Paris at a site called the Place Beaubourg. "Trying to challenge every architectural orthodoxy they could think of, Piano and Rogers pulled out the building's guts—steel frame, escalators, heating ducts, etc.—painted them bright shades of red, green, and blue, and hung them on the outside of the museum," wrote Slate.com writer Christopher Hawthorne.

That building—eventually known as the Centre Georges Pompidou or simply "the Beaubourg"—was widely reviled in some quarters as the folly of a free-spending government, and likened famously by British writer Anthony Burgess to a "$200 million Erector set" in a *New York Times Magazine* article. Despite the jibes, the museum and surrounding plaza instantly became one of the city's top tourist destinations after it opened in 1977. As Piano himself reflected more than two decades later in an interview with Cynthia Grenier for *World and I,* "some love it and some hate it, but it doesn't leave anyone indifferent."

Piano and Rogers would eventually dissolve their partnership and move on to solo practices. On his own, Piano adopted a more sober style, perhaps best exemplified by his first major project in the United States, the Menil Collection, a museum in Houston, Texas, that holds one of the world's top private art collections. Funded entirely by French-American heiress Dominique de Ménil, the museum, which opened in 1987, has been termed "startling in its simplicity," by *Time*'s Richard Lacayo. "A subdued, low-rise museum, the Menil is a machine for delivering light, which it coaxes indoors in just the right amounts through an ingenious roof system of louvers."

In 1998, Piano was awarded the prestigious Pritzker Architecture Prize for his accomplishments, which by then included the terminal for Kansai International Airport in Osaka, Japan, which was the world's largest airport terminal when it opened in 1994 and built entirely on the site of an artificial island. He had also began work on a commission in the southern Italian town of San Giovanni Rotondo that was becoming a major Roman Catholic pilgrimage site for "Padre Pio," the priest who was canonized in 2002 as Saint Pio of Pietrelcina.

Piano also won an important commission in Berlin, Germany's new capital, for the famous Potsdamer Platz, which had been one of the city's major public squares until it was bisected by the Berlin Wall in 1961. Piano created a cinema-casino-theater-hotel complex which became the future site of the Berlin Film Festival for one Potsdamer segment called Marlene-Dietrich-Platz. Visiting the site beforehand, as he always insists upon doing before submitting a proposal, was particularly eerie, he told Grenier in the *World and I* interview. "We found ourselves in a historical place with no historical references. The only references we had were the ghosts of the past hovering about. Not actual ghosts, of course, but there was a kind of dramatic, sinister memory hanging over it all."

While the Pritzker Prize has been bestowed on the world's best-known "star-"chitects, Piano is a rarity among the elite group for having won a major New York city skyscraper commission. In 2000, he was hired by the company that owns the *New York Times* for the job of designing its new headquarters. "Piano is a master of the harmonious sleight of hand," wrote Justin Davidson in *New York* magazine about the 52-story glass tower. "He has made the load-bearing columns appear impossibly delicate and the one-ton steel stays that stabilize the structure seem like skinny wires. The restful lobby garden, with its white birches rising out of moss-covered mounds, disguises a company that virtually runs on stress."

Like the New York Times Building, Piano's new series of buildings for the California Academy of Sciences in San Francisco took nearly a decade to complete. The original neo-classical buildings, a city landmark in Golden Gate Park, were badly damaged in the 1989 Loma Prieta earthquake, but Piano managed to salvage some unique pieces for inclusion in what has been called the world's greenest museum, which opened in late 2008. The site includes a museum of natural history, aquarium, and planetarium, all covered by a 2.5-acre "living roof" made entirely out of plants indigenous to northern California. The undulating green of the roof, which filters rainwater and serves as a cooling system for the building below, echoes the lush forest of the park, but it was part of a construction project whose goal was to work in entirely sustainable materials. Piano described his focus on what he called "the aesthetics of sustainability" to *Time*'s Lacayo: "The 19th century was about new kinds of construction. Steel and so forth. And the 20th century created a language for that. Now architects must develop an aesthetic for our discovery about the fragility of nature."

# Sources

## Periodicals

*New York,* December 3, 2007.
*New York Times,* September 24, 2008.
*New York Times Magazine,* January 23, 1977.

*Smithsonian,* June 1999, p. 62.
*Time,* October 13, 2008, p. 89.
*Times* (London, England), May 16, 2000, p. 16.
*Vanity Fair,* May 2008.
*World and I,* October 1998, p. 100.

## Online

"Renzo Piano: A Celebrity Architect Without All the Glitz," Slate.com (October 22, 2008).

—*Carol Brennan*

# Paul Pierce

**Professional basketball player**

**B**orn October 13, 1977, in Oakland, CA; son of Lorraine; children: Prianna Lee (with fiancée Julie Landrum). *Education:* Attended the University of Kansas, 1995-98.

**Addresses:** *Office*—TD Banknorth Garden, 100 Legends Way, Boston, MA 02114. *Web site*—http://www.paulpierce.net.

## Career

**P**layed for University of Kansas Jayhawks, 1995-98; member of U.S. national basketball team in world championship, 2002; player for Boston Celtics, 1998—.

**Awards:** Named to NBA All-Star team, 2002, 2003, 2004, 2005, 2006, 2008; NBA championship as member of the Boston Celtics, 2008; most valuable player in NBA Finals, 2008.

## Sidelights

**F**or years, Paul Pierce was the best player on the Boston Celtics, yet fans never thought of him in the same light as Larry Bird, the Celtics star of the previous generation, because Pierce had never led the team to a championship. Throughout most of the 2000s, Pierce, nicknamed The Truth, led teams that did not have the talent to contend. That changed in 2007, when Celtics management made big trades to bring more stars to the team. In 2008,

Pierce led Boston to its first National Basketball Association (NBA) championship in two decades and was named most valuable player for the finals.

Pierce grew up in Inglewood, California, and honed his skills on the outdoor basketball courts of Los Angeles. He was an average player in his first two years on the Inglewood High School basketball team, but hard work and a growth spurt elevated his abilities, and he led the team to a division title as a junior. As a senior, he became the top high school prospect in California.

Pierce attended the University of Kansas, where he played under legendary coach Roy Williams. He was the Big Eight's freshman of the year and led the Jayhawks to a 34-2 record as a sophomore. He passed up the chance to enter the NBA in 1997 in order to play his junior year in college. "I felt like I wasn't ready to take that next step," he explained to Josh Barr in the *Washington Post.* "I was having fun just being a kid. I wasn't ready for that big responsibility. I like the atmosphere of Lawrence and the people, the players, the fans and the relationships. When you get to that next step, it's all business." After his junior year, however, Pierce decided to skip his senior year and go pro.

The Celtics chose Pierce as the tenth pick overall in the 1998 NBA draft, almost by accident, after another team traded for a higher pick and snatched up Boston's top prospect. Without much time to think, they chose Pierce. Basketball watchers declared they were surprised that Pierce slipped so far in the draft. Some blamed scouting reports that suggested he had come to pre-draft workouts in less than ideal shape. His draft position seemed to fuel Pierce's competitiveness. He would end his pre-season practices with a shooting drill, firing off nine jump shots and shouting out the names of the nine players drafted before him. "Whatever little thing I can find," Pierce explained to Jackie MacMullan in *Sports Illustrated*, "I use to motivate myself."

Pierce's career with the Celtics took off fast. The coach started him right away, and he scored 19 points or more in ten of his first eleven games. Sometimes playing as a small forward, sometimes as a shooting guard, he averaged 16.5 points a game for the season. Though known for his offensive skill, he also led the team with 1.71 steals per game. He came in third in voting for the league's rookie of the year. The team, however, finished 19-31 in a shortened season. In 1999-2000, his second year, Pierce averaged 19.5 points. "Pierce has become an expert at finding angles, knifing through small cavities in the defense, leaning in, taking advantage of any space he gets on a defender," wrote Jack McCallum in *Sports Illustrated*.

Pierce established good chemistry with the Celtics' other top scorer, Antoine Walker. The two became good friends off the court and made an art out of passing to each other on the court. "The forwards constantly improvise during the game, making eye contact to create give-and-goes and pick-and-rolls," wrote McCallum.

Another element of Pierce's game was his expertise at drawing fouls. He would often initiate contact with an opponent or purposefully scoop a shot from under the defender's arm. He even admitted to drawing a referee's whistle by making noises. "I get in there and yell, Oohh! like I've been mugged real bad," Pierce told McCallum.

In the fall of 2000, before the season began, Pierce had to battle back from a violent injury. A knife-wielding man attacked Pierce in a Boston-area nightclub, stabbing him eleven times in the back, neck, and face. He underwent surgery to repair his lung. "It's something you're not going to forget," Pierce said later (as quoted by Chris Mannix in *Sports Illustrated*). "I feel a lot older from the simple fact I had a brush with death and saw my life flash before my eyes. You grow up ten times as fast."

Only a month after the assault, Pierce had recovered enough to start the first game of the season and score 28 points in the game. He started every game that season, averaging 25.3 points per game, and was named to the NBA All-Star team for the first time. The following year, the Celtics surprised NBA fans by making it into the third round of the playoffs; however, the nightclub incident had caused some to question whether or not Pierce was mature enough to be a team leader. Former Celtic Kevin McHale was quoted (according to Mannix) as saying Pierce "couldn't carry Larry Bird's jock." Pierce played on the United States' team in the 2002 world basketball championships, but his high shot count caused some to call him selfish.

When the Celtics lost in the second round of the 2003 playoffs, team management traded away Walker and looked to rebuild the team with young talent. Though the Walker trade broke up Pierce's top partnership on the court, it also made Pierce the team's undisputed leader. Celtics general manager Danny Ainge declared that he thought that would help push Pierce into the league's elite. "With his work habits I think Paul can catch up with those few guys who are maybe a bit more talented," Ainge told Ian Thomsen in *Sports Illustrated*. "I've never seen a guy with his talent play and work as hard as Paul—and I played with Larry Bird."

Pierce said he was ready to lead. "It's going to help me because I know everybody on the team is going to be watching my every move," he told Thomsen. "I can't have any letdowns, I can't be a bad example for the other guys. I have to watch what I'm saying, what I'm doing. Because that's what a leader's all about."

The team's performance deteriorated. They won 45 games in 2004-05, and in the first round of the playoffs, they lost to the Indiana Pacers. During Game 7 of the series, Pierce yelled at the Celtics' coach, Doc Rivers, angry at Rivers' criticism of his defensive play. During the off-season, trade talk circled around Pierce, and he had his agent talk to the Celtics to deter a rumored trade to the Portland Trail Blazers. Rivers visited Pierce that summer to assure him he was on his side. When the next season began, Pierce acknowledged that he had to maintain a good relationship with his coach for the team to do well.

The Celtics won only 33 games in the 2005-06 season, but it was not Pierce's fault. He reached a career high in scoring, averaging 26.8 points per game. He injured his elbow during the season and underwent surgery in August. The Celtics extended his contract by three years, through the 2010-11 season, at almost $20 million per year. "By making this commitment to me, I think they're making a commitment to be a contending team in these next five years," Pierce told Mannix in *Sports Illustrated*.

But the 2006-07 season was even tougher on Pierce and the Celtics. They were the NBA's second-worst team that season, with a 24-58 record. Pierce averaged 25 points a game that year, but only played in 47 games. At the end, "I had pretty strong thoughts that I wouldn't even be here," Pierce told Thomsen in *Sports Illustrated* the following season. "I was wondering what the plan was, and I was wondering if I was in the plan."

After the season, Pierce went to Ainge and demanded that the team acquire more talent right away. Ainge discarded his strategy of developing young talent and searched for veteran stars. The team made two blockbuster trades, acquiring Kevin Garnett, a former NBA most valuable player, from the Minnesota Timberwolves and Ray Allen, a frequent All-Star, from the Seattle SuperSonics. Having Pierce, Garnett, and Allen on the court together made Boston into a scoring powerhouse and a championship contender.

Pierce was rejuvenated, thrilled to return to the court. "This is the most excited I've been about playing a season," he told Thomsen in *Sports Illustrated*. "I know this type of opportunity doesn't come around for a lot of players. We've got to make the most of it."

Ainge, the general manager, noticed the change in Pierce. "Paul came and gave me a big hug the day we made the [Garnett] trade," Ainge told Thomsen. "He said, 'Never did I think you could bring me these kind of veteran players.' That was probably my favorite moment of the whole thing, to see Paul like a little kid again."

The Celtics ran away with the 2007-08 regular season, finishing with the league's best record. By the start of the playoffs, Pierce ranked among the top ten Celtics of all time in nearly every scoring category, including points, assists, field goals, and three-pointers. The Celtics reached the second round of the playoffs and struggled there against the underdog Atlanta Hawks, taking seven games to beat them.

That victory took them to the conference finals against the Cleveland Cavaliers, who had gone to the finals the year before. Pierce and Cavaliers su-

perstar LeBron James dominated Game 7 with a mammoth scoring duel. Pierce finished with 4 points and James with 45 as the Celtics won, 97-92 "It was basically, get the ball to Paul Pierce and ge the hell out of the way," said Pierce's teammate Gar nett, according to Pablo Torre in *Sports Illustrated*.

In the finals against the Los Angeles Lakers, Pierce again performed in the clutch. In Game 1, he had to be carried off the floor because of a third-quarter knee injury, but he returned a few minutes later and scored eleven more points. In Game 5, though the Celtics lost, Pierce scored 38 points and helped hold Lakers star Kobe Bryant to 8-of-21 shooting.

"He's tough," Bryant said of Pierce (as quoted by Mannix in *Sports Illustrated*). "There's not a lot of players that have a well-rounded offensive game What I mean by that, he's got a good midrange game, long ball, pull up to the hoop, pull up left pull up right. He has the whole package. I enjoy watching him play, I enjoy playing against him, and he's fantastic."

The Celtics won the NBA title with a lopsided 131-92 victory in Game 6. Pierce was awarded the trophy for most valuable player in the finals. It was the team's 17th championship, but its first in two decades. "It means everything," Pierce said (as quoted by Michael Lee in the *Washington Post*). "I'm not living under the shadows of the other greats now. I'm able to make my own history with my time here, and like I said, this is something that I wanted to do. If I was going to be one of the best Celtics to ever play, I had to put up a banner."

## Sources

### Periodicals

*Sports Illustrated*, March 15, 1999, p. 74; November 1, 1999, p. 173; November 26, 2001, p. 48; November 10, 2003, p. 167; December 5, 2005, p. 88, October 23, 2006, p. 110; October 29, 2007, p. 72, June 25, 2008, pp. 30, 54.
*Washington Post*, December 5, 1997, p. B4; June 19, 2008, p. E3.

### Online

"Biography," PaulPierce.net, http://www.paul pierce.net/biography (November 23, 2008).

—*Erick Trickey*

# Amy Poehler

**Actress and comedian**

Born Amy Meredith Poehler, September 16, 1971, in Burlington, MA; daughter of Bill (a teacher) and Eileen (a teacher) Poehler; married Will Arnett (an actor), August 29, 2003; children: Archie. *Education:* Boston College, B.A., 1993.

**Addresses:** *Agent*—Endeavor Agency, 9701 Wilshire Blvd., 10th Fl., Beverly Hills, CA 90212. *Home*—New York, NY.

## Career

Worked as a waitress and as a film double in Chicago, while appearing with Second City and ImprovOlympic, 1993-96; founding member, Upright Citizens Brigade, mid-1990s; appeared in skits for *Late Night with Conan O'Brien*, after 1996; began appearing on *Saturday Night Live*, 2001, then full cast member, 2002-08. Film appearances include: *Loving Manhattan*, 1998; *Tomorrow Night*, 1998; *Deuce Bigalow: Male Gigolo*, 1999; *Wet Hot American Summer*, 2001; *The Devil and Daniel Webster*, 2004; *Envy*, 2004; *Mean Girls*, 2004; *Southland Tales*, 2006; *Blades of Glory*, 2007; *Mr. Woodcock*, 2007; (also writer and producer) *Wild Girls Gone*, 2007; *Baby Mama*, 2008. Television appearances include: *Apt. 2F*, 1997; *Spin City*, 1998; *Undeclared*, 2002; *Arrested Development*, 2004-05; co-creator and voice of Bessie Higgenbottom, *The Mighty B!*, 2008—.

## Sidelights

In 2008 comedian Amy Poehler bid farewell to fellow cast members on *Saturday Night Live* (*SNL*) after a seven-year stint on the long-running NBC

*Michael Loccisano/FilmMagic/Getty Images*

comedy series. A few months earlier, Poehler appeared in *Baby Mama* alongside another *SNL* veteran, Tina Fey, and later that year Poehler inked a deal to appear in her own series for the network. Like Fey, who is the head writer and star of NBC's successful *30 Rock,* Poehler reached a somewhat rare rank in the entertainment business as an attractive female lead who also writes her own comic material. For much of her career, however, Poehler had refused to trade on her looks in order to make her name. "In this business, I don't want to be categorized with the women who are pretty and funny," she told writer Tori Galore in a 1999 interview for *Bust* magazine. "Growing up, I was always attracted to the Gilda Radners of the world who never seemed too pretty to laugh with."

Born in 1971, Poehler was raised in Burlington, Massachusetts, near Boston, with a younger brother. Both parents were high school teachers, and at Burlington High School Poehler was active in student government, soccer, and the drama club. She went on to Boston College with a vague plan to become a teacher, but joining her college's improvisational-comedy troupe sparked a love of performing in front of a live audience with a minimum of scripted material. "I was totally intoxicated," she told *People* writers Jennifer Wulff and Rebecca Paley. "You get one genuine laugh, you just want it again, even if you spend the next ten years being a waitress."

After graduating from college in 1993, Poehler moved to Chicago and joined the famed Second City improv group. She also worked with Improv-Olympic (iO), another well-known Chicago training ground, where she and Fey first met. To make ends meet, she worked as a waitress and as a stand-in on film sets, including a stint as the lighting stand-in for Gina Gershon's character in the 1996 drama *Bound.* She and three male comedians also formed their own comedy group, the Upright Citizens Brigade, and in 1996 they all moved to New York City. Poehler lived in a basement apartment with one of them, recalling in the *People* interview with Wulff and Paley that her first place had "bars on the windows, and you could see people's legs walking by. There were rats, we had an occasional peeping Tom."

The Brigade began a steady weekly gig, and in 1998 were signed to cable network Comedy Central for their series, which featured both sketch comedy and street-scene pranks during its two-year run. Poehler also appeared in skits on *Late Night with Conan O'Brien* during this period of her career, and became fearless about performing physical comedy—which would serve her well on *SNL* a few years down the road. "You can't go halfway," she told Wulff and Paley in *People.* "If you don't allow yourself to look crazy and silly, your vanity will get in the way."

Poehler's guest appearances on series like *Spin City* led to supporting roles in feature films such as *Saving Manhattan* and *Deuce Bigalow: Male Gigolo.* In September of 2001, she began making appearances on *Saturday Night Live,* debuting just days after the terrorist attacks on the United States. "You're just trying to figure out where the bathrooms are, and on top of it, everyone's like, 'Will comedy be able to go on?'" she said about that tough week in an interview with *New York Times* writer Dave Itzkoff. "If you didn't feel small and insignificant before, you definitely did then."

Poehler joined the cast of *SNL* full time in 2002, delivering parodies of such high-profile figures as Michael Jackson, Paula Abdul, Kelly Ripa, and even Hillary Clinton, though two of her most popular characters were Amber, a trailer-park denizen, and Caitlin, the hyper tween. She and Fey made *SNL* history at the start of the 2004-05 season when Poehler replaced Jimmy Fallon as co-anchor of the

show's news segment, "Weekend Update"; in the nearly 30-year history of the show, they were the first female co-anchors of the *SNL* staple faux-news broadcast. Journalists inevitably asked Poehler about the scarcity of successful female comedians or noted that she was a rare female comic with movie-star looks. "You have to be grateful for it and you want it to go away at the same time," she told Itzkoff in the *New York Times.* "If you try to analyze comedy at all, it's deadly. If you try to bring your gender into it, it's unbearable."

In 2002, Poehler was cast in an ill-fated television series from Judd Apatow, who would go on to box-office success with a string of successful comedies. *Undeclared,* like Apatow's other television projects, tanked, but Poehler and the other castmates—among them Seth Rogen and Jason Segal—would achieve fame on subsequent projects. Poehler continued to perform with the Upright Citizens' Brigade on Sunday nights in New York City, which expanded to its own theaters in New York and Los Angeles. She earned her first credit as a screenwriter and producer for the 2007 comedy *Wild Girls Gone,* in which she also appeared alongside other Brigade members. Her first genuine break-out role came in the 2004 Lindsay Lohan comedy *Mean Girls,* which was also Fey's debut as a screenwriter. Fey appeared as a teacher, while Poehler was cast as the mother of Rachel McAdams' character.

By then Poehler had married Canadian actor and comic Will Arnett, who had a starring role as the hapless magician brother in the acclaimed FOX series *Arrested Development.* Poehler appeared in a few episodes of *Arrested Development*'s second season as the seal trainer Arnett's character marries, but as she told a reporter for *Newsweek,* there were no plans for a joint act. "Nothing is more boring than real-life couples," she asserted. "It's deadly."

Poehler and Arnett did agree, however, to appear as a brother-and-sister skating duo in the 2007 comedy *Blades of Glory.* The lead roles were played by Will Ferrell, another *SNL* veteran, and Jon Heder as an unlikely new single-sex skating pair determined to achieve Olympic glory. Their main competition is the sibling duo played by Poehler and Arnett, who appear to have an affection for one another that transcends conventional sibling standards. All four stars trained daily for the roles, but for Poehler it was especially difficult because she had never skated at all before. "I was the worst skater of the bunch," she told a writer for the *New York Post.* "Will was the best skater, being Canadian. And there was a lot of trash talking on the ice, mostly between me and Will Ferrell and Jon Heder. But it's really hard to be tough when you're dressed up like a chandelier in an outfit that plugs in."

In 2008 Poehler appeared in the female-buddy comedy *Baby Mama* alongside Fey. The project was written and directed by Michael McCullers, a former writer for *SNL*, and starred Fey as Kate Holbrook, an executive with a Whole Foods-like health-store chain who, at age 37, decides to hire a surrogate mother to carry her in-vitro-fertilized egg. Poehler played the working-class South Philly woman whose womb she rents, Angie Ostrowiski, who is left without a place to live when she and her boyfriend break up and accepts Kate's invitation to move in. Poehler described *Baby Mama* as "the comedy version of *Reds*," she told *Village Voice* writer Julia Wallace, referring to the 1981 Warren Beatty-Diane Keaton saga of the 1917 Russian Revolution. "Angie, my character, has more in common with Oscar, the doorman, than she does with Kate. They just both understand what it's like to be working really hard for a living. When you have money, you have more choices, and class is a big deal. You have to have money to pay someone if you want to have them carry your baby."

*Baby Mama* received a lukewarm reception from some critics, but *Entertainment Weekly*'s Lisa Schwarzbaum conceded that "Poehler is as improv-sketch loose in her performance as Fey is measured, and both are challenged to a thespian throwdown by a fearsomely funny Sigourney Weaver as the smug head of the surrogacy agency." Writing in the *Los Angeles Times*, Carina Chocano compared the Poehler-Fey pairing to that of Jerry Lewis and Dean Martin, the opposites who made a string of hit comedies in the 1950s. "When Angie first shows up in Kate's life, it's in a pigpen cloud of bad choices and chaos," Chocano wrote. "But McCullers doesn't milk the white-trash bashing for long, and Angie mellows into a three-dimensional character in fairly short order. What she doesn't lose is that lunatic edge that makes her so funny. Next to Fey's even-tempered, good girl, Poehler is a loose cannon."

The year 2008 proved an eventful one for Poehler: Just as *Baby Mama* was released in the spring, she and Arnett announced they were expecting their first child; on October 25 of that year, Poehler gave birth to their son, Archie. In July, NBC released a statement saying that Poehler would not return for what would have been her eighth season of *SNL*, but instead would appear on a new prime-time series for the network from the creators of the American version of *The Office*. Poehler was also the co-creator of an animated kids' series for Nickelodeon, *The Mighty B!*, that debuted in 2008. Its title character, voiced by Poehler, was Bessie Higgenbottom, a Girl Scout with dreams of becoming a superhero. "She's kinda bossy and a motormouth, so it's somewhat autobiographical," Poehler told *Newsweek*.

*SNL* launched the film careers of a long list of male comedians who went on to major stardom, including Bill Murray, Eddie Murphy, Mike Myers, Adam Sandler, and Ferrell. Yet Poehler discovered that as she hit her mid-thirties, the roles she was offered shrank in scope. "I guess I'm not able to play the girlfriend of guys my own age anymore," she said in a *Vanity Fair* article about women in comedy written by Alessandra Stanley. "I play the bitchy older sister. And who doesn't love the bitchy older sister who gets it in the end?" Yet she also acknowledged in other interviews that writing her material, as Fey had done, opened up new avenues. "When you hear the list of comedies in development at studios, they're all about these two guys—these two guys take a road trip, two guys go to dental school, two guys decide to race cars for a living," she told *Time*'s Richard Zoglin. "So it's just about more people writing stories where the woman drives the story and more women developing more stuff for them."

Poehler claims that she and Arnett, thrilled to be working and living in the same city—unlike the first years of their marriage—are happiest at home in their West Village apartment watching television. "I wish I could tell you that we had these crazy comedy competitions of hilariousness, but at the end of the day, all I want is a good cry and an hour-long drama," she told the *New York Post*.

## Sources

*Bust*, Fall 1999.
*Entertainment Weekly*, May 9, 2008, p. 44.
*Los Angeles Times*, April 25, 2008.
*Newsweek*, April 21, 2008, p. 63.
*New York Post*, March 25, 2007, p. 32.
*New York Times*, March 18, 2007.
*People*, April 18, 2005, p. 121.
*Time*, May 30, 2005, p. 8.
*USA Today*, March 23, 2007, p. 1E.
*Vanity Fair*, April 2008.
*Village Voice*, April 22, 2008.

—*Carol Brennan*

# Zac Posen

**Fashion designer**

---

**B**orn October 24, 1980, in New York, NY; son of Stephen (an artist) and Susan (a venture capitalist and attorney) Posen; partner of Brian Callahan (an interior designer and architect). *Education:* Graduated from Parsons School of Design, 1999; graduated from Central St. Martins College of Art and Design, 2001.

**Addresses:** *Office*—Outspoke LLC, 13-17 Laight St., New York, NY 10013.

## Career

**B**egan designing clothes at the age of four; intern, New York Costume Institute, Metropolitan Museum of Art, New York City; intern, Nicole Miller; intern, Tocca; founder and designer, Outspoke LLC, New York City, 2001—; signed 50-50 partnership agreement with Sean "Diddy" Combs, 2004; launched hosiery, handbags, jeans, and racing gloves lines, 2005; launched upscale women's footwear line, 2006; launched signature fragrances, 2007.

**Awards:** André Leon Talley New Look Award for Achievement, Savannah College of Art and Design, 2004; Swarovski's Perry Ellis Award for Womenswear, Council of Fashion Designers of America, 2004; honorary doctorate, Academy of Art University, 2007.

## Sidelights

**I**n the early 2000s, Zac Posen emerged as a leading young American designer. As Lisa Jones Townsel of the *St. Louis Post-Dispatch* said of him, "With an infectious smile and a crown of wavy black hair, Zac Posen ... looks like a precocious child ready to stir up trouble. But as one of the latest wunderkinds in the world of fashion design, Posen stays in the headlines with his flirty flocks and fresh eye." Known for his solid technique, fearlessness, and sense of humor in his work and life, Posen moved from an early trademark of bias-cut styles in his gowns and skirts to bold experimentation in women's wear. After signing a partnership deal with Sean "Diddy" Combs in 2004, Posen further expanded his growing empire into new areas, including hosiery and jeans. Cathy Horyn of the *New York Times* concluded, "Success in fashion is one part talent, one part luck, and one part a tireless ability to hold a gaudy marquee over your head. Posen has all these qualities in excess."

Born on October 24, 1980, in New York City, Posen is the son of Stephen and Susan Posen. His father was an acclaimed abstract painter, and his mother was a venture capitalist turned attorney. Raised in a loft in Soho with his sister Alexandra, Posen was brought up in a creative environment. Among his best friends in childhood were the daughters of artist Julian Schnable, Stella and Lola, and Posen took African dance lessons all of his life. He also studied classical singing from the ages of eight to 18.

Posen was interested in and showed talent for fashion design from an early age. By the time he was four years old, he was designing clothes for his dolls and, by seven, was taking a sewing class. When Posen attended school, he put together interesting outfits such as muffs, antler horns, and a nurse's cape from the 1920s. Because of dyslexia, Posen struggled in academic subjects, except for math, but he had already found his career path. Deciding on fashion as a career by his teens while a student at St. Ann's in Brooklyn, Posen was an intern at the New York Costume Institute at the Metropolitan Museum of Art. There, he worked under curator Richard Martin and was able to meet designers such as John Galliano and Alexander McQueen.

Posen's education became increasingly fashion-oriented. As a high school freshman, he was enrolled in a pre-college program at New York's Parsons School of Design, graduating in 1999. While in school, he was also an intern for designers Nicole Miller and Tocca. Posen then attended London's famed Central St. Martins College of Art and Design from 1999 to 2001. There, he was greatly influenced by Madeline Vionnet, who created the bias cut in 1922. The look became a signature of his early designs.

During his time in London, Posen had one of his dresses appear at the Victoria and Albert Museum for "Curvaceous," a show which focused on the woman's silhouette of the era. His contribution consisted of leather strips and approximately 400 meters of hooks and eyes. Posen also sold pieces to private clients, a practice that continued when he returned to New York in 2001. Later that year, he showed his first collection at the GenArt Fresh Faces Fashion show. The GenArt organization highlights and advises up-and-coming talent not only in fashion but in art and film as well.

Also in 2001, Posen founded his own company, Outspoke LLC, based in New York City, with his sister serving as his creative director and his mother helping run the business. He was the primary designer and soon had his own following. As a designer, Posen set out to create clothes with a specific philosophy. He told the *St. Louis Post-Dispatch*'s Townsel, "We try to make clothing that's timeless, that can't be placed in the past, present or future. We like to make trends but try to find a concise vision of them so they don't go out of season."

At the beginning of 2002, Posen won a $20,000 U.S. Ecco Domani grant for young designers. Posen used this money to create his stunning New York fashion week show in February 2002 called "Artemis." Eva Friede of the Montreal *Gazette* described this, his first solo show, by noting: "There were his famous bias-cut gowns, sexpot suits with witchy collars, and a bias-wrapped red skirt that drew applause, all in the spooky, atmospheric Angel Orensanz centre, New York's oldest synagogue."

While Posen's pieces in this show met with much acclaim and he was considered the toast of fashion week by many critics, not all were impressed. *Vogue* editor at large André Leon Talley told Cathy Horyn of the *New York Times* that "It was a swashbuckling student show. It was disjointed and messy." Horyn added, "But, as Talley points out, that show not only anticipated the craze among young women for flirty dresses with a slight attic quality, but it also demonstrated, even in its messiness, that Posen is driven hardest by technique."

Commenting on his intent with his clothes to the *Gazette*'s Friede, Posen stated "It's really about representing femininity in the most futuristic and modern way, through strength, structure and sensuality." Building on his success, Posen provided dresses for several leading female actresses at the Academy Awards a few weeks later and was signing deals with leading department stores to carry his line. He eventually signed what turned out to be a profitable deal with Bloomingdale's.

Yet Posen knew that his business had to be carefully cultivated, and he had to keep in mind the realities of the industry. While he wanted his creations to be striking and innovative, he also had to make clothes that would sell. Careful in how he presented himself, Posen launched himself and what was becoming his signature sophisticated women's clothes in Britain in the summer of 2002, again to general acclaim.

Over the next few years, Posen's shows became better and better received, with critics such as Horyn noting his growing technical skills, as demonstrated in his draping and use of insets, for example. His 2003 Spring Fashion Week show in New York City, for example, was also well-received. Here, Posen's pieces were inspired by Hollywood glamour of the 1940s and 1950s. Liz Embry of the *Houston Chronicle* commented, "While young, Posen is wise in the ways of fashion. That was made clear at his show ... at Gotham Hall on Broadway. The landmark bank made a breathtaking setting for his beautiful, sensual designs." High-profile models such as Naomi Campbell and Sophie Dahl walked the runway in Posen's creations in the show.

By 2004, Posen was named one of "40 under 40" by *Crain's New York Business*. He was also honored with the New Look award for achievement, an honor traditionally given for lifetime achievement in fashion, but given to Posen as an acknowledgement of his place as emerging greatness in design talent. As he received such accolades, Posen also expanded his business empire by entering into a 50-50 partnership with rap artist/entrepreneur Sean "Diddy" Combs through his Outspoke LLC. This partnership was designed to expand Posen's name and reach.

While Posen was well-known in high-fashion circles, his pieces were available in only about 44 ultrachic shops worldwide by 2004. Combs gave Posen a cash infusion and a bigger distribution network as well as corporate counsel as Combs had his own successful apparel company, Sean John. Posen told the *Chicago Sun-Times*'s Maureen Jenkins, "[Combs] gives incredible advice and has one of the greatest levels of drive. He tells me really to believe in and complete my vision and to listen to it, and not listen to other guiding forces." Combs also inspired Posen in other ways. Posen told Robert Sullivan of *Vogue*, "The definition of what fashion is, is changing to become more lifestyle-oriented, more like what entertainment is. So why wouldn't you partner with someone who has a great passion and great understanding of worldwide culture?"

At his 2005 Spring Fashion Week show, critics believed that Posen showed real growth as he expanded the amount of sportswear and knits in his collection. In the *New York Times*, Horyn commented, "Until now he has been mainly working in his milieu of downtown friends and celebrities, making pretty dresses with insets and fluttery hems. The key look in his spring 2005 collection, though, was a pair of wide black taffeta trousers, treated like a pair of jeans and worn with a cropped tuxedo jacket in cream wool, which was edged in satin and had a great, slouchy look." Other critics praised his bold use of color and pattern as well as tight silhouettes.

With backing from Combs, Posen's company moved into more retail outlets as well as new areas of women's wear, including hosiery (such as limited edition tights with Swarovski crystals), handbags jeans (such as a limited edition with denim company Seven for All Mankind), and racing gloves (made in conjunction with Jaguar) in 2005; upscale women's footwear in 2006; and fragrances in 2007 Future endeavors focused on a men's wear collection, a lower-priced bridge line of women's wear and other products, including the edible, as Posen created a lifestyle brand. As he built that brand, he continued to focus on his core women's wear business and kept an ideal woman in mind. He told Jenkins of the *Chicago Sun-Times*, "The Zac Posen woman is a creative woman, whether she's an artist herself or she's a mother and that's her creation. My clothing is often very architectural and anatomical—it's about modern-day cool goddesses. And it's so important for women to feel good about themselves."

Still focused on women's wear, Posen continued to present challenging collections in 2006 through 2008 His 2006 fall fashion show collection was inspired by the 1960s and 1980s, focusing on forms and shapes to create simple yet elegant women's fashions. Also lauded was Posen's 2007 spring line shown in the September 2006 fashion week. Horyn of the *New York Times* noticed his new maturity. She wrote, "The paradox of Mr. Posen's terrific show ... was that it did not include youthful clothes, at least not the rompers and bubble skirts and crushed down ankle socks we saw from so many of his peers this week.... That's what gave Mr. Posen's show its special charge—you could feel a 25-year-old designer seize his authority."

The pieces in Posen's 2007 fall fashion show were also seen as innovative, as Laura Craik of the London *Evening Standard* noted. She wrote, "The show covered all the themes of New York Fashion Week—pencil skirts, fur, purple—but Posen always does things just a little bit bolder than most of his peers." For his praised spring 2008 collection, Posen took an expectedly daring tactic, being inspired by the film *Days of Heaven,* wheat fields on the Great Plains the Shakers, and early American settlers. While his spring 2009 collection received mixed reviews Horyn of the *New York Times* noted, "The show was trashy and fun.... Many of the itty-bitty silk dresses were adorable, as were filmy leopard-print chiffon dresses and cheeky hot pants worn with a matching soda-pink jacket."

While Posen was firmly established as a fashion icon, he had a plan B. If fashion had not worked out for Posen, he believed he would have worked in the arts. He told Townsel of the *St. Louis Post Dispatch*, "I would have loved to have been a cura tor or filmmaker, but for now I'm focused on my work in fashion and expanding within the brand." Of his potential, Posen told the Montreal *Gazette*'s Friede, "Whatever I do in the future, I'm going to be continuing to create things, whether it's in fashion, film, or composing music—I just think it's the beginning of the career with an open platform for the media to be aware of."

## Sources

### Books

*Complete Marquis Who's Who Biographies,* Marquis Who's Who LLC, 2008.

### Periodicals

Associated Press, September 12, 2007.
*Atlanta Journal-Constitution,* May 15, 2004, p. 1C.
*Chicago Sun-Times,* April 21, 2005, p. 48.
*Evening Standard* (London), February 9, 2007, sec. LL 4, p. 16; April 16, 2007.
*Footwear News,* November 27, 2006, p. 24.
*Gazette* (Montreal, Quebec, Canada), February 26, 2002, p. F1.
*Guardian* (London), July 19, 2002, sec. G2, p. 14.
*Hamilton Spectator* (Ontario, Canada), September 14, 2004, p. G5.
*Houston Chronicle,* September 24, 2002, p. 1; November 17, 2005, p. 1; February 11, 2006, p. 1.
*Newsday* (New York City), September 13, 2008, p. A18.
*New York Times,* February 22, 2004, sec. 6, pt. 2, p. 66; September 13, 2004, p. B9; September 16, 2006, p. B7; February 10, 2007, p. B20; September 13, 2008, p. B7.
*San Francisco Chronicle,* April 22, 2007, p. F1.
*St. Louis Post-Dispatch,* January 3, 2004, p. 26.
*Time,* September 30, 2002, p. 78, p. 80.
*Vogue,* November 2005, p. 180.

—*A. Petruso*

# Paul Potts

## Singer

Born Paul Robert Potts, October 13, 1970, in Bristol, England; son of Roland (a bus driver) and Yvonne (a cashier) Potts; married Julie-Ann Potts, May 2003.

**Addresses:** *Home*—Port Talbot, Wales. *Record company*—Sony/BMG, 550 Madison Ave., New York, NY 10022. *Web site*—http://www.paulpottsofficial.com/.

## Career

Appeared on the Michael Barrymore program *My Kind of Music*, 1999; sang as an amateur with the Bath Opera, performed with the Royal Philharmonic Orchestra, and toured Italy solo, 2000-03; won the grand prize on *Britain's Got Talent* and was signed to a recording contract with BMG, June 2007; toured the United States and appeared on national television programs including *The Oprah Winfrey Show, Good Morning America, The Ellen DeGeneres Show,* and *Today,* 2007; released album *One Chance,* 2007; released album *One Chance: Christmas Edition,* 2007; signed with Deustche Telekom to do advertisements based on his talent-show win, 2008.

## Sidelights

When Paul Potts sang Pavarotti's rendition of Puccini's "Nessun Dorma" on *Britain's Got Talent,* the performance instantly transformed him from a chipped tooth mobile phone salesman into an international star. Facing down the acerbic reality show judge/producer Simon Cowell in a cheap suit and daring to sing opera, this ordinary-looking bloke won the hearts of viewers everywhere. In the process, he revitalized mainstream affection for his chosen field of music.

Born on October 13, 1970, in Bristol, England, Potts is the son of bus driver Roland and supermarket cashier Yvonne Potts. One of four children—three boys and a girl—the future star was chubby and later claimed that he was mercilessly bullied—both physically and verbally—at school for being "different" (as described by Potts on his Web site). When asked how bad the bullying had been, Potts told *Sun* journalist and *Britain's Got Talent* judge Piers Morgan, "Pretty bad. They used to beat me up. I even thought of throwing myself down some stairs one day—not to kill myself but to make people feel sorry for me."

Potts recalls singing since he was practically old enough to talk and enjoys a wide range of musical interests including the works of Queen and Snow Patrol. At age eleven, the youngster did his first actual public vocalizing in a Bristol church choir, but his love of classical music was instigated by an unusual source. "I got into it by watching the movie *E.T.,*" he told Michelle Kung of the *Huffington Post.* "I just wanted to be involved in the music, so I grabbed one of my mum's knitting needles, and pretended I was conducting the music. [Soundtrack conductor] John Williams really had a way with music. From there I moved on to Tchaikovsky, Dvorak, Brahms, all different sorts of composers, and from there, I moved into musicals. I'd also listen to Gilbert and Sullivan, which is a good introduction to opera."

Despite his early passion for the works of Luciano Pavarotti and Jose Carrerras—the latter's version of "Che Gelinda Manina (Your Tiny Hand is Frozen)" from *La Boheme* was a particular favorite—Potts lacked the necessary self-esteem to pursue a career in music. As a result, he kicked around in various menial jobs in Bristol and later in Port Talbot, Wales. It was not until he was 28 years old that Potts let on about his secret musical obsession. Attending a karaoke bar dressed as Pavarotti, complete with fake beard and extra padding in his sweater he sang "Nessun Dorma" to a backing track he had brought from home. Pleased by the response to his performance, he scouted about for a way to get some proper musical training.

Part of his newfound ambition stemmed from his wife, Julie-Ann, whom he had met via an Internet dating site. More of a Bon Jovi fan than an opera buff, Potts's wife encouraged him to chase his dreams, offering support and encouragement every step of the way. In 1999, Potts caught a lucky break on the Michael Barrymore television program *My Kind of Music*. Stating his case and singing his heart out, the aspiring singer won £8,000 (approximately USD $16,000) toward a three-month summer school session in Italy.

The prize money had to be supplemented with his life savings, but the expenditure proved worthwhile. Besides receiving valuable coaching from Mario Melani and Svetlana Sidrova, he got to sing in a master class for Pavarotti himself. Performing an aria by Rudolfo from *La Boheme*, a big phrase rendered him breathless and the famous tenor corrected him. "He didn't really offer me any advice per se," he told Colleen Last of *MSN Entertainment*, "We talked about one of the arias I was singing as part of the course, and he asked me to sing for him. He was a very nice man."

Although Potts could not afford further operatic training in Italy, he kept up his vocal training when he returned to England by bicycling to lessons with coach Ian Comboy, who told the *Guardian*'s Vanessa Thorpe, "The top of his voice is almost totally natural. It does not strain. With most British voices in the Italian mode you can hear that it is still a British voice, but Paul's voice is Italianate."

Joining the amateur Bath Opera company in 1999, he garnered worthwhile stage experience by appearing in productions of *The Marriage of Figaro, Don Giovani,* and *Don Carlos and Turandot.* He also performed with the Royal Philharmonic Orchestra before touring northern Italy as a soloist. These experiences were later questioned by British newspapers when he began to make a splash on *Britain's Got Talent,* a program aimed at giving non-professionals a break. Potts maintains that he never received more than gas money for his early performances. "I've never worked as a professional singer," he states on the BBC Web site. "My four performances with Bath Opera a few years back were all amateur."

However, his budding amateur career nearly came to an abrupt end in 2003 when doctors found a benign tumor during an appendectomy. Barely recovered, he was knocked off his bike and broke his collarbone, and subsequently began to sink into debt. Working as a salesman at the Bridgend branch of the Carphone Warehouse, he hid his singing ambitions from his co-workers until after the first round of the *Britain's Got Talent* competition in 2007.

Competing against a horror magician, male actors dressed as women, and several cute kids, Potts surprised viewers and judges alike. Wearing a budget-priced suit from Tesco—Britain's version of Wal-Mart—and appearing before Simon Cowell, actress Amanda Holden, and journalist Piers Morgan, he emoted through "Nessun Dorma" as if his life depended upon it. The judges, especially the usually sarcastic Cowell, were deeply moved, as was the home viewing audience.

Clips of Potts singing were posted on YouTube, allowing people all over the world to chart his progress on successive shows, and to glory in his becoming the first-ever winner of the competition. In addition to the prize money of £100,000 (roughly USD $200,000), the former salesman was given a recording contract with Cowell's label Sony/BMG. The singer paid off his debts, had his teeth fixed for free, bought some classier suits, and began recording his first album, the appropriately titled *One Chance.*

A mix of pop, seasonal, and operatic tunes recorded in a semi-classical style, *One Chance* hit number one in 20 different countries. In conjunction with appearances on television programs in Britain, Germany, and the United States, Potts toured behind the album, garnering mixed reviews from critics and standing ovations from his fans. In 2008, he signed a lucrative contract with Deutsche Telekom to be included in their mobile phone ads.

Potts, who sang in front of the Queen of England, is in demand for duets and been credited with a rise in opera's mainstream popularity. The biggest news of all came when Cowell's company began laying plans for a movie based on the story of his incredible rise from obscurity to overnight international stardom. "It's very surreal to hear someone wants to make a film about me," he told Last of *MSN Entertainment*, "but I'm trying to take each day as it comes and to welcome each day. But no matter what, I'm not changing who I am."

## Selected discography

*One Chance*, Sony, 2007.
*One Chance: Christmas Edition* (2 disc), Sony, 2007.

## Sources

### Periodicals

*Boston Globe*, March 12, 2008.
*Entertainment Weekly*, June 24, 2008.
*Guardian* (London, England), July 9, 2008.
*Huffington Post*, September 21, 2007.
*Observer* (London, England), June 17, 2007.
*Portsmouth News* (Portsmouth, England), July 17, 2008.
*Sun* (England), April 11, 2008.

### Online

"Artist Biography—Paul Potts," *Billboard*, http://www.billboard.com/bbcom/bio/index.jsp?pid=921343, (August 11, 2008).
"'Britain's Got Talent' winner Potts to spend prize on a new smile," *Mail Online*, http://www.dailymail.co.uk/tvshowbiz/article-462676/Britains-Got-Talent-winner-Potts-to-spend-prize-on-a-new-smile (August 10, 2008).
"Paul Potts Biography," BBC Web site, http://www.bbc.co.uk/wales.music/sites/paul_potts/pages/biography.shtml, (August 10, 2008).
"Paul Potts Biography," Paul Potts Official Web site, http://www.paulpottsofficial.com/article/biography/ (September 25, 2008).
"Paul Potts," Internet Movie Database, http://www.imdb.com/name/nm2698399 (August 11, 2008).
"Paul Potts Interview," MSN Entertainment, http://www.entertainment.uk.msn.com/tv/features/article.aspx?cp-documentid =5512407 (August 20, 2008).
"U.K. Talent Champ: 'Can't believe it,'" MSNBC.com, http://www.msnbc.com/id/19349937.tif/print/1/dispalymode/1098/ (August 21, 2008).

—Ken Burke

# Radiohead

## Alternative-rock group

Members include Colin Greenwood (born June 26, 1969, in Oxford, England), bass, keyboard; Jonny Greenwood (born in 1971 in Oxford, England), guitar, keyboard; Ed O'Brien (born in 1968 in Oxford, England), guitar; Phil Selway (born in 1967 in England), drummer; and Thom Yorke (born October 7, 1968, in Wellingborough, England), vocals.

**Addresses:** *Management*—Grabow Entertainment, 4219 Creekmeadow Dr., Dallas, TX 75287.

## Career

Initially known as On a Friday, the band formed in Abingdon, England, late 1980s; played Oxford, England, club circuit, early 1990s; signed with EMI,

*AP Images*

1991; changed name to Radiohead, 1991; released EP *Drill*, 1992; released first album, *Pablo Honey*, 1993; released *The Bends*, 1995; toured with R.E.M., 1995; released *OK Computer*, 1997; featured in documentary, *Meeting People Is Easy*, 1999; released *Kid A*, 2000; released *Amnesiac*, 2001; released *Hail to the Thief*, 2003; released *In Rainbows* online, 2007; released *In Rainbows* at record stores, 2008.

**Awards:** Grammy Award for best alternative music album, Recording Academy, for *In Rainbows*, 2009.

## Sidelights

The British five-piece band Radiohead rocked the music industry in 2007 when it released its seventh album—*In Rainbows*—directly to fans as a digital download. What was most remarkable about the decision is that Radiohead allowed fans to set the price they wanted to pay for the album, which was released on Radiohead's Web site. A CD version hit record stores several months later, in early 2008. The album went on to earn a Grammy Award for best alternative music album.

Radiohead first made waves in the early 1990s when its grunge-inspired debut single, "Creep," became an unexpected hit. "Creep" is an ode to angst-filled alienation. In it, lead singer Thom Yorke croons, "I wish I was special/But I'm a creep." Many industry critics tagged Radiohead as a probable one-hit wonder, but the band delivered with its 1995 sophomore album *The Bends*, which showed musical depth and caught the attention of alt-rock pioneers R.E.M., who invited Radiohead to open for them during the band's 1995 European and U.S. tours.

Radiohead's members hail from Oxford, England, and have known each other since childhood. Yorke, the band's frontman, was born in Wellingborough, England, in 1968 with a paralyzed left eye. As a youngster, he underwent numerous operations to improve his vision but was left with a distinctive lazy eye, for which he endured endless teasing. Music critics frequently credit Yorke as the driving force behind Radiohead's characteristically turbulent lyrics. By the age of eight, Yorke was infatuated with becoming a rock star. "I decided that when I saw [Queen guitarist] Brian May for the first time on TV," Yorke told David Fricke of *Rolling Stone*. Soon, Yorke acquired his first guitar. By the time he was nine, his family had moved to the Oxford area.

Bassist Colin Greenwood and his little brother, guitarist and keyboardist Jonny, were born in Oxford. The future bass player was born in 1969 and the future guitarist in 1971. Their father was a British army major and they moved often before landing in Abingdon, a town about eight miles south of Oxford. Guitarist Ed O'Brien was born in Oxford in 1968. Drummer Phil Selway, born in 1967, spent his early years in Cambridgeshire, England, but had moved to Abingdon by early adolescence.

The future band mates met at Abingdon School, a boys-only public school. In the late 1980s, they began playing together, calling themselves On a Friday. They chose On a Friday for the name of their band because that was the day they held weekly rehearsals in the school's music room. Though they were young and inexperienced musicians, the teens wrote some competent music back then and are known to rework 20-year-old songs for new albums. "The National Anthem," included on Radiohead's *Kid A* (2000), was written from a piece Yorke composed at age 16.

When it came time for college, the boys parted ways. Yorke went to the University of Exeter, and Colin Greenwood headed to Cambridge University. O'Brien enrolled at the University of Manchester, while Selway chose the University of Liverpool. Jonny Greenwood, who was only 13 when he joined the band, stayed in Abingdon to finish his schooling. On weekends and holidays, the young men made a habit of getting together to write songs and record demo tapes.

By 1991, the four older boys had graduated from college. The band got back together and gained a local following on the Oxford club circuit. In late 1991, the band signed with the British music company EMI. Jonny Greenwood, the youngest member of the band, was enrolled at Oxford Polytechnic but dropped out to focus on the band. At this time, the young men ditched the name On a Friday and adopted Radiohead, which was the title of a Talking Heads song. "There was always a plan to get back together after university," Yorke told Fricke of *Rolling Stone*. "I also wonder what would have happened if we hadn't gone off to college like good little boys. I think we would have freaked if we'd gone straight into the Radiohead thing."

In 1992, Radiohead played more than 130 shows to build up its fan base. The band also worked on its first album, 1993's *Pablo Honey*, which included the unlikely hit "Creep." The song had failed on its initial release in 1992 because British radio stations found it too depressing. "Creep," however, stirred a nerve among U.S. college students, and the video garnered heavy play on MTV, prompting Radiohead to cross the Atlantic and tour in the United States. "Creep" hit No. 2 on *Billboard*'s modern rock chart, increasing sales and pushing *Pablo Honey* to gold status. With the increased attention, "Creep" was re-released in the United Kingdom, this time becoming a top ten hit on the U.K. Singles Chart.

Radiohead followed with *The Bends* in 1995. Filled with epic guitar rock and sonic texturing, the album received critical acclaim, though sales were sluggish. The album's most noted songs were "Fake Plastic Trees," which hit No. 11 on *Billboard*'s Modern Rock Tracks, "High and Dry," and "My Iron Lung." These singles charted well in the U.K. The acoustic ballad "Street Spirit (Fade Out)" hit No. 5 on the U.K. charts.

In 1997, Radiohead released *OK Computer,* a guitar-driven, atmospheric album with songs bemoaning a future in which technology rules. "Fitter Happier" had no vocals, just a computer-generated voice reading phrases. Singles included "Paranoid Android," "Karma Police," and "No Surprises," which all charted in the top ten on the U.K. Singles Chart.

In 2000, readers of *Q* magazine, the British equivalent of *Rolling Stone,* voted *OK Computer* the No. 2 all-time best British rock album. The Beatles' *Revolver* was named No. 1. According to Robert Hilburn of the *Los Angeles Times,* *Q* summed up the album's draw this way: "Aside from being a tremendously stimulating and evocative listen, [the album] was an encapsulation of what it's like to feel terrified by the times.... A work of infinite anguish ... [that ranks with] all the apocalyptic classics in the rock'n'roll pantheon."

When Radiohead embarked on a world tour following the release of *OK Computer,* British filmmaker Grant Gee followed along, capturing the tour for a 1999 documentary, *Meeting People Is Easy.* In the film, Gee captured the band members' insecurities with their newfound stardom. Instead of spotlighting the exhilarating parts of rock'n'roll fame—the high-energy concerts, the fans—Gee focused on the mundane, such as the never-ending interviews, the backstage boredom, and the tedium of life as a road warrior.

In 2000, Radiohead rolled out *Kid A,* an album unlike any of the rock stompers the band had previously produced. The downtempo *Kid A* lacked the steady guitar, drumbeats, and power chords that had driven the band's previous offerings. Instead, Radiohead relied on esoteric sounds from the electronic piano and synthesizer. Radiohead did not re-

lease any singles or videos from the album to increase hype, yet *Kid A* entered the *Billboard* 200 album chart at No. 1 before sales sloughed off. But the album received some poor reviews from critics who called the music inaccessible. In 2001, Radiohead released *Amnesiac.* Many of the songs were recorded or written during the production of *Kid A.* Once again, the album relied on electronic sounds.

In 2003, the band returned to its alt-rock roots with *Hail to the Thief,* which relied more on guitar and piano instead of the electronica that backed the previous two albums, although the sonic influences remained. The album, which peaked at No. 3 on the *Billboard* 200, opened with the song "2+2=5," a reference to George Orwell's thought-provoking book *1984.* The theme of "Big Brother," which Orwell explored in his book, recurs throughout the album. During the 2003-2004 tour that followed the release of *Hail to the Thief,* Radiohead sold out arenas on four continents.

*Hail to the Thief* satisfied Radiohead's contract obligations with EMI, and the band was not eager to resign. With no deadline constraints for another album, Radiohead members took time off to reconnect with family. When they reconvened, they had difficulty finding their groove. "We lost all momentum and it's very, very difficult to get momentum back," Yorke told Jon Pareles of the *New York Times.* "When I say momentum, I don't just mean the physically working everyday, I mean just hanging out and playing each other's music and swapping ideas and stuff. It's something that you take for granted until it's gone."

The band mates played around in the studio but did not feel they were getting anywhere so they decided to hit the road to get a fresh feel. They road-tested new songs and soon found their groove. Bassist Colin Greenwood told Jon Wiederhorn of *Rolling Stone* that creating music in an atmosphere of spontaneity has always worked best for him. He never thinks through solos before playing them. "I don't think I could play anything fresh if I've heard it 100 times before. It wouldn't be dangerous, and there'd be no chance of it going wrong."

In 2007, Radiohead released *In Rainbows* through downloads on its Web site, allowing fans to name their price. Some paid a mere 90 cents for the 10 medium-quality MP3 files comprising the album. Others paid $80 for a package that included two CDs, two vinyl LPs and printed materials. Other fans simply paid what they deemed was a reasonable price. The approach worked for Radiohead, which was banking on the idea that fans would pay a fair price to support the band so members could keep writing songs. In addition, Radiohead received 100 percent of the revenue because there was no middleman. Releasing the album in this manner kept the price down for fans and the profits up for Radiohead.

Many fans considered *In Rainbows* Radiohead's best album yet. Writing in the *New York Times*, Pareles noted that the album is "as bitterly magnificent as the band's best works, with barbed, intricate vamps wrapped around thoughts of death, love, futility, stubbornness and rage." Some songs were familiar to diehard fans. Radiohead had played many of the songs during its 2006 tour, including "Bodysnatchers" and "Nude," the first two singles released. *In Rainbows* went on to win a 2009 Grammy Award for best alternative music album.

When Radiohead hit the road in 2008, members worked to make the tour "green." Radiohead ordered a carbon audit of its 2003 and 2006 North American tours to gain an understanding of the ecological costs of touring. This time around, Radiohead transported its equipment by sea because it was more eco-friendly than air freight. In addition, the group tried to stay on the ground between shows instead of hopping onto jets and focused on playing at venues located on public transportation routes so fans would not have to use so much gas getting to the concerts.

As for the future, the band planned to continue making music, though members have family commitments. Yorke has a son with his partner, Rachel Owens, and Selway has two children. As of early 2009, band members did not delay on songs but tried to stay focused and knock them out while, at the same time, reaching for new heights. "Thom is constantly testing us," guitarist O'Brien told Fricke of *Rolling Stone*. "You think, 'Do I have to keep proving myself?' Yeah, you do. That's why he's such a great bandleader. He keeps you on your toes. But it is a band. I have no doubt that Thom would make amazing music on his own. But we give him the soul."

## Selected discography

*Drill* (EP), Parlophone Records, 1992.
*Pablo Honey,* Capitol, 1993.
*The Bends,* Capitol, 1995.
*OK Computer,* Capitol, 1997.
*Kid A,* Capitol, 2000.
*Amnesiac,* Capitol, 2001.
*I Might Be Wrong: Live Recordings,* Capitol, 2001.
*Hail to the Thief,* Capitol, 2003.
*In Rainbows,* released on Web site, 2007.
*In Rainbows* (re-release), Ato Records/Red, 2008.
*The Best Of (U.S. Limited Edition),* Capitol, 2008.
*The Best Of (U.K. Limited Edition),* EMI Europe, 2008.

## Sources

### Periodicals

*Daily Telegraph,* April 1, 2008, sec. The Arts, p. 25.
*Evening Standard* (London, England), January 17, 2008, p. C24.
*Los Angeles Times,* June 3, 2001, p. 1.
*National Post* (Canada), June 3, 2003, p. AL1.
*New York Times,* June 2, 2006, p. B1; October 11, 2007, p. E1.
*Rolling Stone,* September 7, 1995, p. 19; August 2, 2001, p. 42.

### Online

"Radiohead Finds Sales, Even After Downloads," *New York Times,* http://www.nytimes.com/2008/01/10/arts/music/10radio.html (February 10, 2009).

—Lisa Frick

# Lisa Randall

*Robert Pitts/Landov*

## Physicist

**B**orn June 18, 1962, in New York, NY; daughter of Richard (a sales representative) and Gladys (a teacher) Randall. *Education:* Harvard University, B.A., 1983; Harvard University, Ph.D., 1987.

**Addresses:** *Home*—Cambridge, MA. *Office*—Harvard University, Department of Physics, 17 Oxford St., Cambridge, MA 02138.

## Career

**S**ummer research, Smithsonian Astrophysical Observatory, 1981; summer research, Fermi National Accelerator Laboratory, U.S. Department of Energy, 1982; summer research, IMB, Poughkeepsie, NY, 1982; summer research, Bell Laboratories, 1983; teaching assistant, Harvard University physics department, 1984; President's Fellow, University of California at Berkeley, 1987-89; postdoctoral fellow, Lawrence Berkeley Laboratory, 1989-90; Junior Fellow, Harvard Society of Fellows, 1990-91; assistant professor, Massachusetts Institute of Technology (MIT), 1991-95; Institute for Theoretical Physics, Santa Barbara, CA, 1994; associate professor of physics, MIT, 1995-98; physics professor, Princeton University, 1998-2000; physics professor, MIT, 1998-2001; physics professor, Harvard University, 2001—.

**Awards:** Westinghouse Science Talent Search winner, 1980; Young Investigator Award, National Science Foundation, 1992; Outstanding Junior Investigator Award, Department of Energy, 1992; Premio Caterina Tomassoni e Felice Pietro Chisesi Award, University of Rome, 2003; Klopsteg Award, American Association of Physics Teachers, 2006; Julius Edgar Lilienfeld Prize, American Physical Society, 2007; Elizabeth A. Wood Award, American Crystallographic Association, 2007; named to *Time* magazine's list of the 100 most influential people of 2007; inducted into the National Academy of Sciences, 2008; American Academy of Achievement Golden Plate Award, 2008.

## Sidelights

**H**arvard University physics professor Lisa Randall believes science should be accessible to everyone. She is well-known for her 2005 book *Warped Passages: Unraveling the Mysteries of the Universe's Hidden Dimensions.* Unlike most books published by her peers—which are aimed at the scientific community—Randall's book about exploring the complex mysteries of the universe was aimed at the everyday person. The *New York Times* named it a Notable Book of the Year.

In an interview with Michael Brooks of *New Scientist,* Randall explained why she took time away from research to write a book for the general public. "I wanted to show why physicists think about things like extra dimensions, and how they might tie into 'real' observable phenomena. Another reason is that we have these big particle accelerators and people should know why they are there. We are asking for funding for these things and it's only fair that people should know what the questions are that we're trying to answer with them. I think it is really important to pay back, to explain to people what's going on."

Randall was born in 1962 in New York City to Richard and Gladys Randall. She grew up in the Queens borough of the city. Her father worked as a sales representative for an engineering firm, while her mother took a break from teaching to stay home with Randall and her two sisters. Early on, Randall felt pulled toward mathematics—she liked math because the problems always had definite answers.

"Everything else seemed very subjective," she told *Discover* magazine's Corey S. Powell. "The teachers in English class would say, 'What is the reason that this is an important book?' They'd look for the three good reasons, whereas you might think of some other one. I didn't like the arbitrariness of that."

Randall attended Manhattan's Stuyvesant High School, becoming the first female captain of the school's math team. During her senior year in 1980, she won the famed Westinghouse Science Talent Search competition with an exploration of complex numbers. Randall enrolled at Harvard, earning her bachelor's degree in physics in 1983. She followed with a doctorate in particle physics, also from Harvard, in 1987.

Next, Randall headed to the West Coast to continue her physics research as a President's Fellow at the University of California at Berkeley. By 1990, Randall was back at Harvard on a post-doctoral fellowship and in 1991 she became an assistant physics professor at the Massachusetts Institute of Technology (MIT).

During the summer of 1998, Randall joined forces with Boston University fellow Raman Sundrum, now a physics professor at Johns Hopkins. Sitting together in the ice cream parlor at MIT's student center, they spent hours pondering the laws of physics and the nature of the universe. At the time, Randall had become increasingly intrigued by gravity. She wondered why gravity was so weak on the Earth as compared to the other fundamental forces governing the universe. When asked about this phenomenon, Randall most often uses the example of a paperclip. She notes that a magnet can pick up a paperclip even though the Earth's entire mass of gravity is pulling down on it. Together, Randall and Sundrum focused on solving this mystery.

In the end, they came up with a theory called the Randall-Sundrum models, which they published in two groundbreaking papers, the first in 1999. The model proposes that the universe has more dimensions to it than humans are aware of and that these dimensions could be infinite in nature. In *Warped Passages*, Randall discussed dimensions in depth. She pointed out that scientists know for certain that the dimensions of length, width, height, and time exist, though time is not a dimension humans can "see." In solving the gravity problem, she and Sundrum theorized that the universe has at least one extra dimension beyond these. Randall believes gravity is filtered through this extra dimension and that is why it is so weak on earth.

When Randall and Sundrum published their papers, the theory of an unknown dimension was not new. Other scientists had explored the idea but these theories all surmised that these extra dimensions were tiny—so tiny they had yet to be discovered. The Randall-Sundrum model proposed that this extra dimension is warped and could therefore be infinite. In the end, the equations Randall and Sundrum worked out to solve the gravity problem led Randall to the idea of a warped fifth dimension humans cannot see. Speaking to the *New York Times'* Dennis Overbye, Sundrum said Randall has "unworldly" instincts that allow her to find probable solutions to vexing problems in a way no other scientist has imagined before.

Since publishing her papers on her warped fifth dimension theory, Randall has become one of the most-cited theoretical physicists in the world. "She's an outstanding, well-regarded theorist who's raised some interesting ideas about what's out there," former colleague, MIT physicist and Nobel Prize winner Gerome Friedman told the *Boston Herald*'s Paul Restuccia. "If we see evidence of what she's proposed, it will be extraordinary. It will shake up everything."

Besides teaching at MIT, Randall also spent time at Princeton University as a physics professor from 1998 to 2000. In 2001, she returned to Harvard. Randall holds the notoriety of being the first woman tenured in physics at all three East Coast universities—MIT, Princeton, and Harvard.

In *Warped Passages*, Randall explored her theory of a warped fifth dimension, as well as parallel universes, quantum mechanics, and three-dimensional sinkholes. The material covered in the book was complex, but Randall used creative analogies and fictional vignettes—rather than mathematical equations—to make it more accessible. In addition, she introduced each chapter's topic through the use of pop lyrics, quoting Eminem, the Talking Heads, and *West Side Story.*

Randall began working on the book in earnest in the early 2000s after a rock climbing accident left her bed-ridden for two months. She shattered her heel and had to spend two months with her foot elevated to prevent infection. Despite the accident, rock climbing remains a passion. "Rock climbing is something I love," she told the *San Francisco Chronicle's* Jane Ganahl. "It really clears your head."

Evidence for Randall's theories could come through research conducted at the Large Hadron Collider. Located near Geneva, Switzerland, this multi-billion-dollar atom smasher opened in 2008 and will be used to detect extra-dimensional particles. Some scientists believe that Randall could win the Nobel Prize if evidence for her dimension is found during experiments with the collider.

## Sources

### Books

Randall, Lisa, *Warped Passages: Unraveling the Mysteries of the Universe's Hidden Dimensions*, HarperCollins, 2005.

### Periodicals

*Boston Herald,* November 28, 2005, p. 24.
*Discover,* July 1, 2006, p. 50.
*Guardian* (London, England), July 15, 2005, p. 30.
*New Scientist,* June 18, 2005, p. 48.
*New York Times,* November 1, 2005, p. F1.
*Plain Dealer* (Cleveland, OH), March 19, 2007, p. B2.
*San Francisco Chronicle,* September 1, 2005, p. E1.
*Vogue,* August 2007, pp. 212, 275.

### Online

"Lisa Randall Curriculum Vitae," Harvard University Department of Physics, http://randall.physics.harvard.edu/CV.html (November 7, 2008).

*—Lisa Frick*

# Alex Rigopulos

*Robert Pitts/Landov*

**Chief Executive Officer of Harmonix Music Systems**

---

**B**orn Alexander Peter Rigopulos, c. 1970. *Education:* Massachusetts Institute of Technology, B.S., 1992, M.S., 1994.

**Addresses:** *Office*—Harmonix Music Systems, Inc., 625 Massachusetts Ave., 2nd Fl., Cambridge, MA 02139.

## Career

**C**o-founded Harmonix Music Systems, 1995; chief executive officer, Harmonix Music Systems, 1995—; sold company to MTV Networks/Viacom, 2006.

## Sidelights

**A**lex Rigopulos is the co-founder and chief executive officer of Harmonix Music Systems, the company that created the music-video game phenomena *Guitar Hero* and *Rock Band.* Before they achieved success, Rigopulos and Harmonix co-founder Eran Egozy struggled for almost a decade to develop a product that would catch on with consumers. As Rigopulos told a writer for *Official U.S. Playstation Magazine,* "we both saw a problem in the world that we wanted to solve, which was this: Playing music feels incredibly good, but very few people ever get to experience this because learning to play an instrument is so damned difficult."

Born in the early 1970s, Rigopulos grew up in the Boston area and played in a Led Zeppelin cover band in his teens. He attended the private Deerfield Academy in the Massachusetts city of the same name before entering Massachusetts Institute of Technology (MIT) in Cambridge, one of the most selective colleges in the United States. He studied music composition and earned his undergraduate degree in 1992 before going on to MIT's prestigious graduate program, the MIT Media Lab, which focuses on new frontiers at the intersection of computer science and multimedia. There he met Israeli-born Eran Egozy, who was from a computer science background but had extensive classical-music training.

Rigopulos earned his master's degree from MIT in media arts and sciences in 1994 with a thesis titled "Growing Music From Seeds: Parametric Generation and Control of Seed-Based Music for Interactive Composition and Performance," which featured some novel ideas that would lay the foundation for both *Guitar Hero* and *Rock Band.* In 1995, he and Egozy founded Harmonix Music Systems with the goal of developing an interactive product that would introduce non-musicians to the visceral thrill that musicians achieve from playing live. They drummed up the initial funding from a former fraternity brother of Egozy's who had recently cashed out in the early phase of the dot-com boom.

Harmonix's first product was a CD-ROM computer program called *The Axe: Titans of Classic Rock,* which allowed users to improvise music solos with a joystick device. Introduced in 1997, *The Axe* sold poorly, but did garner some interest in the company from the Walt Disney Corporation; a different version of the product called "CamJam" was installed at the Epcot Center in Orlando, Florida. By this point both Rigopulos and Egozy had run though several rounds of seed money from venture-capital firms, and decided to set up an office in Tokyo, Japan, to be closer to some of the more advanced technologies in the field.

Harmonix's next failure was a joystick on a guitar, which allowed a karaoke performer to play along and had cost the company nearly $7 million to develop and market. Dismayed, Rigopulos and Egozy returned to Cambridge and laid off nearly half their staff of 25. "And to be clear, I don't mean we were earning no money," Rigopulos explained to Don Steinberg in *Inc.* about this pre-*Guitar Hero* era at the company. "I mean we had near zero revenue. We were raising money and spending it, building stuff that no one actually wanted to pay for."

Finally, Rigopulos and Egozy decided to concentrate solely on gaming, and specifically, music-video games. The first product they brought to the market was *Frequency,* which was launched in 2001 on Sony's PlayStation 2 (PS2) console. Again, it failed to catch on with consumers. Writing in *Inc.,* Steinberg described it as "a complex, thinking person's button-masher. You would race down a tunnel whose walls represented instruments—guitar, drums, bass, synthesizer—and press buttons to activate layers of sound. *Frequency* intimidated people."

The sequel to *Frequency* was *Amplitude,* launched in 2003 also on the PS2 platform. That was followed by a deal with Konami, a Japanese company, to create a new karaoke game. *Karaoke Revolution,* which debuted in North America on the PS2 in the fall of 2003. The game incorporated a special headset or microphone that communicated with the software; players scored points for remaining in tune. *Karaoke Revolution* actually gave Rigopulos and Egozy's company their first profits.

A Silicon Valley company called Red Octane contacted Rigopulos and Egozy about coming up with a similar type of game that would use a guitar-like peripheral. The Huang brothers, Red Octane's owners, had earned a small fortune manufacturing dance pads in China for *DanceDance Revolution,* a top-selling interactive music game, and provided the initial funding for *Guitar Hero.*

*Guitar Hero* was released in November of 2005 with a retail price of $70, considered a bit high for the industry. It featured a plastic guitar modeled after a Gibson SG, with large dots of different colors that allowed users to play along with the dots on the screen. There were 47 songs available in the first version, ranging from Blue Öyster Cult's "Godzilla" to the Ramones' "I Wanna Be Sedated." The songs were actually covers performed by a studio band, because the cost of licensing the original tunes would have been prohibitive, and few record labels were interested in the Harmonix project anyway.

Rigopulos and Egozy's creation became one of the best-selling games of 2006, and spawned an entire subgenre of YouTube videos of users filming themselves while playing the game. *Guitar Hero* also set a new sales record in the gaming industry for North America: No other product had hit the $1 billion mark so quickly, and record-company executives were somewhat shocked to notice a spike in online sales for the original versions of the 47 cover songs.

The Huangs' Red Octane was bought by Activision, and the ownership rights to the name *Guitar Hero* went with it. Harmonix remained independent until Rigopulos and Egozy sold it to Viacom in September of 2006 for $175 million. The move by MTV Networks' parent company was considered a clear sign that the record business viewed products like *Guitar Hero* the wave of the future. The major-player status of Viacom and its associated media companies made for a spectacular launch of Rigopulos and Egozy's next release, the multiplayer *Rock Star,* in November of 2007, which featured 51 original songs. Veteran British rockers The Who actually played at the invitation-only launch party for the game, and lead singer Roger Daltrey expressed gratitude to Rigopulos, Egozy, Harmonix staffers, and Viacom visionaries. "We're too old to get on the radio," Daltrey said, according to Steinberg's *Inc.* article. "[Thanks] for you lot. [Thanks] for anything where music's getting heard."

## Sources

*Inc.,* October 2008, p. 124.
*Newsweek,* January 7, 2008, p. 78.
*Official U.S. Playstation Magazine,* May 1, 2003.
*Time,* December 17, 2007, p. 52; April 29, 2008.

—Carol Brennan

# Seth Rogen

## Actor and screenwriter

**B**orn April 15, 1982, in Vancouver, British Columbia, Canada; son of Mark Rogen (a non-profit organizer) and a social worker.

**Addresses:** *Agent*—The Weinstein Company, 5700 Wilshire Blvd., Ste. 600, Los Angeles, CA 90036.

## Career

**A**ctor on television, including: *Freaks and Geeks,* 1999-2000; *North Hollywood,* 2001; *Dawson's Creek,* 2003; *Undeclared,* 2001-03; *Early Bird,* 2005; *Help Me Help You,* 2005; *American Dad,* 2006. Film appearances include: *Donnie Darko,* 2001; *Anchorman: The Legend of Ron Burgundy,* 2004; *The 40-Year-Old Virgin,* 2005; *You, Me, and Dupree,* 2006; *Knocked Up,* 2007; *Superbad,* 2007; *Step Brothers,* 2008; *Fanboys,* 2008; *Pineapple Express,* 2008; *Zack and Miri Make a Porno,* 2008. Voice actor in films and video games, including: *Wake Up, Ron Burgundy: The Lost Movie,* 2004; *Shrek the Third,* 2007; *The Spiderwick Chronicles,* 2008; *Horton Hears a Who!,* 2008; *Kung Fu Panda,* 2008; *Monsters vs. Aliens,* 2009. Writer for television shows, including: *Undeclared,* 2001-02; *Da Ali G Show,* 2003. Writer of screenplays, including: *Superbad,* 2007; *Drillbit Taylor,* 2008; *Pineapple Express,* 2008; *The Green Hornet,* 2009. Producer of films, including: *The 40-Year-Old Virgin,* 2005; *Knocked Up,* 2007; *Superbad,* 2007; *Pineapple Express,* 2008; *Funny People,* 2009; *The Green Hornet,* 2009.

**Awards:** Named Comedy Star of the Year, ShoWest Award, 2008.

## Sidelights

**S**eth Rogen is not the kind of young man who is expected to make it in Hollywood. Overweight, without the handsome looks that are typically relied on to drive box office sales, and intentionally dumpy, the Canadian actor became a surprisingly dominant force in Hollywood, not only as a writer and producer, but as a leading man in romantic comedies. Between 2007 and 2008, Rogen starred in three films, performed small or voice roles in six others, was the writer on three films, and was the producer on three films. Only parts of those lists overlapped. Known for his crass sense of humor, his R-rated approach to comedy and life, his tendency to use drugs and crude jokes to get the laugh, and his unconventional physical appearance, Rogen has created a niche in Hollywood for the kind of films that he has always wanted to watch.

Born in Vancouver, British Columbia, Rogen began his acting career at an early age. By the age of eleven, he was acting in plays in Chinatown, Vancouver, and at age 13, his mother would drive him to a local club, Yuk Yuk's, to do his stand-up comedy routine. Rogen recalled to the A.V. Club that the stand-up routine was actually his parents' idea.

"I knew I just loved comedy, and I think it was my parents who initially brought up the notion of me trying to do stand-up. I think I actually tried writing jokes just at home, just kind of sitting around. But it seemed like a very real way to step into the world of comedy. I felt I could do it, so why not?"

At 16, he auditioned in Los Angeles for Judd Apatow's NBC television show, *Freaks and Geeks*. Despite having a cult following and being well received by critics, *Freaks and Geeks*, a teen show about outcasts in high school, only aired for a single season. But by then, Apatow and Rogen had developed a strong relationship; Rogen, who had dropped out of high school, became something of an apprentice to Apatow, following the writer and director onto his next television show, the short-lived comedy *Undeclared*. Apatow had wanted Rogen to star in the program, but the network felt he did not have the appropriate look for a leading actor. Determined to get Rogen involved with more than just a bit part, Apatow brought Rogen onto the writing staff. Rogen was only 18.

While his youth could have worked against him, Rogen fit in well with the writing staff. "It's uncomfortable for other people when this 18-year-old is ripping out scripts that are among the best," Apatow was quoted as saying by critic Joel Stein in *Time*. But most people managed to forget that Rogen was so much younger. "It didn't occur to me that when he was doing *Freaks and Geeks* he was a teenager. I figured he was actually 40," quipped fellow actor Paul Rudd in the same article.

After *Undeclared*, Rogen planned to focus on writing, assuming—like most of Hollywood—that he was not the type to become a Hollywood actor. But Apatow continued to work with Rogen, sending Rogen and writing partner Evan Greenberg writing exercises and challenges for movie concepts. Along with doing some writing for the Sacha Baron Cohen comedy program *Da Ali G Show*, Rogen did continue to receive small roles. He came back into national attention with *The 40-Year-Old Virgin*. Another Apatow film, the movie featured the storytelling techniques that put Apatow on the map: a sweet story inside a lot of raunchy humor and foul language. Rogen's writing and comedy skills were also put to work. In an interview with Rogen, Will Harris of Bullz-Eye.com reported a conversation the interviewer had with Apatow: "He said you showed everyone up as a writer, and that that was half the reason he hired you onto *The 40-Year-Old Virgin*: so that he could have you on hand to touch up everyone's jokes." Rogen served as Apatow's co-producer, enabling him to take the minor role he

had been given and increase his on-screen time, and the movie's success led them to try something even more daring: casting Rogen as star in Apatow's next romantic comedy.

Like *The 40-Year-Old Virgin*, *Knocked Up* is a story that offers a very sweet-natured center surrounded by crass jokes about sex, drugs, and underachievement. In the film, Rogen plays a do-nothing stoner who has a one-night stand with a woman far out of his league, played by Katherine Heigl. When Heigl's character gets pregnant, the pair decide to keep the baby, and Rogen's character has to deal with being a responsible adult. "He's a self-conscious, cerebral John Belushi, constantly apologizing for his oafishness, desperate to be moral and liked," *Time* Stein wrote of Rogen's performance. Rogen himself was not worried about his first time being the lead actor. "I knew I wouldn't be really carrying the movie, which is nice," he told the A.V. Club. "I knew it was an ensemble, and [Paul] Rudd would be there, and Leslie [Mann], and all the roommates, and ultimately Katherine. I just tried to take it scene by scene. I'm not really a heavier presence in any one scene in *Knocked Up* than I was in *The 40-Year-Old Virgin*. I happen to be in more scenes than other people in the movie, but I'm not carrying it by any means."

Along with *Knocked Up*, Rogen had a much older project come to fruition in 2007. A screenplay that he had initially written with Greenberg when the pair were thirteen was given a green light for filming. The result was *Superbad*. The inspiration for the script came after Rogen and Greenberg had watched a movie together they thought was particularly awful. He and Greenberg thought they could do it better, and so, in the style of Kevin Smith's *Clerks*, which both had enjoyed, they pieced together a script. The 2007 film contains some of the jokes that were in that initial script.

To make 2008 an even bigger year for Rogen, studio executives produced *Drillbit Taylor*, a children's movie Rogen wrote, and financed *Pineapple Express*, an action comedy featuring a lot of drug humor and starring Rogen. In the film, Rogen and James Franco play marijuana addicts who cross a drug dealer. Sony Pictures was reticent about the theme, expressing concern that in one scene marijuana is sold to 12 year olds, but rather than cutting themes that Rogen felt were important to the film—particularly the drugs and violence—he cut some of the more expensive action sequences. The fact that the film could be made so inexpensively gave it the angle it needed to hit the box office. "We were developing a relationship with the studio and in any relationship there's a compromise, as my girlfriend says," Rogen is quoted as telling John Hiscock in the London *Telegraph.*

While Rogen was filming a bit part for the movie *Fanboys,* he was introduced to Kevin Smith, who was filming *Clerks II* at the same time. The pair had long admired each other's work—Rogen grew up with Smith's films as inspiration, and Smith had been impressed with Rogen's work in *The 40-Year-Old Virgin.* When Smith began writing his next film, he created the lead role for Rogen, hoping that he would accept the part. Smith pitched the concept for *Zack and Miri Make a Porno* to Rogen via e-mail, asking him if he would be interested in working on the project. According to the Zach and Miri Web site, Rogen's answer was a prompt yes. "Seth's email said, 'No bull***. When I first got to Los Angeles and an agent asked me what I wanted to do, I said that I wanted to be in a Kevin Smith movie. And that hasn't changed,'" Smith reported. "I was stoked."

Though the title of the film raised some concerns, and the film itself had to fight for an R rating, going through appeals to avoid being labeled NC-17, *Zach and Miri Make a Porno* is a romantic comedy about two down-on-their-luck best friends who decide to make a porno together to pay their rent. In the process of filming, they realize they actually have feelings for each other. The film features serious dramatic scenes as well as over-the-top comedic sex. Smith told the *Edmonton Sun* about the experience of working with Rogen. "He's a good guy," Smith said. "And he does amazing work. Seth is a really strong actor—period!—and not just a strong comedic actor. He really holds his own."

To break still further ground in Hollywood, Rogen and Goldberg penned the script for *The Green Hornet,* based on the old-time radio show hero who has also starred in numerous comic books. Rogen and Goldberg experimented with action in *Pineapple Express,* hoping that the action-comedy would prove they could write a compelling action film. Rogen told Alex Billington of *Entertainment Weekly* that the plan was to make the movie more of a regular action film, rather than delving into the hero's origin story, like many of the comic book movies that have been big blockbuster successes. But comedy would certainly remain a part of the film. "I think it's somewhere in a *True Lies*-type world almost," Rogen told MTV News, referring to the 1994 Arnold Schwarzenegger spy comedy, "with big exciting action but the relationships are all very personal, and that's where a lot of the comedy comes from." Rogen plans to star in the film as Britt Reid, the mil-

lionaire who becomes a masked crime fighter. By the time of the premiere of *Zack and Miri Make a Porno* at the end of 2008, Rogen had lost a lot of weight in preparation for the role. But despite the green light, critics expected that Sony might pull the plug on the film before it could be made, particularly because Stephen Chow, the actor/director they had hoped to bring on board to direct the film, reportedly showed very little interest. In the meantime, Rogen continued to develop other films, pitched a television program, and worked as a voice actor in several children's movies, including *Horton Hears a Who!*, *The Spiderwick Chronicles*, *Kung Fu Panda,* all in 2008, and *Monsters vs. Aliens* in 2009.

While Rogen did not offer a specific formula for the success of his films, he did offer his goals in creating a film: making something he would want to watch. Hiscock in the *Telegraph,* article, quotes him as saying, "If it makes us laugh, we consider it funny; if it entertains us we consider it entertaining," he explained. "We don't want these movies to be stupid and when I go to a movie I like it to have some story and something I am emotionally invested in."

## Sources

### Periodicals

*Daily News* (Bowling Green, KY), November 6, 2008.
*Hollywood Reporter,* November 16, 2007, p. 1.

### Online

A.V. Club, http://www.avclub.com/articles/seth-rogen,14108/ (May 31, 2007).
Bullz-eye.com, http://www.bullz-eye.com/mguide/interviews/2005/seth_rogen.htm (December 6, 2005).
*Edmonton Sun* Online, http://www.edmontonsun.com/Entertainment/Showbiz/2009/02/05/8270361-sun.html (February 12, 2009).
Internet Movie Database, http://www.imdb.com/ (February 12, 2009).
MTV Online, http://splashpage.mtv.com/2008/08/05/seth-rogen-likens-green-hornet-to-true-lies-in-tone/ (February 12, 2009).
Screenhead.com, http://www.screenhead.com/reviews/green-hornet-dead-at-sony/ (February 12, 2009).
*Telegraph* Online, http://www.telegraph.co.uk/culture/film/3558496/Seth-Rogen-Triumph-of-the-supergeek.html (February 12, 2009).

*Time*, May 17, 2007. http://www.time.com/time/magazine/article/0,9171,1622581-1,00.html (February 12, 2009).

*Us* Online, http://www.usmagazine.com/news/seth-rogen-explains-drastic-weight-loss (February 12, 2009).

zackandmiri.com, http://www.zackandmiri.com/ (February 13, 2009).

*—Alana Joli Abbott*

# Mally Roncal

## Makeup artist

**B**orn c. 1972; daughter of Rogelio (a psychiatrist) and Pilar (a gynecologist) Roncal; married Phil Bickett (an investment consultant); children: twins Pilar, Sophie. *Education:* Pre-med major.

**Addresses:** *Office*—Mally Beauty, 14 Country Ct., Monroe, NY 10950-3670.

## Career

**M**akeup artist, late 1990s; spokesperson for Sephora, Revlon, MAC, Almay, Maybelline, and Q-Tip; founded Mally Beauty, 2005.

## Sidelights

**M**akeup artist Mally Roncal's eponymous cosmetic company is somewhat unusual in that it was created entirely with the QVC television-shopping channel customer in mind. Mally Beauty was launched on the cable channel in 2005, and its Filipino-American frontperson is a regular presence and one of the top earners on the network. In Roncal's case, wrote Lisa Napoli in the *New York Times*, QVC's "live, 24/7 TV department store has been the perfect medium, allowing her girls'-night-out enthusiasm to come through in chatty, instructional demonstrations using live models."

Born in the early 1970s, Roncal is the daughter of two doctors. Her father, Rogelio, was born in the Philippines and came to the United States to supplement his medical degree with training in psychiatry

in New York City. He completed his residency in Middletown, New York, and remained in the area as a psychiatrist and substance-abuse specialist. Roncal's mother, Pilar, was a gynecologist, and had been told she would never conceive a child. Roncal was born, but when she was a toddler her mother was diagnosed with breast cancer and given just six months to live. Again, the medical professionals erred, and Roncal's mother lived another 15 years. Mother and daughter enjoyed a close-knit relationship that included overseas travel and clothes shopping. "She was living like every day was the last day of her life," Roncal said of her mother in an interview with *Philippine Daily Inquirer* journalist Carissa Villacorta. "We would go shopping, do makeup, and have lots of fun. She was my inspiration, and I became a makeup artist because I would sit in her dressing room and watch her making up her face. I was fascinated."

Roncal also grew up in Millbrook, New York, a bit further upstate. "Despite the fact that we were the only Filipino family in Millbrook," she told Didi Gluck in *Marie Claire,* "my mother taught me to embrace my ethnicity. To this day, that's my mantra: What makes you different, makes you beautiful." Roncal was so devoted to skin care that she at first considered becoming a dermatologist, but eventually quit her pre-med studies to work full-time as a makeup artist. Entirely self-taught, she began working on fashion shoots and then as a spokesperson for companies like Sephora, Revlon, MAC, Almay, Maybelline, and Q-Tip.

Roncal's breakout year was in 2000, when she began landing jobs for magazine covers and editorial spreads. She also won some prominent clients, among them Beyonce Knowles, Alicia Keys, Jennifer Lopez, Mariah Carey, and Ashlee Simpson-Wentz. Television appearances on CBS' *The Early Show* and Oprah Winfrey's top-rated daytime television show further boosted her profile. The chance to launch her own makeup line came when an industry veteran, Don Pettit, signed on as her business partner. Pettit had worked on the launch of drugstore cosmetic brand Jane while at Estée Lauder, and then founded a brand consulting firm called the Sterling Group.

Some industry professionals raised doubts about Roncal's and Pettit's decision to use the home shopping cable channel as their new brand's launch pad, but Roncal explained that they had looked at the numbers and realized it was the best way to reach the maximum amount of potential customers. "It would have been easy enough to throw our stuff into a department store," she told Napoli in the *New York Times*—although department store cosmetic counter space is an especially hard piece of retail real estate to land. "But Mally Beauty is all about showing makeup artist tricks.... It's a really great study in creative speaking, creative thinking, bringing the product alive for the customer, even though they're just watching you on TV. It's almost as good as walking into that woman's living room."

Mally Beauty debuted on QVC in March of 2005. The line of cosmetics and tools sold for $15 to $95, and sold out all 20,000 units that first day. Just a year later, the company was doing so well that it won counter space at Henri Bendel, the prestigious New York retailer. "We've connected with a great group of consumers through QVC, and we're in their living rooms with QVC," Roncal said in an interview with *WWD*'s Julie Naughton. "I'm also looking forward to being able to touch—literally—our consumers in Bendel's." She also added, "I would never have believed in my wildest dreams that we'd come this far in a year."

Roncal's namesake company remains a privately held company, so sales and revenue figures are estimates, but it was thought to have sold $5 million worth of foundation, blusher, eye shadow, eyelash curlers, and other items during its first year in business. Relentlessly enthusiastic about the makeover experience, Roncal still works the beauty counters and demonstrates on live models on QVC's *Mally Beauty* hours. She also likes to give training sessions to journalists who cover the beauty industry, like *New York Times* writer Natasha Singer, who worked with Roncal and her team during New York Fashion Week in 2006. "If you can learn to do makeup standing up for four hours in a row without a bathroom break while being manhandled by the crowds, think how easy it will be for you to do this at home," Roncal enthused to Singer.

Roncal has twin daughters, Pilar and Sophie, with her husband Phil Bickett, an investment consultant. She hopes to pass on the same pride in her appearance that her own mother instilled in her. "Not to be biased but really, Filipinas are the most beautiful women in the world," she told Villacorta in the *Philippine Daily Inquirer* interview. "There's something about a Filipina as opposed to any other ethnicity: very feminine, very delicate, and we really take pride in our appearance." In the same article, she expressed some dismay when Asian-American clients of hers ask about tricks of the trade for changing the shape of their eyes. "I believe everyone is beautiful and all of our characteristics really lend to celebrating what our nationality is and we should work with that."

## Sources

*Marie Claire*, October 2004, p. 286.
*New York*, June 12, 2006, p. 43.
*New York Times*, February 9, 2006; May 1, 2006, p. F11.
*Philippine Daily Inquirer*, June 4, 2006.
*WWD*, March 31, 2006, p. 7.

—*Carol Brennan*

# Kevin Rudd

## Prime minister of Australia

**B**orn Kevin Michael Rudd, September 21, 1957, in Nambour, Queensland, Australia; son of a farmer and a nurse; married Thérèse Rein (a company owner), 1981; children: Jessica, Nicholas, Marcus. *Education:* Studied at National Taiwan Normal University, 1980; Australian National University, B.A., 1981.

**Addresses:** *Office*—The Hon. Kevin Rudd MP, Prime Minister, P.O. Bos 6022, House of Representatives, Parliament House, Canberra, Australian Capital Territory 2600, Australia.

## Career

**W**ith the Australian Department of Foreign Affairs, 1981-88; chief of staff to the leader of the Australian Labor Party of Queensland, 1989-92; director-general, Office of Cabinet of Queensland, 1991-95; senior China consultant, KPMG Australia, 1996-98; elected to Australian Parliament from the federal seat of Griffith, Queensland, 1998; shadow minister for foreign affairs, 2001-07; shadow minister for international security and for trade, 2005-07; elected chair of the Australian Labor Party, December 2006; became prime minister of Australia, December 2007.

## Sidelights

**K**evin Rudd led his Australian Labor Party to victory at the polls in late 2007 to become the 26th prime minister of Australia. His center-left party's winning margin over its opposition—which had been in power for more than a decade—was so wide that the media instantly dubbed it a "Ruddslide," and political analysts commented that Rudd's victory marked a new era for the nation that is also the world's smallest continent. Rudd's predecessor in the job had been the target of criticism for both his cordial relationship with U.S. President George W. Bush and policies on immigration.

Rudd was born in 1957 in Nambour, Queensland, in the northeast section of the nation. Known as the Sunshine State, Queensland's coastline is adjacent to the Great Barrier Reef and is home to numerous vacation resort towns. As with Australia's five other states, the majority of Queensland's population lives along the coastline, but Rudd grew up in a small inland farming town called Eumundi, where his parents were share-farmers of a 500-acre dairy enterprise. "I had a horse," he told Julia Baird in an interview for the *Sunday Profile,* an Australian Broadcasting Corporation (ABC) program. "My job was to go and get the cattle … I don't recall wearing shoes often." Tragedy beset the family when Rudd was eleven years old and his father suffered fatal injuries in a road accident, but clung to life for six weeks. Afterward, the family was forced to give up their share on the farm, and the adolescent Rudd spent the next few years living with various relatives while his mother trained to become a nurse. For a time, he attended a harsh Roman Catholic boarding school for boys in Brisbane, Queensland's capital.

As a youngster, Rudd was fascinated by China, its history, and culture. In his teen years, he also developed an interest in the Australian Labor Party, which historically had a negligible presence in Queensland. "Television was really important because there I saw the Gough revolution happening on TV," he told Baird, referring to Gough Whitlam, the party's social-progressive leader and prime minister after 1972, "and I read *The Australian*. That just opened the outside world to me in a way which the Internet has done for another generation of Australians," he reflected. At the age of 15, Rudd joined the youth arm of the Australian Labor Party (ALP).

Rudd took a year off after finishing at Nambour State High School and moved to Sydney, Australia's largest city. He entered Australian National University in Canberra and, after a stint as a foreign student at National Taiwan Normal University, earned his first-class honours degree in Asian studies in 1981. Fluent in Mandarin, he obtained a job with Australia's Department of Foreign Affairs and Trade, married a woman he had dated since his first year at college, and moved to Stockholm, Sweden, to work at the Australian embassy there. He was also posted to Beijing, China, but in 1988 chose to enter politics because "I wanted to be able to speak out, to contribute to the national political debate and if you're a public servant or you're an advisor, you cannot," he said in the interview with Baird.

In political terms, Australia operates by a federal system in which power is divided between the six states and the federal government. Still active in the ALP, Rudd went to work for Wayne Goss, the head of the Queensland branch of the ALP, as his chief of staff. In late 1989, Goss was appointed governor of Queensland, and two years later named Rudd to serve as director-general of the Office of Cabinet for Queensland. Under the Australian federal system, governors and their cabinets enjoy broad powers in their respective states, and Rudd was able to enact significant educational reform during his four years as director-general of Goss' cabinet. Keenly interested in Australia's role in the future of the Pacific Rim, Rudd authored a groundbreaking report on education and foreign-language instruction in Queensland's schools whose suggestions were eventually adopted nationwide.

Voters in Queensland ousted Goss' ALP government in 1995, and a year later Rudd took a job with the advisory division of KPMG Australia as its se-

nior China consultant after losing his first election for a seat in the Australian House of Representatives for the Queensland district of Griffith, one of 150 federal electoral districts. He tried again two years later, and won it. The ALP was by then out of power at the national level and was the official opposition party in the bicameral Australian Parliament. The Liberal Party of Australia was the ruling party at the time, and the LPA, as it is known, was headed by a lawyer, John Howard. Despite its name, the Liberal Party functioned as Australia's center-right political voice, and Howard followed a fiscally conservative program that included welfare reform and a drastic revision of the Australian goods and services tax code. During Howard's third term, which began in 2001, there was major public opposition to the prime minister's support for U.S. President George W. Bush's planned war in Iraq as well as resistance to committing Australian troops to that effort. Howard gained some support for policies that were viewed as anti-immigrant, including a so-called "Pacific Solution" that involved the interception of illegal immigrants when they were still at sea but nearing Australia's shores, but only from the most conservative quarters of Australia's voters.

In parliament, Rudd was a vociferous critic of some of Howard's policies, especially the deployment of Australian military personnel to Iraq. In 2001, Rudd's colleagues in the ALP named him the shadow minister for foreign affairs, and four years later he became the shadow minister for international security and trade, too. In December of 2006, he ran for the party leadership post, ousting the incumbent Kim Beazley, who had served in parliament since 1980 and had held several cabinet posts. The ALP was floundering at the time, and though Rudd was considered a relative novice in federal politics, he won the post by promising to lead the party into a new era. At his first speech as ALP leader in April of 2007, he introduced himself to delegates at a party conference with the lines, "I'm Kevin. I'm from Queensland. I'm here to help," according to Tom Bentley in the *New Statesman*.

Thanks to dissatisfaction with the Howard government, the ALP was poised to take a significant lead in Australia's federal elections scheduled for November of 2007—but Rudd's bid to become prime minister was nearly derailed in August when allegations surfaced that he had once visited the upscale New York City strip club Scores. The incident took place four years earlier, when Rudd was in town with another ALP lawmaker for meetings at the United Nations, and was the final stop in an evening out hosted by Col Allan, editor of the *New York Post* and a native of Australia. In his defense,

Rudd said he had not realized what kind of establishment it was when he entered, but left immediately once he did.

A scandal averted, Rudd campaigned on several other issues that resonated more deeply with voters, such as the creation of a national broadband network and greater ties to China and other Pacific Rim powers. On November 24, 2007, Australian voters chose the ALP in record numbers: voter turnout was 94 percent—Australia has compulsory voting, which requires those over the age of 18 to be registered to vote and appear at their local polling station on election day—and nearly a quarter of voters cast their ballots for the ALP, giving it a seven-percent lead over the Liberal Party slate. It was the worst Liberal Party showing in the party's history, and Howard was only the second Australian prime minister ever to be voted out of office.

It was also a relative rarity for a politician from Queensland to lead their party to a federal election victory, and Rudd's ascension to the prime minister's office marked only the second time this had occurred in the past century. Furthermore, the oath of office he took on December 3 was the first by an Australian prime minister that made no mention of the British monarch. Australia is formally known as the Commonwealth of Australia, and in an arrangement similar to that of Canada's, the reigning British sovereign is technically the head of state, while Rudd, as prime minister, is the head of government. Britain's Queen Elizabeth II is represented in government, however, by Australia's Governor-General, who is appointed by her on the advice of the prime minister.

Rudd began his term as prime minister with a first official act that made international headlines: He signed a document called an instrument of ratification for the Kyoto Protocol, the set of international standards on carbon dioxide (greenhouse gas) emissions. Before this, Australia and the United States were the only major powers that had not yet ratified it. Two months later, he delivered a groundbreaking speech on the opening day of Australian Parliament in which he made a formal apology to Australia's aboriginal peoples for past wrongs committed by the government, especially the onetime policy of removing aboriginal children from their homes to church- or government-run boarding schools. Rudd's remarks were heralded in Australia but criticized, too, by some who felt that the government should move forward on the controversial issue of providing financial compensation to those of the "Stolen Generation." A few months later, Canada's prime minister, Stephen Harper, followed

Rudd's lead and also issued an official apology to Canada's First Nations people, concerning a similar program carried out by Canada relatively late in the twentieth century.

In making his cabinet appointments, Rudd again lived up to earlier promises to build a more progressive, tolerant Australia. Julia Gilliard, his deputy prime minister, is the first woman ever to hold the second-in-command job. The new Minister for Climate Change was Penny Wong, Australian's first Asian-born cabinet minister and the first who is openly gay. In 2008 Rudd's government announced a series of reforms that would allow for greater legal rights for same-sex partnerships. There is also talk of possible constitutional reform at a future date, with a revised document that would formally sever Australia's last remaining ties to Britain.

Rudd's wife, Thérèse Rein, runs an international company that contracts with government agencies in Australia, Britain, France, and Germany to provide job-training services for the long-term unemployed. They have three children together: Jessica is an attorney married to Albert Tse, an immigrant from Hong Kong; Nicholas is in college and majoring in law and Chinese; and Marcus is a high school student in Canberra, the federal capital.

Rudd informally adopted his wife's Anglican faith after their marriage, and in a nation where one's religious affiliation is considered a somewhat private matter and nearly a third claim no religious affiliation at all, he has made headlines for openly discussing his Christian faith and its connection to his political views. He describes it as a liberal creed that is both inclusionary and forgiving in its core tenets, and has criticized more conservative politicians who have sought to use its doctrines to pursue policies to the contrary. In 2006, he wrote an essay that appeared in the *Monthly,* a respected magazine that solicits articles from leaders in politics, society, and the arts. In discussing the future of Christianity and its role in the twenty-first century, Rudd argued that it "must always take the side of the marginalised, the vulnerable and the oppressed.... This tradition is very much alive in the prophetic literature of the Old Testament. It is also very much alive in the recorded accounts of Jesus of Nazareth: his engagement with women, gentiles, tax collectors, prostitutes and the poor—all of whom, in the political and social environment of first-century Palestine, were fully paid-up members of the 'marginalised, the vulnerable and the oppressed.'"

## Sources

### Periodicals

*Economist*, December 1, 2007, p. 54; April 26, 2008, p. 60.
*Guardian* (London, England), April 9, 2008, p. 17.
*Independent* (London, England), February 20, 2008, p. 32.
*Monthly*, October 2006.
*New Statesman*, August 20, 2007, p. 28.
*Time International* (South Pacific Edition), April 30, 2007, p. 40.
*Times* (London, England), August 20, 2007, p. 35.

### Online

"The Hon Kevin Rudd MP, Member for Griffith (Qld.)," Parliament of Australia, House of Representatives, http://www.aph.gov.au/house/members/biography.asp?id=83T (June 25, 2008).
"Kevin Rudd: Vision in the Vortex," *Sunday Profile*, Australian Broadcasting Corporation (ABC), http://www.abc.net.au/sundayprofile/stories/s1583524.htm (June 25, 2008).

*—Carol Brennan*

# Paul Rudd

## Actor

**B**orn Paul Stephen Rudd, April 6, 1969, in Passaic, NJ; married Julie Yaeger, February 23, 2003; children: Jack. *Education:* Attended the University of Kansas, late 1980s; graduated from the American Academy of Dramatic Arts—West, Los Angeles, California.

**Addresses:** *Agent*—United Talent Agency, 9560 Wilshire Blvd., Ste. 500, Beverly Hills, CA 90212. *Management*—Brillstein-Grey Entertainment, 9150 Wilshire Blvd., Ste. 350, Beverly Hills, CA 90212. *Publicist*—I/D Public Relations, 8409 Santa Monica Blvd., West Hollywood, CA 90069.

## Career

**A**ctor in films, including: *A Question of Ethics,* 1992; *Jamie's Secret,* 1992; *Clueless,* 1995; *Halloween: The Curse of Michael Myers,* 1995; *Romeo + Juliet,* 1996; *The Size of Watermelons,* 1996; *The Locusts,* 1997; *The Object of My Affection,* 1998; *Overnight Delivery,* 1998; *200 Cigarettes,* 1999; *The Cider House Rules,* 1999; *Gen-X Cops 2: Metal Mayhem,* 2000; *The Château,* 2001; *Reaching Normal,* 2001; *Wet Hot American Summer,* 2001; *House Hunting,* 2003; *The Shape of Things,* 2003; *Two Days,* 2003; *Anchorman: The Legend of Ron Burgundy,* 2004; *P.S.,* 2004; *Tennis, Anyone ...?,* 2004; *The 40-Year-Old Virgin,* 2005; *The Baxter,* 2005; *Diggers,* 2006; *Fast Track,* 2006; *Night at the Museum,* 2006; *The Oh in Ohio,* 2006; *I Could Never Be Your Woman,* 2007; *Knocked Up,* 2007; *Reno 911!: Miami,*
2007; *The Ten,* 2007; *Forgetting Sarah Marshall,* 2008; *Over Her Dead Body,* 2008; *Role Models,* 2008; *I Love You Man,* 2009; *Monsters vs. Aliens* (voice), 2009. Television appearances include: *Sisters,* 1992-95; *The Fire Next Time* (movie), 1993; *Moment of Truth: Stalking Back* (movie), 1993; *Runaway Daughters* (movie), 1994; *Wild Oats,* 1994; *Clueless,* 1996; *Twelfth Night, or What You Will* (special), 1998; *Deadline,* 2000; *The Great Gatsby* (special), 2000; *Strangers with Candy,* Comedy Central, 2000; *Bash: Latter-Day Plays* (special), 2001; *On the Edge* (movie), 2001; *Friends,* NBC, 2002-04; *Stella,* Comedy Central, 2005; *Cheap Seats: Without Ron Parker,* 2006; *Reno 911!,* Comedy Central, 2006-07; *Veronica Mars,* 2007; *Little Britain USA,* 2008. Stage appearances include: *The Last Night of Ballyhoo,* Helen Hayes Theatre, New York City, 1996; *Twelfth Night,* Lincoln Center, New York City, 1998; *bash,* Douglas Fairbanks Theatre, New York City, 1999; *Long Day's Journey into Night,* Lyric Theatre, London, 2000; *The Play What I Wrote,* Lyceum Theatre, New York City, 2003; *Three Days of Rain,* New York City, 2006; *Bloody Poetry,* Globe Theatre; *The Shape of Things,* New York and London productions. Worked as producer on films, including *The Ten,* 2007. Co-wrote screenplays, including *Role Models,* 2008. Worked as creator and executive producer of television series, including *Party Down,* 2009. Also worked as a DJ at bar mitzvahs.

# Sidelights

Actor Paul Rudd became known for his starring turns in film comedies such as 2009's *I Love You, Man* and 2008's *Role Models,* but he already had a long career working on stage, television, and film in roles both dramatic and comedic. Beginning in the early 1990s, Rudd has moved between the genres, acting in New York and London productions of such plays as *The Shape of Things* and *Long Day's Journey into Night.* On television, Rudd appeared in a few television films as well as several taped versions of plays like *Twelfth Night.* He also had regular roles in series such as *Sisters* and *Friends.* Rudd's film career has been equally diverse, from his first high-profile role in 1998's *Object of My Affection* to the 2000 Hong Kong action film *Gen-X Cops 2: Metal Mayhem.* A popular member of the group of actors who work with Judd Apatow, Rudd has come to define a certain type of comic actor in the early 21st century. In general, he told James Christopher of London's *Evening Standard,* "I just try to do roles I don't have regrets about."

Rudd was born on April 6, 1969, in Passaic, New Jersey, the son of British immigrant parents who were both Jewish. He spent his first six years in New Jersey before the family moved to Kansas. Rudd's father worked for TWA as well as a local historical tour guide, and his mother worked as a television station's sales manager. The couple raised their family in Overland Park, Kansas. As a child, Rudd said he felt a bit like an outsider as he attended Broadmoor Junior High and Shawnee Mission High School. While a senior in high school, however, Rudd was class president.

After graduating from high school in 1987, Rudd entered the University of Kansas in Lawrence. There, he studied theater but found he was not a particularly academic student. Rudd continued to train as an actor at the American Academy of Dramatic Arts—West in Los Angeles, from which he graduated. He received additional training at an intense workshop held at the British Drama Academy at Oxford University in England. The workshop was directed by famed actor Ben Kingsley and proved to be formative in Rudd's training as an actor.

Of the experience at the workshop, Rudd told Jim Beckerman of the Bergen County *Record,* "I worked on scenes from *Hamlet,* and it was mind-blowing. We started using props. He really freed us up; he said, Use whatever you want. A ladder and a shovel that just happened to be laying around became weapons. Ben Kingsley had this Evian bottle of wa-

ter that was up there because he was speaking. The bottle turned into some kind of poison. Without thinking, I started picking it up and spitting it at this other guy. It wasn't until after I finished that I said, Oh God, I just took Ben Kingsley's water. It was a little humbling."

While trying to establish himself as an actor, Rudd worked as a DJ at bar mitzvahs. In 1992, Rudd appeared in his first film, *A Question of Ethics,* under the pseudonym Kenny Chin. Rudd spent the next few years primarily working in television, appearing in television movies like 1993's *The Fire Next Time* and 1994's *Runaway Daughters.* He also had a role in a short-lived FOX situation comedy in 1994, *Wild Oats,* and a longer role as Kirby Philby in the cult NBC drama *Sisters* from 1992 to 1995.

The year *Sisters* ended its run, Rudd had roles in two films. He played Josh, the understanding stepbrother to Alicia Silverstone's more flaky teenager, in the hit 1995 comedy *Clueless.* Rudd also appeared in *Halloween: The Curse of Michael Myers.* Over the next few years, Rudd appeared in both Hollywood and independent films. He played Dave Paris, the rival to Leonardo DiCaprio's Romeo for the affections of Clare Dane's Juliet in a stylized interpretation of William Shakespeare's *Romeo + Juliet* as well as more indie fare such as *The Size of Watermelons, The Locusts,* and *Overnight Delivery.* In this time period, Rudd moved from Los Angeles to New York and worked on stage there. In 1996, he landed a supporting role in the play *The Last Night of Ballyhoo,* spending more than a year in the role.

Rudd gained more fame when he was given his first starring role in the 1998 comedy *The Object of My Affection,* the first screenplay written by award-winning playwright Wendy Wasserstein and based on the novel by Stephen McCauley. The film co-starred Jennifer Aniston, who was then a rising star because of her work on *Friends;* the movie demonstrated her ability to act in films. Rudd played George Hanson, a homosexual first-grade teacher who is dumped by his longtime boyfriend, Robert Joley, an academic played by Tim Daly. Hanson moves in with Aniston's character, Nina, and the pair became close friends and have a loving relationship in stark contrast to Nina's relationship with her boorish lawyer boyfriend, Vince (played by John Pankow). Critics raved on Rudd's work in the role, with Caren Weiner of the *New York Times* commenting "In his first starring role, Mr. Rudd ... gives a charming, humane, utterly believable performance."

By the time *Object* was in release, Rudd had returned to the stage with a role in *Twelfth Night, or What You Will.* The director of *Object* was Nicholas

Hytner, who also directed this production at New York's Lincoln Center. Rudd played Duke Orsino, and reprised the role in a PBS televised version of the play. He also appeared Off-Broadway in the production of *bash*, a group of three monologues by playwright Neil LaBute. Next was a small role as a neurotic artist in the popular independent film *200 Cigarettes* and a bigger role as a crippled soldier in the acclaimed film adaptation of the dramatic period novel *The Cider House Rules*, both released in 1999.

In the early 2000s, Rudd's career took a new turn when he took a role as an FBI agent in *Gen-X Cops 2: Metal Mayhem*, a high-profile Hong Kong action film directed by and featuring Benny Chan. While he did not receive star treatment during the production, Rudd admitted he had fun. He told Winnie Chung of Hong Kong's *South China Morning Post*, "It's been a blast." He added, "Let's see, I've been swung across a building four stories up, hung off the side of a building in a harness, performed karate kicks, and I've even gone swimming in Aberdeen harbour, which I am told is more life-threatening than any harness tricks I had to perform. It wasn't so bad, except when I was trying to sleep at night. There was a kind of night-light because the body would have a glow."

Continuing to make challenging choices, Rudd played bitter alcoholic Jamie Tyrone in a 2000 London production of the classic play by Eugene O'Neill, *Long Day's Journey into Night*. He also did work in films such as the raunchy 2001 comedy *Wet Hot American Summer*. In addition, Rudd spent two years on the hit situation comedy *Friends*. From 2002 to 2004, he played straight arrow Mike Hannigan who married one of the show's main characters, ditzy Phoebe Buffay. In 2003, Rudd re-teamed with LaBute to appear in the playwright's second film as a writer/director, *The Shape of Things*. Rudd played Adam, a college-age man who allows his girlfriend, played by Rachel Weisz, to transform him from a fashion failure to a polished male model type. Like his castmates in the film, Rudd appeared in both the original London and New York productions of the play.

While *The Shape of Things* was dark, Rudd continued to make a number of comedic films. He had a supporting sidekick roles in the hit 2005 comedies *Anchorman: The Legend of Ron Burgundy* and *The 40-Year-Old Virgin*. Rudd also appeared in 2006's *The Oh in Ohio*, an indie sex comedy. He played Jack, a high school biology teacher whose marriage to Priscilla (played by Parker Posey) is in trouble because his wife has never had an orgasm. Rudd's

Jack finds fulfillment in sex with a student. Rudd did not limit himself to film for comedy. He also appeared in five episodes of the cult Comedy Central comedy series *Reno 911!* in 2006 and 2007. In addition, Rudd returned to Broadway in a revival of *Three Days of Rain*. The production co-starred Julia Roberts and Bradley Cooper.

After roles in the 2006 drama *Diggers* and the Hollywood blockbuster family comedy *Night at the Museum*, Rudd re-united with director Judd Apatow and the team behind *The 40-Year-Old Virgin* for a supporting role in 2007's hit pregnancy comedy *Knocked Up*. In *Knocked Up*, Rudd played the put upon brother-in-law, and gained more of a public face. He told Barbara Vancheri of the *Pittsburgh Post-Gazette*, "I've noticed a difference just in the number of people who say that they've seen it. It's nice to be part of something like that, I think it really only helps in a career, but once it's kind of out, it's out, and you hope to move on to the next one."

Rudd appeared in several other films released in 2007, including a role in the *Reno 911!* feature film *Reno 911!: Miami*, the ensemble comedic look at the Ten Commandments, *The Ten*, and the Amy Heckerling-directed *I Could Never be Your Woman*. Rudd also worked as a producer on *The Ten*. The film only loosely followed the commandments, and focused more on ten short stories structured around the concepts. Rudd told the *Pittsburgh Post-Gazette's* Vancheri, "It's not a mean-spirited movie, and we're not critiquing anything really." The film ended with a musical number and an acknowledgement about love. Of this aspect, he told Vancheri, "It adds to the whole kind of silliness of it all, and it also seems like the best way that we could end the movie the same way they end the musical *Rent*."

In 2008, Rudd had another supporting role in a film produced by Apatow, *Forgetting Sarah Marshall*. That same year, Rudd co-wrote and co-starred in the comedy *Role Models*. The film focused on two representatives of an energy drink company, played by Rudd and Seann William Scott, who find their lives changed when they are forced to mentor two young boys in the Sturdy Wings program (not unlike Big Brothers-Big Sisters) after an accident on school grounds. Critics generally found the film amusing, though lacking in a consistent plot, and it was a hit globally, drawing $80 million in box-office receipts.

Rudd found more success in 2009 with the hit comedy *I Love You, Man*. As the co-star with Jason Segel, Rudd played Peter Klaven, an awkward groom-to-be who goes in search of male friendship so he can have a best man at his wedding. He eventually bonds with Segel's more loose and confident Sydney Fife. Reviewers and audiences raved about the comedy, touching on the often neglected subject of real, honest male friendships. Rudd also related to the film, telling Cary Darling in the *Fort Worth Star-Telegram*, "That's one of the things I really liked about (*I Love You, Man*) is that neither Jason's or my character are generically male. We're not macho guys in the classic sense of the word. And we are guys who kind of wear our hearts on our sleeves; for all of the silliness, it's not so far removed from people I am friends with."

Also in 2009, Rudd provided a voice for the animated comedy *Monsters vs. Aliens* and appeared in the comedy *Year One*. Of his future as an actor, he told Leah Chernikoff of the New York *Daily News*, "I just happen to have done several comedies in the last few years and I love them, I hope to continue working on them, but I want to do everything—I want to do drama, I want to go back to the theater. The jury is out on action." Rudd knows his success in 2008 and 2009 has opened up possibilities. He told Monica Hesse of the *Washington Post*, "I certainly feel like I have options and opportunities that I never had before. But I'm waiting for the other shoe to drop."

# Sources

## Periodicals

*Atlanta Journal and Constitution,* April 17, 1998, p. 11P.

*Chicago Sun Times,* November 7, 2008, p. A1.

*Daily News* (New York City), March 15, 2009, p. 10.

*Edmonton Journal* (Alberta, Canada), March 20, 2009, p. D3.

*Evening Standard* (London, England), November 9, 2000, p. 38.

*Fort Worth Star-Telegram,* March 18, 2009.

*New York Times,* April 26, 1998, sec. 2, p. 18; July 14, 2006, p. E15.

*Pittsburgh Post-Gazette,* August 31, 2007, p. E1.

*Record* (Bergen County, NJ), April 22, 1998, p. Y1.

*San Francisco Chronicle,* April 17, 1998, p. D1.

*Seattle Times,* May 9, 2003, p. H21.

*South China Morning Post* (Hong Kong), August 10, 2000, p. 5.

*Star-Ledger* (Newark, NJ), March 22, 2009, p. 1.

*USA Today,* June 25, 1999, p. 9E.

*Village Voice,* November 5, 2008.

*Washington Post,* March 19, 2009, p. C1; March 20, 2009, p. C4.

*Western Mail,* September 15, 2007, p. 25.

## Online

"Paul Rudd (I)," Internet Movie Database, http://www.imdb.com/name/nm0748620/ (April 14, 2009).

—A. Petruso

# Mary Doria Russell

Random House

## Author

**B**orn Mary Doria, August 19, 1950, in Elmhurst, IL; daughter of Richard (a county sheriff) and Louise (a nurse) Doria; married Donald Russell (a software engineer), 1970; children: Daniel. *Education:* University of Illinois, B.A., 1972; Northeastern University, Boston, Massachusetts, M.A., 1976; University of Michigan, Ph.D., 1983.

**Addresses:** *Agent*—Dystel & Goderich Literary Management, One Union Square W, Ste. 904, New York, NY 10003. *E-mail*—mary@marydoriarussell. info. *Home*—South Euclid, OH. *Web site*—http://www.marydoriarussell.net/.

## Career

**L**ecturer, Case Western Reserve University, Cleveland, OH, 1983; adjunct professor, anthropology department, Case Western Reserve University, 1986; freelancer specializing in technical writing, early 1990s; novelist, 1996—.

**Awards:** Book of the Month Club's First Fiction Award finalist, 1996, James M. Tiptree Jr. Memorial Award, 1996, British Science Fiction Association Award for best novel, 1997, Arthur C. Clarke Prize for best novel, 1998, John W. Campbell Award for best new writer in science fiction, 1998, Spectrum Classics Hall of Fame winner, 2001, Kurd Lasswitz Preis, Germany, 2001, all for *The Sparrow;* Cleveland Council for the Arts Literature Prize, 1998, American Library Association Readers Choice Award, 1999, Spectrum Classics Hall of Fame award, 2001, all for *Children of God;* named a "Woman of Influence" by *Crain's Cleveland Business,* 2000.

## Sidelights

**T**rained as a paleoanthropologist, Mary Doria Russell taught at Case Western Reserve University until her department was clipped from the budget. Unemployed, Russell turned to novel writing and published *The Sparrow* in 1996. *The Sparrow,* which fuses futuristic space travel, aliens, and a priest in spiritual crisis, quickly achieved critical and popular success. It sold 20,000 copies in hardcover and landed on book-club lists across the United States.

Buoyed by her initial success, Russell continued to write and delved into historical fiction. More than a decade after its publication, *The Sparrow* enjoyed continued sales. "*The Sparrow*'s a perennial seller. It's never been off the radar," bookstore event coordinator Judith Chandler told *Publishers Weekly.* "Mary isn't a women's writer or a men's writer; she has universal appeal. Her works are classics and they're destined to stay in print for a long time."

Russell was born in 1950 in the Chicago suburb of Elmhurst, Illinois. She grew up in Lombard, Illinois, alongside a younger brother. Her father, Richard, was a drill sergeant with the Marine Corps and later served as a county sheriff. Her mother, Louise, spent time with the U.S. Navy Nurse Corps. As a child, Russell was devoutly Catholic. In kindergarten, when asked to bring in something important from her life for show-and-tell, Russell chose a statue of the Virgin Mary. Speaking to Rose Marie Berger of *Sojourners Magazine*, Russell recalled the event, noting she told the class the statue was significant because the Virgin Mary "was the mother of God, and if it weren't for her, there'd be no God, and then there'd be no world." As Russell grew up, she began questioning her faith's teachings and in time became an atheist. Later, she converted to Judaism and has explored religion and faith in her novels.

After graduating from Lombard's Glenbard East High School, Russell earned an undergraduate degree in cultural anthropology from the University of Illinois in 1972. Next, she headed to graduate school, earning a master's degree in social anthropology from Northeastern University in 1976. After earning a doctorate in biological anthropology from the University of Michigan in 1983, Russell took a job as a lecturer at Case Western Reserve University in Cleveland, Ohio, and by 1986 was an adjunct professor in the anthropology department. She completed field work in Croatia and Australia and spent several years lecturing and writing scientific papers on subjects such as bone biology and cannibalism among Neanderthals. While her papers were important within the scientific community, they were not widely read. Since becoming a novelist, Russell has found a much larger audience for her work.

Following budget cuts that eliminated her department at Case Western, Russell found herself without a job in the early 1990s. She worked as a freelance writer for a few years, penning computer manuals. In time, she decided to write a novel. "I would read fiction and think, 'I could do better than that.' So I decided to try my hand at it," she told the *Plain Dealer*'s Donna Marchetti. "It was the first fiction I ever wrote—if you don't count grant proposals."

*The Sparrow* is set in the near future, in a world where the United States is no longer a superpower, having lost its dominance to Japan and Poland. The book's central plot involves a group of human explorers making contact with an extraterrestrial civilization on a fictional planet named Rakhat. The protagonist is a Jesuit missionary named Father Emilio Sandoz, who leads the mission to explore Rakhat and its people. Father Emilio, whose goal in life is to seek oneness with God, is accompanied by a crew with varying religious backgrounds.

Throughout the novel, Russell uses the interplay of these characters to explore faith as the characters begin questioning their own beliefs. The book also explores the nature of cross-cultural contact. In a classic case of cultural misunderstanding, the humans upset the social balance on Rakhat, which has devastating effects.

Russell became so involved in the lives of her characters that she had trouble walking away from the novel at the end of the day. "I'm sorry to say that my family suffered," she told the *Plain Dealer*'s Marchetti. "You have to take people who don't exist as seriously as you do your family. Otherwise, the book won't be a success. It's not always pleasant." To better understand Father Emilio and his intentions, Russell spent a great deal of time reading priest autobiographies.

After 18 months of work, 60 revisions, and 31 rejections, Russell landed an agent for *The Sparrow*. Speaking to James F. McCarty of the *Plain Dealer*, Russell recalled a comment from one of the nearly three dozen agents who initially rejected the manuscript: "Nobody wants to read about priests flying around in outer space." The accepting agent offered the manuscript at auction in August of 1995 and it was snatched up by Villard Books, a Random House imprint, which gave Russell a $75,000 advance. Released in 1996, *The Sparrow* won the James M. Tiptree Jr. Memorial Award for science-fiction writing and was a finalist for the Book of the Month Club's First Fiction Prize. In addition, *Entertainment Weekly* dubbed it one of the top ten books of the year.

Like most science-fiction novels, *The Sparrow* has a far-fetched plot, yet the issues Russell tackles in the storyline are pertinent and accessible to everyone. "I wanted it to work as a mystery, as a love story and an adventure," Russell told the *Plain Dealer*'s McCarty. "I wanted readers to look philosophically at the idea that you can be seduced by the notion that God is leading you and that your life has meaning, that God will remember you."

After the book was finished, Russell continued thinking about Father Emilio and how she left him bitter and heavy-hearted back on the Earth, having lost his faith. She decided to continue his story in *Children of God*, published in 1998. In this sequel, Father Emilio travels back to Rakhat and discovers that the planet is in turmoil—in part due to his prior well-intentioned meddling. Writing in *USA Today*, book critic Leslie Miller said *Children of God* covered complicated moral and spiritual questions with depth and sensitivity. "Hard-core fans of classic science fiction may be disappointed, but those seeking popular fiction with a spiritual core will once again be grateful for Russell's readable approach." *Children of God* was nominated for a Nebula Award, one of science fiction's highest honors. The movie rights for *The Sparrow* and *Children of God* were sold to film producer Addis Wechsler.

In her third novel, 2005's *A Thread of Grace,* Russell broke ties with the science fiction world, setting the story firmly on Earth and back in known time. *A Thread of Grace* explores Jewish refugees trying to survive in Northern Italy during World War II. Russell was inspired to write the book after reading *Benevolence and Betrayal: Five Italian Jewish Families Under Fascism,* a book by Alexander Stille. "I was fascinated, and I knew that had to be my next novel," Russell told the *Columbus Dispatch*'s Margaret Quamme. Russell had become increasingly interested in Italian Jews after converting to the religion in 1993. "I'm Jewish by choice and Italian by heritage," she told the *Ledger*'s Cary McMullen.

*A Thread of Grace* contains a rich fictional narrative and at the same time involves actual events from the waning days of World War II. The novel follows 14-year-old Claudette Blum as she and her father scramble over the Alps and head toward Italy, hoping to find safety from the Nazis there because Italy had recently surrendered to the Allies. Once Blum and her father arrive in Italy, they discover it is no safer for Jews than any other Axis-occupied country. A work of historical fiction, *A Thread of Grace* exposes the true story of a group of Italian citizens who harbored—and saved—thousands of Jews from the Holocaust. Russell told Quamme that the novel's title was derived from a Hebrew saying: "No matter how dark the tapestry God weaves for us, there's always a thread of grace."

True to her nature as an academician, Russell conducted meticulous research before writing the novel, studying everything from aircraft mechanics to the role of the Catholic church in 1940s Europe. *Publishers Weekly* said the novel moved swiftly, "with impressive authority, jostling dialogue, vibrant personalities and meticulous, unexpected historical detail." In keeping with the seeming random nature of Nazi executions, Russell, in choosing the fate of her characters, simply flipped a coin to see whether they would live or die.

In 2008 Russell published her fourth novel, *Dreamers of the Day,* which tells about an early 20th century Ohio spinster and schoolteacher named Agnes. The book follows Agnes through her experience of personal awakening as she sheds her simple lif and heads to Cairo, Egypt. After all of her famil members die in the Great Influenza epidemic o 1918-19, Agnes no longer feels tethered and decide to buy some stylish new clothes and trave. Throughout the novel, Russell plants real-life his torical characters who interact with Agnes. Thes include Winston Churchill, British archaeologis Gertrude Bell, and T. E. Lawrence, a British soldie most often identified as Lawrence of Arabia. Th novel looks into Bell's and Lawrence's dealings i the Middle East, foreshadowing today's volatil situation in the region.

Russell married software engineer Don Russell i 1970. Their son, Daniel, was born in Zagreb, Croatia in 1985. It was Daniel's arrival that forced Russell t begin re-examining her relationship with God. Sh had been an atheist for years but wanted more fc Daniel. "I wanted to raise my son in a solid mora and ethical framework, but I found that I couldn go back to Christianity in any of its forms," she tol *Sojourners Magazine.* Writing *The Sparrow* was par of her journey. As she worked on the book, Russe was contemplating bringing God back into her lif In the end, she converted to Judaism, though sh often identifies as an agnostic.

Over the years, Russell has worked diligently t produce her four novels. Her office is located in he 1929 colonial home, in a modest upstairs room ove looking a wooded ravine. In an interview with *S journers Magazine,* Russell described her work rou tine, saying she prefers to get an early start. Russe drinks two cups of coffee, reads two newspaper: and is up in her office with her third cup of coffe by 8 a.m., ready to work. The first thing she does answer her e-mail. For Russell, fans are not a di: traction—their letters serve as a source c encouragement. "From 9 a.m. to 1 p.m., I'm locke down and working. I edit existing material to be gin, and then try to get a little further in the story, she told *Sojourners Magazine.* Next, she has lunch walks the dogs, and often takes a nap. Then she ready to work until dinnertime.

As 2008 rolled to a close, Russell was busy with ar other novel, a murder mystery tentatively title *Eight to Five, Against.* Like her later novels, this boo is historical fiction. Set on the frontier in Dodg City, Kansas in 1878, the book explores the relatior ship between Wyatt Earp and Doc Holliday, mad famous for their participation in the infamous 188 gunfight at the O.K. Corral. Once again, Russell characters impacted her life. While working on th book, she found herself listening to Chopin an Beethoven because Holliday was a classic pianis Her preference would have been 1980s metal—he favorite bands include Def Leppard and Van Halei

Speaking to the *Tampa Tribune*'s Elaine Morgan, Russell said that she has been successful because she came to writing later in life. "You almost never see a very young, very good writer," Russell said. "Writing requires that you have something to say, not just that you can write good prose. You have to have had a life."

## Selected writings

*The Sparrow,* Villard Books, 1996.
*Children of God,* Villard Books, 1998.
*A Thread of Grace,* Random House, 2005.
*Dreamers of the Day,* Random House, 2008.

## Sources

### Periodicals

*Columbus Dispatch* (OH), February 26, 2005, p. 1E.
*Crain's Cleveland Business* (OH), September 4, 2000, p. W19.

*Daily Herald* (Arlington Heights, IL) September 26, 1996, sec. Neighbor, p. 1.
*Ledger* (Lakeland, FL), April 6, 1998, p. D1.
*Plain Dealer* (Cleveland, OH), October 13, 1996, sec. Sunday, p. 6; March 29, 1998, sec. Arts, p. 10.
*Publishers Weekly,* January 3, 2005, p. 17.
*Sojourners Magazine,* November 2008, p. 34.
*Tampa Tribune* (FL), April 4, 1998, sec. Polk, p. 2.
*USA Today,* April 16, 1998, p. 6D.
*Washington Post,* March 23, 2008, p. BW7.

### Online

"Mary Doria Russell: Bio," Mary Doria Russell Official Website, http://www.marydoriarussell.net/?page_id=3 (November 24, 2008).

*—Lisa Frick*

# Mark Rylance

*AP Images*

## Actor

**B**orn David Mark Rylance Waters, January 18, 1960, in Ashford, Kent, England; son of David and Ann (both English teachers) Waters; married Claire van Kampen, 1992; children: stepdaughter Juliet. *Education:* Graduated from Royal Academy of Dramatic Art.

**Addresses:** *Office*—Longacre Theatre, 220 West 48th St., New York, NY 10036.

## Career

**A**ctor on stage, including: *Desperado Corner*, Citizens Theatre, Glasgow, Scotland, 1981; *The Tempest*, with the Royal Shakespeare Company, 1982; *Hamlet* and *Romeo and Juliet* with the Royal Shakespeare Company, 1989; *Henry V*, Theatre for a New Audience, New York, NY, 1993; *Much Ado about Nothing*, Queens Theatre, 1993; *As You Like It*, Theatre for a New Audience, 1994; *True West*, Donmar Warehouse, 1994; *Macbeth*, Greenwich Theatre, 1995; *Live x 3*, Royal National Theatre, 2000; *Boeing, Boeing*, Comedy Theatre, 2007; *I Am Shakespeare*, United Kingdom tour, 2007; *Peer Gynt*, Guthrie Theater, Minneapolis, MN, 2008; *Boeing, Boeing*, Longacre Theater, New York, NY, 2008. Actor at Shakespeare's Globe Theatre, including: *The Two Gentlemen of Verona*, 1996; *A Chaste Maid in Cheapside*, 1997; *Henry V*, 1997; *The Merchant of Venice*, 1998; *The Honest Whore*, 1998; *Antony and Cleopatra*, 1999; *Hamlet*, 2000; *Cymbeline*, 2001, which also toured in New York, 2002; *The Golden Ass*, 2002; *Twelfth Night*, 2002, which also toured United States in 2003; *Richard II*, 2003, which also appeared on BBC 4; *Measure for Measure*, 2004, which was broadcast in 2005; *The Tempest*, 2005; and *The Storm*, 2005. Film appear-

ances include: *Wallenberg: A Hero's Story*, 1985; *The McGuffin*, 1986; *Hearts of Fire*, 1987; *Incident in Judea*, 1991; *The Grass Arena*, 1991; *Prospero's Books*, 1991; *Institute Benjamenta, or This Dream People Call Human Life*, 1995; *Angels and Insects*, 1995; *Intimacy*, 2001; *The Other Boleyn Girl*, 2008. Television appearances include: *Love Lies Bleeding*, 1993; *Loving*, 1995; *Biography*, 1995; *Leonardo*, 2003; *Richard II*, 2003; *The Government Inspector*, 2005. Artistic director, Shakespeare's Globe, London, England, 1995-2005.

**Awards:** Olivier Award, for Best Actor, *Much Ado about Nothing*, Society of London Theatre, 1994; Olivier Critics Award for *Twelfth Night*, Society of London Theatre, 2002; London Evening Standard Theatre Award for the Globe Season of *Cupid and Psyche*, London Evening Standard, 2002; Best Shakespearean Performance for *Twelfth Night*, London Critics Circle, 2003; BAFTA Award for Best Actor for *The Government Inspector*, BAFTA TV Awards, 2006; Tony Award for best actor for *Boeing, Boeing*, 2008; Drama Desk Award for best actor for *Boeing, Boeing*, 2008.

## Sidelights

**H**ailed as one of the greatest British actors of his generation, Mark Rylance has acted on stage, on television, and in films, achieving critical success in all venues. His distinction as a premiere Shakespearean performer led to his appointment as artistic director for Shakespeare's Globe Theatre in London, England, when the theater was rebuilt close to its original Elizabethan location. His roles have varied from tragic modern men, such as Jay in *Intimacy*, to leading Shakespearean men, including *Hamlet*, to some of Shakespeare's leading ladies, such as Cleopatra of *Antony and Cleopatra* and Olivia in *Twelfth Night*.

Born David Mark Rylance Waters in Ashford, Kent, England, Rylance spent many years growing up in the United States. His family moved to Connecticut in 1962, where his father taught at Choate School. The family later moved to Milwaukee, where his father taught at the University School, a private school that Rylance attended from fourth through twelfth grade. After graduating with his high school diploma from the University School in 1978, Rylance worked at the Guthrie Theater in Minneapolis, Minnesota, as a technician, then traveled to London to study theater. "I had a misconception that everything would make sense when I got back here, that people would be similar and I would feel—like a teenager does—more understood. And that wasn't true at all," Rylance is quoted as saying by Kristin Hohenadel in the *New York Times*. He graduated from the Royal Academy of Dramatic Art and began his career as an actor with the Glasgow Citizens Theatre in 1980.

By 1982, Rylance had become a member of the Royal Shakespeare Company. He was celebrated for his portrayal of Hamlet (a part he has performed more than 400 times in various productions). He took part in such performances as *Peter Pan* in 1984, in which he played the title role, and the 1987 National Theatre production of *The Wandering Jew*, on the set of which he met Claire van Kampen, whom he married. During his tenure with the Royal Shakespeare Company, Rylance began to question Shakespeare's authorship, recognizing the possibility that other writers, perhaps even a team of them, had written the plays with Shakespeare as a front. The company was uncomfortable with Rylance's ideas, and Rylance wanted the freedom to explore nontraditional ways of performing Shakespeare. He and van Kampen founded Phoebus Cart, a new theater company, in 1990. The company performed *The Tempest* on the site of the Old Globe Theater in London with no stage, under open air, in 1991.

In 1995, Rylance became the founding artistic director of Shakespeare's Globe Theatre in London. The building opened in 1997, only 200 yards from the site where Shakespeare's original theater had stood in Elizabethan times. Rylance's goal was to recreate some of the setting of Shakespeare's plays the way they would have been experienced, complete with "groundlings," or standing-room tickets. This new presentation allowed for greater audience involvement, and many directors and actors in the traditional establishment felt the Globe was too much of a spectacle and not enough a serious theater. Rylance's position meant that he was involved, both as an actor and a director, in several plays a year. His contract as director allowed ten weeks off to take on side projects, and Rylance appeared in other productions, including the controversial film *Intimacy*.

Rylance's directorship at the Globe was marked both by successes and criticism. "He has kept the contemporary relevance of Shakespeare in mind, and for several years surpassed the [Royal Shakespeare Company] at staging plays by Shakespeare's contemporaries," wrote Alastair McCaulay in the *Financial Times* of Rylance's achievements. "The general emphasis has been on the direct rapport between actors and audience, often with minimal signs of directorial concepts or even any decided house style." But McCaulay pointed out places where Rylance missed the mark as an artistic director: The Globe brought in too few big name actors, according to the critic, and tried too hard to connect with the audiences in the standing-room area, often to the point where the ticketholders of the least expensive "seats" would laugh at tragedies and comedies without distinction. In addition, Rylance faced difficulties with the board of the theater, due to his charismatic style of leadership and his willingness to question whether all of Shakespeare's plays were actually written by Shakespeare.

Despite quarrels with the board and increasingly scathing reviews from critics, who criticized more as the Globe became more popular, "the whole world" was sorry to see Rylance leave the Globe, according to Dominic Dromgoole, who took on the role of artistic director after Rylance left. Dromgoole recalled the night of Rylance's final performance at the Globe to Cynthia Zarin of the *New Yorker*. He was quoted as saying that Rylance's departure was like the fall of Rome. Mark's part of the creation myth, and that's hard to follow. It was an act of semi-religious worship. People were sobbing in the foyer."

Both during his tenure at the Globe and after he left to resume his career primarily as an actor, Rylance was involved with several "original practices" of Shakespearean productions, in which the entire cast of characters is performed by men. The costumes are built to period specifications with hand-made care, and all music is performed on period instruments. Each show ends in the traditional jig that would have closed most productions in Elizabethan theater.

Rylance pursued his inquiry into Shakespeare's authorship in his play *I Am Shakespeare*. Written by

Rylance after he left the Globe in 2005, the play features the host of an Internet chat show who interviews writers who may have been responsible for Shakespeare's plays, including Francis Bacon and Lady Mary Sidney. Taking the concept one step further, Rylance and actor Derek Jacobi presented audiences with a *Declaration of Reasonable Doubt,* offering evidence toward their claims that Shakespeare had not written all of the works that bear his name. The performed manifesto revealed others who had doubted Shakespeare's authorship, including such notables as Mark Twain, Sigmund Freud, and Charlie Chaplin. Rylance reprised the lead role during the Chichester Festival in the summer of 2007.

In addition to his Shakespearean stage work after leaving the Globe, Rylance has performed in revivals, including *Boeing, Boeing,* a comedy originally performed during the 1960s, but revived in both London and New York in 2007 and 2008. In both revivals, Rylance played the role of Robert, an innocent man who discovers while visiting a friend in Paris that his friend's love life involves three airplane stewardesses and revolves around their flight schedules. Rylance also appeared in the 2008 film *The Other Boleyn Girl,* which debuted in the number four spot at the box office. The film cast Rylance as Thomas Boleyn, the father of Anne Boleyn. "Suddenly, I've gone from being the young dude to being my father," Rylance joked with Zarin of the *New Yorker.*

## Sources

### Periodicals

*Financial Times,* May 31, 2005, p. 13.
*New Yorker,* May 5, 2008, p. 38.
*New York Times,* October 14, 2001, p. AR15.
*Star Tribune* (Minneapolis, MN), October 28, 2005, p. 8F.

### Online

Internet Movie Database, http://www.imdb.com/ (February 11, 2009).

—*Alana Joli Abbot*

# Serzh Sargsyan

*AP Images*

**President of Armenia**

**B**orn Serzh Azaty Sargsyan, June 30, 1954, in Stepanakert, Armenia; son of Azat Avetisi and Nora Vahany (Ohanian) Sargsyan; married Rita Alxandry Dadaian (a kindergarten teacher), June 8, 983; children: daughters Arush, Satenik. *Education:* Earned degree from Yerevan State University, 1979.

**Addresses:** *Office*—Office of the President of Armenia, 26 Baghramian Ave., Yerevan, Armenia.

## Career

**S**erved in the Soviet Army, 1972-74; metalworker, Electro Machinery Factory, 1975-79; held various posts with the Communist Party of Soviet Union (CPSU), 1979-91, including director of the Stepnakert City Communist Party Youth Association Committee, 1979-85, and assistant to the First Secretary of the Nagorno-Karabakh Regional Committee, 986-88; parliamentarian, Supreme Council of Nagorno-Karabakh Republic, 1988-93; elected as a deputy to the Supreme Council of Armenia, 1990; with Intourist, the Soviet state travel bureau, in Nagorno-Karabakh, 1989-91; Nagorno-Karabakh Self-Defense Forces Committee, president, 1991-93; Supreme Council of the Republic of Armenia, parliamentarian, 1991-93; minister of defense, 1993-96, and minister for national security, 1996-99, chief of staff to President Robert Kocharyan, 1999-2007; appointed prime minister of Armenia, 2007; elected president of Armenia, 2008.

## Sidelights

**S**erzh Sargsyan was sworn in as president of Armenia on April 9, 2008, after protests in the capital city of Yerevan spiraled into violent clashes between riot police and demonstrators who asserted his election had been fraudulent. A former Communist Party official and longtime political figure in this landlocked nation wedged at the crossroads of Europe, the Middle East, and Central Asia, Sargsyan and his government as of 2009 had a cordial relationship with the region's most formidable power, Russia. "Until now, Armenia has been a relatively bright example among countries that were once part of the Soviet Union," noted Sabrina Tavernise in the *New York Times.* "Its government allows more dissent than most, and journalists rarely disappear and turn up dead."

Sargsyan was born on June 30, 1954, in Stepanakert, the capital of a small enclave called Nagorno-Karabakh within one of the Soviet Union's constituent republics, Azerbaijan. Nagorno-Karabakh held the status of Autonomous Oblast in a deal struck to allow its Armenian population—who had long been at odds with their Azerbaijani neighbors—to remain in the area. Some of the long history of tension between the Azeris and the Armenians was tied to religion; the Azeri are predominantly Muslim, whereas the Armenian nation was the first in the world to formally adopt Christianity in 300 c.e. when King Tiridates III converted.

In 1971, Sargsyan entered Yerevan State University in the capital of the Armenian Soviet Socialist Republic (SSR), and then he was called up for military duty in the Soviet Army. He spent two years with the army then returned to Yerevan to take a job as a factory metalworker while earning his degree in philosophy. After he graduated in 1979, he held a variety of positions back in Stepanakert with the youth branch of the Communist Party of Soviet Union (CPSU) or with the CPSU's regional Nagorno-Karabakh Committee. After 1988, he was a parliamentarian of the Supreme Council of Nagorno-Karabakh Republic and served in the Supreme Soviet of the Armenian SSR after 1990.

Armenia became independent from the Soviet Union in 1991, but the problem of Nagorno-Karabakh remained. Armenia wanted full reunification with the enclave, but Azerbaijan claimed the territory rightfully belonged to it and that the Armenian population could resettle elsewhere. There had been armed skirmishes before, but after Armenia and Azerbaijan attained full independence from the Soviet Union, an outright war erupted in late 1991. The Armenian side was supported by Russian military aid, whereas veterans of the Soviet-Afghanistan War came to the aid of their Muslim allies in Azerbaijan.

Sargsyan served as president of the Nagorno-Karabakh Self-Defense Forces Committee from 1991 to 1993 while still serving as a parliamentarian with the Supreme Council of the Republic of Armenia. He became Armenia's new minister of defense in the government of Prime Minister Hrant Bagratyan in 1993 and minister for national security in 1996. The Nagorno-Karabakh War had essentially ended by then, with an internationally brokered ceasefire and the former oblast becoming an independent republic, but with a government that is not recognized by any other nation, including Armenia.

Armenia's first president Levon Ter-Petrossian was a classical scholar. First elected in 1991, Ter-Petrossian was forced to resign in 1998 in the wake of a corruption scandal and was succeeded by Robert Kocharyan, whose background was remarkably similar to Sargsyan's: Both were born in Stepanakert in 1954, served in the Soviet Army in the early 1970s, worked in factories before graduating from

Yerevan State University, and were active in shaping military strategy during the Nagorno-Karabakh War. Kocharyan made Sargsyan his chief of staff in 1999. The president also appoints the prime minister, and in 2007 Kocharyan gave Sargsyan this post, a move that was widely seen as his endorsement of Sargsyan in the upcoming presidential election to be held on February 19, 2008. Kocharyan was prevented from standing for another term by Armenia's constitution.

Sargsyan was the candidate of the Hayastani Hanrapetakan Kusaktsutyun (HHK), or Republican Party of Armenia. This was the first political party to be formed in Armenia as it moved into the post-Soviet era, and it is generally considered the party of the oligarchs and big business. In the election Sargsyan, "assisted by a biased media and occasional stuffing of the ballot boxes, won 53 percent of the vote," noted a report that appeared in the *Economist*. "If the election had been conducted fairly, there is a good chance he would have faced a second round and a possible defeat."

Sargsyan's main opponent was Ter-Petrossian, who took 21.5 percent of the vote as an independent candidate. It was a bitter, divisive campaign, with both sides accusing the other of corruption and double-dealing on the Nagorno-Karabakh issue. When the results of the balloting were announced, protests erupted in Yerevan in support of Ter-Petrossian and calling for a new election. The antigovernment demonstrations escalated in number but remained peaceful, and soon encampments began to form. On Saturday, March 1, government troops moved in to oust the demonstrators and secure government buildings surrounding Republic Square after weapons were allegedly found. "Obedient state television showed contrived scenes of police officers and sniffer dogs walking up to small piles of shiny grenades and handguns, nestled like Easter eggs in the grass," noted Tavernise in her *New York Times* report.

Kocharyan used his power as president to declare a 20-day state of emergency on March 1, and Ter-Petrossian was placed under house arrest. About 100 or so opposition leaders were taken into custody, but a core group of protesters fought back outside the French Embassy. Chaos erupted, with cars set aflame, buses commandeered, and stores looted. In all, eight people died—one security officer and seven civilians. When the 20 days ended on Friday, March 21, new protests were staged, flouting a hastily passed law that banned political demonstrations altogether. Again, the riot police were brought in.

Sargsyan was sworn in as president on April 9, 2008, in the Yerevan Opera House. There were fears that the political troubles that took place over the late winter and spring revealed a political instability in Armenia that might be exploited by neighboring Azerbaijan, which might move to retake Nagorno-Karabakh by force.

# Sources

## Books

*Complete Marquis Who's Who Biographies,* Marquis Who's Who LLC, 2008.

## Periodicals

*Economist,* March 8, 2008, p. 61.
*New York Times,* March 2, 2008; March 3, 2008.
*Times* (London, England), March 25, 2008, p. 37.

## Online

"Serzh Sargsyan," President of Armenia, http://www.president.am/president/biography/eng/ (January 26, 2009).

—*Carol Brennan*

# Betsy Saul

**President and co-founder
of Petfinder.com**

**B**orn Betsy Banks c. 1968; daughter of Mike (a college professor) and Joan (an author) Banks; married Jared Saul (a radiologist). *Education:* Earned degree in biology from Missouri Southern State University, 1991; earned graduate degree in forest ecology from Clemson University, c. 1996.

**Addresses:** *Home*—Palm Harbor, FL. *Office*—Petfinder.com, P.O. Box 16385, Tucson, AZ 85732.

## Career

**U**rban forester, State of New Jersey; park ranger, Wrangell-St. Elias National Park, AK; field scientist in South Carolina, Army Corps of Engineers; agriculture extension agent, Rutgers University; co-founder, Petfinder.com, 1996; president, Petfinder.com, 1996—.

**Member:** Board member, Alliance for Contraception in Cats and Dogs.

## Sidelights

**B**etsy Saul launched the Web site Petfinder.com in 1996 as a novel way to connect people with animals in need of a loving home. Within a decade, this searchable online database of potential pets had proved such a success that an estimated 25 percent of all pet adoptions in the United States were engineered via the Web site. In 2006 the site that Saul and her husband had started in their New Jersey home was acquired by Animal Planet Media Enterprises, a division of the Discovery Communications cable-television empire. "When we started, it was estimated that 16 million pets were killed a year in shelters," Saul told a crowd of supporters at Petfinder.com's tenth-anniversary party, according to *Star-Ledger* writer Joan Lowell Smith. "This year, we estimate five million, a dramatic, life-saving improvement."

Born in the late 1960s, Saul grew up in Joplin, Missouri, where her parents' property was also home to crabs, gerbils, snakes, plus the usual dogs and cats. She began volunteering at a local animal shelter at the age of 12, and went on to earn a degree in biology from her hometown's Missouri Southern State University, where her father taught in its education department. Her mother, Joan, is the author of romance novels that include *The Golden Ashtray*.

After graduating in 1991, Saul went on to Clemson University in South Carolina, where she earned a master's in forest ecology. She held a number of jobs related to her field, including park ranger in Alaska, urban forester for the state of New Jersey, and agriculture extension agent for Rutgers University in New Brunswick, New Jersey. She was working full time at Rutgers at the end of 1995 when she and her husband Jared Saul—who was a medical resident in radiology at the time but also had a fair amount of experience with computers and writing code for Web pages—decided to start an Internet site that would connect homeless cats and dogs in area shelters with potential owners.

The idea for Petfinder was based on the Sauls' idea that many people considered adopting a companion animal, but that visiting an animal shelter and being faced with dozens of adorable dogs and cats in cages, all of whom were in need of loving homes, was usually a heartbreaking experience. "I think its very traumatic to go into a shelter, look at animals and then reject them," Saul explained to Ted Sherman in the Newark, New Jersey *Star-Ledger,* one of the first press interviews she gave. "Probably more people would take that first step if they knew they didn't have to leave crying."

Saul and her husband set up Petfinder.com by contacting local animal shelters in New Jersey, and 13 of them agreed to provide daily updates. A bulletin board service (BBS) in Morristown offered to donate some server space to host the site. There had been previous pet-adoption sites in this early era of the World Wide Web, but most were run by and linked to shelters in a specific organization, or were targeted at potential pet parents looking for a certain breed of dog or cat.

Initially, Saul had some doubts about whether people would feel comfortable searching for a pet to adopt online, so she and her husband set a goal of one adoption per month as a measure of their success rate; if that failed, they would abandon the project. Saul initially wrote all the animal profiles herself with the information that the local shelters provided, putting in long hours after her day job.

After Petfinder.com went live in January of 1996, other shelters soon signed on, and it became the first Internet pet-adoption site in the United States that was statewide in scope. Petfinder was free to use, but Saul and her husband eventually landed a sponsor that helped defray some of the costs of running the site. That first advertiser was Petopia.com, an online pet store. In 1998, Petfinder began an expansion process into other states, and a year later Saul left her day job in order to concentrate full time on the site, which had proven immensely successful in matching up potential owners and pets.

Petfinder works by asking users a few basic questions about the type of animal they wish to adopt. It also requires a zip code, and then the search results provide a list of all available pets in the area that meet the user's criteria. After a decade in operation, Petfinder was such a success nationwide—and in Canada, too—that it surpassed the ten-million adoption mark in 2006. This worked out to roughly 8,300 animals adopted monthly, far beyond Saul's original modest goal.

In 2006 Petfinder became part of Discovery Communications, the parent company of the Animal Planet cable channel. The added corporate muscle provided some potentially wonderful new advances, including video capability. "A black cat may not show up that well in a photo, but with video, you can show him being part of a family and having a great personality," Saul enthused in an interview with Karen Lee Stevens for *Cat Watch* magazine. "Video is going to make all the difference in the world for these animals."

With a U.S. housing crisis that began to reach epic proportions after 2007, Saul and Petfinder rose to meet some unexpected new challenges. Because more families were facing foreclosure on their homes and moving into rental housing with no-pet policies, they were sometimes forced to hand over beloved members of their families to animal shelters. Saul became active in various new initiatives to help solve some of these issues, which she does as president of the Petfinder.com Foundation. The nonprofit foundation raises money to help out the 11,000-plus animal-welfare shelters that are members of the Petfinder adoption network and has also launched a special localized foster-care program for pets whose owners are unable to bring their companion animals with them when they are forced to move. "When things are so bad that you're losing your home, it is horrifying to think of abandoning pets, too," she told the *Star-Ledger*'s Smith. "People need to keep grounded, to have something to live for. Pets are part of the family."

## Sources

### Periodicals

*Arizona Daily Star* (Tucson, AZ), February 11, 2003, p. E3.
*Cat Watch,* October 2007, p. 6.
*Newsweek,* March 21, 2005, p. 53.
*New York Times,* September 10, 1998; June 26, 2008.
*Star-Ledger* (Newark, NJ), July 31, 1996, p. 1; November 30, 2003, p. 7; April 9, 2006, p. 6; June 18, 2006, p. 6; December 31, 2006, p. 2; June 26, 2008, p. 52.

### Online

"Board, Staff, & Advisors," Alliance for Contraception in Cats and Dogs, http://www.acc-d.org/Board%20Staff (September 19, 2008).

—*Carol Brennan*

# Sheri Schmelzer

**Entrepreneur**

Born in 1965; married Richard Schmelzer; children: three.

**Addresses:** *Office*—Crocs, Inc., 6328 Monarch Park Pl., Longmont, CO 80503.

## Career

Founder of Jibbitz, 2005; chief design officer of Jibbitz, now a division of Crocs Inc., 2005—. Previously worked as a homemaker.

## Sidelights

Sheri Schmelzer is an accidental entrepreneur. The founder and chief design officer of Jibbitz, a company that creates decorations to fill the holes in Crocs shoes, she created her invention as a craft day idea with her children. The company has since grown phenomenally, employing 42 people and selling more than six million Jibbitz pieces before the company was purchased by Crocs, Inc., in 2006.

"I think that our growth happened so quickly because we hit an untapped market. Nobody had seen anything like it before, so as soon as one or two stores started carrying it, it was like BAM—it took off," Schmelzer explained in an interview on the Ladies Who Launch Web site. When Crocs purchased the company in 2006, Jibbitz was making $2 million per month. The company sold for $10 million up front, with $10 million additional if the company earned out.

Jibbitz began one afternoon in 2005 while Schmelzer was at home with her three children. Her oldest, Lexie, brought out the sewing kit, and Schmelzer began decorating one of 12 pairs of Crocs owned by the family. Several styles of Crocs feature holes that the company says allow feet to breathe. Schmelzer saw them as an opportunity to express individuality. "I grabbed one of the Crocs, pulled some buttons, rhinestones, and fabric out of the kit, and stuck them in the holes. Lexie said, 'Mom, I love that!'" Schmelzer recounted to *Readers Digest.*

Schmelzer's husband, Rich, was a serial entrepreneur, and when he got home that evening, Schmelzer could not wait to show him her work. Rich saw her excitement and believed instantly that they had something they could market. He said that none of the decorated Crocs could leave the house until Schmelzer filed a patent. He completed the paperwork within 48 hours, and Schmelzer began her home-based business almost immediately, designing and crafting trinkets to fit in the holes. The Schmelzers took out money from their home equity line of credit and borrowed funding from a friend to launch the company. Along with contacting local businesses, Schmelzer launched a Web site to sell her decorations. She named the company Jibbitz, after her nickname "flibbertigibbet," referring to her tendency to be very chatty.

The Web site was an instant hit, and soon Schmelzer was getting orders for 200 to 250 Jibbitz a day. Creating them all herself in her basement, Schmelzer had trouble balancing her passion for her new career and her home life. Her husband was very supportive, however, reminding her to take things slowly and spend time with her children. He recommended bringing on more people, moving to an office, and sending some of the manufacturing to China. Schmelzer was resistant to giving up any of her dream to people who might not do the work as well as she could.

It was also a struggle for Schmelzer when her plan did not come together immediately. Her first design did not have the staying power required for daily wear, and customers sent back broken Jibbitz, requesting refunds. It took nine designs until the Jibbitz were sturdy enough, and would fit in any size shoe, despite the difference in hole sizes between children's Crocs and adult styles. Eventually, Schmelzer accepted that she needed more help, and the company moved to an office, which it, in turn, quickly outgrew.

Working with professional designers, customer service operators, and manufacturers in China meant that Schmelzer could keep up with demand for the charms. Maintaining a high level of customer service was very important both to her and to Rich Schmelzer, who became president of the company while Schmelzer served as chief design operator. At first, Schmelzer was leery of giving away even the customer service responsibilities. "We have an amazing crew, but it was hard at first," she confessed in *Readers Digest*. "I wanted to be around the corner listening to their calls to customers, making sure they were saying the right thing. But after doing that for about 48 hours, I had to let go."

Crocs Inc. took an interest in Jibbitz right away, seeing the company as the type of group that provides accessories to cell phones. Crocs and Jibbitz collaborated at the World Shoe Show in Las Vegas in early 2006, running adjoining booths. "They complement our brand well," Tia Mattson of Crocs said in a September 2006 article on the Rocky Mountain News Web site. "It's exciting for us to see how they've grown in response to our growth." Soon, it was more than just an exciting partnership; in October of 2006, Crocs made an offer to buy Jibbitz for $10 million up front, with an addition $10 milliion if Jibbitz earned out. The Schmelzers accepted.

Selling the business was a bittersweet moment for Schmelzer. She had always expected it as a possibility, but was unsure how the purchase would impact the decisions she made in running the company. In the end, Crocs wanted very little change. She explained on the Ladies Who Launch Web site, "They had the attitude that it's stupid to fix something that isn't broken, so they pretty much let us run our company the way we wanted to." The sale enabled Rich Schmelzer to arrange licensing deals with companies such as Marvel and Warner Brothers, featuring characters like Spider-Man and Bugs Bunny.

Despite the purchase, Schmelzer continued to run her company in much the same way. She was there at the office every day, working on ways to make Jibbitz better. She had a space in her office reserved for her children, who came in and drew ideas in her office, which Schmelzer then turns over to her illustrators to create a Jibbitz. The company has also expanded into messenger bags, belts, and cell phone cases. For Schmelzer the ongoing opportunities are a large part of what makes her job enjoyable. As she said on the Rocky Mountain News Web site, "What's fun about it is, you're never done."

## Sources

### Periodicals

*Daily Camera* (Boulder, CO), February 9, 2006; October 2, 2006.
*Denver Post*, October 5, 2006, p. C01.
*Europe Intelligence Wire*, October 3, 2006.
*FSB*, December 2006, p. 18.
*Readers Digest*, June 2008, pp. 57-59.

### Online

"Doodads Fill in the Holes—Crocs-style," Rocky Mountain News Online, http://www.rockymountainnews.com/drmn/other_business/article/0,2777,DRMN_23916_49 68782,00.html (April 21, 2009).
"Instant Company, Crocs Edition," CNN.com, http://money.cnn.com/2006/11/02/magazines/business2/crocs_side.biz2/index.htm (April 21, 2009).
"Sheri Schmelzer: Earning Millions from Crocs Decorations," Women's Home Business Web site, http://www.womenhomebusiness.com/blog/2008/07/sheri-schmelzer-earni ng-millions-from.html (April 21, 2009).
"Sheri Schmelzer," Ladies Who Launch Web site, http://www.ladieswholaunch.com/magazine/f-sheri-schmeltzer/39 (April 21, 2009).
"What Is a Jibbitz?" Entrepreneurs Journey Web site, http://www.entrepreneurs-journey.com/tag/rich-schmelzer/ (April 21, 2009).

*—Alana Joli Abbott*

# Amy Sedaris

## Actress and comedian

**B**orn March 19, 1961, in Endicott, NY; daughter of Lou (an IBM worker) and Sharon Sedaris.

**Addresses:** *Contact*—Jonathan Bluman Paradigm, 10100 Santa Monica Blvd., 25th Fl., Los Angeles, CA 90067. *Home*—New York, NY.

## Career

**A**ctress in films, including: *Commandments*, 1997; *Bad Bosses Go to Hell*, 1997; *Six Days, Seven Nights*, 1998; *Jump Tomorrow*, 2001; *Maid in Manhattan*, 2002; *The School of Rock*, 2003; *Elf*, 2003; *My Baby's Daddy*, 2004; *Strangers with Candy*, 2005; *Stay*, 2005; *Bewitched*, 2005; *Romance and Cigarettes*, 2005; *Chicken Little* (voice), 2005; *Full Grown Men*, 2006; *I Want Someone to Eat Cheese With*, 2006; *Snow Angels*, 2007; *Dedication*, 2007; *Puberty: The Movie* (voice), 2007; *Shrek the Third* (voice), 2007; *Space Buddies* (voice), 2009; *Jennifer's Body*, 2009. Actress, co-writer, and co-creator for television series, including: *Exit 57*, 1995-96; *Strangers with Candy*, 1999-2000. Television guest appearances include: *Just Shoot Me*, 2001; *Sex and the City*, 2002-2003; *Monk*, 2002-2003; *Ed*, 2004; *Law and Order: Special Victims Unit*, 2004; *My Name Is Earl*, 2006; *Andy Barker, P.I.*, 2007; *Rescue Me*, 2007; *Gym Teacher: The Movie*, 2008. Actress and co-author (with brother David Sedaris) of plays, including: *Jamboree*, 1993; *Stump the Host*, 1993; *Stitches*, 1994; *Incident at Cobbler's Knob*, 1994; *One Woman Shoe*, 1995; *The Little Frieda Mysteries*, 1997; *The Book of Liz*, 2001. Stage appearances include: *Froggy, The Country Club*, 1998-99; *The Most Fabulous Story Ever Told*, 1998-99; *Drama Department*, 2001; *Wonder of the World*, 2001-02; *Wigfield: The Can-Do Town That Just May Not* (also co-author), 2003.

**Awards:** Obie Award, for *One Woman Shoe*, 1995; Lucille Lortel Award for Outstanding Featured Actress, League of Off-Broadway Theatres and Producers, 2002.

## Sidelights

**A**ctress, playwright, comic performer, cookbook creator, cheese-ball maker and cupcake baker Amy Sedaris earned a name for herself playing quirky, fringe characters on television, on stage, and in the movies. She catapulted to cult-status fame in the late 1990s for her role as the 47-year-old ex-junkie, ex-con, ex-prostitute high school student Jerri Blank on Comedy Central's *Strangers with Candy*. During the mid-2000s, Sedaris gained notoriety for her frequent guest appearances on *Late Show with David Letterman*, where she wooed audiences with her absurd, stream-of-consciousness ramblings, funny voices, and trademark twisted-up facial expressions. On the show, Sedaris liked to discuss her cheese-ball business; her pet rabbit, Dusty; and her imaginary boyfriend.

Sedaris's ability to create so many personalities—and nail each one—has long fascinated her colleagues. "I don't think of her as a comedian because she doesn't really tell jokes," director and actor Paul Dinello told Christopher Wallenberg in the *Boston Globe*. "She inhabits her character so completely and it's such a transformation that it's like watching a magician at a children's party.... And there's no pretension about what she does. She doesn't consider herself an artist, or consider the art of what she does, although I think other people do."

The fourth of six children, Sedaris was born on March 19, 1961, in Endicott, New York, to Lou and Sharon Sedaris. While Sharon Sedaris was a Protestant, Lou Sedaris was Greek Orthodox and raised his children in the same tradition. Lou Sedaris worked for IBM. Within a few years of Sedaris' birth, he was transferred to Raleigh, North Carolina. As early as elementary school, Sedaris understood there was joy in making others laugh. "Oh, I was always a class clown," Sedaris told Steve Birmingham in the *Austin Chronicle*, "and I remember always getting into trouble in kindergarten and first grade." Sedaris, in fact, had to repeat first grade.

As Sedaris grew up, one of her favorite pastimes was putting on skits for others. With six children in the family, the Sedaris kids practically had their own theater troupe and put on countless home-scripted shows in their living room and back yard. They used wigs, props, and disguise kits. "We always did talent shows," Sedaris told Bob Langford of the *News & Observer*. Sedaris and her siblings spent entire evenings making up skits and capturing them on a tape recorder. As a child, Sedaris was obsessed with others and enjoyed perfecting impersonations of the adults around her. When Christmas or her birthday rolled around, she asked for wigs, makeup, hospital gowns, and uniforms.

For Sedaris, the entire world was a laboratory of people she could watch and imitate. In *Me Talk Pretty One Day*, David Sedaris wrote the following about his sister: "For Amy school was devoted solely to the study of her teachers. She meticulously charted the repetition of their shoes and earrings and was quick to pinpoint their mannerisms. After school, alone in her simulated classroom, she would talk like them, dress like them, and assign herself homework she would never complete." Sedaris also imitated her Girl Scout leader and other adults she found interesting. She loved hanging out at the Raleigh Country Club—not because she liked golf, but because she liked to study the people who frequented the place.

One of Sedaris' favorite pranks was to impersonate her mother. "If someone was coming over to the house and they hadn't met my mom yet, I would dress up and convince them that I was my mother," Sedaris told the *Boston Globe*. "I'd do makeup. I'd do hair. I'd do the dress. The heels. And I would convince them that I was Mrs. Sedaris. I must have been good at it because I convinced a lot of people. And I was only 14 years old."

After graduating from Sanderson High School, Sedaris stayed in Raleigh and worked as a waitress at the Red Lobster and Steak and Ale. For a period, she was employed at the local Winn-Dixie. Sedaris envisioned herself becoming a social worker or getting a job at the nearby women's prison because she liked listening to other people's problems. Sedaris also had a side business with her mother, making the Greek dish spanakopita from scratch and selling it around Raleigh. After one cooking session with her mother, Sedaris returned home to find her Greek immigrant boyfriend unconscious due to a brain aneurysm. Sedaris spent the next three years helping him through rehabilitation. Speaking to Ginia Bellafante of the *New York Times*, Sedaris said the experience taught her not to take any moment for granted. "It has left me now with the feeling that just because I'm in a rocking chair here today does not mean I'll be in a rocking chair tomorrow, because I could be crippled."

In time, Sedaris and her boyfriend separated and she began to feel stuck. Her older brother, David, encouraged her to join him in Chicago. She moved there in the mid-1980s and began taking classes with Second City, a theater and comedy troupe that focuses on improv. Sedaris' classmates at Second City included Paul Dinello, Stephen Colbert, and Chris Farley. The foursome spent two years on the road performing as part of a Second City touring troupe. They hit every state except the two Dakotas. After their tour, Sedaris became a regular on Second City's main stage. Around this time, she also started collaborating with her brother and the two wrote several comedic plays. Using the pen name "The Talent Family," they wrote 1994's *Stitches*, which tells the story of a teen—who has been disfigured in an accident with a boat propeller—who becomes a television celebrity. They also wrote the Obie Award-winning *One Woman Shoe*, a play about welfare recipients, which was staged in New York City in 1995.

In 1993, Sedaris relocated to New York City. Working with Second City pals Colbert and Dinello, whom Sedaris dated for eight years, they developed *Exit 57*, along with help from Mitch Rouse. *Exit 57* was a sketch-comedy series that featured the foursome alongside other comedians. It aired on Comedy Central in 1995 and 1996. Next, the foursome collaborated on the television series, *Strangers with Candy,* a parody of the well-liked after-school specials that were popular in the 1970s and '80s. The series aired on Comedy Central for three seasons, beginning in 1999, and quickly became a cult favorite. The show centered on Sedaris' character, Jerri Blank, a 40-something high school dropout who returns to her hometown and re-enrolls in high school, picking up where she left off some 30 years before. A former junkie, Jerri supported herself as a con artist and prostitute during her time away from her family.

Over the next several years, Sedaris picked up supporting roles on television and in films. She appeared on *Just Shoot Me* in 2001, playing a female double to David Spade's character Finch. In four episodes of *Sex and the City,* airing in 2002 and 2003, Sedaris played Sarah Jessica Parker's agent. She also appeared alongside Jack Black in 2003's *The School of Rock* and earned a role in 2005's *Bewitched.*

In the early 2000s, Sedaris, Colbert, and Dinello collaborated on a book of humor called *Wigfield: The Can-Do Town That Just May Not.* The book was published in 2003. Wigfield, a fictional Midwestern town, is a sad city filled with porn shops, strip clubs, and used auto parts stores. The book—a sort of storybook for grownups—includes photo illustrations of Sedaris, Colbert, and Dinello dressed up as various Wigfield townies. The photos were taken by famed designer Todd Oldham. In *Wigfield,* the threesome cover 22 different characters, with each persona delivering a monologue. The trio adopted the material for the stage and gave several performances while promoting the book in 2003.

In 2005, Sedaris revived her Comedy Central junkie-prostitute alter ego Jerri for a full-length feature titled *Strangers with Candy.* The film was directed by Dinello, with writing credits going to Dinello, Colbert, and Sedaris. Of all the characters Sedaris has played, Jerri remained a favorite. Getting into character required Sedaris to wear a "fat suit" to make her backside flabby. She also got to wear a full wardrobe of turtlenecks and stretch pants. Speaking to the *Boston Globe,* Sedaris described Jerri's mystique this way: "She's the queen of misfits. She's someone who's unattractive but thinks she's attractive. And I think that's why people are drawn to her." Several A-list actors appeared in the film, including Sarah Jessica Parker, Matthew Broderick, Sir Ian Holm, and Kristen Johnston. Oscar winner Philip Seymour Hoffman made a cameo appearance as a school board member. The film was made for $3 million, a small budget by Hollywood standards. The film failed, however, to garner much interest outside the show's already established fan base.

In 2006, Sedaris published *I Like You: Hospitality Under the Influence,* a book of recipes and entertainment tips. The book includes recipes for such dishes as chicken parmesan and brussels sprouts, chicken of the taverns, and Greek foods such as spanakopita and moussaka. According to Jura Koncius of the *Washington Post,* Sedaris wrote the following in the introduction: "This colorfully illustrated book … is my attempt to share with you something I take very seriously: entertaining in my home, my style. It may not be the proper way, or the most traditional, or even legal, but it works for me." In the book, Sedaris dispenses entertainment tips, urging party-givers to set up their ironing board as a bar. Sedaris also notes that coats can be hung over the bathtub on the shower rod. She suggested that marbles be placed in bathroom cabinets to catch nosy guests. The chapter on entertaining senior citizens is printed in extra-large type.

*I Like You* is peppered with photos of Sedaris and her kitchen creations. She dons kitschy 1950s aprons, Saran Wrap, and sprinkles. The pictures were taken in her wacky New York City apartment, which is furnished with pictures of mushrooms and a number of stuffed squirrels. The place is a museum of the absurd, in and of itself. One hallway is wallpapered with candy wrappers. "This is how crazy I am," Sedaris told *Paper*'s Peter Davis. "I took a bunch of wrappers and went over it with packing tape. I was bored one night. It was really hot out, and I had to make five trips to Chinatown because I never bought enough candy." Sedaris' kitchen is decorated with fake meats made out of plastic and papier-mâché. The book also includes a recipe for Sedaris' cupcakes, which she has sold in New York City at a Greenwich Village coffee shop. She also earns extra cash selling her cheese balls at New York's Gourmet Garage.

In 2008, Sedaris hooked up with Dinello again, this time for the television feature *Gym Teacher: The Movie,* which aired on Nickelodeon. Dinello directed the film; Sedaris played a wacky middle-school principal. "I just point her in a direction, wind her up, and magic happens," Dinello told Lynette Rice in *Entertainment Weekly.*

As for the future, it appeared that Sedaris might be returning to television. In late 2008, she signed a deal to write and star in her own comedy series. As usual, she called upon her writing partner Dinello for help. Once they had worked out their ideas, the duo planned to pitch their show to the networks, hoping to be picked up on cable.

# Selected writings

(With Stephen Colbert and Paul Dinello) *Wigfield: The Can-Do Town That Just May Not,* Hyperion, 2003.
*I Like You: Hospitality Under the Influence,* Grand Central, 2006.

# Sources

## Books

*Me Talk Pretty One Day,* Little, Brown, 2000.

## Periodicals

*Boston Globe,* July 5, 2006, p. E1.
*Entertainment Weekly,* June 30/July 7, 2006, p. 56; August 8, 2008, p. 16.
*Globe and Mail* (Canada), October 28, 2006, p. L8.
*News & Observer* (Raleigh, NC), August 23, 1995, p. E18.
*New York Times,* June 22, 2006, p. F1.
*Paper,* June/July 2003, p. 44.
*Washington Post,* November 23, 2006, p. H1.

## Online

"Amy Sedaris on *Strangers with Candy,*" *Austin Chronicle,* http://www.austinchronicle.com/gyrobase/Issue/story?oid=oid%3A388486 (February 13, 2009).
"Chasing Amy," *PaperMag.com,* http://www.papermag.com/?section=article&parid=317&page=1 (February 12, 2009).
"Comedian Amy Sedaris Developing TV Sitcom," Reuters, http://www.reuters.com/article/televisionNews/idUSTRE49E0AS20081015.tif (February 13, 2009).

—*Lisa Frick*

# Glen Senk

## Chief Executive Officer of Urban Outfitters

**B**orn Glen T. Senk, c. 1956. *Education:* New York University, psychology degree, late 1970s; University of Chicago, M.B.A., 1980.

**Addresses:** *Home*—Philadelphia. *Office*—Urban Outfitters, Inc., 5000 S. Broad St., Philadelphia, PA 19112-1495.

## Career

**H**eld management positions at Bloomingdale's, including managing director of Bloomingdale's By Mail, 1980s; chief executive, Habitat International Merchandise and Marketing Group, London, England, 1989-91; senior vice president and general merchandise manager, Williams-Sonoma, 1991-94; president, Anthropologie, 1994—; executive vice president, Urban Outfitters, Inc., 2002-2007; chief executive officer, Urban Outfitters, Inc., 2007—.

## Sidelights

**A**s 2008 drew to a close and retail sales slipped across the United States, Urban Outfitters Inc. bucked the trend and wrapped up the year enjoying a healthy growth in sales. As of January 31, 2009, the company saw sales increase 22 percent to $1.8 billion. The mastermind behind the company's success is CEO Glen Senk. Senk was promoted to the top spot at Urban Outfitters Inc. in 2007. Sales climbed throughout 2007 and 2008. Those who know Senk have not been surprised by his success. "I've known him for ages. He's a brilliant merchant.

He's also got his finger on talent," Bloomingdale's women's fashion executive Stephanie Solomon told the *Philadelphia Inquirer.* "And I trust his intelligence and his foresight."

Urban Outfitters Inc. is a parent company that owns several specialty retailers, including Anthropologie, Free People, and Urban Outfitters, which sell apparel items, and Terrain, a garden store. Senk joined the company in 1994 as president of Anthropologie, a high-end retailer specializing in women's casual clothing and eclectic home accessories. When Senk joined Anthropologie, it was a one-store prototype. Over the course of the next 15 years, Senk used his marketing and merchandising expertise to expand operations. By 2009, there were some 100 Anthropologie outlets across the United States, and the retailer was expanding into London.

Born in the mid-1950s, Senk lived in Brookville, New York, while growing up. An overachiever, Senk spent just four years earning two college degrees—a psychology degree from New York University and a master's degree in business administration from the University of Chicago's Booth School of Business. After earning his graduate degree in 1980, Senk went to work at Bloomingdale's, an upscale department store located in the heart of New York City. At Bloomingdale's, Senk prepared displays and adopted a hands-on management style. Instead of sitting at his desk, he spent 10 to 15 hours a week on the sales floor interacting with shoppers to try to better understand the customer base. In time, Senk was promoted to managing director of Bloomingdale's By Mail, the retailer's national fashion catalog.

From 1989 to 1991, Senk served as chief executive of the Habitat International Merchandise and Marketing Group in London, England. In 1991, he joined home-goods retailer Williams-Sonoma as a senior vice president and general merchandise manager. In 1994, Senk became president of Anthropologie. When Senk joined Anthropologie, the business consisted of a single store in Wayne, Pennsylvania. A decade later, Anthropologie was a 60-store unit, taking in $350 million annually.

Part of Anthropologie's signature is its compelling store environment. Senk considers Anthropologie more than a store; he thinks of it as a destination. Senk attends as much to store ambience as he does to securing quality products because he wants customers to feel as if they have stepped out of their lives and into a new world when they come inside. Many retailers strive to keep each store at each location exactly the same so customers know where to find things. Anthropologie takes the opposite approach: Each store is unique. The stores are designed to tell a narrative that compels customers to walk through the space. Urban Outfitters has followed suit with its stores.

Another difference that sets Anthropologie apart is the store's core philosophy. Anthropologie targets women who are 30 to 45 years old. Instead of carrying a wide assortment of products that will appeal to a variety of people, Anthropologie tries to drive sales by knowing its client base well. "Rather than be all things to all people or mastering a category, we seek to master a specific customer," Senk told WWD's Jean E. Palmieri. "We choose to slice the pie differently. We offer a broad variety of categories, but we're quite edited within each category. Every product we buy, every real estate decision we make, we do through the eyes of the customer." Senk went on to discuss that customer, saying, "She's well-traveled, well-read, she's into cooking, gardening and wine, she has a natural curiosity about the world, she's relatively fit, she gets our references whether it's a small town in Europe, a book or a movie."

Over the years, Senk has conducted focus groups and exit studies to scrutinize customer satisfaction. The stores also hold fitting parties, inviting 20 to 30 women to come in, try on designs, and offer feedback. If need be, Senk changes policies to please customers. During one survey he found that customers did not like the six-garment limit for the dressing rooms or the store policy that forbid friends from going into the dressing rooms. Customers said they preferred to take more items and take their friends in with them. Senk abolished the policy, and customers began holding "fitting parties" back in the dressing rooms. While a lot of business decisions are deliberately calculated, Senk also knows how to take risks. "We drive our business by offering fashion that is unique," Senk told the *Yale Daily News'* Alyssa Nguyen-Phuc. "We'd rather be early and wrong than become stagnant." The store offers everything from $4 bars of soap to $30,000 antiques.

Senk's longtime partner of more than 30 years, Keith Johnson, serves as a buyer for Anthropologie. He focuses not on apparel but on finding unique household products customers might like. Johnson frequents antique stores, bazaars, art shows, and flea markets in the United States, Europe, and Asia. He also searches for things the stores can use to display merchandise, picking up items such as weathered garden furniture and antique wooden cupboards. Anthropologie continually changes its store interiors to keep customers coming back. The concept works because everything in the store is for sale. If a customer likes an antique armoire being used in a display, the customer can buy it.

In his spare time, Senk enjoys horseback riding and is an accomplished equestrian who competes on the East Coast horse show circuit. Senk lives in Philadelphia but has a home in West Palm Beach, Florida, where he keeps horses. He started riding as a child and picked it back up in his 40s.

Over the years, Senk has found that the skills he uses in the equestrian world transfer to the business world, particularly the idea of "reacting." Speaking to Maria Panaritis of the *Philadelphia Inquirer*, Senk put it this way: "The best athletes don't strive for perfection. The best athletes react. I'm a competitive horseback rider. And my trainer's always telling me: 'Don't worry about being perfect. What's important is to constantly react.'"

## Sources

### Periodicals

*Philadelphia Inquirer,* January 6, 2006, p. E1; June 30, 2008, p. C1.

*W,* June 1, 2006, p. 50.

*WWD,* November 17, 2004, p. 31B.

### Online

"Corporate Officers' Biographies," Urban Outfitters, Inc., http://www.urbn.com/profile/officers_bios.jsp (February 4, 2009).

"Fashion Guru Talks Business," *Yale Daily News,* http://www.yaledailynews.com/articles/printarticle/19678 (February 5, 2009).

"Urban Outfitters Reports Holiday Sales Increase," Urban Outfitters Inc., http://phx.corporate-ir. net/phoenix.zhtml?c=115825&p=irol-newsArticle&ID=1241909&highlight= (February 4, 2009).

*—Lisa Frick*

# Richard Serra

**Sculptor**

**B**orn November 2, 1939, in San Francisco, CA; married Nancy Graves (an artist), 1964 (divorced); married Clara Weyergraf (an art historian). *Education:* University of California at Berkeley and at Santa Barbara, B.A., 1961; Yale University, B.F.A. and M.F.A., 1964.

**Addresses:** *Home*—New York and Nova Scotia, Canada. *Gallery*—Gagosian Gallery, 980 Madison Avenue, New York, NY 10075.

## Career

**W**orks have been displayed in private and public collections around the world, including the Castelli Workshop, New York, NY; the Museum of Modern Art, New York, NY; Tate Gallery, London, England; and Gagosian Gallery, New York, NY.

**Awards:** Yale Traveling Fellowship, 1964; Fulbright Scholarship, 1965; elected member, Order of Merit for Science and Art, German government, 2003.

## Sidelights

**A**merican sculptor Richard Serra is well known for his large scale art. While musicians talk about playing heavy metal, Serra actually works with it, creating such works as "Torqued Ellipses," "Charlie Brown," and the controversial "Tilted Arc." Though some of his pieces have been condemned as ugly and inaccessible, museums, including the Museum of Modern Art in New York, have created

Scott Wintrow/Getty Images Entertainment/Getty Images

space particularly to hold Serra's monumental work. Known for his bristling attitude and sharp tongue, Serra has alienated many of his colleagues, while at the same time winning their admiration for his innovation in the field.

Son of a Spanish immigrant and a Russian Jewish woman, Serra was born in San Francisco on November 2, 1939 (some sources say November 29). Early on, he was taught the value of space by his father's discipline: moving piles of sand from one part of the yard to another. His parents encouraged Serra's art, an area in which Serra did not have to compete with his older brother, who was both a talented student and athlete. Though he always enjoyed creating art, he studied English in college and continued taking art courses. During the summer, he worked in a steel mill, which impacted his choice of material as a sculptor later in life. After college, Serra had intended to go on for graduate work in English, but applied for Yale's School of Art instead and was offered a scholarship. Though he came out of Yale with the intention to paint, he wasn't sure how to approach the work. During travels in Europe on a Fullbright scholarship, he was intimidated by the work of Diego Velázquez, and felt he had to leave painting behind. "Velázquez seemed like a bigger thing to deal with," he told Calvin Tomkins of the *New Yorker.* "That sort of nailed the coffin on painting for me. When I got back to Florence, I took everything I had and dumped it in the Arno. I thought I'd better start from scratch, so I started screwing around with sticks and stones and wire and cages and live and stuffed animals."

An Italian art dealer gave Serra his first show in Rome, an exhibit that began Serra's reputation as an avant garde artist. His work in the Rome gallery featured caged animals, both stuffed and alive, one of which was a 97-pound pig. Returning to New York in 1966, Serra immersed himself in the American art scene, studying minimalism and beginning to work with scrap rubber. Three of his films debuted in 1969, the same year that his performance-sculpture, working with malleable lead, debuted at the Castelli workshop. He experimented with splashing hot lead against the wall. The show gathered a lot of attention for Serra internationally, and he began working on free-standing lead prop pieces. Initially, he was hesitant to work with steel, which later became a signature material. "Steel was such a traditional material I wasn't going near it," he told Tomkins. "Picasso, Gonzalez, Calder had all done great things with steel. But then I thought, Well, I can use steel in the way industry uses it—for weight, load bearing, stasis, friction, counterbalance. I knew something about steel, so why not?" He created "Strike" in 1971, a 24-foot-long by eight-feet-high street corner piece, the set-up for which he had to hire industrial riggers. In 1973, he received a contract to create a large outdoor sculpture in St. Louis, for which he built "Quadrilateral," a triangular shaped structure containing eight sheets of ten-foot-high steel.

Serra's style has always been provocative, which occasionally launches him into the center of controversy. His "Tilted Arc," described by Peter Carlson of *People* as "a rusted steel wall 12 feet high and 120 feet long," actually landed Serra in court, defending his work. Originally approved by the federal government in 1980 and funded by the National Endowment for the Arts, the work was installed in 1981. Placed in front of the Jacob K. Javits Federal Building in Manhattan, the sculpture blocked the passage of many federal workers, who felt it was both an eye-sore and an obstruction. In the face of criticism from people who not only did not understand his work but were requesting that it be removed, Serra appeared at a hearing to explain his vision for the piece. Many were unmoved, and a committee was formed to study the testimonies and consider the sculpture's removal. Serra was incensed. "I was told that this was a binding contract with the government, and I believed them," he told Carlson. Despite the 112 people who stood up to defend Serra's work at the hearing, versus the 58

people who spoke against it, "Tilted Arc" was slated to be removed, and Serra launched a lawsuit of $38 million against the government for breach of contract. "Tilted Arc" was eventually removed in 1989.

Despite these troubles, Serra's work continued to be featured around the world. The Museum of Modern Art in New York hosted a retrospective of his career in 1986. Serra continued to produce large-scale sculptures, including his "Weight and Measure" of 1992. Featured at the Tate Gallery in London, the sculpture consists of two large sarcophagi weighing 35 and 39 tons respectively. A Tokyo sculpture called "Wall to Wall" had to be remilled in several places to make sure that all eight steel plates, resting on a two inch base, would connect with the floor for a distance of 36 feet. He began to gain the support of a New York audience in 1997 with his "Torqued Ellipses," several pieces which were displayed at the Dia Art Foundation in Chelsea, NY. They took the shape of twisting, elliptical volumes that Serra's engineer friend Frank Gehry suspected would not stand on their own. Serra proved him wrong, and the works appealed to a wider audience than many of his previous pieces. These monumental sculptures were displayed at the Gagosian Gallery in New York, NY in 2002, weirdly echoing the twisted metal of the World Trade Center only a few blocks away. Noting that Serra had long pushed the boundaries of sculpture, doing new and innovative things, Calvin Tomkins wrote of the Gagosian exhibit in the *New Yorker*, "What amazed me and many others was how far Serra ... had moved beyond the breakout innovations of his most recent show, two years earlier. Once again, it seemed, he was carrying the art of sculpture into new areas, taking great risks and pulling them off, and there was something thrilling and deeply reassuring about that."

With the success of the "Torqued Ellipses," Serra continued to find ways to twist steel into new shapes. He experimented with spirals and bull horns, bands of rippling metal that resemble a Mobius strip, sheets marked with scars from high temperature exposure or rust. He goes to great efforts not to repeat himself. The pieces are intended to rust over time, giving them the appearance, in the long term, of something closer to a natural landscape than worked metal. Serra continues to strive with new ideas, never content to create the same pieces of work over again. "There are a lot of artists who would say that they would make as many of one kind as the market would hold," he told Julie L. Belcove of *W.* "It doesn't interest me. I mean, if I have a chance to make a new piece, why would I want to make something I've already made? Why would anybody?"

When the Museum of Modern Art finished an expansion in 2007, room was created to display Serra's large pieces, and floors in the contemporary galleries were built with the weight of Serra's sculptures in mind. "It's built for me and anybody else that comes after me," Serra told Belcove of *W*. Fellow artist Matthew Barney commented to Belcove, "I think a lot of museums are being built today with Richard in mind." In addition to a retrospective, 20 years after their first exhibit of Serra's work, the Museum of Modern Art incorporated three new works of Serra's. Others were placed in the museum's sculpture garden. To *New York* contributor Karen Rosenberg, the exhibit marked how New Yorkers had finally come to terms with Serra's art after the 1985 hearings against the "Tilted Arc." She wrote, "With this retrospective, the disconnect between the Serra loathed by the public and the Serra lauded by the art world may, finally, be history." The retrospective included some of the early lead work, allowing viewers to get a full feel for the breadth of Serra's career.

Having learned a lesson from the "Tilted Arc," Serra continues to take commissions for his outdoor sculpture work, but includes a "take-it-or-leave-it" clause in his contracts. Collecting one of his works has become something of a status symbol, and his work is displayed throughout the United States and the world, in private and public collections.

One of Serra's philosophies is to make the viewer the subject of the work. Much like the work he saw in Velásquez's paintings, his pieces seek to involve the audience, and their perception, in order to complete the work. "Serra has said that the subject of his sculpture is the viewer's experience in walking through or around it—that what he is doing is not creating static objects but shaping space," wrote Tomkins. Jane Ure-Smith wrote in the *Financial Times* of her experience looking at "Torqued Ellipse" with Serra: "He questions me: From where I stand, can I visualise the shape of parts I cannot see? Answer: No. From any point, can I get a sense of the whole sculpture? I shake my head. 'There's no Gestalt reading, right?' says Serra, in triumph." Richard Lacayo of *Time International* described his own reactions to Serra's post-"Torqued Ellipse" work: "You don't just look at or around any of them. You enter them as you would a temple and absorb them by moving through them." Peter Schjeldahl of the *New Yorker*, who advised audiences to take in the pieces with the perspective of a child in order to appreciate their scope, wrote, "Serra's mostly magnificent retrospective at the Museum of Modern Art proves that he is not only our greatest sculptor but an artist whose subject is greatness befitting our time." Despite his placement of the viewer as part of his work, Serra never expected to appeal to a wide audience, particularly after the disapproval of the masses to his "Tilted Arc." "If at the end of the last century someone had said to me, 'You have a shot at the work being able to communicate to a broad base of people,' I would have said, 'A long shot,'" Serra confessed to Richard Lacayo of *Time International*.

Once frustrated with a government that would destroy work they commissioned, Serra made a second home in Canada, where he found beauty in the light of that region. With his wife Clara, Serra divides his time between New York and Nova Scotia.

## Sources

### Periodicals

*Art in America*, January 2003, p. 134.
*Economist*, October 10, 1992, p. 108.
*Financial Times*, June 2, 2007, p. 16.
*New York*, May 28, 2007, p. 73.
*New Yorker*, August 5, 2002; June 11, 2007, p. 146.
*People*, April 1, 1985, p. 138.
*Time International* (Europe Edition), July 30, 2007, p. 51.
*W*, May 2007, p. 170.

### Online

"Biography of Richard Serra," PBS, http://www.pbs.org/art21/artists/serra/index.html (August 20, 2008).

—Alana Joli Abbott

# Amanda Seyfried

## Actress

**B**orn Amanda Michelle Seyfried, December 3, 1985, in Allentown, PA; daughter of Jack (a pharmacist) and Ann (an occupational therapist) Seyfried. *Education:* Attended Fordham University, 2003.

**Addresses:** *Office*—c/o HBO, 1100 Avenue of the Americas, New York, NY 10036.

## Career

**C**hild model; actress in films, including: *Mean Girls,* 2004; *American Gun,* 2005; *Nine Lives,* 2005; *Alpha Dog,* 2006; *Solstice,* 2007; *Mamma Mia!,* 2008; *Jennifer's Body,* 2009; *A Woman of No Importance,* 2009; *Dear John,* 2009; *Boogie Woogie,* 2009; *Chloe,* 2009. Television appearances include: *Guiding Light,* CBS; *As the World Turns,* CBS, 2000-01; *All My Children,* ABC, 2002-03; *Veronica Mars,* UPN, 2004-06; *Big Love,* HBO, 2006—.

## Sidelights

**A**manda Seyfried first gained attention for her portrayal of the dimwitted Karen in the 2004 teen comedy *Mean Girls.* The Pennsylvania native went on to earn critical acclaim in such diverse projects as the HBO drama *Big Love* and the film adaptation of the hit Broadway musical *Mamma Mia!* Despite her background as a tween and teen model, Seyfried was initially unsure if she was cut out for acting, as she told *Teen Vogue*'s Lauren Waterman. "I'd see myself on a monitor and I would be like, Eww. Who wants to see me? Who wants to listen to that voice? I had no trust in myself that I was made for this."

Seyfried was born on December 3, 1985, in Allentown, Pennsylvania, the second daughter of a pharmacist father and occupational-therapist mother. She began modeling at the age of eleven and appeared in print ads for the retail apparel chain Limited Too, along with Leighton Meester, the future star of the CW's *Gossip Girl.* The income from those jobs helped pay for private vocal lessons, which Seyfried took for several years during her teens. She made her screen debut with a small but uncredited part in the CBS daytime drama *Guiding Light,* and went on to another daytime drama on the network, *As the World Turns,* as Lucy Montgomery in 2000, but was replaced after a few weeks by another actor.

Seyfried had a better run on ABC's *All My Children* from 2002 to 2003 as Joni Stafford, the religious conservative who began dating the popular Jamie Martin character. Most of the network daytime dramas are taped in the New York City area, so Seyfried was able to commute to work while remaining a student at William Allen High School back in Allentown, from which she graduated in 2003. She entered Fordham University in New York City, but soon gave up her studies when an increasing number of film roles began to come her way. The first was *Mean Girls,* the Tina Fey-scripted comedy released in the spring of 2004. Revolving around a somewhat nasty-spirited high-school clique known as the Plastics, the film focuses on the battle between head Plastic Regina George (Rachel McAdams) and new student Cady Heron (Lindsay Lohan). Seyfried was cast as Karen, an airheaded blond; Fey played the teacher who tries to provide guidance to all of the young women. *Mean Girls* did extremely well at the box office and on DVD release and won over critics, too. "Even at its squarest, the movie's mixture of parody and therapy feels kind of ... hip," asserted David Edelstein for Slate.com.

Seyfried later said she had auditioned for the lead part that eventually went to McAdams. "I didn't look mean enough," producers told her, she recalled in an interview with *WWD*'s Elisa Lipsky-Karasz. "Then they said, 'What about Karen?' And I was like, 'OK!' I just wanted to be in a movie." Seyfried gained further attention later that year when the teen television drama *Veronica Mars* debuted on UPN. She was cast as the late Lilly Kane, the fast-living, popular daughter of a business tycoon who was Veronica's best friend. Lilly's sudden death sends Kristen Bell's titular heroine into a career as a private investigator. Seyfried appeared in flashback sequences across eleven episodes of the first two seasons of the series.

In 2005 and 2006, Seyfried had roles in the feature films *American Gun, Nine Lives,* and *Alpha Dog* before beginning work on the first season of the HBO series *Big Love*. The hour-long drama premiered in March of 2006 and attracted a steady viewership with its tale of a polygamist family living almost out in the open in a suburb of Salt Lake City, Utah. Seyfried was cast as Sarah Henrickson, the rebellious eldest daughter of Bill (Bill Paxton) and Barb (Jeanne Tripplehorn) Henrickson, who had a conventional marriage before deciding to adopt the principal of plural marriage.

Seyfried's Sarah dislikes the arrangement whereby her father alternates evenings at the homes of Barb's two "sister-wives," Nicki (Chloë Sevigny) and Margene (Ginnifer Goodwin). She expresses her unhappiness in various ways, including joining a support group for lapsed members of the Church of Jesus Christ of Latter-day Saints, also known as the Mormon Church, and entering into a sexual relationship with a twenty-something journalist she meets there. It seems unclear why her mother, Barb, agreed to the polygamist arrangement in the first place, and "It falls to her suffering teenage daughter Sarah (Amanda Seyfried) to serve as the mouthpiece for

our collective aversion to it," wrote Ginia Bellafante in the *New York Times* in a review of the third-season opener. Seyfried's character "sees the repressive double standards the way no one else around her manages to (and in a dramatic turn early on this season, she is shown to pay a stunningly unfair price for the rebellion she has mounted in the name of her clarity)."

Between filming the 12 *Big Love* episodes for each of the staggered HBO seasons, Seyfried traveled to Greece to shoot the film version of the 1999 Broadway hit musical *Mamma Mia!,* which is built around the music of Swedish pop group Abba. Meryl Streep plays her mother, a hotelier on a small Greek island. Just before her wedding, Seyfried's Sophie invites three of her mother's old boyfriends, one of whom she suspects is her biological father, to attend the ceremony. Finally, Seyfried could put to use her six years of singing lessons; she spent time in Sweden at the estate of Abba's songwriter Benny Andersson to record the tracks. "On my way to his house, I found two four-leaf clovers," she told *Cosmo Girl*'s Rachel Chang. "It was a big thing for me. My grandmother had a huge clover patch in her backyard, and I had been looking my whole life but never found one until that day."

Following *Mamma Mia!,* Seyfried lined up several more film roles. One was in the Diablo Cody-written horror movie *Jennifer's Body,* and another was the screen adaptation of the 1893 Oscar Wilde play *A Woman of No Importance.* Those two works and her turn in *Chloe,* a new project from Canadian filmmaker Atom Egoyan, were slated for 2009 release.

## Sources

### Periodicals

*Cosmo Girl*, August 2008, p. 62.
*New York Times*, January 16, 2009.
*Teen Vogue*, August 2008, p. 142.
*WWD*, October 14, 2005, p. 4.

### Online

"Female Trouble," Slate.com, http://www.slate.com/id/2099693/ (February 9, 2009).

—*Carol Brennan*

# Joan Silber

## Author and educator

**B**orn Joan Karen Silber, June 14, 1945, in Newark, NJ; daughter of Samuel Sanford (a dentist) and Dorothy (a teacher; maiden name, Arlein) Silber. *Education:* Sarah Lawrence College, B.A., 1967; New York University, M.A., 1979.

**Addresses:** *Office*—Sarah Lawrence College, 1 Mead Way, Bronxville, NY 10708-5931. *E-mail*— jsksilber@earthlink.net.

## Career

**W**orked as copy editor, Holt, Rinehart & Wilson, 1967-68; reporter, *New York Free Press,* 1968; worked as a waitress, 1968-71; worked as a sales clerk, 1971-72; assistant teacher in day care center in New York City, 1972; editor of fan magazine *Movie Stars* and *Movie Life* for Ideal Publishing, 1975; reviewer, Kirkus Service, 1976; lawyer's assistant, Warner & Gillers, 1977-78; published first book *Household Words,* 1980; legal proof reader, Women's Action Alliance, 1981; affiliated with the New York University School of Continuing Education, 1981-84; Guggenheim fellowship, 1984-85; writing faculty, Sarah Lawrence College, 1985-90, 1994—; grant, New York Foundation for the Arts, 1986; fellowship, National Endowment for the Arts, 1986; writing faculty, Warren Wilson College's M.F.A. program, 1986—; teacher, 92nd Street Y, 1987-90, 1994-99; published second novel, *In the City,* 1987; published first collection of short stories, *In My Other Life,* 2000; published fourth novel, *The Size of the World,* 2008.

**Member:** Authors Guild, Authors League of America, PEN.

**Awards:** PEN/Hemingway Award for best first novel, Ernest Hemingway Foundation, for *Household Words,* 1980; Pushcart Prize, 2000; O. Henry Prize for "The High Road," 2003; Cohen Award for best short story, *Ploughshares,* for "The High Road," 2003.

## Sidelights

**A**uthor and writing educator Joan Silber is perhaps best known for the National Book Award-nominated short story collection *Ideas of Heaven: A Ring of Short Stories.* Since she began publishing book-length fiction in 1980, she has experienced challenges in her writing career but critics have come to regard her and her work in the highest esteem. As Sherryl Connelly wrote in the New York *Daily News,* "Joan Silber … tells slight tales that resonate because her prose so effortlessly embodies the complexities of the way we live now."

She was born on June 14, 1945, in Newark, New Jersey, the daughter of Samuel and Dorothy Silber. Her father was a dentist who died when Silber was five years old while her mother was a teacher who died when Silber was in her mid-twenties. Silber's grandparents were Russian Jewish immigrants to the United States. After completing high school, Silber entered Sarah Lawrence College, where she studied writing with Jane Cooper and Grace Paley. Silber earned her bachelor of arts degree from Sarah Lawrence in 1967. Until she reached her twenties, Silber wanted to be a poet not a fiction writer, though that situation soon changed.

Upon graduating from college, Silber moved to New York City where she worked as copy editor for the publisher Holt, Rinehart & Wilson from 1967 to 1968. In 1968, she was employed as a reporter for *New York Free Press.* To support herself, Silber also took on menial jobs such as working as a waitress, sales clerk, and assistant teacher in a day care center in the late 1960s and early 1970s.

Returning to publishing in 1975, Silber was the editor of fan magazines *Movie Stars* and *Movie Life* for the New York-based Ideal Publishing. She also wrote book reviews for the Kirkus Service in 1976. Turning to law, Silber was employed as a lawyer's assistant at the New York law firm Warner & Gillers from 1977 to 1978. The following year, Silber earned her master of arts degree from New York University.

In 1980, Silber published her first novel, *Household Words,* a family drama set in the 1940s and 1950s. The story focused on Rhoda Taber, a woman easing toward middle age as she deals with the death of two loved ones and a drifting relationship with her two daughters. She won a PEN/Hemingway Award for best new novel for the book. While launching a writing career, Silber worked as legal proof reader for the Women's Action Alliance in 1981 and was affiliated with the New York University School of Continuing Education from 1981 to 1984.

A Guggenheim fellowship from 1984 to 1985 allowed Silber to focus on writing again. In 1985, she joined the writing faculty of Sarah Lawrence College, where she would remain for the better part of several decades. In 1986, Silber earned a grant from the New York Foundation for the Arts and was given a fellowship by the National Endowment for the Arts. She also began serving on the writing faculty of the Asheville, North Carolina-based Warren Wilson College and its M.F.A. program that year. In 1987, Silber started a three-year stint teaching at the 92nd Street Y. She would teach there again in the 1990s.

Also in 1987, Silber published her second novel, *In the City.* Set in New York City in the mid-1920s, the plot follows the life of young Pauline Samuels who travels from her New Jersey home—where she was raised by Russian Jewish immigrant parents—to live in New York City after graduating from high school. While she hoped to fall in with artists, her job in the garment district and attempts to live an idealized bohemian lifestyle with a Greenwich Village group result in the loss of her virtue.

Critics gave the novel positive, but ultimately mixed reviews. In the *Washington Post Book World,* Jonathan Yardley noted *"In the City* is likable for its earnest-

ness and good intentions, and for the spunkiness of the heroine, but it never gets off the ground." In the *New York Times,* Joyce Johnson commented, "Ms. Silber is at her best in the deft, elegant, wryly economical dissections of Pauline's elastic nature, and in the humor and authenticity with which she portrays the curiosity and self-protective detachment many young girls experience with sex. Yet, at least for this reader, Pauline's very coolness works somewhat against this novel; one misses the energy that comes from intensities of feeling."

After a long break from book-length publications and a focus on her teaching career at Sarah Lawrence College, Warren Wilson College, and the 92nd Street Y throughout the 1990s, Silber published her first collection of short stories, *In My Other Life,* in 2000. Many of the characters in the tales are middle-aged people burdened with a past, often defined by their lives in the late 1970s and early 1980s, but barely surviving the effect of that economic crash. Writing in the *Philadelphia Inquirer,* Rita Giordano praised, "These stories are not melodramas or morality plays. Nor are they flip little nods to life in the fast lane. Silber ... writes with wisdom and a certain restraint about lives of former excess."

The following year, 2001, Silber published her third novel, *Lucky Us.* Unlike her previous novels, this one is set in contemporary times in New York City. It focuses on an ordinary couple, Gabe and Elisa, who meet and begin a romantic relationship, but face challenges along the way including Elisa being diagnosed HIV positive. The chapters move back and forth between their voices, and critics like Dana Kennedy of the *New York Times* called it "an unexpectedly powerful book."

Returning to short stories for her next book, Silber spent three years writing 2004's *Ideas of Heaven: A Ring of Stories.* She was a finalist for the 2004 National Book Award for the collection as well as a finalist for the first Story Prize from the Chisholm Foundation. The disparate first-person tales were carefully, but subtly, woven together, despite spanning centuries and locations. All also focused on the pain of unrequited love and related loss as well as the idea of passion. Critics praised both her writing and the way she constructed *Ideas in Heaven.* For example, Debra Bruno of the *Washington Times* commented, "Miss Silber ... is a lyrical writer. Like William Trevor's writing and Alice Munro's, her prose embraces both particularity and grandeur."

In 2008, Silber published her fourth novel, *The Size of the World.* As with her previous works, she deftly explored a theme in an unusually constructed book.

The novel was constructed as a series of linked short stories, which explored the often hard-to-find link between happiness and place. Each of the six stories features a different first-person narrator living in various places and eras in the twentieth century including Vietnam, Mexico, and Italy during the rule of Benito Mussolini. The novel was nominated for a 2008 Robert Kirsch Award from the *Los Angeles Times.*

Reviewing the novel for the *Washington Post,* Howard Norman noted, "In *The Size of the World* she has succeeded in creating a fictional world that is as far from cozy and adorable as can be. What's more, she is unwavering in her sympathies toward her characters, no matter how they've handled their lives. An hour after finishing *The Size of the World,* I was homesick for them." Similarly, Sherrie Flick of the *Pittsburgh Post-Gazette* praised, "Silber's concise language, inventive dialogue, and far-reaching plot take on the world, and careful readers will see their place in it anew."

As she continued to teach and write well-crafted fiction, Silber admitted food was important to her as a distraction from writing. She told Sarah Adair Frank of *Otium,* "I'm happily fixated on food—my idea of escape reading is to flip through *Gourmet Magazine* or a cookbook, though I don't actually want to bother to make most of the food. A classic way of stalling after lunch, before I write, would be to eat an apple, a cookie, and a piece of chocolate—you can see the escalation in that sequence. A friend, Michael Martone, is collecting a book of essays on rubrics writers live by, and mine was, 'Eat first.'"

## Selected writings

### Novels

*Household Words,* Viking (New York City); 1980, reprinted W.W. Norton (New York City), 2005.
*In the City,* Viking, 1987.

*Lucky Us,* Algonquin (Chapel Hill, NC), 2001.
*The Size of the World,* W.W. Norton, 2008.

### Short Story Collections

*In My Other Life,* Sarabande (Louisville, KY), 2000.
*Ideas of Heaven: A Ring of Stories,* W.W. Norton, 2004.

## Sources

### Books

*Complete Marquis Who's Who Biographies,* Marquis Who's Who LLC, 2009.

### Periodicals

*Christian Science Monitor,* October 26, 2004, p. 16.
*Daily News* (New York City), December 2, 2001, p. 17.
*Los Angeles Times,* March 3, 2009, p. D3.
*New York Times,* March 29, 1987, sec. 7, p. 8; October 28, 2001, sec. 7, p. 22; November 14, 2004, sec. 14CN, p. 9; December 3, 2004, p. E4; July 13, 2008, p. BR9.
*Philadelphia Inquirer,* September 14, 2000.
*Pittsburgh Post-Gazette,* July 20, 2008, p. E5.
*San Diego Union-Tribune Books,* November 6, 2005, p. 7.
*Seattle Times,* June 22, 2008, p. I4.
*Washington Post Book World,* March 18, 1987, p. C2; July 20, 2008, p. BW7.
*Washington Times,* May 16, 2004, p. B7.

### Online

"A Conversation with Joan Silber," *Otium,* http://otium.uchicago.edu/articles/silber_q+a.html (April 25, 2009).
*Contemporary Authors Online,* Thomson Gale, 2006.
"Joan Silber and Scott Withiam, Cohen Awards," *Ploughshares,* http://www.pshares.org/issues/article.cfm?prmarticleid=7755 (April 25, 2009).

—A. Petruso

# Ashlee Simpson-Wentz

## Singer and actress

**B**orn Ashlee Nicole Simpson, October 3, 1984, in Waco, TX; daughter of Joe (a minister and manager) and Tina Simpson; married Pete Wentz (a musician), May 17, 2008.

**Addresses:** *Contact*—Wilhelmina Artist Management, 7257 Beverly Blvd., 2nd Fl., Los Angeles, CA 90036.

## Career

**B**egan career as an actress, c. 1993; appeared as dancer and backup singer on sister Jessica Simpson's tours, c. 1999-2001; resumed acting career, 2001; cast in role on *7th Heaven,* 2002; launched singing career, 2004; released first album, *Autobiography,* 2004; had notorious appearance on *Saturday Night Live,* 2004; released second album, *I Am Me,* 2005; signed endorsement deal with Sketchers, 2006; released third album, *Bittersweet World,* 2008. Television appearances include: *Saved by the Bell: The New Class,* 1993; *Malcolm in the Middle,* 2001; *7th Heaven,* 2002-04; *Newlyweds: Nick & Jessica,* 2003-05; *The Ashlee Simpson Show,* 2004-05. Film appearances include: *The Hot Chick,* 2002; *Raise Your Voice,* 2004; *Undiscovered,* 2005. Stage appearances include: *Chicago,* London, England, 2006.

**Awards:** Female New Artist of the Year Award, *Billboard,* 2004; Fresh Face award, Teen Choice Awards, 2004; Song of the Summer, Teen Choice Awards, for "Pieces of Me," 2004.

Soul Brother/FilmMagic/Getty Images

## Sidelights

**W**ith a pop/rock sound inspired by Janis Joplin, Chrissie Hynde, and Pat Benatar, singer Ashlee Simpson-Wentz had a number-one debut album, *Autobiography* in 2004. Though she had solid singing and acting credentials, Simpson-Wentz spent the early part of her career in the shadow of her older sister, the singer/reality television star Jessica Simpson. Ashlee Simpson-Wentz came into her own over three distinct albums, a regular role on *Seventh Heaven,* and marriage and a pregnancy with fellow musician Pete Wentz.

Born on October 3, 1984, in Waco, Texas, Simpson-Wentz is the daughter of Joe and Tina Simpson. Her father was a minister who later managed his daughters' careers, while her mother raised their family. Simpson-Wentz began dance lessons at the age of three and soon took ballet seriously. She also began an acting career with a guest spot on *Saved by the Bell: The New Class* in 1993.

By the age of eleven, Simpson-Wentz was studying at the School of American Ballet in New York City. She was the youngest person ever admitted to the school. As her older sister's career took off, Simpson-Wentz left the ballet school, moved to Los Angeles with her family, and began dancing on her sister's tours at the age of 14. Simpson-Wentz completed her high school education by being home schooled by her mother. She continued working on her sister's tours and occasionally appeared in commercials until 2001, when she focused exclusively on her own creative pursuits.

Simpson-Wentz resumed television acting in 2001 with a guest appearance on an episode of *Malcolm in the Middle.* In 2002, she appeared in the comedy film *The Hot Chick,* which starred Rob Schneider. Also in 2002, Simpson-Wentz began a two-year stint on the long-running family drama *7th Heaven,* playing Cecilia Smith.

During her time on *7th Heaven,* Simpson-Wentz had a role in the film *Raise Your Voice,* released in 2004. She also appeared in episodes of her sister's reality show on MTV, *Newlyweds: Nick & Jessica,* in 2003, 2004, and 2005. In addition, Simpson-Wentz launched a singing career, first by including a song on the *Freaky Friday* soundtrack, then signing a deal with Geffen Records. She released her full-length debut, *Autobiography,* in the summer of 2004, and the album reached number one on the *Billboard* charts during its first week of release with 398,000 copies sold.

*Autobiography* went on to sell more than a million copies its first month. It was eventually certified platinum, and ultimately sold more than four million copies. She told Jane Stevenson of the *Toronto Sun,* "I had no clue that my album would do that. Everything was so shocking. But it was extremely exciting. Let me tell ya, I was dancing around the room."

The album also produced a hit single, "Pieces of Me," which Simpson-Wentz co-wrote. Another song written by her, "Shadow," was about her position as the younger sister of a pop star. Of the latter song, Simpson-Wentz explained to *USA Today*'s Cesar G. Soriano, "I don't feel like I'm in (Jessica's) shadow any more. We're actually like the closest we've ever been now. I feel like that song is sort of thanking her for helping me find my identity."

While sales were high for *Autobiography,* critics were somewhat dismissive of the album. In the *New York Times,* Jon Pareles wrote, "The album is a thoroughly calculated package, aiming for the same audience that embraces Avril Lavigne and Pink." He added that "*Autobiography* presents Ms. Simpson as a rock

songwriter who is just defiant enough." But Pareles concluded, "Although Ms. Simpson's public image is nearly as much a pop concoction as her sister's is, at least there is a little grit in the recipe."

Because of the success of her singing career, Simpson-Wentz left *7th Heaven* in 2004 to focus on it. She told the *Chattanooga Times Free Press* in June of 2004, "I'm going to do a few episodes to end the character. I know—sad news.... I love the show. It really is such a great show. But with my going on tour and all that stuff, I just can't go on with it."

Simpson-Wentz did not leave television behind entirely, however. To promote *Autobiography,* she launched her own reality series on MTV, *The Ashlee Simpson Show* in June of 2004. The show aired for two seasons in 2004 and 2005. The first season focused on the young singer in her everyday life as she recorded her debut album and launched her music career with the intent of clearly separating her identity from her then much-more-famous sibling. The first episodes of the *The Ashlee Simpson Show* attracted 3.4 million viewers, making it a clear hit for the network.

In October of 2004, Simpson-Wentz had a notorious appearance on *Saturday Night Live.* Because of a voice allegedly weakened due to severe acid reflux, she and her band used a backing track with prerecorded vocals to support her on what was supposed to be a live appearance. Because of an error, the tape for "Pieces of Me" was played instead of the song that should have been starting, "Autobiography." The still raw performer backed off stage while her band played along with the tape until the show cut to commercial. A media frenzy was born.

Simpson-Wentz apologized before the end of the show but did not let the controversy over her use of backing tapes and the way she exited ungracefully bother her. She told Jeffrey Hahne of the Greensboro *News & Record,* "I learned that as far as the whole situation goes, things happen. There are a lot of worse things out there that happen to people and I, if anything, learned about character and I learned about myself and just about keeping your head up, putting your shoulders back, and moving forward." While Simpson-Wentz was able to move past the incident, she was later booed during an appearance at the 2005 Orange Bowl half-time show.

The controversy did not stop Simpson-Wentz from headlining a tour in support of *Autobiography* beginning in February 2005. Later that year, Simpson-

Wentz released her second album, *I Am Me*. Like her first album, *I Am Me* was intended to show Simpson-Wentz as a common girl dealing with everyday problems and trials. Many of the tracks had a confessional quality to them. She told the New York *Daily News*'s Rebecca Louie, "I tried to write exactly about what I was feeling and going through. I am really honest with my fans. I'm human." The fans responded by making *I Am Me* the number one album on *Billboard*'s album chart in its first month of release.

Several songs on *I Am Me* were inspired by the 2004 incident on *Saturday Night Live* and the growth she felt in her aftermath, like the title track, "Catch Me When I Fall," and "Beautifully Broken." Simpson-Wentz even made another appearance to *Saturday Night Live* in October of 2005, where she performed two songs from her new album, including "I Am Me." Simpson-Wentz was confident in her performance and received many compliments on her triumphant return.

Yet the ponderous *I Am Me* did not sell as well as *Autobiography*, and Simpson-Wentz collapsed from exhaustion while performing in Japan on the tour for the album. Still, she pressed forward and even returned to acting again. In 2005, her third film was released, the independent feature *Undiscovered*. In the film, she played Clea. In 2006, Simpson-Wentz appeared as Roxy in a London stage production of the musical *Chicago*.

Simpson-Wentz's performance in *Chicago* was acclaimed by critics and Simpson-Wentz told *Cosmo-GIRL* that her experiences with the show boosted her confidence. She explained to the magazine, "Working on *Chicago* helped me come into my own. We did ten-hour-a-day rehearsals, eight shows a week." She added, "After I did that role I felt like I'd accomplished something.... It taught me to be more comfortable with myself." Simpson-Wentz expanded her business ventures by signing a global endorsement deal with the footwear company Sketchers that year as well.

In 2006, Simpson-Wentz attracted more media attention when it appeared that she had plastic surgery. Before the surgery, she had a distinctive bump on her nose. In May 2006, the bump seemed to have disappeared. Simpson-Wentz did not confirm or deny that she had surgery, and continued to tour the world in support of *I Am Me*. Despite overall poor sales, Simpson-Wentz was happy how the album and tour reflected her growth. She told Nekesa Mumbi Mood of the Associated Press, "I

wanted to start trying new things, and try different kind of styles as well. This album I got to do that, and it's so great to perform that live because there's diversity, and I get to dance around and also there's another side to me that has dealt with breakups and whatnots, and I get to kind of let that all out."

After taking much of 2007 off, Simpson-Wentz began writing and recording her third album. Released in early 2008, *Bittersweet World* showed her fun side with a more dance-pop oriented sound. Such talents as Timbaland, the Neptunes' Chad Hugo, and Kenna worked with Simpson-Wentz to craft a sound that moved away from her more rock/pop-oriented roots on most tracks. While critics were generally dismissive of the record, Jim Farber of the New York *Daily News* pointed out that "There's still no denying that Ashlee Simpson has found her cover-girl face—and cleverly manipulated voice—attached to some of the most youthful and pleasing teen pop of this decade."

Patrick Ferrucci of the *New Haven Register* added, "*Bittersweet World* is her most solid disc yet, a record that's way better than anything her sister has released, which isn't saying much. What makes this album stand out over her previous records is that while the two CDs in her discography try oh so hard to make Simpson feel like an artist, *Bittersweet* is fluff and it doesn't care. And that works because Ashlee's all fluff and she doesn't care."

Shortly before *Bittersweet World* was released, Simpson-Wentz married Pete Wentz, the bass player for the band Fall Out Boy. The couple had been friends for years and began dating in late 2006. After the May of 2008 wedding, she became Ashlee Simpson-Wentz professionally and formally announced that she and her new husband were expecting a baby in November of 2008. Simpson-Wentz then declined to tour in support of the record before the birth of her child.

No matter what happened in her personal or professional life, Simpson-Wentz was not about to let what was said about her affect how she looked at herself. She told Claire Connors of *Shape* in June 2008, "I've had a lot of ups and downs in my life, but I'm learning not to sweat the small stuff. This last year has been about finding strength within myself—not looking to others for it." Simpson-Wentz later added, "I'm happy and definitely more confident than I've ever been before."

## Selected discography

(Contributor) *Freaky Friday Original Soundtrack*, Buena Vista, 2003.
*Autobiography*, Geffen, 2004.

*I Am Me*, Geffen, 2005.
*Bittersweet World*, Geffen, 2008.

# Sources

### Books

*Complete Marquis Who's Who Biographies*, Marquis Who's Who, 2008.

### Periodicals

*Albany Times Union* (Albany, NY), May 29, 2008, p. A2.
Associated Press, May 10, 2006; May 26, 2006.
*Chattanooga Times Free Press* (TN), June 14, 2004, p. D4.
*Chicago Sun-Times*, July 29, 2004, p. 48; April 17, 2008, p. 40.
*CosmoGIRL!*, December 1, 2007, p. 104.
*Daily News* (New York, NY), October 25, 2004, p. 5; October 16, 2005, p. 18; April 22, 2008, p. 35.
*Houston Chronicle*, August 17, 2004, p. 3.
*Los Angeles Times*, April 22, 2008, p. E4.

*New Haven Register* (CT), April 25, 2008.
*New Musical Express*, June 2, 2008.
*News & Record* (Greensboro, NC), March 29, 2005, p. D1.
*New York Post*, October 26, 2004, p. 17.
*New York Times*, July 26, 2004, p. E4; August 1, 2004, sec. 2, p. 23.
*Palm Beach Post* (FL), May 5, 2006, p. 7; May 6, 2006, p. 1D.
*Portland Press Herald* (ME), November 3, 2005, p. D12.
*Shape*, June 2008, p. 52.
*Sunday Telegram* (MA), August 8, 2004, p. G5.
*Toronto Sun*, August 11, 2004, p. 3.
*USA Today*, June 16, 2004, p. 3D.
*WWD*, July 19, 2006, p. 2.
Zaptoit, May 19, 2008; May 29, 2008.

### Online

"Ashlee Simpson-Wentz," Internet Movie Database, http://www.imdb.com/name/nm1249883/ (August 17, 2008).

*—A. Petruso*

# Lanty Smith

## Chairman of Wachovia

**B**orn Lanty L. Smith, December 11, 1942, in Sherrodsville, OH; married Margaret Hays Chandler; children: three. *Education:* Wittenberg University, Springfield, Ohio, B.A.; Duke University, law degree.

**Addresses:** *Office*—Wachovia Corporation, 301 S. College St., Ste. 4000, Charlotte, NC 28288-0013.

## Career

Partner, Jones, Day, Reavis, & Pogue law firm, Cleveland, OH; executive vice-president, Burlington Industries, began 1977; president, Burlington Industries, 1986-87; founder and chief executive officer, Precision Fabrics-Group, began 1988; director, oles Brower Smith & Co., a Greensboro, NC, investment banking firm, began 1998; founder and president, MediWave Star Technology, a Greensboro research and development firm, 1999; Wachovia Corporation, lead independent director, 2000-2008, interim executive officer, 2008, chairman of the board of directors, 2008—; chairman and chief executive officer, Tippet Capital, 2007—.

**Member:** Has served on numerous boards of directors for nonprofit organizations, including: Community Foundation of Greater Greensboro; trustee, Moses H. Cone Memorial Hospital; board of visitors member, Duke University School of Law; trustee, Duke Endowment; Research Triangle Foundation.

**Awards:** Americanism Award, Anti-Defamation League; Greensboro Outstanding Community Service Award, Greensboro, NC.

*John D. Simmons/MCT/Landov*

## Sidelights

**C**hairman of Wachovia Lanty Smith has worked as an executive in a number of industries, from textiles to law and medical device research to merchant banking. Known for his blunt approach and willingness to speak his mind, Smith has been praised for his management style and ability to make difficult decisions under pressure. Smith is well known for his ability to turn around companies in bad times, a quality Wachovia's board of directors hoped to utilize after asking CEO Ken Thompson to retire. The board appointed Smith interim CEO in June of 2008.

A graduate of Wittenberg University in Springfield, Ohio, and an honors graduate of the Duke University School of Law, Smith spent several years in his native state of Ohio working as a lawyer in the firm of Jones, Day, Reavis, and Pogue. After several years, however, he moved to Greensboro, North Carolina, where he became involved in the local community. Smith began his career as an executive in 1977, when he served as executive vice-president at Burlington Industries in Greensboro. He held responsibility for all of Burlington's industrial area, including fabrics, glass, and industrial fabrics. In

1983, Smith became the president of the Burlington Industrial Fabrics Company division, adding those responsibilities to his job and working toward modernizing the division's manufacturing. In 1986, when the chairman and chief executive officer retired, Smith was promoted to president of Burlington and was elected a director. Due to downsizing in 1987, Smith resigned from his position, despite his long relationship with the company. "He has contributed greatly to Burlington, both in staff and in line capacities," CEO Frank S. Greenberg was quoted as saying in the *Daily News Record*. "We appreciate what he has done; he will always have many friends at Burlington."

In fact, Smith was able to purchase a portion of Burlington's assets in 1988. After forming the company Precision Fabrics-Group, Inc., Smith purchased Burlington's Precision Fabrics division and served as the chief executive officer of the new business. At first, the business was very profitable, but soon the industry began losing money on the whole, due to the inexpensive imported textiles flooding the market. Struggling for market share, Smith helped to grow Precision as a business, turning it from a division that was losing money into a profitable company that could produce domestic textiles able to compete with imported products. Despite taking a number of other positions on boards of directors, as well as the title of chief executive at Tippet Capital, an investment and merchant banking firm in Raleigh, Smith remained the chairman at Precision. In 1998, Smith became director at Soles Brower Smith & Co., an investment firm in Greensboro that had previously been struggling. During the first year of Smith's tenure, the company made plans to nearly double the size of its staff. Smith was also one of the founders of MediWave Star Technology, a research and development firm working on medical technology to address cardiac health.

While being involved with several companies on a professional level, Smith also involved himself with a number of nonprofit organizations, making him a civic leader in the Greensboro community. Due to his contributions to the city, he was recognized by being elected a trustee to the Duke Endowment, a foundation that by 2002 had approved grants of more than $116 million and had received awards since its founding of more than $1.8 billion. Smith also received the Americanism Award from the Anti-Defamation League and the Greensboro Outstanding Community Service Award.

In 2000, while still maintaining several of his other positions, Smith joined Wachovia Corporation as the lead independent director. He had begun his re-

lationship with Wachovia, the nation's fourth largest bank, in 1988, when he began serving on the board of directors. Hoping that Smith could do the same for Wachovia that he did for Precision—creating profit in a difficult market—the board appointed Smith as Wachovia's chairman in 2008. "The entire industry is wrestling with major credit issues right now, and Wachovia is certainly not immune," Smith was quoted as saying in the Raleigh *News and Observer*. "But we have a strong underlying business model, and there are a lot of very good people working there. So our focus is to fix the short-term issues and start planning for a very bright long-term future."

Smith offered the bank strength and a solid reputation during a time when Wachovia had suffered considerable losses. "Wherever he is, he's going to stand out as knowledgeable and energetic," William Friday, a long-time acquaintance of Smith, was quoted as saying in the *Charlotte Observer*. "He radiates strength." Joseph Starobin, chief scientist at MediWave and one of the company's co-founders, said in the same article, "His ideas are very strong. Those who work with him respect his guidance."

Though some analysts criticized the choice of Smith due to his close relationship to then CEO Ken Thompson, others felt that he would bring strategic thinking and a calm perspective to the struggling bank. "He's going to look at everything critically," Patrick Burns, co-chief executive of Precision, was quoted as saying in the *Charlotte Observer*. "He's not going to make any hasty short-term decisions. He'll focus on building value long term." Others of Smith's co-workers felt Wachovia could rely on Smith to be honest and upfront. "He's ... lovingly blunt," Piedmont Angel Network executive Lou Anne Flanders-Stec said in the same article. "Sometimes we all need that." John Burness of Duke University echoed the sentiment in the Raleigh *News and Observer*, "He gets to the core of issues. He can be blunt. If you're sitting around the table and talking about a hard issue and somebody brings up a BS point, he'll say, 'That's a BS point.'"

Between May and June of 2008, Wachovia's situation failed to improve, and CEO Ken Thompson was asked to retire. Smith stepped in as the interim CEO from June through July of 2008. Not pointing fingers or offering blame, Smith explained the decision in *Research*, saying, "The board believes new leadership will help to revitalize and reenergize Wachovia and enable it to realize its potential." Smith held the position until Robert Steel, former undersecretary for domestic finance at the U.S. Treasury Department, was hired as CEO. Brad Finkel stein of *Origination News* reported that while Standard & Poor's had given Wachovia a Negative status on their CreditWatch at Thompson's retirement, the analysts acknowledged that Wachovia was showing strong capital increases that could offset the weak earning potential of 2008.

# Sources

### Periodicals

*Charlotte Observer* (Charlotte, NC), May 9, 2008; May 10, 2008; July 10, 2008.
*Daily News Record,* April 5, 1983, p. 11; September 10, 1986, p. 1; December 3, 1987, p. 1; February 18, 1988, p. 15.

*Investment Dealers' Digest,* July 2008.
*News and Observer* (Raleigh, NC), June 8, 2008.
*Origination News,* July 2008, p. 16.
*PR Newswire,* June 3, 2003.
*Research,* July 2008, p. 14.
*Triangle Business Journal,* January 28, 2000, p. 7.

### Online

Wachovia, http://www.wachovia.com/ (February 11, 2009).

—*Alana Joli Abbott*

# Russell P. Smyth

**Chief Executive Officer and President of H&R Block, Inc.**

---

**B**orn c. 1958; married Dawn; children: four. *Education:* Northern Illinois University, B.S., late 1970s, M.B.A., early 1980s.

**Addresses:** *Office*—H&R Block, 1 H&R Block Way, Kansas City, MO 64105.

## Career

**C**areer with McDonald's, began 1984, vice president of the Latin American Group, 1996-99, then international relationship partner for Southeast and Central Asia, 1999-2001, president of Partner Brands, 2001-03, president of European Operations, 2003-05; served as a consultant, equity owner, and active board member for private equity firms and privately held companies, 2005-08; CEO and president, H&R Block, 2008—.

**Awards:** President's Award, McDonald's.

## Sidelights

**I**n 2008, former McDonald's company executive Russell P. Smyth was hired as the chief executive officer and president of tax preparation company H&R Block. The company, which has around 13,000 company-owned and franchised offices, had hopes that Smyth would boost their typically seasonal performance. Though the company had spent many years diversifying into other financial fields, from mortgage lending to investment banking, Smyth's hiring coincided with the company's desire to focus on its primary service: tax preparation. "Russ has excellent experience working with a powerful brand and delivering consistently high quality performance across a vast retail network," H&R Block Chairman Richard Breeden said in *Forbes* Online.

Born Russell P. Smyth around 1958, Smyth is a graduate of North Illinois University, earning both his undergraduate degree and his Master's of Accounting Science. After graduating, he began working on the audit staff of Price Warehouse. Early into his career, he took a job with McDonald's in their finance department, learning the ropes from behind the counter in order to be a better manager. "I cleaned toilets, made fries, and learned to flip burgers," he recalled in the *Kansas City Star*.

Smyth's career with McDonald's lasted 21 years through several positions. He served as vice president of McDonald's Latin American Group and its international relationship partner for Southeast and Central Asia before becoming the president of the Partner Brands Division. That position placed Smyth in charge of McDonald's-owned chain restaurants including Boston Market, Donatos Pizza, Aroma Cafe, Chipotle, and Pret A Manger. From there, Smyth was promoted to president of McDonald's Europe, where he made efforts to change the traditional McDonald's menu to items that would have more appeal for a European audience, adding such items as drinkable yogurt and all-white-meat Chicken McNuggets. The American salad line was also introduced, and quite early on, it met and exceeded the expectations with its European customer base.

Smyth retired from McDonalds in 2005, wanting to spend more time with his family. With his wife and four children living in Chicago, Smyth was frustrated with the amount of time he had to spend abroad and away from his family in his position as president of McDonald's Europe. There was some speculation that Smyth was leaving the company due to underperforming sales in Europe, but other executives assured the press that his reasons were personal. "I regret that he's moving on, but I know he is doing what's right for him, his family, and the direction he wants to take his career, so I respect and support his personal decision," McDonald's president and COO Mike Roberts told *Promo*. Restaurant analyst John Glass told *Nation's Restaurant News* that while Smyth was "much-admired and long-tenured," he felt, "if there was one region that could benefit from a shakeup, it is Europe."

Smyth had been working for small private firms as a consultant and as a board member for three years before taking the job at H&R Block. Like many financial institutions at the end of 2007, H&R Block suffered tremendous losses, largely due to its mortgage lending business Option One. Former chairman and CEO Mark Ernst resigned in November of 2007 and was succeeded as chairman by activist board member Richard Breeden. Seeing problems with the way H&R Block was being run, Breeden and two associates began buying up shares of the company in order to gain more control over the board, hoping to bring the company back to its core business of tax preparation. The board appointed Alan Bennett to serve as interim CEO while the company searched for a new executive, and Smyth replaced Bennett on August 1, 2008.

Smyth announced early on, however, that while the tax preparation service would remain crucial, he also hoped to expand the company's product lines. He declared that H&R Block would not sell the portion of the business which allowed H&R Block to offer prepaid debit cards and lines of credit to customers, one of the popular services that the board had considered selling off. "We have no plans to sell the bank," Smyth revealed in *American Banker*. "We think it's an important part of our strategic plan to grow our retail tax business." But rather than advertising H&R Block as a financial service institution, as his predecessor Ernst had, Smyth made clear that H&R Block would remain a tax company. Smyth also felt that through continuing to offer services like debit cards, H&R Block could be-come a more year-round company and would not depend heavily on its tax-season services. Smyth assured customers and stockholders that once H&R Block had successfully extracted itself from its mortgage business, the company would be in excellent financial shape. He said in the *Kansas City Star*, "The storm has passed and the ship is upright again. Our business plan for next year is done, and we know the key strategies to follow to execute our plan."

While H&R Block prepared fewer tax forms for the 2008 tax season than in previous years, Smyth explained that the company had increased their marketing, particularly to wealthy clients, in the last month before taxes were due. This would mean that the company still earned what they expected, given that more complicated taxes accrue higher fees. That customer base was increasingly important in the 2008 tax season as the retail environment and difficult economy forced lower- and middle-class tax payers to do their own taxes in order to save money.

As he did when he began at McDonald's, Smyth also trained on the front lines at H&R Block, learning what goes on in the day-to-day business and interacting with customers. Smyth continues to serve on the board of directors of Midtronics, Inc., a company that develops technologies for managing batteries. He is also on the Board of Trustees for Lewis University in Romeoville, Illinois.

## Sources

### Periodicals

*Accounting Today*, August 18, 2008, p. 5.
*American Banker*, September 8, 2008, p. 1.
*Crain's Chicago Business*, May 31, 2004, p. 6.
*Kansas City Star*, August 2, 2008.
*Miami Herald*, April 24, 2009.
*Nation's Restaurant News*, December 10, 2001, p. 74; June 20, 2005, p. 1.
*New York Times*, December 4, 2001, p. C4.
*Promo*, June 7, 2005.

### Online

"Board of Directors," H&R Block Web site, http://www.hrblock.com/presscenter/about/bod.jsp (April 28, 2009).
"H&R Block Appoints Russ Smyth Chief Executive Officer," H&R Block Web site, http://www.hrblock.com/press/Article.jsp?articleid=1553 (April 28, 2009).

"H&R Block Names Russ Smyth CEO," The Street. com, http://www.thestreet.com/_googlepi/ newsanalysis/financial-services/1042916 5.html (April 28, 2009).

"H&R Block Orders Up McDonalds' Smyth," *Forbes* Online, http://www.forbes.com/2008/07/28/hr-block-smyth-markets-face-cx_mlm_0725autoface scan02_print.html (April 21, 2009).

"Recession Taxes H&R Block," *Forbes* Online, http://www.forbes.com/2009/03/23/taxes-hr-jackson-taxes-equity-taxes.html?partner= moreover (April 28, 2009).

"Russell P. Smyth," *BusinessWeek* Online, http:// investing.businessweek.com/businessweek/ research/stocks/people/person.asp? personId= 5106047&ric=HRB&previousCapId=21171&pre viousTitle=Intuit%20Inc. (April 28, 2009).

"Russell P. Smyth," *Forbes* Online, http://people. forbes.com/profile/russell-p-smyth/119020 (April 28, 2009).

"Russell P. Smith, President and Chief Executive Officer," H&R Block Web site, http://www.hrblock. com/presscenter/about/profileDetail.jsp?EXEC_ PROFILE_ID=1223 (April 28, 2009).

—*Alana Joli Abbott*

# Peter Som

## Fashion designer

**B**orn c. 1971, in San Francisco, California; son of Helen Fong (an architect). *Education:* Connecticut College, B.A., 1993; graduated from Parsons School of Design, 1997.

**Addresses:** *Home*—New York, NY. *Office*—Peter Som Inc., 260 W. 39th St., 5th Fl., New York, NY 10018.

## Career

**R**eceptionist, British Khaki, mid-1990s; held apprenticeships at Michael Kors and Calvin Klein, mid-1990s; design assistant, Bill Blass, Inc., 1997-99; member of the design staff for Emanuel, the bridge line at Emanuel Ungaro, 1999; launched own women's wear line, 1999; creative director for women's division, Bill Blass, Inc., 2007—.

## Sidelights

**A**merican fashion designer Peter Som landed a coveted but challenging new job just a decade after starting his career when he was named creative director at Bill Blass. Som had worked for Blass—the designer who was both a legend and a leader in American fashion for nearly half a century before his 2002 death—as a newly minted Parsons School of Design graduate back in 1997. The designing job at Blass would not interfere with Som's own eponymous label, which he launched in 1999, but the honor "propelled him into the select group of international talents," asserted *San Francisco*

*Magazine* writer Franklin Melendez, "who pull double duty, running their own labels while overseeing established brands."

Born in the early 1970s, Som grew up in the San Francisco area. His mother, Helen Fong, was a Hong Kong-born architect, and Som grew up in a modernist home filled with pieces from Knoll, the iconic mid-century modern furniture company. His interest in fashion developed at an early age, and he taught himself how to draw the female figure by the basic triangle-circle method so that he could translate his ideas for outfits onto the page. His mother and stepfather encouraged his interest in art, and in his teens Som attended various summer programs at the Rhode Island School of Design and other leading art schools. His first job was with the fast-food chain Jack in the Box, and his first designer purchase, he told Melendez in the *San Francisco Magazine* interview, "was a Dolce & Gabbana coat that was like a big box!"

Som's family lived in Mill Valley, an affluent community just north of San Francisco, and he graduated from a nearby private school, Marin Academy, in 1989. From there he entered Connecticut College, a private liberal arts school whose campus overlooks Long Island Sound. He majored in art history and studio art, and first touched down in New York City when he took a summer internship at British Khaki, a sportswear company that helped revive the preppy-wardrobe staple for the mass market back in the 1980s. It was an excellent introduction to the business, Som explained to Crai Bower, a writer for *Connecticut College Magazine*. "You have to buy unseen garments from overseas, determine what colors won't sell and, most importantly, establish who your customer is. I came back from that internship hell-bent on going to Parsons. I spent my senior year putting together pattern groups and stories every night in my dorm room."

Accepted into the prestigious Parsons School of Design after graduating from Connecticut College in 1993, Som moved to New York City permanently and was hired back at British Khaki as a receptionist during his summers off. In time, the sketches and other work accumulating in his student portfolio were impressive enough to help him land apprenticeships at both Michael Kors and Calvin Klein, which rarely hire students for such positions. When he graduated from Parsons in 1997, he was hired at Bill Blass as the eponymous designer's assistant.

Som spent a year and a half with the Seventh Avenue pioneer, who was one of the first American designers to achieve international success on par with French fashion houses. Blass was also a major influence on American sportswear, incorporating the clean lines of menswear into many of his collections and sparking the fashion for plaid back in the late 1960s in both his men's and women's lines. Som's job at Blass involved copying the designer's larger sketches into a smaller, postcard-sized format used by staff in the pre-production process. He admitted that he was in awe of Blass, who was a well-known fixture on the New York social scene and friends with many of the high-profile women who wore his clothes. His boss, he told *San Francisco Magazine*, "was always a true gentleman. He was never panicked or running around, tearing his hair out. Freaking out is a waste of energy."

Som worked briefly for Emanuel Ungaro, the Italian fashion house, as a designer with Emanuel, its bridge line. He did this while preparing to launch his own line in 1999, and as he recalled in an interview with Meenal Mistry for *W* a few years later, "I would take my full hour of lunch and run to the garment district to meet fabric people and pattern makers and run back and plop down at my desk." He made his first Peter Som collection sales to buyers of small boutiques when he had leased space at a New York trade show. The orders, which he

packed up and shipped himself, helped him reach the goal of launching his own company by the time he turned 30.

Early on, Som's eponymous line earned comparisons to Michael Kors, the successful American designer who founded his line in the early 1980s. Both designers were known for "luxury sportswear with a twist," declared *WWD* writers Miles Socha and Brooke Magnaghi. In Som's early collections, they continued, "everything is clean and crisp, but without any rough edges. Som takes classic, conservative shapes and adds an element of surprise."

Som admitted to making a few mistakes during his first few years in business, and described himself in an interview with Samantha Critchell, a reporter for WRAL-TV in North Carolina, as "naive. I had no five-year plan, no business partner, no clue. I was running on passion and drive." Early in 2002, the U.S. edition of *Vogue* featured him in an article about up-and-coming young American designers, which gave his company a tremendous boost, and over the next few years his collections lured buyers from increasingly prestigious stores, among them Bergdorf Goodman, Neiman Marcus, and Saks Fifth Avenue. While some fashion journalists dismissed his work for what they viewed as an absence of innovation, others commended his designs. Reviewing his Fall 2003 presentation during the biannual runway presentations known as New York Fashion Week, Ginia Bellafante of the *New York Times* called him "a young designer who remains immune to the kind of gimmickry that has afflicted many of his contemporaries."

Som was sometimes grouped with other rising young design stars who were also from an Asian American background. Writing about Som along with Thakoon Panichgul, Derek Lam, and Jeffrey Chow, *Time*'s Kate Betts noted their success might be dubbed "an Asian invasion, except that none of these designers would classify his look in such confining geographic and cultural terms, even though each admits that his work is informed by his roots in unexpected ways." Som admitted that Asian architecture and textile traditions influenced his designs, while pointing out to Betts that "my parents had more pressure on them to become doctors or lawyers. With this generation there is an open-minded feeling in terms of what you can pursue as a career."

In July of 2007, Som was hired by the company that now owned the Bill Blass brand to become the creative director for its women's ready-to-wear line

Since the founder's retirement, a succession of designers had tried to replicate the Blass magic. "All of them struggled, particularly when trying to balance the needs of existing customers with the need to bring in new, younger women," wrote *W*'s Marc Karimzadeh. In late 2006, the company was sold to NexCen Brands, who invited Som to come on board as designer. "Given such turbulence—and the reality that the Bill Blass heyday is now long past and its core devotees long gone from the forefront of fashion, if not from this earth—many industry observers wonder whether the house can regain its relevance," Karimzadeh noted. In an article for *WWD* also by Karimzadeh, Som expressed his excitement about the new challenge. "To me, Bill Blass really represents one of the great American design houses. He had such a clear idea of his vision of streamlined luxury and ready-to-wear. His designs to me represent a woman who is strong and confident, yet not afraid to show that she still has a feminine side."

Som still planned to keep designing his "Peter Som" line, but a few months after the Blass job was announced Som sold a majority stake in his company to NRDC Equity Partners. This retail holding company also owned Lord & Taylor, and its deep pockets would allow the designer to move forward into "everything from home to accessories," he told Melendez in the *San Francisco Magazine* interview. "The sky's the limit now, which is very exciting. Being an independently owned company, you are limited in what you can do."

Som's first pair of collections—one at Bill Blass and the other under his own name—were presented to fashion buyers and press in February of 2008 during New York Fashion Week. For his debut with Blass, "he managed to push things in a more stylish direction than his predecessors," noted *WWD*, "delivering trim suits lacquered in metallics, furs in bright jewel tones and frocks pumped up with oh-so-outré sequins or plumage."

In July of 2008, just a year after taking over at Blass, there were published reports that Som was quitting to concentrate on his own line full-time once again. One part of the story noted that Som quit when NexCen cancelled the Blass runway presentation planned for the next New York Fashion Week in September. "Nexcen has appeared to be on the brink of collapse for some time," reported Amy Odell, who edits the *New York* magazine's fashion blog on its Web site, NYMag.com. "It acted like it was going to sell Bill Blass but then rejected bids for the house last week because they were too low." Then word came that Som and NexCen were merely renegoti-

ating his contract, but that the reports that the runway presentation being cancelled were indeed true. Following up on the story, *Fashion Week Daily* claimed that Bill Blass, which NexCen had acquired in 2006 for $54 million, was being offered to potential buyers for $26 to $28 million. "Rumors abound that, should NexCen fail to find a buyer for Bill Blass, the company will shutter its costly ready-to-wear operations in favor of focusing on its profitable licenses, which earn an estimated $250 million at retail," *Fashion Week Daily* reported.

Whatever may happen at Blass, Som's own eponymous collection remains a steady favorite among fashion cognoscenti. The designer lives in New York City's West Village neighborhood, and at home is where he does "all of my hardcore sketching," he told Bower in the *Connecticut College Magazine* interview. "I just get in the zone by listening to music, whether dance, classical or soundtracks from my old runway shows. I have to imagine my sketch as a real person. I get the attitude down by drawing everything from posture to hair to shoes." In another interview, Som admitted that it was always a little disconcerting to see those sketches come to life. "I see my clothes on the street and they look different than I recall, but different isn't bad," he told Critchell, the WRAL-TV reporter. "It's exciting to me to see what they do, how they wear it, what they wear it with."

## Sources

### Periodicals

*InStyle,* February 2008, p. 100.
*New York Times,* February 14, 2003.
*Palm Beach Daily News,* January 25, 2008, p. A1.
*San Francisco,* March 2008.
*Time,* September 27, 2004, p. 64.
*Vogue,* November 2004, p. 415.
*W,* September 2002, p. 354; October 2007, p. 142.
*WWD,* January 31, 2000, p. 6B; July 27, 2007, p. 2; February 8, 2008, p. 8.

### Online

"Blass Backwards," *Fashion Week Daily,* http://www.fashionweekdaily.com/news/fullstory.sps?iNewsid=6614640 (August 25, 2008).
"Designer Peter Som Sketched Future at a Young Age," WRAL.com, http://www.wral.com/lifestyles/story/3405847/ (August 24, 2008).

"Peter Som Might Be Out at Bill Blass (Updated)," *NYMag.com,* http://nymag.com/daily/fashion/2008/07/peter_som_might_be_out_at_bill.html (August 25, 2008).

"Peter Som '93: A Designing Life," *Connecticut College Magazine,* http://aspen.conncoll.edu/camel web/index.cfm?var3=0&solution=none&circuit =cconline&var5=none&fuseaction=publications &id2=0&var1=0&fuse =none&cwedit=0&var4= 0&var2=0&id=97418062.tif3&action=none&fun ction=view&uid=28&cwedit_submit=false&id3= 0&id1=0&id4=0&id5=0&printerlogo=yes&print er=yes (August 24, 2008).

*—Carol Brennan*

# Shreve Stockton

**Author and photographer**

**B**orn c. 1977. *Education:* Brooks Institute of Photography, B.A., 2001.

**Addresses:** *Home*—Ten Sleep, WY. *Office*—c/o Simon & Schuster, 1230 Avenue of the Americas, 11th Fl., New York, NY 10020.

## Career

**P**hotographer and blogger. Published first book, *Eating Gluten Free: Delicious Recipes and Essential Advice for Everyone Living with Gluten Intolerance,* 2004.

## Sidelights

**S**hreve Stockton chronicled her experiences raising a coyote pup in the 2008 book *The Daily Coyote: A Story of Love, Survival, and Trust in the Wilds of Wyoming.* The book grew out of a Web log, or "blog," Stockton started when the newborn Charlie came to her remote Wyoming home as a gift from her boyfriend. Updated daily with photographs, *The Daily Coyote* blog quickly acquired thousands of followers. Asked by Stuart Jeffries, a writer for London's *Guardian* newspaper, about the appeal of her story, Stockton ventured that it was perhaps because "it's about reconnecting to wildness and freedom. Most people don't have that."

*The Daily Coyote* was not Stockton's first published title. In 2004, she penned a cookbook, *Eating Gluten Free: Delicious Recipes and Essential Advice for Every-*

*one Living with Gluten Intolerance,* after being diagnosed with the autoimmune disorder. She was around 25 years old and living in San Francisco when she began writing it, and had inked the book contract just a few days before a fire destroyed her San Francisco apartment building. She relocated to a remoter part of the city to hunker down and write, and bought a Vespa, a make of motorized scooter from Italy, with the money she saved on rent. Once the book went to press, she decided it was time to move to New York City, where she had previously lived. Her plan was to ship her belongings, but ride her Vespa cross-country, an idea that appalled nearly everyone Stockton knew, for it was rare to see a bike designed for narrow, urban European streets out on the U.S. interstates. She set out in August of 2005, and documented her trip on Vespa Vagabond, her first blog.

The leg of Stockton's trip that took her through Wyoming's Bighorn Mountains deeply impressed her and she later wrote in *The Daily Coyote* book that she "fell in love at first sight.... The landscape around the Bighorns is like an ocean on pause, rolling with the subtle colors of rust and sage and gold, stretching to every horizon." Though she made it to the East Coast, she soon turned back and found a place to live in a remote Wyoming town called Ten Sleep.

Stockton supported herself through various jobs, including working as a substitute teacher and as a ranch hand. She became involved with a local man who was an expert in coyote trapping. Out West, coyotes are considered a nuisance to sheep, cattle, and other livestock that are a vital part of the local economy. Mike, Stockton's boyfriend, was paid by ranchers to hunt and kill the predator animals.

In the spring of 2007, Mike came upon a pair of coyotes who had been killing sheep, then searched for the pups he knew were near because they spend their first three or four weeks of life in a den, usually a burrow the parents have dug. Mike's plan was to toss a gas cartridge in there, which kills the pups instantly, but he found one pup at the edge of the den and scooped it up, wrapped it in a shirt, and put it in his truck before setting off the cartridge. He brought it to Stockton as a gift, but told her, "If you don't want to take care of it, or it gets to be a problem, let me know and I'll drown it in the water tank," she recalled him telling her in her book.

Stockton was entranced by the pup, who was so young that its eyes were barely open and it could not even walk. Like a dog, however, it seemed to love having its belly rubbed, and also cried for its mother through the entire night during his first few days at Stockton's home. She named him Charlie, and began documenting his life in photographs. She fed him goat's milk via syringes, and began taking him outside using a rope harness she had fashioned for her housecat, Eli, with whom Charlie seemed to enjoy an odd détente. She used an old deer antler to teethe him, and soon he began to behave more or less like any domesticated dog—he wore a collar, walked on leash, ate dog food, and obeyed her commands.

In the summer, short on money, Stockton decided to turn the email updates about Charlie into a subscription-only blog. A few months later, her blog was discovered by Heather Armstrong, the blogger who writes the popular Web site Dooce. When Armstrong linked to *The Daily Coyote*, Stockton's numbers began to soar, and soon she was getting 30,000 hits a day, along with fan mail from readers telling her how much they enjoyed reading about Charlie. In December of 2007, author and memoirist Meghan Daum wrote about it in the *Virginian Pilot.* "People are seriously loving this site," remarked Daum. "Stockton's photos are beautiful, but, more important, they capitalize on a triumvirate of cultural fascinations: blogging, living off the grid (Stockton has electricity and DSL but no running water in the winter) and, perhaps most viscerally and ridiculously, having a wild animal as a pet."

Stockton put together a *Daily Coyote* calendar for 2008, but was soon fielding book offers. A year later, Simon & Schuster published the book version, illus-

trated with Stockton's own color photographs. *The Daily Coyote: A Story of Love, Survival, and Trust in the Wilds of Wyoming* won generally positive reviews, with a *Publishers Weekly* contributor finding that "Stockton's journey of sharing her life with a wild animal … makes for a fascinating and rewarding read."

Stockton still runs her subscription blog, located at www.dailycoyote.net. Though she considered reintroducing Charlie into the wild, she bought and built a fence around her property instead so that he could play outside on his own. He still demands a great deal of time and training, especially exercise. "Going on walks with him is such a healthful tool for me," she told Parul Sehgal in a *Publishers Weekly* interview. "It's when we connect and my way of showing him that I'm the one making the decisions. He's just such an incredible catalyst for my evolution as a human being."

## Selected writings

*Eating Gluten Free: Delicious Recipes and Essential Advice for Everyone Living with Gluten Intolerance,* Da Capo Press (Cambridge, MA), 2004.
*The Daily Coyote: A Story of Love, Survival, and Trust in the Wilds of Wyoming,* Simon & Schuster (New York City), 2008.

## Sources

### Books

Stockton, Shreve, *The Daily Coyote: A Story of Love, Survival, and Trust in the Wilds of Wyoming,* Simon & Schuster, 2008, p. 2, p. 26.

### Periodicals

*Booklist,* January 1, 2009, p. 31.
*Entertainment Weekly,* November 21, 2008, p. 123.
*Guardian* (London, England), January 12, 2009, p. 2.
*Publishers Weekly,* January 14, 2008, p. 8; October 27, 2008, p. 42, p. 46.
*Virginian Pilot,* December 28, 2007, p. B7.

—*Carol Brennan*

# Elizabeth Strout

## Author

**B**orn January 6, 1956, in Portland, ME; daughter of Richard (a science professor) and Beverly (a teacher; maiden name, Bean) Strout; married Martin Feinman (an attorney), August 14, 1982; children: Zarina. *Education:* Bates College, Lewiston, ME, B.A., 1977; Syracuse University, J.D., 1982.

**Addresses:** *Agent*—Lisa Bankoff, International Creative Management, 825 Eighth Ave., New York, NY 10019. *Home*—New York, NY.

## Career

**S**taff attorney, Legal Services, Syracuse, NY, after 1982; author, 1980s—; instructor of writing and literature at Manhattan Community College, the New School, and Bard College.

**Awards:** *Los Angeles Times* book award for first fiction, for *Amy and Isabelle*, 1999; *Chicago Tribune* Heartland Prize, for *Amy and Isabelle*, 1999.

## Sidelights

**A**merican writer Elizabeth Strout is the author of three acclaimed novels that explore the lives of small-town residents of Maine, her native state. Though she has lived in New York City for much of her adult life, Strout's prose captures the insularity and hardscrabble character of communities whose populations shrink considerably once the summer season ends. Fellow novelist Joseph O'Neill reviewed one of her works for the *Atlantic Monthly*,

*James Keyser/Time Life Pictures/Getty Images*

and termed Strout "the possessor of an irresistibly companionable, peculiarly American voice: folksy, poetic, but always as precise as a shadow on a brilliant winter day."

Strout was born in 1956 in Portland, Maine's largest city, and grew up in a nearby small town called Harpswell. Her father, Richard, was a science professor and Beverly, her mother, taught school. "Both my parents come from eight or nine generations of Maine people," Strout said in an interview with Alden Mudge for the Web site Bookpage. "Even though I've been in New York for so many years, there's something deeply familiar to me about that kind of small town. There is a way of life up there that's disappearing." During her youth, Strout and her family also lived just across the Maine state line in Durham, New Hampshire. She earned her undergraduate degree from Bates College in Lewiston, Maine, and went on to earn a law degree from Syracuse University in 1982. That same year, she wed attorney Martin Feinman, with whom she has one child, their daughter Zarina.

In Syracuse, Strout worked as a staff attorney for the local legal aid society, but gave up her law career to care for a sick relative and, later, to try her hand at writing fiction. *Redbook* published some of her earliest short stories, such as "Hold Her Tightly," which appeared in its May 1989 issue. Scores more were rejected by other publications, but one submission to the fiction department of the esteemed *New Yorker* magazine prompted an editor there, Daniel Menaker, to personally phone Strout to give her a bit of encouragement, telling her, "I think it's really very good, and I just want to tell you that, whatever you do, don't stop," Menaker said, according to *Newsweek*'s Jeff Giles.

Menaker later went on to a job with Random House, and in that capacity acquired Strout's first novel—which had taken her more than six years to write—at a time when she could not even convince a literary agent to take her as a client. That debut work was *Amy and Isabelle*, which won the *Los Angeles Times* Book Award for First Fiction and the *Chicago Tribune* Heartland Prize in 1999; a year later, it was also shortlisted for the Orange Prize for Fiction, a prestigious British literary award bestowed annually to a novel in English by a female writer. It was also adapted for television by Oprah Winfrey's production company, and the small-screen version of *Amy and Isabelle* aired in March of 2001.

Strout's debut is set in a small Maine town called Shirley Falls. The title characters are a daughter-and-mother pair, and the story opens just as the younger woman reaches the same age as Isabelle was when she became a mother at age 17. As a single parent in a small town, Isabelle lives an isolated life. She works as a secretary at a factory where her more working-class female colleagues resent her for her airs, while Shirley Falls' old-money, Yankee residents also maintain their distance. Though *Amy and Isabelle* chronicles the events of one summer in Maine, Strout explained to Raleigh *News & Observer* writer Bridgette A. Lacy that it's the colder months that give the state's year-round residents their resilience. "Maine has a high level of poverty," she said. "They have many people living with barely enough money. They have very ferocious winters. This winter was just terrible…. The tourists that go up there to see it, they don't see the small houses that can barely be kept warm. They don't see that people only heat just one room in the house."

Though Strout never places *Amy and Isabelle* at a specific time, it seems to be set in the 1970s during one particularly scorching summer. Both a drought and the disappearance of a local girl from a neighboring town dominate the news during these weeks. Teenager Amy resents her mother and begins to rebel. She is caught with one of her high school teachers, a man in his forties, and the tension between mother and daughter erupts into violence. Behind Isabelle's anger, Strout told *Redbook*'s Dawn Raffel, is "Jealousy. As much as she loves her daughter, she still looks at her as the person who is preventing her from having a love life." Strout also debunked the theory "that daughters fear turning into their mothers," she said in the same interview. "I really think mothers get frightened when they see their daughters being too much like them."

*Amy and Isabelle* won terrific reviews. "By focusing on the 'confluence of different longings' that bedevils her characters into harming and helping one another, Strout makes the drab little world of Shirley Falls seem richly important," asserted the *New York Times*' Suzanne Berne, who also termed it "one of those rare, invigorating books that take an apparently familiar world and peer into it with ruthless intimacy, revealing a strange and startling place." Writing in *Time*, Nadya Labi declared that "Strout's insights into the complex psychology between the pair result in a poignant tale about two comings of age…. Strout, with this assured debut, shows compassion for both."

Seven years lapsed between Strout's debut novel and her second, *Abide with Me*, which was published by Random House in 2006. This time, the story is set in 1959 in the small Maine community of West Annett, and revolves around a male protagonist, Reverend Tyler Caskey, a widower and the town's minister. Tyler, still relatively young to have lost a wife, seems debilitated by his grief, and his once-popular sermons began to lose some of their spirit. Left to care for his two daughters, he is unable to cope and ignores the needs of the younger of the pair until a crisis looms. "I was interested in writing about a religious man who is genuine in his religiosity and who gets confronted with such sadness so abruptly that he loses himself," Strout explained in the interview with Mudge for Bookpage. "Not his faith, but his faith in himself."

As *Abide with Me* progresses, the townsfolk of West Annett are abuzz with gossip about Tyler's relationship with his housekeeper, Connie, as the distraught minister explores his moral dark moments with the help of a mental-health professional. Misunderstandings and Tyler's inability to reach out to his youngest daughter lead to an explosive episode, but its resolution, wrote Taylor Antrim in *Vogue*, evinces "Strout's compassion as a novelist, her understanding of how quickly our judgments and prejudices come undone, our suspicion turning to sympathy, our anger to love." A review in the *Financial Times* was equally laudatory, with Melissa Mcclements terming the novel "a gracefully plotted depiction of a man in disintegration. Bit by bit, Tyler loses sight of himself, his community, and his religious calling."

Strout's third novel was *Olive Kitteridge: A Novel in Stories*, which appeared in 2008. As the title hints, its interlocking short stories recount the tale of one longtime resident of Crosby, Maine. Olive has taught math to generations of Crosby's children, and is known for both her fierce commitment to her job and verbal bluntness. Some describe her as difficult, but Oliver prefers to think of herself as a typical plainspoken New Englander. Strout knew that type of person from her own youth in Maine and New Hampshire, she told Dylan Foley in the Newark *Star-Ledger*. "They give themselves carte blanche on being honest. There are people hurt by this. It is almost a childlike disregard for people's feelings."

Olive's much friendlier husband is the town pharmacist, and over the course of the novel their son grows into adulthood and seems a chilling reincarnation of Olive's own dark, moody father, who committed suicide. These forces all converge on Olive in a serious of setbacks—her husband is incapacitated by a stroke, and her son marries and vows never to return to Maine. "Strout's craftsmanship—the way she constructs her stories with rich irony and moments of genuine surprise and intense emotion—is first rate," asserted Deirdre Donahue in a *USA Today* review. The Cleveland *Plain Dealer*'s book editor, Karen R. Long, also commended the author's talent. "Strout, like Sherwood Anderson, is unafraid of small-town darkness—illness, infidelity, suicide and madness—but she keeps her readers above water, too, with scenes of quiet humor and unexpected kindness."

Strout said in the *Star-Ledger* interview that Crosby was not unlike the places where she was raised, which she characterized as "pretty claustrophobic," she told Foley. "For someone like Olive, it's comforting. She has generations of ancestors who have lived there." Many reviewers had commended Strout's portrayal of a woman who is difficult but nevertheless sympathetic to readers—no easy task to achieve for a fiction writer. She told Foley that the math teacher had taken some time to emerge in her imagination, noting that "I had my first Olive episode" some years earlier, she said in the *Star-Ledger* article. "She would come to me at different points, and I came to feel her as an intense presence on the page." Realizing that Olive was perhaps too much of a presence for an entire novel, Strout decided to use a series of short stories instead, which allowed her to present not just Olive's voice, but those of her family members, neighbors, and former students.

Strout lives in the Park Slope neighborhood of Brooklyn, and writes daily at her kitchen table in longhand. In a 2006 article she wrote for the magazine *Real Simple* titled "Sick of Worrying," Strout confessed to years of hypochondria, whose onset came when she was in her twenties, newly married, and caring for her cancer-stricken mother-in-law. "For two years after my mother-in-law died, I was susceptible to any news story on how sick someone got from nibbling unwashed lettuce, or how someone who couldn't shake a cold turned out to have leukemia, or how someone contracted flesh-eating bacteria, as I heard once on TV, from a paper cut on an airplane," she wrote. Though her obsession abated over time, the lingering fear of suffering, unbeknownst, from a chronic disease still persisted, until she finally "realized that to have an imaginary illness, of course, requires an imagination, and that mine has always been particularly active."

## Selected writings

### Novels

*Amy and Isabelle*, Random House (New York City), 1999.
*Abide with Me*, Random House, 2006.
*Olive Kitteridge: A Novel in Stories*, Random House, 2008.

## Sources

### Periodicals

*Atlantic Monthly*, April 2006, p. 101.
*Financial Times*, April 1, 2006, p. 32.
*News & Observer* (Raleigh, NC), April 21, 2008.
*Newsweek*, January 11, 1999, p. 66.
*New Yorker*, April 3, 2006, p. 79.
*New York Times*, March 2, 2001; January 17, 1999.
*Plain Dealer* (Cleveland, OH), April 6, 2008, p. G4.
*Real Simple*, May 2006, p. 71.
*Redbook*, April 1999, p. G6.
*Star-Ledger* (Newark, NJ), March 30, 2008, p. 6.
*Time*, January 11, 1999, p. 101.
*USA Today*, April 24, 2008, p. 7D.
*Vogue*, March 2006, p. 436.

### Online

"Healing Faith," Bookpage, http://www.bookpage.com/0603bp/elizabeth_strout.html (July 24, 2008).

—*Carol Brennan*

# Trudie Styler

## Producer and activist

**B**orn January 6, 1954, in Birmingham, England; daughter of Harry (a farmer turned factory worker) and Pauline (a school meal worker) Styler; married Sting (a rock singer), August 20, 1992; children: Mickey (daughter), Jake, Coco, Giacomo, Katherine (stepdaughter), Joseph (stepson). *Education:* Attended Trent Park College of Education in London, 1970s.

**Addresses:** *Home*—London, England. *Publicist*—Ian Monk Associates, 26-28 Hammersmith Grove, London, W6 7BA.

## Career

**A**ctress in films, including: *Bring on the Night*, 1985; *Mamba*, 1988; *Grotesque*, 1995; *On the QT*, 1999; *Me Without You*, 2001; *Bug*, 2002; *Cheeky*, 2003; *Alpha Male*, 2006; *Living Proof*, 2008. Producer of films, including: *Boys from Brazil*, 1993; *Moving the Mountain*, 1994; *Grotesque*, 1995; *Lock, Stock and Two Smoking Barrels*, 1998; *Snatch*, 2000; *Greenfingers*, 2001; *Cheeky*, 2003; *Stories of Lost Souls*, 2005; *Alpha Male*, 2006; *A Guide to Recognizing Your Saints*, 2006. Director of films, including: *The Sweatbox*, 2002; *Wait*, 2005. Television appearances include: *Agatha Christie's Miss Marple: The Body in the Library*, 1986; *Friends*, 2001; *Confessions of an Ugly Stepsister* (movie), 2002; *Empire* (mini-series), 2005; *Love Soup*, 2005-06. Co-founder, Rainforest Foundation, 1988. Appointed UNICEF United Kingdom ambassador, 2004.

**Awards:** Rainforest Hero Award, Rainforest Action Network, 1994; Humanitarian Award, Hospitality Committee for the United Nations delegations, 1995; Human Rights Champion Award, Amnesty International, 2000; Forces for Nature Award, Natural Resources Defense Council, 2002; Liz Tilberis Humanitarian Award, Environmental Media Association, 2004; Danny Kaye Humanitarian Award, UNICEF, 2005; lifetime achievement award, Environmental Media Association, 2007; partners award (with Bill Clinton and Sting), Oceana, 2008.

## Sidelights

**A** dynamic woman with a multi-faceted career, Trudie Styler has such a busy lifestyle that "it looks like she's juggling chain saws half the day," her rock singer husband, Sting, told *People* writer Bob Meadows. A mother of four, Styler runs her own production company, Xingu Films, while also managing six homes on two continents. She is a red-carpet socialite and fashion trendsetter who has no problem shedding her glamorous image to act in occasional character roles in films and television programs in the United States and Britain.

Styler is also a passionate champion of environmental and human rights. She is an ambassador for UNICEF, and has traveled to troubled areas of the world on behalf of the organization. In 1988, along with Sting, she created the Rainforest Foundation which is dedicated to saving the rainforests and indigenous people of Brazil. Every year she organizes a fund-raiser for the Foundation, recruiting some of the biggest superstars in the music world, including her husband. "She's the strong one in the relationship," Sting remarked to Janine Sharell of CNN.com. "I'm the dizzy blond."

Born on January 6, 1954, Styler grew up in a working class area of Birmingham, England. The middle of three sisters and the shortest of the three, Styler dressed in a wardrobe of outgrown hand-me-downs. Her parents struggled to make ends meet. Her mother worked in a school cafeteria; her father gave up farming, which he loved, to work in a factory.

"I grew up in a council house [public housing], as I expect you know," she said in an interview with the *Observer* writer Geraldine Bedell. "I come from a modest background where paying the rent was problematic. Though there wasn't much money, my mum was generous. She was very religious and she cleaned the church steps, put flowers on the altar, filled her envelopes at Christmas. She always said she didn't mind how we did in exams, as long as we did our best, but what she did care about was giving back for the life we'd been given." Styler credited her mother's example as part of the impetus she now feels, as a wealthy adult, to work for charitable and humanitarian causes.

When Styler was three, she was knocked down by a bread van in the street. The resulting facial injuries prompted her mother to sue the bread company for compensation. The suit was a success. Styler believes her mother had a premonition that her middle daughter would appear before cameras one day, and wanted to be sure her face was properly repaired. Styler still has a strip of white scar tissue across her left cheek. "Strangely the scar in no way detracts from her beauty," Sting wrote in his autobiography *Broken Music* (as quoted by Liz Hoggard in an interview with Styler for the *Independent*), "because she looks to me like a kind of damaged angel."

Styler was extroverted as a young girl. "I was always a showoff," she said to Hoggard. The attention she received from playing a part in a school play was so stimulating that she decided to become an actress. At 14 Styler began studying at the Bristol Old Vic Theatre School, in Bristol, England. She later joined the prestigious Royal Shakespeare Theatre Company. By the late 1970s, she was making guest appearances on several British television series.

Styler's life changed forever in 1982 when she met Gordon Sumner, professionally known as Sting, a singer and bass player in the rock band The Police. At the time, Sting was a "working-class singer," as Guy Adams of the *Independent* described him, who was "just hitting the big time." He lived in the house next door to Styler, in Bayswater, a section of western London, and when the couple met "it was love at first sight." Sting was married at the time to Frances Tomelty, an actress who was a friend of Styler's.

The extra-marital affair between Sting and Styler became public in 1984. This was around the same time as the break-up of The Police, for which Styler was subsequently blamed. She had a hard time getting acting roles during the late 1980s, when she became primarily known as Sting's girlfriend. "My career wasn't going so great, and I was fighting for my own little bit of turf and I felt that I was losing my own personality," she told Sharrell of CNN.com.

Styler began see a greater purpose to her life in 1988 while she was on tour with Sting in South America. During a stopover in Brazil, the couple flew over the Amazonian rainforest and was horrified by what they saw: "huge expanses of charred, smoking wasteland where the forest had been systematically burnt down," Styler recalled in an April 23, 2008, article for the *Huffington Post*. "Of course, we'd heard statistics about how much rainforest was being destroyed but until we saw the decimated land below us that day, stretching for mile upon mile, hour after hour, we had not fully grasped the truth: one of the Earth's most precious resources—and with it the planet itself—is being systematically and ruthlessly destroyed."

Once the plane landed, Sting and Styler met some of the indigenous people in the area whose livelihoods and way of life were being destroyed along with the rainforest. Spurred to act, the couple created the Rainforest Foundation. Going strong some 20 years later, the Foundation has raised enough money to protect more than 115,000 square kilometers of the rainforest, according to Styler, and aims to save nearly one million square miles more. The Foundation also provides financial support for indigenous groups. For the past 15 years, Styler has organized benefits on behalf of the Foundation that have attracted many well-known musicians and raised millions of dollars. In 2008, Billy Joel, James Taylor, and other performers, including Sting, sang at a Rainforest Foundation benefit at New York's Carnegie Hall.

Around the same time as the Foundation began, Styler "reinvented herself as a producer," as Hoggard put it. She started a production company called

Xingu Films, which she named after the Xingu River, a tributary of the Amazon. One of her first productions, *Boys from Brazil,* released in 1993, is a documentary about Brazilian transvestite prostitutes. This was followed by *Moving the Mountain,* a documentary directed by Michael Apted, about the pro-democracy demonstration by Chinese students in Beijing's Tiananmen Square, which was violently crushed by army forces. *Moving the Mountain* won several awards, including the 1994 International Documentary Association Award and the Best Documentary Feature award at the 1994 Vancouver Film Festival.

Styler has also produced several feature films, most notably *Lock, Stock and Two Smoking Barrels,* released in 1998, about four friends who pool their money to play in a high stakes card game, but the game is rigged. They end up owing half a million pounds sterling, and decide to pull off a robbery to pay the debt. The film, a comedy-thriller written and directed by Guy Ritchie, was very well-received in Britain. It led to another Styler-Ritchie collaboration, the less successful *Snatch,* released in 2000.

Meanwhile, in 1992, Styler and Sting were married. Styler produced her own wedding with flair. She wore an expensive Versace gown and rode to the ceremony on a white horse. In the years that have followed, the couple has raised their four children at their primary residence, an estate in Wiltshire, England. Styler has tried to keep her children, who live very privileged lives, from becoming too spoiled. The children's chores on the estate include tending their own gardens. Styler insists they use proper manners. "Maybe I'm a little bit overly conscious of them saying 'please' and 'thank you,' " she told Meadows in *People.* Styler's oldest daughter, Mickey, is often awed by her multi-tasking mother. "She's Wonder Woman, I swear," Mickey Styler-Sumner told Meadows.

Not everyone is a fan of the way Styler runs a household, however. Jane Martin, a chef for Styler and Sting at their Lake House estate near Stonehenge in Salisbury, England, appeared before a British employment tribunal in 2007 and claimed that Styler was verbally abusive to her and fired her unfairly. Styler strongly denied the charges. The tribunal ruled in Martin's favor, claiming she was "cast out and discriminated against" after becoming pregnant (as quoted by the *Times* of South Africa). Styler was said to be devastated by the ruling and rejected the tribunal's findings. She and Sting have appealed the decision and the £25,000 award (approximately USD $50,000).

Styler and Sting also own a home in London, a villa in Tuscany, Italy, a home in New York, and another in California. The couple bought the Lake House in 1991 and decided to turn the property into an organic farm. They began with a few leafy green vegetables and some apple and pear trees. The venture has grown into more than 60 acres of fruits and vegetables, four types of livestock, and honey- and cheese-making facilities. "I love eating from the land," she said to Bedell in the *Observer* interview. "I'm a control freak and I like to know what's gone into the soil." Styler wrote a cookbook with family chef Joseph Sponzo called *The Lake House Cookbook,* published in 1999, which includes 150 recipes based on the farm's bounty.

Not long after cultivating the Lake House property, Styler and Sting began farming on their Tuscan villa. They produce olive oil and honey from the trees and hives on their 900-plus Italian acres. In 2006, organic olive oil and honey from the "Estate di Sumner" went on sale at Harrod's, the renowned department store in London.

When seen in public, Styler cuts a much more glamorous figure than a gentlewoman farmer. "She'll get dirty, but the next day she'll look like an empress," Sting told Meadows. "Any excuse for a party, Trudie will give it." Hoggard described Styler as "the party queen of Manhattan." She and Sting often entertain their many famous friends, including Guy Ritchie and his wife, the pop star Madonna, who were introduced to each other by Styler.

But Styler enjoys putting aside her fancy outfits and makeup for the occasional acting role. "When I'm in public doing the glamorous-wife-of-rock-star persona, I don't want to disappoint," she told Hoggard, "but when I act, I really like to leave that all behind." She was Doris, the mousy, suspicious wife of the butler Fledge (played by Sting) in the 1995 dark British comedy *Grotesque,* which she also produced. (The film was released under the title *Gentlemen Don't Eat Poets* in the United States; its U.S. video title was *Grave Indiscretion.*) More recently, Styler wore a dark wig to play Brede, a manipulative seductress in *Alpha Male,* a 2006 British film that she also produced. Styler has also been seen on television, winning good reviews for her comic turn as Irene, a middle-aged woman fed up with her husband in the British TV series *Love Soup.* Fans of the American TV series *Friends* may recall her 2001 guest appearance on the show, when she appeared as herself.

In 2004 Styler was appointed a UNICEF United Kingdom Ambassador, a role she has undertaken with her usual vigor. She was sent on a fact-finding tour to Ecuador and was appalled to find children living in garbage dumps. Determined to help, she asked Sting to do a benefit concert, which he did in London. Styler has also visited tsunami-affected areas of Sri Lanka and earthquake-ravaged sections of Pakistan. She has pledged her support to create short films for UNICEF's campaign to stop the spread of AIDS in children. In 2005, Styler was awarded the Danny Kaye Humanitarian Award, the most prestigious honor given to a UNICEF ambassador.

As for her future commitments, Styler told Bedell, "I go where my heart takes me and my instinct takes me." Whether it be producing, acting, farming, party-going, mothering, fund-raising, or world traveling, Styler has a large closet of hats—and outfits—to choose from.

## Selected writings

(With Joseph Sponzo) *The Lake House Cookbook,* Clarkson Potter (New York City), 1999.

## Sources

### Periodicals

*Independent* (London, England), August 5, 2006; March 10, 2007.

*Observer* (London, England), February 12, 2006.

*People,* May 24, 2004.

*Times* (South Africa), July 22, 2007.

### Online

"Trudie Styler," Internet Movie Database, http://www.imdb.com/name/nm0836548/ (September 26, 2008).

"Trudie Styler makes a name for herself with environmental benefits," http://www.cnn.com/EVENTS/1996/earth_day/stories/trudie.styler/index.html (July 24, 2008).

"Trudie Styler on the suffering of Ecuadorean tribes," http://dailymail.co.uk/femail/article-466940/Trudie-Styler-suffering-Ecuadorean-tribes.html (July 24, 2008).

"Trudie Styler, UNICEF UK Ambassador," (July 24, 2008).

"Why Sting and I Set Up the Rainforest Foundation Fund," *Huffington Post,* http://www.huffingtonpost.com/trudie-styler/why-sting-and-i-set-up-th_b_98252.html#comments (July 24, 2008).

—*Eve Nagler*

# Kierán Suckling

*Courtesy of Center for Biological Diversity*

**Executive director for the Center for Biological Diversity**

---

**B**orn in 1964 in Boston, MA; son of Maureen Suckling; married Stephanie Buffum (divorced); married Lydia Millet (a novelist), 2003; children: two. *Education:* Studied engineering at the Worcester Polytechnic Institute, Worcester, MA; College of the Holy Cross, Worcester, MA, B.A.; State University of New York at Stony Brook, M.A.

**Addresses:** *Contact*—Center for Biological Diversity, P.O. Box 710, Tucson, AZ 85702-0710. *E-mail*—ksuckling@biologicaldiversity.org. *Home*—Tucson, AZ and Silver City, NM.

## Career

**C**o-founder and executive director, Center for Biological Diversity, Tucson, AZ, 1989—.

## Sidelights

**E**ach year, the number of plants and animals listed on the endangered species list grows significantly, due in part to the work of Kierán Suckling and the Tucson-based Center for Biological Diversity. Since its inception in 1989, the non-profit environmental agency has obtained protection for nearly one-fourth of the more than 1,300 plants and animals listed as endangered or threatened. In addition, the Center has gained a "critical habitat" designation for more than 38 million acres of public land, mostly in efforts to quash logging, grazing, and mining.

While some environmental organizations employ radical civil disobedience and eco-sabotage, the Center for Biological Diversity uses the courts and the Endangered Species Act in its efforts to protect the environment. Speaking to *Range* magazine's J. Zane Walley, Suckling described the process: "The law says that the best possible science is to be used in managing our public lands, so we conduct our own scientific research to show that's not happening, then we litigate. It's an incredible amount of work, but with an honest judge you can shut down a billion-dollar development in a heartbeat." The reason is simple—once a species is listed as endangered, private companies and government agencies are barred from doing anything that will upset its habitat. In essence, all the Center does is force the government to enforce its own laws.

Suckling was born in Boston in 1964. His English father was an engineer who designed power plants. Shortly after Suckling's birth, the family moved to Peru for his father's next project. His parents eventually divorced. Suckling's mother, Maureen, hailed from Ireland and was a deeply devoted Catholic. She named him Kierán (pronounced KIR-un) after Saint Kierán, one of Ireland's apostles. Raised as a Catholic, Suckling developed a childhood fascination with Francis of Assisi, known as the patron saint of animals. St. Francis is famously known for preaching to birds and for urging sanctity for all life. When it was time for Suckling to choose a confirmation name, he went with Francis—and in many ways, Suckling has dedicated his life to carrying out the saint's vision.

Initially, Suckling studied engineering at the Worcester Polytechnic Institute, but as he looked at technology, he began to question its long-term impact on people's lives and the world. He dropped out of the program and enrolled at the College of the Holy Cross, also located in Worcester, Massachusetts, where he earned a bachlor's degree in philosophy before moving on to the State University of New York at Stony Brook where he received a master's in philosophy as well. Putting off his doctoral dissertation—which he has yet to finish—Suckling headed west in the late 1980s to hike around. He noticed pockets where the forests had been clear-cut and became increasingly discouraged by the fast-paced rate of development.

Suckling began his environmental activism by taking part in a logging protest in Montana, then joining the militant environmental activist group Earth First! In 1989, Suckling found work with the U.S. Forest Service counting the Mexican spotted owls who lived among the pines in southwestern New Mexico's Gila National Forest. During this time, he befriended a biologist named Peter Galvin and a physician, Robin Silver, an amateur photographer who was taking pictures of the owls. They became concerned when they realized the U.S. Forest Service intended to allow logging in the owls' nesting habitat. Suckling and Galvin alerted the local newspaper about the situation and were swiftly fired from their jobs.

Intent on saving the owls, the trio teamed up to take on the Forest Service. Silver had filed a lawsuit—invoking the Endangered Species Act—to protect the owls. Initially, the Forest Service and the loggers did not think much of the lawsuit because the Endangered Species Act had yet to actually be enforced in the area. "The managers weren't worried," former Forest Service biologist Leon Fager told Backpacker. "They just wanted to get the cut out and graze the cows."

Working together, the trio gathered data on the nesting sites and worked through the court system to get the owl listed. By 1995, the center's litigation had forced the U.S. Fish & Wildlife Service to designate 4.6 million acres—located on eleven national forests—as critical habitat. A court-ordered injunction halted the proposed logging.

Buoyed by their success, the three men decided to expand their vision, realizing they could use the Endangered Species Act to get areas protected. They called their organization the Greater Gila Biodiversity Project. By the early 1990s, the name had morphed into the Southwest Center for Biological Diversity and in 1999, they dropped the "southwest" designation to reflect their expanded mission.

Serving as executive director, Suckling drives the operation. "Suckling is equal parts Luddite and computer geek; guru and bully; CEO and deep ecologist," Annette McGivney wrote in a profile for Backpacker magazine. "Combine Henry David Thoreau, Bill Gates, and Howard Stern, and you'd come pretty close to capturing Suckling."

The Center's work has halted numerous timber harvests on national forest lands and forced a reduction in the number of grazing allotments on public lands. The Center has also gained protection for hundreds of species, including the Chiricahua leopard frog, the pygmy rabbit, the Northern goshawk, the southwest willow flycatcher, the cactus wren, the California gnat catcher, and a fish called the spikedace.

While environmentalists laud the group's efforts, others say the agency is destroying their way of life. Fifth-generation rancher Jim Chilton has been embattled with the Center and the government trying to keep his grazing allotments. He equates Suckling's work with "ethnic cleansing." As Chilton remarked to Backpacker: "He wants to cleanse the land of us cowboys who have a custom, a culture, a tradition in the West.... Suckling is pushing his ideals and personal desires on a society that does not necessarily share those ideals."

Suckling receives hate e-mail nearly every day. He has had his car defecated on, his tires slashed. None of that fazes him. "Our government and its corporate sponsors have created a system of subsidies that has to be abolished," he told Range magazine. "They turned the lands into a commodity. We have to get public land users off this welfare system. It is not a simple thing to break those chains."

Besides angering ranchers, miners, loggers, and sawmill owners, Suckling's group is despised by many government agencies, which complain that their underfunded budgets are used up in litigation with the Center's lawsuits. Suckling contends that Congress should make the proper funds available so the agencies can do their jobs and protect the environment.

The non-profit Center for Biological Diversity runs off of funds from donations from its 40,000 members. In the past, the Center has received grants from Ted Turner's Foundation, Patagonia, the Center for Deep Ecology, and Bonnie Raitt. As of 2009, the Center had eleven offices in six states. Suckling's goal was to expand until its operations covered the entire United States.

## Sources

### Periodicals

*Backpacker*, February 1, 2003, p. 46.
*New York Times*, August 30, 2001, p. A1.
*Phoenix New Times* (AZ), August 1, 1996.
*Tucson Citizen* (AZ), January 29, 2008, p. 1A.

### Online

"Our Story," Center for Biological Diversity, http://www.biologicaldiversity.org/about/story/index.html (November 15, 2008).
"Playing Outside the Rules," *Range* magazine, http://www.rangemagazine.com/archives/stories/winter99/playing_outside_the_rules.htm (November 15, 2008).

—*Lisa Frick*

# Sugarland

## Country music duo

Frank Micelotta/Getty Images for ACMA

Group formed in 2001 in Atlanta, GA; members include Kristian Bush (born March 14, 1970, in Knoxville, TN; married to Jill; children: Tucker, Camille), mandolin, guitar, singer, songwriter; Jennifer Nettles (born September 12, 1974, in Douglas, GA; married Todd Van Sickle, a club owner; divorced, March 2007), singer, songwriter.

**Addresses:** *Record company*—Mercury Records, 66 Music Sq. W, Nashville, TN 37203-3208. *Web site*—http://www.sugarlandmusic.com.

## Career

Bush was a member of the band Billy Pilgrim and a solo artist; Nettles was a member of bands Soul Miner's Daughter and the Jennifer Nettles Band; Nettles and Bush formed Sugarland, 2001, with Kristen Hall; independently released debut album, *Premium Quality Tunes*, 2003; signed with Mercury, 2004; released first major label album, *Twice the Speed of Life*, 2004; Hall left group, 2006; released first album as a duo, *Enjoy the Ride*, 2006; sued by Hall, 2008; released third album, *Love on the Inside*, 2008.

**Awards:** American Music Award for breakthrough favorite new artist, 2005; Academy of Country Music Award for top new duo/vocal group, 2006.

## Sidelights

The country duo Sugarland emerged from nowhere to become chart-toppers within only a few years of existence. Formed as a trio in 2001 with Kristian Bush, Kristen Hall, and Jennifer Nettles, Sugarland was signed to a major label in 2003 and released its first album, *Twice the Speed of Life*, the following year. Building a buzz on Nettles' strong vocals and a catchy country sound with pop and rock influences, Sugarland was nominated for a Grammy Award for best new artist. Tired of performing endlessly on the road, Hall left the band, but Bush and Nettles kept going as a duo making country music with an edge. Bush told Fred Shuster of the *Richmond Times Dispatch*, "We really believe our audience is just like us—and we're not shy about it. They've shown us that they have no preconceived notions about what country music is. Country has changed—and so has the listener."

Each member of Sugarland had a career in music before forming the group, and all had experience as singer-songwriters. Hall lived in Atlanta for many years. In addition to releasing her own solo albums on the Windham Hill label and spending a brief period in California as a songwriter, she was also a guitar player who once was a guitar tech for the popular folk duo the Indigo Girls. Nettles had her own band, the Jennifer Nettles Band, which played in clubs in the Southeast, and was a member of the regionally popular band, Soul Miner's Daughter. She favored a jazz-pop and country sound, and appeared with one of her bands on the 1999 Lilith Fair Tour.

Bush was born in Tennessee and raised in Sevierville, Tennessee, the hometown of country superstar Dolly Parton. He loved country music, but was drawn to rock as well, especially while attending Avon Old Farms School, a prep school in Connecticut. After college, he formed Billy Pilgrim, an acoustic alternative rock duo once signed to Atlantic Records, for which he played mandolin. He also recorded with other folk/rock musicians, and contributed songs to various movie soundtracks, including *Shallow Hal.*

Hall, Bush, and Nettles formed Sugarland in 2001 in Atlanta. The group began when Hall, who had recently returned to Atlanta after her Los Angeles-based songwriting stint, was writing a song with David LaBruyere. Bush was asked to help out and contributed solid lyrics. Together, they wrote the song "Tennessee," and decided to form a country band. They began forming Sugarland, which added Nettles after auditioning singers that fit in their alternative country vision. Hall had known of Nettles, and Nettles took the opportunity when it was presented.

Bush was impressed by Nettles' talent. He told Devin Grant of the Charleston, South Carolina *Post and Courier*, "There's a certain kind of voice in country; someone you can recognize immediately and someone who isn't faking it. That's the thing I love so much about Dolly Parton or Deana Carter. When we sat down with Jennifer and asked her to try out, we knew right away she was the real thing. That's what a great country voice is supposed to sound like, instead of put on."

Nettles knew that it was not just her voice that would make Sugarland work. The trio needed songwriting chemistry as well. She told Jim Bessman of the BPI Entertainment News Wire, "We're all singer/songwriters and it was very important to make sure before moving forward that we could write with each other. It was the first time for me in a co-writing situation, but it clicked. I got ideas that were fun to write about, and I really enjoyed it."

In 2003, the trio put out their independently released debut album, *Premium Quality Tunes*. The album showed the influence of the Dixie Chicks, Bob Dylan, and Martina McBride. Sugarland's songs had an escapist quality, like "Mississippi" which focused on the fun after a well-earned payday. Bush told Brad Barnes of the *Columbus Ledger-Enquirer*, "A Sugarland song abides by a couple of rules. First of all, it's fun. And second, its emotions align a little more with country—by that I mean the emotions are clear."

With a clearly commercial sound, *Premium Quality Tunes* was intended to garner Sugarland a major label deal. After showing their power and talent at a showcase, the group signed with Mercury's Nashville outlet in 2004. Mercury was part of the powerful Universal Music Group (UMG) Nashville. Sugarland's label believed in them and their sound. UMG Nashville's co-chairman, Luke Lewis, told Nick Marino of the *Atlanta Journal-Constitution*, "We believe that they're a mainstream potential-superstar act. They've got to have a lot of hits to be that.... The great news is that they're already seasoned performers and entertainers, which is not always the case with new artists in Nashville. A lot of them come into town, and they're great singers and great songwriters, but they haven't performed a lot. We kind of have the luxury of having the whole package, so to speak."

Sugarland released their major label debut later in 2004, *Twice the Speed of Life*. It was produced by Garth Fundis, who previously worked with Trisha Yearwood and Alabama, and again featured songs about everyday life, especially as lived in small Southern towns. Most were written by Hall. Reviewing the album, Marino of the *Atlanta Journal-Constitution* commented, "At the end of the day *Twice the Speed* is a true-blue radio-ready country-pop album. It has a truckload of broad, memorable melodies. It brims with positivity and empowerment. It features lyrics about making love in fallen leaves and telling off the boss and standing up when you get knocked down. It's like an episode of *Oprah* set to country music."

The first single off of *Twice the Speed of Life*, "Baby Girl," was a country hit. Other songs from the album, including "Something More" and "Just Might (Make Me Believe)," were also chart toppers. The album went double platinum. Sugarland also gained a large following by constant touring with such acts as Alan Jackson, Brad Paisley, and Sara Evans.

Sugarland emerged in 2004 and 2005 as a major country act that could sell two million copies of its album. They were nominated for three Country Music Association awards in 2005, including single of the year, for "Baby Girl," vocal group of the year, and the Horizon Award for country music newcomer of the year. Sugarland won a 2005 American Music Award for breakthrough favorite new artist, was nominated for five Academy of Country Music Awards in 2006, and was nominated for a 2006 Grammy Award for best new artist.

In early 2006, Sugarland took a break from touring and began working on its second album for Mercury. Shortly thereafter, Hall left the group to focus more on songwriting at her Atlanta home. Reportedly, the group's brutal touring schedule also compelled her to leave the band. Hall later moved to Nashville to further her songwriting career. Bush told Walter Tunis of the Albany, New York *Times Union* a few months after Hall left, "Right now, Kristen is home trying to detox from going on the road for something like 200 shows in a row. But we are all still friends. This was just a life choice that people have to make at certain times."

Bush and Nettles decided to continue Sugarland as a duo—though Hall had co-written the group's hits—and resumed touring in March 2006 by opening for Kenny Chesney and for Brooks & Dunn later in the year. Touring was important to the group, as Nettles explained to Jay Bobbin of the *Buffalo News*, "I think live performance is one of our strengths. We'd all been playing clubs, and other places for many years before we got together, plus it's important that we give people the chance to come and forget their troubles for a while."

Before Sugarland released their next album for Mercury, Nettles gained the group more attention and an unexpected audience by contributing vocals to a song by the long-running hard rock band Bon Jovi. Entitled "Who Says You Can't Go Home," the song reached number one on the *Billboard* country singles chart. In November of 2006, Sugarland released its long-awaited album, *Enjoy the Ride*. Thematically similar to its previous releases, the album was also more confident and with a broader musical sound. The album's first single, "Want To," was a hit even before *Enjoy the Ride* was released.

Critics were generally impressed by *Enjoy the Ride*. Comparing it to *Twice the Speed of Life*, Marino of the *Atlanta Journal-Constitution* noted: "It's radio-friendly country-pop music, simple and catchy. Careful listening, though, reveals a few subtle tweaks to the band's approach. The melodies have gotten slightly earthier, less glossy. Nettles' vocals seem less brittle, more soulful."

The members of Sugarland looked at *Enjoy the Ride* as a new beginning, their first album as a duo. Bush told Patrick Ferrucci of the *New Haven Register*, "It's

like a second first record.... We were a tad bit anxious to start the new record because we were so used to doing things before, when we were a trio. 'Settlin'' was the first thing we wrote; it was the first song we recorded; it's the first song on the record. After we wrote it, Jennifer looked over at me and said, 'You know, this is going to be fine.' But actually, it was like, 'No it's going to be great.'" "Settlin'" became a number-one country hit, as did "Want To." "Stay" was a hit as well.

By early 2007, *Enjoy the Ride* had sold at least a million copies and was a chart hit on both the country and pop album charts. It eventually went double platinum. Sugarland spent most of the year on the road, touring throughout the United States. While they headlined many dates, the duo also opened for Chesney again in larger arenas. Bush told Alan Sculley of the *Sarasota Herald-Tribune* that the songs on *Enjoy the Ride* were meant for such venues. Bush explained, "We imagined, where are we going to sing these songs? We thought to ourselves, 'Well, we're going to be performing these all next year on very large stages. So why not take a page from the John Mellancamp playbook and write them intentionally to play them so they sound great in large places?'"

Continuing to tour into 2008, Sugarland also released a new album in July, the well-received *Love on the Inside*. Its first single, "All I Want to Do," was a hit, and the album debuted at number one. Despite the stress created by a lawsuit from Hall in 2008 seeking her share of the profits from songs she wrote or co-wrote but were released after she left group, the duo was happy with their evolution, as Nettles explained to Janis Fontaine of the Cox News Service. She said, "I definitely think this is the album that I've always wanted to make, and I've never said that before. We're coming into a groove, hitting our stride. We'll continue to evolve and better ourselves in such a way that the best is yet to come."

## Selected discography

*Premium Quality Tunes*, independently released, 2003.
*Twice the Speed of Life*, Mercury, 2004.
*Enjoy the Ride*, Mercury, 2006.
*Love on the Inside*, Mercury, 2008.

## Sources

### Books

*Contemporary Musicians*, vol. 61, Gale Group (Detroit, MI), 2007.

## Periodicals

*Anchorage Daily News* (AK), October 13, 2006, p. H4.

Associated Press, January 20, 2006.

*Atlanta Journal-Constitution,* October 24, 2004, p. 1L; November 5, 2006, p. 1K; August 8, 2008, p. 1D.

*Boston Globe,* December 5, 2007, p. F1.

BPI Entertainment News Wire, October 18, 2004.

*Buffalo News* (NY), November 13, 2005, p. TV2.

*Calgary Sun* (Alberta, Canada), July 12, 2008, p. 49.

*Columbus Ledger-Enquirer,* July 22, 2003.

Cox News Services, July 28, 2008.

*Denver Post,* May 9, 2008, p. D12.

*Los Angeles Times,* July 29, 2008, p. E1; September 11 2008, p. E1.

*New Haven Register* (CT), February 1, 2007.

*New York Times,* November 6, 2006, p. E3.

*Post and Courier* (Charleston, SC), July 10, 2003, p. 4F

PR Newswire, December 8, 2005.

*Richmond Times Dispatch* (VA), November 29, 2007 p. F11.

*Sarasota Herald-Tribune* (FL), May 31, 2007, p. E10.

*Times-Picayune* (New Orleans, LA), May 30, 2007 sec. LIVING, p. 1.

*Times Union* (Albany, NY), September 7, 2006, p. P10

*—A. Petruso*

# Taylor Swift

## Singer and songwriter

AP Images

**B**orn Taylor Alison Swift, December 13, 1989, in Wyomissing, PA; daughter of Scott (a stockbroker and Christmas tree farm operator) and Andrea (a Christmas tree farm operator) Swift.

**Addresses:** *Office*—c/o Troy Tomlinson Sony/ATV Tree Publishing, 8 Music Square West, Nashville, TN 37203.

## Career

**B**egan performing at local events, c. 1999; sought record deal in Nashville, beginning c. 2000; wrote first song, c. 2001; signed publishing deal with Sony/ATV Music, c. 2003; signed recording contract with Big Machine Records, c. 2006; released debut album *Taylor Swift,* 2006; nominated for best new artist Grammy Award, 2008; released sophomore album *Fearless,* 2008.

**Awards:** Breakthrough Video of the Year, Country Music TV, for "Tim McGraw," 2007; Songwriter of the Year Award, Nashville Songwriters Association, 2007; Horizon Award, Country Music Association, 2007; BMI Award for "Tim McGraw," 2007; Video of the Year, Country Music TV, for "Our Song," 2008; Female Video of the Year, Country Music TV, for "Our Song," 2008; Top New Female Vocalist Award, Academy of Country Music, 2008; Superstar of Tomorrow, Young Hollywood Awards, 2008.

## Sidelights

**W**hile still a teen, singer/songwriter Taylor Swift became a country music sensation with two wildly successful albums released before she reached the age of 19. Swift possesses a highly praised talent for songwriting and had a publishing contract several years before landing a record deal. Her universally appealing songs often have themes of love, loss, family, and friendship inspired by her own life and observations regarding the lives of others. Many observers believed Swift would eventually transcend her country pop roots. Sasha Frere-Jones of the *New Yorker* lauded, "Her precociousness isn't about her chart success, but lies in the quality of her work, how fully she's absorbed the lessons of her elders and how little she seems to care which radio format will eventually claim her. Change the beat and the instruments around the voice, and her songs could work anywhere."

Born on December 13, 1989, in Wyomissing, Pennsylvania, Swift is the daughter of Scott and Andrea Swift. Her father was a stockbroker, and her parents also operated a Christmas tree farm in this suburb of Reading. Swift helped the family business by knocking praying mantis pods off of the trees as a child. Music was an important part of Swift's life from an early age as her grandmother Marjorie Finlay was an opera singer who inspired Swift to sing. When Swift was in fourth grade, she won a national poetry writing contest that showed her she could write. She continued to write poetry while she started singing in public. By the age of ten, Swift was performing in local events like county fairs, festivals, and karaoke contests. She was also making demo tapes in search of a contract. Swift visited Nashville for the first time when she was eleven years old, looking for a record deal.

When she was 12 years old, Swift taught herself to play guitar and wrote her first song. She told Bruce DeMara of the *Toronto Star*, "As soon as I picked up a guitar and learned three chords, I started writing songs. Songwriting just came as another form of expression." She added later in the interview, "For me, I was facing a lot of things at school where I found myself on the outside looking in. I was not included. I would go to school some days, a lot of days, and not know who I was going to talk to." Swift concluded, "So the thing that I found to escape from any pain … was writing songs." Swift signed a publishing deal with Sony/ATV Music at the age of 14 and wrote songs after school for the company.

As a songwriter, Swift sometimes focused on life experiences she had not yet had, but only observed. She told Seamus Gallivan of the *Buffalo News*, "I tend to write songs about things going on around me, through observations—how people are thinking, feeling, reacting. I was writing songs about relationships when I was 13, but I wasn't in any relationships. I was writing about things I'd watched in movies or just watching how people communicate."

To support her burgeoning career, the Swift family—which included her younger brother Austin—moved to the Nashville area. Between the ages of 14 and 16, Swift published 140 songs through Sony/ATV. She also soon had her own recording deal with a new label, Big Machine Records, after impressing its president/chief executive officer, Scott Borchetta, in a showcase at the well-known venue the Bluebird Café. Borchetta signed the deal with Swift when she was 15 years old. Swift wrote or co-wrote all eleven tracks for her debut, 2006's *Taylor Swift*. The album was released when she was 16 years old to many positive reviews, eventually sold more than three million copies, and reached triple platinum status.

In the *Buffalo News*, Gallivan commented, "While marked by maturity and broad enough lyrically for mass appeal, the album is built on Swift's youthful

aplomb, and the two million-plus download count on her MySpace page proves that it serves her well.' Another critic, Jessie Aulis of the *Sherbrooke Record*, wrote, "Most of the tunes on the album are very light hearted and deal with typical high school issues such as boys, falling in love, and bad relationships. Even though the themes are simple, the songs have some impressive lyrics and musical arrangements." Other tracks such as "The Outside" focus on loneliness, whereas "Tied Together with a Smile" tackles low self-esteem and eating disorders.

The first single was a hit entitled "Tim McGraw," a ballad which Swift wrote by herself. She explained its origins to John Hayes of the *Pittsburgh Post-Gazette*, "I came up with the title in math class. I was dating this guy who was going off to college and thinking of what would remind him of me. One of the first things that came to mind was Tim McGraw, because we like his songs. But [the song's] not about Tim McGraw. He doesn't have to worry—I'm not a stalker." The video for "Tim McGraw" won the Breakthrough Video of the Year from Country Music TV in 2007. Swift skipped her school's prom to receive the award.

Another track off *Taylor Swift* was her first number-one song on *Billboard*'s Hot Country Songs: "Our Song." By reaching number one, she became only the fifth teen to top this particular *Billboard* chart. In 2008, the video for "Our Song" received two video awards from Country Music TV: video of the year and female video of the year. In addition, "Teardrops on My Guitar" from *Taylor Swift* was also a hit, reaching number two on the charts. It focuses on an unrequited crush on a friend. Of this song, Swift told Mikel Toombs of the *San Diego Union-Tribune*, "I guess this is a good example of how I let my feelings out in songs and sometimes no other way. I love this song because of its honesty and vulnerability."

In support of the triple-platinum *Taylor Swift*, the young singer/songwriter spent much of 2006 and 2007 touring in the United States and Canada. She primarily toured as an opening act for such country stars as Rascal Flatts, Lonestar, Brad Paisley, George Strait, Kenny Chesney, and Tim McGraw. She was still in high school, finishing up her diploma through a home school program run by Aaron Academy that she worked on in the mornings. She focused on her career the rest of the day. Swift went out of her way to meet fans after every show, sometimes even signing autographs while performing. She told Mike Osegueda of the *Fresno Bee*, "Signing autographs and taking pictures with people is the reason I'm here. I've always wanted people to think they're not a burden, and they're not just fans. They're the reason my life is this way. Saying thank you to them is like breathing for me. It's absolutely necessary."

Swift also reached her fans through the Internet, primarily through her popular MySpace page, which was among the most visited pages for a country artist. Her page had more than 12 million plays by July of 2007. She told Marijke Rowland of the Bergen County, New Jersey *Record,* "I think MySpace has worked so well because I didn't want to make [my page] like every other artist's page, with a third-person bio that was completely not personal. Instead of doing that, I wrote a first-person bio about what I like and dislike. It is about what I am as a person, not my accomplishments. It lets them in and lets them know it's me running it, not a company."

Because of her hard work, *Taylor Swift* reached number one on *Billboard*'s Top Country Albums chart in August of 2007. It took 39 weeks for Swift's album to reach number one. Two months later, she re-issued *Taylor Swift* with three new tracks added on ("Invisible," "A Perfectly Good Heart," and "I'm Only Me When I'm with You") as well as a DVD of live performances. Swift explained to Brian Mansfield of *USA Today,* "They're demos I was making when I was just writing in Nashville, when I was like 14 and 15, trying to get a record deal. We wanted to put out new material without putting out a new album so soon." Swift also released a Christmas EP which was an exclusive for Target, *Sounds of the Season: The Taylor Swift Holiday Collection,* in October of 2007. The disc includes such classics as "Santa Baby" and "White Christmas."

Swift's rise led to a Grammy Award nomination for best new artist in early 2008. Though she lost to Amy Winehouse, she considered it an honor to be nominated in that category. A few months later, Swift graduated from high school, though she admitted her experiences were different than her former classmates in Tennessee. She told DeMara of the *Toronto Star,* "All my friends here in Tennessee are getting ready to go off to college next year. And I feel like I've already gone to college ... as far as being away from home, having to learn how to survive, having to learn so many different things about the [music] industry and meeting different people you've never met before. It definitely rounds you out as a human being."

Continuing to tour in 2008 with such country luminaries as Alan Jackson and Rascal Flatts, Swift also landed endorsement deals, such as serving as the face of l.e.i. jeans and lending her name to a line of inexpensive sundresses, both of which were sold at Wal-Mart. She also had her own fashion doll marketed by toymaker Jakks Pacific. In addition, Swift recorded her second album, *Fearless,* which was released in the fall of 2008. As with *Taylor Swift,* she wrote or co-wrote every song on the album. Among them is the hit single "Love Story," which was her take on the Romeo and Juliet story without their deaths at the end.

Discussing "Love Story," Swift told Randy Lewis of the *Los Angeles Times,* "I was going through a situation like that where I could relate. I used to be in high school where you see [a boyfriend] every day. Then I was in a situation where it wasn't so easy for me, and I wrote this song because I could related to the whole Romeo and Juliet thing." Many of her songs on the album focus on romantic relationships and their pitfalls, including "You're Not Sorry," "White Horse," and "You Belong with Me." Like many critics, Lewis praised the album in the *Los Angeles Times,* noting, "As a whole, *Fearless* represents a major advance in her confidence and acumen as a songwriter and evinces complete faith in her conversational vocal style...." The album sold more than 2.1 million copies by mid-January 2009 and spent at least five weeks atop the *Billboard* album charts.

Because of the success of her albums and her youth, Swift enjoyed a strong female following. She welcomed her status as a role model to her fans. She told Keith Groller of the Allentown, Pennsylvania, *Morning Call,* "I take any responsibility as a role model seriously, and I embrace it. I'm not the type of girl who would be partying or drinking anyway. When I look at the crowds at these shows and see so many gorgeous, beautiful young girls singing along and knowing all the words to my songs, I couldn't imagine anything bad happening to them. If I can influence them in a positive way with who I am and how I go about my life, then I'm happy to be a role model."

## Selected discography

*Taylor Swift,* Big Machine Records, 2006.
*Sounds of the Season: The Taylor Swift Holiday Collection* (EP), Big Machine Records, 2007.
*Fearless,* Big Machine Records, 2008.

## Sources

### Books

*Complete Marquis Who's Who Biographies,* Marquis Who's Who, 2008.

## Periodicals

Associated Press, July 26, 2008.

*Billboard,* August 4, 2007; March 22, 2008; January 10, 2009, p. 41; January 17, 2009, p. 37.

*Buffalo News* (NY), October 27, 2006, p. G25.

*Chattanooga Times Free Press* (TN), October 10, 2008.

*Daily News of Los Angeles,* May 1, 2008, p. L1.

*Edmonton Sun* (Alberta, Canada), March 25, 2008, p. 47.

*Fresno Bee* (CA), June 26, 2007, p. E1.

*Los Angeles Times,* October 26, 2008, p. F13; November 20, 2008, p. E2.

*Morning Call* (Allentown, PA), August 30, 2007, p. GO3.

*New Yorker,* November 10, 2008, p. 88.

*Pittsburgh Post-Gazette,* September 23, 2006, p. C5.

*Reading Eagle* (PA), December 7, 2008.

*Record* (Bergen County, NJ), July 6, 2007, p. G14.

*San Diego Union-Tribune,* June 28, 2007, p. Night & Day-15.

*Sherbrooke Record* (Quebec, Canada), February 2, 2007, p. 15.

*Toronto Star,* January 12, 2008, p. E3.

*USA Today,* October 5, 2007, p. 1E.

*Village Voice,* November 19, 2008.

## Online

"Taylor Swift," Internet Movie Database, http://www.imdb.com/name/nm2357847/ (January 21, 2009).

—*A. Petrusc*

# Paulo Szot

*AP Images*

**Actor and opera singer**

**B**orn in 1969 in São Paulo, Brazil. *Education:* Attended Jagiellonian University, Krakow, Poland, late 1980s.

**Addresses:** *Contact*—Zemsky-Green Artists Management, 104 W. 73rd St., Ste. 1, New York, NY 10023.

## Career

**S**ang with the Polish state chorus, early 1990s; made professional debut, São Paulo, Brazil, 1997; debuted with the New York City Opera in *Carmen,* 2003-2004; sang with the National Opera in Bordeaux, France, 2006; sang the role of Belcore in *L'Elisir d'Amore (The Elixir of Love),* New York City Opera, 2006; appeared as Count Almaviva in *Le Nozze di Figaro (The Marriage of Figaro),* Boston Lyric Opera, 2007; made Broadway debut as Emile de Becque in *South Pacific,* 2008-2009; sang in *The Merry Widow,* Opera Marseille, France, 2008-2009; appeared in *Carmen,* Toulouse Opera, France, 2009; sang the lead in Dmitri Shostakovich's satirical opera *The Nose,* Metropolitan Opera, New York, 2009-2010.

**Awards:** Prêmio Carlos Gomes Award, best vocal performance, 2000; Antoinette Perry Award for Excellence in Theater, best leading actor in a musical, 2008, Theatre World Award, best actor in a musical, 2008, Drama Desk Award, outstanding actor in a musical, 2008, Outer Critics Circle Award, outstanding actor in a musical, 2008, all for *South Pacific.*

## Sidelights

**T**rained as an opera singer, Brazilian baritone Paulo Szot spent a dozen years on the opera stage before making his Broadway debut in a 2008 revival of the famed Rodgers and Hammerstein musical *South Pacific.* For the first time in his career, Szot—who was cast in the lead male role—found himself speaking words instead of singing them. "Acting is the most terrifying thing in my whole life," Szot told the *New York Times'* Jesse Green shortly after the musical's premiere. Despite the anxiety, Szot nailed the role. From opening night, the deep-reaching baritone mesmerized audiences. Szot went on to capture a Tony Award for best leading actor in a musical for his performance as Emile de Becque in the Pulitzer Prize-winning musical.

Szot (pronounced SHOT) was born in 1969 in São Paulo, Brazil, and grew up in Ribeirao Pires, a city in southeast Brazil. His Roman Catholic, music-loving parents hailed from Poland but fled to Brazil following World War II after being forced to work at German labor camps during the war. For Szot, piano lessons started at age five, followed by violin at eight. He also took ballet. Szot's interest in dance intensified as a teenager after he saw *A Chorus Line,* a musical about Broadway dancers. He memorized every song from the musical and decided to become a professional dancer.

When Szot was 18, his father secured a scholarship for him to study dance at Jagiellonian University in Krakow, Poland, his father's native country. "So I took a ship, 23 days in a cargo boat, and at first it was tough because everything was different," Szot recalled in an interview with Broadway.com's Kathy Henderson. "I was kind of a spoiled child in Brazil, and in Poland it was communism: They did not have chocolate, they didn't have toilet paper. I wanted to escape, but after a while, I found a wonderful universe of the arts. Brazil is all about football and samba and TV ... and not so much about classical music."

At 21, Szot injured his knee and could no longer dance. A teacher suggested he try singing. After a series of voice lessons, Szot joined the Polish state chorus. In time, another teacher told Szot he was too good to settle for chorus work and urged him to try opera. In 1994, Szot auditioned for the Pavarotti International Voice Competition. Named a finalist, Szot traveled to Philadelphia in 1995 to compete in the contest. He did not win, but the experience convinced him to continue singing.

In 1997, Szot made his professional debut, singing an opera in São Paulo, Brazil. Over the course of the next decade, he sang in some 60 productions, mostly in South America and Europe but also in the United States. Szot made his debut with the New York City Opera during the 2003 and 2004 season, singing Escamillo in *Carmen,* an opera set in 1830s Spain. Later, he returned to the New York City Opera's stage as Belcore in *L'Elisir d'Amore (The Elixir of Love)* and as the lustful Count Almaviva in *Le Nozze di Figaro (The Marriage of Figaro).* In 2006, Szot sang with the National Opera in Bordeaux, France.

In 2007, Szot revived his role as Count Almaviva in a production with the Boston Lyric Opera. During the show's run, Szot auditioned for the part in *South Pacific* at the urging of his agent. Szot did not figure he would get the part. "First of all, I didn't think they would give me the role," Szot told Playbill's Robert Simonson. "I was doing one of the many auditions I do whenever I am in town. I didn't think it would be very probable to hire a Brazilian to do a French role in the United States on Broadway, you know?"

In the end, director Bartlett Sher cast Szot in the lead role of Emile de Becque, a French plantation owner who lives on a South Pacific island and spends the musical trying to woo a young Navy nurse from Arkansas—Ensign Nellie Forbush. In this production, Nellie was played by Kelli O'Hara. The first rehearsal unnerved Szot, who was not used to speaking words. In addition, he was not used to creating characters—in the opera world, there is little room to personalize a character. This freedom left Szot feeling exposed. "In opera you have to come to the first rehearsal completely perfect or you're fired," he told the *New York Times.* "In the musical theater they are not looking for perfection but expression. It would be great to have both together, but sometimes opera singers, and me included, we are only thinking about the perfect singing. In opera you're not your own person and you're never free."

*South Pacific* opened at the Vivian Beaumont Theater in April of 2008 with the cast backed up by a 30-piece orchestra. Rave reviews of the three-hour production followed. Writing in *Variety,* theater critic David Rooney called Szot "a real find." In a review of the musical, Rooney wrote, "The strength of character, quiet masculinity, kindness and mellow intensity Szot brings to the role are all channeled in his velvety voice. His 'Some Enchanted Evening' is more measured than the usual impassioned declaration but all the more stirring for it and his escalating regret in 'This Nearly Was Mine' delivers chills."

At the 2008 Tony Awards, *South Pacific* came away a winner in seven categories. In addition to Szot's award for best performance by an actor in a musical, Sher won the award for best musical director. The awards provided a boon for the show, which was already playing to sold-out theaters. As 2008 came to a close, Szot took a leave from the production to star in *The Merry Widow* at the Opera Marseille in France. He had committed to the show before being cast in *South Pacific.* Again, in March of 2009, he left to appear in a production of *Carmen* at the Toulouse Opera in France. During his absence, bass-baritone David Pittsinger covered his role as Emile.

Booked until 2011, Szot did cancel three jobs so he could perform in *South Pacific.* While his future commitments were all in the opera world, Szot did not rule out the possibility of appearing in another musical. As he told the *New York Times,* "I was wishing for something new in my life. Now I feel I have it. Someday I might like to try out for other Broadway roles."

# Sources

## Periodicals

*New York Times,* April 6, 2008, p. AR1.
*Wall Street Journal,* June 16, 2008, p. B9.

## Online

"Fresh Face: Paulo Szot," Broadway.com, http://www.broadway.com/Paulo-Szot/broadway_news/563043 (February 8, 2009).

"Getting *Pacific,*" Theater Mania, http://www.theatermania.com/broadway/news/02-2008/getting-pacific_1 2884.html (February 9, 2009).

"Playbill.com's Brief Encounter with Paulo Szot," *Playbill,* http://www.playbill.com/celebritybuzz/article/118107.html (February 8, 2009).

"South Pacific," *Variety,* http://www.variety.com/review/VE11179366.tif98.html?categoryid=33&cs=1 (February 9, 2009).

—*Lisa Frick*

# Boris Tadic

## President of Serbia

**B**orn January 15, 1958, in Sarajevo, Yugoslavia; son of Ljuba Tadic (a professor and dissident); married; two children. *Education:* University of Belgrade Faculty of Philosophy, degree in social psychology, c. 1980.

**Addresses:** *Office*—General Secretariat of the President of the Republic of Serbia, Andriev venac 1, 11000 Beograd, Serbia. *Web site*—http://www. predsednik.yu.

## Career

**P**sychology teacher, c. 1980s; military clinical psychologist, c. 1980s; lecturer at University of Belgrade, c. 1990s-2003; member of Democratic Party, 1990—; founder and director of the Center for Development of Democracy and Political Skills, 1997-2002; telecommunications minister of Yugoslavia, November 2000-June 2001; defense minister of Serbia and Montenegro, 2003-2004; leader of Democratic Party of Serbia, 2004—; president of Serbia, 2004—.

## Sidelights

**W**hen Boris Tadic became president of Serbia in 2004, he aimed to remake his nation and reestablish friendly relationships with its neighbors, Europe, and the rest of the world. Western nations embraced Tadic, eager to see Serbia move beyond the extreme nationalism that had dominated the country and fueled the Balkan wars in the 1990s. As Tadic worked to open Serbia to more foreign investment and to join the European Union, he struggled with the aftereffects of the wars, including arrests demanded by an international war crimes court and the burning question of independence for the province of Kosovo. Tadic received a mandate for his internationalist policies in 2008, when Serbian voters reelected him.

Tadic was born on January 15, 1958, in Sarajevo, Yugoslavia (the city later became the capital of Bosnia). His father, Ljuba Tadic, a philosophy professor and dissident, lost his teaching job for opposing the Communist rule of Yugoslav president Josip Broz Tito. Tadic followed his father into academia and activism, studying social psychology at the University of Belgrade's Faculty of Philosophy, then teaching psychology and working as a clinical psychologist for the military. Tadic also became a democracy activist and was arrested and imprisoned several times for his activities in opposing Tito's regime.

In 1990, after the fall of Communism in Eastern Europe, Tadic joined his country's Democratic Party. He founded the Center for the Development of Democracy and Political Skills in 1997 and served as its director. Forming a pro-democracy group in the

Republic of Serbia was risky in the late 1990s. President Slobodan Milosevic championed aggressive Serbian nationalism and tolerated little dissent.

In 2000, Tadic played a role in pushing Milosevic out of office. That year, Milosevic faced challenger Vojislav Kostunica in the presidential election. After the first round of voting, Kostunica insisted that widespread fraud had denied him a majority and a first-round victory, while the government declared that Kostunica had to face Milosevic in a runoff election. Tadic and other opposition politicians organized a general strike that October to support Kostunica and drive Milosevic from office. The government issued a statement on state television threatening Tadic and a co-organizer with arrest. But the protesters prevailed a few days later, forcing Milosevic to resign. A coalition of several democratic parties took over the Yugoslav government. In late 2000 Tadic was named telecommunications minister in the new cabinet. He served until June of 2001.

In March of 2003, Tadic was named to a second cabinet post: defense minister of Serbia and Montenegro, the new name for what remained of the Yugoslavian federal government. He set out to reform the military, providing better food for the soldiers and eliminating a rule that had required them to shower only once a week. He also made the military's general staff directly answerable to him, an important step in maintaining civilian control over the military. Reaching out to Europe and the United States, Tadic announced in October of 2003 that Serbia and Montenegro would send troops to Afghanistan to aid the North Atlantic Treaty Organization (NATO) forces there. He also started a plan to modernize the military in order to make it eligible for NATO's Partnership for Peace program, a step on the path to membership in the military alliance.

Tadic's rise to the presidency came swiftly. He was named leader of the Democratic Party in February of 2004, replacing his friend, Prime Minister Zoran Djindjic, who had been assassinated as retaliation for turning Milosevic over to the war crimes court at The Hague in The Netherlands. That spring, Tadic resigned from the post of defense minister and announced his candidacy for president of Serbia. He promised to make the nation more democratic, friendlier to the rest of Europe, and dedicated to a free-market economy. He argued that bringing Serbia closer to the European Union was the only path to a better life for its citizens.

During his campaign, Tadic appeared in *Taxi,* a popular Serbian reality show on television station B-92, which featured politicians driving cabs and having conversations with the passengers. "You can see how politicians look corrupt from their faces," one passenger was quoted as having complained to Tadic (according to Nicholas Wood of the *New York Times*). "But I don't see that look on your face yet." Tadic's cabbie shift did not go perfectly; he had to stop once to ask for directions, and viewers criticized his appearance as too boring. However, if it did not help his campaign, it did not hurt it either.

Tadic won the presidency in two rounds of voting in May and June of 2004. He won about 54 percent of the vote in the second round, defeating rival Tomislav Nikolic of the Serbian Radical Party. "This election shows the unity of democratic Serbia," Tadic said, as quoted by Wood in the *New York Times*. Tadic proved especially popular among young and professional Serbs, who tended to admire his pragmatic instincts and his calm during political conflicts. His victory was celebrated in Western nations as a step forward in their relationships with Serbia. More than 40 representatives of the European Union and NATO countries attended his July inauguration.

"There has been enough misunderstandings with the world and discord in Serbia," Tadic said in his inaugural speech, according to Wood of the *New York Times*. "We must take big strides forward to make up for lost time." Tadic also promised full cooperation with the international court at The Hague, which was examining war crimes committed in the former Yugoslavia. That stance brought him into conflict with other Serb politicians, including Kostunica, now the prime minister, who argued that Serb defendants should be tried in Serbia. Many accused criminals wanted by the court were still heroes to ultra-nationalist Serbs. However, Tadic reiterated his position in a radio address in October of 2004. It was time for Serbia to "face the truth," he said, according to Wood in the *New York Times*. "It is in our best interests."

Tadic's presidential role was not always so serious. In January of 2005, he met with members of the American rock band R.E.M. before their sold-out concert in Belgrade, Serbia's capital. Tadic told the band he had been a fan of theirs since the early 1980s. The meeting revealed more than Tadic's taste in music: It was an example of his friendliness toward the West and likely a hint at his political conscience, since R.E.M. is known for its social activism. Tadic told the band his favorite song of theirs was "Orange Crush," a protest song against military aggression.

Still, Tadic sometimes took moderately nationalist stances. In February of 2005, Tadic visited Kosovo, a Serbian province that had broken away after a 1999 war. It was under United Nations control and seeking to become an independent country. "Independence for Kosovo is unacceptable for me; I will never endorse it," Tadic repeated in several speeches across Kosovo (according to Wood of the *New York Times*). He thanked ethnic Serbs, a minority in Kosovo, for remaining in the province despite hostility toward them. However, Tadic said he supported continued talks over Kosovo's future status. "Serbia does not want war. It wants peace for its people and for other people," he told a crowd in one town (according to Wood). A year later, Tadic and Kostunica met with Kosovo Albanian leaders in Vienna, Austria, the first official meeting of Serbian and Kosovar leaders since the 1999 war.

During his first term as president, Tadic led several trade delegations in economic talks with other nations and advocated increases in regional trade and reconciliation efforts with other nations from the former Yugoslavia. In 2006, he brought Serbia into the NATO Partnership for Peace program. Meanwhile, his party entered into a coalition in parliament with the party headed by Kostunica, who continued as prime minister.

Tadic's first term ended at a tense time: in early 2008, as Kosovo was preparing to declare independence. Tadic pledged, if re-elected, to have Serbia join the European Union, or EU, as soon as possible. However, the EU was planning to deploy a peacekeeping force to Kosovo to replace the United Nations force there. Kostunica refused to support Tadic for re-election, arguing that if the EU deployed troops in Kosovo, Serbia should not join the organization. Though Tadic also opposed independence for Kosovo, he insisted the issue should not be allowed to derail Serbia's path to joining the EU.

The presidential election was a rematch between Tadic and his 2004 opponent, the Radical Party's Nikolic. In the second-round runoff, held February 3, Tadic defeated Nikolic again, but by a narrow 51 percent to 47 percent. Nikolic's strong showing was taken as a sign that Serbs had grown impatient with their standard of living, which had not improved much during Tadic's presidency. But Tadic's victory was seen as a clear statement that a majority of Serbs wanted to embrace the rest of Europe. Tadic's supporters celebrated by waving European and Serbian flags in the streets of Belgrade.

Three weeks later, on February 17, 2008, Kosovo declared independence. At the United Nations in New York, Tadic protested that the declaration "annuls

international law, tramples upon justice and enthrones injustice," according to Nicholas Kulish and C. J. Chivers of the *New York Times*. He argued that the United Nations mission chief in Kosovo should void the independence declaration and dissolve the Kosovo Assembly, which had approved it. Instead, several Western countries gave Kosovo diplomatic recognition.

Back home, Tadic faced a political crisis. The Kosovo issue had scuttled his party's coalition with Kostunica's party, and the parliament was caught in a stalemate. Tadic responded by calling early parliamentary elections for May. Before the election, in late April, Tadic signed a controversial political and economic agreement with the EU that moved Serbia a step closer to membership in the organization. He received death threats because of his decision.

Serbian voters gave Tadic's Democratic Party a resounding victory in the May elections. It came in first with about 39 percent of the vote, far ahead of the Radical Party's 29 percent and a mere 11 percent for Kostunica's party. "The citizens of Serbia have chosen the European path, and Serbia will be in the EU," Tadic announced, as quoted by Dan Bilefsky of the *New York Times*. "We promise that we will make it." By July, Mirko Cvetkovic, a Democrat, became the new prime minister. The Democratic Party entered into a coalition with the Socialist Party, formerly headed by Milosevic, alarming some Westerners. But Tadic argued the coalition would improve Serbia's national unity and allow political reconciliation.

Tadic had attained unusual power in often-divided Serbia: a clear mandate from the voters to fulfill his goals. In July, Serbian secret police arrested Radovan Karadzic, the most wanted war criminal from the Balkan conflicts, and turned him over to the international criminal court. Karadzic had played a part in the 1995 Srebrenica massacre, and European nations had demanded he be found and arrested. In October, the commander of NATO met with Tadic to pursue more military cooperation with Serbia. As 2009 began, Tadic seemed to have cleared away the political obstacles to moving Serbia closer to Europe and the West.

## Sources

### Periodicals

*Economist*, February 7, 2008; September 18, 2008.

*New York Times,* October 4, 2000; March 26, 2003; October 4, 2003; June 28, 2004; July 12, 2004; September 24, 2004; October 1, 2004; October 6, 2004; January 22, 2005; February 15, 2005; July 11, 2005; July 25, 2006; February 4, 2008; February 19, 2008; March 9, 2008; May 11, 2008; May 12, 2008; July 8, 2008; July 22, 2008; October 21, 2008.

*Washington Post,* July 23, 2008.

**Online**

"President of the Republic of Serbia—Boris Tadic," www.predsednik.yu/mwc/default.asp?c=101000&lng=eng (November 9, 2008).

"Profile: Boris Tadic," BBC News, news.bbc.co.uk/1/hi/world/europe/3806659.stm (November 9, 2008).

*—Erick Trickey*

# John Thain

## Executive

**B**orn John Alexander Thain, May 26, 1955, in Antioch, IL; married Carmen R. Ribera; children: four. *Education:* Massachusetts Institute of Technology, B.S., 1977; Harvard University, M.B.A., 1979.

**Addresses:** *Office*—Merrill Lynch & Co. Inc., 250 Vesey St., Four World Financial Ctr., New York, NY 10080.

## Career

**J**oined Goldman Sachs out of college, c. 1979; partner, Goldman Sachs, 1988; chief financial officer and head of technology and finance operations, Goldman Sachs, 1994-99; director, Goldman Sachs, 1998-2004; president and co-chief operating officer, Goldman Sachs, 1999-2003; president, chief operating officer, Goldman Sachs, 2003-04; CEO, New York Stock Exchange, 2004-06; CEO, NYSE Group Inc., 2006-07; CEO, NYSE Euronext, 2007; chairman, CEO, Merrill Lynch, 2007-08; executive, Bank of America, 2009—.

**Member:** Board, Massachusetts Institute of Technology; board, National Urban League; board, Howard University; international advisory committee, Federal Reserve Bank of New York, 1999—.

**Awards:** Woodrow Wilson Award for Public Service, Woodrow Wilson International Center for Scholars, Smithsonian Institution, 2008.

## Sidelights

**O**ver the course of his 30-year career, John Thain has held high-powered positions with Goldman Sachs, the New York Stock Exchange, and Merrill Lynch, during which time he amassed a vast fortune. In 2007, as head of Merrill Lynch, Thain received $83.1 million, making him the highest-paid CEO of the year. In 2008, Thain orchestrated a merger between Merrill Lynch and Bank of America, creating one of the world's largest financial firms. Through his business transactions, Thain frequently finds himself mentioned in the press and is living a life he never imagined as a child. "I grew up in a small town in the Midwest," he told the *New York Times*'s Landon Thomas Jr. "I never heard of Goldman Sachs growing up, and I never viewed myself as the president of Goldman Sachs or the CEO of the New York Stock Exchange."

The son of a doctor, Thain was born in 1955 in Antioch, Illinois, a small town located between Chicago and Milwaukee. Thain's initial interest lay in science and technology. After high school, he headed east to study at the Massachusetts Institute of Technology. After earning his electrical engineering degree in 1977, Thain enrolled in Harvard

University's Masters of Business Administration program, graduating in 1979. In an interview with *USA Today*'s Del Jones, Thain's Harvard roommate—Staples CEO Ron Sargent—remembered Thain as a frugal "straight arrow" with strong ethics.

After Harvard, Thain went to work at Goldman Sachs, an investment banking and securities firm. Thain worked as an investment banker and later moved into mortgage securities. He proved himself to be an astute businessman and steadily moved up the ranks, becoming a partner in 1988 and chief financial officer and head of technology and finance operations in 1994. Four years later, Thain was made a director and in 1999 he became president. In 2003, he added the title of chief operating officer. Most industry insiders figured he would one day run the company.

In 2004 the New York Stock Exchange (NYSE), seeking a new CEO, lured Thain away from Goldman Sachs. In accepting the position, Thain took a $16 million pay cut. After nearly 25 years at Goldman Sachs, Thain was making more than $20 million a year and had accumulated nearly $300 million in stock. The NYSE offered him a $4 million salary.

Speaking to *Newsweek*'s Richard M. Smith, Thain discussed his decision. Thain said that initially, when the NYSE's John Reed approached him about the job, he said no way. "But over time, Reed convinced me that the New York Stock Exchange was such an important part of the world's financial system, and the problems there were such that I could really make a difference. He said: 'Why don't you give something back to the system?' In the end, I decided to come to the exchange really to do that, and the compensation piece was not in any way relevant."

At the time of Thain's takeover, the 200-year-old NYSE was facing tough criticism on several fronts. Its former chairman and CEO, Dick Grasso, had been ousted over a hefty compensation package that had hit $140 million. In addition, the NYSE was under scrutiny amidst reports that it had lost investors millions of dollars by trading its own accounts ahead of the investors the NYSE was representing.

During his time at the NYSE, Thain was able to build consensus and make positive changes. He is credited with bringing the exchange into the twenty-first century by relying more on electronic trading. In addition, he executed mergers with the upstart electronic trading firms Archipelago and Euronext, thus creating the first trans-Atlantic stock exchange. With those mergers, the non-profit NYSE moved into the publicly traded for-profit sector and began generating cash on its stock. NYSE stock rose 600 percent while Thain was at the helm.

In 2007, after Merrill Lynch was thrown into chaos due to huge losses in the mortgage crisis, the investment bank turned to Thain to fix things. Merrill Lynch made Thain chairman and CEO in September of 2007, handing him a $15 million signing bonus. Thain was given the Herculean task of leading the bank out of financial trouble stemming from poor risk management of mortgage-backed securities. Nine months later, Thain agreed to a $50 billion takeover by Charlotte, North Carolina-based Bank of America. "This isn't necessarily the outcome I would have expected when I took the job," he told the *Guardian*'s Andrew Clark. "We've been consistently cleaning up the balance sheet, repairing the damage that had been done over the last two or three years."

The merger was to be finalized in 2009, thus ending Merrill Lynch's 94-year run. The merger was set to create one of the world's largest financial firms, combining Bank of America's vast retail banking network with Merrill's huge corps of financial advisers. After the merger was announced, Bank of America said Thain would stay on board and be put in charge of global banking, securities, and wealth management in the newly organized company. "I am delighted that John has agreed to join Bank of America," the company's chairman and CEO Kenneth D. Lewis told *New York Times* reporter Michael J. de la Merced. "His experience and expertise will be invaluable as we put our two companies together and move forward as the premier financial services company in the world."

Thain is married to Carmen Ribera Thain; they have four children and several homes. In 2006, Thain purchased a two-bedroom Park Avenue apartment listed for $27.5 million. In addition, he owns a sprawling estate in Westchester County, New York. The property is so large it sits in three towns, boasts five addresses and has a fish-stocked lake. The $10 million mansion that sits on the land has 14 bedrooms and two swimming pools. An amateur beekeeper, Thain maintains several hives on the property.

Thain also believes in service. He sits on the boards of the Massachusetts Institute of Technology, the National Urban League, and Howard University. Since 1999, he has been a member of the Federal

Reserve Bank of New York's international advisory committee. He has also been a member of the French-American Foundation's professional exchange program, during which time he forged relationships with French business and political leaders. Program alumni include former President Bill Clinton, Sen. Hillary Clinton, and Fannie Mae CEO Franklin Raines.

## Sources

### Periodicals

*BusinessWeek,* November 26, 2007, p. 28.
*Evening Standard* (London, England), November 16, 2007, p. 34A.
*Newsweek,* September 17, 2007, p. 20E.
*New York Times,* December 19, 2003, p. A1; November 15, 2007, p. A1; October 3, 2008, p. C8.
*USA Today,* December 19, 2003, p. 3B.

### Online

"Goldman's Thain Trades Money for Fame," *Forbes,* http://www.forbes.com/fdc/welcome_mjx shtml (November 10, 2008).
"Merrill's Thain Was Highest-Paid CEO in 2007: Report," *Market Watch,* http://www.marketwatch com/news/story/merrill-lynchs-thain-tops-ceo story.aspx?guid=7B541D1546-26B2-4CF6-9C60 D3DE508B093E0 (November 10, 2008).
"US Banking: Merrill Lynch Boss to Get $11m Pay off After Nine Months' Work," *Guardian,* http://www.guardian.co.uk/business/2008/sep/18/merrilllynch.executivesalaries (November 10 2008).

—Lisa Fric

# Laura Tohe

## Author

Born Laura Tohe, in Fort Defiance, AZ, c. 1953; daughter of Benson Tohe and Laura Poncho Florence; children: two sons. *Education:* University of New Mexico, B.A., 1975; University of Nebraska, M.A., 1985; University of Nebraska, Ph.D., 1993.

**Addresses:** *Office*—Arizona State University, Department of English, PO Box 870302, Tempe, AZ 85287-0302.

## Career

Editorial assistant, *Prairie Schooner,* 1983; faculty, Women's Studies Department, Arizona State University (ASU), 1994—; assistant professor, Department of English, ASU, 1994-2000; associate professor, Department of English, ASU, 2000—.

**Awards:** Distinguished service award, Goodrich Program, University of Nebraska-Omaha, 1993; poetry of the year award, Wordcraft Circle of Native Writers & Storytellers, for *No Parole Today,* 1999; faculty of the year award, ASU College of Extended Education, 2000.

## Sidelights

Navajo wordsmith Laura Tohe made her mark in the literary world in 1999 with the publication of *No Parole Today,* a collection of stunning memoir-inspired prose and poetry recounting her days at an off-reservation boarding school. Since then, Tohe has published numerous stories, poems and essays in countless literary journals and collections, contributing to a growing body of literature chronicling the Native American experience. Tohe holds the notoriety of writing the lyrics for the first-ever oratorio based on an indigenous creation story. *Enemy Slayer: A Navajo Oratorio* debuted in 2008 in a production by the Phoenix Symphony, prompting a ten-minute standing ovation after its premiere and selling out its second night.

Born on a Diné (Navajo) reservation in Fort Defiance, Arizona, Laura Tohe spent her childhood on reservations in New Mexico and Arizona, often living with members of her extended family. Her mother, Laura Poncho Florence, is descended from the Sleepy Water People clan, while her father, Benson Tohe, is of the Bitter Water clan. Tohe's father was a World War II code-talker. During the war, the U.S. military used Native American code-talkers to transmit messages in a code that, based on their native languages, was virtually uncrackable. Tohe's parents met and married after the war and had four sons and two daughters.

By the mid-1950s, the marriage had fallen apart. Tohe's mother took the children to live on a reservation in northern Arizona. She supported the family by cooking at the local Bureau of Indian Affairs school. They lived in a hogan, the traditional home of the Navajo people. Crafted from wood poles, bark, and earth, the hogan had no plumbing or electricity.

Later, the family lived on a reservation in Crystal, New Mexico, in an isolated area near the mountains. During the winter, they were often snowed in. When the family needed supplies, they had to go to Gallup, New Mexico. Because the roads were primitive and muddy during the day, they had to travel early in the morning before the roads thawed and return late at night after they had frozen over again. Tohe did not mind the treacherous drive. "My mother would tell us stories driving to the shops in town," she recalled in an interview with Gerald M. Gay of the *Arizona Daily Star*. "She would tell us creation stories, stories about our family and stories that her grandmother told her when she was young."

When Tohe hit adolescence, her mother sent her to live at the Albuquerque Indian School campus so she could attend public school because there was no high school near Crystal. The experience proved painful but served as an inspiration for Tohe's breakthrough book, *No Parole Today*. In an e-mail interview with *Newsmakers*, Tohe acknowledged that homesickness was a large part of the experience. "I felt pretty alienated because I didn't know anyone except my brothers and male cousins," she wrote. "In many ways it felt like I was institutionalized since the boarding schools were still modeled after General Henry Pratt's first schools and there was a chain-link fence that surrounded the school. It was like serving a sentence with furloughs to the public school during the day and returned to the campus afterwards."

Pratt pioneered boarding schools for American Indian children in the late nineteenth century—his goal was not education, but assimilation. When Tohe attended boarding school, she found the focus had not really shifted. Teachers at the school pressured the children to speak English and leave their heritage behind. Tohe admitted that she was not always a "good inmate." Once, she stuffed her bed with towels so the house mother would think she was sleeping and she successfully snuck out to party with friends. Other times she was not so lucky. "I sometimes found my name on the roster of offenders," she told *Newsmakers*. In the end, Tohe said, the experience gave her a clear understanding of how institutions work—they "reward those that assimilate and reject those that don't."

In time, Tohe found her way to the University of New Mexico. A young idealist, she decided to become a psychologist so she could return to the res-

ervation and help her people. Deep down in her heart, however, she was conflicted and longed to write. "Growing up on the reservation, I always loved reading and wanted to be a writer. Reading only books by non-native authors convinced me that writing was only for them," Tohe told *Newsmakers*. She ended up with a degree in psychology and a minor in English, graduating in 1975.

After college, Tohe went to live and work with her grandmother, who spent her time as a foster grandparent at the Indian Health Hospital in Gallup, New Mexico. Every day, they hopped into Tohe's red VW bug and drove into Gallup to make their rounds. "My grandmother thought that was fun," she recalled to *Newsmakers*. Later, Tohe moved back to Albuquerque and found a job working with some Indian organizations.

Eventually, the funding ran out and Tohe was without an income. She returned to college, this time following her desire to become a writer. She earned her master's degree in English in 1985 and followed up with her doctorate in English in 1993, both from the University of Nebraska. The following year, she began teaching at Arizona State University, in both the English and women's studies departments.

Tohe's first major publication was 1999's *No Parole Today*, for which she won the Poetry of the Year Award from the Wordcraft Circle of Native Writers & Storytellers. In 2002, she served as co-editor of the anthology *Sister Nations: Native American Women Writers on Community*.

In 2006, San Francisco-based composer Mark Grey asked Tohe to write the libretto—or words—for an oratorio he was composing for the Phoenix Symphony's 60th anniversary. A noted composer, Grey's work debuted at Carnegie Hall in 2003. Oratorios are told in opera fashion but without the staging and costumes. One of the most famous oratorios is Handel's *Messiah*. Oratorios are generally based on biblical stories but Grey wanted to do something different. Initially, Grey was drawn to the idea of composing a David and Goliath-type story based on a Navajo creation story. He began researching Navajo writers and came across Tohe.

Speaking to the *Navajo Times*' Marley Shebala, Grey said he was struck by Tohe's "writing language, how she blends [Navajo] tradition with contemporary in a very beautiful way." He knew that was what his piece needed. "That grounding. The calling of the earth. And she has that in her prose, the way she writes, speaks and lives. The minute I read her work, I knew she was the right person for this project."

After reading Tohe's work, Grey offered her the opportunity to collaborate on the project. They met to discuss the details and decided to create a narrative translated from the story of one of the Twin Heroes of the Navajo people—Enemy Slayer. In Navajo legend, Enemy Slayer is a mythical warrior who was born to protect the Navajo and liberate the world from monsters. Together, they created the Enemy Slayer storyline based on a contemporary veteran returning from war. Tohe wrote the words to accompany Grey's score.

Tohe said that writing the libretto for the oratorio was not as difficult as she thought. Writing poetry had prepared her for the task. Tohe commented in the *Newsmakers* interview, "I've always thought writing poetry is a lot like writing music anyway because I have to pay attention to line length, how the words sound together, tone, theme and the same things that composers work with. When I asked Mark how I should write the libretto, he said, 'write lines this long,' and held out his fingers three inches apart. That's how I started." There were plenty of words to write—Grey composed 230 pages of music for the oratorio.

*Enemy Slayer* debuted in February of 2008, complete with a 76-piece orchestra and 140-member choir backing up a baritone soloist. In the Navajo tradition, the Enemy Way ceremony is used to restore a person back to spiritual and physical health. As Tohe contemplated the project, she knew she did not want to write a literal translation of the story, particularly since this would violate sacred Navajo contexts. Instead, Tohe created a modern adaptation of the story. "The idea was not to make this a literal translation of the myth," Grey explained to the *Arizona Republic*'s Richard Nilsen, "but to follow a ceremonial path through a contemporary lens. Like taking Hamlet and setting it in New York."

The protagonist in *Enemy Slayer* is Seeker, a veteran who wrestles with inner turmoil after returning home from war. The oratorio follows his path as he struggles to find a way back to himself. He has dreadful nightmares about his experiences in the war, which he cannot seem to shake. He turns to substance abuse and contemplates suicide as his family struggles to bring him back into the light. "When I was writing this piece, the war in Iraq was still in the forefront of the news and I wanted to write about that and the terrible costs of war on families, the country, and on those that served in the war," Tohe said in the interview with *Newsmakers*. "I hope that people will appreciate the theme of the oratorio and what it says about the price that we pay spiritually, psychologically, and socially. I didn't have in mind to write only for a Navajo or Native audience, but I wanted to write a piece that bridges a story from the Navajo mythology to the contemporary world. The oratorio is essentially a hybrid of indigenous storytelling and Western musical art form."

The initial reviews were promising. Writing in the *Arizona Republic*, Nilsen said that Tohe's libretto "gives the piece its power." Tohe, for certain, was able to draw on personal experience when writing the libretto. Her father served in World War II and her brother served in Vietnam. Her brother came home so broken he never recovered and died at the age of 40. Following its debut in Phoenix, *Enemy Slayer* was performed at Boulder's Colorado Music Festival in July of 2008 and was scheduled for the stage in Salt Lake City in 2009, as well as at the Brooklyn Philharmonic.

After wrapping up the oratorio, Tohe focused her time on another book, an oral history of Navajo code-talkers. She writes in both English and her native Navajo language. She stays involved with the Navajo community, mostly with writing projects, but she also helped one student raise money for a domestic violence shelter on the reservation. As for the future, Tohe said, she always plans to write but might like to follow other artistic paths such as photography, screenwriting, making clay sculptures, or designing clothes for Native people.

## Selected writings

*Making Friends with Water*, Nosila Press, 1986.
*No Parole Today*, West End Press, 1999.
*Tséyi': Deep in the Rock: Reflections on Canyon de Chelly*, University of Arizona Press, 2005.

## Sources

### Periodicals

*Arizona Daily Star* (Tucson), June 1, 2007, p. E1.
*Arizona Republic* (Phoenix), January 11, 2002, p. 1; April 5, 2002, p. 7; February 3, 2008, p. E1; February 9, 2008, p. E1.
*Paste*, July 2008, p. 37.

### Online

"Curriculum Vitae," Laura Tohe's Web site, http://www.public.asu.edu/tohe (October 7, 2008)

"Enemy Way Inspires Musical Collaboration," *Navajo Times,* http://www.navajotimes.com/entertainment/1026oratorio.php (October 7, 2008).

"A Woman's Place," *ASU Research* magazine, http://www.asu.edu/research/researchmagazine/2003Summer/sum03 (November 7, 2008).

**Other**

Further information was obtained via e-mail correspondence with Laura Tohe in November of 2008.

*—Lisa Frick*

# Dara Torres

## Swimmer

**B**orn Dara Grace Torres, April 15, 1967, in Jupiter, FL; daughter of Edward Torres (a real estate developer) and Marylu Kauder (a former model); married Jeff Gowen (a sports producer), 1990s (divorced); married Itzhak Shasha (a surgeon), 2003 (divorced, 2004); children: Tessa Grace (with David Hoffman). *Education:* University of Florida, bachelor's degree, 1990.

**Addresses:** *Agent*—Evan Morgenstein, PMG Sports, 4502 35th St., Ste. 200, Orlando, FL 32811-6546. *Home*—Parkland, FL. *Office*—c/o USA Swimming Foundation, 1 Olympic Plaza, Colorado Springs, CO 80909.

## Career

**M**ember, U.S. national swim team for the Summer Olympic Games, 1984, 1988, 1996, 2000, 2008. Television reporter, NBC Sports, early 1990s; reporter and commentator for ESPN, Fox News Channel, and TNT; host of *The Clubhouse,* Resort Sports Network, and *Oxygen Sports*; has also appeared on *PGA Tour Sunday*; appeared in swimsuit issue, *Sports Illustrated,* 1994; motivational speaker.

**Awards:** Gold medal, Summer Olympics (Los Angeles, CA), in the 400-meter freestyle relay, 1984; silver medal, Summer Olympics (Seoul, South Korea), in the 400-meter medley relay, and bronze medal, in the 400-meter freestyle relay, 1988; gold medal, Summer Olympics (Barcelona, Spain), in the 400-meter freestyle relay, 1992; two gold medals, Summer Olympics (Sydney, Australia), in the 400-meter freestyle relay and the 400-meter medley relay, and

*Bryan Bedder/Getty Images for WSF*

three bronze medals, in the 50-meter freestyle, 100-meter freestyle, and 100-meter butterfly, 2000; three silver medals, Summer Olympics (Beijing, China), in the 50-meter freestyle, 400-meter freestyle relay, and 400-meter medley relay, 2008.

## Sidelights

**E**very Olympics produces a star, and the 2008 Summer Games in Beijing, China, made Dara Torres a household name. The 41-year-old became the only American swimmer ever to compete in five Olympics, and she also became the first woman over the age of 40 to race in an Olympic pool event. In Beijing Torres set the fastest times of her career, and went home with three new Olympic medals for a career total of 12, including a gold medal she won as a teenager as part of the U.S. women's relay team at the 1984 Los Angeles Games.

Torres was born in 1967 in Jupiter, Florida, the second from the last of six children. Her father, Edward Torres, came from a Sephardic Jewish family and was a real estate developer who later bought the Aladdin Hotel in Las Vegas. Her mother, Marylu, was a former model who had once won the annual Miss Rheingold beauty pageant, a popular East Coast marketing ploy sponsored by the Rheingold brewery.

Torres grew up in affluent Beverly Hills, California, in a nine-bedroom house. Two of her four brothers were swimmers, and she had followed them into classes at the local YMCA by the time she was eight years old. Around this same time, her parents divorced, and when she was ten years old her mother married a professional tennis player, Ed Kauder, who was still playing tournaments in his 50s and was the second-ranked player in his age group.

As one of six children, Torres was intensely competitive with her siblings. "She always wanted the edge on everyone," her mother told *Sports Illustrated* in 1984. "At the dinner table she had to have the biggest portion. In the car she always wanted to be in the front seat. She was competitive from the day she was born." In the water, Torres appeared to have a natural gift, and soon joined the Tandem Swim Club in nearby Culver City. At 12, she set her first national record in her age group with a time of 24.66 seconds for the 50-yard freestyle. Her true breakout moment, however, came in April of 1982 at the Senior Short Course Nationals event in Gainesville, Florida, when she defeated a top-ranked college swimmer with a time of 22.44 seconds in the same event, now called the 50-meter freestyle.

Torres spent some of her high school years at the Westlake School for Girls, a private single-sex academy at the time, but left home at the end of her sophomore year to train in the Orange County community of Mission Viejo, home to a swim club, called the Mission Viejo Nadadores, that had won several national championships. Its coach was Mark Schubert, who also served as an assistant coach for the U.S. national women's team, and it was Torres' goal to earn a spot on it in time for the 1984 Olympics. At the U.S. Olympic trials in June of 1984, she qualified for the relay team with a time of 56.36 seconds in the 100-meter breaststroke.

Over the years, Torres' coaches and trainers often commented upon her seemingly fearless nature, noting that she appeared to be entirely undaunted by the pressure of competition. At the 1984 Summer Olympics in Los Angeles, however, Torres was inside the athletes' tent at the University of Southern California pool as a men's event began. "I remember lifting up the bottom and seeing 17,000 people and I just freaked out," she told *New York Times Magazine* writer Elizabeth Weil. "I got hot, I had to go to the nurse's station, they were putting ice packs on me."

Despite that brief case of nerves, Torres went on to win a gold medal with her teammates in the 400-meter freestyle relay. A year later, she entered the University of Florida, where she developed more disciplined training habits. She swam in National Collegiate Athletic Association (NCAA) events and won 28 titles—the maximum number possible for a college swimmer—and at national indoor championships she began breaking American records in the 50-meter freestyle.

Torres was expected to bring home a medal in the women's 100-meter freestyle at the 1988 Summer Olympics in Seoul, South Korea, but instead finished in seventh place in that event. She did take home a bronze and a silver medal for two relay events at those Games, but later revealed that this was a period of her life when she suffered most intensely from bulimia, an eating disorder that began in her teens. Traumatized over her poor finish in Seoul, she sought professional help for her secret disorder and was able to halt the effects of the harmful behavior.

After graduating from the University of Florida in 1990 with a degree in telecommunications, Torres decided to retire from swimming. As the 1992 Summer Games in Barcelona, Spain, neared, however, she felt the pull of competition once again and resumed her training schedule. She served as cocaptain of the U.S. women's team and won another gold medal in the 400-meter freestyle relay. After Barcelona, however, she vowed to retire from competitive swimming for good and concentrate on her career in television broadcasting. In 1994, she became the first female athlete to appear in *Sports Illustrated*'s top-selling swimsuit issue.

Torres sat out the 1996 Summer Olympics in Atlanta, Georgia. In early 1999, she was out to dinner when her date said, "'Every time you talk about swimming you have this gleam in your eye,'" Torres recalled in an interview with Alex Tresniowski in *People*. "And he said, 'Have you ever thought of making a comeback?'" By that point, Torres had not swam in a race event in nearly seven years, but the comment reignited her competitive streak, and she began training for a spot on the U.S. women's national team that would compete at the 2000 Summer Games in Sydney, Australia.

Sports journalists wrote of Torres's impressive comeback that year, pointing out that at age 33 she was the oldest member of the U.S. swim team. Her star rose even further when she finally won the first individual medals of her Olympic career, taking bronze medals in the 50-meter freestyle, 100-meter freestyle, and 100-meter butterfly; she also took home two more gold medals for relay events. With the close of the Sydney Games, she planned to retire for good. "I felt like I really didn't have anything else to prove to myself," she recalled in the interview with Weil in the *New York Times Magazine.* "Plus, I thought 33 was really old. And I was tired."

The 2004 Summer Olympics in Athens, Greece, came and went without Torres, but a year later, she was pregnant and began swimming again for her daily workout; as she explained to Weil, she experienced bad bouts of morning sickness, and found it preferable to "throw up in the pool gutter than next to the StairMaster." Not surprisingly, she began racing "whoever the middle-aged guy happened to be in the next lane," she told the *New York Times Magazine* writer, and began training in earnest after her daughter was born in April of 2006. Three months later, she entered the Masters World Championships and posted a time in the 50-meter freestyle relay event that qualified her for a spot at the U.S. Olympic trials in June of 2008.

Before the trials, though, Torres began attracting serious attention when she competed at the 2007 U.S. Nationals in Indianapolis in August. She beat several much younger swimmers for a first-place finish in the 100-meter freestyle, and in the 50-meter freestyle she broke her own national record that she had set back in 1981 at age 15. Along with swimmer Michael Phelps, she became one of the top media-covered athletes in the lead-up to the 2008 Beijing Olympics, including a cover photograph accompanying Weil's *New York Times Magazine* profile that revealed an impressive set of abdominal muscles. Most of the attention focused on her age, for at 41 Torres was the first over-40 woman ever to enter an Olympic swim event. Her remarkable times a year earlier in Indianapolis also prompted debate over just how old was old for an athlete; kinesiologists and other sports-science professionals noted that in some types of sports age seemed to play little role in success, and swimming was one of them. In an interview with *People* magazine that appeared during the first week of the 2008 Games, Torres said the only time she truly felt her age was at the U.S. swim team practices, when "I ... have no idea what song is playing on the iPod machine," she admitted to writer Lorenzo Benet. "The kids are all singing and dancing to hip-hop on the pool deck, and I want to put on my classic rock."

Torres won three silver medals in Beijing. The first came on August 10 for the 400-meter women's freestyle relay. A week later, she took second place in the 50-meter freestyle with a time of 24:07:01 seconds. Less than an hour later, she swam in the women's 400-meter medley relay event, and took another silver medal. The only cloud over her achievements of the past year came from a few pundits who speculated that perhaps Torres was using performance-enhancing supplements. To quell the rumors, Torres volunteered to be tested with a more rigorous pilot program recently launched by the U.S. Anti-Doping Agency; all of her tests came back negative. "I've gone beyond the call of duty to prove I'm clean, but you are guilty until proven innocent in this day and age, so what else can I do?" she told Alice Park, a journalist with *Time* magazine. "It's a real bummer.... So many middle-aged women look up to me. I want them to feel proud, like they can do what they set out to do. I would never do anything to disappoint these women."

Torres' wins in Beijing resulted in hundreds of emails and letters from those same fans—many of them athletes and mothers, too—who thanked her for both inspiring them and raising the bar for women's achievements. Random House and Broadway Books signed her to a book deal for her autobiography, slated to appear in the spring of 2009, followed by a health, fitness, and lifestyle tome. In an appearance on *The Tonight Show with Jay Leno* just after her medal-winning performance in Beijing, Torres would not rule out competing in the 2012 Summer Olympics in London, England. "Never say never," the *Honolulu Advertiser,* quoted her as telling Leno. "It's such an adrenaline rush and I love competing."

Torres has been a reporter and announcer for NBC, ESPN, Fox News Channel, and TNT. She has also hosted *The Clubhouse,* a golf show on the Resort Sports Network. Her daughter Tessa's father is Dr. David Hoffman, an infertility specialist. The couple and their daughter live in the South Florida community of Parkland in Broward County. Torres' two earlier marriages, to sports producer Jeff Gowen and surgeon Itzhak Shasha, both ended in divorce. She told *People*'s Benet that Tessa was the reason for her decision to train for the Olympics. "She motivates me because I want her to be proud of me when she gets older, and I'd like her to know that you don't have to put an age limit on your dreams."

## Sources

*Honolulu Advertiser,* August 26, 2008.
*New York Times,* August 9, 2008.
*New York Times Magazine,* June 29, 2008.
*People,* September 18, 2000, p. 201; August 11, 2008, p. 73.
*Sports Illustrated,* June 18, 1984, p. 40; August 25, 2008, p. 74.
*Time,* August 4, 2008, p. 47.

—*Carol Brennan*

# Danilo Turk

*Vincent Kessler/Reuters/Landov*

**President of Slovenia**

---

**B**orn February 19, 1952, in Maribor, Slovenia; married to Barbara Miklic Turk; children: one daughter. *Education:* University of Ljubljana Faculty of Law, Ljubljana, Slovenia, law degree, 1975; Belgrade University, master's degree in law, 1978; University of Ljubljana Faculty of Law, doctorate, 1982.

**Addresses:** *E-mail*—gp.uprsup-rs.si. *Office*—Office of the President of the Republic, Erjavceva 17, SI-1000 Ljubljana, Slovenia. *Web site*—http://www.up-rs.si/up-rs/uprs-eng.nsf.

## Career

**S**ecretary of the Commission for Minorities and Migrants of the Socialist Alliance of the Working People of Slovenia, c. mid to late 1970s; chairman of the commission, early 1980s; became a teacher and academic assistant at the Faculty of Law, University of Ljubljana, Slovenia, 1978; named assistant professor, 1982; named associate professor, 1987; named full professor, 1995; head of Institute of International Law and International Relations, 1983-92; member of Amnesty International, 1975—; member of the United Nations Sub-Commission on Prevention of Discrimination and Protection of Minorities, 1984-1992; chairman of Sub-Commission, 1991; helped establish Slovenia's Human Rights Council, 1987; served as the council's chairman, c. 1990; diplomat in talks between Slovenia and international organizations, 1991; attended Conference of Yugoslavia, 1991-92; Slovenian ambassador to the United Nations, 1992-2000; president of the UN Security Council, 1998-99; UN assistant secretary-general for political affairs, 2000-2005; returned to teaching at

University of Ljubljana Faculty of Law, 2005-2007; named deputy dean of Faculty of Law, 2006; president of Slovenia, 2007—.

## Sidelights

**B**y the time Danilo Turk became president of the small European nation of Slovenia in 2007, he was already an internationally respected figure. Turk emerged as Slovenia's top diplomat soon after it declared independence from Yugoslavia in 1991. As the country's first ambassador to the United Nations, Turk helped the country attain a more prominent international role than its population of two million would suggest. Slovenia was the most peaceful, prosperous, and reliably democratic country to emerge from Yugoslavia's breakup, and the polite, measured Turk represented its character as well as its interests. In 1998 and 2008, during times of international tension, Turk stepped ably into temporary positions of international leadership, first in the UN Security Council, then in the European Union.

Turk was born on February 19, 1952, in Maribor, Slovenia, then part of Yugoslavia. He earned a law degree and a doctorate in law at the University of

Ljubljana, in Slovenia's capital, and a master's degree in law from Belgrade University, the capital of Yugoslavia. In 1978, he became a teacher and assistant at the University of Ljubljana's law school, teaching international law, working his way up to assistant professor in 1982 and associate professor in 1987. A longtime member of the international human-rights group Amnesty International, Turk helped the group investigate rights violations in Yugoslavia in the early 1980s. He served on a United Nations sub-commission on the rights of minorities from 1984 to 1992. He also helped organize the Human Rights Council of Slovenia and later served as its chairman.

After Communism fell out of power in Eastern Europe, Yugoslavia's long-suppressed ethnic identities and tensions were set loose. Leaders of the country's several regions began intense discussions about its future. Turk was named to represent Slovenia in various meetings with United Nations and European officials in the summer of 1991. When Slovenia became the first part of Yugoslavia to declare itself an independent country that year, Turk stepped into the role of diplomat for his new nation. From the fall of 1991 to the summer of 1992, Turk was part of Slovenia's delegation to the Conference of Yugoslavia, which officially declared that the nation had split into several countries.

Years later, Turk defended Slovenia against critics who thought it had broken away too soon and shown little interest in the wars that ravaged much of the rest of the former Yugoslavia in the 1990s. "Slovenia tried for a peaceful dissolution," Turk told Robert Marquand of the *Christian Science Monitor*. "But … we didn't indulge in illusions.… We had to think about our own existence. We didn't want to be part of a larger war that was looming on the horizon. How could we help by being a war victim?"

In 1992, when Slovenia was admitted to the United Nations, Turk became Slovenia's first UN ambassador, a job he held for eight years. Five years into his ambassadorship, Turk led the campaign for Slovenia to win the seat reserved for Eastern Europe on the United Nations Security Council, which addresses international crises. Slovenia won, becoming the first former Yugoslav republic to serve a term on the council. The next year, Turk talked with Barbara Crossette of the *New York Times* about what it takes to win a Security Council seat. "The level of competitiveness has been rising since 1992," Turk said. "A lot of campaigning is going on, and it takes a lot of time and energy." Turk noted that smaller countries' ambassadors often feel a twinge of jealousy toward the five nations with permanent seats on the council: the United States, Great Britain, France, Russia, and China. "That's the comfortable situation of permanent members," Turk said. "Nonpermanent members have to work much harder."

In August of 1998, Turk served a one-month term as president of the Security Council, which temporarily made him an important voice on two issues of international importance. He resisted pressure to delay the Security Council's approval of a plan to try two Libyans for the 1988 bombing of Pan American Flight 103 over Scotland. That same month, the council unanimously renewed economic sanctions against Iraq because it would not cooperate with UN weapons inspectors. "This is a difficult moment," Turk said (as quoted by Ron Kampeas in the *Washington Post*), regarding the time when the Iraqi government broke off talks with inspectors. "It is not easy to have the discussions cut short. It is disturbing." Just before the council's vote, Turk reported that Iraq had not met the conditions for sanctions to be changed. He declared (according to Paul Lewis of the *New York Times*) that Iraq's behavior was "totally unacceptable."

As Slovenia's ambassador, Turk supported UN efforts to address the conflicts in what was left of Yugoslavia, including the 1999 war over Kosovo. In June of 1999, he and other members of the Security Council passed a resolution that ended the war and allowed ethnic Albanian refugees to return to their homes in Kosovo. Until then, the UN had been sidelined, as the Western nations of the North American Treaty Organization had bombed Yugoslavia in order to stop its military operations in Kosovo, while Russia and China had argued other nations should not intervene in Yugoslavia's affairs. "The UN is assuming a leading role, and that is a very important new development," said Turk, according to Patrick Cole of the *Chicago Tribune*. The next year, when Yugoslavia joined the United Nations following strongman Slobodan Milosevic's loss in a presidential election, Turk was among several diplomats who argued that the remaining parts of Yugoslavia might be able to work out their differences instead of splintering further.

In 2000, Turk was named a UN assistant secretary-general for political affairs. He held the position for five years. He helped build democratic rules for governing Kosovo that would include participation by Serbs, a minority in the province. In his last year on the job, he briefed the Security Council on the work of the UN observer mission in Papua New Guinea, which helped create and implement a 2001 peace agreement ending a civil war that cost more than 10,000 lives. In 2005, Turk also diplomatically pressed the Security Council to do more to help the new government in Iraq, which was making a transition to democracy after Saddam Hussein's dictatorship and a military occupation by the United States. "In order for the transition to succeed, advances in the political process will need to be complemented by tangible improvements in the reconstruction, development, and humanitarian area," Turk told the council, according to the States News Service. Turk said a conference about Iraq later that year offered "a new opportunity for the international community to widen and deepen consensus in support [of] Iraq's transition."

Those two addresses were also farewells of sorts. Turk resigned from his job in the summer of 2005 to return to Slovenia. He told a reporter for Slovenian television he was upset that UN Secretary-General Kofi Annan had passed him over for a promotion to the job of under-secretary-general for political affairs. Annan chose Ibrahim Gambari of Nigeria for the job instead. "I believe the decision on who is leading the political affairs secretary must be based on experience," Turk said, as quoted by Agence France Presse. "I am the one that has that experience. People who did not work in the secretary cannot have more experience than me." Turk returned to the Faculty of Law at the University of Ljubljana, where he became a deputy dean.

In 2007, however, Turk decided to run for president of Slovenia, saying he hoped to move the country beyond its fierce political conflicts. "I'm not a professional politician. I was moved to run in this election by my own civic responsibility," Turk told a reporter for Agence France Presse. "I'm a man of good will, compromises, and consensus, and I believe those qualities are missing in Slovenia. I'll try to change that."

The campaign ended up illustrating Turk's complaint about Slovenian politics. After Turk and conservative candidate Lozje Peterle emerged from the first round of voting, Prime Minister Janez Jansa, who supported Peterle, attacked Turk. Jansa claimed Turk had represented Yugoslavia's interests, not Slovenia's, in meetings with the United Nations in 1991, the year Slovenia declared independence.

The attacks did not work. Turk won the second round of presidential voting in November of 2007 with 68 percent of the vote. The election results were considered a sign that Slovenian voters were unhappy with Jansa's conservative government's education, health, and transportation policies, and the

high inflation Slovenia experienced in 2007 after adopting the euro, the European common currency. As president-elect, Turk joined a rally in Ljubljana demanding increases in pensions and salaries for unionized workers, to combat inflation.

Turk's win meant that he and Jansa would have to cooperate. Turk acknowledged the need to do so in his December inaugural address. "I will work on a constructive, harmonized, and balanced collaboration with the government and the parliament in the search for solutions," he said, as quoted by Agence France Presse. In Slovenia, the presidency is mostly ceremonial, but it does include some authority over foreign policy and defense, which Turk asserted during his address. According to Ali Zerdin of the Associated Press, Turk promised he would seek "principled, well-considered positions on all important international issues." A week after Turk's term began, Slovenia began a six-month term as president of the 27-nation European Union. That put Turk in a key international role once again.

Slovenia's biggest challenge as EU president was Kosovo. The breakaway province planned to declare independence from Serbia in early 2008, angering Serbia and Russia. European nations supported independence for Kosovo, but also hoped to start Serbia on a path to joining the EU. At a contentious meeting of European ministers, Slovenia argued that the EU should make Kosovo's independence and Serbia's path to membership separate issues. "We want to make progress but not compromise on principles," Turk told Marquand of the *Christian Science Monitor.* "What I would say [to Serbs] before the elections is that the EU is here, it is open, and it is waiting for you." That February, Boris Tadic, Serbia's pro-European president, won re-election and a mandate to pursue EU membership. Kosovo declared itself an independent country later that month. Serbia signed a political and economic agreement with the EU in late April.

Turk used the EU presidency to press Europe to fight global warming by placing new limits on greenhouse gas emissions. He declared that the EU should become the world's main donor to developing nations. He also advocated admitting Turkey to the EU, a divisive issue.

Speaking to the European Parliament in April, Turk insisted that the EU's talks with Turkey needed to continue. No country "can be precluded from membership only for reasons of political inconvenience or cultural prejudice," said Turk, as quoted by Associated Press Worldstream, alluding to some

Europeans' hesitance at admitting the mostly Muslim nation. "The feeling of exclusion breeds resentment, and resentment breeds instability. We must think about further expansion in the light of the EU's ambition to be a leading global player."

At home, Turk's conflicts with his rival Jansa continued. The men feuded over a matter of protocol: whether Turk's wife or Jansa's fiancée should serve as the official hostess for Laura Bush, wife of U.S. president George W. Bush, when the couple visited Slovenia in July of 2008. They compromised by having both women escort the American first lady.

Slovenian voters resolved the larger conflict in September. They rejected Jansa's bid for re-election, choosing a left-wing coalition in parliamentary elections. In October, Turk spoke to the parliament, urging it to unify in the face of the global economic crisis of late 2008. "We live in times of hope and uncertainty," Turk said, as quoted by Thomson Financial News. "How fast we will be able to ensure conditions for hope and trust to prevail will depend on our joint efforts."

# Sources

## Periodicals

Agence France Presse, June 13, 2005; July 6, 2005; November 11, 2007; December 22, 2007; January 15, 2008; September 22, 2008; November 7, 2008.

Associated Press, June 10, 2008.

Associated Press Worldstream, December 22, 2007; April 23, 2008.

Chicago Tribune, August 27, 1998, p. 3; June 9, 1999, p. 14.

Christian Science Monitor, February 1, 2008, p. 6.

European Report, July 21, 2008.

Global Insight, November 12, 2007; November 20, 2007.

New York Times, August 2, 1998; August 21, 1998; November 12, 2007; February 4, 2008; May 11, 2008.

States News Service, June 16, 2005.

Thomson Financial News Super Focus, October 15, 2008.

Washington Post, August 4, 1998, p. A12; November 2, 2000, p. A25.

## Online

"Biography" President of the Republic of Slovenia, http://www.up-rs.si/up-rs/uprs-eng.nsf/dokumentiweb/Zivljenjepis?OpenDocument (November 9, 2008).

—*Erick Trickey*

# Yulia Tymoshenko

**Prime minister of Ukraine**

**B**orn Yulia Volodymyrivna Telegina, November 27, 1960, in Dnipropetrovsk, Ukraine; daughter of Vladimir Abramovich Grigean and Ludmila Nikolaevna Telegina; married Aleksandr Tymoshenko (a utility company executive), 1979; children: Evgenia. *Education:* Dnipropetrovsk State University, bachelor's degree, 1984; Ph.D., 1999.

**Addresses:** *Office*—c/o Embassy of Ukraine, 3350 M St. NW, Washington, DC 20007. *Web site*—http://www.tymoshenko.com.ua/eng/.

## Career

**E**ngineer-economist with a machinery factory, 1984-89; founded a chain of video-rental stores, 1988; named managing director, Ukrainian Oil Company, 1991; president, United Energy Systems of Ukraine, after 1995; elected to the Ukrainian parliament on the Hromada Party ticket, 1996; became first deputy chief of Hromada Party, 1997; reelected, 1998; leader of the Batkivshchina (All-Ukrainian Union "Fatherland") Party, after 1999; deputy prime minister for fuel and energy, 1999-2001; prime minister, January-September 2005, December 2007—.

## Sidelights

**T**hough she may be little known outside of Europe and Eurasia, Yulia Tymoshenko is undeniably famous in her native Ukraine and one of the most compelling women to enter the political arena anywhere in the world. The famously photogenic prime minister first gained notoriety as one of Ukraine's wealthiest women in the 1990s, and then entered politics as a campaigner for reform. Westerners may know her as the heroine of her country's Orange Revolution of 2004, when images of her wearing her trademark coiled-braid hairstyle captivated the rest of the world in the midst of a deepening political crisis on the streets of Kiev. Since then she has twice served as prime minister, and is widely expected to make a bid for the presidency of the Ukraine in 2009 or 2010.

Born in 1960, Tymoshenko hails from Dnipropetrovsk, an industrial city on the Dnieper River in the eastern part of Ukraine. At the time, Ukraine was part of the Soviet Union, and Tymoshenko spent her first 30 years under a rigid system in which the Communist Party controlled nearly every aspect of its citizens' lives, and traditional Western civil liberties such as freedom of the press were nonexistent. Her mother, who raised her alone after Tymoshenko's father abandoned the family, was a public-transit employee who worked on Dnipropetrovsk's trolley cars.

At Dnipropetrovsk State University, Tymoshenko studied economics and cybernetics and wed a fellow student, Aleksandr Tymoshenko, in 1979. Their daughter, Evgenia, was born a year later. After graduating in 1984, Tymoshenko became an engineer-economist at a Dnipropetrovsk factory that built machinery. A year later, Mikhail Gorbachev came to power in the Soviet Union, and launched a series of reforms that allowed the beginnings of freedom of the press, free enterprise, and even democratic local elections. In 1988, Tymoshenko and her husband opened a video-rental business that quickly expanded into a chain of stores.

In July of 1990, the newly elected legislators of Ukraine's parliament, the *Verkhovna Rada* ("Supreme Council"), voted in favor of declaring the Ukrainian Soviet Socialist Republic a sovereign state, and the following summer issued a formal declaration of independence from the Soviet Union. The first Ukrainian presidential elections took place in December of 1991, and political analysts predicted that with its historically Western Europe-oriented citizenry, abundant natural resources, and heavily industrialized economy, Ukraine would transition quickly to a fully democratic, free-market nation. A deep recession followed, however, and severe shortages of heating oil and even food became commonplace.

In July of 1991, Tymoshenko was made a managing director of the Ukrainian Oil Company (UOC), an oil trading firm. Leonid Kuchma, a former Communist Party official who now supported a more rapid free-market reform program, was elected as the second president of a newly independent Ukraine in 1994. In the heady scramble to sell off government-run entities to private investors, many fortunes were made, Tymoshenko's among them. She reorganized UOC into United Energy Systems of Ukraine (UESU) in 1995, and it became a major importer of natural gas from Russia.

UESU was headquartered in Dnipropetrovsk, Ukraine's third largest city, which was also Kuchma's home base. When he came to office, he brought many allies in Dnipropetrovsk to Kiev with him, among them Pavlo Lazarenko, an acquaintance of Tymoshenko's whom Kuchma appointed prime minister in 1996. With Ukraine now struggling to pay for natural gas from Russia and elsewhere in the former Soviet Union in the new free-market economy, Lazarenko set up a system of smaller gas monopolies that operated regionally and bartered for gas; United Energy Systems was one of the companies that profited from this plan. But Lazarenko soon fell out of favor with Kuchma, and was ousted on corruption charges. He eventually fled the country, and was convicted in U.S. federal court of money laundering, wire fraud, and extortion.

As head of UESU, Tymoshenko accrued a small fortune and became one of the country's new oligarchs, or a cadre of well-connected individuals who are able to exert undue influence on the political process because of their substantial wealth. The press dubbed her the "Gas Princess" and she was rarely seen without a phalanx of bodyguards. But Lazarenko's downfall was accompanied by accusations that UESU had actually stolen gas but then sold it, earning millions in untaxed profits for Tymoshenko and other executives, and that she had paid generous kickbacks to Lazarenko. The rumors were never proven, but would follow her for the rest of her career.

Tymoshenko entered politics in 1996 when she stood for election to the Rada as a member of the Hromada Party and won a seat representing Kirovograd. She rose to an executive position in her party, was reelected in 1998, and became leader of the Batkivshchina (All-Ukrainian Union "Fatherland") Party in 1999. Later that same year, Kuchma appointed a former head of the Ukrainian National Bank, Viktor Yushchenko, to serve as prime minister after Yushchenko's successful introduction of a new currency unit, the *hyrvnia*. Yushchenko led a reformist government that included Tymoshenko as deputy prime minister for fuel and energy. "Because she knew its tricks, Tymoshenko proved an effective reformer of Ukraine's lucrative and filthy energy sector—perhaps too effective," wrote Andrey Slivka in a lengthy *New York Times Magazine* profile. "Her brash reforms brought a huge tranche of Ukraine's shadow economy into the light. But her assaults on the prerogatives of Ukraine's crooked energy titans, her former peers, made her an irritant to the regime."

Kuchma fired Tymoshenko in January of 2001 in a move that was widely viewed as politically motivated. Both the oligarchs and the remnants of the Ukrainian Communist Party had opposed her reforms, and her ties to Lazarenko were also a source of criticism. The charges of corruption resurfaced, and Tymoshenko was arrested in February and spent six weeks in Kiev's hellish Lukyanivka Prison, which dates back to the Tsarist era. The charges of bribery, tax evasion, smuggling, and forgery against her were eventually dropped and she was released.

Still a member of the Rada and now Kuchma's most vocal opponent, Tymoshenko became an anti-corruption crusader and leader of the National Salvation Forum, coalition of groups determined to oust Kuchma from power. That group became a political entity later in 2001 when it reorganized as the Bloc Yulia Tymoshenko (BYuT). It seized upon widespread fears that Kuchma's government was repeating the totalitarian excesses of the Soviet era, and rallied around the mysterious death of journalist Georgi Gongadze in 2000. Audio tapes surfaced that implicated Kuchma in Gongadze's disappearance, and in the secretly recorded conversations Kuchma also vowed to destroy Tymoshenko.

In parliamentary elections in 2002, Tymoshenko's BYuT won eight percent of the vote, while calls for the embattled Kuchma to step down went unheeded. In the coming presidential election in 2004, Kuchma was ineligible to run for a third term, but his handpicked successor was Viktor Yanukovych, another former Communist Party official who was considered a poor choice to lead the country because of a pair of convictions for robbery and assault several years earlier. Yanukovych's leading challenger was Yushchenko, whose Our Ukraine Party had forged a critical alliance with Tymoshenko's increasingly popular BYuT.

Official results of the election were released on November 23, 2004, and deemed Yanukovych the winner. Major protests erupted in Kiev and other cities, with Yushchenko, Tymoshenko, and others claiming that the election tallies had been manipulated to have Kuchma's chosen successor as the winner. Over the next four weeks the demonstrations came to known as Ukraine's Orange Revolution—after the color used in Yushchenko's campaign ads—and on December 26 another vote was held, with Yushchenko winning 52 percent against Yanukovych's 44 percent. The protests continued over the next several days as Kuchma refused to vacate office, and Tymoshenko gained international fame when she urged riot police stationed in front of the presidential building to join "the side of citizens of Ukraine" through a megaphone, according to the *Guardian*'s James Meek. In a stunning move, she convinced the well-armed police to let her and a small delegation into the building to speak directly with Kuchma.

In the end, Kuchma failed to convince Ukraine's Supreme Court to invalidate the second election, and Yushchenko was installed as president. As planned, Tymoshenko became his prime minister, but served for just eight months. Their successful coalition quickly fell apart over disagreements over a plan to re-nationalize some companies that had been privatized back in the 1990s, and Yushchenko dismissed her as prime minister in September of 2005. Two months later, she took part in a first-anniversary rally of the Orange Revolution in Kiev's main square, and wept on the dais as Yushchenko criticized her stint in office.

Tymoshenko became Yushchenko's most formidable political opponent. In parliamentary elections held in March of 2006, her BYuT came in second with 22

percent of the vote, besting Yushchenko's Our Ukraine party, but the surprise winner was Yanukovych's Regions Party. A three-month stalemate ensued, but finally in June a coalition government was formed with members of BYuT, Yushchenko's Our Ukraine Party, and the Socialist Party. It quickly collapsed over internal fissures and Yanukovych became prime minister. Yushchenko, who was still president, dismissed the Rada in April of 2007 and scheduled new legislative elections for September.

In that contest, Tymoshenko's BYuT received 31 percent of the vote, and after another coalition agreement was hammered out between her party and Yushchenko's Our Ukraine, she was sworn in for her second stint as prime minister on December 18, 2007. A scholar of Eastern European politics, Kataryna Wolczuk, profiled Tymoshenko for London's *Independent on Sunday,* and asserted that "her success in the recent elections is therefore bitter-sweet for Yushchenko in their tentatively renewed alliance: Without Tymoshenko, he loses control of parliament; with her on-side, power is in her hands. He is outshone, outwitted and, eventually, may end up out of power because of her."

Ukraine's next presidential contest will take place in 2009 or 2010. Yushchenko is expected to run for a second term, but many believe Tymoshenko, who has attained mass appeal among a broad spectrum of Ukrainian voters, will make her own bid for the office. Even Russia's prime minister, Vladimir Putin—who served for several years as Russia's formidable, authoritarian president—has reportedly been charmed by her. She is still married to Aleksandr Tymoshenko, but he is rarely seen in public with her and the two are thought to have separated. Their daughter was educated at the London School of Economics and in 2005 married Sean Carr of the British rock band Death Valley Screamers.

Tymoshenko's hairstyle, a braid that wraps across the crown of her head, has been widely copied and even prompted a *New York Times* article titled "In a Political Twist, a Hairdo as Manifesto." In it, correspondent Clifford J. Levy wrote that Tymoshenko's coif "curls around her head like a golden crown, a rococo flourish that sets her far apart from the jowly men she has challenged." The style is actually a traditional Ukrainian peasant look and has echoes of the religious iconography of the Orthodox Church. "I do it myself," she told *Times* of London correspondent Andrew Billen in reply to what may be the most frequent question she fields in interviews. "It only takes me seven minutes. If I employed a professional I would need to leave an extra hour in the mornings."

# Sources

*Fortune,* April 3, 2006, p. 39.

*Guardian* (London, England), November 26, 2004, p. 6.

*Independent on Sunday* (London, England), October 28, 2007, p. 24.

*Newsweek International,* April 16, 2007.

*New York Times,* October 7, 2007.

*New York Times Magazine,* January 1, 2006.

*Times* (London, England), May 20, 2006, p. 50.

—*Carol Brennan*

# Nora Volkow

## Research psychiatrist

**B**orn March 27, 1956, in Mexico City, Mexico; daughter of Esteban Volkow Bronstein (a chemist) and Palmira Fernández (a fashion designer); married Stephen Adler (a physicist), c. mid-1980s. *Education:* Modern American School, Mexico City, B.A.; National University of Mexico, Mexico City, M.D., 1981; postdoctoral training, New York University.

**Addresses:** *Office*—National Institute on Drug Abuse, National Institutes of Health, 6001 Executive Blvd., Rm. 5213, Bethesda, MD 20892-9561.

## Career

**R**esearcher, University of Texas—Houston; director of nuclear medicine, Brookhaven National Laboratory, U.S. Department of Energy, then chairman of the medical department, then associate director for life sciences; professor and associate dean, State University of New York—Stony Brook; director, National Institute on Drug Abuse, 2003—. Edited three books, published more than 380 articles in peer-reviewed journals, as well as more than 60 book chapters and manuscripts for non-peer-reviewed journals.

**Awards:** Premio Robins Award, for best medical student in her generation; Laughlin Fellowship Award for outstanding psychiatric residents; selected for membership, Institute of Medicine, National Academy of Sciences; Innovator of the Year, *U.S. News & World Report,* 2000; named as one of the "Top 100 People Who Shape Our World," *Time* magazine, 2007; named one of 20 people to watch, *Newsweek,* 2007.

## Sidelights

**N**ora Volkow, the director of the National Institute on Drug Abuse (NIDA), is a leading researcher in the field of addiction. From drug addiction to cravings for food that drive overeaters, Volkow has made a life study of identifying the brain chemistry that corresponds to addictive behaviors. Her work has led to several awards, including an Innovator of the Year award from *U.S. News & World Report* in 2000 to an Emmy Award, given to NIDA, the National Institute on Alcohol Abuse and Alcoholism, and HBO's joint addiction series in 2007. "We all think we can control our actions," Volkow said to Pat Wingert of *Newsweek.* "But why does one person have such intense cravings that they experience a loss of control, while another person can overpower those desires? I wanted to understand the brain mechanism that makes people lose control."

Volkow grew up in Mexico City, Mexico, where she lived with her family in the home of Leon Trotsky, who was her great-grandfather. She grew up with a passion for animals and animal behavior. As a child, she interfered with an experiment where a monkey was supposed to push a lever to get fresh water;

feeling sympathy for the creature, she found water for him. Later, during medical school, she stole a cat from the laboratory so that it could not be killed for experiments.

Because of her love for living creatures, she was reluctant to experiment on them, until, in 1980, she discovered the field of neuroimaging, or taking pictures of the brain. Her studies in the 1980s led her to prove that cocaine interrupts blood flow to the brain, showing definitively that the drug was anything but harmless. The study led her to prominence in the field of addiction research.

From early in her career, Volkow was interested in obsession and addiction. "It's a pleasure for me to try to understand things that are not obvious. It's a drive," she told Susan Brink of *U.S. News & World Report.* While working as the Associate Director for Life Sciences at Brookhaven National Laboratory—she was the youngest person to be appointed to that position—she studied how obsession and addiction are related to each other inside the brain. Her studies found that addicts, particularly alcoholics, had fewer dopamine receptors, or connections for the brain chemical that triggers happiness.

In 2003, Volkow was appointed the director of the NIDA. Her research at Brookhaven had been funded through NIDA grants, giving her knowledge of how NIDA funding affected research at other institutions. "I'm happy that Volkow accepted this important position to help expand scientific research and share NIDA results with health practitioners and the public," Secretary of the Department of Health and Human Services Tommy Thompson said of Volkow's appointment in *Biotech Week.* Volkow herself was delighted to be able to continue her research—and facilitate the research of others. "I am very excited with this new position, which will give me the opportunity to help fight one of the most serious problems facing our society—that of drug addiction," she said in *Biotech Week.*

In addition to her research, Volkow's duties include expanding ways to get information to the public. Within a year of taking her job, Volkow and her staff launched a Web site geared toward teens that explained the science behind drug abuse. The material, geared toward a variety of grade levels, emphasized the importance of research in discovering both causes and potential cures for addicts. The agency also sent information to 40,000 science teachers across the country, making them aware of the site and explaining the types of materials the agency was making available. In tandem with the site's

launch, NIDA formed a "Back to School" initiative, providing materials to be used in the classroom, including magazines for grades five through nine, a joint effort with children's publisher Scholastic to provide information about drugs and the human body, and a curriculum for high schoolers. All materials were made available free of charge. "We are excited about expanding the resources available to students and teachers on the science behind drug abuse and addiction," Volkow explained on *PR Newswire.* "Beyond their educational value, our materials hold the promise of sparking students' general interest in the biological sciences as a possible career choice, while meeting teachers' needs for engaging curricula that also fulfill national science education objectives."

Volkow has also conducted research that links HIV prevention and drug-abuse prevention, due to connections between drug users and behaviors that make HIV transmission more likely. In addition, one of the beneficial therapies for people infected with HIV is hampered by drug use. NIDA launched a Web site with information on the topic, geared toward teens, due to the lack of concerns many teens were showing about HIV and the corresponding increase of teens infected with the AIDS virus. NIDA also released studies showing the particular risk of HIV infection to African Americans, primarily due to drug use. The agency released a call for research showing the relationships between drug use, abuse, and the prevalence of HIV, for which they pledged to award to approximately ten studies a total of $3 million.

In addition to her continued research on drug addiction, Volkow has expanded her work to include studies on why people overeat. "I could have gone for gambling or sex addiction," she told Jeremy Manier of the *Chicago Tribune.* "But I went for obesity because of the tremendous impact it has." With the same scanning technology used to study the brain's reaction to drugs, Volkow found correspondences between the urge for food and the desires of addicts, particularly among individuals who are "pathologically obese." As in her studies on cocaine in the 1980s, her research on overeating shows a deficiency of dopamine receptors among the obese.

While the correspondences between addiction to food and addiction to drugs might be disturbing for some, Volkow has expressed excitement about the findings. "Just imagine," she said to Pat Wingert of *Newsweek,* "if all the private money being spent to understand and treat obesity could help us understand and treat alcoholics and drug addicts." It also provides her with the opportunity to encourage

NIDA scientists to apply findings in one form of addiction to other areas. She also searches for ways to disrupt the cycle of addiction, whether through drugs that would interrupt a conditioned response or through biofeedback techniques. Much of the research also involves dopamine receptors, as people with many dopamine receptors are less prone to addiction, while addiction reduces the number. Volkow, who was chosen as one of *Time* magazine's 100 people of 2007 and one of *Newsweek*'s 20 people to watch that same year, is dedicated to finding better treatments and aiding people who suffer from addiction of all kinds to overcome them. "This disease robs you of free will," she told Wingert. "The challenge is to find a cure."

## Sources

### Periodicals

*Alcoholism and Drug Abuse Weekly,* December 12, 2005, p. 6; September 10, 2007, p. 8.
*Biotech Week,* February 19, 2003, p. 96.
*Chicago Tribune,* August 26, 2005.
*Clinical Psychiatry News,* March 2003, p. 92.
*Government Computer News,* September 22, 2003, p. 7
*Newsweek,* December 25, 2006, 78.
PR Newswire, October 22, 2003.
*U.S. News and World Report,* December 25, 2000 p. 56.

### Online

"Director's Page," National Institute on Drug Abuse, http://www.nida.nih.gov/about/welcome/volkowpage.html (August 21, 2008).
"Nora Volkow Bio," National Conference of State Legislatures, http://www.ncsl.org/programs/health/forum/chairs/NoraVolkowbio.htm (August 21, 2008).
"The Time 100: Scientists and Thinkers: Nora Volkow," *Time,* http://www.time.com/time/specials/2007/time100/ (May 4, 2007).

—*Alana Joli Abbott*

# Michael Lee West

## Author

## Career

## Sidelights

Born Michael Lee Helton, October 15, 1953, in Lake Providence, LA; daughter of Ralph (a store manager) and Ary Jean Helton; married Willard Mahlon West (a physician); children: Trey, Tyler. *Education:* East Tennessee State University, B.S. (cum laude), 1981.

*Addresses: Home*—Lebanon, TN. *Publisher*—c/o Author Mail, HarperCollins, 10 East 53rd St., 7th Fl., New York, NY 10022.

Worked as a nurse, 1981-84; published writer, 1984—; published first novel, *Crazy Ladies*, 1990; published first nonfiction work, *Consuming Passions: A Food Obsessed Life*, 1999.

*Awards:* Outstanding Alumna, East Tennessee State University, 2000.

The author of several popular novels set in the South, Michael Lee West's work is distinguished by its humor, strong, if not eccentric, female characters, and insider's knowledge of Southern small towns. Her novels, such as *Crazy Ladies* and *American Pie*, are praised by critics for demonstrating her keen writing ability and insightfulness. Of the author, Jeanne F. Brooks wrote in the *San Diego Union-Tribune*, "West, who lives in Tennessee, is writing of a region she knows by heart."

Born in 1953 in Lake Providence, Louisiana, West is the daughter of parents who were natives of Mississippi. As a small child, she spent a significant amount of time in her parents' native state, primarily at her grandmother's home in Liberty. From an early age, West was exposed to vivid storytelling from the women gathered at her grandmother's house, including her aunts and her grandmother herself.

By the age of ten, West was living in Cookeville, Tennessee, where her father purchased then operated a dime store. When she was ten, she developed a lung infection, histoplasmosis, and was forced to spend the summer in bed. West spent that time reading books by Louisa May Alcott as well as such novels as *Peyton Place* and Dr. X's *Intern*. After her maternal grandmother gave her a subscription to *Seventeen* a few years later, West wanted to be a writer herself. She began writing short stories and soon moved on to novels.

When West entered college, she majored in elementary education. Her parents told her that she had to be a teacher or a nurse; however, taking English classes on the side lead her to discover major English poets. West changed her major to English, though her mother pressured her to return to education so she had a career to fall back on if something happened to her husband. West was not married at the time and did not change majors.

However, West soon met and married her husband Will, and left college. In the late 1970s, West returned to school, studying nursing at East Tennessee State University. Again attracted to English as a major, she took copious notes as a student nurse and joined a writing group. Weeks before West was due to graduate, she wanted to change her major back to English, but her husband's reaction compelled her to finish her nursing degree instead. West earned her B.S. cum laude in 1981, and became a registered nurse.

While pursuing a nursing career in which she worked in intensive care at a hospital in Lebanon, Tennessee, a medical-surgical department, and chemotherapy, West continued to write at home. She wrote verse and short stories, much of which was rejected by editors. Despite the lack of interest by publishers, she continued to form her own writing voice.

West quit nursing when she had her second son, Tyler in 1984. As she focused on supporting her sons in their various activities, she continued to work on her writing as well. By the mid-1980s, a few poems and short stories were published. Editors at various magazines like the *New Yorker* and *Redbook* encouraged her literary pursuits.

In 1990, West published her first novel, *Crazy Ladies*. This novel grew out of a short story she began writing in 1988, "When Mama Was Crazy." The story gradually expanded into a full-length novel, featuring the distinctive voices of six women—Miss Gussie, Queenie, Clancy Jane, Bitsy, Violet, and Dorothy—who live in a small town in the South. They deal with and talk about their every day lives over the course of several decades. Each woman has her own section which consists of a very personal journal.

*Crazy Ladies* was praised by many critics, including Benjamin Griffith of the *St. Petersburg Times*. He raved: "Not since Flannery O'Connor's first book has a debut novel by a young Southerner been so filled with wry humor and humanity, as precisely right in its idioms, and so distinctive in its voices as *Crazy Ladies* by Michael Lee West."

West's next novel, *She Flew the Coop: A Novel Concerning Life, Death, Sex, and Recipes in Limoges, Louisiana*, was published in 1994. Also set in the South, this time West focuses on the fictional small town of Limoges, Louisiana, in 1952. In the novel, she explores the daily dramas, tragedies, and triumphs as well as the secrets of Limoges' citizens. As with West's first novel, critics praised her distinctive voice and inventive characterizations.

Reviewing *She Flew the Coop* in the *Washington Post Book World*, Joan Mooney wrote: "West has created a whole world, southern in its recipes and manners, small town in its gossip and interconnections, and utterly individual in the characters, who are so teeming with life you would have to stand back to create some breathing room if you met them."

Similarly well received was West's third novel, *American Pie*. Published in 1996, the book focuses on three sisters—Eleanor, Freddie, and Jo-Nell Mc-Broom—and their grandmother, Minerva Pray. Residents of Tallulah, Tennessee, the book is written in each woman's voice and relates their lives, memories, and complex relationships. As Brooks wrote in the *San Diego Union-Tribune*, "Cracking open *American Pie* is like lifting the lid off a Mason jar of home-canned spiced peaches. What's inside is gold, sweet to the taste—though with a bite—and pure Southern." In the *Richmond Times Dispatch*, Sharon Lloyd Stratton concurred, concluding: "*American Pie* is a well-crafted piece of contemporary Southern fiction, packed with humor and edged with irony."

In 1999, West turned away from fiction to write a hybrid autobiography/cookbook, *Consuming Passions: A Food Obsessed Life*, which emphasizes the link between family and food. Each chapter relates some of her background in humorous fashion and includes many favorite family recipes. As well-received as her novels, West found writing *Consuming Passions* a welcome break from fiction. She told Susan Houston of the Raleigh, North Carolina *News and Observer*, "I had so much fun with it because I'd never written nonfiction before. It was so liberating because I knew how the story ended."

When *Consuming Passions* was published, West was also working on her next novel, a sequel to *Crazy Ladies* entitled *Mad Girls in Love*. Published in 2005, West expands their stories by two more decades but focuses primarily on Bitsy and her often problematic personal life. Other characters from the first book, including Dorothy, also return and share their experiences. While not as lauded as *Crazy Ladies*, Claudia Smith Brinson of the Columbia, South Carolina *State* noted West "will make you laugh. If you enjoy pondering the genetics—or bad luck—of generational eccentricity in the South, if you enjoy hanging out with women who love too much but reap many a tale along the way, this book is for you."

For her next novel, 2007's *Mermaids in the Basement*, West uses California as well as various Southern settings to explore the extended Southern family of screenwriter Renata DeChavnannes. Renata must deal with a potentially unfaithful boyfriend, the deaths of her mother and stepfather, and her father's marriage to his fourth wife. In a letter, her mother also has told her daughter to find out her secrets. Like her previous works, critics found West's novel enjoyable.

Living near Nashville, Tennessee, in a renovated funeral parlor with her family, West planned a third book in the *Crazy Ladies* trilogy and also was considering writing screenplays. Explaining where she gained her sense of humor, she told the *Southern Literary Review*, "My mother says the fairies swiped their real child and replaced her with me. Actually, I get my sense of comedy from Mama. My maternal grandmother was quite lively, too."

## Selected writings

### Novels

*Crazy Ladies*, Longstreet Press (Atlanta, GA), 1990.
*She Flew the Coop: A Novel Concerning Life, Death, Sex, and Recipes in Limoges, Louisiana*, HarperCollins (New York City), 1994.
*American Pie*, HarperCollins, 1996.
*Mad Girls in Love*, HarperCollins, 2005.
*Mermaids in the Basement*, HarperCollins, 2007.

### Memoir

*Consuming Passions: A Food Obsessed Life*, HarperCollins (New York City), 1999.

## Sources

### Books

*Contemporary Authors*, Thomson Gale, 2005.

### Periodicals

*Atlanta Journal and Constitution*, July 15, 1999, p. 5H.
*Booklist*, November 15, 2007, p. 19.
*News and Observer* (Raleigh, NC), August 4, 1999, p. F1.
*New York Times*, July 10, 1994, sec. 7, p. 24.
*Publishers Weekly*, March 15, 1999, p. 53; September 24, 2007, p. 41.
*Richmond Times Dispatch* (VA), October 20, 1996, p. K-4.
*San Diego Union-Tribune*, October 10, 1996, p. 42.
*State* (Columbia, SC), August 3, 2005.
*St. Petersburg Times* (FL), September 23, 1990, p. 6D.
*Virginian-Pilot* (Norfolk, VA), October 13, 1996, p. J2.
*Washington Post Book World*, October 7, 1990, p. X10; July 3, 1994, p. X8.

### Online

"Interview with Michael Lee West," *Southern Literary Review*, http://www.southernlitreview.com/authors/michael_west_interview.htm (October 28, 2008).
"Michael Lee West '81, 2000 Outstanding Alumna," East Tennessee State University Alumni Association, http://www.etsu.edu/alumni/award/00Award_West.asp (October 28, 2008).

—A. Petruso

# Brian Williams

*Michael Loccisano/Getty Images*

**Broadcaster and journalist**

**B**orn Brian Douglas Williams, May 5, 1959, in Elmira, NY; son of Gordon (a retail executive) and Dorothy Williams (married name, Pampel); married Jane Stoddard (a television producer), June 8, 1986; children: Allison, Douglas. *Education:* Attended Brookdale Community College, Catholic University of America, and George Washington University, late 1970s.

**Addresses:** *Home*—New Canaan, CT. *Office*—NBC News, 30 Rockefeller Plz., 3rd Fl., New York, NY, 10112.

## Career

**W**orked at a pancake restaurant and as a volunteer firefighter in Monmouth County, NJ, mid-1970s; White House intern, Carter administration, late 1970s; Congressional liaison aide, National Association of Broadcasters, c. 1981; reporter, KOAM-TV, 1981-82; production assistant, WTTG-TV, Washington, DC, 1982, then general assignment reporter and host of *Panorama*, by 1985; New Jersey correspondent, WCAU-TV, Philadelphia, PA, 1985-87; weekday noon and weekend night anchor, WCBS-TV, New York City, 1987-93; anchor and managing editor, *NBC Nightly News Saturday*, 1993-99; chief White House correspondent, NBC News, Washington, DC, 1994-96; anchor and managing editor, *The News with Brian Williams*, MSNBC/CNBC, 1996-2004; anchor and managing editor, *NBC Nightly News*, 2004—.

**Member:** Board of directors, Congressional Medal of Honor Foundation; Council on Foreign Relations.

**Awards:** Father of Year, National Father's Day Committee, 1996; Man of Year, *GQ* Magazine, 2001; four Edward R. Murrow Awards, Radio-Television News Directors Association, for coverage of Hurricane Katrina, 2005; George Foster Peabody Award, University of Georgia, for *After the Storm: The Long Road Back,* 2005.

## Sidelights

**B**rian Williams succeeded veteran journalist Tom Brokaw as anchor of the *NBC Nightly News* in 2004. The chair he occupies on NBC's flagship evening newscast is inarguably one of the three most-coveted spots in broadcast journalism. While Williams has managed to maintain the No. 1 ratings spot from the Brokaw era, he realizes that there are scores of other ways in which Americans get their news. "We get that we're not telling people for the first time the stories of the day," he told *American Journalism Review* writer Rachel Smolkin. "They understand that. They're coming to us for a recognized brand name, a family of correspondents, people that they know and trust."

Williams was born in 1959 in Elmira, an upstate New York town near the border with Pennsylvania. His father was a store manager who later took a job with the Manhattan-based National Retail Merchants Association when Williams, the last of four children, was ten years old. At that point, the family moved to Middletown, New Jersey, not far from the Jersey shore and with a hill to which the adolescent Williams used to ride his bike to observe the construction of World Trade Center, whose twin towers were the world's tallest buildings at the time. He was fascinated by the three big networks' news anchors—Walter Cronkite of CBS, NBC's Chet Huntley and David Brinkley, and Frank Reynolds and Harry Reasoner of ABC. Their nightly newscasts were watched by half of all U.S. households in 1969 during this era, but have plummeted ever since. Williams came of age in an era when radio and print newspapers were the only other source of news besides these star anchors and the news-gathering organizations behind them, on which the networks lavished huge sums to achieve ratings hegemony.

Williams was raised Roman Catholic and attended Mater Dei High School, where he was an admittedly lackluster student. He worked at a local pancake restaurant and as soon as he was old enough became a volunteer firefighter with the Middletown Township Fire Department, a job he loved. During his career he saved just two lives—a pair of puppies—but he later said the experience proved invaluable to a career in television news. "Going to sleep with my boots, pants, jacket, and helmet next to the bed for so many years is still, to this day, the best training for the life I lead," he told *Esquire*'s Cal Fussman.

Following his graduation from Mater Dei, Williams enrolled at Brookdale Community College, but decided to move to Washington, D.C., on a whim after he and a friend visited the nation's capital for a day. He worked several jobs to help pay his tuition at Catholic University of America, including a stint at Sears and another selling fresh-cut Christmas trees. Restless, he moved on to George Washington University, where he managed to land a coveted White House internship during the administration of President Jimmy Carter. After that point, he quit school altogether, which he would later term "one of the great, great regrets of my life," he told the graduating class of Tulane University in New Orleans when he was invited to deliver the 2007 commencement address.

Williams went to work for the National Association of Broadcasters (NAB), a trade association group of radio and television station owners that was headquartered in Washington. He worked as a Congressional liaison aide, and began to consider a career

in broadcast journalism, which he had dreamed about as a youngster. In 1981, his boss at the NAB helped arrange a tryout at a small television station in Pittsburg, Kansas, called KOAM, whose call letters represented its coverage area at the junction of Kansas, Oklahoma, Arkansas, and Missouri. Williams proved a quick learner in reporting, editing, and delivering stories, but his $168 weekly salary failed to adequately cover his expenses, and he found himself mired in credit-card debt. "There were times when I had absolutely no money to my name," he recalled about this period of his life in the *Esquire* interview. "I had to ask friends for meals. I once went five days without a dollar. To this day, I make sure I always have a folded dollar in my wallet. It's my talisman, my little reminder."

After a little over a year, Williams moved back to Washington and was hired as a production assistant at WTTG-TV, an independent station. He soon worked his way into a position as a general assignment reporter and occasional host of its afternoon talk show, *Panorama,* which had been a career-launching post for tabloid-television journalist Maury Povich. In 1985, Williams was hired by the CBS affiliate in Philadelphia, WCAU-TV, to serve as its New Jersey correspondent. In 1987, he moved on to the CBS affiliate in New York City, WCBS-TV, a move widely considered to be a stepping stone for a correspondent's job with one of the three networks. After two years, he became the permanent co-anchor of its noon news broadcast, and traveled far afield to cover breaking international stories, including the fall of the Berlin Wall. This type of reportage raised his profile even further, and he was discovered by NBC News star Tom Brokaw, anchor of the *NBC Nightly News.*

Williams joined the NBC team as a reporter, and after five months became the regular anchor of the Saturday nightly newscast as well as the permanent substitute for Brokaw when the latter was on vacation or assignment. Early on, many predicted Williams might one day take over for Brokaw, who had been the sole anchor for *NBC Nightly News* since September of 1983. That speculation intensified when NBC News made Williams the chief White House correspondent in 1994.

Williams became a star in his own right with the launch of MSNBC in the summer of 1996. The cable channel was a joint venture between Microsoft and NBC to capitalize on the new- and old-media strengths of both. Williams was given a plum spot as anchor and managing editor of an unprecedented one-hour nightly newscast, *The News with Brian Williams,* which went live on the same day MSNBC was launched on July 15, 1996. Two nights later, TWA Flight 800 went down off the coast of Long Island, and MSNBC broke the story of the crash, which occurred just before Williams' news broadcast was set to start at 9 p.m. Writing in the *New York Times* several days later, Frank Rich commended his coverage of the air disaster, noting that "Williams … loomed on screen to fill air time with scanty information, dropped cues and droning experts. CNN's coverage followed the same old-fashioned TV tradition, except that its stiffly coiffed anchors seemed less human than the affable Mr. Williams. When the story is inexplicable mass death, a TV viewer wants company, not androids."

Williams gained a strong following for his nightly MSNBC newscast, despite some criticism that it veered into tabloid territory with its sensationalistic coverage of the death of Princess Diana and the Clinton White House scandal. "Williams' intelligence comes through in the follow-up questions he asks his guests, in the way he explains and foils some of the fog machines that generate the news," wrote Marjorie Williams in a *Vanity Fair* profile. "He manages to strike a tone that's informal and wise to the ironies of the world, without being smarmy." Predictions that he would some day take over for Brokaw in the broadcast network's flagship newscast had not abated, and he remained the designated fill-in for Brokaw on *NBC Nightly News*. There were also rumors that he was being offered lucrative deals by CNN, ABC, and CBS, but in May of 2002 Brokaw announced he would be leaving *NBC Nightly News* after the 2004 presidential election, and NBC confirmed that Williams would succeed him as anchor after that.

Williams stayed aboard *The News with Brian Williams*, which had by then moved to CNBC, MSNBC/NBC's sister-cable network, until early 2004. He debuted as *NBC Nightly News* anchor on December 2, 2004. His newscast aired live on most NBC affiliates at 6:30 p.m., and was the number-one rated network newscast since 1996. By the end of the first decade of the new century, it remained in first place under Williams' helm despite the challenges presented to it when Katie Couric took over from Dan Rather on the *CBS Evening News* in 2006. It was a much-ballyhooed changing of the guard, with Couric as the first female solo anchor of a traditional network evening newscast. Writing in the *New York Observer*, journalist Rebecca Dana claimed that "Williams is perhaps the last of the old-fashioned news anchors: the raffish cousin to Mr. Brokaw's all-knowing father to Mr. Rather's batty uncle to Mr. Cronkite's saintly Pops."

Williams and his *NBC Nightly News* team collected several important industry honors for their coverage of Hurricane Katrina and its aftermath in 2005, including four Edward R. Murrow Awards and the prestigious George Foster Peabody Award. Williams cut short his family vacation in order to land in New Orleans before the storm hit, and spent Sunday night in the Louisiana Superdome, which city officials had designated as a temporary shelter for residents unable or unwilling to evacuate ahead of the storm. Williams did not stay there in the calamitous week following the catastrophe—when thousands were still in the building without food, water, or even electricity—but he was still there on Monday morning and reported live for NBC's morning newscast, *The Today Show*. Revealing photographs taken by his cell phone camera showed part of the roof gone and rain flooding into the structure.

Williams and other journalists on the scene in the aftermath of the hurricane, when the city's levees broke and entire neighborhoods were underwater, tried and then essentially abandoned their standard objectivity in the face of the disaster and the slow, ineffectual federal response. On Thursday, he conducted an interview with the Federal Emergency Management Agency (FEMA) director Michael Brown, and was famously curt with the White House official, who claimed he had no idea about reports of 25,000 people living in abysmal, unsanitary conditions inside the Superdome. "I get upset about it because I saw things, we all saw things, that [President George W. Bush] didn't and the FEMA director did not," Williams told *Television-Week* writer Allison J. Waldman. "And until you've seen the bodies … floating in the waters in America's 25th largest city, you perhaps may not understand the magnitude of what has taken place there."

Williams appears regularly on *Late Night with David Letterman* and *The Daily Show with Jon Stewart*. On November 3, 2007, he made television history when he became the first network news anchor ever to host *Saturday Night Live*. His salary is believed to be in the ballpark of $10 million a year. He is married to Jane Stoddard, a television producer he met while working at WTTG back in the early 1980s and with whom he has two children. They live in the same Connecticut farmhouse where his wife was raised, which they bought from her parents. In the interview with *Vanity Fair*'s Williams, the news anchor recalled the first time his future wife took him to the New Canaan home where she grew up, saying that at the time, "I thought, I'll never be this lucky. I'll *never* be this lucky."

## Sources

### Periodicals

*American Journalism Review*, August/September 2006.
*Esquire*, July 2005, p. 104.

*New York Observer,* August 27, 2006.

*New York Times,* July 24, 1996; October 27, 2002; December 2, 2004.

*TelevisionWeek,* May 29, 2006, p. 18.

*Vanity Fair,* January 1999; November 2005, p. 176.

*Washington Post,* November 5, 2007, p. C1.

**Online**

"Remarks by Brian Williams—May 19, 2007," Tulane University, http://www.grads.tulane.edu/transcript_brianwilliams.html (April 11, 2009).

—*Carol Brennan*

# Andrea Wong

**Television executive**

Born in 1966, in Northern California. *Education:* Massachusetts Institute of Technology, B.A., 1988; Stanford University, M.B.A.

**Addresses:** *Office*—Lifetime Television, 309 W. 49th St., #C2, New York, NY 10019.

## Career

Researcher, ABC News, 1993; executive assistant to the president, ABC, 1994; vice president and executive assistant to the president, ABC, 1997; vice president, alternative series and specials, ABC, 1998; senior vice president, ABC, 2000; executive vice president, alternative programming, specials and late-night, ABC, 2004; president and chief executive officer, Lifetime Entertainment Services, 2007—.

**Awards:** Honored by Step Up Women's Network, 2008.

## Sidelights

President and CEO of Lifetime Entertainment Services Andrea Wong grew up learning that she shouldn't be afraid to fail. "My parents always allowed me to fail when I was growing up, and that gave me a lot of strength going forward," she explained in an interview with Barbara Kantrowitz for *Newsweek International.* Wong ran for class president in middle school and high school and did not succeed, but learned that even after a failure, she had to keep going. These life lessons became vital

for her as she entered the world of television programming. "For every one hit on television, there are umpteen shows that never or only briefly see the light of day," she continued, noting that while she had succeeded with a number of her programs, she also had many failures. While a student at the Massachusetts Institute of Technology, she also learned the value of solving problems. She learned to break down issues, direct her energy at each part, and solve the parts to solve the whole. "You just have to remain undaunted and realize you will solve them," she explained to Stewart Schley in *Multichannel News.*

Wong first became involved in the television industry as an intern at NBC News while she studied for her M.B.A. at Stanford, University. In 1993, she joined ABC as a researcher for the ABC News program *Primetime Live,* and by 1994, she was named executive assistant to the president. Her career at ABC continued as, in 1997, her duties expanded when she was promoted to vice president and executive assistant to the president, ABC, Inc., and in 1998 Wong became vice president of alternative series and specials. After becoming senior vice president in 2000, she rose to executive vice president of alternative programming, specials, and late-night for ABC in 2004, and continued in that position until she was named the new president and chief executive officer of Lifetime Entertainment Services in 2007.

Wong's work at ABC involved creating a positive brand for non-scripted programming, often called reality television. In 2002, Wong launched *The Bachelor,* and soon after developed sister program *The*

*Bachelorette.* She adapted UK hit *Dancing with the Stars* for an American audience, and the program soon topped the ratings. Other reality programs introduced by Wong include *Extreme Makeover: Home Edition,* which won an Emmy, as well as *Wife Swap* and *Supernanny,* two programs that offer wish fulfillment in domestic environments. Wong was also responsible for bringing the Country Music Awards presentation, the Academy Awards, and the American Music Awards to ABC, rather than other networks.

Lifetime was struggling when Wong took the helm. A cable network designed to appeal to women, Lifetime needed to attract a younger audience to gain viewers. In addition, the marketing department did not have a full staff, making promotion of programs more difficult. At the beginning, Wong made her focus putting new shows on the air, introducing several scripted programs, including the popular *Army Wives* and critically praised *A Side Order of Life.* She also hired people into top marketing positions, and began focusing on creating a staff that would help create a younger image for the network. Along with adding to her marketing team, she hired an executive vice president in ad sales, and new heads of research, scheduling, and movie development, due to many veteran Lifetime staff members leaving the network or retiring.

The fact that *Army Wives* became a success—the most successful show in Lifetime history to that point—gave Wong further leeway in how to approach her new network. "It gave the whole organization a great lift and a great optimism about where we were going. It was just the wind against our backs that we needed to propel us forward," she told an interviewer for *Television Week.*

In addition to the new programming, Wong made redesigning and updating the Lifetime Web presence a priority, again to reach the younger viewers and enhance Lifetime's image as a network that appeals to all women. "I think growing our brand in the digital space is critical to our future," Wong told R. Thomas Umstead in *Multichannel News.* "[We] want to be the leading destination for women for entertainment, for escape, for advocacy on whatever platform they come to. Whether it's linear television, or online or mobile or anywhere else, the Lifetime brand strives to be the destination for women wherever they want content." The increased digital presence could also enhance Lifetime's brand. "The great news for me is Lifetime is an incredibly strong brand," she explained in *Television Week.* "I want to take the brand, bring an increased relevance to today's women to the brand, bring an energy and a vibrancy to it and an optimism to it."

But the changing image of the network also hit some fans negatively, particularly when Wong began introducing more unscripted, reality television shows, replacing the cult favorite *A Side Order of Life.* Her acquisition of *Project Runway* became problematic in the legal arena as well, given that the program's former network claimed to have first rejection rights. The shift was part of an intent to offer more original programs, rather than packaged movies and programming that the network had provided in the past. "I think original programming is critical because it is brand-defining for us," Wong said in an interview with *Broadcasting & Cable.* She also explained that when looking to bring an unscripted program to the network, she sought out "distinctive brands and ideas that look and feel different." She also noted that the unscripted programs on Lifetime could not embrace reality, but that the network's viewers, as she put it to Schley in *Multichannel News,* were seeking "the ultimate escape." Lew Goldstein, co-marketing chief of Lifetime shared with Jon Lafayette of *Television Week,* "Andrea kept using the term 'escape' to define Lifetime," which led to a marketing campaign based on the idea of flying away, depicting an airplane and focusing on travel. "Lifetime has been in your living room, but now we're going to take it to you," Goldstein continued.

In 2008, Wong was honored by the Step Up Women's Network, an organization that supports creating positive role models for girls and women. "Andrea Wong represents everything Step Up strives to promote by utilizing her professional success to give back and make a difference in her community," Daniel Craig, executive director of the organization, said in *PR Newswire.* "Lifetime Networks leads the entertainment industry's focus on positive messaging for women and girls." Wong also received high praise from the former president of entertainment at Lifetime Networks, Susanne Daniels. In *Entertainment Close-up,* Daniels said, "With Andrea's impressive, strategic leadership, Lifetime is destined for even greater success."

## Sources

### Periodicals

*Broadcasting & Cable,* June 16, 2008, p. 3.
*Entertainment Close-up,* June 24, 2008.
*Media Week,* April 28, 2008, p. 6.
*Multichannel News,* December 10, 2007, p. 31; June 23, 2008, p. 25.
*Newsweek International,* October 22, 2007.
*PR Newswire,* May 9, 2008.
*Television Week,* September 3, 2007, p. 4; April 14, 1008, p. 3.

## Online

"Andrea Wong Assumes Role as Newly Appointed President & CEO, Lifetime Entertainment Services," Hearst Corporation Web site, http://www.hearst.com/news/press_042607b.html (August 22, 2008).

*—Alana Joli Abbott*

# Joe Wright

**Director**

**B**orn in London, England, in 1972; son of John (a puppeteer and theater director) and Lyndie (a puppeteer and theater director) Wright. *Education:* Attended Camberwell College of Arts, c. 1990; Central St. Martins College of Art and Design, fine arts degree, after 1990.

**Addresses:** *Agent*—Sue Rogers, International Creative Management, 61 Frith St., London W1D 3JL, England.

## Career

**A**ssociated with Vegetable Vision, a visual-effects company, early 1990s. Director of short films, including: *Crocodile Snap,* 1997; *The End,* 1998. Director for television, including: *Nature Boy* (miniseries), 2000; *Bob & Rose,* 2001; *Bodily Harm* (miniseries), 2002; *Charles II: The Power & the Passion* (miniseries), 2003. Director of feature films, including: *Pride & Prejudice,* 2005; *Atonement,* 2007; *The Soloist,* 2008.

**Awards:** BAFTA Television Award for best drama serial, British Academy of Film and Television Arts, for *Charles II: The Power & the Passion,* 2004; Carl Foreman Award for the most promising newcomer, British Academy of Film and Television Arts, for *Pride & Prejudice,* 2006.

## Sidelights

**B**ritish director Joe Wright's second feature film of his career, *Atonement,* was nominated for a stunning 14 BAFTA awards, the British equivalent of Hollywood's Academy Awards, in 2008. His film adaptation of Ian McEwan's best seller *Atonement* starred Keira Knightley and James McAvoy as doomed lovers in pre-World War II England, and was hailed by critics as a deliciously vivid screen version of a literary gem. "Rarely has a book sprung so vividly to life, but also worked so enthrallingly in pure-movie terms," declared Derek Elley in *Variety.*

Wright was born in 1972 in London, England, to John Wright, a puppeteer who was 65 years old at the time. Wright's parents ran the Little Angel Theatre in the section of greater London known as Islington. Wright's father carved the wooden marionettes himself, operated them, and directed scores of productions that made the 100-seat theater a popular children's attraction in London for decades. Wright and his sister played an active role in the family business, since the home telephone was also Little Angel's box-office number, and he became skilled at booking group reservations at an early age. Though students at his London school often teased him about his parents' line of work, the theater company proved an excellent training ground for a future film director and offered opportunity for exotic travel as Wright and his sister accompanied their parents when the puppet theater made tours abroad.

Wright was diagnosed with dyslexia, a learning disability that made reading difficult, and left school at age 16. After his father died three years later, in 1991, Wright decided to enroll in college. He studied film at Camberwell College of Arts and at his father's alma mater, Central St. Martins College of Art and Design. Though he was probably the only student who had a bit part in an Al Pacino movie at the age of 13—*Revolution,*the 1985 American Revolutionary War drama filmed partly in London—he was indeed "the only one who wanted to make films that actually had a narrative," he told *Observer* writer Jason Solomons about his more avant-garde film school classmates.

For a time Wright worked for a company called Vegetable Vision that produced visual effects for the live shows of the Chemical Brothers, Underworld, and other electronic-music artists. His first directorial efforts were two short films, *Crocodile Snap* and *The End,* in the late 1990s. The miniseries *Nature Boy* in 2000 was his first television job, followed by two more multi-episode made-for-television films, *Bob & Rose* and *Bodily Harm.* In 2003 he helmed a lavishly produced British Broadcasting Corporation (BBC) costume drama, *Charles II: The Power & the Passion,* that aired on BBC1 in November of 2003 with a first-rate cast that included Rufus Sewell and Diana Rigg.

That seventeenth-century period drama led to Wright's next project, *Pride & Prejudice,* which was also his first full-length feature film. The 2005 movie, which starred Keira Knightley in the adaptation of the much-loved Jane Austen novel from 1813, earned Knightley her first Academy Award nomination, and Wright won his first film "BAFTA," as the British Academy of Film and Television Arts awards are known, for Most Promising Newcomer.

Working Title Films hired Wright to direct *Pride & Prejudice,* and they also handed him his next job, a long-awaited screen version of British novelist Ian McEwan's 2001 novel *Atonement.* Its plot centers around 13-year-old Briony Tallis, an aspiring writer from an affluent British family in the late 1930s. She worships her college-age sister Cecilia, and harbors a crush on the young man who grew up on the family's Sussex estate, Robbie, who is nearer to Cecilia's age and also a student at Cambridge University. On a hot English summer day, Briony witnesses several events that confuse her, and her natural inquisitiveness turns intrusive and then inadvertently spiteful after another teenage guest is sexually assaulted. Briony names Robbie as the culprit, and he is sent to prison and then released to serve in the British Army when World War II begins. Cecilia becomes a nurse, as does Briony, but Cecilia refused to have contact with her family after the night Robbie was taken into custody. Briony grows up to become an acclaimed author, but is still haunted decades later by her error in judgment that one summer night.

Following McEwan's novel, *Atonement* is divided into three distinct parts: for the first, on the torrid summer day at the Tallis estate, Wright covered the camera lens with pantyhose to give it an appropriately heated feel; the second segment follows Robbie and two fellow soldiers as they make their way to Dunkirk, a beach in France where more than 300,000 British and French troops were evacuated to safety in 1940 as German forces advanced. The scene at Dunkirk was the most talked-about moment in Wright's film. Conveying the desperation of thousands of stranded forces on a beach as the enemy advanced took a cast of a thousand extras and crew of 300.

*Atonement'*s third segment takes place in the wartime hospital where the now-grown Briony works as a nurse, and was filmed in pale shades of blue and grey with a formalism one critic likened to a Renaissance painting—until the first casualties from the Battle of Dunkirk arrive, and the blood and horror of war flood the screen. An epilogue, with Vanessa Redgrave as the now-elderly Briony, reveals what happened to each of the characters.

*Atonement* opened the 64th annual Venice Film Festival, making the 35-year-old Wright the youngest director in the history of the event to have his or her work chosen for that honor. The critical reception was equally impressive. "What the film brings to the book, apart from excellent performances, are fine images and a powerful period atmosphere," wrote the *Observer'*s Philip French, who asserted that the Dunkirk scene "is a virtuoso long take, lasting five to six minutes, that belongs beside long takes by [Alfred] Hitchcock, [Orson] Welles," and other cinema pioneers.

To the surprise of *Atonement'*s fans, Wright was overlooked at the Academy Award nominations for Best Director. When those Oscar nominations were announced, he was already on the set of his next work, *The Soloist,* starring Jamie Foxx and Robert Downey Jr. The story was based on the real-life biography of Nathaniel Ayers, who was a violin prodigy in his younger years but was later enveloped by schizophrenia and lived on the streets of Los Angeles. Wright admitted to Solomons in the *Observer* interview that "for 12 hours or so I was gutted because everyone seemed so angry about it on my behalf. Then I just looked around and thought: What am I even thinking?"

## Sources

*Entertainment Weekly*, December 7, 2007, p. 54.
*Film Journal International*, November 2005, p. 22.
*New Statesman*, November 24, 2003, p. 47.
*New York Times*, November 4, 2007.

*Observer* (London, England), September 9, 2007; February 10, 2008, p. 36.
*Variety*, January 16, 2006, p. 15; October 23, 2006, p. A2; September 3, 2007, p. 47.

—*Carol Brennan*

# Robert Wyland

## Artist

**B**orn in 1956, in Detroit, MI. *Education:* Attended the Center for Creative Studies.

**Addresses:** *Office*—c/o Wyland Worldwide LLC, 5 Columbia, Aliso Viejo, CA 92656.

## Career

**B**egan painting as a toddler; created first mural, c. 1971; worked for Shrunken Head (a van muralist), c. early 1970s; created first whaling wall, 1981; painted world's largest mural "Planet Ocean" (whaling wall number 33), Long Beach, CA, 1992; painted 17 walls in 17 weeks in 17 different cities on the East Coast of the United States, 1993; founded Wyland Foundation, 1993; painted whaling wall number 86, Tampa, FL, 2000; completed whaling wall number 100, in Beijing, China, 2008.

## Sidelights

**A**rtist Robert Wyland, often referred to just by his last name Wyland, is best known for the 100 murals he painted worldwide of whales between 1977 and 2008. These life-sized murals—dubbed "Whaling Walls"—often adorn buildings and gave him a reputation as a leading environmental marine artist in the United States. Of the murals, which are intended to educate viewers about the environment outside an art gallery, Wyland told the Queensland *Sunday Mail*, "It's a way of making them stop and think. You can't ignore a giant mural." Wyland is also the owner of a number of Wyland Galleries in the United States.

*Jacob Andrzejczak/WireImage/Getty Images*

Born in 1956 in Detroit, Wyland is the son of two auto workers who worked on assembly lines at Chrysler and Chevrolet. His father left the family during his childhood, and his mother brought up Wyland and his three siblings in a garage on welfare. Art was an interest from an early age. Wyland began painting at the age of three or four, using a can of house paint to paint a mural of dinosaurs on the headboard of his parents' bed. By the age of 15, he had created his first mural. At 16, he was drawing portraits of artist Salvador Dali, his idol.

The ocean and its inhabitants became his preferred subject in part because of a youthful love of oceanographer Jacques Cousteau's television specials. Wyland especially became enamored of whales and other large sea creatures. When Wyland was 14 years old, he visited California during a family vacation. There, he observed the migration of California gray whales off the coast. Wyland soon became focused on painting whales, first on canvases, which increased regularly in size, and he became an environmentalist.

Wyland attended art school at the Center for Creative Studies in Detroit, where he majored in painting and sculpture. To pay for his tuition and expenses, he worked for the air-brush artist Shrunken Head, who created van murals that were popular in the 1970s. Murals with environmental themes soon became his trademark, though he spent much of the 1970s as a starving artist. He told John Law of the *Niagara Falls Review,* "In the early 1970s there was no such thing as environmental art. It just so happened I was in the right place at the right time, with Greenpeace and Jacques Cousteau. That captured my imagination and I started painting marine art."

Wyland's first whaling mural was "Gray Whale and Calf," which he painted in 1981 on the side of a hotel in Laguna Beach, California. He came up with the idea for large-scale whale murals when he realized he could not sufficiently capture the majesty of whales on a small canvas. Wyland began painting murals on government buildings, urban office buildings, and clock towers. He told Cathy Hainer of *USA Today,* "I'm trying to paint not only the great whales but the great spirit they possess. By painting them life-sized in public places, I hope to raise people's consciousness and get them involved in protecting the whales."

Wyland's method remained simple over the years. He did not use sketches for his murals, nor did he employ grids. Instead, Wyland visualized the whales swimming in front of him and painted what he saw. As he told John Allemang of the *Globe and Mail* in 1997, "From 20 years of diving, I've got these continuous images in my mind of whales swimming through incredible oceans." He added to Karen Sandstrom of the Cleveland *Plain Dealer,* "When I'm working up close, my mind's eye is way over there, looking at it as if I were far away. It's almost an out-of-body experience."

While his first murals were done completely by himself, Wyland came to rely on his own team as well as volunteers to complete the whaling walls according to his vision. Wyland, however, played a primary role in their creation. Other artists admired his technical skills, with muralist Ron Juncal telling David Washburn of the *San Diego Union-Tribune,* "He is a true magician at working large. Just to go up there with that [spray] gun and start blazing away is not an easy process." Though Wyland charged for the whaling walls early on, they were eventually completed for free, supported by corporate and private sponsors and his own successful art business. As he became a millionaire in the mid-1980s, Wyland spent part of the year working on murals while maintaining studios in California and Hawaii.

Despite the popularity of his work, Wyland sometimes faced legal issues related to his murals. In 1986, for example, he was sued by the Sea Shepherd

Society, a Canadian wildlife conservation group, in the Supreme Court of British Columbia. Wyland was accused of not paying half of his $20,000 fee for painting his thirteenth mural on a Vancouver-based building owned by Canada Life Assurance Company in 1985 to the group. The Sea Shepherd Society claimed that Wyland made an oral agreement to give it these funds, but Wyland stated that he had never had contact with the Sea Shepherd Society. Despite the lawsuit, the company was so pleased with his mural that the building was re-named the Wyland Building.

By the early 1990s, Wyland's standard fee for commercial painting work was $66,000 per day. However, he had begun to complete his whaling walls for free as educational celebrations of the environment. He continued to paint the whale murals in more diverse cities in this time period. In 1990, for example, Wyland painted murals in Tacoma (entitled "Washington Orcas") and the Australian city of Bundaberg. The mural of whales playing took up a whole wall off of the small Australian community's main street. As soon as he completed that whaling wall, Wyland painted a marine mural on the roof of the Sydney aquarium at Darling Harbour.

Two years later, in 1992, Wyland created his biggest whaling wall, number 33, in Long Beach, California. Dubbed "Planet Ocean," it covers the entire external wall of the cylindrical Long Beach Arena. This mural was named the world's largest by the *Guinness Book of World Records.* Wyland used more than 7,000 gallons of paint on the mural, which is ten stories high and incorporates approximately 116,000 square feet.

In the early 1990s, Wyland was building on his fame for commercial purposes by reproducing his murals and paintings as limited edition posters. He also sold whale t-shirts and jewelry and later added postcards and books. Commercialization, however, was not Wyland's goal. He told Karen Kucher of the *San Diego Union-Tribune,* "I believe that if I paint enough of these murals, we will not only save the whales but be able to save their environment, and that's the big picture."

By 1993, it was estimated that more than one billion people per year saw at least one of his whaling walls. That year, Wyland challenged himself by painting 17 walls in 17 weeks in 17 different cities on the East Coast of the United States. The following year, he painted 13 walls in seven weeks, primarily in the western part of North America. These murals included number 55 at the Vancouver Aquarium, which depicts a pod of killer whales; number 65 on the San Diego National Bank building, which depicts migrating California gray whales; and number 66 and number 67 in Mexico City, Mexico. The mural in San Diego alone took about 400 gallons of paint.

While Wyland's murals were popular and desired by many communities, there was sometimes conflict. When the painter wanted to create a mural of a pod of humpback whales on the Milwaukee Public Museum as a gift to the county in 1997, there was public division over whether he should be allowed to do so. Many saw the proposed mural as art, but others derided it as a large-scale billboard or even a possible blot on the landscape that did not fit with both the building and downtown architecture. The county ultimately approved the mural, but on the Courthouse Annex after the museum stated it did not want the whaling wall. Wyland completed the mural (number 72) as part of seven murals in seven cities in seven weeks in the American Midwest and Toronto that year. The Toronto mural (number 70) of eastern humpbacks was created on the Redpath Sugars refinery in Queen's Quay.

By 2000, Wyland was painting number 86 whaling wall in Tampa, Florida. Painted at the Homosassa Springs State Wildlife Park, it features manatees, a subject he painted only a few times. As Wyland neared his goal of 100 murals, he faced several challenging situations. In November of 2004, Wyland threatened legal action against Detroit when the Detroit Board of Zoning Appeals ruled to allow General Motors to erect a billboard over the mural of an endangered humpback whale he painted at Comerica Park in 1997. Wyland protested, citing the federal Visual Artists Rights Act of 1990, and threatened a law suit. After public response in support of Wyland and his art, General Motors dropped the idea a few days later.

A month later, Milwaukee was threatening to tear down the Court Annex, which was falling apart and in the path of what was to be a rebuilt freeway. Wyland again protested, telling them they could not tear down the wall with his mural without his permission. Despite his threats of legal action, he backed down in 2005, said he would not stand in the way of the annex being destroyed, and offered to do another mural in the area.

By the spring of 2006, Wyland was painting number 93, on a building at the Del Mar Fairgrounds, his third whaling wall in San Diego. As Wyland reached

his goal of 100 walls, his commercial business was growing with at least 34 galleries in such places as the Niagara Fallsview Casino resort. His company, Wyland Worldwide, was grossing $100 million annually. He had licensing agreements on a number of products, including sporting equipment, scrubs, and baby clothes, and lent his name and images to such companies as Disney and Campbell. His art was also the focus of a Wyland-theme hotel, which opened in Honolulu, Hawaii, in 2006. In addition, Wyland gave back to the community through his Wyland Foundation (founded in 1993), which promoted ecological conservation efforts in schools. The artist spent a month every year on an educational tour.

Wyland's original goal was to paint 100 whaling walls by the year 2011. He more than met it, painting number 100 in 2008 next to the Great Wall in China shortly before the start of the Summer Olympics at Beijing with the help of 3,000 children. After completing the hundredth mural, Wyland continued to paint and sculpt, oversee his vast business empire, and focus on environmental concerns. While critics often derided his underwater sea scenes and believed he was a better marketer than artist, Wyland was a financial success and made an impact on environmental issues. As he told Allemang of the *Globe and Mail,* "There are two roads an artist can take, to go after the acceptance of the critics or the people. I decided to go for the people."

## Sources

### Books

*Complete Marquis Who's Who Biographies,* Marquis Who's Who LLC, 2006.

### Periodicals

*Art Business News,* August 1, 2008, p. 20.
Associated Press, September 30, 2008.
Associated Press State & Local Wire, November 12, 2004; November 16, 2004; December 3, 2004; November 4, 2005; June 15, 2008.
*Financial Post* (Toronto, Ontario, Canada), February 22, 1986, sec. 2, p. 22.
*Globe and Mail* (Toronto, Ontario, Canada), September 1, 1997, p. C1.
*Highlights for Children,* September 1, 2002, p. 8.
*Milwaukee Journal Sentinel* (WI), June 7, 1997, p. 1; July 18, 1997, p. 1.
*Niagara Falls Review* (Ontario, Canada), August 18, 2006.

*Plain Dealer* (Cleveland, OH), October 4, 1997, p. 1B.

*San Diego Union-Tribune,* September 14, 1994, p. B3; June 20, 2006, p. A1.

*Seattle Times,* October 1, 1992, p. D1.

*Sunday Mail* (Queensland, Australia), September 23, 1990.

*Tampa Tribune* (FL), October 17, 2000, p. 3.

*USA Today,* September 30, 1993, p. 4D.

*Vancouver Sun* (British Columbia, Canada), August 8, 1994, p. C1.

**Online**

"Wyland Whaling Wall," BeachCalifornia.com, http://www.beachcalifornia.com/lbwyland.html (January 1, 2009).

"Wyland Bio," Wyland Marine Life Artist, http://www.wyland.com/brand.cfm (January 1, 2009).

*—A. Petruso*

# Obituaries

## Anne Armstrong

Born Anne Legendre, December 27, 1927, in New Orleans, LA; died of cancer, July 30, 2008, in Houston, TX. Diplomat. Anne Armstrong was a wife, mother, and Texas rancher, but also held several key posts within the Republican Party and was the first woman to serve as U.S. ambassador to the United Kingdom. During the Nixon administration, she became Counselor to the President, a cabinet-level position and another historic first for the well-heeled Texan who possessed some genuinely liberal sensibilities. Armstrong, noted the *New York Times'* William Grimes, "favored a more inclusive Republican party that would reach out to younger voters, ethnic minorities, and women."

Armstrong was born in 1927 in New Orleans, Louisiana, into a family with a coffee-import business that was old French Creole on her father's side. She lived in Brazil as a child because of the family business, and attended the all-female Foxcroft School located deep in Virginia horse country. She was elected student body president and graduated as valedictorian of her 1945 class.

Armstrong graduated from Vassar College in 1949, and moved to New York City to take a job as an editorial assistant at *Harper's Bazaar,* the fashion magazine. Prior to her move, however, she had visited a Vassar classmate's Texas home, and met Tobin Armstrong, scion of a prominent local family and owners of a large parcel of land near Corpus Christi that had been in the family several generations by then. They wed in 1950, and Armstrong went to work as a bookkeeper for the 50,000-acre Armstrong Ranch and its various enterprises. She and her husband also began a family that would eventually number five children.

In the 1948 presidential election, Armstrong volunteered for the Democratic incumbent, Harry S Truman, but switched allegiances to the Republican Party after her marriage. She rose through the local party ranks to a post on the Texas Republican Party's Executive Committee in the early 1960s, and became the state vice chair in 1966. In 1971, U.S. President Richard M. Nixon suggested her name to become the new co-chair of the Republican National Committee, a job she shared with Thomas B. Evans of Delaware for the next two years.

As one of the highest-ranking, non-elected officials in the "Grand Old Party," or GOP, Armstrong wielded a position of enormous influence, especially for a woman in this era. She was an ardent supporter of the Equal Rights Amendment, a proposed constitutional amendment that would have erased all gender biases in legislation and was immensely controversial, for at the time the idea of young American women actually participating in military combat made many uneasy. Armstrong even delivered the keynote address at the 1972 Republican National Convention in Miami Beach, Florida, becoming the first woman of either of the two main political parties ever to do so. "Appealing to Democrats who disapproved of the liberal, anti-war policies championed by their party's presidential nominee, George McGovern," noted Joe Holley in Armstrong's *Washington Post* obituary, "she urged them to find refuge in the Republican Party. In her speech, she said, 'The sudden storm of McGovern has devastated the house of Jackson, of Wilson, Roosevelt, and Kennedy, and millions of Democrats stand homeless in its wake.'"

Later that year, after Nixon won reelection, he offered her an appointment as Counselor to the President, a cabinet-level position that Armstrong used to establish the White House Office of Women's Programs. Because she spoke fluent Spanish, she also served as the administration's liaison to Hispanic voters. During the Watergate debacle that ended Nixon's political career, she was initially a staunch defender of the president until evidence of criminal-level wrongdoing was released to the public during the course of the special investigation. Nixon avoided impeachment by resigning in mid-1974, and Armstrong remained with the new administration under former Vice President Gerald R. Ford as a member of his Council on Wage and Price Stability before he appointed her to become the new U.S. ambassador to the United Kingdom. Again, she was the first woman ever to hold the job, whose predecessors included five U.S. presidents and industry titans such as Andrew W. Mellon and W. Averell Harriman.

At the 1976 Republican National Convention in Kansas City, Missouri, Armstrong's name was drafted as Ford's running mate in the balloting, but Senator Bob Dole of Kansas was chosen by delegates instead. The Ford-Dole ticket lost, and Armstrong left her post as ambassador in March of 1977. She went on to serve as chair of President Ronald Reagan's Foreign Intelligence Advisory Board for much of the 1980s, and Reagan honored her with the nation's highest civilian honor, the Presidential Medal of Freedom, in 1987.

Armstrong was widowed in 2005, and several months later her ranch became the subject of intense media scrutiny when then-Vice President Dick Cheney accidentally fired lead-shot pellets at his 78-year-old friend and hunting-party companion, Harry Whittington, during a quail shoot. Whittington recovered, but journalists noted that the ranch had long been the site of elite private parties whose guest lists were made up of scores of major political figures with a penchant for blood sport.

Stricken with cancer, Armstrong passed away on July 30, 2008, at a hospice-care facility in Houston, Texas, at the age of 80. Five children—John Barclay Armstrong II, Sarita Hixon, Tobin Armstrong Jr., Katharine Armstrong Love, and James L. Armstrong—survive her, as do 13 grandchildren. Her decades of Republican Party service gave her close ties to another prominent Texas family, the Bushes. Her friend George H. W. Bush, U.S. president from 1989 to 1993, described her as "a fantastic shot," according to the *Times* of London. **Sources:** *Los Angeles Times*, July 31, 2008, p. B7; *New York Times*, July 31, 2008, p. C13; *Times* (London), August 4, 2008, p. 51; *Washington Post*, July 31, 2008, p. B7.

—*Carol Brennan*

## Eddy Arnold

Born Richard Edward Arnold, May 15, 1918, in Henderson, TN; died near Nashville, TN, May 8, 2008. Singer. One of the most successful country hit singers in history, Eddy Arnold was a pivotal performers who transformed what had been known as "hillbilly music" into country. Influenced by cowboy singers and popular music, Arnold had a career that spanned seven decades.

From radio shows to television performances, Arnold's appearances evolved over the years, moving from a stereotypical "country bumpkin" role to a more urbane image. The combination of rural background and country flavor with a sophisticated sound became known as "countrypolitan" or the "Nashville Sound," a style Arnold pioneered. "I sing a little country, I sing a little pop and I sing a little folk, and it all goes together," Arnold was quoted as having said in the *Washington Post*.

One of many children in a large farming family, Arnold was interested in music at an early age, introduced to playing guitar by a cousin who loaned him a Sears Roebuck Silvertone instrument. His parents' farm was repossessed during the Depression, and his father became a sharecropper on land that had once belonged to him. When Arnold was eleven, his father died, and Arnold started earning money by singing in public. He performed at church picnics and events, earning as much as a dollar per performance.

At age 12, Arnold took a position with an undertaker, but he continued to perform at local dances or picnics. Recruited to perform in honky tonk clubs in Jackson and on the radio, Arnold was a professional musician by the age of 17, and soon after left home to pursue his career. In 1942, Arnold was hired to perform at the Grand Ole Opry in Nashville, and by the next year, they brought him on as a solo performer. Initially billed "Eddy Arnold, the Tennessee plowboy and his guitar," Arnold performed songs in the style of the "singing cowboy," similar to the tunes that Gene Autry made famous. But he added to this the crooning style of Bing Crosby. Dinah Shore described the sound of his voice like "warm butter and syrup being poured over wonderful buttermilk pancakes," in the *Washington Post*.

Ready to begin a recording career, Arnold signed with Victor Records, which later became RCA. His manager, Col. Tom Parker, later became the manager for Elvis Presley, and the contacts Parker made while working with Arnold aided Parker in promoting Presley's career. Arnold recorded "That's How Much I Love You" in 1946, and it became his first big hit. "What Is Life Without Love," recorded in 1947, became Arnold's first number-one song; six more of Arnold's number-one hits topped the charts by the end of the decade.

Drawing on his success in recording, Arnold left the Opry and began performing on screen. He was one of the few country performers who would make regular appearances on programs with Ed Sullivan, Arthur Godfrey, and Milton Berle. He appeared in *Hoedown* and *Feudin' Rhythm,* two films that came out in 1950. In 1953, Arnold brought his act to Las Vegas, making him one of the first country performers to offer regular shows there. From 1945 to 1954, Arnold had a run of 57 consecutive top-ten hits.

All was not well between Arnold and Parker, however. Arnold, wanting to distance himself from the rural poverty of his youth, wanted to change his image. In addition to appearing only in a tuxedo, Arnold added strings to accompany him, re-recording one of his signature songs, "Cattle Call," with the Hugo Winterhalter Orchestra. The re-branding built Arnold a new audience and made him a star. He was inducted into the Country Music Hall of Fame in 1966.

Over the course of Arnold's career, he sold 80 million records. He hosted a television show and filled in as a guest host for Johnny Carson. "I don't know that that will ever happen again," Kyle Young, director of the Country Music Hall of Fame and Museum told the *Los Angeles Times.* "Think of it: 80 million records sold. That's a number that compares to Garth Brooks' total. He *was* the Garth Brooks, the Kenny Chesney of his time, and his time spanned many years."

Discovering that retirement did not appeal to him, he continued recording throughout the 1980s and 1990s. In 1999, he recorded "Cattle Call" as a duet with LeAnn Rimes. In 2005, Arnold released his final album, *After All These Years,* at the age of 87. "I'd retired and didn't even know if I could still sing. Then I started exercising the voice and found out that I could still do it a little," he was reported as having said in the London *Times.*

Successful in his career, Arnold became very rich, and was often thought to be one of Nashville's wealthiest residents; however, he did not flash his wealth. Arnold was pre-deceased by his wife of 66 years, Sally Gayhart, who passed away in March of 2008. Arnold died at a care facility near Nashville, TN on May 8, 2008, just a week short of his 90th birthday. He is survived by a son and a daughter. **Sources:** *Chicago Tribune,* May 9, 2008, sec. 2 p. 9; *Los Angeles Times,* May 9, 2008, pp. A1, A20-21; *Times* (London), May 9, 2008; *Washington Post,* May 9, 2008, p. B8.

*—Alana Joli Abbott*

## Maurice Bejart

Born Maurice Jean Berger, January 1, 1927, in Marseille, France; died of heart and kidney problems, November 11, 2007, in Lausanne, Switzerland. Ballet director and choreographer. Celebrated in Europe but often criticized in the English speaking world, Maurice Bejart was an innovative and influential choreographer who developed an avant-garde style of dance that rejected traditional ballet stories, characters, and scenery. Many of his dances featured large roles for male dancers, often showcasing masculine eroticism or abandoning traditional gender roles. His dances were both art and social statements, and the size of his productions often required performances to take place in arenas rather than traditional theaters.

Over the course of his career, Bejart created 220 productions. The best known include Bejart's interpretation of Ravel's "Bolero," a production of "The Firebird" placed in the center of the Vietnam Conflict, "The Rite of Spring" interpreted as a mating ritual, and a version of "The Merry Widow" that featured fascist military costumes and a depiction of the Last Supper. Whether due to his social commentary or to his experimental techniques, Bejart "played an essential role in making a large number of people love contemporary dance, without ever ceding to the easy way out or renouncing his deep demands as an artist," Christine Albanel, the Culture Minister of France, said in the *Los Angeles Times.*

The son of philosopher and Oriental scholar Gaston Berger, Maurice Bejart was born Maurice Jean Berger in 1927 in France. His mother, whose maiden name may have been Bejart, died when he was seven years old. Other accounts suggest that Bejart took his stage name by using the maiden name of Molière's wife. Though Bejart had a sickly childhood, his father enrolled him in ballet school as a teen. After high school, he continued to pursue classical dance, studying under Lubov Egorova and Madame Rousanne in Paris. His studies took him to London to study under Vera Volkova.

In many of his early classes, there was a disparity between the number of boys and the number of girls; often, in his youth, he was the only boy in a class of 25 to 30. "It was not right," he was quoted as having said in the *Los Angeles Times.* "Life is a balance between men and women." Noting his emphasis on male dancers in his own productions, he had said, "If I push the boys [as a choreographer], it is because there still needs to be a reaction against the prejudice that it is not good for men to dance."

From 1945 through 1950 he performed with several different ballets, beginning his career as a choreographer with the Royal Swedish Ballet in 1950. Shortly thereafter, he returned to France in order to fulfill his military service, and when he had completed his service in 1953, he co-founded the Ballets de l'Etoile, a company in Paris which he co-directed. In addition, he strove to build a reputation as a freelance choreographer, gaining attention with his 1955 experimental work "Symphonie pour un home seul." The work received attention for its use of "musique concrete," or recorded ambient noise and human sounds, manipulated electronically, which Bejart used to cue movement. The ballet was reviewed by Arnold L. Haskell, quoted in the *Washington Post*, who felt that in the performance, "classical and modern dance vocabularies intermingle. A perfect cohesion is achieved between gesture, rhythm, and sound. This is the masterpiece of a new genre, a work of brutal, hallucinatory power."

In 1959, Bejart was invited by Maurice Huysman, director of the Theatre Royal de la Monnaie in Brussels, Belgium, to choreograph "The Rite of Spring." The piece, with its controversial take on a classical piece of ballet, became his best-known work and won him acclaim in Belgium and beyond. Bejart relocated to Brussels and founded Ballet du XXieme Siecle; his presence at the theater vastly increased attendance, and Bejart was celebrated throughout Europe.

While Bejart's fame grew, so did the criticism of his works. During the 1950s and 1960s, much of the criticism fell on his homoerotic dancing, which he made no attempt to disguise. The shocking nature of the pieces drew negative reactions from many critics, but Bejart himself intended to draw wary eyes. The *Los Angeles Times* quoted him as having explained, "A creator who does not shock is useless. People need reactions. Progress is only achieved by jostling."

In 1960, Bejart was awarded the gold metal at the Festival of Nations in Paris for his work "Le Sacre du Printemps." He worked for a time on a piece with painter Salvador Dali. Throughout the 1960s, in such works as "Romeo and Juliet" and "Messe pour le Temps Present," Bejart continued to focus on male dancing, showcasing sexuality in many of his pieces. In 1970, he founded Mudra Center, a performance academy in Brussels, and in 1978, a branch of the school opened in Senegal.

In 1987, Bejart moved to Lausanne, Switzerland, due to conflicts with the people operating the school, and he founded Bejart Ballet Lausanne. In 1992, he expanded the ballet to include a school similar to the Mudra Center, training many dancers not to mimic his style, but to develop their own. He continued to keep creating dance that would appeal to mass audiences as one of his focuses. According to the London *Times,* "Bejart probably did more than any other choreographer in the past century to win vast new audiences for ballet,"

In addition to his choreography, he created operas, made a film, and wrote two plays, three volumes of an autobiography, and a novel. Bejart continued choreographing new ballets until the month of his death, though he had been in poor health for some time. Bejart died of heart and kidney problems on November 11, 2007. His longtime partner, dancer Jorge Donn, died of AIDS in 1992. Bejart is survived by his sister, Claudette. He was 80 years old. **Sources:** *Los Angeles Times,* November 23, 2007, p. B8; *New York Times,* November 23, 2007, p. C7; *Times* (London), November 23, 2007, p. 83; *Washington Post,* November 23, 2007, p. B6.

—*Alana Joli Abbott*

## Bernie Brillstein

Born Bernard Jules Brillstein, April 26, 1931, in New York, NY; died of chronic obstructive pulmonary disease, August 7, 2008, in Los Angeles, CA. Producer and talent manager. For 52 years, Bernie Brillstein was a dominant presence in Hollywood, from guiding the careers of talents including Gilda Radner, Jim Henson, and John Belushi, to producing such iconic programs as *Saturday Night Live.* He was one of the earliest Hollywood talent representatives to combine his role as a manager with producing, something now common in the industry.

Brillstein was a pivotal figure in Hollywood, known for his larger-than-life appearance. He, "by his own admission, looked like a cross between Santa Claus and Kenny Rogers," described a contributor to the London *Times.* "Bernie was an icon and one of the most successful talent managers in the business," said his long-time partner and former protégé Brad Grey in the *Los Angeles Times.* In his 1999 memoir, *Where Did I Go Right?: You're No One in Hollywood Unless Someone Wants You Dead* (as reported by Vanessa Juarez of *Entertainment Weekly*), Brillstein stated his wish for his tombstone to read "Bernie Brillstein: From *Hee Haw* to *Dangerous Liaisons*," showing the polar opposites of the work he produced: one a lowbrow comedy, the other an award-winning Oscar nominee.

As a child, Brillstein lived with his parents in the Manhattan hotel home of his uncle, Jack Pearl. As a radio and vaudeville performer, Pearl introduced Brillstein to show business early on. Brillstein longed to be a part of his uncle's world, hobnobbing with the stars. He attended New York University, where he studied advertising, and spent two years in the Army before getting his first position in the talent industry: a job in the mailroom of the William Morris Agency in New York.

One of the opportunities William Morris Agency offered to Brillstein was filling in for the managerial assistants. Brillstein took courses at a secretarial school so he could use short hand. He soon became an assistant himself, working in the agency's publicity department, and he continued to climb up the ladder until he held the position of full agent. Lorne Michaels, whom Brillstein worked with on *Saturday Night Live,* described Brillstein's early career in the *Los Angeles Times:* "He was from Manhattan and the nightclub business and a show business that I had sort of seen in the movies. And he was captivating and always funny, really funny, and direct in a kind of language I had never heard before."

But Brillstein was unhappy in Manhattan. When he left William Morris for the fledgling agency Management III in 1967, he was sent to Los Angeles. Brillstein quickly immersed himself in the Hollywood scene, and in 1968, he left Management III to form the Brillstein Company. In his own company, he began "packaging" talent, putting together the television ensemble *Hee Haw.* The variety show, which featured country music and "hillbilly" style humor, appeared on CBS in 1969.

Brillstein also helped Jim Henson create *The Muppet Show,* and turn the Muppets into pop-culture icons with *Sesame Street.* Brillstein was credited with helping to turn the Muppets into entertainment for a mainstream audience, when puppets had previously always been relegated to children's programming. With Brillstein's help and expertise, the Muppets became an industry of their own, as the syndication of *The Muppet Show* paved the way for several movies and scores of products based on the characters.

Michaels also credited Brillstein with being a major force behind *Saturday Night Live,* a show that "took television comedy into a hipper, more daring zone from which it never retreated," wrote Michael Cieply for the *New York Times.* Despite the culture gap between what Michaels was creating and the type of program Brillstein was used to, "at the core he knew about audience and talent and how to put on a show," Michaels explained in the *Los Angeles Times.* "He loved show business, and he was unabashed in how much he loved it."

Along with serving as the executive producer for television programs, including *ALF, The Dana Carvey Show,* and *The Martin Short Show,* Brillstein produced several films. In his memoir, he wrote about a particularly productive two-year period during the late eighties, in which he developed 20 films, "and ended up making six lousy movies, two good movies, and one great movie" (as reported in his *Los Angeles Times* obituary). The great movie was *Dangerous Liaisons,* which was nominated for the Academy Award for best film in 1988. Brillstein also served as the executive director for *The Blues Brothers, Ghostbusters,* and *Dragnet,* among others.

In 1991, Brillstein and Grey partnered to form Brillstein-Grey Entertainment, a management agency and production company that represented clients including Martin Short, Brad Pitt, and Nicholas Cage. In 1996, Brillstein sold his half of the business to Grey, but continued to work at the company until Grey became chairman of Paramount in 2005. Brillstein made a guest appearance on one of the company's television dramas, *The Sopranos,* in 2004.

Brillstein suffered from chronic obstructive pulmonary disease and died on August 7, 2008. He was 77. Married several times, Brillstein is survived by his wife Carrie, two daughters, and three sons. **Sources:** *Entertainment Weekly,* August 22-29, 2008, p. 27; *Los Angeles Times,* August 9, 2008, p. B8; *New York Times,* August 9, 2008, p. A15; *Times* (London), September 1, 2008.

—*Alana Joli Abbott*

## Youssef Chahine

Born January 25, 1926, in Alexandria, Egypt; died of a cerebral hemorrhage, July 27, 2008, in Cairo, Egypt. Filmmaker. Perhaps the Arab world's most prominent filmmaker, Youssef Chahine spent more than 50 years illuminating the thoughts, desires, and struggles of ordinary Egyptians. He infused his 28 films with the tolerant, humanitarian worldview of his hometown of Alexandria and a critical eye toward social injustice and Egyptian leaders. He was "a contrarian, a rebel, an angry commentator, uncowed by censorship nor limited by boundaries," wrote film critic Ibrahim Al Aris (according to Nora Boustany of the *Washington Post*).

Chahine was "a small and wiry figure with inquisitive eyes peering from behind thick glasses resting on an imposing Grecian nose," wrote Boustany in the *Washington Post.* But his slight frame belied his huge talent and central role in Egyptian culture. He was "the visionary dean of the Arab movie industry," Boustany wrote. "He was a master at exposing the decadence of Egypt's upper classes who reveled in lavish social gatherings in bow ties and plunging neck lines … as impoverished Egyptians lived in the shadows, subsisting on fava beans and faith."

Chahine was born in 1926 to a Lebanese father and Greek mother. He spent a year as a student at Victoria College in Egypt then went to the United States to study film at the Pasadena Playhouse in California from 1946 to 1948. He directed his first full-length film, *Baba Amin,* in 1950. His second film, *Son of the Nile,* was nominated for the grand prize at the Cannes Film Festival in France in 1951. Chahine included actor Omar Sharif in his 1954 film *Struggle in the Valley* and is often credited with launching the career of Sharif, who went on to earn international fame.

Chahine's breakthrough film was *Cairo Station,* a complicated psychological drama released in 1958. In the film, Chahine played a disabled newspaper seller at a train station whose desire for a woman who sells soft drinks leads him to murder. Critic Elliott Stein described it as "an idiosyncratic mixture of neorealist social commentary, grotesque horror, and lighthearted comedy" (according to A. O. Scott of the *New York Times*). Many of Chahine's early films are considered classic examples of social realism. His 1969 film *The Land,* about landowners and poor farmers in conflict over the fertile land of the Nile River delta, is sometimes considered his best work.

Alexandria, Chahine's hometown, figured prominently in his films and in his view of the world. A port city on the Mediterranean, Alexandria is considered cosmopolitan and tolerant, with a mix of Christians, Muslims, and Jews of several ethnicities: Italian, Greek, and Lebanese as well as Egyptian. Chahine, a Christian, made Alexandria the subject of four autobiographical films, starting in 1978 with *Alexandria, Why?* With the Alexandria series, Chahine broke free of his earlier realist style and began using sudden changes in tone and musical numbers. The wild shifts were sometimes compared to those of influential Italian filmmaker Federico Fellini. They made Chahine's films hard to categorize, so critics often resorted to calling them eclectic.

Chahine's liberal philosophy led him to criticize both Egypt's authoritarian governments and the country's fundamentalist Islamic movement. Though he was an early supporter of Egyptian

leader Gamal Abdel Nasser's nationalist movement, his 1972 film *The Sparrow* questioned most Arabs' admiration of Nasser and pointed out his failures during the 1967 war with Israel. Chahine's later films often expressed fury at corruption and the rhetoric political leaders used to rally support for disastrous nationalist policies. In 2006, Chahine joined protests against Egyptian president Hosni Mubarak after magistrates declared that the president's re-election had been fraudulent and Mubarak responded with a crackdown on the magistrates and democracy protesters. His last film, *Chaos,* from 2007, harshly criticizes the government for its treatment of democratic activists. However, when Chahine became ill in 2008, Mubarak, in an acknowledgement of Chahine's role in Egyptian culture, helped arrange and pay for his medical treatment.

As Islamic fundamentalists gained more authority in Egyptian culture, they, too, often clashed with Chahine. His 1994 film *The Emigrant,* about the Old Testament figure Joseph, was denounced by Islamic militants, then banned. But the filmmaker did not back down. Instead, in 1997, he released *Destiny,* a film set in the twelfth century that depicts a tolerant Spanish leader being attacked by an extremist Muslim movement.

Chahine's ideals were mixed with a realism, or cynicism, about their reception in Egypt. "If you talk about the Egyptian people, you must know about their problems," he said in an interview with a German Web site (quoted by Scott in the *New York Times*). "Either you are with modernity or you don't know what the hell you're doing." But when the interviewer asked if Egypt would become more free or liberal, Chahine replied, "No, neither in the near nor in the faraway future."

In 1997, the Cannes Film Festival presented Chahine with a lifetime achievement award. It was the climax of decades of admiration of his work by French filmgoers. When Chahine died, Nicolas Sarkozy, president of France, paid tribute to him. Chahine was "very attached to his Egypt but open to the universe," Sarkozy said (quoted by Scott in the *New York Times*), and he sought "to denounce censorship, fanaticism and fundamentalism."

Chahine was stricken by a cerebral hemorrhage in June of 2008. He died on July 27, 2008, at Maadi Military Hospital in Cairo, Egypt, at the age of 82. He is survived by his wife, Colette. **Sources:** *Chicago Tribune,* July 28, 2008, sec. 2, p. 4; *Los Angeles Times,* July 28, 2008, p. B9; *New York Times,* July 28, 2008, p. A17; *Times* (London, England), July 29, 2008, p. 53; *Washington Post,* July 30, 2008, p. B6.

—*Erick Trickey*

# Cyd Charisse

Born Tula Ellice Finklea, March 8, 1922, in Amarillo, TX; died after a heart attack, June 17, 2008, in Los Angeles, CA. Actress and dancer. Cyd Charisse, a film star during Hollywood's golden era, was famed for her fluid grace as a dancer. She appeared in a number of big-budget Hollywood musicals that showcased both her talent and pair of impressively long legs in sequences that partnered her with two of the most famous stars of the 1940s and '50s, Fred Astaire and Gene Kelly. "In the great era of the MGM musical," noted the *Times* of London, "Charisse was the screen's unrivalled female dancer. She had trained in classical ballet and brought to her work an artistic grace that transcended merely accomplished hoofing."

A native of Amarillo, Texas, Charisse was born Tula Ellice Finklea, but her younger brother's attempt to call her "sis" came out as "Sid" instead, a nickname that stuck with her into adulthood. Most reports give her birth date as 1922. As a child, she came down with polio, which in many cases left its youngest victims permanently disabled. She recovered, but began ballet classes for strength training. "I was this tiny, frail little girl, I needed to build up muscle, and I fell in love with dancing from the first lesson," *Los Angeles Times* writer Mary Rourke quoted her as saying.

Charisse proved to have a natural gift for ballet, and around age 12 she began taking classes in the Los Angeles area with Bronislawa Nijinska, a renowned Russian-born teacher and sister of Vaslav Nijinsky, considered one of the greatest male dancers in the history of ballet. At age 14, she began performing with the Ballet Russe de Monte Carlo, a top European company, and used the professional names "Natacha Tulaelis" and "Felia Siderova." She also met a fellow dancer, Nico Charisse, and they were wed in Paris in 1939. Three years later, their son Nicky was born.

Returning to the Los Angeles area, Charisse began appearing as a dancer in Hollywood films. Her first credited role was in a 1946 Judy Garland musical comedy, *The Harvey Girls*, but she gained major notice in another release that same year, *Ziegfeld Follies*, in which she appeared as Astaire's dance partner in one sequence. This film also marked the first use of "Cyd" Charisse as her professional name, a new spelling suggested by Metro Goldwyn-Mayer (MGM) when the studio put her under contract as its resident ballet dancer.

Charisse went on to appear in *The Kissing Bandit* and *East Side, West Side*, was divorced from her first husband, and married singer Tony Martin, all by 1948. She was pregnant with her second son and missed out on the starring role won by Leslie Caron opposite Gene Kelly in the immensely successful movie musical of 1951, *An American in Paris. Singin' in the Rain*, which starred Kelly, Astaire, and Debbie Reynolds, made Charisse a star a year later. She appeared only near the end, in a dance number titled "Broadway Melody," but her *Times* of London obituary cited her as "there to provide, with Kelly, an exhilarating ballet sequence which [had] strictly nothing to do with the rest of the film, but is one of the most dazzling of its many pleasures."

That number made Charisse a household name, and one of Hollywood's most influential directors of movie-musicals, Vincente Minnelli, began casting her in lead roles. The first was *The Band Wagon*, opposite Astaire, followed by the musical adaptation of the Broadway hit *Brigadoon* in 1954, which teamed her again with Kelly. In 1957, she was given the role made famous by Greta Garbo nearly 20 years earlier in *Ninotchka*. The story was updated into a musical titled *Silk Stockings*, which paired Charisse with Astaire. A much more adept dancer than singer, Charisse usually had to have her vocals dubbed in musical numbers.

As the box-office appeal of the big-budget movie musical waned, Charisse moved into purely dramatic parts. "The best of her later straight roles was as the former wife of Kirk Douglas' fading screen star in *Two Weeks in Another Town*," noted her *Times* of London obituary of the 1962 movie. "Shot in Italy, it was one of a number of films Charisse made in Europe after opportunities in Hollywood dried up." For the remainder of her career, she appeared in the occasional film or as a guest star on such television series as *The Love Boat* or *Murder, She Wrote*; she also appeared on the London stage in the 1986 revival of the musical *Charlie Girl* and made her Broadway debut six years later in musical version of *Grand Hotel*. She and her husband co-authored a 1976 biography, *The Two of Us*.

Later in life Charisse revealed that the insurance policy MGM claimed to have taken out on her famously long legs was merely a public-relations stunt. In 2006, she was honored with the National Medal of the Arts and Humanities by President George W. Bush at a White House ceremony. On June 16, 2008, she suffered a heart attack, and died the following day at a Los Angeles hospital. She was 86. Survivors include her husband and sons Nicky Charisse and Tony Martin Jr. To her fans, the two most important men in her life remained Kelly and Astaire, Charisse's equally talented on-screen dance partners. Once asked to differentiate between the two stars, Charisse said that her husband could tell after rehearsals which one she had worked with that day. "If I was black and blue, it was Gene," reported her *New York Times* obituary. "And if it was Fred, I didn't have a scratch." **Sources:** *Chicago Tribune,* June 18, 2008, sec. 2, p. 8; *Los Angeles Times,* June 18, 2008, p. B6; *New York Times,* June 18, 2008; *Times* (London), June 19, 2008, p. 63.

—*Carol Brennan*

## Arthur C. Clarke

Born Arthur Charles Clarke, December 16, 1917, in Minehead, Somerset, England; died of a respiratory ailment, March 19, 2008, in Colombo, Sri Lanka. Author. Arthur C. Clarke was considered the unofficial poet laureate of the space age. His works of science fiction were often thought to be somewhat prophetic, as Clarke predicted advances in technology well before science caught up with his ideas. From space stations and moon landings using a mother ship and landing pod combination to cell phones and the Internet, Clarke depicted technology in his fiction years before it appeared in the news or on the market.

Author of more than 1,000 short stories and essays, Clarke was best known for his collaboration with filmmaker Stanley Kubrick, *2001: A Space Odyssey.* The host of two British television series that carried his name, Clarke was knighted in 1998, nominated for the Nobel Peace Prize in 1994, and received the Unesco Kalinga Prize in 1962 for his factual books on popular science. His famous article from *Wireless World* predicted global communication by bouncing radio signals off of satellites in orbit.

Born in Minehead, Somerset, England in 1917, Clarke was fascinated by science as a young child. Along with keeping a crystal set and Player's cigarette card with a picture of a dinosaur, Clarke constructed a telescope from a cardboard tube and lenses, which he used to observe the moon. He became an avid fan of science fiction at the age of eleven, the year he discovered *Amazing Stories* magazine. Two years later, an issue of *Astounding Stories of Super-Science* "irrevocably changed" his life, according to the *Los Angeles Times.*

Unable to afford college, Clarke moved to London and took a job as an auditor, writing science fiction stories in his off hours. During World War II, Clarke served as an officer in the Royal Air Force (RAF), where he worked as a radar instructor. His position offered him the opportunity to work with a U.S. team on a radar project using microwave beams. It was Clarke's experience working with the RAF that fueled his ideas about extra-terrestrial relays. Clarke submitted an article to *Wireless World,* describing a worldwide communications system. If fixed satellites orbited the earth at 22,300 miles above the Earth, Clarke theorized, radio signals could be bounced off of these satellites to perform global communication. Paid 40 dollars for the article, Clarke was discouraged from patenting the idea, because it was believed to be too far-fetched. Years later, when the geostationary orbit was used for exactly what Clarke had described, scientists from the International Astronomical Union officially named it the Clarke Orbit. Clarke himself referred to the *Wireless World* article as "the most important thing I ever wrote," according to the *New York Times.* In fact, Clarke considered formulating the idea one of his three most important achievements, alongside *2001* and inspiring Gene Roddenberry to create *Star Trek.*

Returning from the RAF, Clarke entered King's College in London, studying physics and mathematics and continuing to write nonfiction articles. But his love for science-fiction remained, and though he gained a reputation for science work with his book *The Exploration in Space* in 1951, he established himself as a fiction writer two years later with his novel *Childhood's End.* The novel, which has been in print continuously since its 1953 publication, depicts a race of aliens seeking to impose peace on a Cold War Earth. The aliens are in actuality preparing humans for the next stage in their evolution, and the story implies that only by becoming something other than human could humanity survive its self-imposed violence. Many of Clarke's novels featured this type of spiritual theme. "Any path to knowledge is a path to God—or Reality, whichever word one prefers to use," Clarke was quoted as having said in the London *Times.*

In 1954, while doing research for a nonfiction book on Australia's Great Barrier Reef, Clarke visited Sri Lanka, off the coast of India, and decided to stay. He settled on the island in 1956, where he became an avid scuba diver. The underwater experience was similar to weightlessness that might be experienced in outer space, and it became more important to him after a bout with polio, and later post-polio syndrome, left him partially paralyzed. Underwater, he still functioned perfectly. He and a partner established a deep-sea diving school in Sri Lanka.

In 1964, filmmaker Stanley Kubrick approached Clarke about working together to create the "proverbial really good science fiction movie," according to the *New York Times*. Their collaboration which consisted of writing both a novel and the script for the film simultaneously, became *2001: A Space Odyssey*, an epic that shows the journey of human consciousness from apes to a Star-Child with godlike powers. Though may viewers were puzzled by the film's meaning—Clarke was once stopped in U.S. customs by a customs officer who would not let him through until he explained the film—*2001* became a cult hit. Many critics considered the work a landmark film, and *2001* was nominated for an Oscar for best screenplay. The film solidified Clarke's reputation. He wrote three sequels to the film, as well as a series of books called the "Rama sequence." Clarke hosted two series on British television, expanding the viewership of science fiction to a general audience. He co-authored later works with science fiction notables Gentry Lee and Stephen Baxter, and his final novel, *The Last Theorem*, was still in progress at the time of his death.

Clarke's work was admired by his peers in science fiction. Ray Bradbury said of Clarke, "He had influenced the world in the best way possible," according to the *Washington Post*. Gregory Benford, one of Clarke's co-authors, told the *Los Angeles Times*, "I'd say he was *the* major hard science-fiction writer ... in the second half of the 20th century." Isaac Asimov, quoted in the *Chicago Tribune*, once wrote, "Nobody has done more in the way of enlightened prediction" than Clarke. Biographer and literary critic George Slusser was quoted in the *Los Angeles Times* as having said, "Clarke incarnates the essence of [science fiction], which is to blend two otherwise opposite activities into a single story, that of the advancement of mankind."

Clarke's work has inspired names for not only the Clarke Orbit, but also an asteroid, spacecraft, and a species of dinosaur. Clarke left no surviving family, but a legacy of works. When asked on his 90th birthday how he wished to be remembered, Clarke said (as quoted in the *Washington Post*), "I want to be remembered most as a writer—one who entertained readers, and, hopefully, stretched their imagination as well." Clarke died on March 19, 2008, in his home in Colombo, Sri Lanka. **Sources:** *Chicago Tribune*, March 19, 2008, sec. 2, p. 11; *Los Angeles Times*, March 19, 2008, pp. A1, A12; *New York Times*, March 19, 2008, p. C12; *Times* (London), March 20, 2008; *Washington Post*, March 19, 2008, p. B7.

—*Alana Joli Abbott*

## Bruce Conner

Born Bruce Guldner Conner, November 18, 1933, in McPherson, KS; died of a liver ailment, July 7, 2008, in San Francisco, CA. Artist. Best remembered as an avant-garde artist who employed public domain film clips the way Beat poets used words, Bruce Conner was a master of found art. An accomplished painter, photographer, and sculptor, Conner utilized film segments from old newsreels, B-movies, educational films, and other sources and recycled them into devastating social and political statements rife with humor, poignancy, and pop culture segues. The two dozen films he crafted between 1958 and 2008 found favor with intellectuals, pop art fanatics, stoners, and serious filmmakers. "For better and sometimes worse," wrote Manohla Dargis of the *New York Times*, "scores of other filmmakers in both the avant-garde and the commercial mainstream have been influenced by Mr. Conner's shocking juxtapositions and propulsive, rhythmically sophisticated montage. MTV should have paid him royalties."

Coner was born and raised in McPherson, Kansas. He claimed to have a vision of himself in an out-of-body experience that sharpened his early artistic vision. As a painter and sculptor, he attended Wichita State University before graduating from the University of Nebraska with a Bachelor of Fine Arts degree in 1956. That same year, a scholarship led him to the Brooklyn Museum Art School and the first exhibition of his paintings. Success in New York would prove a mixed blessing for the artist, who left after one semester to pursue a scholarship at the University of Colorado, where he met Jean Sandstedt. The couple married the following year.

Conner settled in San Francisco during the Beat Generation movement, an era that symbolized creative freedom. Writers and poets such as Jack Kerouac, Alan Ginsberg, and Lawrence Ferlinghetti had used the free-spirited environment as a launching pad for their careers and had thrived. Conner befriended many of these legendary figures, including such visual artists as Jay DeFeo and Wallace Berman. Under the latter's influences, Conner began to make his art from such cast-aside items as furniture, broken dolls, costume jewelry, women's nylons, candles, and old photographs. This technique was called assemblage art. According to Ken Johnson of the *New York Times*, "These works, created between 1957 and 1964, had the aggressive appearance of avant-garde sculpture but at the same time seemed old and musty, like broken-down junk found in found in a forgotten attic or props for a scary Hitchcock-like movie."

Counterculture art seldom paid well, if at all. So, like many other artists, Conner worked with societal refuse because it was the least expensive way he could make his statement. This low-cost technique also helped him establish his film work. After gathering a multitude of film scraps from a local camera store, Conner edited the disjointed segments, spliced them together, and dubbed in lush, romantic music for the 12-minute anti-consumerism screed, *A Movie*. Adam Bernstein of the *Washington Post,* wrote, "A Hallmark of Mr. Conner's work, now common to commercials and music videos, was the use of rapid editing of stock images—scenes of B-list starlets, race-car accidents, soft-core pornography, propaganda films and old Westerns—to create silly, absurd, exotic, lyrical and always disorienting juxtapositions." In the process, the artist made his audiences re-examine the hot button issues of the contemporary era.

Conner never tackled the same subject twice, although his films all shared a unifying technical approach. His 1966 film *Breakaway* featured singer-choreographer Toni Basil dancing nude in a controversial ode to women's liberation. *Report* used images of the Kennedy assassination to rail against crass media desensitization. In many films, he often emphasized his point with music. The New Wave group Devo can be heard in his anti–cold war work *Mongoloid*. David Byrne and Brian Eno's work is featured in *Mea Culpa* and *America Is Waiting*. However, it was the style of Conner's work that proved the greater influence on other filmmakers, most notably Dennis Hopper who mimicked aspects of Conner's style in his 1969 counterculture epic *Easy Rider*. Conner's contributions were more formally acknowledged by the American Film Institute, who presented him with the Maya Deren Independent Film and Video Artists Award in 1988.

Constantly creating, Conner also worked up abstract drawings, ink blots, and photograms, a process that produced ghostly images of ethereal light. When art could not pay the bills, he taught, worked as a janitor, and made jewelry to sell on the street. Yet, for all his hard, obsessive work, Conner enjoyed a reputation as an eclectic artist and a practical joker. Long before his health deteriorated due to drug and alcohol abuse, the artist erroneously announced his own death twice. Many times he refused to put his name on his paintings, signing them instead as "Dennis Hopper." Once he ran a mock campaign for San Francisco supervisor and gave a speech that mentioned nothing but dessert items. When *Art News* ran a feature titled "Hans Hoffman Paints a Picture," the puckish artist countered with his own exhibition, *Bruce Conner Makes a Sandwich.*

After Conner experienced an extensive down period both personally and professionally, his work underwent a serious critical revival starting in 1999, and exhibitions featuring several different eras of his works traveled to museums and galleries nationwide. Moreover, many of his films found a home on YouTube, where young filmmakers can marvel at the concept of found art for free.

The ultimate cult artist, Bruce Conner died of a liver ailment on July 7, 2008. He is survived by his wife Jean, son Robert, and a granddaughter. **Sources:** *Art Monthly,* September 2008, p. 13; *Chicago Tribune,* July 11, 2008, sec. 2, p. 12; *International Contemporary Art 99,* Autumn 2008, p. 5; Internet Movie Database, http://www.imdb.com (February 12, 2009); *Los Angeles Times,* July 10, 2008, p. B8; *New York Times,* July 10, 2008, p. C13; July 12, 2008; *Reason,* October 2008, p. 68; *Washington Post,* July 10, 2008, p. B6.

—*Ken Burke*

## Erik Darling

Born September 25, 1933, in Baltimore, MD; died of lymphoma, August 3, 2008, in Chapel Hill, NC. Folk musician. For more than half a century, folk musician and guitar virtuoso Erik Darling was at the center of the folk scene. Actively involved in the folk revival after World War II, Darling's music also appealed to the mainstream audience. His hits "The Banana Boat Song" and "Walk Right In" hit the top ten charts. He performed with the well-known folk trio the Tarriers, which he helped to found, and took Pete Seeger's place in the band the Weavers, one of the most successful folk groups of its era.

A star performer on both guitar and banjo, with a pleasant tenor voice, Darling shaped the musical style of the groups in which he belonged. According to singer and songwriter Don McLean, who was quoted in the *New York Times,* Darling "was the first guitar gunslinger I came across.... Today you see any number of fabulous guitar players, but back then there were only a handful, and he was one."

Born in Baltimore in 1933, Darling grew up in upstate New York. He was encouraged to learn his father's business, running a local paint store, but Darling was uninterested. When his parents divorced, Darling moved to New York City with his mother. It was there that he first became aware of the folk scene.

Darling once described how he discovered the Sunday performances in Washington Square, stating that he had been told that people played folk songs here, so he took a double-decker bus to see for himself. Still an amateur, Darling declined to join in making music at first, but became a regular part of the crowd. He improved his guitar skills and found others to perform with him. He, along with Bob Carey, was invited to join the Folksay Trio, and with them, he recorded "Tom Dooley." Though their version did not top the charts, a later cover of the song by the Kingston Trio was strongly influenced by their syncopated style.

Darling formed a band called the Tunetellers, another trio. When that group disbanded, Darling and Carey searched for a third member to join their trio the Tarriers. Young actor Alan Arkin left Los Angeles to join the group, and together they made their first top ten hit, "Cindy, Oh Cindy." The group stayed together for several years, coming to prominence with their recording of a Jamaican folk song, "The Banana Boat Song." For their version, they fused a traditional work song with another Jamaican tune, "Hill and Gully Rider." The song was a hit that helped ignite a craze for Calypso music. The Tarriers appeared in the film *Calypso Heat Wave* with such notables as Maya Angelou.

In 1958, Pete Seeger left the Weavers, and the group approached Darling to take his place. Though he at first joined as a temporary member, his songs and styles helped to change the shape of the Weavers, and he stayed with the group for four years. Original Weavers member Fred Hellerman told the *Los Angeles Times,* "Pete never swung the way Erik could swing. His banjo could take command and carry everybody along with it." Darling was a good musical fit for the Weavers, but his politics estranged him from some members of the group, and eventually he left to form a new group, the Rooftop Singers.

Before forming the Rooftop Singers, Darling had discovered "Walk Right In," a song recorded in the 1920s by Gus Cannon's Jug Stompers but largely forgotten. Darling was so taken with the song that he formed the Rooftop Singers specifically to record an updated version. The resulting cover reached number one on the charts, making it Darling's biggest commercial hit, and it increased the popularity of the 12-string guitar.

The Rooftop Singers appeared at the Newport Folk Festival in 1963, along with Bob Dylan, who was changing the face of folk music. Though the group stayed together for four more years, they had no other hits, and the trio style fell out of favor as the face of folk music shifted. Darling recorded a duet album with Pat Street in the late 1960s, after which

he left the music scene for some time. In 1975, Darling reappeared to record the album *The Possible Dream,* then once again dropped out of the industry. Hellerman described this period in the *Los Angeles Times,* "Erik would disappear for awhile and all of a sudden pop up with songs or an album so completely off the wall and different, and of such high quality." In the 1980s, Darling lived in New Mexico, where he began painting, as well as teaching banjo to students such as virtuoso Bela Fleck. In 1994, he resurfaced with *Border Town at Midnight,* inspired by his New Mexico home. His final album, *Child, Child,* was recorded in 2000.

Darling died on August 3, 2008, of lymphoma in Chapel Hill, North Carolina. He was 74. Darling is survived by his former wife, television actress and director Joan Kugell Darling. Two months before his death, his memoir of his career, *I'd Give My Life!: A Journey by Folk Music,* was published. **Sources:** *Chicago Tribune,* August 8, 2008, sec. 2, p. 11; *Los Angeles Times,* August 9, 2008, p. B9; *New York Times,* August 8, 2008, p. C13; *Times* (London), August 13, 2008, p. 53.

—*Alana Joli Abbott*

## Mahmud Darwish

Born March 13, 1942, in Birweh, Palestine (now Israel); died of complications from open heart surgery, August 9, 2008, in Houston, TX. Poet. Mahmud Darwish was recognized as an unofficial poet laureate of Palestine. His poetry spoke as a voice for the Palestinian people, particularly in regards to their plight as an occupied nation. He wrote the symbolic Palestinian Declaration of Independence in 1988, and contributed words to the monumental speech of Yasser Arafat, delivered to the United Nations in 1974.

Arrested several times for his political positions, Darwish lived much of his life in exile from his homeland. Despite his outspoken positions and political association with the Palestine Liberation Organization (PLO), Darwish sometimes struggled with his identity as the national voice of Palestine, and took greater pride in his universal poetry than his political messages. "I don't decide to represent anything except myself," Darwish was quoted as having said by the London *Times.*

Born in 1942 into a large Sunni Muslim family, Darwish began writing poetry at a very early age. In 1948, during the Israeli war for independence,

Darwish's family fled to Lebanon. When they returned a year later, their village was completely gone, replaced with an Israeli settlement. Darwish began speaking out against the Israeli occupation through his poetry as a teen. An early poem, written when he was 14, expressed the unfairness of a Jewish boy having more in life than he and his family. Darwish's father was threatened by the local military governor, who pledged to have Darwish's father fired unless Darwish stopped writing that type of poem.

Unable to earn a college degree in Israel, Darwish joined the Israeli Communist Party, Rakah, and worked as a journalist in Haifa. He edited the newspaper of Rakah, an organization where Jews and Arabs worked together. His first book of poetry, a politically charged collection, was published when he was 19. Darwish rejected the Israeli military rule and was repeatedly placed under house arrest for leaving Haifa without the permit required of Palestinians.

In order to pursue a higher education in political economy, Darwish left Israel for the Soviet Union, where he lived in Moscow and attended university. Later, he moved to Beirut and Cairo, where he worked on *Al-Ahram*, the daily newspaper. During these years, he met Yasser Arafat, who offered him the position of culture minister, which he turned down. He did, however, join the PLO, a move that denied him the possibility of returning to his home in Israel. Moving from Egypt to Lebanon, Darwish stayed active in the PLO, writing the organization's symbolic Palestinian Declaration of Independence.

Despite his efforts on behalf of the PLO, Darwish became disenchanted with the organization. He resigned from the group in 1993, frustrated with the results of the Oslo Accords, which Darwish felt favored Israel and would lead to further violence between Palestinians and Israelis. Shortly thereafter, he was able to return to Israel, settling in Ramallah on the West Bank. Despite being closer to the place where he grew up, Darwish often said he still felt like an outsider, belonging only to a "country of words," according to the London *Times*. Darwish continued to stay active in Palestinian politics, despite his frustration. In 2007, he openly criticized the fighting between Hamas and Fatah, calling it "a public attempt at suicide in the streets," according to the *Los Angeles Times*.

Despite his renown as a political poet, Darwish sometimes struggled with that aspect of his writing. "Sometimes I feel as if I am read before I write," he once said in the *New York Times*. "When I write a poem about my mother, Palestinians think my mother is a symbol for Palestine. But I write as a poet, and my mother is my mother. She's not a symbol." Many of Darwish's poems are recognized as having a universal quality. His works have been translated into more than 20 languages, a greater number than any other contemporary Arab poet. He received awards in several countries, including the 1983 Lenin Peace Prize, the Lannan Foundation Prize for Cultural Freedom, and the Prince Claus Fund, a Dutch cultural award.

The language Darwish chose to compose his poetry also made his work stand out. Rather than writing in modern Arabic, Darwish used the classical form of the language. "He used high language to talk about daily life in a truly exceptional way," fellow poet Ghassan Zaqtan told the *New York Times*. "This is someone who remained at the top of Arabic poetry for 40 years. It was not simply about politics." Syrian poet Adonis, as quoted by the *Washington Post*, wrote that Darwish's role as a Palestinian symbol was "a burden he embraced, which oppressed him and which he tamed and elevated."

Darwish also carried his hope for reconciliation, perhaps through coexistence and pluralism rather than occupation and exclusion, into his career. Darwish served as an editor of the quarterly journal *al-Karmel*, in which he published the poetry of both Israeli and Arab authors. Former Israeli education minister Yossi Sarid recognized Darwish's efforts and suggested including Darwish's work in the national high school curriculum. The suggestion was fought by many politicians and ultimately overruled by then-Prime Minister Ehud Barak.

Darwish died on August 9, 2008, in Houston, Texas, from complications following open heart surgery. Darwish's death was honored through vigils around Ramallah, as well as a three-day mourning period declared by the Palestinian Authority President Mahmoud Abbas. The Palestinian Authority gave Darwish a state funeral, the first since Yasser Arafat's funeral in 2004, in the West Bank. **Sources:** *Los Angeles Times*, August 10, 2008, p. B11; *New York Times*, August 11, 2008, p. A19; *Times* (London), August 14, 2008, p. 56; *Washington Post*, August 13, 2008, p. B6.

—Alana Joli Abbott

# Michael DeBakey

Born September 7, 1908, in Lake Charles, LA; died of natural causes, July 11, 2008, in Houston, TX.

Heart surgeon. Michael DeBakey was the father of modern heart surgery, inventor of several procedures that in the twentieth century and early 2000s save thousands of lives each year. He performed the first coronary artery bypass surgery, invented a pump used in heart-and-lung machines, implanted the first partial artificial heart in a person, performed the first carotid endarterectomy (surgical removal of blockages from the neck's main artery), and invented the Dacron graft (used to repair diseased arteries). He also proposed the concept of mobile army surgical hospitals and in 1939 co-wrote the first American scientific article linking cigarettes to lung cancer. He operated on 60,000 patients and wrote more than 1,500 scientific papers. According to Lawrence K. Altman, writing in the *New York Times*, the *Journal of the American Medical Association* stated in 2005, "Many consider Michael E. DeBakey to be the greatest surgeon ever."

DeBakey was born in Lake Charles, Louisiana, in 1908. His father, Morris, was a pharmacist who also owned farms. DeBakey and his brother and three sisters, all avid readers, studied the *Encyclopedia Britannica,* reading all of it before going to college. DeBakey was inspired to study medicine by working at his father's drugstore. He later credited his mother, Raheeja, with giving him a valuable surgical skill by teaching him to sew. He earned bachelor's and master's degrees at Tulane University in New Orleans, studied at the University of Strasbourg in France and the University of Heidelberg in Germany, then returned to Tulane University for medical school.

As an intern at New Orleans Charity Hospital in 1933, DeBakey saw his first living heart. A victim of a stabbing was brought into the hospital, and DeBakey could see his beating heart through the knife wound. The sight, which would have terrified most people, profoundly inspired him. "I saw it beating and it was beautiful, a work of art, an awe-inspiring sight," he is quoted as saying by Thomas H. Maugh II of the *Los Angeles Times*. "I still have an almost religious sense when I work on the heart. It is something God makes and we have yet to duplicate."

DeBakey was still in medical school in 1934 when he invented the hand-cranked roller pump that keeps blood flowing without touching it or harming red blood cells. He invented this device to help researchers, but soon it was also used in blood transfusions. In 1953, another inventor used the pump as a key piece in the heart-lung machine, which made coronary bypass surgery possible.

After medical school, DeBakey joined the Tulane faculty. He pointed out to his mentor, Alton Ochsner, that all the lung cancer patients in the hospital smoked cigarettes. Lung cancer was on the rise nationwide, but most experts at the time attributed it to the aftereffects of the 1918 influenza epidemic or soldiers' exposure to poison gas in World War I. DeBakey and Ochsner challenged those theories, arguing in a groundbreaking 1939 paper that cigarettes cause lung cancer.

During World War II, DeBakey enlisted in the military and became part of the U.S. surgeon general's European staff. After DeBakey saw that many soldiers died from wounds suffered on the front lines because they were too far from the nearest hospital, he proposed creating medical teams that the military could deploy near battlefields. These mobile army surgical hospitals, implemented during the Korean War, greatly improved wartime medical care (and were made famous in the film and television show *M*A*S*H*).

In 1948, DeBakey joined Baylor University in Houston as chairman of the College of Medicine's surgery department. He began experimenting with ways to repair diseased arteries. He used Dacron, a new synthetic cloth he bought at a department store, to create tubes the size of blood vessels. He implanted the tubes in animals and discovered that their bodies did not reject Dacron but that tissue actually bound to it. In 1954, he sewed the first Dacron graft into a human patient. The invention later saved thousands of lives.

Between the 1950s and the 1970s, DeBakey invented several now-common techniques for operating on damaged hearts and arteries. In 1953, he performed the first carotid endarterectomy, the scraping of plaque from a carotid artery to prevent a stroke. He performed the first coronary artery bypass surgery in 1964, taking a large blood vessel from a patient's leg and using it to bypass the blocked part of his artery. In 1966, he implanted the first left ventricular assist device, a pump that aids a failing heart. Decades later, he invented a similar but much smaller device, known as the MicroMed DeBakey, which was first used in a 1998 surgery and can be used in young children. DeBakey also performed the first multi-organ transplant in 1968, removing a heart, lung, and two kidneys from one donor and implanting them in four patients.

Under DeBakey's leadership, Baylor's College of Medicine was transformed from a mediocre school into a leader in teaching and research. Though very kind to patients, DeBakey treated assistants harshly, castigating and sometimes firing them for minor errors. "If you were on the operating table," he argued (as quoted by Altman of the *New York Times*), "would you want a perfectionist or somebody who cared little for detail?"

DeBakey's first wife, Diana Cooper, was a New Orleans nurse. She died of a heart attack in 1972. Three years later, DeBakey married Katrin Fehlhaber, a German actress. They had a daughter, Olga, in 1977, when DeBakey was 68.

DeBakey received countless awards for his work, including the Legion of Merit for his wartime service, the National Medal of Science, and the country's two highest civilian honors, the Presidential Medal of Freedom and the Congressional Gold Medal. He retired from surgery at age 90, though he continued to assist occasionally in operations. In 2005, DeBakey suffered a torn aorta, a condition he correctly diagnosed in himself after being stricken with pain. Surgeons operated on him, implanting the Dacron graft he invented. He spent a month in intensive care but recovered and returned to his life of writing and travel.

DeBakey died on July 11, 2008, at Methodist Hospital in Houston of natural causes. He was 99. He is survived by his wife, his daughter Olga, two of his four sons from his first marriage, eight grandchildren, and two sisters. **Sources:** *Chicago Tribune,* July 13, 2008, sec. 4, p. 6; *Los Angeles Times,* July 13, 2008, p. A1, pp. A16-17; *New York Times,* July 13, 2008, p. A1, p. A22; *Times* (London), July 14, 2008, p. 49; *Washington Post,* July 13, 2008, p. A1, p. A15.

—Erick Trickey

# Bo Diddley

Born Ellas Otha Bates (some sources say Otha Ellas Bates), December 30, 1928, in McComb, MS; died of heart failure, June 2, 2008, in Archer, FL. Musician. As a performer over the course of five decades, Bo Diddley had a profound, but often unacknowledged, impact on rock and roll. His signature beat, which he called the "freight train" rhythm and others referred to as "shave-and-a-haircut," was not only borrowed by contemporary performers, including Elvis Presley and Buddy Holly, but was used by later rockers, from The Who to David Bowie to the Rolling Stones. His percussive use of the guitar changed the way that musicians looked at the instrument and expanded the instrument's vocabulary, according to Chris Lee of the *Los Angeles Times,* who noted that "Diddley is recognized as one of rock's most influential guitarists."

From his signature look to his distinct sound—created by instruments he designed and intentionally distorted sound equipment—Diddley had a reputa-

tion for being an innovator who was larger than life. Billy Gibbons of ZZ Top said in a statement to the *Chicago Times* that Diddley "constructed the sound we all grew to revolve around." Ron Wood of the Rolling Stones told *Entertainment Weekly,* "Bo set the standards.... Bo didn't follow; we followed him." Wood also is quoted as saying, "From childhood, we all wanted to play like him."

Born to a teenage mother who worked as a sharecropper and a father who died when he was just an infant, if he was present at all, Diddley was named Ellas Otha Bates. He and his mother moved in with a cousin, Gussie McDaniel, who took care of both of them. When McDaniel moved to Chicago from Mississippi, she took Diddley with her, and he took the name Ellas McDaniel, which he used off stage for the rest of his life. His stage name, Bo Diddley, may have come about when he was a child in Chicago. Neighborhood children were said to have called him "ow diddley," which was slang for "bully," because Diddley was involved in many fights, to the point that he considered making a living as a boxer.

But Diddley also spent his early years learning music. He studied violin at the Ebenezer Baptist Church and later turned to guitar. "I looked around and didn't see too many black violinists," Diddley was quoted in the *Washington Post* as having said. The London *Times* also attributed his move away from the violin to a broken finger he suffered, which made violin technique too difficult to continue. Diddley pursued making his living as a boxer, and it may have been at this point in his life that he received his stage name, taking ownership of the Southern slang "you ain't bo diddley," meaning "you're nothing," and "bad bo diddley," meaning "someone who would be dangerous to cross."

While it became clear that Diddley would not succeed in boxing—he lost too often—his family also made it difficult for him to pursue the music he wanted to play. They considered his style to be "the Devil's music," to which Diddley finally countered, "Well, the Devil ain't never paid me," according to the London *Times.* In 1954, he left home to devote his time to his band, playing something that sounded a little like blues and R&B but which was actually quite different. The music drew on the Pentecostal music he had heard as a child in Mississippi alongside Afro-Caribbean rhythms and a percussive style of guitar.

"When I was about 15, I was trying to play like Muddy Waters, but it didn't work," he explained in a 1985 interview, quoted by the *Chicago Times.* "I figured I was on my way to becoming a first-class fool trying to play like Muddy and them. So I invented my own style. I always felt it was better to do your own thing than try to copy someone else, but I had no idea my thing would change rock music."

Diddley performed on street corners with his band, which included at different times Jerome Green on maracas, Roosevelt Jackson on bass, Billy Boy Arnold on harmonica, and Clifton James on drums. Later, the group received gigs in the famous South Side blues tavern the 708 Club. He auditioned at Vee Jay Records, but was turned down. In 1955, when the band had been together eleven years, Chess Records offered him a deal, and he recorded his first two singles, "I'm a Man" and "Bo Diddley." The second song, originally titled "Uncle John" but changed when Diddley began using his stage name (which another story asserts he was given by one of the sound workers at Chess Records), became his signature tune.

"I Am a Man" was a hit on the R&B chart, and Diddley was asked to appear on the *Ed Sullivan Show*. His appearance made him the first African-American artist to perform on the program. Sullivan had asked him to perform "Sixteen Tons," a country number by Merle Travis, but after agreeing, Diddley performed "Bo Diddley" instead. Because it was a live broadcast, Sullivan could not stop him from playing the more raucous number, but as a result, Diddley was never invited back on the program.

Diddley continued until 1967 to perform chart-topping singles, many of them on the self-designed rectangular guitar, which became his signature instrument. Though he had to find other work to pay the bills, in part because he had never received the royalties he was due from his record company, Diddley continued performing. He was invited to tour with British punk band The Clash in 1979, crediting him as an inspiration for garage rock. He performed at the 1985 "Live Aid" benefit concert, at an inaugural gala for George H. W. Bush in 1989, and at the Democratic National Convention for Bill Clinton in 1992. In 1987, he was inducted into the Rock and Roll Hall of Fame, and in 1998 he received a Grammy Award for lifetime achievement.

Due to a stroke while performing in 2007, Diddley retired from performing. He later suffered a heart attack and eventually died of heart failure at the age of 79. Married four times, Diddley is survived by four children, 15 grandchildren, 15 great-grandchildren, and three great-great-grandchildren. He is also survived by his brother Rev. Kenneth

Haynes. **Sources:** *Chicago Tribune*, June 3, 2008, sec. 1, p. 1, p. 14; *Entertainment Weekly*, June 13, 2008, p. 21; *Los Angeles Times*, June 3, 2008, p. A1, p. A13; *Times* (London), June 3, 2008, p. 54; *Washington Post*, June 3, 2008, p. A1, p. A12.

—*Alana Joli Abbott*

## Dith Pran

Born September 27, 1942, in Siem Reap, Cambodia; died of pancreatic cancer, March 30, 2008, in New Brunswick, NJ. Photojournalist. A survivor of the Cambodian holocaust, Dith Pran worked as a photojournalist to reveal the plight of his people. Serving as a translator for foreign journalists during the Cambodian civil war, Dith had no formal training as a journalist, learning how to follow a scoop on the job. As a teammate of Sydney Schanberg, an American journalist working for the *New York Times*, Dith saved the lives of Schanberg and other foreign journalists with his smooth talking and quick thinking. When Schanberg was awarded the Pulitzer Prize for his reporting from Cambodia, Schanberg accepted on behalf of Dith as well.

Forced to work 14 to 18 hours a day with no more than a spoonful of rice rationed to him, Dith avoided execution during the Cambodian genocide by hiding his middle-class, educated background. The story of his heroism in saving Schanberg and other journalists, as well as his struggle to survive under the Khmer Rouge, the communist party of Cambodia, was made into a film, *The Killing Fields*. After coming to America, Dith devoted his life to genocide awareness. He also became a celebrated photographer for the *New York Times*.

When Dith was born in 1942 in Siem Reap, Cambodia, the nation was still part of French Indochina. Dith learned French at school and taught himself to speak English. After finishing school, Dith became an interpreter and translator for the U.S. military, tourists, and visiting film companies. He also found work as a hotel receptionist near Angkor Wat. But as violence in Vietnam escalated, tourism decreased, and the American bombing of Cambodia forced Dith and his family to move to the capital, Phnom Penh.

In the city, Dith extended his translation services to foreign journalists, and soon became a favorite. He was often able to procure hotel rooms, bribe teletype operators to make sure that the journalists met their deadlines, and secure access to parts of Cambodia normally off limits to foreign journalists. In 1972, Dith met Schanberg, and soon began working for the *New York Times* reporter exclusively. Dith developed a sense for what would make a good story and taught himself photography. One of the biggest stories he and Schanberg covered resulted from Dith's bribing a patrol boat crew to take them up river to the site where 400 civilians had been injured or killed by an American bomber that had misidentified the village as a military target.

By spring of 1975, it was increasingly obvious that the Khmer Rouge would take over Phnom Penh. Many Cambodians fled, among them Dith's wife and four children, whom he sent to the United States. Dith stayed to continue working with Schanberg. "He wanted the story of what was happening to get out," Schanberg told the *Washington Post*. The pair expected the violence to subside once the Khmer Rouge were in charge of the capital, but peace never came. On April 17, five days after Dith's family had fled the city, Dith and Schanberg, along with their driver and two other foreign journalists, were confronted by Khmer Rouge soldiers. Dith was told to leave while the others were loaded in a truck, but Dith argued with the soldiers until, he, too, was taken. Though Schanberg had at first thought that Dith was pleading for his own life, he had actually been pleading to stay with the foreign journalists, knowing he was their only chance at survival. Through Dith's smooth talkng and negotiating, he managed to have Schanberg and the others released at the French Embassy, rather than executed.

Though Schanberg tried to get Dith out of the country, Dith was eventually captured. Seeing that many of the intellectuals, particularly those who had been friendly with foreign reporters, were executed, Dith abandoned any signs of his middle-class life and masqueraded as a taxi driver. For the next four and a half years, Dith worked in the fields or at menial jobs. Because the rationed food could not support them, Dith and other villagers ate rats, snakes, and ox blood to keep from starving. Dith once tried to steal additional rice; he was caught, beaten, and sentenced to execution, but was spared at the last moment.

When the Vietnamese invaded Cambodia in 1978, Dith returned to his home village. More than 50 of his family members had been killed, taken to an area just beyond the village that Dith termed "the killing fields," because where the bodies had been left, the grass grew tall and green. Initially appointed a village mayor by the Vietnamese over-

seers, Dith was removed from his position when his history with American journalists was revealed. Dith fled for Thailand, avoiding landmines as well as the Khmer Rouge and Vietnamese soldiers that stood in his way. When he reached the refugee camp, he was treated for malaria, and he found a way to contact Schanberg, who arrived three days later. The *New York Times* arranged for Dith's passage to New York, and Dith was reunited with his family, as well as given a job working as a photographer for the newspaper. Considered a hero, Dith was honored at the White House and became the goodwill ambassador to the office of the United Nations High Commissioner for Refugees.

Dith's story became a feature on the big screen in 1984 as the movie *The Killing Fields*. Dith was portrayed by Haing S. Nagor, a Cambodian doctor turned actor who had also survived the holocaust. Perhaps more than his journalism, the film brought the Cambodian crisis to the public in a personal, dramatic way. *The Killing Fields* received three Academy Awards.

"Pran reminds us of a special category of journalistic heroism—the local partner, the stringer, the interpreter, the driver, the fixer, who knows the ropes, who makes your work possible, who often becomes your friend, who may save your life, who shares little of the glory, and who risks so much more than you do," Bill Keller, executive editor of the *New York Times,* wrote in the same paper. Schanberg also commented in the *New York Times*, "I'm a very lucky man to have had Pran as my reporting partner and even luckier that we came to call each other brother."

Dith became a U.S. citizen in 1986. He founded the Dith Pran Holocaust Awareness Project to insure that the Cambodian holocaust would not be forgotten. He served, alongside Nagor, as a member of the Cambodia Documentation Commission, which was a group committed to seeing Pol Pot, the leader of the Khmer Rouge, tried for justice. Dith is survived by four children from his first marriage, a sister, and eight grandchildren. **Sources:** *Chicago Tribune,* March 31, 2008, sec. 1, p. 12; *Los Angeles Times,* March 31, 2008, pp. A1, A12; *New York Times,* March 31, 2008, p. A19; *Times* (London), March 31, 2008; *Washington Post,* March 31, 2008, p. B6.

—*Alana Joli Abbott*

## Bobby Fischer

Born Robert James Fischer, March 9, 1943, in Chicago, IL; died of kidney failure, January 17, 2008, in

Reykjavik, Iceland. Chess player. First a young genius, then an imperious champion, a ruthless competitor, and vicious recluse, Bobby Fischer dominated the elite levels of chess in the 1960s and 1970s, attracting a huge wave of new fans to the game. He gave chess its most dramatic moment in memory: a thrilling 1972 match in Iceland with Boris Spassky, a psychological combat that became a metaphor and channel for Cold War tensions between the United States and the Soviet Union. When he beat Spassky, Fischer became the only non-Russian to win the world chess championship in three decades and the only American champion of the twentieth century. "It was Bobby Fischer who had, single-handedly, made the world recognize that chess on its highest level was as competitive as football, as thrilling as a duel to the death, as esthetically satisfying as a fine work of art, as intellectually demanding as any form of human activity," wrote Harold C. Schonberg, the *New York Times* reporter who covered the match, in his 1973 book *Grandmasters of Chess* (as quoted by the *New York Times'* Bruce Weber).

Then, at the peak of his career and his fame, Fischer's troubled mind overwhelmed his talent, and he vanished into seclusion. For 20 years, chess fans hoped for his return. When Fischer finally played a rematch with Spassky in 1992, it was a terrible anti-climax. His eccentricities had grown out of control, and his hateful anger and defiance of his country's laws created an international scandal. He spent his last, deeply troubled years as a wanted man in exile.

Fischer was born in Illinois in 1943 to Regina Wender Fischer, a nurse and teacher from Missouri of Polish-Jewish descent. Her husband, German-born physicist Gerhard Fischer, is usually identified as his father, though there is some evidence that his biological father may have actually been a Hungarian-born naval laboratory researcher. Gerhard divorced Regina and left the country when Bobby was two years old, and she raised her son and his older sister, Joan, alone. They moved briefly to Arizona and California, then settled in Brooklyn when Bobby was five.

Joan introduced her brother to chess, buying him a cheap chess set and teaching him the rules. At age eight, he played in a chess event at the Brooklyn Public Library and his skill caught the attention of the club president, who offered him lessons. He joined the Manhattan Chess Club, and by age 12, he was beating some of the best chess players in the country. Opponents, struck by his ruthless style of play and his never-varying wardrobe, nicknamed him "the Boy Robot" and "the Corduroy Killer."

In 1956, Fischer defeated international chess master Donald Byrne with a strategy that included a daring sacrifice of his own queen, a performance so brilliant, *The Chess Review* dubbed it "The Game of the Century." The next year, competing in the 175-person U.S. Open Chess Championship, Fischer tied U.S. champion Arthur B. Bisguier for first place. In January of 1958, at age 14, he beat Bisguier in the U.S. Chess Federation Championship tournament, taking his title. That summer, at age 15, Fischer became the youngest international chess grandmaster ever by taking fifth place in a competition in Yugoslavia.

Genius-level intelligence helped make Fischer a champion; he was said to have an I.Q. of 181. He also studied the game more intensely than anyone else. He knew chess gambits and the styles of chess masters from his time back to the game's invention. He attacked relentlessly and unpredictably, rarely repeating strategies. "He was a classicist," Frank Brady, who played against Fischer and wrote a biography of him, told Joe Holley of the *Washington Post*. "He didn't go into great fireworks and deep sacrifices. He was almost like Bach instead of Beethoven." In 1970, after winning the world five-minute chess championship, Fischer recalled from memory all of his more than 1,000 moves from his 22 games in the tournament.

Even as a youth, Fischer was arrogant, stubborn, and rude. He told an interviewer that women could not achieve greatness in chess. In 1961, he lost a match against Samuel Reshevsky, an Orthodox Jew, because Reshevsky would not play on the Sabbath and Fischer refused to play the rescheduled game the next day, complaining that he was not used to playing in the morning. In 1962, when one chess grandmaster told Fischer that he should see a psychiatrist, Fischer replied that psychiatrists should pay him for the opportunity to examine his mind.

As Fischer's prominence in international chess increased, he became demanding and paranoid. He insisted on special lighting, seating, and rules to enforce quiet at matches. He said Russian players were conspiring to play to draws against each other to wreck his tournament standing. He even claimed his opponents were trying to poison him and bug his hotel rooms. He would withdraw from competing for months, but return and again play with dazzling skill. At one point, he went on a 20-game winning streak against grandmasters.

In 1972, Fischer challenged Spassky, the Russian world chess champion, to a match in Reykjavik, Iceland. No American had won the world championship since the 1800s and Russians had held the title for 35 years, therefore the Fischer-Spassky match became a chessboard proxy for the Cold War. Fischer's eccentric demands heightened the tension. At the last minute, he refused to play, finally relenting after a personal appeal from U.S. National Security Adviser Henry Kissinger and an increase in the prize for the victor.

Fischer lost the first game of the match, then refused to play the second game, forfeiting it to Spassky. He insisted on playing the third game in a small room, with no television or film cameras inside. Spassky agreed. Fischer won the game, then kept winning, taking the lead in the match. The Russians, showing off paranoia of their own, responded by sweeping the hall for bugs and X-raying Fischer's and Spassky's chairs. Fischer won the sixth game with a performance so elegant, even Spassky applauded at the end, and a commentator compared it to a Mozart symphony. Fischer won the match with a score of 12 to 8, won the $250,000 prize, and became world champion.

The drama-filled match transformed chess into a sport as respected as golf or tennis. Membership in the U.S. Chess Federation almost tripled. Americans looked at Fischer as a Cold War hero. President Richard Nixon sent him a telegram congratulating him on his victory. He became as famous for his complete dominance of chess as Babe Ruth in baseball or, later, Michael Jordan in basketball.

However, Fischer's mental instability soon ruined his career. He never defended his title, and in 1975, he forfeited it by refusing to play Russian challenger Anatoly Karpov. He became a recluse, living in South Pasadena, California and shunning publicity. He promoted strange variations on chess: new rules with the major pieces rearranged, a new method of imposing time limits on matches. He did not attend a chess club or event for nearly 20 years. Chess enthusiasts remained fascinated by his seclusion and the prospect of a comeback; a play on this theme took the form of a 1988 book and 1993 movie about chess prodigy Joshua Waitzkin titled *Searching for Bobby Fischer*. The reality of Fischer's life as a hermit was much less romantic. "The rare accounts of his situation all mention cheap rooms in Pasadena and L.A., months of his crashing on former friends and days spent riding the orange city bus between L.A. and Pasadena, analyzing chess games on his pocket set," Ivan Solotaroff wrote in *Esquire* (as quoted by the *New York Times'* Weber).

When Fischer finally mounted a comeback, it was sad and scandalous. He agreed to an unsanctioned 1992 rematch with Spassky at a resort in Yugosla-

via, a few miles from the war raging in neighboring Bosnia. His participation defied U.S. sanctions against Yugoslavia, imposed because of the war. While there, Fischer received a warning letter from the U.S. Treasury Department threatening him with arrest and fines. With reporters watching, he spat on the letter then ranted hatefully about Jews and Russians. Fischer won the match and its $3.5 million prize, but a warrant was issued for his arrest back home. He never returned to the United States.

Between 1992 and his death, Fischer lived in Hungary, Japan, and possibly Switzerland and the Philippines, before settling in Reykjavik, Iceland, the site of his greatest victory. He became more and more hateful toward the United States and toward Jews, even though his mother was Jewish. On a radio broadcast in the Philippines, he declared that the September 11, 2001, terrorist attacks on the United States were "wonderful news" (according to the *Times* of London). He was arrested at an airport in Japan in 2004 on a charge of trying to leave the country with an expired passport; the United States had revoked it. He was detained for nine months while the United States sought his extradition. When Iceland offered him citizenship, Japan released him. He arrived in Reykjavik to cheering crowds. Iceland's ambassador to the United States responded to strong international criticism of Fischer's welcome by saying (according to the *Times* of London) that the former chess champion should be "considered the subject of pity, rather than hatred."

Fischer died of kidney failure on January 17, 2008, at a hospital in Reykjavik. He was 64. He has no known survivors except his longtime companion, Japanese women's chess grandmaster Miyoko Watai. "He was the pride and sorrow of chess," said British grandmaster Raymond Keene (as quoted in the *Chicago Tribune*). "It's tragic that such a great man descended into madness and anti-Semitism." **Sources:** *Chicago Tribune,* January 19, 2008, sec. 4, p. 10; CNN.com, http://www.cnn.com/2008/US/01/18/fischer.obit (January 22, 2008); *Los Angeles Times,* January 19, 2008, pp. A1, A19; *New York Times,* January 19, 2008, pp. A1, A28; *People,* February 4, 2008, p. 131; *Times* (London), January 19, 2008, p. 77; *Washington Post,* January 19, 2008, p. B6.

—*Erick Trickey*

## Dan Fogelberg

Born Daniel Grayling Fogelberg, August 13, 1951, in Peoria, IL; died of prostate cancer, December 16,

2007, in Deer Isle, ME. Musician. Singer and guitarist Dan Fogelberg crafted a string of hits in the mellower, soft-rock genre of pop music that became part of the soundtrack for a generation of young Americans. Fogelberg's "songs ranged from the soul-searching to the sentimental," noted his *Times of London* obituary, "and in the 1970s and 1980s he came to epitomise the sensitive and concerned American singer-songwriter."

Fogelberg was born in 1951 in Peoria, Illinois, and was the last of three sons. His mother Margaret was a talented pianist, and his father was the high school band director at Woodruff High School, from which Fogelberg graduated in 1969. Not surprisingly, musical training began early in the Fogelberg household, and his mother gave him his first piano lessons. By his early teens he had taught himself how to play Hawaiian slide guitar and formed his first band, the Clan, which covered Beatles tunes. With a later ensemble, the Coachmen, he recorded a pair of singles but neither song attracted much notice.

At the University of Illinois's Urbana-Champaign campus, Fogelberg studied theater arts and painting, but his budding career as a guitar-playing folk singer on the coffeehouse circuit began to take precedence over his classes. As his style evolved from folk into a more pop-rock sound in the vein of James Taylor, Fogelberg gained a following in several Midwest college towns. In 1971, he signed on with Irving Azoff, an up-and-coming music manager in Urbana-Champaign who would become one of the most successful record-company executives of the decade. Azoff had already taken a local band called REO Speedwagon to national prominence and would go on to make the Eagles one of the most profitable acts of the 1970s.

At Azoff's suggestion, Fogelberg moved to Nashville and gained some experience as a session musician, which influenced his debut on the Columbia label, *Home Free*. When the record failed to find an audience, Fogelberg was dropped by Columbia. Azoff was still his manager, however, and had little trouble placing Fogelberg with Epic Records. Joe Walsh of the Eagles served as producer for Fogelberg's next LP, *Souvenirs*, which was released in 1974 and had one single that did respectably well on radio, "Part of the Plan."

The turning point in Fogelberg's career came when he opened for the Eagles on their 1975 "One of These Nights" tour. For the next few years he issued a regular stream of soft-rock hits. His fourth LP, 1977's *Nether Lands*, served as a "a near-perfect manifesto of the long-haired, stone-washed denim soft-rock style," his *Times* of London obituary asserted, "alternately lush and poignant but always melodic, with elements of country and folk and dreamlike orchestrations."

In 1978 Fogelberg teamed up with Tim Weisberg, a jazz flautist, for *Twin Sons of Different Mothers*, whose hit single was "The Power of Gold." Fogelberg's 1979 release, *Phoenix*, produced the most successful single of his career: The love song "Longer" reached No. 2 on the U.S. chart and became a wedding staple for years to come. Fans of Fogelberg's music cite the 1981 double LP *Innocent Age* as his most ambitious effort, and a track from this, "Same Old Lang Syne," became another enduring hit for him. Its tale of a meeting a former flame while home for the holidays actually happened to him in Peoria one Christmas.

Fogelberg moved in Southern California musical circles that included the Eagles musicians and Jackson Browne, but in 1982 he left Los Angeles for a 610-acre piece of property near Boulder, Colorado. Subsequent releases had a more traditional country, folk, or bluegrass sound, such as 1985's *High Country Snows* and *River of Souls* from 1993. His last full-length studio release was *Full Circle* in 2003. A year later, he was diagnosed with prostate cancer, and aggressive treatment halted its spread, but only temporarily. He died on December 16, 2007, at his other home in Deer Isle, Maine. His wife, Jean, survives him.

Fogelberg was just 56 when he passed away. Thirty years earlier, at the height of his success, he gave an interview to *Rolling Stone* in which he told writer James Henke that "this pop music isn't going to last forever. You gotta realize that there's a five-year period or so when your peak popularity is—you're lucky if it lasts that long. And then what? So, I'm preparing now to be doing as much music when I'm 60 as what I'm doing now." **Sources:** *Chicago Tribune*, December 17, 2007, sec. 3, p. 10; *Los Angeles Times*, December 17, 2007, p. B9; *New York Times*, December 17, 2007, p. A25; *Rolling Stone*, August 25, 1977; *Times* (London), December 18, 2007, p. 55; *Washington Post*, December 17, 2007, p. B6.

—*Carol Brennan*

## Estelle Getty

Born Estelle Scher, July 25, 1923, in New York, NY; died from complications of Lewy body disease, July

22, 2008, in Los Angeles, CA. Actress. Estelle Getty personified the show-business foot soldier, tackling a long string of supporting parts in plays until her role on the television sitcom *The Golden Girls* made her a star virtually overnight. Blessed with a sure sense of character and comedic timing second to none, Getty was able to deliver her scripted utterances in such a way as to provoke a mixture of shock and delight. Capitalizing upon her television success, Getty co-starred in the 1992 feature film *Stop! Or My Mom Will Shoot*, in which the diminutive actress completely upstaged action superstar Sylvester Stallone.

Born in 1923 in New York City, Getty was the daughter of Polish immigrants Charles and Sarah Scher. Setting her sights on an acting career by age five, during her formative years Estelle honed her comedic skills in Yiddish theater and by performing stand-up comedy at resorts in the Catskill Mountains. The Scher patriarch worked in the glass business, and it was through him that Estelle met the love of her life, Arthur Gettleman. The couple married in 1947 and produced two sons, Carl and Barry. Still determined to act, she shortened her married name to craft her stage moniker, Estelle Getty.

Performing in community theater, Getty took on comedic roles in such reliable plays as *Arsenic and Old Lace* and *Lovers and Other Strangers* with solid turns in such dramatic fare as *The Glass Menagerie* and *Death of a Salesman*. Constantly refining her craft, she performed with the Federal Theatre and the Workshop of the Performing Arts while still running her home and raising her children. "She was a whirlwind as a young mother," her son Barry Gettleman told *People*, "working, auditioning, shopping, cleaning. [And] my mother was a brilliant actress."

Although Getty made notable appearances in such plays as *The Divorce of Judy and Jane* (1971) and *Widows and Children First* (1979), her big break did not come until she played Harvey Fierstein's acerbic mother in *Torch Song Trilogy* in 1981. Having worked together numerous times off-Broadway, Getty and Fierstein found it easy to create and maintain a tempestuous on-stage bond. "It began to strike me as funny to imagine this teeny little thing bossing me around," Fierstein was quoted as saying by Claudia Luther of the *Los Angeles Times*. Critics agreed and Getty was nominated for the Drama Desk Award. However, to her chagrin, Anne Bancroft played her part in the film version.

The success of *Torch Song Trilogy* helped Getty secure a Hollywood agent who lined up small roles in such hit films as *Tootsie, The Chosen, Mask,* and *Protocol*. However, it was television that offered her the role of a lifetime, Sophia Petrillo on *The Golden Girls*.

Getty auditioned three times for *The Golden Girls* before getting the part. When she learned that producers considered her too young to play Bea Arthur's mother—indeed she was 15 and a half months younger—she told a make-up artist, "To you this is just a job," she is quoted as saying in the London *Times*. "To me it's my entire career down the toilet unless you make me look 80." Once hired, she proved a brilliant addition to a groundbreaking sitcom that featured such high-powered TV veterans as Arthur, Rue McClanahan, and Betty White. Enjoyed by audiences both young and old, the program brought into sharp focus the concerns of senior citizens. Initially, the show explained Sophia Petrillo's propensity for politically incorrect one-liners by saying that a stroke had compromised her ability to be tactful. Later in the series it was revealed that Sophia had always been feisty and outspoken.

Playing the character from 1985 to 1995, Getty was nominated for a Best Supporting Actress Emmy Award six times, winning in 1988. The role also earned her a Golden Globe Award and a Golden Apple Award in 1986 as well as the American Comedy Award in 1991 and 1992. So popular was her portrayal that Getty was asked to make guest appearances on other shows as Sophia. Further, she played the character in the spin-off *The Golden Palace* and on the final two seasons of an unrelated sitcom, *Empty Nest*.

Interest in her life and times prompted Getty to write her autobiography, *If I Knew Then What I Know Now ... So What?* in 1986. She also made an exercise videotape for seniors titled *Young at Heart: Body Conditioning with Estelle*. In addition to the already mentioned Sylvester Stallone film, Getty took on numerous television and film parts, including voice-over work for *Stuart Little* and *The Million Dollar Kid*. Plagued by declining health, she retired in 2000. Her husband Arthur died in 2004.

Getty was afflicted with Lewy body dementia, a degenerative brain disorder that has symptoms like those of both Alzheimer's and Parkinson's diseases. In 1992, the AIDS-related death of her nephew Stephen Scher caused the actress to become a strong advocate for gay rights and AIDS research. According to co-star Rue McClanahan, as quoted in *People*, in her later years, Getty "always surrounded herself with young, good-looking gay guys."

Getty offered some tongue-in-cheek advice for aspiring actors. "If there are two things you want to do in life," she is quoted as saying at *Internet Movie Database*, "and one of them is acting ... do the other." Getty died on July 22, 2008, in Hollywood, California, home, just three days before her eighty-fifth birthday. She is survived by her two sons. **Sources:** Broadway.com, http://www.broadway.com/buzz/ buzz_story_print.aspx?id=568906 (February 9, 2009); *Chicago Tribune*, July 12, 2008, sec 2, p. 11; *Contemporary Theatre, Film and Television*, vol. 38, Gale Group, 2002; Internet Movie Database, http://www.imdb. com/name/nm0001268/bio (February 9, 2009); Estelle Getty.com, http://www.estellegetty.com/ credits.html (February 10, 2009); *Los Angeles Times*, July 23, 2008, p. B6; *New York Times*, July 23, 2008, p. A19; *People*, August 11, 2008, pp. 61-62; *Times* (London, England), July 30, 2008, p. 62.

—*Ken Burke*

# Simon Gray

Born Simon James Holliday Gray, October 21, 1936, in Hayling Island, Hampshire, England; died of cancer, August 6, 2008, in London, England. Playwright. Known for his caustic wit and comedies about self-involved intellectuals, Simon Gray was a playwright, novelist, memoirist, and teacher. A smoker from the age of seven, Gray created characters who embraced the same vices that he enjoyed. When forced to give up Scotch for health reasons, Gray switched to champagne, only giving up alcohol all together after a doctor assured him that continuing to drink would lead to a quick death. Despite claiming that alcohol "liberated" his writing, Gray was a meticulous editor, often drafting as many as 40 versions of his scripts before producing a finished edition. "The last draft is always effortless," he was quoted as having said in the *New York Times*. "That's how I know it's finished."

As an academic for most of his adult life, Gray thought of himself first as a teacher. His characters often come from an academic setting and are intellectual in their banter. His later plays became thinner in plot in order to emphasize character studies, particularly in the growing collapse in interpersonal communication. Over the course of his career, Gray completed 40 stage plays, television plays, and screenplays, five novels, and a set of three memoirs.

The son of a pathologist, Gray was born in Hayling Island, England in 1936. In 1939, he and his brother were taken to Canada to live with relatives; his mother said she would stay with them, but left to buy milk and returned to England instead. Gray was miserable in Montreal, finding his relatives abusive and his school situation even worse. In his memoirs he wrote of being molested by his teachers and often beaten by his peers. The experience shaped him into something of a con artist with a talent for petty theft, and when he returned to London as a teen, he was arrested for running a scam using Georgian coins in the London subway system.

He returned to Canada for college, studying at Dalhousie University in Nova Scotia. He earned his doctorate at Trinity College of Cambridge University, and gained a position at Queen Mary, University of London, where he served as a lecturer in drama, poetry, and English literature.

Gray published several novels before he began working as a playwright, a career that came to him as something of a surprise. When a story he had written was sold to television to be adapted, he discovered that the screenwriter who adapted his work would make more on the piece than he had. Gray volunteered to adapt it for screen himself, and built enough confidence from the experience that he created an original play for television. The script was rejected due to the main character, a criminal who wears drag to evade the police. Undeterred, Gray adjusted the screenplay for stage, and *Wise Child*, as it was called, was produced in 1967 with Sir Alec Guinness starring as the main character.

Though *Wise Child* was more successful in London than on Broadway, *Butley*, Gray's second play, was a hit on both sides of the Atlantic. The story of a curmudgeonly college professor, *Butley* is a story that emphasizes what would become a theme in many of Gray's plays: disconnection and loss told through dark humor. The eponymous professor's wife has left him, and though he attempts to connect with a gay male student, he finds both his sexual and his professional life crashing down around him. The play was Gray's first collaboration with director Harold Pinter and star Alan Bates. The three went on to work together in several productions. Bates won a Tony Award for his performance as Butley on Broadway, a role that he reprised in the 1974 film version. His work was so celebrated that it was not until 2006 that the play was revived on Broadway, starring Nathan Lane in the title role.

*Otherwise Engaged,* another play about a detached professor, was Gray's most successful Broadway production. The professor, wishing to listen to his new recording of Wagner's opera *Parsifal*, hangs up on an old college friend who is contemplating suicide. He then suffers a series of interruptions from hostile visitors, each keeping him from escaping his office to listen to his music. The play ran for 309 performances in 1977. Several of Gray's other plays, including *Quartermaine's Terms* and *The Common Pursuit* mine similar settings and themes, all with a morbid humor wound throughout.

Though not as well known for his plays in the early part of the twenty-first century, Gray published a series of three memoirs that chronicled his life and the nature of aging. Using his troubled marriage and divorce, as well as his love of cigarettes and alcohol as his dominant subject matter, Gray wrote about the trials he suffered with both alcoholism and his declining health. Throughout the memoirs, Gray's acerbic wit continues to shine through. He was working on a stage adaptation of his final memoir, *The Last Cigarette*, at the time of his death.

Divorced from his first wife Beryl Kevern, with whom he had two children, Gray is survived by both children and his wife Victoria Rothschild. He died on August 6, 2008, in London, England, after a long battle with both lung cancer and prostate cancer. He was 71. **Sources:** *Los Angeles Times*, August 9, 2008, p. B9; *New York Times*, August 8, 2008, p. C14; *Washington Post*, August 9, 2008, p. B4.

—*Alana Joli Abbott*

## Edmund Hillary

Born Edmund Percival Hillary, July 20, 1919, in Tuakau, New Zealand; died of a heart attack, January 11, 2008, in Auckland, New Zealand. Mountaineer. Sir Edmund Hillary's name has been inextricably linked with Mount Everest since the day in 1953 when he became the first person ever to scale the majestic Himalayan peak. With an elevation of 29,029 feet, Everest is the highest mountain on Earth and was thought to be impossible for even the most experienced of climbers to conquer. "In an era in which exploration, travel, tourism and the Internet have so thoroughly shrunk the world," noted Hillary's *Times* of London obituary, "it is difficult to re-create the sense of unassailable mystery and menace represented in those days by the world's highest peak."

Hillary was born in 1919 in Tuakau, New Zealand, where his father had a beekeeping enterprise. As a young man, Hillary grudgingly entered Auckland University, for he disliked the routine of the classroom and preferred to be out of doors. His first forays in mountaineering came when he scaled New Zealand's peaks, but he soon moved on to more imposing summits in the European Alps. During World War II he served as a navigator with the Royal New Zealand Air Force in the South Pacific. After returning to civilian life he ran his father's apiary business with his brother, Rex, while taking part in various endurance challenges.

Hillary's first Himalayan climb was undertaken with a fellow adventurer named George Lowe in 1951, and while there they were invited to take part in a British-led reconnaissance mission to assess Mount Everest. The immense peak that climbed to a vertical height equal to five and a half miles had been measured as the highest in the world nearly a century before, but several teams of veteran climbers had tried to scale it and failed. Everest's upper reaches were scarce on oxygen and buffeted by strong winds that brought sudden, fearful snow squalls. Moreover, the sole route of access was through Nepal, the mountain kingdom on Everest's southern side, but its government permitted just one expedition a year.

Hillary was chosen as part of the 1953 attempt by the British Royal Geographical Society-Alpine Club. He planned to climb with Lowe as one of a pair of two-man teams, but the expedition's leader, John Hunt, teamed him instead with Tenzing Norgay, a Sherpa from Nepal. The Sherpa people lived in the Himalayas and were acclimatized to the region's harsh conditions; Norgay was one of 35 Sherpa guides hired by the expedition, along with an additional 350 Sherpa porters who carried 18 tons of food and supplies, including supplemental oxygen tanks. Hunt's other designated climbing team was Tom Bourdillon and Charles Evans, who made the initial attempt at scaling Everest's final heights but turned back after a storm erupted and their oxygen apparatus malfunctioned.

Hillary and Norgay set out to make the final ascent to the top of Everest on May 29, 1953. Part of this journey involved what later become known as the "Hillary Step": a 40-foot wall of rock that seemed insurmountable. Hillary found a vertical crack in it and he and Norgay wedged themselves upward through it. Once that obstacle was behind them, the rest of the climb was relatively easy, and when they reached the peak known as the highest point, "we shook hands and then, casting Anglo-Saxon formalities aside, we thumped each other on the back until forced to stop from lack of breath," Hillary recalled in his 1955 book *High Adventure*, according to his *New York Times* obituary.

At the summit, Hillary snapped a photograph of Norgay with his camera, and the Buddhist guide left a small offering of chocolate and biscuits buried in the snow. They spent a quarter-hour there before beginning their equally treacherous descent. It took four days for news of Hillary's achievement to reach the rest of the world, and it was announced on June 2, 1953, the same day that Britain was celebrating the Coronation Day of Queen Elizabeth II. By the time Hillary arrived in Britain to be knighted by the new monarch, he and Norgay had become world-famous.

Hillary returned to the Himalayas several more times, climbing ten more of its peaks and once even leading an official expedition in search of the Abominable Snowman. Forever indebted to Norgay and the other Sherpas, he established the Himalayan Trust, which built schools and health clinics in Nepal. In 1992 he became the first living person who was not the head of state to adorn a piece of New Zealand currency.

Hillary suffered a heart attack in Auckland, New Zealand, and died at the age of 88 on January 11, 2008. Survivors include his wife June and two children, Peter and Sarah, from his first marriage. A second daughter, Belinda, was killed in a 1975 plane crash in Nepal with Hillary's wife Louise. His second wife was the former June Mulgrew, whose husband Peter was a friend of the Hillarys and had died in an infamous 1979 Air New Zealand tourist flight over Antarctica for which Hillary was originally slated to serve as commentator.

Though Hillary usually exhibited a distaste for the pomp and publicity that came with his achievement, he rarely failed to disappoint when reporters asked him about his 1953 feat. "The whole world around us lay spread out like a giant relief map," he told one journalist about reaching the top of Everest, according to his *New York Times* obituary. "I am a lucky man. I have had a dream and it has come true, and that is not a thing that happens often to men." **Sources:** *Chicago Tribune*, January 11, 2008, sec. 1, pp. 1, 9; CNN.com, www.cnn.com/2008/WORLD/asiapcf/01/10/edmund.hillary/index.html; *Los Angeles Times*, January 11, 2008, pp. A1, A4; *New York Times*, January 11, 2008, p. A17; *Times* (London), January 12, 2008, p. 77.

—Carol Brennan

## Patrick Hillery

Born Patrick John Hillery, May 2, 1923, in Miltown Malbay, County Clare, Ireland; died after a short illness, April 12, 2008, in Dublin, Ireland. Politician.

Patrick Hillery served two seven-year terms as president of Ireland in the 1970s and '80s and is credited with guiding his nation toward a peace agreement with the British-ruled Northern Ireland after a long period of civil strife. Though that historic treaty, known as the Good Friday Agreement of 1998, was signed several years after Hillery left office, he is considered to have been instrumental in leading his party, Fianna Fáil, toward a more moderate stance in dealing with sectarian violence.

Hillery was born in 1923, in Miltown Malbay, a town in western County Clare, Ireland. Just a year earlier, Ireland's long battle with its more powerful British-Isles neighbor, England, had ended with a formal separation, which gave the largely Roman Catholic southern counties independence as the Republic of Ireland, while the British-allied, predominantly Protestant northern counties became Northern Ireland, which remained part of the United Kingdom.

Hillery's father was the local doctor in Miltown Malbay, and he followed him into the profession for a time after earning his degree from University College Dublin. In 1951, Hillery won a seat in Ireland's Dáil, or parliament, as the running mate of another County Clare native, Éamon de Valera, who became Ireland's prime minister with the Fianna Fáil win at the polls. De Valera became president of Ireland in 1959, the same year that Hillery was appointed education minister for a notable seven-year stint. In that role, he became a modernizing force, marshalling "all his abundant shrewdness and tact when developing comprehensive schools outside the jurisdiction of the Catholic Church, which had previously been all-powerful in Irish education," noted his *Times* of London obituary. "These schools were to provide the skilled labour force that later attracted foreign investment to Ireland."

Hillery also served stints in Ireland's cabinet as minister for industry and labor minister. He was appointed foreign minister in 1969, coinciding with the onset of yet another round of sectarian strife between Catholics and Protestants throughout Ireland. Irish nationalists rallied round the Irish Republican Army, which carried out a campaign of terrorist acts in both Belfast, the Northern Ireland capital, and as far away as London. On the other side of the struggle was the British government and its formidable military might. In the heated summer of 1970, "after the first British Army house searches in the north provoked further Catholic protests," wrote *New York Times* journalist John F. Burns, Hillery "brushed aside diplomatic protocol to make an unannounced visit to the Catholic stronghold in the Falls Road area of Belfast, further infuriating the British."

As Ireland's foreign minister, Hillery also made a United Nations visit, suggesting a joint British-Irish force or United Nations peacekeepers to help defuse tensions in Ireland and its northern counterpart, both of which were summarily rejected. At the 1971 Fianna Fáil party conference, he led a pitched battle at the podium against hardliners within his own party who wanted to urge armed resistance against British rule. After the infamous Bloody Sunday in January of 1972, when British military forces killed 13 civilians, Hillery traveled to Washington, D.C. to ask for help, and said in a television interview, "I believe the British government have gone mad," according to Burns' *New York Times* tribute.

Hillery played a crucial role in Ireland's entry into the predecessor of the European Union, which was known as the European Economic Community in January of 1973 when Ireland joined the organization. He later became Ireland's representative on the European Commission, but in 1976 was urged to run for president after another political fracas involving Ireland's minister of defense, who had publicly criticized the current president, Cearbhall Ó Dálaigh, while apparently inebriated—an incident which failed to provoke any response or reprimand from the ruling government and caused Ó Dálaigh to resign from office. Hillery ran unopposed in November of 1976 and won the presidency.

As president of Ireland, Hillery had little actual power in comparison to the prime minister, but he was uninterested in political glory. The *Times* of London characterized him as "a hesitant public speaker, and his private charm and warmth did not translate into public charisma. Efforts in the early years to create a more interesting image by, for example, wearing a cape fell rather flat." In early 1982, however, Hillery stood firm when Fianna Fáil leader Charles Haughey wanted to form a new government, which could not be done without presidential approval—one of the few presidential powers accorded to the office. "Hillery refused to take a telephone call from Haughey and dissolved the Dáil," noted the *Times* of London. "The incident established Hillery's credentials as a President above party and set a valuable precedent." A year later, Hillery ran for a second term as president, again unopposed, and won another seven-year term.

Hillery retired from office in 1990. He died after an undisclosed short illness on April 12, 2008, in Dublin, Ireland, at the age of 84. Survivors include his wife Maeve and a son, John. He was predeceased by a daughter, Vivienne, who died in 1987. "Children used to ask me if it was nice to be president, and you would have to say 'yes,'" he once said, according to his *New York Times* obituary. "You know, you couldn't disappoint them." **Sources:** *Chicago Tribune*, April 14, 2008, sec. 2, p. 10; *Los Angeles Times*, April 17, 2008, p. B6; *New York Times*, April 16, 2008, p. A23; *Times* (London), April 14, 2008, p. 48; *Washington Post*, April 13, 2008, p. C8.

—*Carol Brennan*

## L. Rust Hills

Born Lawrence Rust Hills, November 9, 1924, in New York, NY; died of a heart ailment, August 12, 2008, in Belfast, ME. Editor. L. Rust Hills was best known as the fiction editor at *Esquire* during its heyday. His time there coincided with a revival of fortunes for the men's magazine, which had been founded in 1932 but was in the midst of a major redesign and emphasis on cutting-edge journalism by the time Hills took the job in 1957. "In the 1960s *Esquire* was perhaps the nation's most vibrant magazine—sexy, mischievous, irreverent, and hip," asserted Bruce Weber in the *New York Times*, who noted that "Hills' idea of fiction, as well as of the literary life, fit into the ethos of the magazine perfectly."

Hills was born in the borough of Brooklyn in New York City in 1924. His father was a salesperson at a local Sears department store. As a young man, Hills entered the U.S. Merchant Marine Academy at Kings Point, New York, and went on to serve in that branch of the service during World War II. He later attended Kenyon College in Ohio, and received his undergraduate degree from Wesleyan University, Middletown, Connecticut, in 1948, and a master's degree a year later. For a few years, he taught English courses at Columbia University in New York City and Carleton College in Minnesota.

Hills was hired as *Esquire*'s fiction editor in 1957. Back in the 1930s, the magazine had been known for publishing stories from Ernest Hemingway and F. Scott Fitzgerald, among other top American writers, but in its shift to more of a men's fashion magazine *Esquire*'s monthly fiction pages descended into run-of-the-mill adventure tales. To remedy this, Hills sought out up-and-coming young writers and courted some already established names with the goal of making *Esquire* an elite forum once again. One of the first stories to signify this new era was Hills' publication of "The Misfits" from playwright Arthur Miller.

Philip Roth and Saul Bellow were among the writers that Hills published on the pages of the magazine over the next few years, along with John Cheever, William Styron, and William Gaddis. He commissioned a work from Norman Mailer that was serialized in *Esquire* and later became the novel *An American Dream,* one of the controversial writer's most controversial works. Hills also convinced his bosses to run an all-literary issue in 1963, which featured photo-essays on prominent writers and a tongue-in-cheek diagram purported to be the definitive "who's who" on the American literary scene which miffed many and prompted a flurry of letters to the editor and rebuttals in other publications.

Hills left *Esquire* in 1964 to take a job at the *Saturday Evening Post,* a publication with a far more staid reputation. He returned to *Esquire* for an eleven-month stint between 1969 and 1970, and once again in 1978, but remained involved with the magazine until the late 1990s. He continued to search out and champion the work of younger writers, among them Don DeLillo, Raymond Carver, E. Annie Proulx, and Richard Ford.

Hills' role involved editing short stories for publication and condensing soon-to-be-published novels into short story form, a talent at which he was particularly adept. Two of the best-known examples of this came with Styron's 1979 novel *Sophie's Choice,* which won the National Book Award for fiction a year later, and Richard Ford's *Independence Day,* the 1996 Pulitzer-Prize winner. Hills also served as editor of several anthologies of short fiction over the years.

Highly opinionated, Hills was a raffish, thrice-married *bon vivant.* He wrote a collection of essays that appeared in 1972 titled *How to Do Things Right: The Revelations of a Fussy Man,* which was followed by two more "how-to" guides: *How to Retire at 41, or Dropping Out of the Rat Race Without Going Down the Drain,* and *How to Be Good, or the Somewhat Tricky Business of Attaining Moral Virtue in a Society That's Not Just Corrupt But Corrupting, Without Being Completely Out-of-It.* Two decades later the trio of titles was condensed into a single volume and republished.

Hills is also known to generations of would-be writers as the author of a more serious book, *Writing in General and the Short Story in Particular,* first published in 1977 and a standard textbook in college-level creative writing classes in the decades to come. "Everything must work with everything else," he advises short-story crafters in his book, according to his *Washington Post* obituary. "Everything enhances everything else, interrelates with everything else, is inseparable from everything else—and all this is done with a necessary and perfect economy."

Hills' third wife was the writer Joy Williams, with whom he shared retirement homes in Key West, Florida, and Tucson, Arizona. He was visiting Belfast, Maine, on August 12, 2008, when he succumbed to a heart attack at the age of 83. Survivors include Williams; a daughter, Caitlin Hills; and one grandson. Upon news of his death, scores of writers whose work he edited over the years stepped forward to pay tribute. One of them was Gay Talese, who told the *Los Angeles Times'* Dennis McLellan that Hills "wasn't interested in commercial fiction. He was interested in the standards of serious literature, and he tried to, in a commercial magazine, impose upon its pages some of the lofty notions he had about the written word." **Sources:** *Los Angeles Times,* August 16, 2008, p. B6; *New York Times,* August 15, 2008, p. C12; *Washington Post,* August 17, 2008, p. C7.

—*Carol Brennan*

## Hua Guofeng

Born Su Zhu, February 16, 1921, in Jiaocheng, Shanxi Province, China; died after an unspecified illness, August 20, 2008, in Beijing, China. Party leader. Hua Guofeng had a brief tenure as the hand-picked successor to the founder of Communist China, Mao Tse-tung, upon Mao's death in 1976, but fell victim to a series of internal maneuvers within the Chinese Communist Party. A faction of reformers led by Deng Xiaoping wrested power from him and quickly set China on a path toward its impressive position as a global leader at the dawn of the twenty-first century. "On paper, Hua was the most powerful Chinese Communist ruler ever, simultaneously holding China's top party, military, and government titles," noted Mark Magnier in a *Los Angeles Times* obituary. "Hua could have used this to have Deng and other opponents eliminated, throwing the country into further turmoil, but opted not to."

Hua was born Su Zhu in 1921 in Jiaocheng, a town in northern China's Shanxi Province. He participated in the Long March to the south in the mid-1930s, a crucial event in the ultimate victory of Mao's Red Army over the Kuomintang, or Nationalists, several years later. Around the time that Hua formally joined the Communist Party in 1938 he changed his name to an abbreviated form of "China Anti-Japanese National Salvation Vanguard," as many other guerrilla fighters did during this period. He spent eight years in the Red Army, which eventually became the People's Liberation Army (PLA) when the Kuomintang fled to the island of Formosa (now Taiwan) in 1949. Mao became head of a one-party socialist state, the second Communist nation in the world after the Soviet Union.

Hua spent the early part of his career in various party posts in Hunan Province in the south of China. He reportedly gained Mao's attention in the 1950s with an elaborate memorial hall to the leader in Shaoshan, Mao's birthplace. He became a member of the party's Central Committee in 1969, at which point Mao's disastrous Cultural Revolution was already underway. In its attempt to completely overhaul Chinese society, Mao had declared that eliminating class struggle was the party's primary goal. In an effort to root out "bourgeois" elements, several tactics were deployed, including a vast network of public loudspeakers that broadcast party propaganda and "re-education" camps where those suspected of having liberal sympathies were reformed through hard labor. The ten-year Cultural Revolution was a massive upheaval in China, and inadvertently hobbled its economy. Much of it was carried out by the so-called Gang of Four, which consisted of Mao's wife, Jiang Qing, and three senior officials.

In 1970, Hua was elevated to the post of party secretary for Hunan Province, and three years later became a member of the Politburo, or governing body for the Communist political party in China. An aging, ailing Mao named him minister for public security in early 1975, a sign that Hua was being considered as the designated heir to power. In January of 1976, China's prime minister Zhou Enlai died, and Mao named Hua to succeed Zhou. In April, as expected, Hua also took the title of deputy chair of the Chinese Communist Party.

Mao died on September 9, 1976, and Hua assumed the party chairmanship. Four weeks later, he ordered the arrests of the Gang of Four, who were accused of carrying out the worst excesses of the Cultural Revolution. So tenuous was China's internal stability at the time that their arrests were not even announced until two weeks later. Hua is credited with the surprising move, but there remain doubts whether or not the decision to arrest the quartet was actually his. A spectacular show trial followed that was broadcast daily and marked both a legal and symbolic end to end of the Cultural Revolution.

China under Hua still faced many other potential crises: serious economic troubles were compounded by a vast but fractious and uneasy PLA. Reformers within the party eventually prevailed over Hua's cautious continuation of Maoism, and in December of 1978 the Central Committee resolved that the party's goal was no longer eliminating class struggle but instead would be to carry out four important modernizations—in industry, agriculture, defense, and science and technology. This strategy soon made China, with its vast, disciplined workforce, a dominant force in the global economy, especially in the manufacturing sector.

By then Hua had been ousted in an internal party coup by Deng, whom Mao had once banished from Beijing but whom Hua had permitted to return. Hua's loss of power was not immediately apparent outside of China, and he did make a historic visit to Britain and three other Western European nations in the fall of 1979. Less than a year later, however, he was replaced as prime minister by Zhao Ziyang, and in June of 1981 Hua resigned as party chair. Unlike other victims of political struggle among China's power elite, Hua was never arrested, jailed, banished, or died under mysterious circumstances. He remained a member of the Central Committee until 1997.

Hua's death was reported on August 20, 2008, during the Beijing Olympics, the first such Games ever held in China. He was 87 years old and the father of four children, who bear his original surname of Su. Though his rule as China's leader was short, he is considered a transitional figure between the authoritarian Mao and a new generation of Chinese leaders. His willingness to heed the advice of others may have been his greatest strength. "Had he not responded to the urgings of his allies in the Politburo, the murderous factionalism that characterised court politics under Mao would almost certainly have continued," noted his *Times* of London obituary, "and inflicted even more misery, poverty, and oppression on the Chinese people." **Sources:** *Chicago Tribune,* August 21, 2008, sec. 2, p. 9; *Los Angeles Times,* August 21, 2008, p. B6; *New York Times,* August 21, 2008, p. C12; *Times* (London), August 21, 2008, p. 56.

—Carol Brennan

## Michael Kidd

Born Milton Greenwald, August 12, 1915, in New York, NY; died of cancer, December 23, 2007, in Los Angeles, CA. Dancer and choreographer. Honored by the Academy of Motion Picture Arts and Sciences with an award invented to recognize his services, Michael Kidd was a choreographer for film, television, and Broadway performances. Best known for the choreography of *Seven Brides for Seven Brothers*, Kidd was also the director of Emmy nominee *Baryshnikov in Hollywood*, starring Mikhail Baryshnikov, the choreographer of both the stage and film versions of *Guys and Dolls*, which won a Tony on stage, and other Tony winning musicals, including *Finian's Rainbow*, *Can-Can*, *Li'l Abner*, and *Destry Rides Again*.

His dances were noted for their athleticism. "I always use real-life gestures, and most of my dancing is based on real life," Kidd was quoted as having said in the *New York Times*. His philosophy was to make dance intuitive for those watching. The *Los Angeles Times* quoted him as having said, "Dancing should be completely understandable—every move, every turn should mean something, should be crystal clear to the audience." In his 60-year career, Kidd worked with such notables as Fred Astaire, Marlon Brando, Mickey Spillane, Gene Kelly, Barbra Streisand, Julie Andrews, and Danny Kaye.

The son of Russian immigrants, Kidd was born Milton Greenwald in 1915 in the borough of Manhattan in New York City. His father was a barber. Kidd initially intended to become a chemical engineer, but his interest in dance earned him a scholarship for dance courses. During college, he found chemical engineering "too impersonal," according to the *Los Angeles Times*, and he began to pursue his interest in dance more actively.

Attending the School of American Ballet on a scholarship, Kidd became a professional dancer. He first appeared on stage in 1937 as a member of a chorus of Max Reinhardt's *The Eternal Road*, for which he adopted his stage name. In 1938, Kidd joined Lincoln Kirstein's company Ballet Caravan, and soon after starred as the title character *Billy the Kid*. He worked for five years as a solo dancer in ballet, beginning his choreography work with the 1945 ballet, *On Stage!*, in which he also played the leading role. This became the only ballet Kidd ever choreographed: Due to the success of *On Stage*, Kidd was invited to create choreography for Broadway shows. *Finian's Rainbow*, the first Broadway musical Kidd choreographed, won him a Tony award in 1947.

Kidd moved on to choreograph the Broadway production of *Guys and Dolls*, but Hollywood had already begun to take an interest in his work. His first film was *Where's Charley*, a 1952 movie starring Ray Bolger. Shortly thereafter, he was brought on board at Fred Astaire's request to work on *The Band Wagon*, and for the rest of his career, he moved back and forth between Hollywood and Broadway work. In 1954, he worked on two productions simultaneously, the Broadway musical *Can-Can* and the film that became his best known work: *Seven Brides for Seven Brothers*.

Kidd very nearly turned down working on *Seven Brides for Seven Brothers*. He once told the *Los Angeles Times* about his initial reaction: "Here are these slobs living off in the woods. They have no schooling, they are uncouth, there's manure on the floor, the cows come in and out—and they're gonna get up and dance? We'd be laughed out of the theater!" Eventually persuaded, Kidd used his theory of creating dance based on every-day motions to choreograph dances that involved movements like chopping wood. The dances were so athletic that Kidd brought four leading male ballet dancers onto the cast, including Jacques d'Amboise, who described Kidd's style to the *Los Angeles Times* as "a no-holds-barred atomic energy explosion."

But while his dance routines were extremely athletic, Kidd never asked any of his performers to do moves that he himself could not perform. Jacques d'Amboise told CNN.com that Kidd was "willing to do anything himself that he expects of his dancers. And he's a great dancer himself—we respect that." Leading by example, Kidd once reported wearing the high heels of one of his female dancers in order to demonstrate a move he wanted her to perform. Baryshnikov commented of Kidd's direction (as quoted by CNN.com), "I was amazed by his energy and his willingness to reinvent all the time if the situation didn't work."

Kidd performed on stage as well as behind the scenes. He replaced Frank Sinatra in Gene Kelly's *It's Always Fair Weather*, which featured a dance number where he and two other actors danced with trash can lids attached to their shoes. He also acted in the movie *Smile*, but found that he preferred to work behind the camera. Through the 1960s and '70s, Kidd continued to choreograph, produce, and direct on Broadway. He also choreographed several notable movies, including *Hello Dolly!* and *Star!*

Married twice, both times to former dancers, Kidd is survived by his second wife, Shelah Hackett, two daughters from his first marriage, and a son and daughter from his second marriage. He died on December 23, 2007, of cancer. He was 92. **Sources:** *Chicago Tribune*, December 25, 2007, pp. 1, 12; CNN.com, http://www.cnn.com/2007/SHOWBIZ/Movies/12/25/obit.kidd.ap/index.html (December

25, 2007); *Los Angeles Times,* December 25, 2007, p. B8; *New York Times,* December 25, 2007, p. C8; *Times* (London), January 5, 2007, p. 72; *Washington Post,* December 25, 2007, p. B5.

—*Alana Joli Abbott*

## Evel Knievel

Born Robert Craig Knievel, October 17, 1938, in Butte, MT; died of pulmonary fibrosis, November 30, 2007, in Clearwater, FL. Daredevil. Evel Knievel, America's greatest motorcycle daredevil, propelled his star-spangled self through hundreds of stunt jumps, risking his life, breaking his body, and surviving to spin tall tales. The wildly popular 1970s folk hero "combined the daring of Harry Houdini with the bluster of P. T. Barnum," wrote Patricia Sullivan of the *Washington Post.* Revving his bike and peeling up steep ramps, Knievel flew over rows of cars, Mack trucks, and double-decker buses; the fountains outside a Las Vegas casino; and lions, rattlesnakes, and a tank of live sharks. He set a world record for bones broken, and he spent three years in various hospitals recovering from one injury after another.

Born Robert Craig Knievel in 1938 in Montana, the future death-defier discovered his life's work early. "When I was 8, I saw Joey Chitwood's Auto Daredevils at Clark Park, in Butte," he told a *New Yorker* writer (according to Eric Malnic of the *Los Angeles Times*). "A guy jumped a motorcycle over a car. That night, I stole a motorcycle from a neighbor." Knievel told grandiose yarns to build his legend; in another interview, he claimed he stole his first bike at 13. Also shrouded by fibs is the origin of his stage name: he once claimed the Butte police dubbed him "Evil Knievel" when they jailed him for stealing hubcaps. He changed the I in evil to an E to reflect the rhyme.

A talented athlete, the six-foot-tall Knievel competed in track and field, played ice hockey, and won a ski-jumping contest as a teenager. He joined the Army (so a judge would not jail him, he claimed), jumped out of planes 30 times as a paratrooper, and pole-vaulted 14 feet in a soldiers' competition. After his discharge, he played minor-league hockey with the Charlotte Clippers in North Carolina and founded, managed, and played for a semi-pro hockey team in Butte.

According to his own myth-making, Knievel also spent his early adulthood as a successful car thief, card shark, armed robber, and safecracker. By more

sedate accounts, he worked as a hunting guide and raced motorcycles for money. He married his high-school girlfriend, Linda Bork, in 1959.

In 1965, Knievel became co-owner of a Honda motorcycle dealership in Moses Lake, Washington, and decided he needed to do something to bring in business. First, he offered $100 to any customer who could beat him at arm wrestling. Next, he declared he would ride a motorcycle up a ramp, over some parked cars and a box of 100 rattlesnakes, then past a tethered mountain lion. A thousand people showed up to see him do it. His jump fell a little short, and he landed on the snakes, but drove off safely. The crowd was awestruck. "Right then," he said (as quoted by Richard Severo in the *New York Times*), "I knew I could draw a big crowd by jumping over weird stuff."

Knievel quickly formed a touring troupe, Evel Knievel's Motorcycle Daredevils, and traveled the western United States, performing a two-hour show that included cycle jumps through rings of fire. The first time he almost died during a stunt was in Barstow, California, that year. During the shows, another daredevil would gun his bike straight at him going 60 miles per hour. At the last minute, Knievel would jump up, spread-eagled, and the rider would pass under him. In Barstow, he did not leap high enough, and the motorcycle collided with his groin. "A highway patrolman covered my head with a blanket," he claimed (as quoted by Malnic of the *Los Angeles Times*). "He thought I was dead. So did I." Knievel recovered within a month. He went solo in 1966, broke his arm and several ribs in one jump that year, but healed enough to clear 14 cars at once that October.

On New Year's Eve 1967, Knievel vaulted himself and his bike into the pantheon of wild-West American heroism, a cowboy airborne on chrome and leather. In front of 25,000 people and a television audience, Knievel attempted to jump 141 feet over the outdoor fountains at Caesar's Palace in Las Vegas. He made it over the fountains, but crash-landed; his cycle skidded, and he rolled across the pavement, breaking his hip, pelvis, arm, and legs. He spent a month in a coma. When he awoke, he learned he had become a national celebrity.

Throughout the late 1960s and 1970s, Knievel attracted tens of thousands of paid customers to his stunts. He jumped 150 feet over 19 cars in February of 1971, then jumped 20 cars soon after. He entered arenas wearing a cape, boots, and a red, white and blue jumpsuit decorated with American-flag stars and stripes. Patriotic music played during his shows. He reveled in his image as a hero for a nation disillusioned by the Vietnam War and the Watergate scandal. "America was down on its ass when I came along, and it needed somebody who was truthful and honest, somebody who would spill blood and break bones and suffer brain concussions, someone who wasn't phony," he once boasted (as quoted by Malnic in the *Los Angeles Times*).

Many of Knievel's greatest jumps were shown on the popular ABC-TV program *Wide World of Sports.* Millions of kids bought Evel Knievel toys and action figures. Countless mothers scolded their too-careless children with the squelch, "Who do you think you are, Evel Knievel?" Movies, television specials, books, songs, and a rock opera featured him as the main character.

In the mid-1970s, Knievel declared he wanted to jump over the Grand Canyon. But the U.S. Department of the Interior turned him down. He settled for the 1,600-foot-wide Snake River Canyon in Idaho. He bought land on both sides so that he would need no one's permission to cross it, and had a special vehicle built to fire him across. Though he called it the Skycycle, it was more rocket than motorbike, propelled by steam, with a cockpit like those in stunt planes. In September of 1974, 40,000 spectators who had spent $25 each watched his leap from a bluff, while thousands more viewed it on closed-circuit television in theaters across the country. Knievel's rocket shot up a 108-foot ramp at 350 miles per hour and flew above the canyon. But a parachute popped out too early. The rocket drifted down, bounced off the canyon wall twice, then landed safely in some brush.

Fans felt cheated. Many claimed Knievel had lost his nerve. Meanwhile, the press debated whether he was a superhero or a terrible influence. "The witless Knievel is titillating a barbaric appetite for treating violent death as a spectator sport," decried columnist George Will (as quoted by Malnic in the *Los Angeles Times*). "Like pornography, the event is brutalizing, anti-life."

Knievel returned to his motorcycles for ever-more-terrifying leaps. In May of 1975, he made $1 million by jumping 120 feet over 13 English double-decker buses at London's Wembley Stadium. He hit the 13th bus, breaking his hand and pelvis. The same year, he successfully jumped 133 feet over 14 buses at King's Island, an amusement park in Ohio. More than half of all American TV viewers that day watched the performance.

In 1976 in Chicago, Knievel planned a jump over an aquarium tank containing 13 live sharks. But during a practice jump, he crashed again, on the exit ramp. Not only did he break an arm and a collarbone, a nearby cameraman was injured. Some news reports claimed the man lost an eye, which was untrue, but the rumor hurt Knievel's reputation. The shark jump, broadcast in January of 1977 on *Wide World of Sports,* later inspired a similar stunt on the popular TV sitcom *Happy Days,* in which main character Arthur Fonzarelli, another 1970s pop hero, severely injured himself. Just as critics later argued that *Happy Days* was never as good afterward—inspiring the pop culture term "jump the shark," for the moment a pop phenomenon goes from brilliant to bad—so Knievel's shark jump marked the beginning of his career's end.

That same year, the movie *Viva Knievel!,* in which Knievel played himself, flopped. In September, Knievel attacked publicist Sheldon Saltman with a baseball bat as retaliation for his book about Knievel, which claimed he had abused his family and done drugs. Sales of Knievel toys plummeted. Knievel spent six months in jail, and Saltman sued him and won $13 million.

By the time Knievel retired in 1980, he bragged (according to Severo of the *New York Times*) he was "nothing but scar tissue and surgical steel." His body was full of metal: a titanium hip, pins connecting bones and joints, aluminum plates holding his arms together. Doctors had performed 15 major surgeries on him. *Guinness World Records* credited him with having broken his bones more than any other person.

Knievel spent the 1980s in sad obscurity, traveling the United States in a trailer, avoiding his debts. He drank heavily: a fifth of whiskey a day with beer chasers, he claimed. He and his first wife separated in the early 1990s. He was charged in 1995 with battering his new girlfriend, Krystal Kennedy, a woman 30 years younger than himself. But she did not press charges, and she married him in 1999. They eventually divorced, but continued to live together for the rest of his life.

Eventually, Knievel's reputation improved. His son, Robbie, followed in his father's peeling-tire tracks, becoming a motorcycle daredevil himself. He took on stunts his father had not conquered, successfully jumping the Caesar's Palace fountains in 1989 and the Grand Canyon in 1999. Meanwhile, a wave of nostalgia resurrected the elder Knievel's past thrills. The Smithsonian's National Museum of American History celebrated him in 1994 with an exhibit, "America's Legendary Daredevil." It included his jumpsuit, cape, boots, and one of his motorcycles, miraculously undamaged: a Harley Davidson XR-750.

In his later years, Knievel often attended the annual Evel Knievel Days festival in Butte, watching young motorcycle stuntmen he had inspired. He shook off another near-death experience, with hepatitis C, by getting a liver transplant in 1999. He sued rapper Kanye West for his 2006 video for the song "Touch the Sky," in which West dressed up in a red, white, and blue jumpsuit and called himself "Evel Kanyevel." They settled the suit amicably in late November of 2007.

Knievel suffered for years from diabetes and pulmonary fibrosis, an incurable lung-scarring disease. By 2006, he was breathing with the help of an oxygen tank and constantly taking painkillers to cope with his legendary injuries. He died on November 30, 2007, after having trouble breathing, at his condominium in Clearwater, Florida. He is survived by four children, ten grandchildren, and one great-grandchild. "It's been coming for years, but you just don't expect it," said Billy Rundle, Knievel's promoter and friend (as quoted by Malnic in the *Los Angeles Times*). "Superman just doesn't die, right?" **Sources:** CNN.com, www.cnn.com/2007/SHOWBIZ/TV/11/30/obit.knievel/index.html (December 11, 2007); E! Online, http://www.eonline.com/print/index.jsp?uuid=21339ff6-51b7-4705&hyph en;8b4d-9d5994a39bcc&contentType=newsStory (December 11, 2007); *Los Angeles Times*, December 1, 2007, p. A1, p. A21; *New York Times*, December 1, 2007, p. B10; *People*, December 17, 2007, p. 143; *Times* (London), December 3, 2007, p. 53; *Washington Post*, December 1, 2007, p. B5.

—Erick Trickey

## Harvey Korman

Born Harvey Herschel Korman, February 15, 1927, in Chicago, IL; died of complications from the rupture of an abdominal aortic aneurysm, May 29, 2008, in Los Angeles, CA. Actor and comedian. A self-proclaimed "luminous second banana," Harvey Korman was a character actor and comedian who would often delight audiences by being unable to keep a straight face through the antics of his co-stars. A ten-year alum of *The Carol Burnett Show*, Korman was a guest star in dozens of television programs and played character roles in several Mel Brooks films, including *Blazing Saddles*.

Brooks described working with Korman for an article on CNN.com. "You could get rock-solid comedy out of him," Brooks said, calling Korman a "dazzling" comedian. "He could lift the material. He always made it real, always made it work, always believed in characters he was doing." But one of Korman's most notable habits was his tendency to laugh during improvisational sketches, particularly with frequent comedy partner, Tim Conway. "Whatever I said, he'd fall down," Conway told *People*.

Born in Chicago, Illinois, Korman began acting early, performing in school plays in kindergarten and performing on the radio at age 12. His college career was interrupted by a stint in the Navy during World War II, after which he attended the Goodman School of Drama at the Chicago Art Institute. He moved to New York, hoping to make it on Broadway, and attempted to win a role in a stage production for the next 13 years without luck. He and a friend formed a comedy act that was hired to perform two shows; they were fired after they finished the first.

Determined, Korman went to Hollywood, quipping "at least I'd feel warm and comfortable while I failed," according to the *Chicago Tribune*. Like his stint in New York, living in Los Angeles required Korman to find part-time work, including working as a car salesman and a theater doorman. Finally, Korman landed a job working on *The Danny Kaye Show*, a musical variety show, where he became a regular for the last three years of the show's run.

The same year that *The Danny Kaye Show* ended, Carol Burnett launched her own self-titled variety show. Hoping to find someone like Korman to round out her cast, she decided to just ask Korman himself. The pairing was a huge success. Korman and Burnett often played opposite each other in the various comedy sketches that made up *The Carol Burnett Show*. Some of their most famous skits paired them as a married couple: in one, "Ed and Eunice," they were a loving couple beleaguered by the wife's mother (played by Vicki Lawrence); in "Old Folks at Home," they were an argumentative couple plagued by the wife's younger sister (also played by Lawrence). Korman and Burnett parodied *Gone with the Wind* and soap operas, and Korman played a wide variety of characters, including old Yiddish women and romantic heroes. Korman also worked with Conway in a number of sketches, solidifying a comedic partnership.

Korman's role on *The Carol Burnett Show* lasted for ten years, after which Korman was offered his own variety program. Launched in 1977, *The Harvey Korman Show* was short-lived, and *The Carol Burnett Show*, having lost Korman's chemistry with the cast, followed shortly after. "It takes a certain type of person to be a television star," Korman was quoted as having said in the *Washington Post.* "I didn't have whatever that is. I come across as kind of snobbish and maybe a little too bright…. Give me something bizarre to play or put me in a dress and I'm fine."

Korman continued to guest star in a number of television series, including *The Muppet Show, The Love Boat, Perry Mason,* and *Wild, Wild West.* Though he appeared in a small screen Western, it was the large screen *Blazing Saddles* that established him as a film actor. Director and actor Brooks was delighted to work with Korman, if at times he found it difficult. "I used to look past his eyes," Brooks described in the *Los Angeles Times.* "If our eyes met, that's the end of the take. We would break up." Korman performed in three of Brooks' other films, as well as two movies in the "Pink Panther" franchise and *Herbie Goes Bananas.*

Along with his film work, Korman toured with Conway when both actors were in their seventies. Their show *Tim Conway and Harvey Korman: Together Again* ran 120 shows per year, sometimes six or eight performances in a weekend. They performed as recently as December of 2007.

After an abdominal aortic aneurysm, doctors thought Korman would only last days. But several major operations gave Korman several more months to live with his family, until complications from the rupture of the aneurysm led to his death in Los Angeles on May 29, 2008. He was 81 years old. Korman is survived by four children and his second wife, as well as many of the coworkers who admired him. "He was the consummate actor," Burnett told *People.* "I miss him something terrible." **Sources:** *Chicago Tribune,* May 30, 2008, sec. 2 p. 11; CNN.com, http://www.cnn.com/2007/SHOWBIZ/ TV/05/29/korman.obit.ap/index.html (May 30, 2008); E! Online, http://www.eonline.com/ uberblog/b139987_carol_burnett_cohort_harvey_ korman_dies.h tml (May 30, 2008); *Entertainment Weekly,* June 13, 2008, p. 20; *Los Angeles Times,* May 30, 2008, p. B8; *People,* June 16, 2008, p. 86; *Washington Post,* May 30, 2008, p. B7.

—*Alana Joli Abbott*

# Tom Lantos

Born Lantos Tamás Péter, February 1, 1928, in Budapest, Hungary; died of esophageal cancer, Feb-

ruary 11, 2008, in Bethesda, MD. Politican. The only Holocaust survivor ever to serve in U. S. Congress, Rep. Tom Lantos (D-California) was devoted to supporting civil liberties, both in the United States and abroad. His positions on the military were often out of line with his party's platform, but the Democrat believed firmly that Americans must do whatever it took to stop another Holocaust. Lantos was a founder of the Congressional Human Rights Caucus, and worked toward supporting animal rights as well as human rights.

Appointed as the chairman of the House Committee on Foreign Affairs, Lantos commented that his entire life served as a preparation for that position. He became the senior Democratic member of the committee in 2001. Lantos was unafraid of reminding people of his past to support his positions, sometimes offending foreign leaders in the process. In a statement, recorded in the *New York Times,* U.S. President George W. Bush said, "Tom was a living reminder that we must never turn a blind eye to the suffering of the innocent at the hands of evil men."

Born to educators in a middle-class family in Budapest, Hungary, Lantos was 16 years old when the Nazis occupied Hungary. Lantos joined the underground resistance immediately, but was sent to a forced labor camp. Twice, Lantos was able to escape, but he only remained free by being taken in by Swedish diplomat Raoul Wallenberg. Due to his blond hair and blue eyes, Lantos was able to hide his Jewish heritage and deliver messages among Wallenberg's safe houses.

Several of Lantos' family members were killed in the Holocaust. After the war, Lantos tracked down a childhood sweetheart, Annette Tillemann, who had also escaped and was living in Switzerland. Lantos had won a scholarship to study at the University of Washington in Seattle and together they moved to the United States. There, Lantos received both his B.A. and M.A. in economics before moving to the University of California, Berkeley, to earn his Ph.D.

After receiving his Ph.D., Lantos took a position at San Francisco State University, where he taught for 30 years. He served as president of the Millbrae School District board and was occasionally called on as an advisor to Congress in economics and foreign policy. When Leo J. Ryan, the representative of Lantos' district, was killed in Guyana while in office, Republican Bill Royer won the seat in a special election. But in the 1980 elections, Lantos ran against the incumbent, winning narrowly. Though Royer challenged his seat in later elections, and others hoping to take his position criticized Lantos' hawkish stance on military issues, Lantos won reelections by comfortable margins.

In Lantos' early career in Congress, he is credited with successfully moving a bill that gave honorary American citizenship to Wallenberg, who had disappeared under Russian custody at the end of World War II. Lantos became noted for his strong advocacy for human rights. In 1983, Lantos co-founded the Congressional Human Rights Caucus. While he sharply criticized nations, including China, Russia, and Burma, for their frequent human rights violations, Lantos also made inroads in creating dialogue with nations that showed a desire for peace. Lantos supported lifting sanctions against Libya when that nation promised to abandon nuclear, biological, and chemical weapons.

Throughout his career, Lantos was a staunch supporter of Israel, and criticized Saudia Arabia for funding terrorists. He was not afraid to offend people, which sometimes caused problems. As the chairman of the Foreign Affairs Committee, Lantos declared Turkey's mass killings of Armenians during World War I to be genocide. The statement had the potential to severely disrupt Turkish relations with the United States, and consequently a related bill was never passed. Lantos also demanded that the government of Japan offer an apology for the sex slavery promoted by its military during World War I. He was sharply critical of Yahoo executives when they offered the Chinese government the identity of an activist speaking out against Chinese policies (the activist was subsequently arrested). During his tenure on the Congressional Human Rights Caucus, Lantos invited the Dalai Lama to Washington, D.C. and introduced sanctions against the junta in Burma.

One of the few Democrats who supported the invasion of Iraq, feeling that if the United States had stopped Hitler earlier the Holocaust might not have happened, Lantos later became a critic about the direction of the war. He voted against the surge and called for troop withdrawals.

Lantos was not only active in his political life, standing up for human rights, but continued to act outside of the boundaries of his job to promote civil liberties. In 2006, Lantos was among the members of Congress who were arrested at a protest outside the Sudanese Embassy, trying to gain attention for the situation in Darfur. Though he rarely talked about his own World War II experiences, Lantos was one of the five Hungarian Holocaust survivors featured in Steven Spielburg's documentary *The Last*

*Days*. His memories are also recorded in the accompanying book of the same title. The film won the Academy Award for best documentary feature in 1998.

Lantos and his wife asked their two daughters to promise to have many children, in part to make up for the number of family members that were lost during the Holocaust. Holding up their end of the deal, Lantos' daughters had seven and ten children respectively. Lantos is survived by his wife, two daughters, 17 grandchildren, and two great-grandchildren. He died on February 11, 2008, just ten days after his 80th birthday. **Sources:** *Chicago Tribune*, February 12, 2008, sec. 2, p. 11; CNN.com, http://www.cnn.com/2008/POLITICS/02/11/lantos.obit/index.html (February 11, 2008); KTVU Online, http://www.ktvu.com/print/14963111.tif/detail.html (February 11, 2008); *Los Angeles Times*, February 12, 2008, p. B8; *New York Times*, February 12, 2008, p. C13; *Times* (London), February 13, 2008; *Washington Post*, February 12, 2008, p. B6.

—*Alana Joli Abbott*

# Dorian Leigh

Born Dorian Elizabeth Leigh Parker, April 23, 1917, in San Antonio, TX; died from complications due to Alzheimer's disease, July 7, 2008. Model, agency founder, and restaurant owner. If it were not for such models as Dorian Leigh, supermodels such as Cindy Crawford, Giselle Bundchen, and Adriana Lima would not be the celebrities they are in the early 2000s. During the 1940s and 1950s, Leigh was much sought after and became the face for Revlon cosmetics. Her Fire and Ice campaign was one of the company's best, and she drew the praise of many. Both she and her sister, model Suzy Parker, were supermodels before the term came into fashion. Leigh concluded her modeling career in the 1960s and opened one of the first modeling agencies in Europe, located in Paris, France. She ran the agency successfully for eight years, before turning to the restaurant business. She opened Chez Dorian in France, and when that closed, she returned to the United States and started a catering business. She worked with Martha Stewart, before turning to writing. She wrote several cookbooks and her autobiography, before retiring from the spotlight.

Leigh, the eldest of four girls, was born in 1917. When her father, an industrial chemist, created a more viable form of etching acid and the patent made him rich, the family moved to the borough of Queens in New York City. Leigh attended Randolph Macon College in Virginia, where she met and married Marshall Hawkins. The couple had two children, son T. L. Hawkins and daughter Marsha Lynn (who died in the early 1990s). Leigh and Hawkins were divorced in 1937, and after that, Leigh returned to New York and took a calculus class at New York University. She also worked for the Navy doing mechanical drafting.

Leigh also worked for Eastern Aircraft Corporation, designing airplane wings. When a health issue arose, she found work as an apprentice copywriter for Republic Pictures. At age 27, Leigh met Harry Conover of the Harry Conover Agency, who sent her to *Harper's Bazaar* to meet the editor, Diana Vreeland. Conover instructed Leigh to tell Vreeland that she was 19. Upon meeting Vreeland, Leigh was given her first photo shoot, and Vreeland admonished her not to change her "exquisite zigzag eyebrows," according to the *New York Times*.

Before she accepted her first assignment, Leigh asked Vreeland to sign her sister, Suzy, sight unseen. Vreeland agreed. Suzy Parker would become an even more successful model than her sister. Dorian Leigh used her middle name as her last name because her father thought the modeling industry was vulgar, that is, until he saw the pay. Then he was okay with his other daughter using the family name. Leigh began modeling in 1944, landing her first cover in June for *Harper's Bazaar*. She would go on to grace more than 50 covers with a variety of magazines, including *Look*, *McCall's*, and *Vogue*.

It was Leigh's face that made Revlon a popular cosmetic line during the 1950s. When Leigh was chosen for the Fire and Ice and Cherries in the Snow ad campaigns, her career reached new heights, and she became a household name, something unheard of for a model during that time. Leigh was a favorite of such famed photographers as Richard Avedon, Louise Dahl-Wolfe, and Irving Penn. She then signed with the Ford Agency, a company still known in the early 2000s for creating superstar models. According to the *Los Angeles Times*, founder Eileen Ford said Leigh was "truly the best model of our time." At the height of her career, Leigh earned $1 for each minute she worked.

Leigh left modeling in the 1960s. She moved to France and opened her own agency in Paris, one of the first in Europe. The agency was very successful but was forced to close due to embezzlement of funds by her last husband, whom she married in 1964 and divorced two years later. Undeterred,

Leigh turned to cooking and opened a restaurant, Chez Dorian. She also taught at the Paris American Academy and La Varenne Cooking School.

When Leigh's restaurant closed, she returned to the United States and started a catering business. She also worked as a cook for Martha Stewart and sold pâtés to delicatessens, before starting another catering company called Fête Accomplie in 1988. Leigh also released her autobiography, *The Girl Who Had Everything: The Story of the 'Fire and Ice Girl,'* as well as two cookbooks, *Pancakes: From Flapjacks to Crepes* and *Doughnuts: Over Three Dozen Crullers, Fritters and Other Treats*. Leigh moved back to Paris in 1999, but when she was diagnosed with a brain tumor, she returned to the United States, moving into a facility in Falls Church, Virginia.

While her modeling work gave her celebrity status, Leigh's personal life also kept her name in print. In addition to numerous affairs, both real and rumored, she married four times after her first marriage. She had five children in all; four from three of her husbands and a son, Kim Blas Parker (who died of suicide in 1977 at age 21), from her liaison with Alfonso Cabeza de Vaca. On July 7, 2008, Leigh died from complications due to Alzheimer's disease in Falls Church, Virginia. She was 91. She is survived by three of her children, her son, T. L. Hawkins, and her daughters Young Eve Paciello and Miranda Bordat-vanEtten; by four grandchildren; and two great-grandchildren. **Sources:** *Chicago Tribune*, July 10, 2008, sec. 2, p. 8; *Los Angeles Times*, July 11, 2008, p. B7; *New York Times*, July 9, 2008, p. C11; *Times* (London), July 12, 2008, p. 74; *Washington Post*, July 10, 2008, p. B5.

*—Ashyia N. Henderson*

## Ira Levin

Born Ira Marvin Levin, August 27, 1929, in New York, NY; died of a heart attack, November 12, 2007, in New York, NY. Author. As an author of popular fiction, Ira Levin was best known for crafting sinister, psychological thrillers whose movie versions proved equally successful. His most enduring titles are *Rosemary's Baby* and *The Stepford Wives*, each of which featured women who discover horrific malevolence lurking inside their own homes. "Levin was," his *Times* of London obituary asserted, "adept at creating an apparently mundane domestic atmosphere in which it gradually becomes clear to the reader that innocents are being hemmed around by evil from which there appears to be no escape."

Levin was born in New York City in 1929 and grew up in the Bronx and Manhattan boroughs. His father had a successful toy-import company and hoped his son would take over the business, but Levin had made up his mind to become a writer by the time he entered Drake University in Iowa. He spent two years there before returning to New York City in 1948 to complete his education at New York University. In 1950, the year he graduated, he won second place in a scriptwriting contest sponsored by CBS with a drama titled "Leda's Portrait," about an elderly woman in failing health whose caretaker nephew and nurse plot to kill her. It was acquired by the NBC television network and produced for their playhouse series called *Lights Out* in 1951.

Levin's second-place script also landed him a writing job with the network for a time. In 1953 he was drafted into the U.S. Army and spent two years with the Army Signal Corps as a scriptwriter for training films. His first novel, *A Kiss Before Dying*, centered on an amoral young man with an heiress girlfriend. When she becomes pregnant, he knows that her father will likely disinherit her and plots her murder. A few months later, he begins to pursue his slain paramour's sister, but his transgressions follow him, as does a suspicious police detective. The novel won Levin the Edgar Allan Poe Award for best debut novel from the Mystery Writers of America, and was made into a 1956 film that starred Robert Wagner and Joanne Woodward.

Levin also dabbled in writing for the stage. In 1955 his adaptation of *No Time for Sergeants*, a popular novel by Mac Hyman, opened on Broadway and enjoyed a long run. Fourteen years passed between Levin's debut novel and his next book, *Rosemary's Baby*. Published in 1967, the suspenseful tale about a young mother-to-be who begins to believe that her daffy, seemingly harmless next-door neighbors are actually devil worshippers—and that her husband and physician might also be Satanists—sold 2.3 million copies even before the film version arrived in theaters a year later. The screen adaptation was directed by French-Polish *auteur* Roman Polanski, made a star out of a young Mia Farrow, and established "a standard in the gothic macabre that was to create a seemingly inexhaustible taste for satanic themes among filmgoers," noted Levin's *Times* of London obituary.

Levin had less success with his 1970 novel, *This Perfect Day*, a futuristic tale of a man who breaks out of his pre-programmed, pleasant Utopia. Two years later, Levin's *The Stepford Wives* caused a minor sensation when it appeared and was subsequently adapted for the big screen. At a time when scores of U.S. women were exiting unhappy marriages, returning to work or college, or simply demanding some help with the housework and cooking from their families, Levin's *Stepford Wives* were the mysteriously placid women in a fictional suburban community who showed an enthusiastic devotion to household chores and a cheerfully submissive demeanor to their husbands. The perplexed newcomer to this Connecticut town—played by *The Graduate*'s Katharine Ross—eventually discovers that the Stepford men have plotted to replace their human wives with domestic robots. While the film version quickly became a dated, campy classic within a few years, the term "Stepford wife" did enter the vernacular, which pleased Levin enormously.

Levin's next novel was *The Boys from Brazil* and centered on a plot to clone the Nazi leadership and resurrect Adolf Hitler's Third Reich. It was made into a film starring Gregory Peck and Laurence Olivier that was released the same year as Levin's *Deathtrap* opened on Broadway for a four-year run in 1978. Michael Caine and Christopher Reeve appeared in the screen adaptation of the story of an older playwright who plots to eliminate his younger rival. *Sliver* was Levin's final novel, and the 1993 film of the same name starred Sharon Stone as the resident of an apartment building with an unusually high death rate.

Levin died of a heart attack at his New York City home on November 12, 2007, at age 78. He was divorced from his first wife, Gabrielle Aronsohn, in 1968, and a second marriage to Phyllis Finkel in 1979 also ended in divorce. He is survived by three sons from his marriage to Aronsohn—Adam Levin-Delson, Jared Levin, and Nicholas Levin—and by three grandchildren. Though his name was indelibly associated with Polanski's 1968 horror movie, Levin later said he rued its success. "I feel guilty that *Rosemary's Baby* led to *The Exorcist, The Omen*," he said in a *Los Angeles Times* interview, according to his *New York Times* obituary. "A whole generation has been exposed, has more belief in Satan. I don't believe in Satan. And I feel that the strong fundamentalism we have would not be as strong if there hadn't been so many of these books." **Sources:** CNN.com, http://cnn.com/2007/SHOWBIZ/books/11/14/obit.levin.ap/index.html (November 15, 2007); *Los Angeles Times,* November 14, 2007, p. B8; *New York Times,* November 14, 2007, p. C19; *Times* (London), November 15, 2007, p. 68; *Washington Post,* November 14, 2007, p. B7.

—*Carol Brennan*

# Bill Melendez

Born José Cuauhtémoc Melendez, November 15, 1916, in Hermosillo, Sonora, Mexico; died September 2, 2008, in Santa Monica, CA. Animator. In a career that spanned nearly seven decades, animator and director Bill Melendez earned six Emmy Awards, two Peabody Awards, and an Oscar nomination, many of them for his work on Charles M. Schulz's *Peanuts*. Best known for his work bringing Charlie Brown, Snoopy, and the gang to life through animation, Melendez was the only animator Schulz allowed to bring his characters from strip to screen. Melendez animated nearly 50 television specials, four feature films, a Saturday morning cartoon series, and commercials starring the characters. Melendez also provided Snoopy with his yowling, nonsensical voice.

In addition to working with Schulz while the cartoonist was alive, Melendez made sure that the *Peanuts* characters continued to stay in the public eye, animating several specials after Schulz's death in 2000. "Bill Melendez brought his special warmth, charm, and directness to the Charles Schulz characters and brought them to life," filmmaker and animation historian John Canemaker told the *Los Angeles Times*.

Born in Mexico in 1916, Melendez was the son of a Mexican Army officer. Early on, he was eager to draw, creating pictures of horses and cowboys. When he was 12, Melendez and his family moved to Arizona because his mother wanted her sons to speak English. Melendez was placed in the kindergarten class, a humiliating experience that forced him to pick up English very quickly. The family later moved to Los Angeles, where Melendez hoped to become an engineer, but was thwarted by the crashing economy of the Great Depression. He worked a number of jobs before pitching some of his original drawings to Disney. The company recommended formal training, and so Melendez studied at the Chouinard Art Institute. Disney hired him in 1938.

It was an exciting time to work at Disney, due to recent success with their first animated, full-length feature, *Snow White*. While working at Disney, Melendez helped to animate films that would become classics, including *Fantasia, Dumbo,* and *Bambi.* Disney also gave him his nickname: Told that Cuauhtémoc Melendez was too long for the credits screen, he was given the nickname Bill, which is how his name appeared on animation credits from then forward.

One of the few Hispanic animators working at Disney, and in animation in general, Melendez was also involved in animators' rights. In 1941, he left Disney after having helped organize a strike, which led to the recognition of the animators' union. Melendez went on to work with Warner Brothers, animating characters including Bugs Bunny, Daffy Duck, and Porky Pig. In 1948, he joined United Productions of America, a company that was doing new and innovative work in animation. "The animation we were doing was not limited, but stylized," he once recalled (as quoted in the *Los Angeles Times*). "When you analyze Chaplin's shorts, you realize people don't move that way—he stylized his movements. We were going to do the same thing for animation." Melendez worked on a number of shorts, one of which won an Oscar, and served as the director and producer for more than 1,000 commercials.

It was through his commercial work that Melendez first encountered Schulz. Ford had contacted Schulz to use the *Peanuts* character in an advertisement. Schulz was leery of allowing anyone else to work on his characters, but then he saw Melendez's drawings. Rather than using his own embellishments, Melendez stayed very true to Schulz's original style, something that gave the cartoonist faith in Melendez's ability to be true to the characters on screen. The commercials for Ford began a long relationship between Schulz and Melendez that launched the *Peanuts* gang into television programs, an ongoing cartoon series, four movies, and a host of commercials. Due to his success, Melendez was able to form his own studio in 1964, called Bill Melendez Productions.

In 1965, Melendez, Schulz, and collaborator Lee Mendelson created their first television special. *A Charlie Brown Christmas* has aired on CBS every Christmas season since. The format of the half-hour television special became not only the standard for the *Peanuts* programs, but for animated specials in general. *A Charlie Brown Christmas* not only won its creators an Emmy, but effectively established one of the most successful animated franchises in history. The film broke tradition in a number of ways, using real children for the voices of the characters rather than adults playing children, and featuring an upbeat jazz score by Grammy-winner Vince Guaraldi.

*A Charlie Brown Christmas* also created Melendez's secondary career. During the production, Melendez supplied laughs and howls for Snoopy, due to Schulz's insistence that as a dog, Snoopy would not speak in English. Melendez sped up his voice on tape to give the noises a distorted quality, assuming that a voice actor would be hired to voice the final recording. Due to a time shortage, Melendez's voice ended up serving as the final for Snoopy in that film, and in every film thereafter. Melendez continued to receive residuals for his vocal work until his death. Melendez, Schulz, and Mendelson produced the big-screen animated features *A Boy Named Charlie Brown, Snoopy, Come Home, Race for Your Life, Charlie Brown,* and *Bon Voyage, Charlie Brown (and Don't Come Back!!).*

Along with his work on Schulz's characters, Melendez oversaw animated specials based on a number of other syndicated comic strips, including *Garfield* and *Cathy*, as well as animated adaptations of the "Babar" books and C. S. Lewis' *The Lion, the Witch, and the Wardrobe.*

Married for 68 years, Melendez is survived by his wife Helen, two sons, six grandchildren, and eleven great grandchildren. He suffered declining health during the last few years of his life and was 91 years old at the time of his death on September 2, 2008. **Sources:** *Chicago Tribune,* September 5, 2008, sec. 2, p. 13; *Los Angeles Times,* September 4, 2008, p. B7; *New York Times,* September 5, 2008, p. C10; *Times* (London), September 18, 2008, p. 63.

—*Alana Joli Abbott*

## Lydia Mendoza

Born May 21, 1916, in Houston, TX; died of natural causes, December 20, 2007, in San Antonio, TX. Singer. Recognized by her soulful voice accompanied by her signature 12-string guitar, Lydia Mendoza was known not only for her performances, but for the way she pushed the boundaries of music for women of her time. In a career that lasted 50 years, Mendoza was recognized as a pioneer of the Tejano music movement. In the first six years of her career, she recorded more than 200 songs, popularizing Mexican-American music for a wide audience.

Named the "greatest Mexican-American female performer ever to grace a stage" by *Texas Monthly* magazine in 1999 (as quoted in her *Los Angeles Times* obituary), Mendoza was the recipient of a National Medal of Arts and a National Heritage Award. She was celebrated by the Tejano Music Awards, Tejano Conjunto Festival, and inducted into the Texas Women hall of fame. "She was a rebel, in that she did what no other woman artist singer had done

before her; that is, she sang about the 'machismo' culture in a way that set the course for many women today," Lupe Saenez, president of the South Texas Conjunto Association, told the *Los Angeles Times.*

The child of Mexican immigrants, Mendoza was born in Texas in 1916. As a child, she was surrounded by music; at four years old, she attempted to make her own guitar. Cobbled together out of a plank of wood, nails, and rubber bands, the toy made enough sound to make Mendoza happy. By the age of 12, she had learned to play the 12-string guitar, and she learned both violin and mandolin.

Mendoza's family moved back and forth between Mexico and Texas as Mendoza's father looked for jobs. He worked primarily as a railroad mechanic, but when he became too ill to work, Mendoza, her parents, and her sister began to sing on the streets and in restaurants to earn a living. Encouraged by their talents, in 1928 Mendoza's father answered an advertisement from a New York record company looking for Spanish-language musicians. They were paid $140 to record 20 songs in the Blue Bonnett Hotel, calling themselves Cuarteto Carta Blanca after a Monterrey, Mexico, brewery.

For the next several years, the Mendozas lived in San Antonio, performing in restaurants and cantinas, as well as grocery stores and parks. At a performance in Plaza del Zacate, Mendoza charmed the owner of a local radio station and was soon given a weekly slot. She earned $3.50 a week and was offered a recording contract with Bluebird. She toured with her family, continuing to appear in cantinas, often singing solo while her siblings performed variety act numbers. In 1934 her song "Mal Hombre," which means "Evil Man," became a hit in both the United States and Mexico. She continued to tour with her family until World War II, and her recordings increased her popularity with such numbers as "La Valentina" and "Angel de Mis Anhelos."

In 1947, Mendoza and her family returned to touring, but in 1952, one of her siblings got married and her mother died, ending the performances as a family. Mendoza continued to produce records and tour on her own, on both sides of the border, as well as in Cuba and Columbia. As her popularity increased, she received the nicknames "La Alondra de la Frontera," which means "Lark of the Border," as well as "La Cancionera de los Pobres," which means "Singer of the Poor." Her style and content resonated strongly with Mexican-American workers, who often suffered prejudice and discrimination. Mendoza took what was best from both sides of the border and used that in her music. "For Mexicans and Mexican-American communities, the border in those days was a meeting place, not a dividing place, and [Mendoza] reflected those conjoined worlds," folklorist Pat Jasper said in the *Washington Post*.

In the 1960s, Mendoza moved to Houston with her second husband where she became a regular at small nightclubs in the area. Her songs, drawn from nearly 100 years of Mexican-American traditional music, attracted a more diverse crowd as Mendoza made appearances at folk festivals and on university campuses. Her repertoire included more than 1,200 songs.

By the end of her career, Mendoza had recorded more than 800 songs on more than 50 albums for record companies including RCA, Columbia, Azteca, Peerless, El Zarape, and Discos Falcon. She was asked to sing for Jimmy Carter's presidential inauguration in 1977, and was invited back to the White House to receive the National Medal of the Arts in 1999. At that presentation, she was on stage alongside Motown star Aretha Franklin, and was praised by President Bill Clinton as "the first rural American woman performer to garner a large following throughout Latin America," according to the *New York Times*.

Though her height of popularity occurred in the 1950s, Mendoza continued performing until she was forced to retire in 1988 due to a series of strokes. She died on December 20, 2007, at the age of 91. She is survived by her daughter, 13 grandchildren, 12 great-grandchildren, and one great-great-grandchild. **Sources:** *Los Angeles Times*, December 30, 2007, p. B10; *New York Times*, December 24, 2007, p. A16; *Times* (London), January 3, 2008, p. 58; *Washington Post*, December 25, 2007, p. B5.

—*Alana Joli Abbott*

## Igor Moiseyev

Born Igor Alexandrovich Moiseyev, January 21, 1906, in Kiev, in what is now the Ukraine; died November 2, 2007, in Moscow, Russia. Choreographer. A pioneer in combining ballet technique with popular folk dance, Igor Moiseyev was the founder and director of a Russian dance company that overcame national boundaries through movement. He is credited with creating folk dancing as a stage perfor-

mance, rather than as a participatory medium. The Moiseyev Company, which he founded, remains one of the leading artistic groups of Russia.

His philosophy on folk dancing irked some critics, who felt that by changing it to a stage medium he detracted from its authenticity. Moiseyev was unperturbed by such comments, stating in a 1970 interview in the *Los Angeles Times*, "Folklore in the strictest sense is confining. I was never interested in that. I merely take the folk dance and its related customs as a point of departure for fanciful interpretation."

Born in Kiev, Moiseyev was the son of a lawyer and a French woman who worked in fashion. Moiseyev's father spoke fluent French and often traveled to Paris. When Moiseyev was only three, his father was turned over to the Russian Tsarist authorities by the French government. Moiseyev spent a few years in the care of his aunts while his mother pled his father's case. Once his father was released, the family planned to return to France, but World War I made this impossible. In 1915, they settled in Moscow, where Moiseyev's father worked as a French teacher and his mother took work as a seamstress.

As a teen, Moiseyev was enrolled in ballet lessons, studying under Russian ballerina Vera Mosolova. In 1921, Moiseyev entered the Bolshoi Ballet School, and after three years, he became a member of the Bolshoi ballet company, often performing solo dances. He worked closely with Kasyan Goleizovsky, who experimented with form and style. When Goleizovsky was replaced by a more traditional director, Moiseyev and others petitioned for Goleizovsky to return. Though their protest was successful, the new director remained at the helm of the ballet, and Moiseyev stopped receiving lead or solo roles until the director's retirement in 1930. Beginning that year, Moiseyev began creating his own ballets, including his first major work, *Salammbo*, in 1932.

His successes at the Bolshoi gave him opportunities to work beyond the company, and in 1936, Moiseyev was appointed the dance director of the Moscow Theater of Art. That same year, he choreographed a mass acrobatic performance in the Red Square, which became an iconic symbol in Soviet Russia, representing the nation's health and vitality. His work at the Moscow Theater of Art allowed him to create the State Academic Folk Dance Ensemble of the Soviet Union, which featured what would become his signature combination of ballet technique with a folk dance style. Though the company began with many amateurs, soon Moiseyev employed professionally trained dancers, and the troupe became known as the Moiseyev Dance Company.

When the Soviet Union entered World War II, the company was moved from Moscow, but continued to perform throughout the war. Moiseyev developed choreography based on dances from many regions of the Soviet Union, including Russia, the Ukraine, Georgia, Belarus, Armenia, Kazakhstan, Azerbaijan, and Moldova. After World War II ended, the troupe began touring, visiting London and the United States despite tensions between those nations and the Soviet Union. Moiseyev's dancers became something of goodwill ambassadors from the Soviet Union, but they were sometimes met with violent protest. A 1986 performance at the Metropolitan Opera House in New York City was tear gassed—sending 4,000 audience members fleeing—by Russian members of the Jewish Defense League, who opposed Soviet policies.

Moiseyev was seldom directly involved in politics beyond his dances. He celebrated the defense of his hometown by guerilla soldiers in his *Partisans,* but never himself joined the Communist Party. He was unafraid of criticizing Soviet dance restrictions as well, and once was reprimanded by Soviet authorities for complimenting American culture. In the 1960s, he criticized the dependence of Soviet ballet on traditional themes and the unwillingness of the art to depict contemporary issues. At the fall of the Soviet Union in 1991, Moiseyev felt that while his company would be offered more creative freedom, the financial challenges of no longer relying on government stipends would impact the company.

During his world travels, Moiseyev began incorporating other folk traditions into his dances, including Korean fan dancing, rock and roll dance styles from the United States, and folk dance from China, Spain, Cuba, Sicily, and Argentina. His company was featured on the *Toast of the Town,* which would later become *The Ed Sullivan Show.* His many awards included being named People's Artist of the U.S.S.R, the Lenin Prize, three Stalin Prizes, the *Dance Magazine* award in the United States, and the Order of Merit, which he received on his 100th birthday. In his last years, he was seldom seen in public, though he continued to work behind the scenes at the Moiseyev Dance Company.

"Everything I've done, I love," Moiseyev was quoted as having said in the *New York Times.* "If you're not in love, you can't create. And if you're calm when you've created something, you can rest assured that you've created nothing." Moiseyev, who is survived by a daughter and his second wife, died in a hospital in Moscow after several days of unconsciousness. He was 101. **Sources:** *Los Angeles Times,* November 3, 2007, p. B10; *New York Times,* November 3, 2007, p. B12; *Times* (London), November 6, 2007, p. 69.

—Alana Joli Abbott

# Randy Pausch

Born Randolph Frederick Pausch, October 23, 1960, in Baltimore, MD; died of pancreatic cancer, July 25, 2008, in Chesapeake, VA. Professor. The Internet Web site Youtube.com is a popular place to post videos of all kinds of content. This content has ranged from the utterly ridiculous to the most thought-provoking and inspiring. Among the latter is a video featuring Carnegie Mellon University's Randy Pausch (pronounced powsh), a computer science professor. When he revealed that he had only months to live during his "Last Lecture," viewers around the world listened carefully and were inspired by his words. The lecture was posted on Youtube.com, viewed by millions, and became an overnight sensation. Pausch was asked to appear on many television programs, including *The Oprah Winfrey Show,* and he wrote a book, *The Last Lecture,* which was published in April of 2008.

Pausch was born in 1960 in Baltimore, Maryland. His philanthropic parents founded the nonprofit group, Up With Kids. They wanted to encourage him so they allowed him to paint whatever he wanted on his bedroom walls. He drew a quadratic equation, elevator doors, and a rocket ship. He played high school football, and one of his lifetime goals was to play professional football. He graduated from Oakland Mills High School and then completed his undergraduate degree in computer science at Brown University. He later earned his doctorate in computer science from Carnegie Mellon.

Pausch began his teaching career at the University of Virginia. There he created a software system called Alice that is used to introduce people to programming. He also developed specialties in user interfaces, virtual reality, animation, and storytelling. His goal was to help young people have fun while learning something difficult. He said in his lecture, recounted by the *Washington Post,* "Millions of kids are having fun while learning something hard. I can deal with that as a legacy." Pausch sought to become an expert on virtual reality so he could accomplish one of his lifelong goals: writing an entry for the *World Book Encyclopedia*. He was able to meet this goal.

Pausch also wanted to work for the Disney Company as an imaginer. He achieved this dream in 1995 when he incorporated elements of virtual reality for the *Aladdin* ride. In 1997, he joined the faculty at Carnegie Mellon, in Pittsburgh, Pennsylvania. Pausch helped to establish the Entertainment Technology Center, where students learn about all aspects of virtual reality and video gaming. His students won a flight in a NASA training plane that simulates weightlessness, and this being another one of his goals, Pausch went along hoping to participate but was told the experience was for students only. Pausch, undeterred, found a loophole: He achieved his goal by serving as the hometown journalist who covered the story.

Pausch married Jai Glasgow, and the couple had three children. In 2006, he was diagnosed with pancreatic cancer and began to seek treatment to stop its spread. He had been asked to give a "Last Lecture," something colleges and universities have their professors do as a way to impart wisdom to the students. One month before his scheduled lecture, Pausch learned he had two to three months to live. Wanting to say goodbye to his work family as well as leave a legacy for his children, he decided to go through with it.

Pausch began his lecture in front of an audience of more than 400 students, faculty, and other guests. First off, he showed slides of the ten tumors in his liver and announced his doctor's latest prognosis. He followed that by doing a series of pushups. His lecture advised people to remember their childhood dreams and try to fulfill them. He spoke of having accomplished all of his dreams, except for two. He dressed to illustrate his points about living one's dreams and having fun. When Pausch thought his audience did not believe that he did own too-many-to-count stuffed animals he had won over the years (another one of his lifetime goals) at carnivals, he brought out his collection and offered them as gifts to audience members. His lecture was filled with jokes, anecdotes, and the poignant insights of a dying man. He also took the time to have a birthday cake brought out for his wife, since his giving this lecture required him to be away from home over her birthday, probably the last one the couple would share together. Pausch also revealed that he did not do the lecture for closure to his career but as a way to "put myself in a bottle that would one day wash up on the beach for my children," according to the *Los Angeles Times*.

Pausch's lecture first gained attention as *Wall Street* reporter Jeff Zaslow was in the audience to cover the lecture thinking it would make a good story. The lecture had been taped so his wife could show it to their children, but it made its way to the Internet, landing in several places, most significantly on Youtube, where it became an instant hit. Between its debut in December of 2007 and late 2008, more than nine million people had watched the one-hour-and-twenty-minute speech. People from all walks of life and from all over the world viewed it and left comments or wrote letters to Pausch, thanking him for sharing his wisdom.

His newfound fame brought interviews from several shows, including *The Oprah Winfrey Show*, where he was used an uninterrupted ten minutes to give a mini-lecture. Pausch was named by ABC as one of its three Persons of the Year for 2007. *Time* magazine named him as one of the 100 Most Influential People in the World. He was invited to participate in a practice with the Pittsburgh Steelers, which fulfilled one more of his goals, and he was invited to the set of the upcoming *Star Trek* film, where he was given a walk-on role. He also met William Shatner, fulfilling that goal.

This new celebrity status did have one disadvantage: it kept Pausch from spending some of his last days with his family. When asked to expand the lecture into a book, Pausch asked Jeff Zaslow to co-author it and hoped to leave the task to him. A compromise was reached: During his daily bike rides, Pausch dictated into a tape for Zaslow. The book was released in April of 2008 and quickly reached the number-one spot on the charts, where it stayed for weeks.

As quickly as he became an instant celebrity, Pausch faded from the limelight. He spent his last months focused on making final preparations and savoring time with his wife and children. He took his oldest son, Dylan, to ride a dolphin and introduced his other son, Logan, to Mickey Mouse in one last trip to Disney World. Pausch made a trip to Washington to appear before Congress to advocate for additional money for pancreatic cancer research, and in May of 2008, he made a surprise appearance at the Carnegie Mellon graduation. On July 25, 2008, Pausch died of pancreatic cancer in his home in Chesapeake, Virginia. He was 47. He is survived by his wife of eight years, Jai, and his three children, Dylan, Logan, and Chloe, as well as his mother, Virginia, and his sister, Tamara Mason. **Sources:** *Chicago Tribune*, July 26, 2008, sec. 1, p. 1; sec. 1, p. 6; CNN, http://www.cnn.com/2008/SHOWBIZ/books/07/25/obit.pausch/index.html (July 28,

2008); *Los Angeles Times,* July 26, 2008, p. B8; *New York Times,* July 26, 2008, p. A14; *People,* August 11, 2008, p. 54. *Times* (London), July 28, 2008, p. 50; *Washington Post,* July 26, 2008, p. B5.

—*Ashyia N. Henderson*

## Oscar Peterson

Born August 15, 1925, in Montreal, Quebec, Canada; died of kidney failure, December 23, 2007, in Mississauga, Ontario, Canada. Jazz pianist and composer. In a career that spanned seven decades, Oscar Peterson became one of the best-known jazz pianists in the world. Known as technically outstanding but sometimes criticized for his lack of experimentation inside the medium, Peterson received eight Grammy awards, a Lifetime Grammy, the Order of Canada, and was inducted into the International Jazz Hall of Fame. He was the only living person other than a reigning monarch to be featured on a Canadian commemorative stamp.

Referred to by Duke Ellington as the "maharajah of the keyboard" and praised by Count Basie for playing "the best ivory box I've ever heard" (as quoted in the *New York Times*), Peterson started his career as a Canadian teen sensation and continued to tour and perform until the end of his life. His performances influenced a generation of pianists, including fellow Canadian Diana Krall, Herbie Hancock, and Benny Green, with whom Peterson toured in his later years.

Peterson was encouraged at an early age to pursue musical training. His father, a railroad porter, encouraged all five children to pursue careers in music to escape the poverty in which they were raised. After a struggle with tuberculosis when he was young, Peterson could no longer practice on the trumpet and switched to piano, which his older brother, who died from tuberculosis, had preferred.

Peterson took private lessons from Lou Hooper and Paul de Marky, and soon became cocky about his own skills. His father, hoping to deflate Peterson's ego, took him to see virtuoso Art Tatum, and Peterson was so in awe that he gave up piano for two months, certain he would never reach Tatum's level of skill. In later years, however, people often favorably compared Peterson to Tatum, noting the latter's influence on Peterson's technical style.

At 14, Peterson won a competition sponsored by the CBC that led to his regular appearances on radio programs. After receiving his father's permission, he dropped out of high school to pursue a career in music. Peterson's popularity throughout Canada earned him the nickname "Brown Bomber of Boogie-Woogie," due not only to his skill, but also his physical size of six foot three inches and 250 pounds.

In 1944, Peterson made his recording debut with a boogie-woogie version of "I Got Rhythm." He soon after became the only black member of the Johnny Holmes Orchestra, a popular group that toured the United States and Canada. He was heard during a live radio performance by jazz promoter Norman Grantz, who is said to have made the driver of the cab he was riding in take him immediately to the club where Peterson was playing. Grantz encouraged Peterson to expand beyond his boogie-woogie repertoire and develop a reputation as a more serious jazz pianist. To help Peterson accomplish this, Grantz featured him in a 1949 Jazz at the Philharmonic performance at Carnegie Hall. Though he was unbilled, Peterson earned his reputation as a young star with that performance, astonishing jazz celebrities Ella Fitzgerald and Charlie Parker, who were also performing that night.

During the 1950s, Peterson continued to play with Jazz at the Philharmonic, but he also formed his own trio with guitarist Herb Ellis and bassist Ray Brown. The trio "is regarded as one of the finest small ensembles in jazz," according to a critic for the *Washington Post*. Gantz continued to promote Peterson's career for more than 30 years, pairing him with well-known artists including Fitzgerald, Dizzy Gillespie, Clark Terry, and Joe Pass. Over his career, Peterson performed with Billie Holiday, Fred Astaire, and Louis Armstrong.

In addition to his piano performances, Peterson founded a school with members of his trio in Toronto, but was unable to maintain it due to his busy touring schedule. He taught at other schools over the years. He was also a composer, and his piece, "The Canadiana Suite," reflected his deep commitment to his home country, despite his international reputation. His composition, "A Royal Wedding Suite," was written for the wedding of Prince Charles and Lady Diana Spencer.

In 1993, Peterson suffered from a stroke, which restricted motion in his left hand. Though there were fears he might never play again, Peterson underwent extreme physical therapy to regain his mobility. He never completely recovered, but instead developed a new style around his limited motion. "I still can't do some of the things I used to be able to do," he was quoted as having said in the *Los Angeles Times*. "But I've learned to do more things with my right hand. And I've also moved in a direction that has always been important to me, toward concentrating on sound, toward making sure that each note counts." Green said of Peterson's new style, "Oscar can do more with one hand than many pianists can do with two."

Green was also quoted by the *Washington Post* describing Peterson's style: "He says—and he makes it sound so simple—that once he [gauges the key drop of a piano], then he's in complete control of the piano. For the rest of us, of course, there are a lot more steps involved." Peterson himself was quoted in the *New York Times* as having said, "When I sit down to the piano, I don't want any scuffling. I want it to be a love affair."

Despite his recovery from the stroke, his health declined. Married four times, Peterson is survived by his fourth wife, Kelly, and seven of his children. He died at the age of 82 on December 23, 2007, in Mississauga, Ontario, Canada. **Sources:** CNN.com, http://www.cnn.com/2007/SHOWBIZ/Music/12/24/obit.peterson.ap/index.html (December 27, 2007); *Entertainment Weekly*, January 11, 2008, p. 20; *Los Angeles Times*, December 25, 2007, pp. A1, A24-A25; *New York Times*, December 25, 2007, p. C9; *Times* (London), December 26, 2007, p. 66; *Washington Post*, December 25, 2007, pp. A1, A7.

—*Alana Joli Abbott*

## Suzanne Pleshette

Born on January 31, 1937, in Brooklyn Heights, NY; died of respiratory failure, January 19, 2008, in Los Angeles, CA. Actress. Suzanne Pleshette played a multitude of roles over an acting career that spanned nearly six decades, but was best remembered for her role on the top-rated CBS sitcom *The Bob Newhart Show* from 1972 to 1978. As Emily Hartley, the schoolteacher wife of co-star Bob Newhart, "Pleshette's throaty voice and steely gaze made her an unexpectedly perfect foil for" her on-screen spouse, wrote Ken Tucker in *Entertainment Weekly*. "Few TV wives were as enjoyably skeptical as Pleshette's Emily."

Born in 1937, Pleshette grew up in Brooklyn Heights, New York, as an only child. Her father managed a pair of venues that housed big-band performances,

and her mother had once been a dancer. Pleshette's own show-business ambitions were honed at the New York High School of the Performing Arts, followed by stints at Syracuse University and Finch College in Manhattan; she dropped out of the latter to devote herself to Method acting classes. Her television debut came in 1957, and she was cast in her first Broadway production that same year with a role in the murder-tale drama *Compulsion*. A year later, she appeared opposite comedian Jerry Lewis in *The Geisha Boy* for her first big-screen appearance.

Pleshette spent several years working on Broadway, in television plays, and in movies, and in that last category she emerged as a well-regarded performer in several noted teen-oriented movies of the early 1960s. One of them was *Rome Adventure*, which led to a brief 1964 marriage to co-star Troy Donahue, a popular matinee idol of the era. One of her best-known supporting roles came in the 1963 Alfred Hitchcock thriller *The Birds* as the friend of Tippi Hedren's character. After more than a decade of working, she retired when she wed her second husband, oil investor Tom Gallagher, in 1968. Her final bow turned out to be premature, however: As she later told one interviewer, after a few months "my loving husband said, 'You're getting to be awfully boring. Go back to work,'" her *Los Angeles Times* obituary quoted her as saying.

Seeking to avoid a permanent commitment to a series or parts that required her to appear on a movie set at an unnaturally early hour, Pleshette carved out a niche as a frequent guest on the television talk-show circuit, known for her amiable repartee. She was a particular favorite of Johnny Carson, host of NBC's *The Tonight Show*, and was booked for a 1971 appearance on that show with comedian Bob Newhart. David Davis and Lorenzo Music, the creators of a new series in which Newhart was set to star, were watching that night and found Pleshette "was bubble-headed but smart, loving toward her husband but relentless about his imperfections," they told *TV Guide*, according to the *Los Angeles Times*. "We were trying to get away from the standard TV wife, and we knew that whoever we picked would have to be offbeat enough and strong enough to carry the show along with Newhart. We didn't dream Suzanne would accept the part."

Pleshette made her debut as schoolteacher Emily Hartley on the CBS sitcom in 1972, and *The Bob Newhart Show* went on to spend the next six seasons at the top of the Saturday-night ratings. Newhart played Dr. Bob Hartley, a psychiatrist in private practice whose oddball patients and equally eccentric neighbors at both his office and the Chicago high-rise apartment he shared with Pleshette's Emily provided the bulk of the comic fodder. "Emily Hartley's teaching job did not receive much attention," remarked *New York Times* writer Anita Gates, "but the character was confident, sexy and anything but submissive."

Pleshette appeared in scores of other films, television movies, and series. One of her final appearances was as the toxic mother to Karen, Megan Mullaly's character on the hit NBC sitcom *Will & Grace,* by which point the widowed Pleshette had married for a third time, this time to actor Tom Poston, whom she had known for more than 40 years. Poston had co-starred with Newhart in a second television sitcom, *Newhart,* which ran on CBS from 1982 to 1990. In that series, Newhart played Dick Loudon, proprietor of a New England inn, and *Newhart* ended its eight-year run with a stunning turn that the *Chicago Tribune*'s Bob Thomas called "one of the most clever final episodes in TV history." Newhart's Loudon is hit by a stray golf ball, but then awakes "in the bedroom of his *The Bob Newhart Show* home with Ms. Pleshette at his side. He went on to tell her of the crazy dream he'd just had of running an inn filled with a cast of odd characters."

Diagnosed with lung cancer in 2006, Pleshette underwent chemotherapy, and lost Poston the following year. She died from respiratory failure at her Los Angeles home on January 19, 2008, just 12 days before she was to be honored with a star on the Hollywood Walk of Fame, which would have also been her 71st birthday. In one interview from a decade earlier, Pleshette had once said she was grateful to have had as long a career as she had enjoyed. "I'm an actress, and that's why I'm still here," CNN.com quoted her as saying. "Anybody who has the illusion that you can have a career as long as I have and be a star is kidding themselves." **Sources:** *Chicago Tribune,* January 21, 2008, sec. 2, p. 12; CNN.com, http://www.cnn.com/2008/SHOWBIZ/TV/01/20/pleshette.obit.ap/index.html (January 22, 2008); *Entertainment Weekly,* February 1, 2008, p. 10; *Los Angeles Times,* January 20, 2008, p. B13; *New York Times,* January 21, 2008, p. A17; *People,* February 4, 2008, p. 100.

—Carol Brennan

# Sydney Pollack

Born Sydney Irwin Pollack, July 1, 1934, in Lafayette, IN; died of cancer, May 26, 2008, in Pacific Palisades, CA. Filmmaker. In a career that began in acting, turned to directing, and returned to character acting in later years, Sydney Pollack established a reputation for himself as an actor's director. He won awards for his direction on such hit films as *Out of Africa* and *Tootsie.* Noted for featuring big-name stars in his movies, Pollack gained a reputation as a craftsman and a perfectionist.

"He is never satisfied.... His passion is contagious. It inspires everyone around him to dig a little deeper," cinematographer Owen Roizman, who worked with Pollack on five films, was quoted as having said in the *Los Angeles Times.* Michelle Tauber, writing for *People* magazine, noted, "Pollack knew how to put actors in their best light—and they loved him for it."

Born into a Russian-Jewish family in Lafayette, Indiana, Pollack grew up in South Bend, an area Pollack felt was devoid of culture, as well as being anti-Semetic. His parents divorced when he was young, and though his father, a pharmacist, hoped he would become a dentist, Pollack was determined to become an actor. He enrolled in the Neighborhood Playhouse School of Theatre in New York, where he studied under Sandy Meisner. Pollack later became Meisner's assistant, as well as a teacher at the school.

After earning a few small roles on Broadway, Pollack's career was interrupted by his army service from 1957 through 1959. But while he appeared on both Broadway and on television, Pollack saw teaching as his stable income. "I knew I wasn't going to be any great shakes as an actor—the way I looked I would play the soda jerk or the friend of a friend," he was quoted as having said in the *Los Angeles Times.*

In 1961, Pollack took a role in the film *The Young Savages,* which starred Burt Lancaster, who encouraged Pollack to become a director. Through Lancaster's influence, Pollack met with the owner of Universal Pictures and began directing television episodes. He worked on *The Alfred Hitchcock Hour, Ben Casey,* and *The Fugitive* before filming his first feature as a director, *The Slender Thread,* in 1965. Pollack "was young and gifted and enormously talented," Sidney Poitier, who starred in the film, told the *Los Angeles Times.* "He wound up leaving an amazing mark on the American film industry."

After his 1965 film debut, Pollack directed more than 20 films, many of them award winners. He worked with Robert Redford in *This Property is Con-*

demned in 1966, a film that propelled Redford into stardom. Pollack and Redford made seven feature films together, including *The Way We Were* and *Out of Africa,* one of Pollack's most prominent films. Pollack also supported Redford in founding the Sundance Institute, an organization that encourages new and independent filmmakers.

Pollack's landmark film, *They Shoot Horses, Don't They?* was a turning point in his career. Marked by the same sense of what a writer for the London *Times* called "liberalism and social conscience" that distinguished Pollack's earlier works, the film was nominated for nine Oscars, one for best director. The critical reception caused Pollack to be recognized as one of Hollywood's top directors.

Pollack is best known for his films *Out of Africa,* which starred Redford and Meryl Streep, and *Tootsie,* which starred Dustin Hoffman and in which Pollack also had a role on screen. Based on Danish author Isak Dinesen's memoir of life in Kenya in the early twentieth century, *Out of Africa* is a romantic drama depicting Dinesen's experiences and her romance with a big-game hunter. The film won Pollack two Academy Awards, one for best director, the other for best producer. *Out of Africa* also won the Oscar for best picture. *Tootsie* also earned Pollack an Oscar nomination for best director. The comedy stars Dustin Hoffman as an out-of-work actor who, in order to find jobs, disguises himself as a woman. As an actress, Hoffman's character lands a role in a soap opera and falls in love with a female cast member. Pollack directed the film, but also played the role of the exasperated agent. Hoffman and Pollack had creative difficulties over the course of filming, which lent additional tension to the arguments between the two characters.

Pollack continued to work primarily as a director and producer, and has been credited with more than 40 films on which he worked as producer or executive producer. In addition to his behind-the-scenes work, Pollack took on several character roles as an actor later in his life. In films including *Husbands and Wives, Eyes Wide Shut,* and *Michael Clayton,* as well as television shows such as *Will and Grace* and *The Sopranos,* Pollack viewed acting as an opportunity to see how other directors worked.

The recipient of two Oscars and nominated for four more, Pollack was devoted to making films that held meaning for him. He was quoted in the *Los Angeles Times* as having said, "if you have a career like mine, which is so identified with Hollywood, with big studios and stars, you wonder if maybe you shouldn't go off and do what the world thinks of as more personal films with lesser-known people. But I think I've fooled everybody. I've made personal films all along. I just made them in another form." Pollack is survived by his wife, Claire, whom he met when she was studying at the Neighborhood Playhouse, two daughters, and six grandchildren. **Sources:** *Chicago Tribune,* May 27, 2008, sec. 2 p. 5; *Los Angeles Times,* May 27, 2008, pp. A1, A14; *People,* June 9, 2008, p. 122; *Times* (London), May 28, 2008.

—*Alana Joli Abbott*

## Julius B. Richmond

Born Julius Benjamin Richmond, September 26, 1916, in Chicago, IL; died of cancer, July 27, 2008, Brookline, MA. Pediatrician. Julius B. Richmond, a pediatrician and government health expert, founded Head Start, a national preschool program now considered one of the most successful social programs in the United States. As the nation's surgeon general, he also warned of the dangers of smoking cigarettes, a cause he continued to pursue long after his retirement. In 1979, Richmond released the first national health goals for all citizens, helping to solidify the position of the surgeon general as the nation's most prominent public health spokesperson.

Richmond was born in Chicago, Illinois, in 1916. He received a medical degree from the University of Illinois in 1939, spent 18 months in an internship, then joined the Army Air Corps. During World War II, he served as a flight surgeon. After the war, Richmond returned to his alma mater to teach pediatrics.

In 1953, Richmond joined the faculty at the medical college of the State University of New York at Syracuse. There, in the late 1950s, Richmond and his colleague, Betty Caldwell, began to study poverty's effects on children. They found that, because of malnutrition and other factors, poor children's social and psychological development lagged behind others their age. The difference appeared very early, as soon as children began to talk and explore their surroundings. "We discovered that around 18 months there was a decline in cognitive function and responsiveness to adult guidance," Caldwell told Bruce Weber of the *New York Times.* The two researchers found that the problem could be prevented if poor children were given extra attention in a stimulating environment.

Richmond and Caldwell's insight led to the creation of Head Start, the government preschool program that became a centerpiece of President Lyndon B. Johnson's war on poverty. In 1964, Sargent Shriver, the new head of the federal Office of Economic Opportunity, recruited Richmond to join the government and launch the program. Head Start, founded in 1965, enrolled a half-million children in 2,700 communities in its first six months. More than 20 million children have gone through Head Start since. In 1966, Richmond also sponsored the creation of neighborhood health centers across the country.

Stricken with tuberculosis in 1967, Richmond returned to Syracuse to recover. Once he was healthy, he returned to academia, becoming dean of the medical college in Syracuse. He moved to Harvard Medical School in 1971 to study preventive and social medicine, child psychology, and human development.

In 1977, Richmond returned to Washington to become surgeon general and assistant secretary of health under President Jimmy Carter. Richmond did not have the ambitious budget he had been given under the Johnson Administration, but he combined his positions to become both a policymaker and spokesman for the policies he helped implement. In 1979, Richmond released a 1,200-page study of the health effects of smoking cigarettes, a follow-up to a 1964 report by a previous surgeon general, Luther Terry. Richmond's update declared there was "overwhelming proof" that smoking caused lung cancer. In response, Congress replaced a vague health warning on cigarette packs with four specific warnings about dangerous illnesses caused by smoking.

The same year, Richmond released the government's first set of health objectives for the entire nation. His report, "Healthy People: The Surgeon General's Report on Health Promotion and Disease Prevention," advised Americans to consume less sugar, salt, fat, and alcohol, and to exercise moderately, see a doctor regularly, and reduce the risk of dying in auto accidents by wearing seat belts and not speeding. Richmond also developed a strategy to fight infant mortality, launching a campaign to immunize children against diseases such as measles.

Also in 1979, Richmond successfully opposed the Immigration and Naturalization Service's practice of barring gay people from entering the United States. The INS (according to Weber of the *New York Times*) was using a 1952 law that called for anyone "afflicted with … sexual deviation or a mental de-

fect" to be examined by the Public Health Service, then refused entry into the country. Richmond ordered the health service to stop performing the exams on gays, declaring that homosexuality was not a mental defect and could not be identified by medical tests.

After leaving the government in 1981, Richmond returned to Harvard as a professor of health policy. He retired in 1988, but continued to speak out against cigarette smoking. "We are in the midst of the largest man-made epidemic in history, and that is lung cancer," he said (as quoted by Thomas H. Maugh II of the *Los Angeles Times*). Richmond testified in several class-action suits against the tobacco industry, including one involving a flight attendant who had never smoked, but had developed lung cancer because of secondhand smoke on airplanes. The case led to a $300 million settlement that funded the creation of an institute to study smoking-related illnesses. In 2004, Richmond joined three other former surgeons general to offer a nationwide plan to discourage smoking, including a proposed $2 tax on packs of cigarettes.

Richmond died on July 27, 2008, at his home in Brookline, Massachusetts. The cause of his death was cancer. He was 91. He was preceded in death by his first wife, Rhee, and their son, Dale. He is survived by his second wife, Jean; two sons from his first marriage, Barry and Charles; two stepsons, Michael and Steven Berger; nine grandchildren; and five great-grandchildren. **Sources:** *Los Angeles Times*, July 30, 2008, p. B8; *New York Times,* July 30, 2008, p. C14; *Times* (London), August 19, 2008, p. 54; *Washington Post*, July 30, 2008, p. B6.

—*Erick Trickey*

## Tim Russert

Born Timothy John Russert Jr., May 7, 1950, in Buffalo, NY; died of a heart attack, June 13, 2008, in Washington, DC. Journalist. For the 17 years that Tim Russert hosted NBC's *Meet the Press,* withstanding his interviews was a rite of passage for American politicians. Those who gave candid answers to Russert's well-researched questions and persistent follow-ups proved themselves; those who gave vague, evasive answers saw their reputations shrink. Russert was tenacious and tough, but he interrogated guests with a smile that revealed a love of political debate. According to Jacques Steinberg, writing in the *New York Times,* U.S. President George

W. Bush said Russert was "an institution in both news and politics for more than two decades. He was always well-informed and thorough in his interviews. And he was as gregarious off the set as he was prepared on it."

Russert was born in Buffalo, New York, in 1950. His father was a sanitation worker and deliveryman for the *Buffalo News*. Russert majored in political science at John Carroll University in suburban Cleveland, Ohio, and he became the first in his family to graduate from college. He earned a law degree from the Cleveland-Marshall College of Law.

Russert gained his political knowledge firsthand, working as a field organizer in Daniel Patrick Moynihan's 1976 race for the U.S. Senate. He then managed Moynihan's New York City office—while still in his 20s—and served as the senator's special counsel for five years. He then worked for Mario Cuomo's campaign for governor of New York, then served as a counselor to Cuomo after his victory.

In 1984, Russert left politics for journalism, taking a job with NBC as an executive for special news projects. The following year, he scored a major interviewing coup by booking Pope John Paul II on NBC's *Today* show, the pope's first American television appearance. Russert became known for his ability to make complicated political news understandable and exciting. In 1988, he was named NBC's Washington bureau chief. He also became a political commentator on *Today* because network executives liked his political banter during conference calls. NBC News president Michael Gartner named Russert the new moderator of NBC's Sunday public-affairs show, *Meet the Press*, in December of 1991. It was a bold, surprising hire, since Russert did not have a lot of experience on camera. But it paid off.

The show, which dated back to 1948, had a reputation as boring—until Russert livened it up, taking it from third place in the ratings to number one. "[He] chang[ed] it from a sleepy encounter between reporters and Washington newsmakers into an issue-dense program, with Mr. Russert taking on the week's newsmaker," Bill Carter wrote in the *New York Times* (as quoted by Steinberg in his 2008 *New York Times* article). Russert would often confront politicians with their own previous statements by displaying them on screen. He would turn their predictable rhetoric back on them with pointed follow-ups, asking those who complained about the federal deficit which programs they would cut or asking opponents of foreign aid if they would cut off aid to Israel, a top U.S. ally. He once explained that he tried to preempt politicians' usual talking points by incorporating them into his question, forcing them to go further. Political aides began calling *Meet the Press* the "Russert primary," meaning that the show tested and weeded out weak candidates much like primary elections do.

Russert's take on a political event often became the definitive account. On the air on Election Night in 2000, Russert brandished a white dry-erase board and a marker, scribbling combinations of states and their electoral votes, trying to figure out whether George W. Bush or Al Gore would win the presidency. "Florida, Florida, Florida," Russert wrote on it once it became clear that state would decide the race. His white board became an enduring image of that disputed election, which ended in a near-tie in Florida and a grueling recount.

Throughout his career, Russert remained proud of his working-class roots. He wrote a book about his father, titled *Big Russ & Me*, which made the *New York Times* best-seller list. "Tim always would tell everybody that when he asked a question of a guest on *Meet the Press*, he liked to think he asked a question that the guys at the American Legion would ask or understand," comedian Mark Russell, a hometown friend of Russert, told Matea Gold of the *Chicago Tribune*.

During the races for the 2008 presidential nominations, Russert was a moderator for several debates. His persistent questioning of Senator Hillary Clinton was sometimes criticized. But Russert's role as a political analyst was so respected that when he said on May 6 that Senator Barack Obama had attained an insurmountable lead over Clinton in the contest for the Democratic nomination, his declaration was treated as news in itself. Russert relished his central role in covering one of the most dramatic presidential races in his lifetime. "Can you believe we get paid for this year?" he asked his friend, journalist Al Hunt (according to Steinberg of the *New York Times*).

Russert died of a sudden heart attack on June 13, 2008, at the NBC bureau in Washington, D.C., while preparing for the next broadcast of his show; he was 58. "There wasn't a better interviewer on television, a more thoughtful analyst about politics," commented Obama (as quoted by Howard Kurtz of the *Washington Post*). Russert is survived by his wife, Maureen Orth; his son, Luke; his father, Tim Russert; and three sisters. **Sources:** *Chicago Tribune*, June 14, 2008, sec. 1, p. 1, p. 12; *Los Angeles Times*, June 14, 2008, p. A1, p. A21; *New York Times*, June 14, 2008; *People*, June 30, 2008, pp. 46-51; *Times* (London), June 16, 2008, p. 49; *Washington Post*, June 14, 2008, p. A1, p. A6.

—*Erick Trickey*

# Yves Saint Laurent

Born Yves Henri Donat Saint Laurent, August 1, 1936, in Oran, Algeria; died of a brain tumor, June 1, 2008, in Paris, France. Fashion designer. Arguably the most influential fashion designer in the second half of the twentieth century, Yves Saint Laurent revolutionized eveningwear, office attire, and haute couture. His designs during the 1970s changed women's fashion by embracing concepts of women's liberation. A reporter from CNN.com considered Saint Laurent "the last of an era" in fashion.

"It was generally accepted in the world of fashion that no designer had greater impact on how clothing was cut, shaped, and sold," wrote Martin Weil for the *Washington Post.* A *Times* of London contributor referred to Saint Laurent as "omnipotent," quipping, "Once he had made a fashion statement, there was really nothing left for other designers to say."

Born to French parents living in Algeria, Saint Laurent was the son of a wealthy lawyer and and insurance broker. His mother loved fashion, and she encouraged her son's interest at an early age. As a child, Saint Laurent thought he would pursue a career designing sets and costumes for ballet and theater performances, despite his father's encouragement to go into law. Saint Laurent won third prize in the International Wool Secretariat's dress-designing competition, and his mother took him to Paris to introduce him to people in the fashion industry. Michel de Brunhoff, editor-in-chief of French *Vogue,* advised Saint Laurent to earn a university degree and subsequently encouraged him to study at Chambre Syndicale de la Couture.

Bored with school, Saint Laurent entered the International Wool Secretariat's competition again, this time receiving first prize. He began planning a career in theater but was offered a position with Christian Dior, who was then considered the greatest couturier in the world, after de Brunhoff showed Dior the young designer's portfolio. Saint Laurent became Dior's design assistant at the age of 17; according to the *Washington Post,* Dior called Saint Laurent "my right arm." But the *Los Angeles Times* goes a bit further in describing this dependence, quoting Dior as having said, "Yves is my heart, my brain." When Dior died suddenly in 1956, Saint Laurent became the leader of the Dior house.

The *Los Angeles Times* quoted from a 1991 interview that appeared in *Le Figaro* where Saint Laurent said, "I was in a state of complete euphoria preparing that first collection.... I knew I was going to become

famous." The collection debuted in 1958 and was considered a complete success; Saint Laurent was considered a hero to the house of Dior and to all of French fashion. But over the next two years, his clothing became more radical, and critics expressed concern.

Despite having been able to defer his compulsory military service for two years because his job was deemed too important to interrupt, in 1960, Saint Laurent was called into National Service. Less than three weeks into his service, he had a nervous breakdown. His then-lover and future business partner, Pierre Berge, had him transferred to a civilian hospital, where he was treated with experimental drugs. This episode may have caused many of the health and addiction issues that plagued Saint Laurent's later life.

Due to his long recovery, Saint Laurent was replaced at Dior in a breach of contract. With Berge, Saint Laurent challenged the end of his relationship with Dior, and the court ruled that Dior was in the wrong, awarding Saint Laurent $100,000. The money was enough for Saint Laurent to start up his own couture house, which opened in 1961. His first show launched in 1962 and was proclaimed extremely successful. Over the next several years, Saint Laurent's designs had huge impact on the fashion world, from his trapeze dresses to his safari jackets. He drew inspiration from areas untouched by haute couture, from beatniks to peasants, and designed styles using traditional aspects of Russian, Chinese, and African clothing. Along with his high fashion division, he added a ready-to-wear line and, in 1966, opened his first boutique.

In the 1970s, some of Saint Laurent's most influential designs affected both the world of fashion and women's rights. He offered pants suits; a woman's tuxedo, which he named "le smoking"; and other women's clothing based on traditional men's attire. Along with evening wear that included pants, he designed business suits for women to wear in their offices, giving them equal footing to their male co-workers, at least in terms of fashion. It was a bold move during an era when some workplaces prohibited female employees from wearing trousers and women could be turned away from hotels and restaurants if they were not wearing skirts or dresses. In addition, Saint Laurent began designing provocative eveningwear, which implied that women had the same sexual desires and needs as men.

Despite his successes, Saint Laurent struggled with depression, turning to drugs and alcohol and suffering more than one emotional breakdown. It was rumored that he was addicted to tranquilizers. During these low times, however, he was known for having bursts of genius, launching extremely successful collections in periods of manic activity. By the time he retired in 2002, he had rid himself of his drug and alcohol dependencies and proudly announced that at the end of his career, he was sober.

A 1983 retrospective of Saint Laurent's work was showcased at the Museum of Metropolitan Art in New York City, marking the first time a living fashion designer had received the honor. Upon announcing his retirement in 2002, Saint Laurent launched a fashion retrospective at Centre Pompidou in Paris, a museum of contemporary art. The show featured 300 of his designs, once again worn by models down the catwalk.

Mary Rourke, writing in the *Chicago Tribune*, quoted Saint Laurent as saying, "I am extremely proud that women of the world today wear pants suits, pea jackets, and trench coats.... In many ways I feel that I have created the wardrobe of the contemporary woman." Saint Laurent died of a brain tumor at his home in Paris. He was 71. **Sources:** *Chicago Tribune*, June 2, 2008, sec. 1, p. 1, p. 11; CNN.com, http://www.cnn.com/2008/WORLD/europe/06/01/laurent.obit/index.html (March 16, 2009); *Los Angeles Times*, June 2, 2008, p. A1, p. A8; *People*, June 16, 2008, p. 132; *Times* (London), June 3, 2008, p. 53; *Washington Post*, June 2, 2008, p. A1, p. A9.

—*Alana Joli Abbott*

# Roy Scheider

Born Roy Richard Scheider, November 10, 1932, in Orange, NJ; died of complications from multiple myeloma, February 10, 2008, in Little Rock, AR. Actor. American actor Roy Scheider appeared in a string of hit films, but may be best remembered for his role as the embattled police chief of a New England resort town beset by a killer shark in the 1975 thriller *Jaws*. Scheider earned Oscar nominations for two other films of the era—*The French Connection* and *All That Jazz*—but would be indelibly associated with the role of Chief Brody. "With his soft, hurt eyes, rugged features and broken nose," noted his *Times* of London obituary, "Scheider had the look of a trammelled hero."

A native of New Jersey, Scheider was born in 1932 and suffered from rheumatic fever as a child. His father owned a gas station, and Scheider worked there after the age of eight despite his poor health. His physical strength improved immensely in his

teens after he began boxing at the local YMCA, and he even made it to the finals of a Golden Gloves championship match, where his nose was broken by his opponent and never properly fixed. He began college at Rutgers University, but graduated with a degree in history from Pennsylvania's Franklin and Marshall College, where he first appeared on the stage. Afterward, Scheider enlisted in the U.S. Air Force for a three-year stint, and upon returning to civilian life changed his mind about entering law school when the drama department at his alma mater offered him a part in a Shakespeare play, which rekindled his passion for acting.

Scheider made his professional debut at the 1961 New York Shakespeare Festival in its staging of *Romeo and Juliet*. His film debut came three years later in a little-seen 1964 B-movie, *The Curse of the Living Corpse*, and he won what proved to be his breakout role in the 1971 drama *Klute*, in which he played the pimp of a call-girl ring with co-stars Jane Fonda and Donald Sutherland. His first Academy Award nomination, in the Best Supporting Actor category, came for another film that was released that same year, *The French Connection*, which starred Gene Hackman as a New York City narcotics detective determined to bust an international heroin ring.

Emerging director Steven Spielberg cast Scheider in his 1975 beach-resort horror flick *Jaws*, which was based on the novel of the same name by Peter Benchley. The movie proved to be a historic Hollywood benchmark on several fronts: It launched the era of the summer blockbuster, was the first release rolled out nationwide instead of just in selected markets, and became the first movie to break the $100-million box-office barrier. *Jaws* is set on a New England coastal resort island as the busy Fourth of July weekend approaches; Scheider's character, Police Chief Martin Brody, battles with the local mayor about whether or not to close the beaches after shark attacks incite panic, then finally sets out with a scientist (Richard Dreyfuss) to battle the beast himself. Early in the film, when Brody examines the killer shark's first victim, Spielberg's camera "captured Scheider's face, halfway between horror and disbelief, in a pioneering forward tracking zoom out shot which became a signature moment known to film students thereafter as the "Jaws shot," noted a writer for the *Times* of London. "Here the conscience of Brody, probably one of the most fully realised heroes of any Hollywood thriller, is laid open."

The third and final work in Scheider's triumvirate of stellar performances came in 1979 with *All That Jazz*, which was both directed by and based on the life of noted Broadway choreographer Bob Fosse. Its riveting behind-the-scenes look at the making of a Broadway musical meant that Scheider had to learn how to dance, and he was nominated for a second Academy Award for his role, this time in the Best Actor category. "Equipped with Mr. Fosse's Mephistophelean beard and manic drive," *New York Times* journalist Dave Kehr asserted, "Scheider's character, Joe Gideon, gobbled amphetamines in an attempt to stage a new Broadway show while completing the editing of a film (and pursuing a parade of alluring young women)—a monumental act of self-abuse that leads to open-heart surgery."

Scheider continued to work in film during the 1980s and '90s, but usually in supporting roles. He returned to Broadway, and also did television work, including a starring role in the cult-favorite NBC series *SeaQuest DSV*. Near his Long Island home in the community of Sag Harbor, he co-founded the Hayground School, and was also active in environmental and anti-war causes. He and his second wife, Brenda Siemer, spent time in Florence, Italy, where he was a key figure in the renovation of an old factory into a historic park, tourist center, and film soundstage.

By the time the 30th anniversary celebrations for *Jaws* occurred in 2005, Scheider had already been diagnosed with multiple myeloma, a cancer of the bloodstream. In January of 2008 he underwent a bone-marrow transplant at the University of Arkansas for Medical Sciences, a leading treatment center for the disease, but came down with a staph infection and died there on February 10, 2008, at the age of 75. Survivors include Siemer and his two children from that marriage, Christian Verrier Scheider and Molly Mae Scheider; Maximilia Connelly Lord, his daughter from his first marriage to Cynthia Bebout, predeceased him in 2006. Despite his career-making role as Chief Brody in *Jaws,* Scheider was "underappreciated" by Hollywood, *French Connection* director William Friedkin told *Entertainment Weekly*'s Gregory Kirschling. Friedkin continued, "*All That Jazz* will stand the test of time. It really is one of the finest performances by an American actor in a movie." **Sources:** *Chicago Tribune,* February 11, 2008, sec. 2, p. 12; *Entertainment Weekly,* February 22, 2008, p. 13; *Los Angeles Times,* February 11, 2008, p. B7; *New York Times,* February 11, 2008, p. A21; *People,* February 25, 2008, p. 124; *Times* (London), February 12, 2008, p. 53.

—Carol Brennan

# Irena Sendler

Born Irena Krzyzanowski, February 15, 1910, in Warsaw, Poland; died of pneumonia, May 12, 2008, in Warsaw, Poland. Social worker. During World War II, Irena Sendler risked her life to save more than 2,000 Jewish children in Warsaw, Poland, whose parents would later die in concentration camps. Sendler, a social worker in the city who worked for a secret underground organization, spirited the children out of the Warsaw Ghetto and placed them in homes or orphanages in the countryside under false names. "I saw the Polish nation drowning," Sendler would later say about her heroism—a term she disdained—according to the *Times* of London. "And those in the most difficult position were the Jews. And among them those most vulnerable were the children. So I had to help."

Sendler was born in 1910 in Warsaw and grew up in nearby Otwock, where her father, a physician, died seven years later from typhus after being one of the few medical professionals who would attend to Jewish patients, who were particularly hard-hit by the outbreak. Conditions for Jews in the predominantly Roman Catholic nation would worsen considerably after 1939, when Nazi Germany invaded Poland and began implementing harsh anti-Semitic statutes. Such laws were already in force in Germany and Austria, and the German authorities also began building large-scale prison camps, with mass-extermination ovens and gas chambers, on Polish soil.

Sendler was a married 29-year-old social worker with Warsaw's social welfare office when the war began. Her first acts of defiance involved helping Jews and opponents of the Nazi regime flee to safety. When the city's Jewish population was walled into the infamous Warsaw Ghetto and sealed by checkpoints, Sendler organized a secret humanitarian program among her friends and colleagues. She brought in food and medical supplies, aided by her municipal-government pass that gave her relatively easy access through the heavily armed checkpoints.

In the summer of 1942, German authorities began mass deportations out of the Ghetto to concentration camps, where Jews were used as slave labor until they either starved to death or were systematically killed off in poison-gas chambers when they became too frail to work. A few months later, Sendler became head of the children's division of an aid organization, *Rada Pomocy Zydom,* or Council for Aid to Jews, which was known by its code name "Zegota." Her task was to relocate children from the Ghetto, smuggling them to safety and then placing them with sympathizers elsewhere. Some children went to farm families in the countryside, while others were placed in orphanages, but they all received new identity documents stating they were Gentiles, or non-Jews. Sendler brought the children out of the Ghetto via ingenious means: sometimes Warsaw's sewer system was used, and there were also some buildings on the borders of the Ghetto that had secret basements.

There was a second, even more fearsome task for Sendler: she had to keep meticulous records of the children's real names and temporary homes, so that when the war ended they could be reunited with their families. She did this by writing in code on cigarette papers, which she then buried in glass jars in a friend's yard. The worst part of her job, she would later say, was convincing the parents. "The one question every parent asked me was 'Can you guarantee they will live?'" her *Los Angeles Times* obituary quoted her as saying. "We had to admit honestly that we could not, as we did not even know if we would succeed in leaving the ghetto that day. The only guarantee was that the children would most likely die if they stayed."

In Nazi-occupied Poland, aiding a Jew was punishable by death. Sendler's activities attracted the attention of the Gestapo, the Nazi secret police agency, and she was arrested in October of 1943. In prison, she was beaten and tortured, but refused to divulge any details of her work or the names of her fellow humanitarians. She was sentenced to death, but the Polish government in exile in London, which funded Zegota, managed to bribe a guard and Sendler was able to escape. Her name was still on the list of those who were to be shot that day, however, so she was forced to live underground for the remainder of the war.

Poland was liberated by Allied forces from the Soviet Union on their way to defeat Nazi Germany. The true extent of the Nazi plan to exterminate Europe's Jewish population was revealed in the final weeks of the war, during the spring of 1945, and Sendler was devastated to learn that many of the children she helped were now truly orphans. After the war, she remained in the field of social work under the new Communist regime and lived in relative obscurity. That changed in 1965 when the State of Israel honored her as one of the "Righteous Among the Nations" by Yad Vashem, the Holocaust Martyrs' and Heroes' Remembrance Authority.

Word of Sendler's heroism during the war was further spread after the year 2000 thanks to a play written by four high school students in Kansas who were fascinated by her story. *Life in a Jar* has been performed at schools across the United States and Europe, and for several years proceeds from dona-

tions collected after the performances paid for Sendler's nursing home care in Warsaw, where she died on May 12, 2008, at the age of 98. Her survivors include a daughter and granddaughter, but many of the children she helped also considered her a parent of sorts. Two years earlier, one of those rescued infants, Elzbieta Ficowska, read a statement by Sendler at a Polish Senate ceremony honoring Sendler's wartime work. Sendler was too frail to attend herself, but her response asserted that "every child saved with my help and the help of all the wonderful secret messengers, who today are no longer living, is the justification of my existence on this earth," according to the *Times* of London, "and not a title to glory." **Sources:** *Chicago Tribune,* May 13, 2008, sec. 2, p. 5; *Los Angeles Times,* May 13, 2008, pp. A1, A15; *Times* (London), May 13, 2008, p. 57.

*—Carol Brennan*

## Ian Smith

Born Ian Douglas Smith, April 8, 1919, in Selukwe, Rhodesia; died after suffering a stroke, November 20, 2007, in Cape Town, South Africa. Politician. As prime minister of the central African nation of Rhodesia for 14 years, Ian Smith led a bitter and protracted struggle to prevent the nation's four million blacks from gaining a political voice. Smith's infamous Unilateral Declaration of Independence (UDI) in 1965 asserted Rhodesian independence from Britain, but a brutal guerrilla war erupted seven years later, and the Smith government finally capitulated in 1979. A year later, Rhodesia was renamed Zimbabwe.

Smith was born in 1919 in Selukwe, a town in what was then called Southern Rhodesia, which was populated by British and Scottish farming families like his own. As a young man he studied commerce at Rhodes University in South Africa, an institution named after Cecil John Rhodes, the diamond-mining magnate and founder of Rhodesia. During World War II Smith served with the Royal Air Force as a fighter pilot and survived two crashes; the first left his face badly damaged and he required reconstructive surgery, and the second placed him behind enemy lines in Italy, which he escaped by walking across the Alps. Following the war he returned to Selukwe and established himself as a cattle farmer.

Smith's political career began when he was elected to Rhodesia's legislative assembly in 1948. A few years later, the country was divided into three separate entities of Northern Rhodesia, Southern Rhodesia, and Nyasaland, and he emerged as one of the most vocal opponents of Britain's plan to grant black Africans political rights in its colonies in preparation for full independence. In 1962 he joined a breakaway faction within his own party calling itself the Rhodesian Front (RF). Over the next few years the RF gained widespread support among many of the 250,000 whites who were opposed to giving Rhodesia's four million blacks any political rights.

Smith became head of the RF and Rhodesia's prime minister after a 1964 party coup. His government led a concerted effort to jail, exile, or otherwise silence the country's emerging black nationalist leaders. Britain, however, still maintained legal authority over Rhodesia, and sought to forge a compromise; one proposal would have given blacks increasing political representation over the next three decades, with the goal of full citizenship rights by the year 2000. Smith rebuffed this and other conciliatory measures, and after the RF won elections in May of 1965, he formulated a plan of action.

Six months later, Smith's government announced Rhodesia's Unilateral Declaration of Independence (UDI). Based in part on the 1776 Declaration of Independence signed by representatives of the 13 North American colonies, the UDI pushed Rhodesia to front-page news around the world, and marked the first time since the American Revolutionary War that a British colony was in revolt against the Crown.

Not surprisingly, Britain considered the UDI an illegal act, and successfully sought economic sanctions by the United Nations against Rhodesia. Smith, however, had forged alliances with both South Africa—another recalcitrant white-ruled nation on the continent—and with nearby Mozambique and Angola, which were still under Portuguese colonial authority, and these measures kept the Rhodesian economy afloat and even prospering for a time. On three separate occasions the British government attempted to broker a solution, but relations disintegrated into outright diplomatic hostility.

In 1972 black Rhodesian guerrillas launched a rocket attack on a white-owned farm that served as the opening volley in a seven-year-long guerrilla war. An estimated 30,000 people died, most of them civilians or members of two insurgency groups, the Zimbabwean African People's Union (ZAPU) and the Zimbabwean African National Union (ZANU). When Portugal's socialist dictatorship fell in 1974 and it lost control of Mozambique a year later, the new black nationalist government welcomed ZANU fighters and permitted them to use Mozambique as their base of attack. In 1976, U.S. Secretary of State Henry N. Kissinger met with Smith in South Africa and forced him to accept an ultimatum.

In 1978, Smith agreed to a transitional government with himself at the helm of an executive council and a year later the newly named nation of Zimbabwe-Rhodesia came into existence. In late 1979, the Lancaster House Conference in London resulted in the final capitulation of Smith's government to majority rule. The new arrangement called for the first free elections to be held in February of 1980, with 20 of the 100 seats in the assembly allotted to white candidates. Smith and other RF members won them, with Robert Mugabe's ZANU Party winning the majority of the remaining 80 seats. Rhodesia ceased to exist on April 18, 1980.

Smith remained active in politics for the next few years, but was suspended from Zimbabwe's parliament in 1987 for speaking out publicly in favor of apartheid in South Africa, the last remaining bastion of white minority rule on the continent. Soon afterward, Mugabe abolished the 20-seat allotment for white Zimbabweans in the assembly. The Mugabe government, meanwhile, grew increasingly despotic, and in 2002 Smith was stripped of his citizenship and moved to South Africa.

Smith died in a nursing home near Cape Town, South Africa, on November 20, 2007, following a stroke. He was 88. His wife, Jane Watt, whom he wed in 1948, predeceased him, as did their son, Alec. Mugabe clung to power despite calls for him to step down; the prosperous nation he had inherited at the 1980 handover was by now on the brink of economic ruin. In his later years Smith often claimed that blacks in Zimbabwe had better access to education, housing, and health care under his regime than they had under Mugabe's. "There are millions of black people who say things were better when I was in control," the *New York Times* quoted Smith as saying in 2004. "I have challenged Mugabe to walk down the street with me and see who has most support. I have much better relations with black people than he does." **Sources:** *Los Angeles Times,* November 21, 2007, p. B9; *New York Times,* November 21, 2007, p. C16; *Times* (London), November 21, 2007, p. 70; *Washington Post,* November 21, 2007, p. B7.

—*Carol Brennan*

# Tony Snow

Born Robert Anthony Snow, June 1, 1955, in Berea, KY; died of colon cancer, July 12, 2008, in Washington, DC. Press secretary and journalist. Tony Snow was already a nationally known figure in 2006 when he became press secretary for U.S. president George W. Bush. He had spent decades as a journalist, writing commentary for conservative newspapers, then joining Fox News as host of its Sunday interview show. Snow's candor, cordiality, and journalistic reputation helped him establish a good working relationship with White House reporters and defend Bush effectively, even as the president's policies became increasingly unpopular. After Snow was diagnosed with cancer, his determination to continue his work added to the admiration for him among the press and the public.

Snow was born in 1955 in Berea, Kentucky. His father was a high school teacher and administrator, his mother a nurse. He graduated from Davidson College in North Carolina in 1977. Over the next two years, he taught in Kenya and Ohio, worked as a social worker for the mentally ill in North Carolina, and studied economics and philosophy at the University of Chicago.

In 1979, Snow went into journalism, becoming an editorial writer for the *Greensboro Record* in North Carolina. He went on to write for newspapers in Norfolk and Newport News, Virginia, then in 1984 became the deputy editorial editor for the *Detroit News*, where he wrote a regular column that was published in newspapers nationwide. He met his wife, Jill, at the *News*; she was the editor's secretary. They married in 1987, the same year he was named editorial page editor of the *Washington Times*, the conservative newspaper in the nation's capital.

Snow worked for U.S. President George H. W. Bush as a speechwriter starting in 1991, though he later moved to a less prominent job in the media affairs office. After Bush left office, Snow returned to journalism and commentary, this time on radio and TV. He worked as a substitute host for radio personalities Rush Limbaugh and Diane Rehm and did commentary on the radio network NPR and the TV networks CNN and ABC.

In 1996, Snow became host of the Sunday morning public affairs show on the conservative cable network Fox News. That job, which he held for seven years, made him a nationally known figure. After Chris Wallace replaced him on the show in 2003, Snow became a radio talk show host for Fox. His

show was broadcast on 125 radio stations across the United States. Like many conservative talk radio personalities during the 2000s, Snow often criticized U.S. President George W. Bush, arguing that he was not conservative enough. He once called Bush an "impotent" leader (according to Peter Wallsten of the *Los Angeles Times*) and said conservatives considered him "something of an embarrassment."

In February of 2005, Snow was diagnosed with colon cancer, the same disease that had killed his mother. He chose aggressive treatment for it. He underwent six months of chemotherapy, and his colon was removed.

The next year, Snow made a surprising career move. He went to work for the president he had criticized. Bush and his advisors decided they needed new spokespeople to reinvigorate their administration and the Republican Party in the face of rising criticism from both Democrats and conservatives. In April of 2006, Bush named Snow his press secretary. The president laughed off Snow's past criticisms of him. "I asked him about those comments," Bush told reporters (according to Peter Baker of the *Washington Post*), "and he said, 'You should have heard what I said about the other guy.'"

Snow worked to improve Bush's standing with the public and with White House reporters. "Parlaying skills honed during years at Fox News, he offered a daily televised defense of the embattled president that was robust and at times even combative while repairing strained relations with a press corps frustrated by years of rote talking points," wrote Peter Baker of the *Washington Post*. "He enjoyed the give-and-take of a tough briefing, but his smile, upbeat energy and glib repartee seemed to take the edge off sometimes rough rhetoric."

In a departure from past press secretaries' roles, Snow also took his spokesperson job far outside the White House press room, appearing on television and conservative talk radio to make the case for Bush's policies. He even went on CNN to debate host Lou Dobbs, a strong critic of Bush's proposal to allow millions of undocumented immigrant workers to remain in the United States legally. Snow also worked to raise money for Republican candidates, which previous presidential press secretaries had not done out of fear of appearing partisan.

In March of 2007, Snow learned his cancer had returned and spread to his liver. He took a five-week health leave for treatment then returned to his job. "Why sit around and bemoan your fate?" he explained (according to Wallsten of the *Los Angeles Times*). "Go ahead and get in there, and while you're at it, enjoy every moment that you're alive."

Snow left the press secretary job that September, after 17 months, saying he wanted to make more money to support his family. Though he made $168,000 a year as press secretary, he figured he could make more on the lucrative lecture circuit. He also became a political commentator for CNN.

Snow died on July 12, 2008, at a hospital in Washington, DC, of colon cancer. He was 53. He is survived by his wife, Jill, and three children, Kendall, Kristi, and Robbie. "It was a joy to watch Tony at the podium each day," Bush said (in a statement quoted by Sheryl Gay Stolberg of the *New York Times*). "He brought wit, grace, and a great love of country to his work." **Sources:** *Los Angeles Times*, July 13, 2008, p. B11; *New York Times*, July 13, 2008, p. A21; *People*, July 28, 2008, p. 78; *Times* (London), September 5, 2008, p. 69; *Washington Post*, July 13, 2008, p. A1, p. A7.

—*Erick Trickey*

## Aleksandr Solzhenitsyn

Born Aleksandr Isayevich Solzhenitsyn, December 11, 1918, in Kislovodsk, U.S.S.R.; died from heart failure, August 3, 2008, in Moscow, Russia. Author. Dissident author Aleksandr Solzhenitsyn was acclaimed as one of the Russian language's greatest literary heroes of all time. His works exposed brutal conditions inside Soviet-era penal camps, where he himself had spent nearly a decade. "Solzhenitsyn wrote about subjects rarely tackled in Soviet or Russian literature, such as the uprising by prisoners against the authorities," noted his *Times* of London obituary, "and he did so in a vivid language permeated with the slang and vocabulary that developed in that vast network of penal labour and prison camps which has come to be known as the Gulag."

Solzhenitsyn was born in December of 1918, a little more than a year after the Bolshevik Revolution ousted an autocratic tsarist dynasty and instituted a one-party socialist state. He came from Kislovodsk, a town in the Caucasus region of the U.S.S.R., and never met his army-officer father, who died shortly before he was born. In the city of Rostov-on-Don, where a young Solzhenitsyn was raised, his mother worked as a typist and he dreamed of becoming a writer.

At Rostov University, Solzhenitsyn studied mathematics, earning his degree in 1941, and immediately enlisted in the Red Army, which was in the midst of World War II at the time. As commander of a reconnaissance unit he traveled westward with the army as it fought Nazi Germany, but in the final months of the war he incautiously made remarks about Soviet leader Josef Stalin in a letter to a school friend. The communiqué was intercepted by authorities and Solzhenitsyn was arrested and convicted on charges of publishing anti-Soviet propaganda in the summer of 1945. He was given a sentence of eight years.

Some of Solzhenitsyn's confinement was spent at Special Prison No. 16, a research facility where other educated professionals were also incarcerated. Solzhenitsyn worked on a voice-recognition project while there, but was deemed insubordinate in attitude and sent to a much harsher facility in Kazakhstan. Here he was expected to engage in truly punishing hard labor on a very meager diet, as were thousands of his fellow inmates. In between long shifts as a mineworker or as a bricklayer, he found time to write on small scraps of paper—the contents of which he memorized before destroying.

Freed in 1953, Solzhenitsyn became a high school science teacher in a town in Kazakhstan, the only place he was permitted to live. His first marriage, to a fellow student back in 1940, had by then ended, and he was diagnosed with cancer but initially was not permitted to travel to a larger city for medical treatment. Authorities finally relented, and he would later write about this lonely, frightening period of his life in his 1967 novel *Cancer Ward*, in which the tumors represent the internal burdens carried by all citizens in a repressive state.

Solzhenitsyn recovered, and in the late 1950s was permitted to return to Russia, the main Soviet republic, where he remarried first wife. Stalin died in 1953 and a few years later there was a palpable lessening of censorship rules. Solzhenitsyn submitted the manuscript of a short story set in the gulag to a leading literary journal called *Novy Mir*, and whether or not the novella *One Day in the Life of Ivan Denisovich* was to be published was actually debated at the highest levels of the Politburo, the central governing committee of the ruling Communist Party. It was deemed a politically correct work, for it fit in with current leader Nikita Khrushchev's campaign to discredit his predecessor.

*One Day in the Life of Ivan Denisovich* caused a sensation when it appeared in the November 1962 issue of *Novy Mir*, and translated versions quickly appeared in the West and made Solzhenitsyn an international literary star. Within a few years, however, the political climate shifted once again, and Solzhenitsyn was deemed a threat. His next two works were smuggled out of the country on microfilm and published abroad, again to major acclaim. These were *The First Circle* and *The Cancer Ward*. In 1970 he was recognized with the Nobel Prize in Literature by the Swedish Academy, but Soviet authorities refused to allow him to leave the country for the awards ceremony in Stockholm.

Solzhenitsyn was also embroiled in a private domestic drama after falling in love with another woman, with whom he had the first two of his three sons. His first wife balked at granting him a divorce, but finally did; she later wrote a spurious memoir of their marriage that was part of the official campaign to discredit him. In 1973, he was finally divorced, and the first part of his master opus, *The Gulag Archipelago*, was published abroad. This was the first installment of what would be a voluminous history of the Soviet penal system, presented in a fictionalized account of one victim but also bolstered by heart-wrenching first-person accounts. U.S. diplomat George F. Kennan, considered the policy architect of the cold war, "described it as 'the greatest and most powerful single indictment of a political regime ever to be leveled in modern times,'" according to Solzhenitsyn's *New York Times* obituary.

Solzhenitsyn was arrested on February 12, 1974, stripped of his Russian citizenship, and put on a plane to West Germany. He eventually settled on a remote 50-acre property in Cavendish, Vermont, with his wife and sons, where he wrote for hours in simple wooden cabin and spent decades as one of New England's most reclusive literary icons. He remained critical of the Soviet state, but also leveled charges against the West and its democracies, too. The Soviet Union collapsed in 1991, and three years later he returned via a train trip that was filmed by the British Broadcasting Corporation as a television documentary. Feted once again by the state, he saw all of his works published in Russia and even hosted a television talk show for a time. He died of heart failure at the age of 89 in Moscow on August 3, 2008. He is survived by his wife, Natalia Svetlova, and his sons Yermolai, Ignat, and Stepan. **Sources:** *Chicago Tribune,* August 4, 2008, sec. 1, pp. 1, 14; *Los Angeles Times,* August 4, 2008, pp. A1, A13; *New York Times,* August 4, 2008, pp. A1, A16; *Times (London),* August 5, 2008, p. 50; *Washington Post,* August 4, 2008, pp. A1, A12.

—*Carol Brennan*

## Jo Stafford

Born Jo Elizabeth Stafford, November 12, 1917, in Coalinga, CA; died of congestive heart failure, July 16, 2008, in Los Angeles, CA. Singer. One of the best loved singers of the 1940s and 1950s, Jo Stafford began her rise to fame during the Big Band era, achieving chart success as part of the Pied Pipers vocal group before the Tommy Dorsey Orchestra showcased her as a solo artist. Aided by such top-flight arrangers as Johnny Mercer and husband Paul Weston, she produced an astounding 87 Top 40 hits between 1944 and 1956, including such chart-toppers as "Candy," "You Belong to Me," "Make Love to Me!" and her duet with Gordon McRae, "My Darling, My Darling." Yet despite enduring popularity and the consistent high quality of her work, the singer's only Grammy award was earned with a comedy album on which she deliberately sang off-pitch.

Born in 1917 in Coalinga, California, she was the daughter of Grover Cleveland Stafford and Anna York. Prior to Stafford's birth, the elder Stafford moved the family from their farm in Gainesboro, Tennessee, to the oil fields of the San Joaquin Valley. The third of four children—Christine and Pauline were 11 and 14 years older at the time of her birth—young Jo received five years of voice lessons from KNX announcer Foster Rucker, who taught her the extraordinary breath control she would display throughout her career. At age 12, she made her debut singing "Believe Me If All Those Endearing Young Charms," and at age 16, she sang an aria from the opera *Rigoletto* at the Long Beach Terrace Theater. After completing high school, the budding vocalist joined her siblings in a harmony trio patterned after the popular Boswell Sisters called the Stafford Sisters.

Stafford sang with her sisters on local radio, appearing three nights a week on a 15-minute program for KHJ and five nights a week in the hour-long *Crockett Family of Kentucky* for KNK. This experience led to work as back-up vocalists for Twentieth Century Fox film studio on such musicals as *Alexander's Ragtime Band* and *A Damsel in Distress*. During delays in soundtrack recording, Stafford began harmonizing with members of all-male groups, the Esquires and the Rhythm Kings, achieving a rich, pleasing blend. Subsequently, when Stafford's sister Pauline married, which ended the family trio, Jo helped form a new group called the Pied Pipers.

Originally an octet, the Pied Pipers consisted of Stafford, future husband John Huddleston, Hal Cooper, Chuck Lowry, Bud Hervey, George Tait, Woody

Newbury, and Dick Whittinghill. Heard by Paul Weston and Alex Stordahl, then arrangers for Tommy Dorsey's Orchestra, the singing group was hired in 1938 as regulars on Dorsey's network radio program for Raleigh-Kool cigarettes. After only two months, the Pipers were fired by a British sponsor who thought their swinging repertoire was too racy. Quickly, the group returned to Los Angeles, became a quartet and struggled—briefly renamed Poverty Inc.—until Dorsey rehired them in 1940. Recording for the Victor label, the Pipers created quite a commercial splash, providing vocals for such Dorsey hits as "My! My!," "You've Got Me This Way," and "Let's Get Away from It All." Moreover, they backed young Frank Sinatra on such seminal hits as "I'll Never Smile Again," "Stardust," "Do I Worry," and "There Are Such Things." During this early run with the Pipers, Stafford was also the featured vocalist on Dorsey's "Yes, Indeed!," which ranked number four in 1941.

When Dorsey attempted to fire Lowry from the group, the Pipers left his employ, and Weston brought them to the newly formed Capitol Records in 1944. After two major hits ("Mairzy Doats" and "The Trolley Song,") Stafford—who had divorced Huddelston in 1943—departed to pursue a solo career. While she worked with Red Ingle and Johnny Mercer, her Capitol sides became a staple of pop radio playlists and established her as a top star in her own right. Popular among soldiers serving overseas, she was dubbed "G. I. Joe," but Stafford countered with the tongue-in-cheek suggestion that she be re-dubbed "Miss Out Going Freight."

Eschewing the nightclub route that most singers preferred, Stafford stayed viable through appearances on numerous network radio programs, including the *Carnation Contented Hour, Club Fifteen, The Railroad Hour, The Bob Crosby Show, The Chesterfield Supper Club,* and her own starring vehicle *The Jo Stafford Show.* Her international appeal was greatly enhanced when she was a host for Radio Luxembourg and Voice of America.

Ending her run with Capitol in 1950, Stafford signed with Columbia and began a fresh assault on the pop charts under the direction of producer Mitch Miller. In addition to pop fare ala "If" and "Shrimp Boats," the songstress capitalized on her predilection for country music by hitting the Top Ten with the Hank Williams-penned "Hey Good Lookin'" and "Jambalaya." Stafford also cut popular duets with such established male stars as Gordon McRae, Frankie Laine, Johnny Mercer, and Dick Haymes. Although she remained a popular star until her retirement, the advent of rock 'n' roll curtailed Stafford's hit-making abilities after 1956.

In addition to appearances on major variety programs, Stafford hosted her own 15-minute television variety program on CBS from 1954 through 1955, performing with an orchestra led by her husband Paul Weston, whom she had married in 1952. After returning to Capitol Records in 1961, Stafford also hosted the syndicated variety series *The Jo Stafford Show,* which was taped in London.

Ironically, Stafford—who was blessed with perfect pitch—won her only Grammy Award in 1960 when she and Weston assumed the identities of Jonathan and Darlene Edwards. A seemingly tone-deaf couple, the Edwards' comically slaughtered great hits and standards alike with sharp and flat notes delivered with deadpan precision. Rediscovered by the *Dr. Demento* radio show during the 1970s, Jonathan and Darlene Edwards recorded a delightfully discordant rendition of the Bee Gees' hit "Staying Alive" in 1982. It too became an instant comedy classic.

Stafford's career slowed during the mid-1960s, and she officially retired in 1975. Along with Weston she remained involved with such philanthropic organizations as SHARE and the Crippled Children Societies of California. After Weston died in 1996, Stafford withdrew from public life. She died on July 16, 2008, of congestive heart failure at the age of 90. One of the great voices of a bygone era, she is survived by her daughter Amy, a singer; son Tim, a musician/record producer; and four grandchildren.

**Sources:** Allmusic.com, http://www.allmusic.com/cg/amg.dll?p=amg&sql=11:dftxqw5ldhe (January 27, 2009); *Chicago Tribune,* July 19, 2008, sec. 1, p. 21; *Contemporary Musicians.* vol. 24, Gale Group, 1999; Internet Movie Database, http://www.imdb.com/name/nm0821300/bio (January 27, 2009); Lackman, Ron, *The Encyclopedia of American Radio,* Checkmark Books, 2000; *Los Angeles Times,* July 18, 2008, p. B6; *New York Times,* July 19, 2008, p. A15; *Times* (London), July 19, 2008, p. 68; Warner, Jay, *The Da Capo Book of American Singing Groups,* Da Capo Press, 1992; Whitburn, Joel, *The Billboard Book of Top 40 Hits,* Billboard Books, 2000; Whitburn, Joel, *Joel Whitburn's Pop Memories 1890–1954,* Record Research, 1986.

—*Ken Burke*

## Suharto

Born June 8, 1921, in Kemusu, Indonesia; died of heart, lung, and kidney problems, January 27, 2008, n Jakarta, Indonesia. Politician. Suharto, longtime president of Indonesia and one of the twentieth century's longest-reigning dictators, modernized his nation at a terrible price. He gained and held power through brutal force. Estimates of the number of Indonesians killed by the armed forces he commanded ranged from a half-million to two million. Yet Western nations considered him an ally, because he fought Communism and brought stability and economic growth to Indonesia, the world's fourth-largest country by population, a sprawling Southeast Asian nation made up of thousands of islands. During his 32 years in office, Suharto and his family allegedly siphoned billions of dollars of government money into companies they owned. In 1998, after Suharto failed to respond decisively to the East Asian economic crisis, massive protests forced him to resign and allow Indonesia to progress to democracy.

Suharto was born in 1921 in Kemusu, a village on the island of Java, which was part of the Dutch East Indies at the time. (Like many Javanese, he had only a single name.) His father was a local irrigation official. Suharto had only a junior high school education, and although he briefly took an apprenticeship at a bank in 1940, he was entirely a creature of the military. In 1940, he joined the Royal Netherlands East Indies Army, where he rose to the rank of sergeant. After Japan invaded the island in 1942, he joined a local police force, then the Fatherland Defense Corps, an army of Indonesian nationalists that supported the Japanese as a step toward independence. When Japan surrendered to Allied forces in August of 1945, at the close of World War II, and Indonesia declared independence, Suharto enlisted in what would become the Indonesian national army, which fought an intermittent war of independence against the Dutch for the next four years. Suharto eventually became a lieutenant colonel and successfully commanded a brigade in a battle with Dutch forces.

In 1959, Suharto, then a full colonel, was removed from command of a division under suspicion of smuggling. But after a year at an army college, he was promoted to general. He commanded the forces that took the western half of New Guinea from the Dutch. In 1963, he was named to a powerful post: commander of the army's strategic reserve forces in the Indonesian capital, Jakarta.

On October 1, 1965, rebels in the army murdered six generals as the first step in a coup attempt against Indonesia's president, Sukarno. Why Suharto was not assassinated with the other generals that night remained a subject of controversy his entire life. Suharto was said to have escaped death because he was visiting one of his children in the hospital that night, but many observers speculated he was involved in the plot; however, after the murders, Suharto moved quickly to suppress the coup attempt, taking effective control of the country in the process. While leaving Sukarno in the presidency as a figurehead, Suharto rearranged Indonesian politics, completely and violently.

Indonesia's Communist Party, which the president had tolerated and even encouraged, was blamed for the coup attempt. The army, which Suharto controlled, gave out arms to citizens and encouraged them to murder suspected Communists, many of them ethnic Chinese. Between a half-million and one million people died in the violence. Accounts from the time reported that Suharto dispatched army officials to organize the massacres. Scholars believe up to 750,000 people were arrested during the military crackdown after the coup and that 55,000 to 100,000 people were accused of supporting Communism and imprisoned without trial for years.

Over the next three years, Suharto consolidated his power. In March of 1966, Sukarno, the president, granted Suharto supreme authority over the country. In 1967, the People's Consultative Assembly named Suharto acting president, and the assembly officially elected him to succeed Sukarno in 1968. Suharto was reelected every five years for the next three decades.

Suharto acted boldly to set Indonesia on a new path. He resolved a confrontation with neighboring Malaysia and increased cooperation with other Southeast Asian nations. He moved Indonesia away from its once-friendly relations with Communist nations and cultivated closer relationships with the United States and Japan. The nation, bankrupt when Suharto took power, soon saw economic growth, built in part on exporting rice and oil. The annual average income of Indonesians rose from $50 in 1965 to more than $1,000 in 1996. Dire poverty, which affected 56 percent of the population when he took over, fell to 12 percent by the time he stepped down. Literacy rates and average life spans of Indonesians rose during his rule.

However, Suharto's regime often turned to murder to hold and expand its power. When East Timor declared independence from the Netherlands in 1975, Indonesia invaded it. The occupation, which lasted decades, cost 200,000 lives in a nation of 700,000 people. In the early 1980s, across Indonesia, death squads organized by army special forces killed 4,000 to 9,000 people, some of them political operatives, others criminals.

Indonesians grew increasingly unhappy with the massive wealth Suharto's family acquired. His children controlled the country's toll roads and the companies that dominated the airline, oil, and advertising industries. His wife, Siti Hartinah Suharto, known as Madame Tien, became nicknamed "Madame Tien Percent," because of the widespread belief that she extracted commissions from business deals. One leading Indonesian scholar estimated that 80 percent of large government projects were awarded to Suharto's family or friends.

After his 1993 reelection, Suharto cracked down on the country's press, which was criticizing him and calling for reform. Younger Indonesians and Islamic politicians joined the criticism of his rule. Mass demonstrations against his regime were held in 1994. Riots broke out in 1996; Suharto responded by ordering the military to shoot anyone causing a disturbance.

When East Asia plunged into an economic crisis in 1997, more unrest resulted as Indonesians protested a huge fall in the value of the country's currency and spiking prices for essentials such as fuel and cooking oil. Suharto dithered over economic reforms, but the ruling elite reelected him president in March of 1998 anyway. The nation revolted. Waves of student protests swept the country, some degenerating into riots. More than 500 students died in the street conflicts. Finally, after his cabinet resigned and students occupied the parliament building, Suharto resigned on May 21, 1998. "I am sorry for my mistakes," he told the nation (according to Marilyn Berger of the *New York Times*). His deputy, B. J. Habibie, took over as president, with free elections following soon after.

A government investigation of Suharto's business practices led to his arrest in May of 2000 on charges of embezzling up to $570 million during his 32 years in power; however, court-appointed doctors announced that Suharto was unable to stand trial because of several strokes. The case was dropped, triggering more demonstrations and riots. In 2007, prosecutors sued Suharto, again accusing him of embezzlement and seeking damages of $1.1 billion. That same year, Suharto was named at the top of a list, compiled by the United Nations and World Bank, of former world leaders who had stolen from the governments they led. The list cited an estimate that Suharto had embezzled $15 to $35 billion.

Suharto spent the last several years of his life secluded in his Jakarta home. In an interview two months before he died, he denied ever engaging in corruption. He was admitted to a hospital on January 4, 2008, with several illnesses, including low blood pressure and anemia. He died of heart, lung, and kidney problems on January 28, 2008, in Jakarta. He is survived by six children, eleven grandchildren, and one great-grandchild. **Sources:** *Los Angeles Times*, January 28, 2008, p. B7; *New York Times*, January 28, 2008, p. A20; *Times* (London), January 28, 2008, p. 49.

—*Erick Trickey*

## Germaine Tillion

Born Germaine Marie Rosine Tillion, May 30, 1907, in Allègre, Haute-Loire, France; died April 18, 2008, in St.-Mande, France. Anthropologist and French Resistance fighter. Germaine Tillion was a noted anthropologist and member of the French Resistance during World War II who spent three years in a Nazi concentration camp. One of France's most prominent intellectuals of the postwar era, Tillion became involved in Algeria's struggle for independence in the 1950s as the colony battled to be free of French control, and was later honored with the Grand Croix of the Legion d'Honneur, becoming only the fifth French woman ever to receive it.

Tillion was born in 1907 in Allègre, a city in France's Haute-Loire department, where her father served as a local magistrate. Her mother was an art historian and later a travel guide editor in Paris, where the family moved after Tillion's father died. In 1932 Tillion earned her degree from the Institut d'Ethnologie, and two years later embarked upon the first of four lengthy trips to Algeria, one of France's colonial holdings in North Africa, where she studied Berber culture in a remote mountain region. Back in France after the outbreak of World War II in 1939, she was devastated by the French government's swift surrender to Nazi Germany in the spring of the following year.

A few months later, Tillion joined one of the first organized resistance groups against the Nazi occupiers that collectively became known as the French Resistance movement. Her group was comprised of colleagues at the Museum of Man in Paris, and carried out exceedingly dangerous work to rescue French Jews and sabotage the German war effort. Two members of her group were discovered and executed, and in August of 1942 she herself was arrested at Paris's Gare de Lyon train station. Sent to the infamous Fresnes prison near Paris, she was later deported to Ravensbruck, a concentration camp in eastern Germany. Her mother, who had also aided the Resistance, was there too, and died in the gas chamber just a few months before the camp was liberated by Allied forces. While there, Tillion "learned that she had been designated to disappear without a trace, with the label NN, under Hitler's Nacht und Nebel (night and fog) decree on the fate of Resistance workers," noted her *New York Times* obituary.

Tillion later wrote a memoir of her time at Ravensbruck that bore the title of the camp. "If I survived," she wrote in it, according to the *Times* of London, "it was largely and mainly out of luck, and then from anger, the desire to reveal these crimes and, finally, because of a coalition of friendship—for I had lost the visceral desire to live." After the war, she returned to her work as an anthropologist, and her experiences in Algeria led to a government appointment to return to the North African colony in 1954 and report on the troubling situation there, as Algerians launched what would prove to be an agonizing eight-year war for independence.

Tillion's 1957 book *L'Algerie* was praised by distinguished French-Algerian writer Albert Camus, but roused the ire of some of Tillion's left-wing associates in France because she urged some type of continuing association between the two lands, arguing that Algeria should not be simply abandoned. Her views piqued the interest of leaders of the Algerian independence movement, and she found herself in an unofficial intermediary role between Algeria's National Liberation Front (FLN) and the French government during another visit. At the time, she did not know she was meeting with one of FLN's leaders, but later recalled that Yacef Saadi said to her, "You see that we are neither criminals nor murderers," to which she replied, "You are murderers," according to her *New York Times* obituary. Nevertheless, Tillion did manage to persuade Saadi to halt a bombing campaign in exchange for a promise from the French government to end the torture and execution of captured Algerian rebels.

From 1958 to 1980 Tillion taught at the School for Advanced Studies in the Social Sciences in Paris. In addition to her memoir *Ravensbruck* and books on Algeria, she also authored a groundbreaking study of patriarchy in Mediterranean world, *Le harem et les cousins,* which was published in 1966. In 2000, a volume of her collected early writings, *Il etait une fois l'ethnographie* ("Once Upon a Time There Was Ethnography") appeared, but much of her data and notebooks from the 1930s had vanished after her arrest at the Paris train station. Later in life she was a prominent supporter for the rights of illegal and legal immigrants in France from North Africa and elsewhere.

Tillion died at the age of 100 on April 18, 2008, at her home in St.-Mande, France. Never married and childless, she left no immediate survivors, but her legacy as one of France's most prominent intellectuals was assured. Of her chosen field, ethnology, she once asserted that "From the start it taught me to respect other people's culture," the *Times* of London quoted her as saying. "We are all walled gardens that must, paradoxically, communicate with others. You need to open the doors a bit, and always keep a corner where weeds can grow." **Sources:** *Guardian* (London), April 24, 2008, p. 36; *Los Angeles Times,* April 28, 2008, p. B7; *New York Times,* April 25, 2008, p. A25; *Times* (London), April 24, 2008, p. 61; *Washington Post,* April 21, 2008, p. B6.

—Carol Brennan

## Ike Turner

Born Izear Luster Turner, Jr. or Ike Wister Turner (sources differ), November 5, 1931, in Clarksdale, MS; died of an accidental cocaine overdose, December 12, 2007, in San Marcos, CA. Musician. Known early in his career as one of the musicians who gave birth to the rock'n'roll style, Ike Turner became best known for his reputedly abusive relationship with ex-wife Tina Turner. A songwriter, bandleader, talent scout, producer, and R&B musician, Turner was inducted into the Rock and Roll Hall of Fame and was the recipient of Grammy awards, both during his collaboration with his ex-wife and as a solo artist.

With a career that spanned more than six decades, Turner was best known for his performances during the late 1960s and early 1970s, when he and Tina led the band the Ike and Tina Turner Revue. Their music hit the Top 40 charts, and when they were featured as an opening act for the Rolling Stones, they found their music reaching the wider rock audience, as well as continuing to earn respect in the R&B world.

Turner was the son of a seamstress and minister, but was raised by his mother after his father was beaten to death by a racist mob. He was often in trouble as a child, involved in selling moonshine whiskey before he was a teenager. His mother bought him his first piano when he was nine years old, and he studied with Pinetop Perkins, learning to play boogie-woogie and blues. He taught himself how to play guitar. Turner began performing as a back-up musician at the age of eleven, and formed his own band soon after. Along with performing music, Turner also spent time at the local radio station, where the DJs taught him how to cue up records and segue from one to the next.

Turner's band, first called the Top Hatters and later called the Kings of Rhythm, played in clubs from the Delta region of Mississippi to Memphis, Tennessee. B. B. King took an interest in the group, helping them to secure regular weekend performances and encouraging them to record with Memphis Recording Service, which later became the well-known Sun Studios. The group wrote a song—Turner composing the introduction and first verse while the band collaborated on the rest—that became an instant hit. "Rocket 88" hit number one on the Billboard R&B chart and became known as the "record that marked the birth of rock'n'roll," according to a London *Times* article. But while the song was a huge success, Turner received little credit: Instead of being credited to Ike Turner and the Kings of Rhythm, it was listed as being performed by Jackie Brenston and the Delta Cats. Brenston was the group's saxophonist and vocalist for the song. Turner received only $20 for the work, despite it going on to sell a half a million copies.

Despite the lack of credit, Turner got work as a session guitarist, then moved to East St. Louis where he became a bandleader in local clubs, as well as a talent scout. He was performing with the 1958 incarnation of the Kings of Rhythm when he was approached by 17-year-old singer Anna Mae Bullock, who wanted to sing with them. Though at first he turned her away, she was persistent, and stories differ as to whether she convinced him or simply took the microphone. The audience was blown away by her performance, as was Turner, who brought her into the group as a regular performer and eventually renamed her Tina Turner. The pair were married in 1962, and they performed a number of hits together, including "A Fool for Love" and "It's Gonna Work Out Fine." As their popularity grew, the band was renamed the Ike and Tina Turner Revue and grew to include a number of female back-up singers called the Ike-ettes.

While they had chemistry on stage and seemed to be enjoying their success in public, their lives were darker behind the scenes. Tina accused Turner of being abusive and controlling, and though they stayed together for several years, she finally left him in 1976. To declare her independence, she refused to take any money from the divorce settlement, instead beginning her own successful solo career. Turner's life spiraled downward. He had already been involved with cocaine, and his drug use increased as his relationship and career fell apart. His studio was destroyed in a 1982 fire, and in 1990 Turner was imprisoned on drug charges.

The prison sentence forced him to miss his induction into the Rock and Roll Hall of Fame, which he perceived as a slight against his career. The *Los Angeles Times* reported that "when his award was shipped to him, it arrived broken." After Turner's release, his luck seemed to turn around when hip-hop artists Salt-N-Peppa sampled one of his songs and he received a windfall. He wrote an autobiography, sharing his side of the story that Tina had written about years earlier, trying to reclaim his reputation after it was tarnished in the movie based on her autobiography, *What's Love Got to Do with It?*

In 2001, Turner reformed the Kings of Rhythm and re-recorded their original "Rocket 88." His album *Here and Now* was nominated for a Grammy, and he toured around the world. His next solo album, *Risin' with the Blues*, won the Grammy for best traditional blues album.

Despite the negative reputation he received from the media, Turner remained unrepentant. He once told the *Los Angeles Times*, "I regret that I've screwed up my life, but I'm not ashamed of nothing I did." He was, however, frustrated with the lack of recognition he received for his musicianship outside of the industry. "You can go ask Snoop Dogg or Eminem, you can ask the Rolling Stones or [Eric] Clapton, or you can ask anybody—*anybody*—they all know my contribution to music, but it hasn't been in print about what I've done or what I've contributed until now," he was quoted as having said in the *Los Angeles Times*.

In later years Turner spoke in schools about the dangers of substance abuse, and though he spoke of his pride in having left addiction behind after his jail sentence, the San Diego County Medical Examiner's Office reported that Turner died of an accidental cocaine overdose. Turner, who was 76 when he died at his home in San Marcos, California, is survived by four of his children. **Sources:** CNN.com, http://www.cnn.com/2007/SHOWBIZ/ Music/12/12/obit.ike.turner.ap/index.htm (December 17, 2007); http://www.cnn.com/2008/ SHOWBIZ/Music/01/16/iketurner.cpcaome/index. html (January 16, 2008); *Los Angeles Times*, December 13, 2007, p. B8; *New York Times*, December 13, 2007, p. C15; *Times* (London), December 14, 2007, p. 76.

*—Alana Joli Abbot*

# Jerry Wexler

Born Gerald Wexler, January 10, 1917, in New York, NY; died of congestive heart failure, August 15, 2008, in Sarasota, FL. Record producer. Jerry Wexler, one of the most influential producers in the music industry, coined the phrase rhythm and blues to describe predominantly African-American music being created during the 1950s. The artists he produced included such notables as Ray Charles, Aretha Franklin, Wilson Pickett, and Big Joe Turner. He also signed on rock artists Led Zeppelin and Bob Dylan, though his heart was always in soul music rather than rock and roll.

"He played a major role in bringing black music to the masses, and in the evolution of rhythm and blues to soul music," Jim Henke, vice president and chief curator for the Rock and Roll Hall of Fame (which inducted Wexler in 1987) was quoted as having said in the *New York Times*. "Beyond that, he really developed the role of the record producer. Jerry did a lot more than just turn on a tape recorder. He left his stamp on a lot of great music. He had a commercial ear as well as a critical ear."

Wexler was born in New York City in 1917, the son of a Polish immigrant who worked as a window cleaner. His mother hoped that he would become a writer, but Wexler had other ideas. He disdained school, preferring to spend time in pool halls and record stores. Wexler frequented the jazz scene, going to Harlem to visit jazz clubs. In an effort to set him on the path she had chosen, Wexler's mother sent him to Kansas State College of Agriculture and Applied Science (now Kansas State University). Rather than growing academically, Wexler expanded his music horizons by traveling to Kansas City, Missouri, to explore the blues scene.

After serving two years stateside in the Army during World War II, Wexler returned to Kansas State to complete his degree in journalism. He then moved back to New York and found odd jobs, helping his father wash windows, before he was hired by Broadcast Music, Inc. (BMI) as a song plugger. Shortly thereafter, he was hired by *Billboard* magazine as a cub reporter.

In the late 1940s, *Billboard* released the top charts for music by African-American artists under a chart labeled "Race Records." Some of the staffers at *Billboard*, including Wexler, felt the term was offensive and inappropriate, and they sought a different name. "One guy said this and one guy said that, and I said, 'Rhythm and blues,' and they said: 'Oh, that sounds pretty good. Let's do that.'" Wexler once said (as quoted in the *New York Times*). "In the next issue, that section came out as Rhythm and Blues instead of Race." Wexler recalled in his autobiography, as quoted in the *Los Angeles Times*, "I was happy when it stuck; it defined a new genre of music. The handle worked its way into our language and has managed to survive four decades."

It was also during Wexler's tenure at *Billboard* that he discovered his gift for an attuned ear, and for recognizing an artist's talent and style. He met Patti Page and recommended that she perform the song "The Tennessee Waltz." After he hummed her a few bars, she was convinced, and she later recorded the song, which sold three million copies. Wexler was hired by Big Three, part of MGM Records, but in 1953, he was offered a minor partnership at Atlantic, a fledgling record label that specialized in rhythm and blues, which he accepted.

For the next decade, Wexler worked closely with Atlantic partner Ahmet Ertegun to turn Atlantic Records from a small label into a dominant and influential force in the industry. Ertegun provided a genteel attitude, while Wexler used his gruff outlook to move the music business forward. He brought Ray Charles on to the label, and Wexler and Ertegun co-produced Charles' "I've Got a Woman," his first number-one hit, in 1955. Wexler also brought Aretha Franklin over from Columbia records, encouraging her to sing not only gospel, but sexy, sultry numbers as well. That change resulted in hits like "Respect" and "Chain of Fools." Wexler's ear for music and his way of encouraging and shaping his performers led Charles to be called "King of Soul," and Franklin the "Queen of Soul." Wexler and Ertegun were so hands-on with their production approach that they introduced the phrase "produced by" on records, something that, until then, had not been acknowledged in the industry.

In the 1970s, Wexler and Ertegun's interests began to diverge: Wexler was more interested in music from the Southern style, and Ertegun was more interested in pursuing rock and roll artists. The pair sold Atlantic to Warner Brothers in 1968, and Wexler left Atlantic in 1975 to work directly for the parent company. While pursuing soul musicians and producing artists such as Dusty Springfield, Wexler introduced the idea of recording on location, inspiring his artists to immerse themselves in the appropriate environment for their music.

During the 1970s and 1980s, Wexler worked with Willie Nelson, resurrecting the artist's struggling career. He produced Bob Dylan's first Born-Again

Christian album, despite his own identity as an atheist Jew. Wexler also produced such notables as Linda Ronstadt, Dire Straits, Carlos Santana, and George Michael.

Wexler died on August 15, 2008; he was 91. He was married three times; his first two marriages ended in divorce. Wexler is survived by third wife Jean Arnold, a playwright-novelist, his daughter, Lisa, and his son, Paul. **Sources:** *Chicago Tribune,* August 16, 2008, sec. 1, p. 20; CNN.com, http://www.cnn.com/2008/SHOWBIZ/TV/08/15/jerry.wexler.ap/index.html (August 15, 2008); *Los Angeles Times,* August 16, 2008, p. B6; *New York Times,* August 16, 2008, p. B20; *Times* (London), August 18, 2008, p. 52.

—*Alana Joli Abbott*

## Richard Wright

Born Richard William Wright, July 28, 1943, in Pinner, Middlesex, England; died of cancer, September 15, 2008, in London, England. Musician. A founding member of the rock band Pink Floyd, Richard Wright was an influential musician whose thick chords and chaotic melodies on both piano and organ shaped not only the psychedelic scene in London, but impacted rock music for years to come. Shaping his style with the jazz he loved as a child, Wright wrote or co-wrote many of the songs that made Pink Floyd famous. He performed with the group as their keyboardist as well as sometimes serving as the lead singer.

Though a falling out with band member Roger Waters forced him to leave Pink Floyd for a period during the 1980s, Wright performed with the group for the majority of his career. Only one of Pink Floyd's albums does not feature Wright as a performer. Because he was not featured as prominently in the media as other band members, his influence was sometimes forgotten by critics. As Pink Floyd guitarist David Gilmour reminisced in the *Chicago Tribune,* Wright "was gentle, unassuming and private but his soulful voice and playing were vital, magical components of our most recognized Pink Floyd Sound. I have never played with anyone quite like him."

The son of a bio-chemist, Wright was born in Pinner, Middlesex, an area in northwest London. At an early age, he taught himself how to play piano, and learned to play trumpet, trombone, and guitar by the time he was ten. He attended Haberdasher's Aske's School, where he further developed his interests in classical and jazz music. Jazz was his true passion and, in his teens, he began spending time at London jazz clubs, watching artists such as Kenny Ball and Humphrey Lyttelton.

When Wright was 17 he attended the Regent Street School of Architecture, where he met fellow musicians Roger Waters and Nick Mason. They formed a small band, Sigma 6, and began performing rhythm and blues music. When they met Syd Barrett, their music really began to come together in a new and inventive way. Inspired partially by his own psychedelic drug use and mental health issues, which would force him into early retirement, Barrett led the group in an improvisational style that featured the guitar, keyboards, and bass more prominently. The four together formed the Pink Floyd Sound, named after American jazz musicians Pink Anderson and Floyd Council. They later dropped the last word and became Pink Floyd.

The band hit the new London scene at the perfect time. The "underground" movement was just beginning, and the group became celebrities in the psychedelic scene. Their first album, *The Piper at the Gates of Dawn,* was an instant success. With music that was whimsical and free-form, and that heavily featured Wright's keyboards, the album used sound techniques that were ground-breaking. The record also heralded a shift in the band's membership. Barrett's use of LSD and his fragile mental state made him unreliable, and the other members of the band sent him on his way, replacing him with guitarist David Gilmour. The new Pink Floyd continued to press their music forward beyond the rock norm, using complex compositions with jazz and classical influences. They rejected the model of the three-minute, three-chord single and combined short numbers with long, extended pieces on their albums throughout the 1960s and 1970s. They performed with full orchestras and built a post-psychedelic sound that continued to shape contemporary rock music.

Their most pivotal album, *Dark Side of the Moon,* spent 741 weeks on the Billboard album chart, longer than any other album in history. Though the concept of the album came from Waters, Wright was a huge influence, from his integration of the saxophone in several numbers to his vocal duet with Gilmour in "Time," one of the album's best known songs. *Dark Side of the Moon* was followed by two other successful albums before the group recorded *The Wall,* which stayed at the number-one spot for 15 weeks, making it the third best-selling album of all time. Wright himself was baffled by the group's popularity; the *Los Angeles Times* quoted him as having said, "I know we've made some great songs and great music, but I can't tell you why we're so popular."

Like Barrett, Wright was influenced by his drug usage; by the time Pink Floyd recorded *The Wall*, Wright struggled with a heavy cocaine addiction. This led to friction between him and the other band members, particularly Waters. Eventually Waters, who by then had taken charge of the group, became fed up with Wright's unreliability. Waters threatened not to release *The Wall* unless Wright resigned or accepted being fired. Wright continued on with the band, but only in the capacity of a salaried back-up performer, rather than a full band member. Wright toured with Pink Floyd during their concerts for *The Wall*, but then left the band in the early 1980s. Wright did not appear on Pink Floyd's subsequent album, *The Final Cut*, though he did record a solo album of his own, titled *Wet Dreams*.

Waters left Pink Floyd after *The Final Cut*, and though he declared the band dead, Gilmour and Mason resolved to keep the band alive and invited Wright back. After a legal battle surrounding whether or not the group could continue to be called Pink Floyd, the group recorded *A Momentary Lapse of Reason*, and later, *The Division Bell*. Though the group remained divided for decades, and Wright and Waters went 14 years without speaking, the four performers were reunited in 2005 at the Live 8 London concert, where they performed together a final time.

Wright was married three times, and is survived by his third wife, Millie, two sons, a daughter, and a grandson. **Sources:** *Chicago Tribune,* September 16, 2008, sec. 2, p. 5; *Los Angeles Times,* September 16, 2008, p. B9; *New York Times,* September 16, 2008, p. C13; *Times* (London), September 16, 2008, p. 60.

—*Alana Joli Abbott*

# 2009 Nationality Index

This index lists all newsmakers alphabetically under their respective nationalities. Indexes in softbound issues allow access to the current year's entries; indexes in annual hardbound volumes are cumulative, covering the entire *Newsmakers* series.

Listee names are followed by a year and issue number; thus **1996**:3 indicates that an entry on that individual appears in both 1996, Issue 3, and the 1996 cumulation. For access to newsmakers appearing earlier than the current softbound issue, see the previous year's cumulation.

**AFGHAN**
Karzai, Hamid 1955(?)- **2002**:3

**ALGERIAN**
Zeroual, Liamine 1951- **1996**:2

**AMERICAN**
Aaliyah 1979-2001 **2001**:3
Abbey, Edward 1927-1989
Obituary **1989**:3
Abbott, George 1887-1995
Obituary **1995**:3
Abbott, Jim 1967- **1988**:3
Abdul, Paula 1962- **1990**:3
Abercrombie, Josephine 1925- **1987**:2
Abernathy, Ralph 1926-1990
Obituary **1990**:3
Abraham, S. Daniel 1924- **2003**:3
Abraham, Spencer 1952- **1991**:4
Abrams, Elliott 1948- **1987**:1
Abrams, J. J. 1966- **2007**:3
Abramson, Lyn 1950- **1986**:3
Abzug, Bella 1920-1998 **1998**:2
Achtenberg, Roberta **1993**:4
Ackerman, Will 1949- **1987**:4
Acuff, Roy 1903-1992
Obituary **1993**:2
Adair, Red 1915- **1987**:3
Adams, Amy 1974- **2008**:4
Adams, Don 1923-2005
Obituary **2007**:1
Adams, Patch 1945(?)- **1999**:2
Adams, Scott 1957- **1996**:4
Adams, Yolanda 1961- **2008**:2
Adams-Geller, Paige 1969(?)- **2006**:4
Addams, Charles 1912-1988
Obituary **1989**:1
Adler, Jonathan 1966- **2006**:3
Adu, Freddy 1989- **2005**:3
Affleck, Ben 1972- **1999**:1
AFI **2007**:3
Agassi, Andre 1970- **1990**:2
Agatston, Arthur 1947- **2005**:1
Agee, Tommie 1942-2001
Obituary **2001**:4
Agnew, Spiro Theodore 1918-1996

Obituary **1997**:1
Aguilera, Christina 1980- **2000**:4
Aiello, Danny 1933- **1990**:4
Aikman, Troy 1966- **1994**:2
Ailes, Roger 1940- **1989**:3
Ailey, Alvin 1931-1989 **1989**:2
Obituary **1990**:2
Ainge, Danny 1959- **1987**:1
Akers, John F. 1934- **1988**:3
Akers, Michelle 1966- **1996**:1
Akin, Phil
Brief entry **1987**:3
Alba, Jessica 1981- **2001**:2
Albee, Edward 1928- **1997**:1
Albert, Eddie 1906-2005
Obituary **2006**:3
Albert, Marv 1943- **1994**:3
Albert, Stephen 1941- **1986**:1
Albom, Mitch 1958- **1999**:3
Albrecht, Chris 1952(?)- **2005**:4
Albright, Madeleine 1937- **1994**:3
Alda, Robert 1914-1986
Obituary **1986**:3
Alexander, Jane 1939- **1994**:2
Alexander, Jason 1962(?)- **1993**:3
Alexander, Lamar 1940- **1991**:2
Alexie, Sherman 1966- **1998**:4
Ali, Laila 1977- **2001**:2
Ali, Muhammad 1942- **1997**:2
Alioto, Joseph L. 1916-1998
Obituary **1998**:3
Allaire, Jeremy 1971- **2006**:4
Allaire, Paul 1938- **1995**:1
Allard, Linda 1940- **2003**:2
Allen, Bob 1935- **1992**:4
Allen, Debbie 1950- **1998**:2
Allen, Joan 1956- **1998**:1
Allen, John 1930- **1992**:1
Allen, Mel 1913-1996
Obituary **1996**:4
Allen, Ray 1975- **2002**:1
Allen, Steve 1921-2000
Obituary **2001**:2
Allen, Tim 1953- **1993**:1
Allen, Woody 1935- **1994**:1
Allen Jr., Ivan 1911-2003
Obituary **2004**:3

Alley, Kirstie 1955- **1990**:3
Allred, Gloria 1941- **1985**:2
Allyson, June 1917-2006
Obituary **2007**:3
Alsop, Marin 1956- **2008**:3
Alter, Hobie
Brief entry **1985**:1
Altman, Robert 1925- **1993**:2
Altman, Sidney 1939- **1997**:2
Alvarez, Aida **1999**:2
Ambrose, Stephen 1936- **2002**:3
Ameche, Don 1908-1993
Obituary **1994**:2
Amory, Cleveland 1917-1998
Obituary **1999**:2
Amos, Tori 1963- **1995**:1
Amos, Wally 1936- **2000**:1
Amsterdam, Morey 1912-1996
Obituary **1997**:1
Anastas, Robert
Brief entry **1985**:2
Ancier, Garth 1957- **1989**:1
Anderson, Brad 1949- **2007**:3
Anderson, Gillian 1968- **1997**:1
Anderson, Harry 1951(?)- **1988**:2
Anderson, Laurie 1947- **2000**:2
Anderson, Marion 1897-1993
Obituary **1993**:4
Anderson, Poul 1926-2001
Obituary **2002**:3
Anderson, Tom and Chris
DeWolfe **2007**:2
Andreessen, Marc 1972- **1996**:2
Andrews, Lori B. 1952- **2005**:3
Andrews, Maxene 1916-1995
Obituary **1996**:2
Angelos, Peter 1930- **1995**:4
Angelou, Maya 1928- **1993**:4
Angier, Natalie 1958- **2000**:3
Aniston, Jennifer 1969- **2000**:3
Annenberg, Walter 1908- **1992**:3
Anthony, Earl 1938-2001
Obituary **2002**:3
Anthony, Marc 1969- **2000**:3
Antonini, Joseph 1941- **1991**:2
Apatow, Judd 1967- **2006**:3
Apple, Fiona 1977- **2006**:3

Applegate, Christina 1972- **2000**:4
Applewhite, Marshall Herff
  1931-1997
  Obituary **1997**:3
Arad, Avi 1948- **2003**:2
Archer, Dennis 1942- **1994**:4
Arden, Eve 1912(?)-1990
  Obituary **1991**:2
Aretsky, Ken 1941- **1988**:1
Arison, Ted 1924- **1990**:3
Arkin, Alan 1934- **2007**:4
Arkoff, Samuel Z. 1918-2001
  Obituary **2002**:4
Arledge, Roone 1931- **1992**:2
Arlen, Harold 1905-1986
  Obituary **1986**:3
Arman 1928- **1993**:1
Armstrong, Anne 1927-2008
  Obituary **2009**:4
Armstrong, C. Michael 1938- **2002**:1
Armstrong, Henry 1912-1988
  Obituary **1989**:1
Armstrong, Lance 1971- **2000**:1
Arnaz, Desi 1917-1986
  Obituary **1987**:1
Arnold, Eddy 1918-2008
  Obituary **2009**:2
Arnold, Tom 1959- **1993**:2
Aronson, Jane 1951- **2009**:3
Arquette, Patricia 1968- **2001**:3
Arquette, Rosanna 1959- **1985**:2
Arrau, Claudio 1903-1991
  Obituary **1992**:1
Arrested Development **1994**:2
Arthur, Jean 1901(?)-1991
  Obituary **1992**:1
Ash, Mary Kay 1915(?)- **1996**:1
Ashanti 1980- **2004**:1
Ashcroft, John 1942- **2002**:4
Ashe, Arthur 1943-1993
  Obituary **1993**:3
Aspin, Les 1938-1995
  Obituary **1996**:1
Astaire, Fred 1899-1987
  Obituary **1987**:4
Astin, Sean 1971- **2005**:1
Astor, Brooke 1902-2007
  Obituary **2008**:4
Astor, Mary 1906-1987
  Obituary **1988**:1
Atkins, Robert C. 1930-2003
  Obituary **2004**:2
Atwater, Lee 1951-1991 **1989**:4
  Obituary **1991**:4
Aucoin, Kevyn 1962- **2001**:3
Auerbach, Red 1911-2006
  Obituary **2008**:1
Aurre, Laura
  Brief entry **1986**:3
Austin, Stone Cold Steve
  1964- **2001**:3
Autry, Gene 1907-1998
  Obituary **1999**:1
Avedon, Richard 1923- **1993**:4
Axelrod, Julius 1912-2004
  Obituary **2006**:1
Axthelm, Pete 1943(?)-1991
  Obituary **1991**:3
Aykroyd, Dan 1952- **1989**:3
Azaria, Hank 1964- **2001**:3
Azinger, Paul 1960- **1995**:2
Babbitt, Bruce 1938- **1994**:1

Babilonia, Tai 1959- **1997**:2
Bacall, Lauren 1924- **1997**:3
Backstreet Boys **2001**:3
Backus, Jim 1913-1989
  Obituary **1990**:1
Backus, John W. 1924-2007
  Obituary **2008**:2
Bacon, Kevin 1958- **1995**:3
Badgley, Mark and James
  Mischka **2004**:3
Badu, Erykah 1971- **2000**:4
Baez, Joan 1941- **1998**:3
Bahcall, John N. 1934-2005
  Obituary **2006**:4
Bailey, F. Lee 1933- **1995**:4
Bailey, Pearl 1918-1990
  Obituary **1991**:1
Baird, Bill
  Brief entry **1987**:2
Baiul, Oksana 1977- **1995**:3
Baker, Anita 1958- **1987**:4
Baker, James A. III 1930- **1991**:2
Baker, Kathy
  Brief entry **1986**:1
Bakker, Robert T. 1950(?)- **1991**:3
Bakula, Scott 1954- **2003**:1
Baldessari, John 1931(?)- **1991**:4
Baldrige, Malcolm 1922-1987
  Obituary **1988**:1
Baldwin, Alec 1958- **2002**:2
Baldwin, James 1924-1987
  Obituary **1988**:2
Ball, Alan 1957- **2005**:1
Ball, Edward 1959- **1999**:2
Ball, Lucille 1911-1989
  Obituary **1989**:3
Ball, Michael 1964(?)- **2007**:3
Ballard, Robert D. 1942- **1998**:4
Ballmer, Steven 1956- **1997**:2
Bancroft, Anne 1931-2005
  Obituary **2006**:3
Banks, Dennis J. 193- **1986**:4
Banks, Jeffrey 1953- **1998**:2
Banks, Russell 1940- **2009**:2
Banks, Tyra 1973- **1996**:3
Barad, Jill 1951- **1994**:2
Baraka, Amiri 1934- **2000**:3
Baranski, Christine 1952- **2001**:2
Barber, Red 1908-1992
  Obituary **1993**:2
Barber, Tiki 1975- **2007**:1
Barbera, Joseph 1911- **1988**:2
Barkin, Ellen 1955- **1987**:3
Barkley, Charles 1963- **1988**:2
Barks, Carl 1901-2000
  Obituary **2001**:2
Barksdale, James L. 1943- **1998**:2
Barnes, Brenda C. 1955(?)- **2007**:4
Barnes, Ernie 1938- **1997**:4
Barney **1993**:4
Barnouin, Kim 1971-. See Kim
  Barnouin and Rory Freedman
Barr, Roseanne 1953(?)- **1989**:1
Barrett, Craig R. 1939- **1999**:4
Barry, Dave 1947(?)- **1991**:2
Barry, Lynda 1956(?)- **1992**:1
Barry, Marion 1936- **1991**:1
Barrymore, Drew 1975- **1995**:3
Barshefsky, Charlene 1951(?)- **2000**:4
Baryshnikov, Mikhail
  Nikolaevich 1948- **1997**:3
Basie, Count 1904(?)-1984

  Obituary **1985**:1
Basinger, Kim 1953- **1987**:2
Bass, Karen 1953- **2009**:3
Bassett, Angela 1959(?)- **1994**:4
Bateman, Jason 1969- **2005**:3
Bateman, Justine 1966- **1988**:4
Bates, Kathy 1949(?)- **1991**:4
Battle, Kathleen 1948- **1998**:1
Bauer, Eddie 1899-1986
  Obituary **1986**:3
Baumgartner, Bruce
  Brief entry **1987**:3
Baxter, Anne 1923-1985
  Obituary **1986**:1
Baxter, Pamela 1949- **2009**:4
Bayley, Corrine
  Brief entry **1986**:4
Beal, Deron 1968(?)- **2005**:3
Beals, Jennifer 1963- **2005**:2
Beals, Vaughn 1928- **1988**:2
Beame, Abraham 1906-2001
  Obituary **2001**:4
Bean, Alan L. 1932- **1986**:2
Beattie, Owen
  Brief entry **1985**:2
Beatty, Warren 1937- **2000**:1
Bechdel, Alison 1960- **2007**:3
Beck 1970- **2000**:2
Becker, Brian 1957(?)- **2004**:4
Bedford, Deborah 1958- **2006**:3
Beene, Geoffrey 1927-2004
  Obituary **2005**:4
Beers, Charlotte 1935- **1999**:3
Begaye, Kelsey 1950(?)- **1999**:3
Beinecke, Frances 1960(?)- **2007**:4
Bell, Art 1945- **2000**:1
Bell, Ricky 1955-1984
  Obituary **1985**:1
Bellamy, Carol 1942- **2001**:2
Belle, Albert 1966- **1996**:4
Bellissimo, Wendy 1967(?)- **2007**:1
Bellow, Saul 1915-2005
  Obituary **2006**:2
Belluzzo, Rick 1953- **2001**:3
Belushi, Jim 1954- **1986**:2
Belzer, Richard 1944- **1985**:3
Ben & Jerry **1991**:3
Benatar, Pat 1953- **1986**:1
Benchley, Peter 1940-2006
  Obituary **2007**:1
Benes, Francine 1946- **2008**:2
Bening, Annette 1958(?)- **1992**:1
Bennett, Joan 1910-1990
  Obituary **1991**:2
Bennett, Michael 1943-1987
  Obituary **1988**:1
Bennett, Tony 1926- **1994**:4
Bennett, William 1943- **1990**:1
Benoit, Joan 1957- **1986**:3
Benson, Ezra Taft 1899-1994
  Obituary **1994**:4
Bentley, Dierks 1975- **2007**:3
Bentsen, Lloyd 1921- **1993**:3
Bergalis, Kimberly 1968(?)-1991
  Obituary **1992**:3
Bergen, Candice 1946- **1990**:1
Berger, Sandy 1945- **2000**:1
Berkley, Seth 1956- **2002**:3
Berle, Milton 1908-2002
  Obituary **2003**:2
Berle, Peter A.A.
  Brief entry **1987**:3

Berlin, Irving 1888-1989
  Obituary **1990**:1
Berliner, Andy and Rachel **2008**:2
Berman, Gail 1957(?)- **2006**:1
Berman, Jennifer and Laura **2003**:2
Bern, Dorrit J. 1950(?)- **2006**:3
Bernanke, Ben 1953- **2008**:3
Bernardi, Herschel 1923-1986
  Obituary **1986**:4
Bernardin, Cardinal Joseph
  1928-1996 **1997**:2
Bernhard, Sandra 1955(?)- **1989**:4
Bernsen, Corbin 1955- **1990**:2
Bernstein, Elmer 1922-2004
  Obituary **2005**:4
Bernstein, Leonard 1918-1990
  Obituary **1991**:1
Berresford, Susan V. 1943- **1998**:4
Berry, Chuck 1926- **2001**:2
Berry, Halle 1968- **1996**:2
Bethe, Hans 1906-2005
  Obituary **2006**:2
Bettelheim, Bruno 1903-1990
  Obituary **1990**:3
Beyonce 1981- **2009**:3
Bezos, Jeff 1964- **1998**:4
Bialik, Mayim 1975- **1993**:3
Bias, Len 1964(?)-1986
  Obituary **1986**:3
Bibliowicz, Jessica 1959- **2009**:3
Biden, Joe 1942- **1986**:3
Bieber, Owen 1929- **1986**:1
Biehl, Amy 1967(?)-1993
  Obituary **1994**:1
Bigelow, Kathryn 1952(?)- **1990**:4
Bikoff, J. Darius 1962(?)- **2007**:3
Bikoff, James L.
  Brief entry **1986**:2
Billington, James 1929- **1990**:3
Birch, Thora 1982- **2002**:4
Bird, Brad 1956(?)- **2005**:4
Bird, Larry 1956- **1990**:3
Bishop, Andre 1948- **2000**:1
Bishop, Joey 1918-2007
  Obituary **2008**:4
Bissell, Patrick 1958-1987
  Obituary **1988**:2
Bixby, Bill 1934-1993
  Obituary **1994**:2
Black, Carole 1945- **2003**:1
Black, Cathleen 1944- **1998**:4
Black, Jack 1969- **2002**:3
Black Eyed Peas **2006**:2
Blackmun, Harry A. 1908-1999
  Obituary **1999**:3
Blackstone, Harry Jr. 1934-1997
  Obituary **1997**:4
Blaine, David 1973- **2003**:3
Blair, Bonnie 1964- **1992**:3
Blakey, Art 1919-1990
  Obituary **1991**:1
Blanc, Mel 1908-1989
  Obituary **1989**:4
Blass, Bill 1922-2002
  Obituary **2003**:3
Bledsoe, Drew 1972- **1995**:1
Blige, Mary J. 1971- **1995**:3
Bloch, Erich 1925- **1987**:4
Bloch, Henry 1922- **1988**:4
Bloch, Ivan 1940- **1986**:3
Block, Herbert 1909-2001
  Obituary **2002**:4

Bloodworth-Thomason,
  Linda 1947- **1994**:1
Bloomberg, Michael 1942- **1997**:1
Blume, Judy 1936- **1998**:4
Blumenthal, Susan J. 1951(?)- **2007**:3
Bly, Robert 1926- **1992**:4
Blyth, Myrna 1939- **2002**:4
Bochco, Steven 1943- **1989**:1
Boehner, John A. 1949- **2006**:4
Boggs, Wade 1958- **1989**:3
Bogosian, Eric 1953- **1990**:4
Bohbot, Michele 1959(?)- **2004**:2
Boiardi, Hector 1897-1985
  Obituary **1985**:3
Boies, David 1941- **2002**:1
Boitano, Brian 1963- **1988**:3
Bolger, Ray 1904-1987
  Obituary **1987**:2
Bollinger, Lee C. 1946- **2003**:2
Bolton, Michael 1953(?)- **1993**:2
Bombeck, Erma 1927-1996
  Obituary **1996**:4
Bonds, Barry 1964- **1993**:3
Bonet, Lisa 1967- **1989**:2
Bonilla, Bobby 1963- **1992**:2
Bon Jovi, Jon 1962- **1987**:4
Bonner, Robert 1942(?)- **2003**:4
Bono, Sonny 1935-1998 **1992**:2
  Obituary **1998**:2
Bontecou, Lee 1931- **2004**:4
Boone, Mary 1951- **1985**:1
Booth, Shirley 1898-1992
  Obituary **1993**:2
Bopp, Thomas 1949- **1997**:3
Borofsky, Jonathan 1942- **2006**:4
Bose, Amar
  Brief entry **1986**:4
Bosworth, Brian 1965- **1989**:1
Bosworth, Kate 1983- **2006**:3
Botstein, Leon 1946- **1985**:3
Boudreau, Louis 1917-2001
  Obituary **2002**:3
Bourdain, Anthony 1956- **2008**:3
Bowe, Riddick 1967(?)- **1993**:2
Bowen, Julie 1970- **2007**:1
Bowles, Paul 1910-1999
  Obituary **2000**:3
Bowman, Scotty 1933- **1998**:4
Boxcar Willie 1931-1999
  Obituary **1999**:4
Boxer, Barbara 1940- **1995**:1
Boyer, Herbert Wayne 1936- **1985**:1
Boyington, Gregory Pappy
  1912-1988
  Obituary **1988**:2
Boyle, Gertrude 1924- **1995**:3
Boyle, Lara Flynn 1970- **2003**:4
Boyle, Peter 1935- **2002**:3
Boyle, T. C. 1948- **2007**:2
Boynton, Sandra 1953- **2004**:1
Bradford, Barbara Taylor
  1933- **2002**:4
Bradley, Bill 1943- **2000**:2
Bradley, Ed 1941-2006
  Obituary **2008**:1
Bradley, Todd 1958- **2003**:3
Bradley, Tom 1917-1998
  Obituary **1999**:1
Bradshaw, John 1933- **1992**:1
Brady, Sarah and James S. **1991**:4
Brady, Tom 1977- **2002**:4
Brady, Wayne 1972- **2008**:3

Braff, Zach 1975- **2005**:2
Brando, Marlon 1924-2004
  Obituary **2005**:3
Brandy 1979- **1996**:4
Bratt, Benjamin 1963- **2009**:3
Braun, Carol Moseley 1947- **1993**:1
Bravo, Ellen 1944- **1998**:2
Bravo, Rose Marie 1951(?)- **2005**:3
Braxton, Toni 1967- **1994**:3
Brazile, Donna 1959- **2001**:1
Breathed, Berkeley 1957- **2005**:3
Bremen, Barry 1947- **1987**:3
Bremer, L. Paul 1941- **2004**:2
Brennan, Edward A. 1934- **1989**:1
Brennan, Robert E. 1943(?)- **1988**:1
Brennan, William 1906-1997
  Obituary **1997**:4
Brenneman, Amy 1964- **2002**:1
Breyer, Stephen Gerald 1938- **1994**:4
Bridges, Lloyd 1913-1998
  Obituary **1998**:3
Brillstein, Bernie 1931-2008
  Obituary **2009**:4
Brinker, Nancy 1946- **2007**:1
Brinkley, David 1920-2003
  Obituary **2004**:3
Bristow, Lonnie 1930- **1996**:1
Brite, Poppy Z. 1967- **2005**:1
Brockovich-Ellis, Erin 1960- **2003**:3
Brody, Adrien 1973- **2006**:3
Brokaw, Tom 1940- **2000**:3
Bronfman, Edgar, Jr. 1955- **1994**:4
Bronson, Charles 1921-2003
  Obituary **2004**:4
Brooks, Albert 1948(?)- **1991**:4
Brooks, Diana D. 1950- **1990**:1
Brooks, Garth 1962- **1992**:1
Brooks, Gwendolyn
  1917-2000 **1998**:1
  Obituary **2001**:2
Brooks, Mel 1926- **2003**:1
Brosius, Christopher **2007**:1
Brower, David 1912- **1990**:4
Brown, Bobbi 1957- **2001**:4
Brown, Dan 1964- **2004**:4
Brown, Dee 1908-2002
  Obituary **2004**:1
Brown, Edmund G., Sr. 1905-1996
  Obituary **1996**:3
Brown, Howard and Karen
  Stewart **2007**:3
Brown, J. Carter 1934-2002
  Obituary **2003**:3
Brown, James 1928(?)- **1991**:4
Brown, Jerry 1938- **1992**:4
Brown, Jim 1936- **1993**:2
Brown, John Seely 1940- **2004**:1
Brown, Judie 1944- **1986**:2
Brown, Les 1912-2001
  Obituary **2001**:3
Brown, Les 1945- **1994**:3
Brown, Paul 1908-1991
  Obituary **1992**:1
Brown, Ron 1941- **1990**:3
Brown, Ron 1941-1996
  Obituary **1996**:4
Brown, Ruth 1928-2006
  Obituary **2008**:1
Brown, Willie 1934- **1996**:4
Brown, Willie L. 1934- **1985**:2
Browner, Carol M. 1955- **1994**:1
Browning, Edmond

Brief entry **1986**:2
Bruckheimer, Jerry 1945- **2007**:2
Bryant, Kobe 1978- **1998**:3
Brynner, Yul 1920(?)-1985
    Obituary **1985**:4
Buchanan, Pat 1938- **1996**:3
Buchwald, Art 1925-2007
    Obituary **2008**:2
Buck, Linda 1956(?)- **2004**:2
Buckley, Betty 1947- **1996**:2
Buckley, Jeff 1966-1997
    Obituary **1997**:4
Buffett, Jimmy 1946- **1999**:3
Buffett, Warren 1930- **1995**:2
Bujones, Fernando 1955-2005
    Obituary **2007**:1
Bullock, Sandra 1967- **1995**:4
Bundy, McGeorge 1919-1996
    Obituary **1997**:1
Bundy, William P. 1917-2000
    Obituary **2001**:2
Bunshaft, Gordon 1909-1990 **1989**:3
    Obituary **1991**:1
Burch, Tory 1966- **2009**:3
Burck, Wade
    Brief entry **1986**:1
Burger, Warren E. 1907-1995
    Obituary **1995**:4
Burk, Martha 1941- **2004**:1
Burnett, Carol 1933- **2000**:3
Burnison, Chantal Simone
    1950(?)- **1988**:3
Burns, Charles R.
    Brief entry **1988**:1
Burns, Edward 1968- **1997**:1
Burns, George 1896-1996
    Obituary **1996**:3
Burns, Ken 1953- **1995**:2
Burns, Robin 1953(?)- **1991**:2
Burr, Donald Calvin 1941- **1985**:3
Burroughs, William S. 1914- **1994**:2
Burroughs, William S. 1914-1997
    Obituary **1997**:4
Burrows, James 1940- **2005**:3
Burstyn, Ellen 1932- **2001**:4
Burton, Jake 1954- **2007**:1
Burton, Tim 1959- **1993**:1
Burum, Stephen H.
    Brief entry **1987**:2
Buscaglia, Leo 1924-1998
    Obituary **1998**:4
Buscemi, Steve 1957- **1997**:4
Busch, August A. III 1937- **1988**:2
Busch, August Anheuser, Jr.
    1899-1989
    Obituary **1990**:2
Busch, Charles 1954- **1998**:3
Busch, Kurt 1978- **2006**:1
Bush, Barbara 1925- **1989**:3
Bush, George W., Jr. 1946- **1996**:4
Bush, Jeb 1953- **2003**:1
Bush, Millie 1987- **1992**:1
Bushnell, Candace 1959(?)- **2004**:2
Bushnell, Nolan 1943- **1985**:1
Buss, Jerry 1933- **1989**:3
Butcher, Susan 1954- **1991**:1
Butler, Brett 1958(?)- **1995**:1
Butler, Octavia E. 1947- **1999**:3
Butterfield, Paul 1942-1987
    Obituary **1987**:3
Buttons, Red 1919-2006
    Obituary **2007**:3

Bynes, Amanda 1986- **2005**:1
Caan, James 1939- **2004**:4
Cabot, Meg 1967- **2008**:4
Caen, Herb 1916-1997
    Obituary **1997**:4
Caesar, Adolph 1934-1986
    Obituary **1986**:3
Cage, John 1912-1992
    Obituary **1993**:1
Cage, Nicolas 1964- **1991**:1
Cagney, James 1899-1986
    Obituary **1986**:2
Cain, Herman 1945- **1998**:3
Calhoun, Rory 1922-1999
    Obituary **1999**:4
Caliguiri, Richard S. 1931-1988
    Obituary **1988**:3
Callaway, Ely 1919-2001
    Obituary **2002**:3
Calloway, Cab 1908-1994
    Obituary **1995**:2
Calloway, D. Wayne 1935- **1987**:3
Cameron, David
    Brief entry **1988**:1
Cammermeyer, Margarethe
    1942- **1995**:2
Campanella, Roy 1921-1993
    Obituary **1994**:1
Campbell, Bebe Moore 1950- **1996**:2
Campbell, Ben Nighthorse
    1933- **1998**:3
Campbell, Bill **1997**:1
Campbell, Erica 1972-. See Mary
    Mary
Campbell, Tina 1972-. See Mary
    Mary
Canfield, Alan B.
    Brief entry **1986**:3
Cannon, Nick 1980- **2006**:4
Cantrell, Ed
    Brief entry **1985**:3
Caplan, Arthur L. 1950- **2000**:2
Capriati, Jennifer 1976- **1991**:1
Caras, Roger 1928-2001
    Obituary **2002**:1
Caray, Harry 1914(?)-1998 **1988**:3
    Obituary **1998**:3
Carcaterra, Lorenzo 1954- **1996**:1
Card, Andrew H., Jr. 1947- **2003**:2
Carell, Steve 1963- **2006**:4
Carey, Drew 1958- **1997**:4
Carey, Mariah 1970(?)- **1991**:3
Carey, Ron 1936- **1993**:3
Carlin, George 1937- **1996**:3
Carlino, Cristina 1961(?)- **2008**:4
Carlisle, Belinda 1958- **1989**:3
Carlson, Richard 1961- **2002**:1
Carmona, Richard 1949- **2003**:2
Carnahan, Jean 1933- **2001**:2
Carnahan, Mel 1934-2000
    Obituary **2001**:2
Carney, Art 1918-2003
    Obituary **2005**:1
Carpenter, Mary-Chapin
    1958(?)- **1994**:1
Carradine, John 1906-1988
    Obituary **1989**:2
Carson, Ben 1951- **1998**:2
Carson, Johnny 1925-2005
    Obituary **2006**:1
Carson, Lisa Nicole 1969- **1999**:3
Carter, Amy 1967- **1987**:4

Carter, Benny 1907-2003
    Obituary **2004**:3
Carter, Billy 1937-1988
    Obituary **1989**:1
Carter, Chris 1956- **2000**:1
Carter, Gary 1954- **1987**:1
Carter, Jimmy 1924- **1995**:1
Carter, Joe 1960- **1994**:2
Carter, Nell 1948-2003
    Obituary **2004**:2
Carter, Ron 1937- **1987**:3
Carter, Rubin 1937- **2000**:3
Carter, Stephen L. **2008**:2
Carter, Vince 1977- **2001**:4
Cartwright, Carol Ann 1941- **2009**:4
Caruso, David 1956(?)- **1994**:3
Carver, Raymond 1938-1988
    Obituary **1989**:1
Carvey, Dana 1955- **1994**:1
Case, Steve 1958- **1995**:4
Casey, William 1913-1987
    Obituary **1987**:3
Cash, Johnny 1932- **1995**:3
Cash, June Carter 1929-2003
    Obituary **2004**:2
Cassavetes, John 1929-1989
    Obituary **1989**:2
Cassidy, Mike 1963(?)- **2006**:1
Cassini, Oleg 1913-2006
    Obituary **2007**:2
Castelli, Leo 1907-1999
    Obituary **2000**:1
Castellucci, Cecil 1969- **2008**:3
Castillo, Ana 1953- **2000**:4
Catlett, Elizabeth 1915(?)- **1999**:3
Cattrall, Kim 1956- **2003**:3
Caulfield, Joan 1922(?)-1991
    Obituary **1992**:1
Cavazos, Lauro F. 1927- **1989**:2
Caviezel, Jim 1968- **2005**:3
Centrello, Gina 1959(?)- **2008**:3
Cerf, Vinton G. 1943- **1999**:2
Chabon, Michael 1963- **2002**:1
Chaing Kai-Shek, Madame
    1898-2003
    Obituary **2005**:1
Chamberlain, Joba 1985- **2008**:3
Chamberlain, Wilt 1936-1999
    Obituary **2000**:2
Chamberlin, Wendy 1948- **2002**:4
Chancellor, John
    Obituary **1997**:1
Chaney, John 1932- **1989**:1
Channing, Stockard 1946- **1991**:3
Chao, Elaine L. 1953- **2007**:3
Chapman, Tracy 1964- **1989**:2
Chappell, Tom 1943- **2002**:3
Chappelle, Dave 1973- **2005**:3
Charisse, Cyd 1922-2008
    Obituary **2009**:3
Charles, Ray 1930-2004
    Obituary **2005**:3
Charron, Paul 1942- **2004**:1
Chase, Chevy 1943- **1990**:1
Chase, Debra Martin 1956- **2009**:1
Chast, Roz 1955- **1992**:4
Chastain, Brandi 1968- **2001**:3
Chatham, Russell 1939- **1990**:1
Chaudhari, Praveen 1937- **1989**:4
Chavez, Cesar 1927-1993
    Obituary **1993**:4
Chavez, Linda 1947- **1999**:3

Chavez-Thompson, Linda 1944-
**1999**:1
Chavis, Benjamin 1948- **1993**:4
Cheadle, Don 1964- **2002**:1
Cheatham, Adolphus Doc 1905-1997
Obituary **1997**:4
Cheek, James Edward
Brief entry **1987**:1
Chen, Steve and Chad Hurley
**2007**:2
Chenault, Kenneth I. 1951- **1999**:3
Cheney, Dick 1941- **1991**:3
Cheney, Lynne V. 1941- **1990**:4
Cher 1946- **1993**:1
Chesney, Kenny 1968- **2008**:2
Chia, Sandro 1946- **1987**:2
Chihuly, Dale 1941- **1995**:2
Chiklis, Michael 1963- **2003**:3
Child, Julia 1912- **1999**:4
Chisholm, Shirley 1924-2005
Obituary **2006**:1
Chittister, Joan D. 1936- **2002**:2
Chizen, Bruce 1955(?)- **2004**:2
Cho, Margaret 1970- **1995**:2
Chouinard, Yvon 1938(?)- **2002**:2
Christensen, Kate 1962- **2009**:4
Christopher, Warren 1925- **1996**:3
Chu, Paul C.W. 1941- **1988**:2
Chung, Connie 1946- **1988**:4
Chyna 1970- **2001**:4
Cisneros, Henry 1947- **1987**:2
Claiborne, Liz 1929- **1986**:3
Clancy, Tom 1947- **1998**:4
Clark, J. E.
Brief entry **1986**:1
Clark, Jim 1944- **1997**:1
Clark, Kenneth B. 1914-2005
Obituary **2006**:3
Clark, Marcia 1954(?)- **1995**:1
Clark, Mary Higgins 1929- **2000**:4
Clark, Maxine 1949- **2009**:4
Clarke, Richard A. 1951(?)- **2002**:2
Clarke, Stanley 1951- **1985**:4
Clarkson, Kelly 1982- **2003**:3
Clarkson, Patricia 1959- **2005**:3
Clavell, James 1924(?)-1994
Obituary **1995**:1
Clay, Andrew Dice 1958- **1991**:1
Cleaver, Eldridge 1935-1998
Obituary **1998**:4
Clemens, Roger 1962- **1991**:4
Clements, George 1932- **1985**:1
Cleveland, James 1932(?)-1991
Obituary **1991**:3
Cliburn, Van 1934- **1995**:1
Clinton, Bill 1946- **1992**:1
Clinton, Hillary Rodham
1947- **1993**:2
Clooney, George 1961- **1996**:4
Clooney, Rosemary 1928-2002
Obituary **2003**:4
Close, Glenn 1947- **1988**:3
Clowes, Daniel 1961- **2007**:1
Clyburn, James 1940- **1999**:4
Cobain, Kurt 1967-1944
Obituary **1994**:3
Coburn, James 1928-2002
Obituary **2004**:1
Coca, Imogene 1908-2001
Obituary **2002**:2
Cochran, Johnnie 1937- **1996**:1
Coco, James 1929(?)-1987

Obituary **1987**:2
Codrescu, Andreaa 1946- **1997**:3
Cody, Diablo 1978- **2009**:1
Coen, Joel and Ethan **1992**:1
Coffin, William Sloane, Jr.
1924- **1990**:3
Cohen, William S. 1940- **1998**:1
Colasanto, Nicholas 1923(?)-1985
Obituary **1985**:2
Colbert, Stephen 1964- **2007**:4
Colby, William E. 1920-1996
Obituary **1996**:4
Cole, Anne 1930(?)- **2007**:3
Cole, Johnetta B. 1936- **1994**:3
Cole, Kenneth 1954(?)- **2003**:1
Cole, Natalie 1950- **1992**:4
Coleman, Dabney 1932- **1988**:3
Coleman, Sheldon, Jr. 1953- **1990**:2
Coles, Robert 1929(?)- **1995**:1
Collier, Sophia 1956(?)- **2001**:2
Collins, Albert 1932-1993
Obituary **1994**:2
Collins, Billy 1941- **2002**:2
Collins, Cardiss 1931- **1995**:3
Collins, Eileen 1956- **1995**:3
Collins, Kerry 1972- **2002**:3
Colwell, Rita Rossi 1934- **1999**:3
Combs, Sean Puffy 1970- **1998**:4
Commager, Henry Steele 1902-1998
Obituary **1998**:3
Como, Perry 1912-2001
Obituary **2002**:2
Condit, Phil 1941- **2001**:3
Condon, Bill 1955- **2007**:3
Condon, Richard 1915-1996
Obituary **1996**:4
Conigliaro, Tony 1945-1990
Obituary **1990**:3
Connally, John 1917-1993
Obituary **1994**:1
Connelly, Jennifer 1970- **2002**:4
Connelly, Michael 1956- **2007**:1
Conner, Bruce 1933-2008
Obituary **2009**:3
Conner, Dennis 1943- **1987**:2
Connerly, Ward 1939- **2000**:2
Connick, Harry, Jr. 1967- **1991**:1
Conrad, Pete 1930-1999
Obituary **2000**:1
Convy, Bert 1934(?)-1991
Obituary **1992**:1
Conyers, John, Jr. 1929- **1999**:1
Cook, Robin 1940- **1996**:3
Cooke, Alistair 1908-2004
Obituary **2005**:3
Coolio 1963- **1996**:4
Cooper, Alexander 1936- **1988**:4
Cooper, Anderson 1967- **2006**:1
Cooper, Chris 1951- **2004**:1
Cooper, Cynthia **1999**:1
Cooper, Stephen F. 1946- **2005**:4
Coors, William K.
Brief entry **1985**:1
Copeland, Al 1944(?)- **1988**:3
Copland, Aaron 1900-1990
Obituary **1991**:2
Copperfield, David 1957- **1986**:3
Coppola, Carmine 1910-1991
Obituary **1991**:4
Coppola, Francis Ford 1939- **1989**:4
Coppola, Sofia 1971- **2004**:3
Corbett, John 1962- **2004**:1

Corea, Chick 1941- **1986**:3
Cornum, Rhonda 1954- **2006**:3
Cornwell, Patricia 1956- **2003**:1
Corwin, Jeff 1967- **2005**:1
Cosby, Bill 1937- **1999**:2
Cosell, Howard 1918-1995
Obituary **1995**:4
Costas, Bob 1952- **1986**:4
Costner, Kevin 1955- **1989**:4
Couples, Fred 1959- **1994**:4
Couric, Katherine 1957- **1991**:4
Courier, Jim 1970- **1993**:2
Courtney, Erica 1957- **2009**:3
Cousteau, Jean-Michel 1938- **1988**:2
Covey, Stephen R. 1932- **1994**:4
Cowley, Malcolm 1898-1989
Obituary **1989**:3
Cox, Courteney 1964- **1996**:2
Cox, Richard Joseph
Brief entry **1985**:1
Cozza, Stephen 1985- **2001**:1
Craig, James 1956- **2001**:1
Crais, Robert 1954(?)- **2007**:4
Cram, Donald J. 1919-2001
Obituary **2002**:2
Crandall, Robert L. 1935- **1992**:1
Craven, Wes 1939- **1997**:3
Crawford, Broderick 1911-1986
Obituary **1986**:3
Crawford, Cheryl 1902-1986
Obituary **1987**:1
Crawford, Cindy 1966- **1993**:3
Cray, Robert 1953- **1988**:2
Cray, Seymour R. 1925-1996
Brief entry **1986**:3
Obituary **1997**:2
Creamer, Paula 1986- **2006**:2
Crenna, Richard 1926-2003
Obituary **2004**:1
Crichton, Michael 1942- **1995**:3
Cronkite, Walter Leland 1916- **1997**:3
Crosby, David 1941- **2000**:4
Crothers, Scatman 1910-1986
Obituary **1987**:1
Crow, Sheryl 1964- **1995**:2
Crowe, Cameron 1957- **2001**:2
Cruise, Tom 1962(?)- **1985**:4
Crumb, R. 1943- **1995**:4
Crump, Scott 1954(?)- **2008**:1
Cruz, Nilo 1961(?)- **2004**:4
Cruzan, Nancy 1957(?)-1990
Obituary **1991**:3
Crystal, Billy 1947- **1985**:3
Cugat, Xavier 1900-1990
Obituary **1991**:2
Culkin, Macaulay 1980(?)- **1991**:3
Cunningham, Merce 1919- **1998**:1
Cunningham, Michael 1952- **2003**:4
Cunningham, Randall 1963- **1990**:1
Cunningham, Reverend William
1930-1997
Obituary **1997**:4
Cuomo, Mario 1932- **1992**:2
Curran, Charles E. 1934- **1989**:2
Curren, Tommy
Brief entry **1987**:4
Curry, Ann 1956- **2001**:1
Curtis, Ben 1977- **2004**:2
Curtis, Jamie Lee 1958- **1995**:1
Cusack, John 1966- **1999**:3
Cyrus, Billy Ray 1961(?)- **1993**:1
Cyrus, Miley 1992- **2008**:3

Dafoe, Willem 1955- **1988**:1

Dahmer, Jeffrey 1959-1994
  Obituary **1995**:2

Daily, Bishop Thomas V.
  1927- **1990**:4

D'Alessio, Kitty
  Brief entry **1987**:3

Daly, Carson 1973- **2002**:4

D'Amato, Al 1937- **1996**:1

Damon, Johnny 1973- **2005**:4

Damon, Matt 1970- **1999**:1

Danes, Claire 1979- **1999**:4

Dangerfield, Rodney 1921-2004
  Obituary **2006**:1

Daniels, Faith 1958- **1993**:3

Daniels, Jeff 1955- **1989**:4

Danticat, Edwidge 1969- **2005**:4

Danza, Tony 1951- **1989**:1

D'Arby, Terence Trent 1962- **1988**:4

Darden, Christopher 1957(?)- **1996**:4

Darling, Erik 1933-2008
  Obituary **2009**:4

Daschle, Tom 1947- **2002**:3

Davenport, Lindsay 1976- **1999**:2

David, George 1942- **2005**:1

David, Larry 1948- **2003**:4

Davis, Angela 1944- **1998**:3

Davis, Bette 1908-1989
  Obituary **1990**:1

Davis, Eric 1962- **1987**:4

Davis, Geena 1957- **1992**:1

Davis, Miles 1926-1991
  Obituary **1992**:2

Davis, Noel **1990**:3

Davis, Ossie 1917-2005
  Obituary **2006**:1

Davis, Paige 1969- **2004**:2

Davis, Patti 1952- **1995**:1

Davis, Raymond, Jr. 1914-2006
  Obituary **2007**:3

Davis, Sammy, Jr. 1925-1990
  Obituary **1990**:4

Davis, Terrell 1972- **1998**:2

Dawson, Rosario 1979- **2007**:2

Day, Dennis 1917-1988
  Obituary **1988**:4

Day, Pat 1953- **1995**:2

Dean, Howard 1948- **2005**:4

Dean, Laura 1945- **1989**:4

Dearden, John Cardinal 1907-1988
  Obituary **1988**:4

DeBakey, Michael 1908-2008
  Obituary **2009**:3

DeBartolo, Edward J., Jr.
  1946- **1989**:3

DeCarava, Roy 1919- **1996**:3

De Cordova, Frederick 1910- **1985**:2

Dee, Sandra 1942-2005
  Obituary **2006**:2

Deen, Paula 1947- **2008**:3

Dees, Morris 1936- **1992**:1

DeGeneres, Ellen **1995**:3

de Kooning, Willem
  1904-1997 **1994**:4
  Obituary **1997**:3

De La Hoya, Oscar 1973- **1998**:2

Delany, Dana 1956- **2008**:4

Delany, Sarah 1889-1999
  Obituary **1999**:3

de la Renta, Oscar 1932- **2005**:4

DeLay, Tom 1947- **2000**:1

Dell, Michael 1965- **1996**:2

DeLuca, Fred 1947- **2003**:3

De Matteo, Drea 1973- **2005**:2

DeMayo, Neda 1960(?)- **2006**:2

de Mille, Agnes 1905-1993
  Obituary **1994**:2

Deming, W. Edwards
  1900-1993 **1992**:2
  Obituary **1994**:2

Demme, Jonathan 1944- **1992**:4

Dempsey, Patrick 1966- **2006**:1

De Niro, Robert 1943- **1999**:1

Dennehy, Brian 1938- **2002**:1

Dennis, Sandy 1937-1992
  Obituary **1992**:4

Denver, Bob 1935-2005
  Obituary **2006**:4

Denver, John 1943-1997
  Obituary **1998**:1

De Palma, Brian 1940- **2007**:3

de Passe, Suzanne 1946(?)- **1990**:4

Depp, Johnny 1963(?)- **1991**:3

Dern, Laura 1967- **1992**:3

Dershowitz, Alan 1938(?)- **1992**:1

Desormeaux, Kent 1970- **1990**:2

Destiny's Child **2001**:3

Deutch, John 1938- **1996**:4

Devine, John M. 1944- **2003**:2

DeVita, Vincent T., Jr. 1935- **1987**:3

De Vito, Danny 1944- **1987**:1

Diamond, I.A.L. 1920-1988
  Obituary **1988**:3

Diamond, Selma 1921(?)-1985
  Obituary **1985**:2

Diaz, Cameron 1972- **1999**:1

DiBello, Paul
  Brief entry **1986**:4

DiCaprio, Leonardo Wilhelm
  1974- **1997**:2

Dickerson, Nancy H.
  1927-1997 **1998**:2

Dickey, James 1923-1997 **1998**:2

Dickinson, Brian 1937- **1998**:2

Dickinson, Janice 1953- **2005**:2

Diddley, Bo 1928-2008
  Obituary **2009**:3

Diebenkorn, Richard 1922-1993
  Obituary **1993**:3

Diemer, Walter E.
  1904(?)-1998 **1998**:2

Diesel, Vin 1967- **2004**:1

DiFranco, Ani 1970(?)- **1997**:1

Diggs, Taye 1971- **2000**:1

Diller, Barry 1942- **1991**:1

Diller, Elizabeth and Ricardo
  Scofidio **2004**:3

Dillon, Matt 1964- **1992**:2

DiMaggio, Joe 1914-1999
  Obituary **1999**:3

Di Meola, Al 1954- **1986**:4

Dinkins, David N. 1927- **1990**:2

Disney, Lillian 1899-1997
  Obituary **1998**:3

Disney, Roy E. 1930- **1986**:3

Dith Pran 1942-2008
  Obituary **2009**:2

Divine 1946-1988
  Obituary **1988**:3

Dixie Chicks **2001**:2

Doctorow, E. L. 1931- **2007**:1

Doherty, Shannen 1971(?)- **1994**:2

Dolan, Terry 1950-1986 **1985**:2

Dolan, Tom 1975- **2001**:2

Dolby, Ray Milton
  Brief entry **1986**:1

Dole, Bob 1923- **1994**:2

Dole, Elizabeth Hanford
  1936- **1990**:1

Dolenz, Micky 1945- **1986**:4

Domar, Alice 1958- **2007**:1

Donahue, Tim 1950(?)- **2004**:3

Donahue, Troy 1936-2001
  Obituary **2002**:4

Donghia, Angelo R. 1935-1985
  Obituary **1985**:2

Donnellan, Nanci **1995**:2

Dorati, Antal 1906-1988
  Obituary **1989**:2

Dorris, Michael 1945-1997
  Obituary **1997**:3

Dorsey, Thomas A. 1899-1993
  Obituary **1993**:3

Doubleday, Nelson, Jr. 1933- **1987**:1

Douglas, Buster 1960(?)- **1990**:4

Douglas, Marjory Stoneman
  1890-1998 **1993**:1
  Obituary **1998**:4

Douglas, Michael 1944- **1986**:2

Douglas, Mike 1925-2006
  Obituary **2007**:4

Dove, Rita 1952- **1994**:3

Dowd, Maureen Brigid 1952- **1997**:1

Downey, Bruce 1947- **2003**:1

Downey, Morton, Jr. 1932- **1988**:4

Downey, Robert, Jr. 1965- **2007**:1

Dr. Demento 1941- **1986**:1

Dr. Dre 1965(?)- **1994**:3

Dravecky, Dave 1956- **1992**:1

Drescher, Fran 1957(?)- **1995**:3

Drexler, Clyde 1962- **1992**:4

Drexler, Millard S. 1944- **1990**:3

Dreyfuss, Richard 1947- **1996**:3

Drysdale, Don 1936-1993
  Obituary **1994**:1

Duarte, Henry 1963(?)- **2003**:3

Dubrof, Jessica 1989-1996
  Obituary **1996**:4

Duchovny, David 1960- **1998**:3

Dudley, Jane 1912-2001
  Obituary **2002**:4

Duff, Hilary 1987- **2004**:4

Duffy, Karen 1962- **1998**:1

Dukakis, Michael 1933- **1988**:3

Dukakis, Olympia 1931- **1996**:4

Duke, David 1951(?)- **1990**:2

Duke, Doris 1912-1993
  Obituary **1994**:2

Duke, Red
  Brief entry **1987**:1

Dunagan, Deanna 1940- **2009**:2

Duncan, Tim 1976- **2000**:1

Duncan, Todd 1903-1998
  Obituary **1998**:3

Dunham, Carroll 1949- **2003**:4

Dunham, Katherine 1909-2006
  Obituary **2007**:2

Dunlap, Albert J. **1997**:2

Dunne, Dominick 1925- **1997**:1

Dunst, Kirsten 1982- **2001**:4

Dunwoody, Ann 1953- **2009**:2

Dupri, Jermaine 1972- **1999**:1

Durocher, Leo 1905-1991
  Obituary **1992**:2

Durrell, Gerald 1925-1995
  Obituary **1995**:3

Duval, David 1971- **2000**:3
Duvall, Camille
  Brief entry **1988**:1
Duvall, Robert 1931- **1999**:3
Dworkin, Andrea 1946-2005
  Obituary **2006**:2
Dykstra, Lenny 1963- **1993**:4
Dylan, Bob 1941- **1998**:1
Earle, Sylvia 1935- **2001**:1
Earnhardt, Dale 1951-2001
  Obituary **2001**:4
Earnhardt, Dale, Jr. 1974- **2004**:4
Eastwood, Clint 1930- **1993**:3
Eaton, Robert J. 1940- **1994**:2
Eazy-E 1963(?)-1995
  Obituary **1995**:3
Eberhart, Richard 1904-2005
  Obituary **2006**:3
Ebersole, Christine 1953- **2007**:2
Ebert, Roger 1942- **1998**:3
Ebsen, Buddy 1908-2003
  Obituary **2004**:3
Eckert, Robert A. 1955(?)- **2002**:3
Eckhart, Aaron 1968- **2009**:2
Ecko, Marc 1972- **2006**:3
Eckstine, Billy 1914-1993
  Obituary **1993**:4
Edelman, Marian Wright
  1939- **1990**:4
Ederle, Gertrude 1905-2003
  Obituary **2005**:1
Edmonds, Kenneth Babyface
  1958(?)- **1995**:3
Edwards, Bob 1947- **1993**:2
Edwards, Harry 1942- **1989**:4
Efron, Zac 1987- **2008**:2
Eggers, Dave 1970- **2001**:3
Ehrlichman, John 1925-1999
  Obituary **1999**:3
Eilberg, Amy
  Brief entry **1985**:3
Eisenman, Peter 1932- **1992**:4
Eisenstaedt, Alfred 1898-1995
  Obituary **1996**:1
Eisner, Michael 1942- **1989**:2
Eisner, Will 1917-2005
  Obituary **2006**:1
Elders, Joycelyn 1933- **1994**:1
Eldridge, Roy 1911-1989
  Obituary **1989**:3
Elfman, Jenna 1971- **1999**:4
Ellerbee, Linda 1944- **1993**:3
Elliott, Missy 1971- **2003**:4
Ellis, David 1971- **2009**:4
Ellis, Perry 1940-1986
  Obituary **1986**:3
Ellison, Larry 1944- **2004**:2
Ellison, Ralph 1914-1994
  Obituary **1994**:4
Ellroy, James 1948- **2003**:4
Elway, John 1960- **1990**:3
Eminem 1974- **2001**:2
Engelbreit, Mary 1952(?)- **1994**:3
Engibous, Thomas J. 1953- **2003**:3
Engler, John 1948- **1996**:3
Engles, Gregg L. 1957- **2007**:3
Englund, Richard 1932(?)-1991
  Obituary **1991**:3
Engstrom, Elmer W. 1901-1984
  Obituary **1985**:2
Ensler, Eve 1954(?)- **2002**:4
Ephron, Henry 1912-1992

Obituary **1993**:2
Ephron, Nora 1941- **1992**:3
Epps, Omar 1973- **2000**:4
Epstein, Jason 1928- **1991**:1
Epstein, Theo 1973- **2003**:4
Erdrich, Louise 1954- **2005**:3
Ertegun, Ahmet 1923- **1986**:3
Ervin, Sam 1896-1985
  Obituary **1985**:2
Esiason, Boomer 1961- **1991**:1
Estefan, Gloria **1991**:4
Estes, Pete 1916-1988
  Obituary **1988**:3
Estevez, Emilio 1962- **1985**:4
Estrich, Susan 1953- **1989**:1
Etheridge, Melissa 1961(?)- **1995**:4
Evanovich, Janet 1943- **2005**:2
Evans, Dale 1912-2001
  Obituary **2001**:3
Evans, Janet 1971- **1989**:1
Evans, Joni 1942- **1991**:4
Evans, Nancy 1950- **2000**:4
Evans, Robert 1930- **2004**:1
Eve 1978- **2004**:3
Evers-Williams, Myrlie 1933- **1995**:4
Ewing, Patrick 1962- **1985**:3
Eyler, John. H., Jr. 1948(?)- **2001**:3
Factor, Max 1904-1996
  Obituary **1996**:4
Fagan, Garth 1940- **2000**:1
Fairbanks, Douglas, Jr. 1909-2000
  Obituary **2000**:4
Fairstein, Linda 1948(?)- **1991**:1
Falconer, Ian 1960(?)- **2003**:1
Falkenberg, Nanette 1951- **1985**:2
Fallon, Jimmy 1974- **2003**:1
Faludi, Susan 1959- **1992**:4
Falwell, Jerry 1933-2007
  Obituary **2008**:3
Fanning, Dakota 1994- **2005**:2
Fanning, Shawn 1980- **2001**:1
Farley, Chris 1964-1997 **1998**:2
Farmer, James 1920-1999
  Obituary **2000**:1
Farrakhan, Louis 1933- **1990**:4
Farrell, Perry 1960- **1992**:2
Farrell, Suzanne 1945- **1996**:3
Farrow, Mia 1945- **1998**:3
Fassa, Lynda 1963(?)- **2008**:4
Fast, Howard 1914-2003
  Obituary **2004**:2
Faubus, Orval 1910-1994
  Obituary **1995**:2
Fauci, Anthony S. 1940- **2004**:1
Faulkner, Shannon 1975- **1994**:4
Faust, Drew Gilpin 1947- **2008**:1
Favre, Brett Lorenzo 1969- **1997**:2
Favreau, Jon 1966- **2002**:3
Fawcett, Farrah 1947- **1998**:4
Fehr, Donald 1948- **1987**:2
Feinstein, Dianne 1933- **1993**:3
Feld, Eliot 1942- **1996**:1
Feld, Kenneth 1948- **1988**:2
Feldman, Sandra 1939- **1987**:3
Feldshuh, Tovah 1952- **2005**:3
Fell, Norman 1924-1998
  Obituary **1999**:2
Fender, Leo 1909-1991
  Obituary **1992**:1
Fenley, Molissa 1954- **1988**:3
Fenwick, Millicent H.
  Obituary **1993**:2

Fernandez, Joseph 1935- **1991**:3
Ferraro, Geraldine 1935- **1998**:3
Ferrell, Trevor
  Brief entry **1985**:2
Ferrell, Will 1968- **2004**:4
Ferrera, America 1984- **2006**:2
Fertel, Ruth 1927- **2000**:2
Fetchit, Stepin 1892(?)-1985
  Obituary **1986**:1
Fey, Tina 1970- **2005**:3
Fieger, Geoffrey 1950- **2001**:3
Field, Patricia 1942(?)- **2002**:2
Field, Sally 1946- **1995**:3
Fielder, Cecil 1963- **1993**:2
Fields, Debbi 1956- **1987**:3
Fields, Evelyn J. 1949- **2001**:3
Fierstein, Harvey 1954- **2004**:2
Filo, David and Jerry Yang **1998**:3
Finley, Karen 1956- **1992**:4
Finnamore, Suzanne 1959- **2009**:1
Fiorina, Carleton S. 1954- **2000**:1
Fireman, Paul
  Brief entry **1987**:2
Firestone, Roy 1953- **1988**:2
Fischer, Bobby 1943-2008
  Obituary **2009**:1
Fish, Hamilton 1888-1991
  Obituary **1991**:3
Fishburne, Laurence 1961(?)- **1995**:3
Fisher, Carrie 1956- **1991**:1
Fisher, Mary 1948- **1994**:3
Fisher, Mel 1922(?)- **1985**:4
Fitzgerald, A. Ernest 1926- **1986**:2
Fitzgerald, Ella 1917-1996
  Obituary **1996**:4
Fitzgerald, Patrick 1960- **2006**:4
Flanders, Ed 1934-1995
  Obituary **1995**:3
Flatley, Michael 1958- **1997**:3
Flavor Flav 1959- **2007**:3
Fleischer, Ari 1960- **2003**:1
Fleiss, Mike 1964- **2003**:4
Fleming, Art 1925(?)-1995
  Obituary **1995**:4
Fleming, Claudia 1959- **2004**:1
Fleming, Renee **2001**:4
Flockhart, Calista 1964- **1998**:4
Flood, Curt 1938-1997
  Obituary **1997**:2
Florio, James J. 1937- **1991**:2
Flutie, Doug 1962- **1999**:2
Flynn, Ray 1939- **1989**:1
Flynt, Larry 1942- **1997**:3
Fogelberg, Dan 1951-2007
  Obituary **2009**:1
Foley, Thomas S. 1929- **1990**:1
Folkman, Judah 1933- **1999**:1
Fomon, Robert M. 1925- **1985**:3
Fonda, Bridget 1964- **1995**:1
Foo Fighters **2006**:2
Foote, Shelby 1916- **1991**:2
Forbes, Malcolm S. 1919-1990
  Obituary **1990**:3
Forbes, Steve 1947- **1996**:2
Ford, Faith 1964- **2005**:3
Ford, Gerald R. 1913-2007
  Obituary **2008**:2
Ford, Glenn 1916-2006
  Obituary **2007**:4
Ford, Harrison 1942- **1990**:2
Ford, Henry II 1917-1987
  Obituary **1988**:1

Ford, Tennessee Ernie 1919-1991
  Obituary **1992**:2
Ford, Tom 1962- **1999**:3
Ford, William Clay, Jr. 1957- **1999**:1
Foreman, Dave 1947(?)- **1990**:3
Foreman, George 1949- **2004**:2
Forsythe, William 1949- **1993**:2
Foss, Joe 1915- **1990**:3
Fosse, Bob 1927-1987
  Obituary **1988**:1
Fossett, Steve 1944- **2007**:2
Fossey, Dian 1932-1985
  Obituary **1986**:1
Foster, David 1950(?)- **1988**:2
Foster, Jodie 1962- **1989**:2
Foster, Phil 1914-1985
  Obituary **1985**:3
Foster, Sutton 1975- **2003**:2
Foster, Tabatha 1985-1988
  Obituary **1988**:3
Foster, Vincent 1945(?)-1993
  Obituary **1994**:1
Fox, Matthew 1940- **1992**:2
Fox, Matthew 1966- **2006**:1
Fox, Vivica 1964- **1999**:1
Foxworthy, Jeff 1958- **1996**:1
Foxx, Jamie 1967- **2001**:1
Foxx, Redd 1922-1991
  Obituary **1992**:2
France, Johnny
  Brief entry **1987**:1
Francis, Philip L. 1946- **2007**:4
Franciscus, James 1934-1991
  Obituary **1992**:1
Frank, Barney 1940- **1989**:2
Frank, Robert 1924- **1995**:2
Franken, Al 1952(?)- **1996**:3
Frankenheimer, John 1930-2002
  Obituary **2003**:4
Frankenthaler, Helen 1928- **1990**:1
Frankfort, Lew 1946- **2008**:2
Franklin, Aretha 1942- **1998**:3
Franklin, Melvin 1942-1995
  Obituary **1995**:3
Franks, Tommy 1945- **2004**:1
Franz, Dennis 1944- **1995**:2
Franzen, Jonathan 1959- **2002**:3
Fraser, Brendan 1967- **2000**:1
Fraser, Claire M. 1955- **2005**:2
Frazier, Charles 1950- **2003**:2
Freedman, Rory 1971-. See Kim
  Barnouin and Rory Freedman
Freeh, Louis J. 1950- **1994**:2
Freeman, Cliff 1941- **1996**:1
Freeman, Morgan 1937- **1990**:4
Freleng, Friz 1906(?)-1995
  Obituary **1995**:4
French, Tana 1973- **2009**:3
Freston, Kathy 1965- **2009**:3
Friedan, Betty 1921- **1994**:2
Friedman, Milton 1912-2006
  Obituary **2008**:1
Friend, Patricia A. 1946- **2003**:3
Frist, Bill 1952- **2003**:4
Fudge, Ann 1951- **2000**:3
Fulbright, J. William 1905-1995
  Obituary **1995**:3
Fulghum, Robert 1937- **1996**:1
Funt, Allen 1914-1999
  Obituary **2000**:1
Furman, Rosemary
  Brief entry **1986**:4

Furyk, Jim 1970- **2004**:2
Futrell, Mary Hatwood 1940- **1986**:1
Futter, Ellen V. 1949- **1995**:1
Gabor, Eva 1921(?)-1995
  Obituary **1996**:1
Gacy, John Wayne 1942-1994
  Obituary **1994**:4
Gaines, William M. 1922-1992
  Obituary **1993**:1
Gale, Robert Peter 1945- **1986**:4
Galindo, Rudy 1969- **2001**:2
Gallagher, Peter 1955- **2004**:3
Gallo, Robert 1937- **1991**:1
Galvin, John R. 1929- **1990**:1
Galvin, Martin
  Brief entry **1985**:3
Gandolfini, James 1961- **2001**:3
Gandy, Kim 1954(?)- **2002**:2
Ganzi, Victor 1947- **2003**:3
Garbo, Greta 1905-1990
  Obituary **1990**:3
Garcia, Andy 1956- **1999**:3
Garcia, Cristina 1958- **1997**:4
Garcia, Jerry 1942-1995 **1988**:3
  Obituary **1996**:1
Garcia, Joe
  Brief entry **1986**:4
Gardner, Ava Lavinia 1922-1990
  Obituary **1990**:2
Gardner, David and Tom **2001**:4
Gardner, Randy 1957- **1997**:2
Garner, Jennifer 1972- **2003**:1
Garnett, Kevin 1976- **2000**:3
Garofalo, Janeane 1964- **1996**:4
Garr, Teri 1949- **1988**:4
Garrison, Jim 1922-1992
  Obituary **1993**:2
Garson, Greer 1903-1996
  Obituary **1996**:4
Garzarelli, Elaine M. 1951- **1992**:3
Gates, Bill 1955- **1987**:4
Gates, Robert M. 1943- **1992**:2
Gathers, Hank 1967(?)-1990
  Obituary **1990**:3
Gault, Willie 1960- **1991**:2
Gayle, Helene 1955- **2008**:2
Gebbie, Kristine 1944(?)- **1994**:2
Geffen, David 1943- **1985**:3
Gehry, Frank O. 1929- **1987**:1
Geisel, Theodor 1904-1991
  Obituary **1992**:2
Geithner, Timothy F. 1961- **2009**:4
Gellar, Sarah Michelle 1977- **1999**:3
Geller, Margaret Joan 1947- **1998**:2
Gentine, Lou 1947- **2008**:2
George, Elizabeth 1949- **2003**:3
Gephardt, Richard 1941- **1987**:3
Gerba, Charles 1945- **1999**:4
Gerberding, Julie 1955- **2004**:1
Gere, Richard 1949- **1994**:3
Gergen, David 1942- **1994**:1
Gerstner, Lou 1942- **1993**:4
Gertz, Alison 1966(?)-1992
  Obituary **1993**:2
Gerulaitis, Vitas 1954-1994
  Obituary **1995**:1
Getty, Estelle 1923-2008
  Obituary **2009**:3
Getz, Stan 1927-1991
  Obituary **1991**:4
Giamatti, A. Bartlett
  1938-1989 **1988**:4

  Obituary **1990**:1
Giamatti, Paul 1967- **2009**:4
Giannulli, Mossimo 1963- **2002**:3
Gibson, Althea 1927-2003
  Obituary **2004**:4
Gibson, Kirk 1957- **1985**:2
Gibson, William Ford, III
  1948- **1997**:2
Gifford, Kathie Lee 1953- **1992**:2
Gilbert, Walter 1932- **1988**:3
Gilford, Jack 1907-1990
  Obituary **1990**:4
Gill, Vince 1957- **1995**:2
Gillespie, Dizzy 1917-1993
  Obituary **1993**:2
Gillespie, Marcia 1944- **1999**:4
Gillett, George 1938- **1988**:1
Gilruth, Robert 1913-2000
  Obituary **2001**:1
Gingrich, Newt 1943- **1991**:1
Ginsberg, Allen 1926-1997
  Obituary **1997**:3
Ginsberg, Ian 1962(?)- **2006**:4
Ginsburg, Ruth Bader 1933- **1993**:4
Gioia, Dana 1950- **2008**:4
Gish, Lillian 1893-1993
  Obituary **1993**:4
Giuliani, Rudolph 1944- **1994**:2
Glaser, Elizabeth 1947-1994
  Obituary **1995**:2
Glass, David 1935- **1996**:1
Glass, Ira 1959- **2008**:2
Glass, Philip 1937- **1991**:4
Glasser, Ira 1938- **1989**:1
Glaus, Troy 1976- **2003**:3
Glazman, Lev and Alina
  Roytberg **2007**:4
Gleason, Jackie 1916-1987
  Obituary **1987**:4
Glenn, John 1921- **1998**:3
Gless, Sharon 1944- **1989**:3
Glover, Danny 1947- **1998**:4
Glover, Savion 1973- **1997**:1
Gobel, George 1920(?)-1991
  Obituary **1991**:4
Gober, Robert 1954- **1996**:3
Goetz, Bernhard Hugo
  1947(?)- **1985**:3
Goizueta, Roberto 1931-1997 **1996**:1
  Obituary **1998**:1
Gold, Thomas 1920-2004
  Obituary **2005**:3
Goldberg, Gary David 1944- **1989**:4
Goldberg, Leonard 1934- **1988**:4
Goldberg, Whoopi 1955- **1993**:3
Goldblum, Jeff 1952- **1988**:1
Golden, Thelma 1965- **2003**:3
Goldhaber, Fred
  Brief entry **1986**:3
Goldman, William 1931- **2001**:1
Goldman-Rakic, Patricia
  1937- **2002**:4
Goldwater, Barry 1909-1998
  Obituary **1998**:4
Gomez, Lefty 1909-1989
  Obituary **1989**:3
Gooden, Dwight 1964- **1985**:2
Gooding, Cuba, Jr. 1968- **1997**:3
Goodman, Benny 1909-1986
  Obituary **1986**:3
Goodman, Drew and Myra **2007**:4
Goodman, John 1952- **1990**:3

Goody, Joan 1935- **1990**:2
Goody, Sam 1904-1991
   Obituary **1992**:1
Gorder, Genevieve 1974- **2005**:4
Gordon, Dexter 1923-1990 **1987**:1
Gordon, Gale 1906-1995
   Obituary **1996**:1
Gordon, James 1941- **2009**:4
Gordon, Jeff 1971- **1996**:1
Gordon, Michael 1951(?)- **2005**:1
Gore, Albert, Jr. 1948(?)- **1993**:2
Gore, Albert, Sr. 1907-1998
   Obituary **1999**:2
Gore, Tipper 1948- **1985**:4
Goren, Charles H. 1901-1991
   Obituary **1991**:4
Gorman, Leon
   Brief entry **1987**:1
Gossett, Louis, Jr. 1936- **1989**:3
Gottlieb, William 1917-2006
   Obituary **2007**:2
Gould, Chester 1900-1985
   Obituary **1985**:2
Gould, Gordon 1920- **1987**:1
Gould, Stephen Jay 1941-2002
   Obituary **2003**:3
Goulet, Robert 1933-2007
   Obituary **2008**:4
Grace, J. Peter 1913- **1990**:2
Grace, Topher 1978- **2005**:4
Graden, Brian 1963- **2004**:2
Grafton, Sue 1940- **2000**:2
Graham, Bill 1931-1991 **1986**:4
   Obituary **1992**:2
Graham, Billy 1918- **1992**:1
Graham, Donald 1945- **1985**:4
Graham, Heather 1970- **2000**:1
Graham, Katharine Meyer
   1917- **1997**:3
   Obituary **2002**:3
Graham, Lauren 1967- **2003**:4
Graham, Martha 1894-1991
   Obituary **1991**:4
Gramm, Phil 1942- **1995**:2
Grammer, Kelsey 1955(?)- **1995**:1
Granato, Cammi 1971- **1999**:3
Grandin, Temple 1947- **2006**:1
Grange, Red 1903-1991
   Obituary **1991**:3
Grant, Amy 1961(?)- **1985**:4
Grant, Cary 1904-1986
   Obituary **1987**:1
Grant, Charity
   Brief entry **1985**:2
Grant, Rodney A. **1992**:1
Graves, Michael 1934- **2000**:1
Graves, Nancy 1940- **1989**:3
Graves, Ron 1967- **2009**:3
Gray, Hanna 1930- **1992**:4
Gray, John 1952(?)- **1995**:3
Gray, Macy 1970(?)- **2002**:1
Gray, Spalding 1941-2004
   Obituary **2005**:2
Grazer, Brian 1951- **2006**:4
Graziano, Rocky 1922-1990
   Obituary **1990**:4
Green, Richard R. 1936- **1988**:3
Greenberg, Hank 1911-1986
   Obituary **1986**:4
Greenberg, Robert 1940(?)- **2003**:2
Green Day **1995**:4
Greene, Brian 1963- **2003**:4

Greenspan, Alan 1926- **1992**:2
Greenwald, Julie 1970- **2008**:1
Gregorian, Vartan 1934- **1990**:3
Gregory, Cynthia 1946- **1990**:2
Gregory, Dick 1932- **1990**:3
Gregory, Rogan 1972- **2008**:2
Grier, Pam 1949- **1998**:3
Griffey, Ken Jr. 1969- **1994**:1
Griffin, Merv 1925-2008
   Obituary **2008**:4
Griffith, Melanie 1957- **1989**:2
Griffiths, Martha 1912-2003
   Obituary **2004**:2
Grisham, John 1955- **1994**:4
Groban, Josh 1981- **2009**:1
Grodin, Charles 1935- **1997**:3
Groening, Matt 1955(?)- **1990**:4
Gross, Terry 1951- **1998**:3
Grove, Andrew S. 1936- **1995**:3
Grucci, Felix 1905- **1987**:1
Gruden, Jon 1963- **2003**:4
Grusin, Dave
   Brief entry **1987**:2
Guccione, Bob 1930- **1986**:1
Guccione, Bob, Jr. 1956- **1991**:4
Guest, Christopher 1948- **2004**:2
Guggenheim, Charles 1924-2002
   Obituary **2003**:4
Gumbel, Bryant 1948- **1990**:2
Gumbel, Greg 1946- **1996**:4
Gund, Agnes 1938- **1993**:2
Gunn, Hartford N., Jr. 1926-1986
   Obituary **1986**:2
Gupta, Sanjay 1969- **2009**:4
Gutmann, Amy 1949- **2008**:4
Guyer, David
   Brief entry **1988**:1
Gwynn, Tony 1960- **1995**:1
Gyllenhaal, Jake 1980- **2005**:3
Gyllenhaal, Maggie 1977- **2009**:2
Haas, Robert D. 1942- **1986**:4
Hackett, Buddy 1924-2003
   Obituary **2004**:3
Hackman, Gene 1931- **1989**:3
Hackney, Sheldon 1933- **1995**:1
Hagelstein, Peter
   Brief entry **1986**:3
Hagen, Uta 1919-2004
   Obituary **2005**:2
Hagler, Marvelous
   Marvin 1954- **1985**:2
Hahn, Jessica 1960- **1989**:4
Hair, Jay D. 1945- **1994**:3
Ha Jin 1956- **2000**:3
Hakuta, Ken
   Brief entry **1986**:1
Halberstam, David 1934-2007
   Obituary **2008**:3
Haldeman, H. R. 1926-1993
   Obituary **1994**:2
Hale, Alan 1957- **1997**:3
Hale, Clara 1905-1992
   Obituary **1993**:3
Hale, Victoria 1961(?)- **2008**:4
Haley, Alex 1924-1992
   Obituary **1992**:3
Hall, Anthony Michael 1968- **1986**:3
Hall, Arsenio 1955- **1990**:2
Hall, Gus 1910-2000
   Obituary **2001**:2
Halston 1932-1990
   Obituary **1990**:3

Hamels, Cole 1983- **2009**:4
Hamilton, Laurell K. 1963- **2008**:2
Hamilton, Margaret 1902-1985
   Obituary **1985**:3
Hamilton, Scott 1958- **1998**:2
Hamm, Jon 1971- **2009**:2
Hamm, Mia 1972- **2000**:1
Hamm, Paul 1982- **2005**:1
Hammer, Armand 1898-1990
   Obituary **1991**:3
Hammer, Jan 1948- **1987**:3
Hammer, M. C. **1991**:2
Hammond, E. Cuyler 1912-1986
   Obituary **1987**:1
Hammond, John 1910-1987
   Obituary **1988**:2
Hampton, Lionel 1908-2002
   Obituary **2003**:4
Hanauer, Chip 1954- **1986**:2
Hancock, Herbie 1940- **1985**:1
Hand, Elizabeth 1957- **2007**:2
Handler, Chelsea 1975- **2009**:3
Handler, Daniel 1970- **2003**:3
Handler, Ruth 1916-2002
   Obituary **2003**:3
Hanks, Tom 1956- **1989**:2
Hanna, William 1910-2001
   Obituary **2002**:1
Hannah, Daryl 1961- **1987**:4
Hannigan, Alyson 1974- **2007**:3
Harbert, Ted 1955- **2007**:2
Hardaway, Anfernee 1971- **1996**:2
Harden, Marcia Gay 1959- **2002**:4
Haring, Keith 1958-1990
   Obituary **1990**:3
Harker, Patrick T. 1958- **2001**:2
Harkes, John 1967- **1996**:4
Harmon, Mark 1951- **1987**:1
Harmon, Tom 1919-1990
   Obituary **1990**:3
Harriman, Pamela 1920- **1994**:4
Harriman, W. Averell 1891-1986
   Obituary **1986**:4
Harris, Barbara **1996**:3
Harris, Barbara 1930- **1989**:3
Harris, E. Lynn 1955- **2004**:2
Harris, Ed 1950- **2002**:2
Harris, Emmylou 1947- **1991**:3
Harris, Katherine 1957- **2001**:3
Harris, Patricia Roberts 1924-1985
   Obituary **1985**:2
Harris, Thomas 1940(?)- **2001**:1
Harry, Deborah 1945- **1990**:1
Hart, Carey 1975- **2006**:4
Hart, Johnny 1931-2007
   Obituary **2008**:2
Hart, Kitty Carlisle 1910-2007
   Obituary **2008**:2
Hart, Mary
   Brief entry **1988**:1
Hart, Melissa Joan 1976- **2002**:1
Hart, Mickey 1944(?)- **1991**:2
Hartman, Phil 1948-1998 **1996**:2
   Obituary **1998**:4
Harvard, Beverly 1950- **1995**:2
Harvey, Paul 1918- **1995**:3
Harwell, Ernie 1918- **1997**:3
Haseltine, William A. 1944- **1999**:2
Hassenfeld, Stephen 1942- **1987**:4
Hastert, Dennis 1942- **1999**:3
Hastings, Reed 1961(?)- **2006**:2

Hatch, Orin G. 1934- **2000**:2
Hatch, Richard 1961- **2001**:1
Hatcher, Teri 1964- **2005**:4
Hatem, George 1910(?)-1988
  Obituary **1989**:1
Hathaway, Anne 1982- **2007**:2
Hawk, Tony 1968- **2001**:4
Hawke, Ethan 1971(?)- **1995**:4
Hawkins, Jeff and Donna
  Dubinsky **2000**:2
Hawkins, Screamin' Jay 1929-1999
  Obituary **2000**:3
Hawn, Goldie Jeanne 1945- **1997**:2
Hayes, Helen 1900-1993
  Obituary **1993**:4
Hayes, Isaac 1942- **1998**:4
Hayes, Robert M. 1952- **1986**:3
Hayes, Woody 1913-1987
  Obituary **1987**:2
Haysbert, Dennis 1954- **2007**:1
Hayse, Bruce 1949(?)- **2004**:3
Hayworth, Rita 1918-1987
  Obituary **1987**:3
Headroom, Max 1985- **1986**:4
Healey, Jack 1938(?)- **1990**:1
Healy, Bernadine 1944- **1993**:1
Healy, Timothy S. 1923- **1990**:2
Heard, J.C. 1917-1988
  Obituary **1989**:1
Hearst, Randolph A. 1915-2000
  Obituary **2001**:3
Heat-Moon, William
  Least 1939- **2000**:2
Heche, Anne 1969- **1999**:1
Heckerling, Amy 1954- **1987**:2
Heckert, Richard E.
  Brief entry **1987**:3
Hefner, Christie 1952- **1985**:1
Heid, Bill
  Brief entry **1987**:2
Heifetz, Jascha 1901-1987
  Obituary **1988**:2
Heigl, Katharine 1978- **2008**:3
Heinz, H.J. 1908-1987
  Obituary **1987**:2
Heinz, John 1938-1991
  Obituary **1991**:4
Held, Al 1928-2005
  Obituary **2006**:4
Helgenberger, Marg 1958- **2002**:2
Heller, Joseph 1923-1999
  Obituary **2000**:2
Heller, Walter 1915-1987
  Obituary **1987**:4
Helms, Bobby 1936-1997
  Obituary **1997**:4
Helms, Jesse 1921- **1998**:1
Helmsley, Leona 1920- **1988**:1
Heloise 1951- **2001**:4
Helton, Todd 1973- **2001**:1
Hemingway, Margaux 1955-1996
  Obituary **1997**:1
Henderson, Rickey 1958- **2002**:3
Hennessy, John L. 1952- **2002**:2
Henning, Doug 1947-1999
  Obituary **2000**:3
Henry, Carl F.H. 1913-2003
  Obituary **2005**:1
Hensel Twins **1996**:4
Henson, Brian 1964(?)- **1992**:1
Henson, Jim 1936-1990 **1989**:1
  Obituary **1990**:4

Hepburn, Katharine 1909- **1991**:2
Herbert, Don 1917-2007
  Obituary **2008**:3
Hernandez, Lazaro and Jack
  McCollough **2008**:4
Hernandez, Willie 1954- **1985**:1
Hero, Peter 1942- **2001**:2
Hershberger, Sally 1961(?)- **2006**:4
Hershey, Barbara 1948- **1989**:1
Hershiser, Orel 1958- **1989**:2
Herz, Rachel 1963- **2008**:1
Herzog, Doug 1960(?)- **2002**:4
Heston, Charlton 1924- **1999**:4
Hewitt, Jennifer Love 1979- **1999**:2
Hewlett, William 1913-2001
  Obituary **2001**:4
Heyer, Steven J. 1952- **2007**:1
Hiaasen, Carl 1953- **2007**:2
Highsmith, Patricia 1921-1995
  Obituary **1995**:3
Hilbert, Stephen C. 1946- **1997**:4
Hilfiger, Tommy 1952- **1993**:3
Hill, Andrew 1931-2007
  Obituary **2008**:3
Hill, Anita 1956- **1994**:1
Hill, Faith 1967- **2000**:1
Hill, George Roy 1921-2002
  Obituary **2004**:1
Hill, Grant 1972- **1995**:3
Hill, J. Edward 1938- **2006**:2
Hill, Lauryn 1975- **1999**:3
Hill, Lynn 1961(?)- **1991**:2
Hillegass, Clifton Keith 1918- **1989**:4
Hills, Carla 1934- **1990**:3
Hills, L. Rust 1924-2008
  Obituary **2009**:4
Hines, Gregory 1946- **1992**:4
Hinton, Milt 1910-2000
  Obituary **2001**:3
Hirschhorn, Joel
  Brief entry **1986**:1
Hirshberg, Gary 1954(?)- **2007**:2
Hirt, Al 1922-1999
  Obituary **1999**:4
Hiss, Alger 1904-1996
  Obituary **1997**:2
Ho, Don 1930-2007
  Obituary **2008**:2
Hockfield, Susan 1951- **2009**:2
Hodges, Carl 1937- **2008**:1
Hoff, Syd 1912-2004
  Obituary **2005**:3
Hoffa, Jim, Jr. 1941- **1999**:2
Hoffman, Abbie 1936-1989
  Obituary **1989**:3
Hoffman, Dustin 1937- **2005**:4
Hoffman, Philip Seymour
  1967- **2006**:3
Hoffs, Susanna 1962(?)- **1988**:2
Hogan, Ben 1912-1997
  Obituary **1997**:4
Hogan, Hulk 1953- **1987**:3
Holbrooke, Richard 1941(?)- **1996**:2
Holden, Betsy 1955- **2003**:2
Holder, Jr., Eric H. 1951- **2009**:4
Holl, Steven 1947- **2003**:1
Hollander, Joel 1956(?)- **2006**:4
Holliday, Chad 1948- **2006**:4
Holmes, John C. 1945-1988
  Obituary **1988**:3
Holtz, Lou 1937- **1986**:4
Holyfield, Evander 1962- **1991**:3

Hooker, John Lee 1917- **1998**:1
  Obituary **2002**:3
hooks, bell 1952- **2000**:2
Hootie and the Blowfish **1995**:4
Hope, Bob 1903-2003
  Obituary **2004**:4
Horne, Lena 1917- **1998**:4
Horner, Jack 1946- **1985**:2
Hornsby, Bruce 1954(?)- **1989**:3
Horovitz, Adam 1968(?)- **1988**:3
Horowitz, Paul 1942- **1988**:2
Horowitz, Vladimir 1903-1989
  Obituary **1990**:1
Horrigan, Edward, Jr. 1929- **1989**:1
Horvath, David and Sun-Min
  Kim **2008**:4
Horwich, Frances 1908-2001
  Obituary **2002**:3
Hosseini, Khaled 1965- **2008**:3
Houseman, John 1902-1988
  Obituary **1989**:1
Housenbold, Jeffrey 1969- **2009**:2
Houston, Cissy 1933- **1999**:3
Houston, Whitney 1963- **1986**:3
Howard, Desmond
  Kevin 1970- **1997**:2
Howard, Ron **1997**:2
Howser, Dick 1936-1987
  Obituary **1987**:4
Hubbard, Freddie 1938- **1988**:4
Hudson, Dawn 1957- **2008**:1
Hudson, Jennifer 1981- **2008**:1
Hudson, Kate 1979- **2001**:2
Hudson, Rock 1925-1985
  Obituary **1985**:4
Huerta, Dolores 1930- **1998**:1
Huffman, Felicity 1962- **2006**:2
Hughes, Cathy 1947- **1999**:1
Hughes, Karen 1957- **2001**:2
Hughes, Mark 1956- **1985**:3
Hughes, Sarah 1985- **2002**:4
Hughley, D.L. 1964- **2001**:1
Huizenga, Wayne 1938(?)- **1992**:1
Hull, Jane Dee 1935- **1999**:2
Hullinger, Charlotte
  Brief entry **1985**:1
Hundt, Reed Eric 1948- **1997**:2
Hunt, Helen 1963- **1994**:4
Hunter, Catfish 1946-1999
  Obituary **2000**:1
Hunter, Evan 1926-2005
  Obituary **2006**:4
Hunter, Holly 1958- **1989**:4
Hunter, Howard 1907- **1994**:4
Hunter, Madeline 1916(?)- **1991**:2
Hurt, William 1950- **1986**:1
Huston, Anjelica 1952(?)- **1989**:3
Huston, John 1906-1987
  Obituary **1988**:1
Hutton, Timothy 1960- **1986**:3
Hwang, David Henry 1957- **1999**:1
Hyatt, Joel 1950- **1985**:3
Hyde, Henry 1924- **1999**:1
Hynde, Chrissie 1951- **1991**:1
Iacocca, Lee 1924- **1993**:1
Ice Cube 1969- **1999**:2
Ice-T **1992**:3
Ifill, Gwen 1955- **2002**:4
Iger, Bob 1951- **2006**:1
Iglesias, Enrique 1975- **2000**:1
Ilitch, Mike 1929- **1993**:4
Immelt, Jeffrey R. 1956- **2001**:2

Imus, Don 1940- **1997**:1
Inatome, Rick 1953- **1985**:4
Indigo Girls **1994**:4
Ingersoll, Ralph II 1946- **1988**:2
Inkster, Juli 1960- **2000**:2
Inman, Bobby Ray 1931- **1985**:1
Iovine, Jimmy 1953- **2006**:3
Ireland, Patricia 1946(?)- **1992**:2
Irvin, Michael 1966- **1996**:3
Irving, John 1942- **2006**:2
Irwin, Bill **1988**:3
Irwin, Hale 1945- **2005**:2
Irwin, James 1930-1991
   Obituary **1992**:1
Isaacson, Portia
   Brief entry **1986**:1
Isaacson, Walter 1952- **2003**:2
Ito, Lance 1950(?)- **1995**:3
Iverson, Allen 1975- **2001**:4
Ives, Burl 1909-1995
   Obituary **1995**:4
Ivins, Molly 1942(?)- **1993**:4
Jablonski, Nina G. 1953- **2009**:3
Jackson, Alan 1958- **2003**:1
Jackson, Bo 1962- **1986**:3
Jackson, Cordell 1923- **1992**:4
Jackson, Janet 1966(?)- **1990**:4
Jackson, Jesse 1941- **1996**:1
Jackson, Jesse, Jr. 1965- **1998**:3
Jackson, Lisa P. 1962- **2009**:4
Jackson, Michael 1958- **1996**:2
Jackson, Phil 1945- **1996**:3
Jackson, Samuel L. 1949(?)- **1995**:4
Jackson, Thomas Penfield
   1937- **2000**:2
Jacobs, Joe 1945(?)- **1994**:1
Jacobs, Marc 1963- **2002**:3
Jacobson, Nina 1965- **2009**:2
Jacuzzi, Candido 1903-1986
   Obituary **1987**:1
Jahn, Helmut 1940- **1987**:3
James, Etta 1938- **1995**:2
James, Jesse 1969- **2004**:4
James, LeBron 1984- **2007**:3
James, Rick 1948-2004
   Obituary **2005**:4
Jamison, Judith 1944- **1990**:3
Janklow, Morton 1930- **1989**:3
Janney, Allison 1959- **2003**:3
Janzen, Daniel H. 1939- **1988**:4
Jarmusch, Jim 1953- **1998**:3
Jarrett, Keith 1945- **1992**:4
Jarvik, Robert K. 1946- **1985**:1
Jay, Ricky 1949(?)- **1995**:1
Jay-Z 1970- **2006**:1
Jefferts Schori, Katharine
   1954- **2007**:2
Jeffords, James 1934- **2002**:2
Jeffrey, Mildred 1910-2004
   Obituary **2005**:2
Jemison, Mae C. 1956- **1993**:1
Jen, Gish 1955- **2000**:1
Jenkins, Sally 1960(?)- **1997**:2
Jennings, Waylon 1937-2002
   Obituary **2003**:2
Jeter, Derek 1974- **1999**:4
Jewel 1974- **1999**:2
Jillian, Ann 1951- **1986**:4
Jindal, Bobby 1971- **2006**:1
Jobs, Steve 1955- **2000**:1
Joel, Billy 1949- **1994**:3
Joffrey, Robert 1930-1988

   Obituary **1988**:3
Johansson, Scarlett 1984- **2005**:4
John, Daymond 1968- **2000**:1
Johnson, Abigail 1961- **2005**:3
Johnson, Betsey 1942- **1996**:2
Johnson, Beverly 1952- **2005**:2
Johnson, Diane 1934- **2004**:3
Johnson, Don 1949- **1986**:1
Johnson, Earvin Magic 1959- **1988**:4
Johnson, Jack 1975- **2006**:4
Johnson, Jimmie 1975- **2007**:2
Johnson, Jimmy 1943- **1993**:3
Johnson, John H. 1918-2005
   Obituary **2005**:4
Johnson, Kevin 1966(?)- **1991**:1
Johnson, Keyshawn 1972- **2000**:4
Johnson, Lady Bird 1912-2007
   Obituary **2008**:4
Johnson, Larry 1969- **1993**:3
Johnson, Michael **2000**:1
Johnson, Philip 1906- **1989**:2
Johnson, Randy 1963- **1996**:2
Johnson, Robert L. 1946- **2000**:4
Johnson, Shawn 1992- **2009**:2
Jolie, Angelina 1975- **2000**:2
Jonas Brothers **2008**:4
Jones, Arthur A. 1924(?)- **1985**:3
Jones, Bill T. **1991**:4
Jones, Cherry 1956- **1999**:3
Jones, Chuck 1912- **2001**:2
Jones, E. Fay 1921-2004
   Obituary **2005**:4
Jones, Edward P. 1950- **2005**:1
Jones, Etta 1928-2001
   Obituary **2002**:4
Jones, Gayl 1949- **1999**:4
Jones, Jerry 1942- **1994**:4
Jones, Marion 1975- **1998**:4
Jones, Norah 1979- **2004**:1
Jones, Quincy 1933- **1990**:4
Jones, Sarah 1974(?)- **2005**:2
Jones, Tommy Lee 1947(?)- **1994**:2
Jong, Erica 1942- **1998**:3
Jonze, Spike 1961(?)- **2000**:3
Jordan, Barbara 1936-1996
   Obituary **1996**:3
Jordan, Charles M. 1927- **1989**:4
Jordan, James 1936(?)-1993
   Obituary **1994**:1
Jordan, King 1943(?)- **1990**:1
Jordan, Michael 1963- **1987**:2
Jordan, Vernon, Jr. 1935- **2002**:3
Jorgensen, Christine 1926-1989
   Obituary **1989**:4
Joseph, Wendy Evans
   1955(?)- **2006**:2
Jovovich, Milla 1975- **2002**:1
Joyce, William 1957- **2006**:1
Joyner, Florence Griffith
   1959-1998 **1989**:2
   Obituary **1999**:1
Joyner-Kersee, Jackie 1962- **1993**:1
Judd, Ashley 1968- **1998**:1
Judge, Mike 1963(?)- **1994**:2
Judkins, Reba
   Brief entry **1987**:3
Julavits, Heidi 1968- **2007**:4
July, Miranda 1974- **2008**:2
Junck, Mary E. 1948(?)- **2003**:4
Jurgensen, Karen 1949(?)- **2004**:3
Justin, John Jr. 1917- **1992**:2
Justiz, Manuel J. 1948- **1986**:4

Kael, Pauline 1919-2001 **2000**:4
   Obituary **2002**:4
Kahane, Meir 1932-1990
   Obituary **1991**:2
Kahn, Madeline 1942-1999
   Obituary **2000**:2
Kallen, Jackie 1946(?)- **1994**:1
Kamali, Norma 1945- **1989**:1
Kamen, Dean 1951(?)- **2003**:1
Kanakaredes, Melina 1967- **2007**:1
Kandel, Eric 1929- **2005**:2
Kanokogi, Rusty
   Brief entry **1987**:1
Kapor, Mitch 1950- **1990**:3
Karan, Donna 1948- **1988**:1
Karmazin, Mel 1943- **2006**:1
Kasem, Casey 1933(?)- **1987**:1
Kashuk, Sonia 1959(?)- **2002**:4
Kaskey, Ray
   Brief entry **1987**:2
Kassebaum, Nancy 1932- **1991**:1
Kathwari, M. Farooq 1944- **2005**:4
Katz, Alex 1927- **1990**:3
Katz, Lillian 1927- **1987**:4
Katzenberg, Jeffrey 1950- **1995**:3
Kaufman, Charlie 1958- **2005**:1
Kaufman, Elaine **1989**:4
Kavner, Julie 1951- **1992**:3
Kaye, Danny 1913-1987
   Obituary **1987**:2
Kaye, Nora 1920-1987
   Obituary **1987**:4
Kaye, Sammy 1910-1987
   Obituary **1987**:4
Kazan, Elia 1909-2003
   Obituary **2004**:4
Keating, Charles H., Jr. 1923- **1990**:4
Keaton, Diane 1946- **1997**:1
Keaton, Michael 1951- **1989**:4
Keeling, Charles 1928-2005
   Obituary **2006**:3
Keeshan, Bob 1927-2004
   Obituary **2005**:2
Keitel, Harvey 1939- **1994**:3
Keith, Brian 1921-1997
   Obituary **1997**:4
Keith, Louis 1935- **1988**:2
Kelleher, Herb 1931- **1995**:1
Kellerman, Jonathan 1949- **2009**:1
Kelley, DeForest 1929-1999
   Obituary **2000**:1
Kelley, Virginia 1923-1994
   Obituary **1994**:3
Kelly, Ellsworth 1923- **1992**:1
Kelly, Gene 1912-1996
   Obituary **1996**:3
Kelly, Jim 1960- **1991**:4
Kelly, Maureen 1972(?)- **2007**:3
Kelly, Patrick 1954(?)-1990
   Obituary **1990**:2
Kelly, R. 1968- **1997**:3
Kelly, William R. 1905-1998 **1998**:2
Kemp, Jack 1935- **1990**:4
Kemp, Jan 1949- **1987**:2
Kemp, Shawn 1969- **1995**:1
Kendricks, Eddie 1939-1992
   Obituary **1993**:2
Kennan, George 1904-2005
   Obituary **2006**:2
Kennedy, John F., Jr.
   1960-1999 **1990**:1
   Obituary **1999**:4

Kennedy, Rose 1890-1995
Obituary **1995**:3
Kennedy, Weldon 1938- **1997**:3
Kenny G 1957(?)- **1994**:4
Keno, Leigh and Leslie
1957(?)- **2001**:2
Kent, Corita 1918-1986
Obituary **1987**:1
Keough, Donald Raymond
1926- **1986**:1
Keplinger, Dan 1973- **2001**:1
Kerger, Paula A. 1957- **2007**:2
Kerkorian, Kirk 1917- **1996**:2
Kerr, Clark 1911-2003
Obituary **2005**:1
Kerr, Cristie 1977- **2008**:2
Kerr, Jean 1922-2003
Obituary **2004**:1
Kerr, Walter 1913-1996
Obituary **1997**:1
Kerrey, Bob 1943- **1986**:1
Kerrigan, Nancy 1969- **1994**:3
Kerry, John 1943- **2005**:2
Kesey, Ken 1935-2001
Obituary **2003**:1
Kessler, David 1951- **1992**:1
Ketcham, Hank 1920-2001
Obituary **2002**:2
Kevorkian, Jack 1928(?)- **1991**:3
Keyes, Alan 1950- **1996**:2
Keys, Alicia 1981- **2006**:1
Kidd, Jason 1973- **2003**:2
Kidd, Michael 1915-2007
Obituary **2009**:1
Kid Rock 1972- **2001**:1
Kilborn, Craig 1964- **2003**:2
Kilby, Jack 1923- **2002**:2
Kiley, Dan 1912-2004
Obituary **2005**:2
Kilgore, Marcia 1968- **2006**:3
Kilmer, Val **1991**:4
Kilpatrick, Kwame 1970- **2009**:2
Kilts, James M. 1948- **2001**:3
Kim, Eugenia 1974(?)- **2006**:1
Kim Barnouin and Rory Freedman
1971- **2009**:4
Kimmel, Jimmy 1967- **2009**:2
Kimsey, James V. 1940(?)- **2001**:1
King, Alan 1927-2004
Obituary **2005**:3
King, Bernice 1963- **2000**:2
King, Coretta Scott 1927- **1999**:3
King, Don 1931- **1989**:1
King, Larry 1933- **1993**:1
King, Mary-Claire 1946- **1998**:3
King, Stephen 1947- **1998**:1
Kingsborough, Donald
Brief entry **1986**:2
Kingsley, Patricia 1932- **1990**:2
Kingsolver, Barbara 1955- **2005**:1
Kinison, Sam 1954(?)-1992
Obituary **1993**:1
Kinney, Jeff 1971- **2009**:3
Kiraly, Karch
Brief entry **1987**:1
Kirk, David 1956(?)- **2004**:1
Kirkpatrick, Jeane 1926-2006
Obituary **2008**:1
Kissinger, Henry 1923- **1999**:4
Kissling, Frances 1943- **1989**:2
Kistler, Darci 1964- **1993**:1
Kitaj, R. B. 1932-2007

Obituary **2008**:4
Kite, Tom 1949- **1990**:3
Klass, Perri 1958- **1993**:2
Klein, Calvin 1942- **1996**:2
Kline, Kevin 1947- **2000**:1
Kloss, Henry E.
Brief entry **1985**:2
Kluge, John 1914- **1991**:1
Knievel, Evel 1938-2007
Obituary **2009**:1
Knievel, Robbie 1963- **1990**:1
Knight, Bobby 1940- **1985**:3
Knight, Philip H. 1938- **1994**:1
Knight, Ted 1923-1986
Obituary **1986**:4
Knight, Wayne 1956- **1997**:1
Knotts, Don 1924-2006
Obituary **2007**:1
Knowles, John 1926-2001
Obituary **2003**:1
Koch, Bill 1940- **1992**:3
Koch, Jim 1949- **2004**:3
Kohnstamm, Abby 1954- **2001**:1
Koogle, Tim 1951- **2000**:4
Koons, Jeff 1955(?)- **1991**:4
Koontz, Dean 1945- **1999**:3
Koop, C. Everett 1916- **1989**:3
Kopits, Steven E.
Brief entry **1987**:1
Koplovitz, Kay 1945- **1986**:3
Kopp, Wendy **1993**:3
Koppel, Ted 1940- **1989**:1
Kordich, Jay 1923- **1993**:2
Koresh, David 1960(?)-1993
Obituary **1993**:4
Korman, Harvey 1927-2008
Obituary **2009**:2
Kornberg, Arthur 1918(?)- **1992**:1
Kors, Michael 1959- **2000**:4
Kostabi, Mark 1960- **1989**:4
Kostova, Elizabeth 1964- **2006**:2
Kovacevich, Dick 1943- **2004**:3
Kozinski, Alex 1950- **2002**:2
Kozol, Jonathan 1936- **1992**:1
Kramer, Larry 1935- **1991**:2
Kramer, Stanley 1913-2001
Obituary **2002**:1
Krantz, Judith 1928- **2003**:1
Krause, Peter 1965- **2009**:2
Kravitz, Lenny 1964(?)- **1991**:1
Krim, Mathilde 1926- **1989**:2
Kroc, Ray 1902-1984
Obituary **1985**:1
Krol, John 1910-1996
Obituary **1996**:3
Kroll, Alexander S. 1938- **1989**:3
Krone, Julie 1963(?)- **1989**:2
Kruk, John 1961- **1994**:4
Krupp, Fred 1954- **2008**:3
Krzyzewski, Mike 1947- **1993**:2
Kubler-Ross, Elisabeth 1926-2004
Obituary **2005**:4
Kubrick, Stanley 1928-1999
Obituary **1999**:3
Kudrow, Lisa 1963(?)- **1996**:1
Kullman, Ellen 1956- **2009**:4
Kulp, Nancy 1921-1991
Obituary **1991**:3
Kunitz, Stanley J. 1905- **2001**:2
Kunstler, William 1919-1995
Obituary **1996**:1
Kunstler, William 1920(?)- **1992**:3

Kuralt, Charles 1934-1997
Obituary **1998**:3
Kurzban, Ira 1949- **1987**:2
Kurzweil, Raymond 1948- **1986**:3
Kushner, Tony 1956- **1995**:2
Kutcher, Ashton 1978- **2003**:4
Kwoh, Yik San 1946(?)- **1988**:2
Kyser, Kay 1906(?)-1985
Obituary **1985**:3
LaBeouf, Shia 1986- **2008**:1
Lachey, Nick and Jessica
Simpson **2004**:4
LaDuke, Winona 1959- **1995**:2
Laettner, Christian 1969- **1993**:1
Lafley, A. G. 1947- **2003**:4
LaFontaine, Pat 1965- **1985**:1
Lagasse, Emeril 1959- **1998**:3
Lahiri, Jhumpa 1967- **2001**:3
Lahti, Christine 1950- **1988**:2
Laimbeer, Bill 1957- **2004**:3
Lake, Ricki 1968(?)- **1994**:4
Lalas, Alexi 1970- **1995**:1
Lam, Derek 1966- **2009**:2
Lamb, Wally 1950- **1999**:1
Lamour, Dorothy 1914-1996
Obituary **1997**:1
L'Amour, Louis 1908-1988
Obituary **1988**:4
Lancaster, Burt 1913-1994
Obituary **1995**:1
Land, Edwin H. 1909-1991
Obituary **1991**:3
Lander, Toni 1931-1985
Obituary **1985**:4
Landers, Ann 1918-2002
Obituary **2003**:3
Landon, Alf 1887-1987
Obituary **1988**:1
Landon, Michael 1936-1991
Obituary **1992**:1
Landrieu, Mary L. 1955- **2002**:2
Landry, Tom 1924-2000
Obituary **2000**:3
Lane, Burton 1912-1997
Obituary **1997**:2
Lane, Diane 1965- **2006**:2
Lane, Nathan 1956- **1996**:4
Lang, Eugene M. 1919- **1990**:3
Lange, Jessica 1949- **1995**:4
Lange, Liz 1967(?)- **2003**:4
Langella, Frank 1940- **2008**:3
Langer, Robert 1948- **2003**:4
Langevin, James R. 1964- **2001**:2
Langston, J. William
Brief entry **1986**:2
Lanier, Jaron 1961(?)- **1993**:4
Lansbury, Angela 1925- **1993**:1
Lansdale, Edward G. 1908-1987
Obituary **1987**:2
Lansing, Sherry 1944- **1995**:4
Lantos, Tom 1928-2008
Obituary **2009**:2
Lanza, Robert 1956- **2004**:3
LaPaglia, Anthony 1959- **2004**:4
Lardner Jr., Ring 1915-2000
Obituary **2001**:2
Larian, Isaac 1954- **2008**:1
Larroquette, John 1947- **1986**:2
Larson, Jonathan 1961(?)-1996
Obituary **1997**:2
LaSalle, Eriq 1962- **1996**:4
Lasseter, John 1957- **2007**:2

Lauder, Estee 1908(?)- **1992**:2
Lauper, Cyndi 1953- **1985**:1
Lauren, Ralph 1939- **1990**:1
Lawless, Lucy 1968- **1997**:4
Lawrence, Martin 1966(?)- **1993**:4
Laybourne, Geraldine 1947- **1997**:1
Lazarus, Charles 1923- **1992**:4
Lazarus, Shelly 1947- **1998**:3
Lear, Frances 1923- **1988**:3
Leary, Denis 1958- **1993**:3
Leary, Timothy 1920-1996
    Obituary **1996**:4
LeBlanc, Matt 1967- **2005**:4
Lederman, Leon Max 1922- **1989**:4
Lee, Brandon 1965(?)-1993
    Obituary **1993**:4
Lee, Chang-Rae 1965- **2005**:1
Lee, Henry C. 1938- **1997**:1
Lee, Jason 1970- **2006**:4
Lee, Pamela 1967(?)- **1996**:4
Lee, Peggy 1920-2002
    Obituary **2003**:1
Lee, Sandra 1966- **2008**:3
Lee, Spike 1957- **1988**:4
Legend, John 1978- **2007**:1
Leguizamo, John 1965- **1999**:1
Lehane, Dennis 1965- **2001**:4
Leibovitz, Annie 1949- **1988**:4
Leigh, Dorian 1917-2008
    Obituary **2009**:3
Leigh, Janet 1927-2004
    Obituary **2005**:4
Leigh, Jennifer Jason 1962- **1995**:2
Lelyveld, Joseph S. 1937- **1994**:4
Lemmon, Jack 1925- **1998**:4
    Obituary **2002**:3
Lemon, Ted
    Brief entry **1986**:4
LeMond, Greg 1961- **1986**:4
L'Engle, Madeleine 1918-2007
    Obituary **2008**:4
Leno, Jay 1950- **1987**:1
Leonard, Elmore 1925- **1998**:4
Leonard, Sugar Ray 1956- **1989**:4
Leopold, Luna 1915-2006
    Obituary **2007**:1
Lepore, Nanette 1964(?)- **2006**:4
Lerner, Michael 1943- **1994**:2
Lerner, Sandy 1955(?)- **2005**:1
Leslie, Lisa 1972- **1997**:4
Letterman, David 1947- **1989**:3
Levi, Zachary 1980- **2009**:4
Levin, Gerald 1939- **1995**:2
Levin, Ira 1929-2007
    Obituary **2009**:1
Levine, Arnold 1939- **2002**:3
Levine, James 1943- **1992**:3
Levinson, Arthur D. 1950- **2008**:3
Levinson, Barry 1932- **1989**:3
Levitt, Arthur 1931- **2004**:2
Lewis, Edward B. 1918-2004
    Obituary **2005**:4
Lewis, Edward T. 1940- **1999**:4
Lewis, Henry 1932-1996
    Obituary **1996**:3
Lewis, Huey 1951- **1987**:3
Lewis, John 1920-2001
    Obituary **2002**:1
Lewis, Juliette 1973- **1999**:3
Lewis, Kenneth D. 1947- **2009**:2
Lewis, Loida Nicolas 1942- **1998**:3
Lewis, Ray 1975- **2001**:3

Lewis, Reggie 1966(?)-1993
    Obituary **1994**:1
Lewis, Reginald F. 1942-1993 **1988**:4
    Obituary **1993**:3
Lewis, Richard 1948(?)- **1992**:1
Lewis, Shari 1934-1998 **1993**:1
    Obituary **1999**:1
LeWitt, Sol 1928- **2001**:2
Lewitzky, Bella 1916-2004
    Obituary **2005**:3
Leyland, Jim 1944- **1998**:2
Lhuillier, Monique 1971(?)- **2007**:4
Liberace 1919-1987
    Obituary **1987**:2
Libeskind, Daniel 1946- **2004**:1
Lichtenstein, Roy 1923-1997 **1994**:1
    Obituary **1998**:1
Lieberman, Joseph 1942- **2001**:1
Lightner, Candy 1946- **1985**:1
Liguori, Peter 1960- **2005**:2
Lilly, John C. 1915-2001
    Obituary **2002**:4
Lil Wayne 1982- **2009**:3
Lim, Phillip 1974(?)- **2008**:1
Liman, Arthur 1932- **1989**:4
Liman, Doug 1965- **2007**:1
Limbaugh, Rush **1991**:3
Lin, Maya 1960(?)- **1990**:3
Lincoln, Blanche 1960- **2003**:1
Lindbergh, Anne Morrow 1906-2001
    Obituary **2001**:4
Lindros, Eric 1973- **1992**:1
Lindsay, John V. 1921-2000
    Obituary **2001**:3
Lindsay-Abaire, David
    1970(?)- **2008**:2
Lines, Ray 1960(?)- **2004**:1
Ling, Bai 1970- **2000**:3
Ling, Lisa 1973- **2004**:2
Linklater, Richard 1960- **2007**:2
Linney, Laura 1964- **2009**:4
Lipinski, Tara 1982- **1998**:3
Lipkis, Andy
    Brief entry **1985**:3
Lipsig, Harry H. 1901- **1985**:1
Lipton, Martin 1931- **1987**:3
Lisick, Beth 1969(?)- **2006**:2
Lithgow, John 1945- **1985**:2
Little, Benilde 1959(?)- **2006**:2
Little, Cleavon 1939-1992
    Obituary **1993**:2
Litzenburger, Liesel 1967(?)- **2008**:1
Liu, Lucy 1968- **2000**:4
Lively, Blake 1987- **2009**:1
Livingston, Ron 1968- **2007**:2
LL Cool J 1968- **1998**:2
Lobell, Jeanine 1964(?)- **2002**:3
Locklear, Heather 1961- **1994**:3
Lodge, Henry Cabot 1902-1985
    Obituary **1985**:1
Loewe, Frederick 1901-1988
    Obituary **1988**:2
Lofton, Kenny 1967- **1998**:1
Logan, Joshua 1908-1988
    Obituary **1988**:4
Lohan, Lindsay 1986- **2005**:3
Long, Nia 1970- **2001**:3
Long, Shelley 1950(?)- **1985**:1
Longo, Robert 1953(?)- **1990**:4
Lopes, Lisa 1971-2002
    Obituary **2003**:3
Lopez, George 1963- **2003**:4

Lopez, Jennifer 1970- **1998**:4
Lopez, Mario 1973- **2009**:3
Lopez, Nancy 1957- **1989**:3
Lord, Bette Bao 1938- **1994**:1
Lord, Jack 1920-1998 **1998**:2
Lord, Winston
    Brief entry **1987**:4
Lords, Traci 1968- **1995**:4
Lott, Trent 1941- **1998**:1
Louganis, Greg 1960- **1995**:3
Louis-Dreyfus, Julia 1961(?)- **1994**:1
Louv, Richard 1949- **2006**:2
Love, Courtney 1964(?)- **1995**:1
Love, Susan 1948- **1995**:2
Loveless, Patty 1957- **1998**:2
Lovett, Lyle 1958(?)- **1994**:1
Lovley, Derek 1954(?)- **2005**:3
Lowe, Edward 1921- **1990**:2
Lowe, Rob 1964(?)- **1990**:4
Lowell, Mike 1974- **2003**:2
Lowry, Adam and Eric Ryan **2008**:1
Loy, Myrna 1905-1993
    Obituary **1994**:2
Lucas, George 1944- **1999**:4
Lucci, Susan 1946(?)- **1999**:4
Luce, Clare Boothe 1903-1987
    Obituary **1988**:1
Lucid, Shannon 1943- **1997**:1
Lucke, Lewis 1951(?)- **2004**:4
Ludacris 1977- **2007**:4
Ludlum, Robert 1927-2001
    Obituary **2002**:1
Lukas, D. Wayne 1936(?)- **1986**:2
Lupino, Ida 1918(?)-1995
    Obituary **1996**:1
LuPone, Patti 1949- **2009**:2
Lutz, Robert A. 1932- **1990**:1
Lynch, David 1946- **1990**:4
Lyne, Susan 1950- **2005**:4
Lynn, Loretta 1935(?)- **2001**:1
Mac, Bernie 1957- **2003**:1
MacCready, Paul 1925- **1986**:4
MacDonald, Laurie and Walter
    Parkes **2004**:1
MacDowell, Andie 1958(?)- **1993**:4
MacFarlane, Seth 1973- **2006**:1
Mack, John J. 1944- **2006**:3
Mackey, John 1953- **2008**:2
MacKinnon, Catharine 1946- **1993**:2
MacMurray, Fred 1908-1991
    Obituary **1992**:2
MacNelly, Jeff 1947-2000
    Obituary **2000**:4
MacRae, Gordon 1921-1986
    Obituary **1986**:2
Macy, William H. **1999**:3
Madden, Chris 1948- **2006**:1
Madden, John 1936- **1995**:1
Madden, Steve 1958- **2007**:2
Maddux, Greg 1966- **1996**:2
Madonna 1958- **1985**:2
Maglich, Bogdan C. 1928- **1990**:1
Magliozzi, Tom and Ray **1991**:4
Maguire, Tobey 1975- **2002**:2
Maher, Bill 1956- **1996**:2
Mahony, Roger M. 1936- **1988**:2
Maida, Adam Cardinal 1930- **1998**:2
Mailer, Norman 1923- **1998**:1
Maiman, Theodore 1927-2007
    Obituary **2008**:3
Majerle, Dan 1965- **1993**:4
Malda, Rob 1976- **2007**:3

Malkovich, John 1953- **1988**:2
Malloy, Edward Monk 1941- **1989**:4
Malone, John C. 1941- **1988**:3
Malone, Karl 1963- **1990**:1
Maltby, Richard, Jr. 1937- **1996**:3
Mamet, David 1947- **1998**:4
Manchin, Joe 1947- **2006**:4
Mancini, Henry 1924-1994
   Obituary **1994**:4
Manheimer, Heidi 1963- **2009**:3
Mankiller, Wilma P.
   Brief entry **1986**:2
Mann, Sally 1951- **2001**:2
Manning, Eli 1981- **2008**:4
Manning, Peyton 1976- **2007**:4
Mansfield, Mike 1903-2001
   Obituary **2002**:4
Mansion, Gracie
   Brief entry **1986**:3
Manson, JoAnn E. 1953- **2008**:3
Manson, Marilyn 1969- **1999**:4
Mantegna, Joe 1947- **1992**:1
Mantle, Mickey 1931-1995
   Obituary **1996**:1
Mapplethorpe, Robert 1946-1989
   Obituary **1989**:3
Maraldo, Pamela J. 1948(?)- **1993**:4
Maravich, Pete 1948-1988
   Obituary **1988**:2
Marchand, Nancy 1928-2000
   Obituary **2001**:1
Marchetto, Marisa Acocella
   1962(?)- **2007**:3
Marcus, Stanley 1905-2002
   Obituary **2003**:1
Mardin, Brice 1938- **2007**:4
Margolis, Bobby 1948(?)- **2007**:2
Marier, Rebecca 1974- **1995**:4
Marin, Cheech 1946- **2000**:1
Marineau, Philip 1946- **2002**:4
Maris, Roger 1934-1985
   Obituary **1986**:1
Mark, Mary Ellen 1940- **2006**:2
Marky Mark 1971- **1993**:3
Maroon 5 **2008**:1
Marriott, J. Willard 1900-1985
   Obituary **1985**:4
Marriott, J. Willard, Jr. 1932- **1985**:4
Marsalis, Branford 1960- **1988**:3
Marsalis, Wynton 1961- **1997**:4
Marshall, Penny 1942- **1991**:3
Marshall, Susan 1958- **2000**:4
Marshall, Thurgood 1908-1993
   Obituary **1993**:3
Martin, Agnes 1912-2004
   Obituary **2006**:1
Martin, Billy 1928-1989 **1988**:4
   Obituary **1990**:2
Martin, Casey 1972- **2002**:1
Martin, Dean 1917-1995
   Obituary **1996**:2
Martin, Dean Paul 1952(?)-1987
   Obituary **1987**:3
Martin, Judith 1938- **2000**:3
Martin, Lynn 1939- **1991**:4
Martin, Mary 1913-1990
   Obituary **1991**:2
Martin, Steve 1945- **1992**:2
Martinez, Bob 1934- **1992**:1
Marvin, Lee 1924-1987
   Obituary **1988**:1
Mary Mary 1972- **2009**:4

Mas Canosa, Jorge 1939-1997 **1998**:2
Mashouf, Manny 1938(?)- **2008**:1
Master P 1970- **1999**:4
Masters, William H. 1915-2001
   Obituary **2001**:4
Matalin, Mary 1953- **1995**:2
Mathews, Dan 1965- **1998**:3
Mathias, Bob 1930-2006
   Obituary **2007**:4
Mathis, Clint 1976- **2003**:1
Matlin, Marlee 1965- **1992**:2
Matlovich, Leonard P. 1944(?)-1988
   Obituary **1988**:4
Matthau, Walter 1920- **2000**:3
Matthews, Dave 1967- **1999**:3
Mattingly, Don 1961- **1986**:2
Matuszak, John 1951(?)-1989
   Obituary **1989**:4
Mauldin, Bill 1921-2003
   Obituary **2004**:2
Maxwell, Hamish 1926- **1989**:4
Mayer, John 1977- **2007**:4
Mayes, Frances 1940(?)- **2004**:3
Maynard, Joyce 1953- **1999**:4
McAuliffe, Christa 1948-1986
   Obituary **1986**:3
McCain, John S. 1936- **1998**:4
McCall, Nathan 1955- **1994**:4
McCarron, Chris 1955- **1995**:4
McCarthy, Carolyn 1944- **1998**:4
McCarthy, Cormac 1933- **2008**:1
McCarthy, Jenny 1972- **1997**:4
McCartney, Bill 1940- **1995**:3
McCartney, Linda 1942-1998
   Obituary **1998**:4
McCloskey, J. Michael 1934- **1988**:2
McCloskey, James 1944(?)- **1993**:1
McCloy, John J. 1895-1989
   Obituary **1989**:3
McColough, C. Peter 1922- **1990**:2
McConaughey, Matthew David
   1969- **1997**:1
McCourt, Frank 1930- **1997**:4
McCrea, Joel 1905-1990
   Obituary **1991**:1
McDermott, Alice 1953- **1999**:2
McDonald, Camille 1953(?)- **2004**:1
McDonnell, Mary 1952- **2008**:2
McDonnell, Patrick 1956- **2009**:4
McDonnell, Sanford N. 1922- **1988**:4
McDonough, William 1951- **2003**:1
McDormand, Frances 1957- **1997**:3
McDougall, Ron 1942- **2001**:4
McDuffie, Robert 1958- **1990**:2
McElligott, Thomas J. 1943- **1987**:4
McEntire, Reba 1954- **1987**:3
McFarlane, Todd 1961- **1999**:1
McFerrin, Bobby 1950- **1989**:1
McGillis, Kelly 1957- **1989**:3
McGinley, Ryan 1977- **2009**:1
McGinley, Ted 1958- **2004**:4
McGowan, William 1927- **1985**:2
McGowan, William G. 1927-1992
   Obituary **1993**:1
McGrath, Judy 1953- **2006**:1
McGraw, Phil 1950- **2005**:2
McGraw, Tim 1966- **2000**:3
McGraw, Tug 1944-2004
   Obituary **2005**:1
McGreevey, James 1957- **2005**:2
McGruder, Aaron 1974- **2005**:4
McGuire, Dorothy 1918-2001

   Obituary **2002**:4
McGwire, Mark 1963- **1999**:1
McIntyre, Richard
   Brief entry **1986**:2
McKee, Lonette 1952(?)- **1996**:1
McKenna, Terence **1993**:3
McKinney, Cynthia A. 1955- **1997**:1
McKinney, Stewart B. 1931-1987
   Obituary **1987**:4
McLaughlin, Betsy 1962(?)- **2004**:3
McMahon, Jim 1959- **1985**:4
McMahon, Vince, Jr. 1945(?)- **1985**:4
McMillan, Terry 1951- **1993**:2
McMillen, Tom 1952- **1988**:4
McMurtry, James 1962- **1990**:2
McMurtry, Larry 1936- **2006**:4
McNamara, Robert S. 1916- **1995**:4
McNealy, Scott 1954- **1999**:4
McNerney, W. James 1949- **2006**:3
McRae, Carmen 1920(?)-1994
   Obituary **1995**:2
McSally, Martha 1966(?)- **2002**:4
McVeigh, Timothy 1968-2001
   Obituary **2002**:2
Meadows, Audrey 1925-1996
   Obituary **1996**:3
Meier, Richard 1934- **2001**:4
Meisel, Steven 1954- **2002**:4
Melendez, Bill 1916-2008
   Obituary **2009**:4
Mellinger, Frederick 1924(?)-1990
   Obituary **1990**:4
Mello, Dawn 1938(?)- **1992**:2
Mellon, Paul 1907-1999
   Obituary **1999**:3
Melman, Richard
   Brief entry **1986**:1
Melton, Douglas 1954- **2008**:3
Meltzer, Brad 1970- **2005**:4
Mendoza, Lydia 1916-2007
   Obituary **2009**:1
Mengers, Sue 1938- **1985**:3
Menninger, Karl 1893-1990
   Obituary **1991**:1
Menuhin, Yehudi 1916-1999
   Obituary **1999**:3
Merchant, Ismail 1936-2005
   Obituary **2006**:3
Merchant, Natalie 1963- **1996**:3
Meredith, Burgess 1909-1997
   Obituary **1998**:1
Merkerson, S. Epatha 1952- **2006**:4
Merrick, David 1912-2000
   Obituary **2000**:4
Merrill, James 1926-1995
   Obituary **1995**:3
Merritt, Justine
   Brief entry **1985**:3
Messick, Dale 1906-2005
   Obituary **2006**:2
Messing, Debra 1968- **2004**:4
Metallica **2004**:2
Meyer, Stephenie 1973- **2009**:1
Meyers, Nancy 1949- **2006**:1
Mfume, Kweisi 1948- **1996**:3
Michelman, Kate 1942- **1998**:4
Michener, James A. 1907-1997
   Obituary **1998**:1
Mickelson, Phil 1970- **2004**:4
Midler, Bette 1945- **1989**:4
Mikan, George 1924-2005
   Obituary **2006**:3

Mikulski, Barbara 1936- **1992**:4
Milano, Alyssa 1972- **2002**:3
Milbrett, Tiffeny 1972- **2001**:1
Milburn, Rodney Jr.
  1950-1997 **1998**:2
Millan, Cesar 1969- **2007**:4
Milland, Ray 1908(?)-1986
  Obituary **1986**:2
Millard, Barbara J.
  Brief entry **1985**:3
Miller, Andre 1976- **2003**:3
Miller, Ann 1923-2004
  Obituary **2005**:2
Miller, Arthur 1915- **1999**:4
Miller, Bebe 1950- **2000**:2
Miller, Bode 1977- **2002**:4
Miller, Dennis 1953- **1992**:4
Miller, Frank 1957- **2008**:2
Miller, Merton H. 1923-2000
  Obituary **2001**:1
Miller, Nicole 1951(?)- **1995**:4
Miller, Rand 1959(?)- **1995**:4
Miller, Reggie 1965- **1994**:4
Miller, Roger 1936-1992
  Obituary **1993**:2
Miller, Sue 1943- **1999**:3
Mills, Malia 1966- **2003**:1
Mills, Wilbur 1909-1992
  Obituary **1992**:4
Milosz, Czeslaw 1911-2004
  Obituary **2005**:4
Minner, Ruth Ann 1935- **2002**:2
Minnesota Fats 1900(?)-1996
  Obituary **1996**:3
Minsky, Marvin 1927- **1994**:3
Misrach, Richard 1949- **1991**:2
Mitchell, Arthur 1934- **1995**:1
Mitchell, George J. 1933- **1989**:3
Mitchell, John 1913-1988
  Obituary **1989**:2
Mitchell, Joni 1943- **1991**:4
Mitchelson, Marvin 1928- **1989**:2
Mitchum, Robert 1917-1997
  Obituary **1997**:4
Mizrahi, Isaac 1961- **1991**:1
Moakley, Joseph 1927-2001
  Obituary **2002**:2
Moby 1965- **2000**:1
Modano, Mike 1970- **2008**:2
Mohajer, Dineh 1972- **1997**:3
Molinari, Susan 1958- **1996**:4
Monaghan, Tom 1937- **1985**:1
Mondavi, Robert 1913- **1989**:2
Monica 1980- **2004**:2
Mo'Nique 1967- **2008**:1
Monk, Art 1957- **1993**:2
Monroe, Bill 1911-1996
  Obituary **1997**:1
Monroe, Rose Will 1920-1997
  Obituary **1997**:4
Montana, Joe 1956- **1989**:2
Montgomery, Elizabeth 1933-1995
  Obituary **1995**:4
Moody, John 1943- **1985**:3
Moody, Rick 1961- **2002**:2
Moog, Robert 1934-2005
  Obituary **2006**:4
Moon, Warren 1956- **1991**:3
Moonves, Les 1949- **2004**:2
Moore, Ann 1950- **2009**:1
Moore, Archie 1913-1998
  Obituary **1999**:2

Moore, Clayton 1914-1999
  Obituary **2000**:3
Moore, Demi 1963(?)- **1991**:4
Moore, Julianne 1960- **1998**:1
Moore, Mandy 1984- **2004**:2
Moore, Mary Tyler 1936- **1996**:2
Moore, Michael 1954(?)- **1990**:3
Moore, Rachel 1965- **2008**:2
Moose, Charles 1953(?)- **2003**:4
Moreno, Arturo 1946- **2005**:2
Morgan, Dodge 1932(?)- **1987**:1
Morgan, Robin 1941- **1991**:1
Morgan, Tracy 1968- **2009**:3
Morita, Noriyuki Pat 1932- **1987**:3
Moritz, Charles 1936- **1989**:3
Morris, Dick 1948- **1997**:3
Morris, Doug 1938- **2005**:1
Morris, Henry M. 1918-2006
  Obituary **2007**:2
Morris, Kathryn 1969- **2006**:4
Morris, Mark 1956- **1991**:1
Morrison, Sterling 1942-1995
  Obituary **1996**:1
Morrison, Toni 1931- **1998**:1
Morrison, Trudi
  Brief entry **1986**:2
Morrow, Rob 1962- **2006**:4
Mortensen, Viggo 1958- **2003**:3
Mosbacher, Georgette
  1947(?)- **1994**:2
Mos Def 1973- **2005**:4
Mosley, Walter 1952- **2003**:4
Moss, Cynthia 1940- **1995**:2
Moss, Randy 1977- **1999**:3
Motherwell, Robert 1915-1991
  Obituary **1992**:1
Mott, William Penn, Jr. 1909- **1986**:1
Mottola, Tommy 1949- **2002**:1
Mourning, Alonzo 1970- **1994**:2
Moyers, Bill 1934- **1991**:4
Moynihan, Daniel Patrick 1927-2003
  Obituary **2004**:2
Mulcahy, Anne M. 1952- **2003**:2
Muldowney, Shirley 1940- **1986**:1
Mulkey-Robertson, Kim
  1962- **2006**:1
Mullis, Kary 1944- **1995**:3
Mumford, Lewis 1895-1990
  Obituary **1990**:2
Muniz, Frankie 1985- **2001**:4
Murdoch, Rupert 1931- **1988**:4
Murkoff, Heidi 1958- **2009**:3
Murphy, Brittany 1977- **2005**:1
Murphy, Eddie 1961- **1989**:2
Murphy, Kathleen A. **2009**:2
Murray, Arthur 1895-1991
  Obituary **1991**:3
Murray, Bill 1950- **2002**:4
Musburger, Brent 1939- **1985**:1
Muskie, Edmund S. 1914-1996
  Obituary **1996**:3
Mydans, Carl 1907-2004
  Obituary **2005**:4
Nader, Ralph 1934- **1989**:4
Nagin, Ray 1956- **2007**:1
Nair, Mira 1957- **2007**:4
Nance, Jack 1943(?)-1996
  Obituary **1997**:3
Napolitano, Janet 1957- **1997**:1
Nardelli, Robert 1948- **2008**:4
Nas 1973- **2009**:2
Natsios, Andrew 1949- **2005**:1

Nauman, Bruce 1941- **1995**:4
Navratilova, Martina 1956- **1989**:1
Neal, James Foster 1929- **1986**:2
Nechita, Alexandra 1985- **1996**:4
Neeleman, David 1959- **2003**:3
Ne-Yo 1982- **2009**:4
Neiman, LeRoy 1927- **1993**:3
Nelson, Byron 1912-2006
  Obituary **2007**:4
Nelson, Gaylord A. 1914-2005
  Obituary **2006**:3
Nelson, Harriet 1909(?)-1994
  Obituary **1995**:1
Nelson, Rick 1940-1985
  Obituary **1986**:1
Nelson, Willie 1933- **1993**:4
Nemerov, Howard 1920-1991
  Obituary **1992**:1
Neuharth, Allen H. 1924- **1986**:1
Nevelson, Louise 1900-1988
  Obituary **1988**:3
Newhouse, Samuel I., Jr.
  1927- **1997**:1
New Kids on the Block **1991**:2
Newman, Arnold 1918- **1993**:1
Newman, Joseph 1936- **1987**:1
Newman, Paul 1925- **1995**:3
Newman, Ryan 1977- **2005**:1
Newsom, Gavin 1967- **2009**:3
Newton, Huey 1942-1989
  Obituary **1990**:1
Nichols, Mike 1931- **1994**:4
Nicholson, Jack 1937- **1989**:2
Nielsen, Jerri 1951(?)- **2001**:3
Nipon, Albert
  Brief entry **1986**:4
Nirvana **1992**:4
Nissel, Angela 1974- **2006**:4
Nixon, Bob 1954(?)- **2006**:4
Nixon, Pat 1912-1993
  Obituary **1994**:1
Nixon, Richard 1913-1994
  Obituary **1994**:4
Nolan, Lloyd 1902-1985
  Obituary **1985**:4
Nolte, Nick 1941- **1992**:4
Noonan, Peggy 1950- **1990**:3
North, Alex 1910- **1986**:3
North, Oliver 1943- **1987**:4
Northrop, Peggy 1954- **2009**:2
Norton, Andre 1912-2005
  Obituary **2006**:2
Norton, Edward 1969- **2000**:2
Norville, Deborah 1958- **1990**:3
Notorious B.I.G. 1973(?)-1997
  Obituary **1997**:3
Noyce, Robert N. 1927- **1985**:4
'N Sync **2001**:4
Nunn, Sam 1938- **1990**:2
Nussbaum, Karen 1950- **1988**:3
Nye, Bill 1955- **1997**:2
Nyro, Laura 1947-1997
  Obituary **1997**:3
Oates, Joyce Carol 1938- **2000**:1
Obama, Barack 1961- **2007**:4
O'Brien, Conan 1963(?)- **1994**:1
O'Connor, Cardinal John
  1920- **1990**:3
O'Connor, Carroll 1924-2001
  Obituary **2002**:3
O'Connor, Donald 1925-2003
  Obituary **2004**:4

O'Connor, John 1920-2000
  Obituary **2000**:4
O'Connor, Sandra Day 1930- **1991**:1
O'Day, Anita 1919-2006
  Obituary **2008**:1
O'Donnell, Rosie 1962- **1994**:3
O'Keefe, Sean 1956- **2005**:2
Olajuwon, Akeem 1963- **1985**:1
Oldham, Todd 1961- **1995**:4
O'Leary, Hazel 1937- **1993**:4
Olin, Ken 1955(?)- **1992**:3
Oliver, Daniel 1939- **1988**:2
Olmos, Edward James 1947- **1990**:1
Olopade, Olufunmilayo
  1957(?)- **2006**:3
Olsen, Kenneth H. 1926- **1986**:4
Olsen, Mary-Kate and Ashley
  1986- **2002**:1
Olsen, Sigrid 1953- **2007**:1
Olson, Billy 1958- **1986**:3
Olson, Johnny 1910(?)-1985
  Obituary **1985**:4
O'Malley, Susan 1962(?)- **1995**:2
Onassis, Jacqueline Kennedy
  1929-1994
  Obituary **1994**:4
O'Neal, Shaquille 1972- **1992**:1
O'Neil, Buck 1911-2006
  Obituary **2007**:4
O'Neill, Paul H. 1935- **2001**:4
O'Neill, Tip 1912-1994
  Obituary **1994**:3
Ono, Yoko 1933- **1989**:2
Orbach, Jerry 1935-2004
  Obituary **2006**:1
Orbison, Roy 1936-1988
  Obituary **1989**:2
O'Reilly, Bill 1949- **2001**:2
Orman, Suze 1951(?)- **2003**:1
Ormandy, Eugene 1899-1985
  Obituary **1985**:2
Ornish, Dean 1953- **2004**:2
Orr, Kay 1939- **1987**:4
Osborne, Joan 1962- **1996**:4
Osgood, Charles 1933- **1996**:2
Osteen, Joel 1963- **2006**:2
O'Steen, Van
  Brief entry **1986**:3
Ostin, Mo 1927- **1996**:2
Ostroff, Dawn 1960- **2006**:4
Otte, Ruth 1949- **1992**:4
OutKast **2004**:4
Ovitz, Michael 1946- **1990**:1
Owens, Buck 1929-2006
  Obituary **2007**:2
Owens, Delia and Mark **1993**:3
Oz, Mehmet 1960- **2007**:2
Paar, Jack 1918-2004
  Obituary **2005**:2
Pacelle, Wayne 1965- **2009**:4
Pacino, Al 1940- **1993**:4
Pack, Ellen 1963(?)- **2001**:2
Packard, David 1912-1996
  Obituary **1996**:3
Page, Geraldine 1924-1987
  Obituary **1987**:4
Pagels, Elaine 1943- **1997**:1
Paglia, Camille 1947- **1992**:3
Paige, Emmett, Jr.
  Brief entry **1986**:4
Paige, Rod 1933- **2003**:2
Paisley, Brad 1972- **2008**:3

Pakula, Alan 1928-1998
  Obituary **1999**:2
Palahniuk, Chuck 1962- **2004**:1
Palance, Jack 1919-2006
  Obituary **2008**:1
Paley, William S. 1901-1990
  Obituary **1991**:2
Palin, Sarah 1964- **2009**:1
Palmeiro, Rafael 1964- **2005**:1
Palmer, Jim 1945- **1991**:2
Palmer, Violet 1964(?)- **2005**:2
Palmisano, Samuel J. 1952(?)- **2003**:1
Paltrow, Gwyneth 1972- **1997**:1
Panetta, Leon 1938- **1995**:1
Panettiere, Hayden 1989- **2008**:4
Panichgul, Thakoon 1974- **2009**:4
Panofsky, Wolfgang 1919-2007
  Obituary **2008**:4
Pantoliano, Joe 1951- **2002**:3
Papp, Joseph 1921-1991
  Obituary **1992**:2
Paretsky, Sara 1947- **2002**:4
Parker, Brant 1920-2007
  Obituary **2008**:2
Parker, Colonel Tom 1929-1997
  Obituary **1997**:2
Parker, Mary-Louise 1964- **2002**:2
Parker, Sarah Jessica 1965- **1999**:2
Parker, Suzy 1932-2003
  Obituary **2004**:2
Parker, Trey and Matt Stone **1998**:2
Parker, Willie 1980- **2009**:3
Parks, Bert 1914-1992
  Obituary **1992**:3
Parks, Gordon 1912-2006
  Obituary **2006**:2
Parks, Rosa 1913-2005
  Obituary **2007**:1
Parks, Suzan-Lori 1964- **2003**:2
Parsons, David 1959- **1993**:4
Parsons, Gary 1950(?)- **2006**:2
Parsons, Richard 1949- **2002**:4
Parton, Dolly 1946- **1999**:4
Pascal, Amy 1958- **2003**:3
Pass, Joe 1929-1994
  Obituary **1994**:4
Pastorius, Jaco 1951-1987
  Obituary **1988**:1
Pataki, George 1945- **1995**:2
Patchett, Ann 1963- **2003**:2
Paterno, Joe 1926- **1995**:4
Patrick, Danica 1982- **2003**:3
Patrick, Robert 1959- **2002**:1
Patterson, Richard North
  1947- **2001**:4
Patton, John 1947(?)- **2004**:4
Pauley, Jane 1950- **1999**:1
Pauling, Linus 1901-1994
  Obituary **1995**:1
Paulsen, Pat 1927-1997
  Obituary **1997**:4
Paulucci, Jeno
  Brief entry **1986**:3
Pausch, Randy 1960-2008
  Obituary **2009**:3
Pavin, Corey 1959- **1996**:4
Paxton, Bill 1955- **1999**:3
Payne, Alexander 1961- **2005**:4
Payton, Lawrence 1938(?)-1997
  Obituary **1997**:4
Payton, Walter 1954-1999
  Obituary **2000**:2

Pearl, Minnie 1912-1996
  Obituary **1996**:3
Pearl Jam **1994**:2
Peck, Gregory 1916-2003
  Obituary **2004**:3
Pedersen, William 1938(?)- **1989**:4
Peebles, R. Donahue 1960- **2003**:2
Peete, Calvin 1943- **1985**:4
Peete, Holly Robinson 1964- **2005**:2
Pei, I.M. 1917- **1990**:4
Peller, Clara 1902(?)-1987
  Obituary **1988**:1
Pelosi, Nancy 1940- **2004**:2
Peltier, Leonard 1944- **1995**:2
Peluso, Michelle 1971(?)- **2007**:4
Pendleton, Clarence M. 1930-1988
  Obituary **1988**:4
Penn, Kal 1977- **2009**:1
Penn, Sean 1960- **1987**:2
Penn & Teller **1992**:1
Pennington, Ty 1965- **2005**:4
Penske, Roger 1937- **1988**:3
Pep, Willie 1922-2006
  Obituary **2008**:1
Pepper, Claude 1900-1989
  Obituary **1989**:4
Percy, Walker 1916-1990
  Obituary **1990**:4
Perdue, Frank 1920-2005
  Obituary **2006**:2
Perelman, Ronald 1943- **1989**:2
Perez, Rosie **1994**:2
Perkins, Anthony 1932-1992
  Obituary **1993**:2
Perkins, Carl 1932-1998 **1998**:2
Perlman, Steve 1961(?)- **1998**:2
Perot, H. Ross 1930- **1992**:4
Perry, Carrie Saxon 1932(?)- **1989**:2
Perry, Harold A. 1917(?)-1991
  Obituary **1992**:1
Perry, Luke 1966(?)- **1992**:3
Perry, Matthew 1969- **1997**:2
Perry, Tyler 1969- **2006**:1
Perry, William 1927- **1994**:4
Pesci, Joe 1943- **1992**:4
Peter, Valentine J. 1934- **1988**:2
Peters, Bernadette 1948- **2000**:1
Peters, Mary E. 1948- **2008**:3
Peters, Tom 1942- **1998**:1
Petersen, Donald Eugene
  1926- **1985**:1
Peterson, Cassandra 1951- **1988**:1
Peterson, Roger Tory 1908-1996
  Obituary **1997**:1
Petty, Tom 1952- **1988**:1
Peyton, Elizabeth 1965- **2007**:1
Pfeiffer, Michelle 1957- **1990**:2
Phair, Liz 1967- **1995**:3
Phelan, John Joseph, Jr. 1931- **1985**:4
Phelps, Michael 1985- **2009**:2
Phifer, Mekhi 1975- **2004**:1
Philbin, Regis 1933- **2000**:2
Phillips, John 1935-2001
  Obituary **2002**:1
Phillips, Julia 1944- **1992**:1
Phillips, Sam 1923-2003
  Obituary **2004**:4
Phoenix, Joaquin 1974- **2000**:4
Phoenix, River 1970-1993 **1990**:2
  Obituary **1994**:2
Piazza, Mike 1968- **1998**:4
Pickett, Wilson 1941-2006

Obituary **2007**:1
Picoult, Jodi 1966- **2008**:1
Pierce, David Hyde 1959- **1996**:3
Pierce, Frederick S. 1934(?)- **1985**:3
Pierce, Mary 1975- **1994**:4
Pierce, Paul 1977- **2009**:2
Pilatus, Robert 1966(?)-1998
Obituary **1998**:3
Pilkey, Dav 1966- **2001**:1
Pincay, Laffit, Jr. 1946- **1986**:3
Pinchot, Bronson 1959(?)- **1987**:4
Pink 1979- **2004**:3
Pinker, Steven A. 1954- **2000**:1
Pinkett Smith, Jada 1971- **1998**:3
Pipher, Mary 1948(?)- **1996**:4
Pippen, Scottie 1965- **1992**:2
Pirro, Jeanine 1951- **1998**:2
Pitt, Brad 1964- **1995**:2
Pittman, Robert W. 1953- **1985**:1
Piven, Jeremy 1965- **2007**:3
Plater-Zyberk, Elizabeth
1950- **2005**:2
Plato, Dana 1964-1999
Obituary **1999**:4
Pleshette, Suzanne 1937-2008
Obituary **2009**:2
Plimpton, George 1927-2003
Obituary **2004**:4
Plotkin, Mark 1955(?)- **1994**:3
Poehler, Amy 1971- **2009**:1
Poitier, Sidney 1927- **1990**:3
Politkovskaya, Anna 1958-2006
Obituary **2007**:4
Pollack, Sydney 1934-2008
Obituary **2009**:2
Popcorn, Faith
Brief entry **1988**:1
Pope, Generoso 1927-1988 **1988**:4
Porco, Carolyn 1953- **2005**:4
Porter, Sylvia 1913-1991
Obituary **1991**:4
Portman, John 1924- **1988**:2
Portman, Natalie 1981- **2000**:3
Posen, Zac 1980- **2009**:3
Post, Peggy 1940(?)- **2001**:4
Poston, Tom 1921-2007
Obituary **2008**:3
Potok, Anna Maximilian
Brief entry **1985**:2
Potok, Chaim 1929-2002
Obituary **2003**:4
Potter, Michael 1960(?)- **2003**:3
Potts, Annie 1952- **1994**:1
Pough, Richard Hooper 1904- **1989**:1
Pouillon, Nora 1943- **2005**:1
Povich, Maury 1939(?)- **1994**:3
Powell, Colin 1937- **1990**:1
Powell, Lewis F. 1907-1998
Obituary **1999**:1
Pratt, Jane 1963(?)- **1999**:1
Predock, Antoine 1936- **1993**:2
Preminger, Otto 1906-1986
Obituary **1986**:3
Presley, Lisa Marie 1968- **2004**:3
Presley, Pricilla 1945- **2001**:1
Presser, Jackie 1926-1988
Obituary **1988**:4
Pressler, Paul 1956(?)- **2003**:4
Preston, Billy 1946-2006
Obituary **2007**:3
Preston, Robert 1918-1987
Obituary **1987**:3

Prevor, Barry and Steven
Shore **2006**:2
Price, Vincent 1911-1993
Obituary **1994**:2
Pride, Charley 1938(?)- **1998**:1
Priestly, Jason 1970(?)- **1993**:2
Prince 1958- **1995**:3
Prince, Faith 1959(?)- **1993**:2
Prinze, Freddie, Jr. 1976- **1999**:3
Pritzker, A.N. 1896-1986
Obituary **1986**:2
Probst, Larry 1951(?)- **2005**:1
Proctor, Barbara Gardner
1933(?)- **1985**:3
Profet, Margie 1958- **1994**:4
Proulx, E. Annie 1935- **1996**:1
Prowse, Juliet 1937-1996
Obituary **1997**:1
Prusiner, Stanley 1942- **1998**:2
Pryce, Deborah 1951- **2006**:3
Pryor, Richard **1999**:3
Public Enemy **1992**:1
Puccio, Thomas P. 1944- **1986**:4
Puck, Theodore 1916-2005
Obituary **2007**:1
Puck, Wolfgang 1949- **1990**:1
Puckett, Kirby 1960-2006
Obituary **2007**:2
Puente, Tito 1923-2000
Obituary **2000**:4
Pujols, Albert 1980- **2005**:3
Puleston, Dennis 1905-2001
Obituary **2002**:2
Puryear, Martin 1941- **2002**:4
Puzo, Mario 1920-1999
Obituary **2000**:1
Pynchon, Thomas 1937- **1997**:4
Quaid, Dennis 1954- **1989**:4
Quayle, Dan 1947- **1989**:2
Queen Latifah 1970(?)- **1992**:2
Queer Eye for the Straight Guy
cast **2004**:3
Questrom, Allen 1940- **2001**:4
Quill, Timothy E. 1949- **1997**:3
Quindlen, Anna 1952- **1993**:1
Quinlan, Karen Ann 1954-1985
Obituary **1985**:2
Quinn, Anthony 1915-2001
Obituary **2002**:2
Quinn, Jane Bryant 1939(?)- **1993**:4
Quinn, Martha 1959- **1986**:4
Quivers, Robin 1953(?)- **1995**:4
Rabbitt, Eddie 1941-1998
Obituary **1998**:4
Radecki, Thomas
Brief entry **1986**:2
Radner, Gilda 1946-1989
Obituary **1989**:4
Radocy, Robert
Brief entry **1986**:3
Raimi, Sam 1959- **1999**:2
Raimondi, John
Brief entry **1987**:4
Raines, Franklin 1949- **1997**:4
Raitt, Bonnie 1949- **1990**:2
Raitt, John 1917-2005
Obituary **2006**:2
Ramey, Estelle R. 1917-2006
Obituary **2007**:4
Ramirez, Manny 1972- **2005**:4
Ramo, Roberta Cooper 1942- **1996**:1
Ramone, Joey 1951-2001

Obituary **2002**:2
Rand, A. Barry 1944- **2000**:3
Randall, Lisa 1962- **2009**:2
Randall, Tony 1920-2004
Obituary **2005**:3
Randi, James 1928- **1990**:2
Raphael, Sally Jessy 1943- **1992**:4
Rapp, C.J.
Brief entry **1987**:3
Rascal Flatts **2007**:1
Rashad, Phylicia 1948- **1987**:3
Raskin, Jef 1943(?)- **1997**:4
Rauschenberg, Robert 1925- **1991**:2
Raven 1985- **2005**:1
Rawlings, Mike 1954- **2003**:1
Rawls, Lou 1933-2006
Obituary **2007**:1
Ray, James Earl 1928-1998
Obituary **1998**:4
Ray, Rachael 1968- **2007**:1
Raye, Martha 1916-1994
Obituary **1995**:1
Raymond, Lee R. 1930- **2000**:3
Reagan, Ronald 1911-2004
Obituary **2005**:3
Reasoner, Harry 1923-1991
Obituary **1992**:1
Redenbacher, Orville 1907-1995
Obituary **1996**:1
Redfield, James 1952- **1995**:2
Redford, Robert 1937- **1993**:2
Redig, Patrick 1948- **1985**:3
Redman, Joshua 1969- **1999**:2
Redmond, Tim 1947- **2008**:1
Redstone, Sumner 1923- **1994**:1
Reed, Dean 1939(?)-1986
Obituary **1986**:3
Reed, Donna 1921-1986
Obituary **1986**:1
Reed, Ralph 1961(?)- **1995**:1
Reed, Robert 1933(?)-1992
Obituary **1992**:4
Reese, Della 1931- **1999**:2
Reeve, Christopher 1952- **1997**:2
Reeves, Keanu 1964- **1992**:1
Reeves, Steve 1926-2000
Obituary **2000**:4
Regan, Judith 1953- **2003**:1
Rehnquist, William H. 1924- **2001**:2
Reich, Robert 1946- **1995**:4
Reichs, Kathleen J. 1948- **2007**:3
Reid, Harry 1939- **2006**:1
Reilly, Charles Nelson
Obituary **2008**:3
Reilly, John C. 1965- **2003**:4
Reiner, Rob 1947- **1991**:2
Reiser, Paul 1957- **1995**:2
Remick, Lee 1936(?)-1991
Obituary **1992**:1
Reno, Janet 1938- **1993**:3
Retton, Mary Lou 1968- **1985**:2
Reubens, Paul 1952- **1987**:2
Rey, Margret E. 1906-1996
Obituary **1997**:2
Reynolds, Paula Rosput 1956- **2008**:4
Reznor, Trent 1965- **2000**:2
Ribicoff, Abraham 1910-1998
Obituary **1998**:3
Ricci, Christina 1980- **1999**:1
Rice, Anne 1941- **1995**:1
Rice, Condoleezza 1954- **2002**:1
Rice, Jerry 1962- **1990**:4

Rich, Buddy 1917-1987
   Obituary **1987**:3
Rich, Charlie 1932-1995
   Obituary **1996**:1
Richards, Ann 1933- **1991**:2
Richards, Michael 1949(?)- **1993**:4
Richmond, Julius B. 1916-2008
   Obituary **2009**:4
Richter, Charles Francis 1900-1985
   Obituary **1985**:4
Rickover, Hyman 1900-1986
   Obituary **1986**:4
Riddle, Nelson 1921-1985
   Obituary **1985**:4
Ridge, Tom 1945- **2002**:2
Rifkin, Jeremy 1945- **1990**:3
Riggio, Leonard S. 1941- **1999**:4
Riggs, Bobby 1918-1995
   Obituary **1996**:2
Rigopulos, Alex 1970- **2009**:4
Riley, Pat 1945- **1994**:3
Riley, Richard W. 1933- **1996**:3
Rimes, LeeAnn 1982- **1997**:4
Riney, Hal 1932- **1989**:1
Ringgold, Faith 1930- **2000**:3
Ringwald, Molly 1968- **1985**:4
Riordan, Richard 1930- **1993**:4
Ripa, Kelly 1970- **2002**:2
Ripken, Cal, Jr. 1960- **1986**:2
Ripken, Cal, Sr. 1936(?)-1999
   Obituary **1999**:4
Ritchie, Dennis and Kenneth
   Thompson **2000**:1
Ritter, John 1948- **2003**:4
Ritts, Herb 1954(?)- **1992**:4
Rivera, Geraldo 1943- **1989**:1
Rivers, Joan 1933- **2005**:3
Rizzo, Frank 1920-1991
   Obituary **1992**:1
Robards, Jason 1922-2000
   Obituary **2001**:3
Robb, Charles S. 1939- **1987**:2
Robbins, Harold 1916-1997
   Obituary **1998**:1
Robbins, Jerome 1918-1998
   Obituary **1999**:1
Robbins, Tim 1959- **1993**:1
Roberts, Brian L. 1959- **2002**:4
Roberts, Cokie 1943- **1993**:4
Roberts, Doris 1930- **2003**:4
Roberts, Julia 1967- **1991**:3
Roberts, Steven K. 1952(?)- **1992**:1
Roberts, Xavier 1955- **1985**:3
Robertson, Pat 1930- **1988**:2
Robinson, David 1965- **1990**:4
Robinson, Earl 1910(?)-1991
   Obituary **1992**:1
Robinson, Eddie 1919-2007
   Obituary **2008**:2
Robinson, Frank 1935- **1990**:2
Robinson, Max 1939-1988
   Obituary **1989**:2
Robinson, Sugar Ray 1921-1989
   Obituary **1989**:3
Robinson, V. Gene 1947- **2004**:4
Roche, Kevin 1922- **1985**:1
Rock, Chris 1967(?)- **1998**:1
Rock, John
   Obituary **1985**:1
Rock, The 1972- **2001**:2
Rockwell, David 1956- **2003**:3
Roddenberry, Gene 1921-1991

Obituary **1992**:2
Roddick, Andy 1982- **2004**:3
Rodin, Judith 1945(?)- **1994**:4
Rodman, Dennis 1961- **1991**:3
Rodriguez, Alex 1975- **2001**:2
Rodriguez, Narciso 1961- **2005**:1
Rodriguez, Robert 1968- **2005**:1
Roedy, Bill 1949(?)- **2003**:2
Roemer, Buddy 1943- **1991**:4
Rogers, Adrian 1931- **1987**:4
Rogers, Fred 1928- **2000**:4
Rogers, Ginger 1911(?)-1995
   Obituary **1995**:4
Rogers, Roy 1911-1998
   Obituary **1998**:4
Rogers, William P. 1913-2001
   Obituary **2001**:4
Roizen, Michael 1946- **2007**:4
Roker, Al 1954- **2003**:1
Roker, Roxie 1929(?)-1995
   Obituary **1996**:2
Rolle, Esther 1922-1998
   Obituary **1999**:2
Rollins, Henry 1961- **2007**:3
Rollins, Howard E., Jr. 1950- **1986**:1
Romano, Ray 1957- **2001**:4
Romijn, Rebecca 1972- **2007**:1
Romo, Tony 1980- **2008**:3
Roncal, Mally 1972- **2009**:4
Rooney, Art 1901-1988
   Obituary **1989**:1
Roosevelt, Franklin D., Jr. 1914-1988
   Obituary **1989**:1
Rose, Axl 1962(?)- **1992**:1
Rose, Charlie 1943- **1994**:2
Rose, Pete 1941- **1991**:1
Rosenberg, Evelyn 1942- **1988**:2
Rosenberg, Steven 1940- **1989**:1
Rosendahl, Bruce R.
   Brief entry **1986**:4
Rosenfeld, Irene 1953- **2008**:3
Rosenthal, Joseph 1911-2006
   Obituary **2007**:4
Rosenzweig, Ilene 1965(?)- **2004**:1
Rosgen, Dave 1942(?)- **2005**:2
Ros-Lehtinen, Ileana 1952- **2000**:2
Ross, Herbert 1927-2001
   Obituary **2002**:4
Ross, Percy
   Brief entry **1986**:2
Ross, Steven J. 1927-1992
   Obituary **1993**:3
Rossellini, Isabella 1952- **2001**:4
Rossner, Judith 1935-2005
   Obituary **2006**:4
Rosten, Leo 1908-1997
   Obituary **1997**:3
Roth, Philip 1933- **1999**:1
Roth, William Victor, Jr. 1921-2003
   Obituary **2005**:1
Rothenberg, Susan 1945- **1995**:3
Rothstein, Ruth **1988**:2
Rothwax, Harold 1930- **1996**:3
Rourke, Mickey 1956- **1988**:4
Rouse, James 1914-1996
   Obituary **1996**:4
Rove, Karl 1950- **2006**:2
Rowan, Carl 1925-2000
   Obituary **2001**:2
Rowan, Dan 1922-1987
   Obituary **1988**:1
Rowe, Jack 1944- **2005**:2

Rowland, Pleasant **1992**:3
Rowley, Coleen 1955(?)- **2004**:2
Rowley, Cynthia 1958- **2002**:1
Roybal-Allard, Lucille 1941- **1999**:4
Royko, Mike 1932-1997
   Obituary **1997**:4
Rozelle, Pete 1926-1996
   Obituary **1997**:2
Rubin, Jerry 1938-1994
   Obituary **1995**:2
Rudd, Paul 1969- **2009**:4
Rudner, Rita 1956- **1993**:2
Rudnick, Paul 1957(?)- **1994**:3
Rudolph, Wilma 1940-1994
   Obituary **1995**:2
Ruehl, Mercedes 195(?)- **1992**:4
Ruffin, David 1941-1991
   Obituary **1991**:4
Rumsfeld, Donald 1932- **2004**:1
Runyan, Marla 1969- **2001**:1
RuPaul 1961(?)- **1996**:1
Ruppe, Loret Miller 1936- **1986**:2
Rusk, Dean 1909-1994
   Obituary **1995**:2
Russell, Keri 1976- **2000**:1
Russell, Kurt 1951- **2007**:4
Russell, Mary 1950- **2009**:2
Russell, Nipsey 1924-2005
   Obituary **2007**:1
Russert, Tim 1950-2008
   Obituary **2009**:3
Russo, Patricia 1952- **2008**:4
Russo, Rene 1954- **2000**:2
Russo, Richard 1949- **2002**:3
Rutan, Burt 1943- **1987**:2
Ryan, Meg 1962(?)- **1994**:1
Ryan, Nolan 1947- **1989**:4
Ryder, Winona 1971- **1991**:2
Saberhagen, Bret 1964- **1986**:1
Sachs, Jeffrey D. 1954- **2004**:4
Safire, William 1929- **2000**:3
Sagal, Katey 1954- **2005**:2
Sagan, Carl 1934-1996
   Obituary **1997**:2
Sagansky, Jeff 1952- **1993**:2
Sajak, Pat
   Brief entry **1985**:4
Salbi, Zainab 1969(?)- **2008**:3
Salerno-Sonnenberg,
   Nadja 1961(?)- **1988**:4
Salk, Jonas 1914-1995 **1994**:4
   Obituary **1995**:4
Salzman, Mark 1959- **2002**:1
Sammons, Mary 1946- **2007**:4
Sample, Bill
   Brief entry **1986**:2
Sampras, Pete 1971- **1994**:1
Sams, Craig 1944- **2007**:3
Sanchez, Loretta 1960- **2000**:3
Sanders, Barry 1968- **1992**:1
Sanders, Bernie 1941(?)- **1991**:4
Sanders, Deion 1967- **1992**:4
Sandler, Adam 1966- **1999**:2
Sanger, Steve 1946- **2002**:3
Saporta, Vicki
   Brief entry **1987**:3
Sapphire 1951(?)- **1996**:4
Saralegui, Cristina 1948- **1999**:2
Sarandon, Susan 1946- **1995**:3
Sarazen, Gene 1902-1999
   Obituary **1999**:4
Satcher, David 1941- **2001**:4

Satriani, Joe 1957(?)- **1989**:3
Saul, Betsy 1968- **2009**:2
Savage, Fred 1976- **1990**:1
Savalas, Telly 1924-1994
    Obituary **1994**:3
Sawyer, Diane 1945- **1994**:4
Scalia, Antonin 1936- **1988**:2
Scardino, Marjorie 1947- **2002**:1
Scavullo, Francesco 1921-2004
    Obituary **2005**:1
Schaap, Dick 1934-2001
    Obituary **2003**:1
Schaefer, William Donald
    1921- **1988**:1
Schank, Roger 1946- **1989**:2
Scheck, Barry 1949- **2000**:4
Scheider, Roy 1932-2008
    Obituary **2009**:2
Schembechler, Bo 1929(?)- **1990**:3
Schenk, Dale 1957(?)- **2002**:2
Schiavo, Mary 1955- **1998**:2
Schilling, Curt 1966- **2002**:3
Schirra, Wally 1923-2007
    Obituary **2008**:3
Schlessinger, David
    Brief entry **1985**:1
Schlessinger, Laura 1947(?)- **1996**:3
Schmelzer, Sheri 1965- **2009**:4
Schmidt, Eric 1955- **2002**:4
Schmidt, Mike 1949- **1988**:3
Schnabel, Julian 1951- **1997**:1
Schneider, Rob 1965- **1997**:4
Schoenfeld, Gerald 1924- **1986**:2
Scholz, Tom 1949- **1987**:2
Schott, Marge 1928- **1985**:4
Schreiber, Liev 1967- **2007**:2
Schroeder, Barbet 1941- **1996**:1
Schroeder, William J. 1932-1986
    Obituary **1986**:4
Schultes, Richard Evans 1915-2001
    Obituary **2002**:1
Schultz, Howard 1953- **1995**:3
Schulz, Charles 1922-2000
    Obituary **2000**:3
Schulz, Charles M. 1922- **1998**:1
Schumacher, Joel 1929- **2004**:3
Schuman, Patricia Glass
    1943- **1993**:2
Schwab, Charles 1937(?)- **1989**:3
Schwartz, Allen 1945(?)- **2008**:2
Schwartz, David 1936(?)- **1988**:3
Schwarzenegger, Arnold
    1947- **1991**:1
Schwarzkopf, Norman 1934- **1991**:3
Schwimmer, David 1966(?)- **1996**:2
Schwinn, Edward R., Jr.
    Brief entry **1985**:4
Scorsese, Martin 1942- **1989**:1
Scott, Gene
    Brief entry **1986**:1
Scott, George C. 1927-1999
    Obituary **2000**:2
Scott, H. Lee, Jr. 1949- **2008**:3
Scott, Randolph 1898(?)-1987
    Obituary **1987**:2
Sculley, John 1939- **1989**:4
Seacrest, Ryan 1976- **2004**:4
Sears, Barry 1947- **2004**:2
Sebelius, Kathleen 1948- **2008**:4
Sebold, Alice 1963(?)- **2005**:4
Secretariat 1970-1989
    Obituary **1990**:1

Sedaris, Amy 1961- **2009**:3
Sedaris, David 1956- **2005**:3
Sedelmaier, Joe 1933- **1985**:3
Sedgwick, Kyra 1965- **2006**:2
Segal, Shelli 1955(?)- **2005**:3
Seger, Bob 1945- **1987**:1
Seidelman, Susan 1953(?)- **1985**:4
Seidenberg, Ivan 1946- **2004**:1
Seinfeld, Jerry 1954- **1992**:4
Selena 1971-1995
    Obituary **1995**:4
Selig, Bud 1934- **1995**:2
Semel, Terry 1943- **2002**:2
Senk, Glen 1956- **2009**:3
Seo, Danny 1977- **2008**:3
Serra, Richard 1939- **2009**:1
Serrano, Andres 1950- **2000**:4
Serros, Michele 1967(?)- **2008**:2
Sethi, Simran 1971(?)- **2008**:1
Sevareid, Eric 1912-1992
    Obituary **1993**:1
Sevigny, Chloe 1974- **2001**:4
Seyfried, Amanda 1985- **2009**:3
Shabazz, Betty 1936-1997
    Obituary **1997**:4
Shaich, Ron 1953- **2004**:4
Shakur, Tupac 1971-1996
    Obituary **1997**:1
Shalala, Donna 1941- **1992**:3
Shalikashvili, John 1936- **1994**:2
Shandling, Garry 1949- **1995**:1
Shanley, John Patrick 1950- **2006**:1
Sharkey, Ray 1953-1993
    Obituary **1994**:1
Sharpe, Sterling 1965- **1994**:3
Sharpton, Al 1954- **1991**:2
Shaw, Artie 1910-2004
    Obituary **2006**:1
Shaw, Carol 1958(?)- **2002**:1
Shaw, William 1934(?)- **2000**:3
Shawn, Dick 1924(?)-1987
    Obituary **1987**:3
Shawn, William 1907-1992
    Obituary **1993**:3
Shea, Jim, Jr. 1968- **2002**:4
Sheedy, Ally 1962- **1989**:1
Sheehan, Daniel P. 1945(?)- **1989**:1
Sheen, Charlie 1965- **2001**:2
Sheen, Martin 1940- **2002**:1
Sheffield, Gary 1968- **1998**:1
Sheindlin, Judith 1942(?)- **1999**:1
Sheldon, Sidney 1917-2007
    Obituary **2008**:2
Shepard, Alan 1923-1998
    Obituary **1999**:1
Shepard, Sam 1943- **1996**:4
Shepherd, Cybill 1950- **1996**:3
Sherman, Cindy 1954- **1992**:3
Sherman, Russell 1930- **1987**:4
Shields, Brooke 1965- **1996**:3
Shields, Carol 1935-2003
    Obituary **2004**:3
Shilts, Randy 1951-1994 **1993**:4
    Obituary **1994**:3
Shimomura, Tsutomu 1965- **1996**:1
Shirley, Donna 1941- **1999**:1
Shocked, Michelle 1963(?)- **1989**:4
Shoemaker, Bill 1931-2003
    Obituary **2004**:4
Shore, Dinah 1917-1994
    Obituary **1994**:3
Shreve, Anita 1946(?)- **2003**:4

Shriver, Lionel 1957- **2008**:4
Shriver, Maria
    Brief entry **1986**:2
Shue, Andrew 1964- **1994**:4
Shula, Don 1930- **1992**:2
Shyamalan, M. Night 1970- **2003**:2
Sidney, Ivan
    Brief entry **1987**:2
Sidransky, David 1960- **2002**:4
Siebert, Muriel 1932(?)- **1987**:2
Sigmund, Barbara Boggs 1939-1990
    Obituary **1991**:1
Silber, Joan 1945- **2009**:4
Silber, John 1926- **1990**:1
Silverman, Jonathan 1966- **1997**:2
Silverman, Sarah 1970- **2008**:1
Silvers, Phil 1912-1985
    Obituary **1985**:4
Silverstein, Shel 1932-1999
    Obituary **1999**:4
Silverstone, Alicia 1976- **1997**:4
Simmons, Adele Smith 1941- **1988**:4
Simmons, Russell and Kimora
    Lee **2003**:2
Simmons, Ruth 1945- **1995**:2
Simon, Lou Anna K. 1947- **2005**:4
Simon, Paul 1928-2003
    Obituary **2005**:1
Simon, Paul 1942(?)- **1992**:2
Simone, Nina 1933-2003
    Obituary **2004**:2
Simpson, Lorna 1960- **2008**:1
Simpson, Wallis 1896-1986
    Obituary **1986**:3
Simpson-Wentz, Ashlee 1984- **2009**:1
Sinatra, Frank 1915-1998
    Obituary **1998**:4
Sinclair, Mary 1918- **1985**:2
Singer, Bryan 1965- **2007**:3
Singer, Isaac Bashevis 1904-1991
    Obituary **1992**:1
Singer, Margaret Thaler 1921-2003
    Obituary **2005**:1
Singleton, John 1968- **1994**:3
Sinise, Gary 1955(?)- **1996**:1
Sirica, John 1904-1992
    Obituary **1993**:2
Siskel, Gene 1946-1999
    Obituary **1999**:3
Skaist-Levy, Pam and Gela
    Taylor **2005**:1
Skelton, Red 1913-1997
    Obituary **1998**:1
Skinner, B.F. 1904-1990
    Obituary **1991**:1
Skinner, Sam 1938- **1992**:3
Slater, Christian 1969- **1994**:1
Slater, Rodney E. 1955- **1997**:4
Slatkin, Harry 1961(?)- **2006**:2
Slick, Grace 1939- **2001**:2
Slotnick, Barry
    Brief entry **1987**:4
Smale, John G. 1927- **1987**:3
Smigel, Robert 1959(?)- **2001**:3
Smiley, Jane 1949- **1995**:4
Smith, Anna Deavere 1950- **2002**:2
Smith, Anna Nicole 1967-2007
    Obituary **2008**:2
Smith, Buffalo Bob 1917-1998
    Obituary **1999**:1
Smith, Emmitt **1994**:1
Smith, Frederick W. 1944- **1985**:4

Smith, Howard K. 1914-2002
    Obituary **2003**:2
Smith, Jack 1938- **1994**:3
Smith, Jeff 1939(?)- **1991**:4
Smith, Jerry 1943-1986
    Obituary **1987**:1
Smith, Jimmy 1928-2005
    Obituary **2006**:2
Smith, Kate 1907(?)-1986
    Obituary **1986**:3
Smith, Kevin 1970- **2000**:4
Smith, Lanty 1942- **2009**:3
Smith, Roger 1925- **1990**:3
Smith, Samantha 1972-1985
    Obituary **1985**:3
Smith, Will 1968- **1997**:2
Smith, Willi 1948-1987
    Obituary **1987**:3
Smits, Jimmy 1956- **1990**:1
Smoot, George F. 1945- **1993**:3
Smyth, Russell P. 1958- **2009**:4
Snead, Sam 1912-2002
    Obituary **2003**:3
Snider, Dee 1955- **1986**:1
Snider, Stacey 1961(?)- **2002**:4
Snipes, Wesley 1962- **1993**:1
Snoop Doggy Dogg 1972(?)- **1995**:2
Snow, Hank 1914-1999
    Obituary **2000**:3
Snow, John W. 1939- **2006**:2
Snow, Tony 1955-2008
    Obituary **2009**:3
Snowe, Olympia 1947- **1995**:3
Snyder, Jimmy 1919-1996
    Obituary **1996**:4
Snyder, Mitch 1944(?)-1990
    Obituary **1991**:1
Snyder, Ron 1956(?)- **2007**:4
Sobieski, Leelee 1982- **2002**:3
Sobol, Donald J. 1924- **2004**:4
Soderbergh, Steven 1963- **2001**:4
Som, Peter 1971- **2009**:1
Somers, Suzanne 1946- **2000**:1
Sondheim, Stephen 1930- **1994**:4
Sontag, Susan 1933-2004
    Obituary **2006**:1
Soren, David
    Brief entry **1986**:3
Sorkin, Aaron 1961- **2003**:2
Sorvino, Mira 1970(?)- **1996**:3
Sothern, Ann 1909-2001
    Obituary **2002**:1
Souter, David 1939- **1991**:3
Southern, Terry 1926-1995
    Obituary **1996**:2
Sowell, Thomas 1930- **1998**:3
Spacek, Sissy 1949- **2003**:1
Spacey, Kevin 1959- **1996**:4
Spade, David 1965- **1999**:2
Spade, Kate 1962- **2003**:1
Spader, James 1960- **1991**:2
Spahn, Warren 1921-2003
    Obituary **2005**:1
Spears, Britney 1981- **2000**:3
Spector, Phil 1940- **1989**:1
Spelke, Elizabeth 1949- **2003**:1
Spelling, Aaron 1923-2006
    Obituary **2007**:3
Spelling, Tori 1973- **2008**:3
Spellings, Margaret 1957- **2005**:4
Spergel, David 1961- **2004**:1
Spheeris, Penelope 1945(?)- **1989**:2

Spiegelman, Art 1948- **1998**:3
Spielberg, Steven 1947- **1993**:4
Spillane, Mickey 1918-2006
    Obituary **2007**:3
Spitzer, Eliot 1959- **2007**:2
Spock, Benjamin 1903-1998 **1995**:2
    Obituary **1998**:3
Spong, John 1931- **1991**:3
Spray, Ed 1941- **2004**:1
Sprewell, Latrell 1970- **1999**:4
Sprouse, Stephen 1953-2004
    Obituary **2005**:2
St. James, Lyn 1947- **1993**:2
Stack, Robert 1919-2003
    Obituary **2004**:2
Stafford, Jo 1917-2008
    Obituary **2009**:3
Stahl, Lesley 1941- **1997**:1
Stallings, George A., Jr. 1948- **1990**:1
Stallone, Sylvester 1946- **1994**:2
Stamos, John 1963- **2008**:1
Staples, Roebuck Pops 1915-2000
    Obituary **2001**:3
Stapleton, Maureen 1925-2006
    Obituary **2007**:2
Stargell, Willie 1940-2001
    Obituary **2002**:1
Starr, Kenneth 1946- **1998**:3
Steel, Danielle 1947- **1999**:2
Steel, Dawn 1946-1997 **1990**:1
    Obituary **1998**:2
Steele, Shelby 1946- **1991**:2
Stefani, Gwen 1969- **2005**:4
Steger, Will 1945(?)- **1990**:4
Steig, William 1907-2003
    Obituary **2004**:4
Steiger, Rod 1925-2002
    Obituary **2003**:4
Stein, Ben 1944- **2001**:1
Steinberg, Leigh 1949- **1987**:3
Steinbrenner, George 1930- **1991**:1
Steinem, Gloria 1934- **1996**:2
Stella, Frank 1936- **1996**:2
Stempel, Robert 1933- **1991**:3
Stephanopoulos, George
    1961- **1994**:3
Sterling, Bruce 1954- **1995**:4
Stern, David 1942- **1991**:4
Stern, Howard 1954- **1988**:2
Stern, Isaac 1920-2001
    Obituary **2002**:4
Stevens, Anne 1949(?)- **2006**:3
Stevens, Eileen 1939- **1987**:3
Stevenson, McLean 1929-1996
    Obituary **1996**:2
Stewart, Dave 1957- **1991**:1
Stewart, Jimmy 1908-1997
    Obituary **1997**:4
Stewart, Jon 1962- **2001**:2
Stewart, Julia 1955- **2008**:3
Stewart, Martha 1942(?)- **1992**:1
Stewart, Payne 1957-1999
    Obituary **2000**:2
Stewart, Potter 1915-1985
    Obituary **1986**:1
Stewart, Tony 1971- **2003**:4
Stiles, Julia 1981- **2002**:3
Stiller, Ben 1965- **1999**:1
Stine, R. L. 1943- **2003**:1
Stockton, John Houston 1962- **1997**:3
Stockton, Shreve 1977- **2009**:4
Stofflet, Ty

Brief entry **1987**:1
Stokes, Carl 1927-1996
    Obituary **1996**:4
Stone, I.F. 1907-1989
    Obituary **1990**:1
Stone, Irving 1903-1989
    Obituary **1990**:2
Stone, Oliver 1946- **1990**:4
Stone, Sharon 1958- **1993**:4
Stonesifer, Patty 1956- **1997**:1
Strait, George 1952- **1998**:3
Strange, Curtis 1955- **1988**:4
Strauss, Robert 1918- **1991**:4
Streep, Meryl 1949- **1990**:2
Street, Picabo 1971- **1999**:3
Streisand, Barbra 1942- **1992**:2
Stritch, Elaine 1925- **2002**:4
Stroh, Peter W. 1927- **1985**:2
Stroman, Susan **2000**:4
Strout, Elizabeth 1956- **2009**:1
Strug, Kerri 1977- **1997**:3
Studi, Wes 1944(?)- **1994**:3
Styne, Jule 1905-1994
    Obituary **1995**:1
Styron, William 1925-2006
    Obituary **2008**:1
Suarez, Xavier
    Brief entry **1986**:2
Suckling, Kierán 1964- **2009**:2
Sugarland 1970- **2009**:2
Sui, Anna 1955(?)- **1995**:1
Sullivan, Leon 1922-2001
    Obituary **2002**:2
Sullivan, Louis 1933- **1990**:4
Sulzberger, Arthur O., Jr.
    1951- **1998**:3
Summitt, Pat 1952- **2004**:1
Sun Ra 1914(?)-1993
    Obituary **1994**:1
Sununu, John 1939- **1989**:2
Susskind, David 1920-1987
    Obituary **1987**:2
Swaggart, Jimmy 1935- **1987**:3
Swank, Hilary 1974- **2000**:3
Swanson, Mary Catherine
    1944- **2002**:2
Swayze, John Cameron 1906-1995
    Obituary **1996**:1
Sweeney, John J. 1934- **2000**:3
Swift, Jane 1965(?)- **2002**:1
Swift, Taylor 1989- **2009**:3
Swoopes, Sheryl 1971- **1998**:2
Sykes, Wanda 1964- **2007**:4
System of a Down **2006**:4
Szent-Gyoergyi, Albert 1893-1986
    Obituary **1987**:2
T. I. 1980- **2008**:1
Tafel, Richard 1962- **2000**:4
Tagliabue, Paul 1940- **1990**:2
Tan, Amy 1952- **1998**:3
Tandy, Jessica 1901-1994 **1990**:4
    Obituary **1995**:1
Tannen, Deborah 1945- **1995**:1
Tanny, Vic 1912(?)-1985
    Obituary **1985**:3
Tarantino, Quentin 1963(?)- **1995**:1
Tarkenian, Jerry 1930- **1990**:4
Tartakovsky, Genndy 1970- **2004**:4
Tartikoff, Brandon 1949-1997 **1985**:2
    Obituary **1998**:1
Tartt, Donna 1963- **2004**:3
Taylor, Jeff 1960- **2001**:3

Taylor, Lawrence 1959- **1987**:3
Taylor, Lili 1967- **2000**:2
Taylor, Maxwell 1901-1987
    Obituary **1987**:3
Taylor, Paul 1930- **1992**:3
Taylor, Susan L. 1946- **1998**:2
Tellem, Nancy 1953(?)- **2004**:4
Tenet, George 1953- **2000**:3
Terry, Randall **1991**:4
Tesh, John 1952- **1996**:3
Testaverde, Vinny 1962- **1987**:2
Teter, Hannah 1987- **2006**:4
Thain, John 1955- **2009**:2
Thalheimer, Richard 1948-
    Brief entry **1988**:3
Tharp, Twyla 1942- **1992**:4
Thiebaud, Wayne 1920- **1991**:1
Thomas, Clarence 1948- **1992**:2
Thomas, Danny 1914-1991
    Obituary **1991**:3
Thomas, Dave **1986**:2
    Obituary **2003**:1
Thomas, Debi 1967- **1987**:2
Thomas, Derrick 1967-2000
    Obituary **2000**:3
Thomas, Edmond J. 1943(?)- **2005**:1
Thomas, Frank 1968- **1994**:3
Thomas, Helen 1920- **1988**:4
Thomas, Isiah 1961- **1989**:2
Thomas, Michael Tilson 1944- **1990**:3
Thomas, Michel 1911(?)- **1987**:4
Thomas, Thurman 1966- **1993**:1
Thomas-Graham, Pamela
    1963- **2007**:1
Thompson, Fred 1942- **1998**:2
Thompson, Hunter S. 1939- **1992**:1
Thompson, John 1941- **1988**:3
Thompson, John W. 1949- **2005**:1
Thompson, Lonnie 1948- **2003**:3
Thompson, Starley
    Brief entry **1987**:3
Thomson, James 1958- **2002**:3
Thornton, Billy Bob 1956(?)- **1997**:4
Thurman, Uma 1970- **1994**:2
Thurmond, Strom 1902-2003
    Obituary **2004**:3
Tiffany 1972- **1989**:1
Tillman, Robert L. 1944(?)- **2004**:1
Tillstrom, Burr 1917-1985
    Obituary **1986**:1
Tilly, Jennifer 1958(?)- **1997**:2
Timbaland 1971- **2007**:4
Timberlake, Justin 1981- **2008**:4
Tisch, Laurence A. 1923- **1988**:2
Tito, Dennis 1940(?)- **2002**:1
TLC **1996**:1
Toguri, Iva 1916-2006
    Obituary **2007**:4
Tohe, Laura 1953- **2009**:2
Tom and Ray Magliozzi **1991**:4
Tomei, Marisa 1964- **1995**:2
Tompkins, Susie
    Brief entry **1987**:2
Tone-Loc 1966- **1990**:3
Toomer, Ron 1930- **1990**:1
Toone, Bill
    Brief entry **1987**:2
Torme, Mel 1925-1999
    Obituary **1999**:4
Torre, Joseph Paul 1940- **1997**:1
Torres, Dara 1967- **2009**:1
Totenberg, Nina 1944- **1992**:2

Tower, John 1926-1991
    Obituary **1991**:4
Townsend, Kathleen Kennedy
    1951- **2001**:3
Trask, Amy 1961- **2003**:3
Traub, Marvin
    Brief entry **1987**:3
Travis, Randy 1959- **1988**:4
Travolta, John 1954- **1995**:2
Tretheway, Natasha 1966- **2008**:3
Treybig, James G. 1940- **1988**:3
Tribe, Laurence H. 1941- **1988**:1
Tritt, Travis 1964(?)- **1995**:1
Trotman, Alex 1933- **1995**:4
Trotter, Charlie 1960- **2000**:4
Troutt, Kenny A. 1948- **1998**:1
Trudeau, Garry 1948- **1991**:2
Truitt, Anne 1921- **1993**:1
Trump, Donald 1946- **1989**:2
Tsongas, Paul Efthemios 1941-1997
    Obituary **1997**:2
Tucci, Stanley 1960- **2003**:2
Tuck, Lily 1938- **2006**:1
Tucker, Chris 1973(?)- **1999**:1
Tucker, Forrest 1919-1986
    Obituary **1987**:1
Tully, Tim 1954(?)- **2004**:3
Tune, Tommy 1939- **1994**:2
Tunick, Spencer 1967- **2008**:1
Ture, Kwame 1941-1998
    Obituary **1999**:2
Turlington, Christy 1969(?)- **2001**:4
Turner, Ike 1931-2007
    Obituary **2009**:1
Turner, Janine 1962- **1993**:2
Turner, Kathleen 1954(?)- **1985**:3
Turner, Lana 1921-1995
    Obituary **1996**:1
Turner, Ted 1938- **1989**:1
Turner, Tina 1939- **2000**:3
Turturro, John 1957- **2002**:2
Tutwiler, Margaret 1950- **1992**:4
Twitty, Conway 1933-1993
    Obituary **1994**:1
Twombley, Cy 1928(?)- **1995**:1
Tyler, Anne 1941- **1995**:4
Tyler, Liv 1978- **1997**:2
Tyler, Richard 1948(?)- **1995**:3
Tyner, Rob 1945(?)-1991
    Obituary **1992**:2
Tyson, Don 1930- **1995**:3
Tyson, Laura D'Andrea 1947- **1994**:1
Tyson, Mike 1966- **1986**:4
Udall, Mo 1922-1998
    Obituary **1999**:2
Underwood, Carrie 1983- **2008**:1
Union, Gabrielle 1972- **2004**:2
Unitas, Johnny 1933-2002
    Obituary **2003**:4
Unz, Ron 1962(?)- **1999**:1
Updike, John 1932- **2001**:2
Upshaw, Dawn 1960- **1991**:2
Upshaw, Gene 1945- **1988**:1
Urich, Robert 1947- **1988**:1
    Obituary **2003**:3
Usher 1979- **2005**:1
Vagelos, P. Roy 1929- **1989**:4
Valdes-Rodriguez, Alisa 1969- **2005**:4
Valente, Benita 1934(?)- **1985**:3
Valenti, Jack 1921-2007
    Obituary **2008**:3
Valvo, Carmen Marc 1954- **2003**:4

Van Allen, James 1914-2006
    Obituary **2007**:4
Van Andel, Jay 1924-2004
    Obituary **2006**:1
Vandross, Luther 1951-2005
    Obituary **2006**:3
Van Duyn, Mona 1921- **1993**:2
Van Dyken, Amy 1973- **1997**:1
Van Halen, Edward 1957- **1985**:2
Vanilla Ice 1967(?)- **1991**:3
Van Sant, Gus 1952- **1992**:2
Van Slyke, Andy 1960- **1992**:4
Varney, Jim 1949-2000
    Brief entry **1985**:4
    Obituary **2000**:3
Varone, Doug 1956- **2001**:2
Varvatos, John 1956(?)- **2006**:2
Vaughan, Sarah 1924-1990
    Obituary **1990**:3
Vaughan, Stevie Ray 1956(?)-1990
    Obituary **1991**:1
Vaughn, Mo 1967- **1999**:2
Vaughn, Vince 1970- **1999**:2
Veeck, Bill 1914-1986
    Obituary **1986**:1
Vega, Suzanne 1959- **1988**:1
Venter, J. Craig 1946- **2001**:1
Ventura, Jesse 1951- **1999**:2
Venturi, Robert 1925- **1994**:4
Verdi-Fletcher, Mary 1955- **1998**:2
Verdon, Gwen 1925-2000
    Obituary **2001**:2
Vickrey, William S. 1914-1996
    Obituary **1997**:2
Vidal, Gore 1925- **1996**:2
Vieira, Meredith 1953- **2001**:3
Vincent, Fay 1938- **1990**:2
Vinton, Will
    Brief entry **1988**:1
Violet, Arlene 1943- **1985**:3
Vischer, Phil 1966- **2002**:2
Vitale, Dick 1939- **1988**:4
Vitetta, Ellen S. 1942(?)- **2005**:4
Vitousek, Peter 1949- **2003**:1
Vogel, Paula 1951- **1999**:2
Voight, Jon 1938- **2002**:3
Volkow, Nora 1956- **2009**:1
Von D, Kat 1982- **2008**:3
Vonnegut, Kurt 1922- **1998**:4
von Trapp, Maria 1905-1987
    Obituary **1987**:3
vos Savant, Marilyn 1946- **1988**:2
Vreeland, Diana 1903(?)-1989
    Obituary **1990**:1
Wachner, Linda 1946- **1988**:3
Waddell, Thomas F. 1937-1987
    Obituary **1988**:2
Wade, Dwyane 1982- **2007**:1
Wagner, Catherine F. 1953- **2002**:3
Wagoner, Porter 1927-2007
    Obituary **2008**:4
Waitt, Ted 1963(?)- **1997**:4
Waldron, Hicks B. 1923- **1987**:3
Walgreen, Charles III
    Brief entry **1987**:4
Walker, Alice 1944- **1999**:1
Walker, Jay 1955- **2004**:2
Walker, Junior 1942(?)-1995
    Obituary **1996**:2
Walker, Kara 1969- **1999**:2
Walker, Nancy 1922-1992
    Obituary **1992**:3

Wallace, Ben 1974- **2004**:3
Wallace, George 1919-1998
   Obituary **1999**:1
Wallace, Irving 1916-1990
   Obituary **1991**:1
Wallis, Hal 1898(?)-1986
   Obituary **1987**:1
Walls, Jeannette 1960(?)- **2006**:3
Walsh, Bill 1931- **1987**:4
Walters, Barbara 1931- **1998**:3
Walton, Sam 1918-1992 **1986**:2
   Obituary **1993**:1
Wang, An 1920-1990 **1986**:1
   Obituary **1990**:3
Wang, Vera 1949- **1998**:4
Wapner, Joseph A. 1919- **1987**:1
Ward, Sela 1956- **2001**:3
Warden, Jack 1920-2006
   Obituary **2007**:3
Warhol, Andy 1927(?)-1987
   Obituary **1987**:2
Wariner, Jeremy 1984- **2006**:3
Warner, Kurt 1971- **2000**:3
Warren, Robert Penn 1905-1989
   Obituary **1990**:1
Washington, Alonzo 1967- **2000**:1
Washington, Denzel 1954- **1993**:2
Washington, Grover, Jr. 1943- **1989**:1
Washington, Harold 1922-1987
   Obituary **1988**:1
Wasserman, Lew 1913-2002
   Obituary **2003**:3
Wasserstein, Wendy 1950- **1991**:3
Waterman, Cathy 1950(?)- **2002**:2
Waters, Alice 1944- **2006**:3
Waters, John 1946- **1988**:3
Waters, Maxine 1938- **1998**:4
Waterston, Sam 1940- **2006**:1
Watkins, Sherron 1959- **2003**:1
Watson, Elizabeth 1949- **1991**:2
Watterson, Bill 1958(?)- **1990**:3
Wattleton, Faye 1943- **1989**:1
Watts, J.C. 1957- **1999**:2
Wayans, Damon 1960- **1998**:4
Wayans, Keenen Ivory
   1958(?)- **1991**:1
Wayne, David 1914-1995
   Obituary **1995**:3
Weaver, Sigourney 1949- **1988**:3
Webb, Wellington E. 1941- **2000**:3
Webber, Chris 1973- **1994**:1
Weber, Pete 1962- **1986**:3
Wegman, William 1942(?)- **1991**:1
Weicker, Lowell P., Jr. 1931- **1993**:1
Weil, Andrew 1942- **1997**:4
Weill, Sandy 1933- **1990**:4
Weinberger, Caspar 1917-2006
   Obituary **2007**:2
Weiner, Jennifer 1970- **2006**:3
Weinstein, Bob and Harvey **2000**:4
Weintraub, Jerry 1937- **1986**:1
Weitz, Bruce 1943- **1985**:4
Welch, Bob 1956- **1991**:3
Welch, Jack 1935- **1993**:3
Weldon, William 1948- **2007**:4
Wells, David 1963- **1999**:3
Wells, Linda 1958- **2002**:3
Wells, Mary 1943-1992
   Obituary **1993**:1
Wells, Sharlene
   Brief entry **1985**:1
Wellstone, Paul 1944-2002

Obituary **2004**:1
Welty, Eudora 1909-2001
   Obituary **2002**:3
Wenner, Jann 1946- **1993**:1
Wescott, Seth 1976- **2006**:4
West, Cornel 1953- **1994**:2
West, Dorothy 1907- **1996**:1
West, Dottie 1932-1991
   Obituary **1992**:2
West, Kanye 1977- **2006**:1
West, Michael Lee 1953- **2009**:2
Westmoreland, William C. 1914-2005
   Obituary **2006**:4
Wexler, Jerry 1917-2008
   Obituary **2009**:4
Wexler, Nancy S. 1945- **1992**:3
Whaley, Suzy 1966- **2003**:4
Whedon, Joss 1964- **2006**:3
Whelan, Tensie 1960- **2007**:1
Whelan, Wendy 1967(?)- **1999**:3
Whipple, Fred L. 1906-2004
   Obituary **2005**:4
Whitaker, Forest 1961- **1996**:2
White, Barry 1944-2003
   Obituary **2004**:3
White, Bill 1934- **1989**:3
White, Byron 1917-2002
   Obituary **2003**:3
White, Jaleel 1976- **1992**:3
White, Julie 1961- **2008**:2
White, Reggie 1961- **1993**:4
White, Ryan 1972(?)-1990
   Obituary **1990**:3
Whitestone, Heather 1973(?)- **1995**:1
White Stripes, The **2006**:1
Whiting, Susan 1956- **2007**:4
Whitman, Christine Todd 1947(?)-
   **1994**:3
Whitman, Meg 1957- **2000**:3
Whitmire, Kathy 1946- **1988**:2
Whitney, Patrick 1952(?)- **2006**:1
Whitson, Peggy 1960- **2003**:3
Whittle, Christopher 1947- **1989**:3
Wiesel, Elie 1928- **1998**:1
Wiest, Dianne 1948- **1995**:2
Wigand, Jeffrey 1943(?)- **2000**:4
Wigler, Michael
   Brief entry **1985**:1
Wilder, Billy 1906-2002
   Obituary **2003**:2
Wilder, L. Douglas 1931- **1990**:3
Wildmon, Donald 1938- **1988**:4
Wilkens, Lenny 1937- **1995**:2
Williams, Anthony 1952- **2000**:4
Williams, Brian 1959- **2009**:4
Williams, Doug 1955- **1988**:2
Williams, Edward Bennett 1920-1988
   Obituary **1988**:4
Williams, G. Mennen 1911-1988
   Obituary **1988**:2
Williams, Hosea 1926-2000
   Obituary **2001**:2
Williams, Joe 1918-1999
   Obituary **1999**:4
Williams, Pharrell 1973- **2005**:3
Williams, Ricky 1977- **2000**:2
Williams, Robin 1952- **1988**:4
Williams, Serena 1981- **1999**:4
Williams, Ted 1918-2002
   Obituary **2003**:4
Williams, Treat 1951- **2004**:3
Williams, Vanessa L. 1963- **1999**:2

Williams, Venus 1980- **1998**:2
Williams, Willie L. 1944(?)- **1993**:1
Williamson, Marianne
   1953(?)- **1991**:4
Willis, Bruce 1955- **1986**:4
Willson, S. Brian 1942(?)- **1989**:3
Wilson, August 1945- **2002**:2
Wilson, Brian 1942- **1996**:1
Wilson, Carl 1946-1998 **1998**:2
Wilson, Cassandra 1955- **1996**:3
Wilson, Edward O. 1929- **1994**:4
Wilson, Flip 1933-1998
   Obituary **1999**:2
Wilson, Gretchen 1970- **2006**:3
Wilson, Jerry
   Brief entry **1986**:2
Wilson, Owen 1968- **2002**:3
Wilson, Pete 1933- **1992**:3
Wilson, William Julius 1935- **1997**:1
Winans, CeCe 1964- **2000**:1
Winfield, Paul 1941-2004
   Obituary **2005**:2
Winfrey, Oprah 1954- **1986**:4
Winger, Debra 1955- **1994**:3
Winick, Judd 1970- **2005**:3
Winokur, Marissa Jaret 1973- **2005**:1
Winston, George 1949(?)- **1987**:1
Winter, Paul 1939- **1990**:2
Winters, Shelley 1920-2006
   Obituary **2007**:1
Wise, Robert 1914-2005
   Obituary **2006**:4
Wiseman, Len 1973- **2008**:2
Witherspoon, Reese 1976- **2002**:1
Witkin, Joel-Peter 1939- **1996**:1
Witten, Edward 1951- **2006**:2
Woertz, Patricia A. 1953- **2007**:3
Wolf, Naomi 1963(?)- **1994**:3
Wolf, Stephen M. 1941- **1989**:3
Wolfe, Tom 1930- **1999**:2
Wolff, Tobias 1945- **2005**:1
Wolfman Jack 1938-1995
   Obituary **1996**:1
Womack, Lee Ann 1966- **2002**:1
Wong, Andrea 1966- **2009**:1
Wong, B.D. 1962- **1998**:1
Wood, Elijah 1981- **2002**:4
Woodard, Lynette 1959(?)- **1986**:2
Woodcock, Leonard 1911-2001
   Obituary **2001**:4
Woodruff, Robert Winship 1889-1985
   Obituary **1985**:1
Woods, James 1947- **1988**:3
Woods, Tiger 1975- **1995**:4
Woodson, Ron 1965- **1996**:4
Woodwell, George S. 1928- **1987**:2
Worth, Irene 1916-2002
   Obituary **2003**:2
Worthy, James 1961- **1991**:2
Wren, John 1952(?)- **2007**:2
Wright, Steven 1955- **1986**:3
Wright, Will 1960- **2003**:4
Wrigley, William, Jr. 1964(?)- **2002**:2
Wu, Harry 1937- **1996**:1
Wyatt, Jane 1910-2006
   Obituary **2008**:1
Wyland, Robert 1956- **2009**:3
Wyle, Noah 1971- **1997**:3
Wyman, Jane 1917-2007
   Obituary **2008**:4
Wynette, Tammy 1942-1998
   Obituary **1998**:3

Wynn, Keenan 1916-1986
  Obituary **1987**:1
Wynn, Stephen A. 1942- **1994**:3
Wynonna 1964- **1993**:3
Xzibit 1974- **2005**:4
Yamaguchi, Kristi 1971- **1992**:3
Yamasaki, Minoru 1912-1986
  Obituary **1986**:2
Yankovic, Frank 1915-1998
  Obituary **1999**:2
Yankovic, Weird Al 1959- **1985**:4
Yard, Molly **1991**:4
Yeager, Chuck 1923- **1998**:1
Yearwood, Trisha 1964- **1999**:1
Yetnikoff, Walter 1933- **1988**:1
Yoakam, Dwight 1956- **1992**:4
Yokich, Stephen P. 1935- **1995**:4
York, Dick 1923-1992
  Obituary **1992**:4
Young, Coleman A. 1918-1997
  Obituary **1998**:1
Young, Loretta 1913-2000
  Obituary **2001**:1
Young, Robert 1907-1998
  Obituary **1999**:1
Young, Steve 1961- **1995**:2
Youngblood, Johnny Ray
  1948- **1994**:1
Youngman, Henny 1906(?)-1998
  Obituary **1998**:3
Zagat, Tim and Nina **2004**:3
Zahn, Paula 1956(?)- **1992**:3
Zamboni, Frank J.
  Brief entry **1986**:4
Zamora, Pedro 1972-1994
  Obituary **1995**:2
Zanker, Bill
  Brief entry **1987**:3
Zanuck, Lili Fini 1954- **1994**:2
Zappa, Frank 1940-1993
  Obituary **1994**:2
Zech, Lando W.
  Brief entry **1987**:4
Zellweger, Renee 1969- **2001**:1
Zemeckis, Robert 1952- **2002**:1
Zerhouni, Elias A. 1951- **2004**:3
Zetcher, Arnold B. 1940- **2002**:1
Zevon, Warren 1947-2003
  Obituary **2004**:4
Ziff, William B., Jr. 1930- **1986**:4
Zigler, Edward 1930- **1994**:1
Zinnemann, Fred 1907-1997
  Obituary **1997**:3
Zinni, Anthony 1943- **2003**:1
Ziskin, Laura 1950- **2008**:2
Zito, Barry 1978- **2003**:3
Zucker, Jeff 1965(?)- **1993**:3
Zucker, Jerry 1950- **2002**:2
Zuckerberg, Mark 1984- **2008**:2
Zuckerman, Mortimer 1937- **1986**:3
Zwilich, Ellen 1939- **1990**:1

**ANGOLAN**
  Savimbi, Jonas 1934- **1986**:2

**ARGENTINIAN**
  Barenboim, Daniel 1942- **2001**:1
  Bocca, Julio 1967- **1995**:3
  Duhalde, Eduardo 1941- **2003**:3

Fernández de Kirchner, Cristina
  1953- **2009**:1
Herrera, Paloma 1975- **1996**:2
Maradona, Diego 1961(?)- **1991**:3
Pelli, Cesar 1927(?)- **1991**:4
Sabatini, Gabriela
  Brief entry **1985**:4
Timmerman, Jacobo 1923-1999
  Obituary **2000**:3

**ARMENIAN**
  Sargsyan, Serzh 1954- **2009**:3

**AUSTRALIAN**
  Allen, Peter 1944-1992
    Obituary **1993**:1
  Allenby, Robert 1971- **2007**:1
  Anderson, Judith 1899(?)-1992
    Obituary **1992**:3
  Baker, Simon 1969- **2009**:4
  Bee Gees, The **1997**:4
  Blanchett, Cate 1969- **1999**:3
  Bloom, Natalie 1971- **2007**:1
  Bond, Alan 1938- **1989**:2
  Bradman, Sir Donald 1908-2001
    Obituary **2002**:1
  Byrne, Rhonda 1955- **2008**:2
  Clavell, James 1924(?)-1994
    Obituary **1995**:1
  Freeman, Cathy 1973- **2001**:3
  Gibb, Andy 1958-1988
    Obituary **1988**:3
  Gibson, Mel 1956- **1990**:1
  Helfgott, David 1937(?)- **1997**:2
  Hewitt, Lleyton 1981- **2002**:2
  Hughes, Robert 1938- **1996**:4
  Humphries, Barry 1934- **1993**:1
  Hutchence, Michael 1960-1997
    Obituary **1998**:1
  Irwin, Steve 1962- **2001**:2
  Jackman, Hugh 1968- **2004**:4
  Kidman, Nicole 1967- **1992**:4
  Klensch, Elsa **2001**:4
  Larbalestier, Justine 1968(?)- **2008**:4
  Ledger, Heath 1979- **2006**:3
  Luhrmann, Baz 1962- **2002**:3
  McMahon, Julian 1968- **2006**:1
  Minogue, Kylie 1968- **2003**:4
  Mueck, Ron 1958- **2008**:3
  Murdoch, Rupert 1931- **1988**:4
  Norman, Greg 1955- **1988**:3
  Powter, Susan 1957(?)- **1994**:3
  Rafter, Patrick 1972- **2001**:1
  Rudd, Kevin 1957- **2009**:1
  Rush, Geoffrey 1951- **2002**:1
  Summers, Anne 1945- **1990**:2
  Travers, P.L. 1899(?)-1996
    Obituary **1996**:4
  Tyler, Richard 1948(?)- **1995**:3
  Urban, Keith 1967- **2006**:3
  Webb, Karrie 1974- **2000**:4

**AUSTRIAN**
  Brabeck-Letmathe, Peter
    1944- **2001**:4
  Brandauer, Klaus Maria 1944- **1987**:3
  Djerassi, Carl 1923- **2000**:4
  Drucker, Peter F. 1909- **1992**:3
  Falco

Brief entry **1987**:2
Frankl, Viktor E. 1905-1997
  Obituary **1998**:1
Hrabal, Bohumil 1914-1997
  Obituary **1997**:3
Jelinek, Elfriede 1946- **2005**:3
Lamarr, Hedy 1913-2000
  Obituary **2000**:3
Lang, Helmut 1956- **1999**:2
Lorenz, Konrad 1903-1989
  Obituary **1989**:3
Mateschitz, Dietrich 1944- **2008**:1
Perutz, Max 1914-2002
  Obituary **2003**:2
Porsche, Ferdinand 1909-1998
  Obituary **1998**:4
Pouillon, Nora 1943- **2005**:1
Puck, Wolfgang 1949- **1990**:1
Strobl, Fritz 1972- **2003**:3
von Karajan, Herbert 1908-1989
  Obituary **1989**:4
von Trapp, Maria 1905-1987
  Obituary **1987**:3
Wiesenthal, Simon 1908-2005
  Obituary **2006**:4

**BANGLADESHI**
  Nasrin, Taslima 1962- **1995**:1
  Yunus, Muhammad 1940- **2007**:3

**BARBADIAN**
  Rihanna 1988- **2008**:4

**BELARUSSIAN**
  Lukashenko, Alexander 1954- **2006**:4

**BELGIAN**
  Clijsters, Kim 1983- **2006**:3
  Henin-Hardenne, Justine 1982- **2004**
    :4
  Hepburn, Audrey 1929-1993
    Obituary **1993**:2
  Verhofstadt, Guy 1953- **2006**:3
  von Furstenberg, Diane 1946- **1994**:2

**BOLIVIAN**
  Morales, Evo 1959- **2007**:2
  Sanchez de Lozada, Gonzalo 1930-
    **2004**:3

**BOSNIAN**
  Izetbegovic, Alija 1925- **1996**:4

**BRAZILIAN**
  Bundchen, Gisele 1980- **2009**:1
  Cardoso, Fernando Henrique
    1931- **1996**:4
  Castaneda, Carlos 1931-1998
    Obituary **1998**:4
  Collor de Mello, Fernando
    1949- **1992**:4
  Fittipaldi, Emerson 1946- **1994**:2
  Ronaldinho 1980- **2007**:3
  Ronaldo 1976- **1999**:2
  Salgado, Sebastiao 1944- **1994**:2
  Senna, Ayrton 1960(?)-1994 **1991**:4

Obituary **1994**:4
Silva, Luiz Inacio Lula da
1945- **2003**:4
Szot, Paulo 1969- **2009**:3
Xuxa 1963(?)- **1994**:2

**BRITISH**
Adamson, George 1906-1989
Obituary **1990**:2
Adele 1988- **2009**:4
Baddeley, Hermione 1906(?)-1986
Obituary **1986**:4
Beckett, Wendy (Sister) 1930- **1998**:3
Boyle, Danny 1956- **2009**:4
Branson, Richard 1951- **1987**:1
Chatwin, Bruce 1940-1989
Obituary **1989**:2
Clarke, Arthur C. 1917-2008
Obituary **2009**:2
Cleese, John 1939- **1989**:2
Cummings, Sam 1927- **1986**:3
Dalton, Timothy 1946- **1988**:4
Davison, Ian Hay 1931- **1986**:1
Day-Lewis, Daniel 1957- **1989**:4
Dench, Judi 1934- **1999**:4
Egan, John 1939- **1987**:2
Emin, Tracey 1963- **2009**:2
Eno, Brian 1948- **1986**:2
Ferguson, Sarah 1959- **1990**:3
Fiennes, Ranulph 1944- **1990**:3
Foster, Norman 1935- **1999**:4
Gift, Roland 1960(?)- **1990**:2
Goodall, Jane 1934- **1991**:1
Gray, Simon 1936-2008
Obituary **2009**:4
Hamilton, Hamish 1900-1988
Obituary **1988**:4
Harrison, Rex 1908-1990
Obituary **1990**:4
Hawking, Stephen W. 1942- **1990**:1
Hawkins, Sally 1976- **2009**:4
Hockney, David 1937- **1988**:3
Hoskins, Bob 1942- **1989**:1
Hounsfield, Godfrey 1919- **1989**:2
Howard, Trevor 1916-1988
Obituary **1988**:2
Ireland, Jill 1936-1990
Obituary **1990**:4
Ive, Jonathan 1967- **2009**:2
Knopfler, Mark 1949- **1986**:2
Laing, R.D. 1927-1989
Obituary **1990**:1
Lawrence, Ruth
Brief entry **1986**:3
Leach, Robin 1942(?)-
Brief entry **1985**:4
Lennox, Annie 1954- **1985**:4
Livingstone, Ken 1945- **1988**:3
Lloyd Webber, Andrew 1948- **1989**:1
Macmillan, Harold 1894-1986
Obituary **1987**:2
MacMillan, Kenneth 1929-1992
Obituary **1993**:2
Maxwell, Robert 1923- **1990**:1
Michael, George 1963- **1989**:2
Milne, Christopher Robin 1920-1996
Obituary **1996**:4
Moore, Henry 1898-1986
Obituary **1986**:4
Murdoch, Iris 1919-1999
Obituary **1999**:4
Norrington, Roger 1934- **1989**:4

Oldman, Gary 1958- **1998**:1
Olivier, Laurence 1907-1989
Obituary **1989**:4
Philby, Kim 1912-1988
Obituary **1988**:3
Radiohead **2009**:3
Rattle, Simon 1955- **1989**:4
Redgrave, Vanessa 1937- **1989**:2
Rhodes, Zandra 1940- **1986**:2
Roddick, Anita 1943(?)- **1989**:4
Runcie, Robert 1921-2000 **1989**:4
Obituary **2001**:1
Rylance, Mark 1960- **2009**:3
Saatchi, Charles 1943- **1987**:3
Steptoe, Patrick 1913-1988
Obituary **1988**:3
Stevens, James
Brief entry **1988**:1
Thatcher, Margaret 1925- **1989**:2
Tudor, Antony 1908(?)-1987
Obituary **1987**:4
Ullman, Tracey 1961- **1988**:3
Wilson, Peter C. 1913-1984
Obituary **1985**:2
Wintour, Anna 1949- **1990**:4
Wright, Richard 1943-2008
Obituary **2009**:4

**BRUNEI**
Bolkiah, Sultan Muda Hassanal
1946- **1985**:4

**BULGARIAN**
Christo 1935- **1992**:3
Dimitrova, Ghena 1941- **1987**:1

**BURMESE**
Suu Kyi, Aung San 1945(?)- **1996**:2

**CAMBODIAN**
Lon Nol
Obituary **1986**:1
Pol Pot 1928-1998
Obituary **1998**:4

**CAMEROONIAN**
Biya, Paul 1933- **2006**:1

**CANADIAN**
Altman, Sidney 1939- **1997**:2
Arbour, Louise 1947- **2005**:1
Atwood, Margaret 1939- **2001**:2
Balsillie, Jim and Mike
Lazaridis **2006**:4
Barenaked Ladies **1997**:2
Black, Conrad 1944- **1986**:2
Bouchard, Lucien 1938- **1999**:2
Bourassa, Robert 1933-1996
Obituary **1997**:1
Bourque, Raymond Jean
1960- **1997**:3
Burr, Raymond 1917-1993
Obituary **1994**:1
Campbell, Kim 1947- **1993**:4
Campbell, Neve 1973- **1998**:2
Campeau, Robert 1923- **1990**:1
Candy, John 1950-1994 **1988**:2
Obituary **1994**:3
Carrey, Jim 1962- **1995**:1
Cavanagh, Tom 1968- **2003**:1

Cerovsek, Corey
Brief entry **1987**:4
Charney, Dov 1969- **2008**:2
Cherry, Don 1934- **1993**:4
Chretien, Jean 1934- **1990**:4
Christensen, Hayden 1981- **2003**:3
Coffey, Paul 1961- **1985**:4
Copps, Sheila 1952- **1986**:4
Cronenberg, David 1943- **1992**:3
Cronyn, Hume 1911-2003
Obituary **2004**:3
Crosby, Sidney 1987- **2006**:3
Dewhurst, Colleen 1924-1991
Obituary **1992**:2
Dion, Celine 1970(?)- **1995**:3
Doherty, Denny 1940-2007
Obituary **2008**:2
Eagleson, Alan 1933- **1987**:4
Ebbers, Bernie 1943- **1998**:1
Egoyan, Atom 1960- **2000**:2
Erickson, Arthur 1924- **1989**:3
Fonyo, Steve
Brief entry **1985**:4
Foster, David 1950(?)- **1988**:2
Fox, Michael J. 1961- **1986**:1
Frank, Robert 1924- **1995**:2
Frye, Northrop 1912-1991
Obituary **1991**:3
Fuhr, Grant 1962- **1997**:3
Furtado, Nelly 1978- **2007**:2
Garneau, Marc 1949- **1985**:1
Gatien, Peter
Brief entry **1986**:1
Giguere, Jean-Sebastien 1977- **2004**:2
Gilmour, Doug 1963- **1994**:3
Gold, Christina A. 1947- **2008**:1
Graham, Nicholas 1960(?)- **1991**:4
Granholm, Jennifer 1959- **2003**:3
Green, Tom 1972- **1999**:4
Greene, Graham 1952- **1997**:2
Greene, Lorne 1915-1987
Obituary **1988**:1
Gretzky, Wayne 1961- **1989**:2
Haggis, Paul 1953- **2006**:4
Haney, Chris
Brief entry **1985**:1
Harper, Stephen J. 1959- **2007**:3
Harris, Michael Deane 1945- **1997**:2
Hayakawa, Samuel Ichiye 1906-1992
Obituary **1992**:3
Hennessy, Jill 1969- **2003**:2
Hextall, Ron 1964- **1988**:2
Hull, Brett 1964- **1991**:4
Jennings, Peter Charles 1938- **1997**:2
Johnson, Pierre Marc 1946- **1985**:4
Jones, Jenny 1946- **1998**:2
Juneau, Pierre 1922- **1988**:3
Jung, Andrea **2000**:2
Karsh, Yousuf 1908-2002
Obituary **2003**:4
Keeler, Ruby 1910-1993
Obituary **1993**:4
Kent, Arthur 1954- **1991**:4
Kielburger, Craig 1983- **1998**:1
Kilgore, Marcia 1968- **2006**:3
Korchinsky, Mike 1961- **2004**:2
Lalonde, Marc 1929- **1985**:1
Lang, K.D. 1961- **1988**:4
Lanois, Daniel 1951- **1991**:1
Lavigne, Avril 1984- **2005**:2
Lemieux, Claude 1965- **1996**:1
Lemieux, Mario 1965- **1986**:4

Leaavesque, Reneaa
    Obituary **1988**:1
Levy, Eugene 1946- **2004**:3
Lewis, Stephen 1937- **1987**:2
Mandel, Howie 1955- **1989**:1
Markle, C. Wilson 1938- **1988**:1
Martin, Paul 1938- **2004**:4
McKinnell, Henry 1943(?)- **2002**:3
McLachlan, Sarah 1968- **1998**:4
McLaren, Norman 1914-1987
    Obituary **1987**:2
McLaughlin, Audrey 1936- **1990**:3
McTaggart, David 1932(?)- **1989**:4
Messier, Mark 1961- **1993**:1
Morgentaler, Henry 1923- **1986**:3
Morissette, Alanis 1974- **1996**:2
Moss, Carrie-Anne 1967- **2004**:3
Mulroney, Brian 1939- **1989**:2
Munro, Alice 1931- **1997**:1
Myers, Mike 1964(?)- **1992**:3
Nickelback **2007**:2
O'Donnell, Bill
    Brief entry **1987**:4
O'Hara, Catherine 1954- **2007**:4
Ondaatje, Philip Michael
    1943- **1997**:3
Paquin, Anna 1982- **2009**:4
Parizeau, Jacques 1930- **1995**:1
Peckford, Brian 1942- **1989**:1
Peterson, David 1943- **1987**:1
Peterson, Oscar 1925-2007
    Obituary **2009**:1
Pocklington, Peter H. 1941- **1985**:2
Pratt, Christopher 1935- **1985**:3
Raffi 1948- **1988**:1
Randi, James 1928- **1990**:2
Reisman, Simon 1919- **1987**:4
Reitman, Ivan 1946- **1986**:3
Reuben, Gloria 1964- **1999**:4
Rhea, Caroline 1964- **2004**:1
Richard, Maurice 1921-2000
    Obituary **2000**:4
Richards, Lloyd 1919-2006
    Obituary **2007**:3
Rogen, Seth 1982- **2009**:3
Roy, Patrick 1965- **1994**:2
Rypien, Mark 1962- **1992**:3
Sainte-Marie, Buffy 1941- **2000**:1
Sakic, Joe 1969- **2002**:1
Shaffer, Paul 1949- **1987**:1
Shields, Carol 1935-2003
    Obituary **2004**:3
Short, Martin 1950- **1986**:1
Stephens, Arran and Ratana **2008**:4
Strong, Maurice 1929- **1993**:1
Sutherland, Kiefer 1966- **2002**:4
Tilghman, Shirley M. 1946- **2002**:1
Trudeau, Pierre 1919-2000
    Obituary **2001**:1
Twain, Shania 1965- **1996**:3
Vander Zalm, William 1934- **1987**:3
Vardalos, Nia 1962- **2003**:4
Vickrey, William S. 1914-1996
    Obituary **1997**:2
Villeneuve, Jacques 1971- **1997**:1
Weir, Mike 1970- **2004**:1
Whitehead, Robert 1916-2002
    Obituary **2003**:3
Williams, Lynn 1924- **1986**:4
Wilson, Bertha
    Brief entry **1986**:1
Wood, Sharon

Brief entry **1988**:1
Young, Neil 1945- **1991**:2
Yzerman, Steve 1965- **1991**:2

**CENTRAL AFRICAN**
    Bozize, Francois 1946- **2006**:3

**CHADIAN**
    Deby, Idriss 1952- **2002**:2

**CHILEAN**
    Arrau, Claudio 1903-1991
        Obituary **1992**:1
    Bachelet, Michelle 1951- **2007**:3
    Lagos, Ricardo 1938- **2005**:3
    Pinochet, Augusto 1915- **1999**:2

**CHINESE**
    Chaing Kai-Shek, Madame
        1898-2003
        Obituary **2005**:1
    Chan, Jackie 1954- **1996**:1
    Chen, Joan 1961- **2000**:2
    Chen, T.C.
        Brief entry **1987**:3
    Deng Xiaoping 1904-1997 **1995**:1
        Obituary **1997**:3
    Fang Lizhi 1937- **1988**:1
    Gao Xingjian 1940- **2001**:2
    Gong Li 1965- **1998**:4
    Guo Jingjing 1981- **2009**:2
    Hatem, George 1910(?)-1988
        Obituary **1989**:1
    Hou Hsiao-hsien 1947- **2000**:2
    Hua Guofeng 1921-2008
        Obituary **2009**:4
    Hu Jintao 1942- **2004**:1
    Hu Yaobang 1915-1989
        Obituary **1989**:4
    Hwang, David Henry 1957- **1999**:1
    Jiang Quing 1914-1991
        Obituary **1992**:1
    Jiang Zemin 1926- **1996**:1
    Lee, Ang 1954- **1996**:3
    Lee, Henry C. 1938- **1997**:1
    Li, Jet 1963- **2005**:3
    Lord, Bette Bao 1938- **1994**:1
    Lucid, Shannon 1943- **1997**:1
    Ma, Jack 1964- **2007**:1
    Ma, Pony 1971(?)- **2006**:3
    Tan Dun 1957- **2002**:1
    Weihui, Zhou 1973- **2001**:1
    Wei Jingsheng 1950- **1998**:2
    Woo, John 1945(?)- **1994**:2
    Wu, Harry 1937- **1996**:1
    Wu Yi 1938- **2005**:2
    Yao Ming 1980- **2004**:1
    Ye Jianying 1897-1986
        Obituary **1987**:1
    Yen, Samuel 1927- **1996**:4
    Zhang, Ziyi 1979- **2006**:2
    Zhao Ziyang 1919- **1989**:1

**COLOMBIAN**
    Botero, Fernando 1932- **1994**:3
    Garcia Marquez, Gabriel
        1928- **2005**:2
    Juanes 1972- **2004**:4
    Leguizamo, John 1965- **1999**:1
    Pastrana, Andres 1954- **2002**:1
    Schroeder, Barbet 1941- **1996**:1

Shakira 1977- **2002**:3
Uribe, Alvaro 1952- **2003**:3

**CONGOLESE**
    Kabila, Joseph 1971- **2003**:2
    Kabila, Laurent 1939- **1998**:1
        Obituary **2001**:3
    Mobutu Sese Seko 1930-1998
        Obituary **1998**:4

**COSTA RICAN**
    Arias Sanchez, Oscar 1941- **1989**:3

**COTE D'IVOIRIAN**
    Gbagbo, Laurent 1945- **2003**:2

**CROATIAN**
    Ivanisevic, Goran 1971- **2002**:1
    Mesic, Stipe 1934- **2005**:4
    Tudjman, Franjo 1922- **1996**:2
    Tudjman, Franjo 1922-1999
        Obituary **2000**:2

**CUBAN**
    Acosta, Carlos 1973(?)- **1997**:4
    Canseco, Jose 1964- **1990**:2
    Castro, Fidel 1926- **1991**:4
    Cruz, Celia 1925-2003
        Obituary **2004**:3
    Cugat, Xavier 1900-1990
        Obituary **1991**:2
    Estefan, Gloria **1991**:4
    Garcia, Andy 1956- **1999**:3
    Garcia, Cristina 1958- **1997**:4
    Goizueta, Roberto 1931-1997 **1996**:1
        Obituary **1998**:1
    Gutierrez, Carlos M. 1953- **2001**:4
    Murano, Elsa 1959- **2009**:1
    Palmeiro, Rafael 1964- **2005**:1
    Saralegui, Cristina 1948- **1999**:2
    Zamora, Pedro 1972-1994
        Obituary **1995**:2

**CYPRIAN**
    Chalayan, Hussein 1970- **2003**:2
    Kyprianou, Spyros 1932-2002
        Obituary **2003**:2

**CZECH**
    Albright, Madeleine 1937- **1994**:3
    Hammer, Jan 1948- **1987**:3
    Hasek, Dominik 1965- **1998**:3
    Havel, Vaclav 1936- **1990**:3
    Hingis, Martina 1980- **1999**:1
    Hrabal, Bohumil 1914-1997
        Obituary **1997**:3
    Jagr, Jaromir 1972- **1995**:4
    Klima, Petr 1964- **1987**:1
    Kukoc, Toni 1968- **1995**:4
    Maxwell, Robert 1923-1991
        Obituary **1992**:2
    Porizkova, Paulina
        Brief entry **1986**:4
    Reisz, Karel 1926-2002
        Obituary **2004**:1
    Serkin, Rudolf 1903-1991
        Obituary **1992**:1
    Stoppard, Tom 1937- **1995**:4
    Trump, Ivana 1949- **1995**:2
    Zatopek, Emil 1922-2000

Obituary **2001**:3

## DANISH

Borge, Victor 1909-2000
  Obituary **2001**:3
Hau, Lene Vestergaard 1959- **2006**:4
Kristiansen, Kjeld Kirk 1948(?)- **1988**
  :3
Lander, Toni 1931-1985
  Obituary **1985**:4
Rasmussen, Anders Fogh
  1953- **2006**:1

## DJIBOUTI

Guelleh, Ismail Omar 1947- **2006**:2

## DOMINICAN

Fernández, Leonel 1953- **2009**:2
Sosa, Sammy 1968- **1999**:1

## DOMINICAN REPUBLICAN

Balaguer, Joaquin 1907-2002
  Obituary **2003**:4
de la Renta, Oscar 1932- **2005**:4
Pujols, Albert 1980- **2005**:3
Ramirez, Manny 1972- **2005**:4
Soriano, Alfonso 1976- **2008**:1

## DUTCH

Appel, Karel 1921-2006
  Obituary **2007**:2
de Hoop Scheffer, Jaap 1948- **2005**:1
de Kooning, Willem
  1904-1997 **1994**:4
  Obituary **1997**:3
Duisenberg, Wim 1935-2005
  Obituary **2006**:4
Heineken, Alfred 1923-2002
  Obituary **2003**:1
Juliana 1909-2004
  Obituary **2005**:3
Koolhaas, Rem 1944- **2001**:1
Matadin, Vinoodh and Inez van
  Lamsweerde **2007**:4
Parker, Colonel Tom 1929-1997
  Obituary **1997**:2

## ECUADORAN

Correa, Rafael 1963- **2008**:1

## EGYPTIAN

Chahine, Youssef 1926-2008
  Obituary **2009**:3
ElBaradei, Mohamed 1942- **2006**:3
Ghali, Boutros Boutros 1922- **1992**:3
Mahfouz, Naguib 1911-2006
  Obituary **2007**:4
Mubarak, Hosni 1928- **1991**:4
Rahman, Sheik Omar Abdel- 1938-
  **1993**:3

## ENGLISH

Adams, Douglas 1952-2001
  Obituary **2002**:2
Ali, Monica 1967- **2007**:4
Altea, Rosemary 1946- **1996**:3
Amanpour, Christiane 1958- **1997**:2
Ambler, Eric 1909-1998
  Obituary **1999**:2
Ames, Roger 1950(?)- **2005**:2

Amis, Kingsley 1922-1995
  Obituary **1996**:2
Amis, Martin 1949- **2008**:3
Andrews, Julie 1935- **1996**:1
Ashcroft, Peggy 1907-1991
  Obituary **1992**:1
Ashwell, Rachel 1960(?)- **2004**:2
Atkinson, Rowan 1955- **2004**:3
Banksy 1975(?)- **2007**:2
Barker, Clive 1952- **2003**:3
Barker, Pat 1943- **2009**:1
Baron Cohen, Sacha 1971- **2007**:3
Barrett, Syd 1946-2006
  Obituary **2007**:3
Bates, Alan 1934-2003
  Obituary **2005**:1
Beckham, David 1975- **2003**:1
Bee Gees, The **1997**:4
Bell, Gabrielle 1975(?)- **2007**:4
Berners-Lee, Tim 1955(?)- **1997**:4
Blair, Tony 1953- **1996**:3
Bloom, Orlando 1977- **2004**:2
Bonham Carter, Helena 1966- **1998**:4
Bowie, David 1947- **1998**:2
Broadbent, Jim 1949- **2008**:4
Brown, Gordon 1951- **2008**:3
Brown, Tina 1953- **1992**:1
Burgess, Anthony 1917-1993
  Obituary **1994**:2
Burnett, Mark 1960- **2003**:1
Bush, Kate 1958- **1994**:3
Caine, Michael 1933- **2000**:4
Campbell, Naomi 1970- **2000**:2
Carey, George 1935- **1992**:3
Charles, Prince of Wales
  1948- **1995**:3
Child, Lee 1954- **2007**:3
Choo, Jimmy 1957(?)- **2006**:3
Christie, Julie 1941- **2008**:4
Clapton, Eric 1945- **1993**:3
Coldplay **2004**:4
Collins, Jackie 1941- **2004**:4
Comfort, Alex 1920-2000
  Obituary **2000**:4
Cook, Peter 1938-1995
  Obituary **1995**:2
Cooke, Alistair 1908-2004
  Obituary **2005**:3
Costello, Elvis 1954(?)- **1994**:4
Cowell, Simon 1959- **2003**:4
Craig, Daniel 1968- **2008**:1
Crawford, Michael 1942- **1994**:2
Crick, Francis 1916-2004
  Obituary **2005**:4
Crisp, Quentin 1908-1999
  Obituary **2000**:3
Cushing, Peter 1913-1994
  Obituary **1995**:1
Davis, Crispin 1949- **2004**:1
Dee, Janie 1966(?)- **2001**:4
Diana, Princess of Wales
  1961-1997 **1993**:1
  Obituary **1997**:4
Dido 1971- **2004**:4
Driver, Minnie 1971- **2000**:1
Duran Duran **2005**:3
Dyson, James 1947- **2005**:4
Elliott, Denholm 1922-1992
  Obituary **1993**:2
Entwistle, John 1944-2002
  Obituary **2003**:3
Everett, Rupert 1959- **2003**:1

Everything But The Girl **1996**:4
Faldo, Nick 1957- **1993**:3
Fforde, Jasper 1961- **2006**:3
Fielding, Helen 1959- **2000**:4
Fiennes, Ralph 1962- **1996**:2
Finney, Albert 1936- **2003**:3
Fonteyn, Margot 1919-1991
  Obituary **1991**:3
Freud, Lucian 1922- **2000**:4
Frieda, John 1951- **2004**:1
Fuller, Simon 1960- **2008**:2
Furse, Clara 1957- **2008**:2
Galliano, John 1960- **2005**:2
Gielgud, John 1904-2000
  Obituary **2000**:4
Goldsworthy, Andy 1956- **2007**:2
Gordon, Michael 1951(?)- **2005**:1
Grant, Hugh 1960- **1995**:3
Gray, David 1970- **2001**:4
Green, Philip 1952- **2008**:2
Greene, Graham 1904-1991
  Obituary **1991**:4
Guinness, Alec 1914-2000
  Obituary **2001**:1
Haddon, Mark 1962- **2005**:2
Hadid, Zaha 1950- **2005**:3
Hamilton, Lewis 1985- **2008**:4
Harris, Richard 1930-2002
  Obituary **2004**:1
Harrison, George 1943-2001
  Obituary **2003**:1
Harvey, Polly Jean 1970(?)- **1995**:4
Headroom, Max 1985- **1986**:4
Hebard, Caroline 1944- **1998**:2
Hemming, Nikki 1967- **2009**:1
Hempleman-Adams,
  David 1956- **2004**:3
Hicks, India 1967- **2008**:2
Hill, Benny 1925-1992
  Obituary **1992**:3
Hindmarch, Anya 1969- **2008**:2
Hollinghurst, Alan 1954- **2006**:1
Hornby, Nick 1957- **2002**:2
Houser, Sam 1972(?)- **2004**:4
Hoyle, Sir Fred 1915-2001
  Obituary **2002**:4
Hughes, Ted 1930-1998
  Obituary **1999**:2
Hume, Basil Cardinal 1923-1999
  Obituary **2000**:1
Humphry, Derek 1931(?)- **1992**:2
Hurley, Elizabeth **1999**:2
Irons, Jeremy 1948- **1991**:4
Izzard, Eddie 1963- **2008**:1
Jacques, Brian 1939- **2002**:2
Jagger, Jade 1971- **2005**:1
John, Elton 1947- **1995**:4
Kerr, Deborah 1921-2007
  Obituary **2008**:4
Kidd, Jemma 1974- **2009**:1
Kinsella, Sophie 1969- **2005**:2
Knightley, Keira 1985- **2005**:2
Lane, Ronnie 1946-1997
  Obituary **1997**:4
Lasdun, Denys 1914-2001
  Obituary **2001**:4
Laurie, Hugh 1959- **2007**:2
Law, Jude 1971- **2000**:3
Lawson, Nigella 1960- **2003**:2
Leach, Penelope 1937- **1992**:4
Leakey, Mary Douglas 1913-1996
  Obituary **1997**:2

le Carre, John 1931- **2000**:1
Lessing, Doris 1919- **2008**:4
LeVay, Simon 1943- **1992**:2
Lewis, Lennox 1965- **2000**:2
Lively, Penelope 1933- **2007**:4
Lupino, Ida 1918(?)-1995
    Obituary **1996**:1
Lyne, Adrian 1941- **1997**:2
MacArthur, Ellen 1976- **2005**:3
Major, John 1943- **1991**:2
Malone, Jo 1964(?)- **2004**:3
Marber, Patrick 1964- **2007**:4
Marsden, Brian 1937- **2004**:4
McCall Smith, Alexander
    1948- **2005**:2
McCartney, Paul 1942- **2002**:4
McCartney, Stella 1971- **2001**:3
McDonagh, Martin 1970- **2007**:3
McDowall, Roddy 1928-1998
    Obituary **1999**:1
McEwan, Ian 1948- **2004**:2
McKellen, Ian 1939- **1994**:1
Mercury, Freddie 1946-1991
    Obituary **1992**:2
Milligan, Spike 1918-2002
    Obituary **2003**:2
Minghella, Anthony 1954- **2004**:3
Mirren, Helen 1945- **2005**:1
Molina, Alfred 1953- **2005**:3
Montagu, Ashley 1905-1999
    Obituary **2000**:2
Moore, Dudley 1935-2002
    Obituary **2003**:2
Morrissey 1959- **2005**:2
Moss, Kate 1974- **1995**:3
Newkirk, Ingrid 1949- **1992**:3
Newton-John, Olivia 1948- **1998**:4
Nolan, Christopher 1970(?)- **2006**:3
Northam, Jeremy 1961- **2003**:2
Nunn, Trevor 1940- **2000**:2
Oasis **1996**:3
Ogilvy, David 1911-1999
    Obituary **2000**:1
Oliver, Jamie 1975- **2002**:3
Osborne, John 1929-1994
    Obituary **1995**:2
Osbournes, The **2003**:4
Owen, Clive 1964- **2006**:2
Owen-Jones, Lindsay 1946(?)- **2004**:2
Palmer, Robert 1949-2003
    Obituary **2004**:4
Park, Nick 1958- **1997**:3
Patten, Christopher 1944- **1993**:3
Pegg, Simon 1970- **2009**:1
Penrose, Roger 1931- **1991**:4
Pleasence, Donald 1919-1995
    Obituary **1995**:3
Pople, John 1925-2004
    Obituary **2005**:2
Porter, George 1920-2002
    Obituary **2003**:4
Potts, Paul 1970- **2009**:1
Princess Margaret, Countess of
    Snowdon 1930-2002
    Obituary **2003**:2
Pullman, Philip 1946- **2003**:2
Queen Elizabeth the Queen Mother
    1900-2002
    Obituary **2003**:2
Radcliffe, Daniel 1989- **2007**:4
Ramsay, Gordon 1966- **2008**:2
Redgrave, Lynn 1943- **1999**:3

Reisz, Karel 1926-2002
    Obituary **2004**:1
Rendell, Ruth 1930- **2007**:2
Rice, Peter 1967(?)- **2007**:2
Richards, Keith 1943- **1993**:3
Ritchie, Guy 1968- **2001**:3
Robinson, Peter 1950- **2007**:4
Ronson, Charlotte 1977(?)- **2007**:3
Roth, Tim 1961- **1998**:2
Saatchi, Maurice 1946- **1995**:4
Sacks, Oliver 1933- **1995**:4
Schlesinger, John 1926-2003
    Obituary **2004**:3
Scott, Ridley 1937- **2001**:1
Seal 1962(?)- **1994**:4
Sentamu, John 1949- **2006**:2
Seymour, Jane 1951- **1994**:4
Smith, Paul 1946- **2002**:4
Smith, Zadie 1975- **2003**:4
Spice Girls **2008**:3
Springer, Jerry 1944- **1998**:4
Springfield, Dusty 1939-1999
    Obituary **1999**:3
Stewart, Patrick 1940- **1996**:1
Stewart, Rod 1945- **2007**:1
Sting 1951- **1991**:4
Stone, Joss 1987- **2006**:2
Stoppard, Tom 1937- **1995**:4
Strummer, Joe 1952-2002
    Obituary **2004**:1
Styler, Trudie 1954- **2009**:1
Sullivan, Andrew 1964(?)- **1996**:1
Swinton, Tilda 1960- **2008**:4
Taylor, Elizabeth 1932- **1993**:3
Taylor, Graham 1958(?)- **2005**:3
Temperley, Alice 1975- **2008**:2
Thompson, Emma 1959- **1993**:2
Tilberis, Elizabeth 1947(?)- **1994**:3
Trotman, Alex 1933- **1995**:4
Uchida, Mitsuko 1949(?)- **1989**:3
Ustinov, Peter 1921-2004
    Obituary **2005**:3
Ware, Lancelot 1915-2000
    Obituary **2001**:1
Watson, Emily 1967- **2001**:1
Watts, Naomi 1968- **2006**:1
Weisz, Rachel 1971- **2006**:4
Westwood, Vivienne 1941- **1998**:3
Wiles, Andrew 1953(?)- **1994**:1
Wilkinson, Tom 1948- **2003**:2
Wilmut, Ian 1944- **1997**:3
Winehouse, Amy 1983- **2008**:1
Winslet, Kate 1975- **2002**:4
Wright, Joe 1972- **2009**:1

**ESTONIAN**
Ilves, Toomas Hendrik 1953- **2007**:4

**FIJI ISLANDER**
Mara, Ratu Sir Kamisese 1920-2004
    Obituary **2005**:3
Singh, Vijay 1963- **2000**:4

**FILIPINO**
Aquino, Corazon 1933- **1986**:2
Lewis, Loida Nicolas 1942- **1998**:3
Macapagal-Arroyo, Gloria
    1947- **2001**:4
Marcos, Ferdinand 1917-1989
    Obituary **1990**:1
Natori, Josie 1947- **1994**:3

Ramos, Fidel 1928- **1995**:2
Salonga, Lea 1971- **2003**:3
Sin, Jaime 1928-2005
    Obituary **2006**:3

**FINNISH**
Halonen, Tarja 1943- **2006**:4
Kekkonen, Urho 1900-1986
    Obituary **1986**:4
Ollila, Jorma 1950- **2003**:4
Torvalds, Linus 1970(?)- **1999**:3

**FRENCH**
Adjani, Isabelle 1955- **1991**:1
Agnes B 1941- **2002**:3
Albou, Sophie 1967- **2007**:2
Arnault, Bernard 1949- **2000**:4
Bangalter, Thomas 1975-. See Daft
    Punk
Baulieu, Etienne-Emile 1926- **1990**:1
Becaud, Gilbert 1927-2001
    Obituary **2003**:1
Bejart, Maurice 1927-2007
    Obituary **2009**:1
Besse, Georges 1927-1986
    Obituary **1987**:1
Binoche, Juliette 1965- **2001**:3
Bourgeois, Louise 1911- **1994**:1
Brando, Cheyenne 1970-1995
    Obituary **1995**:4
Bruni, Carla 1967- **2009**:3
Calment, Jeanne 1875-1997
    Obituary **1997**:4
Cardin, Pierre 1922- **2003**:3
Cartier-Bresson, Henri 1908-2004
    Obituary **2005**:4
Chagall, Marc 1887-1985
    Obituary **1985**:2
Chirac, Jacques 1932- **1995**:4
Colbert, Claudette 1903-1996
    Obituary **1997**:1
Conseil, Dominique
    Nils 1962(?)- **2007**:2
Cotillard, Marion 1975- **2009**:1
Cousteau, Jacques-Yves
    1910-1997 **1998**:2
Cousteau, Jean-Michel 1938- **1988**:2
Cresson, Edith 1934- **1992**:1
Daft Punk 1975- **2009**:4
de Homem-Christo, Guy-Manuel
    1975-. See Daft Punk
Delors, Jacques 1925- **1990**:2
Deneuve, Catherine 1943- **2003**:2
Depardieu, Gerard 1948- **1991**:2
Derrida, Jacques 1930-2005
    Obituary **2006**:1
Dubuffet, Jean 1901-1985
    Obituary **1985**:4
Duras, Marguerite 1914-1996
    Obituary **1996**:3
Fekkai, Frederic 1959(?)- **2003**:2
Gaultier, Jean-Paul 1952- **1998**:1
Ghosn, Carlos 1954- **2008**:3
Godard, Jean-Luc 1930- **1998**:1
Grappelli, Stephane 1908-1997
    Obituary **1998**:1
Guillem, Sylvie 1965(?)- **1988**:2
Indurain, Miguel 1964- **1994**:1
Klarsfeld, Beate 1939- **1989**:1
Kouchner, Bernard 1939- **2005**:3
Lacroix, Christian 1951- **2005**:2
Lefebvre, Marcel 1905- **1988**:4

Louboutin, Christian 1963- **2006**:1
Malle, Louis 1932-1995
  Obituary **1996**:2
Marceau, Marcel 1923-2007
  Obituary **2008**:4
Mauresmo, Amelie 1979- **2007**:2
Mercier, Laura 1959(?)- **2002**:2
Millepied, Benjamin 1977(?)- **2006**:4
Mitterrand, Francois 1916-1996
  Obituary **1996**:2
Nars, Francois 1959- **2003**:1
Parker, Tony 1982- **2008**:1
Petrossian, Christian
  Brief entry **1985**:3
Picasso, Paloma 1949- **1991**:1
Ponty, Jean-Luc 1942- **1985**:4
Prost, Alain 1955- **1988**:1
Rampal, Jean-Pierre 1922- **1989**:2
Reza, Yasmina 1959(?)- **1999**:2
Rothschild, Philippe de 1902-1988
  Obituary **1988**:2
Rykiel, Sonia 1930- **2000**:3
Saint Laurent, Yves 1936-2008
  Obituary **2009**:3
Sarkozy, Nicolas 1955- **2008**:4
Simone, Nina 1933-2003
  Obituary **2004**:2
Starck, Philippe 1949- **2004**:1
Tautou, Audrey 1978- **2004**:2
Thom, Rene 1923-2002
  Obituary **2004**:1
Thomas, Michel 1911(?)- **1987**:4
Tillion, Germaine 1907-2008
  Obituary **2009**:2
Touitou, Jean 1952(?)- **2008**:4
Ungaro, Emanuel 1933- **2001**:3
Villechaize, Herve 1943(?)-1993
  Obituary **1994**:1
Xenakis, Iannis 1922-2001
  Obituary **2001**:4

**GABONESE**
Bozize, Francois 1946- **2006**:3

**GEORGIAN**
Saakashvili, Mikhail 1967- **2008**:4

**GERMAN**
Barbie, Klaus 1913-1991
  Obituary **1992**:2
Becker, Boris
  Brief entry **1985**:3
Bernhard, Wolfgang 1960- **2007**:1
Bethe, Hans 1906-2005
  Obituary **2006**:2
Beuys, Joseph 1921-1986
  Obituary **1986**:3
Blobel, Gunter 1936- **2000**:4
Boyle, Gertrude 1924- **1995**:3
Brandt, Willy 1913-1992
  Obituary **1993**:2
Breitschwerdt, Werner 1927- **1988**:4
Casper, Gerhard 1937- **1993**:1
Dietrich, Marlene 1901-1992
  Obituary **1992**:4
Etzioni, Amitai 1929- **1994**:3
Fischer, Joschka 1948- **2005**:2
Frank, Anthony M. 1931(?)- **1992**:1
Graf, Steffi 1969- **1987**:4

Grass, Gunter 1927- **2000**:2
Gursky, Andreas 1955- **2002**:2
Hahn, Carl H. 1926- **1986**:4
Hess, Rudolph 1894-1987
  Obituary **1988**:1
Honecker, Erich 1912-1994
  Obituary **1994**:4
Kiefer, Anselm 1945- **1990**:2
Kinski, Klaus 1926-1991 **1987**:2
  Obituary **1992**:2
Klarsfeld, Beate 1939- **1989**:1
Klemperer, Werner 1920-2000
  Obituary **2001**:3
Klum, Heidi 1973- **2006**:3
Kohl, Helmut 1930- **1994**:1
Krogner, Heinz 1941(?)- **2004**:2
Lagerfeld, Karl 1938- **1999**:4
Max, Peter 1937- **1993**:2
Mengele, Josef 1911-1979
  Obituary **1985**:2
Mutter, Anne-Sophie 1963- **1990**:3
Newton, Helmut 1920- **2002**:1
Nowitzki, Dirk 1978- **2007**:2
Nuesslein-Volhard, Christiane
  1942- **1998**:1
Pfeiffer, Eckhard 1941- **1998**:4
Pilatus, Robert 1966(?)-1998
  Obituary **1998**:3
Polke, Sigmar 1941- **1999**:4
Rey, Margret E. 1906-1996
  Obituary **1997**:2
Richter, Gerhard 1932- **1997**:2
Sander, Jil 1943- **1995**:2
Schily, Otto
  Brief entry **1987**:4
Schrempp, Juergen 1944- **2000**:2
Schroder, Gerhard 1944- **1999**:1
Schumacher, Michael 1969- **2005**:2
Schwarzkopf, Elisabeth 1915-2006
  Obituary **2007**:3
Tillmans, Wolfgang 1968- **2001**:4
Von Hellermann, Sophie
  1975- **2006**:3
Werner, Ruth 1907-2000
  Obituary **2001**:1
Witt, Katarina 1966(?)- **1991**:3
Zetsche, Dieter 1953- **2002**:3

**GHANIAN**
Annan, Kofi 1938- **1999**:1
Chambas, Mohammed ibn 1950-
  **2003**:3
Kufuor, John Agyekum 1938- **2005**:4

**GREECE**
Karamanlis, Costas 1956- **2009**:1

**GREEK**
George and Lena Korres 1971- **2009**
  :1
Huffington, Arianna 1950- **1996**:2
Papandreou, Andrea 1919-1996
  Obituary **1997**:1
Stefanidis, John 1937- **2007**:3

**GUATEMALAN**
Berger, Oscar 1946- **2004**:4
Menchu, Rigoberta 1960(?)- **1993**:2

**GUINEA-BISSAUNI**
Makeba, Miriam 1934- **1989**:2
Ture, Kwame 1941-1998
  Obituary **1999**:2

**GUYANESE**
Jagdeo, Bharrat 1964- **2008**:1

**HAITIAN**
Aristide, Jean-Bertrand 1953- **1991**:3
Cedras, Raoul 1950- **1994**:4
Danticat, Edwidge 1969- **2005**:4
Preaaval, Reneaa 1943- **1997**:2

**HONG KONGER**
Chow, Stephen 1962- **2006**:1
Chow Yun-fat 1955- **1999**:4
Lee, Martin 1938- **1998**:2

**HUNGARIAN**
Dorati, Antal 1906-1988
  Obituary **1989**:2
Fodor, Eugene 1906(?)-1991
  Obituary **1991**:3
Gabor, Eva 1921(?)-1995
  Obituary **1996**:1
Grove, Andrew S. 1936- **1995**:3
Ligeti, Gyorgy 1923-2006
  Obituary **2007**:3
Polgar, Judit 1976- **1993**:3
Solti, Georg 1912-1997
  Obituary **1998**:1

**ICELANDIC**
Bjork 1965- **1996**:1
Finnbogadoaattir, Vigdiaas
  Brief entry **1986**:2

**INDIAN**
Chopra, Deepak 1947- **1996**:3
Devi, Phoolan 1955(?)- **1986**:1
  Obituary **2002**:3
Durrell, Gerald 1925-1995
  Obituary **1995**:3
Gandhi, Indira 1917-1984
  Obituary **1985**:1
Gandhi, Rajiv 1944-1991
  Obituary **1991**:4
Gandhi, Sonia 1947- **2000**:2
Gowda, H. D. Deve 1933- **1997**:1
Iyengar, B.K.S. 1918- **2005**:1
Mahesh Yogi, Maharishi
  1911(?)- **1991**:3
Mehta, Zubin 1938(?)- **1994**:3
Mittal, Lakshmi 1950- **2007**:2
Mother Teresa 1910-1997 **1993**:1
  Obituary **1998**:1
Musharraf, Pervez 1943- **2000**:2
Narayan, R.K. 1906-2001
  Obituary **2002**:2
Nooyi, Indra 1955- **2004**:3
Prowse, Juliet 1937-1996
  Obituary **1997**:1
Rajneesh, Bhagwan Shree 1931-1990
  Obituary **1990**:2
Ram, Jagjivan 1908-1986
  Obituary **1986**:4
Rao, P. V. Narasimha 1921- **1993**:2

Rushdie, Salman 1947- **1994**:1
Sharma, Nisha 1982(?)- **2004**:2
Vajpayee, Atal Behari 1926- **1998**:4
Wahid, Abdurrahman 1940- **2000**:3

## INDONESIAN

Habibie, Bacharuddin Jusuf
1936- **1999**:3
Suharto 1921-2008
Obituary **2009**:2
Megawati Sukarnoputri 1947- **2000**:1

## IRANIAN

Ahmadinejad, Mahmoud 1956- **2007**:1
Ebadi, Shirin 1947- **2004**:3
Khatami, Mohammed 1943- **1997**:4
Khomeini, Ayatollah Ruhollah
1900(?)-1989
Obituary **1989**:4
Rafsanjani, Ali Akbar Hashemi
1934(?)- **1987**:3
Satrapi, Marjane 1969- **2006**:3
Schroeder, Barbet 1941- **1996**:1

## IRAQI

al-Ani, Jananne 1966- **2008**:4
Hussein, Saddam 1937- **1991**:1
Kamel, Hussein 1954- **1996**:1
Saatchi, Maurice 1946- **1995**:4
Salbi, Zainab 1969(?)- **2008**:3

## IRISH

Adams, Gerald 1948- **1994**:1
Ahern, Bertie 1951- **1999**:3
Ahern, Cecelia 1981- **2008**:4
Beckett, Samuel Barclay 1906-1989
Obituary **1990**:2
Best, George 1946-2005
Obituary **2007**:1
Bono 1960- **1988**:4
Branagh, Kenneth 1960- **1992**:2
Brosnan, Pierce 1952- **2000**:3
Byrne, Gabriel 1950- **1997**:4
de Valois, Dame Ninette 1898-2001
Obituary **2002**:1
Doyle, Roddy 1958- **2008**:1
Enya 1962(?)- **1992**:3
Farrell, Colin 1976- **2004**:1
Geldof, Bob 1954(?)- **1985**:3
Heaney, Seamus 1939- **1996**:2
Herzog, Chaim 1918-1997
Obituary **1997**:3
Hillery, Patrick 1923-2008
Obituary **2009**:2
Hume, John 1938- **1987**:1
Huston, John 1906-1987
Obituary **1988**:1
Jordan, Neil 1950(?)- **1993**:3
Keyes, Marian 1963- **2006**:2
McCourt, Frank 1930- **1997**:4
McGahern, John 1934-2006
Obituary **2007**:2
McGuinness, Martin 1950(?)- **1985**:4
Neeson, Liam 1952- **1993**:4
O'Connor, Sinead 1967- **1990**:4
O'Sullivan, Maureen 1911-1998
Obituary **1998**:4
Power, Samantha 1970- **2005**:4

Rhys Meyers, Jonathan 1977- **2007**:1
Robinson, Mary 1944- **1993**:1
Trimble, David 1944- **1999**:1
U2 **2002**:4

## ISRAELI

Arens, Moshe 1925- **1985**:1
Arison, Ted 1924- **1990**:3
Barak, Ehud 1942- **1999**:4
Begin, Menachem 1913-1992
Obituary **1992**:3
Elbaz, Alber 1961- **2008**:1
Herzog, Chaim 1918-1997
Obituary **1997**:3
Levinger, Moshe 1935- **1992**:1
Levy, David 1938- **1987**:2
Mintz, Shlomo 1957- **1986**:2
Netanyahu, Benjamin 1949- **1996**:4
Peres, Shimon 1923- **1996**:3
Rabin, Leah 1928-2000
Obituary **2001**:2
Rabin, Yitzhak 1922-1995 **1993**:1
Obituary **1996**:2
Shcharansky, Anatoly 1948- **1986**:2
Weizman, Ezer 1924-2005
Obituary **2006**:3

## ITALIAN

Agnelli, Giovanni 1921- **1989**:4
Armani, Giorgio 1934(?)- **1991**:2
Bartoli, Cecilia 1966- **1994**:1
Benetton, Luciano 1935- **1988**:1
Benigni, Roberto 1952- **1999**:2
Berio, Luciano 1925-2003
Obituary **2004**:2
Berlusconi, Silvio 1936(?)- **1994**:4
Capra, Frank 1897-1991
Obituary **1992**:2
Cavalli, Roberto 1940- **2004**:4
Ciampi, Carlo Azeglio 1920- **2004**:3
Clemente, Francesco 1952- **1992**:2
Coppola, Carmine 1910-1991
Obituary **1991**:4
De Luca, Guerrino 1952- **2007**:1
Dolce, Domenico and Stefano
Gabbana **2005**:4
Fabio 1961(?)- **1993**:4
Fabris, Enrico 1981- **2006**:4
Fano, Ugo 1912-2001
Obituary **2001**:4
Fellini, Federico 1920-1993
Obituary **1994**:2
Ferrari, Enzo 1898-1988 **1988**:4
Ferre, Gianfranco 1944-2007
Obituary **2008**:3
Ferretti, Alberta 1950(?)- **2004**:1
Ferri, Alessandra 1963- **1987**:2
Fo, Dario 1926- **1998**:1
Gardenia, Vincent 1922-1992
Obituary **1993**:2
Gassman, Vittorio 1922-2000
Obituary **2001**:1
Gucci, Maurizio
Brief entry **1985**:4
Lamborghini, Ferrucio 1916-1993
Obituary **1993**:3
Leone, Sergio 1929-1989
Obituary **1989**:4
Masina, Giulietta 1920-1994
Obituary **1994**:3
Mastroianni, Marcello 1914-1996
Obituary **1997**:2

Michelangeli, Arturo Benedetti
1920- **1988**:2
Montand, Yves 1921-1991
Obituary **1992**:2
Pavarotti, Luciano 1935- **1997**:4
Piano, Renzo 1937- **2009**:2
Ponti, Carlo 1912-2007
Obituary **2008**:2
Pozzi, Lucio 1935- **1990**:2
Prada, Miuccia 1950(?)- **1996**:1
Rizzoli, Paola 1943(?)- **2004**:3
Rosso, Renzo 1955- **2005**:2
Sinopoli, Giuseppe 1946- **1988**:1
Staller, Ilona 1951- **1988**:3
Tomba, Alberto 1966- **1992**:3
Valli, Giambattista 1966- **2008**:3
Versace, Donatella 1955- **1999**:1
Versace, Gianni 1946-1997
Brief entry **1988**:1
Obituary **1998**:2
Zanardi, Alex 1966- **1998**:2
Zeffirelli, Franco 1923- **1991**:3

## JAMAICAN

Bolt, Usain 1986- **2009**:2
Dekker, Desmond 1941-2006
Obituary **2007**:2
Marley, Ziggy 1968- **1990**:4
Tosh, Peter 1944-1987
Obituary **1988**:2

## JAPANESE

Akihito, Emperor of Japan
1933- **1990**:1
Ando, Tadao 1941- **2005**:4
Aoki, Rocky 1940- **1990**:2
Arakawa, Shizuka 1981- **2006**:4
Doi, Takako
Brief entry **1987**:4
Hirohito, Emperor of Japan
1901-1989
Obituary **1989**:2
Honda, Soichiro 1906-1991
Obituary **1986**:1
Hosokawa, Morihiro 1938- **1994**:1
Isozaki, Arata 1931- **1990**:2
Itami, Juzo 1933-1997 **1998**:2
Katayama, Yutaka 1909- **1987**:1
Koizumi, Junichiro 1942- **2002**:1
Kuma, Kengo 1954- **2009**:1
Kurokawa, Kisho 1934-2007
Obituary **2008**:4
Kurosawa, Akira 1910-1998 **1991**:1
Obituary **1999**:1
Kutaragi, Ken 1950- **2005**:3
Mako 1933-2006
Obituary **2007**:3
Masako, Crown Princess
1963- **1993**:4
Matsuhisa, Nobuyuki 1949- **2002**:3
Matsui, Hideki 1974- **2007**:4
Mitarai, Fujio 1935- **2002**:4
Miyake, Issey 1939- **1985**:2
Miyazaki, Hayao 1941- **2006**:2
Miyazawa, Kiichi 1919- **1992**:2
Mori, Yoshiro 1937- **2000**:4
Morita, Akio 1921- **1989**:4
Morita, Akio 1921-1999
Obituary **2000**:2
Murakami, Haruki 1949- **2008**:3
Murakami, Takashi 1962- **2004**:2

Nagako, Empress Dowager
1903-2000
Obituary **2001**:1
Nara, Yoshitomo 1959- **2006**:2
Nomo, Hideo 1968- **1996**:2
Obuchi, Keizo 1937- **1999**:2
Obuchi, Keizo 1937-2000
Obituary **2000**:4
Oe, Kenzaburo 1935- **1997**:1
Sasakawa, Ryoichi
Brief entry **1988**:1
Shimomura, Tsutomu 1965- **1996**:1
Suzuki, Ichiro 1973- **2002**:2
Suzuki, Sin'ichi 1898-1998
Obituary **1998**:3
Takada, Kenzo 1938- **2003**:2
Takei, Kei 1946- **1990**:2
Takeshita, Noburu 1924-2000
Obituary **2001**:1
Tanaka, Tomoyuki 1910-1997
Obituary **1997**:3
Tange, Kenzo 1913-2005
Obituary **2006**:2
Taniguchi, Yoshio 1937- **2005**:4
Toyoda, Eiji 1913- **1985**:2
Uchida, Mitsuko 1949(?)- **1989**:3
Umeki, Miyoshi 1929-2007
Obituary **2008**:4
Yamamoto, Kenichi 1922- **1989**:1

**JORDANIAN**
Abdullah II, King 1962- **2002**:4
al-Abdullah, Rania 1970- **2001**:1
Hussein I, King 1935-1999 **1997**:3
Obituary **1999**:3

**KAZAKHSTANI**
Nazarbayev, Nursultan 1940- **2006**:4

**KENYAN**
Kibaki, Mwai 1931- **2003**:4
Maathai, Wangari 1940- **2005**:3
Moi, Daniel arap 1924- **1993**:2

**KOREAN**
Chung Ju Yung 1915-2001
Obituary **2002**:1
Kim Dae Jung 1925- **1998**:3
Kim Il Sung 1912-1994
Obituary **1994**:4
Kim Jong Il 1942- **1995**:2
Lee Jong-Wook 1945- **2005**:1
Lee Myung-bak 1941- **2009**:2
Pak, Se Ri 1977- **1999**:4
Roh Moo-hyun 1946- **2005**:1

**KOSOVOAN**
Rugova, Ibrahim 1944-2006
Obituary **2007**:1

**KYRGYZSTANI**
Bakiyev, Kurmanbek 1949- **2007**:1

**LATVIAN**
Baryshnikov, Mikhail Nikolaevich
1948- **1997**:3

**LEBANESE**
Berri, Nabih 1939(?)- **1985**:2
Haladjian, Rafi 1962(?)- **2008**:3
Jumblatt, Walid 1949(?)- **1987**:4
Sarkis, Elias 1924-1985
Obituary **1985**:3

**LIBERIAN**
Doe, Samuel 1952-1990
Obituary **1991**:1
Sirleaf, Ellen Johnson 1938- **2007**:3

**LIBYAN**
Qaddhafi, Muammar 1942- **1998**:3

**LITHUANIAN**
Landsbergis, Vytautas 1932- **1991**:3

**MACEDONIAN**
Trajkovski, Boris 1956-2004
Obituary **2005**:2

**MADAGASCAN**
Ravalomanana, Marc 1950(?)- **2003**:1

**MALAWI**
Banda, Hastings 1898- **1994**:3

**MALAYSIAN**
Badawi, Abdullah Ahmad 1939-
**2009**:3
Choo, Jimmy 1957(?)- **2006**:3
Lum, Olivia 1961- **2009**:1
Ngau, Harrison **1991**:3
Yeang, Ken 1948- **2008**:3
Yeoh, Michelle 1962- **2003**:2

**MEXICAN**
Alvarez Bravo, Manuel 1902-2002
Obituary **2004**:1
Catlett, Elizabeth 1915(?)- **1999**:3
Colosio, Luis Donaldo 1950-1994
**1994**:3
Cuaron, Alfonso 1961- **2008**:2
Esquivel, Juan 1918- **1996**:2
Felix, Maria 1914-2002
Obituary **2003**:2
Fox, Vicente 1942- **2001**:1
Garcia, Amalia 1951- **2005**:3
Graham, Robert 1938- **1993**:4
Hayek, Salma 1968- **1999**:1
Kahlo, Frida 1907-1954 **1991**:3
Ochoa, Lorena 1981- **2007**:4
Paz, Octavio 1914- **1991**:2
Salinas, Carlos 1948- **1992**:1
Santana, Carlos 1947- **2000**:2
Tamayo, Rufino 1899-1991
Obituary **1992**:1
Zedillo, Ernesto 1951- **1995**:1

**MONACO**
Albert, Prince of Monaco 1958- **2006**
:2
Rainier III, Prince of Monaco
1923-2005

Obituary **2006**:2

**MONGOLIAN**
Enkhbayar, Nambaryn 1958- **2007**:1

**MOROCCAN**
Elbaz, Alber 1961- **2008**:1
King Hassan II 1929-1999
Obituary **2000**:1
Lalami, Laila **2007**:1

**MOZAMBICAN**
Chissano, Joaquim 1939- **1987**:4
Dhlakama, Afonso 1953- **1993**:3
Guebuza, Armando 1943- **2008**:4
Machel, Samora 1933-1986
Obituary **1987**:1

**NAMIBIAN**
Nujoma, Sam 1929- **1990**:4

**NEPALI**
Shah, Gyanendra 1947- **2006**:1

**NEW ZEALANDER**
Campion, Jane **1991**:4
Castle-Hughes, Keisha 1990- **2004**:4
Crowe, Russell 1964- **2000**:4
Frame, Janet 1924-2004
Obituary **2005**:2
Hillary, Edmund 1919-2008
Obituary **2009**:1
Jackson, Peter 1961- **2004**:4
Kleinpaste, Ruud 1952- **2006**:2
Shipley, Jenny 1952- **1998**:3

**NICARAGUAN**
Astorga, Nora 1949(?)-1988 **1988**:2
Cruz, Arturo 1923- **1985**:1
Obando, Miguel 1926- **1986**:4
Ortega, Daniel 1945- **2008**:2
Robelo, Alfonso 1940(?)- **1988**:1

**NIGERIAN**
Abacha, Sani 1943- **1996**:3
Babangida, Ibrahim Badamosi
1941- **1992**:4
Obasanjo, Olusegun 1937(?)- **2000**:2
Okoye, Christian 1961- **1990**:2
Olajuwon, Akeem 1963- **1985**:1
Olopade, Olufunmilayo
1957(?)- **2006**:3
Sade 1959- **1993**:2
Saro-Wiwa, Ken 1941-1995
Obituary **1996**:2
Yar'Adua, Umaru 1951- **2008**:3

**NORWEGIAN**
Brundtland, Gro Harlem
1939- **2000**:1
Cammermeyer, Margarethe
1942- **1995**:2
Olav, King of Norway 1903-1991

Obituary **1991**:3
Stoltenberg, Jens 1959- **2006**:4

## PAKISTANI
Bhutto, Benazir 1953- **1989**:4
Zia ul-Haq, Mohammad 1924-1988
Obituary **1988**:4

## PALESTINIAN
Abbas, Mahmoud 1935- **2008**:4
Arafat, Yasser 1929- **1989**:3
Darwish, Mahmud 1942-2008
Obituary **2009**:4
Freij, Elias 1920- **1986**:4
Habash, George 1925(?)- **1986**:1
Husseini, Faisal 1940- **1998**:4
Nidal, Abu 1937- **1987**:1
Sharon, Ariel 1928- **2001**:4
Terzi, Zehdi Labib 1924- **1985**:3

## PANAMANIAN
Blades, Ruben 1948- **1998**:2

## PARAGUAYAN
Stroessner, Alfredo 1912-2006
Obituary **2007**:4

## PERUVIAN
Fujimori, Alberto 1938- **1992**:4
Garcia, Alan 1949- **2007**:4
Perez de Cuellar, Javier 1920- **1991**:3
Testino, Mario 1954- **2002**:1

## POLISH
Begin, Menachem 1913-1992
Obituary **1992**:3
Eisenstaedt, Alfred 1898-1995
Obituary **1996**:1
John Paul II, Pope 1920- **1995**:3
Kaczynski, Lech 1949- **2007**:2
Kieslowski, Krzysztof 1941-1996
Obituary **1996**:3
Kosinski, Jerzy 1933-1991
Obituary **1991**:4
Masur, Kurt 1927- **1993**:4
Niezabitowska, Malgorzata
1949(?)- **1991**:3
Rosten, Leo 1908-1997
Obituary **1997**:3
Sabin, Albert 1906-1993
Obituary **1993**:4
Sendler, Irena 1910-2008
Obituary **2009**:2
Singer, Isaac Bashevis 1904-1991
Obituary **1992**:1
Walesa, Lech 1943- **1991**:2

## PORTUGUESE
Saramago, Jose 1922- **1999**:1

## PUERTO RICAN
Alvarez, Aida **1999**:2
Del Toro, Benicio 1967- **2001**:4
Ferrer, Jose 1912-1992
Obituary **1992**:3
Julia, Raul 1940-1994
Obituary **1995**:1
Martin, Ricky 1971- **1999**:4

Novello, Antonia 1944- **1991**:2
Trinidad, Felix 1973- **2000**:4

## ROMANIAN
Basescu, Traian 1951- **2006**:2
Ceausescu, Nicolae 1918-1989
Obituary **1990**:2
Codrescu, Andreaa 1946- **1997**:3

## RUSSIAN
Brodsky, Joseph 1940-1996
Obituary **1996**:3
Gorbachev, Raisa 1932-1999
Obituary **2000**:2
Gordeeva, Ekaterina 1972- **1996**:4
Grinkov, Sergei 1967-1995
Obituary **1996**:2
Kasparov, Garry 1963- **1997**:4
Kasyanov, Mikhail 1957- **2001**:1
Konstantinov, Vladimir 1967- **1997**:4
Kournikova, Anna 1981- **2000**:3
Lapidus, Morris 1902-2001
Obituary **2001**:4
Lebed, Alexander 1950- **1997**:1
Medvedev, Dmitry 1965- **2009**:4
Moiseyev, Igor 1906-2007
Obituary **2009**:1
Ovechkin, Alexander 1985- **2009**:2
Primakov, Yevgeny 1929- **1999**:3
Putin, Vladimir 1952- **2000**:3
Rostropovich, Mstislav 1927-2007
Obituary **2008**:3
Safin, Marat 1980- **2001**:3
Sarraute, Nathalie 1900-1999
Obituary **2000**:2
Schneerson, Menachem Mendel
1902-1994 **1992**:4
Obituary **1994**:4
Sharapova, Maria 1987- **2005**:2
Solzhenitsyn, Aleksandr 1918-2008
Obituary **2009**:4
Titov, Gherman 1935-2000
Obituary **2001**:3

## RWANDAN
Kagame, Paul 1957- **2001**:4

## SALVADORAN
Duarte, Jose Napoleon 1925-1990
Obituary **1990**:3

## SAUDI
Fahd, King of Saudi Arabia
1923(?)-2005
Obituary **2006**:4

## SCOTTISH
Coldplay **2004**:4
Connery, Sean 1930- **1990**:4
Ferguson, Craig 1962- **2005**:4
Ferguson, Niall 1964- **2006**:1
Franchitti, Dario 1973- **2008**:1
Macquarrie, John 1919-2007
Obituary **2008**:3
McGregor, Ewan 1971(?)- **1998**:2
Mina, Denise 1966- **2006**:1
Paolozzi, Eduardo 1924-2005
Obituary **2006**:3

Ramsay, Mike 1950(?)- **2002**:1
Rowling, J.K. 1965- **2000**:1

## SENEGALESE
Senghor, Leopold 1906-2001
Obituary **2003**:1

## SERBIAN
Djokovic, Novak 1987- **2008**:4
Tadic, Boris 1958- **2009**:3

## SLOVENIAN
Turk, Danilo 1952- **2009**:3

## SOMALIAN
Iman 1955- **2001**:3

## SOUTH AFRICAN
Barnard, Christiaan 1922-2001
Obituary **2002**:4
Blackburn, Molly 1931(?)-1985
Obituary **1985**:4
Botha, P. W. 1916-2006
Obituary **2008**:1
Buthelezi, Mangosuthu Gatsha
1928- **1989**:3
Coetzee, J. M. 1940- **2004**:4
de Klerk, F.W. 1936- **1990**:1
Duncan, Sheena
Brief entry **1987**:1
Fugard, Athol 1932- **1992**:3
Hani, Chris 1942-1993
Obituary **1993**:4
Horn, Mike 1966- **2009**:3
Makeba, Miriam 1934- **1989**:2
Mandela, Nelson 1918- **1990**:3
Mandela, Winnie 1934- **1989**:3
Matthews, Dave 1967- **1999**:3
Mbeki, Thabo 1942- **1999**:4
Oppenheimer, Harry 1908-2000
Obituary **2001**:3
Paton, Alan 1903-1988
Obituary **1988**:3
Ramaphosa, Cyril 1953- **1988**:2
Sisulu, Walter 1912-2003
Obituary **2004**:2
Slovo, Joe 1926- **1989**:2
Suzman, Helen 1917- **1989**:3
Tambo, Oliver 1917- **1991**:3
Theron, Charlize 1975- **2001**:4
Treurnicht, Andries 1921- **1992**:2
Woods, Donald 1933-2001
Obituary **2002**:3

## SOVIET
Asimov, Isaac 1920-1992
Obituary **1992**:3
Chernenko, Konstantin 1911-1985
Obituary **1985**:1
Dalai Lama 1935- **1989**:1
Dubinin, Yuri 1930- **1987**:4
Dzhanibekov, Vladimir 1942- **1988**:1
Erte 1892-1990
Obituary **1990**:4
Federov, Sergei 1969- **1995**:1
Godunov, Alexander 1949-1995
Obituary **1995**:4
Gorbachev, Mikhail 1931- **1985**:2

Grebenshikov, Boris 1953- **1990**:1
Gromyko, Andrei 1909-1989
   Obituary **1990**:2
Karadzic, Radovan 1945- **1995**:3
Milosevic, Slobodan 1941- **1993**:2
Molotov, Vyacheslav Mikhailovich
   1890-1986
   Obituary **1987**:1
Nureyev, Rudolf 1938-1993
   Obituary **1993**:2
Sakharov, Andrei Dmitrievich
   1921-1989
   Obituary **1990**:2
Smirnoff, Yakov 1951- **1987**:2
Vidov, Oleg 194- **1987**:4
Yeltsin, Boris 1931- **1991**:1
Zhirinovsky, Vladimir 1946- **1994**:2

**SPANISH**
Almodovar, Pedro 1951- **2000**:3
Banderas, Antonio 1960- **1996**:2
Bardem, Javier 1969- **2008**:4
Blahnik, Manolo 1942- **2000**:2
Calatrava, Santiago 1951- **2005**:1
Carreras, Jose 1946- **1995**:2
Cela, Camilo Jose 1916-2001
   Obituary **2003**:1
Chillida, Eduardo 1924-2002
   Obituary **2003**:4
Cruz, Penelope 1974- **2001**:4
Dali, Salvador 1904-1989
   Obituary **1989**:2
de Pinies, Jamie
   Brief entry **1986**:3
Domingo, Placido 1941- **1993**:2
Juan Carlos I 1938- **1993**:1
Lopez de Arriortua, Jose Ignacio
   1941- **1993**:4
Miro, Joan 1893-1983
   Obituary **1985**:1
Moneo, Jose Rafael 1937- **1996**:4
Montoya, Carlos 1903-1993
   Obituary **1993**:4
Nadal, Rafael 1986- **2009**:1
Samaranch, Juan Antonio
   1920- **1986**:2
Segovia, Andreaas 1893-1987
   Obituary **1987**:3
Wences, Senor 1896-1999
   Obituary **1999**:4

**SRI LANKAN**
Bandaranaike, Sirimavo 1916-2000
   Obituary **2001**:2
Ondaatje, Philip Michael
   1943- **1997**:3
Wickramasinghe, Ranil 1949- **2003**:2

**SUDANESE**
al-Bashir, Omar 1944- **2009**:1
Turabi, Hassan 1932(?)- **1995**:4

**SWEDISH**
Bergman, Ingmar 1918- **1999**:4
Cardigans, The **1997**:4
Carlsson, Arvid 1923- **2001**:2

Garbo, Greta 1905-1990
   Obituary **1990**:3
Hallstrom, Lasse 1946- **2002**:3
Lidstrom, Nicklas 1970- **2009**:1
Lindbergh, Pelle 1959-1985
   Obituary **1985**:4
Lindgren, Astrid 1907-2002
   Obituary **2003**:1
Nilsson, Birgit 1918-2005
   Obituary **2007**:1
Olin, Lena 1956- **1991**:2
Palme, Olof 1927-1986
   Obituary **1986**:2
Persson, Stefan 1947- **2004**:1
Renvall, Johan
   Brief entry **1987**:4
Sorenstam, Annika 1970- **2001**:1

**SWISS**
del Ponte, Carla 1947- **2001**:1
Federer, Roger 1981- **2004**:2
Frank, Robert 1924- **1995**:2
Vasella, Daniel 1953- **2005**:3
Vollenweider, Andreas 1953- **1985**:2

**SYRIAN**
al-Assad, Bashar 1965- **2004**:2
Assad, Hafez 1930-2000
   Obituary **2000**:4
Assad, Hafez al- 1930(?)- **1992**:1
Assad, Rifaat 1937(?)- **1986**:3

**TAHITIAN**
Brando, Cheyenne 1970-1995
   Obituary **1995**:4

**TAIWANESE**
Chen Shui-bian 1950(?)- **2001**:2
Ho, David 1952- **1997**:2
Lee Teng-hui 1923- **2000**:1
Ma Ying-jeou 1950- **2009**:4

**TANZANIAN**
Nyerere, Julius 1922(?)-1999
   Obituary **2000**:2

**THAI**
Thaksin Shinawatra 1949- **2005**:4

**TRINIDADIAN**
Ture, Kwame 1941-1998
   Obituary **1999**:2

**TUNISIAN**
Azria, Max 1949- **2001**:4

**TURKISH**
Ecevit, Bulent 1925-2006
   Obituary **2008**:1
Gul, Abdullah 1950- **2009**:4
Ocalan, Abdullah 1948(?)- **1999**:4
Pamuk, Orhan 1952- **2007**:3

**UGANDAN**
Amin, Idi 1925(?)-2003
   Obituary **2004**:4
Museveni, Yoweri 1944- **2002**:1

**UKRAINIAN**
Baiul, Oksana 1977- **1995**:3
Tymoshenko, Yulia 1960- **2009**:1
Yushchenko, Viktor 1954- **2006**:1

**URUGUAYAN**
Vazquez, Tabare 1940- **2006**:2

**UZBEKISTANI**
Karimov, Islam 1938- **2006**:3

**VENEZUELAN**
Hernandez, Felix 1986- **2008**:2
Herrera, Carolina 1939- **1997**:1
Perez, Carlos Andre 1922- **1990**:2
Santana, Johan 1979- **2008**:1

**VIETNAMESE**
Dong, Pham Van 1906-2000
   Obituary **2000**:4
Le Duan 1908(?)-1986
   Obituary **1986**:4
Le Duc Tho 1911-1990
   Obituary **1991**:1

**WELSH**
Bale, Christian 1974- **2001**:3
Dahl, Roald 1916-1990
   Obituary **1991**:2
Hopkins, Anthony 1937- **1992**:4
Jenkins, Roy Harris 1920-2003
   Obituary **2004**:1
Jones, Tom 1940- **1993**:4
Macdonald, Julien 1973(?)- **2005**:3
William, Prince of Wales 1982- **2001**
   :3
Zeta-Jones, Catherine
   1969- **1999**:4

**YEMENI**
Saleh, Ali Abdullah 1942- **2001**:3

**YUGOSLAVIAN**
Filipovic, Zlata 1981(?)- **1994**:4
Kostunica, Vojislav 1944- **2001**:1
Pogorelich, Ivo 1958- **1986**:4
Seles, Monica 1974(?)- **1991**:3

**ZAIRAN**
Mobutu Sese Seko 1930-1997 **1993**:4
   Obituary **1998**:1

**ZAMBIAN**
Chiluba, Frederick 1943- **1992**:3

**ZIMBABWEAN**
Mugabe, Robert 1924- **1988**:4
Smith, Ian 1919-2007
   Obituary **2009**:1

# 2009 Occupation Index

This index lists all newsmakers alphabetically by their occupations or fields of primary activity. Indexes in softbound issues allow access to the current year's entries; indexes in annual hardbound volumes are cumulative, covering the entire *Newsmakers* series.

Listee names are followed by a year and issue number; thus **1996**:3 indicates that an entry on that individual appears in both 1996, Issue 3, and the 1996 cumulation. For access to newsmakers appearing earlier than the current softbound issue, see the previous year's cumulation.

## ART AND DESIGN

Adams, Scott 1957- **1996**:4
Adams-Geller, Paige 1969(?)- **2006**:4
Addams, Charles 1912-1988
　Obituary **1989**:1
Adler, Jonathan 1966- **2006**:3
Agnes B 1941- **2002**:3
al-Ani, Jananne 1966- **2008**:4
Albou, Sophie 1967- **2007**:2
Allard, Linda 1940- **2003**:2
Alvarez Bravo, Manuel 1902-2002
　Obituary **2004**:1
Anderson, Laurie 1947- **2000**:2
Ando, Tadao 1941- **2005**:4
Appel, Karel 1921-2006
　Obituary **2007**:2
Arman 1928- **1993**:1
Armani, Giorgio 1934(?)- **1991**:2
Ashwell, Rachel 1960(?)- **2004**:2
Aucoin, Kevyn 1962- **2001**:3
Avedon, Richard 1923- **1993**:4
Azria, Max 1949- **2001**:4
Badgley, Mark and James
　Mischka **2004**:3
Baldessari, John 1931(?)- **1991**:4
Ball, Michael 1964(?)- **2007**:3
Banks, Jeffrey 1953- **1998**:2
Banksy 1975(?)- **2007**:2
Barbera, Joseph 1911- **1988**:2
Barks, Carl 1901-2000
　Obituary **2001**:2
Barnes, Ernie 1938- **1997**:4
Barry, Lynda 1956(?)- **1992**:1
Bean, Alan L. 1932- **1986**:2
Beene, Geoffrey 1927-2004
　Obituary **2005**:4
Bell, Gabrielle 1975(?)- **2007**:4
Bellissimo, Wendy 1967(?)- **2007**:1
Beuys, Joseph 1921-1986
　Obituary **1986**:3
Bird, Brad 1956(?)- **2005**:4
Blahnik, Manolo 1942- **2000**:2
Blass, Bill 1922-2002
　Obituary **2003**:3
Bohbot, Michele 1959(?)- **2004**:2
Bontecou, Lee 1931- **2004**:4
Boone, Mary 1951- **1985**:1

Borofsky, Jonathan 1942- **2006**:4
Botero, Fernando 1932- **1994**:3
Bourgeois, Louise 1911- **1994**:1
Bowie, David 1947- **1998**:2
Boynton, Sandra 1953- **2004**:1
Breathed, Berkeley 1957- **2005**:3
Brown, Bobbi 1957- **2001**:4
Brown, Howard and Karen
　Stewart **2007**:3
Brown, J. Carter 1934-2002
　Obituary **2003**:3
Bundchen, Gisele 1980- **2009**:1
Bunshaft, Gordon 1909-1990 **1989**:3
　Obituary **1991**:1
Burch, Tory 1966- **2009**:3
Calatrava, Santiago 1951- **2005**:1
Cameron, David
　Brief entry **1988**:1
Campbell, Ben Nighthorse
　1933- **1998**:1
Campbell, Naomi 1970- **2000**:2
Cardin, Pierre 1922- **2003**:3
Cartier-Bresson, Henri 1908-2004
　Obituary **2005**:4
Cassini, Oleg 1913-2006
　Obituary **2007**:2
Castelli, Leo 1907-1999
　Obituary **2000**:1
Catlett, Elizabeth 1915(?)- **1999**:3
Cavalli, Roberto 1940- **2004**:4
Chagall, Marc 1887-1985
　Obituary **1985**:2
Chalayan, Hussein 1970- **2003**:2
Chast, Roz 1955- **1992**:4
Chatham, Russell 1939- **1990**:1
Chia, Sandro 1946- **1987**:2
Chihuly, Dale 1941- **1995**:2
Chillida, Eduardo 1924-2002
　Obituary **2003**:4
Choo, Jimmy 1957(?)- **2006**:3
Christo 1935- **1992**:3
Claiborne, Liz 1929- **1986**:3
Clemente, Francesco 1952- **1992**:2
Cole, Anne 1930(?)- **2007**:3
Cole, Kenneth 1954(?)- **2003**:1
Conner, Bruce 1933-2008
　Obituary **2009**:3

Cooper, Alexander 1936- **1988**:4
Courtney, Erica 1957- **2009**:3
Crumb, R. 1943- **1995**:4
Dali, Salvador 1904-1989
　Obituary **1989**:2
Davis, Paige 1969- **2004**:2
DeCarava, Roy 1919- **1996**:3
de Kooning, Willem
　1904-1997 **1994**:4
　Obituary **1997**:3
de la Renta, Oscar 1932- **2005**:4
Diebenkorn, Richard 1922-1993
　Obituary **1993**:4
Diller, Elizabeth and Ricardo
　Scofidio **2004**:3
Dith Pran 1942-2008
　Obituary **2009**:2
Dolce, Domenico and Stefano
　Gabbana **2005**:4
Donghia, Angelo R. 1935-1985
　Obituary **1985**:2
Duarte, Henry 1963(?)- **2003**:3
Dubuffet, Jean 1901-1985
　Obituary **1985**:4
Dunham, Carroll 1949- **2003**:4
Ecko, Marc 1972- **2006**:3
Eisenman, Peter 1932- **1992**:4
Eisenstaedt, Alfred 1898-1995
　Obituary **1996**:1
Eisner, Will 1917-2005
　Obituary **2006**:1
Elbaz, Alber 1961- **2008**:1
Ellis, David 1971- **2009**:4
Ellis, Perry 1940-1986
　Obituary **1986**:3
Emin, Tracey 1963- **2009**:2
Engelbreit, Mary 1952(?)- **1994**:3
Erickson, Arthur 1924- **1989**:3
Erte 1892-1990
　Obituary **1990**:4
Eve 1978- **2004**:3
Fekkai, Frederic 1959(?)- **2003**:2
Ferre, Gianfranco 1944-2007
　Obituary **2008**:3
Ferretti, Alberta 1950(?)- **2004**:1
Field, Patricia 1942(?)- **2002**:2
Finley, Karen 1956- **1992**:4

Fisher, Mary 1948- **1994**:3
Ford, Tom 1962- **1999**:3
Foster, Norman 1935- **1999**:4
Frank, Robert 1924- **1995**:2
Frankenthaler, Helen 1928- **1990**:1
Freud, Lucian 1922- **2000**:4
Frieda, John 1951- **2004**:1
Gaines, William M. 1922-1992
    Obituary **1993**:1
Galliano, John 1960- **2005**:2
Gaultier, Jean-Paul 1952- **1998**:1
Gehry, Frank O. 1929- **1987**:1
Giannulli, Mossimo 1963- **2002**:3
Gioia, Dana 1950- **2008**:4
Gober, Robert 1954- **1996**:3
Golden, Thelma 1965- **2003**:3
Goldsworthy, Andy 1956- **2007**:2
Goody, Joan 1935- **1990**:2
Gorder, Genevieve 1974- **2005**:4
Gordon, Michael 1951(?)- **2005**:1
Gottlieb, William 1917-2006
    Obituary **2007**:2
Gould, Chester 1900-1985
    Obituary **1985**:2
Graham, Nicholas 1960(?)- **1991**:4
Graham, Robert 1938- **1993**:4
Graves, Michael 1934- **2000**:1
Graves, Nancy 1940- **1989**:3
Greenberg, Robert 1940(?)- **2003**:2
Gregory, Rogan 1972- **2008**:2
Groening, Matt 1955(?)- **1990**:4
Guccione, Bob 1930- **1986**:1
Gund, Agnes 1938- **1993**:2
Gursky, Andreas 1955- **2002**:2
Hadid, Zaha 1950- **2005**:3
Halston 1932-1990
    Obituary **1990**:3
Handford, Martin **1991**:3
Haring, Keith 1958-1990
    Obituary **1990**:3
Hart, Johnny 1931-2007
    Obituary **2008**:2
Held, Al 1928-2005
    Obituary **2006**:4
Hernandez, Lazaro and Jack
    McCollough **2008**:4
Hershberger, Sally 1961(?)- **2006**:4
Hicks, India 1967- **2008**:2
Hilfiger, Tommy 1952- **1993**:3
Hindmarch, Anya 1969- **2008**:2
Hockney, David 1937- **1988**:3
Hoff, Syd 1912-2004
    Obituary **2005**:3
Holl, Steven 1947- **2003**:1
Hughes, Robert 1938- **1996**:4
Isozaki, Arata 1931- **1990**:2
Jacobs, Marc 1963- **2002**:3
Jagger, Jade 1971- **2005**:1
Jahn, Helmut 1940- **1987**:3
Johnson, Betsey 1942- **1996**:2
Johnson, Philip 1906- **1989**:2
Jones, E. Fay 1921-2004
    Obituary **2005**:4
Jordan, Charles M. 1927- **1989**:4
Joseph, Wendy Evans
    1955(?)- **2006**:2
Judge, Mike 1963(?)- **1994**:2
July, Miranda 1974- **2008**:2
Kahlo, Frida 1907-1954 **1991**:3
Kamali, Norma 1945- **1989**:1
Karan, Donna 1948- **1988**:1
Karsh, Yousuf 1908-2002

Obituary **2003**:4
Kashuk, Sonia 1959(?)- **2002**:4
Kaskey, Ray
    Brief entry **1987**:2
Katz, Alex 1927- **1990**:3
Kelly, Ellsworth 1923- **1992**:1
Kelly, Patrick 1954(?)-1990
    Obituary **1990**:2
Kent, Corita 1918-1986
    Obituary **1987**:1
Keplinger, Dan 1973- **2001**:1
Ketcham, Hank 1920-2001
    Obituary **2002**:2
Kidd, Jemma 1974- **2009**:1
Kiefer, Anselm 1945- **1990**:2
Kiley, Dan 1912-2004
    Obituary **2005**:2
Kim, Eugenia 1974(?)- **2006**:1
Kinney, Jeff 1971- **2009**:3
Kitaj, R. B. 1932-2007
    Obituary **2008**:4
Klein, Calvin 1942- **1996**:2
Koolhaas, Rem 1944- **2001**:1
Koons, Jeff 1955(?)- **1991**:4
Kors, Michael 1959- **2000**:4
Kostabi, Mark 1960- **1989**:4
Kuma, Kengo 1954- **2009**:1
Kurokawa, Kisho 1934-2007
    Obituary **2008**:4
Lacroix, Christian 1951- **2005**:2
Lagerfeld, Karl 1938- **1999**:4
Lam, Derek 1966- **2009**:2
Lang, Helmut 1956- **1999**:2
Lange, Liz 1967(?)- **2003**:4
Lapidus, Morris 1902-2001
    Obituary **2001**:4
Lasdun, Denys 1914-2001
    Obituary **2001**:4
Lauren, Ralph 1939- **1990**:1
Leibovitz, Annie 1949- **1988**:4
Leigh, Dorian 1917-2008
    Obituary **2009**:3
Lepore, Nanette 1964(?)- **2006**:4
LeWitt, Sol 1928- **2001**:2
Lhuillier, Monique 1971(?)- **2007**:4
Libeskind, Daniel 1946- **2004**:1
Lichtenstein, Roy 1923-1997 **1994**:1
    Obituary **1998**:1
Lim, Phillip 1974(?)- **2008**:1
Lin, Maya 1960(?)- **1990**:3
Lobell, Jeanine 1964(?)- **2002**:3
Longo, Robert 1953(?)- **1990**:4
Louboutin, Christian 1963- **2006**:1
Macdonald, Julien 1973(?)- **2005**:3
MacFarlane, Seth 1973- **2006**:1
MacNelly, Jeff 1947-2000
    Obituary **2000**:4
Madden, Chris 1948- **2006**:1
Mann, Sally 1951- **2001**:2
Mansion, Gracie
    Brief entry **1986**:3
Mapplethorpe, Robert 1946-1989
    Obituary **1989**:3
Mardin, Brice 1938- **2007**:4
Mark, Mary Ellen 1940- **2006**:2
Martin, Agnes 1912-2004
    Obituary **2006**:1
Matadin, Vinoodh and Inez van
    Lamsweerde **2007**:4
Mauldin, Bill 1921-2003
    Obituary **2004**:2
Max, Peter 1937- **1993**:2

McCartney, Linda 1942-1998
    Obituary **1998**:4
McCartney, Stella 1971- **2001**:3
McDonnell, Patrick 1956- **2009**:4
McDonough, William 1951- **2003**:1
McFarlane, Todd 1961- **1999**:1
McGinley, Ryan 1977- **2009**:1
McGruder, Aaron 1974- **2005**:4
Meier, Richard 1934- **2001**:4
Meisel, Steven 1954- **2002**:4
Melendez, Bill 1916-2008
    Obituary **2009**:4
Mellinger, Frederick 1924(?)-1990
    Obituary **1990**:4
Mercier, Laura 1959(?)- **2002**:2
Messick, Dale 1906-2005
    Obituary **2006**:2
Miller, Nicole 1951(?)- **1995**:4
Mills, Malia 1966- **2003**:1
Miro, Joan 1893-1983
    Obituary **1985**:1
Misrach, Richard 1949- **1991**:2
Miyake, Issey 1939- **1985**:2
Miyazaki, Hayao 1941- **2006**:2
Mizrahi, Isaac 1961- **1991**:1
Moneo, Jose Rafael 1937- **1996**:4
Moore, Henry 1898-1986
    Obituary **1986**:4
Motherwell, Robert 1915-1991
    Obituary **1992**:1
Mueck, Ron 1958- **2008**:3
Mumford, Lewis 1895-1990
    Obituary **1990**:2
Murakami, Takashi 1962- **2004**:2
Mydans, Carl 1907-2004
    Obituary **2005**:4
Nara, Yoshitomo 1959- **2006**:2
Nars, Francois 1959- **2003**:1
Natori, Josie 1947- **1994**:3
Nauman, Bruce 1941- **1995**:4
Nechita, Alexandra 1985- **1996**:4
Neiman, LeRoy 1927- **1993**:3
Nevelson, Louise 1900-1988
    Obituary **1988**:3
Newman, Arnold 1918- **1993**:1
Newton, Helmut 1920- **2002**:1
Nipon, Albert
    Brief entry **1986**:4
Ogilvy, David 1911-1999
    Obituary **2000**:1
Oldham, Todd 1961- **1995**:4
Olsen, Sigrid 1953- **2007**:1
Ono, Yoko 1933- **1989**:2
Panichgul, Thakoon 1974- **2009**:4
Paolozzi, Eduardo 1924-2005
    Obituary **2006**:3
Parker, Brant 1920-2007
    Obituary **2008**:2
Parker, Suzy 1932-2003
    Obituary **2004**:2
Parks, Gordon 1912-2006
    Obituary **2006**:2
Pedersen, William 1938(?)- **1989**:4
Pei, I.M. 1917- **1990**:4
Pelli, Cesar 1927(?)- **1991**:4
Penn & Teller **1992**:1
Pennington, Ty 1965- **2005**:4
Peyton, Elizabeth 1965- **2007**:1
Piano, Renzo 1937- **2009**:2
Picasso, Paloma 1949- **1991**:1
Plater-Zyberk, Elizabeth
    1950- **2005**:2

Polke, Sigmar 1941- **1999**:4
Portman, John 1924- **1988**:2
Posen, Zac 1980- **2009**:3
Potok, Anna Maximilian
  Brief entry **1985**:2
Pozzi, Lucio 1935- **1990**:2
Prada, Miuccia 1950(?)- **1996**:1
Pratt, Christopher 1935- **1985**:3
Predock, Antoine 1936- **1993**:2
Puryear, Martin 1941- **2002**:4
Queer Eye for the Straight Guy
  cast **2004**:3
Radocy, Robert
  Brief entry **1986**:3
Raimondi, John
  Brief entry **1987**:4
Raskin, Jef 1943(?)- **1997**:4
Rauschenberg, Robert 1925- **1991**:2
Rhodes, Zandra 1940- **1986**:2
Richter, Gerhard 1932- **1997**:2
Ringgold, Faith 1930- **2000**:3
Ritts, Herb 1954(?)- **1992**:4
Roberts, Xavier 1955- **1985**:3
Roche, Kevin 1922- **1985**:1
Rockwell, David 1956- **2003**:3
Rodriguez, Narciso 1961- **2005**:1
Roncal, Mally 1972- **2009**:4
Ronson, Charlotte 1977(?)- **2007**:3
Rosenberg, Evelyn 1942- **1988**:2
Rosenthal, Joseph 1911-2006
  Obituary **2007**:4
Rosenzweig, Ilene 1965(?)- **2004**:1
Rosso, Renzo 1955- **2005**:2
Rothenberg, Susan 1945- **1995**:3
Rouse, James 1914-1996
  Obituary **1996**:4
Rowley, Cynthia 1958- **2002**:1
Rykiel, Sonia 1930- **2000**:3
Saatchi, Charles 1943- **1987**:3
Saint Laurent, Yves 1936-2008
  Obituary **2009**:3
Salgado, Sebastiao 1944- **1994**:2
Scavullo, Francesco 1921-2004
  Obituary **2005**:1
Schnabel, Julian 1951- **1997**:1
Schulz, Charles 1922-2000
  Obituary **2000**:3
Schulz, Charles M. 1922- **1998**:1
Schwartz, Allen 1945(?)- **2008**:2
Segal, Shelli 1955(?)- **2005**:3
Serra, Richard 1939- **2009**:1
Serrano, Andres 1950- **2000**:4
Shaw, Carol 1958(?)- **2002**:1
Sherman, Cindy 1954- **1992**:3
Simpson, Lorna 1960- **2008**:1
Skaist-Levy, Pam and Gela
  Taylor **2005**:1
Slick, Grace 1939- **2001**:2
Smith, Paul 1946- **2002**:4
Smith, Willi 1948-1987
  Obituary **1987**:3
Som, Peter 1971- **2009**:1
Spade, Kate 1962- **2003**:1
Spiegelman, Art 1948- **1998**:3
Sprouse, Stephen 1953-2004
  Obituary **2005**:2
Starck, Philippe 1949- **2004**:1
Stefani, Gwen 1969- **2005**:4
Stefanidis, John 1937- **2007**:3
Stella, Frank 1936- **1996**:2
Stockton, Shreve 1977- **2009**:4
Sui, Anna 1955(?)- **1995**:1

Takada, Kenzo 1938- **2003**:2
Tamayo, Rufino 1899-1991
  Obituary **1992**:1
Tange, Kenzo 1913-2005
  Obituary **2006**:2
Taniguchi, Yoshio 1937- **2005**:4
Temperley, Alice 1975- **2008**:2
Testino, Mario 1954- **2002**:1
Thiebaud, Wayne 1920- **1991**:1
Tillmans, Wolfgang 1968- **2001**:4
Tompkins, Susie
  Brief entry **1987**:2
Touitou, Jean 1952(?)- **2008**:4
Trudeau, Garry 1948- **1991**:2
Truitt, Anne 1921- **1993**:1
Tunick, Spencer 1967- **2008**:1
Twombley, Cy 1928(?)- **1995**:1
Tyler, Richard 1948(?)- **1995**:3
Ungaro, Emanuel 1933- **2001**:3
Valli, Giambattista 1966- **2008**:3
Valvo, Carmen Marc 1954- **2003**:4
Venturi, Robert 1925- **1994**:4
Versace, Donatella 1955- **1999**:1
Versace, Gianni 1946-1997
  Brief entry **1988**:1
  Obituary **1998**:2
Von D, Kat 1982- **2008**:3
von Furstenberg, Diane 1946- **1994**:2
Von Hellermann, Sophie
  1975- **2006**:3
Vreeland, Diana 1903(?)-1989
  Obituary **1990**:1
Wagner, Catherine F. 1953- **2002**:3
Walker, Kara 1969- **1999**:2
Wang, Vera 1949- **1998**:4
Warhol, Andy 1927(?)-1987
  Obituary **1987**:2
Washington, Alonzo 1967- **2000**:1
Waterman, Cathy 1950(?)- **2002**:2
Watterson, Bill 1958(?)- **1990**:3
Wegman, William 1942(?)- **1991**:1
Westwood, Vivienne 1941- **1998**:3
Whitney, Patrick 1952(?)- **2006**:1
Wilson, Peter C. 1913-1984
  Obituary **1985**:2
Winick, Judd 1970- **2005**:3
Wintour, Anna 1949- **1990**:4
Witkin, Joel-Peter 1939- **1996**:1
Wyland, Robert 1956- **2009**:3
Yamasaki, Minoru 1912-1986
  Obituary **1986**:2
Yeang, Ken 1948- **2008**:3

**BUSINESS**
Abraham, S. Daniel 1924- **2003**:3
Ackerman, Will 1949- **1987**:4
Adams-Geller, Paige 1969(?)- **2006**:4
Adler, Jonathan 1966- **2006**:3
Agnelli, Giovanni 1921- **1989**:4
Ailes, Roger 1940- **1989**:3
Akers, John F. 1934- **1988**:3
Akin, Phil
  Brief entry **1987**:3
Albou, Sophie 1967- **2007**:2
Albrecht, Chris 1952(?)- **2005**:4
Allaire, Jeremy 1971- **2006**:4
Allaire, Paul 1938- **1995**:1
Allard, Linda 1940- **2003**:2
Allen, Bob 1935- **1992**:4
Allen, John 1930- **1992**:1
Alter, Hobie

Brief entry **1985**:1
Alvarez, Aida **1999**:2
Ames, Roger 1950(?)- **2005**:2
Amos, Wally 1936- **2000**:1
Ancier, Garth 1957- **1989**:1
Anderson, Brad 1949- **2007**:3
Anderson, Tom and Chris
  DeWolfe **2007**:2
Andreessen, Marc 1972- **1996**:2
Annenberg, Walter 1908- **1992**:3
Antonini, Joseph 1941- **1991**:2
Aoki, Rocky 1940- **1990**:2
Arad, Avi 1948- **2003**:2
Aretsky, Ken 1941- **1988**:1
Arison, Ted 1924- **1990**:3
Arledge, Roone 1931- **1992**:2
Armstrong, C. Michael 1938- **2002**:1
Arnault, Bernard 1949- **2000**:4
Ash, Mary Kay 1915(?)- **1996**:1
Ashwell, Rachel 1960(?)- **2004**:2
Aurre, Laura
  Brief entry **1986**:3
Ball, Michael 1964(?)- **2007**:3
Ballmer, Steven 1956- **1997**:2
Balsillie, Jim and Mike
  Lazaridis **2006**:4
Banks, Jeffrey 1953- **1998**:2
Barad, Jill 1951- **1994**:2
Barksdale, James L. 1943- **1998**:2
Barnes, Brenda C. 1955(?)- **2007**:4
Barrett, Craig R. 1939- **1999**:4
Bauer, Eddie 1899-1986
  Obituary **1986**:3
Baxter, Pamela 1949- **2009**:4
Beals, Vaughn 1928- **1988**:2
Becker, Brian 1957(?)- **2004**:4
Beene, Geoffrey 1927-2004
  Obituary **2005**:4
Beers, Charlotte 1935- **1999**:3
Bellissimo, Wendy 1967(?)- **2007**:1
Ben & Jerry **1991**:3
Benetton, Luciano 1935- **1988**:1
Berliner, Andy and Rachel **2008**:2
Berlusconi, Silvio 1936(?)- **1994**:4
Berman, Gail 1957(?)- **2006**:1
Bern, Dorrit J. 1950(?)- **2006**:3
Bernhard, Wolfgang 1960- **2007**:1
Besse, Georges 1927-1986
  Obituary **1987**:1
Bezos, Jeff 1964- **1998**:4
Bibliowicz, Jessica 1959- **2009**:3
Bieber, Owen 1929- **1986**:1
Bikoff, J. Darius 1962(?)- **2007**:3
Bikoff, James L.
  Brief entry **1986**:2
Black, Carole 1945- **2003**:1
Black, Cathleen 1944- **1998**:4
Black, Conrad 1944- **1986**:2
Bloch, Henry 1922- **1988**:4
Bloch, Ivan 1940- **1986**:3
Bloom, Natalie 1971- **2007**:1
Bloomberg, Michael 1942- **1997**:1
Bohbot, Michele 1959(?)- **2004**:2
Boiardi, Hector 1897-1985
  Obituary **1985**:3
Bolkiah, Sultan Muda Hassanal
  1946- **1985**:4
Bond, Alan 1938- **1989**:2
Bose, Amar
  Brief entry **1986**:4
Boyer, Herbert Wayne 1936- **1985**:1
Boyle, Gertrude 1924- **1995**:3

Boynton, Sandra 1953- **2004**:1
Brabeck-Letmathe, Peter
	1944- **2001**:4
Bradley, Todd 1958- **2003**:3
Branson, Richard 1951- **1987**:1
Bravo, Ellen 1944- **1998**:2
Bravo, Rose Marie 1951(?)- **2005**:3
Breitschwerdt, Werner 1927- **1988**:4
Brennan, Edward A. 1934- **1989**:1
Brennan, Robert E. 1943(?)- **1988**:1
Bronfman, Edgar, Jr. 1955- **1994**:4
Brooks, Diana D. 1950- **1990**:1
Brosius, Christopher **2007**:1
Brown, Howard and Karen
	Stewart **2007**:3
Brown, John Seely 1940- **2004**:1
Brown, Tina 1953- **1992**:1
Buffett, Jimmy 1946- **1999**:3
Buffett, Warren 1930- **1995**:2
Burch, Tory 1966- **2009**:3
Burnison, Chantal Simone
	1950(?)- **1988**:3
Burns, Robin 1953(?)- **1991**:2
Burr, Donald Calvin 1941- **1985**:3
Burton, Jake 1954- **2007**:1
Busch, August A. III 1937- **1988**:2
Busch, August Anheuser, Jr.
	1899-1989
	Obituary **1990**:2
Bushnell, Nolan 1943- **1985**:1
Buss, Jerry 1933- **1989**:3
Cain, Herman 1945- **1998**:3
Callaway, Ely 1919-2001
	Obituary **2002**:3
Calloway, D. Wayne 1935- **1987**:3
Campeau, Robert 1923- **1990**:1
Canfield, Alan B.
	Brief entry **1986**:3
Carlino, Cristina 1961(?)- **2008**:4
Carter, Billy 1937-1988
	Obituary **1989**:1
Case, Steve 1958- **1995**:4
Cassidy, Mike 1963(?)- **2006**:1
Cassini, Oleg 1913-2006
	Obituary **2007**:2
Centrello, Gina 1959(?)- **2008**:3
Chalayan, Hussein 1970- **2003**:2
Chappell, Tom 1943- **2002**:3
Charney, Dov 1969- **2008**:2
Charron, Paul 1942- **2004**:1
Chen, Steve and Chad
	Hurley **2007**:2
Chenault, Kenneth I. 1951- **1999**:3
Chizen, Bruce 1955(?)- **2004**:2
Choo, Jimmy 1957(?)- **2006**:3
Chouinard, Yvon 1938(?)- **2002**:2
Chung Ju Yung 1915-2001
	Obituary **2002**:1
Claiborne, Liz 1929- **1986**:3
Clark, Jim 1944- **1997**:1
Clark, Maxine 1949- **2009**:4
Cole, Anne 1930(?)- **2007**:3
Cole, Kenneth 1954(?)- **2003**:1
Coleman, Sheldon, Jr. 1953- **1990**:2
Collier, Sophia 1956(?)- **2001**:2
Combs, Sean Puffy 1970- **1998**:4
Condit, Phil 1941- **2001**:3
Conseil, Dominique Nils
	1962(?)- **2007**:2
Cooper, Alexander 1936- **1988**:4
Cooper, Stephen F. 1946- **2005**:4
Coors, William K.

Brief entry **1985**:1
Copeland, Al 1944(?)- **1988**:3
Covey, Stephen R. 1932- **1994**:4
Cox, Richard Joseph
	Brief entry **1985**:1
Craig, James 1956- **2001**:1
Craig, Sid and Jenny **1993**:4
Crandall, Robert L. 1935- **1992**:1
Crawford, Cheryl 1902-1986
	Obituary **1987**:1
Cray, Seymour R. 1925-1996
	Brief entry **1986**:3
	Obituary **1997**:2
Crump, Scott 1954(?)- **2008**:1
Cummings, Sam 1927- **1986**:3
D'Alessio, Kitty
	Brief entry **1987**:3
David, George 1942- **2005**:1
Davis, Crispin 1949- **2004**:1
Davison, Ian Hay 1931- **1986**:1
DeBartolo, Edward J., Jr.
	1946- **1989**:3
de la Renta, Oscar 1932- **2005**:4
Dell, Michael 1965- **1996**:2
DeLuca, Fred 1947- **2003**:3
De Luca, Guerrino 1952- **2007**:1
Deming, W. Edwards
	1900-1993 **1992**:2
	Obituary **1994**:2
de Passe, Suzanne 1946(?)- **1990**:4
Devine, John M. 1944- **2003**:2
Diemer, Walter E.
	1904(?)-1998 **1998**:2
DiFranco, Ani 1970(?)- **1997**:1
Diller, Barry 1942- **1991**:1
Disney, Lillian 1899-1997
	Obituary **1998**:3
Disney, Roy E. 1930- **1986**:3
Dolby, Ray Milton
	Brief entry **1986**:1
Dolce, Domenico and Stefano
	Gabbana **2005**:4
Donahue, Tim 1950(?)- **2004**:3
Doubleday, Nelson, Jr. 1933- **1987**:1
Downey, Bruce 1947- **2003**:1
Drexler, Millard S. 1944- **1990**:3
Drucker, Peter F. 1909- **1992**:3
Duisenberg, Wim 1935-2005
	Obituary **2006**:4
Dunlap, Albert J. **1997**:2
Dupri, Jermaine 1972- **1999**:1
Dyson, James 1947- **2005**:4
Eagleson, Alan 1933- **1987**:4
Eaton, Robert J. 1940- **1994**:2
Ebbers, Bernie 1943- **1998**:1
Eckert, Robert A. 1955(?)- **2002**:3
Ecko, Marc 1972- **2006**:3
Egan, John 1939- **1987**:2
Eisner, Michael 1942- **1989**:2
Elbaz, Alber 1961- **2008**:1
Ellis, Perry 1940-1986
	Obituary **1986**:3
Ellison, Larry 1944- **2004**:2
Engibous, Thomas J. 1953- **2003**:3
Engles, Gregg L. 1957- **2007**:3
Engstrom, Elmer W. 1901-1984
	Obituary **1985**:2
Epstein, Jason 1928- **1991**:1
Ertegun, Ahmet 1923- **1986**:3
Estes, Pete 1916-1988
	Obituary **1988**:3
Evans, Nancy 1950- **2000**:4

Eyler, John. H., Jr. 1948(?)- **2001**:3
Factor, Max 1904-1996
	Obituary **1996**:4
Fassa, Lynda 1963(?)- **2008**:4
Fekkai, Frederic 1959(?)- **2003**:2
Feld, Kenneth 1948- **1988**:2
Fender, Leo 1909-1991
	Obituary **1992**:1
Ferrari, Enzo 1898-1988 **1988**:4
Ferre, Gianfranco 1944-2007
	Obituary **2008**:3
Ferretti, Alberta 1950(?)- **2004**:1
Fertel, Ruth 1927- **2000**:2
Fields, Debbi 1956- **1987**:3
Fiorina, Carleton S. 1954- **2000**:1
Fireman, Paul
	Brief entry **1987**:2
Fisher, Mel 1922(?)- **1985**:4
Fleming, Claudia 1959- **2004**:1
Flynt, Larry 1942- **1997**:3
Fodor, Eugene 1906(?)-1991
	Obituary **1991**:3
Fomon, Robert M. 1925- **1985**:3
Forbes, Malcolm S. 1919-1990
	Obituary **1990**:3
Ford, Henry II 1917-1987
	Obituary **1988**:1
Ford, William Clay, Jr. 1957- **1999**:1
Foreman, George 1949- **2004**:2
Francis, Philip L. 1946- **2007**:4
Frank, Anthony M. 1931(?)- **1992**:1
Frankfort, Lew 1946- **2008**:2
Freeman, Cliff 1941- **1996**:1
Frieda, John 1951- **2004**:1
Fudge, Ann 1951- **2000**:3
Furse, Clara 1957- **2008**:2
Galliano, John 1960- **2005**:2
Ganzi, Victor 1947- **2003**:3
Garcia, Joe
	Brief entry **1986**:4
Garzarelli, Elaine M. 1951- **1992**:3
Gates, Bill 1955- **1987**:4
Gatien, Peter
	Brief entry **1986**:1
Gaultier, Jean-Paul 1952- **1998**:1
Gentine, Lou 1947- **2008**:2
George and Lena Korres
	1971- **2009**:1
Gerstner, Lou 1942- **1993**:4
Ghosn, Carlos 1954- **2008**:3
Gilbert, Walter 1932- **1988**:3
Gillett, George 1938- **1988**:1
Ginsberg, Ian 1962(?)- **2006**:4
Glass, David 1935- **1996**:1
Glazman, Lev and Alina
	Roytberg **2007**:4
Goizueta, Roberto 1931-1997 **1996**:1
	Obituary **1998**:1
Gold, Christina A. 1947- **2008**:1
Goldberg, Leonard 1934- **1988**:4
Goodman, Drew and Myra **2007**:4
Goody, Sam 1904-1991
	Obituary **1992**:1
Gordon, Michael 1951(?)- **2005**:1
Gorman, Leon
	Brief entry **1987**:1
Grace, J. Peter 1913- **1990**:2
Graden, Brian 1963- **2004**:2
Graham, Bill 1931-1991 **1986**:4
	Obituary **1992**:2
Graham, Donald 1945- **1985**:4

Graham, Katharine Meyer
1917- **1997**:3
  Obituary **2002**:3
Graham, Nicholas 1960(?)- **1991**:4
Graves, Ron 1967- **2009**:3
Green, Philip 1952- **2008**:2
Greenberg, Robert 1940(?)- **2003**:2
Greenwald, Julie 1970- **2008**:1
Gregory, Dick 1932- **1990**:3
Gregory, Rogan 1972- **2008**:2
Griffin, Merv 1925-2008
  Obituary **2008**:4
Grove, Andrew S. 1936- **1995**:3
Grucci, Felix 1905- **1987**:1
Gucci, Maurizio
  Brief entry **1985**:4
Guccione, Bob 1930- **1986**:1
Gund, Agnes 1938- **1993**:2
Gutierrez, Carlos M. 1953- **2001**:4
Haas, Robert D. 1942- **1986**:4
Hahn, Carl H. 1926- **1986**:4
Hakuta, Ken
  Brief entry **1986**:1
Hamilton, Hamish 1900-1988
  Obituary **1988**:4
Hammer, Armand 1898-1990
  Obituary **1991**:3
Handler, Ruth 1916-2002
  Obituary **2003**:3
Haney, Chris
  Brief entry **1985**:1
Harbert, Ted 1955- **2007**:2
Hart, Carey 1975- **2006**:4
Haseltine, William A. 1944- **1999**:2
Hassenfeld, Stephen 1942- **1987**:4
Hastings, Reed 1961(?)- **2006**:2
Hawkins, Jeff and Donna
  Dubinsky **2000**:2
Hearst, Randolph A. 1915-2000
  Obituary **2001**:3
Heckert, Richard E.
  Brief entry **1987**:3
Hefner, Christie 1952- **1985**:1
Heineken, Alfred 1923-2002
  Obituary **2003**:1
Heinz, H.J. 1908-1987
  Obituary **1987**:2
Helmsley, Leona 1920- **1988**:1
Hemming, Nikki 1967- **2009**:1
Hernandez, Lazaro and Jack
  McCollough **2008**:4
Herrera, Carolina 1939- **1997**:1
Hershberger, Sally 1961(?)- **2006**:4
Herzog, Doug 1960(?)- **2002**:4
Heyer, Steven J. 1952- **2007**:1
Hilbert, Stephen C. 1946- **1997**:4
Hilfiger, Tommy 1952- **1993**:3
Hillegass, Clifton Keith 1918- **1989**:4
Hindmarch, Anya 1969- **2008**:2
Hirshberg, Gary 1954(?)- **2007**:2
Holbrooke, Richard 1941(?)- **1996**:2
Holden, Betsy 1955- **2003**:2
Hollander, Joel 1956(?)- **2006**:4
Holliday, Chad 1948- **2006**:4
Honda, Soichiro 1906-1991
  Obituary **1986**:1
Horrigan, Edward, Jr. 1929- **1989**:1
Horvath, David and Sun-Min
  Kim **2008**:4
Housenbold, Jeffrey 1969- **2009**:2
Houser, Sam 1972(?)- **2004**:4
Hudson, Dawn 1957- **2008**:1

Hughes, Cathy 1947- **1999**:1
Hughes, Mark 1956- **1985**:3
Huizenga, Wayne 1938(?)- **1992**:1
Hyatt, Joel 1950- **1985**:3
Iacocca, Lee 1924- **1993**:1
Iger, Bob 1951- **2006**:1
Ilitch, Mike 1929- **1993**:4
Iman 1955- **2001**:3
Immelt, Jeffrey R. 1956- **2001**:2
Inatome, Rick 1953- **1985**:4
Ingersoll, Ralph II 1946- **1988**:2
Iovine, Jimmy 1953- **2006**:3
Isaacson, Portia
  Brief entry **1986**:1
Ive, Jonathan 1967- **2009**:2
Jacuzzi, Candido 1903-1986
  Obituary **1987**:1
Jagger, Jade 1971- **2005**:1
James, Jesse 1969- **2004**:4
Janklow, Morton 1930- **1989**:3
Jay-Z 1970- **2006**:1
Jobs, Steve 1955- **2000**:1
John, Daymond 1968- **2000**:1
Johnson, Abigail 1961- **2005**:3
Johnson, John H. 1918-2005
  Obituary **2005**:4
Johnson, Lady Bird 1912-2007
  Obituary **2008**:4
Johnson, Robert L. 1946- **2000**:4
Jones, Arthur A. 1924(?)- **1985**:3
Jones, Jerry 1942- **1994**:4
Jordan, Charles M. 1927- **1989**:4
Jordan, James 1936(?)-1993
  Obituary **1994**:1
Junck, Mary E. 1948(?)- **2003**:4
Juneau, Pierre 1922- **1988**:3
Jung, Andrea **2000**:2
Jurgensen, Karen 1949(?)- **2004**:3
Justin, John Jr. 1917- **1992**:2
Kapor, Mitch 1950- **1990**:3
Karmazin, Mel 1943- **2006**:1
Katayama, Yutaka 1909- **1987**:1
Kathwari, M. Farooq 1944- **2005**:4
Katz, Lillian 1927- **1987**:4
Katzenberg, Jeffrey 1950- **1995**:3
Kaufman, Elaine **1989**:4
Keating, Charles H., Jr. 1923- **1990**:4
Kelleher, Herb 1931- **1995**:1
Kelly, Maureen 1972(?)- **2007**:3
Kelly, R. 1968- **1997**:3
Kelly, William R. 1905-1998 **1998**:2
Keough, Donald Raymond
  1926- **1986**:1
Kerkorian, Kirk 1917- **1996**:2
Kerrey, Bob 1943- **1986**:1
Kidd, Jemma 1974- **2009**:1
Kilgore, Marcia 1968- **2006**:3
Kilts, James M. 1948- **2001**:3
Kim, Eugenia 1974(?)- **2006**:1
King, Don 1931- **1989**:1
Kingsborough, Donald
  Brief entry **1986**:2
Kingsley, Patricia 1932- **1990**:2
Klein, Calvin 1942- **1996**:2
Kloss, Henry E.
  Brief entry **1985**:2
Kluge, John 1914- **1991**:1
Knight, Philip H. 1938- **1994**:1
Koch, Bill 1940- **1992**:3
Koch, Jim 1949- **2004**:3
Kohnstamm, Abby 1954- **2001**:1
Koogle, Tim 1951- **2000**:4

Koplovitz, Kay 1945- **1986**:3
Korchinsky, Mike 1961- **2004**:2
Kordich, Jay 1923- **1993**:2
Kovacevich, Dick 1943- **2004**:3
Kristiansen, Kjeld Kirk
  1948(?)- **1988**:3
Kroc, Ray 1902-1984
  Obituary **1985**:1
Krogner, Heinz 1941(?)- **2004**:2
Kroll, Alexander S. 1938- **1989**:3
Kullman, Ellen 1956- **2009**:4
Kurzweil, Raymond 1948- **1986**:3
Kutaragi, Ken 1950- **2005**:3
Lacroix, Christian 1951- **2005**:2
Lafley, A. G. 1947- **2003**:4
Laimbeer, Bill 1957- **2004**:3
Lam, Derek 1966- **2009**:2
Lamborghini, Ferrucio 1916-1993
  Obituary **1993**:3
Land, Edwin H. 1909-1991
  Obituary **1991**:3
Lang, Eugene M. 1919- **1990**:3
Lansing, Sherry 1944- **1995**:4
Larian, Isaac 1954- **2008**:1
Lauder, Estee 1908(?)- **1992**:2
Lauren, Ralph 1939- **1990**:1
Laybourne, Geraldine 1947- **1997**:1
Lazarus, Charles 1923- **1992**:4
Lazarus, Shelly 1947- **1998**:3
Lear, Frances 1923- **1988**:3
Leigh, Dorian 1917-2008
  Obituary **2009**:3
Lelyveld, Joseph S. 1937- **1994**:4
Lemon, Ted
  Brief entry **1986**:4
Lepore, Nanette 1964(?)- **2006**:4
Lerner, Sandy 1955(?)- **2005**:1
Levin, Gerald 1939- **1995**:2
Levinson, Arthur D. 1950- **2008**:3
Lewis, Kenneth D. 1947- **2009**:2
Lewis, Loida Nicolas 1942- **1998**:3
Lewis, Reginald F. 1942-1993 **1988**:4
  Obituary **1993**:3
Lhuillier, Monique 1971(?)- **2007**:4
Liguori, Peter 1960- **2005**:2
Lim, Phillip 1974(?)- **2008**:1
Lines, Ray 1960(?)- **2004**:1
Lopez de Arriortua, Jose Ignacio
  1941- **1993**:4
Louboutin, Christian 1963- **2006**:1
Lowe, Edward 1921- **1990**:2
Lowry, Adam and Eric Ryan **2008**:1
Lum, Olivia 1961- **2009**:1
Lutz, Robert A. 1932- **1990**:1
Lyne, Susan 1950- **2005**:4
Ma, Jack 1964- **2007**:1
Ma, Pony 1971(?)- **2006**:3
Macdonald, Julien 1973(?)- **2005**:3
Mack, John J. 1944- **2006**:3
Mackey, John 1953- **2008**:2
Madden, Chris 1948- **2006**:1
Madden, Steve 1958- **2007**:2
Malone, Jo 1964(?)- **2004**:3
Malone, John C. 1941- **1988**:3
Manheimer, Heidi 1963- **2009**:3
Marcus, Stanley 1905-2002
  Obituary **2003**:1
Margolis, Bobby 1948(?)- **2007**:2
Marineau, Philip 1946- **2002**:4
Markle, C. Wilson 1938- **1988**:1
Marriott, J. Willard 1900-1985
  Obituary **1985**:4

Marriott, J. Willard, Jr. 1932- **1985**:4
Mas Canosa, Jorge 1939-1997 **1998**:2
Mashouf, Manny 1938(?)- **2008**:1
Master P 1970- **1999**:4
Mateschitz, Dietrich 1944- **2008**:1
Matsuhisa, Nobuyuki 1949- **2002**:3
Maxwell, Hamish 1926- **1989**:4
Maxwell, Robert 1923- **1990**:1
Maxwell, Robert 1923-1991
    Obituary **1992**:2
McCloy, John J. 1895-1989
    Obituary **1989**:3
McColough, C. Peter 1922- **1990**:2
McDonald, Camille 1953(?)- **2004**:1
McDonnell, Sanford N. 1922- **1988**:4
McDougall, Ron 1942- **2001**:4
McElligott, Thomas J. 1943- **1987**:4
McGowan, William 1927- **1985**:2
McGowan, William G. 1927-1992
    Obituary **1993**:1
McGrath, Judy 1953- **2006**:1
McIntyre, Richard
    Brief entry **1986**:2
McKinnell, Henry 1943(?)- **2002**:3
McLaughlin, Betsy 1962(?)- **2004**:3
McMahon, Vince, Jr. 1945(?)- **1985**:4
McNamara, Robert S. 1916- **1995**:4
McNealy, Scott 1954- **1999**:4
McNerney, W. James 1949- **2006**:3
Mellinger, Frederick 1924(?)-1990
    Obituary **1990**:4
Mello, Dawn 1938(?)- **1992**:2
Melman, Richard
    Brief entry **1986**:1
Mengers, Sue 1938- **1985**:3
Millard, Barbara J.
    Brief entry **1985**:3
Miller, Merton H. 1923-2000
    Obituary **2001**:1
Miller, Rand 1959(?)- **1995**:4
Mitarai, Fujio 1935- **2002**:4
Mittal, Lakshmi 1950- **2007**:2
Mohajer, Dineh 1972- **1997**:3
Monaghan, Tom 1937- **1985**:1
Mondavi, Robert 1913- **1989**:2
Moody, John 1943- **1985**:3
Moonves, Les 1949- **2004**:2
Moore, Ann 1950- **2009**:1
Moreno, Arturo 1946- **2005**:2
Morgan, Dodge 1932(?)- **1987**:1
Morita, Akio 1921- **1989**:4
Morita, Akio 1921-1999
    Obituary **2000**:2
Moritz, Charles 1936- **1989**:3
Morris, Doug 1938- **2005**:1
Mosbacher, Georgette
    1947(?)- **1994**:2
Mulcahy, Anne M. 1952- **2003**:2
Murakami, Takashi 1962- **2004**:2
Murdoch, Rupert 1931- **1988**:4
Murphy, Kathleen A. **2009**:2
Murray, Arthur 1895-1991
    Obituary **1991**:3
Nardelli, Robert 1948- **2008**:4
Nars, Francois 1959- **2003**:1
Neeleman, David 1959- **2003**:3
Neuharth, Allen H. 1924- **1986**:1
Newhouse, Samuel I., Jr.
    1927- **1997**:1
Nipon, Albert
    Brief entry **1986**:4
Nooyi, Indra 1955- **2004**:3

Noyce, Robert N. 1927- **1985**:4
Nussbaum, Karen 1950- **1988**:3
Ollila, Jorma 1950- **2003**:4
Olsen, Kenneth H. 1926- **1986**:4
Olsen, Sigrid 1953- **2007**:1
Oppenheimer, Harry 1908-2000
    Obituary **2001**:3
Orman, Suze 1951(?)- **2003**:1
Ostin, Mo 1927- **1996**:2
Otte, Ruth 1949- **1992**:4
Ovitz, Michael 1946- **1990**:1
Owen-Jones, Lindsay 1946(?)- **2004**:2
Packard, David 1912-1996
    Obituary **1996**:3
Palmisano, Samuel J. 1952(?)- **2003**:1
Panichgul, Thakoon 1974- **2009**:4
Parsons, Gary 1950(?)- **2006**:2
Paulucci, Jeno
    Brief entry **1986**:3
Peebles, R. Donahue 1960- **2003**:2
Peller, Clara 1902(?)-1987
    Obituary **1988**:1
Peluso, Michelle 1971(?)- **2007**:4
Penske, Roger 1937- **1988**:3
Perdue, Frank 1920-2005
    Obituary **2006**:2
Perelman, Ronald 1943- **1989**:2
Perot, H. Ross 1930- **1992**:4
Persson, Stefan 1947- **2004**:1
Peters, Tom 1942- **1998**:1
Petersen, Donald Eugene
    1926- **1985**:1
Petrossian, Christian
    Brief entry **1985**:3
Pfeiffer, Eckhard 1941- **1998**:4
Phelan, John Joseph, Jr. 1931- **1985**:4
Phillips, Sam 1923-2003
    Obituary **2004**:4
Pierce, Frederick S. 1934(?)- **1985**:3
Pittman, Robert W. 1953- **1985**:1
Pocklington, Peter H. 1941- **1985**:2
Popcorn, Faith
    Brief entry **1988**:1
Pope, Generoso 1927-1988 **1988**:4
Porizkova, Paulina
    Brief entry **1986**:4
Porsche, Ferdinand 1909-1998
    Obituary **1998**:4
Porter, Sylvia 1913-1991
    Obituary **1991**:4
Portman, John 1924- **1988**:2
Posen, Zac 1980- **2009**:3
Potter, Michael 1960(?)- **2003**:3
Pouillon, Nora 1943- **2005**:1
Prada, Miuccia 1950(?)- **1996**:1
Pratt, Jane 1963(?)- **1999**:1
Presser, Jackie 1926-1988
    Obituary **1988**:4
Pressler, Paul 1956(?)- **2003**:4
Prevor, Barry and Steven
    Shore **2006**:2
Pritzker, A.N. 1896-1986
    Obituary **1986**:2
Probst, Larry 1951(?)- **2005**:1
Proctor, Barbara Gardner
    1933(?)- **1985**:3
Puck, Wolfgang 1949- **1990**:1
Questrom, Allen 1940- **2001**:4
Quinn, Jane Bryant 1939(?)- **1993**:4
Radocy, Robert
    Brief entry **1986**:3
Ramsay, Gordon 1966- **2008**:2

Rand, A. Barry 1944- **2000**:3
Rapp, C.J.
    Brief entry **1987**:3
Rawlings, Mike 1954- **2003**:1
Raymond, Lee R. 1930- **2000**:3
Redenbacher, Orville 1907-1995
    Obituary **1996**:1
Redmond, Tim 1947- **2008**:1
Redstone, Sumner 1923- **1994**:1
Regan, Judith 1953- **2003**:1
Reynolds, Paula Rosput 1956- **2008**:4
Rhodes, Zandra 1940- **1986**:2
Rice, Peter 1967(?)- **2007**:2
Riggio, Leonard S. 1941- **1999**:4
Rigopulos, Alex 1970- **2009**:4
Riney, Hal 1932- **1989**:1
Riordan, Richard 1930- **1993**:4
Roberts, Xavier 1955- **1985**:3
Roddick, Anita 1943(?)- **1989**:4
Rodriguez, Narciso 1961- **2005**:1
Roedy, Bill 1949(?)- **2003**:2
Roncal, Mally 1972- **2009**:4
Ronson, Charlotte 1977(?)- **2007**:3
Rooney, Art 1901-1988
    Obituary **1989**:1
Roosevelt, Franklin D., Jr. 1914-1988
    Obituary **1989**:1
Rosenfeld, Irene 1953- **2008**:3
Ross, Percy
    Brief entry **1986**:2
Ross, Steven J. 1927-1992
    Obituary **1993**:3
Rossellini, Isabella 1952- **2001**:4
Rosso, Renzo 1955- **2005**:2
Rothschild, Philippe de 1902-1988
    Obituary **1988**:2
Rothstein, Ruth **1988**:2
Rowe, Jack 1944- **2005**:2
Rowland, Pleasant **1992**:3
Rowley, Coleen 1955(?)- **2004**:2
Russo, Patricia 1952- **2008**:4
Saatchi, Maurice 1946- **1995**:4
Sachs, Jeffrey D. 1954- **2004**:4
Sagansky, Jeff 1952- **1993**:2
Saint Laurent, Yves 1936-2008
    Obituary **2009**:3
Sammons, Mary 1946- **2007**:4
Sams, Craig 1944- **2007**:3
Sander, Jil 1943- **1995**:2
Sanger, Steve 1946- **2002**:3
Sasakawa, Ryoichi
    Brief entry **1988**:1
Scardino, Marjorie 1947- **2002**:1
Schlessinger, David
    Brief entry **1985**:1
Schmelzer, Sheri 1965- **2009**:4
Schoenfeld, Gerald 1924- **1986**:2
Schott, Marge 1928- **1985**:4
Schrempp, Juergen 1944- **2000**:2
Schultz, Howard 1953- **1995**:3
Schwab, Charles 1937(?)- **1989**:3
Schwartz, Allen 1945(?)- **2008**:2
Schwinn, Edward R., Jr.
    Brief entry **1985**:4
Scott, H. Lee, Jr. 1949- **2008**:3
Sculley, John 1939- **1989**:4
Sedelmaier, Joe 1933- **1985**:3
Segal, Shelli 1955(?)- **2005**:3
Seidenberg, Ivan 1946- **2004**:1
Senk, Glen 1956- **2009**:3
Shaich, Ron 1953- **2004**:4
Siebert, Muriel 1932(?)- **1987**:2

Simmons, Russell and Kimora Lee **2003**:2
Skaist-Levy, Pam and Gela Taylor **2005**:1
Slatkin, Harry 1961(?)- **2006**:2
Smale, John G. 1927- **1987**:3
Smith, Frederick W. 1944- **1985**:4
Smith, Jack 1938- **1994**:3
Smith, Lanty 1942- **2009**:3
Smith, Roger 1925- **1990**:3
Smyth, Russell P. 1958- **2009**:4
Snider, Stacey 1961(?)- **2002**:4
Snyder, Ron 1956(?)- **2007**:4
Som, Peter 1971- **2009**:1
Spade, Kate 1962- **2003**:1
Spector, Phil 1940- **1989**:1
Spray, Ed 1941- **2004**:1
Sprouse, Stephen 1953-2004
Obituary **2005**:2
Starck, Philippe 1949- **2004**:1
Steel, Dawn 1946-1997 **1990**:1
Obituary **1998**:2
Steinberg, Leigh 1949- **1987**:3
Steinbrenner, George 1930- **1991**:1
Stempel, Robert 1933- **1991**:3
Stephens, Arran and Ratana **2008**:4
Stern, David 1942- **1991**:4
Stevens, Anne 1949(?)- **2006**:3
Stewart, Julia 1955- **2008**:3
Stewart, Martha 1942(?)- **1992**:1
Stonesifer, Patty 1956- **1997**:1
Stroh, Peter W. 1927- **1985**:2
Strong, Maurice 1929- **1993**:1
Sullivan, Andrew 1964(?)- **1996**:1
Summers, Anne 1945- **1990**:2
Tagliabue, Paul 1940- **1990**:2
Takada, Kenzo 1938- **2003**:2
Tanny, Vic 1912(?)-1985
Obituary **1985**:3
Tartikoff, Brandon 1949-1997 **1985**:2
Obituary **1998**:1
Tellem, Nancy 1953(?)- **2004**:4
Temperley, Alice 1975- **2008**:2
Thain, John 1955- **2009**:2
Thalheimer, Richard 1948-
Brief entry **1988**:3
Thomas, Dave **1986**:2
Obituary **2003**:1
Thomas, Michel 1911(?)- **1987**:4
Thomas-Graham, Pamela 1963- **2007**:1
Thompson, John W. 1949- **2005**:1
Tilberis, Elizabeth 1947(?)- **1994**:3
Tillman, Robert L. 1944(?)- **2004**:1
Timberlake, Justin 1981- **2008**:4
Tisch, Laurence A. 1923- **1988**:2
Tompkins, Susie
Brief entry **1987**:2
Touitou, Jean 1952(?)- **2008**:4
Toyoda, Eiji 1913- **1985**:2
Trask, Amy 1961- **2003**:3
Traub, Marvin
Brief entry **1987**:3
Treybig, James G. 1940- **1988**:3
Trotman, Alex 1933- **1995**:4
Trotter, Charlie 1960- **2000**:4
Troutt, Kenny A. 1948- **1998**:1
Trump, Donald 1946- **1989**:2
Trump, Ivana 1949- **1995**:2
Turlington, Christy 1969(?)- **2001**:4
Turner, Ted 1938- **1989**:1
Tyler, Richard 1948(?)- **1995**:3
Tyson, Don 1930- **1995**:3

Unz, Ron 1962(?)- **1999**:1
Upshaw, Gene 1945- **1988**:1
Vagelos, P. Roy 1929- **1989**:4
Valli, Giambattista 1966- **2008**:3
Van Andel, Jay 1924-2004
Obituary **2006**:1
Varvatos, John 1956(?)- **2006**:2
Vasella, Daniel 1953- **2005**:3
Veeck, Bill 1914-1986
Obituary **1986**:1
Versace, Donatella 1955- **1999**:1
Versace, Gianni 1946-1997
Brief entry **1988**:1
Obituary **1998**:2
Vinton, Will
Brief entry **1988**:1
Vischer, Phil 1966- **2002**:2
Von D, Kat 1982- **2008**:3
von Furstenberg, Diane 1946- **1994**:2
Wachner, Linda 1946- **1988**:3
Waitt, Ted 1963(?)- **1997**:4
Waldron, Hicks B. 1923- **1987**:3
Walgreen, Charles III
Brief entry **1987**:4
Walker, Jay 1955- **2004**:2
Walton, Sam 1918-1992 **1986**:2
Obituary **1993**:1
Wang, An 1920-1990 **1986**:1
Obituary **1990**:3
Ware, Lancelot 1915-2000
Obituary **2001**:1
Waters, Alice 1944- **2006**:3
Watkins, Sherron 1959- **2003**:1
Weill, Sandy 1933- **1990**:4
Weinstein, Bob and Harvey **2000**:4
Weintraub, Jerry 1937- **1986**:1
Welch, Jack 1935- **1993**:3
Weldon, William 1948- **2007**:4
Westwood, Vivienne 1941- **1998**:3
Whiting, Susan 1956- **2007**:4
Whitman, Meg 1957- **2000**:3
Whittle, Christopher 1947- **1989**:3
Williams, Edward Bennett 1920-1988
Obituary **1988**:4
Williams, Lynn 1924- **1986**:4
Wilson, Jerry
Brief entry **1986**:2
Wilson, Peter C. 1913-1984
Obituary **1985**:2
Wintour, Anna 1949- **1990**:4
Woertz, Patricia A. 1953- **2007**:3
Wolf, Stephen M. 1941- **1989**:3
Wong, Andrea 1966- **2009**:1
Woodcock, Leonard 1911-2001
Obituary **2001**:4
Woodruff, Robert Winship 1889-1985
Obituary **1985**:1
Wren, John 1952(?)- **2007**:2
Wrigley, William, Jr. 1964(?)- **2002**:2
Wynn, Stephen A. 1942- **1994**:3
Yamamoto, Kenichi 1922- **1989**:1
Yetnikoff, Walter 1933- **1988**:1
Yunus, Muhammad 1940- **2007**:3
Zagat, Tim and Nina **2004**:3
Zamboni, Frank J.
Brief entry **1986**:4
Zanker, Bill
Brief entry **1987**:3
Zetcher, Arnold B. 1940- **2002**:1
Zetsche, Dieter 1953- **2002**:3
Ziff, William B., Jr. 1930- **1986**:4
Zuckerman, Mortimer 1937- **1986**:3

**DANCE**
Abdul, Paula 1962- **1990**:3
Acosta, Carlos 1973(?)- **1997**:4
Ailey, Alvin 1931-1989 **1989**:2
Obituary **1990**:2
Allen, Debbie 1950- **1998**:2
Astaire, Fred 1899-1987
Obituary **1987**:4
Baryshnikov, Mikhail Nikolaevich 1948- **1997**:3
Bejart, Maurice 1927-2007
Obituary **2009**:1
Bennett, Michael 1943-1987
Obituary **1988**:1
Bissell, Patrick 1958-1987
Obituary **1988**:2
Bocca, Julio 1967- **1995**:3
Bujones, Fernando 1955-2005
Obituary **2007**:1
Campbell, Neve 1973- **1998**:2
Charisse, Cyd 1922-2008
Obituary **2009**:3
Cunningham, Merce 1919- **1998**:1
Davis, Sammy, Jr. 1925-1990
Obituary **1990**:4
Dean, Laura 1945- **1989**:4
de Mille, Agnes 1905-1993
Obituary **1994**:2
de Valois, Dame Ninette 1898-2001
Obituary **2002**:1
Dudley, Jane 1912-2001
Obituary **2002**:4
Dunham, Katherine 1909-2006
Obituary **2007**:2
Englund, Richard 1932(?)-1991
Obituary **1991**:3
Fagan, Garth 1940- **2000**:1
Farrell, Suzanne 1945- **1996**:3
Feld, Eliot 1942- **1996**:1
Fenley, Molissa 1954- **1988**:3
Ferri, Alessandra 1963- **1987**:2
Flatley, Michael 1958- **1997**:3
Fonteyn, Margot 1919-1991
Obituary **1991**:3
Forsythe, William 1949- **1993**:2
Fosse, Bob 1927-1987
Obituary **1988**:1
Garr, Teri 1949- **1988**:4
Glover, Savion 1973- **1997**:1
Godunov, Alexander 1949-1995
Obituary **1995**:4
Graham, Martha 1894-1991
Obituary **1991**:4
Gregory, Cynthia 1946- **1990**:2
Guillem, Sylvie 1965(?)- **1988**:2
Herrera, Paloma 1975- **1996**:2
Hewitt, Jennifer Love 1979- **1999**:2
Hines, Gregory 1946- **1992**:4
Jackson, Janet 1966(?)- **1990**:4
Jamison, Judith 1944- **1990**:3
Joffrey, Robert 1930-1988
Obituary **1988**:3
Jones, Bill T. **1991**:4
Kaye, Nora 1920-1987
Obituary **1987**:4
Keeler, Ruby 1910-1993
Obituary **1993**:4
Kelly, Gene 1912-1996
Obituary **1996**:3
Kidd, Michael 1915-2007

Obituary **2009**:1
Kistler, Darci 1964- **1993**:1
Lander, Toni 1931-1985
   Obituary **1985**:4
Lewitzky, Bella 1916-2004
   Obituary **2005**:3
MacMillan, Kenneth 1929-1992
   Obituary **1993**:2
Madonna 1958- **1985**:2
Marshall, Susan 1958- **2000**:4
Millepied, Benjamin 1977(?)- **2006**:4
Miller, Ann 1923-2004
   Obituary **2005**:2
Miller, Bebe 1950- **2000**:2
Mitchell, Arthur 1934- **1995**:1
Moiseyev, Igor 1906-2007
   Obituary **2009**:1
Moore, Rachel 1965- **2008**:2
Morris, Mark 1956- **1991**:1
Murray, Arthur 1895-1991
   Obituary **1991**:3
North, Alex 1910- **1986**:3
Nureyev, Rudolf 1938-1993
   Obituary **1993**:2
Parker, Sarah Jessica 1965- **1999**:2
Parsons, David 1959- **1993**:4
Perez, Rosie **1994**:2
Prowse, Juliet 1937-1996
   Obituary **1997**:1
Rauschenberg, Robert 1925- **1991**:2
Renvall, Johan
   Brief entry **1987**:4
Robbins, Jerome 1918-1998
   Obituary **1999**:1
Rogers, Ginger 1911(?)-1995
   Obituary **1995**:4
Stroman, Susan **2000**:4
Takei, Kei 1946- **1990**:2
Taylor, Paul 1930- **1992**:3
Tharp, Twyla 1942- **1992**:4
Tudor, Antony 1908(?)-1987
   Obituary **1987**:4
Tune, Tommy 1939- **1994**:2
Varone, Doug 1956- **2001**:2
Verdi-Fletcher, Mary 1955- **1998**:2
Verdon, Gwen 1925-2000
   Obituary **2001**:2
Whelan, Wendy 1967(?)- **1999**:3

## EDUCATION

Abramson, Lyn 1950- **1986**:3
Alexander, Lamar 1940- **1991**:2
Bakker, Robert T. 1950(?)- **1991**:3
Bayley, Corrine
   Brief entry **1986**:4
Billington, James 1929- **1990**:3
Bollinger, Lee C. 1946- **2003**:2
Botstein, Leon 1946- **1985**:3
Bush, Millie 1987- **1992**:1
Campbell, Bebe Moore 1950- **1996**:2
Cartwright, Carol Ann 1941- **2009**:4
Casper, Gerhard 1937- **1993**:1
Cavazos, Lauro F. 1927- **1989**:2
Cheek, James Edward
   Brief entry **1987**:1
Cheney, Lynne V. 1941- **1990**:4
Clements, George 1932- **1985**:1
Cole, Johnetta B. 1936- **1994**:3
Coles, Robert 1929(?)- **1995**:1
Commager, Henry Steele 1902-1998
   Obituary **1998**:3
Curran, Charles E. 1934- **1989**:2

Davis, Angela 1944- **1998**:3
Delany, Sarah 1889-1999
   Obituary **1999**:3
Deming, W. Edwards 1900-1993
   **1992**:2
   Obituary **1994**:2
Dershowitz, Alan 1938(?)- **1992**:1
Dove, Rita 1952- **1994**:3
Drucker, Peter F. 1909- **1992**:3
Eberhart, Richard 1904-2005
   Obituary **2006**:3
Edelman, Marian Wright
   1939- **1990**:4
Edwards, Harry 1942- **1989**:4
Etzioni, Amitai 1929- **1994**:3
Faust, Drew Gilpin 1947- **2008**:1
Feldman, Sandra 1939- **1987**:3
Ferguson, Niall 1964- **2006**:1
Fernandez, Joseph 1935- **1991**:3
Folkman, Judah 1933- **1999**:1
Fox, Matthew 1940- **1992**:2
Friedman, Milton 1912-2006
   Obituary **2008**:1
Fulbright, J. William 1905-1995
   Obituary **1995**:3
Futrell, Mary Hatwood 1940- **1986**:1
Futter, Ellen V. 1949- **1995**:1
Ghali, Boutros Boutros 1922- **1992**:3
Giamatti, A. Bartlett
   1938-1989 **1988**:4
   Obituary **1990**:1
Goldhaber, Fred
   Brief entry **1986**:3
Gray, Hanna 1930- **1992**:4
Green, Richard R. 1936- **1988**:3
Gregorian, Vartan 1934- **1990**:3
Gund, Agnes 1938- **1993**:2
Gutmann, Amy 1949- **2008**:4
Hackney, Sheldon 1933- **1995**:1
Hair, Jay D. 1945- **1994**:3
Harker, Patrick T. 1958- **2001**:2
Hayakawa, Samuel Ichiye 1906-1992
   Obituary **1992**:3
Healy, Bernadine 1944- **1993**:1
Healy, Timothy S. 1923- **1990**:2
Heaney, Seamus 1939- **1996**:2
Heller, Walter 1915-1987
   Obituary **1987**:4
Hennessy, John L. 1952- **2002**:2
Hill, Anita 1956- **1994**:1
Hill, J. Edward 1938- **2006**:2
Hillegass, Clifton Keith 1918- **1989**:4
Hockfield, Susan 1951- **2009**:2
Horwich, Frances 1908-2001
   Obituary **2002**:3
Hunter, Madeline 1916(?)- **1991**:2
Jablonski, Nina G. 1953- **2009**:3
Janzen, Daniel H. 1939- **1988**:4
Jones, Edward P. 1950- **2005**:1
Jordan, King 1943(?)- **1990**:1
Justiz, Manuel J. 1948- **1986**:4
Kandel, Eric 1929- **2005**:2
Kellerman, Jonathan 1949- **2009**:1
Kemp, Jan 1949- **1987**:2
Kerr, Clark 1911-2003
   Obituary **2005**:1
King, Mary-Claire 1946- **1998**:3
Kopp, Wendy **1993**:3
Kozol, Jonathan 1936- **1992**:1
Lagasse, Emeril 1959- **1998**:3
Lamb, Wally 1950- **1999**:1
Lang, Eugene M. 1919- **1990**:3

Langston, J. William
   Brief entry **1986**:2
Lawrence, Ruth
   Brief entry **1986**:3
Laybourne, Geraldine 1947- **1997**:1
Leach, Penelope 1937- **1992**:4
Lee, Chang-Rae 1965- **2005**:1
Lerner, Michael 1943- **1994**:2
Levine, Arnold 1939- **2002**:3
MacKinnon, Catharine 1946- **1993**:2
Malloy, Edward Monk 1941- **1989**:4
Manson, JoAnn E. 1953- **2008**:3
Marier, Rebecca 1974- **1995**:4
McAuliffe, Christa 1948-1986
   Obituary **1985**:4
McCall Smith, Alexander
   1948- **2005**:2
McMillan, Terry 1951- **1993**:2
Melton, Douglas 1954- **2008**:3
Morrison, Toni 1931- **1998**:1
Mumford, Lewis 1895-1990
   Obituary **1990**:2
Murano, Elsa 1959- **2009**:1
Nemerov, Howard 1920-1991
   Obituary **1992**:1
Nye, Bill 1955- **1997**:2
O'Keefe, Sean 1956- **2005**:2
Owens, Delia and Mark **1993**:3
Pagels, Elaine 1943- **1997**:1
Paglia, Camille 1947- **1992**:3
Paige, Rod 1933- **2003**:2
Parizeau, Jacques 1930- **1995**:1
Pausch, Randy 1960-2008
   Obituary **2009**:3
Peter, Valentine J. 1934- **1988**:2
Riley, Richard W. 1933- **1996**:3
Rodin, Judith 1945(?)- **1994**:4
Rosendahl, Bruce R.
   Brief entry **1986**:4
Rowland, Pleasant **1992**:3
Scheck, Barry 1949- **2000**:4
Schuman, Patricia Glass
   1943- **1993**:2
Shalala, Donna 1941- **1992**:3
Sherman, Russell 1930- **1987**:4
Silber, Joan 1945- **2009**:4
Silber, John 1926- **1990**:1
Simmons, Adele Smith 1941- **1988**:4
Simmons, Ruth 1945- **1995**:2
Simon, Lou Anna K. 1947- **2005**:4
Singer, Margaret Thaler 1921-2003
   Obituary **2005**:1
Smoot, George F. 1945- **1993**:3
Sowell, Thomas 1930- **1998**:3
Spellings, Margaret 1957- **2005**:4
Spock, Benjamin 1903-1998 **1995**:2
   Obituary **1998**:3
Steele, Shelby 1946- **1991**:2
Strout, Elizabeth 1956- **2009**:1
Swanson, Mary Catherine
   1944- **2002**:2
Tannen, Deborah 1945- **1995**:1
Thiebaud, Wayne 1920- **1991**:1
Thomas, Michel 1911(?)- **1987**:4
Tilghman, Shirley M. 1946- **2002**:1
Tohe, Laura 1953- **2009**:2
Tretheway, Natasha 1966- **2008**:3
Tribe, Laurence H. 1941- **1988**:1
Tyson, Laura D'Andrea 1947- **1994**:1
Unz, Ron 1962(?)- **1999**:1
Van Duyn, Mona 1921- **1993**:2
Vickrey, William S. 1914-1996

Obituary **1997**:2
Warren, Robert Penn 1905-1989
  Obituary **1990**:1
West, Cornel 1953- **1994**:2
Wexler, Nancy S. 1945- **1992**:3
Whitney, Patrick 1952(?)- **2006**:1
Wiesel, Elie 1928- **1998**:1
Wigand, Jeffrey 1943(?)- **2000**:4
Wiles, Andrew 1953(?)- **1994**:1
Wilson, Edward O. 1929- **1994**:4
Wilson, William Julius 1935- **1997**:1
Wolff, Tobias 1945- **2005**:1
Wu, Harry 1937- **1996**:1
Zanker, Bill
  Brief entry **1987**:3
Zigler, Edward 1930- **1994**:1

FILM

Abbott, George 1887-1995
  Obituary **1995**:3
Abrams, J. J. 1966- **2007**:3
Adams, Amy 1974- **2008**:4
Adjani, Isabelle 1955- **1991**:1
Affleck, Ben 1972- **1999**:1
Aiello, Danny 1933- **1990**:4
Albert, Eddie 1906-2005
  Obituary **2006**:3
Alda, Robert 1914-1986
  Obituary **1986**:3
Alexander, Jane 1939- **1994**:2
Alexander, Jason 1962(?)- **1993**:3
Allen, Debbie 1950- **1998**:2
Allen, Joan 1956- **1998**:1
Allen, Woody 1935- **1994**:1
Alley, Kirstie 1955- **1990**:3
Allyson, June 1917-2006
  Obituary **2007**:3
Almodovar, Pedro 1951- **2000**:3
Altman, Robert 1925- **1993**:2
Ameche, Don 1908-1993
  Obituary **1994**:2
Anderson, Judith 1899(?)-1992
  Obituary **1992**:3
Andrews, Julie 1935- **1996**:1
Aniston, Jennifer 1969- **2000**:3
Apatow, Judd 1967- **2006**:3
Applegate, Christina 1972- **2000**:4
Arad, Avi 1948- **2003**:2
Arden, Eve 1912(?)-1990
  Obituary **1991**:2
Arkin, Alan 1934- **2007**:4
Arkoff, Samuel Z. 1918-2001
  Obituary **2002**:4
Arlen, Harold 1905-1986
  Obituary **1986**:3
Arnaz, Desi 1917-1986
  Obituary **1987**:1
Arnold, Tom 1959- **1993**:2
Arquette, Patricia 1968- **2001**:3
Arquette, Rosanna 1959- **1985**:2
Arthur, Jean 1901(?)-1991
  Obituary **1992**:1
Ashcroft, Peggy 1907-1991
  Obituary **1992**:1
Astaire, Fred 1899-1987
  Obituary **1987**:4
Astin, Sean 1971- **2005**:1
Astor, Mary 1906-1987
  Obituary **1988**:1
Atkinson, Rowan 1955- **2004**:3
Autry, Gene 1907-1998
  Obituary **1999**:1

Aykroyd, Dan 1952- **1989**:3
Bacall, Lauren 1924- **1997**:3
Backus, Jim 1913-1989
  Obituary **1990**:1
Bacon, Kevin 1958- **1995**:3
Baddeley, Hermione 1906(?)-1986
  Obituary **1986**:4
Bailey, Pearl 1918-1990
  Obituary **1991**:1
Bakula, Scott 1954- **2003**:1
Baldwin, Alec 1958- **2002**:2
Bale, Christian 1974- **2001**:3
Ball, Alan 1957- **2005**:1
Ball, Lucille 1911-1989
  Obituary **1989**:3
Bancroft, Anne 1931-2005
  Obituary **2006**:3
Banderas, Antonio 1960- **1996**:2
Banks, Tyra 1973- **1996**:3
Bardem, Javier 1969- **2008**:4
Barker, Clive 1952- **2003**:3
Barkin, Ellen 1955- **1987**:3
Baron Cohen, Sacha 1971- **2007**:3
Barr, Roseanne 1953(?)- **1989**:1
Barrymore, Drew 1975- **1995**:3
Baryshnikov, Mikhail Nikolaevich
  1948- **1997**:3
Basinger, Kim 1953- **1987**:2
Bassett, Angela 1959(?)- **1994**:4
Bateman, Jason 1969- **2005**:3
Bateman, Justine 1966- **1988**:4
Bates, Alan 1934-2003
  Obituary **2005**:1
Bates, Kathy 1949(?)- **1991**:4
Baxter, Anne 1923-1985
  Obituary **1986**:1
Beals, Jennifer 1963- **2005**:2
Beatty, Warren 1937- **2000**:1
Belushi, Jim 1954- **1986**:2
Benigni, Roberto 1952- **1999**:2
Bening, Annette 1958(?)- **1992**:1
Bennett, Joan 1910-1990
  Obituary **1991**:2
Bergen, Candice 1946- **1990**:1
Bergman, Ingmar 1918- **1999**:4
Berman, Gail 1957(?)- **2006**:1
Bernardi, Herschel 1923-1986
  Obituary **1986**:4
Bernhard, Sandra 1955(?)- **1989**:4
Bernsen, Corbin 1955- **1990**:2
Berry, Halle 1968- **1996**:2
Beyonce 1981- **2009**:3
Bialik, Mayim 1975- **1993**:3
Bigelow, Kathryn 1952(?)- **1990**:4
Binoche, Juliette 1965- **2001**:3
Birch, Thora 1982- **2002**:4
Bird, Brad 1956(?)- **2005**:4
Bishop, Joey 1918-2007
  Obituary **2008**:4
Black, Jack 1969- **2002**:3
Blades, Ruben 1948- **1998**:2
Blanc, Mel 1908-1989
  Obituary **1989**:4
Blanchett, Cate 1969- **1999**:3
Bloom, Orlando 1977- **2004**:2
Bogosian, Eric 1953- **1990**:4
Bolger, Ray 1904-1987
  Obituary **1987**:2
Bonet, Lisa 1967- **1989**:2
Bonham Carter, Helena 1966- **1998**:4
Booth, Shirley 1898-1992
  Obituary **1993**:2

Bosworth, Kate 1983- **2006**:3
Bowen, Julie 1970- **2007**:1
Bowie, David 1947- **1998**:2
Boyle, Danny 1956- **2009**:4
Boyle, Lara Flynn 1970- **2003**:4
Boyle, Peter 1935- **2002**:3
Braff, Zach 1975- **2005**:2
Branagh, Kenneth 1960- **1992**:2
Brandauer, Klaus Maria 1944- **1987**:3
Brando, Marlon 1924-2004
  Obituary **2005**:3
Bratt, Benjamin 1963- **2009**:3
Bridges, Lloyd 1913-1998
  Obituary **1998**:3
Brillstein, Bernie 1931-2008
  Obituary **2009**:4
Broadbent, Jim 1949- **2008**:4
Brody, Adrien 1973- **2006**:3
Bronson, Charles 1921-2003
  Obituary **2004**:4
Brooks, Albert 1948(?)- **1991**:4
Brooks, Mel 1926- **2003**:1
Brosnan, Pierce 1952- **2000**:3
Brown, James 1928(?)- **1991**:4
Brown, Jim 1936- **1993**:2
Brown, Ruth 1928-2006
  Obituary **2008**:1
Bruckheimer, Jerry 1945- **2007**:2
Brynner, Yul 1920(?)-1985
  Obituary **1985**:4
Buckley, Betty 1947- **1996**:2
Bullock, Sandra 1967- **1995**:4
Burnett, Carol 1933- **2000**:3
Burns, Edward 1968- **1997**:1
Burns, George 1896-1996
  Obituary **1996**:3
Burns, Ken 1953- **1995**:2
Burr, Raymond 1917-1993
  Obituary **1994**:1
Burstyn, Ellen 1932- **2001**:4
Burton, Tim 1959- **1993**:1
Burum, Stephen H.
  Brief entry **1987**:2
Buscemi, Steve 1957- **1997**:4
Buttons, Red 1919-2006
  Obituary **2007**:3
Bynes, Amanda 1986- **2005**:1
Byrne, Gabriel 1950- **1997**:4
Caan, James 1939- **2004**:4
Caesar, Adolph 1934-1986
  Obituary **1986**:3
Cage, Nicolas 1964- **1991**:1
Cagney, James 1899-1986
  Obituary **1986**:2
Caine, Michael 1933- **2000**:4
Calhoun, Rory 1922-1999
  Obituary **1999**:4
Campbell, Naomi 1970- **2000**:2
Campbell, Neve 1973- **1998**:2
Campion, Jane **1991**:4
Candy, John 1950-1994 **1988**:2
  Obituary **1994**:3
Cannon, Nick 1980- **2006**:4
Capra, Frank 1897-1991
  Obituary **1992**:2
Carell, Steve 1963- **2006**:4
Carey, Drew 1958- **1997**:4
Carlin, George 1937- **1996**:3
Carney, Art 1918-2003
  Obituary **2005**:1
Carradine, John 1906-1988
  Obituary **1989**:2

Carrey, Jim 1962- **1995**:1
Carson, Lisa Nicole 1969- **1999**:3
Caruso, David 1956(?)- **1994**:3
Carvey, Dana 1955- **1994**:1
Cassavetes, John 1929-1989
  Obituary **1989**:2
Castellucci, Cecil 1969- **2008**:3
Castle-Hughes, Keisha 1990- **2004**:4
Cattrall, Kim 1956- **2003**:3
Caulfield, Joan 1922(?)-1991
  Obituary **1992**:1
Cavanagh, Tom 1968- **2003**:1
Caviezel, Jim 1968- **2005**:3
Chahine, Youssef 1926-2008
  Obituary **2009**:3
Chan, Jackie 1954- **1996**:1
Channing, Stockard 1946- **1991**:3
Chappelle, Dave 1973- **2005**:3
Charisse, Cyd 1922-2008
  Obituary **2009**:3
Chase, Chevy 1943- **1990**:1
Chase, Debra Martin 1956- **2009**:1
Cheadle, Don 1964- **2002**:1
Chen, Joan 1961- **2000**:2
Cher 1946- **1993**:1
Chiklis, Michael 1963- **2003**:3
Chow, Stephen 1962- **2006**:1
Chow Yun-fat 1955- **1999**:4
Christensen, Hayden 1981- **2003**:3
Christie, Julie 1941- **2008**:4
Clarkson, Patricia 1959- **2005**:3
Clay, Andrew Dice 1958- **1991**:1
Cleese, John 1939- **1989**:2
Close, Glenn 1947- **1988**:3
Coburn, James 1928-2002
  Obituary **2004**:1
Coco, James 1929(?)-1987
  Obituary **1987**:2
Cody, Diablo 1978- **2009**:1
Coen, Joel and Ethan **1992**:1
Colbert, Claudette 1903-1996
  Obituary **1997**:1
Colbert, Stephen 1964- **2007**:4
Coleman, Dabney 1932- **1988**:3
Condon, Bill 1955- **2007**:3
Connelly, Jennifer 1970- **2002**:4
Connery, Sean 1930- **1990**:4
Connick, Harry, Jr. 1967- **1991**:1
Cooper, Chris 1951- **2004**:1
Coppola, Carmine 1910-1991
  Obituary **1991**:4
Coppola, Francis Ford 1939- **1989**:4
Coppola, Sofia 1971- **2004**:3
Corbett, John 1962- **2004**:1
Cosby, Bill 1937- **1999**:2
Costner, Kevin 1955- **1989**:4
Cotillard, Marion 1975- **2009**:1
Cox, Courteney 1964- **1996**:2
Craig, Daniel 1968- **2008**:1
Craven, Wes 1939- **1997**:3
Crawford, Broderick 1911-1986
  Obituary **1986**:3
Crenna, Richard 1926-2003
  Obituary **2004**:1
Crichton, Michael 1942- **1995**:3
Cronenberg, David 1943- **1992**:3
Cronyn, Hume 1911-2003
  Obituary **2004**:3
Crothers, Scatman 1910-1986
  Obituary **1987**:1
Crowe, Cameron 1957- **2001**:2
Crowe, Russell 1964- **2000**:4

Cruise, Tom 1962(?)- **1985**:4
Cruz, Penelope 1974- **2001**:4
Crystal, Billy 1947- **1985**:3
Cuaron, Alfonso 1961- **2008**:2
Culkin, Macaulay 1980(?)- **1991**:3
Curtis, Jamie Lee 1958- **1995**:1
Cusack, John 1966- **1999**:3
Cushing, Peter 1913-1994
  Obituary **1995**:1
Dafoe, Willem 1955- **1988**:1
Dalton, Timothy 1946- **1988**:4
Damon, Matt 1970- **1999**:1
Danes, Claire 1979- **1999**:4
Dangerfield, Rodney 1921-2004
  Obituary **2006**:1
Daniels, Jeff 1955- **1989**:4
Danza, Tony 1951- **1989**:1
David, Larry 1948- **2003**:4
Davis, Bette 1908-1989
  Obituary **1990**:1
Davis, Geena 1957- **1992**:1
Davis, Ossie 1917-2005
  Obituary **2006**:1
Davis, Sammy, Jr. 1925-1990
  Obituary **1990**:4
Dawson, Rosario 1979- **2007**:2
Day, Dennis 1917-1988
  Obituary **1988**:4
Day-Lewis, Daniel 1957- **1989**:4
De Cordova, Frederick 1910- **1985**:2
Dee, Sandra 1942-2005
  Obituary **2006**:2
DeGeneres, Ellen **1995**:3
Delany, Dana 1956- **2008**:4
Del Toro, Benicio 1967- **2001**:4
De Matteo, Drea 1973- **2005**:2
Demme, Jonathan 1944- **1992**:4
Dempsey, Patrick 1966- **2006**:1
Dench, Judi 1934- **1999**:4
Deneuve, Catherine 1943- **2003**:2
De Niro, Robert 1943- **1999**:1
Dennehy, Brian 1938- **2002**:1
Dennis, Sandy 1937-1992
  Obituary **1992**:4
De Palma, Brian 1940- **2007**:3
Depardieu, Gerard 1948- **1991**:2
Depp, Johnny 1963(?)- **1991**:3
Dern, Laura 1967- **1992**:3
De Vito, Danny 1944- **1987**:1
Diamond, I.A.L. 1920-1988
  Obituary **1988**:3
Diamond, Selma 1921(?)-1985
  Obituary **1985**:2
Diaz, Cameron 1972- **1999**:1
DiCaprio, Leonardo Wilhelm
  1974- **1997**:2
Diesel, Vin 1967- **2004**:1
Dietrich, Marlene 1901-1992
  Obituary **1992**:4
Diggs, Taye 1971- **2000**:1
Diller, Barry 1942- **1991**:1
Dillon, Matt 1964- **1992**:2
Disney, Roy E. 1930- **1986**:3
Divine 1946-1988
  Obituary **1988**:3
Doherty, Shannen 1971(?)- **1994**:2
Donahue, Troy 1936-2001
  Obituary **2002**:4
Douglas, Michael 1944- **1986**:2
Downey, Robert, Jr. 1965- **2007**:1
Drescher, Fran 1957(?)- **1995**:3
Dreyfuss, Richard 1947- **1996**:3

Driver, Minnie 1971- **2000**:1
Duchovny, David 1960- **1998**:3
Duff, Hilary 1987- **2004**:4
Duffy, Karen 1962- **1998**:1
Dukakis, Olympia 1931- **1996**:4
Dunagan, Deanna 1940- **2009**:2
Dunst, Kirsten 1982- **2001**:4
Duvall, Robert 1931- **1999**:3
Eastwood, Clint 1930- **1993**:3
Ebersole, Christine 1953- **2007**:2
Ebsen, Buddy 1908-2003
  Obituary **2004**:3
Eckhart, Aaron 1968- **2009**:2
Efron, Zac 1987- **2008**:2
Egoyan, Atom 1960- **2000**:2
Eisner, Michael 1942- **1989**:2
Elliott, Denholm 1922-1992
  Obituary **1993**:2
Ephron, Henry 1912-1992
  Obituary **1993**:2
Ephron, Nora 1941- **1992**:3
Epps, Omar 1973- **2000**:4
Estevez, Emilio 1962- **1985**:4
Evans, Robert 1930- **2004**:1
Eve 1978- **2004**:3
Everett, Rupert 1959- **2003**:1
Fairbanks, Douglas, Jr. 1909-2000
  Obituary **2000**:4
Fallon, Jimmy 1974- **2003**:1
Fanning, Dakota 1994- **2005**:2
Farley, Chris 1964-1997 **1998**:2
Farrell, Colin 1976- **2004**:1
Farrow, Mia 1945- **1998**:3
Favreau, Jon 1966- **2002**:3
Fawcett, Farrah 1947- **1998**:4
Feldshuh, Tovah 1952- **2005**:3
Felix, Maria 1914-2002
  Obituary **2003**:2
Fell, Norman 1924-1998
  Obituary **1999**:2
Fellini, Federico 1920-1993
  Obituary **1994**:2
Ferguson, Craig 1962- **2005**:4
Ferrell, Will 1968- **2004**:4
Ferrer, Jose 1912-1992
  Obituary **1992**:3
Ferrera, America 1984- **2006**:2
Fetchit, Stepin 1892(?)-1985
  Obituary **1986**:1
Fey, Tina 1970- **2005**:3
Fforde, Jasper 1961- **2006**:3
Field, Sally 1946- **1995**:3
Fiennes, Ralph 1962- **1996**:2
Fierstein, Harvey 1954- **2004**:2
Finney, Albert 1936- **2003**:3
Fishburne, Laurence 1961(?)- **1995**:3
Fisher, Carrie 1956- **1991**:1
Flanders, Ed 1934-1995
  Obituary **1995**:3
Fleiss, Mike 1964- **2003**:4
Fleming, Art 1925(?)-1995
  Obituary **1995**:4
Flockhart, Calista 1964- **1998**:4
Fonda, Bridget 1964- **1995**:1
Ford, Faith 1964- **2005**:3
Ford, Glenn 1916-2006
  Obituary **2007**:4
Ford, Harrison 1942- **1990**:2
Fosse, Bob 1927-1987
  Obituary **1988**:1
Foster, Jodie 1962- **1989**:2
Fox, Michael J. 1961- **1986**:1

Fox, Vivica 1964- **1999**:1
Franciscus, James 1934-1991
    Obituary **1992**:1
Frank, Robert 1924- **1995**:2
Frankenheimer, John 1930-2002
    Obituary **2003**:4
Franz, Dennis 1944- **1995**:2
Fraser, Brendan 1967- **2000**:1
Freeman, Morgan 1937- **1990**:4
Freleng, Friz 1906(?)-1995
    Obituary **1995**:4
Fugard, Athol 1932- **1992**:3
Gabor, Eva 1921(?)-1995
    Obituary **1996**:1
Gallagher, Peter 1955- **2004**:3
Garbo, Greta 1905-1990
    Obituary **1990**:3
Garcia, Andy 1956- **1999**:3
Gardenia, Vincent 1922-1992
    Obituary **1993**:2
Gardner, Ava Lavinia 1922-1990
    Obituary **1990**:2
Garner, Jennifer 1972- **2003**:1
Garofalo, Janeane 1964- **1996**:4
Garr, Teri 1949- **1988**:4
Garson, Greer 1903-1996
    Obituary **1996**:4
Gassman, Vittorio 1922-2000
    Obituary **2001**:1
Geffen, David 1943- **1985**:3
Gellar, Sarah Michelle 1977- **1999**:3
Gere, Richard 1949- **1994**:3
Getty, Estelle 1923-2008
    Obituary **2009**:3
Giamatti, Paul 1967- **2009**:4
Gibson, Mel 1956- **1990**:1
Gielgud, John 1904-2000
    Obituary **2000**:4
Gift, Roland 1960(?)- **1990**:2
Gilford, Jack 1907-1990
    Obituary **1990**:4
Gish, Lillian 1893-1993
    Obituary **1993**:4
Gleason, Jackie 1916-1987
    Obituary **1987**:4
Gless, Sharon 1944- **1989**:3
Glover, Danny 1947- **1998**:4
Gobel, George 1920(?)-1991
    Obituary **1991**:4
Godard, Jean-Luc 1930- **1998**:1
Godunov, Alexander 1949-1995
    Obituary **1995**:4
Goldberg, Leonard 1934- **1988**:4
Goldberg, Whoopi 1955- **1993**:3
Goldblum, Jeff 1952- **1988**:1
Gong Li 1965- **1998**:4
Gooding, Cuba, Jr. 1968- **1997**:3
Goodman, John 1952- **1990**:3
Gordon, Dexter 1923-1990 **1987**:1
Gordon, Gale 1906-1995
    Obituary **1996**:1
Gossett, Louis, Jr. 1936- **1989**:3
Goulet, Robert 1933-2007
    Obituary **2008**:4
Grace, Topher 1978- **2005**:4
Graham, Heather 1970- **2000**:1
Graham, Lauren 1967- **2003**:4
Grant, Cary 1904-1986
    Obituary **1987**:1
Grant, Hugh 1960- **1995**:3
Grant, Rodney A. **1992**:1
Gray, Spalding 1941-2004

Obituary **2005**:2
Grazer, Brian 1951- **2006**:4
Greene, Graham 1952- **1997**:2
Greene, Lorne 1915-1987
    Obituary **1988**:1
Grier, Pam 1949- **1998**:3
Griffith, Melanie 1957- **1989**:2
Grodin, Charles 1935- **1997**:3
Grusin, Dave
    Brief entry **1987**:2
Guest, Christopher 1948- **2004**:2
Guggenheim, Charles 1924-2002
    Obituary **2003**:4
Guinness, Alec 1914-2000
    Obituary **2001**:1
Gyllenhaal, Jake 1980- **2005**:3
Gyllenhaal, Maggie 1977- **2009**:2
Hackett, Buddy 1924-2003
    Obituary **2004**:3
Hackman, Gene 1931- **1989**:3
Hagen, Uta 1919-2004
    Obituary **2005**:2
Haggis, Paul 1953- **2006**:4
Hall, Anthony Michael 1968- **1986**:3
Hall, Arsenio 1955- **1990**:2
Hallstrom, Lasse 1946- **2002**:3
Hamilton, Margaret 1902-1985
    Obituary **1985**:3
Hamm, Jon 1971- **2009**:2
Hammer, Jan 1948- **1987**:3
Hanks, Tom 1956- **1989**:2
Hannah, Daryl 1961- **1987**:4
Hannigan, Alyson 1974- **2007**:3
Harden, Marcia Gay 1959- **2002**:4
Hargitay, Mariska 1964- **2006**:2
Harmon, Mark 1951- **1987**:1
Harris, Ed 1950- **2002**:2
Harris, Richard 1930-2002
    Obituary **2004**:1
Harrison, Rex 1908-1990
    Obituary **1990**:4
Harry, Deborah 1945- **1990**:1
Hart, Kitty Carlisle 1910-2007
    Obituary **2008**:2
Hartman, Phil 1948-1998 **1996**:2
    Obituary **1998**:4
Harwell, Ernie 1918- **1997**:3
Hatcher, Teri 1964- **2005**:4
Hathaway, Anne 1982- **2007**:2
Hawke, Ethan 1971(?)- **1995**:4
Hawkins, Sally 1976- **2009**:4
Hawn, Goldie Jeanne 1945- **1997**:2
Hayek, Salma 1968- **1999**:1
Hayes, Helen 1900-1993
    Obituary **1993**:4
Hayes, Isaac 1942- **1998**:4
Haysbert, Dennis 1954- **2007**:1
Hayworth, Rita 1918-1987
    Obituary **1987**:3
Heche, Anne 1969- **1999**:1
Heckerling, Amy 1954- **1987**:2
Heigl, Katharine 1978- **2008**:3
Hemingway, Margaux 1955-1996
    Obituary **1997**:1
Hennessy, Jill 1969- **2003**:2
Henson, Brian 1964(?)- **1992**:1
Henson, Jim 1936-1990 **1989**:1
    Obituary **1990**:4
Hepburn, Audrey 1929-1993
    Obituary **1993**:2
Hepburn, Katharine 1909- **1991**:2
Hershey, Barbara 1948- **1989**:1

Heston, Charlton 1924- **1999**:4
Hewitt, Jennifer Love 1979- **1999**:2
Hill, George Roy 1921-2002
    Obituary **2004**:1
Hill, Lauryn 1975- **1999**:3
Hines, Gregory 1946- **1992**:4
Hoffman, Dustin 1937- **2005**:4
Hoffman, Philip Seymour
    1967- **2006**:3
Holmes, John C. 1945-1988
    Obituary **1988**:3
Hope, Bob 1903-2003
    Obituary **2004**:4
Hopkins, Anthony 1937- **1992**:4
Horne, Lena 1917- **1998**:4
Hoskins, Bob 1942- **1989**:1
Hou Hsiao-hsien 1947- **2000**:2
Houseman, John 1902-1988
    Obituary **1989**:1
Howard, Ron **1997**:2
Howard, Trevor 1916-1988
    Obituary **1988**:2
Hudson, Jennifer 1981- **2008**:1
Hudson, Kate 1979- **2001**:2
Hudson, Rock 1925-1985
    Obituary **1985**:4
Huffman, Felicity 1962- **2006**:2
Humphries, Barry 1934- **1993**:1
Hunt, Helen 1963- **1994**:4
Hunter, Holly 1958- **1989**:4
Hurley, Elizabeth **1999**:2
Hurt, William 1950- **1986**:1
Huston, Anjelica 1952(?)- **1989**:3
Huston, John 1906-1987
    Obituary **1988**:1
Hutton, Timothy 1960- **1986**:3
Ice Cube 1969- **1999**:2
Ice-T **1992**:3
Ireland, Jill 1936-1990
    Obituary **1990**:4
Irons, Jeremy 1948- **1991**:4
Irving, John 1942- **2006**:2
Itami, Juzo 1933-1997 **1998**:2
Ives, Burl 1909-1995
    Obituary **1995**:4
Izzard, Eddie 1963- **2008**:1
Jackman, Hugh 1968- **2004**:4
Jackson, Peter 1961- **2004**:4
Jackson, Samuel L. 1949(?)- **1995**:4
Jacobson, Nina 1965- **2009**:2
Janney, Allison 1959- **2003**:3
Jarmusch, Jim 1953- **1998**:3
Jay, Ricky 1949(?)- **1995**:1
Jillian, Ann 1951- **1986**:4
Johansson, Scarlett 1984- **2005**:4
Johnson, Beverly 1952- **2005**:2
Johnson, Don 1949- **1986**:1
Jolie, Angelina 1975- **2000**:2
Jones, Cherry 1956- **1999**:3
Jones, Tommy Lee 1947(?)- **1994**:2
Jonze, Spike 1961(?)- **2000**:3
Jordan, Neil 1950(?)- **1993**:3
Jovovich, Milla 1975- **2002**:1
Joyce, William 1957- **2006**:1
Judd, Ashley 1968- **1998**:1
Julia, Raul 1940-1994
    Obituary **1995**:1
Kahn, Madeline 1942-1999
    Obituary **2000**:2
Kanakaredes, Melina 1967- **2007**:1
Kasem, Casey 1933(?)- **1987**:1
Katzenberg, Jeffrey 1950- **1995**:3

Kaufman, Charlie 1958- **2005**:1
Kavner, Julie 1951- **1992**:3
Kaye, Danny 1913-1987
   Obituary **1987**:2
Kazan, Elia 1909-2003
   Obituary **2004**:4
Keaton, Diane 1946- **1997**:1
Keaton, Michael 1951- **1989**:4
Keeler, Ruby 1910-1993
   Obituary **1993**:4
Keitel, Harvey 1939- **1994**:3
Keith, Brian 1921-1997
   Obituary **1997**:4
Kelly, Gene 1912-1996
   Obituary **1996**:3
Kerr, Deborah 1921-2007
   Obituary **2008**:4
Kidman, Nicole 1967- **1992**:4
Kilmer, Val **1991**:4
Kimmel, Jimmy 1967- **2009**:2
King, Alan 1927-2004
   Obituary **2005**:3
King, Stephen 1947- **1998**:1
Kinski, Klaus 1926-1991 **1987**:2
   Obituary **1992**:2
Kline, Kevin 1947- **2000**:1
Knight, Wayne 1956- **1997**:1
Knightley, Keira 1985- **2005**:2
Knotts, Don 1924-2006
   Obituary **2007**:1
Kramer, Larry 1935- **1991**:2
Kramer, Stanley 1913-2001
   Obituary **2002**:1
Krause, Peter 1965- **2009**:2
Kubrick, Stanley 1928-1999
   Obituary **1999**:3
Kulp, Nancy 1921-1991
   Obituary **1991**:3
Kurosawa, Akira 1910-1998 **1991**:1
   Obituary **1999**:1
Kutcher, Ashton 1978- **2003**:4
LaBeouf, Shia 1986- **2008**:1
Lahti, Christine 1950- **1988**:2
Lake, Ricki 1968(?)- **1994**:4
Lamarr, Hedy 1913-2000
   Obituary **2000**:3
Lamour, Dorothy 1914-1996
   Obituary **1997**:1
Lancaster, Burt 1913-1994
   Obituary **1995**:1
Lane, Diane 1965- **2006**:2
Lane, Nathan 1956- **1996**:4
Lange, Jessica 1949- **1995**:4
Langella, Frank 1940- **2008**:3
Lansbury, Angela 1925- **1993**:1
Lansing, Sherry 1944- **1995**:4
LaPaglia, Anthony 1959- **2004**:4
Lardner Jr., Ring 1915-2000
   Obituary **2001**:2
Larroquette, John 1947- **1986**:2
Lasseter, John 1957- **2007**:2
Laurie, Hugh 1959- **2007**:2
Law, Jude 1971- **2000**:3
Lawless, Lucy 1968- **1997**:4
Lawrence, Martin 1966(?)- **1993**:4
Leary, Denis 1958- **1993**:3
LeBlanc, Matt 1967- **2005**:4
Ledger, Heath 1979- **2006**:3
Lee, Ang 1954- **1996**:3
Lee, Brandon 1965(?)-1993
   Obituary **1993**:4
Lee, Jason 1970- **2006**:4

Lee, Pamela 1967(?)- **1996**:4
Lee, Spike 1957- **1988**:4
Leguizamo, John 1965- **1999**:1
Leigh, Janet 1927-2004
   Obituary **2005**:4
Leigh, Jennifer Jason 1962- **1995**:2
Lemmon, Jack 1925- **1998**:4
   Obituary **2002**:3
Leno, Jay 1950- **1987**:1
Leone, Sergio 1929-1989
   Obituary **1989**:4
Levi, Zachary 1980- **2009**:4
Levinson, Barry 1932- **1989**:3
Levy, Eugene 1946- **2004**:3
Lewis, Juliette 1973- **1999**:3
Lewis, Richard 1948(?)- **1992**:1
Li, Jet 1963- **2005**:3
Liberace 1919-1987
   Obituary **1987**:2
Liman, Doug 1965- **2007**:1
Ling, Bai 1970- **2000**:3
Linklater, Richard 1960- **2007**:2
Linney, Laura 1964- **2009**:4
Lithgow, John 1945- **1985**:2
Little, Cleavon 1939-1992
   Obituary **1993**:2
Liu, Lucy 1968- **2000**:4
Lively, Blake 1987- **2009**:1
Livingston, Ron 1968- **2007**:2
LL Cool J 1968- **1998**:2
Lloyd Webber, Andrew 1948- **1989**:1
Locklear, Heather 1961- **1994**:3
Loewe, Frederick 1901-1988
   Obituary **1988**:2
Logan, Joshua 1908-1988
   Obituary **1988**:4
Lohan, Lindsay 1986- **2005**:3
Long, Nia 1970- **2001**:3
Long, Shelley 1950(?)- **1985**:1
Lopez, Jennifer 1970- **1998**:4
Lord, Jack 1920-1998 **1998**:2
Lords, Traci 1968- **1995**:4
Louis-Dreyfus, Julia 1961(?)- **1994**:1
Lovett, Lyle 1958(?)- **1994**:1
Lowe, Rob 1964(?)- **1990**:4
Loy, Myrna 1905-1993
   Obituary **1994**:2
Lucas, George 1944- **1999**:4
Ludacris 1977- **2007**:4
Luhrmann, Baz 1962- **2002**:3
Lupino, Ida 1918(?)-1995
   Obituary **1996**:1
LuPone, Patti 1949- **2009**:2
Lynch, David 1946- **1990**:4
Lyne, Adrian 1941- **1997**:2
Mac, Bernie 1957- **2003**:1
MacDonald, Laurie and Walter
   Parkes **2004**:1
MacDowell, Andie 1958(?)- **1993**:4
MacMurray, Fred 1908-1991
   Obituary **1992**:2
MacRae, Gordon 1921-1986
   Obituary **1986**:2
Macy, William H. **1999**:3
Madonna 1958- **1985**:2
Maguire, Tobey 1975- **2002**:2
Maher, Bill 1956- **1996**:2
Mako 1933-2006
   Obituary **2007**:3
Malkovich, John 1953- **1988**:2
Malle, Louis 1932-1995
   Obituary **1996**:2

Mamet, David 1947- **1998**:4
Mancini, Henry 1924-1994
   Obituary **1994**:4
Mandel, Howie 1955- **1989**:1
Mantegna, Joe 1947- **1992**:1
Marber, Patrick 1964- **2007**:4
Marin, Cheech 1946- **2000**:1
Markle, C. Wilson 1938- **1988**:1
Marsalis, Branford 1960- **1988**:3
Marshall, Penny 1942- **1991**:3
Martin, Dean 1917-1995
   Obituary **1996**:2
Martin, Dean Paul 1952(?)-1987
   Obituary **1987**:3
Martin, Steve 1945- **1992**:2
Marvin, Lee 1924-1987
   Obituary **1988**:1
Masina, Giulietta 1920-1994
   Obituary **1994**:3
Mastroianni, Marcello 1914-1996
   Obituary **1997**:2
Matlin, Marlee 1965- **1992**:2
Matthau, Walter 1920- **2000**:3
Matuszak, John 1951(?)-1989
   Obituary **1989**:4
McConaughey, Matthew David
   1969- **1997**:1
McCrea, Joel 1905-1990
   Obituary **1991**:1
McDonagh, Martin 1970- **2007**:3
McDonnell, Mary 1952- **2008**:2
McDormand, Frances 1957- **1997**:3
McDowall, Roddy 1928-1998
   Obituary **1999**:1
McGillis, Kelly 1957- **1989**:3
McGinley, Ted 1958- **2004**:4
McGregor, Ewan 1971(?)- **1998**:2
McGuire, Dorothy 1918-2001
   Obituary **2002**:4
McKee, Lonette 1952(?)- **1996**:1
McKellen, Ian 1939- **1994**:1
McLaren, Norman 1914-1987
   Obituary **1987**:2
McMahon, Julian 1968- **2006**:1
Meadows, Audrey 1925-1996
   Obituary **1996**:3
Merchant, Ismail 1936-2005
   Obituary **2006**:3
Meredith, Burgess 1909-1997
   Obituary **1998**:1
Merkerson, S. Epatha 1952- **2006**:4
Messing, Debra 1968- **2004**:4
Meyers, Nancy 1949- **2006**:1
Midler, Bette 1945- **1989**:4
Milano, Alyssa 1972- **2002**:3
Milland, Ray 1908(?)-1986
   Obituary **1986**:2
Miller, Ann 1923-2004
   Obituary **2005**:2
Miller, Frank 1957- **2008**:2
Milligan, Spike 1918-2002
   Obituary **2003**:2
Minghella, Anthony 1954- **2004**:3
Minogue, Kylie 1968- **2003**:4
Mirren, Helen 1945- **2005**:1
Mitchum, Robert 1917-1997
   Obituary **1997**:4
Miyazaki, Hayao 1941- **2006**:2
Molina, Alfred 1953- **2005**:3
Mo'Nique 1967- **2008**:1
Montand, Yves 1921-1991
   Obituary **1992**:2

Montgomery, Elizabeth 1933-1995
  Obituary **1995**:4
Moore, Clayton 1914-1999
  Obituary **2000**:3
Moore, Demi 1963(?)- **1991**:4
Moore, Dudley 1935-2002
  Obituary **2003**:2
Moore, Julianne 1960- **1998**:1
Moore, Mandy 1984- **2004**:2
Moore, Mary Tyler 1936- **1996**:2
Moore, Michael 1954(?)- **1990**:3
Morgan, Tracy 1968- **2009**:3
Morita, Noriyuki Pat 1932- **1987**:3
Morris, Kathryn 1969- **2006**:4
Morrow, Rob 1962- **2006**:4
Mortensen, Viggo 1958- **2003**:3
Mos Def 1973- **2005**:4
Moss, Carrie-Anne 1967- **2004**:3
Murphy, Brittany 1977- **2005**:1
Murphy, Eddie 1961- **1989**:2
Murray, Bill 1950- **2002**:4
Myers, Mike 1964(?)- **1992**:3
Nair, Mira 1957- **2007**:4
Nance, Jack 1943(?)-1996
  Obituary **1997**:3
Neeson, Liam 1952- **1993**:4
Nelson, Harriet 1909(?)-1994
  Obituary **1995**:1
Nelson, Rick 1940-1985
  Obituary **1986**:1
Nelson, Willie 1933- **1993**:4
Newman, Paul 1925- **1995**:3
Newton-John, Olivia 1948- **1998**:4
Nichols, Mike 1931- **1994**:4
Nicholson, Jack 1937- **1989**:2
Nixon, Bob 1954(?)- **2006**:4
Nolan, Christopher 1970(?)- **2006**:3
Nolan, Lloyd 1902-1985
  Obituary **1985**:4
Nolte, Nick 1941- **1992**:4
North, Alex 1910- **1986**:3
Northam, Jeremy 1961- **2003**:2
Norton, Edward 1969- **2000**:2
O'Connor, Donald 1925-2003
  Obituary **2004**:4
O'Donnell, Rosie 1962- **1994**:3
O'Hara, Catherine 1954- **2007**:4
Oldman, Gary 1958- **1998**:1
Olin, Ken 1955(?)- **1992**:3
Olin, Lena 1956- **1991**:2
Olivier, Laurence 1907-1989
  Obituary **1989**:4
Olmos, Edward James 1947- **1990**:1
O'Sullivan, Maureen 1911-1998
  Obituary **1998**:4
Ovitz, Michael 1946- **1990**:1
Owen, Clive 1964- **2006**:2
Paar, Jack 1918-2004
  Obituary **2005**:2
Pacino, Al 1940- **1993**:4
Page, Geraldine 1924-1987
  Obituary **1987**:4
Pakula, Alan 1928-1998
  Obituary **1999**:2
Palance, Jack 1919-2006
  Obituary **2008**:1
Paltrow, Gwyneth 1972- **1997**:1
Panettiere, Hayden 1989- **2008**:4
Pantoliano, Joe 1951- **2002**:3
Paquin, Anna 1982- **2009**:4
Park, Nick 1958- **1997**:3
Parker, Mary-Louise 1964- **2002**:2

Parker, Sarah Jessica 1965- **1999**:2
Parker, Trey and Matt Stone **1998**:2
Parks, Bert 1914-1992
  Obituary **1992**:3
Parks, Gordon 1912-2006
  Obituary **2006**:2
Pascal, Amy 1958- **2003**:3
Patrick, Robert 1959- **2002**:1
Paxton, Bill 1955- **1999**:3
Payne, Alexander 1961- **2005**:4
Peck, Gregory 1916-2003
  Obituary **2004**:3
Peete, Holly Robinson 1964- **2005**:2
Pegg, Simon 1970- **2009**:1
Penn, Kal 1977- **2009**:1
Penn, Sean 1960- **1987**:2
Perez, Rosie 1994:2
Perkins, Anthony 1932-1992
  Obituary **1993**:2
Perry, Luke 1966(?)- **1992**:3
Perry, Matthew 1969- **1997**:2
Perry, Tyler 1969- **2006**:1
Pesci, Joe 1943- **1992**:4
Peters, Bernadette 1948- **2000**:1
Peterson, Cassandra 1951- **1988**:1
Pfeiffer, Michelle 1957- **1990**:2
Phifer, Mekhi 1975- **2004**:1
Phillips, Julia 1944- **1992**:1
Phoenix, Joaquin 1974- **2000**:4
Phoenix, River 1970-1993 **1990**:2
  Obituary **1994**:2
Picasso, Paloma 1949- **1991**:1
Pinchot, Bronson 1959(?)- **1987**:4
Pinkett Smith, Jada 1971- **1998**:3
Pitt, Brad 1964- **1995**:2
Piven, Jeremy 1965- **2007**:3
Pleasence, Donald 1919-1995
  Obituary **1995**:3
Pleshette, Suzanne 1937-2008
  Obituary **2009**:2
Plimpton, George 1927-2003
  Obituary **2004**:4
Poehler, Amy 1971- **2009**:1
Poitier, Sidney 1927- **1990**:3
Pollack, Sydney 1934-2008
  Obituary **2009**:2
Ponti, Carlo 1912-2007
  Obituary **2008**:2
Portman, Natalie 1981- **2000**:3
Potts, Annie 1952- **1994**:1
Preminger, Otto 1906-1986
  Obituary **1986**:3
Presley, Pricilla 1945- **2001**:1
Preston, Robert 1918-1987
  Obituary **1987**:3
Price, Vincent 1911-1993
  Obituary **1994**:2
Prince 1958- **1995**:3
Prinze, Freddie, Jr. 1976- **1999**:3
Prowse, Juliet 1937-1996
  Obituary **1997**:1
Pryor, Richard **1999**:3
Puzo, Mario 1920-1999
  Obituary **2000**:1
Quaid, Dennis 1954- **1989**:4
Queen Latifah 1970(?)- **1992**:2
Quinn, Anthony 1915-2001
  Obituary **2002**:2
Radcliffe, Daniel 1989- **2007**:4
Radner, Gilda 1946-1989
  Obituary **1989**:4
Raimi, Sam 1959- **1999**:2

Randall, Tony 1920-2004
  Obituary **2005**:3
Raven 1985- **2005**:1
Rawls, Lou 1933-2006
  Obituary **2007**:1
Raye, Martha 1916-1994
  Obituary **1995**:1
Reagan, Ronald 1911-2004
  Obituary **2005**:3
Redford, Robert 1937- **1993**:2
Redgrave, Lynn 1943- **1999**:3
Redgrave, Vanessa 1937- **1989**:2
Reed, Donna 1921-1986
  Obituary **1986**:1
Reese, Della 1931- **1999**:2
Reeve, Christopher 1952- **1997**:2
Reeves, Keanu 1964- **1992**:1
Reeves, Steve 1926-2000
  Obituary **2000**:4
Reilly, John C. 1965- **2003**:4
Reiner, Rob 1947- **1991**:2
Reiser, Paul 1957- **1995**:2
Reisz, Karel 1926-2002
  Obituary **2004**:1
Reitman, Ivan 1946- **1986**:3
Remick, Lee 1936(?)-1991
  Obituary **1992**:1
Reuben, Gloria 1964- **1999**:4
Reubens, Paul 1952- **1987**:2
Rhys Meyers, Jonathan 1977- **2007**:1
Ricci, Christina 1980- **1999**:1
Rice, Peter 1967(?)- **2007**:2
Richards, Michael 1949(?)- **1993**:4
Riddle, Nelson 1921-1985
  Obituary **1985**:4
Ringwald, Molly 1968- **1985**:4
Ritchie, Guy 1968- **2001**:3
Ritter, John 1948- **2003**:4
Robards, Jason 1922-2000
  Obituary **2001**:3
Robbins, Jerome 1918-1998
  Obituary **1999**:1
Robbins, Tim 1959- **1993**:1
Roberts, Doris 1930- **2003**:4
Roberts, Julia 1967- **1991**:3
Rock, Chris 1967(?)- **1998**:1
Rodriguez, Robert 1968- **2005**:1
Rogen, Seth 1982- **2009**:3
Rogers, Ginger 1911(?)-1995
  Obituary **1995**:4
Rogers, Roy 1911-1998
  Obituary **1998**:4
Roker, Roxie 1929(?)-1995
  Obituary **1996**:2
Rolle, Esther 1922-1998
  Obituary **1999**:2
Rollins, Henry 1961- **2007**:3
Rollins, Howard E., Jr. 1950- **1986**:1
Romijn, Rebecca 1972- **2007**:1
Ross, Herbert 1927-2001
  Obituary **2002**:4
Roth, Tim 1961- **1998**:2
Rourke, Mickey 1956- **1988**:4
Rowan, Dan 1922-1987
  Obituary **1988**:1
Rudd, Paul 1969- **2009**:4
Rudner, Rita 1956- **1993**:2
Rudnick, Paul 1957(?)- **1994**:3
Ruehl, Mercedes 195(?)- **1992**:4
RuPaul 1961(?)- **1996**:1
Rush, Geoffrey 1951- **2002**:1
Russell, Kurt 1951- **2007**:4

Russell, Nipsey 1924-2005
 Obituary **2007**:1
Russo, Rene 1954- **2000**:2
Ryan, Meg 1962(?)- **1994**:1
Ryder, Winona 1971- **1991**:2
Sagal, Katey 1954- **2005**:2
Salonga, Lea 1971- **2003**:3
Sandler, Adam 1966- **1999**:2
Sarandon, Susan 1946- **1995**:3
Savage, Fred 1976- **1990**:1
Savalas, Telly 1924-1994
 Obituary **1994**:3
Scheider, Roy 1932-2008
 Obituary **2009**:2
Schlesinger, John 1926-2003
 Obituary **2004**:3
Schneider, Rob 1965- **1997**:4
Schreiber, Liev 1967- **2007**:2
Schroeder, Barbet 1941- **1996**:1
Schumacher, Joel 1929- **2004**:3
Schwarzenegger, Arnold
 1947- **1991**:1
Schwimmer, David 1966(?)- **1996**:2
Scorsese, Martin 1942- **1989**:1
Scott, George C. 1927-1999
 Obituary **2000**:2
Scott, Randolph 1898(?)-1987
 Obituary **1987**:2
Scott, Ridley 1937- **2001**:1
Sedaris, Amy 1961- **2009**:3
Sedgwick, Kyra 1965- **2006**:2
Seidelman, Susan 1953(?)- **1985**:4
Sevigny, Chloe 1974- **2001**:4
Seyfried, Amanda 1985- **2009**:3
Seymour, Jane 1951- **1994**:4
Shaffer, Paul 1949- **1987**:1
Shanley, John Patrick 1950- **2006**:1
Sharkey, Ray 1953-1993
 Obituary **1994**:1
Shawn, Dick 1924(?)-1987
 Obituary **1987**:3
Sheedy, Ally 1962- **1989**:1
Sheen, Martin 1940- **2002**:1
Sheldon, Sidney 1917-2007
 Obituary **2008**:2
Shepard, Sam 1943- **1996**:4
Shields, Brooke 1965- **1996**:3
Shore, Dinah 1917-1994
 Obituary **1994**:3
Short, Martin 1950- **1986**:1
Shue, Andrew 1964- **1994**:4
Shyamalan, M. Night 1970- **2003**:2
Silverman, Jonathan 1966- **1997**:2
Silverman, Sarah 1970- **2008**:1
Silvers, Phil 1912-1985
 Obituary **1985**:4
Silverstone, Alicia 1976- **1997**:4
Sinatra, Frank 1915-1998
 Obituary **1998**:4
Singer, Bryan 1965- **2007**:3
Singleton, John 1968- **1994**:3
Sinise, Gary 1955(?)- **1996**:1
Siskel, Gene 1946-1999
 Obituary **1999**:3
Slater, Christian 1969- **1994**:1
Smirnoff, Yakov 1951- **1987**:2
Smith, Kevin 1970- **2000**:4
Smith, Will 1968- **1997**:2
Smits, Jimmy 1956- **1990**:1
Snipes, Wesley 1962- **1993**:1
Sobieski, Leelee 1982- **2002**:3
Soderbergh, Steven 1963- **2001**:4

Sondheim, Stephen 1930- **1994**:4
Sorkin, Aaron 1961- **2003**:2
Sorvino, Mira 1970(?)- **1996**:3
Sothern, Ann 1909-2001
 Obituary **2002**:1
Southern, Terry 1926-1995
 Obituary **1996**:2
Spacek, Sissy 1949- **2003**:1
Spacey, Kevin 1959- **1996**:4
Spade, David 1965- **1999**:2
Spader, James 1960- **1991**:2
Spelling, Tori 1973- **2008**:3
Spheeris, Penelope 1945(?)- **1989**:2
Spielberg, Steven 1947- **1993**:4
Stack, Robert 1919-2003
 Obituary **2004**:2
Staller, Ilona 1951- **1988**:3
Stallone, Sylvester 1946- **1994**:2
Stamos, John 1963- **2008**:1
Stapleton, Maureen 1925-2006
 Obituary **2007**:2
Steel, Dawn 1946-1997 **1990**:1
 Obituary **1998**:2
Stefani, Gwen 1969- **2005**:4
Steiger, Rod 1925-2002
 Obituary **2003**:4
Stevenson, McLean 1929-1996
 Obituary **1996**:3
Stewart, Jimmy 1908-1997
 Obituary **1997**:4
Stewart, Patrick 1940- **1996**:1
Stiles, Julia 1981- **2002**:3
Stiller, Ben 1965- **1999**:1
Sting 1951- **1991**:4
Stone, Oliver 1946- **1990**:4
Stone, Sharon 1958- **1993**:4
Stoppard, Tom 1937- **1995**:4
Streep, Meryl 1949- **1990**:2
Streisand, Barbra 1942- **1992**:2
Strummer, Joe 1952-2002
 Obituary **2004**:1
Studi, Wes 1944(?)- **1994**:3
Styler, Trudie 1954- **2009**:1
Styne, Jule 1905-1994
 Obituary **1995**:1
Susskind, David 1920-1987
 Obituary **1987**:2
Sutherland, Kiefer 1966- **2002**:4
Swank, Hilary 1974- **2000**:3
Swinton, Tilda 1960- **2008**:4
Sykes, Wanda 1964- **2007**:4
Tanaka, Tomoyuki 1910-1997
 Obituary **1997**:3
Tandy, Jessica 1901-1994 **1990**:4
 Obituary **1995**:1
Tarantino, Quentin 1963(?)- **1995**:1
Tautou, Audrey 1978- **2004**:2
Taylor, Elizabeth 1932- **1993**:3
Taylor, Lili 1967- **2000**:2
Theron, Charlize 1975- **2001**:4
Thiebaud, Wayne 1920- **1991**:1
Thompson, Emma 1959- **1993**:2
Thompson, Fred 1942- **1998**:2
Thornton, Billy Bob 1956(?)- **1997**:4
Thurman, Uma 1970- **1994**:2
Tilly, Jennifer 1958(?)- **1997**:2
Timberlake, Justin 1981- **2008**:4
Tomei, Marisa 1964- **1995**:2
Travolta, John 1954- **1995**:2
Tucci, Stanley 1960- **2003**:2
Tucker, Chris 1973(?)- **1999**:1
Tucker, Forrest 1919-1986

 Obituary **1987**:1
Turner, Janine 1962- **1993**:2
Turner, Kathleen 1954(?)- **1985**:3
Turner, Lana 1921-1995
 Obituary **1996**:1
Turturro, John 1957- **2002**:2
Tyler, Liv 1978- **1997**:2
Ullman, Tracey 1961- **1988**:3
Umeki, Miyoshi 1929-2007
 Obituary **2008**:4
Union, Gabrielle 1972- **2004**:2
Urich, Robert 1947- **1988**:1
 Obituary **2003**:3
Usher 1979- **2005**:1
Ustinov, Peter 1921-2004
 Obituary **2005**:3
Valenti, Jack 1921-2007
 Obituary **2008**:3
Vanilla Ice 1967(?)- **1991**:3
Van Sant, Gus 1952- **1992**:2
Vardalos, Nia 1962- **2003**:4
Varney, Jim 1949-2000
 Brief entry **1985**:4
 Obituary **2000**:3
Vaughn, Vince 1970- **1999**:2
Ventura, Jesse 1951- **1999**:2
Vidal, Gore 1925- **1996**:2
Vidov, Oleg 194- **1987**:4
Villechaize, Herve 1943(?)-1993
 Obituary **1994**:1
Vincent, Fay 1938- **1990**:2
Voight, Jon 1938- **2002**:3
Walker, Nancy 1922-1992
 Obituary **1992**:3
Wallis, Hal 1898(?)-1986
 Obituary **1987**:1
Warden, Jack 1920-2006
 Obituary **2007**:3
Warhol, Andy 1927(?)-1987
 Obituary **1987**:2
Washington, Denzel 1954- **1993**:2
Wasserman, Lew 1913-2002
 Obituary **2003**:3
Waters, John 1946- **1988**:3
Waterston, Sam 1940- **2006**:1
Watson, Emily 1967- **2001**:1
Watts, Naomi 1968- **2006**:1
Wayans, Damon 1960- **1998**:4
Wayans, Keenen Ivory
 1958(?)- **1991**:1
Wayne, David 1914-1995
 Obituary **1995**:3
Weaver, Sigourney 1949- **1988**:3
Wegman, William 1942(?)- **1991**:1
Weinstein, Bob and Harvey **2000**:4
Weintraub, Jerry 1937- **1986**:1
Weisz, Rachel 1971- **2006**:4
Whedon, Joss 1964- **2006**:3
Whitaker, Forest 1961- **1996**:2
White, Julie 1961- **2008**:2
Wiest, Dianne 1948- **1995**:2
Wilder, Billy 1906-2002
 Obituary **2003**:2
Wilkinson, Tom 1948- **2003**:2
Williams, Robin 1952- **1988**:4
Williams, Treat 1951- **2004**:3
Williams, Vanessa L. 1963- **1999**:2
Willis, Bruce 1955- **1986**:4
Wilson, Owen 1968- **2002**:3
Winfield, Paul 1941-2004
 Obituary **2005**:2
Winfrey, Oprah 1954- **1986**:4

Winger, Debra 1955- **1994**:3
Winokur, Marissa Jaret 1973- **2005**:1
Winslet, Kate 1975- **2002**:4
Winters, Shelley 1920-2006
  Obituary **2007**:1
Wise, Robert 1914-2005
  Obituary **2006**:4
Wiseman, Len 1973- **2008**:2
Witherspoon, Reese 1976- **2002**:1
Wolfman Jack 1938-1995
  Obituary **1996**:1
Wong, B.D. 1962- **1998**:1
Woo, John 1945(?)- **1994**:2
Wood, Elijah 1981- **2002**:4
Woods, James 1947- **1988**:3
Wright, Joe 1972- **2009**:1
Wyle, Noah 1971- **1997**:3
Wyman, Jane 1917-2007
  Obituary **2008**:4
Wynn, Keenan 1916-1986
  Obituary **1987**:1
Xzibit 1974- **2005**:4
Yeoh, Michelle 1962- **2003**:2
Young, Loretta 1913-2000
  Obituary **2001**:1
Young, Robert 1907-1998
  Obituary **1999**:1
Zanuck, Lili Fini 1954- **1994**:2
Zeffirelli, Franco 1923- **1991**:3
Zellweger, Renee 1969- **2001**:1
Zemeckis, Robert 1952- **2002**:1
Zeta-Jones, Catherine 1969- **1999**:4
Zhang, Ziyi 1979- **2006**:2
Ziskin, Laura 1950- **2008**:2
Zucker, Jerry 1950- **2002**:2

**LAW**
Abzug, Bella 1920-1998 **1998**:2
Achtenberg, Roberta **1993**:4
Allred, Gloria 1941- **1985**:2
Andrews, Lori B. 1952- **2005**:3
Angelos, Peter 1930- **1995**:4
Archer, Dennis 1942- **1994**:4
Astorga, Nora 1949(?)-1988 **1988**:2
Babbitt, Bruce 1938- **1994**:1
Bailey, F. Lee 1933- **1995**:4
Baker, James A. III 1930- **1991**:2
Bikoff, James L.
  Brief entry **1986**:2
Blackmun, Harry A. 1908-1999
  Obituary **1999**:3
Boies, David 1941- **2002**:1
Bradley, Tom 1917-1998
  Obituary **1999**:1
Brennan, William 1906-1997
  Obituary **1997**:4
Breyer, Stephen Gerald 1938- **1994**:4
Brown, Willie 1934- **1996**:4
Brown, Willie L. 1934- **1985**:2
Burger, Warren E. 1907-1995
  Obituary **1995**:4
Burnison, Chantal Simone
  1950(?)- **1988**:3
Campbell, Kim 1947- **1993**:4
Cantrell, Ed
  Brief entry **1985**:3
Carter, Stephen L. **2008**:2
Casey, William 1913-1987
  Obituary **1987**:3
Casper, Gerhard 1937- **1993**:1
Chase, Debra Martin 1956- **2009**:1
Clark, Marcia 1954(?)- **1995**:1

Clinton, Bill 1946- **1992**:1
Clinton, Hillary Rodham
  1947- **1993**:2
Cochran, Johnnie 1937- **1996**:1
Colby, William E. 1920-1996
  Obituary **1996**:4
Cuomo, Mario 1932- **1992**:2
Darden, Christopher 1957(?)- **1996**:4
Dees, Morris 1936- **1992**:1
del Ponte, Carla 1947- **2001**:1
Dershowitz, Alan 1938(?)- **1992**:1
Deutch, John 1938- **1996**:4
Dole, Elizabeth Hanford
  1936- **1990**:1
Dukakis, Michael 1933- **1988**:3
Eagleson, Alan 1933- **1987**:4
Ehrlichman, John 1925-1999
  Obituary **1999**:3
Ervin, Sam 1896-1985
  Obituary **1985**:2
Estrich, Susan 1953- **1989**:1
Fairstein, Linda 1948(?)- **1991**:1
Fehr, Donald 1948- **1987**:2
Fieger, Geoffrey 1950- **2001**:3
Fitzgerald, Patrick 1960- **2006**:4
Florio, James J. 1937- **1991**:2
Foster, Vincent 1945(?)-1993
  Obituary **1994**:1
France, Johnny
  Brief entry **1987**:1
Freeh, Louis J. 1950- **1994**:2
Fulbright, J. William 1905-1995
  Obituary **1995**:3
Furman, Rosemary
  Brief entry **1986**:4
Garrison, Jim 1922-1992
  Obituary **1993**:2
Ginsburg, Ruth Bader 1933- **1993**:4
Giuliani, Rudolph 1944- **1994**:2
Glasser, Ira 1938- **1989**:1
Gore, Albert, Sr. 1907-1998
  Obituary **1999**:2
Grisham, John 1955- **1994**:4
Harvard, Beverly 1950- **1995**:2
Hayes, Robert M. 1952- **1986**:3
Hill, Anita 1956- **1994**:1
Hills, Carla 1934- **1990**:3
Hirschhorn, Joel
  Brief entry **1986**:1
Hoffa, Jim, Jr. 1941- **1999**:2
Hyatt, Joel 1950- **1985**:3
Ireland, Patricia 1946(?)- **1992**:2
Ito, Lance 1950(?)- **1995**:3
Janklow, Morton 1930- **1989**:3
Kennedy, John F., Jr.
  1960-1999 **1990**:1
  Obituary **1999**:4
Kennedy, Weldon 1938- **1997**:3
Kunstler, William 1919-1995
  Obituary **1996**:1
Kunstler, William 1920(?)- **1992**:3
Kurzban, Ira 1949- **1987**:2
Lee, Henry C. 1938- **1997**:1
Lee, Martin 1938- **1998**:2
Lewis, Loida Nicolas 1942- **1998**:3
Lewis, Reginald F. 1942-1993 **1988**:4
  Obituary **1993**:3
Lightner, Candy 1946- **1985**:1
Liman, Arthur 1932- **1989**:4
Lipsig, Harry H. 1901- **1985**:1
Lipton, Martin 1931- **1987**:3
MacKinnon, Catharine 1946- **1993**:2

Marshall, Thurgood 1908-1993
  Obituary **1993**:3
McCloskey, James 1944(?)- **1993**:1
Mitchell, George J. 1933- **1989**:3
Mitchell, John 1913-1988
  Obituary **1989**:2
Mitchelson, Marvin 1928- **1989**:2
Morrison, Trudi
  Brief entry **1986**:2
Nader, Ralph 1934- **1989**:4
Napolitano, Janet 1957- **1997**:1
Neal, James Foster 1929- **1986**:2
O'Connor, Sandra Day 1930- **1991**:1
O'Leary, Hazel 1937- **1993**:4
O'Steen, Van
  Brief entry **1986**:3
Panetta, Leon 1938- **1995**:1
Pirro, Jeanine 1951- **1998**:2
Powell, Lewis F. 1907-1998
  Obituary **1999**:1
Puccio, Thomas P. 1944- **1986**:4
Quayle, Dan 1947- **1989**:2
Raines, Franklin 1949- **1997**:4
Ramaphosa, Cyril 1953- **1988**:2
Ramo, Roberta Cooper 1942- **1996**:1
Rehnquist, William H. 1924- **2001**:2
Reno, Janet 1938- **1993**:3
Rothwax, Harold 1930- **1996**:3
Scalia, Antonin 1936- **1988**:2
Scheck, Barry 1949- **2000**:4
Schily, Otto
  Brief entry **1987**:4
Sheehan, Daniel P. 1945(?)- **1989**:1
Sheindlin, Judith 1942(?)- **1999**:1
Sirica, John 1904-1992
  Obituary **1993**:2
Skinner, Sam 1938- **1992**:3
Slater, Rodney E. 1955- **1997**:4
Slotnick, Barry
  Brief entry **1987**:4
Souter, David 1939- **1991**:3
Spitzer, Eliot 1959- **2007**:2
Starr, Kenneth 1946- **1998**:3
Steinberg, Leigh 1949- **1987**:3
Stern, David 1942- **1991**:4
Stewart, Potter 1915-1985
  Obituary **1986**:1
Strauss, Robert 1918- **1991**:4
Tagliabue, Paul 1940- **1990**:2
Thomas, Clarence 1948- **1992**:2
Thompson, Fred 1942- **1998**:2
Tribe, Laurence H. 1941- **1988**:1
Vincent, Fay 1938- **1990**:2
Violet, Arlene 1943- **1985**:3
Wapner, Joseph A. 1919- **1987**:1
Watson, Elizabeth 1949- **1991**:2
White, Byron 1917-2002
  Obituary **2003**:3
Williams, Edward Bennett 1920-1988
  Obituary **1988**:4
Williams, Willie L. 1944(?)- **1993**:1
Wilson, Bertha
  Brief entry **1986**:1

**MUSIC**
Aaliyah 1979-2001 **2001**:3
Abdul, Paula 1962- **1990**:3
Ackerman, Will 1949- **1987**:4
Acuff, Roy 1903-1992
  Obituary **1993**:2
Adams, Yolanda 1961- **2008**:2
Adele 1988- **2009**:4

AFI **2007**:3

Aguilera, Christina 1980- **2000**:4

Albert, Stephen 1941- **1986**:1

Allen, Peter 1944-1992

    Obituary **1993**:1

Alsop, Marin 1956- **2008**:3

Ames, Roger 1950(?)- **2005**:2

Amos, Tori 1963- **1995**:1

Anderson, Marion 1897-1993

    Obituary **1993**:4

Andrews, Julie 1935- **1996**:1

Andrews, Maxene 1916-1995

    Obituary **1996**:2

Anthony, Marc 1969- **2000**:3

Apple, Fiona 1977- **2006**:3

Arlen, Harold 1905-1986

    Obituary **1986**:3

Arnaz, Desi 1917-1986

    Obituary **1987**:1

Arnold, Eddy 1918-2008

    Obituary **2009**:2

Arrau, Claudio 1903-1991

    Obituary **1992**:1

Arrested Development **1994**:2

Ashanti 1980- **2004**:1

Astaire, Fred 1899-1987

    Obituary **1987**:4

Autry, Gene 1907-1998

    Obituary **1999**:1

Backstreet Boys **2001**:3

Badu, Erykah 1971- **2000**:4

Baez, Joan 1941- **1998**:3

Bailey, Pearl 1918-1990

    Obituary **1991**:1

Baker, Anita 1958- **1987**:4

Bangalter, Thomas 1975-. See Daft Punk

Barenboim, Daniel 1942- **2001**:1

Barrett, Syd 1946-2006

    Obituary **2007**:3

Bartoli, Cecilia 1966- **1994**:1

Basie, Count 1904(?)-1984

    Obituary **1985**:1

Battle, Kathleen 1948- **1998**:1

Beastie Boys, The **1999**:1

Becaud, Gilbert 1927-2001

    Obituary **2003**:1

Beck 1970- **2000**:2

Bee Gees, The **1997**:4

Benatar, Pat 1953- **1986**:1

Bennett, Tony 1926- **1994**:4

Bentley, Dierks 1975- **2007**:3

Berio, Luciano 1925-2003

    Obituary **2004**:2

Berlin, Irving 1888-1989

    Obituary **1990**:1

Bernhard, Sandra 1955(?)- **1989**:4

Bernstein, Elmer 1922-2004

    Obituary **2005**:4

Bernstein, Leonard 1918-1990

    Obituary **1991**:1

Berry, Chuck 1926- **2001**:2

Beyonce 1981- **2009**:3

Bjork 1965- **1996**:1

Black Eyed Peas **2006**:2

Blades, Ruben 1948- **1998**:2

Blakey, Art 1919-1990

    Obituary **1991**:1

Blige, Mary J. 1971- **1995**:3

Bolton, Michael 1953(?)- **1993**:2

Bon Jovi, Jon 1962- **1987**:4

Bono 1960- **1988**:4

Bono, Sonny 1935-1998 **1992**:2

    Obituary **1998**:2

Borge, Victor 1909-2000

    Obituary **2001**:3

Botstein, Leon 1946- **1985**:3

Bowie, David 1947- **1998**:2

Bowles, Paul 1910-1999

    Obituary **2000**:3

Boxcar Willie 1931-1999

    Obituary **1999**:4

Boyz II Men **1995**:1

Brandy 1979- **1996**:4

Branson, Richard 1951- **1987**:1

Braxton, Toni 1967- **1994**:3

Brooks, Garth 1962- **1992**:1

Brown, James 1928(?)- **1991**:4

Brown, Les 1912-2001

    Obituary **2001**:3

Brown, Ruth 1928-2006

    Obituary **2008**:1

Bruni, Carla 1967- **2009**:3

Buckley, Jeff 1966-1997

    Obituary **1997**:4

Buffett, Jimmy 1946- **1999**:3

Bush, Kate 1958- **1994**:3

Butterfield, Paul 1942-1987

    Obituary **1987**:3

Cage, John 1912-1992

    Obituary **1993**:1

Calloway, Cab 1908-1994

    Obituary **1995**:2

Campbell, Erica 1972-. See Mary Mary

Campbell, Tina 1972-. See Mary Mary

Cannon, Nick 1980- **2006**:4

Cardigans, The **1997**:4

Carey, Mariah 1970(?)- **1991**:3

Carlisle, Belinda 1958- **1989**:3

Carpenter, Mary-Chapin 1958(?)- **1994**:1

Carreras, Jose 1946- **1995**:2

Carter, Benny 1907-2003

    Obituary **2004**:3

Carter, Nell 1948-2003

    Obituary **2004**:2

Carter, Ron 1937- **1987**:3

Cash, Johnny 1932- **1995**:3

Cash, June Carter 1929-2003

    Obituary **2004**:2

Castellucci, Cecil 1969- **2008**:3

Cerovsek, Corey

    Brief entry **1987**:4

Chapman, Tracy 1964- **1989**:2

Charles, Ray 1930-2004

    Obituary **2005**:3

Cheatham, Adolphus Doc 1905-1997

    Obituary **1997**:4

Cher 1946- **1993**:1

Chesney, Kenny 1968- **2008**:2

Clapton, Eric 1945- **1993**:3

Clarke, Stanley 1951- **1985**:4

Clarkson, Kelly 1982- **2003**:3

Cleveland, James 1932(?)-1991

    Obituary **1991**:3

Cliburn, Van 1934- **1995**:1

Clooney, Rosemary 1928-2002

    Obituary **2003**:4

Cobain, Kurt 1967-1944

    Obituary **1994**:3

Coldplay **2004**:4

Cole, Natalie 1950- **1992**:4

Collins, Albert 1932-1993

    Obituary **1994**:2

Combs, Sean Puffy 1970- **1998**:4

Como, Perry 1912-2001

    Obituary **2002**:2

Connick, Harry, Jr. 1967- **1991**:1

Coolio 1963- **1996**:4

Copland, Aaron 1900-1990

    Obituary **1991**:2

Coppola, Carmine 1910-1991

    Obituary **1991**:4

Corea, Chick 1941- **1986**:3

Costello, Elvis 1954(?)- **1994**:4

Cowell, Simon 1959- **2003**:4

Crawford, Michael 1942- **1994**:2

Cray, Robert 1953- **1988**:2

Crosby, David 1941- **2000**:4

Crothers, Scatman 1910-1986

    Obituary **1987**:1

Crow, Sheryl 1964- **1995**:2

Crowe, Russell 1964- **2000**:4

Cruz, Celia 1925-2003

    Obituary **2004**:3

Cugat, Xavier 1900-1990

    Obituary **1991**:2

Cyrus, Billy Ray 1961(?)- **1993**:1

Cyrus, Miley 1992- **2008**:3

Daft Punk 1975- **2009**:4

D'Arby, Terence Trent 1962- **1988**:4

Darling, Erik 1933-2008

    Obituary **2009**:4

Davis, Miles 1926-1991

    Obituary **1992**:2

Davis, Sammy, Jr. 1925-1990

    Obituary **1990**:4

Day, Dennis 1917-1988

    Obituary **1988**:4

Dean, Laura 1945- **1989**:4

de Homem-Christo, Guy-Manuel 1975-. See Daft Punk

Dekker, Desmond 1941-2006

    Obituary **2007**:2

Denver, John 1943-1997

    Obituary **1998**:1

de Passe, Suzanne 1946(?)- **1990**:4

Destiny's Child **2001**:3

Diddley, Bo 1928-2008

    Obituary **2009**:3

Dido 1971- **2004**:4

DiFranco, Ani 1970(?)- **1997**:1

Di Meola, Al 1954- **1986**:4

Dimitrova, Ghena 1941- **1987**:1

Dion, Celine 1970(?)- **1995**:3

Dixie Chicks **2001**:2

Doherty, Denny 1940-2007

    Obituary **2008**:2

Dolenz, Micky 1945- **1986**:4

Domingo, Placido 1941- **1993**:2

Dorati, Antal 1906-1988

    Obituary **1989**:2

Dorsey, Thomas A. 1899-1993

    Obituary **1993**:3

Douglas, Mike 1925-2006

    Obituary **2007**:4

Dr. Demento 1941- **1986**:1

Dr. Dre 1965(?)- **1994**:3

Duff, Hilary 1987- **2004**:4

Duncan, Todd 1903-1998

    Obituary **1998**:3

Dupri, Jermaine 1972- **1999**:1

Duran Duran **2005**:3

Dylan, Bob 1941- **1998**:1

Eazy-E 1963(?)-1995
  Obituary **1995**:3
Eckstine, Billy 1914-1993
  Obituary **1993**:4
Edmonds, Kenneth Babyface
  1958(?)- **1995**:3
Eldridge, Roy 1911-1989
  Obituary **1989**:3
Elliott, Missy 1971- **2003**:4
Eminem 1974- **2001**:2
Eno, Brian 1948- **1986**:2
Entwistle, John 1944-2002
  Obituary **2003**:3
En Vogue **1994**:1
Enya 1962(?)- **1992**:3
Ertegun, Ahmet 1923- **1986**:3
Esquivel, Juan 1918- **1996**:2
Estefan, Gloria **1991**:4
Etheridge, Melissa 1961(?)- **1995**:4
Eve 1978- **2004**:3
Everything But The Girl **1996**:4
Falco
  Brief entry **1987**:2
Farrell, Perry 1960- **1992**:2
Fender, Leo 1909-1991
  Obituary **1992**:1
Fitzgerald, Ella 1917-1996
  Obituary **1996**:4
Flavor Flav 1959- **2007**:3
Fleming, Renee **2001**:4
Fogelberg, Dan 1951-2007
  Obituary **2009**:1
Foo Fighters **2006**:2
Ford, Tennessee Ernie 1919-1991
  Obituary **1992**:2
Foster, David 1950(?)- **1988**:2
Franklin, Aretha 1942- **1998**:3
Franklin, Melvin 1942-1995
  Obituary **1995**:3
Fuller, Simon 1960- **2008**:2
Furtado, Nelly 1978- **2007**:2
Garbage **2002**:3
Garcia, Jerry 1942-1995 **1988**:3
  Obituary **1996**:1
Geffen, David 1943- **1985**:3
Geldof, Bob 1954(?)- **1985**:3
Getz, Stan 1927-1991
  Obituary **1991**:4
Gibb, Andy 1958-1988
  Obituary **1988**:3
Gifford, Kathie Lee 1953- **1992**:2
Gift, Roland 1960(?)- **1990**:2
Gill, Vince 1957- **1995**:2
Gillespie, Dizzy 1917-1993
  Obituary **1993**:2
Glass, Philip 1937- **1991**:4
Goodman, Benny 1909-1986
  Obituary **1986**:3
Goody, Sam 1904-1991
  Obituary **1992**:1
Gordon, Dexter 1923-1990 **1987**:1
Gore, Tipper 1948- **1985**:4
Goulet, Robert 1933-2007
  Obituary **2008**:4
Graham, Bill 1931-1991 **1986**:4
  Obituary **1992**:2
Grant, Amy 1961(?)- **1985**:4
Grappelli, Stephane 1908-1997
  Obituary **1998**:1
Gray, David 1970- **2001**:4
Gray, Macy 1970(?)- **2002**:1
Grebenshikov, Boris 1953- **1990**:1

Green Day **1995**:4
Greenwald, Julie 1970- **2008**:1
Groban, Josh 1981- **2009**:1
Grusin, Dave
  Brief entry **1987**:2
Guccione, Bob, Jr. 1956- **1991**:4
Guest, Christopher 1948- **2004**:2
Hammer, Jan 1948- **1987**:3
Hammer, M. C. **1991**:2
Hammond, John 1910-1987
  Obituary **1988**:2
Hampton, Lionel 1908-2002
  Obituary **2003**:4
Hancock, Herbie 1940- **1985**:1
Harris, Emmylou 1947- **1991**:3
Harrison, George 1943-2001
  Obituary **2003**:1
Harry, Deborah 1945- **1990**:1
Hart, Mary
  Brief entry **1988**:1
Hart, Mickey 1944(?)- **1991**:2
Harvey, Polly Jean 1970(?)- **1995**:4
Hawkins, Screamin' Jay 1929-1999
  Obituary **2000**:3
Hayes, Isaac 1942- **1998**:4
Heard, J.C. 1917-1988
  Obituary **1989**:1
Heid, Bill
  Brief entry **1987**:2
Heifetz, Jascha 1901-1987
  Obituary **1988**:2
Helfgott, David 1937(?)- **1997**:2
Helms, Bobby 1936-1997
  Obituary **1997**:4
Hewitt, Jennifer Love 1979- **1999**:2
Hill, Andrew 1931-2007
  Obituary **2008**:3
Hill, Faith 1967- **2000**:1
Hill, Lauryn 1975- **1999**:3
Hinton, Milt 1910-2000
  Obituary **2001**:3
Hirt, Al 1922-1999
  Obituary **1999**:4
Ho, Don 1930-2007
  Obituary **2008**:2
Hoffs, Susanna 1962(?)- **1988**:2
Hooker, John Lee 1917- **1998**:1
  Obituary **2002**:3
Hootie and the Blowfish **1995**:4
Horne, Lena 1917- **1998**:4
Hornsby, Bruce 1954(?)- **1989**:3
Horovitz, Adam 1968(?)- **1988**:3
Horowitz, Vladimir 1903-1989
  Obituary **1990**:1
Houston, Cissy 1933- **1999**:3
Houston, Whitney 1963- **1986**:3
Hubbard, Freddie 1938- **1988**:4
Hudson, Jennifer 1981- **2008**:1
Hutchence, Michael 1960-1997
  Obituary **1998**:1
Hynde, Chrissie 1951- **1991**:1
Ice Cube 1969- **1999**:2
Ice-T **1992**:3
Iglesias, Enrique 1975- **2000**:1
Indigo Girls **1994**:4
Iovine, Jimmy 1953- **2006**:3
Ives, Burl 1909-1995
  Obituary **1995**:4
Jackson, Alan 1958- **2003**:1
Jackson, Cordell 1923- **1992**:4
Jackson, Janet 1966(?)- **1990**:4
Jackson, Michael 1958- **1996**:2

James, Etta 1938- **1995**:2
James, Rick 1948-2004
  Obituary **2005**:4
Jarrett, Keith 1945- **1992**:4
Jay-Z 1970- **2006**:1
Jennings, Waylon 1937-2002
  Obituary **2003**:2
Jewel 1974- **1999**:2
Joel, Billy 1949- **1994**:3
John, Elton 1947- **1995**:4
Johnson, Jack 1975- **2006**:4
Jonas Brothers **2008**:4
Jones, Etta 1928-2001
  Obituary **2002**:4
Jones, Jenny 1946- **1998**:2
Jones, Norah 1979- **2004**:1
Jones, Quincy 1933- **1990**:4
Jones, Tom 1940- **1993**:4
Juanes 1972- **2004**:4
Kaye, Sammy 1910-1987
  Obituary **1987**:4
Kelly, R. 1968- **1997**:3
Kendricks, Eddie 1939-1992
  Obituary **1993**:2
Kenny G 1957(?)- **1994**:4
Keys, Alicia 1981- **2006**:1
Kid Rock 1972- **2001**:1
Kilmer, Val **1991**:4
King, Coretta Scott 1927- **1999**:3
Knopfler, Mark 1949- **1986**:2
Kravitz, Lenny 1964(?)- **1991**:1
Kronos Quartet **1993**:1
Kurzweil, Raymond 1948- **1986**:3
Kyser, Kay 1906(?)-1985
  Obituary **1985**:3
Lachey, Nick and Jessica
  Simpson **2004**:4
Lane, Burton 1912-1997
  Obituary **1997**:2
Lane, Ronnie 1946-1997
  Obituary **1997**:4
Lang, K.D. 1961- **1988**:4
Lanois, Daniel 1951- **1991**:1
Larson, Jonathan 1961(?)-1996
  Obituary **1997**:2
Lauper, Cyndi 1953- **1985**:1
Lavigne, Avril 1984- **2005**:2
Lee, Peggy 1920-2002
  Obituary **2003**:1
Legend, John 1978- **2007**:1
Lennox, Annie 1954- **1985**:4
Levine, James 1943- **1992**:3
Lewis, Henry 1932-1996
  Obituary **1996**:3
Lewis, Huey 1951- **1987**:3
Lewis, John 1920-2001
  Obituary **2002**:1
Liberace 1919-1987
  Obituary **1987**:2
Ligeti, Gyorgy 1923-2006
  Obituary **2007**:3
Lil Wayne 1982- **2009**:3
Living Colour **1993**:3
LL Cool J 1968- **1998**:2
Lloyd Webber, Andrew 1948- **1989**:1
Loewe, Frederick 1901-1988
  Obituary **1988**:2
Lohan, Lindsay 1986- **2005**:3
Lopes, Lisa 1971-2002
  Obituary **2003**:3
Lords, Traci 1968- **1995**:4
Love, Courtney 1964(?)- **1995**:1

Loveless, Patty 1957- **1998**:2
Lovett, Lyle 1958(?)- **1994**:1
Ludacris 1977- **2007**:4
Lynn, Loretta 1935(?)- **2001**:1
MacRae, Gordon 1921-1986
    Obituary **1986**:2
Madonna 1958- **1985**:2
Makeba, Miriam 1934- **1989**:2
Mancini, Henry 1924-1994
    Obituary **1994**:4
Manson, Marilyn 1969- **1999**:4
Marky Mark 1971- **1993**:3
Marley, Ziggy 1968- **1990**:4
Maroon 5 **2008**:1
Marsalis, Branford 1960- **1988**:3
Marsalis, Wynton 1961- **1997**:4
Martin, Dean 1917-1995
    Obituary **1996**:2
Martin, Dean Paul 1952(?)-1987
    Obituary **1987**:3
Martin, Ricky 1971- **1999**:4
Mary Mary 1972- **2009**:4
Master P 1970- **1999**:4
Masur, Kurt 1927- **1993**:4
Matthews, Dave 1967- **1999**:3
Mayer, John 1977- **2007**:4
McCartney, Linda 1942-1998
    Obituary **1998**:4
McCartney, Paul 1942- **2002**:4
McDuffie, Robert 1958- **1990**:2
McEntire, Reba 1954- **1987**:3
McFerrin, Bobby 1950- **1989**:1
McGraw, Tim 1966- **2000**:3
McLachlan, Sarah 1968- **1998**:4
McMurtry, James 1962- **1990**:2
McRae, Carmen 1920(?)-1994
    Obituary **1995**:2
Mehta, Zubin 1938(?)- **1994**:3
Mendoza, Lydia 1916-2007
    Obituary **2009**:1
Menuhin, Yehudi 1916-1999
    Obituary **1999**:3
Merchant, Natalie 1963- **1996**:3
Mercury, Freddie 1946-1991
    Obituary **1992**:2
Metallica **2004**:2
Michael, George 1963- **1989**:2
Michelangeli, Arturo Benedetti
    1920- **1988**:2
Midler, Bette 1945- **1989**:4
Miller, Roger 1936-1992
    Obituary **1993**:2
Minogue, Kylie 1968- **2003**:4
Mintz, Shlomo 1957- **1986**:2
Mitchell, Joni 1943- **1991**:4
Moby 1965- **2000**:1
Monica 1980- **2004**:2
Monroe, Bill 1911-1996
    Obituary **1997**:1
Montand, Yves 1921-1991
    Obituary **1992**:2
Montoya, Carlos 1903-1993
    Obituary **1993**:4
Moog, Robert 1934-2005
    Obituary **2006**:4
Moore, Dudley 1935-2002
    Obituary **2003**:2
Moore, Mandy 1984- **2004**:2
Morissette, Alanis 1974- **1996**:2
Morris, Doug 1938- **2005**:1
Morrison, Sterling 1942-1995
    Obituary **1996**:1

Morrissey 1959- **2005**:2
Mos Def 1973- **2005**:4
Mottola, Tommy 1949- **2002**:1
Mutter, Anne-Sophie 1963- **1990**:3
Nas 1973- **2009**:2
Ne-Yo 1982- **2009**:4
Nelson, Rick 1940-1985
    Obituary **1986**:1
Nelson, Willie 1933- **1993**:4
New Kids on the Block **1991**:2
Newton-John, Olivia 1948- **1998**:4
Nickelback **2007**:2
Nilsson, Birgit 1918-2005
    Obituary **2007**:1
Nirvana **1992**:4
No Doubt **1997**:3
Norrington, Roger 1934- **1989**:4
North, Alex 1910- **1986**:3
Notorious B.I.G. 1973(?)-1997
    Obituary **1997**:3
'N Sync **2001**:4
Nyro, Laura 1947-1997
    Obituary **1997**:3
Oasis **1996**:3
O'Connor, Sinead 1967- **1990**:4
O'Day, Anita 1919-2006
    Obituary **2008**:1
Ono, Yoko 1933- **1989**:2
Orbison, Roy 1936-1988
    Obituary **1989**:2
Ormandy, Eugene 1899-1985
    Obituary **1985**:2
Osborne, Joan 1962- **1996**:4
Osbournes, The **2003**:4
Ostin, Mo 1927- **1996**:2
OutKast **2004**:4
Owens, Buck 1929-2006
    Obituary **2007**:2
Paisley, Brad 1972- **2008**:3
Palmer, Robert 1949-2003
    Obituary **2004**:4
Parker, Colonel Tom 1929-1997
    Obituary **1997**:2
Parton, Dolly 1946- **1999**:4
Pass, Joe 1929-1994
    Obituary **1994**:4
Pastorius, Jaco 1951-1987
    Obituary **1988**:1
Pavarotti, Luciano 1935- **1997**:4
Payton, Lawrence 1938(?)-1997
    Obituary **1997**:4
Pearl, Minnie 1912-1996
    Obituary **1996**:3
Pearl Jam **1994**:2
Perkins, Carl 1932-1998 **1998**:2
Peterson, Oscar 1925-2007
    Obituary **2009**:1
Petty, Tom 1952- **1988**:1
Phair, Liz 1967- **1995**:3
Phillips, John 1935-2001
    Obituary **2002**:1
Phillips, Sam 1923-2003
    Obituary **2004**:4
Pickett, Wilson 1941-2006
    Obituary **2007**:1
Pilatus, Robert 1966(?)-1998
    Obituary **1998**:3
Pink 1979- **2004**:3
Pittman, Robert W. 1953- **1985**:1
Pogorelich, Ivo 1958- **1986**:4
Ponty, Jean-Luc 1942- **1985**:4
Potts, Paul 1970- **2009**:1

Presley, Lisa Marie 1968- **2004**:3
Preston, Billy 1946-2006
    Obituary **2007**:3
Preston, Robert 1918-1987
    Obituary **1987**:3
Pride, Charley 1938(?)- **1998**:1
Prince 1958- **1995**:3
Public Enemy **1992**:1
Puente, Tito 1923-2000
    Obituary **2000**:4
Queen Latifah 1970(?)- **1992**:2
Quinn, Martha 1959- **1986**:4
Rabbitt, Eddie 1941-1998
    Obituary **1998**:4
Radiohead **2009**:3
Raffi 1948- **1988**:1
Raitt, Bonnie 1949- **1990**:2
Ramone, Joey 1951-2001
    Obituary **2002**:2
Rampal, Jean-Pierre 1922- **1989**:2
Rascal Flatts **2007**:1
Rashad, Phylicia 1948- **1987**:3
Raskin, Jef 1943(?)- **1997**:4
Rattle, Simon 1955- **1989**:4
Raven 1985- **2005**:1
Rawls, Lou 1933-2006
    Obituary **2007**:1
Red Hot Chili Peppers **1993**:1
Redman, Joshua 1969- **1999**:2
Reed, Dean 1939(?)-1986
    Obituary **1986**:3
Reese, Della 1931- **1999**:2
Reznor, Trent 1965- **2000**:2
Rich, Buddy 1917-1987
    Obituary **1987**:3
Rich, Charlie 1932-1995
    Obituary **1996**:1
Richards, Keith 1943- **1993**:3
Riddle, Nelson 1921-1985
    Obituary **1985**:4
Rihanna 1988- **2008**:4
Rimes, LeeAnn 1982- **1997**:4
Robbins, Jerome 1918-1998
    Obituary **1999**:1
Robinson, Earl 1910(?)-1991
    Obituary **1992**:1
Roedy, Bill 1949(?)- **2003**:2
Rogers, Roy 1911-1998
    Obituary **1998**:4
Rollins, Henry 1961- **2007**:3
Rose, Axl 1962(?)- **1992**:1
Rostropovich, Mstislav 1927-2007
    Obituary **2008**:3
Ruffin, David 1941-1991
    Obituary **1991**:4
RuPaul 1961(?)- **1996**:1
Sade 1959- **1993**:2
Sagal, Katey 1954- **2005**:2
Sainte-Marie, Buffy 1941- **2000**:1
Salerno-Sonnenberg, Nadja
    1961(?)- **1988**:4
Salonga, Lea 1971- **2003**:3
Santana, Carlos 1947- **2000**:2
Satriani, Joe 1957(?)- **1989**:3
Scholz, Tom 1949- **1987**:2
Schwarzkopf, Elisabeth 1915-2006
    Obituary **2007**:3
Seal 1962(?)- **1994**:4
Seger, Bob 1945- **1987**:1
Segovia, Andreaas 1893-1987
    Obituary **1987**:3
Selena 1971-1995

Obituary **1995**:4
Serkin, Rudolf 1903-1991
  Obituary **1992**:1
Shaffer, Paul 1949- **1987**:1
Shakira 1977- **2002**:3
Shakur, Tupac 1971-1996
  Obituary **1997**:1
Shaw, Artie 1910-2004
  Obituary **2006**:1
Sherman, Russell 1930- **1987**:4
Shocked, Michelle 1963(?)- **1989**:4
Shore, Dinah 1917-1994
  Obituary **1994**:3
Simmons, Russell and Kimora Lee
  **2003**:2
Simon, Paul 1942(?)- **1992**:2
Simone, Nina 1933-2003
  Obituary **2004**:2
Simpson-Wentz, Ashlee 1984- **2009**:1
Sinatra, Frank 1915-1998
  Obituary **1998**:4
Sinopoli, Giuseppe 1946- **1988**:1
Smith, Jimmy 1928-2005
  Obituary **2006**:2
Smith, Kate 1907(?)-1986
  Obituary **1986**:3
Smith, Will 1968- **1997**:2
Snider, Dee 1955- **1986**:1
Snoop Doggy Dogg 1972(?)- **1995**:2
Snow, Hank 1914-1999
  Obituary **2000**:3
Solti, Georg 1912-1997
  Obituary **1998**:1
Sondheim, Stephen 1930- **1994**:4
Spears, Britney 1981- **2000**:3
Spector, Phil 1940- **1989**:1
Spice Girls **2008**:3
Springfield, Dusty 1939-1999
  Obituary **1999**:3
Stafford, Jo 1917-2008
  Obituary **2009**:3
Staples, Roebuck Pops 1915-2000
  Obituary **2001**:3
Stefani, Gwen 1969- **2005**:4
Stern, Isaac 1920-2001
  Obituary **2002**:4
Stewart, Rod 1945- **2007**:1
Sting 1951- **1991**:4
Stone, Joss 1987- **2006**:2
Strait, George 1952- **1998**:3
Streisand, Barbra 1942- **1992**:2
Strummer, Joe 1952-2002
  Obituary **2004**:1
Styne, Jule 1905-1994
  Obituary **1995**:1
Sugarland 1970- **2009**:2
Sun Ra 1914(?)-1993
  Obituary **1994**:1
Suzuki, Sin'ichi 1898-1998
  Obituary **1998**:3
Swift, Taylor 1989- **2009**:3
System of a Down **2006**:4
Szot, Paulo 1969- **2009**:3
T. I. 1980- **2008**:1
Tan Dun 1957- **2002**:1
Tesh, John 1952- **1996**:3
Thomas, Michael Tilson 1944- **1990**:3
Tiffany 1972- **1989**:1
Timbaland 1971- **2007**:4
Timberlake, Justin 1981- **2008**:4
TLC **1996**:1
Tone-Loc 1966- **1990**:3

Torme, Mel 1925-1999
  Obituary **1999**:4
Tosh, Peter 1944-1987
  Obituary **1988**:2
Travis, Randy 1959- **1988**:4
Tritt, Travis 1964(?)- **1995**:1
Tune, Tommy 1939- **1994**:2
Turner, Ike 1931-2007
  Obituary **2009**:1
Turner, Tina 1939- **2000**:3
Twain, Shania 1965- **1996**:3
Twitty, Conway 1933-1993
  Obituary **1994**:1
Tyner, Rob 1945(?)-1991
  Obituary **1992**:2
U2 **2002**:4
Uchida, Mitsuko 1949(?)- **1989**:3
Ullman, Tracey 1961- **1988**:3
Underwood, Carrie 1983- **2008**:1
Upshaw, Dawn 1960- **1991**:2
Urban, Keith 1967- **2006**:3
Usher 1979- **2005**:1
Valente, Benita 1934(?)- **1985**:3
Vandross, Luther 1951-2005
  Obituary **2006**:2
Van Halen, Edward 1957- **1985**:2
Vanilla Ice 1967(?)- **1991**:3
Vaughan, Sarah 1924-1990
  Obituary **1990**:3
Vaughan, Stevie Ray 1956(?)-1990
  Obituary **1991**:1
Vega, Suzanne 1959- **1988**:1
Vollenweider, Andreas 1953- **1985**:2
von Karajan, Herbert 1908-1989
  Obituary **1989**:4
von Trapp, Maria 1905-1987
  Obituary **1987**:3
Wagoner, Porter 1927-2007
  Obituary **2008**:4
Walker, Junior 1942(?)-1995
  Obituary **1996**:2
Washington, Grover, Jr. 1943- **1989**:1
Wasserman, Lew 1913-2002
  Obituary **2003**:3
Weintraub, Jerry 1937- **1986**:1
Wells, Mary 1943-1992
  Obituary **1993**:1
West, Dottie 1932-1991
  Obituary **1992**:2
West, Kanye 1977- **2006**:1
Wexler, Jerry 1917-2008
  Obituary **2009**:4
White, Barry 1944-2003
  Obituary **2004**:3
White Stripes, The **2006**:1
Williams, Joe 1918-1999
  Obituary **1999**:4
Williams, Pharrell 1973- **2005**:3
Williams, Vanessa L. 1963- **1999**:2
Willis, Bruce 1955- **1986**:4
Wilson, Brian 1942- **1996**:1
Wilson, Carl 1946-1998 **1998**:2
Wilson, Cassandra 1955- **1996**:3
Wilson, Gretchen 1970- **2006**:3
Winans, CeCe 1964- **2000**:1
Winehouse, Amy 1983- **2008**:1
Winston, George 1949(?)- **1987**:1
Winter, Paul 1939- **1990**:2
Womack, Lee Ann 1966- **2002**:1
Wright, Richard 1943-2008
  Obituary **2009**:4
Wynette, Tammy 1942-1998

Obituary **1998**:3
Wynonna 1964- **1993**:3
Xenakis, Iannis 1922-2001
  Obituary **2001**:4
Xzibit 1974- **2005**:4
Yankovic, Frank 1915-1998
  Obituary **1999**:2
Yankovic, Weird Al 1959- **1985**:4
Yearwood, Trisha 1964- **1999**:1
Yoakam, Dwight 1956- **1992**:4
Young, Neil 1945- **1991**:2
Zappa, Frank 1940-1993
  Obituary **1994**:2
Zevon, Warren 1947-2003
  Obituary **2004**:4
Zinnemann, Fred 1907-1997
  Obituary **1997**:3
Zwilich, Ellen 1939- **1990**:1

**POLITICS AND
GOVERNMENT--FOREIGN**
Abacha, Sani 1943- **1996**:3
Abbas, Mahmoud 1935- **2008**:4
Abdullah II, King 1962- **2002**:4
Adams, Gerald 1948- **1994**:1
Ahern, Bertie 1951- **1999**:3
Ahmadinejad, Mahmoud
  1956- **2007**:1
Akihito, Emperor of Japan 1933-
  **1990**:1
al-Abdullah, Rania 1970- **2001**:1
al-Assad, Bashar 1965- **2004**:2
al-Bashir, Omar 1944- **2009**:1
Albert, Prince of Monaco
  1958- **2006**:2
Albright, Madeleine 1937- **1994**:3
Amin, Idi 1925(?)-2003
  Obituary **2004**:4
Annan, Kofi 1938- **1999**:1
Aquino, Corazon 1933- **1986**:2
Arafat, Yasser 1929- **1989**:3
Arens, Moshe 1925- **1985**:1
Arias Sanchez, Oscar 1941- **1989**:3
Aristide, Jean-Bertrand 1953- **1991**:3
Assad, Hafez 1930-2000
  Obituary **2000**:4
Assad, Hafez al- 1930(?)- **1992**:1
Assad, Rifaat 1937(?)- **1986**:3
Astorga, Nora 1949(?)-1988 **1988**:2
Babangida, Ibrahim Badamosi
  1941- **1992**:4
Bachelet, Michelle 1951- **2007**:3
Badawi, Abdullah Ahmad
  1939- **2009**:3
Bakiyev, Kurmanbek 1949- **2007**:1
Balaguer, Joaquin 1907-2002
  Obituary **2003**:4
Banda, Hastings 1898- **1994**:3
Bandaranaike, Sirimavo 1916-2000
  Obituary **2001**:2
Barak, Ehud 1942- **1999**:4
Barbie, Klaus 1913-1991
  Obituary **1992**:2
Basescu, Traian 1951- **2006**:2
Begin, Menachem 1913-1992
  Obituary **1992**:3
Berger, Oscar 1946- **2004**:4
Berlusconi, Silvio 1936(?)- **1994**:4
Berri, Nabih 1939(?)- **1985**:2
Bhutto, Benazir 1953- **1989**:4
Biya, Paul 1933- **2006**:1
Blair, Tony 1953- **1996**:3

Bolkiah, Sultan Muda Hassanal 1946- **1985**:4

Botha, P. W. 1916-2006
Obituary **2008**:1

Bouchard, Lucien 1938- **1999**:2

Bourassa, Robert 1933-1996
Obituary **1997**:1

Bozize, Francois 1946- **2006**:3

Brandt, Willy 1913-1992
Obituary **1993**:2

Brown, Gordon 1951- **2008**:3

Brundtland, Gro Harlem 1939- **2000**:1

Buthelezi, Mangosuthu Gatsha 1928- **1989**:3

Campbell, Kim 1947- **1993**:4

Cardoso, Fernando Henrique 1931- **1996**:4

Castro, Fidel 1926- **1991**:4

Ceausescu, Nicolae 1918-1989
Obituary **1990**:2

Cedras, Raoul 1950- **1994**:4

Chaing Kai-Shek, Madame 1898-2003
Obituary **2005**:1

Chambas, Mohammed ibn 1950- **2003**:3

Chen Shui-bian 1950(?)- **2001**:2

Chernenko, Konstantin 1911-1985
Obituary **1985**:1

Chiluba, Frederick 1943- **1992**:3

Chirac, Jacques 1932- **1995**:4

Chissano, Joaquim 1939- **1987**:4

Chretien, Jean 1934- **1990**:4

Ciampi, Carlo Azeglio 1920- **2004**:3

Collor de Mello, Fernando 1949- **1992**:4

Colosio, Luis Donaldo 1950-1994 **1994**:3

Copps, Sheila 1952- **1986**:4

Correa, Rafael 1963- **2008**:1

Cresson, Edith 1934- **1992**:1

Cruz, Arturo 1923- **1985**:1

Dalai Lama 1935- **1989**:1

Deby, Idriss 1952- **2002**:2

de Hoop Scheffer, Jaap 1948- **2005**:1

de Klerk, F.W. 1936- **1990**:1

Delors, Jacques 1925- **1990**:2

Deng Xiaoping 1904-1997 **1995**:1
Obituary **1997**:3

de Pinies, Jamie
Brief entry **1986**:3

Devi, Phoolan 1955(?)- **1986**:1
Obituary **2002**:3

Dhlakama, Afonso 1953- **1993**:3

Doe, Samuel 1952-1990
Obituary **1991**:1

Doi, Takako
Brief entry **1987**:4

Dong, Pham Van 1906-2000
Obituary **2000**:4

Duarte, Jose Napoleon 1925-1990
Obituary **1990**:3

Dubinin, Yuri 1930- **1987**:4

Duhalde, Eduardo 1941- **2003**:3

Ecevit, Bulent 1925-2006
Obituary **2008**:1

Enkhbayar, Nambaryn 1958- **2007**:1

Fahd, King of Saudi Arabia 1923(?)-2005
Obituary **2006**:4

Ferguson, Sarah 1959- **1990**:3

Fernández, Leonel 1953- **2009**:2

Fernández de Kirchner, Cristina 1953- **2009**:1

Finnbogadoaattir, Vigdiaas
Brief entry **1986**:2

Fischer, Joschka 1948- **2005**:2

Fox, Vicente 1942- **2001**:1

Freij, Elias 1920- **1986**:4

Fujimori, Alberto 1938- **1992**:4

Galvin, Martin
Brief entry **1985**:3

Gandhi, Indira 1917-1984
Obituary **1985**:1

Gandhi, Rajiv 1944-1991
Obituary **1991**:4

Gandhi, Sonia 1947- **2000**:2

Garcia, Alan 1949- **2007**:4

Garcia, Amalia 1951- **2005**:3

Garneau, Marc 1949- **1985**:1

Gbagbo, Laurent 1945- **2003**:2

Ghali, Boutros Boutros 1922- **1992**:3

Gorbachev, Mikhail 1931- **1985**:2

Gorbachev, Raisa 1932-1999
Obituary **2000**:2

Gowda, H. D. Deve 1933- **1997**:1

Gromyko, Andrei 1909-1989
Obituary **1990**:2

Guebuza, Armando 1943- **2008**:4

Guelleh, Ismail Omar 1947- **2006**:2

Gul, Abdullah 1950- **2009**:4

Habash, George 1925(?)- **1986**:1

Habibie, Bacharuddin Jusuf 1936- **1999**:3

Halonen, Tarja 1943- **2006**:4

Hani, Chris 1942-1993
Obituary **1993**:4

Harper, Stephen J. 1959- **2007**:3

Harriman, Pamela 1920- **1994**:4

Harris, Michael Deane 1945- **1997**:2

Havel, Vaclav 1936- **1990**:3

Herzog, Chaim 1918-1997
Obituary **1997**:3

Hess, Rudolph 1894-1987
Obituary **1988**:1

Hillery, Patrick 1923-2008
Obituary **2009**:2

Hirohito, Emperor of Japan 1901-1989
Obituary **1989**:2

Honecker, Erich 1912-1994
Obituary **1994**:4

Hosokawa, Morihiro 1938- **1994**:1

Hua Guofeng 1921-2008
Obituary **2009**:4

Hu Jintao 1942- **2004**:1

Hume, John 1938- **1987**:1

Hussein, Saddam 1937- **1991**:1

Husseini, Faisal 1940- **1998**:4

Hussein I, King 1935-1999 **1997**:3
Obituary **1999**:3

Hu Yaobang 1915-1989
Obituary **1989**:4

Ilves, Toomas Hendrik 1953- **2007**:4

Izetbegovic, Alija 1925- **1996**:4

Jagdeo, Bharrat 1964- **2008**:1

Jenkins, Roy Harris 1920-2003
Obituary **2004**:1

Jiang Quing 1914-1991
Obituary **1992**:1

Jiang Zemin 1926- **1996**:1

Johnson, Pierre Marc 1946- **1985**:4

Juan Carlos I 1938- **1993**:1

Juliana 1909-2004
Obituary **2005**:3

Jumblatt, Walid 1949(?)- **1987**:4

Juneau, Pierre 1922- **1988**:3

Kabila, Joseph 1971- **2003**:2

Kabila, Laurent 1939- **1998**:1
Obituary **2001**:3

Kaczynski, Lech 1949- **2007**:2

Kagame, Paul 1957- **2001**:4

Kamel, Hussein 1954- **1996**:1

Karadzic, Radovan 1945- **1995**:3

Karamanlis, Costas 1956- **2009**:1

Karimov, Islam 1938- **2006**:3

Karzai, Hamid 1955(?)- **2002**:3

Kasyanov, Mikhail 1957- **2001**:1

Kekkonen, Urho 1900-1986
Obituary **1986**:4

Khatami, Mohammed 1943- **1997**:4

Khomeini, Ayatollah Ruhollah 1900(?)-1989
Obituary **1989**:4

Kibaki, Mwai 1931- **2003**:4

Kim Dae Jung 1925- **1998**:3

Kim Il Sung 1912-1994
Obituary **1994**:4

Kim Jong Il 1942- **1995**:2

King Hassan II 1929-1999
Obituary **2000**:1

Kohl, Helmut 1930- **1994**:1

Koizumi, Junichiro 1942- **2002**:1

Kostunica, Vojislav 1944- **2001**:1

Kouchner, Bernard 1939- **2005**:3

Kufuor, John Agyekum 1938- **2005**:4

Kyprianou, Spyros 1932-2002
Obituary **2003**:2

Lagos, Ricardo 1938- **2005**:3

Lalonde, Marc 1929- **1985**:1

Landsbergis, Vytautas 1932- **1991**:3

Lebed, Alexander 1950- **1997**:1

Le Duan 1908(?)-1986
Obituary **1986**:4

Le Duc Tho 1911-1990
Obituary **1991**:1

Lee, Martin 1938- **1998**:2

Lee Jong-Wook 1945- **2005**:1

Lee Myung-bak 1941- **2009**:2

Lee Teng-hui 1923- **2000**:1

Leaavesque, Reneaa
Obituary **1988**:1

Levy, David 1938- **1987**:2

Lewis, Stephen 1937- **1987**:2

Livingstone, Ken 1945- **1988**:3

Lon Nol
Obituary **1986**:1

Lukashenko, Alexander 1954- **2006**:4

Macapagal-Arroyo, Gloria 1947- **2001**:4

Machel, Samora 1933-1986
Obituary **1987**:1

Macmillan, Harold 1894-1986
Obituary **1987**:2

Major, John 1943- **1991**:2

Mandela, Nelson 1918- **1990**:3

Mandela, Winnie 1934- **1989**:3

Mara, Ratu Sir Kamisese 1920-2004
Obituary **2005**:3

Marcos, Ferdinand 1917-1989
Obituary **1990**:1

Martin, Paul 1938- **2004**:4

Masako, Crown Princess 1963- **1993**:4

Mas Canosa, Jorge 1939-1997 **1998**:2

Ma Ying-jeou 1950- **2009**:4
Mbeki, Thabo 1942- **1999**:4
McGuinness, Martin 1950(?)- **1985**:4
McLaughlin, Audrey 1936- **1990**:3
Medvedev, Dmitry 1965- **2009**:4
Megawati Sukarnoputri 1947- **2000**:1
Mesic, Stipe 1934- **2005**:4
Milosevic, Slobodan 1941- **1993**:2
Mitterrand, Francois 1916-1996
    Obituary **1996**:2
Miyazawa, Kiichi 1919- **1992**:2
Mobutu Sese Seko 1930-1997 **1993**:4
    Obituary **1998**:1
Mobutu Sese Seko 1930-1998
    Obituary **1998**:4
Moi, Daniel arap 1924- **1993**:2
Molotov, Vyacheslav Mikhailovich
    1890-1986
    Obituary **1987**:1
Morales, Evo 1959- **2007**:2
Mori, Yoshiro 1937- **2000**:4
Mubarak, Hosni 1928- **1991**:4
Mugabe, Robert 1924- **1988**:4
Mulroney, Brian 1939- **1989**:2
Museveni, Yoweri 1944- **2002**:1
Musharraf, Pervez 1943- **2000**:2
Nagako, Empress Dowager
    1903-2000
    Obituary **2001**:1
Nazarbayev, Nursultan 1940- **2006**:4
Netanyahu, Benjamin 1949- **1996**:4
Nidal, Abu 1937- **1987**:1
Niezabitowska, Malgorzata
    1949(?)- **1991**:3
Nujoma, Sam 1929- **1990**:4
Nyerere, Julius 1922(?)-1999
    Obituary **2000**:2
Obando, Miguel 1926- **1986**:4
Obasanjo, Olusegun 1937(?)- **2000**:2
Obuchi, Keizo 1937- **1999**:2
Obuchi, Keizo 1937-2000
    Obituary **2000**:4
Ocalan, Abdullah 1948(?)- **1999**:4
Olav, King of Norway 1903-1991
    Obituary **1991**:3
Ortega, Daniel 1945- **2008**:2
Palme, Olof 1927-1986
    Obituary **1986**:2
Papandreou, Andrea 1919-1996
    Obituary **1997**:1
Parizeau, Jacques 1930- **1995**:1
Pastrana, Andres 1954- **2002**:1
Paton, Alan 1903-1988
    Obituary **1988**:3
Patten, Christopher 1944- **1993**:3
Paz, Octavio 1914- **1991**:2
Peckford, Brian 1942- **1989**:1
Peres, Shimon 1923- **1996**:3
Perez, Carlos Andre 1922- **1990**:2
Perez de Cuellar, Javier 1920- **1991**:3
Peterson, David 1943- **1987**:1
Philby, Kim 1912-1988
    Obituary **1988**:3
Pinochet, Augusto 1915- **1999**:2
Pol Pot 1928-1998
    Obituary **1998**:4
Preaaval, Reneaa 1943- **1997**:2
Primakov, Yevgeny 1929- **1999**:3
Princess Margaret, Countess of
    Snowdon 1930-2002
    Obituary **2003**:2
Putin, Vladimir 1952- **2000**:3

Qaddhafi, Muammar 1942- **1998**:3
Queen Elizabeth the Queen Mother
    1900-2002
    Obituary **2003**:2
Rabin, Leah 1928-2000
    Obituary **2001**:2
Rabin, Yitzhak 1922-1995 **1993**:1
    Obituary **1996**:2
Rafsanjani, Ali Akbar Hashemi
    1934(?)- **1987**:3
Rahman, Sheik Omar Abdel-
    1938- **1993**:3
Rainier III, Prince of Monaco
    1923-2005
    Obituary **2006**:2
Ram, Jagjivan 1908-1986
    Obituary **1986**:4
Ramos, Fidel 1928- **1995**:2
Rao, P. V. Narasimha 1921- **1993**:2
Rasmussen, Anders Fogh 1953- **2006**
    :1
Ravalomanana, Marc 1950(?)- **2003**:1
Reisman, Simon 1919- **1987**:4
Robelo, Alfonso 1940(?)- **1988**:1
Robinson, Mary 1944- **1993**:1
Roh Moo-hyun 1946- **2005**:1
Rudd, Kevin 1957- **2009**:1
Rugova, Ibrahim 1944-2006
    Obituary **2007**:1
Saakashvili, Mikhail 1967- **2008**:4
Saleh, Ali Abdullah 1942- **2001**:3
Salinas, Carlos 1948- **1992**:1
Sanchez de Lozada, Gonzalo
    1930- **2004**:3
Sargsyan, Serzh 1954- **2009**:3
Sarkis, Elias 1924-1985
    Obituary **1985**:3
Sarkozy, Nicolas 1955- **2008**:4
Saro-Wiwa, Ken 1941-1995
    Obituary **1996**:2
Savimbi, Jonas 1934- **1986**:2
Schily, Otto
    Brief entry **1987**:4
Schroder, Gerhard 1944- **1999**:1
Shah, Gyanendra 1947- **2006**:1
Sharon, Ariel 1928- **2001**:4
Shipley, Jenny 1952- **1998**:3
Silva, Luiz Inacio Lula da
    1945- **2003**:4
Simpson, Wallis 1896-1986
    Obituary **1986**:3
Sirleaf, Ellen Johnson 1938- **2007**:3
Sisulu, Walter 1912-2003
    Obituary **2004**:2
Slovo, Joe 1926- **1989**:2
Smith, Ian 1919-2007
    Obituary **2009**:1
Staller, Ilona 1951- **1988**:3
Stoltenberg, Jens 1959- **2006**:4
Strauss, Robert 1918- **1991**:4
Stroessner, Alfredo 1912-2006
    Obituary **2007**:4
Suharto 1921-2008
    Obituary **2009**:2
Suu Kyi, Aung San 1945(?)- **1996**:2
Suzman, Helen 1917- **1989**:3
Tadic, Boris 1958- **2009**:3
Takeshita, Noboru 1924-2000
    Obituary **2001**:1
Tambo, Oliver 1917- **1991**:3
Terzi, Zehdi Labib 1924- **1985**:3
Thaksin Shinawatra 1949- **2005**:4

Thatcher, Margaret 1925- **1989**:2
Trajkovski, Boris 1956-2004
    Obituary **2005**:2
Treurnicht, Andries 1921- **1992**:2
Trimble, David 1944- **1999**:1
Trudeau, Pierre 1919-2000
    Obituary **2001**:1
Tudjman, Franjo 1922- **1996**:2
Tudjman, Franjo 1922-1999
    Obituary **2000**:2
Turabi, Hassan 1932(?)- **1995**:4
Turk, Danilo 1952- **2009**:3
Tymoshenko, Yulia 1960- **2009**:1
Uribe, Alvaro 1952- **2003**:3
Vajpayee, Atal Behari 1926- **1998**:4
Vander Zalm, William 1934- **1987**:3
Vazquez, Tabare 1940- **2006**:2
Verhofstadt, Guy 1953- **2006**:3
Wahid, Abdurrahman 1940- **2000**:3
Walesa, Lech 1943- **1991**:2
Wei Jingsheng 1950- **1998**:2
Weizman, Ezer 1924-2005
    Obituary **2006**:3
Werner, Ruth 1907-2000
    Obituary **2001**:1
Wickramasinghe, Ranil 1949- **2003**:2
William, Prince of Wales 1982- **2001**
    :3
Wilson, Bertha
    Brief entry **1986**:1
Wu Yi 1938- **2005**:2
Yar'Adua, Umaru 1951- **2008**:3
Ye Jianying 1897-1986
    Obituary **1987**:1
Yeltsin, Boris 1931- **1991**:1
Yushchenko, Viktor 1954- **2006**:1
Zedillo, Ernesto 1951- **1995**:1
Zeroual, Liamine 1951- **1996**:2
Zhao Ziyang 1919- **1989**:1
Zhirinovsky, Vladimir 1946- **1994**:2
Zia ul-Haq, Mohammad 1924-1988
    Obituary **1988**:4

**POLITICS AND GOVERNMENT--U.S.**
Abraham, Spencer 1952- **1991**:4
Abrams, Elliott 1948- **1987**:1
Abzug, Bella 1920-1998 **1998**:2
Achtenberg, Roberta **1993**:4
Agnew, Spiro Theodore 1918-1996
    Obituary **1997**:1
Ailes, Roger 1940- **1989**:3
Albright, Madeleine 1937- **1994**:3
Alexander, Lamar 1940- **1991**:2
Alioto, Joseph L. 1916-1998
    Obituary **1998**:3
Allen Jr., Ivan 1911-2003
    Obituary **2004**:3
Alvarez, Aida **1999**:2
Archer, Dennis 1942- **1994**:4
Armstrong, Anne 1927-2008
    Obituary **2009**:4
Ashcroft, John 1942- **2002**:4
Aspin, Les 1938-1995
    Obituary **1996**:1
Atwater, Lee 1951-1991 **1989**:4
    Obituary **1991**:4
Babbitt, Bruce 1938- **1994**:1
Baker, James A. III 1930- **1991**:2
Baldrige, Malcolm 1922-1987
    Obituary **1988**:1
Banks, Dennis J. 193- **1986**:4
Barry, Marion 1936- **1991**:1

Barshefsky, Charlene 1951(?)- **2000**:4
Bass, Karen 1953- **2009**:3
Beame, Abraham 1906-2001
    Obituary **2001**:4
Begaye, Kelsey 1950(?)- **1999**:3
Bennett, William 1943- **1990**:1
Benson, Ezra Taft 1899-1994
    Obituary **1994**:4
Bentsen, Lloyd 1921- **1993**:3
Berger, Sandy 1945- **2000**:1
Berle, Peter A.A.
    Brief entry **1987**:3
Bernanke, Ben 1953- **2008**:3
Biden, Joe 1942- **1986**:3
Boehner, John A. 1949- **2006**:4
Bonner, Robert 1942(?)- **2003**:4
Bono, Sonny 1935-1998 **1992**:2
    Obituary **1998**:2
Boxer, Barbara 1940- **1995**:1
Boyington, Gregory Pappy
    1912-1988
    Obituary **1988**:2
Bradley, Bill 1943- **2000**:2
Bradley, Tom 1917-1998
    Obituary **1999**:1
Brady, Sarah and James S. **1991**:4
Braun, Carol Moseley 1947- **1993**:1
Brazile, Donna 1959- **2001**:1
Bremer, L. Paul 1941- **2004**:2
Brennan, William 1906-1997
    Obituary **1997**:4
Brown, Edmund G., Sr. 1905-1996
    Obituary **1996**:3
Brown, Jerry 1938- **1992**:4
Brown, Ron 1941- **1990**:3
Brown, Ron 1941-1996
    Obituary **1996**:4
Brown, Willie 1934- **1996**:4
Brown, Willie L. 1934- **1985**:2
Browner, Carol M. 1955- **1994**:1
Buchanan, Pat 1938- **1996**:3
Bundy, McGeorge 1919-1996
    Obituary **1997**:1
Bundy, William P. 1917-2000
    Obituary **2001**:2
Bush, Barbara 1925- **1989**:3
Bush, George W., Jr. 1946- **1996**:4
Bush, Jeb 1953- **2003**:1
Caliguiri, Richard S. 1931-1988
    Obituary **1988**:3
Campbell, Ben Nighthorse
    1933- **1998**:1
Campbell, Bill **1997**:1
Card, Andrew H., Jr. 1947- **2003**:2
Carey, Ron 1936- **1993**:3
Carmona, Richard 1949- **2003**:2
Carnahan, Jean 1933- **2001**:2
Carnahan, Mel 1934-2000
    Obituary **2001**:2
Carter, Billy 1937-1988
    Obituary **1989**:1
Carter, Jimmy 1924- **1995**:1
Casey, William 1913-1987
    Obituary **1987**:3
Cavazos, Lauro F. 1927- **1989**:2
Chamberlin, Wendy 1948- **2002**:4
Chao, Elaine L. 1953- **2007**:3
Chavez, Linda 1947- **1999**:3
Chavez-Thompson, Linda
    1944- **1999**:1
Cheney, Dick 1941- **1991**:3
Cheney, Lynne V. 1941- **1990**:4

Chisholm, Shirley 1924-2005
    Obituary **2006**:1
Christopher, Warren 1925- **1996**:3
Cisneros, Henry 1947- **1987**:2
Clark, J. E.
    Brief entry **1986**:1
Clinton, Bill 1946- **1992**:1
Clinton, Hillary Rodham
    1947- **1993**:2
Clyburn, James 1940- **1999**:4
Cohen, William S. 1940- **1998**:1
Collins, Cardiss 1931- **1995**:3
Connally, John 1917-1993
    Obituary **1994**:1
Conyers, John, Jr. 1929- **1999**:1
Cornum, Rhonda 1954- **2006**:3
Cuomo, Mario 1932- **1992**:2
D'Amato, Al 1937- **1996**:1
Daschle, Tom 1947- **2002**:3
Dean, Howard 1948- **2005**:4
DeLay, Tom 1947- **2000**:1
Dinkins, David N. 1927- **1990**:2
Dolan, Terry 1950-1986 **1985**:2
Dole, Bob 1923- **1994**:2
Dole, Elizabeth Hanford
    1936- **1990**:1
Dukakis, Michael 1933- **1988**:3
Duke, David 1951(?)- **1990**:2
Dunwoody, Ann 1953- **2009**:2
Ehrlichman, John 1925-1999
    Obituary **1999**:3
Elders, Joycelyn 1933- **1994**:1
Engler, John 1948- **1996**:3
Ervin, Sam 1896-1985
    Obituary **1985**:2
Estrich, Susan 1953- **1989**:1
Falkenberg, Nanette 1951- **1985**:2
Farmer, James 1920-1999
    Obituary **2000**:1
Farrakhan, Louis 1933- **1990**:4
Faubus, Orval 1910-1994
    Obituary **1995**:2
Feinstein, Dianne 1933- **1993**:3
Fenwick, Millicent H.
    Obituary **1993**:2
Ferraro, Geraldine 1935- **1998**:3
Fish, Hamilton 1888-1991
    Obituary **1991**:3
Fitzgerald, A. Ernest 1926- **1986**:2
Fleischer, Ari 1960- **2003**:1
Florio, James J. 1937- **1991**:2
Flynn, Ray 1939- **1989**:1
Foley, Thomas S. 1929- **1990**:1
Forbes, Steve 1947- **1996**:2
Ford, Gerald R. 1913-2007
    Obituary **2008**:2
Foster, Vincent 1945(?)-1993
    Obituary **1994**:1
Frank, Anthony M. 1931(?)- **1992**:1
Frank, Barney 1940- **1989**:2
Franks, Tommy 1945- **2004**:1
Frist, Bill 1952- **2003**:4
Fulbright, J. William 1905-1995
    Obituary **1995**:3
Galvin, John R. 1929- **1990**:1
Garrison, Jim 1922-1992
    Obituary **1993**:2
Gates, Robert M. 1943- **1992**:2
Gebbie, Kristine 1944(?)- **1994**:2
Geithner, Timothy F. 1961- **2009**:4
Gephardt, Richard 1941- **1987**:3
Gergen, David 1942- **1994**:1

Gingrich, Newt 1943- **1991**:1
Giuliani, Rudolph 1944- **1994**:2
Glenn, John 1921- **1998**:3
Goldwater, Barry 1909-1998
    Obituary **1998**:4
Gore, Albert, Jr. 1948(?)- **1993**:2
Gore, Albert, Sr. 1907-1998
    Obituary **1999**:2
Gramm, Phil 1942- **1995**:2
Granholm, Jennifer 1959- **2003**:3
Greenspan, Alan 1926- **1992**:2
Griffiths, Martha 1912-2003
    Obituary **2004**:2
Haldeman, H. R. 1926-1993
    Obituary **1994**:2
Hall, Gus 1910-2000
    Obituary **2001**:2
Harriman, Pamela 1920- **1994**:4
Harriman, W. Averell 1891-1986
    Obituary **1986**:4
Harris, Katherine 1957- **2001**:3
Harris, Patricia Roberts 1924-1985
    Obituary **1985**:2
Hastert, Dennis 1942- **1999**:3
Hatch, Orin G. 1934- **2000**:2
Hayakawa, Samuel Ichiye 1906-1992
    Obituary **1992**:3
Heinz, John 1938-1991
    Obituary **1991**:4
Heller, Walter 1915-1987
    Obituary **1987**:4
Helms, Jesse 1921- **1998**:1
Hills, Carla 1934- **1990**:3
Hiss, Alger 1904-1996
    Obituary **1997**:2
Holbrooke, Richard 1941(?)- **1996**:2
Holder, Jr., Eric H. 1951- **2009**:4
Hughes, Karen 1957- **2001**:2
Hull, Jane Dee 1935- **1999**:2
Hundt, Reed Eric 1948- **1997**:2
Hyde, Henry 1924- **1999**:1
Inman, Bobby Ray 1931- **1985**:1
Jackson, Jesse 1941- **1996**:1
Jackson, Jesse, Jr. 1965- **1998**:3
Jackson, Lisa P. 1962- **2009**:4
Jackson, Thomas Penfield
    1937- **2000**:2
Jeffords, James 1934- **2002**:2
Jeffrey, Mildred 1910-2004
    Obituary **2005**:2
Jindal, Bobby 1971- **2006**:1
Johnson, Lady Bird 1912-2007
    Obituary **2008**:4
Jordan, Barbara 1936-1996
    Obituary **1996**:3
Kassebaum, Nancy 1932- **1991**:1
Kemp, Jack 1935- **1990**:4
Kennan, George 1904-2005
    Obituary **2006**:2
Kennedy, Rose 1890-1995
    Obituary **1995**:3
Kerrey, Bob 1943- **1986**:1
Kerry, John 1943- **2005**:2
Kessler, David 1951- **1992**:1
Keyes, Alan 1950- **1996**:2
Kilpatrick, Kwame 1970- **2009**:2
Kirkpatrick, Jeane 1926-2006
    Obituary **2008**:1
Kissinger, Henry 1923- **1999**:4
Koop, C. Everett 1916- **1989**:3
Landon, Alf 1887-1987
    Obituary **1988**:1

Landrieu, Mary L. 1955- **2002**:2
Langevin, James R. 1964- **2001**:2
Lansdale, Edward G. 1908-1987
  Obituary **1987**:2
Lantos, Tom 1928-2008
  Obituary **2009**:2
Levitt, Arthur 1931- **2004**:2
Lieberman, Joseph 1942- **2001**:1
Liman, Arthur 1932- **1989**:4
Lincoln, Blanche 1960- **2003**:1
Lindsay, John V. 1921-2000
  Obituary **2001**:3
Lodge, Henry Cabot 1902-1985
  Obituary **1985**:1
Lord, Winston
  Brief entry **1987**:4
Lott, Trent 1941- **1998**:1
Luce, Clare Boothe 1903-1987
  Obituary **1988**:1
Lucke, Lewis 1951(?)- **2004**:4
Manchin, Joe 1947- **2006**:4
Mankiller, Wilma P.
  Brief entry **1986**:2
Mansfield, Mike 1903-2001
  Obituary **2002**:4
Martin, Lynn 1939- **1991**:4
Martinez, Bob 1934- **1992**:1
Matalin, Mary 1953- **1995**:2
Mathias, Bob 1930-2006
  Obituary **2007**:4
McCain, John S. 1936- **1998**:4
McCarthy, Carolyn 1944- **1998**:4
McCloy, John J. 1895-1989
  Obituary **1989**:3
McGreevey, James 1957- **2005**:2
McKinney, Cynthia A. 1955- **1997**:1
McKinney, Stewart B. 1931-1987
  Obituary **1987**:4
McMillen, Tom 1952- **1988**:4
McNamara, Robert S. 1916- **1995**:4
Mfume, Kweisi 1948- **1996**:3
Mikulski, Barbara 1936- **1992**:4
Mills, Wilbur 1909-1992
  Obituary **1992**:4
Minner, Ruth Ann 1935- **2002**:2
Mitchell, George J. 1933- **1989**:3
Mitchell, John 1913-1988
  Obituary **1989**:2
Moakley, Joseph 1927-2001
  Obituary **2002**:2
Molinari, Susan 1958- **1996**:4
Morris, Dick 1948- **1997**:3
Morrison, Trudi
  Brief entry **1986**:2
Mott, William Penn, Jr. 1909- **1986**:1
Moyers, Bill 1934- **1991**:4
Moynihan, Daniel Patrick 1927-2003
  Obituary **2004**:2
Muskie, Edmund S. 1914-1996
  Obituary **1996**:3
Nagin, Ray 1956- **2007**:1
Natsios, Andrew 1949- **2005**:1
Neal, James Foster 1929- **1986**:2
Nelson, Gaylord A. 1914-2005
  Obituary **2006**:3
Newsom, Gavin 1967- **2009**:3
Newton, Huey 1942-1989
  Obituary **1990**:1
Nixon, Pat 1912-1993
  Obituary **1994**:1
Nixon, Richard 1913-1994
  Obituary **1994**:4

Noonan, Peggy 1950- **1990**:3
North, Oliver 1943- **1987**:4
Novello, Antonia 1944- **1991**:2
Nunn, Sam 1938- **1990**:2
Obama, Barack 1961- **2007**:4
O'Leary, Hazel 1937- **1993**:4
Oliver, Daniel 1939- **1988**:2
Onassis, Jacqueline Kennedy
  1929-1994
  Obituary **1994**:4
O'Neill, Paul H. 1935- **2001**:4
O'Neill, Tip 1912-1994
  Obituary **1994**:3
Orr, Kay 1939- **1987**:4
Paige, Emmett, Jr.
  Brief entry **1986**:4
Paige, Rod 1933- **2003**:2
Palin, Sarah 1964- **2009**:1
Panetta, Leon 1938- **1995**:1
Pataki, George 1945- **1995**:2
Pelosi, Nancy 1940- **2004**:2
Pendleton, Clarence M. 1930-1988
  Obituary **1988**:4
Pepper, Claude 1900-1989
  Obituary **1989**:4
Perot, H. Ross 1930- **1992**:4
Perry, Carrie Saxon 1932(?)- **1989**:2
Perry, William 1927- **1994**:4
Peters, Mary E. 1948- **2008**:3
Powell, Colin 1937- **1990**:1
Powell, Lewis F. 1907-1998
  Obituary **1999**:1
Pryce, Deborah 1951- **2006**:3
Quayle, Dan 1947- **1989**:2
Raines, Franklin 1949- **1997**:4
Reagan, Ronald 1911-2004
  Obituary **2005**:3
Reed, Ralph 1961(?)- **1995**:1
Reich, Robert 1946- **1995**:4
Reid, Harry 1939- **2006**:1
Reno, Janet 1938- **1993**:3
Ribicoff, Abraham 1910-1998
  Obituary **1998**:3
Rice, Condoleezza 1954- **2002**:1
Richards, Ann 1933- **1991**:2
Rickover, Hyman 1900-1986
  Obituary **1986**:4
Ridge, Tom 1945- **2002**:2
Riordan, Richard 1930- **1993**:4
Rizzo, Frank 1920-1991
  Obituary **1992**:1
Robb, Charles S. 1939- **1987**:2
Robertson, Pat 1930- **1988**:2
Roemer, Buddy 1943- **1991**:4
Rogers, William P. 1913-2001
  Obituary **2001**:4
Roosevelt, Franklin D., Jr. 1914-1988
  Obituary **1989**:1
Ros-Lehtinen, Ileana 1952- **2000**:2
Roth, William Victor, Jr. 1921-2003
  Obituary **2005**:1
Rove, Karl 1950- **2006**:2
Roybal-Allard, Lucille 1941- **1999**:4
Rumsfeld, Donald 1932- **2004**:1
Rusk, Dean 1909-1994
  Obituary **1995**:2
Sanchez, Loretta 1960- **2000**:3
Sanders, Bernie 1941(?)- **1991**:4
Satcher, David 1941- **2001**:4
Scalia, Antonin 1936- **1988**:2
Schaefer, William Donald
  1921- **1988**:1

Schiavo, Mary 1955- **1998**:2
Schwarzenegger, Arnold
  1947- **1991**:1
Schwarzkopf, Norman 1934- **1991**:3
Sebelius, Kathleen 1948- **2008**:4
Senghor, Leopold 1906-2001
  Obituary **2003**:1
Shalikashvili, John 1936- **1994**:2
Sheehan, Daniel P. 1945(?)- **1989**:1
Sidney, Ivan
  Brief entry **1987**:2
Sigmund, Barbara Boggs 1939-1990
  Obituary **1991**:1
Simon, Paul 1928-2003
  Obituary **2005**:1
Skinner, Sam 1938- **1992**:3
Slater, Rodney E. 1955- **1997**:4
Snow, John W. 1939- **2006**:2
Snow, Tony 1955-2008
  Obituary **2009**:3
Snowe, Olympia 1947- **1995**:3
Spellings, Margaret 1957- **2005**:4
Spitzer, Eliot 1959- **2007**:2
Starr, Kenneth 1946- **1998**:3
Stephanopoulos, George
  1961- **1994**:3
Stewart, Potter 1915-1985
  Obituary **1986**:1
Stokes, Carl 1927-1996
  Obituary **1996**:4
Strauss, Robert 1918- **1991**:4
Suarez, Xavier
  Brief entry **1986**:2
Sullivan, Louis 1933- **1990**:4
Sununu, John 1939- **1989**:2
Swift, Jane 1965(?)- **2002**:1
Taylor, Maxwell 1901-1987
  Obituary **1987**:3
Tenet, George 1953- **2000**:3
Thomas, Clarence 1948- **1992**:2
Thomas, Edmond J. 1943(?)- **2005**:1
Thomas, Helen 1920- **1988**:4
Thompson, Fred 1942- **1998**:2
Thurmond, Strom 1902-2003
  Obituary **2004**:3
Tower, John 1926-1991
  Obituary **1991**:4
Townsend, Kathleen Kennedy
  1951- **2001**:3
Tsongas, Paul Efthemios 1941-1997
  Obituary **1997**:2
Tutwiler, Margaret 1950- **1992**:4
Tyson, Laura D'Andrea 1947- **1994**:1
Udall, Mo 1922-1998
  Obituary **1999**:2
Ventura, Jesse 1951- **1999**:2
Violet, Arlene 1943- **1985**:3
Wallace, George 1919-1998
  Obituary **1999**:1
Washington, Harold 1922-1987
  Obituary **1988**:1
Waters, Maxine 1938- **1998**:4
Watts, J.C. 1957- **1999**:2
Webb, Wellington E. 1941- **2000**:3
Weicker, Lowell P., Jr. 1931- **1993**:1
Weinberger, Caspar 1917-2006
  Obituary **2007**:2
Wellstone, Paul 1944-2002
  Obituary **2004**:1
Westmoreland, William C. 1914-2005
  Obituary **2006**:4

Whitman, Christine Todd
    1947(?)- **1994**:3
Whitmire, Kathy 1946- **1988**:2
Wilder, L. Douglas 1931- **1990**:3
Williams, Anthony 1952- **2000**:4
Williams, G. Mennen 1911-1988
    Obituary **1988**:2
Wilson, Pete 1933- **1992**:3
Yard, Molly **1991**:4
Young, Coleman A. 1918-1997
    Obituary **1998**:1
Zech, Lando W.
    Brief entry **1987**:4
Zerhouni, Elias A. 1951- **2004**:3
Zinni, Anthony 1943- **2003**:1

## RADIO

Adams, Yolanda 1961- **2008**:2
Albert, Marv 1943- **1994**:3
Albom, Mitch 1958- **1999**:3
Ameche, Don 1908-1993
    Obituary **1994**:2
Autry, Gene 1907-1998
    Obituary **1999**:1
Backus, Jim 1913-1989
    Obituary **1990**:1
Barber, Red 1908-1992
    Obituary **1993**:2
Becker, Brian 1957(?)- **2004**:4
Bell, Art 1945- **2000**:1
Blanc, Mel 1908-1989
    Obituary **1989**:4
Campbell, Bebe Moore 1950- **1996**:2
Caray, Harry 1914(?)-1998 **1988**:3
    Obituary **1998**:3
Carson, Johnny 1925-2005
    Obituary **2006**:1
Cherry, Don 1934- **1993**:4
Codrescu, Andreaa 1946- **1997**:3
Cosell, Howard 1918-1995
    Obituary **1995**:4
Costas, Bob 1952- **1986**:4
Crenna, Richard 1926-2003
    Obituary **2004**:1
Day, Dennis 1917-1988
    Obituary **1988**:4
Denver, Bob 1935-2005
    Obituary **2006**:4
Donnellan, Nanci **1995**:2
Douglas, Mike 1925-2006
    Obituary **2007**:4
Dr. Demento 1941- **1986**:1
Durrell, Gerald 1925-1995
    Obituary **1995**:3
Edwards, Bob 1947- **1993**:2
Fleming, Art 1925(?)-1995
    Obituary **1995**:4
Ford, Tennessee Ernie 1919-1991
    Obituary **1992**:2
Glass, Ira 1959- **2008**:2
Gobel, George 1920(?)-1991
    Obituary **1991**:4
Goodman, Benny 1909-1986
    Obituary **1986**:3
Gordon, Gale 1906-1995
    Obituary **1996**:1
Graham, Billy 1918- **1992**:1
Granato, Cammi 1971- **1999**:3
Grange, Red 1903-1991
    Obituary **1991**:3
Greene, Lorne 1915-1987
    Obituary **1988**:1

Griffin, Merv 1925-2008
    Obituary **2008**:4
Gross, Terry 1951- **1998**:3
Harmon, Tom 1919-1990
    Obituary **1990**:3
Harvey, Paul 1918- **1995**:3
Harwell, Ernie 1918- **1997**:3
Hill, George Roy 1921-2002
    Obituary **2004**:1
Hollander, Joel 1956(?)- **2006**:4
Hope, Bob 1903-2003
    Obituary **2004**:4
Houseman, John 1902-1988
    Obituary **1989**:1
Hughes, Cathy 1947- **1999**:1
Imus, Don 1940- **1997**:1
Ives, Burl 1909-1995
    Obituary **1995**:4
Karmazin, Mel 1943- **2006**:1
Kasem, Casey 1933(?)- **1987**:1
Keyes, Alan 1950- **1996**:2
Kimmel, Jimmy 1967- **2009**:2
King, Larry 1933- **1993**:1
Kyser, Kay 1906(?)-1985
    Obituary **1985**:3
Leaavesque, Reneaa
    Obituary **1988**:1
Limbaugh, Rush **1991**:3
Magliozzi, Tom and Ray **1991**:4
Milligan, Spike 1918-2002
    Obituary **2003**:2
Nelson, Harriet 1909(?)-1994
    Obituary **1995**:1
Olson, Johnny 1910(?)-1985
    Obituary **1985**:4
Osgood, Charles 1933- **1996**:2
Paar, Jack 1918-2004
    Obituary **2005**:2
Paley, William S. 1901-1990
    Obituary **1991**:2
Parks, Bert 1914-1992
    Obituary **1992**:3
Parsons, Gary 1950(?)- **2006**:2
Porter, Sylvia 1913-1991
    Obituary **1991**:4
Quivers, Robin 1953(?)- **1995**:4
Raphael, Sally Jessy 1943- **1992**:4
Raye, Martha 1916-1994
    Obituary **1995**:1
Reagan, Ronald 1911-2004
    Obituary **2005**:3
Riddle, Nelson 1921-1985
    Obituary **1985**:4
Roberts, Cokie 1943- **1993**:4
Rollins, Henry 1961- **2007**:3
Saralegui, Cristina 1948- **1999**:2
Schlessinger, Laura 1947(?)- **1996**:3
Seacrest, Ryan 1976- **2004**:4
Sedaris, David 1956- **2005**:3
Sevareid, Eric 1912-1992
    Obituary **1993**:1
Shore, Dinah 1917-1994
    Obituary **1994**:3
Smith, Buffalo Bob 1917-1998
    Obituary **1999**:1
Smith, Kate 1907(?)-1986
    Obituary **1986**:3
Stern, Howard 1954- **1988**:2
Swayze, John Cameron 1906-1995
    Obituary **1996**:1
Toguri, Iva 1916-2006
    Obituary **2007**:4

Tom and Ray Magliozzi **1991**:4
Totenberg, Nina 1944- **1992**:2
Wolfman Jack 1938-1995
    Obituary **1996**:1
Young, Robert 1907-1998
    Obituary **1999**:1

## RELIGION

Abernathy, Ralph 1926-1990
    Obituary **1990**:3
Altea, Rosemary 1946- **1996**:3
Applewhite, Marshall Herff
    1931-1997
    Obituary **1997**:3
Aristide, Jean-Bertrand 1953- **1991**:3
Beckett, Wendy (Sister) 1930- **1998**:3
Benson, Ezra Taft 1899-1994
    Obituary **1994**:4
Bernardin, Cardinal Joseph
    1928-1996 **1997**:2
Berri, Nabih 1939(?)- **1985**:2
Browning, Edmond
    Brief entry **1986**:2
Burns, Charles R.
    Brief entry **1988**:1
Carey, George 1935- **1992**:3
Chavis, Benjamin 1948- **1993**:4
Chittister, Joan D. 1936- **2002**:2
Chopra, Deepak 1947- **1996**:3
Clements, George 1932- **1985**:1
Cleveland, James 1932(?)-1991
    Obituary **1991**:3
Coffin, William Sloane, Jr.
    1924- **1990**:3
Cunningham, Reverend William
    1930-1997
    Obituary **1997**:4
Curran, Charles E. 1934- **1989**:2
Daily, Bishop Thomas V.
    1927- **1990**:4
Dalai Lama 1935- **1989**:1
Dearden, John Cardinal 1907-1988
    Obituary **1988**:4
Dorsey, Thomas A. 1899-1993
    Obituary **1993**:3
Eilberg, Amy
    Brief entry **1985**:3
Falwell, Jerry 1933-2007
    Obituary **2008**:3
Farrakhan, Louis 1933- **1990**:4
Fox, Matthew 1940- **1992**:2
Fulghum, Robert 1937- **1996**:1
Graham, Billy 1918- **1992**:1
Grant, Amy 1961(?)- **1985**:4
Hahn, Jessica 1960- **1989**:4
Harris, Barbara **1996**:3
Harris, Barbara 1930- **1989**:3
Healy, Timothy S. 1923- **1990**:2
Henry, Carl F.H. 1913-2003
    Obituary **2005**:1
Huffington, Arianna 1950- **1996**:2
Hume, Basil Cardinal 1923-1999
    Obituary **2000**:1
Hunter, Howard 1907- **1994**:4
Irwin, James 1930-1991
    Obituary **1992**:1
Jackson, Jesse 1941- **1996**:1
Jefferts Schori, Katharine
    1954- **2007**:2
John Paul II, Pope 1920- **1995**:3
Jumblatt, Walid 1949(?)- **1987**:4
Kahane, Meir 1932-1990

Obituary **1991**:2
Khomeini, Ayatollah Ruhollah
1900(?)-1989
Obituary **1989**:4
Kissling, Frances 1943- **1989**:2
Koresh, David 1960(?)-1993
Obituary **1993**:4
Krol, John 1910-1996
Obituary **1996**:3
Lefebvre, Marcel 1905- **1988**:4
Levinger, Moshe 1935- **1992**:1
Macquarrie, John 1919-2007
Obituary **2008**:3
Mahesh Yogi, Maharishi 1911(?)-
**1991**:3
Mahony, Roger M. 1936- **1988**:2
Maida, Adam Cardinal 1930- **1998**:2
Malloy, Edward Monk 1941- **1989**:4
McCloskey, James 1944(?)- **1993**:1
Morris, Henry M. 1918-2006
Obituary **2007**:2
Mother Teresa 1910-1997 **1993**:1
Obituary **1998**:1
Obando, Miguel 1926- **1986**:4
O'Connor, Cardinal John
1920- **1990**:3
O'Connor, John 1920-2000
Obituary **2000**:4
Osteen, Joel 1963- **2006**:2
Perry, Harold A. 1917(?)-1991
Obituary **1992**:1
Peter, Valentine J. 1934- **1988**:2
Rafsanjani, Ali Akbar Hashemi
1934(?)- **1987**:3
Rahman, Sheik Omar Abdel-
1938- **1993**:3
Rajneesh, Bhagwan Shree 1931-1990
Obituary **1990**:2
Reed, Ralph 1961(?)- **1995**:1
Reese, Della 1931- **1999**:2
Robertson, Pat 1930- **1988**:2
Robinson, V. Gene 1947- **2004**:4
Rogers, Adrian 1931- **1987**:4
Runcie, Robert 1921-2000 **1989**:4
Obituary **2001**:1
Schneerson, Menachem Mendel
1902-1994 **1992**:4
Obituary **1994**:4
Scott, Gene
Brief entry **1986**:1
Sentamu, John 1949- **2006**:2
Sharpton, Al 1954- **1991**:2
Shaw, William 1934(?)- **2000**:3
Sin, Jaime 1928-2005
Obituary **2006**:3
Smith, Jeff 1939(?)- **1991**:4
Spong, John 1931- **1991**:3
Stallings, George A., Jr. 1948- **1990**:1
Swaggart, Jimmy 1935- **1987**:3
Taylor, Graham 1958(?)- **2005**:3
Turabi, Hassan 1932(?)- **1995**:4
Violet, Arlene 1943- **1985**:3
Wildmon, Donald 1938- **1988**:4
Williamson, Marianne
1953(?)- **1991**:4
Youngblood, Johnny Ray
1948- **1994**:1

**SCIENCE**

Abramson, Lyn 1950- **1986**:3
Adams, Patch 1945(?)- **1999**:2
Adamson, George 1906-1989

Obituary **1990**:2
Agatston, Arthur 1947- **2005**:1
Allen, John 1930- **1992**:1
Altman, Sidney 1939- **1997**:2
Aronson, Jane 1951- **2009**:3
Atkins, Robert C. 1930-2003
Obituary **2004**:2
Axelrod, Julius 1912-2004
Obituary **2006**:1
Bahcall, John N. 1934-2005
Obituary **2006**:4
Bakker, Robert T. 1950(?)- **1991**:3
Ballard, Robert D. 1942- **1998**:4
Barnard, Christiaan 1922-2001
Obituary **2002**:4
Baulieu, Étienne-Emile 1926- **1990**:1
Bayley, Corrine
Brief entry **1986**:4
Bean, Alan L. 1932- **1986**:2
Beattie, Owen
Brief entry **1985**:2
Benes, Francine 1946- **2008**:2
Berkley, Seth 1956- **2002**:3
Berle, Peter A.A.
Brief entry **1987**:3
Berman, Jennifer and Laura **2003**:2
Bethe, Hans 1906-2005
Obituary **2006**:2
Bettelheim, Bruno 1903-1990
Obituary **1990**:3
Blobel, Gunter 1936- **2000**:4
Bloch, Erich 1925- **1987**:4
Blumenthal, Susan J. 1951(?)- **2007**:3
Boyer, Herbert Wayne 1936- **1985**:1
Brinker, Nancy 1946- **2007**:1
Bristow, Lonnie 1930- **1996**:1
Brown, John Seely 1940- **2004**:1
Buck, Linda 1956(?)- **2004**:2
Burnison, Chantal Simone
1950(?)- **1988**:3
Carlsson, Arvid 1923- **2001**:2
Carson, Ben 1951- **1998**:2
Cerf, Vinton G. 1943- **1999**:2
Chaudhari, Praveen 1937- **1989**:4
Chu, Paul C.W. 1941- **1988**:2
Coles, Robert 1929(?)- **1995**:1
Collins, Eileen 1956- **1995**:3
Colwell, Rita Rossi 1934- **1999**:3
Comfort, Alex 1920-2000
Obituary **2000**:4
Conrad, Pete 1930-1999
Obituary **2000**:1
Cousteau, Jacques-Yves
1910-1997 **1998**:2
Cousteau, Jean-Michel 1938- **1988**:2
Cram, Donald J. 1919-2001
Obituary **2002**:2
Cray, Seymour R. 1925-1996
Brief entry **1986**:3
Obituary **1997**:2
Crick, Francis 1916-2004
Obituary **2005**:4
Davis, Noel **1990**:3
Davis, Raymond, Jr. 1914-2006
Obituary **2007**:3
DeBakey, Michael 1908-2008
Obituary **2009**:3
DeVita, Vincent T., Jr. 1935- **1987**:3
Diemer, Walter E.
1904(?)-1998 **1998**:2
Djerassi, Carl 1923- **2000**:4
Domar, Alice 1958- **2007**:1

Douglas, Marjory Stoneman
1890-1998 **1993**:1
Obituary **1998**:4
Downey, Bruce 1947- **2003**:1
Duke, Red
Brief entry **1987**:1
Durrell, Gerald 1925-1995
Obituary **1995**:3
Earle, Sylvia 1935- **2001**:1
Fang Lizhi 1937- **1988**:1
Fano, Ugo 1912-2001
Obituary **2001**:4
Fauci, Anthony S. 1940- **2004**:1
Fields, Evelyn J. 1949- **2001**:3
Fiennes, Ranulph 1944- **1990**:3
Fisher, Mel 1922(?)- **1985**:4
Folkman, Judah 1933- **1999**:1
Fossey, Dian 1932-1985
Obituary **1986**:1
Foster, Tabatha 1985-1988
Obituary **1988**:3
Fraser, Claire M. 1955- **2005**:2
Friedman, Milton 1912-2006
Obituary **2008**:1
Futter, Ellen V. 1949- **1995**:1
Gale, Robert Peter 1945- **1986**:4
Gallo, Robert 1937- **1991**:1
Garneau, Marc 1949- **1985**:1
Gayle, Helene 1955- **2008**:2
Geller, Margaret Joan 1947- **1998**:2
George and Lena Korres
1971- **2009**:1
Gerba, Charles 1945- **1999**:4
Gerberding, Julie 1955- **2004**:1
Gilbert, Walter 1932- **1988**:3
Gilruth, Robert 1913-2000
Obituary **2001**:1
Glenn, John 1921- **1998**:3
Gold, Thomas 1920-2004
Obituary **2005**:3
Goldman-Rakic, Patricia
1937- **2002**:4
Goodall, Jane 1934- **1991**:1
Gordon, James 1941- **2009**:4
Gould, Gordon 1920- **1987**:1
Gould, Stephen Jay 1941-2002
Obituary **2003**:3
Grandin, Temple 1947- **2006**:1
Greene, Brian 1963- **2003**:4
Gupta, Sanjay 1969- **2009**:4
Hagelstein, Peter
Brief entry **1986**:3
Hair, Jay D. 1945- **1994**:3
Hale, Alan 1957- **1997**:3
Hale, Victoria 1961(?)- **2008**:4
Hammond, E. Cuyler 1912-1986
Obituary **1987**:1
Haseltine, William A. 1944- **1999**:2
Hatem, George 1910(?)-1988
Obituary **1989**:1
Hau, Lene Vestergaard 1959- **2006**:4
Hawking, Stephen W. 1942- **1990**:1
Healy, Bernadine 1944- **1993**:1
Herbert, Don 1917-2007
Obituary **2008**:3
Herz, Rachel 1963- **2008**:1
Hill, J. Edward 1938- **2006**:2
Ho, David 1952- **1997**:2
Hodges, Carl 1937- **2008**:1
Horner, Jack 1946- **1985**:2
Horowitz, Paul 1942- **1988**:2
Hounsfield, Godfrey 1919- **1989**:2

Hoyle, Sir Fred 1915-2001
    Obituary **2002**:4
Irwin, James 1930-1991
    Obituary **1992**:1
Jablonski, Nina G. 1953- **2009**:3
Jacobs, Joe 1945(?)- **1994**:1
Janzen, Daniel H. 1939- **1988**:4
Jarvik, Robert K. 1946- **1985**:1
Jemison, Mae C. 1956- **1993**:1
Jorgensen, Christine 1926-1989
    Obituary **1989**:4
Kandel, Eric 1929- **2005**:2
Keeling, Charles 1928-2005
    Obituary **2006**:3
Keith, Louis 1935- **1988**:2
Kellerman, Jonathan 1949- **2009**:1
Kessler, David 1951- **1992**:1
Kevorkian, Jack 1928(?)- **1991**:3
King, Mary-Claire 1946- **1998**:3
Klass, Perri 1958- **1993**:2
Kleinpaste, Ruud 1952- **2006**:2
Koop, C. Everett 1916- **1989**:3
Kopits, Steven E.
    Brief entry **1987**:1
Kornberg, Arthur 1918(?)- **1992**:1
Krim, Mathilde 1926- **1989**:2
Kubler-Ross, Elisabeth 1926-2004
    Obituary **2005**:4
Kwoh, Yik San 1946(?)- **1988**:2
Laing, R.D. 1927-1989
    Obituary **1990**:1
Langer, Robert 1948- **2003**:4
Langston, J. William
    Brief entry **1986**:2
Lanza, Robert 1956- **2004**:3
Leakey, Mary Douglas 1913-1996
    Obituary **1997**:2
Leakey, Richard 1944- **1994**:2
Lederman, Leon Max 1922- **1989**:4
Leopold, Luna 1915-2006
    Obituary **2007**:1
LeVay, Simon 1943- **1992**:2
Levine, Arnold 1939- **2002**:3
Lewis, Edward B. 1918-2004
    Obituary **2005**:4
Lilly, John C. 1915-2001
    Obituary **2002**:4
Lorenz, Konrad 1903-1989
    Obituary **1989**:3
Love, Susan 1948- **1995**:2
Lovley, Derek 1954(?)- **2005**:3
Lucid, Shannon 1943- **1997**:1
Maglich, Bogdan C. 1928- **1990**:1
Maiman, Theodore 1927-2007
    Obituary **2008**:3
Manson, JoAnn E. 1953- **2008**:3
Marsden, Brian 1937- **2004**:4
Masters, William H. 1915-2001
    Obituary **2001**:4
McIntyre, Richard
    Brief entry **1986**:2
Melton, Douglas 1954- **2008**:3
Menninger, Karl 1893-1990
    Obituary **1991**:1
Minsky, Marvin 1927- **1994**:3
Montagu, Ashley 1905-1999
    Obituary **2000**:2
Moog, Robert 1934-2005
    Obituary **2006**:4
Morgentaler, Henry 1923- **1986**:3
Moss, Cynthia 1940- **1995**:2
Mullis, Kary 1944- **1995**:3

Ngau, Harrison **1991**:3
Nielsen, Jerri 1951(?)- **2001**:3
Novello, Antonia 1944- **1991**:2
Nuesslein-Volhard, Christiane
    1942- **1998**:1
Nye, Bill 1955- **1997**:2
O'Keefe, Sean 1956- **2005**:2
Olopade, Olufunmilayo
    1957(?)- **2006**:3
Ornish, Dean 1953- **2004**:2
Owens, Delia and Mark **1993**:3
Oz, Mehmet 1960- **2007**:2
Panofsky, Wolfgang 1919-2007
    Obituary **2008**:4
Patton, John 1947(?)- **2004**:4
Pauling, Linus 1901-1994
    Obituary **1995**:1
Penrose, Roger 1931- **1991**:4
Perutz, Max 1914-2002
    Obituary **2003**:2
Peterson, Roger Tory 1908-1996
    Obituary **1997**:1
Pinker, Steven A. 1954- **2000**:1
Plotkin, Mark 1955(?)- **1994**:3
Pople, John 1925-2004
    Obituary **2005**:2
Porco, Carolyn 1953- **2005**:4
Porter, George 1920-2002
    Obituary **2003**:4
Pough, Richard Hooper 1904- **1989**:1
Profet, Margie 1958- **1994**:4
Prusiner, Stanley 1942- **1998**:2
Puck, Theodore 1916-2005
    Obituary **2007**:1
Quill, Timothy E. 1949- **1997**:3
Radecki, Thomas
    Brief entry **1986**:2
Ramey, Estelle R. 1917-2006
    Obituary **2007**:4
Randall, Lisa 1962- **2009**:2
Redenbacher, Orville 1907-1995
    Obituary **1996**:1
Redig, Patrick 1948- **1985**:3
Richmond, Julius B. 1916-2008
    Obituary **2009**:4
Richter, Charles Francis 1900-1985
    Obituary **1985**:4
Rifkin, Jeremy 1945- **1990**:3
Rizzoli, Paola 1943(?)- **2004**:3
Rock, John
    Obituary **1985**:1
Roizen, Michael 1946- **2007**:4
Rosenberg, Steven 1940- **1989**:1
Rosendahl, Bruce R.
    Brief entry **1986**:4
Rosgen, Dave 1942(?)- **2005**:2
Russell, Mary 1950- **2009**:2
Sabin, Albert 1906-1993
    Obituary **1993**:4
Sacks, Oliver 1933- **1995**:4
Sagan, Carl 1934-1996
    Obituary **1997**:2
Sakharov, Andrei Dmitrievich
    1921-1989
    Obituary **1990**:2
Salk, Jonas 1914-1995 **1994**:4
    Obituary **1995**:4
Schank, Roger 1946- **1989**:2
Schenk, Dale 1957(?)- **2002**:2
Schirra, Wally 1923-2007
    Obituary **2008**:3
Schroeder, William J. 1932-1986

Obituary **1986**:4
Schultes, Richard Evans 1915-2001
    Obituary **2002**:1
Sears, Barry 1947- **2004**:2
Shepard, Alan 1923-1998
    Obituary **1999**:1
Shimomura, Tsutomu 1965- **1996**:1
Shirley, Donna 1941- **1999**:1
Sidransky, David 1960- **2002**:4
Singer, Margaret Thaler 1921-2003
    Obituary **2005**:1
Skinner, B.F. 1904-1990
    Obituary **1991**:1
Smoot, George F. 1945- **1993**:3
Soren, David
    Brief entry **1986**:3
Spelke, Elizabeth 1949- **2003**:1
Spergel, David 1961- **2004**:1
Spock, Benjamin 1903-1998 **1995**:2
    Obituary **1998**:3
Steger, Will 1945(?)- **1990**:4
Steptoe, Patrick 1913-1988
    Obituary **1988**:3
Sullivan, Louis 1933- **1990**:4
Szent-Gyoergyi, Albert 1893-1986
    Obituary **1987**:2
Thom, Rene 1923-2002
    Obituary **2004**:1
Thompson, Lonnie 1948- **2003**:3
Thompson, Starley
    Brief entry **1987**:3
Thomson, James 1958- **2002**:3
Tillion, Germaine 1907-2008
    Obituary **2009**:2
Toone, Bill
    Brief entry **1987**:2
Tully, Tim 1954(?)- **2004**:3
Vagelos, P. Roy 1929- **1989**:4
Van Allen, James 1914-2006
    Obituary **2007**:4
Venter, J. Craig 1946- **2001**:1
Vickrey, William S. 1914-1996
    Obituary **1997**:2
Vitetta, Ellen S. 1942(?)- **2005**:4
Volkow, Nora 1956- **2009**:1
Waddell, Thomas F. 1937-1987
    Obituary **1988**:2
Weil, Andrew 1942- **1997**:4
Wexler, Nancy S. 1945- **1992**:3
Whipple, Fred L. 1906-2004
    Obituary **2005**:4
Whitson, Peggy 1960- **2003**:3
Wigand, Jeffrey 1943(?)- **2000**:4
Wigler, Michael
    Brief entry **1985**:1
Wiles, Andrew 1953(?)- **1994**:1
Wilmut, Ian 1944- **1997**:3
Wilson, Edward O. 1929- **1994**:4
Witten, Edward 1951- **2006**:2
Woodwell, George S. 1928- **1987**:2
Yeager, Chuck 1923- **1998**:1
Yen, Samuel 1927- **1996**:4
Zech, Lando W.
    Brief entry **1987**:4

**SOCIAL ISSUES**
Abbey, Edward 1927-1989
    Obituary **1989**:3
Abernathy, Ralph 1926-1990
    Obituary **1990**:3
Ali, Muhammad 1942- **1997**:2
Allred, Gloria 1941- **1985**:2

Amory, Cleveland 1917-1998
  Obituary **1999**:2
Anastas, Robert
  Brief entry **1985**:2
Andrews, Lori B. 1952- **2005**:3
Arbour, Louise 1947- **2005**:1
Aristide, Jean-Bertrand 1953- **1991**:3
Aronson, Jane 1951- **2009**:3
Astor, Brooke 1902-2007
  Obituary **2008**:4
Baez, Joan 1941- **1998**:3
Baird, Bill
  Brief entry **1987**:2
Baldwin, James 1924-1987
  Obituary **1988**:2
Ball, Edward 1959- **1999**:2
Banks, Dennis J. 193- **1986**:4
Bayley, Corrine
  Brief entry **1986**:4
Beal, Deron 1968(?)- **2005**:3
Beinecke, Frances 1960(?)- **2007**:4
Bellamy, Carol 1942- **2001**:2
Ben & Jerry **1991**:3
Bergalis, Kimberly 1968(?)-1991
  Obituary **1992**:3
Berliner, Andy and Rachel **2008**:2
Berresford, Susan V. 1943- **1998**:4
Biehl, Amy 1967(?)-1993
  Obituary **1994**:1
Blackburn, Molly 1931(?)-1985
  Obituary **1985**:4
Block, Herbert 1909-2001
  Obituary **2002**:4
Bly, Robert 1926- **1992**:4
Bradshaw, John 1933- **1992**:1
Brady, Sarah and James S. **1991**:4
Bravo, Ellen 1944- **1998**:2
Breathed, Berkeley 1957- **2005**:3
Bristow, Lonnie 1930- **1996**:1
Brockovich-Ellis, Erin 1960- **2003**:3
Brooks, Gwendolyn
  1917-2000 **1998**:1
  Obituary **2001**:2
Brower, David 1912- **1990**:4
Brown, Howard and Karen
  Stewart **2007**:3
Brown, Jim 1936- **1993**:2
Brown, Judie 1944- **1986**:2
Burk, Martha 1941- **2004**:1
Bush, Barbara 1925- **1989**:3
Cammermeyer, Margarethe
  1942- **1995**:2
Caplan, Arthur L. 1950- **2000**:2
Caras, Roger 1928-2001
  Obituary **2002**:1
Carter, Amy 1967- **1987**:4
Carter, Rubin 1937- **2000**:3
Chavez, Cesar 1927-1993
  Obituary **1993**:4
Chavez-Thompson, Linda
  1944- **1999**:1
Chavis, Benjamin 1948- **1993**:4
Clark, Kenneth B. 1914-2005
  Obituary **2006**:3
Cleaver, Eldridge 1935-1998
  Obituary **1998**:4
Clements, George 1932- **1985**:1
Clinton, Hillary Rodham
  1947- **1993**:2
Coffin, William Sloane, Jr.
  1924- **1990**:3
Cole, Johnetta B. 1936- **1994**:3

Coles, Robert 1929(?)- **1995**:1
Connerly, Ward 1939- **2000**:2
Conseil, Dominique Nils
  1962(?)- **2007**:2
Coors, William K.
  Brief entry **1985**:1
Corwin, Jeff 1967- **2005**:1
Cozza, Stephen 1985- **2001**:1
Crisp, Quentin 1908-1999
  Obituary **2000**:3
Cruzan, Nancy 1957(?)-1990
  Obituary **1991**:3
Davis, Angela 1944- **1998**:3
Dees, Morris 1936- **1992**:1
DeMayo, Neda 1960(?)- **2006**:2
Devi, Phoolan 1955(?)- **1986**:1
  Obituary **2002**:3
Dickinson, Brian 1937- **1998**:2
Dorris, Michael 1945-1997
  Obituary **1997**:3
Douglas, Marjory Stoneman
  1890-1998 **1993**:1
  Obituary **1998**:4
Downey, Morton, Jr. 1932- **1988**:4
Duncan, Sheena
  Brief entry **1987**:1
Dworkin, Andrea 1946-2005
  Obituary **2006**:2
Ebadi, Shirin 1947- **2004**:3
Edelman, Marian Wright
  1939- **1990**:4
Edwards, Harry 1942- **1989**:4
ElBaradei, Mohamed 1942- **2006**:3
Elders, Joycelyn 1933- **1994**:1
Ellison, Ralph 1914-1994
  Obituary **1994**:4
Ensler, Eve 1954(?)- **2002**:4
Etzioni, Amitai 1929- **1994**:3
Evers-Williams, Myrlie 1933- **1995**:4
Falkenberg, Nanette 1951- **1985**:2
Faludi, Susan 1959- **1992**:4
Farrakhan, Louis 1933- **1990**:4
Fassa, Lynda 1963(?)- **2008**:4
Faubus, Orval 1910-1994
  Obituary **1995**:2
Faulkner, Shannon 1975- **1994**:4
Ferguson, Niall 1964- **2006**:1
Ferrell, Trevor
  Brief entry **1985**:2
Filipovic, Zlata 1981(?)- **1994**:4
Finley, Karen 1956- **1992**:4
Fisher, Mary 1948- **1994**:3
Fonyo, Steve
  Brief entry **1985**:4
Foreman, Dave 1947(?)- **1990**:3
Francis, Philip L. 1946- **2007**:4
Friedan, Betty 1921- **1994**:2
Friend, Patricia A. 1946- **2003**:3
Galvin, Martin
  Brief entry **1985**:3
Gandy, Kim 1954(?)- **2002**:2
Garcia, Jerry 1942-1995 **1988**:3
  Obituary **1996**:1
Gayle, Helene 1955- **2008**:2
Gebbie, Kristine 1944(?)- **1994**:2
Geldof, Bob 1954(?)- **1985**:3
George and Lena Korres
  1971- **2009**:1
Gertz, Alison 1966(?)-1992
  Obituary **1993**:2
Glaser, Elizabeth 1947-1994
  Obituary **1995**:2

Glasser, Ira 1938- **1989**:1
Goetz, Bernhard Hugo
  1947(?)- **1985**:3
Goldhaber, Fred
  Brief entry **1986**:3
Goodall, Jane 1934- **1991**:1
Goodman, Drew and Myra **2007**:4
Gore, Tipper 1948- **1985**:4
Grandin, Temple 1947- **2006**:1
Grant, Charity
  Brief entry **1985**:2
Greenberg, Hank 1911-1986
  Obituary **1986**:4
Gregory, Rogan 1972- **2008**:2
Guyer, David
  Brief entry **1988**:1
Hackney, Sheldon 1933- **1995**:1
Hahn, Jessica 1960- **1989**:4
Hale, Clara 1905-1992
  Obituary **1993**:3
Hayes, Robert M. 1952- **1986**:3
Hayse, Bruce 1949(?)- **2004**:3
Healey, Jack 1938(?)- **1990**:1
Hebard, Caroline 1944- **1998**:2
Hefner, Christie 1952- **1985**:1
Hepburn, Audrey 1929-1993
  Obituary **1993**:2
Hero, Peter 1942- **2001**:2
Hindmarch, Anya 1969- **2008**:2
Hirshberg, Gary 1954(?)- **2007**:2
Hoffman, Abbie 1936-1989
  Obituary **1989**:3
Hudson, Rock 1925-1985
  Obituary **1985**:4
Huerta, Dolores 1930- **1998**:1
Huffington, Arianna 1950- **1996**:2
Hullinger, Charlotte
  Brief entry **1985**:1
Hume, John 1938- **1987**:1
Humphry, Derek 1931(?)- **1992**:2
Ireland, Jill 1936-1990
  Obituary **1990**:4
Ireland, Patricia 1946(?)- **1992**:2
Iyengar, B.K.S. 1918- **2005**:1
Jackson, Jesse 1941- **1996**:1
Jacobs, Joe 1945(?)- **1994**:1
Jeffrey, Mildred 1910-2004
  Obituary **2005**:2
Jordan, King 1943(?)- **1990**:1
Jordan, Vernon, Jr. 1935- **2002**:3
Jorgensen, Christine 1926-1989
  Obituary **1989**:4
Judkins, Reba
  Brief entry **1987**:3
Kathwari, M. Farooq 1944- **2005**:4
Kennedy, Rose 1890-1995
  Obituary **1995**:3
Kevorkian, Jack 1928(?)- **1991**:3
Kielburger, Craig 1983- **1998**:1
King, Bernice 1963- **2000**:2
King, Coretta Scott 1927- **1999**:3
Kingsolver, Barbara 1955- **2005**:1
Kissling, Frances 1943- **1989**:2
Klarsfeld, Beate 1939- **1989**:1
Korchinsky, Mike 1961- **2004**:2
Kouchner, Bernard 1939- **2005**:3
Kozinski, Alex 1950- **2002**:2
Kozol, Jonathan 1936- **1992**:1
Kramer, Larry 1935- **1991**:2
Krim, Mathilde 1926- **1989**:2
Krupp, Fred 1954- **2008**:3
Kunstler, William 1919-1995

Obituary **1996**:1
Kurzban, Ira 1949- **1987**:2
LaDuke, Winona 1959- **1995**:2
Lang, Eugene M. 1919- **1990**:3
Leary, Timothy 1920-1996
    Obituary **1996**:4
Lerner, Sandy 1955(?)- **2005**:1
LeVay, Simon 1943- **1992**:2
Lightner, Candy 1946- **1985**:1
Lines, Ray 1960(?)- **2004**:1
Lipkis, Andy
    Brief entry **1985**:3
Lodge, Henry Cabot 1902-1985
    Obituary **1985**:1
Lord, Bette Bao 1938- **1994**:1
Louv, Richard 1949- **2006**:2
Lowry, Adam and Eric Ryan **2008**:1
Lum, Olivia 1961- **2009**:1
Maathai, Wangari 1940- **2005**:3
Mackey, John 1953- **2008**:2
MacKinnon, Catharine 1946- **1993**:2
Mahony, Roger M. 1936- **1988**:2
Makeba, Miriam 1934- **1989**:2
Mandela, Nelson 1918- **1990**:3
Mandela, Winnie 1934- **1989**:3
Mankiller, Wilma P.
    Brief entry **1986**:2
Maraldo, Pamela J. 1948(?)- **1993**:4
Marier, Rebecca 1974- **1995**:4
Martinez, Bob 1934- **1992**:1
Mathews, Dan 1965- **1998**:3
Matlovich, Leonard P. 1944(?)-1988
    Obituary **1988**:4
Mauldin, Bill 1921-2003
    Obituary **2004**:2
McCall, Nathan 1955- **1994**:4
McCartney, Bill 1940- **1995**:3
McCloskey, J. Michael 1934- **1988**:2
McDonnell, Patrick 1956- **2009**:4
McGuinness, Martin 1950(?)- **1985**:4
McKinnell, Henry 1943(?)- **2002**:3
McSally, Martha 1966(?)- **2002**:4
McTaggart, David 1932(?)- **1989**:4
McVeigh, Timothy 1968-2001
    Obituary **2002**:2
Menchu, Rigoberta 1960(?)- **1993**:2
Mengele, Josef 1911-1979
    Obituary **1985**:2
Menninger, Karl 1893-1990
    Obituary **1991**:1
Merritt, Justine
    Brief entry **1985**:3
Michelman, Kate 1942- **1998**:4
Monroe, Rose Will 1920-1997
    Obituary **1997**:4
Moose, Charles 1953(?)- **2003**:4
Morgentaler, Henry 1923- **1986**:3
Mother Teresa 1910-1997 **1993**:1
    Obituary **1998**:1
Mott, William Penn, Jr. 1909- **1986**:1
Mumford, Lewis 1895-1990
    Obituary **1990**:2
Nader, Ralph 1934- **1989**:4
Nasrin, Taslima 1962- **1995**:1
Newkirk, Ingrid 1949- **1992**:3
Ngau, Harrison **1991**:3
Nidal, Abu 1937- **1987**:1
Nixon, Bob 1954(?)- **2006**:4
Pacelle, Wayne 1965- **2009**:4
Parks, Rosa 1913-2005
    Obituary **2007**:1
Paton, Alan 1903-1988

Obituary **1988**:3
Peebles, R. Donahue 1960- **2003**:2
Peltier, Leonard 1944- **1995**:1
Pendleton, Clarence M. 1930-1988
    Obituary **1988**:4
Politkovskaya, Anna 1958-2006
    Obituary **2007**:4
Power, Samantha 1970- **2005**:4
Pritzker, A.N. 1896-1986
    Obituary **1986**:2
Puleston, Dennis 1905-2001
    Obituary **2002**:2
Quill, Timothy E. 1949- **1997**:3
Quinlan, Karen Ann 1954-1985
    Obituary **1985**:2
Radecki, Thomas
    Brief entry **1986**:2
Ramaphosa, Cyril 1953- **1988**:2
Redmond, Tim 1947- **2008**:1
Reeve, Christopher 1952- **1997**:2
Ross, Percy
    Brief entry **1986**:2
Rothstein, Ruth **1988**:2
Rowley, Coleen 1955(?)- **2004**:2
Rubin, Jerry 1938-1994
    Obituary **1995**:2
Ruppe, Loret Miller 1936- **1986**:2
Sachs, Jeffrey D. 1954- **2004**:4
Sakharov, Andrei Dmitrievich
    1921-1989
    Obituary **1990**:2
Salbi, Zainab 1969(?)- **2008**:3
Sample, Bill
    Brief entry **1986**:2
Sams, Craig 1944- **2007**:3
Saro-Wiwa, Ken 1941-1995
    Obituary **1996**:2
Sasakawa, Ryoichi
    Brief entry **1988**:1
Saul, Betsy 1968- **2009**:2
Schiavo, Mary 1955- **1998**:2
Sendler, Irena 1910-2008
    Obituary **2009**:2
Seo, Danny 1977- **2008**:3
Shabazz, Betty 1936-1997
    Obituary **1997**:4
Sharma, Nisha 1982(?)- **2004**:2
Sharpton, Al 1954- **1991**:2
Shcharansky, Anatoly 1948- **1986**:2
Shilts, Randy 1951-1994 **1993**:4
    Obituary **1994**:3
Shocked, Michelle 1963(?)- **1989**:4
Sidney, Ivan
    Brief entry **1987**:2
Sinclair, Mary 1918- **1985**:2
Singer, Margaret Thaler 1921-2003
    Obituary **2005**:1
Slotnick, Barry
    Brief entry **1987**:4
Slovo, Joe 1926- **1989**:2
Smith, Samantha 1972-1985
    Obituary **1985**:3
Snyder, Mitch 1944(?)-1990
    Obituary **1991**:1
Sontag, Susan 1933-2004
    Obituary **2006**:1
Spong, John 1931- **1991**:3
Steele, Shelby 1946- **1991**:2
Steinem, Gloria 1934- **1996**:2
Stephens, Arran and Ratana **2008**:4
Steptoe, Patrick 1913-1988
    Obituary **1988**:3

Stevens, Eileen 1939- **1987**:3
Stevens, James
    Brief entry **1988**:1
Strong, Maurice 1929- **1993**:1
Strummer, Joe 1952-2002
    Obituary **2004**:1
Suckling, Kierán 1964- **2009**:2
Sullivan, Leon 1922-2001
    Obituary **2002**:2
Sullivan, Louis 1933- **1990**:4
Summers, Anne 1945- **1990**:2
Suu Kyi, Aung San 1945(?)- **1996**:2
Sweeney, John J. 1934- **2000**:3
Szent-Gyoergyi, Albert 1893-1986
    Obituary **1987**:2
Tafel, Richard 1962- **2000**:4
Tambo, Oliver 1917- **1991**:3
Tannen, Deborah 1945- **1995**:1
Terry, Randall **1991**:4
Thomas, Clarence 1948- **1992**:2
Tillion, Germaine 1907-2008
    Obituary **2009**:2
Ture, Kwame 1941-1998
    Obituary **1999**:2
Unz, Ron 1962(?)- **1999**:1
Verdi-Fletcher, Mary 1955- **1998**:2
Vitousek, Peter 1949- **2003**:1
Waddell, Thomas F. 1937-1987
    Obituary **1988**:2
Waters, Alice 1944- **2006**:3
Wattleton, Faye 1943- **1989**:1
Wei Jingsheng 1950- **1998**:2
Wells, Sharlene
    Brief entry **1985**:1
West, Cornel 1953- **1994**:2
Whelan, Tensie 1960- **2007**:1
White, Ryan 1972(?)-1990
    Obituary **1990**:3
Whitestone, Heather 1973(?)- **1995**:1
Wiesenthal, Simon 1908-2005
    Obituary **2006**:4
Wigand, Jeffrey 1943(?)- **2000**:4
Wildmon, Donald 1938- **1988**:4
Williams, Hosea 1926-2000
    Obituary **2001**:2
Williamson, Marianne
    1953(?)- **1991**:4
Willson, S. Brian 1942(?)- **1989**:3
Wilmut, Ian 1944- **1997**:3
Wilson, William Julius 1935- **1997**:1
Wolf, Naomi 1963(?)- **1994**:3
Woodruff, Robert Winship 1889-1985
    Obituary **1985**:1
Wu, Harry 1937- **1996**:1
Yard, Molly **1991**:4
Yeang, Ken 1948- **2008**:3
Yokich, Stephen P. 1935- **1995**:4
Youngblood, Johnny Ray
    1948- **1994**:1
Yunus, Muhammad 1940- **2007**:3
Zamora, Pedro 1972-1994
    Obituary **1995**:2
Zech, Lando W.
    Brief entry **1987**:4
Zigler, Edward 1930- **1994**:1


**SPORTS**
Abbott, Jim 1967- **1988**:3
Abercrombie, Josephine 1925- **1987**:2
Adu, Freddy 1989- **2005**:3

Agassi, Andre 1970- **1990**:2
Agee, Tommie 1942-2001
    Obituary **2001**:4
Aikman, Troy 1966- **1994**:2
Ainge, Danny 1959- **1987**:1
Akers, Michelle 1966- **1996**:1
Albert, Marv 1943- **1994**:3
Albom, Mitch 1958- **1999**:3
Ali, Laila 1977- **2001**:2
Ali, Muhammad 1942- **1997**:2
Allen, Mel 1913-1996
    Obituary **1996**:4
Allen, Ray 1975- **2002**:1
Allenby, Robert 1971- **2007**:1
Alter, Hobie
    Brief entry **1985**:1
Angelos, Peter 1930- **1995**:4
Anthony, Earl 1938-2001
    Obituary **2002**:3
Aoki, Rocky 1940- **1990**:2
Arakawa, Shizuka 1981- **2006**:4
Armstrong, Henry 1912-1988
    Obituary **1989**:1
Armstrong, Lance 1971- **2000**:1
Ashe, Arthur 1943-1993
    Obituary **1993**:3
Auerbach, Red 1911-2006
    Obituary **2008**:1
Austin, Stone Cold Steve
    1964- **2001**:3
Axthelm, Pete 1943(?)-1991
    Obituary **1991**:3
Azinger, Paul 1960- **1995**:2
Babilonia, Tai 1959- **1997**:2
Baiul, Oksana 1977- **1995**:3
Baker, Kathy
    Brief entry **1986**:1
Barber, Tiki 1975- **2007**:1
Barkley, Charles 1963- **1988**:2
Barnes, Ernie 1938- **1997**:4
Baumgartner, Bruce
    Brief entry **1987**:3
Becker, Boris
    Brief entry **1985**:3
Beckham, David 1975- **2003**:1
Bell, Ricky 1955-1984
    Obituary **1985**:1
Belle, Albert 1966- **1996**:4
Benoit, Joan 1957- **1986**:3
Best, George 1946-2005
    Obituary **2007**:1
Bias, Len 1964(?)-1986
    Obituary **1986**:3
Bird, Larry 1956- **1990**:3
Blair, Bonnie 1964- **1992**:3
Bledsoe, Drew 1972- **1995**:1
Boggs, Wade 1958- **1989**:3
Boitano, Brian 1963- **1988**:3
Bolt, Usain 1986- **2009**:2
Bonds, Barry 1964- **1993**:3
Bonilla, Bobby 1963- **1992**:2
Bosworth, Brian 1965- **1989**:1
Boudreau, Louis 1917-2001
    Obituary **2002**:3
Bourque, Raymond Jean
    1960- **1997**:3
Bowe, Riddick 1967(?)- **1993**:2
Bowman, Scotty 1933- **1998**:4
Bradman, Sir Donald 1908-2001
    Obituary **2002**:1
Brady, Tom 1977- **2002**:4
Bremen, Barry 1947- **1987**:3

Brown, Jim 1936- **1993**:2
Brown, Paul 1908-1991
    Obituary **1992**:1
Bryant, Kobe 1978- **1998**:3
Burton, Jake 1954- **2007**:1
Busch, August Anheuser, Jr.
    1899-1989
    Obituary **1990**:2
Busch, Kurt 1978- **2006**:1
Buss, Jerry 1933- **1989**:3
Butcher, Susan 1954- **1991**:1
Callaway, Ely 1919-2001
    Obituary **2002**:3
Campanella, Roy 1921-1993
    Obituary **1994**:1
Canseco, Jose 1964- **1990**:2
Capriati, Jennifer 1976- **1991**:1
Caray, Harry 1914(?)-1998 **1988**:3
    Obituary **1998**:3
Carter, Gary 1954- **1987**:1
Carter, Joe 1960- **1994**:2
Carter, Rubin 1937- **2000**:3
Carter, Vince 1977- **2001**:4
Chamberlain, Joba 1985- **2008**:3
Chamberlain, Wilt 1936-1999
    Obituary **2000**:2
Chaney, John 1932- **1989**:1
Chastain, Brandi 1968- **2001**:3
Chen, T.C.
    Brief entry **1987**:3
Cherry, Don 1934- **1993**:4
Chyna 1970- **2001**:4
Clemens, Roger 1962- **1991**:4
Clijsters, Kim 1983- **2006**:3
Coffey, Paul 1961- **1985**:4
Collins, Kerry 1972- **2002**:3
Conigliaro, Tony 1945-1990
    Obituary **1990**:3
Conner, Dennis 1943- **1987**:2
Cooper, Cynthia **1999**:1
Copeland, Al 1944(?)- **1988**:3
Cosell, Howard 1918-1995
    Obituary **1995**:4
Costas, Bob 1952- **1986**:4
Couples, Fred 1959- **1994**:4
Courier, Jim 1970- **1993**:2
Creamer, Paula 1986- **2006**:2
Crosby, Sidney 1987- **2006**:3
Cunningham, Randall 1963- **1990**:1
Curren, Tommy
    Brief entry **1987**:4
Curtis, Ben 1977- **2004**:2
Damon, Johnny 1973- **2005**:4
Danza, Tony 1951- **1989**:1
Davenport, Lindsay 1976- **1999**:2
Davis, Eric 1962- **1987**:4
Davis, Terrell 1972- **1998**:2
Day, Pat 1953- **1995**:2
DeBartolo, Edward J., Jr.
    1946- **1989**:3
De La Hoya, Oscar 1973- **1998**:2
Desormeaux, Kent 1970- **1990**:2
DiBello, Paul
    Brief entry **1986**:4
DiMaggio, Joe 1914-1999
    Obituary **1999**:3
Djokovic, Novak 1987- **2008**:4
Dolan, Tom 1975- **2001**:2
Donnellan, Nanci **1995**:2
Doubleday, Nelson, Jr. 1933- **1987**:1
Douglas, Buster 1960(?)- **1990**:4
Dravecky, Dave 1956- **1992**:1

Drexler, Clyde 1962- **1992**:4
Drysdale, Don 1936-1993
    Obituary **1994**:1
Duncan, Tim 1976- **2000**:1
Durocher, Leo 1905-1991
    Obituary **1992**:2
Duval, David 1971- **2000**:3
Duvall, Camille
    Brief entry **1988**:1
Dykstra, Lenny 1963- **1993**:4
Eagleson, Alan 1933- **1987**:4
Earnhardt, Dale 1951-2001
    Obituary **2001**:4
Earnhardt, Dale, Jr. 1974- **2004**:4
Ederle, Gertrude 1905-2003
    Obituary **2005**:1
Edwards, Harry 1942- **1989**:4
Elway, John 1960- **1990**:3
Epstein, Theo 1973- **2003**:4
Esiason, Boomer 1961- **1991**:1
Evans, Janet 1971- **1989**:1
Ewing, Patrick 1962- **1985**:3
Fabris, Enrico 1981- **2006**:4
Faldo, Nick 1957- **1993**:3
Favre, Brett Lorenzo 1969- **1997**:2
Federer, Roger 1981- **2004**:2
Federov, Sergei 1969- **1995**:1
Fehr, Donald 1948- **1987**:2
Ferrari, Enzo 1898-1988 **1988**:4
Fielder, Cecil 1963- **1993**:2
Fiennes, Ranulph 1944- **1990**:3
Firestone, Roy 1953- **1988**:2
Fischer, Bobby 1943-2008
    Obituary **2009**:1
Fittipaldi, Emerson 1946- **1994**:2
Flood, Curt 1938-1997
    Obituary **1997**:2
Flutie, Doug 1962- **1999**:2
Foreman, George 1949- **2004**:2
Foss, Joe 1915- **1990**:3
Fossett, Steve 1944- **2007**:2
Franchitti, Dario 1973- **2008**:1
Freeman, Cathy 1973- **2001**:3
Fuhr, Grant 1962- **1997**:3
Furyk, Jim 1970- **2004**:2
Galindo, Rudy 1969- **2001**:2
Garcia, Joe
    Brief entry **1986**:4
Gardner, Randy 1957- **1997**:2
Garnett, Kevin 1976- **2000**:3
Gathers, Hank 1967(?)-1990
    Obituary **1990**:3
Gault, Willie 1960- **1991**:2
Gerulaitis, Vitas 1954-1994
    Obituary **1995**:1
Giamatti, A. Bartlett
    1938-1989 **1988**:4
    Obituary **1990**:1
Gibson, Althea 1927-2003
    Obituary **2004**:4
Gibson, Kirk 1957- **1985**:2
Giguere, Jean-Sebastien 1977- **2004**:2
Gilmour, Doug 1963- **1994**:3
Glaus, Troy 1976- **2003**:3
Gomez, Lefty 1909-1989
    Obituary **1989**:3
Gooden, Dwight 1964- **1985**:2
Gordeeva, Ekaterina 1972- **1996**:4
Gordon, Jeff 1971- **1996**:1
Graf, Steffi 1969- **1987**:4
Granato, Cammi 1971- **1999**:3
Grange, Red 1903-1991

Obituary **1991**:3
Graziano, Rocky 1922-1990
Obituary **1990**:4
Greenberg, Hank 1911-1986
Obituary **1986**:4
Gretzky, Wayne 1961- **1989**:2
Griffey, Ken Jr. 1969- **1994**:1
Grinkov, Sergei 1967-1995
Obituary **1996**:2
Gruden, Jon 1963- **2003**:4
Gumbel, Greg 1946- **1996**:4
Guo Jingjing 1981- **2009**:2
Gwynn, Tony 1960- **1995**:1
Hagler, Marvelous Marvin
1954- **1985**:2
Hamels, Cole 1983- **2009**:4
Hamilton, Lewis 1985- **2008**:4
Hamilton, Scott 1958- **1998**:2
Hamm, Mia 1972- **2000**:1
Hamm, Paul 1982- **2005**:1
Hanauer, Chip 1954- **1986**:2
Hardaway, Anfernee 1971- **1996**:2
Harkes, John 1967- **1996**:4
Harmon, Tom 1919-1990
Obituary **1990**:3
Hart, Carey 1975- **2006**:4
Harwell, Ernie 1918- **1997**:3
Hasek, Dominik 1965- **1998**:3
Hawk, Tony 1968- **2001**:4
Hayes, Woody 1913-1987
Obituary **1987**:2
Helton, Todd 1973- **2001**:1
Hempleman-Adams, David
1956- **2004**:3
Henderson, Rickey 1958- **2002**:3
Henin-Hardenne, Justine
1982- **2004**:4
Hernandez, Felix 1986- **2008**:2
Hernandez, Willie 1954- **1985**:1
Hershiser, Orel 1958- **1989**:2
Hewitt, Lleyton 1981- **2002**:2
Hextall, Ron 1964- **1988**:2
Hill, Grant 1972- **1995**:3
Hill, Lynn 1961(?)- **1991**:2
Hillary, Edmund 1919-2008
Obituary **2009**:1
Hingis, Martina 1980- **1999**:1
Hogan, Ben 1912-1997
Obituary **1997**:4
Hogan, Hulk 1953- **1987**:3
Holtz, Lou 1937- **1986**:4
Holyfield, Evander 1962- **1991**:3
Horn, Mike 1966- **2009**:3
Howard, Desmond
Kevin 1970- **1997**:2
Howser, Dick 1936-1987
Obituary **1987**:4
Hughes, Sarah 1985- **2002**:4
Hull, Brett 1964- **1991**:4
Hunter, Catfish 1946-1999
Obituary **2000**:1
Indurain, Miguel 1964- **1994**:1
Inkster, Juli 1960- **2000**:2
Irvin, Michael 1966- **1996**:3
Irwin, Hale 1945- **2005**:2
Ivanisevic, Goran 1971- **2002**:1
Iverson, Allen 1975- **2001**:4
Jackson, Bo 1962- **1986**:3
Jackson, Phil 1945- **1996**:3
Jagr, Jaromir 1972- **1995**:4
James, LeBron 1984- **2007**:3
Jenkins, Sally 1960(?)- **1997**:2

Jeter, Derek 1974- **1999**:4
Johnson, Earvin Magic 1959- **1988**:4
Johnson, Jimmie 1975- **2007**:2
Johnson, Jimmy 1943- **1993**:3
Johnson, Kevin 1966(?)- **1991**:1
Johnson, Keyshawn 1972- **2000**:4
Johnson, Larry 1969- **1993**:3
Johnson, Michael **2000**:1
Johnson, Randy 1963- **1996**:2
Johnson, Shawn 1992- **2009**:2
Jones, Jerry 1942- **1994**:4
Jones, Marion 1975- **1998**:4
Jordan, Michael 1963- **1987**:2
Joyner, Florence Griffith
1959-1998 **1989**:2
Obituary **1999**:1
Joyner-Kersee, Jackie 1962- **1993**:1
Kallen, Jackie 1946(?)- **1994**:1
Kanokogi, Rusty
Brief entry **1987**:1
Kasparov, Garry 1963- **1997**:4
Kelly, Jim 1960- **1991**:4
Kemp, Jack 1935- **1990**:4
Kemp, Jan 1949- **1987**:2
Kemp, Shawn 1969- **1995**:1
Kerr, Cristie 1977- **2008**:2
Kerrigan, Nancy 1969- **1994**:3
Kidd, Jason 1973- **2003**:2
King, Don 1931- **1989**:1
Kiraly, Karch
Brief entry **1987**:1
Kite, Tom 1949- **1990**:3
Klima, Petr 1964- **1987**:1
Knievel, Evel 1938-2007
Obituary **2009**:1
Knievel, Robbie 1963- **1990**:1
Knight, Bobby 1940- **1985**:3
Koch, Bill 1940- **1992**:3
Konstantinov, Vladimir 1967- **1997**:4
Kournikova, Anna 1981- **2000**:3
Kroc, Ray 1902-1984
Obituary **1985**:1
Krone, Julie 1963(?)- **1989**:2
Kruk, John 1961- **1994**:4
Krzyzewski, Mike 1947- **1993**:2
Kukoc, Toni 1968- **1995**:4
Laettner, Christian 1969- **1993**:1
LaFontaine, Pat 1965- **1985**:1
Laimbeer, Bill 1957- **2004**:3
Lalas, Alexi 1970- **1995**:1
Landry, Tom 1924-2000
Obituary **2000**:3
Lemieux, Claude 1965- **1996**:1
Lemieux, Mario 1965- **1986**:4
LeMond, Greg 1961- **1986**:4
Leonard, Sugar Ray 1956- **1989**:4
Leslie, Lisa 1972- **1997**:4
Lewis, Lennox 1965- **2000**:2
Lewis, Ray 1975- **2001**:3
Lewis, Reggie 1966(?)-1993
Obituary **1994**:1
Leyland, Jim 1944- **1998**:2
Lidstrom, Nicklas 1970- **2009**:1
Lindbergh, Pelle 1959-1985
Obituary **1985**:4
Lindros, Eric 1973- **1992**:1
Lipinski, Tara 1982- **1998**:3
Lofton, Kenny 1967- **1998**:1
Lopez, Nancy 1957- **1989**:3
Louganis, Greg 1960- **1995**:3
Lowell, Mike 1974- **2003**:2
Lukas, D. Wayne 1936(?)- **1986**:2

MacArthur, Ellen 1976- **2005**:3
Madden, John 1936- **1995**:1
Maddux, Greg 1966- **1996**:2
Majerle, Dan 1965- **1993**:4
Malone, Karl 1963- **1990**:1
Manning, Eli 1981- **2008**:4
Manning, Peyton 1976- **2007**:4
Mantle, Mickey 1931-1995
Obituary **1996**:1
Maradona, Diego 1961(?)- **1991**:3
Maravich, Pete 1948-1988
Obituary **1988**:2
Maris, Roger 1934-1985
Obituary **1986**:1
Martin, Billy 1928-1989 **1988**:4
Obituary **1990**:2
Martin, Casey 1972- **2002**:1
Mathias, Bob 1930-2006
Obituary **2007**:4
Mathis, Clint 1976- **2003**:1
Matsui, Hideki 1974- **2007**:4
Mattingly, Don 1961- **1986**:2
Matuszak, John 1951(?)-1989
Obituary **1989**:4
Mauresmo, Amelie 1979- **2007**:2
McCarron, Chris 1955- **1995**:4
McCartney, Bill 1940- **1995**:3
McGraw, Tug 1944-2004
Obituary **2005**:1
McGwire, Mark 1963- **1999**:1
McMahon, Jim 1959- **1985**:4
McMahon, Vince, Jr. 1945(?)- **1985**:4
Messier, Mark 1961- **1993**:1
Mickelson, Phil 1970- **2004**:4
Mikan, George 1924-2005
Obituary **2006**:3
Milbrett, Tiffeny 1972- **2001**:1
Milburn, Rodney Jr.
1950-1997 **1998**:2
Miller, Andre 1976- **2003**:3
Miller, Bode 1977- **2002**:4
Miller, Reggie 1965- **1994**:4
Minnesota Fats 1900(?)-1996
Obituary **1996**:3
Modano, Mike 1970- **2008**:2
Monaghan, Tom 1937- **1985**:1
Monk, Art 1957- **1993**:2
Montana, Joe 1956- **1989**:2
Moon, Warren 1956- **1991**:3
Moore, Archie 1913-1998
Obituary **1999**:2
Moreno, Arturo 1946- **2005**:2
Morgan, Dodge 1932(?)- **1987**:1
Moss, Randy 1977- **1999**:3
Mourning, Alonzo 1970- **1994**:2
Muldowney, Shirley 1940- **1986**:1
Mulkey-Robertson, Kim
1962- **2006**:1
Musburger, Brent 1939- **1985**:1
Nadal, Rafael 1986- **2009**:1
Navratilova, Martina 1956- **1989**:1
Nelson, Byron 1912-2006
Obituary **2007**:4
Newman, Paul 1925- **1995**:3
Newman, Ryan 1977- **2005**:1
Nomo, Hideo 1968- **1996**:2
Norman, Greg 1955- **1988**:3
Nowitzki, Dirk 1978- **2007**:2
Ochoa, Lorena 1981- **2007**:4
O'Donnell, Bill
Brief entry **1987**:4
Okoye, Christian 1961- **1990**:2

Olajuwon, Akeem 1963- **1985**:1
Olson, Billy 1958- **1986**:3
O'Malley, Susan 1962(?)- **1995**:2
O'Neal, Shaquille 1972- **1992**:1
O'Neil, Buck 1911-2006
Obituary **2007**:4
Ovechkin, Alexander 1985- **2009**:2
Pak, Se Ri 1977- **1999**:4
Palmeiro, Rafael 1964- **2005**:1
Palmer, Jim 1945- **1991**:2
Palmer, Violet 1964(?)- **2005**:2
Parker, Tony 1982- **2008**:1
Parker, Willie 1980- **2009**:3
Paterno, Joe 1926- **1995**:4
Patrick, Danica 1982- **2003**:3
Pavin, Corey 1959- **1996**:4
Payton, Walter 1954-1999
Obituary **2000**:2
Peete, Calvin 1943- **1985**:4
Penske, Roger 1937- **1988**:3
Pep, Willie 1922-2006
Obituary **2008**:1
Phelps, Michael 1985- **2009**:2
Piazza, Mike 1968- **1998**:4
Pierce, Mary 1975- **1994**:4
Pierce, Paul 1977- **2009**:2
Pincay, Laffit, Jr. 1946- **1986**:3
Pippen, Scottie 1965- **1992**:2
Pocklington, Peter H. 1941- **1985**:2
Polgar, Judit 1976- **1993**:3
Prost, Alain 1955- **1988**:1
Puckett, Kirby 1960-2006
Obituary **2007**:2
Pujols, Albert 1980- **2005**:3
Rafter, Patrick 1972- **2001**:1
Ramirez, Manny 1972- **2005**:4
Retton, Mary Lou 1968- **1985**:2
Rice, Jerry 1962- **1990**:4
Richard, Maurice 1921-2000
Obituary **2000**:4
Riggs, Bobby 1918-1995
Obituary **1996**:2
Riley, Pat 1945- **1994**:3
Ripken, Cal, Jr. 1960- **1986**:2
Ripken, Cal, Sr. 1936(?)-1999
Obituary **1999**:4
Roberts, Steven K. 1952(?)- **1992**:1
Robinson, David 1965- **1990**:4
Robinson, Eddie 1919-2007
Obituary **2008**:2
Robinson, Frank 1935- **1990**:2
Robinson, Sugar Ray 1921-1989
Obituary **1989**:3
Roddick, Andy 1982- **2004**:3
Rodman, Dennis 1961- **1991**:3
Rodriguez, Alex 1975- **2001**:2
Romo, Tony 1980- **2008**:3
Ronaldinho 1980- **2007**:3
Ronaldo 1976- **1999**:2
Rooney, Art 1901-1988
Obituary **1989**:1
Rose, Pete 1941- **1991**:1
Roy, Patrick 1965- **1994**:2
Rozelle, Pete 1926-1996
Obituary **1997**:2
Rudolph, Wilma 1940-1994
Obituary **1995**:2
Runyan, Marla 1969- **2001**:1
Ryan, Nolan 1947- **1989**:4
Rypien, Mark 1962- **1992**:3
Sabatini, Gabriela
Brief entry **1985**:4

Saberhagen, Bret 1964- **1986**:1
Safin, Marat 1980- **2001**:3
Sakic, Joe 1969- **2002**:1
Samaranch, Juan Antonio
1920- **1986**:2
Sampras, Pete 1971- **1994**:1
Sanders, Barry 1968- **1992**:1
Sanders, Deion 1967- **1992**:4
Santana, Johan 1979- **2008**:1
Sarazen, Gene 1902-1999
Obituary **1999**:4
Schaap, Dick 1934-2001
Obituary **2003**:1
Schembechler, Bo 1929(?)- **1990**:3
Schilling, Curt 1966- **2002**:3
Schmidt, Mike 1949- **1988**:3
Schott, Marge 1928- **1985**:4
Schumacher, Michael 1969- **2005**:2
Schwarzenegger, Arnold
1947- **1991**:1
Secretariat 1970-1989
Obituary **1990**:1
Seles, Monica 1974(?)- **1991**:3
Selig, Bud 1934- **1995**:2
Senna, Ayrton 1960(?)-1994 **1991**:4
Obituary **1994**:4
Sharapova, Maria 1987- **2005**:2
Sharpe, Sterling 1965- **1994**:3
Shea, Jim, Jr. 1968- **2002**:4
Sheffield, Gary 1968- **1998**:1
Shoemaker, Bill 1931-2003
Obituary **2004**:4
Shula, Don 1930- **1992**:2
Singh, Vijay 1963- **2000**:4
Smith, Emmitt **1994**:1
Smith, Jerry 1943-1986
Obituary **1987**:1
Snead, Sam 1912-2002
Obituary **2003**:3
Snyder, Jimmy 1919-1996
Obituary **1996**:4
Sorenstam, Annika 1970- **2001**:1
Soriano, Alfonso 1976- **2008**:1
Sosa, Sammy 1968- **1999**:1
Spahn, Warren 1921-2003
Obituary **2005**:1
Sprewell, Latrell 1970- **1999**:4
St. James, Lyn 1947- **1993**:2
Stargell, Willie 1940-2001
Obituary **2002**:1
Steger, Will 1945(?)- **1990**:4
Steinberg, Leigh 1949- **1987**:3
Steinbrenner, George 1930- **1991**:1
Stern, David 1942- **1991**:4
Stewart, Dave 1957- **1991**:1
Stewart, Payne 1957-1999
Obituary **2000**:2
Stewart, Tony 1971- **2003**:4
Stockton, John Houston 1962- **1997**:3
Stofflet, Ty
Brief entry **1987**:1
Strange, Curtis 1955- **1988**:4
Street, Picabo 1971- **1999**:3
Strobl, Fritz 1972- **2003**:3
Strug, Kerri 1977- **1997**:3
Summitt, Pat 1952- **2004**:1
Suzuki, Ichiro 1973- **2002**:2
Swoopes, Sheryl 1971- **1998**:2
Tagliabue, Paul 1940- **1990**:2
Tarkenian, Jerry 1930- **1990**:4
Taylor, Lawrence 1959- **1987**:3
Testaverde, Vinny 1962- **1987**:2

Teter, Hannah 1987- **2006**:4
Thomas, Debi 1967- **1987**:2
Thomas, Derrick 1967-2000
Obituary **2000**:3
Thomas, Frank 1968- **1994**:3
Thomas, Isiah 1961- **1989**:2
Thomas, Thurman 1966- **1993**:1
Thompson, John 1941- **1988**:3
Tomba, Alberto 1966- **1992**:3
Torre, Joseph Paul 1940- **1997**:1
Torres, Dara 1967- **2009**:1
Trask, Amy 1961- **2003**:3
Trinidad, Felix 1973- **2000**:4
Turner, Ted 1938- **1989**:1
Tyson, Mike 1966- **1986**:4
Unitas, Johnny 1933-2002
Obituary **2003**:4
Upshaw, Gene 1945- **1988**:1
Van Dyken, Amy 1973- **1997**:1
Van Slyke, Andy 1960- **1992**:4
Vaughn, Mo 1967- **1999**:2
Veeck, Bill 1914-1986
Obituary **1986**:1
Ventura, Jesse 1951- **1999**:2
Villeneuve, Jacques 1971- **1997**:1
Vincent, Fay 1938- **1990**:2
Vitale, Dick 1939- **1988**:4
Waddell, Thomas F. 1937-1987
Obituary **1988**:2
Wade, Dwyane 1982- **2007**:1
Wallace, Ben 1974- **2004**:3
Walsh, Bill 1931- **1987**:4
Wariner, Jeremy 1984- **2006**:3
Warner, Kurt 1971- **2000**:3
Webb, Karrie 1974- **2000**:4
Webber, Chris 1973- **1994**:1
Weber, Pete 1962- **1986**:3
Weir, Mike 1970- **2004**:1
Welch, Bob 1956- **1991**:3
Wells, David 1963- **1999**:3
Wescott, Seth 1976- **2006**:4
Whaley, Suzy 1966- **2003**:4
White, Bill 1934- **1989**:3
White, Byron 1917-2002
Obituary **2003**:3
White, Reggie 1961- **1993**:4
Wilkens, Lenny 1937- **1995**:2
Williams, Doug 1955- **1988**:2
Williams, Edward Bennett 1920-1988
Obituary **1988**:4
Williams, Ricky 1977- **2000**:2
Williams, Serena 1981- **1999**:4
Williams, Ted 1918-2002
Obituary **2003**:4
Williams, Venus 1980- **1998**:2
Witt, Katarina 1966(?)- **1991**:3
Woodard, Lynette 1959(?)- **1986**:2
Woods, Tiger 1975- **1995**:4
Woodson, Ron 1965- **1996**:4
Worthy, James 1961- **1991**:2
Yamaguchi, Kristi 1971- **1992**:3
Yao Ming 1980- **2004**:1
Young, Steve 1961- **1995**:2
Yzerman, Steve 1965- **1991**:2
Zamboni, Frank J.
Brief entry **1986**:4
Zanardi, Alex 1966- **1998**:2
Zatopek, Emil 1922-2000
Obituary **2001**:3
Zito, Barry 1978- **2003**:3

## TECHNOLOGY

Adair, Red 1915- **1987**:3
Allaire, Jeremy 1971- **2006**:4
Allaire, Paul 1938- **1995**:1
Anderson, Tom and Chris
   DeWolfe **2007**:2
Andreessen, Marc 1972- **1996**:2
Backus, John W. 1924-2007
   Obituary **2008**:2
Balsillie, Jim and Mike
   Lazaridis **2006**:4
Barksdale, James L. 1943- **1998**:2
Beal, Deron 1968(?)- **2005**:3
Belluzzo, Rick 1953- **2001**:3
Berners-Lee, Tim 1955(?)- **1997**:4
Bezos, Jeff 1964- **1998**:4
Bird, Brad 1956(?)- **2005**:4
Bloch, Erich 1925- **1987**:4
Bose, Amar
   Brief entry **1986**:4
Boyer, Herbert Wayne 1936- **1985**:1
Bradley, Todd 1958- **2003**:3
Burum, Stephen H.
   Brief entry **1987**:2
Bushnell, Nolan 1943- **1985**:1
Butterfield, Stewart and Caterina
   Fake **2007**:3
Case, Steve 1958- **1995**:4
Cassidy, Mike 1963(?)- **2006**:1
Cerf, Vinton G. 1943- **1999**:2
Chaudhari, Praveen 1937- **1989**:4
Chen, Steve and Chad
   Hurley **2007**:2
Chizen, Bruce 1955(?)- **2004**:2
Clarke, Richard A. 1951(?)- **2002**:2
Cray, Seymour R. 1925-1996
   Brief entry **1986**:3
   Obituary **1997**:2
David, George 1942- **2005**:1
Davis, Noel **1990**:3
Dell, Michael 1965- **1996**:2
De Luca, Guerrino 1952- **2007**:1
Dolby, Ray Milton
   Brief entry **1986**:1
Donahue, Tim 1950(?)- **2004**:3
Dunlap, Albert J. **1997**:2
Dzhanibekov, Vladimir 1942- **1988**:1
Ellison, Larry 1944- **2004**:2
Engibous, Thomas J. 1953- **2003**:3
Engstrom, Elmer W. 1901-1984
   Obituary **1985**:2
Evans, Nancy 1950- **2000**:4
Fanning, Shawn 1980- **2001**:1
Fender, Leo 1909-1991
   Obituary **1992**:1
Filo, David and Jerry Yang **1998**:3
Gardner, David and Tom **2001**:4
Garneau, Marc 1949- **1985**:1
Gates, Bill 1955- **1987**:4
Gould, Gordon 1920- **1987**:1
Hagelstein, Peter
   Brief entry **1986**:3
Haladjian, Rafi 1962(?)- **2008**:3
Hemming, Nikki 1967- **2009**:1
Hewlett, William 1913-2001
   Obituary **2001**:4
Hounsfield, Godfrey 1919- **1989**:2
Housenbold, Jeffrey 1969- **2009**:2
Inman, Bobby Ray 1931- **1985**:1
Irwin, James 1930-1991
   Obituary **1992**:1
Ive, Jonathan 1967- **2009**:2

Jacuzzi, Candido 1903-1986
   Obituary **1987**:1
Jarvik, Robert K. 1946- **1985**:1
Jemison, Mae C. 1956- **1993**:1
Kamen, Dean 1951(?)- **2003**:1
Kilby, Jack 1923- **2002**:2
Kimsey, James V. 1940(?)- **2001**:1
Kloss, Henry E.
   Brief entry **1985**:2
Koch, Bill 1940- **1992**:3
Kurzweil, Raymond 1948- **1986**:3
Kutaragi, Ken 1950- **2005**:3
Kwoh, Yik San 1946(?)- **1988**:2
Lalami, Laila **2007**:1
Lamborghini, Ferrucio 1916-1993
   Obituary **1993**:3
Land, Edwin H. 1909-1991
   Obituary **1991**:3
Langer, Robert 1948- **2003**:4
Lanier, Jaron 1961(?)- **1993**:4
Ma, Jack 1964- **2007**:1
Ma, Pony 1971(?)- **2006**:3
MacCready, Paul 1925- **1986**:4
Malda, Rob 1976- **2007**:3
McGowan, William 1927- **1985**:2
McLaren, Norman 1914-1987
   Obituary **1987**:2
McNealy, Scott 1954- **2009**:3
Minsky, Marvin 1927- **1994**:3
Moody, John 1943- **1985**:3
Morita, Akio 1921- **1989**:4
Morita, Akio 1921-1999
   Obituary **2000**:2
Newman, Joseph 1936- **1987**:1
Noyce, Robert N. 1927- **1985**:4
Ollila, Jorma 1950- **2003**:4
Pack, Ellen 1963(?)- **2001**:2
Palmisano, Samuel J. 1952(?)- **2003**:1
Parsons, Richard 1949- **2002**:4
Peluso, Michelle 1971(?)- **2007**:4
Perlman, Steve 1961(?)- **1998**:2
Perry, William 1927- **1994**:4
Pfeiffer, Eckhard 1941- **1998**:4
Probst, Larry 1951(?)- **2005**:1
Ramsay, Mike 1950(?)- **2002**:1
Raskin, Jef 1943(?)- **1997**:4
Rifkin, Jeremy 1945- **1990**:3
Rigopulos, Alex 1970- **2009**:4
Ritchie, Dennis and Kenneth
   Thompson **2000**:1
Roberts, Brian L. 1959- **2002**:4
Roberts, Steven K. 1952(?)- **1992**:1
Rutan, Burt 1943- **1987**:2
Schank, Roger 1946- **1989**:2
Schmidt, Eric 1955- **2002**:4
Scholz, Tom 1949- **1987**:2
Schroeder, William J. 1932-1986
   Obituary **1986**:4
Sculley, John 1939- **1989**:4
Seidenberg, Ivan 1946- **2004**:1
Semel, Terry 1943- **2002**:2
Shirley, Donna 1941- **1999**:1
Sinclair, Mary 1918- **1985**:2
Taylor, Jeff 1960- **2001**:3
Thomas, Edmond J. 1943(?)- **2005**:1
Thompson, John W. 1949- **2005**:1
Tito, Dennis 1940(?)- **2002**:1
Titov, Gherman 1935-2000
   Obituary **2001**:3
Tom and Ray Magliozzi **1991**:4
Toomer, Ron 1930- **1990**:1
Torvalds, Linus 1970(?)- **1999**:3

Treybig, James G. 1940- **1988**:3
Walker, Jay 1955- **2004**:2
Wang, An 1920-1990 **1986**:1
   Obituary **1990**:3
Wright, Will 1960- **2003**:4
Yamamoto, Kenichi 1922- **1989**:1
Zuckerberg, Mark 1984- **2008**:2

## TELEVISION

Abrams, J. J. 1966- **2007**:3
Adams, Amy 1974- **2008**:4
Adams, Don 1923-2005
   Obituary **2007**:1
Affleck, Ben 1972- **1999**:1
Alba, Jessica 1981- **2001**:2
Albert, Eddie 1906-2005
   Obituary **2006**:3
Albert, Marv 1943- **1994**:3
Albom, Mitch 1958- **1999**:3
Albrecht, Chris 1952(?)- **2005**:4
Alda, Robert 1914-1986
   Obituary **1986**:3
Alexander, Jane 1939- **1994**:2
Alexander, Jason 1962(?)- **1993**:3
Allen, Debbie 1950- **1998**:2
Allen, Steve 1921-2000
   Obituary **2001**:2
Allen, Tim 1953- **1993**:1
Alley, Kirstie 1955- **1990**:3
Allyson, June 1917-2006
   Obituary **2007**:3
Altman, Robert 1925- **1993**:2
Amanpour, Christiane 1958- **1997**:2
Ameche, Don 1908-1993
   Obituary **1994**:2
Amsterdam, Morey 1912-1996
   Obituary **1997**:1
Ancier, Garth 1957- **1989**:1
Anderson, Gillian 1968- **1997**:1
Anderson, Harry 1951(?)- **1988**:2
Anderson, Judith 1899(?)-1992
   Obituary **1992**:3
Andrews, Julie 1935- **1996**:1
Angelou, Maya 1928- **1993**:4
Aniston, Jennifer 1969- **2000**:3
Apatow, Judd 1967- **2006**:3
Applegate, Christina 1972- **2000**:4
Arden, Eve 1912(?)-1990
   Obituary **1991**:2
Arkin, Alan 1934- **2007**:4
Arledge, Roone 1931- **1992**:2
Arlen, Harold 1905-1986
   Obituary **1986**:3
Arnaz, Desi 1917-1986
   Obituary **1987**:1
Arnold, Tom 1959- **1993**:2
Arquette, Rosanna 1959- **1985**:2
Astin, Sean 1971- **2005**:1
Atkinson, Rowan 1955- **2004**:3
Autry, Gene 1907-1998
   Obituary **1999**:1
Axthelm, Pete 1943(?)-1991
   Obituary **1991**:3
Aykroyd, Dan 1952- **1989**:3
Azaria, Hank 1964- **2001**:3
Bacall, Lauren 1924- **1997**:3
Backus, Jim 1913-1989
   Obituary **1990**:1
Bacon, Kevin 1958- **1995**:3
Baddeley, Hermione 1906(?)-1986
   Obituary **1986**:4
Bailey, Pearl 1918-1990

Obituary **1991**:1
Baker, Simon 1969- **2009**:4
Bakula, Scott 1954- **2003**:1
Ball, Alan 1957- **2005**:1
Ball, Lucille 1911-1989
Obituary **1989**:3
Baranski, Christine 1952- **2001**:2
Barbera, Joseph 1911- **1988**:2
Bardem, Javier 1969- **2008**:4
Barkin, Ellen 1955- **1987**:3
Barney **1993**:4
Baron Cohen, Sacha 1971- **2007**:3
Barr, Roseanne 1953(?)- **1989**:1
Barrymore, Drew 1975- **1995**:3
Basinger, Kim 1953- **1987**:2
Bassett, Angela 1959(?)- **1994**:4
Bateman, Jason 1969- **2005**:3
Bateman, Justine 1966- **1988**:4
Baxter, Anne 1923-1985
Obituary **1986**:1
Beals, Jennifer 1963- **2005**:2
Beatty, Warren 1937- **2000**:1
Belushi, Jim 1954- **1986**:2
Belzer, Richard 1944- **1985**:3
Bergen, Candice 1946- **1990**:1
Berle, Milton 1908-2002
Obituary **2003**:2
Berman, Gail 1957(?)- **2006**:1
Bernardi, Herschel 1923-1986
Obituary **1986**:4
Bernsen, Corbin 1955- **1990**:2
Bernstein, Leonard 1918-1990
Obituary **1991**:1
Berry, Halle 1968- **1996**:2
Bialik, Mayim 1975- **1993**:3
Bird, Brad 1956(?)- **2005**:4
Bishop, Joey 1918-2007
Obituary **2008**:4
Bixby, Bill 1934-1993
Obituary **1994**:2
Black, Carole 1945- **2003**:1
Blades, Ruben 1948- **1998**:2
Blaine, David 1973- **2003**:3
Blanc, Mel 1908-1989
Obituary **1989**:4
Blanchett, Cate 1969- **1999**:3
Bloodworth-Thomason,
Linda 1947- **1994**:1
Bloom, Orlando 1977- **2004**:2
Bochco, Steven 1943- **1989**:1
Bolger, Ray 1904-1987
Obituary **1987**:2
Bonet, Lisa 1967- **1989**:2
Bono, Sonny 1935-1998 **1992**:2
Obituary **1998**:2
Booth, Shirley 1898-1992
Obituary **1993**:2
Bourdain, Anthony 1956- **2008**:3
Bowen, Julie 1970- **2007**:1
Boyle, Lara Flynn 1970- **2003**:4
Boyle, Peter 1935- **2002**:3
Bradley, Ed 1941-2006
Obituary **2008**:1
Bradshaw, John 1933- **1992**:1
Brady, Wayne 1972- **2008**:3
Braff, Zach 1975- **2005**:2
Brandy 1979- **1996**:4
Bratt, Benjamin 1963- **2009**:3
Brenneman, Amy 1964- **2002**:1
Bridges, Lloyd 1913-1998
Obituary **1998**:3
Brinkley, David 1920-2003

Obituary **2004**:3
Broadbent, Jim 1949- **2008**:4
Brokaw, Tom 1940- **2000**:3
Bronson, Charles 1921-2003
Obituary **2004**:4
Brooks, Mel 1926- **2003**:1
Brosnan, Pierce 1952- **2000**:3
Brown, Les 1945- **1994**:3
Brown, Ruth 1928-2006
Obituary **2008**:1
Bruckheimer, Jerry 1945- **2007**:2
Buckley, Betty 1947- **1996**:2
Bullock, Sandra 1967- **1995**:4
Burnett, Carol 1933- **2000**:3
Burnett, Mark 1960- **2003**:1
Burns, George 1896-1996
Obituary **1996**:3
Burns, Ken 1953- **1995**:2
Burr, Raymond 1917-1993
Obituary **1994**:1
Burrows, James 1940- **2005**:3
Butler, Brett 1958(?)- **1995**:1
Buttons, Red 1919-2006
Obituary **2007**:3
Bynes, Amanda 1986- **2005**:1
Byrne, Rhonda 1955- **2008**:2
Caan, James 1939- **2004**:4
Caine, Michael 1933- **2000**:4
Calhoun, Rory 1922-1999
Obituary **1999**:4
Campbell, Neve 1973- **1998**:2
Campion, Jane **1991**:4
Candy, John 1950-1994 **1988**:2
Obituary **1994**:3
Cannon, Nick 1980- **2006**:4
Carell, Steve 1963- **2006**:4
Carey, Drew 1958- **1997**:4
Carlin, George 1937- **1996**:3
Carney, Art 1918-2003
Obituary **2005**:1
Carrey, Jim 1962- **1995**:1
Carson, Johnny 1925-2005
Obituary **2006**:1
Carson, Lisa Nicole 1969- **1999**:3
Carter, Chris 1956- **2000**:1
Carter, Nell 1948-2003
Obituary **2004**:2
Caruso, David 1956(?)- **1994**:3
Carvey, Dana 1955- **1994**:1
Cassavetes, John 1929-1989
Obituary **1989**:2
Cattrall, Kim 1956- **2003**:3
Caulfield, Joan 1922(?)-1991
Obituary **1992**:1
Cavanagh, Tom 1968- **2003**:1
Caviezel, Jim 1968- **2005**:3
Chancellor, John
Obituary **1997**:1
Channing, Stockard 1946- **1991**:3
Chappelle, Dave 1973- **2005**:3
Chase, Chevy 1943- **1990**:1
Chase, Debra Martin 1956- **2009**:1
Chavez, Linda 1947- **1999**:3
Cher 1946- **1993**:1
Cherry, Don 1934- **1993**:4
Chiklis, Michael 1963- **2003**:3
Child, Julia 1912- **1999**:4
Cho, Margaret 1970- **1995**:2
Chow Yun-fat 1955- **1999**:4
Christensen, Hayden 1981- **2003**:3
Chung, Connie 1946- **1988**:4
Clarkson, Kelly 1982- **2003**:3

Clarkson, Patricia 1959- **2005**:3
Clay, Andrew Dice 1958- **1991**:1
Cleese, John 1939- **1989**:2
Clooney, George 1961- **1996**:4
Close, Glenn 1947- **1988**:3
Coca, Imogene 1908-2001
Obituary **2002**:2
Coco, James 1929(?)-1987
Obituary **1987**:2
Colasanto, Nicholas 1923(?)-1985
Obituary **1985**:2
Colbert, Stephen 1964- **2007**:4
Coleman, Dabney 1932- **1988**:3
Condon, Bill 1955- **2007**:3
Connery, Sean 1930- **1990**:4
Convy, Bert 1934(?)-1991
Obituary **1992**:1
Cook, Peter 1938-1995
Obituary **1995**:2
Cooke, Alistair 1908-2004
Obituary **2005**:3
Cooper, Anderson 1967- **2006**:1
Cooper, Chris 1951- **2004**:1
Copperfield, David 1957- **1986**:3
Coppola, Francis Ford 1939- **1989**:4
Corbett, John 1962- **2004**:1
Corwin, Jeff 1967- **2005**:1
Cosby, Bill 1937- **1999**:2
Cosell, Howard 1918-1995
Obituary **1995**:4
Costas, Bob 1952- **1986**:4
Couric, Katherine 1957- **1991**:4
Cousteau, Jacques-Yves
1910-1997 **1998**:2
Cowell, Simon 1959- **2003**:4
Cox, Courteney 1964- **1996**:2
Cox, Richard Joseph
Brief entry **1985**:1
Craig, Daniel 1968- **2008**:1
Crais, Robert 1954(?)- **2007**:4
Crawford, Broderick 1911-1986
Obituary **1986**:3
Crawford, Cindy 1966- **1993**:3
Crawford, Michael 1942- **1994**:2
Crenna, Richard 1926-2003
Obituary **2004**:1
Crichton, Michael 1942- **1995**:3
Cronkite, Walter Leland 1916- **1997**:3
Crothers, Scatman 1910-1986
Obituary **1987**:1
Crystal, Billy 1947- **1985**:3
Curry, Ann 1956- **2001**:1
Curtis, Jamie Lee 1958- **1995**:1
Cushing, Peter 1913-1994
Obituary **1995**:1
Cyrus, Miley 1992- **2008**:3
Dalton, Timothy 1946- **1988**:4
Daly, Carson 1973- **2002**:4
Damon, Matt 1970- **1999**:1
Danes, Claire 1979- **1999**:4
Dangerfield, Rodney 1921-2004
Obituary **2006**:1
Daniels, Faith 1958- **1993**:3
Daniels, Jeff 1955- **1989**:4
Danza, Tony 1951- **1989**:1
David, Larry 1948- **2003**:4
Davis, Bette 1908-1989
Obituary **1990**:1
Davis, Geena 1957- **1992**:1
Davis, Paige 1969- **2004**:2
Davis, Sammy, Jr. 1925-1990
Obituary **1990**:4

Day, Dennis 1917-1988
  Obituary **1988**:4
De Cordova, Frederick 1910- **1985**:2
Deen, Paula 1947- **2008**:3
DeGeneres, Ellen **1995**:3
Delany, Dana 1956- **2008**:4
De Matteo, Drea 1973- **2005**:2
Dempsey, Patrick 1966- **2006**:1
Denver, Bob 1935-2005
  Obituary **2006**:4
Depardieu, Gerard 1948- **1991**:2
Depp, Johnny 1963(?)- **1991**:3
De Vito, Danny 1944- **1987**:1
Dewhurst, Colleen 1924-1991
  Obituary **1992**:2
Diamond, Selma 1921(?)-1985
  Obituary **1985**:2
DiCaprio, Leonardo Wilhelm
  1974- **1997**:2
Dickerson, Nancy H.
  1927-1997 **1998**:2
Dickinson, Janice 1953- **2005**:2
Diller, Barry 1942- **1991**:1
Disney, Roy E. 1930- **1986**:3
Doherty, Shannen 1971(?)- **1994**:2
Dolenz, Micky 1945- **1986**:4
Douglas, Michael 1944- **1986**:2
Douglas, Mike 1925-2006
  Obituary **2007**:4
Downey, Morton, Jr. 1932- **1988**:4
Downey, Robert, Jr. 1965- **2007**:1
Drescher, Fran 1957(?)- **1995**:3
Duchovny, David 1960- **1998**:3
Duff, Hilary 1987- **2004**:4
Duffy, Karen 1962- **1998**:1
Dukakis, Olympia 1931- **1996**:4
Duke, Red
  Brief entry **1987**:1
Dunagan, Deanna 1940- **2009**:2
Durrell, Gerald 1925-1995
  Obituary **1995**:3
Duvall, Robert 1931- **1999**:3
Eastwood, Clint 1930- **1993**:3
Ebersole, Christine 1953- **2007**:2
Ebert, Roger 1942- **1998**:3
Ebsen, Buddy 1908-2003
  Obituary **2004**:3
Eckhart, Aaron 1968- **2009**:2
Efron, Zac 1987- **2008**:2
Eisner, Michael 1942- **1989**:2
Elfman, Jenna 1971- **1999**:4
Ellerbee, Linda 1944- **1993**:3
Elliott, Denholm 1922-1992
  Obituary **1993**:2
Engstrom, Elmer W. 1901-1984
  Obituary **1985**:2
Evans, Dale 1912-2001
  Obituary **2001**:3
Eve 1978- **2004**:3
Fallon, Jimmy 1974- **2003**:1
Fanning, Dakota 1994- **2005**:2
Farley, Chris 1964-1997 **1998**:2
Fawcett, Farrah 1947- **1998**:4
Feldshuh, Tovah 1952- **2005**:3
Fell, Norman 1924-1998
  Obituary **1999**:2
Ferguson, Craig 1962- **2005**:4
Ferrell, Will 1968- **2004**:4
Ferrer, Jose 1912-1992
  Obituary **1992**:3
Ferrera, America 1984- **2006**:2
Fey, Tina 1970- **2005**:3

Field, Sally 1946- **1995**:3
Finney, Albert 1936- **2003**:3
Firestone, Roy 1953- **1988**:2
Fishburne, Laurence 1961(?)- **1995**:3
Fisher, Carrie 1956- **1991**:1
Flanders, Ed 1934-1995
  Obituary **1995**:3
Flavor Flav 1959- **2007**:3
Fleiss, Mike 1964- **2003**:4
Fleming, Art 1925(?)-1995
  Obituary **1995**:4
Flockhart, Calista 1964- **1998**:4
Fonda, Bridget 1964- **1995**:1
Ford, Faith 1964- **2005**:3
Ford, Glenn 1916-2006
  Obituary **2007**:4
Ford, Tennessee Ernie 1919-1991
  Obituary **1992**:2
Fosse, Bob 1927-1987
  Obituary **1988**:1
Foster, Jodie 1962- **1989**:2
Foster, Phil 1914-1985
  Obituary **1985**:3
Fox, Matthew 1966- **2006**:1
Fox, Michael J. 1961- **1986**:1
Fox, Vivica 1964- **1999**:1
Foxworthy, Jeff 1958- **1996**:1
Foxx, Jamie 1967- **2001**:1
Foxx, Redd 1922-1991
  Obituary **1992**:2
Franciscus, James 1934-1991
  Obituary **1992**:1
Frankenheimer, John 1930-2002
  Obituary **2003**:4
Franz, Dennis 1944- **1995**:2
Freeman, Morgan 1937- **1990**:4
Freleng, Friz 1906(?)-1995
  Obituary **1995**:4
Fuller, Simon 1960- **2008**:2
Funt, Allen 1914-1999
  Obituary **2000**:1
Gabor, Eva 1921(?)-1995
  Obituary **1996**:1
Gallagher, Peter 1955- **2004**:3
Gandolfini, James 1961- **2001**:3
Garcia, Andy 1956- **1999**:3
Gardenia, Vincent 1922-1992
  Obituary **1993**:2
Garner, Jennifer 1972- **2003**:1
Garofalo, Janeane 1964- **1996**:4
Gellar, Sarah Michelle 1977- **1999**:3
Gere, Richard 1949- **1994**:3
Getty, Estelle 1923-2008
  Obituary **2009**:3
Gifford, Kathie Lee 1953- **1992**:2
Gilford, Jack 1907-1990
  Obituary **1990**:4
Gillett, George 1938- **1988**:1
Gish, Lillian 1893-1993
  Obituary **1993**:4
Glass, Ira 1959- **2008**:2
Gleason, Jackie 1916-1987
  Obituary **1987**:4
Gless, Sharon 1944- **1989**:3
Glover, Danny 1947- **1998**:4
Gobel, George 1920(?)-1991
  Obituary **1991**:4
Goldberg, Gary David 1944- **1989**:4
Goldberg, Leonard 1934- **1988**:4
Goldberg, Whoopi 1955- **1993**:3
Goldblum, Jeff 1952- **1988**:1
Goodman, John 1952- **1990**:3

Gorder, Genevieve 1974- **2005**:4
Gordon, Gale 1906-1995
  Obituary **1996**:1
Goren, Charles H. 1901-1991
  Obituary **1991**:4
Gossett, Louis, Jr. 1936- **1989**:3
Grace, Topher 1978- **2005**:4
Graden, Brian 1963- **2004**:2
Graham, Billy 1918- **1992**:1
Graham, Lauren 1967- **2003**:4
Grammer, Kelsey 1955(?)- **1995**:1
Grange, Red 1903-1991
  Obituary **1991**:3
Grant, Rodney A. **1992**:1
Grazer, Brian 1951- **2006**:4
Graziano, Rocky 1922-1990
  Obituary **1990**:4
Green, Tom 1972- **1999**:4
Greene, Graham 1952- **1997**:2
Greene, Lorne 1915-1987
  Obituary **1988**:1
Griffin, Merv 1925-2008
  Obituary **2008**:4
Griffith, Melanie 1957- **1989**:2
Grodin, Charles 1935- **1997**:3
Groening, Matt 1955(?)- **1990**:4
Guest, Christopher 1948- **2004**:2
Gumbel, Bryant 1948- **1990**:2
Gumbel, Greg 1946- **1996**:4
Gunn, Hartford N., Jr. 1926-1986
  Obituary **1986**:2
Gyllenhaal, Jake 1980- **2005**:3
Gyllenhaal, Maggie 1977- **2009**:2
Hackett, Buddy 1924-2003
  Obituary **2004**:3
Hackman, Gene 1931- **1989**:3
Haggis, Paul 1953- **2006**:4
Haley, Alex 1924-1992
  Obituary **1992**:3
Hall, Anthony Michael 1968- **1986**:3
Hall, Arsenio 1955- **1990**:2
Hamilton, Margaret 1902-1985
  Obituary **1985**:3
Hamilton, Scott 1958- **1998**:2
Hamm, Jon 1971- **2009**:2
Hammer, Jan 1948- **1987**:3
Handler, Chelsea 1975- **2009**:3
Hanks, Tom 1956- **1989**:2
Hanna, William 1910-2001
  Obituary **2002**:1
Hannigan, Alyson 1974- **2007**:3
Harbert, Ted 1955- **2007**:2
Hargitay, Mariska 1964- **2006**:2
Harmon, Mark 1951- **1987**:1
Hart, Carey 1975- **2006**:4
Hart, Kitty Carlisle 1910-2007
  Obituary **2008**:2
Hart, Mary
  Brief entry **1988**:1
Hart, Melissa Joan 1976- **2002**:1
Hartman, Phil 1948-1998 **1996**:2
  Obituary **1998**:4
Hatch, Richard 1961- **2001**:1
Hatcher, Teri 1964- **2005**:4
Hathaway, Anne 1982- **2007**:2
Hawn, Goldie Jeanne 1945- **1997**:2
Hayek, Salma 1968- **1999**:1
Hayes, Helen 1900-1993
  Obituary **1993**:4
Hayes, Isaac 1942- **1998**:4
Haysbert, Dennis 1954- **2007**:1
Headroom, Max 1985- **1986**:4

Heche, Anne 1969- **1999**:1
Hefner, Christie 1952- **1985**:1
Heigl, Katharine 1978- **2008**:3
Helgenberger, Marg 1958- **2002**:2
Hennessy, Jill 1969- **2003**:2
Henning, Doug 1947-1999
   Obituary **2000**:3
Henson, Brian 1964(?)- **1992**:1
Henson, Jim 1936-1990 **1989**:1
   Obituary **1990**:4
Hepburn, Katharine 1909- **1991**:2
Herbert, Don 1917-2007
   Obituary **2008**:3
Hershey, Barbara 1948- **1989**:1
Heston, Charlton 1924- **1999**:4
Hewitt, Jennifer Love 1979- **1999**:2
Hill, Benny 1925-1992
   Obituary **1992**:3
Hill, George Roy 1921-2002
   Obituary **2004**:1
Hill, Lauryn 1975- **1999**:3
Hoffman, Dustin 1937- **2005**:4
Hoffman, Philip Seymour
   1967- **2006**:3
Hope, Bob 1903-2003
   Obituary **2004**:4
Horwich, Frances 1908-2001
   Obituary **2002**:3
Hoskins, Bob 1942- **1989**:1
Houseman, John 1902-1988
   Obituary **1989**:1
Houston, Cissy 1933- **1999**:3
Howard, Ron **1997**:2
Howard, Trevor 1916-1988
   Obituary **1988**:2
Hudson, Jennifer 1981- **2008**:1
Hudson, Rock 1925-1985
   Obituary **1985**:4
Huffington, Arianna 1950- **1996**:2
Huffman, Felicity 1962- **2006**:2
Hughley, D.L. 1964- **2001**:1
Humphries, Barry 1934- **1993**:1
Hunt, Helen 1963- **1994**:4
Hunter, Holly 1958- **1989**:4
Hurley, Elizabeth **1999**:2
Hurt, William 1950- **1986**:1
Huston, Anjelica 1952(?)- **1989**:3
Hutton, Timothy 1960- **1986**:3
Ifill, Gwen 1955- **2002**:4
Iger, Bob 1951- **2006**:1
Ireland, Jill 1936-1990
   Obituary **1990**:4
Irons, Jeremy 1948- **1991**:4
Irwin, Steve 1962- **2001**:2
Isaacson, Walter 1952- **2003**:2
Itami, Juzo 1933-1997 **1998**:2
Izzard, Eddie 1963- **2008**:1
Jackson, Janet 1966(?)- **1990**:4
Jackson, Samuel L. 1949(?)- **1995**:4
James, Jesse 1969- **2004**:4
Janney, Allison 1959- **2003**:3
Jennings, Peter Charles 1938- **1997**:2
Jillian, Ann 1951- **1986**:4
Johnson, Beverly 1952- **2005**:2
Johnson, Don 1949- **1986**:1
Jonas Brothers **2008**:4
Jones, Cherry 1956- **1999**:3
Jones, Chuck 1912- **2001**:2
Jones, Jenny 1946- **1998**:2
Jones, Tom 1940- **1993**:4
Jones, Tommy Lee 1947(?)- **1994**:2
Joyce, William 1957- **2006**:1

Judd, Ashley 1968- **1998**:1
Judge, Mike 1963(?)- **1994**:2
Julia, Raul 1940-1994
   Obituary **1995**:1
Juneau, Pierre 1922- **1988**:3
Kahn, Madeline 1942-1999
   Obituary **2000**:2
Kanakaredes, Melina 1967- **2007**:1
Kasem, Casey 1933(?)- **1987**:1
Katzenberg, Jeffrey 1950- **1995**:3
Kaufman, Charlie 1958- **2005**:1
Kavner, Julie 1951- **1992**:3
Kaye, Danny 1913-1987
   Obituary **1987**:2
Kaye, Sammy 1910-1987
   Obituary **1987**:4
Keaton, Michael 1951- **1989**:4
Keeshan, Bob 1927-2004
   Obituary **2005**:2
Keitel, Harvey 1939- **1994**:3
Keith, Brian 1921-1997
   Obituary **1997**:4
Kelley, DeForest 1929-1999
   Obituary **2000**:1
Keno, Leigh and Leslie
   1957(?)- **2001**:2
Kent, Arthur 1954- **1991**:4
Kerger, Paula A. 1957- **2007**:2
Kidman, Nicole 1967- **1992**:4
Kilborn, Craig 1964- **2003**:2
Kimmel, Jimmy 1967- **2009**:2
King, Alan 1927-2004
   Obituary **2005**:3
King, Larry 1933- **1993**:1
King, Stephen 1947- **1998**:1
Kinison, Sam 1954(?)-1992
   Obituary **1993**:1
Kleinpaste, Ruud 1952- **2006**:2
Klemperer, Werner 1920-2000
   Obituary **2001**:3
Klensch, Elsa **2001**:4
Kloss, Henry E.
   Brief entry **1985**:2
Klum, Heidi 1973- **2006**:3
Knight, Ted 1923-1986
   Obituary **1986**:4
Knight, Wayne 1956- **1997**:1
Knightley, Keira 1985- **2005**:2
Knotts, Don 1924-2006
   Obituary **2007**:1
Koplovitz, Kay 1945- **1986**:3
Koppel, Ted 1940- **1989**:1
Kordich, Jay 1923- **1993**:2
Korman, Harvey 1927-2008
   Obituary **2009**:2
Krause, Peter 1965- **2009**:2
Kudrow, Lisa 1963(?)- **1996**:1
Kulp, Nancy 1921-1991
   Obituary **1991**:3
Kuralt, Charles 1934-1997
   Obituary **1998**:3
Kutcher, Ashton 1978- **2003**:4
LaBeouf, Shia 1986- **2008**:1
Lachey, Nick and Jessica
   Simpson **2004**:4
Lagasse, Emeril 1959- **1998**:3
Lahti, Christine 1950- **1988**:2
Lake, Ricki 1968(?)- **1994**:4
Landon, Michael 1936-1991
   Obituary **1992**:1
Lane, Diane 1965- **2006**:2
Lange, Jessica 1949- **1995**:4

Langella, Frank 1940- **2008**:3
Lansbury, Angela 1925- **1993**:1
LaPaglia, Anthony 1959- **2004**:4
Larroquette, John 1947- **1986**:2
LaSalle, Eriq 1962- **1996**:4
Laurie, Hugh 1959- **2007**:2
Lawless, Lucy 1968- **1997**:4
Lawrence, Martin 1966(?)- **1993**:4
Lawson, Nigella 1960- **2003**:2
Laybourne, Geraldine 1947- **1997**:1
Leach, Penelope 1937- **1992**:4
Leach, Robin 1942(?)-
   Brief entry **1985**:4
Leary, Denis 1958- **1993**:3
LeBlanc, Matt 1967- **2005**:4
Ledger, Heath 1979- **2006**:3
Lee, Jason 1970- **2006**:4
Lee, Pamela 1967(?)- **1996**:4
Lee, Sandra 1966- **2008**:3
Leguizamo, John 1965- **1999**:1
Leigh, Jennifer Jason 1962- **1995**:2
Lemmon, Jack 1925- **1998**:4
   Obituary **2002**:3
Leno, Jay 1950- **1987**:1
Letterman, David 1947- **1989**:3
Levi, Zachary 1980- **2009**:4
Levinson, Arthur D. 1950- **2008**:3
Levinson, Barry 1932- **1989**:3
Levy, Eugene 1946- **2004**:3
Lewis, Juliette 1973- **1999**:3
Lewis, Richard 1948(?)- **1992**:1
Lewis, Shari 1934-1998 **1993**:1
   Obituary **1999**:1
Liberace 1919-1987
   Obituary **1987**:2
Liguori, Peter 1960- **2005**:2
Liman, Doug 1965- **2007**:1
Ling, Lisa 1973- **2004**:2
Linney, Laura 1964- **2009**:4
Little, Cleavon 1939-1992
   Obituary **1993**:2
Liu, Lucy 1968- **2000**:4
Lively, Blake 1987- **2009**:1
Livingston, Ron 1968- **2007**:2
LL Cool J 1968- **1998**:2
Locklear, Heather 1961- **1994**:3
Lohan, Lindsay 1986- **2005**:3
Long, Shelley 1950(?)- **1985**:1
Lopez, George 1963- **2003**:4
Lopez, Jennifer 1970- **1998**:4
Lopez, Mario 1973- **2009**:3
Lord, Jack 1920-1998 **1998**:2
Lords, Traci 1968- **1995**:4
Louis-Dreyfus, Julia 1961(?)- **1994**:1
Loy, Myrna 1905-1993
   Obituary **1994**:2
Lucci, Susan 1946(?)- **1999**:4
Ludacris 1977- **2007**:4
Lupino, Ida 1918(?)-1995
   Obituary **1996**:1
LuPone, Patti 1949- **2009**:2
Lynch, David 1946- **1990**:4
Mac, Bernie 1957- **2003**:1
MacFarlane, Seth 1973- **2006**:1
MacMurray, Fred 1908-1991
   Obituary **1992**:2
MacRae, Gordon 1921-1986
   Obituary **1986**:2
Macy, William H. **1999**:3
Madden, Chris 1948- **2006**:1
Madden, John 1936- **1995**:1
Maher, Bill 1956- **1996**:2

Mako 1933-2006
  Obituary **2007**:3
Malkovich, John 1953- **1988**:2
Malone, John C. 1941- **1988**:3
Mandel, Howie 1955- **1989**:1
Mantegna, Joe 1947- **1992**:1
Marber, Patrick 1964- **2007**:4
Marchand, Nancy 1928-2000
  Obituary **2001**:1
Martin, Dean 1917-1995
  Obituary **1996**:2
Martin, Mary 1913-1990
  Obituary **1991**:2
Martin, Steve 1945- **1992**:2
Matlin, Marlee 1965- **1992**:2
Matthau, Walter 1920- **2000**:3
McCarthy, Jenny 1972- **1997**:4
McDonnell, Mary 1952- **2008**:2
McDormand, Frances 1957- **1997**:3
McDowall, Roddy 1928-1998
  Obituary **1999**:1
McGillis, Kelly 1957- **1989**:3
McGinley, Ted 1958- **2004**:4
McGraw, Phil 1950- **2005**:2
McGregor, Ewan 1971(?)- **1998**:2
McKee, Lonette 1952(?)- **1996**:1
McKellen, Ian 1939- **1994**:1
McMahon, Julian 1968- **2006**:1
Meadows, Audrey 1925-1996
  Obituary **1996**:3
Meltzer, Brad 1970- **2005**:4
Meredith, Burgess 1909-1997
  Obituary **1998**:1
Merkerson, S. Epatha 1952- **2006**:4
Messing, Debra 1968- **2004**:4
Midler, Bette 1945- **1989**:4
Milano, Alyssa 1972- **2002**:3
Millan, Cesar 1969- **2007**:4
Milland, Ray 1908(?)-1986
  Obituary **1986**:2
Miller, Dennis 1953- **1992**:4
Milligan, Spike 1918-2002
  Obituary **2003**:2
Minogue, Kylie 1968- **2003**:4
Mirren, Helen 1945- **2005**:1
Mitchum, Robert 1917-1997
  Obituary **1997**:4
Molina, Alfred 1953- **2005**:3
Mo'Nique 1967- **2008**:1
Montgomery, Elizabeth 1933-1995
  Obituary **1995**:4
Moonves, Les 1949- **2004**:2
Moore, Clayton 1914-1999
  Obituary **2000**:3
Moore, Demi 1963(?)- **1991**:4
Moore, Dudley 1935-2002
  Obituary **2003**:2
Moore, Julianne 1960- **1998**:1
Moore, Mary Tyler 1936- **1996**:2
Morgan, Tracy 1968- **2009**:3
Morita, Noriyuki Pat 1932- **1987**:3
Morris, Kathryn 1969- **2006**:4
Morrow, Rob 1962- **2006**:4
Mortensen, Viggo 1958- **2003**:3
Mos Def 1973- **2005**:4
Moss, Carrie-Anne 1967- **2004**:3
Moyers, Bill 1934- **1991**:4
Muniz, Frankie 1985- **2001**:4
Murdoch, Rupert 1931- **1988**:4
Murphy, Brittany 1977- **2005**:1
Murphy, Eddie 1961- **1989**:2
Musburger, Brent 1939- **1985**:1

Myers, Mike 1964(?)- **1992**:3
Nance, Jack 1943(?)-1996
  Obituary **1997**:3
Neeson, Liam 1952- **1993**:4
Nelson, Harriet 1909(?)-1994
  Obituary **1995**:1
Nelson, Rick 1940-1985
  Obituary **1986**:1
Nelson, Willie 1933- **1993**:4
Newton-John, Olivia 1948- **1998**:4
Nichols, Mike 1931- **1994**:4
Nissel, Angela 1974- **2006**:4
Nixon, Bob 1954(?)- **2006**:4
Nolan, Lloyd 1902-1985
  Obituary **1985**:4
Nolte, Nick 1941- **1992**:4
Northam, Jeremy 1961- **2003**:2
Norville, Deborah 1958- **1990**:3
Nye, Bill 1955- **1997**:2
O'Brien, Conan 1963(?)- **1994**:1
O'Connor, Carroll 1924-2001
  Obituary **2002**:3
O'Donnell, Rosie 1962- **1994**:3
O'Hara, Catherine 1954- **2007**:4
Oldman, Gary 1958- **1998**:1
Olin, Ken 1955(?)- **1992**:3
Oliver, Jamie 1975- **2002**:3
Olivier, Laurence 1907-1989
  Obituary **1989**:4
Olmos, Edward James 1947- **1990**:1
Olsen, Mary-Kate and Ashley
  1986- **2002**:1
Olson, Johnny 1910(?)-1985
  Obituary **1985**:4
Orbach, Jerry 1935-2004
  Obituary **2006**:1
O'Reilly, Bill 1949- **2001**:2
Osbournes, The **2003**:4
Osgood, Charles 1933- **1996**:2
Ostroff, Dawn 1960- **2006**:4
O'Sullivan, Maureen 1911-1998
  Obituary **1998**:4
Otte, Ruth 1949- **1992**:4
Ovitz, Michael 1946- **1990**:1
Owen, Clive 1964- **2006**:2
Owens, Buck 1929-2006
  Obituary **2007**:2
Paar, Jack 1918-2004
  Obituary **2005**:2
Palance, Jack 1919-2006
  Obituary **2008**:1
Paley, William S. 1901-1990
  Obituary **1991**:2
Palmer, Jim 1945- **1991**:2
Panettiere, Hayden 1989- **2008**:4
Pantoliano, Joe 1951- **2002**:3
Paquin, Anna 1982- **2009**:4
Park, Nick 1958- **1997**:3
Parker, Sarah Jessica 1965- **1999**:2
Parker, Trey and Matt Stone **1998**:2
Parks, Bert 1914-1992
  Obituary **1992**:3
Pauley, Jane 1950- **1999**:1
Paulsen, Pat 1927-1997
  Obituary **1997**:4
Paxton, Bill 1955- **1999**:3
Peete, Holly Robinson 1964- **2005**:2
Pegg, Simon 1970- **2009**:1
Peller, Clara 1902(?)-1987
  Obituary **1988**:1
Penn, Kal 1977- **2009**:1
Penn, Sean 1960- **1987**:2

Pennington, Ty 1965- **2005**:4
Perez, Rosie **1994**:2
Perry, Luke 1966(?)- **1992**:3
Perry, Matthew 1969- **1997**:2
Peterson, Cassandra 1951- **1988**:1
Pfeiffer, Michelle 1957- **1990**:2
Phifer, Mekhi 1975- **2004**:1
Philbin, Regis 1933- **2000**:2
Phoenix, River 1970-1993 **1990**:2
  Obituary **1994**:2
Pierce, David Hyde 1959- **1996**:3
Pierce, Frederick S. 1934(?)- **1985**:3
Pinchot, Bronson 1959(?)- **1987**:4
Pinkett Smith, Jada 1971- **1998**:3
Pitt, Brad 1964- **1995**:2
Pittman, Robert W. 1953- **1985**:1
Plato, Dana 1964-1999
  Obituary **1999**:4
Pleasence, Donald 1919-1995
  Obituary **1995**:3
Pleshette, Suzanne 1937-2008
  Obituary **2009**:2
Plimpton, George 1927-2003
  Obituary **2004**:4
Poehler, Amy 1971- **2009**:1
Poitier, Sidney 1927- **1990**:3
Pollack, Sydney 1934-2008
  Obituary **2009**:2
Poston, Tom 1921-2007
  Obituary **2008**:3
Potts, Annie 1952- **1994**:1
Povich, Maury 1939(?)- **1994**:3
Powter, Susan 1957(?)- **1994**:3
Price, Vincent 1911-1993
  Obituary **1994**:2
Priestly, Jason 1970(?)- **1993**:2
Prince, Faith 1959(?)- **1993**:2
Prinze, Freddie, Jr. 1976- **1999**:3
Pryor, Richard **1999**:3
Quaid, Dennis 1954- **1989**:4
Queen Latifah 1970(?)- **1992**:2
Queer Eye for the Straight Guy
  cast **2004**:3
Quinn, Martha 1959- **1986**:4
Quivers, Robin 1953(?)- **1995**:4
Radcliffe, Daniel 1989- **2007**:4
Radecki, Thomas
  Brief entry **1986**:2
Radner, Gilda 1946-1989
  Obituary **1989**:4
Raimi, Sam 1959- **1999**:2
Ramsay, Gordon 1966- **2008**:2
Randall, Tony 1920-2004
  Obituary **2005**:3
Randi, James 1928- **1990**:2
Raphael, Sally Jessy 1943- **1992**:4
Rashad, Phylicia 1948- **1987**:3
Raven 1985- **2005**:1
Rawls, Lou 1933-2006
  Obituary **2007**:1
Ray, Rachael 1968- **2007**:1
Raye, Martha 1916-1994
  Obituary **1995**:1
Reasoner, Harry 1923-1991
  Obituary **1992**:1
Redgrave, Lynn 1943- **1999**:3
Redgrave, Vanessa 1937- **1989**:2
Reed, Donna 1921-1986
  Obituary **1986**:1
Reed, Robert 1933(?)-1992
  Obituary **1992**:4
Reese, Della 1931- **1999**:2

Reeve, Christopher 1952- **1997**:2
Reilly, Charles Nelson
  Obituary **2008**:3
Reiner, Rob 1947- **1991**:2
Reiser, Paul 1957- **1995**:2
Remick, Lee 1936(?)-1991
  Obituary **1992**:1
Reuben, Gloria 1964- **1999**:4
Reubens, Paul 1952- **1987**:2
Rhea, Caroline 1964- **2004**:1
Rhys Meyers, Jonathan 1977- **2007**:1
Ricci, Christina 1980- **1999**:1
Richards, Michael 1949(?)- **1993**:4
Riddle, Nelson 1921-1985
  Obituary **1985**:4
Ripa, Kelly 1970- **2002**:2
Ritter, John 1948- **2003**:4
Rivera, Geraldo 1943- **1989**:1
Rivers, Joan 1933- **2005**:3
Robbins, Tim 1959- **1993**:1
Roberts, Cokie 1943- **1993**:4
Roberts, Doris 1930- **2003**:4
Roberts, Julia 1967- **1991**:3
Robertson, Pat 1930- **1988**:2
Robinson, Max 1939-1988
  Obituary **1989**:2
Rock, Chris 1967(?)- **1998**:1
Rock, The 1972- **2001**:2
Roddenberry, Gene 1921-1991
  Obituary **1992**:2
Rogen, Seth 1982- **2009**:3
Rogers, Fred 1928- **2000**:4
Rogers, Roy 1911-1998
  Obituary **1998**:4
Roker, Al 1954- **2003**:1
Roker, Roxie 1929(?)-1995
  Obituary **1996**:2
Rolle, Esther 1922-1998
  Obituary **1999**:2
Rollins, Henry 1961- **2007**:3
Rollins, Howard E., Jr. 1950- **1986**:1
Romano, Ray 1957- **2001**:4
Romijn, Rebecca 1972- **2007**:1
Rose, Charlie 1943- **1994**:2
Rourke, Mickey 1956- **1988**:4
Rowan, Dan 1922-1987
  Obituary **1988**:1
Rudd, Paul 1969- **2009**:4
Rudner, Rita 1956- **1993**:2
Russell, Keri 1976- **2000**:1
Russell, Kurt 1951- **2007**:4
Russell, Nipsey 1924-2005
  Obituary **2007**:1
Russert, Tim 1950-2008
  Obituary **2009**:3
Ryan, Meg 1962(?)- **1994**:1
Sagal, Katey 1954- **2005**:2
Sagansky, Jeff 1952- **1993**:2
Sajak, Pat
  Brief entry **1985**:4
Sandler, Adam 1966- **1999**:2
Saralegui, Cristina 1948- **1999**:2
Sarandon, Susan 1946- **1995**:3
Savage, Fred 1976- **1990**:1
Savalas, Telly 1924-1994
  Obituary **1994**:3
Sawyer, Diane 1945- **1994**:4
Schaap, Dick 1934-2001
  Obituary **2003**:1
Schneider, Rob 1965- **1997**:4
Schreiber, Liev 1967- **2007**:2
Schwimmer, David 1966(?)- **1996**:2

Scott, Gene
  Brief entry **1986**:1
Seacrest, Ryan 1976- **2004**:4
Sedaris, Amy 1961- **2009**:3
Sedelmaier, Joe 1933- **1985**:3
Sedgwick, Kyra 1965- **2006**:2
Seinfeld, Jerry 1954- **1992**:4
Sethi, Simran 1971(?)- **2008**:1
Sevareid, Eric 1912-1992
  Obituary **1993**:1
Seyfried, Amanda 1985- **2009**:3
Seymour, Jane 1951- **1994**:4
Shaffer, Paul 1949- **1987**:1
Shandling, Garry 1949- **1995**:1
Sharkey, Ray 1953-1993
  Obituary **1994**:1
Shawn, Dick 1924(?)-1987
  Obituary **1987**:3
Sheedy, Ally 1962- **1989**:1
Sheen, Charlie 1965- **2001**:2
Sheindlin, Judith 1942(?)- **1999**:1
Sheldon, Sidney 1917-2007
  Obituary **2008**:2
Shepherd, Cybill 1950- **1996**:3
Shields, Brooke 1965- **1996**:3
Shore, Dinah 1917-1994
  Obituary **1994**:3
Short, Martin 1950- **1986**:1
Shriver, Maria
  Brief entry **1986**:2
Shue, Andrew 1964- **1994**:4
Silverman, Jonathan 1966- **1997**:2
Silverman, Sarah 1970- **2008**:1
Silvers, Phil 1912-1985
  Obituary **1985**:4
Silverstone, Alicia 1976- **1997**:4
Simpson-Wentz, Ashlee 1984- **2009**:1
Singer, Bryan 1965- **2007**:3
Sinise, Gary 1955(?)- **1996**:1
Siskel, Gene 1946-1999
  Obituary **1999**:3
Skelton, Red 1913-1997
  Obituary **1998**:1
Slater, Christian 1969- **1994**:1
Smigel, Robert 1959(?)- **2001**:3
Smirnoff, Yakov 1951- **1987**:2
Smith, Anna Nicole 1967-2007
  Obituary **2008**:2
Smith, Buffalo Bob 1917-1998
  Obituary **1999**:1
Smith, Howard K. 1914-2002
  Obituary **2003**:2
Smith, Jeff 1939(?)- **1991**:4
Smith, Kate 1907(?)-1986
  Obituary **1986**:3
Smits, Jimmy 1956- **1990**:1
Snipes, Wesley 1962- **1993**:1
Somers, Suzanne 1946- **2000**:1
Sondheim, Stephen 1930- **1994**:4
Sorkin, Aaron 1961- **2003**:2
Southern, Terry 1926-1995
  Obituary **1996**:2
Spade, David 1965- **1999**:2
Spelling, Aaron 1923-2006
  Obituary **2007**:3
Spelling, Tori 1973- **2008**:3
Spheeris, Penelope 1945(?)- **1989**:2
Spielberg, Steven 1947- **1993**:4
Spray, Ed 1941- **2004**:1
Springer, Jerry 1944- **1998**:4
Stack, Robert 1919-2003
  Obituary **2004**:2

Stamos, John 1963- **2008**:1
Stapleton, Maureen 1925-2006
  Obituary **2007**:2
Stein, Ben 1944- **2001**:1
Stern, Howard 1954- **1988**:2
Stevenson, McLean 1929-1996
  Obituary **1996**:3
Stewart, Jon 1962- **2001**:2
Stewart, Martha 1942(?)- **1992**:1
Stewart, Patrick 1940- **1996**:1
Stiller, Ben 1965- **1999**:1
Stone, Sharon 1958- **1993**:4
Stoppard, Tom 1937- **1995**:4
Streisand, Barbra 1942- **1992**:2
Studi, Wes 1944(?)- **1994**:3
Susskind, David 1920-1987
  Obituary **1987**:2
Sutherland, Kiefer 1966- **2002**:4
Swaggart, Jimmy 1935- **1987**:3
Swayze, John Cameron 1906-1995
  Obituary **1996**:1
Swinton, Tilda 1960- **2008**:4
Sykes, Wanda 1964- **2007**:4
Tandy, Jessica 1901-1994 **1990**:4
  Obituary **1995**:1
Tartakovsky, Genndy 1970- **2004**:4
Tartikoff, Brandon 1949-1997 **1985**:2
  Obituary **1998**:1
Tautou, Audrey 1978- **2004**:2
Taylor, Elizabeth 1932- **1993**:3
Tellem, Nancy 1953(?)- **2004**:4
Tesh, John 1952- **1996**:3
Thomas, Danny 1914-1991
  Obituary **1991**:3
Thompson, Emma 1959- **1993**:2
Thornton, Billy Bob 1956(?)- **1997**:4
Tillstrom, Burr 1917-1985
  Obituary **1986**:1
Tilly, Jennifer 1958(?)- **1997**:2
Timberlake, Justin 1981- **2008**:4
Tisch, Laurence A. 1923- **1988**:2
Tomei, Marisa 1964- **1995**:2
Totenberg, Nina 1944- **1992**:2
Travolta, John 1954- **1995**:2
Trotter, Charlie 1960- **2000**:4
Trudeau, Garry 1948- **1991**:2
Tucci, Stanley 1960- **2003**:2
Tucker, Chris 1973(?)- **1999**:1
Tucker, Forrest 1919-1986
  Obituary **1987**:1
Turner, Janine 1962- **1993**:2
Turner, Lana 1921-1995
  Obituary **1996**:1
Turner, Ted 1938- **1989**:1
Ullman, Tracey 1961- **1988**:3
Umeki, Miyoshi 1929-2007
  Obituary **2008**:4
Underwood, Carrie 1983- **2008**:1
Urich, Robert 1947- **1988**:1
  Obituary **2003**:3
Usher 1979- **2005**:1
Ustinov, Peter 1921-2004
  Obituary **2005**:3
Vanilla Ice 1967(?)- **1991**:3
Vardalos, Nia 1962- **2003**:4
Varney, Jim 1949-2000
  Brief entry **1985**:4
  Obituary **2000**:3
Vaughn, Vince 1970- **1999**:2
Ventura, Jesse 1951- **1999**:2
Vidal, Gore 1925- **1996**:2
Vieira, Meredith 1953- **2001**:3

Villechaize, Herve 1943(?)-1993
  Obituary **1994**:1
Vitale, Dick 1939- **1988**:4
Von D, Kat 1982- **2008**:3
Wagoner, Porter 1927-2007
  Obituary **2008**:4
Walker, Nancy 1922-1992
  Obituary **1992**:3
Walters, Barbara 1931- **1998**:3
Wapner, Joseph A. 1919- **1987**:1
Ward, Sela 1956- **2001**:3
Warden, Jack 1920-2006
  Obituary **2007**:3
Washington, Denzel 1954- **1993**:2
Wasserman, Lew 1913-2002
  Obituary **2003**:3
Waterston, Sam 1940- **2006**:1
Wayans, Damon 1960- **1998**:4
Wayans, Keenen Ivory
  1958(?)- **1991**:1
Wayne, David 1914-1995
  Obituary **1995**:3
Weisz, Rachel 1971- **2006**:4
Weitz, Bruce 1943- **1985**:4
Whedon, Joss 1964- **2006**:3
Whitaker, Forest 1961- **1996**:2
White, Jaleel 1976- **1992**:3
White, Julie 1961- **2008**:2
Whiting, Susan 1956- **2007**:4
Whittle, Christopher 1947- **1989**:3
Wilkinson, Tom 1948- **2003**:2
Williams, Brian 1959- **2009**:4
Williams, Robin 1952- **1988**:4
Williams, Treat 1951- **2004**:3
Williams, Vanessa L. 1963- **1999**:2
Willis, Bruce 1955- **1986**:4
Wilson, Flip 1933-1998
  Obituary **1999**:2
Winfield, Paul 1941-2004
  Obituary **2005**:2
Winfrey, Oprah 1954- **1986**:4
Winger, Debra 1955- **1994**:3
Winokur, Marissa Jaret 1973- **2005**:1
Wolfman Jack 1938-1995
  Obituary **1996**:1
Wong, Andrea 1966- **2009**:1
Wong, B.D. 1962- **1998**:1
Woods, James 1947- **1988**:3
Wright, Steven 1955- **1986**:3
Wyatt, Jane 1910-2006
  Obituary **2008**:1
Wyle, Noah 1971- **1997**:3
Wyman, Jane 1917-2007
  Obituary **2008**:4
Wynn, Keenan 1916-1986
  Obituary **1987**:1
Xuxa 1963(?)- **1994**:2
Xzibit 1974- **2005**:4
Yetnikoff, Walter 1933- **1988**:1
York, Dick 1923-1992
  Obituary **1992**:4
Young, Robert 1907-1998
  Obituary **1999**:1
Youngman, Henny 1906(?)-1998
  Obituary **1998**:3
Zahn, Paula 1956(?)- **1992**:3
Zamora, Pedro 1972-1994
  Obituary **1995**:2
Zeta-Jones, Catherine 1969- **1999**:4
Zucker, Jeff 1965(?)- **1993**:3

**THEATER**

Abbott, George 1887-1995
  Obituary **1995**:3
Adjani, Isabelle 1955- **1991**:1
Albee, Edward 1928- **1997**:1
Albert, Eddie 1906-2005
  Obituary **2006**:3
Alda, Robert 1914-1986
  Obituary **1986**:3
Alexander, Jane 1939- **1994**:2
Alexander, Jason 1962(?)- **1993**:3
Allen, Joan 1956- **1998**:1
Allen, Peter 1944-1992
  Obituary **1993**:1
Ameche, Don 1908-1993
  Obituary **1994**:2
Andrews, Julie 1935- **1996**:1
Angelou, Maya 1928- **1993**:4
Arden, Eve 1912(?)-1990
  Obituary **1991**:2
Arkin, Alan 1934- **2007**:4
Ashcroft, Peggy 1907-1991
  Obituary **1992**:1
Atkinson, Rowan 1955- **2004**:3
Aykroyd, Dan 1952- **1989**:3
Bacall, Lauren 1924- **1997**:3
Bacon, Kevin 1958- **1995**:3
Baddeley, Hermione 1906(?)-1986
  Obituary **1986**:4
Bailey, Pearl 1918-1990
  Obituary **1991**:1
Ball, Alan 1957- **2005**:1
Bancroft, Anne 1931-2005
  Obituary **2006**:3
Barkin, Ellen 1955- **1987**:3
Barry, Lynda 1956(?)- **1992**:1
Bassett, Angela 1959(?)- **1994**:4
Bates, Alan 1934-2003
  Obituary **2005**:1
Bates, Kathy 1949(?)- **1991**:4
Becker, Brian 1957(?)- **2004**:4
Beckett, Samuel Barclay 1906-1989
  Obituary **1990**:2
Belushi, Jim 1954- **1986**:2
Bening, Annette 1958(?)- **1992**:1
Bennett, Joan 1910-1990
  Obituary **1991**:2
Bennett, Michael 1943-1987
  Obituary **1988**:1
Bernardi, Herschel 1923-1986
  Obituary **1986**:4
Bernhard, Sandra 1955(?)- **1989**:4
Bernstein, Leonard 1918-1990
  Obituary **1991**:1
Bishop, Andre 1948- **2000**:1
Bishop, Joey 1918-2007
  Obituary **2008**:4
Blackstone, Harry Jr. 1934-1997
  Obituary **1997**:4
Blanchett, Cate 1969- **1999**:3
Bloch, Ivan 1940- **1986**:3
Bloom, Orlando 1977- **2004**:2
Bogosian, Eric 1953- **1990**:4
Bolger, Ray 1904-1987
  Obituary **1987**:2
Bonham Carter, Helena 1966- **1998**:4
Booth, Shirley 1898-1992
  Obituary **1993**:2
Bowen, Julie 1970- **2007**:1
Bowie, David 1947- **1998**:2
Brady, Wayne 1972- **2008**:3
Branagh, Kenneth 1960- **1992**:2

Brandauer, Klaus Maria 1944- **1987**:3
Brando, Marlon 1924-2004
  Obituary **2005**:3
Broadbent, Jim 1949- **2008**:4
Brooks, Mel 1926- **2003**:1
Brown, Ruth 1928-2006
  Obituary **2008**:1
Brynner, Yul 1920(?)-1985
  Obituary **1985**:4
Buckley, Betty 1947- **1996**:2
Bullock, Sandra 1967- **1995**:4
Burck, Wade
  Brief entry **1986**:1
Burr, Raymond 1917-1993
  Obituary **1994**:1
Busch, Charles 1954- **1998**:3
Byrne, Gabriel 1950- **1997**:4
Caan, James 1939- **2004**:4
Caesar, Adolph 1934-1986
  Obituary **1986**:3
Cagney, James 1899-1986
  Obituary **1986**:2
Caine, Michael 1933- **2000**:4
Candy, John 1950-1994 **1988**:2
  Obituary **1994**:3
Carney, Art 1918-2003
  Obituary **2005**:1
Carrey, Jim 1962- **1995**:1
Carson, Lisa Nicole 1969- **1999**:3
Carter, Nell 1948-2003
  Obituary **2004**:2
Cassavetes, John 1929-1989
  Obituary **1989**:2
Caulfield, Joan 1922(?)-1991
  Obituary **1992**:1
Cavanagh, Tom 1968- **2003**:1
Caviezel, Jim 1968- **2005**:3
Channing, Stockard 1946- **1991**:3
Christie, Julie 1941- **2008**:4
Clarkson, Patricia 1959- **2005**:3
Close, Glenn 1947- **1988**:3
Coco, James 1929(?)-1987
  Obituary **1987**:2
Connery, Sean 1930- **1990**:4
Convy, Bert 1934(?)-1991
  Obituary **1992**:1
Cook, Peter 1938-1995
  Obituary **1995**:2
Cooper, Chris 1951- **2004**:1
Coppola, Carmine 1910-1991
  Obituary **1991**:4
Costner, Kevin 1955- **1989**:4
Craig, Daniel 1968- **2008**:1
Crawford, Broderick 1911-1986
  Obituary **1986**:3
Crawford, Cheryl 1902-1986
  Obituary **1987**:1
Crawford, Michael 1942- **1994**:2
Crisp, Quentin 1908-1999
  Obituary **2000**:3
Cronyn, Hume 1911-2003
  Obituary **2004**:3
Cruz, Nilo 1961(?)- **2004**:4
Culkin, Macaulay 1980(?)- **1991**:3
Cusack, John 1966- **1999**:3
Cushing, Peter 1913-1994
  Obituary **1995**:1
Dafoe, Willem 1955- **1988**:1
Dalton, Timothy 1946- **1988**:4
Daniels, Jeff 1955- **1989**:4
Davis, Ossie 1917-2005
  Obituary **2006**:1

Davis, Paige 1969- **2004**:2
Dawson, Rosario 1979- **2007**:2
Day-Lewis, Daniel 1957- **1989**:4
Dee, Janie 1966(?)- **2001**:4
Delany, Dana 1956- **2008**:4
Dench, Judi 1934- **1999**:4
De Niro, Robert 1943- **1999**:1
Dennis, Sandy 1937-1992
    Obituary **1992**:4
Denver, Bob 1935-2005
    Obituary **2006**:4
Depardieu, Gerard 1948- **1991**:2
Dern, Laura 1967- **1992**:3
De Vito, Danny 1944- **1987**:1
Dewhurst, Colleen 1924-1991
    Obituary **1992**:2
Diggs, Taye 1971- **2000**:1
Douglas, Michael 1944- **1986**:2
Dukakis, Olympia 1931- **1996**:4
Dunagan, Deanna 1940- **2009**:2
Duncan, Todd 1903-1998
    Obituary **1998**:3
Duvall, Robert 1931- **1999**:3
Ebersole, Christine 1953- **2007**:2
Ebsen, Buddy 1908-2003
    Obituary **2004**:3
Eckhart, Aaron 1968- **2009**:2
Efron, Zac 1987- **2008**:2
Elliott, Denholm 1922-1992
    Obituary **1993**:2
Ephron, Henry 1912-1992
    Obituary **1993**:2
Fawcett, Farrah 1947- **1998**:4
Feld, Kenneth 1948- **1988**:2
Feldshuh, Tovah 1952- **2005**:3
Ferguson, Craig 1962- **2005**:4
Ferrer, Jose 1912-1992
    Obituary **1992**:3
Fiennes, Ralph 1962- **1996**:2
Fierstein, Harvey 1954- **2004**:2
Finney, Albert 1936- **2003**:3
Fishburne, Laurence 1961(?)- **1995**:3
Fisher, Carrie 1956- **1991**:1
Flanders, Ed 1934-1995
    Obituary **1995**:3
Flockhart, Calista 1964- **1998**:4
Fo, Dario 1926- **1998**:1
Ford, Faith 1964- **2005**:3
Fosse, Bob 1927-1987
    Obituary **1988**:1
Foster, Sutton 1975- **2003**:2
Freeman, Morgan 1937- **1990**:4
Fugard, Athol 1932- **1992**:3
Gabor, Eva 1921(?)-1995
    Obituary **1996**:1
Gallagher, Peter 1955- **2004**:3
Gardenia, Vincent 1922-1992
    Obituary **1993**:2
Garr, Teri 1949- **1988**:4
Geffen, David 1943- **1985**:3
Gere, Richard 1949- **1994**:3
Gielgud, John 1904-2000
    Obituary **2000**:4
Gilford, Jack 1907-1990
    Obituary **1990**:4
Gleason, Jackie 1916-1987
    Obituary **1987**:4
Glover, Danny 1947- **1998**:4
Glover, Savion 1973- **1997**:1
Gobel, George 1920(?)-1991
    Obituary **1991**:4
Goldberg, Whoopi 1955- **1993**:3

Goldblum, Jeff 1952- **1988**:1
Gossett, Louis, Jr. 1936- **1989**:3
Goulet, Robert 1933-2007
    Obituary **2008**:4
Grammer, Kelsey 1955(?)- **1995**:1
Grant, Cary 1904-1986
    Obituary **1987**:1
Grant, Hugh 1960- **1995**:3
Gray, Simon 1936-2008
    Obituary **2009**:4
Gray, Spalding 1941-2004
    Obituary **2005**:2
Greene, Graham 1952- **1997**:2
Gregory, Dick 1932- **1990**:3
Gyllenhaal, Jake 1980- **2005**:3
Gyllenhaal, Maggie 1977- **2009**:2
Hagen, Uta 1919-2004
    Obituary **2005**:2
Hall, Anthony Michael 1968- **1986**:3
Hamilton, Margaret 1902-1985
    Obituary **1985**:3
Harris, Richard 1930-2002
    Obituary **2004**:1
Harrison, Rex 1908-1990
    Obituary **1990**:4
Hart, Kitty Carlisle 1910-2007
    Obituary **2008**:2
Hathaway, Anne 1982- **2007**:2
Havel, Vaclav 1936- **1990**:3
Hawke, Ethan 1971(?)- **1995**:4
Hayes, Helen 1900-1993
    Obituary **1993**:4
Hennessy, Jill 1969- **2003**:2
Henning, Doug 1947-1999
    Obituary **2000**:3
Hepburn, Katharine 1909- **1991**:2
Hill, George Roy 1921-2002
    Obituary **2004**:1
Hines, Gregory 1946- **1992**:4
Hoffman, Dustin 1937- **2005**:4
Hoffman, Philip Seymour
    1967- **2006**:3
Hopkins, Anthony 1937- **1992**:4
Horne, Lena 1917- **1998**:4
Hoskins, Bob 1942- **1989**:1
Houseman, John 1902-1988
    Obituary **1989**:1
Houston, Cissy 1933- **1999**:3
Huffman, Felicity 1962- **2006**:2
Humphries, Barry 1934- **1993**:1
Hunt, Helen 1963- **1994**:4
Hunter, Holly 1958- **1989**:4
Hurt, William 1950- **1986**:1
Hwang, David Henry 1957- **1999**:1
Irons, Jeremy 1948- **1991**:4
Irwin, Bill **1988**:3
Itami, Juzo 1933-1997 **1998**:2
Ives, Burl 1909-1995
    Obituary **1995**:4
Izzard, Eddie 1963- **2008**:1
Jackman, Hugh 1968- **2004**:4
Jackson, Samuel L. 1949(?)- **1995**:4
Janney, Allison 1959- **2003**:3
Jay, Ricky 1949(?)- **1995**:1
Jillian, Ann 1951- **1986**:4
Johansson, Scarlett 1984- **2005**:4
Jones, Cherry 1956- **1999**:3
Jones, Sarah 1974(?)- **2005**:2
Jones, Tommy Lee 1947(?)- **1994**:2
Julia, Raul 1940-1994
    Obituary **1995**:1
Kahn, Madeline 1942-1999

    Obituary **2000**:2
Kanakaredes, Melina 1967- **2007**:1
Kavner, Julie 1951- **1992**:3
Kaye, Danny 1913-1987
    Obituary **1987**:2
Kaye, Nora 1920-1987
    Obituary **1987**:4
Kazan, Elia 1909-2003
    Obituary **2004**:4
Keeler, Ruby 1910-1993
    Obituary **1993**:4
Keitel, Harvey 1939- **1994**:3
Kerr, Deborah 1921-2007
    Obituary **2008**:4
Kerr, Jean 1922-2003
    Obituary **2004**:1
Kilmer, Val **1991**:4
King, Alan 1927-2004
    Obituary **2005**:3
Kinski, Klaus 1926-1991 **1987**:2
    Obituary **1992**:2
Kline, Kevin 1947- **2000**:1
Kramer, Larry 1935- **1991**:2
Krause, Peter 1965- **2009**:2
Kushner, Tony 1956- **1995**:2
Lahti, Christine 1950- **1988**:2
Lane, Burton 1912-1997
    Obituary **1997**:2
Lane, Nathan 1956- **1996**:4
Lange, Jessica 1949- **1995**:4
Langella, Frank 1940- **2008**:3
Lansbury, Angela 1925- **1993**:1
Larson, Jonathan 1961(?)-1996
    Obituary **1997**:2
Lawless, Lucy 1968- **1997**:4
Leary, Denis 1958- **1993**:3
Leigh, Jennifer Jason 1962- **1995**:2
Lithgow, John 1945- **1985**:2
Little, Cleavon 1939-1992
    Obituary **1993**:2
Lloyd Webber, Andrew 1948- **1989**:1
Loewe, Frederick 1901-1988
    Obituary **1988**:2
Logan, Joshua 1908-1988
    Obituary **1988**:4
Lord, Jack 1920-1998 **1998**:2
LuPone, Patti 1949- **2009**:2
MacRae, Gordon 1921-1986
    Obituary **1986**:2
Macy, William H. **1999**:3
Maher, Bill 1956- **1996**:2
Malkovich, John 1953- **1988**:2
Maltby, Richard, Jr. 1937- **1996**:3
Mamet, David 1947- **1998**:4
Mantegna, Joe 1947- **1992**:1
Marber, Patrick 1964- **2007**:4
Marceau, Marcel 1923-2007
    Obituary **2008**:4
Marshall, Penny 1942- **1991**:3
Martin, Mary 1913-1990
    Obituary **1991**:2
McDonagh, Martin 1970- **2007**:3
McDonnell, Mary 1952- **2008**:2
McDormand, Frances 1957- **1997**:3
McDowall, Roddy 1928-1998
    Obituary **1999**:1
McGillis, Kelly 1957- **1989**:3
McGregor, Ewan 1971(?)- **1998**:2
McKee, Lonette 1952(?)- **1996**:1
McKellen, Ian 1939- **1994**:1
McMahon, Julian 1968- **2006**:1
Merkerson, S. Epatha 1952- **2006**:4

Merrick, David 1912-2000
  Obituary **2000**:4
Messing, Debra 1968- **2004**:4
Midler, Bette 1945- **1989**:4
Minghella, Anthony 1954- **2004**:3
Mirren, Helen 1945- **2005**:1
Molina, Alfred 1953- **2005**:3
Montand, Yves 1921-1991
  Obituary **1992**:2
Montgomery, Elizabeth 1933-1995
  Obituary **1995**:4
Moore, Dudley 1935-2002
  Obituary **2003**:2
Moore, Mary Tyler 1936- **1996**:2
Morrow, Rob 1962- **2006**:4
Mos Def 1973- **2005**:4
Moss, Carrie-Anne 1967- **2004**:3
Neeson, Liam 1952- **1993**:4
Newman, Paul 1925- **1995**:3
Nichols, Mike 1931- **1994**:4
Nolan, Lloyd 1902-1985
  Obituary **1985**:4
Nolte, Nick 1941- **1992**:4
North, Alex 1910- **1986**:3
Northam, Jeremy 1961- **2003**:2
Nunn, Trevor 1940- **2000**:2
O'Donnell, Rosie 1962- **1994**:3
Oldman, Gary 1958- **1998**:1
Olin, Ken 1955(?)- **1992**:3
Olin, Lena 1956- **1991**:2
Olivier, Laurence 1907-1989
  Obituary **1989**:4
Orbach, Jerry 1935-2004
  Obituary **2006**:1
Osborne, John 1929-1994
  Obituary **1995**:2
O'Sullivan, Maureen 1911-1998
  Obituary **1998**:4
Owen, Clive 1964- **2006**:2
Pacino, Al 1940- **1993**:4
Page, Geraldine 1924-1987
  Obituary **1987**:4
Papp, Joseph 1921-1991
  Obituary **1992**:2
Parks, Suzan-Lori 1964- **2003**:2
Paulsen, Pat 1927-1997
  Obituary **1997**:4
Peck, Gregory 1916-2003
  Obituary **2004**:3
Penn, Sean 1960- **1987**:2
Penn & Teller **1992**:1
Perkins, Anthony 1932-1992
  Obituary **1993**:2
Perry, Tyler 1969- **2006**:1
Peters, Bernadette 1948- **2000**:1
Pfeiffer, Michelle 1957- **1990**:2
Picasso, Paloma 1949- **1991**:1
Pinchot, Bronson 1959(?)- **1987**:4
Piven, Jeremy 1965- **2007**:3
Pleasence, Donald 1919-1995
  Obituary **1995**:3
Poitier, Sidney 1927- **1990**:3
Poston, Tom 1921-2007
  Obituary **2008**:3
Preminger, Otto 1906-1986
  Obituary **1986**:3
Preston, Robert 1918-1987
  Obituary **1987**:3
Price, Vincent 1911-1993
  Obituary **1994**:2
Prince, Faith 1959(?)- **1993**:2
Quaid, Dennis 1954- **1989**:4

Radcliffe, Daniel 1989- **2007**:4
Radner, Gilda 1946-1989
  Obituary **1989**:4
Raitt, John 1917-2005
  Obituary **2006**:2
Randall, Tony 1920-2004
  Obituary **2005**:3
Rashad, Phylicia 1948- **1987**:3
Raye, Martha 1916-1994
  Obituary **1995**:1
Redford, Robert 1937- **1993**:2
Redgrave, Lynn 1943- **1999**:3
Redgrave, Vanessa 1937- **1989**:2
Reeves, Keanu 1964- **1992**:1
Reilly, Charles Nelson
  Obituary **2008**:3
Reilly, John C. 1965- **2003**:4
Reitman, Ivan 1946- **1986**:3
Reza, Yasmina 1959(?)- **1999**:2
Richards, Lloyd 1919-2006
  Obituary **2007**:3
Richards, Michael 1949(?)- **1993**:4
Ritter, John 1948- **2003**:4
Robbins, Jerome 1918-1998
  Obituary **1999**:1
Roberts, Doris 1930- **2003**:4
Roker, Roxie 1929(?)-1995
  Obituary **1996**:2
Rolle, Esther 1922-1998
  Obituary **1999**:2
Rudd, Paul 1969- **2009**:4
Rudner, Rita 1956- **1993**:2
Rudnick, Paul 1957(?)- **1994**:3
Ruehl, Mercedes 195(?)- **1992**:4
Rylance, Mark 1960- **2009**:3
Salonga, Lea 1971- **2003**:3
Sarandon, Susan 1946- **1995**:3
Schoenfeld, Gerald 1924- **1986**:2
Schreiber, Liev 1967- **2007**:2
Schwimmer, David 1966(?)- **1996**:2
Scott, George C. 1927-1999
  Obituary **2000**:2
Seymour, Jane 1951- **1994**:4
Shaffer, Paul 1949- **1987**:1
Shanley, John Patrick 1950- **2006**:1
Shawn, Dick 1924(?)-1987
  Obituary **1987**:3
Sheldon, Sidney 1917-2007
  Obituary **2008**:2
Shepard, Sam 1943- **1996**:4
Short, Martin 1950- **1986**:1
Silvers, Phil 1912-1985
  Obituary **1985**:4
Sinise, Gary 1955(?)- **1996**:1
Slater, Christian 1969- **1994**:1
Smith, Anna Deavere 1950- **2002**:2
Snipes, Wesley 1962- **1993**:1
Sondheim, Stephen 1930- **1994**:4
Spacey, Kevin 1959- **1996**:4
Stamos, John 1963- **2008**:1
Stapleton, Maureen 1925-2006
  Obituary **2007**:2
Steiger, Rod 1925-2002
  Obituary **2003**:4
Stewart, Jimmy 1908-1997
  Obituary **1997**:4
Stewart, Patrick 1940- **1996**:1
Stiller, Ben 1965- **1999**:1
Sting 1951- **1991**:4
Stoppard, Tom 1937- **1995**:4
Streep, Meryl 1949- **1990**:2
Streisand, Barbra 1942- **1992**:2

Stritch, Elaine 1925- **2002**:4
Styne, Jule 1905-1994
  Obituary **1995**:1
Susskind, David 1920-1987
  Obituary **1987**:2
Swinton, Tilda 1960- **2008**:4
Szot, Paulo 1969- **2009**:3
Tandy, Jessica 1901-1994 **1990**:4
  Obituary **1995**:1
Taylor, Elizabeth 1932- **1993**:3
Taylor, Lili 1967- **2000**:2
Thompson, Emma 1959- **1993**:2
Tomei, Marisa 1964- **1995**:2
Tucci, Stanley 1960- **2003**:2
Tune, Tommy 1939- **1994**:2
Ullman, Tracey 1961- **1988**:3
Umeki, Miyoshi 1929-2007
  Obituary **2008**:4
Urich, Robert 1947- **1988**:1
  Obituary **2003**:3
Ustinov, Peter 1921-2004
  Obituary **2005**:3
Vardalos, Nia 1962- **2003**:4
Vogel, Paula 1951- **1999**:2
Walker, Nancy 1922-1992
  Obituary **1992**:3
Washington, Denzel 1954- **1993**:2
Wasserstein, Wendy 1950- **1991**:3
Waterston, Sam 1940- **2006**:1
Watts, Naomi 1968- **2006**:1
Wayne, David 1914-1995
  Obituary **1995**:3
Weaver, Sigourney 1949- **1988**:3
Weisz, Rachel 1971- **2006**:4
Weitz, Bruce 1943- **1985**:4
Wences, Senor 1896-1999
  Obituary **1999**:4
Whitaker, Forest 1961- **1996**:2
White, Julie 1961- **2008**:2
Whitehead, Robert 1916-2002
  Obituary **2003**:3
Wiest, Dianne 1948- **1995**:2
Wilkinson, Tom 1948- **2003**:2
Williams, Treat 1951- **2004**:3
Willis, Bruce 1955- **1986**:4
Winfield, Paul 1941-2004
  Obituary **2005**:2
Winokur, Marissa Jaret 1973- **2005**:1
Wong, B.D. 1962- **1998**:1
Woods, James 1947- **1988**:3
Worth, Irene 1916-2002
  Obituary **2003**:2
Wyatt, Jane 1910-2006
  Obituary **2008**:1
Wyle, Noah 1971- **1997**:3
Youngman, Henny 1906(?)-1998
  Obituary **1998**:3
Zeffirelli, Franco 1923- **1991**:3

**WRITING**
Adams, Douglas 1952-2001
  Obituary **2002**:2
Adams, Scott 1957- **1996**:4
Ahern, Cecelia 1981- **2008**:4
Albom, Mitch 1958- **1999**:3
Alexie, Sherman 1966- **1998**:4
Ali, Monica 1967- **2007**:4
Amanpour, Christiane 1958- **1997**:2
Ambler, Eric 1909-1998
  Obituary **1999**:2
Ambrose, Stephen 1936- **2002**:3
Amis, Kingsley 1922-1995

Obituary **1996**:2
Amis, Martin 1949- **2008**:3
Amory, Cleveland 1917-1998
    Obituary **1999**:2
Anderson, Poul 1926-2001
    Obituary **2002**:3
Angelou, Maya 1928- **1993**:4
Angier, Natalie 1958- **2000**:3
Asimov, Isaac 1920-1992
    Obituary **1992**:3
Atkins, Robert C. 1930-2003
    Obituary **2004**:2
Atwood, Margaret 1939- **2001**:2
Axthelm, Pete 1943(?)-1991
    Obituary **1991**:3
Bacall, Lauren 1924- **1997**:3
Bakker, Robert T. 1950(?)- **1991**:3
Baldwin, James 1924-1987
    Obituary **1988**:2
Ball, Edward 1959- **1999**:2
Banks, Russell 1940- **2009**:2
Baraka, Amiri 1934- **2000**:3
Barber, Red 1908-1992
    Obituary **1993**:2
Barker, Clive 1952- **2003**:3
Barker, Pat 1943- **2009**:1
Barnouin, Kim 1971-. See Kim
    Barnouin and Rory Freedman
Barry, Dave 1947(?)- **1991**:2
Barry, Lynda 1956(?)- **1992**:1
Bechdel, Alison 1960- **2007**:3
Beckett, Samuel Barclay 1906-1989
    Obituary **1990**:2
Bedford, Deborah 1958- **2006**:3
Bell, Gabrielle 1975(?)- **2007**:4
Bellow, Saul 1915-2005
    Obituary **2006**:2
Benchley, Peter 1940-2006
    Obituary **2007**:1
Bloodworth-Thomason,
    Linda 1947- **1994**:1
Blume, Judy 1936- **1998**:4
Bly, Robert 1926- **1992**:4
Blyth, Myrna 1939- **2002**:4
Bombeck, Erma 1927-1996
    Obituary **1996**:4
Bourdain, Anthony 1956- **2008**:3
Bowles, Paul 1910-1999
    Obituary **2000**:3
Boyle, T. C. 1948- **2007**:2
Boynton, Sandra 1953- **2004**:1
Bradford, Barbara Taylor
    1933- **2002**:4
Bradshaw, John 1933- **1992**:1
Branagh, Kenneth 1960- **1992**:2
Breathed, Berkeley 1957- **2005**:3
Brite, Poppy Z. 1967- **2005**:1
Brodsky, Joseph 1940-1996
    Obituary **1996**:3
Brokaw, Tom 1940- **2000**:3
Brooks, Gwendolyn
    1917-2000 **1998**:1
    Obituary **2001**:2
Brown, Dan 1964- **2004**:4
Brown, Dee 1908-2002
    Obituary **2004**:1
Brown, Tina 1953- **1992**:1
Buchwald, Art 1925-2007
    Obituary **2008**:2
Buffett, Jimmy 1946- **1999**:3
Burgess, Anthony 1917-1993
    Obituary **1994**:2

Burroughs, William S. 1914- **1994**:2
Burroughs, William S. 1914-1997
    Obituary **1997**:4
Buscaglia, Leo 1924-1998
    Obituary **1998**:4
Busch, Charles 1954- **1998**:3
Bush, Millie 1987- **1992**:1
Bushnell, Candace 1959(?)- **2004**:2
Butler, Octavia E. 1947- **1999**:3
Byrne, Gabriel 1950- **1997**:4
Byrne, Rhonda 1955- **2008**:2
Cabot, Meg 1967- **2008**:4
Caen, Herb 1916-1997
    Obituary **1997**:4
Campbell, Bebe Moore 1950- **1996**:2
Caplan, Arthur L. 1950- **2000**:2
Carcaterra, Lorenzo 1954- **1996**:1
Carey, George 1935- **1992**:3
Carlson, Richard 1961- **2002**:1
Carter, Stephen L. **2008**:2
Carver, Raymond 1938-1988
    Obituary **1989**:1
Castaneda, Carlos 1931-1998
    Obituary **1998**:4
Castellucci, Cecil 1969- **2008**:3
Castillo, Ana 1953- **2000**:4
Cela, Camilo Jose 1916-2001
    Obituary **2003**:1
Chabon, Michael 1963- **2002**:1
Chatwin, Bruce 1940-1989
    Obituary **1989**:2
Chavez, Linda 1947- **1999**:3
Cheney, Lynne V. 1941- **1990**:4
Child, Julia 1912- **1999**:4
Child, Lee 1954- **2007**:3
Chopra, Deepak 1947- **1996**:3
Christensen, Kate 1962- **2009**:4
Clancy, Tom 1947- **1998**:4
Clark, Mary Higgins 1929- **2000**:4
Clarke, Arthur C. 1917-2008
    Obituary **2009**:2
Clavell, James 1924(?)-1994
    Obituary **1995**:1
Cleaver, Eldridge 1935-1998
    Obituary **1998**:4
Clowes, Daniel 1961- **2007**:1
Codrescu, Andreaa 1946- **1997**:3
Cody, Diablo 1978- **2009**:1
Coetzee, J. M. 1940- **2004**:4
Colbert, Stephen 1964- **2007**:4
Cole, Johnetta B. 1936- **1994**:3
Coles, Robert 1929(?)- **1995**:1
Collins, Billy 1941- **2002**:2
Collins, Jackie 1941- **2004**:4
Comfort, Alex 1920-2000
    Obituary **2000**:4
Condon, Richard 1915-1996
    Obituary **1996**:4
Connelly, Michael 1956- **2007**:1
Cook, Robin 1940- **1996**:3
Cornwell, Patricia 1956- **2003**:1
Cosby, Bill 1937- **1999**:2
Covey, Stephen R. 1932- **1994**:4
Cowley, Malcolm 1898-1989
    Obituary **1989**:3
Crais, Robert 1954(?)- **2007**:4
Crichton, Michael 1942- **1995**:3
Cronenberg, David 1943- **1992**:3
Cruz, Nilo 1961(?)- **2004**:4
Cunningham, Michael 1952- **2003**:4
Dahl, Roald 1916-1990
    Obituary **1991**:2

Dangerfield, Rodney 1921-2004
    Obituary **2006**:1
Danticat, Edwidge 1969- **2005**:4
Darden, Christopher 1957(?)- **1996**:4
Darwish, Mahmud 1942-2008
    Obituary **2009**:4
David, Larry 1948- **2003**:4
Davis, Patti 1952- **1995**:1
Deen, Paula 1947- **2008**:3
Delany, Sarah 1889-1999
    Obituary **1999**:3
Derrida, Jacques 1930-2005
    Obituary **2006**:1
Dershowitz, Alan 1938(?)- **1992**:1
Diamond, I.A.L. 1920-1988
    Obituary **1988**:3
Diamond, Selma 1921(?)-1985
    Obituary **1985**:2
Dickey, James 1923-1997 **1998**:2
Dickinson, Brian 1937- **1998**:2
Dickinson, Janice 1953- **2005**:2
Djerassi, Carl 1923- **2000**:4
Doctorow, E. L. 1931- **2007**:1
Dorris, Michael 1945-1997
    Obituary **1997**:3
Douglas, Marjory Stoneman
    1890-1998 **1993**:1
    Obituary **1998**:4
Dove, Rita 1952- **1994**:3
Dowd, Maureen Brigid 1952- **1997**:1
Doyle, Roddy 1958- **2008**:1
Drucker, Peter F. 1909- **1992**:3
Dunne, Dominick 1925- **1997**:1
Duras, Marguerite 1914-1996
    Obituary **1996**:3
Durrell, Gerald 1925-1995
    Obituary **1995**:3
Dworkin, Andrea 1946-2005
    Obituary **2006**:2
Eberhart, Richard 1904-2005
    Obituary **2006**:3
Ebert, Roger 1942- **1998**:3
Edwards, Bob 1947- **1993**:2
Eggers, Dave 1970- **2001**:3
Eisner, Will 1917-2005
    Obituary **2006**:1
Elliott, Missy 1971- **2003**:4
Ellison, Ralph 1914-1994
    Obituary **1994**:4
Ellroy, James 1948- **2003**:4
Ephron, Nora 1941- **1992**:3
Epstein, Jason 1928- **1991**:1
Erdrich, Louise 1954- **2005**:3
Etzioni, Amitai 1929- **1994**:3
Evanovich, Janet 1943- **2005**:2
Evans, Joni 1942- **1991**:4
Evans, Robert 1930- **2004**:1
Fabio 1961(?)- **1993**:4
Falconer, Ian 1960(?)- **2003**:1
Faludi, Susan 1959- **1992**:4
Fast, Howard 1914-2003
    Obituary **2004**:2
Ferguson, Niall 1964- **2006**:1
Fforde, Jasper 1961- **2006**:3
Fielding, Helen 1959- **2000**:4
Filipovic, Zlata 1981(?)- **1994**:4
Finnamore, Suzanne 1959- **2009**:1
Fish, Hamilton 1888-1991
    Obituary **1991**:3
Fisher, Carrie 1956- **1991**:1
Flynt, Larry 1942- **1997**:3
Fo, Dario 1926- **1998**:1

Fodor, Eugene 1906(?)-1991
  Obituary **1991**:3
Foote, Shelby 1916- **1991**:2
Forbes, Steve 1947- **1996**:2
Foxworthy, Jeff 1958- **1996**:1
Frame, Janet 1924-2004
  Obituary **2005**:2
Franken, Al 1952(?)- **1996**:3
Frankl, Viktor E. 1905-1997
  Obituary **1998**:1
Franzen, Jonathan 1959- **2002**:3
Frazier, Charles 1950- **2003**:2
Freedman, Rory 1971-. See Kim
  Barnouin and Rory Freedman
French, Tana 1973- **2009**:3
Freston, Kathy 1965- **2009**:3
Friedan, Betty 1921- **1994**:2
Frye, Northrop 1912-1991
  Obituary **1991**:3
Fugard, Athol 1932- **1992**:3
Fulbright, J. William 1905-1995
  Obituary **1995**:3
Fulghum, Robert 1937- **1996**:1
Gaines, William M. 1922-1992
  Obituary **1993**:1
Gao Xingjian 1940- **2001**:2
Garcia, Cristina 1958- **1997**:4
Garcia Marquez, Gabriel
  1928- **2005**:2
Geisel, Theodor 1904-1991
  Obituary **1992**:2
George, Elizabeth 1949- **2003**:3
Gibson, William Ford, III
  1948- **1997**:2
Gillespie, Marcia 1944- **1999**:4
Ginsberg, Allen 1926-1997
  Obituary **1997**:3
Goldman, William 1931- **2001**:1
Gore, Albert, Jr. 1948(?)- **1993**:2
Goren, Charles H. 1901-1991
  Obituary **1991**:4
Gottlieb, William 1917-2006
  Obituary **2007**:2
Grafton, Sue 1940- **2000**:2
Graham, Billy 1918- **1992**:1
Graham, Katharine Meyer
  1917- **1997**:3
  Obituary **2002**:3
Grandin, Temple 1947- **2006**:1
Grass, Gunter 1927- **2000**:2
Gray, John 1952(?)- **1995**:3
Gray, Simon 1936-2008
  Obituary **2009**:4
Gray, Spalding 1941-2004
  Obituary **2005**:2
Greene, Graham 1904-1991
  Obituary **1991**:4
Grisham, John 1955- **1994**:4
Grodin, Charles 1935- **1997**:3
Guccione, Bob, Jr. 1956- **1991**:4
Gupta, Sanjay 1969- **2009**:4
Haddon, Mark 1962- **2005**:2
Ha Jin 1956- **2000**:3
Halberstam, David 1934-2007
  Obituary **2008**:3
Haley, Alex 1924-1992
  Obituary **1992**:3
Hamilton, Laurell K. 1963- **2008**:2
Hand, Elizabeth 1957- **2007**:2
Handford, Martin **1991**:3
Handler, Chelsea 1975- **2009**:3
Handler, Daniel 1970- **2003**:3

Harris, E. Lynn 1955- **2004**:2
Harris, Thomas 1940(?)- **2001**:1
Hart, Johnny 1931-2007
  Obituary **2008**:2
Hart, Mickey 1944(?)- **1991**:2
Havel, Vaclav 1936- **1990**:3
Hayakawa, Samuel Ichiye 1906-1992
  Obituary **1992**:3
Heaney, Seamus 1939- **1996**:2
Heat-Moon, William Least
  1939- **2000**:2
Heller, Joseph 1923-1999
  Obituary **2000**:2
Heloise 1951- **2001**:4
Henry, Carl F.H. 1913-2003
  Obituary **2005**:1
Herzog, Chaim 1918-1997
  Obituary **1997**:3
Hiaasen, Carl 1953- **2007**:2
Hicks, India 1967- **2008**:2
Highsmith, Patricia 1921-1995
  Obituary **1995**:3
Hills, L. Rust 1924-2008
  Obituary **2009**:4
Hoff, Syd 1912-2004
  Obituary **2005**:3
Hollinghurst, Alan 1954- **2006**:1
hooks, bell 1952- **2000**:2
Horn, Mike 1966- **2009**:3
Hornby, Nick 1957- **2002**:2
Hosseini, Khaled 1965- **2008**:3
Hrabal, Bohumil 1914-1997
  Obituary **1997**:3
Hughes, Robert 1938- **1996**:4
Hughes, Ted 1930-1998
  Obituary **1999**:2
Humphries, Barry 1934- **1993**:1
Humphry, Derek 1931(?)- **1992**:2
Hunter, Evan 1926-2005
  Obituary **2006**:4
Hwang, David Henry 1957- **1999**:1
Ice-T **1992**:3
Irving, John 1942- **2006**:2
Ivins, Molly 1942(?)- **1993**:4
Jablonski, Nina G. 1953- **2009**:3
Jacques, Brian 1939- **2002**:2
Jay, Ricky 1949(?)- **1995**:1
Jelinek, Elfriede 1946- **2005**:3
Jen, Gish 1955- **2000**:1
Jenkins, Sally 1960(?)- **1997**:2
Jennings, Peter Charles 1938- **1997**:2
Jewel 1974- **1999**:2
Johnson, Beverly 1952- **2005**:2
Johnson, Diane 1934- **2004**:3
Jones, Edward P. 1950- **2005**:1
Jones, Gayl 1949- **1999**:4
Jones, Jenny 1946- **1998**:2
Jong, Erica 1942- **1998**:3
Jordan, Neil 1950(?)- **1993**:3
Joyce, William 1957- **2006**:1
Julavits, Heidi 1968- **2007**:4
July, Miranda 1974- **2008**:2
Jurgensen, Karen 1949(?)- **2004**:3
Kael, Pauline 1919-2001 **2000**:4
  Obituary **2002**:4
Kahane, Meir 1932-1990
  Obituary **1991**:2
Kasparov, Garry 1963- **1997**:4
Kazan, Elia 1909-2003
  Obituary **2004**:4
Kellerman, Jonathan 1949- **2009**:1

Kennedy, John F., Jr.
  1960-1999 **1990**:1
  Obituary **1999**:4
Kent, Arthur 1954- **1991**:4
Kerr, Jean 1922-2003
  Obituary **2004**:1
Kerr, Walter 1913-1996
  Obituary **1997**:1
Kesey, Ken 1935-2001
  Obituary **2003**:1
Keyes, Marian 1963- **2006**:2
Kieslowski, Krzysztof 1941-1996
  Obituary **1996**:3
Kim Barnouin and Rory Freedman
  1971- **2009**:4
King, Alan 1927-2004
  Obituary **2005**:3
King, Coretta Scott 1927- **1999**:3
King, Larry 1933- **1993**:1
King, Stephen 1947- **1998**:1
Kingsolver, Barbara 1955- **2005**:1
Kinney, Jeff 1971- **2009**:3
Kinsella, Sophie 1969- **2005**:2
Kirk, David 1956(?)- **2004**:1
Klass, Perri 1958- **1993**:2
Kleinpaste, Ruud 1952- **2006**:2
Knowles, John 1926-2001
  Obituary **2003**:1
Koontz, Dean 1945- **1999**:3
Kordich, Jay 1923- **1993**:2
Kosinski, Jerzy 1933-1991
  Obituary **1991**:4
Kostova, Elizabeth 1964- **2006**:2
Kozol, Jonathan 1936- **1992**:1
Kramer, Larry 1935- **1991**:2
Krantz, Judith 1928- **2003**:1
Kunitz, Stanley J. 1905- **2001**:2
Lahiri, Jhumpa 1967- **2001**:3
Lalami, Laila **2007**:1
Lamb, Wally 1950- **1999**:1
L'Amour, Louis 1908-1988
  Obituary **1988**:4
Landers, Ann 1918-2002
  Obituary **2003**:3
Landsbergis, Vytautas 1932- **1991**:3
Larbalestier, Justine 1968(?)- **2008**:4
Lawson, Nigella 1960- **2003**:2
Leach, Penelope 1937- **1992**:4
le Carre, John 1931- **2000**:1
Lee, Chang-Rae 1965- **2005**:1
Lee, Sandra 1966- **2008**:3
Lehane, Dennis 1965- **2001**:4
Lelyveld, Joseph S. 1937- **1994**:4
L'Engle, Madeleine 1918-2007
  Obituary **2008**:4
Leonard, Elmore 1925- **1998**:4
Lerner, Michael 1943- **1994**:2
Lessing, Doris 1919- **2008**:4
Levin, Ira 1929-2007
  Obituary **2009**:1
Levy, Eugene 1946- **2004**:3
Lewis, Edward T. 1940- **1999**:4
Lindbergh, Anne Morrow 1906-2001
  Obituary **2001**:4
Lindgren, Astrid 1907-2002
  Obituary **2003**:1
Lindsay-Abaire, David
  1970(?)- **2008**:2
Lisick, Beth 1969(?)- **2006**:2
Little, Benilde 1959(?)- **2006**:2
Litzenburger, Liesel 1967(?)- **2008**:1
Lively, Penelope 1933- **2007**:4

Logan, Joshua 1908-1988
  Obituary **1988**:4
Lord, Bette Bao 1938- **1994**:1
Louv, Richard 1949- **2006**:2
Ludlum, Robert 1927-2001
  Obituary **2002**:1
Lupino, Ida 1918(?)-1995
  Obituary **1996**:1
Madden, Chris 1948- **2006**:1
Mahfouz, Naguib 1911-2006
  Obituary **2007**:4
Mailer, Norman 1923- **1998**:1
Mamet, David 1947- **1998**:4
Marchetto, Marisa Acocella 1962(?)-
  **2007**:3
Martin, Judith 1938- **2000**:3
Mayes, Frances 1940(?)- **2004**:3
Maynard, Joyce 1953- **1999**:4
McCall, Nathan 1955- **1994**:4
McCall Smith, Alexander
  1948- **2005**:2
McCarthy, Cormac 1933- **2008**:1
McCourt, Frank 1930- **1997**:4
McDermott, Alice 1953- **1999**:2
McDonnell, Patrick 1956- **2009**:4
McEwan, Ian 1948- **2004**:2
McGahern, John 1934-2006
  Obituary **2007**:2
McGraw, Phil 1950- **2005**:2
McKenna, Terence **1993**:3
McMillan, Terry 1951- **1993**:2
McMurtry, Larry 1936- **2006**:4
McNamara, Robert S. 1916- **1995**:4
Melendez, Bill 1916-2008
  Obituary **2009**:4
Meltzer, Brad 1970- **2005**:4
Menchu, Rigoberta 1960(?)- **1993**:2
Menninger, Karl 1893-1990
  Obituary **1991**:1
Merrill, James 1926-1995
  Obituary **1995**:3
Meyer, Stephenie 1973- **2009**:1
Michener, James A. 1907-1997
  Obituary **1998**:1
Millan, Cesar 1969- **2007**:4
Miller, Arthur 1915- **1999**:4
Miller, Frank 1957- **2008**:2
Miller, Sue 1943- **1999**:3
Milne, Christopher Robin 1920-1996
  Obituary **1996**:4
Milosz, Czeslaw 1911-2004
  Obituary **2005**:4
Mina, Denise 1966- **2006**:1
Mo'Nique 1967- **2008**:1
Montagu, Ashley 1905-1999
  Obituary **2000**:2
Moody, Rick 1961- **2002**:2
Moore, Michael 1954(?)- **1990**:3
Morgan, Robin 1941- **1991**:1
Morris, Henry M. 1918-2006
  Obituary **2007**:2
Morrison, Toni 1931- **1998**:1
Mortensen, Viggo 1958- **2003**:3
Mosley, Walter 1952- **2003**:4
Moyers, Bill 1934- **1991**:4
Munro, Alice 1931- **1997**:1
Murakami, Haruki 1949- **2008**:3
Murdoch, Iris 1919-1999
  Obituary **1999**:4
Murkoff, Heidi 1958- **2009**:3
Narayan, R.K. 1906-2001
  Obituary **2002**:2

Nasrin, Taslima 1962- **1995**:1
Nemerov, Howard 1920-1991
  Obituary **1992**:1
Newkirk, Ingrid 1949- **1992**:3
Niezabitowska, Malgorzata 1949(?)-
  **1991**:3
Nissel, Angela 1974- **2006**:4
Noonan, Peggy 1950- **1990**:3
Northrop, Peggy 1954- **2009**:2
Norton, Andre 1912-2005
  Obituary **2006**:2
Oates, Joyce Carol 1938- **2000**:1
Obama, Barack 1961- **2007**:4
O'Brien, Conan 1963(?)- **1994**:1
Oe, Kenzaburo 1935- **1997**:1
Onassis, Jacqueline Kennedy
  1929-1994
  Obituary **1994**:4
Ondaatje, Philip Michael
  1943- **1997**:3
Ornish, Dean 1953- **2004**:2
Osborne, John 1929-1994
  Obituary **1995**:2
Osteen, Joel 1963- **2006**:2
Owens, Delia and Mark **1993**:3
Oz, Mehmet 1960- **2007**:4
Pagels, Elaine 1943- **1997**:1
Paglia, Camille 1947- **1992**:3
Palahniuk, Chuck 1962- **2004**:1
Pamuk, Orhan 1952- **2007**:3
Paretsky, Sara 1947- **2002**:4
Parker, Brant 1920-2007
  Obituary **2008**:2
Parks, Suzan-Lori 1964- **2003**:2
Patchett, Ann 1963- **2003**:2
Patterson, Richard North
  1947- **2001**:4
Paz, Octavio 1914- **1991**:2
Percy, Walker 1916-1990
  Obituary **1990**:4
Peters, Tom 1942- **1998**:1
Phillips, Julia 1944- **1992**:1
Picoult, Jodi 1966- **2008**:1
Pilkey, Dav 1966- **2001**:1
Pipher, Mary 1948(?)- **1996**:4
Plimpton, George 1927-2003
  Obituary **2004**:4
Politkovskaya, Anna 1958-2006
  Obituary **2007**:4
Porter, Sylvia 1913-1991
  Obituary **1991**:4
Post, Peggy 1940(?)- **2001**:4
Potok, Chaim 1929-2002
  Obituary **2003**:4
Pouillon, Nora 1943- **2005**:1
Powter, Susan 1957(?)- **1994**:3
Pratt, Jane 1963(?)- **1999**:1
Proulx, E. Annie 1935- **1996**:1
Pullman, Philip 1946- **2003**:2
Pynchon, Thomas 1937- **1997**:4
Quindlen, Anna 1952- **1993**:1
Quinn, Jane Bryant 1939(?)- **1993**:4
Ramsay, Gordon 1966- **2008**:2
Redfield, James 1952- **1995**:2
Reichs, Kathleen J. 1948- **2007**:3
Rendell, Ruth 1930- **2007**:2
Rey, Margret E. 1906-1996
  Obituary **1997**:2
Reza, Yasmina 1959(?)- **1999**:2
Rice, Anne 1941- **1995**:1
Ringgold, Faith 1930- **2000**:3
Robbins, Harold 1916-1997

Obituary **1998**:1
Roberts, Cokie 1943- **1993**:4
Roberts, Steven K. 1952(?)- **1992**:1
Robinson, Peter 1950- **2007**:4
Roddenberry, Gene 1921-1991
  Obituary **1992**:2
Roizen, Michael 1946- **2007**:4
Rosenzweig, Ilene 1965(?)- **2004**:1
Rossner, Judith 1935-2005
  Obituary **2006**:4
Rosten, Leo 1908-1997
  Obituary **1997**:3
Roth, Philip 1933- **1999**:1
Rowan, Carl 1925-2000
  Obituary **2001**:2
Rowland, Pleasant **1992**:3
Rowling, J.K. 1965- **2000**:1
Royko, Mike 1932-1997
  Obituary **1997**:4
Rudnick, Paul 1957(?)- **1994**:3
Rushdie, Salman 1947- **1994**:1
Russell, Mary 1950- **2009**:2
Russo, Richard 1949- **2002**:3
Sacks, Oliver 1933- **1995**:4
Safire, William 1929- **2000**:3
Salk, Jonas 1914-1995 **1994**:4
  Obituary **1995**:4
Salzman, Mark 1959- **2002**:1
Sapphire 1951(?)- **1996**:4
Saramago, Jose 1922- **1999**:1
Saro-Wiwa, Ken 1941-1995
  Obituary **1996**:2
Sarraute, Nathalie 1900-1999
  Obituary **2000**:2
Satrapi, Marjane 1969- **2006**:3
Schaap, Dick 1934-2001
  Obituary **2003**:1
Schroeder, Barbet 1941- **1996**:1
Schulz, Charles M. 1922- **1998**:1
Sears, Barry 1947- **2004**:2
Sebold, Alice 1963(?)- **2005**:4
Sedaris, Amy 1961- **2009**:3
Sedaris, David 1956- **2005**:3
Senghor, Leopold 1906-2001
  Obituary **2003**:1
Serros, Michele 1967(?)- **2008**:2
Sethi, Simran 1971(?)- **2008**:1
Sevareid, Eric 1912-1992
  Obituary **1993**:1
Shanley, John Patrick 1950- **2006**:1
Shawn, William 1907-1992
  Obituary **1993**:3
Sheldon, Sidney 1917-2007
  Obituary **2008**:2
Shepard, Sam 1943- **1996**:4
Shields, Carol 1935-2003
  Obituary **2004**:3
Shilts, Randy 1951-1994 **1993**:4
  Obituary **1994**:3
Shreve, Anita 1946(?)- **2003**:4
Shriver, Lionel 1957- **2008**:4
Silber, Joan 1945- **2009**:4
Silverstein, Shel 1932-1999
  Obituary **1999**:4
Singer, Isaac Bashevis 1904-1991
  Obituary **1992**:1
Siskel, Gene 1946-1999
  Obituary **1999**:3
Skinner, B.F. 1904-1990
  Obituary **1991**:1
Smiley, Jane 1949- **1995**:4
Smith, Kevin 1970- **2000**:4

Smith, Zadie 1975- **2003**:4
Sobol, Donald J. 1924- **2004**:4
Solzhenitsyn, Aleksandr 1918-2008
　Obituary **2009**:4
Sontag, Susan 1933-2004
　Obituary **2006**:1
Southern, Terry 1926-1995
　Obituary **1996**:2
Sowell, Thomas 1930- **1998**:3
Spiegelman, Art 1948- **1998**:3
Spillane, Mickey 1918-2006
　Obituary **2007**:3
Spock, Benjamin 1903-1998 **1995**:2
　Obituary **1998**:3
Spong, John 1931- **1991**:3
Stahl, Lesley 1941- **1997**:1
Steel, Danielle 1947- **1999**:2
Steele, Shelby 1946- **1991**:2
Stefanidis, John 1937- **2007**:3
Steig, William 1907-2003
　Obituary **2004**:4
Steinem, Gloria 1934- **1996**:2
Sterling, Bruce 1954- **1995**:4
Stewart, Martha 1942(?)- **1992**:1
Stine, R. L. 1943- **2003**:1
Stockton, Shreve 1977- **2009**:4
Stone, I.F. 1907-1989
　Obituary **1990**:1
Stone, Irving 1903-1989
　Obituary **1990**:2
Stoppard, Tom 1937- **1995**:4
Strout, Elizabeth 1956- **2009**:1
Studi, Wes 1944(?)- **1994**:3
Styron, William 1925-2006

　Obituary **2008**:1
Sullivan, Andrew 1964(?)- **1996**:1
Sulzberger, Arthur O., Jr.
　1951- **1998**:3
Sykes, Wanda 1964- **2007**:4
Tan, Amy 1952- **1998**:3
Tannen, Deborah 1945- **1995**:1
Tartt, Donna 1963- **2004**:3
Taylor, Graham 1958(?)- **2005**:3
Taylor, Susan L. 1946- **1998**:2
Thompson, Hunter S. 1939- **1992**:1
Thornton, Billy Bob 1956(?)- **1997**:4
Tilberis, Elizabeth 1947(?)- **1994**:3
Timmerman, Jacobo 1923-1999
　Obituary **2000**:3
Tohe, Laura 1953- **2009**:2
Totenberg, Nina 1944- **1992**:2
Travers, P.L. 1899(?)-1996
　Obituary **1996**:4
Tretheway, Natasha 1966- **2008**:3
Trudeau, Garry 1948- **1991**:2
Tuck, Lily 1938- **2006**:1
Tyler, Anne 1941- **1995**:4
Updike, John 1932- **2001**:2
Ustinov, Peter 1921-2004
　Obituary **2005**:3
Valdes-Rodriguez, Alisa 1969- **2005**:4
Van Duyn, Mona 1921- **1993**:2
Vardalos, Nia 1962- **2003**:4
Vidal, Gore 1925- **1996**:2
Vogel, Paula 1951- **1999**:2
Vonnegut, Kurt 1922- **1998**:4
von Trapp, Maria 1905-1987
　Obituary **1987**:3

vos Savant, Marilyn 1946- **1988**:2
Walker, Alice 1944- **1999**:1
Wallace, Irving 1916-1990
　Obituary **1991**:1
Walls, Jeannette 1960(?)- **2006**:3
Warren, Robert Penn 1905-1989
　Obituary **1990**:1
Wasserstein, Wendy 1950- **1991**:3
Waters, John 1946- **1988**:3
Weihui, Zhou 1973- **2001**:1
Weil, Andrew 1942- **1997**:4
Weiner, Jennifer 1970- **2006**:3
Wells, Linda 1958- **2002**:3
Welty, Eudora 1909-2001
　Obituary **2002**:3
Wenner, Jann 1946- **1993**:1
West, Cornel 1953- **1994**:2
West, Dorothy 1907- **1996**:1
West, Michael Lee 1953- **2009**:2
Wiesel, Elie 1928- **1998**:1
Williams, Brian 1959- **2009**:4
Wilson, August 1945- **2002**:2
Wilson, Edward O. 1929- **1994**:4
Winick, Judd 1970- **2005**:3
Wolf, Naomi 1963(?)- **1994**:3
Wolfe, Tom 1930- **1999**:2
Wolff, Tobias 1945- **2005**:1
Woods, Donald 1933-2001
　Obituary **2002**:3
Yeang, Ken 1948- **2008**:3
Zinnemann, Fred 1907-1997
　Obituary **1997**:3

# 2009 Subject Index

This index lists all newsmakers by subjects, company names, products, organizations, issues, awards, and professional specialties. Indexes in softbound issues allow access to the current year's entries; indexes in annual hardbound volumes are cumulative, covering the entire *Newsmakers* series.

Listee names are followed by a year and issue number; thus **1996**:3 indicates that an entry on that individual appears in both 1996, Issue 3, and the 1996 cumulation. For access to newsmakers appearing earlier than the current softbound issue, see the previous year's cumulation.

**ABC Television**
 Arledge, Roone 1931- **1992**:2
 Diller, Barry 1942- **1991**:1
 Funt, Allen 1914-1999
  Obituary **2000**:1
 Philbin, Regis 1933- **2000**:2
 Pierce, Frederick S. 1934(?)- **1985**:3

**Abortion**
 Allred, Gloria 1941- **1985**:2
 Baird, Bill
  Brief entry **1987**:2
 Baulieu, Etienne-Emile 1926- **1990**:1
 Brown, Judie 1944- **1986**:2
 Falkenberg, Nanette 1951- **1985**:2
 Kissling, Frances 1943- **1989**:2
 Morgentaler, Henry 1923- **1986**:3
 Terry, Randall **1991**:4
 Wattleton, Faye 1943- **1989**:1
 Yard, Molly **1991**:4

**Abscam**
 Neal, James Foster 1929- **1986**:2
 Puccio, Thomas P. 1944- **1986**:4

**Academy Awards**
 Affleck, Ben 1972- **1999**:1
 Allen, Woody 1935- **1994**:1
 Almodovar, Pedro 1951- **2000**:3
 Ameche, Don 1908-1993
  Obituary **1994**:2
 Andrews, Julie 1935- **1996**:1
 Arkin, Alan 1934- **2007**:4
 Arlen, Harold 1905-1986
  Obituary **1986**:3
 Arthur, Jean 1901(?)-1991
  Obituary **1992**:1
 Ashcroft, Peggy 1907-1991
  Obituary **1992**:1
 Astor, Mary 1906-1987
  Obituary **1988**:1
 Ball, Alan 1957- **2005**:1
 Bancroft, Anne 1931-2005
  Obituary **2006**:3
 Barbera, Joseph 1911- **1988**:2

Bardem, Javier 1969- **2008**:4
Baryshnikov, Mikhail Nikolaevich
 1948- **1997**:3
Bates, Kathy 1949(?)- **1991**:4
Baxter, Anne 1923-1985
 Obituary **1986**:1
Beatty, Warren 1937- **2000**:1
Benigni, Roberto 1952- **1999**:2
Bergman, Ingmar 1918- **1999**:4
Berlin, Irving 1888-1989
 Obituary **1990**:1
Bernstein, Elmer 1922-2004
 Obituary **2005**:4
Binoche, Juliette 1965- **2001**:3
Bird, Brad 1956(?)- **2005**:4
Booth, Shirley 1898-1992
 Obituary **1993**:2
Boyle, Danny 1956- **2009**:4
Brando, Marlon 1924-2004
 Obituary **2005**:3
Broadbent, Jim 1949- **2008**:4
Brody, Adrien 1973- **2006**:3
Brooks, Mel 1926- **2003**:1
Brynner, Yul 1920(?)-1985
 Obituary **1985**:4
Burstyn, Ellen 1932- **2001**:4
Buttons, Red 1919-2006
 Obituary **2007**:3
Cagney, James 1899-1986
 Obituary **1986**:2
Caine, Michael 1933- **2000**:4
Capra, Frank 1897-1991
 Obituary **1992**:2
Carney, Art 1918-2003
 Obituary **2005**:1
Cassavetes, John 1929-1989
 Obituary **1989**:2
Cher 1946- **1993**:1
Christie, Julie 1941- **2008**:4
Coburn, James 1928-2002
 Obituary **2004**:1
Condon, Bill 1955- **2007**:3
Connelly, Jennifer 1970- **2002**:4
Connery, Sean 1930- **1990**:4
Cooper, Chris 1951- **2004**:1
Copland, Aaron 1900-1990

 Obituary **1991**:2
Coppola, Carmine 1910-1991
 Obituary **1991**:4
Coppola, Francis Ford 1939- **1989**:4
Coppola, Sofia 1971- **2004**:3
Crawford, Broderick 1911-1986
 Obituary **1986**:3
Damon, Matt 1970- **1999**:1
Davis, Bette 1908-1989
 Obituary **1990**:1
Davis, Geena 1957- **1992**:1
Del Toro, Benicio 1967- **2001**:4
Demme, Jonathan 1944- **1992**:4
Dench, Judi 1934- **1999**:4
De Niro, Robert 1943- **1999**:1
Dennis, Sandy 1937-1992
 Obituary **1992**:4
Diamond, I.A.L. 1920-1988
 Obituary **1988**:3
Douglas, Michael 1944- **1986**:2
Duvall, Robert 1931- **1999**:3
Eastwood, Clint 1930- **1993**:3
Elliott, Denholm 1922-1992
 Obituary **1993**:2
Fellini, Federico 1920-1993
 Obituary **1994**:2
Ferrer, Jose 1912-1992
 Obituary **1992**:3
Field, Sally 1946- **1995**:3
Fosse, Bob 1927-1987
 Obituary **1988**:1
Gielgud, John 1904-2000
 Obituary **2000**:4
Gish, Lillian 1893-1993
 Obituary **1993**:4
Goldberg, Whoopi 1955- **1993**:3
Goldman, William 1931- **2001**:1
Gooding, Cuba, Jr. 1968- **1997**:3
Gossett, Louis, Jr. 1936- **1989**:3
Grant, Cary 1904-1986
 Obituary **1987**:1
Grazer, Brian 1951- **2006**:4
Guggenheim, Charles 1924-2002
 Obituary **2003**:4
Hackman, Gene 1931- **1989**:3
Haggis, Paul 1953- **2006**:4

Hanks, Tom 1956- **1989**:2
Harden, Marcia Gay 1959- **2002**:4
Hawn, Goldie Jeanne 1945- **1997**:2
Hayes, Helen 1900-1993
    Obituary **1993**:4
Hayes, Isaac 1942- **1998**:4
Hepburn, Audrey 1929-1993
    Obituary **1993**:2
Hepburn, Katharine 1909- **1991**:2
Heston, Charlton 1924- **1999**:4
Hill, George Roy 1921-2002
    Obituary **2004**:1
Hoffman, Dustin 1937- **2005**:4
Hoffman, Philip Seymour
    1967- **2006**:3
Hope, Bob 1903-2003
    Obituary **2004**:4
Hopkins, Anthony 1937- **1992**:4
Houseman, John 1902-1988
    Obituary **1989**:1
Hudson, Jennifer 1981- **2008**:1
Hurt, William 1950- **1986**:1
Huston, Anjelica 1952(?)- **1989**:3
Huston, John 1906-1987
    Obituary **1988**:1
Hutton, Timothy 1960- **1986**:3
Irons, Jeremy 1948- **1991**:4
Irving, John 1942- **2006**:2
Ives, Burl 1909-1995
    Obituary **1995**:4
Jackson, Peter 1961- **2004**:4
Jones, Chuck 1912- **2001**:2
Jones, Tommy Lee 1947(?)- **1994**:2
Jordan, Neil 1950(?)- **1993**:3
Kaye, Danny 1913-1987
    Obituary **1987**:2
Kazan, Elia 1909-2003
    Obituary **2004**:4
Keaton, Diane 1946- **1997**:1
Kline, Kevin 1947- **2000**:1
Kubrick, Stanley 1928-1999
    Obituary **1999**:3
Kurosawa, Akira 1910-1998 **1991**:1
    Obituary **1999**:1
Lange, Jessica 1949- **1995**:4
Lardner Jr., Ring 1915-2000
    Obituary **2001**:2
Lasseter, John 1957- **2007**:2
Lemmon, Jack 1925- **1998**:4
    Obituary **2002**:3
Levinson, Barry 1932- **1989**:3
Lithgow, John 1945- **1985**:2
Loy, Myrna 1905-1993
    Obituary **1994**:2
Lucas, George 1944- **1999**:4
Malle, Louis 1932-1995
    Obituary **1996**:2
Mancini, Henry 1924-1994
    Obituary **1994**:4
Marvin, Lee 1924-1987
    Obituary **1988**:1
Matlin, Marlee 1965- **1992**:2
Matthau, Walter 1920- **2000**:3
McCartney, Paul 1942- **2002**:4
McDonagh, Martin 1970- **2007**:3
McDormand, Frances 1957- **1997**:3
McDowall, Roddy 1928-1998
    Obituary **1999**:1
McLaren, Norman 1914-1987
    Obituary **1987**:2
McMurtry, Larry 1936- **2006**:4
Milland, Ray 1908(?)-1986

Obituary **1986**:2
Minghella, Anthony 1954- **2004**:3
Miyazaki, Hayao 1941- **2006**:2
Newman, Paul 1925- **1995**:3
Nichols, Mike 1931- **1994**:4
Nicholson, Jack 1937- **1989**:2
North, Alex 1910- **1986**:3
Pacino, Al 1940- **1993**:4
Page, Geraldine 1924-1987
    Obituary **1987**:4
Pakula, Alan 1928-1998
    Obituary **1999**:2
Palance, Jack 1919-2006
    Obituary **2008**:1
Paquin, Anna 1982- **2009**:4
Park, Nick 1958- **1997**:3
Payne, Alexander 1961- **2005**:4
Peck, Gregory 1916-2003
    Obituary **2004**:3
Pesci, Joe 1943- **1992**:4
Phillips, Julia 1944- **1992**:1
Poitier, Sidney 1927- **1990**:3
Pollack, Sydney 1934-2008
    Obituary **2009**:2
Prince 1958- **1995**:3
Puzo, Mario 1920-1999
    Obituary **2000**:1
Quinn, Anthony 1915-2001
    Obituary **2002**:2
Redford, Robert 1937- **1993**:2
Redgrave, Vanessa 1937- **1989**:2
Reed, Donna 1921-1986
    Obituary **1986**:1
Riddle, Nelson 1921-1985
    Obituary **1985**:4
Robards, Jason 1922-2000
    Obituary **2001**:3
Robbins, Jerome 1918-1998
    Obituary **1999**:1
Rogers, Ginger 1911(?)-1995
    Obituary **1995**:4
Rollins, Howard E., Jr. 1950- **1986**:1
Ruehl, Mercedes 195(?)- **1992**:4
Rush, Geoffrey 1951- **2002**:1
Sainte-Marie, Buffy 1941- **2000**:1
Schlesinger, John 1926-2003
    Obituary **2004**:3
Scott, George C. 1927-1999
    Obituary **2000**:2
Shanley, John Patrick 1950- **2006**:1
Sheldon, Sidney 1917-2007
    Obituary **2008**:2
Sinatra, Frank 1915-1998
    Obituary **1998**:4
Soderbergh, Steven 1963- **2001**:4
Sorvino, Mira 1970(?)- **1996**:3
Spacek, Sissy 1949- **2003**:1
Spacey, Kevin 1959- **1996**:4
Stallone, Sylvester 1946- **1994**:2
Stapleton, Maureen 1925-2006
    Obituary **2007**:2
Steiger, Rod 1925-2002
    Obituary **2003**:4
Streep, Meryl 1949- **1990**:2
Streisand, Barbra 1942- **1992**:2
Styne, Jule 1905-1994
    Obituary **1995**:1
Swank, Hilary 1974- **2000**:3
Swinton, Tilda 1960- **2008**:4
Tan Dun 1957- **2002**:1
Tandy, Jessica 1901-1994 **1990**:4
    Obituary **1995**:1

Taylor, Elizabeth 1932- **1993**:3
Thompson, Emma 1959- **1993**:2
Tomei, Marisa 1964- **1995**:2
Trudeau, Garry 1948- **1991**:2
Umeki, Miyoshi 1929-2007
    Obituary **2008**:4
Ustinov, Peter 1921-2004
    Obituary **2005**:3
Vinton, Will
    Brief entry **1988**:1
Voight, Jon 1938- **2002**:3
Wallis, Hal 1898(?)-1986
    Obituary **1987**:1
Washington, Denzel 1954- **1993**:2
Weisz, Rachel 1971- **2006**:4
Wiest, Dianne 1948- **1995**:2
Wilder, Billy 1906-2002
    Obituary **2003**:2
Winters, Shelley 1920-2006
    Obituary **2007**:1
Wise, Robert 1914-2005
    Obituary **2006**:4
Wyman, Jane 1917-2007
    Obituary **2008**:4
Zanuck, Lili Fini 1954- **1994**:2
Zemeckis, Robert 1952- **2002**:1

## Acoustics
Kloss, Henry E.
    Brief entry **1985**:2

## Acquired Immune Deficiency Syndrome [AIDS]
Ashe, Arthur 1943-1993
    Obituary **1993**:3
Bennett, Michael 1943-1987
    Obituary **1988**:1
Bergalis, Kimberly 1968(?)-1991
    Obituary **1992**:3
Berkley, Seth 1956- **2002**:3
Dolan, Terry 1950-1986 **1985**:2
Eazy-E 1963(?)-1995
    Obituary **1995**:3
Fisher, Mary 1948- **1994**:3
Gallo, Robert 1937- **1991**:1
Gebbie, Kristine 1944(?)- **1994**:2
Gertz, Alison 1966(?)-1992
    Obituary **1993**:2
Glaser, Elizabeth 1947-1994
    Obituary **1995**:2
Halston 1932-1990
    Obituary **1990**:3
Haring, Keith 1958-1990
    Obituary **1990**:3
Ho, David 1952- **1997**:2
Holmes, John C. 1945-1988
    Obituary **1988**:3
Hudson, Rock 1925-1985
    Obituary **1985**:4
Kramer, Larry 1935- **1991**:2
Krim, Mathilde 1926- **1989**:2
Kushner, Tony 1956- **1995**:2
Liberace 1919-1987
    Obituary **1987**:2
Louganis, Greg 1960- **1995**:3
Mapplethorpe, Robert 1946-1989
    Obituary **1989**:3
Matlovich, Leonard P. 1944(?)-1988
    Obituary **1988**:4
McKinney, Stewart B. 1931-1987
    Obituary **1987**:4
Mullis, Kary 1944- **1995**:3

Robinson, Max 1939-1988
Obituary **1989**:2
Shilts, Randy 1951-1994 **1993**:4
Obituary **1994**:3
Smith, Jerry 1943-1986
Obituary **1987**:1
Taylor, Elizabeth 1932- **1993**:3
Waddell, Thomas F. 1937-1987
Obituary **1988**:2
White, Ryan 1972(?)-1990
Obituary **1990**:3
Zamora, Pedro 1972-1994
Obituary **1995**:2

**Adolph Coors Co.**
Coors, William K.
Brief entry **1985**:1

**Adoption**
Aronson, Jane 1951- **2009**:3
Clements, George 1932- **1985**:1

**Advertising**
Ailes, Roger 1940- **1989**:3
Beers, Charlotte 1935- **1999**:3
Freeman, Cliff 1941- **1996**:1
Kroll, Alexander S. 1938- **1989**:3
Lazarus, Shelly 1947- **1998**:3
McElligott, Thomas J. 1943- **1987**:4
Ogilvy, David 1911-1999
Obituary **2000**:1
O'Steen, Van
Brief entry **1986**:3
Peller, Clara 1902(?)-1987
Obituary **1988**:1
Proctor, Barbara Gardner 1933(?)-
**1985**:3
Riney, Hal 1932- **1989**:1
Saatchi, Charles 1943- **1987**:3
Saatchi, Maurice 1946- **1995**:4
Sedelmaier, Joe 1933- **1985**:3
Vinton, Will
Brief entry **1988**:1
Whittle, Christopher 1947- **1989**:3
Wren, John 1952(?)- **2007**:2

**African National Congress [ANC]**
Buthelezi, Mangosuthu Gatsha
1928- **1989**:3
Hani, Chris 1942-1993
Obituary **1993**:4
Mandela, Nelson 1918- **1990**:3
Mbeki, Thabo 1942- **1999**:4
Sisulu, Walter 1912-2003
Obituary **2004**:2
Slovo, Joe 1926- **1989**:2
Tambo, Oliver 1917- **1991**:3

**Agriculture**
Davis, Noel **1990**:3

**AIDS Coalition to Unleash Power**
**[ACT-UP]**
Kramer, Larry 1935- **1991**:2

**AIM**
Peltier, Leonard 1944- **1995**:1

**A.J. Canfield Co.**
Canfield, Alan B.
Brief entry **1986**:3

**Albert Nipon, Inc.**
Nipon, Albert
Brief entry **1986**:4

**Alcohol abuse**
Anastas, Robert
Brief entry **1985**:2
Bradshaw, John 1933- **1992**:1
Lightner, Candy 1946- **1985**:1
MacRae, Gordon 1921-1986
Obituary **1986**:2
Mantle, Mickey 1931-1995
Obituary **1996**:1
Welch, Bob 1956- **1991**:3

**Alternative medicine**
Jacobs, Joe 1945(?)- **1994**:1
Weil, Andrew 1942- **1997**:4

**Alvin Ailey Dance Theatre**
Jamison, Judith 1944- **1990**:3

**Amazon.com, Inc.**
Bezos, Jeff 1964- **1998**:4

**American Academy and Institute of**
**Arts and Letters**
Brooks, Gwendolyn
1917-2000 **1998**:1
Obituary **2001**:2
Buchwald, Art 1925-2007
Obituary **2008**:2
Cunningham, Merce 1919- **1998**:1
Dickey, James 1923-1997 **1998**:2
Foster, Norman 1935- **1999**:4
Graves, Michael 1934- **2000**:1
Mamet, David 1947- **1998**:4
Roth, Philip 1933- **1999**:1
Vonnegut, Kurt 1922- **1998**:4
Walker, Alice 1944- **1999**:1
Wolfe, Tom 1930- **1999**:2

**American Airlines**
Crandall, Robert L. 1935- **1992**:1

**American Ballet Theatre [ABT]**
Bissell, Patrick 1958-1987
Obituary **1988**:2
Bocca, Julio 1967- **1995**:3
Bujones, Fernando 1955-2005
Obituary **2007**:1
Englund, Richard 1932(?)-1991
Obituary **1991**:3
Feld, Eliot 1942- **1996**:1
Ferri, Alessandra 1963- **1987**:2
Godunov, Alexander 1949-1995
Obituary **1995**:4
Gregory, Cynthia 1946- **1990**:2
Herrera, Paloma 1975- **1996**:2
Kaye, Nora 1920-1987
Obituary **1987**:4
Lander, Toni 1931-1985
Obituary **1985**:4
Moore, Rachel 1965- **2008**:2
Parker, Sarah Jessica 1965- **1999**:2
Renvall, Johan
Brief entry **1987**:4
Robbins, Jerome 1918-1998
Obituary **1999**:1
Tudor, Antony 1908(?)-1987
Obituary **1987**:4

**American Book Awards**
Alexie, Sherman 1966- **1998**:4
Baraka, Amiri 1934- **2000**:3
Child, Julia 1912- **1999**:4
Erdrich, Louise 1954- **2005**:3
Kissinger, Henry 1923- **1999**:4
Walker, Alice 1944- **1999**:1
Wolfe, Tom 1930- **1999**:2

**American Civil Liberties Union [ACLU]**
Abzug, Bella 1920-1998 **1998**:2
Glasser, Ira 1938- **1989**:1

**American Express**
Chenault, Kenneth I. 1951- **1999**:3
Weill, Sandy 1933- **1990**:4

**American Federation of Labor and**
**Congress of Industrial Organizations**
Chavez-Thompson, Linda 1944-
**1999**:1
Sweeney, John J. 1934- **2000**:3

**American Indian Movement [AIM]**
Banks, Dennis J. 193- **1986**:4

**American Library Association [ALA]**
Blume, Judy 1936- **1998**:4
Heat-Moon, William Least 1939-
**2000**:2
Schuman, Patricia Glass 1943- **1993**
:2
Steel, Danielle 1947- **1999**:2

**American Life League [ALL]**
Brown, Judie 1944- **1986**:2

**American Medical Association [AMA]**
Bristow, Lonnie 1930- **1996**:1
Hill, J. Edward 1938- **2006**:2

**Amer-I-can minority empowerment**
**program**
Brown, Jim 1936- **1993**:2

**American Museum of Natural History**
Futter, Ellen V. 1949- **1995**:1

**American Music Awards**
Adams, Yolanda 1961- **2008**:2
Ashanti 1980- **2004**:1
Badu, Erykah 1971- **2000**:4
Beyonce 1981- **2009**:3
Boyz II Men **1995**:1
Brooks, Garth 1962- **1992**:1
Campbell, Erica 1972- (
See Mary Mary)
Campbell, Tina 1972- (
See Mary Mary)
Cole, Natalie 1950- **1992**:4
Franklin, Aretha 1942- **1998**:3
Jackson, Alan 1958- **2003**:1
Jackson, Michael 1958- **1996**:2
Jay-Z 1970- **2006**:1
Jewel 1974- **1999**:2
Keys, Alicia 1981- **2006**:1

Loveless, Patty 1957- **1998**:2
Mary Mary 1972- **2009**:4
McEntire, Reba 1954- **1987**:3
Newton-John, Olivia 1948- **1998**:4
Nickelback **2007**:2
Parton, Dolly 1946- **1999**:4
Rihanna 1988- **2008**:4
Spears, Britney 1981- **2000**:3
Spice Girls **2008**:3
Strait, George 1952- **1998**:3
Sugarland 1970- **2009**:2
Timberlake, Justin 1981- **2008**:4
Turner, Tina 1939- **2000**:3
Wilson, Gretchen 1970- **2006**:3
Yoakam, Dwight 1956- **1992**:4

**American Power Boat Association [APBA]**
Copeland, Al 1944(?)- **1988**:3
Hanauer, Chip 1954- **1986**:2

**America Online [AOL]**
Case, Steve 1958- **1995**:4
Kimsey, James V. 1940(?)- **2001**:1

**America's Cup**
Bond, Alan 1938- **1989**:2
Conner, Dennis 1943- **1987**:2
Turner, Ted 1938- **1989**:1

**Amnesty International**
Healey, Jack 1938(?)- **1990**:1
Wiesel, Elie 1928- **1998**:1

**Anaheim Angels baseball team**
Glaus, Troy 1976- **2003**:3
Moreno, Arturo 1946- **2005**:2
Vaughn, Mo 1967- **1999**:2

**Anheuser-Busch, Inc.**
Busch, August A. III 1937- **1988**:2
Busch, August Anheuser, Jr.
1899-1989
Obituary **1990**:2

**Animal rights**
Amory, Cleveland 1917-1998
Obituary **1999**:2
Caras, Roger 1928-2001
Obituary **2002**:1
DeMayo, Neda 1960(?)- **2006**:2
Grandin, Temple 1947- **2006**:1
Hurley, Elizabeth **1999**:2
McDonnell, Patrick 1956- **2009**:4
Newkirk, Ingrid 1949- **1992**:3
Pacelle, Wayne 1965- **2009**:4
Steel, Danielle 1947- **1999**:2
Suckling, Kierán 1964- **2009**:2

**Animal training**
Burck, Wade
Brief entry **1986**:1
Butcher, Susan 1954- **1991**:1

**Anthropology**
Beattie, Owen
Brief entry **1985**:2
Castaneda, Carlos 1931-1998
Obituary **1998**:4

Cole, Johnetta B. 1936- **1994**:3
Jablonski, Nina G. 1953- **2009**:3
Leakey, Richard 1944- **1994**:2
Montagu, Ashley 1905-1999
Obituary **2000**:2
Reichs, Kathleen J. 1948- **2007**:3
Tillion, Germaine 1907-2008
Obituary **2009**:2

**Apartheid**
Biehl, Amy 1967(?)-1993
Obituary **1994**:1
Blackburn, Molly 1931(?)-1985
Obituary **1985**:4
Botha, P. W. 1916-2006
Obituary **2008**:1
Buthelezi, Mangosuthu Gatsha
1928- **1989**:3
Carter, Amy 1967- **1987**:4
de Klerk, F.W. 1936- **1990**:1
Duncan, Sheena
Brief entry **1987**:1
Fugard, Athol 1932- **1992**:3
Hoffman, Abbie 1936-1989
Obituary **1989**:3
Makeba, Miriam 1934- **1989**:2
Mandela, Winnie 1934- **1989**:3
Paton, Alan 1903-1988
Obituary **1988**:3
Ramaphosa, Cyril 1953- **1988**:2
Suzman, Helen 1917- **1989**:3
Tambo, Oliver 1917- **1991**:3
Treurnicht, Andries 1921- **1992**:2
Woods, Donald 1933-2001
Obituary **2002**:3

**Apple Computer, Inc.**
Ive, Jonathan 1967- **2009**:2
Jobs, Steve 1955- **2000**:1
Perlman, Steve 1961(?)- **1998**:2
Raskin, Jef 1943(?)- **1997**:4
Sculley, John 1939- **1989**:4

**Archaeology**
Soren, David
Brief entry **1986**:3

**Architecture**
Ando, Tadao 1941- **2005**:4
Bunshaft, Gordon 1909-1990 **1989**:3
Obituary **1991**:1
Calatrava, Santiago 1951- **2005**:1
Cooper, Alexander 1936- **1988**:4
Diller, Elizabeth and Ricardo
Scofidio **2004**:3
Eisenman, Peter 1932- **1992**:4
Erickson, Arthur 1924- **1989**:3
Foster, Norman 1935- **1999**:4
Gehry, Frank O. 1929- **1987**:1
Goody, Joan 1935- **1990**:2
Graves, Michael 1934- **2000**:1
Hadid, Zaha 1950- **2005**:3
Holl, Steven 1947- **2003**:1
Isozaki, Arata 1931- **1990**:2
Jahn, Helmut 1940- **1987**:3
Johnson, Philip 1906- **1989**:2
Jones, E. Fay 1921-2004
Obituary **2005**:4
Joseph, Wendy Evans
1955(?)- **2006**:2
Kiefer, Anselm 1945- **1990**:2

Kiley, Dan 1912-2004
Obituary **2005**:2
Kurokawa, Kisho 1934-2007
Obituary **2008**:4
Lapidus, Morris 1902-2001
Obituary **2001**:4
Lasdun, Denys 1914-2001
Obituary **2001**:4
Libeskind, Daniel 1946- **2004**:1
Lin, Maya 1960(?)- **1990**:3
McDonough, William 1951- **2003**:1
Meier, Richard 1934- **2001**:4
Moneo, Jose Rafael 1937- **1996**:4
Mumford, Lewis 1895-1990
Obituary **1990**:2
Pedersen, William 1938(?)- **1989**:4
Pei, I.M. 1917- **1990**:4
Pelli, Cesar 1927(?)- **1991**:4
Piano, Renzo 1937- **2009**:2
Plater-Zyberk, Elizabeth
1950- **2005**:2
Portman, John 1924- **1988**:2
Predock, Antoine 1936- **1993**:2
Roche, Kevin 1922- **1985**:1
Rockwell, David 1956- **2003**:3
Rouse, James 1914-1996
Obituary **1996**:4
Tange, Kenzo 1913-2005
Obituary **2006**:2
Taniguchi, Yoshio 1937- **2005**:4
Venturi, Robert 1925- **1994**:4
Yamasaki, Minoru 1912-1986
Obituary **1986**:2
Yeang, Ken 1948- **2008**:3

**Argus Corp. Ltd.**
Black, Conrad 1944- **1986**:2

**Arizona state government**
Hull, Jane Dee 1935- **1999**:2

**Arkansas state government**
Clinton, Bill 1946- **1992**:1

**Artificial heart**
Jarvik, Robert K. 1946- **1985**:1
Schroeder, William J. 1932-1986
Obituary **1986**:4

**Artificial intelligence**
Minsky, Marvin 1927- **1994**:3

**Association of Southeast Asian Nations**
Bolkiah, Sultan Muda Hassanal
1946- **1985**:4

**Astronautics**
Bean, Alan L. 1932- **1986**:2
Collins, Eileen 1956- **1995**:3
Conrad, Pete 1930-1999
Obituary **2000**:1
Dzhanibekov, Vladimir 1942- **1988**:1
Garneau, Marc 1949- **1985**:1
Glenn, John 1921- **1998**:3
Lucid, Shannon 1943- **1997**:1
McAuliffe, Christa 1948-1986
Obituary **1985**:4
Whitson, Peggy 1960- **2003**:3

**Astronomy**
Bahcall, John N. 1934-2005
Obituary **2006**:4
Bopp, Thomas 1949- **1997**:3

Geller, Margaret Joan 1947- **1998**:2
Hale, Alan 1957- **1997**:3
Hawking, Stephen W. 1942- **1990**:1
Hoyle, Sir Fred 1915-2001
    Obituary **2002**:4
Marsden, Brian 1937- **2004**:4
Smoot, George F. 1945- **1993**:3

**AT&T**
    Allen, Bob 1935- **1992**:4
    Armstrong, C. Michael 1938- **2002**:1

**Atari**
    Bushnell, Nolan 1943- **1985**:1
    Kingsborough, Donald
      Brief entry **1986**:2
    Perlman, Steve 1961(?)- **1998**:2

**Atlanta Braves baseball team**
    Lofton, Kenny 1967- **1998**:1
    Maddux, Greg 1966- **1996**:2
    Sanders, Deion 1967- **1992**:4
    Spahn, Warren 1921-2003
      Obituary **2005**:1
    Turner, Ted 1938- **1989**:1

**Atlanta Falcons football team**
    Sanders, Deion 1967- **1992**:4

**Atlanta Hawks basketball team**
    Maravich, Pete 1948-1988
      Obituary **1988**:2
    McMillen, Tom 1952- **1988**:4
    Turner, Ted 1938- **1989**:1
    Wilkens, Lenny 1937- **1995**:2

**Atlantic Records**
    Ertegun, Ahmet 1923- **1986**:3
    Greenwald, Julie 1970- **2008**:1

**Automobile racing**
    Busch, Kurt 1978- **2006**:1
    Earnhardt, Dale, Jr. 1974- **2004**:4
    Ferrari, Enzo 1898-1988 **1988**:4
    Fittipaldi, Emerson 1946- **1994**:2
    Franchitti, Dario 1973- **2008**:1
    Gordon, Jeff 1971- **1996**:1
    Johnson, Jimmie 1975- **2007**:2
    Muldowney, Shirley 1940- **1986**:1
    Newman, Paul 1925- **1995**:3
    Newman, Ryan 1977- **2005**:1
    Penske, Roger 1937- **1988**:3
    Porsche, Ferdinand 1909-1998
      Obituary **1998**:4
    Prost, Alain 1955- **1988**:1
    Schumacher, Michael 1969- **2005**:2
    Senna, Ayrton 1960(?)-1994 **1991**:4
      Obituary **1994**:4
    St. James, Lyn 1947- **1993**:2
    Villeneuve, Jacques 1971- **1997**:1
    Zanardi, Alex 1966- **1998**:2

**Aviation**
    Burr, Donald Calvin 1941- **1985**:3
    Dubrof, Jessica 1989-1996
      Obituary **1996**:4
    Fossett, Steve 1944- **2007**:2
    Lindbergh, Anne Morrow 1906-2001
      Obituary **2001**:4
    MacCready, Paul 1925- **1986**:4

Martin, Dean Paul 1952(?)-1987
    Obituary **1987**:3
Moody, John 1943- **1985**:3
Rutan, Burt 1943- **1987**:2
Schiavo, Mary 1955- **1998**:2
Wolf, Stephen M. 1941- **1989**:3
Yeager, Chuck 1923- **1998**:1

**Avis Rent A Car**
    Rand, A. Barry 1944- **2000**:3

**Avon Products, Inc.**
    Gold, Christina A. 1947- **2008**:1
    Jung, Andrea **2000**:2
    Waldron, Hicks B. 1923- **1987**:3

**Bad Boy Records**
    Combs, Sean Puffy 1970- **1998**:4

**Ballet West**
    Lander, Toni 1931-1985
      Obituary **1985**:4

**Ballooning**
    Aoki, Rocky 1940- **1990**:2

**Baltimore, Md., city government**
    Schaefer, William Donald
      1921- **1988**:1

**Baltimore Orioles baseball team**
    Angelos, Peter 1930- **1995**:4
    Palmeiro, Rafael 1964- **2005**:1
    Palmer, Jim 1945- **1991**:2
    Ripken, Cal, Jr. 1960- **1986**:2
    Ripken, Cal, Sr. 1936(?)-1999
      Obituary **1999**:4
    Robinson, Frank 1935- **1990**:2
    Williams, Edward Bennett 1920-1988
      Obituary **1988**:4

**Band Aid**
    Geldof, Bob 1954(?)- **1985**:3

**Bard College**
    Botstein, Leon 1946- **1985**:3

**Barnes & Noble, Inc.**
    Riggio, Leonard S. 1941- **1999**:4

**Baseball**
    Abbott, Jim 1967- **1988**:3
    Ainge, Danny 1959- **1987**:1
    Barber, Red 1908-1992
      Obituary **1993**:2
    Boggs, Wade 1958- **1989**:3
    Bonds, Barry 1964- **1993**:3
    Campanella, Roy 1921-1993
      Obituary **1994**:1
    Canseco, Jose 1964- **1990**:2
    Caray, Harry 1914(?)-1998 **1988**:3
      Obituary **1998**:3
    Carter, Gary 1954- **1987**:1
    Carter, Joe 1960- **1994**:2
    Chamberlain, Joba 1985- **2008**:3
    Clemens, Roger 1962- **1991**:4
    Damon, Johnny 1973- **2005**:4
    Davis, Eric 1962- **1987**:4

DiMaggio, Joe 1914-1999
    Obituary **1999**:3
Doubleday, Nelson, Jr. 1933- **1987**:1
Dravecky, Dave 1956- **1992**:1
Drysdale, Don 1936-1993
    Obituary **1994**:1
Durocher, Leo 1905-1991
    Obituary **1992**:2
Dykstra, Lenny 1963- **1993**:4
Edwards, Harry 1942- **1989**:4
Fehr, Donald 1948- **1987**:2
Fielder, Cecil 1963- **1993**:2
Giamatti, A. Bartlett
    1938-1989 **1988**:4
    Obituary **1990**:1
Gibson, Kirk 1957- **1985**:2
Glaus, Troy 1976- **2003**:3
Gomez, Lefty 1909-1989
    Obituary **1989**:3
Gooden, Dwight 1964- **1985**:2
Greenberg, Hank 1911-1986
    Obituary **1986**:4
Griffey, Ken Jr. 1969- **1994**:1
Gwynn, Tony 1960- **1995**:1
Hamels, Cole 1983- **2009**:4
Helton, Todd 1973- **2001**:1
Hernandez, Felix 1986- **2008**:2
Hernandez, Willie 1954- **1985**:1
Howser, Dick 1936-1987
    Obituary **1987**:4
Hunter, Catfish 1946-1999
    Obituary **2000**:1
Jackson, Bo 1962- **1986**:3
Johnson, Randy 1963- **1996**:2
Kroc, Ray 1902-1984
    Obituary **1985**:1
Kruk, John 1961- **1994**:4
Leyland, Jim 1944- **1998**:2
Lofton, Kenny 1967- **1998**:1
Lowell, Mike 1974- **2003**:2
Maddux, Greg 1966- **1996**:2
Mantle, Mickey 1931-1995
    Obituary **1996**:1
Maris, Roger 1934-1985
    Obituary **1986**:1
Martin, Billy 1928-1989 **1988**:4
    Obituary **1990**:2
Matsui, Hideki 1974- **2007**:4
Mattingly, Don 1961- **1986**:2
McGraw, Tug 1944-2004
    Obituary **2005**:1
McGwire, Mark 1963- **1999**:1
Monaghan, Tom 1937- **1985**:1
Moreno, Arturo 1946- **2005**:2
Nomo, Hideo 1968- **1996**:2
O'Neil, Buck 1911-2006
    Obituary **2007**:4
Palmeiro, Rafael 1964- **2005**:1
Palmer, Jim 1945- **1991**:2
Piazza, Mike 1968- **1998**:4
Puckett, Kirby 1960-2006
    Obituary **2007**:2
Pujols, Albert 1980- **2005**:3
Ramirez, Manny 1972- **2005**:4
Ripken, Cal, Jr. 1960- **1986**:2
Robinson, Frank 1935- **1990**:2
Rose, Pete 1941- **1991**:1
Ryan, Nolan 1947- **1989**:4
Saberhagen, Bret 1964- **1986**:1
Sanders, Deion 1967- **1992**:4
Santana, Johan 1979- **2008**:1
Schembechler, Bo 1929(?)- **1990**:3

Schilling, Curt 1966- **2002**:3
Schmidt, Mike 1949- **1988**:3
Schott, Marge 1928- **1985**:4
Selig, Bud 1934- **1995**:2
Sheffield, Gary 1968- **1998**:1
Soriano, Alfonso 1976- **2008**:1
Sosa, Sammy 1968- **1999**:1
Spahn, Warren 1921-2003
  Obituary **2005**:1
Steinbrenner, George 1930- **1991**:1
Stewart, Dave 1957- **1991**:1
Thomas, Frank 1968- **1994**:3
Van Slyke, Andy 1960- **1992**:4
Vaughn, Mo 1967- **1999**:2
Veeck, Bill 1914-1986
  Obituary **1986**:1
Vincent, Fay 1938- **1990**:2
Welch, Bob 1956- **1991**:3
Wells, David 1963- **1999**:3
White, Bill 1934- **1989**:3
Williams, Ted 1918-2002
  Obituary **2003**:4
Zito, Barry 1978- **2003**:3

**Basketball**
Ainge, Danny 1959- **1987**:1
Allen, Ray 1975- **2002**:1
Auerbach, Red 1911-2006
  Obituary **2008**:1
Barkley, Charles 1963- **1988**:2
Bias, Len 1964(?)-1986
  Obituary **1986**:3
Bird, Larry 1956- **1990**:3
Carter, Vince 1977- **2001**:4
Chaney, John 1932- **1989**:1
Cooper, Cynthia **1999**:1
Drexler, Clyde 1962- **1992**:4
Ewing, Patrick 1962- **1985**:3
Gathers, Hank 1967(?)-1990
  Obituary **1990**:3
Hardaway, Anfernee 1971- **1996**:2
Jackson, Phil 1945- **1996**:3
James, LeBron 1984- **2007**:3
Johnson, Earvin Magic 1959- **1988**:4
Johnson, Kevin 1966(?)- **1991**:1
Johnson, Larry 1969- **1993**:3
Jordan, Michael 1963- **1987**:2
Kemp, Shawn 1969- **1995**:1
Kidd, Jason 1973- **2003**:2
Knight, Bobby 1940- **1985**:3
Krzyzewski, Mike 1947- **1993**:2
Kukoc, Toni 1968- **1995**:4
Laettner, Christian 1969- **1993**:1
Laimbeer, Bill 1957- **2004**:3
Leslie, Lisa 1972- **1997**:4
Lewis, Reggie 1966(?)-1993
  Obituary **1994**:1
Majerle, Dan 1965- **1993**:4
Malone, Karl 1963- **1990**:1
Maravich, Pete 1948-1988
  Obituary **1988**:2
McMillen, Tom 1952- **1988**:4
Mikan, George 1924-2005
  Obituary **2006**:3
Miller, Andre 1976- **2003**:3
Miller, Reggie 1965- **1994**:4
Mourning, Alonzo 1970- **1994**:2
Mulkey-Robertson, Kim
  1962- **2006**:1
Nowitzki, Dirk 1978- **2007**:2
Olajuwon, Akeem 1963- **1985**:1
O'Malley, Susan 1962(?)- **1995**:2
O'Neal, Shaquille 1972- **1992**:1

Palmer, Violet 1964(?)- **2005**:2
Parker, Tony 1982- **2008**:1
Pierce, Paul 1977- **2009**:2
Riley, Pat 1945- **1994**:3
Robinson, David 1965- **1990**:4
Rodman, Dennis 1961- **1991**:3
Stern, David 1942- **1991**:4
Stockton, John Houston 1962- **1997**:3
Summitt, Pat 1952- **2004**:1
Swoopes, Sheryl 1971- **1998**:2
Tarkenian, Jerry 1930- **1990**:4
Thomas, Isiah 1961- **1989**:2
Thompson, John 1941- **1988**:3
Vitale, Dick 1939- **1988**:4
Wade, Dwyane 1982- **2007**:1
Wallace, Ben 1974- **2004**:3
Webber, Chris 1973- **1994**:1
Wilkens, Lenny 1937- **1995**:2
Woodard, Lynette 1959(?)- **1986**:2
Worthy, James 1961- **1991**:2
Yao Ming 1980- **2004**:1

**Beatrice International**
Lewis, Reginald F. 1942-1993 **1988**:4
  Obituary **1993**:3

**Benetton Group**
Benetton, Luciano 1935- **1988**:1

**Benihana of Tokyo, Inc.**
Aoki, Rocky 1940- **1990**:2

**Berkshire Hathaway, Inc.**
Buffett, Warren 1930- **1995**:2

**Bethlehem, Jordan, city government**
Freij, Elias 1920- **1986**:4

**Bicycling**
Armstrong, Lance 1971- **2000**:1
Indurain, Miguel 1964- **1994**:1
LeMond, Greg 1961- **1986**:4
Roberts, Steven K. 1952(?)- **1992**:1

**Billiards**
Minnesota Fats 1900(?)-1996
  Obituary **1996**:3

**Bill T. Jones/Arnie Zane & Company**
Jones, Bill T. **1991**:4

**Biodiversity**
Wilson, Edward O. 1929- **1994**:4

**Bioethics**
Andrews, Lori B. 1952- **2005**:3
Bayley, Corrine
  Brief entry **1986**:4
Caplan, Arthur L. 1950- **2000**:2

**Biogen, Inc.**
Gilbert, Walter 1932- **1988**:3

**Biosphere 2**
Allen, John 1930- **1992**:1

**Biotechnology**
Gilbert, Walter 1932- **1988**:3
Haseltine, William A. 1944- **1999**:2

**Birds**
Berle, Peter A.A.
  Brief entry **1987**:3
Pough, Richard Hooper 1904- **1989**:1
Redig, Patrick 1948- **1985**:3
Toone, Bill
  Brief entry **1987**:2

**Birth control**
Baird, Bill
  Brief entry **1987**:2
Baulieu, Etienne-Emile 1926- **1990**:1
Djerassi, Carl 1923- **2000**:4
Falkenberg, Nanette 1951- **1985**:2
Morgentaler, Henry 1923- **1986**:3
Rock, John
  Obituary **1985**:1
Wattleton, Faye 1943- **1989**:1

**Black Panther Party**
Cleaver, Eldridge 1935-1998
  Obituary **1998**:4
Newton, Huey 1942-1989
  Obituary **1990**:1
Ture, Kwame 1941-1998
  Obituary **1999**:2

**Black Sash**
Duncan, Sheena
  Brief entry **1987**:1

**Blockbuster Video**
Huizenga, Wayne 1938(?)- **1992**:1

**Bloomingdale's**
Campeau, Robert 1923- **1990**:1
Traub, Marvin
  Brief entry **1987**:3

**Boat racing**
Aoki, Rocky 1940- **1990**:2
Conner, Dennis 1943- **1987**:2
Copeland, Al 1944(?)- **1988**:3
Hanauer, Chip 1954- **1986**:2
Turner, Ted 1938- **1989**:1

**Bodybuilding**
Powter, Susan 1957(?)- **1994**:3
Reeves, Steve 1926-2000
  Obituary **2000**:4
Schwarzenegger, Arnold
  1947- **1991**:1

**Body Shops International**
Roddick, Anita 1943(?)- **1989**:4

**Bose Corp.**
Bose, Amar
  Brief entry **1986**:4

**Boston, Mass., city government**
Flynn, Ray 1939- **1989**:1
Frank, Barney 1940- **1989**:2

**Boston Bruins hockey team**
Bourque, Raymond Jean 1960- **1997**
:3

**Boston Celtics basketball team**
Ainge, Danny 1959- **1987**:1
Auerbach, Red 1911-2006
  Obituary **2008**:1

Bird, Larry 1956- **1990**:3
Lewis, Reggie 1966(?)-1993
  Obituary **1994**:1
Maravich, Pete 1948-1988
  Obituary **1988**:2
Pierce, Paul 1977- **2009**:2

**Boston Properties Co.**
Zuckerman, Mortimer 1937- **1986**:3

**Boston Red Sox baseball team**
Boggs, Wade 1958- **1989**:3
Clemens, Roger 1962- **1991**:4
Conigliaro, Tony 1945-1990
  Obituary **1990**:3
Damon, Johnny 1973- **2005**:4
Epstein, Theo 1973- **2003**:4
Henderson, Rickey 1958- **2002**:3
Ramirez, Manny 1972- **2005**:4
Vaughn, Mo 1967- **1999**:2
Williams, Ted 1918-2002
  Obituary **2003**:4

**Boston University**
Silber, John 1926- **1990**:1

**Bowling**
Anthony, Earl 1938-2001
  Obituary **2002**:3
Weber, Pete 1962- **1986**:3

**Boxing**
Abercrombie, Josephine 1925- **1987**:2
Ali, Laila 1977- **2001**:2
Armstrong, Henry 1912-1988
  Obituary **1989**:1
Bowe, Riddick 1967(?)- **1993**:2
Carter, Rubin 1937- **2000**:3
Danza, Tony 1951- **1989**:1
De La Hoya, Oscar 1973- **1998**:2
Douglas, Buster 1960(?)- **1990**:4
Foreman, George 1949- **2004**:2
Graziano, Rocky 1922-1990
  Obituary **1990**:4
Hagler, Marvelous Marvin 1954-
  **1985**:2
Holyfield, Evander 1962- **1991**:3
Kallen, Jackie 1946(?)- **1994**:1
King, Don 1931- **1989**:1
Leonard, Sugar Ray 1956- **1989**:4
Lewis, Lennox 1965- **2000**:2
Moore, Archie 1913-1998
  Obituary **1999**:2
Pep, Willie 1922-2006
  Obituary **2008**:1
Robinson, Sugar Ray 1921-1989
  Obituary **1989**:3
Trinidad, Felix 1973- **2000**:4
Tyson, Mike 1966- **1986**:4

**Boys Town**
Peter, Valentine J. 1934- **1988**:2

**BrainReserve**
Popcorn, Faith
  Brief entry **1988**:1

**Branch Davidians religious sect**
Koresh, David 1960(?)-1993
  Obituary **1993**:4

**Brewing**
Busch, August A. III 1937- **1988**:2
Coors, William K.
  Brief entry **1985**:1
Stroh, Peter W. 1927- **1985**:2

**Bridge**
Goren, Charles H. 1901-1991
  Obituary **1991**:4

**British Columbia provincial government**
Vander Zalm, William 1934- **1987**:3

**British royal family**
Charles, Prince of Wales
  1948- **1995**:3
Diana, Princess of Wales
  1961-1997 **1993**:1
  Obituary **1997**:4
Ferguson, Sarah 1959- **1990**:3
Princess Margaret, Countess of
  Snowdon 1930-2002
  Obituary **2003**:2
Queen Elizabeth the Queen Mother
  1900-2002
  Obituary **2003**:2
William, Prince of Wales
  1982- **2001**:3

**Broadcasting**
Albert, Marv 1943- **1994**:3
Allen, Mel 1913-1996
  Obituary **1996**:4
Ancier, Garth 1957- **1989**:1
Barber, Red 1908-1992
  Obituary **1993**:2
Bell, Art 1945- **2000**:1
Brown, James 1928(?)- **1991**:4
Caray, Harry 1914(?)-1998 **1988**:3
  Obituary **1998**:3
Cherry, Don 1934- **1993**:4
Chung, Connie 1946- **1988**:4
Cosell, Howard 1918-1995
  Obituary **1995**:4
Costas, Bob 1952- **1986**:4
Couric, Katherine 1957- **1991**:4
Daniels, Faith 1958- **1993**:3
Dickerson, Nancy H.
  1927-1997 **1998**:2
Donnellan, Nanci **1995**:2
Dr. Demento 1941- **1986**:1
Drysdale, Don 1936-1993
  Obituary **1994**:1
Edwards, Bob 1947- **1993**:2
Ellerbee, Linda 1944- **1993**:3
Firestone, Roy 1953- **1988**:2
Gillett, George 1938- **1988**:1
Goldberg, Leonard 1934- **1988**:4
Grange, Red 1903-1991
  Obituary **1991**:3
Gumbel, Bryant 1948- **1990**:2
Gunn, Hartford N., Jr. 1926-1986
  Obituary **1986**:2
Harvey, Paul 1918- **1995**:3
Hollander, Joel 1956(?)- **2006**:4
Imus, Don 1940- **1997**:1
Jones, Jenny 1946- **1998**:2
Kasem, Casey 1933(?)- **1987**:1
Kent, Arthur 1954- **1991**:4
King, Larry 1933- **1993**:1

Kluge, John 1914- **1991**:1
Koppel, Ted 1940- **1989**:1
Kuralt, Charles 1934-1997
  Obituary **1998**:3
Madden, John 1936- **1995**:1
Moyers, Bill 1934- **1991**:4
Murdoch, Rupert 1931- **1988**:4
Musburger, Brent 1939- **1985**:1
Norville, Deborah 1958- **1990**:3
Osgood, Charles 1933- **1996**:2
Paley, William S. 1901-1990
  Obituary **1991**:2
Pauley, Jane 1950- **1999**:1
Pierce, Frederick S. 1934(?)- **1985**:3
Povich, Maury 1939(?)- **1994**:3
Quivers, Robin 1953(?)- **1995**:4
Reasoner, Harry 1923-1991
  Obituary **1992**:1
Riley, Pat 1945- **1994**:3
Rivera, Geraldo 1943- **1989**:1
Roberts, Cokie 1943- **1993**:4
Robertson, Pat 1930- **1988**:2
Russert, Tim 1950-2008
  Obituary **2009**:3
Sawyer, Diane 1945- **1994**:4
Sevareid, Eric 1912-1992
  Obituary **1993**:1
Shriver, Maria
  Brief entry **1986**:2
Snyder, Jimmy 1919-1996
  Obituary **1996**:4
Stahl, Lesley 1941- **1997**:1
Stern, Howard 1954- **1988**:2
Swaggart, Jimmy 1935- **1987**:3
Tartikoff, Brandon 1949-1997 **1985**:2
  Obituary **1998**:1
Totenberg, Nina 1944- **1992**:2
Turner, Ted 1938- **1989**:1
Vitale, Dick 1939- **1988**:4
Walters, Barbara 1931- **1998**:3
Zahn, Paula 1956(?)- **1992**:3
Zucker, Jeff 1965(?)- **1993**:3

**Brokerage**
Brennan, Robert E. 1943(?)- **1988**:1
Fomon, Robert M. 1925- **1985**:3
Phelan, John Joseph, Jr. 1931- **1985**:4
Schwab, Charles 1937(?)- **1989**:3
Siebert, Muriel 1932(?)- **1987**:2

**Brooklyn Dodgers baseball team**
Campanella, Roy 1921-1993
  Obituary **1994**:1
Drysdale, Don 1936-1993
  Obituary **1994**:1

**Brown University**
Gregorian, Vartan 1934- **1990**:3

**Buddhism**
Dalai Lama 1935- **1989**:1

**Buffalo Bills football team**
Flutie, Doug 1962- **1999**:2
Kelly, Jim 1960- **1991**:4
Thomas, Thurman 1966- **1993**:1

**Buffalo Sabres**
Hasek, Dominik 1965- **1998**:3

**Cabbage Patch Kids**
Roberts, Xavier 1955- **1985**:3

**Cable Ace Awards**
   Blades, Ruben 1948- **1998**:2
   Carey, Drew 1958- **1997**:4
   Cuaron, Alfonso 1961- **2008**:2
   Fierstein, Harvey 1954- **2004**:2
   Graden, Brian 1963- **2004**:2
   Maher, Bill 1956- **1996**:2
   Rock, Chris 1967(?)- **1998**:1

**Cable News Network (CNN)**
   Amanpour, Christiane 1958- **1997**:2
   Cooper, Anderson 1967- **2006**:1
   Gupta, Sanjay 1969- **2009**:4
   Isaacson, Walter 1952- **2003**:2

**Cable television**
   Albrecht, Chris 1952(?)- **2005**:4
   Cox, Richard Joseph
      Brief entry **1985**:1
   Firestone, Roy 1953- **1988**:2
   Harbert, Ted 1955- **2007**:2
   Headroom, Max 1985- **1986**:4
   Hefner, Christie 1952- **1985**:1
   Johnson, Robert L. 1946- **2000**:4
   Koplovitz, Kay 1945- **1986**:3
   Malone, John C. 1941- **1988**:3
   Murdoch, Rupert 1931- **1988**:4
   Otte, Ruth 1949- **1992**:4
   Pittman, Robert W. 1953- **1985**:1
   Quinn, Martha 1959- **1986**:4
   Roberts, Brian L. 1959- **2002**:4
   Robertson, Pat 1930- **1988**:2
   Vitale, Dick 1939- **1988**:4

**Caldecott Book Awards**
   Falconer, Ian 1960(?)- **2003**:1
   Pilkey, Dav 1966- **2001**:1
   Ringgold, Faith 1930- **2000**:3
   Steig, William 1907-2003
      Obituary **2004**:4

**California Angels baseball team**
   Abbott, Jim 1967- **1988**:3
   Autry, Gene 1907-1998
      Obituary **1999**:1
   Conigliaro, Tony 1945-1990
      Obituary **1990**:3
   Ryan, Nolan 1947- **1989**:4

**California state government**
   Brown, Edmund G., Sr. 1905-1996
      Obituary **1996**:3
   Brown, Jerry 1938- **1992**:4
   Brown, Willie L. 1934- **1985**:2
   Roybal-Allard, Lucille 1941- **1999**:4
   Wilson, Pete 1933- **1992**:3

**Camping equipment**
   Bauer, Eddie 1899-1986
      Obituary **1986**:3
   Coleman, Sheldon, Jr. 1953- **1990**:2

**Canadian Broadcasting Corp. [CBC]**
   Juneau, Pierre 1922- **1988**:3

**Cancer research**
   DeVita, Vincent T., Jr. 1935- **1987**:3
   Folkman, Judah 1933- **1999**:1
   Fonyo, Steve
      Brief entry **1985**:4

Gale, Robert Peter 1945- **1986**:4
   Hammond, E. Cuyler 1912-1986
      Obituary **1987**:1
   King, Mary-Claire 1946- **1998**:3
   Krim, Mathilde 1926- **1989**:2
   Love, Susan 1948- **1995**:2
   Rosenberg, Steven 1940- **1989**:1
   Szent-Gyoergyi, Albert 1893-1986
      Obituary **1987**:2
   Wigler, Michael
      Brief entry **1985**:1

**Cannes Film Festival**
   Brando, Marlon 1924-2004
      Obituary **2005**:3
   Egoyan, Atom 1960- **2000**:2
   Hou Hsiao-hsien 1947- **2000**:2
   July, Miranda 1974- **2008**:2
   Mirren, Helen 1945- **2005**:1
   Nair, Mira 1957- **2007**:4
   Smith, Kevin 1970- **2000**:4

**Carnival Cruise Lines**
   Arison, Ted 1924- **1990**:3

**Car repair**
   Magliozzi, Tom and Ray **1991**:4

**Cartoons**
   Addams, Charles 1912-1988
      Obituary **1989**:1
   Barbera, Joseph 1911- **1988**:2
   Barry, Lynda 1956(?)- **1992**:1
   Bechdel, Alison 1960- **2007**:3
   Blanc, Mel 1908-1989
      Obituary **1989**:4
   Chast, Roz 1955- **1992**:4
   Disney, Roy E. 1930- **1986**:3
   Freleng, Friz 1906(?)-1995
      Obituary **1995**:4
   Gaines, William M. 1922-1992
      Obituary **1993**:1
   Gould, Chester 1900-1985
      Obituary **1985**:2
   Groening, Matt 1955(?)- **1990**:4
   Hart, Johnny 1931-2007
      Obituary **2008**:2
   Judge, Mike 1963(?)- **1994**:2
   Kinney, Jeff 1971- **2009**:3
   MacFarlane, Seth 1973- **2006**:1
   MacNelly, Jeff 1947-2000
      Obituary **2000**:4
   Marchetto, Marisa Acocella 1962(?)- **2007**:3
   Mauldin, Bill 1921-2003
      Obituary **2004**:2
   McDonnell, Patrick 1956- **2009**:4
   Melendez, Bill 1916-2008
      Obituary **2009**:4
   Messick, Dale 1906-2005
      Obituary **2006**:2
   Parker, Brant 1920-2007
      Obituary **2008**:2
   Parker, Trey and Matt Stone **1998**:2
   Schulz, Charles 1922-2000
      Obituary **2000**:3
   Schulz, Charles M. 1922- **1998**:1
   Spiegelman, Art 1948- **1998**:3
   Tartakovsky, Genndy 1970- **2004**:4
   Trudeau, Garry 1948- **1991**:2
   Watterson, Bill 1958(?)- **1990**:3

**Catholic Church**
   Beckett, Wendy (Sister) 1930- **1998**:3
   Bernardin, Cardinal Joseph 1928-1996 **1997**:2
   Burns, Charles R.
      Brief entry **1988**:1
   Clements, George 1932- **1985**:1
   Cunningham, Reverend William 1930-1997
      Obituary **1997**:4
   Curran, Charles E. 1934- **1989**:2
   Daily, Bishop Thomas V. 1927- **1990**:4
   Dearden, John Cardinal 1907-1988
      Obituary **1988**:4
   Fox, Matthew 1940- **1992**:2
   Healy, Timothy S. 1923- **1990**:2
   Hume, Basil Cardinal 1923-1999
      Obituary **2000**:1
   John Paul II, Pope 1920- **1995**:3
   Kissling, Frances 1943- **1989**:2
   Krol, John 1910-1996
      Obituary **1996**:3
   Lefebvre, Marcel 1905- **1988**:4
   Mahony, Roger M. 1936- **1988**:2
   Maida, Adam Cardinal 1930- **1998**:2
   Obando, Miguel 1926- **1986**:4
   O'Connor, Cardinal John 1920- **1990**:3
   O'Connor, John 1920-2000
      Obituary **2000**:4
   Peter, Valentine J. 1934- **1988**:2
   Rock, John
      Obituary **1985**:1
   Sin, Jaime 1928-2005
      Obituary **2006**:3
   Stallings, George A., Jr. 1948- **1990**:1

**CAT Scanner**
   Hounsfield, Godfrey 1919- **1989**:2

**Cattle rustling**
   Cantrell, Ed
      Brief entry **1985**:3

**Caviar**
   Petrossian, Christian
      Brief entry **1985**:3

**CBS, Inc.**
   Bradley, Ed 1941-2006
      Obituary **2008**:1
   Buttons, Red 1919-2006
      Obituary **2007**:3
   Cox, Richard Joseph
      Brief entry **1985**:1
   Cronkite, Walter Leland 1916- **1997**:3
   Moonves, Les 1949- **2004**:2
   Paley, William S. 1901-1990
      Obituary **1991**:2
   Reasoner, Harry 1923-1991
      Obituary **1992**:1
   Sagansky, Jeff 1952- **1993**:2
   Tellem, Nancy 1953(?)- **2004**:4
   Tisch, Laurence A. 1923- **1988**:2
   Yetnikoff, Walter 1933- **1988**:1

**Center for Equal Opportunity**
   Chavez, Linda 1947- **1999**:3

**Centers for Living**
   Williamson, Marianne 1953(?)- **1991**:4

**Central America**
Astorga, Nora 1949(?)-1988 **1988**:2
Cruz, Arturo 1923- **1985**:1
Obando, Miguel 1926- **1986**:4
Robelo, Alfonso 1940(?)- **1988**:1

**Central Intelligence Agency [CIA]**
Carter, Amy 1967- **1987**:4
Casey, William 1913-1987
Obituary **1987**:3
Colby, William E. 1920-1996
Obituary **1996**:4
Deutch, John 1938- **1996**:4
Gates, Robert M. 1943- **1992**:2
Inman, Bobby Ray 1931- **1985**:1
Tenet, George 1953- **2000**:3

**Centurion Ministries**
McCloskey, James 1944(?)- **1993**:1

**Cesar Awards**
Adjani, Isabelle 1955- **1991**:1
Deneuve, Catherine 1943- **2003**:2
Depardieu, Gerard 1948- **1991**:2
Tautou, Audrey 1978- **2004**:2

**Chanel, Inc.**
D'Alessio, Kitty
Brief entry **1987**:3
Lagerfeld, Karl 1938- **1999**:4

**Chantal Pharmacentical Corp.**
Burnison, Chantal Simone
1950(?)- **1988**:3

**Charlotte Hornets basketball team**
Bryant, Kobe 1978- **1998**:3
Johnson, Larry 1969- **1993**:3
Mourning, Alonzo 1970- **1994**:2

**Chef Boy-ar-dee**
Boiardi, Hector 1897-1985
Obituary **1985**:3

**Chess**
Kasparov, Garry 1963- **1997**:4
Polgar, Judit 1976- **1993**:3

**Chicago, Ill., city government**
Washington, Harold 1922-1987
Obituary **1988**:1

**Chicago Bears football team**
McMahon, Jim 1959- **1985**:4
Payton, Walter 1954-1999
Obituary **2000**:2

**Chicago Blackhawks**
Hasek, Dominik 1965- **1998**:3

**Chicago Bulls basketball team**
Jackson, Phil 1945- **1996**:3
Jordan, Michael 1963- **1987**:2
Kukoc, Toni 1968- **1995**:4
Pippen, Scottie 1965- **1992**:2

**Chicago Cubs baseball team**
Caray, Harry 1914(?)-1998 **1988**:3
Obituary **1998**:3
Soriano, Alfonso 1976- **2008**:1

Sosa, Sammy 1968- **1999**:1

**Chicago White Sox baseball team**
Caray, Harry 1914(?)-1998 **1988**:3
Obituary **1998**:3
Leyland, Jim 1944- **1998**:2
Thomas, Frank 1968- **1994**:3
Veeck, Bill 1914-1986
Obituary **1986**:1

**Child care**
Hale, Clara 1905-1992
Obituary **1993**:3
Leach, Penelope 1937- **1992**:4
Spock, Benjamin 1903-1998 **1995**:2
Obituary **1998**:3

**Children's Defense Fund [CDF]**
Clinton, Hillary Rodham
1947- **1993**:2
Edelman, Marian Wright
1939- **1990**:4

**Chimpanzees**
Goodall, Jane 1934- **1991**:1

**Choreography**
Abdul, Paula 1962- **1990**:3
Ailey, Alvin 1931-1989 **1989**:2
Obituary **1990**:2
Astaire, Fred 1899-1987
Obituary **1987**:4
Bennett, Michael 1943-1987
Obituary **1988**:1
Cunningham, Merce 1919- **1998**:1
Dean, Laura 1945- **1989**:4
de Mille, Agnes 1905-1993
Obituary **1994**:2
Feld, Eliot 1942- **1996**:1
Fenley, Molissa 1954- **1988**:3
Forsythe, William 1949- **1993**:2
Fosse, Bob 1927-1987
Obituary **1988**:1
Glover, Savion 1973- **1997**:1
Graham, Martha 1894-1991
Obituary **1991**:4
Jamison, Judith 1944- **1990**:3
Joffrey, Robert 1930-1988
Obituary **1988**:3
Jones, Bill T. **1991**:4
Lewitzky, Bella 1916-2004
Obituary **2005**:3
MacMillan, Kenneth 1929-1992
Obituary **1993**:2
Mitchell, Arthur 1934- **1995**:1
Morris, Mark 1956- **1991**:1
Nureyev, Rudolf 1938-1993
Obituary **1993**:2
Parsons, David 1959- **1993**:4
Ross, Herbert 1927-2001
Obituary **2002**:4
Takei, Kei 1946- **1990**:2
Taylor, Paul 1930- **1992**:3
Tharp, Twyla 1942- **1992**:4
Tudor, Antony 1908(?)-1987
Obituary **1987**:4
Tune, Tommy 1939- **1994**:2
Varone, Doug 1956- **2001**:2

**Christian Coalition**
Reed, Ralph 1961(?)- **1995**:1

**Christic Institute**
Sheehan, Daniel P. 1945(?)- **1989**:1

**Chrysler Motor Corp.**
Eaton, Robert J. 1940- **1994**:2
Iacocca, Lee 1924- **1993**:1
Lutz, Robert A. 1932- **1990**:1
Nardelli, Robert 1948- **2008**:4

**Church of England**
Carey, George 1935- **1992**:3
Runcie, Robert 1921-2000 **1989**:4
Obituary **2001**:1

**Cincinatti Bengals football team**
Esiason, Boomer 1961- **1991**:1

**Cincinnati Reds baseball team**
Davis, Eric 1962- **1987**:4
Rose, Pete 1941- **1991**:1
Schott, Marge 1928- **1985**:4

**Cinematography**
Burum, Stephen H.
Brief entry **1987**:2
Markle, C. Wilson 1938- **1988**:1
McLaren, Norman 1914-1987
Obituary **1987**:2

**Civil rights**
Abernathy, Ralph 1926-1990
Obituary **1990**:3
Abzug, Bella 1920-1998 **1998**:2
Allen Jr., Ivan 1911-2003
Obituary **2004**:3
Allred, Gloria 1941- **1985**:2
Aquino, Corazon 1933- **1986**:2
Baldwin, James 1924-1987
Obituary **1988**:2
Banks, Dennis J. 193- **1986**:4
Blackburn, Molly 1931(?)-1985
Obituary **1985**:4
Buthelezi, Mangosuthu Gatsha
1928- **1989**:3
Chavez, Linda 1947- **1999**:3
Chavis, Benjamin 1948- **1993**:4
Clements, George 1932- **1985**:1
Connerly, Ward 1939- **2000**:2
Davis, Angela 1944- **1998**:3
Dees, Morris 1936- **1992**:1
Delany, Sarah 1889-1999
Obituary **1999**:3
Duncan, Sheena
Brief entry **1987**:1
Farmer, James 1920-1999
Obituary **2000**:1
Faubus, Orval 1910-1994
Obituary **1995**:2
Glasser, Ira 1938- **1989**:1
Griffiths, Martha 1912-2003
Obituary **2004**:2
Harris, Barbara 1930- **1989**:3
Healey, Jack 1938(?)- **1990**:1
Hoffman, Abbie 1936-1989
Obituary **1989**:3
Hume, John 1938- **1987**:1
Jordan, Vernon, Jr. 1935- **2002**:3
King, Bernice 1963- **2000**:2
King, Coretta Scott 1927- **1999**:3
Kunstler, William 1920(?)- **1992**:3

Makeba, Miriam 1934- **1989**:2
Mandela, Winnie 1934- **1989**:3
Marshall, Thurgood 1908-1993
    Obituary **1993**:3
McGuinness, Martin 1950(?)- **1985**:4
Parks, Rosa 1913-2005
    Obituary **2007**:1
Pendleton, Clarence M. 1930-1988
    Obituary **1988**:4
Ram, Jagjivan 1908-1986
    Obituary **1986**:4
Shabazz, Betty 1936-1997
    Obituary **1997**:4
Sharpton, Al 1954- **1991**:2
Shcharansky, Anatoly 1948- **1986**:2
Simone, Nina 1933-2003
    Obituary **2004**:2
Slovo, Joe 1926- **1989**:2
Stallings, George A., Jr. 1948- **1990**:1
Steele, Shelby 1946- **1991**:2
Sullivan, Leon 1922-2001
    Obituary **2002**:2
Suzman, Helen 1917- **1989**:3
Ture, Kwame 1941-1998
    Obituary **1999**:2
Washington, Harold 1922-1987
    Obituary **1988**:1
West, Cornel 1953- **1994**:2
Williams, G. Mennen 1911-1988
    Obituary **1988**:2
Williams, Hosea 1926-2000
    Obituary **2001**:2
Wu, Harry 1937- **1996**:1

**Civil War**
    Foote, Shelby 1916- **1991**:2

**Claymation**
    Park, Nick 1958- **1997**:3
    Vinton, Will
        Brief entry **1988**:1

**Cleveland Ballet Dancing Wheels**
    Verdi-Fletcher, Mary 1955- **1998**:2

**Cleveland Browns football team**
    Brown, Jim 1936- **1993**:2

**Cleveland Cavaliers basketball team**
    James, LeBron 1984- **2007**:3
    Wilkens, Lenny 1937- **1995**:2

**Cleveland city government**
    Stokes, Carl 1927-1996
        Obituary **1996**:4

**Cleveland Indians baseball team**
    Belle, Albert 1966- **1996**:4
    Boudreau, Louis 1917-2001
        Obituary **2002**:3
    Greenberg, Hank 1911-1986
        Obituary **1986**:4
    Lofton, Kenny 1967- **1998**:1
    Veeck, Bill 1914-1986
        Obituary **1986**:1

**Cliff's Notes**
    Hillegass, Clifton Keith 1918- **1989**:4

**Climatology**
    Thompson, Starley
        Brief entry **1987**:3

**Clio Awards**
    Proctor, Barbara Gardner 1933(?)-
        **1985**:3
    Riney, Hal 1932- **1989**:1
    Rivers, Joan 1933- **2005**:3
    Sedelmaier, Joe 1933- **1985**:3

**Cloning**
    Lanza, Robert 1956- **2004**:3
    Wilmut, Ian 1944- **1997**:3

**Coaching**
    Bowman, Scotty 1933- **1998**:4
    Brown, Paul 1908-1991
        Obituary **1992**:1
    Chaney, John 1932- **1989**:1
    Hayes, Woody 1913-1987
        Obituary **1987**:2
    Holtz, Lou 1937- **1986**:4
    Howser, Dick 1936-1987
        Obituary **1987**:4
    Jackson, Phil 1945- **1996**:3
    Johnson, Jimmy 1943- **1993**:3
    Knight, Bobby 1940- **1985**:3
    Leyland, Jim 1944- **1998**:2
    Lukas, D. Wayne 1936(?)- **1986**:2
    Martin, Billy 1928-1989 **1988**:4
        Obituary **1990**:2
    McCartney, Bill 1940- **1995**:3
    Paterno, Joe 1926- **1995**:4
    Schembechler, Bo 1929(?)- **1990**:3
    Shula, Don 1930- **1992**:2
    Tarkenian, Jerry 1930- **1990**:4
    Walsh, Bill 1931- **1987**:4

**Coca-Cola Co.**
    Goizueta, Roberto 1931-1997 **1996**:1
        Obituary **1998**:1
    Keough, Donald Raymond
        1926- **1986**:1
    Woodruff, Robert Winship 1889-1985
        Obituary **1985**:1

**Coleman Co.**
    Coleman, Sheldon, Jr. 1953- **1990**:2

**Colorado Avalanche hockey team**
    Lemieux, Claude 1965- **1996**:1

**Colorization**
    Markle, C. Wilson 1938- **1988**:1

**Columbia Pictures**
    Pascal, Amy 1958- **2003**:3
    Steel, Dawn 1946-1997 **1990**:1
        Obituary **1998**:2
    Vincent, Fay 1938- **1990**:2

**Columbia Sportswear**
    Boyle, Gertrude 1924- **1995**:3

**Comedy**
    Adams, Don 1923-2005
        Obituary **2007**:1
    Alexander, Jason 1962(?)- **1993**:3
    Allen, Steve 1921-2000
        Obituary **2001**:2
    Allen, Tim 1953- **1993**:1
    Allen, Woody 1935- **1994**:1

Anderson, Harry 1951(?)- **1988**:2
Arnold, Tom 1959- **1993**:2
Atkinson, Rowan 1955- **2004**:3
Baron Cohen, Sacha 1971- **2007**:3
Barr, Roseanne 1953(?)- **1989**:1
Bateman, Jason 1969- **2005**:3
Belushi, Jim 1954- **1986**:2
Belzer, Richard 1944- **1985**:3
Benigni, Roberto 1952- **1999**:2
Berle, Milton 1908-2002
    Obituary **2003**:2
Bernhard, Sandra 1955(?)- **1989**:4
Bishop, Joey 1918-2007
    Obituary **2008**:4
Black, Jack 1969- **2002**:3
Bogosian, Eric 1953- **1990**:4
Borge, Victor 1909-2000
    Obituary **2001**:3
Brooks, Albert 1948(?)- **1991**:4
Brooks, Mel 1926- **2003**:1
Burns, George 1896-1996
    Obituary **1996**:3
Burrows, James 1940- **2005**:3
Busch, Charles 1954- **1998**:3
Butler, Brett 1958(?)- **1995**:1
Buttons, Red 1919-2006
    Obituary **2007**:3
Candy, John 1950-1994 **1988**:2
    Obituary **1994**:3
Carey, Drew 1958- **1997**:4
Carney, Art 1918-2003
    Obituary **2005**:1
Carrey, Jim 1962- **1995**:1
Carvey, Dana 1955- **1994**:1
Chappelle, Dave 1973- **2005**:3
Chase, Chevy 1943- **1990**:1
Cho, Margaret 1970- **1995**:2
Clay, Andrew Dice 1958- **1991**:1
Cleese, John 1939- **1989**:2
Colbert, Stephen 1964- **2007**:4
Cook, Peter 1938-1995
    Obituary **1995**:2
Cosby, Bill 1937- **1999**:2
Crystal, Billy 1947- **1985**:3
Dangerfield, Rodney 1921-2004
    Obituary **2006**:1
DeGeneres, Ellen **1995**:3
Diamond, Selma 1921(?)-1985
    Obituary **1985**:2
Dr. Demento 1941- **1986**:1
Fallon, Jimmy 1974- **2003**:1
Farley, Chris 1964-1997 **1998**:2
Fey, Tina 1970- **2005**:3
Ford, Faith 1964- **2005**:3
Foster, Phil 1914-1985
    Obituary **1985**:3
Foxworthy, Jeff 1958- **1996**:1
Foxx, Jamie 1967- **2001**:1
Foxx, Redd 1922-1991
    Obituary **1992**:2
Franken, Al 1952(?)- **1996**:3
Gleason, Jackie 1916-1987
    Obituary **1987**:4
Gobel, George 1920(?)-1991
    Obituary **1991**:4
Goldberg, Whoopi 1955- **1993**:3
Gordon, Gale 1906-1995
    Obituary **1996**:1
Gregory, Dick 1932- **1990**:3
Hackett, Buddy 1924-2003
    Obituary **2004**:3
Hall, Arsenio 1955- **1990**:2

Handler, Chelsea 1975- **2009**:3
Hill, Benny 1925-1992
    Obituary **1992**:3
Hope, Bob 1903-2003
    Obituary **2004**:4
Hughley, D.L. 1964- **2001**:1
Humphries, Barry 1934- **1993**:1
Irwin, Bill **1988**:3
Izzard, Eddie 1963- **2008**:1
Jones, Jenny 1946- **1998**:2
Kinison, Sam 1954(?)-1992
    Obituary **1993**:1
Knotts, Don 1924-2006
    Obituary **2007**:1
Korman, Harvey 1927-2008
    Obituary **2009**:2
Lawrence, Martin 1966(?)- **1993**:4
Leary, Denis 1958- **1993**:3
Leguizamo, John 1965- **1999**:1
Leno, Jay 1950- **1987**:1
Letterman, David 1947- **1989**:3
Lewis, Richard 1948(?)- **1992**:1
Lisick, Beth 1969(?)- **2006**:2
Lopez, George 1963- **2003**:4
Mac, Bernie 1957- **2003**:1
Mandel, Howie 1955- **1989**:1
Martin, Steve 1945- **1992**:2
McCarthy, Jenny 1972- **1997**:4
Miller, Dennis 1953- **1992**:4
Milligan, Spike 1918-2002
    Obituary **2003**:2
Mo'Nique 1967- **2008**:1
Morgan, Tracy 1968- **2009**:3
Morita, Noriyuki Pat 1932- **1987**:3
Murphy, Eddie 1961- **1989**:2
Murray, Bill 1950- **2002**:4
Myers, Mike 1964(?)- **1992**:3
O'Brien, Conan 1963(?)- **1994**:1
O'Donnell, Rosie 1962- **1994**:3
O'Hara, Catherine 1954- **2007**:4
Parker, Trey and Matt Stone **1998**:2
Paulsen, Pat 1927-1997
    Obituary **1997**:4
Penn & Teller **1992**:1
Peterson, Cassandra 1951- **1988**:1
Poehler, Amy 1971- **2009**:1
Pryor, Richard **1999**:3
Reiser, Paul 1957- **1995**:2
Reubens, Paul 1952- **1987**:2
Rhea, Caroline 1964- **2004**:1
Richards, Michael 1949(?)- **1993**:4
Rivers, Joan 1933- **2005**:3
Rock, Chris 1967(?)- **1998**:1
Rogen, Seth 1982- **2009**:3
Rogers, Ginger 1911(?)-1995
    Obituary **1995**:4
Rowan, Dan 1922-1987
    Obituary **1988**:1
Rudner, Rita 1956- **1993**:2
Russell, Nipsey 1924-2005
    Obituary **2007**:1
Sandler, Adam 1966- **1999**:2
Schneider, Rob 1965- **1997**:4
Seinfeld, Jerry 1954- **1992**:4
Shandling, Garry 1949- **1995**:1
Shawn, Dick 1924(?)-1987
    Obituary **1987**:3
Short, Martin 1950- **1986**:1
Silverman, Sarah 1970- **2008**:1
Silvers, Phil 1912-1985
    Obituary **1985**:4
Skelton, Red 1913-1997

Obituary **1998**:1
Smigel, Robert 1959(?)- **2001**:3
Smirnoff, Yakov 1951- **1987**:2
Spade, David 1965- **1999**:2
Sykes, Wanda 1964- **2007**:4
Tucker, Chris 1973(?)- **1999**:1
Wayans, Keenen Ivory
    1958(?)- **1991**:1
Williams, Robin 1952- **1988**:4
Wilson, Flip 1933-1998
    Obituary **1999**:2
Wright, Steven 1955- **1986**:3
Yankovic, Weird Al 1959- **1985**:4
Youngman, Henny 1906(?)-1998
    Obituary **1998**:3

**Comic Books**
    Arad, Avi 1948- **2003**:2
    Barks, Carl 1901-2000
        Obituary **2001**:2
    Bell, Gabrielle 1975(?)- **2007**:4
    Dawson, Rosario 1979- **2007**:2
    Eisner, Will 1917-2005
        Obituary **2006**:1
    Meltzer, Brad 1970- **2005**:4
    Miller, Frank 1957- **2008**:2
    Picoult, Jodi 1966- **2008**:1
    Smith, Kevin 1970- **2000**:4
    Washington, Alonzo 1967- **2000**:1
    Winick, Judd 1970- **2005**:3

**Committee for the Scientific
Investigation of Claims of the
Paranormal**
    Randi, James 1928- **1990**:2

**Committee to Halt Useless College
Killings [CHUCK]**
    Stevens, Eileen 1939- **1987**:3

**Communitarianism**
    Etzioni, Amitai 1929- **1994**:3

**Compaq Computer Corp.**
    Pfeiffer, Eckhard 1941- **1998**:4

**CompuServe Inc.**
    Bloch, Henry 1922- **1988**:4
    Ebbers, Bernie 1943- **1998**:1

**ComputerLand Corp.**
    Millard, Barbara J.
        Brief entry **1985**:3

**Computers**
    Akers, John F. 1934- **1988**:3
    Andreessen, Marc 1972- **1996**:2
    Backus, John W. 1924-2007
        Obituary **2008**:2
    Barrett, Craig R. 1939- **1999**:4
    Berners-Lee, Tim 1955(?)- **1997**:4
    Case, Steve 1958- **1995**:4
    Cerf, Vinton G. 1943- **1999**:2
    Cray, Seymour R. 1925-1996
        Brief entry **1986**:3
        Obituary **1997**:2
    Dell, Michael 1965- **1996**:2
    De Luca, Guerrino 1952- **2007**:1
    Gates, Bill 1955- **1987**:4
    Grove, Andrew S. 1936- **1995**:3

Hawkins, Jeff and Donna
    Dubinsky **2000**:2
Headroom, Max 1985- **1986**:4
Hounsfield, Godfrey 1919- **1989**:2
Inatome, Rick 1953- **1985**:4
Inman, Bobby Ray 1931- **1985**:1
Isaacson, Portia
    Brief entry **1986**:1
Kapor, Mitch 1950- **1990**:3
Kurzweil, Raymond 1948- **1986**:3
Lanier, Jaron 1961(?)- **1993**:4
McNealy, Scott 1954- **1999**:4
Millard, Barbara J.
    Brief entry **1985**:3
Miller, Rand 1959(?)- **1995**:4
Noyce, Robert N. 1927- **1985**:4
Olsen, Kenneth H. 1926- **1986**:4
Packard, David 1912-1996
    Obituary **1996**:3
Raskin, Jef 1943(?)- **1997**:4
Ritchie, Dennis and Kenneth
    Thompson **2000**:1
Roberts, Steven K. 1952(?)- **1992**:1
Schank, Roger 1946- **1989**:2
Sculley, John 1939- **1989**:4
Shimomura, Tsutomu 1965- **1996**:1
Sterling, Bruce 1954- **1995**:4
Torvalds, Linus 1970(?)- **1999**:3
Treybig, James G. 1940- **1988**:3
Wang, An 1920-1990 **1986**:1
    Obituary **1990**:3

**Conducting (musical)**
    Alsop, Marin 1956- **2008**:3
    Bernstein, Leonard 1918-1990
        Obituary **1991**:1
    Dorati, Antal 1906-1988
        Obituary **1989**:2
    Goodman, Benny 1909-1986
        Obituary **1986**:3
    Levine, James 1943- **1992**:3
    Lewis, Henry 1932-1996
        Obituary **1996**:3
    Mehta, Zubin 1938(?)- **1994**:3
    Menuhin, Yehudi 1916-1999
        Obituary **1999**:3
    Norrington, Roger 1934- **1989**:4
    Ormandy, Eugene 1899-1985
        Obituary **1985**:2
    Rattle, Simon 1955- **1989**:4
    Riddle, Nelson 1921-1985
        Obituary **1985**:4
    Rostropovich, Mstislav 1927-2007
        Obituary **2008**:3
    Solti, Georg 1912-1997
        Obituary **1998**:1
    Thomas, Michael Tilson 1944- **1990**:3
    von Karajan, Herbert 1908-1989
        Obituary **1989**:4

**Congressional Medal of Honor**
    Hope, Bob 1903-2003
        Obituary **2004**:4
    Kerrey, Bob 1943- **1986**:1
    Parks, Rosa 1913-2005
        Obituary **2007**:1
    Shepard, Alan 1923-1998
        Obituary **1999**:1

**Connecticut state government**
    Lieberman, Joseph 1942- **2001**:1
    Perry, Carrie Saxon 1932(?)- **1989**:2
    Ribicoff, Abraham 1910-1998

Obituary **1998**:3
Weicker, Lowell P., Jr. 1931- **1993**:1

**Conseco, Inc.**
Hilbert, Stephen C. 1946- **1997**:4

**Conservation (wildlife)**
Adamson, George 1906-1989
Obituary **1990**:2
Babbitt, Bruce 1938- **1994**:1
Brower, David 1912- **1990**:4
Corwin, Jeff 1967- **2005**:1
Douglas, Marjory Stoneman
1890-1998 **1993**:1
Obituary **1998**:4
Durrell, Gerald 1925-1995
Obituary **1995**:3
Foreman, Dave 1947(?)- **1990**:3
Goodall, Jane 1934- **1991**:1
Hair, Jay D. 1945- **1994**:3
Hayse, Bruce 1949(?)- **2004**:3
Moss, Cynthia 1940- **1995**:2
Owens, Delia and Mark **1993**:3
Wilson, Edward O. 1929- **1994**:4

**Conservative Judaism**
Eilberg, Amy
Brief entry **1985**:3

**Conservative Party (Great Britain)**
Major, John 1943- **1991**:2
Thatcher, Margaret 1925- **1989**:2

**Consumer protection**
Nader, Ralph 1934- **1989**:4

**Cooking**
Bourdain, Anthony 1956- **2008**:3
Deen, Paula 1947- **2008**:3
Ford, Faith 1964- **2005**:3
Lawson, Nigella 1960- **2003**:2
Lee, Sandra 1966- **2008**:3
Matsuhisa, Nobuyuki 1949- **2002**:3
Oliver, Jamie 1975- **2002**:3
Pouillon, Nora 1943- **2005**:1
Ramsay, Gordon 1966- **2008**:2
Ray, Rachael 1968- **2007**:1
Trotter, Charlie 1960- **2000**:4
Waters, Alice 1944- **2006**:3

**Cosmetics**
Ash, Mary Kay 1915(?)- **1996**:1
Aucoin, Kevyn 1962- **2001**:3
Baxter, Pamela 1949- **2009**:4
Bloom, Natalie 1971- **2007**:1
Carlino, Cristina 1961(?)- **2008**:4
Iman 1955- **2001**:3
Kashuk, Sonia 1959(?)- **2002**:4
Kelly, Maureen 1972(?)- **2007**:3
Lerner, Sandy 1955(?)- **2005**:1
Lobell, Jeanine 1964(?)- **2002**:3
Manheimer, Heidi 1963- **2009**:3
Mercier, Laura 1959(?)- **2002**:2
Mohajer, Dineh 1972- **1997**:3
Nars, Francois 1959- **2003**:1
Owen-Jones, Lindsay 1946(?)- **2004**:2
Roncal, Mally 1972- **2009**:4
Shaw, Carol 1958(?)- **2002**:1

**Coty Awards**
Beene, Geoffrey 1927-2004
Obituary **2005**:4
Blass, Bill 1922-2002

Obituary **2003**:3
de la Renta, Oscar 1932- **2005**:4
Ellis, Perry 1940-1986
Obituary **1986**:3
Halston 1932-1990
Obituary **1990**:3
Johnson, Betsey 1942- **1996**:2
Kamali, Norma 1945- **1989**:1
Karan, Donna 1948- **1988**:1
Klein, Calvin 1942- **1996**:2
Lauren, Ralph 1939- **1990**:1
Smith, Willi 1948-1987
Obituary **1987**:3

**Council of Economic Advisers**
Tyson, Laura D'Andrea 1947- **1994**:1

**Counseling**
Bradshaw, John 1933- **1992**:1
Gray, John 1952(?)- **1995**:3

**Counterfeiting**
Bikoff, James L.
Brief entry **1986**:2

**Country Music Awards**
Bentley, Dierks 1975- **2007**:3
Brooks, Garth 1962- **1992**:1
Carpenter, Mary-Chapin
1958(?)- **1994**:1
Chesney, Kenny 1968- **2008**:2
Harris, Emmylou 1947- **1991**:3
Hill, Faith 1967- **2000**:1
Jackson, Alan 1958- **2003**:1
Loveless, Patty 1957- **1998**:2
McEntire, Reba 1954- **1987**:3
McGraw, Tim 1966- **2000**:3
Nelson, Willie 1933- **1993**:4
Newton-John, Olivia 1948- **1998**:4
Paisley, Brad 1972- **2008**:3
Parton, Dolly 1946- **1999**:4
Pride, Charley 1938(?)- **1998**:1
Rascal Flatts **2007**:1
Spacek, Sissy 1949- **2003**:1
Strait, George 1952- **1998**:3
Sugarland 1970- **2009**:2
Travis, Randy 1959- **1988**:4
Twitty, Conway 1933-1993
Obituary **1994**:1
Underwood, Carrie 1983- **2008**:1
Urban, Keith 1967- **2006**:3
Wagoner, Porter 1927-2007
Obituary **2008**:4
Wilson, Gretchen 1970- **2006**:3
Womack, Lee Ann 1966- **2002**:1
Wynette, Tammy 1942-1998
Obituary **1998**:3
Wynonna 1964- **1993**:3
Yearwood, Trisha 1964- **1999**:1

**Creation Spirituality**
Altea, Rosemary 1946- **1996**:3
Fox, Matthew 1940- **1992**:2

**Creative Artists Agency**
Ovitz, Michael 1946- **1990**:1

**Cy Young Award**
Clemens, Roger 1962- **1991**:4
Hernandez, Willie 1954- **1985**:1
Hershiser, Orel 1958- **1989**:2

Johnson, Randy 1963- **1996**:2
Maddux, Greg 1966- **1996**:2
Palmer, Jim 1945- **1991**:2
Saberhagen, Bret 1964- **1986**:1
Santana, Johan 1979- **2008**:1

**Daimler-Benz AG [Mercedes-Benz]**
Breitschwerdt, Werner 1927- **1988**:4

**DaimlerChrysler Corp.**
Schrempp, Juergen 1944- **2000**:2
Zetsche, Dieter 1953- **2002**:3

**Dallas Cowboys football team**
Aikman, Troy 1966- **1994**:2
Irvin, Michael 1966- **1996**:3
Johnson, Jimmy 1943- **1993**:3
Jones, Jerry 1942- **1994**:4
Landry, Tom 1924-2000
Obituary **2000**:3
Romo, Tony 1980- **2008**:3
Smith, Emmitt **1994**:1

**Dance Theatre of Harlem**
Fagan, Garth 1940- **2000**:1
Mitchell, Arthur 1934- **1995**:1

**Dell Computer Corp.**
Dell, Michael 1965- **1996**:2

**Democratic National Committee [DNC]**
Brown, Ron 1941- **1990**:3
Brown, Ron 1941-1996
Obituary **1996**:4
Dean, Howard 1948- **2005**:4
Waters, Maxine 1938- **1998**:4

**Denver Broncos football team**
Barnes, Ernie 1938- **1997**:4
Davis, Terrell 1972- **1998**:2
Elway, John 1960- **1990**:3

**Department of Commerce**
Baldrige, Malcolm 1922-1987
Obituary **1988**:1
Brown, Ron 1941-1996
Obituary **1996**:4

**Department of Defense**
Cohen, William S. 1940- **1998**:1
Perry, William 1927- **1994**:4

**Department of Education**
Cavazos, Lauro F. 1927- **1989**:2
Riley, Richard W. 1933- **1996**:3

**Department of Energy**
O'Leary, Hazel 1937- **1993**:4

**Department of Health, Education, and Welfare [HEW]**
Harris, Patricia Roberts 1924-1985
Obituary **1985**:2
Ribicoff, Abraham 1910-1998
Obituary **1998**:3

**Department of Health and Human Services [HHR]**
Kessler, David 1951- **1992**:1
Sullivan, Louis 1933- **1990**:4

**Department of Housing and Urban Development [HUD]**
    Achtenberg, Roberta **1993**:4
    Harris, Patricia Roberts 1924-1985
        Obituary **1985**:2
    Kemp, Jack 1935- **1990**:4
    Morrison, Trudi
        Brief entry **1986**:2

**Department of Labor**
    Dole, Elizabeth Hanford 1936- **1990**:1
    Martin, Lynn 1939- **1991**:4

**Department of State**
    Christopher, Warren 1925- **1996**:3
    Muskie, Edmund S. 1914-1996
        Obituary **1996**:3

**Department of the Interior**
    Babbitt, Bruce 1938- **1994**:1

**Department of Transportation**
    Dole, Elizabeth Hanford 1936- **1990**:1
    Schiavo, Mary 1955- **1998**:2

**Depression**
    Abramson, Lyn 1950- **1986**:3

**Desilu Productions**
    Arnaz, Desi 1917-1986
        Obituary **1987**:1
    Ball, Lucille 1911-1989
        Obituary **1989**:3

**Detroit city government**
    Archer, Dennis 1942- **1994**:4
    Maida, Adam Cardinal 1930- **1998**:2
    Young, Coleman A. 1918-1997
        Obituary **1998**:1

**Detroit Lions football team**
    Ford, William Clay, Jr. 1957- **1999**:1
    Sanders, Barry 1968- **1992**:1
    White, Byron 1917-2002
        Obituary **2003**:3

**Detroit Pistons basketball team**
    Hill, Grant 1972- **1995**:3
    Laimbeer, Bill 1957- **2004**:3
    Rodman, Dennis 1961- **1991**:3
    Thomas, Isiah 1961- **1989**:2
    Vitale, Dick 1939- **1988**:4
    Wallace, Ben 1974- **2004**:3

**Detroit Red Wings hockey team**
    Bowman, Scotty 1933- **1998**:4
    Federov, Sergei 1969- **1995**:1
    Ilitch, Mike 1929- **1993**:4
    Klima, Petr 1964- **1987**:1
    Konstantinov, Vladimir 1967- **1997**:4
    Yzerman, Steve 1965- **1991**:2

**Detroit Tigers baseball team**
    Fielder, Cecil 1963- **1993**:2
    Gibson, Kirk 1957- **1985**:2
    Greenberg, Hank 1911-1986

        Obituary **1986**:4
    Harwell, Ernie 1918- **1997**:3
    Hernandez, Willie 1954- **1985**:1
    Ilitch, Mike 1929- **1993**:4
    Monaghan, Tom 1937- **1985**:1
    Schembechler, Bo 1929(?)- **1990**:3

**Diets**
    Agatston, Arthur 1947- **2005**:1
    Atkins, Robert C. 1930-2003
        Obituary **2004**:2
    Gregory, Dick 1932- **1990**:3
    Ornish, Dean 1953- **2004**:2
    Powter, Susan 1957(?)- **1994**:3
    Sears, Barry 1947- **2004**:2

**Digital Equipment Corp. [DEC]**
    Olsen, Kenneth H. 1926- **1986**:4

**Dilbert cartoon**
    Adams, Scott 1957- **1996**:4

**Dinosaurs**
    Bakker, Robert T. 1950(?)- **1991**:3
    Barney **1993**:4
    Crichton, Michael 1942- **1995**:3
    Henson, Brian 1964(?)- **1992**:1

**Diplomacy**
    Abrams, Elliott 1948- **1987**:1
    Albright, Madeleine 1937- **1994**:3
    Astorga, Nora 1949(?)-1988 **1988**:2
    Baker, James A. III 1930- **1991**:2
    Begin, Menachem 1913-1992
        Obituary **1992**:3
    Berri, Nabih 1939(?)- **1985**:2
    Carter, Jimmy 1924- **1995**:1
    de Pinies, Jamie
        Brief entry **1986**:3
    Dubinin, Yuri 1930- **1987**:4
    Ghali, Boutros Boutros 1922- **1992**:3
    Gromyko, Andrei 1909-1989
        Obituary **1990**:2
    Harriman, Pamela 1920- **1994**:4
    Harriman, W. Averell 1891-1986
        Obituary **1986**:4
    Harris, Patricia Roberts 1924-1985
        Obituary **1985**:2
    Holbrooke, Richard 1941(?)- **1996**:2
    Jumblatt, Walid 1949(?)- **1987**:4
    Kekkonen, Urho 1900-1986
        Obituary **1986**:4
    Keyes, Alan 1950- **1996**:2
    Kim Dae Jung 1925- **1998**:3
    Lansdale, Edward G. 1908-1987
        Obituary **1987**:2
    Le Duc Tho 1911-1990
        Obituary **1991**:1
    Lewis, Stephen 1937- **1987**:2
    Lodge, Henry Cabot 1902-1985
        Obituary **1985**:1
    Lord, Winston
        Brief entry **1987**:4
    Luce, Clare Boothe 1903-1987
        Obituary **1988**:1
    Masako, Crown Princess 1963- **1993**:4
    McCloy, John J. 1895-1989
        Obituary **1989**:3
    Molotov, Vyacheslav Mikhailovich 1890-1986

        Obituary **1987**:1
    Palme, Olof 1927-1986
        Obituary **1986**:2
    Paz, Octavio 1914- **1991**:2
    Perez de Cuellar, Javier 1920- **1991**:3
    Strauss, Robert 1918- **1991**:4
    Taylor, Maxwell 1901-1987
        Obituary **1987**:3
    Terzi, Zehdi Labib 1924- **1985**:3
    Williams, G. Mennen 1911-1988
        Obituary **1988**:2
    Zeroual, Liamine 1951- **1996**:2
    Zhao Ziyang 1919- **1989**:1

**Discovery Channel**
    Otte, Ruth 1949- **1992**:4

**Disney/ABC Cable Networks**
    Cyrus, Miley 1992- **2008**:3
    Efron, Zac 1987- **2008**:2
    Jonas Brothers **2008**:4
    Laybourne, Geraldine 1947- **1997**:1

**DNA Testing**
    Scheck, Barry 1949- **2000**:4

**Documentaries**
    Burns, Ken 1953- **1995**:2
    Moore, Michael 1954(?)- **1990**:3

**Dolby Laboratories, Inc.**
    Dolby, Ray Milton
        Brief entry **1986**:1

**Domino's Pizza**
    Monaghan, Tom 1937- **1985**:1

**Donghia Companies**
    Donghia, Angelo R. 1935-1985
        Obituary **1985**:2

**Doubleday Mystery Guild**
    Grafton, Sue 1940- **2000**:2

**Drama Desk Awards**
    Allen, Debbie 1950- **1998**:2
    Allen, Joan 1956- **1998**:1
    Bishop, Andre 1948- **2000**:1
    Brooks, Mel 1926- **2003**:1
    Crisp, Quentin 1908-1999
        Obituary **2000**:3
    Dunagan, Deanna 1940- **2009**:2
    Ebersole, Christine 1953- **2007**:2
    Fagan, Garth 1940- **2000**:1
    Fierstein, Harvey 1954- **2004**:2
    Foster, Sutton 1975- **2003**:2
    Hoffman, Dustin 1937- **2005**:4
    Janney, Allison 1959- **2003**:3
    Kline, Kevin 1947- **2000**:1
    Lane, Nathan 1956- **1996**:4
    Langella, Frank 1940- **2008**:3
    LaPaglia, Anthony 1959- **2004**:4
    LuPone, Patti 1949- **2009**:2
    McDonagh, Martin 1970- **2007**:3
    Nunn, Trevor 1940- **2000**:2
    Peters, Bernadette 1948- **2000**:1
    Rylance, Mark 1960- **2009**:3
    Salonga, Lea 1971- **2003**:3
    Shanley, John Patrick 1950- **2006**:1

Smith, Anna Deavere 1950- **2002**:2
Spacey, Kevin 1959- **1996**:4
Szot, Paulo 1969- **2009**:3
Waterston, Sam 1940- **2006**:1
Wong, B.D. 1962- **1998**:1

**DreamWorks SKG**
Jacobson, Nina 1965- **2009**:2
Katzenberg, Jeffrey 1950- **1995**:3
Ostin, Mo 1927- **1996**:2
Spielberg, Steven 1947- **1993**:4

**Drug abuse**
Barrymore, Drew 1975- **1995**:3
Bennett, William 1943- **1990**:1
Bradshaw, John 1933- **1992**:1
Burroughs, William S. 1914-1997
Obituary **1997**:4
Hirschhorn, Joel
Brief entry **1986**:1
Phoenix, River 1970-1993 **1990**:2
Obituary **1994**:2

**Drunk driving**
Anastas, Robert
Brief entry **1985**:2
Lightner, Candy 1946- **1985**:1

**Druze**
Jumblatt, Walid 1949(?)- **1987**:4

**Duds 'n' Suds**
Akin, Phil
Brief entry **1987**:3

**Duke University basketball team**
Krzyzewski, Mike 1947- **1993**:2

**Dun & Bradstreet**
Moritz, Charles 1936- **1989**:3

**Dwarfism**
Kopits, Steven E.
Brief entry **1987**:1

**E. F. Hutton Group, Inc.**
Fomon, Robert M. 1925- **1985**:3

**Earth First!**
Foreman, Dave 1947(?)- **1990**:3
Hayse, Bruce 1949(?)- **2004**:3

**eBay**
Whitman, Meg 1957- **2000**:3

**Ecology**
Abbey, Edward 1927-1989
Obituary **1989**:3
Allen, John 1930- **1992**:1
Brower, David 1912- **1990**:4
Foreman, Dave 1947(?)- **1990**:3
Janzen, Daniel H. 1939- **1988**:4
Lipkis, Andy
Brief entry **1985**:3
McCloskey, J. Michael 1934- **1988**:2
McIntyre, Richard
Brief entry **1986**:2
McTaggart, David 1932(?)- **1989**:4

Mott, William Penn, Jr. 1909- **1986**:1
Nader, Ralph 1934- **1989**:4
Plotkin, Mark 1955(?)- **1994**:3
Wilson, Edward O. 1929- **1994**:4
Woodwell, George S. 1928- **1987**:2

**Economics**
Bernanke, Ben 1953- **2008**:3
Delors, Jacques 1925- **1990**:2
Garzarelli, Elaine M. 1951- **1992**:3
Greenspan, Alan 1926- **1992**:2
Heller, Walter 1915-1987
Obituary **1987**:4
Kim Dae Jung 1925- **1998**:3
Lalonde, Marc 1929- **1985**:1
Parizeau, Jacques 1930- **1995**:1
Porter, Sylvia 1913-1991
Obituary **1991**:4
Reisman, Simon 1919- **1987**:4
Sachs, Jeffrey D. 1954- **2004**:4
Sowell, Thomas 1930- **1998**:3
Tyson, Laura D'Andrea 1947- **1994**:1
Yunus, Muhammad 1940- **2007**:3

**Edmonton Oilers hockey team**
Coffey, Paul 1961- **1985**:4
Gretzky, Wayne 1961- **1989**:2
Pocklington, Peter H. 1941- **1985**:2

**E.I. DuPont de Nemours & Co.**
Heckert, Richard E.
Brief entry **1987**:3
Holliday, Chad 1948- **2006**:4

**E.I. DuPont de Nemours & Co.**
Kullman, Ellen 1956- **2009**:4

**Emmy Awards**
Abrams, J. J. 1966- **2007**:3
Adams, Don 1923-2005
Obituary **2007**:1
Albert, Marv 1943- **1994**:3
Alexander, Jane 1939- **1994**:2
Alexander, Jason 1962(?)- **1993**:3
Allen, Debbie 1950- **1998**:2
Anderson, Judith 1899(?)-1992
Obituary **1992**:3
Apatow, Judd 1967- **2006**:3
Arledge, Roone 1931- **1992**:2
Aykroyd, Dan 1952- **1989**:3
Azaria, Hank 1964- **2001**:3
Ball, Lucille 1911-1989
Obituary **1989**:3
Bancroft, Anne 1931-2005
Obituary **2006**:3
Baranski, Christine 1952- **2001**:2
Barbera, Joseph 1911- **1988**:2
Berle, Milton 1908-2002
Obituary **2003**:2
Bernstein, Elmer 1922-2004
Obituary **2005**:4
Bochco, Steven 1943- **1989**:1
Boyle, Peter 1935- **2002**:3
Bradley, Ed 1941-2006
Obituary **2008**:1
Brady, Wayne 1972- **2008**:3
Burnett, Carol 1933- **2000**:3
Burnett, Mark 1960- **2003**:1
Burrows, James 1940- **2005**:3
Carney, Art 1918-2003
Obituary **2005**:1

Carter, Chris 1956- **2000**:1
Carter, Nell 1948-2003
Obituary **2004**:2
Chase, Chevy 1943- **1990**:1
Chiklis, Michael 1963- **2003**:3
Child, Julia 1912- **1999**:4
Clarkson, Patricia 1959- **2005**:3
Coca, Imogene 1908-2001
Obituary **2002**:2
Coco, James 1929(?)-1987
Obituary **1987**:2
Colbert, Stephen 1964- **2007**:4
Cooke, Alistair 1908-2004
Obituary **2005**:3
Copperfield, David 1957- **1986**:3
Corwin, Jeff 1967- **2005**:1
Cosby, Bill 1937- **1999**:2
Cronkite, Walter Leland 1916- **1997**:3
Davis, Bette 1908-1989
Obituary **1990**:1
De Cordova, Frederick 1910- **1985**:2
Delany, Dana 1956- **2008**:4
De Matteo, Drea 1973- **2005**:2
De Vito, Danny 1944- **1987**:1
Dewhurst, Colleen 1924-1991
Obituary **1992**:2
Douglas, Mike 1925-2006
Obituary **2007**:4
Fey, Tina 1970- **2005**:3
Field, Patricia 1942(?)- **2002**:2
Field, Sally 1946- **1995**:3
Finney, Albert 1936- **2003**:3
Flanders, Ed 1934-1995
Obituary **1995**:3
Fosse, Bob 1927-1987
Obituary **1988**:1
Foster, Jodie 1962- **1989**:2
Frankenheimer, John 1930-2002
Obituary **2003**:4
Franz, Dennis 1944- **1995**:2
Freleng, Friz 1906(?)-1995
Obituary **1995**:4
Gandolfini, James 1961- **2001**:3
Gellar, Sarah Michelle 1977- **1999**:3
Getty, Estelle 1923-2008
Obituary **2009**:3
Giamatti, Paul 1967- **2009**:4
Gless, Sharon 1944- **1989**:3
Gobel, George 1920(?)-1991
Obituary **1991**:4
Goldberg, Gary David 1944- **1989**:4
Goldberg, Leonard 1934- **1988**:4
Gossett, Louis, Jr. 1936- **1989**:3
Goulet, Robert 1933-2007
Obituary **2008**:4
Grammer, Kelsey 1955(?)- **1995**:1
Griffin, Merv 1925-2008
Obituary **2008**:4
Grodin, Charles 1935- **1997**:3
Guest, Christopher 1948- **2004**:2
Gupta, Sanjay 1969- **2009**:4
Haggis, Paul 1953- **2006**:4
Hanks, Tom 1956- **1989**:2
Hartman, Phil 1948-1998 **1996**:2
Obituary **1998**:4
Heche, Anne 1969- **1999**:1
Heigl, Katharine 1978- **2008**:3
Helgenberger, Marg 1958- **2002**:2
Henning, Doug 1947-1999
Obituary **2000**:3
Hopkins, Anthony 1937- **1992**:4
Howard, Trevor 1916-1988

Obituary **1988**:2
Huffman, Felicity 1962- **2006**:2
Izzard, Eddie 1963- **2008**:1
Janney, Allison 1959- **2003**:3
Jennings, Peter Charles 1938- **1997**:2
Johnson, Don 1949- **1986**:1
Jones, Tommy Lee 1947(?)- **1994**:2
Joyce, William 1957- **2006**:1
Kavner, Julie 1951- **1992**:3
Kaye, Danny 1913-1987
    Obituary **1987**:2
Keeshan, Bob 1927-2004
    Obituary **2005**:2
Kimmel, Jimmy 1967- **2009**:2
Knight, Ted 1923-1986
    Obituary **1986**:4
Knotts, Don 1924-2006
    Obituary **2007**:1
Koppel, Ted 1940- **1989**:1
Kuralt, Charles 1934-1997
    Obituary **1998**:3
LaBeouf, Shia 1986- **2008**:1
LaPaglia, Anthony 1959- **2004**:4
Larroquette, John 1947- **1986**:2
Lemmon, Jack 1925- **1998**:4
    Obituary **2002**:3
Letterman, David 1947- **1989**:3
Levinson, Barry 1932- **1989**:3
Levy, Eugene 1946- **2004**:3
Lewis, Shari 1934-1998 **1993**:1
    Obituary **1999**:1
Liberace 1919-1987
    Obituary **1987**:2
Linney, Laura 1964- **2009**:4
Lucci, Susan 1946(?)- **1999**:4
MacFarlane, Seth 1973- **2006**:1
Malkovich, John 1953- **1988**:2
Mantegna, Joe 1947- **1992**:1
McFarlane, Todd 1961- **1999**:1
Melendez, Bill 1916-2008
    Obituary **2009**:4
Meredith, Burgess 1909-1997
    Obituary **1998**:1
Merkerson, S. Epatha 1952- **2006**:4
Messing, Debra 1968- **2004**:4
Midler, Bette 1945- **1989**:4
Miller, Arthur 1915- **1999**:4
Mirren, Helen 1945- **2005**:1
Moore, Julianne 1960- **1998**:1
Moore, Mary Tyler 1936- **1996**:2
Murray, Bill 1950- **2002**:4
Myers, Mike 1964(?)- **1992**:3
North, Alex 1910- **1986**:3
O'Brien, Conan 1963(?)- **1994**:1
O'Connor, Carroll 1924-2001
    Obituary **2002**:3
O'Connor, Donald 1925-2003
    Obituary **2004**:4
Olmos, Edward James 1947- **1990**:1
Olson, Johnny 1910(?)-1985
    Obituary **1985**:4
Page, Geraldine 1924-1987
    Obituary **1987**:4
Palance, Jack 1919-2006
    Obituary **2008**:1
Paulsen, Pat 1927-1997
    Obituary **1997**:4
Piven, Jeremy 1965- **2007**:3
Poston, Tom 1921-2007
    Obituary **2008**:3
Pryor, Richard **1999**:3
Randall, Tony 1920-2004

Obituary **2005**:3
Ray, Rachael 1968- **2007**:1
Redgrave, Vanessa 1937- **1989**:2
Ritter, John 1948- **2003**:4
Rivera, Geraldo 1943- **1989**:1
Rivers, Joan 1933- **2005**:3
Roberts, Doris 1930- **2003**:4
Rock, Chris 1967(?)- **1998**:1
Rolle, Esther 1922-1998
    Obituary **1999**:2
Rollins, Howard E., Jr. 1950- **1986**:1
Romano, Ray 1957- **2001**:4
Rose, Charlie 1943- **1994**:2
Saralegui, Cristina 1948- **1999**:2
Schulz, Charles M. 1922- **1998**:1
Scott, George C. 1927-1999
    Obituary **2000**:2
Seymour, Jane 1951- **1994**:4
Sheldon, Sidney 1917-2007
    Obituary **2008**:2
Silvers, Phil 1912-1985
    Obituary **1985**:4
Sinatra, Frank 1915-1998
    Obituary **1998**:4
Sorkin, Aaron 1961- **2003**:2
Springer, Jerry 1944- **1998**:4
Stack, Robert 1919-2003
    Obituary **2004**:2
Stapleton, Maureen 1925-2006
    Obituary **2007**:2
Stein, Ben 1944- **2001**:1
Stiller, Ben 1965- **1999**:1
Streep, Meryl 1949- **1990**:2
Susskind, David 1920-1987
    Obituary **1987**:2
Tharp, Twyla 1942- **1992**:4
Tillstrom, Burr 1917-1985
    Obituary **1986**:1
Vieira, Meredith 1953- **2001**:3
Vonnegut, Kurt 1922- **1998**:4
Walker, Nancy 1922-1992
    Obituary **1992**:3
Walters, Barbara 1931- **1998**:3
Ward, Sela 1956- **2001**:3
Warden, Jack 1920-2006
    Obituary **2007**:3
Waterston, Sam 1940- **2006**:1
Weitz, Bruce 1943- **1985**:4
Wilson, Flip 1933-1998
    Obituary **1999**:2
Winfield, Paul 1941-2004
    Obituary **2005**:2
Witt, Katarina 1966(?)- **1991**:3
Woods, James 1947- **1988**:3
Wyatt, Jane 1910-2006
    Obituary **2008**:1
Young, Robert 1907-1998
    Obituary **1999**:1

**Encore Books**
    Schlessinger, David
        Brief entry **1985**:1

**Energy Machine**
    Newman, Joseph 1936- **1987**:1

**Entrepreneurs**
    Akin, Phil
        Brief entry **1987**:3
    Allen, John 1930- **1992**:1
    Alter, Hobie
        Brief entry **1985**:1

Aoki, Rocky 1940- **1990**:2
Arison, Ted 1924- **1990**:3
Aurre, Laura
    Brief entry **1986**:3
Bauer, Eddie 1899-1986
    Obituary **1986**:3
Ben & Jerry **1991**:3
Berlusconi, Silvio 1936(?)- **1994**:4
Black, Conrad 1944- **1986**:2
Bloomberg, Michael 1942- **1997**:1
Boiardi, Hector 1897-1985
    Obituary **1985**:3
Bose, Amar
    Brief entry **1986**:4
Branson, Richard 1951- **1987**:1
Buffett, Warren 1930- **1995**:2
Burr, Donald Calvin 1941- **1985**:3
Bushnell, Nolan 1943- **1985**:1
Campeau, Robert 1923- **1990**:1
Clark, Jim 1944- **1997**:1
Covey, Stephen R. 1932- **1994**:4
Craig, Sid and Jenny **1993**:4
Cray, Seymour R. 1925-1996
    Brief entry **1986**:3
    Obituary **1997**:2
Cummings, Sam 1927- **1986**:3
Dell, Michael 1965- **1996**:2
DiFranco, Ani 1970(?)- **1997**:1
Ertegun, Ahmet 1923- **1986**:3
Garcia, Joe
    Brief entry **1986**:4
Gates, Bill 1955- **1987**:4
Gatien, Peter
    Brief entry **1986**:1
Gillett, George 1938- **1988**:1
Graham, Bill 1931-1991 **1986**:4
    Obituary **1992**:2
Guccione, Bob 1930- **1986**:1
Haney, Chris
    Brief entry **1985**:1
Herrera, Carolina 1939- **1997**:1
Hilbert, Stephen C. 1946- **1997**:4
Honda, Soichiro 1906-1991
    Obituary **1986**:1
Hughes, Mark 1956- **1985**:3
Hyatt, Joel 1950- **1985**:3
Ilitch, Mike 1929- **1993**:4
Inatome, Rick 1953- **1985**:4
Isaacson, Portia
    Brief entry **1986**:1
Jacuzzi, Candido 1903-1986
    Obituary **1987**:1
Jones, Arthur A. 1924(?)- **1985**:3
Katz, Lillian 1927- **1987**:4
Kerkorian, Kirk 1917- **1996**:2
Kingsborough, Donald
    Brief entry **1986**:2
Knight, Philip H. 1938- **1994**:1
Koplovitz, Kay 1945- **1986**:3
Kurzweil, Raymond 1948- **1986**:3
Mahesh Yogi, Maharishi
    1911(?)- **1991**:3
Markle, C. Wilson 1938- **1988**:1
Marriott, J. Willard 1900-1985
    Obituary **1985**:4
McGowan, William 1927- **1985**:2
McIntyre, Richard
    Brief entry **1986**:2
Melman, Richard
    Brief entry **1986**:1
Monaghan, Tom 1937- **1985**:1
Moody, John 1943- **1985**:3

Morgan, Dodge 1932(?)- **1987**:1
Murdoch, Rupert 1931- **1988**:4
Murray, Arthur 1895-1991
    Obituary **1991**:3
Olsen, Kenneth H. 1926- **1986**:4
Paulucci, Jeno
    Brief entry **1986**:3
Penske, Roger 1937- **1988**:3
Pocklington, Peter H. 1941- **1985**:2
Radocy, Robert
    Brief entry **1986**:3
Roberts, Xavier 1955- **1985**:3
Roddick, Anita 1943(?)- **1989**:4
Sasakawa, Ryoichi
    Brief entry **1988**:1
Schlessinger, David
    Brief entry **1985**:1
Smith, Frederick W. 1944- **1985**:4
Tanny, Vic 1912(?)-1985
    Obituary **1985**:3
Thalheimer, Richard 1948-
    Brief entry **1988**:3
Thomas, Michel 1911(?)- **1987**:4
Tompkins, Susie
    Brief entry **1987**:2
Trump, Donald 1946- **1989**:2
Trump, Ivana 1949- **1995**:2
Waitt, Ted 1963(?)- **1997**:4
Wilson, Jerry
    Brief entry **1986**:2
Wilson, Peter C. 1913-1984
    Obituary **1985**:2
Wynn, Stephen A. 1942- **1994**:3
Zanker, Bill
    Brief entry **1987**:3

**Environmentalism**
Albert, Eddie 1906-2005
    Obituary **2006**:3
Beinecke, Frances 1960(?)- **2007**:4
Ben & Jerry **1991**:3
Benchley, Peter 1940-2006
    Obituary **2007**:1
Brockovich-Ellis, Erin 1960- **2003**:3
Brower, David 1912- **1990**:4
Brown, Howard and Karen
    Stewart **2007**:3
Denver, John 1943-1997
    Obituary **1998**:1
Douglas, Marjory Stoneman
    1890-1998 **1993**:1
    Obituary **1998**:4
Foreman, Dave 1947(?)- **1990**:3
Goodman, Drew and Myra **2007**:4
Gore, Albert, Jr. 1948(?)- **1993**:2
Hair, Jay D. 1945- **1994**:3
Hayse, Bruce 1949(?)- **2004**:3
Hodges, Carl 1937- **2008**:1
Johnson, Lady Bird 1912-2007
    Obituary **2008**:4
Korchinsky, Mike 1961- **2004**:2
Krupp, Fred 1954- **2008**:3
Lowry, Adam and Eric Ryan **2008**:1
Maathai, Wangari 1940- **2005**:3
McDonough, William 1951- **2003**:1
Nelson, Gaylord A. 1914-2005
    Obituary **2006**:3
Ngau, Harrison **1991**:3
Nixon, Bob 1954(?)- **2006**:4
Plotkin, Mark 1955(?)- **1994**:3
Puleston, Dennis 1905-2001
    Obituary **2002**:2
Redmond, Tim 1947- **2008**:1

Sams, Craig 1944- **2007**:3
Seo, Danny 1977- **2008**:3
Sethi, Simran 1971(?)- **2008**:1
Stephens, Arran and Ratana **2008**:4
Strong, Maurice 1929- **1993**:1
Strummer, Joe 1952-2002
    Obituary **2004**:1
Styler, Trudie 1954- **2009**:1
Suckling, Kierán 1964- **2009**:2
Vitousek, Peter 1949- **2003**:1
Whelan, Tensie 1960- **2007**:1
Yeang, Ken 1948- **2008**:3

**Environmental Protection Agency [EPA]**
Browner, Carol M. 1955- **1994**:1
Jackson, Lisa P. 1962- **2009**:4

**Episcopal Church**
Browning, Edmond
    Brief entry **1986**:2
Harris, Barbara **1996**:3
Harris, Barbara 1930- **1989**:3
Jefferts Schori, Katharine 1954- **2007**:2
Spong, John 1931- **1991**:3

**Espionage**
Philby, Kim 1912-1988
    Obituary **1988**:3

**Esprit clothing**
Krogner, Heinz 1941(?)- **2004**:2
Tompkins, Susie
    Brief entry **1987**:2

**Essence magazine**
Gillespie, Marcia 1944- **1999**:4
Lewis, Edward T. 1940- **1999**:4
Taylor, Susan L. 1946- **1998**:2

**Estee Lauder**
Baxter, Pamela 1949- **2009**:4
Burns, Robin 1953(?)- **1991**:2
Lauder, Estee 1908(?)- **1992**:2

**Ethnobotany**
Plotkin, Mark 1955(?)- **1994**:3

**European Commission**
Delors, Jacques 1925- **1990**:2

**Euthanasia**
Cruzan, Nancy 1957(?)-1990
    Obituary **1991**:3
Humphry, Derek 1931(?)- **1992**:2
Kevorkian, Jack 1928(?)- **1991**:3

**Excel Communications**
Troutt, Kenny A. 1948- **1998**:1

**Exploration**
Ballard, Robert D. 1942- **1998**:4
Fiennes, Ranulph 1944- **1990**:3
Hempleman-Adams, David 1956- **2004**:3
Horn, Mike 1966- **2009**:3
Steger, Will 1945(?)- **1990**:4

**ExxonMobil Oil**
Raymond, Lee R. 1930- **2000**:3

**Fabbrica Italiana Automobili Torino SpA [Fiat]**
Agnelli, Giovanni 1921- **1989**:4

**Faith Center Church**
Scott, Gene
    Brief entry **1986**:1

**Fallon McElligott**
McElligott, Thomas J. 1943- **1987**:4

**Famous Amos Chocolate Chip Cookies**
Amos, Wally 1936- **2000**:1

**Fashion**
Adams-Geller, Paige 1969(?)- **2006**:4
Agnes B 1941- **2002**:3
Albou, Sophie 1967- **2007**:2
Allard, Linda 1940- **2003**:2
Armani, Giorgio 1934(?)- **1991**:2
Avedon, Richard 1923- **1993**:4
Bacall, Lauren 1924- **1997**:3
Badgley, Mark and James
    Mischka **2004**:3
Ball, Michael 1964(?)- **2007**:3
Banks, Jeffrey 1953- **1998**:2
Beene, Geoffrey 1927-2004
    Obituary **2005**:4
Benetton, Luciano 1935- **1988**:1
Blahnik, Manolo 1942- **2000**:2
Blass, Bill 1922-2002
    Obituary **2003**:3
Bohbot, Michele 1959(?)- **2004**:2
Bravo, Rose Marie 1951(?)- **2005**:3
Brown, Howard and Karen
    Stewart **2007**:3
Bruni, Carla 1967- **2009**:3
Burch, Tory 1966- **2009**:3
Cameron, David
    Brief entry **1988**:1
Cardin, Pierre 1922- **2003**:3
Cassini, Oleg 1913-2006
    Obituary **2007**:2
Cavalli, Roberto 1940- **2004**:4
Chalayan, Hussein 1970- **2003**:2
Charney, Dov 1969- **2008**:2
Charron, Paul 1942- **2004**:1
Choo, Jimmy 1957(?)- **2006**:3
Claiborne, Liz 1929- **1986**:3
Cole, Anne 1930(?)- **2007**:3
Cole, Kenneth 1954(?)- **2003**:1
Crawford, Cindy 1966- **1993**:3
D'Alessio, Kitty
    Brief entry **1987**:3
de la Renta, Oscar 1932- **2005**:4
Dickinson, Janice 1953- **2005**:2
Dolce, Domenico and Stefano
    Gabbana **2005**:4
Duarte, Henry 1963(?)- **2003**:3
Ecko, Marc 1972- **2006**:3
Elbaz, Alber 1961- **2008**:1
Ellis, Perry 1940-1986
    Obituary **1986**:3
Erte 1892-1990
    Obituary **1990**:4
Eve 1978- **2004**:3
Ferre, Gianfranco 1944-2007
    Obituary **2008**:3
Ferretti, Alberta 1950(?)- **2004**:1
Ford, Tom 1962- **1999**:3
Frankfort, Lew 1946- **2008**:2

Galliano, John 1960- **2005**:2
Gaultier, Jean-Paul 1952- **1998**:1
Giannulli, Mossimo 1963- **2002**:3
Green, Philip 1952- **2008**:2
Gregory, Rogan 1972- **2008**:2
Gucci, Maurizio
  Brief entry **1985**:4
Haas, Robert D. 1942- **1986**:4
Halston 1932-1990
  Obituary **1990**:3
Hernandez, Lazaro and Jack
  McCollough **2008**:4
Herrera, Carolina 1939- **1997**:1
Hilfiger, Tommy 1952- **1993**:3
Hindmarch, Anya 1969- **2008**:2
Jacobs, Marc 1963- **2002**:3
Johnson, Betsey 1942- **1996**:2
Johnson, Beverly 1952- **2005**:2
Kamali, Norma 1945- **1989**:1
Karan, Donna 1948- **1988**:1
Kelly, Patrick 1954(?)-1990
  Obituary **1990**:2
Kim, Eugenia 1974(?)- **2006**:1
Klein, Calvin 1942- **1996**:2
Klensch, Elsa **2001**:4
Korchinsky, Mike 1961- **2004**:2
Kors, Michael 1959- **2000**:4
Krogner, Heinz 1941(?)- **2004**:2
Lacroix, Christian 1951- **2005**:2
Lagerfeld, Karl 1938- **1999**:4
Lam, Derek 1966- **2009**:2
Lang, Helmut 1956- **1999**:2
Lange, Liz 1967(?)- **2003**:4
Lauren, Ralph 1939- **1990**:1
Leigh, Dorian 1917-2008
  Obituary **2009**:3
Lepore, Nanette 1964(?)- **2006**:4
Lhuillier, Monique 1971(?)- **2007**:4
Lim, Phillip 1974(?)- **2008**:1
Louboutin, Christian 1963- **2006**:1
Macdonald, Julien 1973(?)- **2005**:3
Madden, Steve 1958- **2007**:2
Margolis, Bobby 1948(?)- **2007**:2
Mashouf, Manny 1938(?)- **2008**:1
Matadin, Vinoodh and Inez van
  Lamsweerde **2007**:4
McLaughlin, Betsy 1962(?)- **2004**:3
Mellinger, Frederick 1924(?)-1990
  Obituary **1990**:4
Mello, Dawn 1938(?)- **1992**:2
Miller, Nicole 1951(?)- **1995**:4
Mills, Malia 1966- **2003**:1
Miyake, Issey 1939- **1985**:2
Mizrahi, Isaac 1961- **1991**:1
Murakami, Takashi 1962- **2004**:2
Natori, Josie 1947- **1994**:3
Nipon, Albert
  Brief entry **1986**:4
Oldham, Todd 1961- **1995**:4
Olsen, Sigrid 1953- **2007**:1
Panichgul, Thakoon 1974- **2009**:4
Parker, Suzy 1932-2003
  Obituary **2004**:2
Persson, Stefan 1947- **2004**:1
Picasso, Paloma 1949- **1991**:1
Porizkova, Paulina
  Brief entry **1986**:4
Posen, Zac 1980- **2009**:3
Potok, Anna Maximilian
  Brief entry **1985**:2
Prada, Miuccia 1950(?)- **1996**:1
Pressler, Paul 1956(?)- **2003**:4

Queer Eye for the Straight Guy
  cast **2004**:3
Rhodes, Zandra 1940- **1986**:2
Rodriguez, Narciso 1961- **2005**:1
Ronson, Charlotte 1977(?)- **2007**:3
Rosso, Renzo 1955- **2005**:2
Rykiel, Sonia 1930- **2000**:3
Saint Laurent, Yves 1936-2008
  Obituary **2009**:3
Sander, Jil 1943- **1995**:2
Scavullo, Francesco 1921-2004
  Obituary **2005**:1
Schwartz, Allen 1945(?)- **2008**:2
Segal, Shelli 1955(?)- **2005**:3
Skaist-Levy, Pam and Gela
  Taylor **2005**:1
Smith, Paul 1946- **2002**:4
Smith, Willi 1948-1987
  Obituary **1987**:3
Snyder, Ron 1956(?)- **2007**:4
Som, Peter 1971- **2009**:1
Spade, Kate 1962- **2003**:1
Sprouse, Stephen 1953-2004
  Obituary **2005**:2
Stefani, Gwen 1969- **2005**:4
Sui, Anna 1955(?)- **1995**:1
Takada, Kenzo 1938- **2003**:2
Temperley, Alice 1975- **2008**:2
Thomas-Graham, Pamela
  1963- **2007**:1
Tilberis, Elizabeth 1947(?)- **1994**:3
Timberlake, Justin 1981- **2008**:4
Tompkins, Susie
  Brief entry **1987**:2
Touitou, Jean 1952(?)- **2008**:4
Trump, Ivana 1949- **1995**:2
Tyler, Richard 1948(?)- **1995**:3
Valli, Giambattista 1966- **2008**:3
Valvo, Carmen Marc 1954- **2003**:4
Varvatos, John 1956(?)- **2006**:2
Versace, Donatella 1955- **1999**:1
Versace, Gianni 1946-1997
  Brief entry **1988**:1
  Obituary **1998**:2
von Furstenberg, Diane 1946- **1994**:2
Wachner, Linda 1946- **1988**:3
Wang, Vera 1949- **1998**:4
Westwood, Vivienne 1941- **1998**:3

**Federal Bureau of Investigation [FBI]**
  Freeh, Louis J. 1950- **1994**:2
  Kennedy, Weldon 1938- **1997**:3
  Rowley, Coleen 1955(?)- **2004**:2

**Federal Communications Commission
(FCC)**
  Hundt, Reed Eric 1948- **1997**:2
  Thomas, Edmond J. 1943(?)- **2005**:1

**Federal Express Corp.**
  Smith, Frederick W. 1944- **1985**:4

**Federal Reserve System**
  Greenspan, Alan 1926- **1992**:2

**Federal Trade Commission [FTC]**
  Oliver, Daniel 1939- **1988**:2

**Film Criticism**
  Kael, Pauline 1919-2001 **2000**:4
  Obituary **2002**:4

**Fire fighting**
  Adair, Red 1915- **1987**:3

**Fireworks**
  Grucci, Felix 1905- **1987**:1

**First Jersey Securities**
  Brennan, Robert E. 1943(?)- **1988**:1

**Florida Marlins baseball team**
  Leyland, Jim 1944- **1998**:2
  Lowell, Mike 1974- **2003**:2
  Sheffield, Gary 1968- **1998**:1

**Food and Drug Administration [FDA]**
  Kessler, David 1951- **1992**:1

**Football**
  Aikman, Troy 1966- **1994**:2
  Barnes, Ernie 1938- **1997**:4
  Bell, Ricky 1955-1984
    Obituary **1985**:1
  Bledsoe, Drew 1972- **1995**:1
  Bosworth, Brian 1965- **1989**:1
  Brown, Jim 1936- **1993**:2
  Brown, Paul 1908-1991
    Obituary **1992**:1
  Cunningham, Randall 1963- **1990**:1
  Davis, Terrell 1972- **1998**:2
  Elway, John 1960- **1990**:3
  Esiason, Boomer 1961- **1991**:1
  Flutie, Doug 1962- **1999**:2
  Gault, Willie 1960- **1991**:2
  Grange, Red 1903-1991
    Obituary **1991**:3
  Hayes, Woody 1913-1987
    Obituary **1987**:2
  Holtz, Lou 1937- **1986**:4
  Irvin, Michael 1966- **1996**:3
  Jackson, Bo 1962- **1986**:3
  Johnson, Jimmy 1943- **1993**:3
  Johnson, Keyshawn 1972- **2000**:4
  Jones, Jerry 1942- **1994**:4
  Kelly, Jim 1960- **1991**:4
  Kemp, Jack 1935- **1990**:4
  Landry, Tom 1924-2000
    Obituary **2000**:3
  Lewis, Ray 1975- **2001**:3
  Madden, John 1936- **1995**:1
  Manning, Eli 1981- **2008**:4
  Manning, Peyton 1976- **2007**:4
  Matuszak, John 1951(?)-1989
    Obituary **1989**:4
  McMahon, Jim 1959- **1985**:4
  Monk, Art 1957- **1993**:2
  Montana, Joe 1956- **1989**:2
  Moon, Warren 1956- **1991**:3
  Moss, Randy 1977- **1999**:3
  Okoye, Christian 1961- **1990**:2
  Parker, Willie 1980- **2009**:3
  Payton, Walter 1954-1999
    Obituary **2000**:2
  Rice, Jerry 1962- **1990**:4
  Robinson, Eddie 1919-2007
    Obituary **2008**:2
  Romo, Tony 1980- **2008**:3
  Rypien, Mark 1962- **1992**:3
  Sanders, Barry 1968- **1992**:1
  Sanders, Deion 1967- **1992**:4
  Schembechler, Bo 1929(?)- **1990**:3
  Sharpe, Sterling 1965- **1994**:3

Shula, Don 1930- **1992**:2
Smith, Emmitt **1994**:1
Smith, Jerry 1943-1986
  Obituary **1987**:1
Tagliabue, Paul 1940- **1990**:2
Taylor, Lawrence 1959- **1987**:3
Testaverde, Vinny 1962- **1987**:2
Thomas, Derrick 1967-2000
  Obituary **2000**:3
Thomas, Thurman 1966- **1993**:1
Trask, Amy 1961- **2003**:3
Unitas, Johnny 1933-2002
  Obituary **2003**:4
Upshaw, Gene 1945- **1988**:1
Walsh, Bill 1931- **1987**:4
Warner, Kurt 1971- **2000**:3
White, Reggie 1961- **1993**:4
Williams, Doug 1955- **1988**:2
Young, Steve 1961- **1995**:2

**Forbes, Inc.**
  Forbes, Steve 1947- **1996**:2

**Ford Foundation**
  Berresford, Susan V. 1943- **1998**:4

**Ford Motor Co.**
  Devine, John M. 1944- **2003**:2
  Ford, Henry II 1917-1987
    Obituary **1988**:1
  Ford, William Clay, Jr. 1957- **1999**:1
  Lutz, Robert A. 1932- **1990**:1
  McNamara, Robert S. 1916- **1995**:4
  Petersen, Donald Eugene 1926- **1985**:1
  Stevens, Anne 1949(?)- **2006**:3
  Trotman, Alex 1933- **1995**:4

**Fox Broadcasting Co.**
  Ancier, Garth 1957- **1989**:1
  Berman, Gail 1957(?)- **2006**:1
  Carter, Chris 1956- **2000**:1
  Diller, Barry 1942- **1991**:1
  Murdoch, Rupert 1931- **1988**:4
  Wayans, Keenen Ivory
    1958(?)- **1991**:1

**Frederick's of Hollywood**
  Mellinger, Frederick 1924(?)-1990
    Obituary **1990**:4

**Freedom House**
  Lord, Bette Bao 1938- **1994**:1

**Friends of the Earth [FOE]**
  Brower, David 1912- **1990**:4
  Ngau, Harrison **1991**:3

**Friends of the Everglades**
  Douglas, Marjory Stoneman
    1890-1998 **1993**:1
    Obituary **1998**:4

**Future Computing, Inc.**
  Isaacson, Portia
    Brief entry **1986**:1

**Gallaudet University**
  Jordan, King 1943(?)- **1990**:1

**Gannett Co., Inc.**
  Neuharth, Allen H. 1924- **1986**:1

**Gap Inc.**
  Drexler, Millard S. 1944- **1990**:3
  Pressler, Paul 1956(?)- **2003**:4

**Garth Fagan Dance**
  Fagan, Garth 1940- **2000**:1

**Gateway 2000**
  Waitt, Ted 1963(?)- **1997**:4

**Gay rights**
  Achtenberg, Roberta **1993**:4
  Cammermeyer, Margarethe
    1942- **1995**:2
  Crisp, Quentin 1908-1999
    Obituary **2000**:3
  Frank, Barney 1940- **1989**:2
  Goldhaber, Fred
    Brief entry **1986**:3
  Matlovich, Leonard P. 1944(?)-1988
    Obituary **1988**:4
  Newsom, Gavin 1967- **2009**:3
  Robinson, V. Gene 1947- **2004**:4
  Tafel, Richard 1962- **2000**:4

**Genentech, Inc.**
  Boyer, Herbert Wayne 1936- **1985**:1

**General Electric Co.**
  Fudge, Ann 1951- **2000**:3
  Immelt, Jeffrey R. 1956- **2001**:2
  Welch, Jack 1935- **1993**:3

**General Motors Corp. [GM]**
  Devine, John M. 1944- **2003**:2
  Estes, Pete 1916-1988
    Obituary **1988**:3
  Jordan, Charles M. 1927- **1989**:4
  Lutz, Robert A. 1932- **1990**:1
  Moore, Michael 1954(?)- **1990**:3
  Smith, Jack 1938- **1994**:3
  Smith, Roger 1925- **1990**:3
  Stempel, Robert 1933- **1991**:3

**Genetics**
  Boyer, Herbert Wayne 1936- **1985**:1
  Gilbert, Walter 1932- **1988**:3
  Haseltine, William A. 1944- **1999**:2
  King, Mary-Claire 1946- **1998**:3
  Kornberg, Arthur 1918(?)- **1992**:1
  Krim, Mathilde 1926- **1989**:2
  Lewis, Edward B. 1918-2004
    Obituary **2005**:4
  Nuesslein-Volhard, Christiane
    1942- **1998**:1
  Rifkin, Jeremy 1945- **1990**:3
  Rosenberg, Steven 1940- **1989**:1
  Wigler, Michael
    Brief entry **1985**:1

**Genome Corp.**
  Gilbert, Walter 1932- **1988**:3

**Geology**
  Rosendahl, Bruce R.
    Brief entry **1986**:4

**Georgetown University**
  Healy, Timothy S. 1923- **1990**:2

**Georgetown University basketball team**
  Thompson, John 1941- **1988**:3

**Gesundheit! Institute**
  Adams, Patch 1945(?)- **1999**:2

**Gianni Versace Group**
  Versace, Donatella 1955- **1999**:1
  Versace, Gianni 1946-1997
    Brief entry **1988**:1
    Obituary **1998**:2

**Gillett Group**
  Gillett, George 1938- **1988**:1

**Golden Globe Awards**
  Abrams, J. J. 1966- **2007**:3
  Affleck, Ben 1972- **1999**:1
  Arkin, Alan 1934- **2007**:4
  Bacall, Lauren 1924- **1997**:3
  Bakula, Scott 1954- **2003**:1
  Bardem, Javier 1969- **2008**:4
  Baron Cohen, Sacha 1971- **2007**:3
  Bateman, Jason 1969- **2005**:3
  Beatty, Warren 1937- **2000**:1
  Bernstein, Elmer 1922-2004
    Obituary **2005**:4
  Blanchett, Cate 1969- **1999**:3
  Boyle, Danny 1956- **2009**:4
  Broadbent, Jim 1949- **2008**:4
  Bronson, Charles 1921-2003
    Obituary **2004**:4
  Burnett, Carol 1933- **2000**:3
  Caine, Michael 1933- **2000**:4
  Carell, Steve 1963- **2006**:4
  Carter, Chris 1956- **2000**:1
  Cattrall, Kim 1956- **2003**:3
  Cheadle, Don 1964- **2002**:1
  Cher 1946- **1993**:1
  Chiklis, Michael 1963- **2003**:3
  Christie, Julie 1941- **2008**:4
  Connelly, Jennifer 1970- **2002**:4
  Cooper, Chris 1951- **2004**:1
  Coppola, Sofia 1971- **2004**:3
  Cosby, Bill 1937- **1999**:2
  Curtis, Jamie Lee 1958- **1995**:1
  Damon, Matt 1970- **1999**:1
  Danes, Claire 1979- **1999**:4
  Dench, Judi 1934- **1999**:4
  De Niro, Robert 1943- **1999**:1
  Dennehy, Brian 1938- **2002**:1
  Depardieu, Gerard 1948- **1991**:2
  Downey, Robert, Jr. 1965- **2007**:1
  Duvall, Robert 1931- **1999**:3
  Elfman, Jenna 1971- **1999**:4
  Farrow, Mia 1945- **1998**:3
  Fell, Norman 1924-1998
    Obituary **1999**:2
  Fiennes, Ralph 1962- **1996**:2
  Finney, Albert 1936- **2003**:3
  Flockhart, Calista 1964- **1998**:4
  Ford, Glenn 1916-2006
    Obituary **2007**:4
  Garner, Jennifer 1972- **2003**:1
  Getty, Estelle 1923-2008
    Obituary **2009**:3
  Giamatti, Paul 1967- **2009**:4
  Goldberg, Whoopi 1955- **1993**:3

Hallstrom, Lasse 1946- **2002**:3
Hamm, Jon 1971- **2009**:2
Hanks, Tom 1956- **1989**:2
Hargitay, Mariska 1964- **2006**:2
Harris, Ed 1950- **2002**:2
Hatcher, Teri 1964- **2005**:4
Hawkins, Sally 1976- **2009**:4
Heston, Charlton 1924- **1999**:4
Hoffman, Dustin 1937- **2005**:4
Hoffman, Philip Seymour
    1967- **2006**:3
Hudson, Jennifer 1981- **2008**:1
Huffman, Felicity 1962- **2006**:2
Irons, Jeremy 1948- **1991**:4
Jackson, Peter 1961- **2004**:4
Johnson, Don 1949- **1986**:1
Jolie, Angelina 1975- **2000**:2
Keaton, Diane 1946- **1997**:1
Lansbury, Angela 1925- **1993**:1
Laurie, Hugh 1959- **2007**:2
Leigh, Janet 1927-2004
    Obituary **2005**:4
Lemmon, Jack 1925- **1998**:4
    Obituary **2002**:3
Linney, Laura 1964- **2009**:4
Lucas, George 1944- **1999**:4
Luhrmann, Baz 1962- **2002**:3
Matlin, Marlee 1965- **1992**:2
Matthau, Walter 1920- **2000**:3
Merkerson, S. Epatha 1952- **2006**:4
Minghella, Anthony 1954- **2004**:3
Moore, Dudley 1935-2002
    Obituary **2003**:2
Moore, Mary Tyler 1936- **1996**:2
Norton, Edward 1969- **2000**:2
O'Connor, Donald 1925-2003
    Obituary **2004**:4
Owen, Clive 1964- **2006**:2
Pakula, Alan 1928-1998
    Obituary **1999**:2
Paquin, Anna 1982- **2009**:4
Payne, Alexander 1961- **2005**:4
Peters, Bernadette 1948- **2000**:1
Redgrave, Lynn 1943- **1999**:3
Rhys Meyers, Jonathan 1977- **2007**:1
Ritter, John 1948- **2003**:4
Roberts, Julia 1967- **1991**:3
Russell, Keri 1976- **2000**:1
Sheen, Martin 1940- **2002**:1
Spacek, Sissy 1949- **2003**:1
Streisand, Barbra 1942- **1992**:2
Sutherland, Kiefer 1966- **2002**:4
Swank, Hilary 1974- **2000**:3
Taylor, Lili 1967- **2000**:2
Thompson, Emma 1959- **1993**:2
Ullman, Tracey 1961- **1988**:3
Washington, Denzel 1954- **1993**:2
Waterston, Sam 1940- **2006**:1
Weisz, Rachel 1971- **2006**:4

**Golden State Warriors basketball team**
Sprewell, Latrell 1970- **1999**:4
Webber, Chris 1973- **1994**:1

**Golf**
Allenby, Robert 1971- **2007**:1
Azinger, Paul 1960- **1995**:2
Baker, Kathy
    Brief entry **1986**:1
Callaway, Ely 1919-2001
    Obituary **2002**:3
Chen, T.C.

Brief entry **1987**:3
Couples, Fred 1959- **1994**:4
Creamer, Paula 1986- **2006**:2
Curtis, Ben 1977- **2004**:2
Duval, David 1971- **2000**:3
Faldo, Nick 1957- **1993**:3
Furyk, Jim 1970- **2004**:2
Hogan, Ben 1912-1997
    Obituary **1997**:4
Irwin, Hale 1945- **2005**:2
Kerr, Cristie 1977- **2008**:2
Kite, Tom 1949- **1990**:3
Lopez, Nancy 1957- **1989**:3
Martin, Casey 1972- **2002**:1
Mickelson, Phil 1970- **2004**:4
Nelson, Byron 1912-2006
    Obituary **2007**:4
Norman, Greg 1955- **1988**:3
Ochoa, Lorena 1981- **2007**:4
Pak, Se Ri 1977- **1999**:4
Pavin, Corey 1959- **1996**:4
Peete, Calvin 1943- **1985**:4
Sarazen, Gene 1902-1999
    Obituary **1999**:4
Singh, Vijay 1963- **2000**:4
Snead, Sam 1912-2002
    Obituary **2003**:3
Strange, Curtis 1955- **1988**:4
Webb, Karrie 1974- **2000**:4
Weir, Mike 1970- **2004**:1
Whaley, Suzy 1966- **2003**:4
Woods, Tiger 1975- **1995**:4

**Gorillas**
Fossey, Dian 1932-1985
    Obituary **1986**:1

**Gospel music**
Adams, Yolanda 1961- **2008**:2
Dorsey, Thomas A. 1899-1993
    Obituary **1993**:3
Franklin, Aretha 1942- **1998**:3
Houston, Cissy 1933- **1999**:3
Reese, Della 1931- **1999**:2
Staples, Roebuck Pops 1915-2000
    Obituary **2001**:3

**Grammy Awards**
Adams, Yolanda 1961- **2008**:2
Adele 1988- **2009**:4
Aguilera, Christina 1980- **2000**:4
Anderson, Marion 1897-1993
    Obituary **1993**:4
Anthony, Marc 1969- **2000**:3
Apple, Fiona 1977- **2006**:3
Arrested Development **1994**:2
Ashanti 1980- **2004**:1
Badu, Erykah 1971- **2000**:4
Baker, Anita 1958- **1987**:4
Bangalter, Thomas 1975- (
See Daft Punk)
Battle, Kathleen 1948- **1998**:1
Beck 1970- **2000**:2
Bee Gees, The **1997**:4
Benatar, Pat 1953- **1986**:1
Bennett, Tony 1926- **1994**:4
Berry, Chuck 1926- **2001**:2
Beyonce 1981- **2009**:3
Blades, Ruben 1948- **1998**:2
Bolton, Michael 1953(?)- **1993**:2
Bono 1960- **1988**:4
Boyz II Men **1995**:1

Brandy 1979- **1996**:4
Braxton, Toni 1967- **1994**:3
Brown, James 1928(?)- **1991**:4
Brown, Ruth 1928-2006
    Obituary **2008**:1
Campbell, Erica 1972- (
See Mary Mary)
Campbell, Tina 1972- (
See Mary Mary)
Carey, Mariah 1970(?)- **1991**:3
Carpenter, Mary-Chapin
    1958(?)- **1994**:1
Carter, Benny 1907-2003
    Obituary **2004**:3
Cash, Johnny 1932- **1995**:3
Cash, June Carter 1929-2003
    Obituary **2004**:2
Chapman, Tracy 1964- **1989**:2
Charles, Ray 1930-2004
    Obituary **2005**:3
Clapton, Eric 1945- **1993**:3
Cleveland, James 1932(?)-1991
    Obituary **1991**:3
Coldplay **2004**:4
Cole, Natalie 1950- **1992**:4
Collins, Albert 1932-1993
    Obituary **1994**:2
Corea, Chick 1941- **1986**:3
Cosby, Bill 1937- **1999**:2
Cray, Robert 1953- **1988**:2
Crosby, David 1941- **2000**:4
Crow, Sheryl 1964- **1995**:2
Cruz, Celia 1925-2003
    Obituary **2004**:3
Daft Punk 1975- **2009**:4
Dangerfield, Rodney 1921-2004
    Obituary **2006**:1
de Homem-Christo, Guy-Manuel
    1975- (
See Daft Punk)
Destiny's Child **2001**:3
Diddley, Bo 1928-2008
    Obituary **2009**:3
Di Meola, Al 1954- **1986**:4
Dion, Celine 1970(?)- **1995**:3
Dixie Chicks **2001**:2
Duran Duran **2005**:3
Dylan, Bob 1941- **1998**:1
Edmonds, Kenneth Babyface
    1958(?)- **1995**:3
Elliott, Missy 1971- **2003**:4
Eminem 1974- **2001**:2
Ertegun, Ahmet 1923- **1986**:3
Etheridge, Melissa 1961(?)- **1995**:4
Eve 1978- **2004**:3
Farrell, Perry 1960- **1992**:2
Foo Fighters **2006**:2
Ford, Tennessee Ernie 1919-1991
    Obituary **1992**:2
Foster, David 1950(?)- **1988**:2
Franklin, Aretha 1942- **1998**:3
Franklin, Melvin 1942-1995
    Obituary **1995**:3
Furtado, Nelly 1978- **2007**:2
Getz, Stan 1927-1991
    Obituary **1991**:4
Gill, Vince 1957- **1995**:2
Goldberg, Whoopi 1955- **1993**:3
Goodman, Benny 1909-1986
    Obituary **1986**:3
Goulet, Robert 1933-2007
    Obituary **2008**:4

Grant, Amy 1961(?)- **1985**:4
Gray, Macy 1970(?)- **2002**:1
Green Day **1995**:4
Hammer, Jan 1948- **1987**:3
Hammer, M. C. **1991**:2
Hancock, Herbie 1940- **1985**:1
Harris, Emmylou 1947- **1991**:3
Harrison, George 1943-2001
   Obituary **2003**:1
Hayes, Isaac 1942- **1998**:4
Hill, Lauryn 1975- **1999**:3
Hirt, Al 1922-1999
   Obituary **1999**:4
Hooker, John Lee 1917- **1998**:1
   Obituary **2002**:3
Horne, Lena 1917- **1998**:4
Hornsby, Bruce 1954(?)- **1989**:3
Houston, Cissy 1933- **1999**:3
Houston, Whitney 1963- **1986**:3
Hubbard, Freddie 1938- **1988**:4
Iglesias, Enrique 1975- **2000**:1
Indigo Girls **1994**:4
Jackson, Michael 1958- **1996**:2
James, Rick 1948-2004
   Obituary **2005**:4
Jay-Z 1970- **2006**:1
Jennings, Waylon 1937-2002
   Obituary **2003**:2
Joel, Billy 1949- **1994**:3
John, Elton 1947- **1995**:4
Jones, Norah 1979- **2004**:1
Kenny G 1957(?)- **1994**:4
Keys, Alicia 1981- **2006**:1
Knopfler, Mark 1949- **1986**:2
Kronos Quartet **1993**:1
Lauper, Cyndi 1953- **1985**:1
Lee, Peggy 1920-2002
   Obituary **2003**:1
Legend, John 1978- **2007**:1
Levy, Eugene 1946- **2004**:3
Lil Wayne 1982- **2009**:3
Living Colour **1993**:3
LL Cool J 1968- **1998**:2
Ludacris 1977- **2007**:4
Lynn, Loretta 1935(?)- **2001**:1
Marin, Cheech 1946- **2000**:1
Maroon 5 **2008**:1
Marsalis, Wynton 1961- **1997**:4
Martin, Ricky 1971- **1999**:4
Martin, Steve 1945- **1992**:2
Mary Mary 1972- **2009**:4
Mayer, John 1977- **2007**:4
McCartney, Paul 1942- **2002**:4
McEntire, Reba 1954- **1987**:3
McFerrin, Bobby 1950- **1989**:1
McLachlan, Sarah 1968- **1998**:4
Menuhin, Yehudi 1916-1999
   Obituary **1999**:3
Metallica **2004**:2
Midler, Bette 1945- **1989**:4
Miller, Roger 1936-1992
   Obituary **1993**:2
Mitchell, Joni 1943- **1991**:4
Monica 1980- **2004**:2
Moog, Robert 1934-2005
   Obituary **2006**:4
Morissette, Alanis 1974- **1996**:2
Murphy, Eddie 1961- **1989**:2
Ne-Yo 1982- **2009**:4
Nelson, Willie 1933- **1993**:4
Newton-John, Olivia 1948- **1998**:4
Orbison, Roy 1936-1988

Obituary **1989**:2
Osbournes, The **2003**:4
OutKast **2004**:4
Paisley, Brad 1972- **2008**:3
Palmer, Robert 1949-2003
   Obituary **2004**:4
Parton, Dolly 1946- **1999**:4
Pass, Joe 1929-1994
   Obituary **1994**:4
Peterson, Oscar 1925-2007
   Obituary **2009**:1
Pink 1979- **2004**:3
Pride, Charley 1938(?)- **1998**:1
Prince 1958- **1995**:3
Pryor, Richard **1999**:3
Puente, Tito 1923-2000
   Obituary **2000**:4
Radiohead **2009**:3
Raitt, Bonnie 1949- **1990**:2
Rascal Flatts **2007**:1
Rattle, Simon 1955- **1989**:4
Rawls, Lou 1933-2006
   Obituary **2007**:1
Reznor, Trent 1965- **2000**:2
Riddle, Nelson 1921-1985
   Obituary **1985**:4
Rihanna 1988- **2008**:4
Rimes, LeeAnn 1982- **1997**:4
Rollins, Henry 1961- **2007**:3
Sade 1959- **1993**:2
Santana, Carlos 1947- **2000**:2
Selena 1971-1995
   Obituary **1995**:4
Shakira 1977- **2002**:3
Silverstein, Shel 1932-1999
   Obituary **1999**:4
Simon, Paul 1942(?)- **1992**:2
Sinatra, Frank 1915-1998
   Obituary **1998**:4
Smith, Will 1968- **1997**:2
Solti, Georg 1912-1997
   Obituary **1998**:1
Sondheim, Stephen 1930- **1994**:4
Stafford, Jo 1917-2008
   Obituary **2009**:3
Stefani, Gwen 1969- **2005**:4
Stewart, Rod 1945- **2007**:1
Sting 1951- **1991**:4
Streisand, Barbra 1942- **1992**:2
System of a Down **2006**:4
T. I. 1980- **2008**:1
Timbaland 1971- **2007**:4
Timberlake, Justin 1981- **2008**:4
Torme, Mel 1925-1999
   Obituary **1999**:4
Tosh, Peter 1944-1987
   Obituary **1988**:2
Travis, Randy 1959- **1988**:4
Turner, Ike 1931-2007
   Obituary **2009**:1
Turner, Tina 1939- **2000**:3
Twain, Shania 1965- **1996**:3
U2 **2002**:4
Underwood, Carrie 1983- **2008**:1
Urban, Keith 1967- **2006**:3
Usher 1979- **2005**:1
Vandross, Luther 1951-2005
   Obituary **2006**:3
Vaughan, Stevie Ray 1956(?)-1990
   Obituary **1991**:1
Wagoner, Porter 1927-2007
   Obituary **2008**:4

Washington, Grover, Jr. 1943- **1989**:1
West, Kanye 1977- **2006**:1
White, Barry 1944-2003
   Obituary **2004**:3
White Stripes, The **2006**:1
Williams, Joe 1918-1999
   Obituary **1999**:4
Williams, Pharrell 1973- **2005**:3
Williams, Robin 1952- **1988**:4
Wilson, Flip 1933-1998
   Obituary **1999**:2
Wilson, Gretchen 1970- **2006**:3
Winans, CeCe 1964- **2000**:1
Wynonna 1964- **1993**:3
Yankovic, Frank 1915-1998
   Obituary **1999**:2
Yearwood, Trisha 1964- **1999**:1
Zevon, Warren 1947-2003
   Obituary **2004**:4

**Grand Ole Opry**
Bentley, Dierks 1975- **2007**:3
Snow, Hank 1914-1999
   Obituary **2000**:3
Wagoner, Porter 1927-2007
   Obituary **2008**:4

**Grand Prix racing**
Prost, Alain 1955- **1988**:1

**Green Bay Packers football team**
Favre, Brett Lorenzo 1969- **1997**:2
Howard, Desmond Kevin
   1970- **1997**:2
Sharpe, Sterling 1965- **1994**:3
White, Reggie 1961- **1993**:4

**Greenpeace International**
McTaggart, David 1932(?)- **1989**:4

**Greens party (West Germany)**
Schily, Otto
   Brief entry **1987**:4

**GRP Records, Inc.**
Grusin, Dave
   Brief entry **1987**:2

**Gucci**
Ford, Tom 1962- **1999**:3

**Gucci Shops, Inc.**
Gucci, Maurizio
   Brief entry **1985**:4
Mello, Dawn 1938(?)- **1992**:2

**Gulf + Western**
Diller, Barry 1942- **1991**:1

**Gun control**
Brady, Sarah and James S. **1991**:4

**Gymnastics**
Hamm, Paul 1982- **2005**:1
Johnson, Shawn 1992- **2009**:2
Retton, Mary Lou 1968- **1985**:2
Strug, Kerri 1977- **1997**:3

**H & R Block, Inc.**
Bloch, Henry 1922- **1988**:4

**Hampshire College**
Simmons, Adele Smith 1941- **1988**:4

**Handicap rights**
Brady, Sarah and James S. **1991**:4
Dickinson, Brian 1937- **1998**:2

**Hanna-Barbera Productions**
Barbera, Joseph 1911- **1988**:2
Hanna, William 1910-2001
Obituary **2002**:1

**Hard Candy**
Mohajer, Dineh 1972- **1997**:3

**Harlem Globetrotters basketball team**
Woodard, Lynette 1959(?)- **1986**:2

**Harley-Davidson Motor Co., Inc.**
Beals, Vaughn 1928- **1988**:2

**Hartford, Conn., city government**
Perry, Carrie Saxon 1932(?)- **1989**:2

**Hasbro, Inc.**
Hassenfeld, Stephen 1942- **1987**:4

**Hasidism**
Schneerson, Menachem Mendel 1902-1994 **1992**:4
Obituary **1994**:4

**Hasty Pudding Theatricals**
Beatty, Warren 1937- **2000**:1
Burnett, Carol 1933- **2000**:3
Hanks, Tom 1956- **1989**:2
Peters, Bernadette 1948- **2000**:1

**Hearst Magazines**
Black, Cathleen 1944- **1998**:4
Ganzi, Victor 1947- **2003**:3

**Heisman Trophy**
Flutie, Doug 1962- **1999**:2
Howard, Desmond Kevin 1970- **1997**:2
Jackson, Bo 1962- **1986**:3
Testaverde, Vinny 1962- **1987**:2
Williams, Ricky 1977- **2000**:2

**Helmsley Hotels, Inc.**
Helmsley, Leona 1920- **1988**:1

**Hemlock Society**
Humphry, Derek 1931(?)- **1992**:2

**Herbalife International**
Hughes, Mark 1956- **1985**:3

**Hereditary Disease Foundation**
Wexler, Nancy S. 1945- **1992**:3

**Herut Party (Israel)**
Levy, David 1938- **1987**:2

**Hewlett-Packard**
Fiorina, Carleton S. 1954- **2000**:1
Hewlett, William 1913-2001
Obituary **2001**:4

**High Flight Foundation**
Irwin, James 1930-1991
Obituary **1992**:1

**Hitchhiking**
Heid, Bill
Brief entry **1987**:2

**Hobie Cat**
Alter, Hobie
Brief entry **1985**:1
Hasek, Dominik 1965- **1998**:3

**Hockey**
Bourque, Raymond Jean 1960- **1997**:3
Cherry, Don 1934- **1993**:4
Coffey, Paul 1961- **1985**:4
Crosby, Sidney 1987- **2006**:3
Eagleson, Alan 1933- **1987**:4
Federov, Sergei 1969- **1995**:1
Fuhr, Grant 1962- **1997**:3
Giguere, Jean-Sebastien 1977- **2004**:2
Gilmour, Doug 1963- **1994**:3
Granato, Cammi 1971- **1999**:3
Gretzky, Wayne 1961- **1989**:2
Hextall, Ron 1964- **1988**:2
Hull, Brett 1964- **1991**:4
Jagr, Jaromir 1972- **1995**:4
Klima, Petr 1964- **1987**:1
Konstantinov, Vladimir 1967- **1997**:4
LaFontaine, Pat 1965- **1985**:1
Lemieux, Claude 1965- **1996**:1
Lemieux, Mario 1965- **1986**:4
Lindbergh, Pelle 1959-1985
Obituary **1985**:4
Lindros, Eric 1973- **1992**:1
Messier, Mark 1961- **1993**:1
Modano, Mike 1970- **2008**:2
Ovechkin, Alexander 1985- **2009**:2
Pocklington, Peter H. 1941- **1985**:2
Richard, Maurice 1921-2000
Obituary **2000**:4
Roy, Patrick 1965- **1994**:2
Sakic, Joe 1969- **2002**:1
Yzerman, Steve 1965- **1991**:2
Zamboni, Frank J.
Brief entry **1986**:4

**Honda Motor Co.**
Honda, Soichiro 1906-1991
Obituary **1986**:1

**Hong Kong government**
Lee, Martin 1938- **1998**:2
Patten, Christopher 1944- **1993**:3

**Horror fiction**
Barker, Clive 1952- **2003**:3
Brite, Poppy Z. 1967- **2005**:1
Harris, Thomas 1940(?)- **2001**:1
King, Stephen 1947- **1998**:1
Koontz, Dean 1945- **1999**:3
Stine, R. L. 1943- **2003**:1

**Horse racing**
Day, Pat 1953- **1995**:2
Desormeaux, Kent 1970- **1990**:2
Krone, Julie 1963(?)- **1989**:2

Packard, David 1912-1996
Obituary **1996**:3

Lukas, D. Wayne 1936(?)- **1986**:2
McCarron, Chris 1955- **1995**:4
Mellon, Paul 1907-1999
Obituary **1999**:3
O'Donnell, Bill
Brief entry **1987**:4
Pincay, Laffit, Jr. 1946- **1986**:3
Secretariat 1970-1989
Obituary **1990**:1
Shoemaker, Bill 1931-2003
Obituary **2004**:4

**Houston, Tex., city government**
Watson, Elizabeth 1949- **1991**:2
Whitmire, Kathy 1946- **1988**:2

**Houston Astros baseball team**
Lofton, Kenny 1967- **1998**:1
Ryan, Nolan 1947- **1989**:4

**Houston Oilers football team**
Moon, Warren 1956- **1991**:3

**Houston Rockets basketball team**
Olajuwon, Akeem 1963- **1985**:1
Yao Ming 1980- **2004**:1

**Hugo Awards**
Asimov, Isaac 1920-1992
Obituary **1992**:3

**Human Genome Sciences, Inc. [HGS]**
Haseltine, William A. 1944- **1999**:2

**Huntington's disease**
Wexler, Nancy S. 1945- **1992**:3

**Hustler Magazine**
Flynt, Larry 1942- **1997**:3

**Hyatt Legal Services**
Bloch, Henry 1922- **1988**:4
Hyatt, Joel 1950- **1985**:3

**Hydroponics**
Davis, Noel **1990**:3

**Ice cream**
Ben & Jerry **1991**:3

**Ice skating**
Arakawa, Shizuka 1981- **2006**:4
Baiul, Oksana 1977- **1995**:3
Gordeeva, Ekaterina 1972- **1996**:4
Grinkov, Sergei 1967-1995
Obituary **1996**:2
Hamilton, Scott 1958- **1998**:2
Hughes, Sarah 1985- **2002**:4
Kerrigan, Nancy 1969- **1994**:3
Lipinski, Tara 1982- **1998**:3
Thomas, Debi 1967- **1987**:2
Witt, Katarina 1966(?)- **1991**:3
Yamaguchi, Kristi 1971- **1992**:3
Zamboni, Frank J.
Brief entry **1986**:4

**Imani Temple**
Stallings, George A., Jr. 1948- **1990**:1

**Immigration**
Kurzban, Ira 1949- **1987**:2
Lewis, Loida Nicolas 1942- **1998**:3
Mahony, Roger M. 1936- **1988**:2

**Imposters**
Bremen, Barry 1947- **1987**:3

**Inacomp Computer Centers, Inc.**
Inatome, Rick 1953- **1985**:4

**Indiana Pacers basketball team**
Miller, Reggie 1965- **1994**:4

**Indiana University basketball team**
Knight, Bobby 1940- **1985**:3

**Indonesia**
Wahid, Abdurrahman 1940- **2000**:3

**Insurance**
Davison, Ian Hay 1931- **1986**:1
Hilbert, Stephen C. 1946- **1997**:4

**Integrated circuit**
Noyce, Robert N. 1927- **1985**:4

**Intel Corp.**
Barrett, Craig R. 1939- **1999**:4
Grove, Andrew S. 1936- **1995**:3
Noyce, Robert N. 1927- **1985**:4

**Interarms Corp.**
Cummings, Sam 1927- **1986**:3

**International Anticounterfeiting
Coalition [IACC]**
Bikoff, James L.
Brief entry **1986**:2

**International Brotherhood of Teamsters**
Carey, Ron 1936- **1993**:3
Hoffa, Jim, Jr. 1941- **1999**:2
Presser, Jackie 1926-1988
Obituary **1988**:4
Saporta, Vicki
Brief entry **1987**:3

**International Business Machines Corp.
[IBM Corp.]**
Akers, John F. 1934- **1988**:3
Chaudhari, Praveen 1937- **1989**:4
Gerstner, Lou 1942- **1993**:4
Kohnstamm, Abby 1954- **2001**:1
Palmisano, Samuel J. 1952(?)- **2003**:1

**International Creative Management
Associates**
Mengers, Sue 1938- **1985**:3

**International Olympic Committee [IOC]**
Eagleson, Alan 1933- **1987**:4
Samaranch, Juan Antonio 1920- **1986**
:2

**Internet**
Allaire, Jeremy 1971- **2006**:4

Anderson, Tom and Chris DeWolfe
**2007**:2
Beal, Deron 1968(?)- **2005**:3
Berners-Lee, Tim 1955(?)- **1997**:4
Butterfield, Stewart and Caterina
Fake **2007**:3
Chen, Steve and Chad
Hurley **2007**:2
Clark, Jim 1944- **1997**:1
Ebbers, Bernie 1943- **1998**:1
Evans, Nancy 1950- **2000**:4
Fanning, Shawn 1980- **2001**:1
Filo, David and Jerry Yang **1998**:3
Gardner, David and Tom **2001**:4
Haladjian, Rafi 1962(?)- **2008**:3
Housenbold, Jeffrey 1969- **2009**:2
Koogle, Tim 1951- **2000**:4
Ma, Jack 1964- **2007**:1
Malda, Rob 1976- **2007**:3
Nissel, Angela 1974- **2006**:4
Pack, Ellen 1963(?)- **2001**:2
Peluso, Michelle 1971(?)- **2007**:4
Pirro, Jeanine 1951- **1998**:2
Schmidt, Eric 1955- **2002**:4
Stockton, Shreve 1977- **2009**:4
Taylor, Jeff 1960- **2001**:3
Zuckerberg, Mark 1984- **2008**:2

**Investment banking**
Fomon, Robert M. 1925- **1985**:3

**Irish Northern Aid Committee
[NORAID]**
Galvin, Martin
Brief entry **1985**:3

**Irish Republican Army [IRA]**
Adams, Gerald 1948- **1994**:1
Galvin, Martin
Brief entry **1985**:3
McGuinness, Martin 1950(?)- **1985**:4

**Jacuzzi Bros., Inc.**
Jacuzzi, Candido 1903-1986
Obituary **1987**:1

**Jaguar Cars PLC**
Egan, John 1939- **1987**:2

**Jane magazine**
Pratt, Jane 1963(?)- **1999**:1

**Jewish Defense League**
Kahane, Meir 1932-1990
Obituary **1991**:2

**Joe Boxer Corp.**
Graham, Nicholas 1960(?)- **1991**:4

**Joffrey Ballet**
Joffrey, Robert 1930-1988
Obituary **1988**:3

**Jolt Cola**
Rapp, C.J.
Brief entry **1987**:3

**Judo**
Kanokogi, Rusty
Brief entry **1987**:1

**Juno Awards**
Furtado, Nelly 1978- **2007**:2
Lavigne, Avril 1984- **2005**:2
McLachlan, Sarah 1968- **1998**:4
Nickelback **2007**:2
Sainte-Marie, Buffy 1941- **2000**:1
Timbaland 1971- **2007**:4

**Justin Industries**
Justin, John Jr. 1917- **1992**:2

**Kansas City Chiefs football team**
Okoye, Christian 1961- **1990**:2
Thomas, Derrick 1967-2000
Obituary **2000**:3

**Kansas City Royals baseball team**
Howser, Dick 1936-1987
Obituary **1987**:4
Jackson, Bo 1962- **1986**:3
Saberhagen, Bret 1964- **1986**:1

**Kelly Services**
Kelly, William R. 1905-1998 **1998**:2

**Khmer Rouge**
Lon Nol
Obituary **1986**:1

**Kitty Litter**
Lowe, Edward 1921- **1990**:2

**Kloss Video Corp.**
Kloss, Henry E.
Brief entry **1985**:2

**K Mart Corp.**
Antonini, Joseph 1941- **1991**:2
Stewart, Martha 1942(?)- **1992**:1

**Kraft General Foods**
Fudge, Ann 1951- **2000**:3
Holden, Betsy 1955- **2003**:2
Rosenfeld, Irene 1953- **2008**:3

**Ku Klux Klan**
Duke, David 1951(?)- **1990**:2

**Labor**
Bieber, Owen 1929- **1986**:1
Carey, Ron 1936- **1993**:3
Eagleson, Alan 1933- **1987**:4
Fehr, Donald 1948- **1987**:2
Feldman, Sandra 1939- **1987**:3
Hoffa, Jim, Jr. 1941- **1999**:2
Huerta, Dolores 1930- **1998**:1
Kielburger, Craig 1983- **1998**:1
Martin, Lynn 1939- **1991**:4
Nussbaum, Karen 1950- **1988**:3
Presser, Jackie 1926-1988
Obituary **1988**:4
Ramaphosa, Cyril 1953- **1988**:2
Rothstein, Ruth **1988**:2
Saporta, Vicki
Brief entry **1987**:3
Steinberg, Leigh 1949- **1987**:3
Upshaw, Gene 1945- **1988**:1
Williams, Lynn 1924- **1986**:4

**Labour Party (Great Britain)**
Blair, Tony 1953- **1996**:3
Jenkins, Roy Harris 1920-2003
Obituary **2004**:1
Livingstone, Ken 1945- **1988**:3
Maxwell, Robert 1923- **1990**:1

**Ladies Professional Golf Association [LPGA]**
Baker, Kathy
Brief entry **1986**:1
Creamer, Paula 1986- **2006**:2
Inkster, Juli 1960- **2000**:2
Kerr, Cristie 1977- **2008**:2
Lopez, Nancy 1957- **1989**:3
Ochoa, Lorena 1981- **2007**:4
Pak, Se Ri 1977- **1999**:4
Sorenstam, Annika 1970- **2001**:1
Webb, Karrie 1974- **2000**:4
Whaley, Suzy 1966- **2003**:4

**Language instruction**
Thomas, Michel 1911(?)- **1987**:4

**Lasers**
Gould, Gordon 1920- **1987**:1
Hagelstein, Peter
Brief entry **1986**:3
Maiman, Theodore 1927-2007
Obituary **2008**:3

**Law enforcement**
Cantrell, Ed
Brief entry **1985**:3
France, Johnny
Brief entry **1987**:1
Harvard, Beverly 1950- **1995**:2
Rizzo, Frank 1920-1991
Obituary **1992**:1
Watson, Elizabeth 1949- **1991**:2
Williams, Willie L. 1944(?)- **1993**:1

**Learning Annex**
Zanker, Bill
Brief entry **1987**:3

**Lear's magazine**
Lear, Frances 1923- **1988**:3

**Lego toy system**
Kristiansen, Kjeld Kirk
1948(?)- **1988**:3

**Lenin Peace Prize**
Kekkonen, Urho 1900-1986
Obituary **1986**:4

**Lettuce Entertain You Enterprises, Inc.**
Melman, Richard
Brief entry **1986**:1

**Leukemia research**
Gale, Robert Peter 1945- **1986**:4

**Levi Strauss & Co.**
Haas, Robert D. 1942- **1986**:4
Marineau, Philip 1946- **2002**:4

**Liberal Democratic Party (Japan)**
Miyazawa, Kiichi 1919- **1992**:2

**Liberal Party (Canada)**
Chretien, Jean 1934- **1990**:4
Peterson, David 1943- **1987**:1

**Liberal Party (South Africa)**
Paton, Alan 1903-1988
Obituary **1988**:3

**Library of Congress**
Billington, James 1929- **1990**:3
Dickey, James 1923-1997 **1998**:2
Van Duyn, Mona 1921- **1993**:2

**Likud Party (Israel)**
Netanyahu, Benjamin 1949- **1996**:4

**Lillian Vernon Corp.**
Katz, Lillian 1927- **1987**:4

**Limelight clubs**
Gatien, Peter
Brief entry **1986**:1

**Lincoln Savings and Loan**
Keating, Charles H., Jr. 1923- **1990**:4

**Linguistics**
Tannen, Deborah 1945- **1995**:1

**Literacy**
Bush, Millie 1987- **1992**:1
Kozol, Jonathan 1936- **1992**:1

**Little Caesars pizza restaurants**
Ilitch, Mike 1929- **1993**:4

**Little People's Research Fund**
Kopits, Steven E.
Brief entry **1987**:1

**Live Aid**
Bono 1960- **1988**:4
Dylan, Bob 1941- **1998**:1
Geldof, Bob 1954(?)- **1985**:3
Graham, Bill 1931-1991 **1986**:4
Obituary **1992**:2

**L.L. Bean Co.**
Gorman, Leon
Brief entry **1987**:1

**Lloyd's of London**
Davison, Ian Hay 1931- **1986**:1

**Loews Corp.**
Tisch, Laurence A. 1923- **1988**:2

**Log Cabin Republicans**
Tafel, Richard 1962- **2000**:4

**Lone Ranger**
Moore, Clayton 1914-1999
Obituary **2000**:3

**Los Angeles city government**
Bradley, Tom 1917-1998
Obituary **1999**:1
Riordan, Richard 1930- **1993**:4

**Los Angeles Dodgers baseball team**
Hershiser, Orel 1958- **1989**:2
Nomo, Hideo 1968- **1996**:2
Welch, Bob 1956- **1991**:3

**Los Angeles Express football team**
Young, Steve 1961- **1995**:2

**Los Angeles Kings hockey team**
Gretzky, Wayne 1961- **1989**:2

**Los Angeles Lakers basketball team**
Bryant, Kobe 1978- **1998**:3
Buss, Jerry 1933- **1989**:3
Chamberlain, Wilt 1936-1999
Obituary **2000**:2
Johnson, Earvin Magic 1959- **1988**:4
Riley, Pat 1945- **1994**:3
Worthy, James 1961- **1991**:2

**Los Angeles Museum of Contemporary Art**
Isozaki, Arata 1931- **1990**:2

**Los Angeles Raiders football team**
Gault, Willie 1960- **1991**:2
Upshaw, Gene 1945- **1988**:1

**Los Angeles Sparks basketball team**
Leslie, Lisa 1972- **1997**:4

**Louisiana Legislature**
Duke, David 1951(?)- **1990**:2

**Louisiana state government**
Roemer, Buddy 1943- **1991**:4

**Luis Vuitton**
Arnault, Bernard 1949- **2000**:4

**Magic**
Anderson, Harry 1951(?)- **1988**:2
Blackstone, Harry Jr. 1934-1997
Obituary **1997**:4
Blaine, David 1973- **2003**:3
Copperfield, David 1957- **1986**:3
Henning, Doug 1947-1999
Obituary **2000**:3
Jay, Ricky 1949(?)- **1995**:1

**Maine State Government**
Muskie, Edmund S. 1914-1996
Obituary **1996**:3

**Major League Baseball Players Association**
Fehr, Donald 1948- **1987**:2
Selig, Bud 1934- **1995**:2

**Malawi Congress Party [MCP]**
Banda, Hastings 1898- **1994**:3

**Marriott Corp.**
Marriott, J. Willard 1900-1985
Obituary **1985**:4
Marriott, J. Willard, Jr. 1932- **1985**:4

**Martial arts**
Chan, Jackie 1954- **1996**:1
Lee, Brandon 1965(?)-1993
Obituary **1993**:4

Li, Jet 1963- **2005**:3

**Maryland state government**
Schaefer, William Donald 1921- **1988**:1

**Massachusetts state government**
Dukakis, Michael 1933- **1988**:3
Flynn, Ray 1939- **1989**:1
Frank, Barney 1940- **1989**:2
Moakley, Joseph 1927-2001
Obituary **2002**:2

**Mathematics**
Hawking, Stephen W. 1942- **1990**:1
Lawrence, Ruth
Brief entry **1986**:3
Penrose, Roger 1931- **1991**:4
Pople, John 1925-2004
Obituary **2005**:2
Thom, Rene 1923-2002
Obituary **2004**:1
Wiles, Andrew 1953(?)- **1994**:1

**Mattel, Inc.**
Barad, Jill 1951- **1994**:2
Eckert, Robert A. 1955(?)- **2002**:3
Handler, Ruth 1916-2002
Obituary **2003**:3

**Max Factor and Company**
Factor, Max 1904-1996
Obituary **1996**:4

**Maximilian Furs, Inc.**
Potok, Anna Maximilian
Brief entry **1985**:2

**Mazda Motor Corp.**
Yamamoto, Kenichi 1922- **1989**:1

**McDonald's Restaurants**
Kroc, Ray 1902-1984
Obituary **1985**:1

**McDonnell Douglas Corp.**
McDonnell, Sanford N. 1922- **1988**:4

**MCI Communications Corp.**
Cerf, Vinton G. 1943- **1999**:2
McGowan, William 1927- **1985**:2
McGowan, William G. 1927-1992
Obituary **1993**:1

**Medicine**
Adams, Patch 1945(?)- **1999**:2
Baulieu, Etienne-Emile 1926- **1990**:1
Bayley, Corrine
Brief entry **1986**:4
Blumenthal, Susan J. 1951(?)- **2007**:3
Carson, Ben 1951- **1998**:2
Crichton, Michael 1942- **1995**:3
DeVita, Vincent T., Jr. 1935- **1987**:3
Duke, Red
Brief entry **1987**:1
Elders, Joycelyn 1933- **1994**:1
Foster, Tabatha 1985-1988
Obituary **1988**:3

Gale, Robert Peter 1945- **1986**:4
Gallo, Robert 1937- **1991**:1
Hatem, George 1910(?)-1988
Obituary **1989**:1
Healy, Bernadine 1944- **1993**:1
Hill, J. Edward 1938- **2006**:2
Hounsfield, Godfrey 1919- **1989**:2
Jacobs, Joe 1945(?)- **1994**:1
Jarvik, Robert K. 1946- **1985**:1
Jemison, Mae C. 1956- **1993**:1
Jorgensen, Christine 1926-1989
Obituary **1989**:4
Keith, Louis 1935- **1988**:2
Kevorkian, Jack 1928(?)- **1991**:3
Klass, Perri 1958- **1993**:2
Koop, C. Everett 1916- **1989**:3
Kopits, Steven E.
Brief entry **1987**:1
Kwoh, Yik San 1946(?)- **1988**:2
Langston, J. William
Brief entry **1986**:2
Lorenz, Konrad 1903-1989
Obituary **1989**:3
Morgentaler, Henry 1923- **1986**:3
Novello, Antonia 1944- **1991**:2
Olopade, Olufunmilayo 1957(?)- **2006**:3
Oz, Mehmet 1960- **2007**:2
Radocy, Robert
Brief entry **1986**:3
Rock, John
Obituary **1985**:1
Rosenberg, Steven 1940- **1989**:1
Rothstein, Ruth **1988**:2
Sabin, Albert 1906-1993
Obituary **1993**:4
Sacks, Oliver 1933- **1995**:4
Schroeder, William J. 1932-1986
Obituary **1986**:4
Spock, Benjamin 1903-1998 **1995**:2
Obituary **1998**:3
Steptoe, Patrick 1913-1988
Obituary **1988**:3
Sullivan, Louis 1933- **1990**:4
Szent-Gyoergyi, Albert 1893-1986
Obituary **1987**:2
Vagelos, P. Roy 1929- **1989**:4
Weil, Andrew 1942- **1997**:4
Wigler, Michael
Brief entry **1985**:1

**Men's issues**
Bly, Robert 1926- **1992**:4
McCartney, Bill 1940- **1995**:3

**Merck & Co.**
Vagelos, P. Roy 1929- **1989**:4

**Metromedia, Inc.**
Kluge, John 1914- **1991**:1

**Miami, Fla., city government**
Suarez, Xavier
Brief entry **1986**:2

**Miami Dolphins football team**
Shula, Don 1930- **1992**:2

**Michigan state government**
Engler, John 1948- **1996**:3
Williams, G. Mennen 1911-1988
Obituary **1988**:2

**Microelectronics and Computer Technologies Corp.**
Inman, Bobby Ray 1931- **1985**:1

**Microsoft Corp.**
Ballmer, Steven 1956- **1997**:2
Belluzzo, Rick 1953- **2001**:3
Gates, Bill 1955- **1987**:4
Stonesifer, Patty 1956- **1997**:1

**Middle East**
Arafat, Yasser 1929- **1989**:3
Arens, Moshe 1925- **1985**:1
Assad, Hafez al- 1930(?)- **1992**:1
Begin, Menachem 1913-1992
Obituary **1992**:3
Berri, Nabih 1939(?)- **1985**:2
Freij, Elias 1920- **1986**:4
Ghali, Boutros Boutros 1922- **1992**:3
Hussein, Saddam 1937- **1991**:1
Hussein I, King 1935-1999 **1997**:3
Obituary **1999**:3
Jumblatt, Walid 1949(?)- **1987**:4
Khatami, Mohammed 1943- **1997**:4
Khomeini, Ayatollah Ruhollah 1900(?)-1989
Obituary **1989**:4
Levy, David 1938- **1987**:2
Nidal, Abu 1937- **1987**:1
Rafsanjani, Ali Akbar Hashemi 1934(?)- **1987**:3
Redgrave, Vanessa 1937- **1989**:2
Sarkis, Elias 1924-1985
Obituary **1985**:3
Schwarzkopf, Norman 1934- **1991**:3
Terzi, Zehdi Labib 1924- **1985**:3

**Military**
Abacha, Sani 1943- **1996**:3
Arens, Moshe 1925- **1985**:1
Aspin, Les 1938-1995
Obituary **1996**:1
Babangida, Ibrahim Badamosi 1941- **1992**:4
Boyington, Gregory Pappy 1912-1988
Obituary **1988**:2
Cammermeyer, Margarethe 1942- **1995**:2
Cedras, Raoul 1950- **1994**:4
Cornum, Rhonda 1954- **2006**:3
Doe, Samuel 1952-1990
Obituary **1991**:1
Dunwoody, Ann 1953- **2009**:2
Dzhanibekov, Vladimir 1942- **1988**:1
Fitzgerald, A. Ernest 1926- **1986**:2
Franks, Tommy 1945- **2004**:1
Galvin, John R. 1929- **1990**:1
Garneau, Marc 1949- **1985**:1
Hess, Rudolph 1894-1987
Obituary **1988**:1
Hope, Bob 1903-2003
Obituary **2004**:4
Hussein, Saddam 1937- **1991**:1
Inman, Bobby Ray 1931- **1985**:1
Jumblatt, Walid 1949(?)- **1987**:4
Lansdale, Edward G. 1908-1987
Obituary **1987**:2
Le Duan 1908(?)-1986
Obituary **1986**:4
Le Duc Tho 1911-1990
Obituary **1991**:1

Marier, Rebecca 1974- **1995**:4
McCain, John S. 1936- **1998**:4
McSally, Martha 1966(?)- **2002**:4
North, Oliver 1943- **1987**:4
Paige, Emmett, Jr.
  Brief entry **1986**:4
Pinochet, Augusto 1915- **1999**:2
Powell, Colin 1937- **1990**:1
Rickover, Hyman 1900-1986
  Obituary **1986**:4
Schwarzkopf, Norman 1934- **1991**:3
Shalikashvili, John 1936- **1994**:2
Taylor, Maxwell 1901-1987
  Obituary **1987**:3
Ventura, Jesse 1951- **1999**:2
Westmoreland, William C. 1914-2005
  Obituary **2006**:4
Willson, S. Brian 1942(?)- **1989**:3
Yeager, Chuck 1923- **1998**:1
Ye Jianying 1897-1986
  Obituary **1987**:1
Zech, Lando W.
  Brief entry **1987**:4
Zia ul-Haq, Mohammad 1924-1988
  Obituary **1988**:4

**Milwaukee Brewers baseball team**
  Sheffield, Gary 1968- **1998**:1
  Veeck, Bill 1914-1986
    Obituary **1986**:1

**Minimalist art**
  Richter, Gerhard 1932- **1997**:2

**Minnesota state government**
  Ventura, Jesse 1951- **1999**:2
  Wellstone, Paul 1944-2002
    Obituary **2004**:1

**Minnesota Timberwolves basketball team**
  Garnett, Kevin 1976- **2000**:3
  Laettner, Christian 1969- **1993**:1

**Minnesota Vikings football team**
  Moss, Randy 1977- **1999**:3
  Payton, Walter 1954-1999
    Obituary **2000**:2

**Miramax**
  Weinstein, Bob and Harvey **2000**:4

**Miss America Pageant**
  Wells, Sharlene
    Brief entry **1985**:1
  Williams, Vanessa L. 1963- **1999**:2

**Miss Manners**
  Martin, Judith 1938- **2000**:3

**Mister Rogers**
  Rogers, Fred 1928- **2000**:4

**Modeling**
  Brando, Cheyenne 1970-1995
    Obituary **1995**:4
  Bruni, Carla 1967- **2009**:3
  Campbell, Naomi 1970- **2000**:2
  Crawford, Cindy 1966- **1993**:3

Diaz, Cameron 1972- **1999**:1
Dickinson, Janice 1953- **2005**:2
Fabio 1961(?)- **1993**:4
Fawcett, Farrah 1947- **1998**:4
Hurley, Elizabeth **1999**:2
Johnson, Beverly 1952- **2005**:2
Klum, Heidi 1973- **2006**:3
Leigh, Dorian 1917-2008
  Obituary **2009**:3
Leslie, Lisa 1972- **1997**:4
MacDowell, Andie 1958(?)- **1993**:4
Marky Mark 1971- **1993**:3
McCarthy, Jenny 1972- **1997**:4
Moss, Kate 1974- **1995**:3
Parker, Suzy 1932-2003
  Obituary **2004**:2
Romijn, Rebecca 1972- **2007**:1
Smith, Anna Nicole 1967-2007
  Obituary **2008**:2

**Molecular biology**
  Gilbert, Walter 1932- **1988**:3
  Kornberg, Arthur 1918(?)- **1992**:1
  Levinson, Arthur D. 1950- **2008**:3
  Melton, Douglas 1954- **2008**:3
  Mullis, Kary 1944- **1995**:3
  Sidransky, David 1960- **2002**:4

**Montreal Canadiens hockey team**
  Lemieux, Claude 1965- **1996**:1
  Richard, Maurice 1921-2000
    Obituary **2000**:4
  Roy, Patrick 1965- **1994**:2

**Monty Python**
  Cleese, John 1939- **1989**:2
  Milligan, Spike 1918-2002
    Obituary **2003**:2

**Mormon Church**
  Benson, Ezra Taft 1899-1994
    Obituary **1994**:4
  Hunter, Howard 1907- **1994**:4

**Mothers Against Drunk Driving [MADD]**
  Lightner, Candy 1946- **1985**:1
  Potts, Annie 1952- **1994**:1

**Motivational speakers**
  Brown, Les 1945- **1994**:3
  Peters, Tom 1942- **1998**:1

**Motorcycles**
  Beals, Vaughn 1928- **1988**:2
  Hart, Carey 1975- **2006**:4
  James, Jesse 1969- **2004**:4
  Knievel, Robbie 1963- **1990**:1

**Motown Records**
  de Passe, Suzanne 1946(?)- **1990**:4
  Franklin, Melvin 1942-1995
    Obituary **1995**:3
  Kendricks, Eddie 1939-1992
    Obituary **1993**:2
  Payton, Lawrence 1938(?)-1997
    Obituary **1997**:4
  Ruffin, David 1941-1991
    Obituary **1991**:4
  Wells, Mary 1943-1992
    Obituary **1993**:1

**Mountain climbing**
  Wood, Sharon
    Brief entry **1988**:1

**Moving Earth (dance company)**
  Takei, Kei 1946- **1990**:2

**Mozambique Liberation Front [FRELIMO]**
  Chissano, Joaquim 1939- **1987**:4
  Machel, Samora 1933-1986
    Obituary **1987**:1

**Mrs. Fields Cookies, Inc.**
  Fields, Debbi 1956- **1987**:3

**Ms. magazine**
  Gillespie, Marcia 1944- **1999**:4
  Morgan, Robin 1941- **1991**:1
  Steinem, Gloria 1934- **1996**:2
  Summers, Anne 1945- **1990**:2

**MTV Networks, Inc.**
  Daly, Carson 1973- **2002**:4
  Duffy, Karen 1962- **1998**:1
  Duran Duran **2005**:3
  Graden, Brian 1963- **2004**:2
  Kutcher, Ashton 1978- **2003**:4
  Laybourne, Geraldine 1947- **1997**:1
  McGrath, Judy 1953- **2006**:1
  Osbournes, The **2003**:4
  Pittman, Robert W. 1953- **1985**:1
  Quinn, Martha 1959- **1986**:4
  Roedy, Bill 1949(?)- **2003**:2
  Sethi, Simran 1971(?)- **2008**:1

**Multiple birth research**
  Keith, Louis 1935- **1988**:2

**Muppets**
  Henson, Brian 1964(?)- **1992**:1
  Henson, Jim 1936-1990 **1989**:1
    Obituary **1990**:4

**Museum of Modern Art (New York City)**
  Gund, Agnes 1938- **1993**:2
  Taniguchi, Yoshio 1937- **2005**:4

**NAACP**
  Chavis, Benjamin 1948- **1993**:4

**National Abortion Rights Action League [NARAL]**
  Falkenberg, Nanette 1951- **1985**:2
  Michelman, Kate 1942- **1998**:4

**National Academy of Science**
  Djerassi, Carl 1923- **2000**:4
  Van Allen, James 1914-2006
    Obituary **2007**:4

**National Aeronautics and Space Administration [NASA]**
  Bean, Alan L. 1932- **1986**:2
  Collins, Eileen 1956- **1995**:3
  Conrad, Pete 1930-1999

Obituary **2000**:1
Garneau, Marc 1949- **1985**:1
Glenn, John 1921- **1998**:3
Jemison, Mae C. 1956- **1993**:1
Lucid, Shannon 1943- **1997**:1
McAuliffe, Christa 1948-1986
Obituary **1985**:4
O'Keefe, Sean 1956- **2005**:2
Schirra, Wally 1923-2007
Obituary **2008**:3
Shepard, Alan 1923-1998
Obituary **1999**:1

**National Association for the Advancement of Colored People [NAACP]**
Adams, Yolanda 1961- **2008**:2
Chavis, Benjamin 1948- **1993**:4
Evers-Williams, Myrlie 1933- **1995**:4
Johnson, Robert L. 1946- **2000**:4
LL Cool J 1968- **1998**:2
Mfume, Kweisi 1948- **1996**:3
Parks, Rosa 1913-2005
Obituary **2007**:1

**National Audubon Society**
Berle, Peter A.A.
Brief entry **1987**:3

**National Baptist Convention**
Shaw, William 1934(?)- **2000**:3

**National Basketball Association [NBA]**
Auerbach, Red 1911-2006
Obituary **2008**:1
Bryant, Kobe 1978- **1998**:3
Duncan, Tim 1976- **2000**:1
Garnett, Kevin 1976- **2000**:3
Laimbeer, Bill 1957- **2004**:3
Malone, Karl 1963- **1990**:1
Mikan, George 1924-2005
Obituary **2006**:3
O'Malley, Susan 1962(?)- **1995**:2
Parker, Tony 1982- **2008**:1
Stockton, John Houston 1962- **1997**:3
Wallace, Ben 1974- **2004**:3
Yao Ming 1980- **2004**:1

**National Cancer Institute**
DeVita, Vincent T., Jr. 1935- **1987**:3
King, Mary-Claire 1946- **1998**:3
Rosenberg, Steven 1940- **1989**:1

**National Center for Atmospheric Research**
Thompson, Starley
Brief entry **1987**:3

**National Coalition for the Homeless**
Hayes, Robert M. 1952- **1986**:3

**National Coalition on Television Violence [NCTV]**
Radecki, Thomas
Brief entry **1986**:2

**National Commission on Excellence**
Justiz, Manuel J. 1948- **1986**:4

**National Conservative Political Action Committee [NCPAC]**
Dolan, Terry 1950-1986 **1985**:2

**National Education Association [NEA]**
Chavez, Linda 1947- **1999**:3
Futrell, Mary Hatwood 1940- **1986**:1

**National Endowment for the Arts**
Alexander, Jane 1939- **1994**:2
Alexie, Sherman 1966- **1998**:4
Anderson, Laurie 1947- **2000**:2
Bishop, Andre 1948- **2000**:1
Brooks, Gwendolyn
1917-2000 **1998**:1
Obituary **2001**:2
Castillo, Ana 1953- **2000**:4
Cruz, Nilo 1961(?)- **2004**:4
Erdrich, Louise 1954- **2005**:3
Fagan, Garth 1940- **2000**:1
Gioia, Dana 1950- **2008**:4
Jones, Gayl 1949- **1999**:4
Lewitzky, Bella 1916-2004
Obituary **2005**:3
Marshall, Susan 1958- **2000**:4
Miller, Bebe 1950- **2000**:2
Oates, Joyce Carol 1938- **2000**:1
Parks, Suzan-Lori 1964- **2003**:2
Reeve, Christopher 1952- **1997**:2
Ringgold, Faith 1930- **2000**:3
Serrano, Andres 1950- **2000**:4
Wagner, Catherine F. 1953- **2002**:3
Wolff, Tobias 1945- **2005**:1

**National Endowment for the Humanities [NEH]**
Cheney, Lynne V. 1941- **1990**:4
Hackney, Sheldon 1933- **1995**:1

**National Federation for Decency**
Wildmon, Donald 1938- **1988**:4

**National Football League [NFL]**
Favre, Brett Lorenzo 1969- **1997**:2
Flutie, Doug 1962- **1999**:2
Howard, Desmond Kevin
1970- **1997**:2
Moss, Randy 1977- **1999**:3
Shula, Don 1930- **1992**:2
Tagliabue, Paul 1940- **1990**:2

**National Football League Players Association**
Upshaw, Gene 1945- **1988**:1

**National Hockey League Players Association [NHLPA]**
Bourque, Raymond Jean 1960- **1997**:3
Eagleson, Alan 1933- **1987**:4
Fuhr, Grant 1962- **1997**:3

**National Hot Rod Association [NHRA]**
Muldowney, Shirley 1940- **1986**:1

**National Institute of Education**
Justiz, Manuel J. 1948- **1986**:4

**National Institutes of Health [NIH]**
Healy, Bernadine 1944- **1993**:1
Jacobs, Joe 1945(?)- **1994**:1
Zerhouni, Elias A. 1951- **2004**:3

**National Organization for Women [NOW]**
Abzug, Bella 1920-1998 **1998**:2
Friedan, Betty 1921- **1994**:2
Gandy, Kim 1954(?)- **2002**:2

Ireland, Patricia 1946(?)- **1992**:2
Yard, Molly **1991**:4

**National Park Service**
Mott, William Penn, Jr. 1909- **1986**:1

**National Public Radio [NPR]**
Codrescu, Andreaa 1946- **1997**:3
Edwards, Bob 1947- **1993**:2
Gross, Terry 1951- **1998**:3
Magliozzi, Tom and Ray **1991**:4
Maynard, Joyce 1953- **1999**:4
Roberts, Cokie 1943- **1993**:4
Tom and Ray Magliozzi **1991**:4
Totenberg, Nina 1944- **1992**:2

**National Restaurant Association**
Cain, Herman 1945- **1998**:3

**National Rifle Association [NRA]**
Foss, Joe 1915- **1990**:3
Helms, Jesse 1921- **1998**:1
Heston, Charlton 1924- **1999**:4

**National Science Foundation [NSF]**
Bloch, Erich 1925- **1987**:4
Colwell, Rita Rossi 1934- **1999**:3
Geller, Margaret Joan 1947- **1998**:2

**National Security Agency**
Inman, Bobby Ray 1931- **1985**:1

**National Union for the Total Independence of Angola [UNITA]**
Savimbi, Jonas 1934- **1986**:2

**National Union of Mineworkers [NUM]**
Ramaphosa, Cyril 1953- **1988**:2

**National Wildlife Federation [NWF]**
Hair, Jay D. 1945- **1994**:3

**Nation of Islam**
Cleaver, Eldridge 1935-1998
Obituary **1998**:4
Farrakhan, Louis 1933- **1990**:4
Shabazz, Betty 1936-1997
Obituary **1997**:4

**Native American issues**
Banks, Dennis J. 193- **1986**:4
Begaye, Kelsey 1950(?)- **1999**:3
Brown, Dee 1908-2002
Obituary **2004**:1
Campbell, Ben Nighthorse
1933- **1998**:1
Castaneda, Carlos 1931-1998
Obituary **1998**:4
Grant, Rodney A. **1992**:1
Greene, Graham 1952- **1997**:2
LaDuke, Winona 1959- **1995**:2
Mankiller, Wilma P.
Brief entry **1986**:2
Peltier, Leonard 1944- **1995**:1
Sidney, Ivan
Brief entry **1987**:2
Studi, Wes 1944(?)- **1994**:3
Tohe, Laura 1953- **2009**:2

**Nautilus Sports/Medical Industries**
  Jones, Arthur A. 1924(?)- **1985**:3

**Navajo Nation**
  Begaye, Kelsey 1950(?)- **1999**:3

**Nazi Party**
  Hess, Rudolph 1894-1987
    Obituary **1988**:1
  Klarsfeld, Beate 1939- **1989**:1
  Mengele, Josef 1911-1979
    Obituary **1985**:2

**NBC Television Network**
  Brokaw, Tom 1940- **2000**:3
  Curry, Ann 1956- **2001**:1
  Gumbel, Greg 1946- **1996**:4
  Tartikoff, Brandon 1949-1997 **1985**:2
    Obituary **1998**:1
  Williams, Brian 1959- **2009**:4

**Nebraska state government**
  Kerrey, Bob 1943- **1986**:1
  Orr, Kay 1939- **1987**:4

**Nebula Awards**
  Asimov, Isaac 1920-1992
    Obituary **1992**:3
  Brooks, Mel 1926- **2003**:1
  Hand, Elizabeth 1957- **2007**:2

**Negro American League**
  O'Neil, Buck 1911-2006
    Obituary **2007**:4
  Pride, Charley 1938(?)- **1998**:1

**Netscape Communications Corp.**
  Andreessen, Marc 1972- **1996**:2
  Barksdale, James L. 1943- **1998**:2
  Clark, Jim 1944- **1997**:1

**Neurobiology**
  Goldman-Rakic, Patricia
    1937- **2002**:4
  Hockfield, Susan 1951- **2009**:2
  Kandel, Eric 1929- **2005**:2
  LeVay, Simon 1943- **1992**:2
  Tully, Tim 1954(?)- **2004**:3

**New Democratic Party (Canada) [NDP]**
  Lewis, Stephen 1937- **1987**:2
  McLaughlin, Audrey 1936- **1990**:3

**New England Patriots football team**
  Bledsoe, Drew 1972- **1995**:1
  Brady, Tom 1977- **2002**:4

**Newfoundland provincial government**
  Peckford, Brian 1942- **1989**:1

**New Hampshire state government**
  Sununu, John 1939- **1989**:2

**New Jersey Devils hockey team**
  Lemieux, Claude 1965- **1996**:1

**New Orleans Saints football team**
  Williams, Ricky 1977- **2000**:2

**New York City Ballet**
  Kistler, Darci 1964- **1993**:1
  Millepied, Benjamin 1977(?)- **2006**:4
  Whelan, Wendy 1967(?)- **1999**:3

**New York City Board of Education**
  Green, Richard R. 1936- **1988**:3

**New York City government**
  Dinkins, David N. 1927- **1990**:2
  Fairstein, Linda 1948(?)- **1991**:1
  Giuliani, Rudolph 1944- **1994**:2
  Kennedy, John F., Jr.
    1960-1999 **1990**:1
    Obituary **1999**:4

**New York City public schools**
  Fernandez, Joseph 1935- **1991**:3

**New Yorker magazine**
  Brown, Tina 1953- **1992**:1
  Chast, Roz 1955- **1992**:4
  Hoff, Syd 1912-2004
    Obituary **2005**:3
  Shawn, William 1907-1992
    Obituary **1993**:3
  Steig, William 1907-2003
    Obituary **2004**:4

**New York Giants football team**
  Barber, Tiki 1975- **2007**:1
  Collins, Kerry 1972- **2002**:3
  Manning, Eli 1981- **2008**:4
  Taylor, Lawrence 1959- **1987**:3

**New York Islanders hockey team**
  LaFontaine, Pat 1965- **1985**:1

**New York Knicks basketball team**
  Bradley, Bill 1943- **2000**:2
  Ewing, Patrick 1962- **1985**:3
  McMillen, Tom 1952- **1988**:4
  Riley, Pat 1945- **1994**:3
  Sprewell, Latrell 1970- **1999**:4

**New York Mets baseball team**
  Agee, Tommie 1942-2001
    Obituary **2001**:4
  Bonilla, Bobby 1963- **1992**:2
  Carter, Gary 1954- **1987**:1
  Doubleday, Nelson, Jr. 1933- **1987**:1
  Gooden, Dwight 1964- **1985**:2
  McGraw, Tug 1944-2004
    Obituary **2005**:1
  Piazza, Mike 1968- **1998**:4
  Ryan, Nolan 1947- **1989**:4

**New York Philharmonic Orchestra**
  Masur, Kurt 1927- **1993**:4

**New York Public Library**
  Gregorian, Vartan 1934- **1990**:3
  Healy, Timothy S. 1923- **1990**:2

**New York Rangers hockey team**
  Messier, Mark 1961- **1993**:1

**New York State Government**
  Cuomo, Mario 1932- **1992**:2
  Florio, James J. 1937- **1991**:2
  Pataki, George 1945- **1995**:2

  Rothwax, Harold 1930- **1996**:3

**New York Stock Exchange**
  Fomon, Robert M. 1925- **1985**:3
  Phelan, John Joseph, Jr. 1931- **1985**:4
  Siebert, Muriel 1932(?)- **1987**:2

**New York Times**
  Dowd, Maureen Brigid 1952- **1997**:1
  Lelyveld, Joseph S. 1937- **1994**:4
  Sulzberger, Arthur O., Jr.
    1951- **1998**:3

**New York Titans football team**
  Barnes, Ernie 1938- **1997**:4

**New York Yankees baseball team**
  Chamberlain, Joba 1985- **2008**:3
  DiMaggio, Joe 1914-1999
    Obituary **1999**:3
  Gomez, Lefty 1909-1989
    Obituary **1989**:3
  Howser, Dick 1936-1987
    Obituary **1987**:4
  Jeter, Derek 1974- **1999**:4
  Mantle, Mickey 1931-1995
    Obituary **1996**:1
  Maris, Roger 1934-1985
    Obituary **1986**:1
  Martin, Billy 1928-1989 **1988**:4
    Obituary **1990**:2
  Matsui, Hideki 1974- **2007**:4
  Mattingly, Don 1961- **1986**:2
  Steinbrenner, George 1930- **1991**:1
  Torre, Joseph Paul 1940- **1997**:1
  Wells, David 1963- **1999**:3

**Nike, Inc.**
  Hamm, Mia 1972- **2000**:1
  Knight, Philip H. 1938- **1994**:1

**Nissan Motor Co.**
  Ghosn, Carlos 1954- **2008**:3
  Katayama, Yutaka 1909- **1987**:1

**Nobel Prize**
  Altman, Sidney 1939- **1997**:2
  Arias Sanchez, Oscar 1941- **1989**:3
  Axelrod, Julius 1912-2004
    Obituary **2006**:1
  Beckett, Samuel Barclay 1906-1989
    Obituary **1990**:2
  Begin, Menachem 1913-1992
    Obituary **1992**:3
  Bellow, Saul 1915-2005
    Obituary **2006**:2
  Blobel, Gunter 1936- **2000**:4
  Carlsson, Arvid 1923- **2001**:2
  Cela, Camilo Jose 1916-2001
    Obituary **2003**:1
  Coetzee, J. M. 1940- **2004**:4
  Cram, Donald J. 1919-2001
    Obituary **2002**:2
  Crick, Francis 1916-2004
    Obituary **2005**:4
  Davis, Raymond, Jr. 1914-2006
    Obituary **2007**:3
  Ebadi, Shirin 1947- **2004**:3
  ElBaradei, Mohamed 1942- **2006**:3
  Fo, Dario 1926- **1998**:1

Friedman, Milton 1912-2006
Obituary **2008**:1
Gao Xingjian 1940- **2001**:2
Garcia Marquez, Gabriel
1928- **2005**:2
Grass, Gunter 1927- **2000**:2
Heaney, Seamus 1939- **1996**:2
Hounsfield, Godfrey 1919- **1989**:2
Jelinek, Elfriede 1946- **2005**:3
Kandel, Eric 1929- **2005**:2
Kilby, Jack 1923- **2002**:2
Kissinger, Henry 1923- **1999**:4
Kornberg, Arthur 1918(?)- **1992**:1
Lederman, Leon Max 1922- **1989**:4
Lessing, Doris 1919- **2008**:4
Lewis, Edward B. 1918-2004
Obituary **2005**:4
Lorenz, Konrad 1903-1989
Obituary **1989**:3
Mahfouz, Naguib 1911-2006
Obituary **2007**:4
Menchu, Rigoberta 1960(?)- **1993**:2
Milosz, Czeslaw 1911-2004
Obituary **2005**:4
Morrison, Toni 1931- **1998**:1
Mother Teresa 1910-1997 **1993**:1
Obituary **1998**:1
Mullis, Kary 1944- **1995**:3
Nuesslein-Volhard, Christiane
1942- **1998**:1
Oe, Kenzaburo 1935- **1997**:1
Pamuk, Orhan 1952- **2007**:3
Pauling, Linus 1901-1994
Obituary **1995**:1
Paz, Octavio 1914- **1991**:2
Perutz, Max 1914-2002
Obituary **2003**:2
Pople, John 1925-2004
Obituary **2005**:2
Porter, George 1920-2002
Obituary **2003**:4
Prusiner, Stanley 1942- **1998**:2
Sakharov, Andrei Dmitrievich
1921-1989
Obituary **1990**:2
Saramago, Jose 1922- **1999**:1
Singer, Isaac Bashevis 1904-1991
Obituary **1992**:1
Suu Kyi, Aung San 1945(?)- **1996**:2
Szent-Gyoergyi, Albert 1893-1986
Obituary **1987**:2
Trimble, David 1944- **1999**:1
Walesa, Lech 1943- **1991**:2
Wiesel, Elie 1928- **1998**:1
Yunus, Muhammad 1940- **2007**:3

**No Limit (record label)**
Master P 1970- **1999**:4

**North Atlantic Treaty Organization
[NATO]**
de Hoop Scheffer, Jaap 1948- **2005**:1
Galvin, John R. 1929- **1990**:1

**NPR**
Tom and Ray Magliozzi **1991**:4

**Nuclear energy**
Gale, Robert Peter 1945- **1986**:4
Hagelstein, Peter
Brief entry **1986**:3

Lederman, Leon Max 1922- **1989**:4
Maglich, Bogdan C. 1928- **1990**:1
Merritt, Justine
Brief entry **1985**:3
Nader, Ralph 1934- **1989**:4
Palme, Olof 1927-1986
Obituary **1986**:2
Rickover, Hyman 1900-1986
Obituary **1986**:4
Sinclair, Mary 1918- **1985**:2
Smith, Samantha 1972-1985
Obituary **1985**:3
Zech, Lando W.
Brief entry **1987**:4

**Nuclear Regulatory Commission [NRC]**
Zech, Lando W.
Brief entry **1987**:4

**Oakland A's baseball team**
Canseco, Jose 1964- **1990**:2
Caray, Harry 1914(?)-1998 **1988**:3
Obituary **1998**:3
Stewart, Dave 1957- **1991**:1
Welch, Bob 1956- **1991**:3
Zito, Barry 1978- **2003**:3

**Oakland Raiders football team**
Matuszak, John 1951(?)-1989
Obituary **1989**:4
Trask, Amy 1961- **2003**:3
Upshaw, Gene 1945- **1988**:1

**Obie Awards**
Albee, Edward 1928- **1997**:1
Arkin, Alan 1934- **2007**:4
Baldwin, Alec 1958- **2002**:2
Bergman, Ingmar 1918- **1999**:4
Close, Glenn 1947- **1988**:3
Coco, James 1929(?)-1987
Obituary **1987**:2
Daniels, Jeff 1955- **1989**:4
Dewhurst, Colleen 1924-1991
Obituary **1992**:2
Diller, Elizabeth and Ricardo
Scofidio **2004**:3
Dukakis, Olympia 1931- **1996**:4
Duvall, Robert 1931- **1999**:3
Ebersole, Christine 1953- **2007**:2
Ensler, Eve 1954(?)- **2002**:4
Fierstein, Harvey 1954- **2004**:2
Fo, Dario 1926- **1998**:1
Fugard, Athol 1932- **1992**:3
Gray, Spalding 1941-2004
Obituary **2005**:2
Hoffman, Dustin 1937- **2005**:4
Hurt, William 1950- **1986**:1
Hwang, David Henry 1957- **1999**:1
Irwin, Bill **1988**:3
Kline, Kevin 1947- **2000**:1
Langella, Frank 1940- **2008**:3
Leguizamo, John 1965- **1999**:1
McDonagh, Martin 1970- **2007**:3
McDonnell, Mary 1952- **2008**:2
Merkerson, S. Epatha 1952- **2006**:4
Miller, Arthur 1915- **1999**:4
Pacino, Al 1940- **1993**:4
Parks, Suzan-Lori 1964- **2003**:2
Schreiber, Liev 1967- **2007**:2
Sedaris, Amy 1961- **2009**:3
Shanley, John Patrick 1950- **2006**:1

Shepard, Sam 1943- **1996**:4
Streep, Meryl 1949- **1990**:2
Tune, Tommy 1939- **1994**:2
Turturro, John 1957- **2002**:2
Vogel, Paula 1951- **1999**:2
Washington, Denzel 1954- **1993**:2
Waterston, Sam 1940- **2006**:1
White, Julie 1961- **2008**:2
Woods, James 1947- **1988**:3

**Occidental Petroleum Corp.**
Hammer, Armand 1898-1990
Obituary **1991**:3

**Oceanography**
Cousteau, Jacques-Yves
1910-1997 **1998**:2
Cousteau, Jean-Michel 1938- **1988**:2
Fisher, Mel 1922(?)- **1985**:4

**Office of National Drug Control Policy**
Bennett, William 1943- **1990**:1
Martinez, Bob 1934- **1992**:1

**Ogilvy & Mather Advertising**
Lazarus, Shelly 1947- **1998**:3

**Ohio State University football team**
Hayes, Woody 1913-1987
Obituary **1987**:2

**Oil**
Adair, Red 1915- **1987**:3
Aurre, Laura
Brief entry **1986**:3
Hammer, Armand 1898-1990
Obituary **1991**:3
Jones, Jerry 1942- **1994**:4

**Olympic games**
Abbott, Jim 1967- **1988**:3
Ali, Muhammad 1942- **1997**:2
Arakawa, Shizuka 1981- **2006**:4
Armstrong, Lance 1971- **2000**:1
Baiul, Oksana 1977- **1995**:3
Baumgartner, Bruce
Brief entry **1987**:3
Benoit, Joan 1957- **1986**:3
Blair, Bonnie 1964- **1992**:3
Boitano, Brian 1963- **1988**:3
Bolt, Usain 1986- **2009**:2
Bradley, Bill 1943- **2000**:2
Conner, Dennis 1943- **1987**:2
Davenport, Lindsay 1976- **1999**:2
De La Hoya, Oscar 1973- **1998**:2
DiBello, Paul
Brief entry **1986**:4
Dolan, Tom 1975- **2001**:2
Drexler, Clyde 1962- **1992**:4
Eagleson, Alan 1933- **1987**:4
Edwards, Harry 1942- **1989**:4
Evans, Janet 1971- **1989**:1
Ewing, Patrick 1962- **1985**:3
Fabris, Enrico 1981- **2006**:4
Freeman, Cathy 1973- **2001**:3
Gault, Willie 1960- **1991**:2
Graf, Steffi 1969- **1987**:4
Granato, Cammi 1971- **1999**:3
Grinkov, Sergei 1967-1995
Obituary **1996**:2

Guo Jingjing 1981- **2009**:2
Hamilton, Scott 1958- **1998**:2
Hamm, Mia 1972- **2000**:1
Hamm, Paul 1982- **2005**:1
Holyfield, Evander 1962- **1991**:3
Hughes, Sarah 1985- **2002**:4
Johnson, Michael **2000**:1
Johnson, Shawn 1992- **2009**:2
Jordan, Michael 1963- **1987**:2
Joyner, Florence Griffith
    1959-1998 **1989**:2
    Obituary **1999**:1
Joyner-Kersee, Jackie 1962- **1993**:1
Kerrigan, Nancy 1969- **1994**:3
Kiraly, Karch
    Brief entry **1987**:1
Knight, Bobby 1940- **1985**:3
Laettner, Christian 1969- **1993**:1
LaFontaine, Pat 1965- **1985**:1
Lalas, Alexi 1970- **1995**:1
Leonard, Sugar Ray 1956- **1989**:4
Leslie, Lisa 1972- **1997**:4
Lewis, Lennox 1965- **2000**:2
Lindbergh, Pelle 1959-1985
    Obituary **1985**:4
Lipinski, Tara 1982- **1998**:3
Louganis, Greg 1960- **1995**:3
Mathias, Bob 1930-2006
    Obituary **2007**:4
Milbrett, Tiffeny 1972- **2001**:1
Milburn, Rodney Jr.
    1950-1997 **1998**:2
Miller, Bode 1977- **2002**:4
Mulkey-Robertson, Kim
    1962- **2006**:1
Phelps, Michael 1985- **2009**:2
Retton, Mary Lou 1968- **1985**:2
Rudolph, Wilma 1940-1994
    Obituary **1995**:2
Runyan, Marla 1969- **2001**:1
Samaranch, Juan Antonio
    1920- **1986**:2
Shea, Jim, Jr. 1968- **2002**:4
Street, Picabo 1971- **1999**:3
Strobl, Fritz 1972- **2003**:3
Strug, Kerri 1977- **1997**:3
Summitt, Pat 1952- **2004**:1
Swoopes, Sheryl 1971- **1998**:2
Teter, Hannah 1987- **2006**:4
Thomas, Debi 1967- **1987**:2
Thompson, John 1941- **1988**:3
Tomba, Alberto 1966- **1992**:3
Torres, Dara 1967- **2009**:1
Van Dyken, Amy 1973- **1997**:1
Waddell, Thomas F. 1937-1987
    Obituary **1988**:2
Wariner, Jeremy 1984- **2006**:3
Wescott, Seth 1976- **2006**:4
Witt, Katarina 1966(?)- **1991**:3
Woodard, Lynette 1959(?)- **1986**:2
Yamaguchi, Kristi 1971- **1992**:3

**Ontario provincial government**
    Peterson, David 1943- **1987**:1

**ON Technology**
    Kapor, Mitch 1950- **1990**:3

**Opera**
    Anderson, Marion 1897-1993
        Obituary **1993**:4
    Bartoli, Cecilia 1966- **1994**:1

Battle, Kathleen 1948- **1998**:1
Berio, Luciano 1925-2003
    Obituary **2004**:2
Carreras, Jose 1946- **1995**:2
Domingo, Placido 1941- **1993**:2
Fleming, Renee **2001**:4
Nilsson, Birgit 1918-2005
    Obituary **2007**:1
Pavarotti, Luciano 1935- **1997**:4
Potts, Paul 1970- **2009**:1
Schwarzkopf, Elisabeth 1915-2006
    Obituary **2007**:3
Upshaw, Dawn 1960- **1991**:2
Zeffirelli, Franco 1923- **1991**:3

**Operation Rescue**
    Terry, Randall **1991**:4

**Orlando Magic basketball team**
    Hardaway, Anfernee 1971- **1996**:2

**Painting**
    Appel, Karel 1921-2006
        Obituary **2007**:2
    Banksy 1975(?)- **2007**:2
    Bean, Alan L. 1932- **1986**:2
    Botero, Fernando 1932- **1994**:3
    Chagall, Marc 1887-1985
        Obituary **1985**:2
    Chatham, Russell 1939- **1990**:1
    Chia, Sandro 1946- **1987**:2
    Conner, Bruce 1933-2008
        Obituary **2009**:3
    Dali, Salvador 1904-1989
        Obituary **1989**:2
    de Kooning, Willem
        1904-1997 **1994**:4
        Obituary **1997**:3
    Diebenkorn, Richard 1922-1993
        Obituary **1993**:4
    Dubuffet, Jean 1901-1985
        Obituary **1985**:4
    Ellis, David 1971- **2009**:4
    Emin, Tracey 1963- **2009**:2
    Frankenthaler, Helen 1928- **1990**:1
    Freud, Lucian 1922- **2000**:4
    Graves, Nancy 1940- **1989**:3
    Haring, Keith 1958-1990
        Obituary **1990**:3
    Held, Al 1928-2005
        Obituary **2006**:4
    Hockney, David 1937- **1988**:3
    Kahlo, Frida 1907-1954 **1991**:3
    Katz, Alex 1927- **1990**:3
    Kelly, Ellsworth 1923- **1992**:1
    Kiefer, Anselm 1945- **1990**:2
    Kitaj, R. B. 1932-2007
        Obituary **2008**:4
    Kostabi, Mark 1960- **1989**:4
    Lichtenstein, Roy 1923-1997 **1994**:1
        Obituary **1998**:1
    Longo, Robert 1953(?)- **1990**:4
    Mardin, Brice 1938- **2007**:4
    Martin, Agnes 1912-2004
        Obituary **2006**:1
    Miro, Joan 1893-1983
        Obituary **1985**:1
    Motherwell, Robert 1915-1991
        Obituary **1992**:1
    Murakami, Takashi 1962- **2004**:2
    Nechita, Alexandra 1985- **1996**:4
    Neiman, LeRoy 1927- **1993**:3

Ono, Yoko 1933- **1989**:2
Peyton, Elizabeth 1965- **2007**:1
Polke, Sigmar 1941- **1999**:4
Pozzi, Lucio 1935- **1990**:2
Pratt, Christopher 1935- **1985**:3
Rauschenberg, Robert 1925- **1991**:2
Rothenberg, Susan 1945- **1995**:3
Schnabel, Julian 1951- **1997**:1
Stella, Frank 1936- **1996**:2
Tamayo, Rufino 1899-1991
    Obituary **1992**:1
Thiebaud, Wayne 1920- **1991**:1
Twombley, Cy 1928(?)- **1995**:1
Von Hellermann, Sophie
    1975- **2006**:3
Warhol, Andy 1927(?)-1987
    Obituary **1987**:2
Wegman, William 1942(?)- **1991**:1
Wyland, Robert 1956- **2009**:3

**Pakistan People's Party**
    Bhutto, Benazir 1953- **1989**:4

**Paleontology**
    Bakker, Robert T. 1950(?)- **1991**:3
    Gould, Stephen Jay 1941-2002
        Obituary **2003**:3
    Horner, Jack 1946- **1985**:2

**Palestine Liberation Organization [PLO]**
    Abbas, Mahmoud 1935- **2008**:4
    Arafat, Yasser 1929- **1989**:3
    Darwish, Mahmud 1942-2008
        Obituary **2009**:4
    Habash, George 1925(?)- **1986**:1
    Husseini, Faisal 1940- **1998**:4
    Hussein I, King 1935-1999 **1997**:3
        Obituary **1999**:3
    Redgrave, Vanessa 1937- **1989**:2
    Terzi, Zehdi Labib 1924- **1985**:3

**Palimony**
    Marvin, Lee 1924-1987
        Obituary **1988**:1
    Mitchelson, Marvin 1928- **1989**:2

**Palm Computing**
    Hawkins, Jeff and Donna Dubinsky
        **2000**:2

**Paralegals**
    Furman, Rosemary
        Brief entry **1986**:4

**Paramount Pictures**
    Diller, Barry 1942- **1991**:1
    Lansing, Sherry 1944- **1995**:4
    Steel, Dawn 1946-1997 **1990**:1
        Obituary **1998**:2

**Parents' Music Resource Center
[PMRC]**
    Gore, Tipper 1948- **1985**:4
    Snider, Dee 1955- **1986**:1

**Parents of Murdered Children**
    Hullinger, Charlotte
        Brief entry **1985**:1

**Paris Opera Ballet Company**
    Guillem, Sylvie 1965(?)- **1988**:2

**Parkinson's disease**
Ali, Muhammad 1942- **1997**:2
Langston, J. William
Brief entry **1986**:2

**Parks**
Mott, William Penn, Jr. 1909- **1986**:1

**Parsons Dance Company**
Parsons, David 1959- **1993**:4

**Parti Quebecois**
Johnson, Pierre Marc 1946- **1985**:4
Leaavesque, Reneaa
Obituary **1988**:1
Parizeau, Jacques 1930- **1995**:1

**Paul Taylor Dance Company**
Taylor, Paul 1930- **1992**:3

**Peabody Awards**
Child, Julia 1912- **1999**:4
Duncan, Todd 1903-1998
Obituary **1998**:3
Gross, Terry 1951- **1998**:3
Herbert, Don 1917-2007
Obituary **2008**:3
Keeshan, Bob 1927-2004
Obituary **2005**:2
Kuralt, Charles 1934-1997
Obituary **1998**:3
Melendez, Bill 1916-2008
Obituary **2009**:4
Miller, Arthur 1915- **1999**:4
O'Connor, Donald 1925-2003
Obituary **2004**:4
Osgood, Charles 1933- **1996**:2
Schulz, Charles M. 1922- **1998**:1

**Peace Corps**
Ruppe, Loret Miller 1936- **1986**:2

**Pennsylvania State University**
Paterno, Joe 1926- **1995**:4

**Penthouse International Ltd.**
Guccione, Bob 1930- **1986**:1

**People Express Airlines**
Burr, Donald Calvin 1941- **1985**:3

**People for the Ethical Treatment of Animals [PETA]**
Mathews, Dan 1965- **1998**:3
McCartney, Linda 1942-1998
Obituary **1998**:4
Newkirk, Ingrid 1949- **1992**:3

**People Organized and Working for Economic Rebirth [POWER]**
Farrakhan, Louis 1933- **1990**:4

**People's Choice Awards**
Almodovar, Pedro 1951- **2000**:3
Applegate, Christina 1972- **2000**:4
Burnett, Carol 1933- **2000**:3
Rihanna 1988- **2008**:4
Somers, Suzanne 1946- **2000**:1

Timberlake, Justin 1981- **2008**:4

**Pepsico, Inc.**
Calloway, D. Wayne 1935- **1987**:3
Nooyi, Indra 1955- **2004**:3
Sculley, John 1939- **1989**:4

**Performance art**
Beuys, Joseph 1921-1986
Obituary **1986**:3
Bogosian, Eric 1953- **1990**:4
Ellis, David 1971- **2009**:4
Finley, Karen 1956- **1992**:4
Irwin, Bill **1988**:3
Ono, Yoko 1933- **1989**:2
Penn & Teller **1992**:1
Pozzi, Lucio 1935- **1990**:2

**Perry Ellis Award**
Cameron, David
Brief entry **1988**:1
Hernandez, Lazaro and Jack McCollough **2008**:4
Kim, Eugenia 1974(?)- **2006**:1
Lam, Derek 1966- **2009**:2
Posen, Zac 1980- **2009**:3
Rowley, Cynthia 1958- **2002**:1
Spade, Kate 1962- **2003**:1
Varvatos, John 1956(?)- **2006**:2

**Persian Gulf War**
Amanpour, Christiane 1958- **1997**:2
Hussein I, King 1935-1999 **1997**:3
Obituary **1999**:3
Kent, Arthur 1954- **1991**:4
Powell, Colin 1937- **1990**:1
Schwarzkopf, Norman 1934- **1991**:3

**Philadelphia Eagles football team**
Cunningham, Randall 1963- **1990**:1

**Philadelphia 76ers basketball team**
Barkley, Charles 1963- **1988**:2
Chamberlain, Wilt 1936-1999
Obituary **2000**:2
Iverson, Allen 1975- **2001**:4

**Philadelphia Flyers hockey team**
Hextall, Ron 1964- **1988**:2
Lindbergh, Pelle 1959-1985
Obituary **1985**:4

**Philadelphia Phillies baseball team**
Dykstra, Lenny 1963- **1993**:4
Hamels, Cole 1983- **2009**:4
Kruk, John 1961- **1994**:4
McGraw, Tug 1944-2004
Obituary **2005**:1
Schmidt, Mike 1949- **1988**:3
Williams, Ricky 1977- **2000**:2

**Philanthropy**
Annenberg, Walter 1908- **1992**:3
Astor, Brooke 1902-2007
Obituary **2008**:4
Bolkiah, Sultan Muda Hassanal 1946- **1985**:4
Duke, Doris 1912-1993
Obituary **1994**:2

Ferrell, Trevor
Brief entry **1985**:2
Haas, Robert D. 1942- **1986**:4
Hammer, Armand 1898-1990
Obituary **1991**:3
Heinz, H.J. 1908-1987
Obituary **1987**:2
Hero, Peter 1942- **2001**:2
Judkins, Reba
Brief entry **1987**:3
Kaye, Danny 1913-1987
Obituary **1987**:2
Lang, Eugene M. 1919- **1990**:3
Lerner, Sandy 1955(?)- **2005**:1
Marriott, J. Willard 1900-1985
Obituary **1985**:4
Mellon, Paul 1907-1999
Obituary **1999**:3
Menuhin, Yehudi 1916-1999
Obituary **1999**:3
Pritzker, A.N. 1896-1986
Obituary **1986**:2
Ross, Percy
Brief entry **1986**:2
Sasakawa, Ryoichi
Brief entry **1988**:1
Stevens, James
Brief entry **1988**:1
Thomas, Danny 1914-1991
Obituary **1991**:3

**Philip Morris Companies, Inc.**
Maxwell, Hamish 1926- **1989**:4
Wigand, Jeffrey 1943(?)- **2000**:4

**Phoenix Suns basketball team**
Johnson, Kevin 1966(?)- **1991**:1
Majerle, Dan 1965- **1993**:4

**Photography**
al-Ani, Jananne 1966- **2008**:4
Alvarez Bravo, Manuel 1902-2002
Obituary **2004**:1
Avedon, Richard 1923- **1993**:4
Butterfield, Stewart and Caterina Fake **2007**:3
Cartier-Bresson, Henri 1908-2004
Obituary **2005**:4
DeCarava, Roy 1919- **1996**:3
Dith Pran 1942-2008
Obituary **2009**:2
Eisenstaedt, Alfred 1898-1995
Obituary **1996**:1
Frank, Robert 1924- **1995**:2
Gottlieb, William 1917-2006
Obituary **2007**:2
Hockney, David 1937- **1988**:3
Karsh, Yousuf 1908-2002
Obituary **2003**:4
Land, Edwin H. 1909-1991
Obituary **1991**:3
Leibovitz, Annie 1949- **1988**:4
Mann, Sally 1951- **2001**:2
Mapplethorpe, Robert 1946-1989
Obituary **1989**:3
Mark, Mary Ellen 1940- **2006**:2
Matadin, Vinoodh and Inez van Lamsweerde **2007**:4
McCartney, Linda 1942-1998
Obituary **1998**:4
McDowall, Roddy 1928-1998
Obituary **1999**:1

Meisel, Steven 1954- **2002**:4
Misrach, Richard 1949- **1991**:2
Mydans, Carl 1907-2004
  Obituary **2005**:4
Nars, Francois 1959- **2003**:1
Newman, Arnold 1918- **1993**:1
Newton, Helmut 1920- **2002**:1
Parks, Gordon 1912-2006
  Obituary **2006**:2
Ritts, Herb 1954(?)- **1992**:4
Rosenthal, Joseph 1911-2006
  Obituary **2007**:4
Salgado, Sebastiao 1944- **1994**:2
Scavullo, Francesco 1921-2004
  Obituary **2005**:1
Sherman, Cindy 1954- **1992**:3
Simpson, Lorna 1960- **2008**:1
Testino, Mario 1954- **2002**:1
Tillmans, Wolfgang 1968- **2001**:4
Tunick, Spencer 1967- **2008**:1
Wegman, William 1942(?)- **1991**:1
Witkin, Joel-Peter 1939- **1996**:1

**Physical fitness**
  Hughes, Mark 1956- **1985**:3
  Jones, Arthur A. 1924(?)- **1985**:3
  Powter, Susan 1957(?)- **1994**:3
  Schwarzenegger, Arnold
    1947- **1991**:1
  Tanny, Vic 1912(?)-1985
    Obituary **1985**:3
  Wilson, Jerry
    Brief entry **1986**:2

**Physics**
  Bethe, Hans 1906-2005
    Obituary **2006**:2
  Chaudhari, Praveen 1937- **1989**:4
  Chu, Paul C.W. 1941- **1988**:2
  Davis, Raymond, Jr. 1914-2006
    Obituary **2007**:3
  Fang Lizhi 1937- **1988**:1
  Fano, Ugo 1912-2001
    Obituary **2001**:4
  Hau, Lene Vestergaard 1959- **2006**:4
  Hawking, Stephen W. 1942- **1990**:1
  Horowitz, Paul 1942- **1988**:2
  Lederman, Leon Max 1922- **1989**:4
  Maglich, Bogdan C. 1928- **1990**:1
  Maiman, Theodore 1927-2007
    Obituary **2008**:3
  Panofsky, Wolfgang 1919-2007
    Obituary **2008**:4
  Penrose, Roger 1931- **1991**:4
  Randall, Lisa 1962- **2009**:2
  Sakharov, Andrei Dmitrievich
    1921-1989
    Obituary **1990**:2
  Witten, Edward 1951- **2006**:2

**PhytoFarms**
  Davis, Noel **1990**:3

**Pittsburgh, Pa., city government**
  Caliguiri, Richard S. 1931-1988
    Obituary **1988**:3

**Pittsburgh Penguins hockey team**
  Jagr, Jaromir 1972- **1995**:4
  Lemieux, Mario 1965- **1986**:4

**Pittsburgh Pirates baseball team**
  Leyland, Jim 1944- **1998**:2
  Stargell, Willie 1940-2001

  Obituary **2002**:1

**Pittsburgh Steelers football team**
  Parker, Willie 1980- **2009**:3
  Rooney, Art 1901-1988
    Obituary **1989**:1
  White, Byron 1917-2002
    Obituary **2003**:3
  Woodson, Ron 1965- **1996**:4

**Pixar Animation Studios**
  Jobs, Steve 1955- **2000**:1
  Varney, Jim 1949-2000
    Brief entry **1985**:4
    Obituary **2000**:3

**Pixillation**
  McLaren, Norman 1914-1987
    Obituary **1987**:2

**Pizza Kwik, Ltd.**
  Paulucci, Jeno
    Brief entry **1986**:3

**Pizza Time Theatres, Inc.**
  Bushnell, Nolan 1943- **1985**:1

**Planned Parenthood Federation of
America**
  Maraldo, Pamela J. 1948(?)- **1993**:4
  Wattleton, Faye 1943- **1989**:1

**Playboy Enterprises**
  Hefner, Christie 1952- **1985**:1
  Ingersoll, Ralph II 1946- **1988**:2
  Melman, Richard
    Brief entry **1986**:1

**Pleasant Company**
  Rowland, Pleasant **1992**:3

**Poetry**
  Angelou, Maya 1928- **1993**:4
  Bly, Robert 1926- **1992**:4
  Brooks, Gwendolyn
    1917-2000 **1998**:1
    Obituary **2001**:2
  Burroughs, William S. 1914-1997
    Obituary **1997**:4
  Codrescu, Andreaa 1946- **1997**:3
  Collins, Billy 1941- **2002**:2
  Darwish, Mahmud 1942-2008
    Obituary **2009**:4
  Dickey, James 1923-1997 **1998**:2
  Dove, Rita 1952- **1994**:3
  Dylan, Bob 1941- **1998**:1
  Eberhart, Richard 1904-2005
    Obituary **2006**:3
  Ginsberg, Allen 1926-1997
    Obituary **1997**:3
  Gioia, Dana 1950- **2008**:4
  Heaney, Seamus 1939- **1996**:2
  Hughes, Ted 1930-1998
    Obituary **1999**:2
  Jewel 1974- **1999**:2
  Jones, Sarah 1974(?)- **2005**:2
  Kunitz, Stanley J. 1905- **2001**:2
  Milligan, Spike 1918-2002
    Obituary **2003**:2

Milosz, Czeslaw 1911-2004
  Obituary **2005**:4
Mortensen, Viggo 1958- **2003**:3
Nemerov, Howard 1920-1991
  Obituary **1992**:1
Paz, Octavio 1914- **1991**:2
Sapphire 1951(?)- **1996**:4
Senghor, Leopold 1906-2001
  Obituary **2003**:1
Tohe, Laura 1953- **2009**:2
Tretheway, Natasha 1966- **2008**:3
Van Duyn, Mona 1921- **1993**:2
Walker, Alice 1944- **1999**:1

**Polaroid Corp.**
  Land, Edwin H. 1909-1991
    Obituary **1991**:3

**Pole vaulting**
  Olson, Billy 1958- **1986**:3

**Pop art**
  Castelli, Leo 1907-1999
    Obituary **2000**:1
  Lichtenstein, Roy 1923-1997 **1994**:1
    Obituary **1998**:1
  Paolozzi, Eduardo 1924-2005
    Obituary **2006**:3
  Richter, Gerhard 1932- **1997**:2
  Warhol, Andy 1927(?)-1987
    Obituary **1987**:2

**Popular Front for the Liberation of
Palestine [PFLP]**
  Habash, George 1925(?)- **1986**:1

**Pornography**
  Dworkin, Andrea 1946-2005
    Obituary **2006**:2
  Flynt, Larry 1942- **1997**:3

**Portland, Ore., city government**
  Clark, J. E.
    Brief entry **1986**:1

**Portland Trail Blazers basketball team**
  Drexler, Clyde 1962- **1992**:4
  Wilkens, Lenny 1937- **1995**:2

**Presidential Medal of Freedom**
  Annenberg, Walter 1908- **1992**:3
  Cagney, James 1899-1986
    Obituary **1986**:2
  Cheek, James Edward
    Brief entry **1987**:1
  Copland, Aaron 1900-1990
    Obituary **1991**:2
  Cronkite, Walter Leland 1916- **1997**:3
  DeBakey, Michael 1908-2008
    Obituary **2009**:3
  Ellison, Ralph 1914-1994
    Obituary **1994**:4
  Ford, Gerald R. 1913-2007
    Obituary **2008**:2
  Fulbright, J. William 1905-1995
    Obituary **1995**:3
  Kissinger, Henry 1923- **1999**:4
  Luce, Clare Boothe 1903-1987
    Obituary **1988**:1
  Ormandy, Eugene 1899-1985

Obituary **1985**:2
Parks, Rosa 1913-2005
    Obituary **2007**:1
Rickover, Hyman 1900-1986
    Obituary **1986**:4
Rumsfeld, Donald 1932- **2004**:1
Salk, Jonas 1914-1995 **1994**:4
    Obituary **1995**:4
Sinatra, Frank 1915-1998
    Obituary **1998**:4
Smith, Kate 1907(?)-1986
    Obituary **1986**:3
Strauss, Robert 1918- **1991**:4
Wasserman, Lew 1913-2002
    Obituary **2003**:3
Wiesenthal, Simon 1908-2005
    Obituary **2006**:4

**President's Council for Physical Fitness**
    Schwarzenegger, Arnold
    1947- **1991**:1

**Primerica**
    Weill, Sandy 1933- **1990**:4

**Princeton, N.J., city government**
    Sigmund, Barbara Boggs 1939-1990
    Obituary **1991**:1

**Pritzker Prize**
    Ando, Tadao 1941- **2005**:4
    Bunshaft, Gordon 1909-1990 **1989**:3
        Obituary **1991**:1
    Foster, Norman 1935- **1999**:4
    Hadid, Zaha 1950- **2005**:3
    Johnson, Philip 1906- **1989**:2
    Koolhaas, Rem 1944- **2001**:1
    Piano, Renzo 1937- **2009**:2
    Pritzker, A.N. 1896-1986
        Obituary **1986**:2
    Roche, Kevin 1922- **1985**:1
    Tange, Kenzo 1913-2005
        Obituary **2006**:2
    Venturi, Robert 1925- **1994**:4

**Procter & Gamble Co.**
    Lafley, A. G. 1947- **2003**:4
    Smale, John G. 1927- **1987**:3

**Proctor & Gardner Advertising, Inc.**
    Proctor, Barbara Gardner
    1933(?)- **1985**:3

**Professional Bowlers Association [PBA]**
    Weber, Pete 1962- **1986**:3

**Professional Flair**
    Verdi-Fletcher, Mary 1955- **1998**:2

**Professional Golfers Association [PGA]**
    Azinger, Paul 1960- **1995**:2
    Chen, T.C.
        Brief entry **1987**:3
    Couples, Fred 1959- **1994**:4
    Curtis, Ben 1977- **2004**:2
    Furyk, Jim 1970- **2004**:2
    Irwin, Hale 1945- **2005**:2
    Nelson, Byron 1912-2006
        Obituary **2007**:4

Norman, Greg 1955- **1988**:3
Peete, Calvin 1943- **1985**:4
Sarazen, Gene 1902-1999
    Obituary **1999**:4
Singh, Vijay 1963- **2000**:4
Stewart, Payne 1957-1999
    Obituary **2000**:2
Strange, Curtis 1955- **1988**:4
Weir, Mike 1970- **2004**:1

**Progress and Freedom Foundation**
    Huffington, Arianna 1950- **1996**:2

**Project Head Start**
    Zigler, Edward 1930- **1994**:1

**Promise Keepers**
    McCartney, Bill 1940- **1995**:3

**Psychedelic drugs**
    Castaneda, Carlos 1931-1998
        Obituary **1998**:4
    Leary, Timothy 1920-1996
        Obituary **1996**:4
    McKenna, Terence **1993**:3

**Psychiatry**
    Bettelheim, Bruno 1903-1990
        Obituary **1990**:3
    Coles, Robert 1929(?)- **1995**:1
    Frankl, Viktor E. 1905-1997
        Obituary **1998**:1
    Gordon, James 1941- **2009**:4
    Laing, R.D. 1927-1989
        Obituary **1990**:1
    Menninger, Karl 1893-1990
        Obituary **1991**:1

**Psychology**
    Clark, Kenneth B. 1914-2005
        Obituary **2006**:3
    Herz, Rachel 1963- **2008**:1
    Pinker, Steven A. 1954- **2000**:1

**Public Broadcasting Service [PBS]**
    Barney **1993**:4
    Cooke, Alistair 1908-2004
        Obituary **2005**:3
    Gunn, Hartford N., Jr. 1926-1986
        Obituary **1986**:2
    Kerger, Paula A. 1957- **2007**:2
    Lewis, Shari 1934-1998 **1993**:1
        Obituary **1999**:1
    Rogers, Fred 1928- **2000**:4
    Rose, Charlie 1943- **1994**:2
    Trotter, Charlie 1960- **2000**:4

**Public relations**
    Kingsley, Patricia 1932- **1990**:2

**Publishing**
    Annenberg, Walter 1908- **1992**:3
    Black, Conrad 1944- **1986**:2
    Brown, Tina 1953- **1992**:1
    Centrello, Gina 1959(?)- **2008**:3
    Davis, Crispin 1949- **2004**:1
    Doubleday, Nelson, Jr. 1933- **1987**:1
    Epstein, Jason 1928- **1991**:1
    Evans, Joni 1942- **1991**:4

Forbes, Malcolm S. 1919-1990
    Obituary **1990**:3
Forbes, Steve 1947- **1996**:2
Gaines, William M. 1922-1992
    Obituary **1993**:1
Graham, Donald 1945- **1985**:4
Guccione, Bob 1930- **1986**:1
Guccione, Bob, Jr. 1956- **1991**:4
Hamilton, Hamish 1900-1988
    Obituary **1988**:4
Hefner, Christie 1952- **1985**:1
Hillegass, Clifton Keith 1918- **1989**:4
Ingersoll, Ralph II 1946- **1988**:2
Kennedy, John F., Jr.
    1960-1999 **1990**:1
    Obituary **1999**:4
Lear, Frances 1923- **1988**:3
Levin, Gerald 1939- **1995**:2
Lewis, Edward T. 1940- **1999**:4
Macmillan, Harold 1894-1986
    Obituary **1987**:2
Maxwell, Robert 1923- **1990**:1
Maxwell, Robert 1923-1991
    Obituary **1992**:2
Morgan, Dodge 1932(?)- **1987**:1
Morgan, Robin 1941- **1991**:1
Murdoch, Rupert 1931- **1988**:4
Neuharth, Allen H. 1924- **1986**:1
Newhouse, Samuel I., Jr.
    1927- **1997**:1
Onassis, Jacqueline Kennedy
    1929-1994
    Obituary **1994**:4
Pope, Generoso 1927-1988 **1988**:4
Pratt, Jane 1963(?)- **1999**:1
Regan, Judith 1953- **2003**:1
Rowland, Pleasant **1992**:3
Steinem, Gloria 1934- **1996**:2
Sullivan, Andrew 1964(?)- **1996**:1
Summers, Anne 1945- **1990**:2
Tilberis, Elizabeth 1947(?)- **1994**:3
Wenner, Jann 1946- **1993**:1
Whittle, Christopher 1947- **1989**:3
Wintour, Anna 1949- **1990**:4
Ziff, William B., Jr. 1930- **1986**:4
Zuckerman, Mortimer 1937- **1986**:3
Zwilich, Ellen 1939- **1990**:1

**Pulitzer Prize**
    Abbott, George 1887-1995
        Obituary **1995**:3
    Albee, Edward 1928- **1997**:1
    Albert, Stephen 1941- **1986**:1
    Angier, Natalie 1958- **2000**:3
    Barry, Dave 1947(?)- **1991**:2
    Bellow, Saul 1915-2005
        Obituary **2006**:2
    Bennett, Michael 1943-1987
        Obituary **1988**:1
    Block, Herbert 1909-2001
        Obituary **2002**:4
    Breathed, Berkeley 1957- **2005**:3
    Brooks, Gwendolyn
        1917-2000 **1998**:1
        Obituary **2001**:2
    Buchwald, Art 1925-2007
        Obituary **2008**:2
    Caen, Herb 1916-1997
        Obituary **1997**:4
    Chabon, Michael 1963- **2002**:1
    Coles, Robert 1929(?)- **1995**:1
    Copland, Aaron 1900-1990
        Obituary **1991**:2

Cruz, Nilo 1961(?)- **2004**:4
Cunningham, Michael 1952- **2003**:4
Dove, Rita 1952- **1994**:3
Eberhart, Richard 1904-2005
    Obituary **2006**:3
Ebert, Roger 1942- **1998**:3
Faludi, Susan 1959- **1992**:4
Geisel, Theodor 1904-1991
    Obituary **1992**:2
Halberstam, David 1934-2007
    Obituary **2008**:3
Haley, Alex 1924-1992
    Obituary **1992**:3
Jones, Edward P. 1950- **2005**:1
Kennan, George 1904-2005
    Obituary **2006**:2
Kushner, Tony 1956- **1995**:2
Lahiri, Jhumpa 1967- **2001**:3
Lelyveld, Joseph S. 1937- **1994**:4
Lindsay-Abaire, David
    1970(?)- **2008**:2
Logan, Joshua 1908-1988
    Obituary **1988**:4
Mailer, Norman 1923- **1998**:1
Mamet, David 1947- **1998**:4
Marsalis, Wynton 1961- **1997**:4
Mauldin, Bill 1921-2003
    Obituary **2004**:2
McCarthy, Cormac 1933- **2008**:1
McCourt, Frank 1930- **1997**:4
McMurtry, Larry 1936- **2006**:4
Merrill, James 1926-1995
    Obituary **1995**:3
Michener, James A. 1907-1997
    Obituary **1998**:1
Miller, Arthur 1915- **1999**:4
Morrison, Toni 1931- **1998**:1
Papp, Joseph 1921-1991
    Obituary **1992**:2
Parks, Suzan-Lori 1964- **2003**:2
Power, Samantha 1970- **2005**:4
Proulx, E. Annie 1935- **1996**:1
Quindlen, Anna 1952- **1993**:1
Rosenthal, Joseph 1911-2006
    Obituary **2007**:4
Roth, Philip 1933- **1999**:1
Royko, Mike 1932-1997
    Obituary **1997**:4
Safire, William 1929- **2000**:3
Shanley, John Patrick 1950- **2006**:1
Shepard, Sam 1943- **1996**:4
Shields, Carol 1935-2003
    Obituary **2004**:3
Smiley, Jane 1949- **1995**:4
Sondheim, Stephen 1930- **1994**:4
Styron, William 1925-2006
    Obituary **2008**:1
Tretheway, Natasha 1966- **2008**:3
Trudeau, Garry 1948- **1991**:2
Tyler, Anne 1941- **1995**:4
Updike, John 1932- **2001**:2
Van Duyn, Mona 1921- **1993**:2
Vogel, Paula 1951- **1999**:2
Walker, Alice 1944- **1999**:1
Wasserstein, Wendy 1950- **1991**:3
Welty, Eudora 1909-2001
    Obituary **2002**:3
Wilson, August 1945- **2002**:2
Wilson, Edward O. 1929- **1994**:4

**Quebec provincial government**
    Bouchard, Lucien 1938- **1999**:2
    Johnson, Pierre Marc 1946- **1985**:4

Leaavesque, Reneaa
    Obituary **1988**:1

**Radical Party (Italy)**
    Staller, Ilona 1951- **1988**:3

**Radio One, Inc.**
    Hughes, Cathy 1947- **1999**:1

**Random House publishers**
    Evans, Joni 1942- **1991**:4

**RCA Corp.**
    Engstrom, Elmer W. 1901-1984
        Obituary **1985**:2

**Real estate**
    Bloch, Ivan 1940- **1986**:3
    Buss, Jerry 1933- **1989**:3
    Campeau, Robert 1923- **1990**:1
    Portman, John 1924- **1988**:2
    Trump, Donald 1946- **1989**:2

**Reebok U.S.A. Ltd., Inc.**
    Fireman, Paul
        Brief entry **1987**:2

**Renaissance Motion Pictures**
    Raimi, Sam 1959- **1999**:2

**RENAMO [Resistanica Nacional Mocambican]**
    Dhlakama, Afonso 1953- **1993**:3

**Renault, Inc.**
    Besse, Georges 1927-1986
        Obituary **1987**:1
    Ghosn, Carlos 1954- **2008**:3

**Republican National Committee**
    Abraham, Spencer 1952- **1991**:4
    Atwater, Lee 1951-1991 **1989**:4
        Obituary **1991**:4
    Molinari, Susan 1958- **1996**:4

**Restaurants**
    Aoki, Rocky 1940- **1990**:2
    Aretsky, Ken 1941- **1988**:1
    Bushnell, Nolan 1943- **1985**:1
    Copeland, Al 1944(?)- **1988**:3
    Fertel, Ruth 1927- **2000**:2
    Kaufman, Elaine **1989**:4
    Kerrey, Bob 1943- **1986**:1
    Kroc, Ray 1902-1984
        Obituary **1985**:1
    Lagasse, Emeril 1959- **1998**:3
    Melman, Richard
        Brief entry **1986**:1
    Petrossian, Christian
        Brief entry **1985**:3
    Pouillon, Nora 1943- **2005**:1
    Puck, Wolfgang 1949- **1990**:1
    Shaich, Ron 1953- **2004**:4
    Thomas, Dave **1986**:2
        Obituary **2003**:1
    Timberlake, Justin 1981- **2008**:4
    Waters, Alice 1944- **2006**:3
    Zagat, Tim and Nina **2004**:3

**Retailing**
    Adams-Geller, Paige 1969(?)- **2006**:4
    Albou, Sophie 1967- **2007**:2
    Anderson, Brad 1949- **2007**:3
    Ball, Michael 1964(?)- **2007**:3
    Barnes, Brenda C. 1955(?)- **2007**:4
    Baxter, Pamela 1949- **2009**:4
    Bern, Dorrit J. 1950(?)- **2006**:3
    Bravo, Rose Marie 1951(?)- **2005**:3
    Brown, Howard and Karen Stewart
        **2007**:3
    Burch, Tory 1966- **2009**:3
    Cassini, Oleg 1913-2006
        Obituary **2007**:2
    Charney, Dov 1969- **2008**:2
    Charron, Paul 1942- **2004**:1
    Choo, Jimmy 1957(?)- **2006**:3
    Clark, Maxine 1949- **2009**:4
    Cole, Anne 1930(?)- **2007**:3
    Courtney, Erica 1957- **2009**:3
    Drexler, Millard S. 1944- **1990**:3
    Ecko, Marc 1972- **2006**:3
    Elbaz, Alber 1961- **2008**:1
    Fassa, Lynda 1963(?)- **2008**:4
    Francis, Philip L. 1946- **2007**:4
    Frankfort, Lew 1946- **2008**:2
    Ginsberg, Ian 1962(?)- **2006**:4
    Glazman, Lev and Alina
        Roytberg **2007**:4
    Goodman, Drew and Myra **2007**:4
    Green, Philip 1952- **2008**:2
    Greenwald, Julie 1970- **2008**:1
    Gregory, Rogan 1972- **2008**:2
    Hernandez, Lazaro and Jack
        McCollough **2008**:4
    Hindmarch, Anya 1969- **2008**:2
    Horvath, David and Sun-Min
        Kim **2008**:4
    Lam, Derek 1966- **2009**:2
    Larian, Isaac 1954- **2008**:1
    Lepore, Nanette 1964(?)- **2006**:4
    Lhuillier, Monique 1971(?)- **2007**:4
    Lim, Phillip 1974(?)- **2008**:1
    Madden, Steve 1958- **2007**:2
    Manheimer, Heidi 1963- **2009**:3
    Marcus, Stanley 1905-2002
        Obituary **2003**:1
    Margolis, Bobby 1948(?)- **2007**:2
    Mashouf, Manny 1938(?)- **2008**:1
    Mateschitz, Dietrich 1944- **2008**:1
    Olsen, Sigrid 1953- **2007**:1
    Panichgul, Thakoon 1974- **2009**:4
    Persson, Stefan 1947- **2004**:1
    Posen, Zac 1980- **2009**:3
    Prevor, Barry and Steven
        Shore **2006**:2
    Rigopulos, Alex 1970- **2009**:4
    Roncal, Mally 1972- **2009**:4
    Ronson, Charlotte 1977(?)- **2007**:3
    Saint Laurent, Yves 1936-2008
        Obituary **2009**:3
    Sams, Craig 1944- **2007**:3
    Schmelzer, Sheri 1965- **2009**:4
    Schwartz, Allen 1945(?)- **2008**:2
    Senk, Glen 1956- **2009**:3
    Snyder, Ron 1956(?)- **2007**:4
    Som, Peter 1971- **2009**:1
    Stephens, Arran and Ratana **2008**:4
    Temperley, Alice 1975- **2008**:2
    Thomas-Graham, Pamela
        1963- **2007**:1
    Touitou, Jean 1952(?)- **2008**:4

Valli, Giambattista 1966- **2008**:3

**Reuben Awards**
Gould, Chester 1900-1985
Obituary **1985**:2
Schulz, Charles 1922-2000
Obituary **2000**:3

**Revlon, Inc.**
Bosworth, Kate 1983- **2006**:3
Duffy, Karen 1962- **1998**:1
Perelman, Ronald 1943- **1989**:2

**Rhode Island state government**
Violet, Arlene 1943- **1985**:3

**Richter Scale**
Richter, Charles Francis 1900-1985
Obituary **1985**:4

**Ringling Brothers and Barnum & Bailey Circus**
Burck, Wade
Brief entry **1986**:1
Feld, Kenneth 1948- **1988**:2

**RJR Nabisco, Inc.**
Horrigan, Edward, Jr. 1929- **1989**:1

**Robotics**
Kwoh, Yik San 1946(?)- **1988**:2

**Rock Climbing**
Hill, Lynn 1961(?)- **1991**:2

**Rockman**
Scholz, Tom 1949- **1987**:2

**Roller Coasters**
Toomer, Ron 1930- **1990**:1

**Rolling Stone magazine**
Wenner, Jann 1946- **1993**:1

**Rotary engine**
Yamamoto, Kenichi 1922- **1989**:1

**Running**
Benoit, Joan 1957- **1986**:3
Bolt, Usain 1986- **2009**:2
Joyner, Florence Griffith 1959-1998 **1989**:2
Obituary **1999**:1
Knight, Philip H. 1938- **1994**:1
Zatopek, Emil 1922-2000
Obituary **2001**:3

**Russian Federation**
Putin, Vladimir 1952- **2000**:3
Yeltsin, Boris 1931- **1991**:1

**Sailing**
Alter, Hobie
Brief entry **1985**:1
Conner, Dennis 1943- **1987**:2
Koch, Bill 1940- **1992**:3
Morgan, Dodge 1932(?)- **1987**:1

**San Antonio, Tex., city government**
Cisneros, Henry 1947- **1987**:2

**San Antonio Spurs basketball team**
Duncan, Tim 1976- **2000**:1
Parker, Tony 1982- **2008**:1
Robinson, David 1965- **1990**:4

**San Diego Chargers football team**
Barnes, Ernie 1938- **1997**:4
Bell, Ricky 1955-1984
Obituary **1985**:1
Unitas, Johnny 1933-2002
Obituary **2003**:4

**San Diego Padres baseball team**
Dravecky, Dave 1956- **1992**:1
Gwynn, Tony 1960- **1995**:1
Kroc, Ray 1902-1984
Obituary **1985**:1
Sheffield, Gary 1968- **1998**:1

**SANE/FREEZE**
Coffin, William Sloane, Jr. 1924- **1990**:3

**San Francisco city government**
Alioto, Joseph L. 1916-1998
Obituary **1998**:3
Brown, Willie 1934- **1996**:4

**San Francisco 49ers football team**
DeBartolo, Edward J., Jr. 1946- **1989**:3
Montana, Joe 1956- **1989**:2
Rice, Jerry 1962- **1990**:4
Walsh, Bill 1931- **1987**:4
Young, Steve 1961- **1995**:2

**San Francisco Giants baseball team**
Bonds, Barry 1964- **1993**:3
Dravecky, Dave 1956- **1992**:1

**Save the Children Federation**
Guyer, David
Brief entry **1988**:1

**Schottco Corp.**
Schott, Marge 1928- **1985**:4

**Schwinn Bicycle Co.**
Schwinn, Edward R., Jr.
Brief entry **1985**:4

**Science fiction**
Anderson, Poul 1926-2001
Obituary **2002**:3
Asimov, Isaac 1920-1992
Obituary **1992**:3
Butler, Octavia E. 1947- **1999**:3
Clarke, Arthur C. 1917-2008
Obituary **2009**:2
Hand, Elizabeth 1957- **2007**:2
Kelley, DeForest 1929-1999
Obituary **2000**:1
Lucas, George 1944- **1999**:4
Norton, Andre 1912-2005
Obituary **2006**:2

Sterling, Bruce 1954- **1995**:4

**Sculpture**
Appel, Karel 1921-2006
Obituary **2007**:2
Beuys, Joseph 1921-1986
Obituary **1986**:3
Bontecou, Lee 1931- **2004**:4
Borofsky, Jonathan 1942- **2006**:4
Botero, Fernando 1932- **1994**:3
Bourgeois, Louise 1911- **1994**:1
Chia, Sandro 1946- **1987**:2
Chillida, Eduardo 1924-2002
Obituary **2003**:4
Christo 1935- **1992**:3
Conner, Bruce 1933-2008
Obituary **2009**:3
Dubuffet, Jean 1901-1985
Obituary **1985**:4
Dunham, Carroll 1949- **2003**:4
Ellis, David 1971- **2009**:4
Gober, Robert 1954- **1996**:3
Goldsworthy, Andy 1956- **2007**:2
Graham, Robert 1938- **1993**:4
Graves, Nancy 1940- **1989**:3
Kaskey, Ray
Brief entry **1987**:2
Kelly, Ellsworth 1923- **1992**:1
Kiefer, Anselm 1945- **1990**:2
Lin, Maya 1960(?)- **1990**:3
Moore, Henry 1898-1986
Obituary **1986**:4
Mueck, Ron 1958- **2008**:3
Murakami, Takashi 1962- **2004**:2
Nevelson, Louise 1900-1988
Obituary **1988**:3
Ono, Yoko 1933- **1989**:2
Paolozzi, Eduardo 1924-2005
Obituary **2006**:3
Puryear, Martin 1941- **2002**:4
Raimondi, John
Brief entry **1987**:4
Rauschenberg, Robert 1925- **1991**:2
Rosenberg, Evelyn 1942- **1988**:2
Serra, Richard 1939- **2009**:1
Tamayo, Rufino 1899-1991
Obituary **1992**:1
Truitt, Anne 1921- **1993**:1

**Seagram Co.**
Bronfman, Edgar, Jr. 1955- **1994**:4

**Sears, Roebuck & Co.**
Brennan, Edward A. 1934- **1989**:1

**Seattle Mariners baseball team**
Griffey, Ken Jr. 1969- **1994**:1
Hernandez, Felix 1986- **2008**:2
Johnson, Randy 1963- **1996**:2
Suzuki, Ichiro 1973- **2002**:2

**Seattle Seahawks football team**
Bosworth, Brian 1965- **1989**:1

**Seattle Supersonics basketball team**
Kemp, Shawn 1969- **1995**:1
Wilkens, Lenny 1937- **1995**:2

**Second City comedy troupe**
Aykroyd, Dan 1952- **1989**:3
Belushi, Jim 1954- **1986**:2
Candy, John 1950-1994 **1988**:2

Obituary **1994**:3
Fey, Tina 1970- **2005**:3
Levy, Eugene 1946- **2004**:3
Radner, Gilda 1946-1989
Obituary **1989**:4
Short, Martin 1950- **1986**:1

**Sedelmaier Film Productions**
Sedelmaier, Joe 1933- **1985**:3

**Seismology**
Richter, Charles Francis 1900-1985
Obituary **1985**:4

**Senate Armed Services Committee**
Cohen, William S. 1940- **1998**:1
Goldwater, Barry 1909-1998
Obituary **1998**:4
McCain, John S. 1936- **1998**:4
Nunn, Sam 1938- **1990**:2
Tower, John 1926-1991
Obituary **1991**:4

**Sharper Image, The**
Thalheimer, Richard 1948-
Brief entry **1988**:3

**Shiites**
Berri, Nabih 1939(?)- **1985**:2
Khomeini, Ayatollah Ruhollah
1900(?)-1989
Obituary **1989**:4
Rafsanjani, Ali Akbar Hashemi
1934(?)- **1987**:3

**ShoWest Awards**
Cuaron, Alfonso 1961- **2008**:2
Driver, Minnie 1971- **2000**:1
LaBeouf, Shia 1986- **2008**:1
Lane, Diane 1965- **2006**:2
Ledger, Heath 1979- **2006**:3
Meyers, Nancy 1949- **2006**:1
Rogen, Seth 1982- **2009**:3
Swank, Hilary 1974- **2000**:3
Yeoh, Michelle 1962- **2003**:2

**Shubert Organization**
Schoenfeld, Gerald 1924- **1986**:2

**Sierra Club**
McCloskey, J. Michael 1934- **1988**:2

**Sinn Fein**
Adams, Gerald 1948- **1994**:1
McGuinness, Martin 1950(?)- **1985**:4

**Skiing**
DiBello, Paul
Brief entry **1986**:4
Miller, Bode 1977- **2002**:4
Street, Picabo 1971- **1999**:3
Strobl, Fritz 1972- **2003**:3
Tomba, Alberto 1966- **1992**:3

**Sled dog racing**
Butcher, Susan 1954- **1991**:1

**Small Business Administration [SBA]**
Alvarez, Aida **1999**:2

**Smith College**
Simmons, Ruth 1945- **1995**:2

**Smoking**
Horrigan, Edward, Jr. 1929- **1989**:1
Maxwell, Hamish 1926- **1989**:4

**Soccer**
Adu, Freddy 1989- **2005**:3
Akers, Michelle 1966- **1996**:1
Beckham, David 1975- **2003**:1
Best, George 1946-2005
Obituary **2007**:1
Chastain, Brandi 1968- **2001**:3
Harkes, John 1967- **1996**:4
Lalas, Alexi 1970- **1995**:1
Maradona, Diego 1961(?)- **1991**:3
Mathis, Clint 1976- **2003**:1
Ronaldinho 1980- **2007**:3
Ronaldo 1976- **1999**:2

**Social Democratic and Labour Party
[SDLP]**
Hume, John 1938- **1987**:1

**Socialism**
Castro, Fidel 1926- **1991**:4
Sanders, Bernie 1941(?)- **1991**:4

**Socialist Party (France)**
Cresson, Edith 1934- **1992**:1

**Softball**
Stofflet, Ty
Brief entry **1987**:1

**Soloflex, Inc.**
Wilson, Jerry
Brief entry **1986**:2

**Sony Corp.**
Kutaragi, Ken 1950- **2005**:3
Morita, Akio 1921- **1989**:4
Morita, Akio 1921-1999
Obituary **2000**:2
Mottola, Tommy 1949- **2002**:1

**So So Def Recordings, Inc.**
Dupri, Jermaine 1972- **1999**:1

**Sotheby & Co.**
Brooks, Diana D. 1950- **1990**:1
Wilson, Peter C. 1913-1984
Obituary **1985**:2

**Southern Baptist Convention**
Rogers, Adrian 1931- **1987**:4

**South West African People's
Organization [SWAPO]**
Nujoma, Sam 1929- **1990**:4

**Southwest Airlines**
Kelleher, Herb 1931- **1995**:1

**Soviet-American relations**
Chernenko, Konstantin 1911-1985
Obituary **1985**:1
Dubinin, Yuri 1930- **1987**:4
Dzhanibekov, Vladimir 1942- **1988**:1
Gale, Robert Peter 1945- **1986**:4
Gorbachev, Mikhail 1931- **1985**:2
Grebenshikov, Boris 1953- **1990**:1
Gromyko, Andrei 1909-1989
Obituary **1990**:2
Hammer, Armand 1898-1990
Obituary **1991**:3
Harriman, W. Averell 1891-1986
Obituary **1986**:4
Putin, Vladimir 1952- **2000**:3
Sakharov, Andrei Dmitrievich
1921-1989
Obituary **1990**:2
Smith, Samantha 1972-1985
Obituary **1985**:3
Vidov, Oleg 194- **1987**:4

**Speed skating**
Blair, Bonnie 1964- **1992**:3
Fabris, Enrico 1981- **2006**:4

**Spinal-cord injuries**
Reeve, Christopher 1952- **1997**:2

**Spin magazine**
Guccione, Bob, Jr. 1956- **1991**:4

**St. Louis Blues hockey team**
Fuhr, Grant 1962- **1997**:3
Hull, Brett 1964- **1991**:4

**St. Louis Browns baseball team**
Veeck, Bill 1914-1986
Obituary **1986**:1

**St. Louis Cardinals baseball team**
Busch, August A. III 1937- **1988**:2
Busch, August Anheuser, Jr.
1899-1989
Obituary **1990**:2
McGwire, Mark 1963- **1999**:1
Pujols, Albert 1980- **2005**:3

**St. Louis Rams football team**
Warner, Kurt 1971- **2000**:3

**Starbucks Coffee Co.**
Schultz, Howard 1953- **1995**:3

**Strategic Defense Initiative**
Hagelstein, Peter
Brief entry **1986**:3

**Stroh Brewery Co.**
Stroh, Peter W. 1927- **1985**:2

**Students Against Drunken Driving
[SADD]**
Anastas, Robert
Brief entry **1985**:2
Lightner, Candy 1946- **1985**:1

**Submarines**
Rickover, Hyman 1900-1986
Obituary **1986**:4
Zech, Lando W.
Brief entry **1987**:4

**Suicide**
  Applewhite, Marshall Herff
  1931-1997
    Obituary **1997**:3
  Dorris, Michael 1945-1997
    Obituary **1997**:3
  Hutchence, Michael 1960-1997
    Obituary **1998**:1
  Quill, Timothy E. 1949- **1997**:3

**Sunbeam Corp.**
  Dunlap, Albert J. **1997**:2

**Sundance Institute**
  Redford, Robert 1937- **1993**:2

**Sun Microsystems, Inc.**
  McNealy, Scott 1954- **1999**:4

**Sunshine Foundation**
  Sample, Bill
    Brief entry **1986**:2

**Superconductors**
  Chaudhari, Praveen 1937- **1989**:4
  Chu, Paul C.W. 1941- **1988**:2

**Supreme Court of Canada**
  Wilson, Bertha
    Brief entry **1986**:1

**Surfing**
  Curren, Tommy
    Brief entry **1987**:4
  Johnson, Jack 1975- **2006**:4

**Swimming**
  Ederle, Gertrude 1905-2003
    Obituary **2005**:1
  Evans, Janet 1971- **1989**:1
  Phelps, Michael 1985- **2009**:2
  Torres, Dara 1967- **2009**:1
  Van Dyken, Amy 1973- **1997**:1

**Tampa Bay Buccaneers football team**
  Bell, Ricky 1955-1984
    Obituary **1985**:1
  Gruden, Jon 1963- **2003**:4
  Johnson, Keyshawn 1972- **2000**:4
  Testaverde, Vinny 1962- **1987**:2
  Williams, Doug 1955- **1988**:2
  Young, Steve 1961- **1995**:2

**Tandem Computers, Inc.**
  Treybig, James G. 1940- **1988**:3

**Teach for America**
  Kopp, Wendy **1993**:3

**Tectonics**
  Rosendahl, Bruce R.
    Brief entry **1986**:4

**Teddy Ruxpin**
  Kingsborough, Donald
    Brief entry **1986**:2

**Tele-Communications, Inc.**
  Malone, John C. 1941- **1988**:3

**Televangelism**
  Graham, Billy 1918- **1992**:1
  Hahn, Jessica 1960- **1989**:4
  Robertson, Pat 1930- **1988**:2
  Rogers, Adrian 1931- **1987**:4
  Swaggart, Jimmy 1935- **1987**:3

**Temple University basketball team**
  Chaney, John 1932- **1989**:1

**Tennis**
  Agassi, Andre 1970- **1990**:2
  Ashe, Arthur 1943-1993
    Obituary **1993**:3
  Becker, Boris
    Brief entry **1985**:3
  Capriati, Jennifer 1976- **1991**:1
  Clijsters, Kim 1983- **2006**:3
  Courier, Jim 1970- **1993**:2
  Davenport, Lindsay 1976- **1999**:2
  Djokovic, Novak 1987- **2008**:4
  Federer, Roger 1981- **2004**:2
  Gerulaitis, Vitas 1954-1994
    Obituary **1995**:1
  Gibson, Althea 1927-2003
    Obituary **2004**:4
  Graf, Steffi 1969- **1987**:4
  Henin-Hardenne, Justine
  1982- **2004**:4
  Hewitt, Lleyton 1981- **2002**:2
  Hingis, Martina 1980- **1999**:1
  Ivanisevic, Goran 1971- **2002**:1
  Kournikova, Anna 1981- **2000**:3
  Mauresmo, Amelie 1979- **2007**:2
  Navratilova, Martina 1956- **1989**:1
  Pierce, Mary 1975- **1994**:4
  Riggs, Bobby 1918-1995
    Obituary **1996**:2
  Roddick, Andy 1982- **2004**:3
  Sabatini, Gabriela
    Brief entry **1985**:4
  Safin, Marat 1980- **2001**:3
  Sampras, Pete 1971- **1994**:1
  Seles, Monica 1974(?)- **1991**:3
  Sharapova, Maria 1987- **2005**:2
  Williams, Serena 1981- **1999**:4
  Williams, Venus 1980- **1998**:2

**Test tube babies**
  Steptoe, Patrick 1913-1988
    Obituary **1988**:3

**Texas Rangers baseball team**
  Rodriguez, Alex 1975- **2001**:2
  Ryan, Nolan 1947- **1989**:4

**Texas State Government**
  Bush, George W., Jr. 1946- **1996**:4
  Richards, Ann 1933- **1991**:2

**Therapeutic Recreation Systems**
  Radocy, Robert
    Brief entry **1986**:3

**Timberline Reclamations**
  McIntyre, Richard
    Brief entry **1986**:2

**Time Warner Inc.**
  Ho, David 1952- **1997**:2
  Levin, Gerald 1939- **1995**:2
  Ross, Steven J. 1927-1992

    Obituary **1993**:3

**TLC Beatrice International**
  Lewis, Loida Nicolas 1942- **1998**:3

**TLC Group L.P.**
  Lewis, Reginald F. 1942-1993 **1988**:4
    Obituary **1993**:3

**9 to 5**
  Bravo, Ellen 1944- **1998**:2
  Nussbaum, Karen 1950- **1988**:3

**Today Show**
  Couric, Katherine 1957- **1991**:4
  Gumbel, Bryant 1948- **1990**:2
  Norville, Deborah 1958- **1990**:3

**Tony Awards**
  Abbott, George 1887-1995
    Obituary **1995**:3
  Alda, Robert 1914-1986
    Obituary **1986**:3
  Alexander, Jane 1939- **1994**:2
  Alexander, Jason 1962(?)- **1993**:3
  Allen, Debbie 1950- **1998**:2
  Allen, Joan 1956- **1998**:1
  Arkin, Alan 1934- **2007**:4
  Bacall, Lauren 1924- **1997**:3
  Bailey, Pearl 1918-1990
    Obituary **1991**:1
  Bancroft, Anne 1931-2005
    Obituary **2006**:3
  Bates, Alan 1934-2003
    Obituary **2005**:1
  Bennett, Michael 1943-1987
    Obituary **1988**:1
  Bloch, Ivan 1940- **1986**:3
  Booth, Shirley 1898-1992
    Obituary **1993**:2
  Brooks, Mel 1926- **2003**:1
  Brown, Ruth 1928-2006
    Obituary **2008**:1
  Brynner, Yul 1920(?)-1985
    Obituary **1985**:4
  Buckley, Betty 1947- **1996**:2
  Burnett, Carol 1933- **2000**:3
  Carter, Nell 1948-2003
    Obituary **2004**:2
  Channing, Stockard 1946- **1991**:3
  Close, Glenn 1947- **1988**:3
  Crawford, Cheryl 1902-1986
    Obituary **1987**:1
  Crawford, Michael 1942- **1994**:2
  Cronyn, Hume 1911-2003
    Obituary **2004**:3
  Dench, Judi 1934- **1999**:4
  Dennis, Sandy 1937-1992
    Obituary **1992**:4
  Dewhurst, Colleen 1924-1991
    Obituary **1992**:2
  Dunagan, Deanna 1940- **2009**:2
  Ebersole, Christine 1953- **2007**:2
  Fagan, Garth 1940- **2000**:1
  Ferrer, Jose 1912-1992
    Obituary **1992**:3
  Fiennes, Ralph 1962- **1996**:2
  Fierstein, Harvey 1954- **2004**:2
  Fishburne, Laurence 1961(?)- **1995**:3
  Flanders, Ed 1934-1995
    Obituary **1995**:3

Fosse, Bob 1927-1987
    Obituary **1988**:1
Foster, Sutton 1975- **2003**:2
Gleason, Jackie 1916-1987
    Obituary **1987**:4
Glover, Savion 1973- **1997**:1
Goulet, Robert 1933-2007
    Obituary **2008**:4
Hagen, Uta 1919-2004
    Obituary **2005**:2
Harrison, Rex 1908-1990
    Obituary **1990**:4
Hepburn, Katharine 1909- **1991**:2
Hines, Gregory 1946- **1992**:4
Hoffman, Dustin 1937- **2005**:4
Hwang, David Henry 1957- **1999**:1
Irons, Jeremy 1948- **1991**:4
Jackman, Hugh 1968- **2004**:4
Kahn, Madeline 1942-1999
    Obituary **2000**:2
Keaton, Diane 1946- **1997**:1
Kline, Kevin 1947- **2000**:1
Kushner, Tony 1956- **1995**:2
Lane, Nathan 1956- **1996**:4
Langella, Frank 1940- **2008**:3
Lansbury, Angela 1925- **1993**:1
LaPaglia, Anthony 1959- **2004**:4
Lithgow, John 1945- **1985**:2
LuPone, Patti 1949- **2009**:2
Mantegna, Joe 1947- **1992**:1
Matthau, Walter 1920- **2000**:3
McKellen, Ian 1939- **1994**:1
Merrick, David 1912-2000
    Obituary **2000**:4
Midler, Bette 1945- **1989**:4
Miller, Arthur 1915- **1999**:4
Moore, Dudley 1935-2002
    Obituary **2003**:2
Nichols, Mike 1931- **1994**:4
Nunn, Trevor 1940- **2000**:2
Orbach, Jerry 1935-2004
    Obituary **2006**:1
Pacino, Al 1940- **1993**:4
Papp, Joseph 1921-1991
    Obituary **1992**:2
Parker, Mary-Louise 1964- **2002**:2
Peters, Bernadette 1948- **2000**:1
Preston, Robert 1918-1987
    Obituary **1987**:3
Prince, Faith 1959(?)- **1993**:2
Reilly, Charles Nelson
    Obituary **2008**:3
Reza, Yasmina 1959(?)- **1999**:2
Richards, Lloyd 1919-2006
    Obituary **2007**:3
Robbins, Jerome 1918-1998
    Obituary **1999**:1
Ruehl, Mercedes 195(?)- **1992**:4
Rylance, Mark 1960- **2009**:3
Salonga, Lea 1971- **2003**:3
Schreiber, Liev 1967- **2007**:2
Shanley, John Patrick 1950- **2006**:1
Sheldon, Sidney 1917-2007
    Obituary **2008**:2
Sondheim, Stephen 1930- **1994**:4
Spacey, Kevin 1959- **1996**:4
Stapleton, Maureen 1925-2006
    Obituary **2007**:2
Stoppard, Tom 1937- **1995**:4
Stritch, Elaine 1925- **2002**:4
Stroman, Susan **2000**:4
Styne, Jule 1905-1994

Obituary **1995**:1
Szot, Paulo 1969- **2009**:3
Tune, Tommy 1939- **1994**:2
Verdon, Gwen 1925-2000
    Obituary **2001**:2
Wasserstein, Wendy 1950- **1991**:3
Wayne, David 1914-1995
    Obituary **1995**:3
White, Julie 1961- **2008**:2
Whitehead, Robert 1916-2002
    Obituary **2003**:3
Winokur, Marissa Jaret 1973- **2005**:1
Wong, B.D. 1962- **1998**:1
Worth, Irene 1916-2002
    Obituary **2003**:2

**Toronto Blue Jays baseball team**
    Ainge, Danny 1959- **1987**:1
    Carter, Joe 1960- **1994**:2
    Wells, David 1963- **1999**:3

**Toronto Maple Leafs hockey team**
    Gilmour, Doug 1963- **1994**:3

**Tour de France**
    Armstrong, Lance 1971- **2000**:1
    Indurain, Miguel 1964- **1994**:1
    LeMond, Greg 1961- **1986**:4

**Toyota Motor Corp.**
    Toyoda, Eiji 1913- **1985**:2

**Toys and games**
    Barad, Jill 1951- **1994**:2
    Bushnell, Nolan 1943- **1985**:1
    Hakuta, Ken
        Brief entry **1986**:1
    Haney, Chris
        Brief entry **1985**:1
    Hassenfeld, Stephen 1942- **1987**:4
    Kingsborough, Donald
        Brief entry **1986**:2
    Kristiansen, Kjeld Kirk
        1948(?)- **1988**:3
    Lazarus, Charles 1923- **1992**:4
    Roberts, Xavier 1955- **1985**:3
    Rowland, Pleasant **1992**:3

**Toys R Us**
    Eyler, John. H., Jr. 1948(?)- **2001**:3
    Lazarus, Charles 1923- **1992**:4

**Track and field**
    Bolt, Usain 1986- **2009**:2
    Johnson, Michael **2000**:1
    Jones, Marion 1975- **1998**:4
    Joyner, Florence Griffith
        1959-1998 **1989**:2
        Obituary **1999**:1
    Wariner, Jeremy 1984- **2006**:3

**Trade negotiation**
    Hills, Carla 1934- **1990**:3
    Reisman, Simon 1919- **1987**:4

**Tradex**
    Hakuta, Ken
        Brief entry **1986**:1

**Travel**
    Arison, Ted 1924- **1990**:3
    Fodor, Eugene 1906(?)-1991
        Obituary **1991**:3

Steger, Will 1945(?)- **1990**:4

**Treasure Salvors, Inc.**
    Fisher, Mel 1922(?)- **1985**:4

**TreePeople**
    Lipkis, Andy
        Brief entry **1985**:3

**Trevor's Campaign**
    Ferrell, Trevor
        Brief entry **1985**:2

**Trivial Pursuit**
    Haney, Chris
        Brief entry **1985**:1

**Twentieth Century-Fox Film Corp.**
    Diller, Barry 1942- **1991**:1
    Goldberg, Leonard 1934- **1988**:4

**U2**
    Bono 1960- **1988**:4
    U2 **2002**:4

**UFW**
    Chavez, Cesar 1927-1993
        Obituary **1993**:4

**Ultralight aircraft**
    MacCready, Paul 1925- **1986**:4
    Moody, John 1943- **1985**:3

**Uncle Noname (cookie company)**
    Amos, Wally 1936- **2000**:1

**UNICEF**
    Bellamy, Carol 1942- **2001**:2
    Hepburn, Audrey 1929-1993
        Obituary **1993**:2
    Styler, Trudie 1954- **2009**:1
    Ustinov, Peter 1921-2004
        Obituary **2005**:3

**Union Pacific Railroad**
    Harriman, W. Averell 1891-1986
        Obituary **1986**:4

**United Airlines**
    Friend, Patricia A. 1946- **2003**:3
    Wolf, Stephen M. 1941- **1989**:3

**United Auto Workers [UAW]**
    Bieber, Owen 1929- **1986**:1
    Woodcock, Leonard 1911-2001
        Obituary **2001**:4
    Yokich, Stephen P. 1935- **1995**:4

**United Farm Workers [UFW]**
    Chavez, Cesar 1927-1993
        Obituary **1993**:4
    Huerta, Dolores 1930- **1998**:1

**United Federation of Teachers**
    Feldman, Sandra 1939- **1987**:3

**United Nations [UN]**
    Albright, Madeleine 1937- **1994**:3
    Annan, Kofi 1938- **1999**:1
    Arbour, Louise 1947- **2005**:1

Astorga, Nora 1949(?)-1988 **1988**:2
Bailey, Pearl 1918-1990
  Obituary **1991**:1
de Pinies, Jamie
  Brief entry **1986**:3
Fulbright, J. William 1905-1995
  Obituary **1995**:3
Ghali, Boutros Boutros 1922- **1992**:3
Gromyko, Andrei 1909-1989
  Obituary **1990**:2
Kirkpatrick, Jeane 1926-2006
  Obituary **2008**:1
Kouchner, Bernard 1939- **2005**:3
Lewis, Stephen 1937- **1987**:2
Lodge, Henry Cabot 1902-1985
  Obituary **1985**:1
Perez de Cuellar, Javier 1920- **1991**:3
Terzi, Zehdi Labib 1924- **1985**:3

**United Petroleum Corp.**
Aurre, Laura
  Brief entry **1986**:3

**United Press International [UPI]**
Thomas, Helen 1920- **1988**:4

**United Steelworkers of America [USW]**
Williams, Lynn 1924- **1986**:4

**University Network**
Scott, Gene
  Brief entry **1986**:1

**University of Chicago**
Friedman, Milton 1912-2006
  Obituary **2008**:1
Gray, Hanna 1930- **1992**:4

**University of Colorado football team**
McCartney, Bill 1940- **1995**:3

**University of Las Vegas at Nevada basketball team**
Tarkenian, Jerry 1930- **1990**:4

**University of Michigan football team**
Harmon, Tom 1919-1990
  Obituary **1990**:3
McCartney, Bill 1940- **1995**:3
Schembechler, Bo 1929(?)- **1990**:3

**University of Notre Dame**
Holtz, Lou 1937- **1986**:4
Malloy, Edward Monk 1941- **1989**:4

**University of Pennsylvania**
Gutmann, Amy 1949- **2008**:4
Rodin, Judith 1945(?)- **1994**:4

**University of Tennessee**
Alexander, Lamar 1940- **1991**:2

**University of Wisconsin**
Shalala, Donna 1941- **1992**:3

**UNIX**
Ritchie, Dennis and Kenneth
Thompson **2000**:1

**Untouchables**
Ram, Jagjivan 1908-1986
  Obituary **1986**:4

**Urban design**
Cooper, Alexander 1936- **1988**:4

**U.S. Civil Rights Commission**
Pendleton, Clarence M. 1930-1988
  Obituary **1988**:4

**U.S. Department of Transportation**
Peters, Mary E. 1948- **2008**:3
Slater, Rodney E. 1955- **1997**:4

**U.S. House of Representatives**
Abzug, Bella 1920-1998 **1998**:2
Aspin, Les 1938-1995
  Obituary **1996**:1
Bono, Sonny 1935-1998 **1992**:2
  Obituary **1998**:2
Clyburn, James 1940- **1999**:4
Collins, Cardiss 1931- **1995**:3
Conyers, John, Jr. 1929- **1999**:1
DeLay, Tom 1947- **2000**:1
Fenwick, Millicent H.
  Obituary **1993**:2
Ferraro, Geraldine 1935- **1998**:3
Foley, Thomas S. 1929- **1990**:1
Frank, Barney 1940- **1989**:2
Fulbright, J. William 1905-1995
  Obituary **1995**:3
Gephardt, Richard 1941- **1987**:3
Gingrich, Newt 1943- **1991**:1
Gore, Albert, Sr. 1907-1998
  Obituary **1999**:2
Hastert, Dennis 1942- **1999**:3
Hyde, Henry 1924- **1999**:1
Jackson, Jesse, Jr. 1965- **1998**:3
Jordan, Barbara 1936-1996
  Obituary **1996**:3
Langevin, James R. 1964- **2001**:2
McCarthy, Carolyn 1944- **1998**:4
McKinney, Cynthia A. 1955- **1997**:1
McKinney, Stewart B. 1931-1987
  Obituary **1987**:4
McMillen, Tom 1952- **1988**:4
Mfume, Kweisi 1948- **1996**:3
Mills, Wilbur 1909-1992
  Obituary **1992**:4
O'Neill, Tip 1912-1994
  Obituary **1994**:3
Pelosi, Nancy 1940- **2004**:2
Pepper, Claude 1900-1989
  Obituary **1989**:4
Quayle, Dan 1947- **1989**:2
Ros-Lehtinen, Ileana 1952- **2000**:2
Roybal-Allard, Lucille 1941- **1999**:4
Sanchez, Loretta 1960- **2000**:3
Sanders, Bernie 1941(?)- **1991**:4
Udall, Mo 1922-1998
  Obituary **1999**:2
Waters, Maxine 1938- **1998**:4
Watts, J.C. 1957- **1999**:2

**U.S. National Security Adviser**
Berger, Sandy 1945- **2000**:1

**U.S. Office of Management and Budget**
Raines, Franklin 1949- **1997**:4

**U.S. Postal Service**
Frank, Anthony M. 1931(?)- **1992**:1

**U.S. Public Health Service**
Koop, C. Everett 1916- **1989**:3
Novello, Antonia 1944- **1991**:2
Sullivan, Louis 1933- **1990**:4

**U.S. Senate**
Abrams, Elliott 1948- **1987**:1
Biden, Joe 1942- **1986**:3
Boxer, Barbara 1940- **1995**:1
Bradley, Bill 1943- **2000**:2
Braun, Carol Moseley 1947- **1993**:1
Campbell, Ben Nighthorse
  1933- **1998**:1
Cohen, William S. 1940- **1998**:1
D'Amato, Al 1937- **1996**:1
Dole, Bob 1923- **1994**:2
Ervin, Sam 1896-1985
  Obituary **1985**:2
Feinstein, Dianne 1933- **1993**:3
Fulbright, J. William 1905-1995
  Obituary **1995**:3
Glenn, John 1921- **1998**:3
Goldwater, Barry 1909-1998
  Obituary **1998**:4
Hatch, Orin G. 1934- **2000**:2
Heinz, John 1938-1991
  Obituary **1991**:4
Helms, Jesse 1921- **1998**:1
Jackson, Jesse 1941- **1996**:1
Kassebaum, Nancy 1932- **1991**:1
Kemp, Jack 1935- **1990**:4
Lott, Trent 1941- **1998**:1
McCain, John S. 1936- **1998**:4
Mikulski, Barbara 1936- **1992**:4
Mitchell, George J. 1933- **1989**:3
Morrison, Trudi
  Brief entry **1986**:2
Muskie, Edmund S. 1914-1996
  Obituary **1996**:3
Nunn, Sam 1938- **1990**:2
Pepper, Claude 1900-1989
  Obituary **1989**:4
Quayle, Dan 1947- **1989**:2
Ribicoff, Abraham 1910-1998
  Obituary **1998**:3
Snowe, Olympia 1947- **1995**:3
Thompson, Fred 1942- **1998**:2
Tower, John 1926-1991
  Obituary **1991**:4

**U.S. Supreme Court**
Blackmun, Harry A. 1908-1999
  Obituary **1999**:3
Brennan, William 1906-1997
  Obituary **1997**:4
Breyer, Stephen Gerald 1938- **1994**:4
Burger, Warren E. 1907-1995
  Obituary **1995**:4
Flynt, Larry 1942- **1997**:3
Ginsburg, Ruth Bader 1933- **1993**:4
Marshall, Thurgood 1908-1993
  Obituary **1993**:3
O'Connor, Sandra Day 1930- **1991**:1
Powell, Lewis F. 1907-1998
  Obituary **1999**:1
Rehnquist, William H. 1924- **2001**:2
Scalia, Antonin 1936- **1988**:2
Souter, David 1939- **1991**:3
Stewart, Potter 1915-1985

Obituary **1986**:1
Thomas, Clarence 1948- **1992**:2

**U.S. Trade Representative**
Barshefsky, Charlene 1951(?)- **2000**:4

**U.S. Treasury**
Bentsen, Lloyd 1921- **1993**:3

**USA Network**
Herzog, Doug 1960(?)- **2002**:4
Koplovitz, Kay 1945- **1986**:3

**Utah Jazz basketball team**
Malone, Karl 1963- **1990**:1
Maravich, Pete 1948-1988
Obituary **1988**:2
Stockton, John Houston 1962- **1997**:3

**Vampires**
Kostova, Elizabeth 1964- **2006**:2
Rice, Anne 1941- **1995**:1

**Vanity Fair magazine**
Brown, Tina 1953- **1992**:1

**Venezuela**
Perez, Carlos Andre 1922- **1990**:2

**Veterinary medicine**
Redig, Patrick 1948- **1985**:3

**Viacom, Inc.**
Karmazin, Mel 1943- **2006**:1
Redstone, Sumner 1923- **1994**:1

**Vietnam War**
Dong, Pham Van 1906-2000
Obituary **2000**:4

**Vigilantism**
Goetz, Bernhard Hugo
1947(?)- **1985**:3
Slotnick, Barry
Brief entry **1987**:4

**Virgin Holdings Group Ltd.**
Branson, Richard 1951- **1987**:1

**Virginia state government**
Robb, Charles S. 1939- **1987**:2
Wilder, L. Douglas 1931- **1990**:3

**Virtual reality**
Lanier, Jaron 1961(?)- **1993**:4

**Vogue magazine**
Wintour, Anna 1949- **1990**:4

**Volkswagenwerk AG**
Bernhard, Wolfgang 1960- **2007**:1
Hahn, Carl H. 1926- **1986**:4
Lopez de Arriortua, Jose Ignacio
1941- **1993**:4

**Volleyball**
Kiraly, Karch
Brief entry **1987**:1

**Voyager aircraft**
Rutan, Burt 1943- **1987**:2

**Wacky WallWalker**
Hakuta, Ken
Brief entry **1986**:1

**Wall Street Analytics, Inc.**
Unz, Ron 1962(?)- **1999**:1

**Wallyball**
Garcia, Joe
Brief entry **1986**:4

**Wal-Mart Stores, Inc.**
Glass, David 1935- **1996**:1
Scott, H. Lee, Jr. 1949- **2008**:3
Walton, Sam 1918-1992 **1986**:2
Obituary **1993**:1

**Walt Disney Productions**
Disney, Roy E. 1930- **1986**:3
Eisner, Michael 1942- **1989**:2
Iger, Bob 1951- **2006**:1
Katzenberg, Jeffrey 1950- **1995**:3

**Wang Laboratories, Inc.**
Wang, An 1920-1990 **1986**:1
Obituary **1990**:3

**War crimes**
Barbie, Klaus 1913-1991
Obituary **1992**:2
Hess, Rudolph 1894-1987
Obituary **1988**:1
Karadzic, Radovan 1945- **1995**:3
Klarsfeld, Beate 1939- **1989**:1
Mengele, Josef 1911-1979
Obituary **1985**:2
Milosevic, Slobodan 1941- **1993**:2

**Warnaco**
Wachner, Linda 1946- **1988**:3

**Washington, D.C., city government**
Barry, Marion 1936- **1991**:1
Williams, Anthony 1952- **2000**:4

**Washington Bullets basketball team**
McMillen, Tom 1952- **1988**:4
O'Malley, Susan 1962(?)- **1995**:2

**Washington Post**
Graham, Donald 1945- **1985**:4
Graham, Katharine Meyer 1917-
**1997**:3
Obituary **2002**:3

**Washington Redskins football team**
Monk, Art 1957- **1993**:2
Rypien, Mark 1962- **1992**:3
Smith, Jerry 1943-1986
Obituary **1987**:1
Williams, Doug 1955- **1988**:2
Williams, Edward Bennett 1920-1988
Obituary **1988**:4

**Watergate**
Dickerson, Nancy H.
1927-1997 **1998**:2
Ehrlichman, John 1925-1999

Obituary **1999**:3
Ervin, Sam 1896-1985
Obituary **1985**:2
Graham, Katharine Meyer 1917-
**1997**:3
Obituary **2002**:3
Haldeman, H. R. 1926-1993
Obituary **1994**:2
Mitchell, John 1913-1988
Obituary **1989**:2
Neal, James Foster 1929- **1986**:2
Nixon, Richard 1913-1994
Obituary **1994**:4
Thompson, Fred 1942- **1998**:2

**Water skiing**
Duvall, Camille
Brief entry **1988**:1

**Wayne's World**
Myers, Mike 1964(?)- **1992**:3

**WebTV Networks Inc.**
Perlman, Steve 1961(?)- **1998**:2

**Wendy's International**
Thomas, Dave **1986**:2
Obituary **2003**:1

**Who Wants to be a Millionaire**
Philbin, Regis 1933- **2000**:2

**Windham Hill Records**
Ackerman, Will 1949- **1987**:4

**Wine making**
Lemon, Ted
Brief entry **1986**:4
Mondavi, Robert 1913- **1989**:2
Rothschild, Philippe de 1902-1988
Obituary **1988**:2

**Women's issues**
Allred, Gloria 1941- **1985**:2
Baez, Joan 1941- **1998**:3
Boxer, Barbara 1940- **1995**:1
Braun, Carol Moseley 1947- **1993**:1
Burk, Martha 1941- **2004**:1
Butler, Brett 1958(?)- **1995**:1
Cresson, Edith 1934- **1992**:1
Davis, Angela 1944- **1998**:3
Doi, Takako
Brief entry **1987**:4
Faludi, Susan 1959- **1992**:4
Faulkner, Shannon 1975- **1994**:4
Ferraro, Geraldine 1935- **1998**:3
Finley, Karen 1956- **1992**:4
Finnbogadoaattir, Vigdiaas
Brief entry **1986**:2
Flynt, Larry 1942- **1997**:3
Friedan, Betty 1921- **1994**:2
Furman, Rosemary
Brief entry **1986**:4
Grant, Charity
Brief entry **1985**:2
Griffiths, Martha 1912-2003
Obituary **2004**:2
Harris, Barbara 1930- **1989**:3
Hill, Anita 1956- **1994**:1
Ireland, Jill 1936-1990

Obituary **1990**:4
Jong, Erica 1942- **1998**:3
Kanokogi, Rusty
  Brief entry **1987**:1
Love, Susan 1948- **1995**:2
MacKinnon, Catharine 1946- **1993**:2
Marier, Rebecca 1974- **1995**:4
Mikulski, Barbara 1936- **1992**:4
Monroe, Rose Will 1920-1997
  Obituary **1997**:4
Morgan, Robin 1941- **1991**:1
Nasrin, Taslima 1962- **1995**:1
Nussbaum, Karen 1950- **1988**:3
Paglia, Camille 1947- **1992**:3
Profet, Margie 1958- **1994**:4
Ramey, Estelle R. 1917-2006
  Obituary **2007**:4
Salbi, Zainab 1969(?)- **2008**:3
Steinem, Gloria 1934- **1996**:2
Summers, Anne 1945- **1990**:2
Wattleton, Faye 1943- **1989**:1
Wolf, Naomi 1963(?)- **1994**:3
Yard, Molly **1991**:4

**Women's National Basketball
Association [WNBA]**
Cooper, Cynthia **1999**:1
Laimbeer, Bill 1957- **2004**:3
Swoopes, Sheryl 1971- **1998**:2

**Woods Hole Research Center**
Woodwell, George S. 1928- **1987**:2

**World Bank**
McCloy, John J. 1895-1989
  Obituary **1989**:3
McNamara, Robert S. 1916- **1995**:4

**World Cup**
Hamm, Mia 1972- **2000**:1

**World Health Organization**
Brundtland, Gro Harlem
  1939- **2000**:1

**World of Wonder, Inc.**
Kingsborough, Donald
  Brief entry **1986**:2

**World Wrestling Federation [WWF]**
Austin, Stone Cold Steve 1964- **2001**
  :3
Chyna 1970- **2001**:4
Hogan, Hulk 1953- **1987**:3
McMahon, Vince, Jr. 1945(?)- **1985**:4
Rock, The 1972- **2001**:2
Ventura, Jesse 1951- **1999**:2

**W.R. Grace & Co.**
Grace, J. Peter 1913- **1990**:2

**Wrestling**
Austin, Stone Cold Steve
  1964- **2001**:3
Baumgartner, Bruce

Brief entry **1987**:3
Chyna 1970- **2001**:4
Hogan, Hulk 1953- **1987**:3
McMahon, Vince, Jr. 1945(?)- **1985**:4
Rock, The 1972- **2001**:2
Ventura, Jesse 1951- **1999**:2

**Xerox**
Allaire, Paul 1938- **1995**:1
Brown, John Seely 1940- **2004**:1
McColough, C. Peter 1922- **1990**:2
Mulcahy, Anne M. 1952- **2003**:2
Rand, A. Barry 1944- **2000**:3

**Yahoo!**
Filo, David and Jerry Yang **1998**:3
Koogle, Tim 1951- **2000**:4
Semel, Terry 1943- **2002**:2

**Young & Rubicam, Inc.**
Kroll, Alexander S. 1938- **1989**:3

**Zamboni ice machine**
Zamboni, Frank J.
  Brief entry **1986**:4

**Ziff Corp**
Ziff, William B., Jr. 1930- **1986**:4

**Zimbabwe African National Union
[ZANU]**
Mugabe, Robert 1924- **1988**:4

# Cumulative Newsmakers Index

This index lists all newsmakers included in the entire *Newsmakers* series.

Listee names are followed by a year and issue number; thus **1996**:3 indicates that an entry on that individual appears in both 1996, Issue 3, and the 1996 cumulation.

Aaliyah 1979-2001 ............................ **2001**:3
Abacha, Sani 1943- ......................... **1996**:3
Abbas, Mahmoud 1935- ................ **2008**:4
Abbey, Edward 1927-1989
    Obituary ........................................ **1989**:3
Abbott, George 1887-1995
    Obituary ........................................ **1995**:3
Abbott, Jim 1967- ............................ **1988**:3
Abbruzzese, Dave
    See Pearl Jam
Abdel-Rahman, Sheik Omar
    See Rahman, Sheik Omar Abdel-
Abdul, Paula 1962- ......................... **1990**:3
Abdullah II, King 1962- ................. **2002**:4
Abercrombie, Josephine 1925- ....... **1987**:2
Abernathy, Ralph 1926-1990
    Obituary ........................................ **1990**:3
Abraham, S. Daniel 1924- .............. **2003**:3
Abraham, Spencer 1952- ................ **1991**:4
Abrams, Elliott 1948- ..................... **1987**:1
Abrams, J. J. 1966- .......................... **2007**:3
Abramson, Lyn 1950- ..................... **1986**:3
Abzug, Bella 1920-1998 ................. **1998**:2
Achtenberg, Roberta ...................... **1993**:4
Ackerman, G. William
    See Ackerman, Will
Ackerman, Will 1949- ..................... **1987**:4
Acosta, Carlos 1973(?)- .................. **1997**:4
Acuff, Roy 1903-1992
    Obituary ........................................ **1993**:2
Adair, Paul Neal
    See Adair, Red
Adair, Red 1915- ............................. **1987**:3
Adams, Amy 1974- .......................... **2008**:4
Adams, Don 1923-2005
    Obituary ........................................ **2007**:1
Adams, Douglas 1952-2001
    Obituary ........................................ **2002**:2
Adams, Gerald 1948- ...................... **1994**:1
Adams, Patch 1945(?)- .................... **1999**:2
Adams, Scott 1957- ......................... **1996**:4
Adams, Yolanda 1961- .................... **2008**:2
Adams-Geller, Paige 1969(?)- ........ **2006**:4
Adamson, George 1906-1989
    Obituary ........................................ **1990**:2
Addams, Charles 1912-1988
    Obituary ........................................ **1989**:1
Adele 1988- ..................................... **2009**:4
Adjani, Isabelle 1955- ..................... **1991**:1

Adler, Jonathan 1966- .................... **2006**:3
Adu, Freddy 1989- .......................... **2005**:3
Adu, Helen Folasade
    See Sade
Affleck, Ben 1972- .......................... **1999**:1
AFI ................................................... **2007**:3
Agassi, Andre 1970- ....................... **1990**:2
Agatston, Arthur 1947- .................. **2005**:1
Agee, Tommie 1942-2001
    Obituary ........................................ **2001**:4
Agnelli, Giovanni 1921- ................. **1989**:4
Agnes B 1941- ................................. **2002**:3
Agnew, Spiro Theodore 1918-1996
    Obituary ........................................ **1997**:1
Aguilera, Christina 1980- ............... **2000**:4
Ahern, Bertie 1951- ........................ **1999**:3
Ahern, Cecelia 1981- ...................... **2008**:4
Ahmadinejad, Mahmoud 1956- .... **2007**:1
Aiello, Danny 1933- ........................ **1990**:4
Aikman, Troy 1966- ........................ **1994**:2
Ailes, Roger 1940- .......................... **1989**:3
Ailey, Alvin 1931-1989 ................... **1989**:2
    Obituary ........................................ **1990**:2
Ainge, Daniel Ray
    See Ainge, Danny
Ainge, Danny 1959- ........................ **1987**:1
Akers, John F. 1934- ....................... **1988**:3
Akers, Michelle 1966- ..................... **1996**:1
Akihito, Emperor of Japan 1933- .. **1990**:1
Akin, Phil
    Brief entry ..................................... **1987**:3
al-Abdullah, Rania 1970- ............... **2001**:1
al-Ani, Jananne 1966- ..................... **2008**:4
al-Assad, Bashar 1965- ................... **2004**:2
al-Assad, Hafez
    See Assad, Hafez al-
al-Assad, Rifaat
    See Assad, Rifaat
Alba, Jessica 1981- .......................... **2001**:2
al-Banna, Sabri Khalil
    See Nidal, Abu
al-Bashir, Omar 1944- .................... **2009**:1
Albee, Edward 1928- ...................... **1997**:1
Albert, Eddie 1906-2005
    Obituary ........................................ **2006**:3
Albert, Marv 1943- ......................... **1994**:3
Albert, Prince of Monaco 1958- .... **2006**:2
Albert, Stephen 1941- ..................... **1986**:1
Albom, Mitch 1958- ........................ **1999**:3

Albou, Sophie 1967- ....................... **2007**:2
Albrecht, Chris 1952(?)- ................. **2005**:4
Albright, Madeleine 1937- ............. **1994**:3
Alda, Robert 1914-1986
    Obituary ........................................ **1986**:3
Alexander, Jane 1939- .................... **1994**:2
Alexander, Jason 1962(?)- .............. **1993**:3
Alexander, Lamar 1940- ................. **1991**:2
Alexie, Sherman 1966- ................... **1998**:4
Ali, Laila 1977- ............................... **2001**:2
Ali, Monica 1967- ........................... **2007**:4
Ali, Muhammad 1942- .................... **1997**:2
Ali, Nadirah
    See Arrested Development
Ali, Toni
    See Arrested Development
Alioto, Joseph L. 1916-1998
    Obituary ........................................ **1998**:3
Allaire, Jeremy 1971- ..................... **2006**:4
Allaire, Paul 1938- .......................... **1995**:1
Allard, Linda 1940- ........................ **2003**:2
Allen, Bob 1935- ............................. **1992**:4
Allen, Debbie 1950- ........................ **1998**:2
Allen, Joan 1956- ............................ **1998**:1
Allen, John 1930- ............................ **1992**:1
Allen, Mel 1913-1996
    Obituary ........................................ **1996**:4
Allen, Peter 1944-1992
    Obituary ........................................ **1993**:1
Allen, Ray 1975- ............................. **2002**:1
Allen, Robert Eugene
    See Allen, Bob
Allen, Steve 1921-2000
    Obituary ........................................ **2001**:2
Allen, Tim 1953- ............................. **1993**:1
Allen, Woody 1935- ........................ **1994**:1
Allenby, Robert 1971- .................... **2007**:1
Allen Jr., Ivan 1911-2003
    Obituary ........................................ **2004**:3
Alley, Kirstie 1955- ........................ **1990**:3
Allman, Cher
    See Cher
Allred, Gloria 1941- ....................... **1985**:2
Allyson, June 1917-2006
    Obituary ........................................ **2007**:3
al-Majid, Hussein Kamel Hassan
    See Kamel, Hussein
Almodovar, Pedro 1951- ................ **2000**:3
Alsop, Marin 1956- ........................ **2008**:3

Altea, Rosemary 1946- .................. **1996**:3
Alter, Hobie
   Brief entry ...................................... **1985**:1
Altman, Robert 1925- ..................... **1993**:2
Altman, Sidney 1939- ..................... **1997**:2
al-Turabi, Hassan
   See Turabi, Hassan
Alvarez, Aida ................................... **1999**:2
Alvarez Bravo, Manuel 1902-2002
   Obituary ......................................... **2004**:1
Amanpour, Christiane 1958- ......... **1997**:2
Ambler, Eric 1909-1998
   Obituary ......................................... **1999**:2
Ambrose, Stephen 1936- ................ **2002**:3
Ameche, Don 1908-1993
   Obituary ......................................... **1994**:2
Ament, Jeff
   See Pearl Jam
Ames, Roger 1950(?)- ..................... **2005**:2
Amin, Idi 1925(?)-2003
   Obituary ......................................... **2004**:4
Amis, Kingsley 1922-1995
   Obituary ......................................... **1996**:2
Amis, Martin 1949- ......................... **2008**:3
Amory, Cleveland 1917-1998
   Obituary ......................................... **1999**:2
Amos, Tori 1963- ............................. **1995**:1
Amos, Wally 1936- .......................... **2000**:1
Amsterdam, Morey 1912-1996
   Obituary ......................................... **1997**:1
Anastas, Robert
   Brief entry ...................................... **1985**:2
Ancier, Garth 1957- ......................... **1989**:1
Anderson, Brad 1949- ..................... **2007**:3
Anderson, Gillian 1968- .................. **1997**:1
Anderson, Harry 1951(?)- ............. **1988**:2
Anderson, Judith 1899(?)-1992
   Obituary ......................................... **1992**:3
Anderson, Laurie 1947- .................. **2000**:2
Anderson, Marion 1897-1993
   Obituary ......................................... **1993**:4
Anderson, Pamela
   See Lee, Pamela
Anderson, Poul 1926-2001
   Obituary ......................................... **2002**:3
Anderson, Tom and Chris
   DeWolfe ........................................ **2007**:2
Ando, Tadao 1941- .......................... **2005**:4
Andreessen, Marc 1972- ................. **1996**:2
Andrews, Julie 1935- ...................... **1996**:1
Andrews, Lori B. 1952- ................... **2005**:3
Andrews, Maxene 1916-1995
   Obituary ......................................... **1996**:2
Angelos, Peter 1930- ....................... **1995**:4
Angelou, Maya 1928- ...................... **1993**:4
Angier, Natalie 1958- ...................... **2000**:3
Aniston, Jennifer 1969- ................... **2000**:3
Annan, Kofi 1938- ........................... **1999**:1
Annenberg, Walter 1908- ............... **1992**:3
Anthony, Earl 1938-2001
   Obituary ......................................... **2002**:3
Anthony, Marc 1969- ...................... **2000**:3
Antonini, Joseph 1941- ................... **1991**:2
Aoki, Hiroaki
   See Aoki, Rocky
Aoki, Rocky 1940- ........................... **1990**:2
Apatow, Judd 1967- ........................ **2006**:3
Appel, Karel 1921-2006
   Obituary ......................................... **2007**:2
Apple, Fiona 1977- .......................... **2006**:3
Applegate, Christina 1972- ............ **2000**:4

Applewhite, Marshall Herff 1931-1997
   Obituary ......................................... **1997**:3
Aquino, Corazon 1933- ................... **1986**:2
Arad, Avi 1948- ............................... **2003**:2
Arafat, Yasser 1929- ........................ **1989**:3
Arakawa, Shizuka 1981- ................. **2006**:4
Arbour, Louise 1947- ...................... **2005**:1
Archer, Dennis 1942- ...................... **1994**:4
Arden, Eve 1912(?)-1990
   Obituary ......................................... **1991**:2
Arens, Moshe 1925- ........................ **1985**:1
Aretsky, Ken 1941- .......................... **1988**:1
Arias Sanchez, Oscar 1941- ........... **1989**:3
Arison, Ted 1924- ............................ **1990**:3
Aristide, Jean-Bertrand 1953- ........ **1991**:3
Arkin, Alan 1934- ............................ **2007**:4
Arkoff, Samuel Z. 1918-2001
   Obituary ......................................... **2002**:4
Arledge, Roone 1931- ..................... **1992**:2
Arlen, Harold 1905-1986
   Obituary ......................................... **1986**:3
Arman 1928- .................................... **1993**:1
Armani, Giorgio 1934(?)- ............... **1991**:2
Armstrong, Anne 1927-2008
   Obituary ......................................... **2009**:4
Armstrong, C. Michael 1938- ........ **2002**:1
Armstrong, Henry 1912-1988
   Obituary ......................................... **1989**:1
Armstrong, Lance 1971- .................. **2000**:1
Armstrong, William 1972-
   See Green Day
Arnault, Bernard 1949- ................... **2000**:4
Arnaz, Desi 1917-1986
   Obituary ......................................... **1987**:1
Arnold, Eddy 1918-2008
   Obituary ......................................... **2009**:2
Arnold, Tom 1959- .......................... **1993**:2
Aronson, Jane 1951- ........................ **2009**:3
Arquette, Patricia 1968- .................. **2001**:3
Arquette, Rosanna 1959- ................ **1985**:2
Arrau, Claudio 1903-1991
   Obituary ......................................... **1992**:1
Arrested Development ..................... **1994**:2
Arriortua, Jose Ignacio Lopez de
   See Lopez de Arriortua, Jose Ignacio
Arthur, Jean 1901(?)-1991
   Obituary ......................................... **1992**:1
Arthurs, Paul Bonehead
   See Oasis
Asad, Hafiz al-
   See Assad, Hafez al-
Ash, Mary Kay
   See Ash, Mary Kay
Ash, Mary Kay 1915(?)- .................. **1996**:1
Ashanti 1980- ................................... **2004**:1
Ashcroft, John 1942- ....................... **2002**:4
Ashcroft, Peggy 1907-1991
   Obituary ......................................... **1992**:1
Ashe, Arthur 1943-1993
   Obituary ......................................... **1993**:3
Ashwell, Rachel 1960(?)- ............... **2004**:2
Asimov, Isaac 1920-1992
   Obituary ......................................... **1992**:3
Aspin, Les 1938-1995
   Obituary ......................................... **1996**:1
Assad, Hafez 1930-2000
   Obituary ......................................... **2000**:4
Assad, Hafez al- 1930(?)- ............... **1992**:1
Assad, Rifaat 1937(?)- ..................... **1986**:3
Astaire, Fred 1899-1987
   Obituary ......................................... **1987**:4

Astaire, Frederick Austerlitz
   See Astaire, Fred
Astin, Sean 1971- ............................. **2005**:1
Astor, Brooke 1902-2007
   Obituary ......................................... **2008**:4
Astor, Mary 1906-1987
   Obituary ......................................... **1988**:1
Astorga, Nora 1949(?)-1988 ........... **1988**:2
Atkins, Robert C. 1930-2003
   Obituary ......................................... **2004**:2
Atkinson, Rowan 1955- .................. **2004**:3
Atwater, Harvey Leroy
   See Atwater, Lee
Atwater, Lee 1951-1991 .................. **1989**:4
   Obituary ......................................... **1991**:4
Atwood, Margaret 1939- ................. **2001**:2
Aucoin, Kevyn 1962- ....................... **2001**:3
Auerbach, Red 1911-2006
   Obituary ......................................... **2008**:1
Aurre, Laura
   Brief entry ...................................... **1986**:3
Austin, Stone Cold Steve 1964- ..... **2001**:3
Autry, Gene 1907-1998
   Obituary ......................................... **1999**:1
Avedon, Richard 1923- ................... **1993**:4
Axelrod, Julius 1912-2004
   Obituary ......................................... **2006**:1
Axthelm, Pete 1943(?)-1991
   Obituary ......................................... **1991**:3
Aykroyd, Dan 1952- ........................ **1989**:3
Azaria, Hank 1964- ......................... **2001**:3
Azinger, Paul 1960- ......................... **1995**:2
Azria, Max 1949- ............................. **2001**:4
Babangida, Ibrahim Badamosi
   1941- ............................................... **1992**:4
Babbitt, Bruce 1938- ........................ **1994**:1
Babilonia, Tai 1959- ........................ **1997**:2
Bacall, Lauren 1924- ....................... **1997**:3
Bachelet, Michelle 1951- ................. **2007**:3
Backstreet Boys .............................. **2001**:3
Backus, Jim 1913-1989
   Obituary ......................................... **1990**:1
Backus, John W. 1924-2007
   Obituary ......................................... **2008**:2
Bacon, Kevin 1958- ......................... **1995**:3
Badawi, Abdullah Ahmad 1939- ... **2009**:3
Baddeley, Hermione 1906(?)-1986
   Obituary ......................................... **1986**:4
Badgley, Mark and James
   Mischka ......................................... **2004**:3
Badu, Erykah 1971- ......................... **2000**:4
Baez, Joan 1941- .............................. **1998**:3
Bahcall, John N. 1934-2005
   Obituary ......................................... **2006**:4
Bailey, F. Lee 1933- ......................... **1995**:4
Bailey, Pearl 1918-1990
   Obituary ......................................... **1991**:1
Baird, Bill
   Brief entry ...................................... **1987**:2
Baird, William Ritchie, Jr.
   See Baird, Bill
Baiul, Oksana 1977- ........................ **1995**:3
Baker, Anita 1958- .......................... **1987**:4
Baker, James A. III 1930- ................ **1991**:2
Baker, Kathy
   Brief entry ...................................... **1986**:1
Baker, Simon 1969- ......................... **2009**:4
Bakiyev, Kurmanbek 1949- ........... **2007**:1
Bakker, Robert T. 1950(?)- ............. **1991**:3
Bakula, Scott 1954- ......................... **2003**:1
Balaguer, Joaquin 1907-2002
   Obituary ......................................... **2003**:4

Baldessari, John 1931(?)- ............... **1991**:4
Baldrige, Howard Malcolm
   See Baldrige, Malcolm
Baldrige, Malcolm 1922-1987
   Obituary ......................... **1988**:1
Baldwin, Alec 1958- ...................... **2002**:2
Baldwin, James 1924-1987
   Obituary ......................... **1988**:2
Bale, Christian 1974- ..................... **2001**:3
Ball, Alan 1957- ............................. **2005**:1
Ball, Edward 1959- ........................ **1999**:2
Ball, Lucille 1911-1989
   Obituary ......................... **1989**:3
Ball, Michael 1964(?)- .................... **2007**:3
Ballard, Robert D. 1942- ................ **1998**:4
Ballmer, Steven 1956- .................... **1997**:2
Balsillie, Jim and Mike Lazaridis .. **2006**:4
Balzary, Michael
   See Red Hot Chili Peppers
Bancroft, Anne 1931-2005
   Obituary ......................... **2006**:3
Banda, Hastings 1898- ................... **1994**:3
Bandaranaike, Sirimavo 1916-2000
   Obituary ......................... **2001**:2
Banderas, Antonio 1960- ............... **1996**:2
Bangalter, Thomas 1975-
   See Daft Punk
Banks, Dennis J. 193- ..................... **1986**:4
Banks, Jeffrey 1953- ....................... **1998**:2
Banks, Russell 1940- ...................... **2009**:2
Banks, Tyra 1973- .......................... **1996**:3
Banksy 1975(?)- .............................. **2007**:2
Barad, Jill 1951- ............................. **1994**:2
Barak, Ehud 1942- ......................... **1999**:4
Baraka, Amiri 1934- ....................... **2000**:3
Baranski, Christine 1952- ............... **2001**:2
Barber, Red 1908-1992
   Obituary ......................... **1993**:2
Barber, Tiki 1975- .......................... **2007**:1
Barber, Walter Lanier
   See Barber, Red
Barbera, Joseph 1911- .................... **1988**:2
Barbie, Klaus 1913-1991
   Obituary ......................... **1992**:2
Bardem, Javier 1969- ..................... **2008**:4
Barenaked Ladies ........................... **1997**:2
Barenboim, Daniel 1942- ............... **2001**:1
Barker, Clive 1952- ......................... **2003**:3
Barker, Pat 1943- ........................... **2009**:1
Barkin, Ellen 1955- ........................ **1987**:3
Barkley, Charles 1963- ................... **1988**:2
Barks, Carl 1901-2000
   Obituary ......................... **2001**:2
Barksdale, James L. 1943- .............. **1998**:2
Barnard, Christiaan 1922-2001
   Obituary ......................... **2002**:4
Barnes, Brenda C. 1955(?)- ............ **2007**:4
Barnes, Ernie 1938- ....................... **1997**:4
Barney .......................................... **1993**:4
Barnouin, Kim 1971-
   See Kim Barnouin and Rory Freedman
Barnwell, Tim (Headliner)
   See Arrested Development
Baron Cohen, Sacha 1971- ............ **2007**:3
Barr, Roseanne 1953(?)- ................ **1989**:1
Barrett, Craig R. 1939- ................... **1999**:4
Barrett, Syd 1946-2006
   Obituary ......................... **2007**:3
Barry, Dave 1947(?)- ...................... **1991**:2
Barry, Lynda 1956(?)- .................... **1992**:1
Barry, Marion 1936- ....................... **1991**:1
Barrymore, Drew 1975- .................. **1995**:3

Barshefsky, Charlene 1951(?)- ........ **2000**:4
Bartoli, Cecilia 1966- ..................... **1994**:1
Baryshnikov, Mikhail Nikolaevich 1948-
   .................................... **1997**:3
Basescu, Traian 1951- .................... **2006**:2
Basie, Count 1904(?)-1984
   Obituary ......................... **1985**:1
Basie, William James
   See Basie, Count
Basinger, Kim 1953- ....................... **1987**:2
Bass, Karen 1953- .......................... **2009**:3
Bassett, Angela 1959(?)- ................ **1994**:4
Bateman, Jason 1969- .................... **2005**:3
Bateman, Justine 1966- .................. **1988**:4
Bates, Alan 1934-2003
   Obituary ......................... **2005**:1
Bates, Kathy 1949(?)- ..................... **1991**:4
Battle, Kathleen 1948- .................... **1998**:1
Bauer, Eddie 1899-1986
   Obituary ......................... **1986**:3
Baulieu, Etienne-Emile 1926- ........ **1990**:1
Baumgartner, Bruce
   Brief entry ...................... **1987**:3
Baxter, Anne 1923-1985
   Obituary ......................... **1986**:1
Baxter, Pamela 1949- ..................... **2009**:4
Bayley, Corrine
   Brief entry ...................... **1986**:4
Beal, Deron 1968(?)- ...................... **2005**:3
Beals, Jennifer 1963- ...................... **2005**:2
Beals, Vaughn 1928- ...................... **1988**:2
Beame, Abraham 1906-2001
   Obituary ......................... **2001**:4
Bean, Alan L. 1932- ....................... **1986**:2
Beastie Boys, The .......................... **1999**:1
Beattie, Owen
   Brief entry ...................... **1985**:2
Beatty, Warren 1937- ..................... **2000**:1
Becaud, Gilbert 1927-2001
   Obituary ......................... **2003**:1
Bechdel, Alison 1960- .................... **2007**:3
Beck 1970- ..................................... **2000**:2
Becker, Boris
   Brief entry ...................... **1985**:3
Becker, Brian 1957(?)- ................... **2004**:4
Beckett, Samuel Barclay 1906-1989
   Obituary ......................... **1990**:2
Beckett, Wendy (Sister) 1930- ........ **1998**:3
Beckham, David 1975- .................... **2003**:1
Bedford, Deborah 1958- ................. **2006**:3
Bee Gees, The ................................ **1997**:4
Beene, Geoffrey 1927-2004
   Obituary ......................... **2005**:4
Beers, Charlotte 1935- ................... **1999**:3
Begaye, Kelsey 1950(?)- ................. **1999**:3
Begin, Menachem 1913-1992
   Obituary ......................... **1992**:3
Beinecke, Frances 1960(?)- ............ **2007**:4
Bejart, Maurice 1927-2007
   Obituary ......................... **2009**:1
Bell, Art 1945- ............................... **2000**:1
Bell, Gabrielle 1975(?)- .................. **2007**:4
Bell, Ricky 1955-1984
   Obituary ......................... **1985**:1
Bellamy, Carol 1942- ..................... **2001**:2
Belle, Albert 1966- ......................... **1996**:4
Bellissimo, Wendy 1967(?)- ........... **2007**:1
Bellow, Saul 1915-2005
   Obituary ......................... **2006**:2
Belluzzo, Rick 1953- ...................... **2001**:3
Belushi, James
   See Belushi, Jim

Belushi, Jim 1954- ......................... **1986**:2
Belzer, Richard 1944- .................... **1985**:3
Ben & Jerry .................................... **1991**:3
Benatar, Pat 1953- ......................... **1986**:1
Benchley, Peter 1940-2006
   Obituary ......................... **2007**:1
Benes, Francine 1946- .................... **2008**:2
Benetton, Luciano 1935- ................ **1988**:1
Benigni, Roberto 1952- .................. **1999**:2
Bening, Annette 1958(?)- ............... **1992**:1
Bennett, Joan 1910-1990
   Obituary ......................... **1991**:2
Bennett, Michael 1943-1987
   Obituary ......................... **1988**:1
Bennett, Tony 1926- ...................... **1994**:4
Bennett, William 1943- .................. **1990**:1
Benoit, Joan 1957- ......................... **1986**:3
Benson, Ezra Taft 1899-1994
   Obituary ......................... **1994**:4
Bentley, Dierks 1975- .................... **2007**:3
Bentsen, Lloyd 1921- ..................... **1993**:3
Bergalis, Kimberly 1968(?)-1991
   Obituary ......................... **1992**:3
Bergen, Candice 1946- ................... **1990**:1
Berger, Oscar 1946- ....................... **2004**:4
Berger, Sandy 1945- ...................... **2000**:1
Bergman, Ingmar 1918- ................. **1999**:4
Berio, Luciano 1925-2003
   Obituary ......................... **2004**:2
Berkley, Seth 1956- ........................ **2002**:3
Berle, Milton 1908-2002
   Obituary ......................... **2003**:2
Berle, Peter A.A.
   Brief entry ...................... **1987**:3
Berlin, Irving 1888-1989
   Obituary ......................... **1990**:1
Berliner, Andy and Rachel ............. **2008**:2
Berlusconi, Silvio 1936(?)- ............. **1994**:4
Berman, Gail 1957(?)- .................... **2006**:1
Berman, Jennifer and Laura ........... **2003**:2
Bern, Dorrit J. 1950(?)- .................. **2006**:3
Bernanke, Ben 1953- ..................... **2008**:3
Bernardi, Herschel 1923-1986
   Obituary ......................... **1986**:4
Bernardin, Cardinal Joseph
   1928-1996 ....................... **1997**:2
Berners-Lee, Tim 1955(?)- ............. **1997**:4
Bernhard, Sandra 1955(?)- ............ **1989**:4
Bernhard, Wolfgang 1960- ............ **2007**:1
Bernsen, Corbin 1955- ................... **1990**:2
Bernstein, Elmer 1922-2004
   Obituary ......................... **2005**:4
Bernstein, Leonard 1918-1990
   Obituary ......................... **1991**:1
Berresford, Susan V. 1943- ............ **1998**:4
Berri, Nabih 1939(?)- ..................... **1985**:2
Berry, Chuck 1926- ....................... **2001**:2
Berry, Halle 1968- ......................... **1996**:2
Besse, Georges 1927-1986
   Obituary ......................... **1987**:1
Best, George 1946-2005
   Obituary ......................... **2007**:1
Bethe, Hans 1906-2005
   Obituary ......................... **2006**:2
Bettelheim, Bruno 1903-1990
   Obituary ......................... **1990**:3
Beuys, Joseph 1921-1986
   Obituary ......................... **1986**:3
Beyonce 1981- ............................... **2009**:3
Bezos, Jeff 1964- ........................... **1998**:4
Bhraonain, Eithne Ni
   See Enya

Bhutto, Benazir 1953- ...................... **1989**:4
Bialik, Mayim 1975- ......................... **1993**:3
Bias, Len 1964(?)-1986
  Obituary ..................................... **1986**:3
Bias, Leonard
  See Bias, Len
Bibliowicz, Jessica 1959- ............... **2009**:3
Biden, Joe 1942- ............................. **1986**:3
Biden, Joseph Robinette, Jr.
  See Biden, Joe
Bieber, Owen 1929- ........................ **1986**:1
Biehl, Amy 1967(?)-1993
  Obituary ..................................... **1994**:1
Bigelow, Kathryn 1952(?)- .............. **1990**:4
Bikoff, J. Darius 1962(?)- ................. **2007**:3
Bikoff, James L.
  Brief entry ................................. **1986**:2
Billington, James 1929- ................... **1990**:3
Binoche, Juliette 1965- ................... **2001**:3
Birch, Thora 1982- .......................... **2002**:4
Bird, Brad 1956(?)- .......................... **2005**:4
Bird, Larry 1956- ............................. **1990**:3
Birnbaum, Nathan
  See Burns, George
Bishop, Andre 1948- ....................... **2000**:1
Bishop, Joey 1918-2007
  Obituary ..................................... **2008**:4
Bissell, Patrick 1958-1987
  Obituary ..................................... **1988**:2
Bissell, Walter Patrick
  See Bissell, Patrick
Bixby, Bill 1934-1993
  Obituary ..................................... **1994**:2
Biya, Paul 1933- .............................. **2006**:1
Bjork 1965- ...................................... **1996**:1
Black, Carole 1945- ......................... **2003**:1
Black, Cathleen 1944- ...................... **1998**:4
Black, Conrad 1944- ......................... **1986**:2
Black, Jack 1969- ............................. **2002**:3
Blackburn, Molly 1931(?)-1985
  Obituary ..................................... **1985**:4
Black Eyed Peas ............................... **2006**:2
Blackmun, Harry A. 1908-1999
  Obituary ..................................... **1999**:3
Blackstone, Harry Jr. 1934-1997
  Obituary ..................................... **1997**:4
Blades, Ruben 1948- ........................ **1998**:2
Blahnik, Manolo 1942- .................... **2000**:2
Blaine, David 1973- ......................... **2003**:3
Blair, Anthony Charles Lynton
  See Blair, Tony
Blair, Bonnie 1964- .......................... **1992**:3
Blair, Tony 1953- ............................. **1996**:3
Blakey, Art 1919-1990
  Obituary ..................................... **1991**:1
Blanc, Mel 1908-1989
  Obituary ..................................... **1989**:4
Blanchett, Cate 1969- ...................... **1999**:3
Blass, Bill 1922-2002
  Obituary ..................................... **2003**:3
Blau, Jeno
  See Ormandy, Eugene
Bledsoe, Drew 1972- ....................... **1995**:1
Blige, Mary J. 1971- ........................ **1995**:3
Blobel, Gunter 1936- ....................... **2000**:4
Bloch, Erich 1925- ........................... **1987**:4
Bloch, Henry 1922- .......................... **1988**:4
Bloch, Ivan 1940- ............................ **1986**:3
Block, Herbert 1909-2001
  Obituary ..................................... **2002**:4
Bloodworth-Thomason, Linda
  1947- ......................................... **1994**:1

Bloom, Natalie 1971- ...................... **2007**:1
Bloom, Orlando 1977- ..................... **2004**:2
Bloomberg, Michael 1942- .............. **1997**:1
Blount, Herman
  See Sun Ra
Blume, Judy 1936- ........................... **1998**:4
Blumenthal, Susan J. 1951(?)- ........ **2007**:3
Bly, Robert 1926- ............................. **1992**:4
Blyth, Myrna 1939- .......................... **2002**:4
Bocca, Julio 1967- ............................ **1995**:3
Bochco, Steven 1943- ...................... **1989**:1
Boehner, John A. 1949- ................... **2006**:4
Boggs, Wade 1958- .......................... **1989**:3
Bogosian, Eric 1953- ....................... **1990**:4
Bohbot, Michele 1959(?)- ............... **2004**:2
Boiardi, Hector
  See Boiardi, Hector
Boiardi, Hector 1897-1985
  Obituary ..................................... **1985**:3
Boies, David 1941- ........................... **2002**:1
Boitano, Brian 1963- ........................ **1988**:3
Bolger, Ray 1904-1987
  Obituary ..................................... **1987**:2
Bolger, Raymond Wallace
  See Bolger, Ray
Bolkiah, Sultan Muda
  Hassanal 1946- ......................... **1985**:4
Bollea, Terry Gene
  See Hogan, Hulk
Bollinger, Lee C. 1946- .................... **2003**:2
Bolt, Usain 1986- ............................. **2009**:2
Bolton, Michael 1953(?)- ................. **1993**:2
Bombeck, Erma 1927-1996
  Obituary ..................................... **1996**:4
Bond, Alan 1938- ............................. **1989**:2
Bonds, Barry 1964- .......................... **1993**:3
Bonet, Lisa 1967- ............................. **1989**:2
Bonham Carter, Helena 1966- ....... **1998**:4
Bonilla, Bobby 1963- ....................... **1992**:2
Bonilla, Roberto Martin Antonio
  See Bonilla, Bobby
Bon Jovi, Jon 1962- ......................... **1987**:4
Bonner, Robert 1942(?)- .................. **2003**:4
Bono 1960- ...................................... **1988**:4
Bono, Cher
  See Cher
Bono, Salvatore Philip
  See Bono, Sonny
Bono, Sonny 1935-1998 ................... **1992**:2
  Obituary ..................................... **1998**:2
Bontecou, Lee 1931- ........................ **2004**:4
Boone, Mary 1951- .......................... **1985**:1
Booth, Shirley 1898-1992
  Obituary ..................................... **1993**:2
Bopp, Thomas 1949- ....................... **1997**:3
Borge, Victor 1909-2000
  Obituary ..................................... **2001**:3
Borofsky, Jonathan 1942- ............... **2006**:4
Bose, Amar
  Brief entry ................................. **1986**:4
Bosworth, Brian 1965- ..................... **1989**:1
Bosworth, Kate 1983- ...................... **2006**:3
Botero, Fernando 1932- ................... **1994**:3
Botha, P. W. 1916-2006
  Obituary ..................................... **2008**:1
Botstein, Leon 1946- ....................... **1985**:3
Bouchard, Lucien 1938- .................. **1999**:2
Boudreau, Louis 1917-2001
  Obituary ..................................... **2002**:3
Bourassa, Robert 1933-1996
  Obituary ..................................... **1997**:1
Bourdain, Anthony 1956- ............... **2008**:3

Bourgeois, Louise 1911- ................. **1994**:1
Bourque, Raymond Jean 1960- ...... **1997**:3
Boutros Ghali, Boutros
  See Ghali, Boutros Boutros
Bowe, Riddick 1967(?)- ................... **1993**:2
Bowen, Julie 1970- .......................... **2007**:1
Bowie, David 1947- .......................... **1998**:2
Bowles, Paul 1910-1999
  Obituary ..................................... **2000**:3
Bowman, Scotty 1933- ..................... **1998**:4
Boxcar Willie 1931-1999
  Obituary ..................................... **1999**:4
Boxer, Barbara 1940- ....................... **1995**:1
Boyer, Herbert Wayne 1936- .......... **1985**:1
Boyington, Gregory Pappy 1912-1988
  Obituary ..................................... **1988**:2
Boyle, Danny 1956- ......................... **2009**:4
Boyle, Gertrude 1924- ..................... **1995**:3
Boyle, Lara Flynn 1970- .................. **2003**:4
Boyle, Peter 1935- ........................... **2002**:3
Boyle, T. C. 1948- ............................ **2007**:2
Boynton, Sandra 1953- .................... **2004**:1
Boyz II Men ..................................... **1995**:1
Bozize, Francois 1946- .................... **2006**:3
Brabeck-Letmathe, Peter 1944- ...... **2001**:4
Bradford, Barbara Taylor 1933- ..... **2002**:4
Bradley, Bill 1943- ........................... **2000**:2
Bradley, Ed 1941-2006
  Obituary ..................................... **2008**:1
Bradley, Todd 1958- ........................ **2003**:3
Bradley, Tom 1917-1998
  Obituary ..................................... **1999**:1
Bradman, Sir Donald 1908-2001
  Obituary ..................................... **2002**:1
Bradshaw, John 1933- ..................... **1992**:1
Brady, James S.
  See Brady, Sarah and James S.
Brady, Sarah
  See Brady, Sarah and James S.
Brady, Sarah and James S. ............. **1991**:4
Brady, Tom 1977- ............................ **2002**:4
Brady, Wayne 1972- ........................ **2008**:3
Braff, Zach 1975- ............................. **2005**:2
Branagh, Kenneth 1960- ................. **1992**:2
Brandauer, Klaus Maria 1944- ....... **1987**:3
Brando, Cheyenne 1970-1995
  Obituary ..................................... **1995**:4
Brando, Marlon 1924-2004
  Obituary ..................................... **2005**:3
Brandt, Willy 1913-1992
  Obituary ..................................... **1993**:2
Brandy 1979- ................................... **1996**:4
Branson, Richard 1951- ................... **1987**:1
Bratt, Benjamin 1963- ..................... **2009**:1
Braun, Carol Moseley 1947- ........... **1993**:1
Bravo, Ellen 1944- ........................... **1998**:2
Bravo, Miguel Obando y
  See Obando, Miguel
Bravo, Rose Marie 1951(?)- ............. **2005**:3
Braxton, Toni 1967- ......................... **1994**:3
Brazile, Donna 1959- ....................... **2001**:1
Breathed, Berkeley 1957- ................ **2005**:3
Breitschwerdt, Werner 1927- .......... **1988**:4
Bremen, Barry 1947- ....................... **1987**:3
Bremer, L. Paul 1941- ...................... **2004**:2
Brennan, Edward A. 1934- .............. **1989**:1
Brennan, Robert E. 1943(?)- ........... **1988**:1
Brennan, William 1906-1997
  Obituary ..................................... **1997**:4
Brenneman, Amy 1964- ................... **2002**:1
Breyer, Stephen Gerald 1938- ........ **1994**:4

Bridges, Lloyd 1913-1998
  Obituary ........................ **1998**:3
Brillstein, Bernie 1931-2008
  Obituary ........................ **2009**:4
Brinker, Nancy 1946- ........................ **2007**:1
Brinkley, David 1920-2003
  Obituary ........................ **2004**:3
Bristow, Lonnie 1930- ........................ **1996**:1
Brite, Poppy Z. 1967- ........................ **2005**:1
Broadbent, Jim 1949- ........................ **2008**:4
Broadus, Calvin
  See Snoop Doggy Dogg
Brockovich-Ellis, Erin 1960- .......... **2003**:3
Brodsky, Joseph 1940-1996
  Obituary ........................ **1996**:3
Brody, Adrien 1973- ........................ **2006**:3
Brokaw, Tom 1940- ........................ **2000**:3
Bronfman, Edgar, Jr. 1955- .......... **1994**:4
Bronson, Charles 1921-2003
  Obituary ........................ **2004**:4
Brooks, Albert 1948(?)- ........................ **1991**:4
Brooks, Diana D. 1950- ........................ **1990**:1
Brooks, Garth 1962- ........................ **1992**:1
Brooks, Gwendolyn 1917-2000 ...... **1998**:1
  Obituary ........................ **2001**:2
Brooks, Mel 1926- ........................ **2003**:1
Brosius, Christopher ........................ **2007**:1
Brosnan, Pierce 1952- ........................ **2000**:3
Brower, David 1912- ........................ **1990**:4
Brown, Bobbi 1957- ........................ **2001**:4
Brown, Dan 1964- ........................ **2004**:4
Brown, Dee 1908-2002
  Obituary ........................ **2004**:1
Brown, Edmund G., Sr. 1905-1996
  Obituary ........................ **1996**:3
Brown, Edmund Gerald, Jr.
  See Brown, Jerry
Brown, Gordon 1951- ........................ **2008**:3
Brown, Howard and Karen
  Stewart ........................ **2007**:3
Brown, J. Carter 1934-2002
  Obituary ........................ **2003**:3
Brown, James 1928(?)- ........................ **1991**:4
Brown, James Nathaniel
  See Brown, Jim
Brown, Jerry 1938- ........................ **1992**:4
Brown, Jim 1936- ........................ **1993**:2
Brown, John Seely 1940- ........................ **2004**:1
Brown, Judie 1944- ........................ **1986**:2
Brown, Les 1912-2001
  Obituary ........................ **2001**:3
Brown, Les 1945- ........................ **1994**:3
Brown, Leslie Calvin
  See Brown, Les
Brown, Pat
  See Brown, Edmund G., Sr.
Brown, Paul 1908-1991
  Obituary ........................ **1992**:1
Brown, Ron 1941- ........................ **1990**:3
Brown, Ron 1941-1996
  Obituary ........................ **1996**:4
Brown, Ruth 1928-2006
  Obituary ........................ **2008**:1
Brown, Tina 1953- ........................ **1992**:1
Brown, Willie 1934- ........................ **1996**:4
Brown, Willie L. 1934- ........................ **1985**:2
Browner, Carol M. 1955- ........................ **1994**:1
Browning, Edmond
  Brief entry ........................ **1986**:2
Bruckheimer, Jerry 1945- ........................ **2007**:2
Brundtland, Gro Harlem 1939- ..... **2000**:1
Bruni, Carla 1967- ........................ **2009**:3

Bryan, Mark 1967(?)-
  See Hootie and the Blowfish
Bryant, Kobe 1978- ........................ **1998**:3
Brynner, Yul 1920(?)-1985
  Obituary ........................ **1985**:4
Buchanan, Pat 1938- ........................ **1996**:3
Buchanan, Patrick J.
  See Buchanan, Pat
Buchwald, Art 1925-2007
  Obituary ........................ **2008**:2
Buck, Linda 1956(?)- ........................ **2004**:2
Buckley, Betty 1947- ........................ **1996**:2
Buckley, Jeff 1966-1997
  Obituary ........................ **1997**:4
Buffett, Jimmy 1946- ........................ **1999**:3
Buffett, Warren 1930- ........................ **1995**:2
Buhaina, Abdullah Ibn
  See Blakey, Art
Bujones, Fernando 1955-2005
  Obituary ........................ **2007**:1
Bullock, Sandra 1967- ........................ **1995**:4
Bulsara, Frederick
  See Mercury, Freddie
Bundchen, Gisele 1980- ........................ **2009**:1
Bundy, McGeorge 1919-1996
  Obituary ........................ **1997**:1
Bundy, William P. 1917-2000
  Obituary ........................ **2001**:2
Bunshaft, Gordon 1909-1990 ......... **1989**:3
  Obituary ........................ **1991**:1
Burch, Tory 1966- ........................ **2009**:3
Burck, Wade
  Brief entry ........................ **1986**:1
Burger, Warren E. 1907-1995
  Obituary ........................ **1995**:4
Burgess, Anthony 1917-1993
  Obituary ........................ **1994**:2
Burk, Martha 1941- ........................ **2004**:1
Burnett, Carol 1933- ........................ **2000**:3
Burnett, Mark 1960- ........................ **2003**:1
Burnison, Chantal Simone
  1950(?)- ........................ **1988**:3
Burns, Charles R.
  Brief entry ........................ **1988**:1
Burns, Edward 1968- ........................ **1997**:1
Burns, George 1896-1996
  Obituary ........................ **1996**:3
Burns, Ken 1953- ........................ **1995**:2
Burns, Robin 1953(?)- ........................ **1991**:2
Burns, Tex
  See L'Amour, Louis
Burr, Donald Calvin 1941- ........... **1985**:3
Burr, Raymond 1917-1993
  Obituary ........................ **1994**:1
Burrell, Stanely Kirk
  See Hammer, M. C.
Burroughs, William S. 1914- ......... **1994**:2
Burroughs, William S. 1914-1997
  Obituary ........................ **1997**:4
Burrows, James 1940- ........................ **2005**:3
Burstyn, Ellen 1932- ........................ **2001**:4
Burton, Jake 1954- ........................ **2007**:1
Burton, Tim 1959- ........................ **1993**:1
Burum, Stephen H.
  Brief entry ........................ **1987**:2
Buscaglia, Leo 1924-1998
  Obituary ........................ **1998**:4
Buscemi, Steve 1957- ........................ **1997**:4
Busch, August A. III 1937- ........... **1988**:2
Busch, August Anheuser, Jr. 1899-1989
  Obituary ........................ **1990**:2
Busch, Charles 1954- ........................ **1998**:3

Busch, Kurt 1978- ........................ **2006**:1
Bush, Barbara 1925- ........................ **1989**:3
Bush, George W., Jr. 1946- .............. **1996**:4
Bush, Jeb 1953- ........................ **2003**:1
Bush, Kate 1958- ........................ **1994**:3
Bush, Millie 1987- ........................ **1992**:1
Bushnell, Candace 1959(?)- ........... **2004**:2
Bushnell, Nolan 1943- ........................ **1985**:1
Buss, Jerry 1933- ........................ **1989**:3
Butcher, Susan 1954- ........................ **1991**:1
Buthelezi, Mangosuthu Gatsha
  1928- ........................ **1989**:3
Butler, Brett 1958(?)- ........................ **1995**:1
Butler, Octavia E. 1947- ........................ **1999**:3
Butterfield, Paul 1942-1987
  Obituary ........................ **1987**:3
Butterfield, Stewart and Caterina
  Fake ........................ **2007**:3
Buttons, Red 1919-2006
  Obituary ........................ **2007**:3
Bynes, Amanda 1986- ........................ **2005**:1
Byrne, Gabriel 1950- ........................ **1997**:4
Byrne, Rhonda 1955- ........................ **2008**:2
Caan, James 1939- ........................ **2004**:4
Cabot, Meg 1967- ........................ **2008**:4
Caen, Herb 1916-1997
  Obituary ........................ **1997**:4
Caesar, Adolph 1934-1986
  Obituary ........................ **1986**:3
Cage, John 1912-1992
  Obituary ........................ **1993**:1
Cage, Nicolas 1964- ........................ **1991**:1
Cagney, James 1899-1986
  Obituary ........................ **1986**:2
Cain, Herman 1945- ........................ **1998**:3
Caine, Michael 1933- ........................ **2000**:4
Calatrava, Santiago 1951- .............. **2005**:1
Calhoun, Rory 1922-1999
  Obituary ........................ **1999**:4
Calhoun, William
  See Living Colour
Caliguiri, Richard S. 1931-1988
  Obituary ........................ **1988**:3
Callaway, Ely 1919-2001
  Obituary ........................ **2002**:3
Calloway, Cab 1908-1994
  Obituary ........................ **1995**:2
Calloway, D. Wayne 1935- ............. **1987**:3
Calloway, David Wayne
  See Calloway, D. Wayne
Calment, Jeanne 1875-1997
  Obituary ........................ **1997**:4
Cameron, David
  Brief entry ........................ **1988**:1
Cammermeyer, Margarethe
  1942- ........................ **1995**:2
Campanella, Roy 1921-1993
  Obituary ........................ **1994**:1
Campbell, Avril Phaedra
  See Campbell, Kim
Campbell, Bebe Moore 1950- ........ **1996**:2
Campbell, Ben Nighthorse 1933- .. **1998**:1
Campbell, Bill ........................ **1997**:1
Campbell, Erica 1972-
  See Mary Mary
Campbell, Kim 1947- ........................ **1993**:4
Campbell, Naomi 1970- ........................ **2000**:2
Campbell, Neve 1973- ........................ **1998**:2
Campbell, Tina 1972-
  See Mary Mary
Campeau, Robert 1923- ........................ **1990**:1
Campion, Jane ........................ **1991**:4

Candy, John 1950-1994 .................. **1988**:2
  Obituary ....................... **1994**:3
Canfield, Alan B.
  Brief entry ..................... **1986**:3
Cannon, Nick 1980- ..................... **2006**:4
Canseco, Jose 1964- ...................... **1990**:2
Cantrell, Ed
  Brief entry ..................... **1985**:3
Caplan, Arthur L. 1950- ................. **2000**:2
Capra, Frank 1897-1991
  Obituary ....................... **1992**:2
Capriati, Jennifer 1976- .................. **1991**:1
Carabina, Harry Christopher
  See Caray, Harry
Caras, Roger 1928-2001
  Obituary ....................... **2002**:1
Caray, Harry 1914(?)-1998 ............. **1988**:3
  Obituary ....................... **1998**:3
Carcaterra, Lorenzo 1954- .............. **1996**:1
Card, Andrew H., Jr. 1947- ........... **2003**:2
Cardigans, The ........................... **1997**:4
Cardin, Pierre 1922- ...................... **2003**:3
Cardoso, Fernando Henrique
  1931- ......................... **1996**:4
Carell, Steve 1963- ...................... **2006**:4
Carey, Drew 1958- ...................... **1997**:4
Carey, George 1935- ..................... **1992**:3
Carey, Mariah 1970(?)- .................. **1991**:3
Carey, Ron 1936- ........................ **1993**:3
Carlin, George 1937- .................... **1996**:3
Carlino, Cristina 1961(?)- ............. **2008**:4
Carlisle, Belinda 1958- .................. **1989**:3
Carlos, King Juan
  See Juan Carlos I
Carlos I, Juan
  See Juan Carlos I
Carlson, Richard 1961- .................. **2002**:1
Carlsson, Arvid 1923- ................... **2001**:2
Carmichael, Stokely
  See Ture, Kwame
Carmona, Richard 1949- ................ **2003**:2
Carnahan, Jean 1933- ................... **2001**:2
Carnahan, Mel 1934-2000
  Obituary ....................... **2001**:2
Carney, Art 1918-2003
  Obituary ....................... **2005**:1
Carpenter, Mary-Chapin 1958(?)- . **1994**:1
Carradine, John 1906-1988
  Obituary ....................... **1989**:2
Carreras, Jose 1946- ..................... **1995**:2
Carrey, Jim 1962- ........................ **1995**:1
Carson, Ben 1951- ....................... **1998**:2
Carson, Johnny 1925-2005
  Obituary ....................... **2006**:1
Carson, Lisa Nicole 1969- ............. **1999**:3
Carter, Amy 1967- ....................... **1987**:4
Carter, Benny 1907-2003
  Obituary ....................... **2004**:3
Carter, Billy 1937-1988
  Obituary ....................... **1989**:1
Carter, Chris 1956- ...................... **2000**:1
Carter, Gary 1954- ....................... **1987**:1
Carter, James Earl, Jr.
  See Carter, Jimmy
Carter, Jimmy 1924- ..................... **1995**:1
Carter, Joe 1960- ......................... **1994**:2
Carter, Nell 1948-2003
  Obituary ....................... **2004**:2
Carter, Ron 1937- ........................ **1987**:3
Carter, Ronald
  See Carter, Ron
Carter, Rubin 1937- ...................... **2000**:3

Carter, Stephen L. ...................... **2008**:2
Carter, Vince 1977- ..................... **2001**:4
Cartier-Bresson, Henri 1908-2004
  Obituary ....................... **2005**:4
Cartwright, Carol Ann 1941- ........ **2009**:4
Caruso, David 1956(?)- ................. **1994**:3
Carver, Raymond 1938-1988
  Obituary ....................... **1989**:1
Carvey, Dana 1955- ..................... **1994**:1
Carville, James 1944-
  See Matalin, Mary
Case, Steve 1958- ........................ **1995**:4
Casey, William 1913-1987
  Obituary ....................... **1987**:3
Cash, Johnny 1932- ..................... **1995**:3
Cash, June Carter 1929-2003
  Obituary ....................... **2004**:2
Casper, Gerhard 1937- .................. **1993**:1
Cassavetes, John 1929-1989
  Obituary ....................... **1989**:2
Cassidy, Mike 1963(?)- ................. **2006**:1
Cassini, Oleg 1913-2006
  Obituary ....................... **2007**:2
Castaneda, Carlos 1931-1998
  Obituary ....................... **1998**:4
Castelli, Leo 1907-1999
  Obituary ....................... **2000**:1
Castellucci, Cecil 1969- ................ **2008**:3
Castillo, Ana 1953- ...................... **2000**:4
Castle-Hughes, Keisha 1990- ........ **2004**:4
Castro, Fidel 1926- ...................... **1991**:4
Catlett, Elizabeth 1915(?)- ........... **1999**:3
Cattrall, Kim 1956- ...................... **2003**:3
Caulfield, Joan 1922(?)-1991
  Obituary ....................... **1992**:1
Cavalli, Roberto 1940- .................. **2004**:4
Cavanagh, Tom 1968- ................... **2003**:1
Cavazos, Lauro F. 1927- ............... **1989**:2
Caviezel, Jim 1968- ...................... **2005**:3
Cavoukian, Raffi
  See Raffi
Ceausescu, Nicolae 1918-1989
  Obituary ....................... **1990**:2
Cedras, Raoul 1950- ..................... **1994**:4
Cela, Camilo Jose 1916-2001
  Obituary ....................... **2003**:1
Centrello, Gina 1959(?)- ............... **2008**:3
Cerf, Vinton G. 1943- .................. **1999**:2
Cerovsek, Corey
  Brief entry ..................... **1987**:4
Chabon, Michael 1963- ................. **2002**:1
Chagall, Marc 1887-1985
  Obituary ....................... **1985**:2
Chahine, Youssef 1926-2008
  Obituary ....................... **2009**:3
Chaing Kai-Shek, Madame 1898-2003
  Obituary ....................... **2005**:1
Chalayan, Hussein 1970- ............... **2003**:2
Chambas, Mohammed ibn 1950- .. **2003**:3
Chamberlain, Joba 1985- ............... **2008**:3
Chamberlain, Wilt 1936-1999
  Obituary ....................... **2000**:2
Chamberlin, Wendy 1948- ............. **2002**:4
Chan, Jackie 1954- ...................... **1996**:1
Chancellor, John
  Obituary ....................... **1997**:1
Chaney, John 1932- ...................... **1989**:1
Channing, Stockard 1946- ............. **1991**:3
Chao, Elaine L. 1953- ................... **2007**:3
Chapman, Tracy 1964- .................. **1989**:2
Chappell, Tom 1943- .................... **2002**:3
Chappelle, Dave 1973- .................. **2005**:3

Charisse, Cyd 1922-2008
  Obituary ....................... **2009**:3
Charles, Prince of Wales 1948- ...... **1995**:3
Charles, Ray 1930-2004
  Obituary ....................... **2005**:3
Charney, Dov 1969- ..................... **2008**:2
Charron, Paul 1942- ..................... **2004**:1
Chase, Chevy 1943- ..................... **1990**:1
Chase, Debra Martin 1956- ........... **2009**:1
Chast, Roz 1955- ........................ **1992**:4
Chastain, Brandi 1968- ................. **2001**:3
Chatham, Russell 1939- ................ **1990**:1
Chatwin, Bruce 1940-1989
  Obituary ....................... **1989**:2
Chatwin, Charles Bruce
  See Chatwin, Bruce
Chauchoin, Lily Claudette
  See Colbert, Claudette
Chaudhari, Praveen 1937- ............. **1989**:4
Chavez, Cesar 1927-1993
  Obituary ....................... **1993**:4
Chavez, Linda 1947- .................... **1999**:3
Chavez-Thompson, Linda 1944- ... **1999**:1
Chavis, Benjamin 1948- ................ **1993**:4
Cheadle, Don 1964- ..................... **2002**:1
Cheatham, Adolphus Doc 1905-1997
  Obituary ....................... **1997**:4
Cheek, James Edward
  Brief entry ..................... **1987**:1
Chen, Joan 1961- ........................ **2000**:2
Chen, Steve and Chad Hurley ........ **2007**:2
Chen, T.C.
  Brief entry ..................... **1987**:3
Chen, Tze-chung
  See Chen, T.C.
Chenault, Kenneth I. 1951- ........... **1999**:3
Cheney, Dick 1941- ...................... **1991**:3
Cheney, Lynne V. 1941- ................ **1990**:4
Chen Shui-bian 1950(?)- ............... **2001**:2
Cher 1946- ................................ **1993**:1
Chernenko, Konstantin 1911-1985
  Obituary ....................... **1985**:1
Cherry, Don 1934- ....................... **1993**:4
Chesney, Kenny 1968- .................. **2008**:2
Chia, Sandro 1946- ...................... **1987**:2
Chihuly, Dale 1941- ..................... **1995**:2
Chiklis, Michael 1963- .................. **2003**:3
Child, Julia 1912- ........................ **1999**:4
Child, Lee 1954- ......................... **2007**:3
Chillida, Eduardo 1924-2002
  Obituary ....................... **2003**:4
Chiluba, Frederick 1943- ............... **1992**:3
Chirac, Jacques 1932- ................... **1995**:4
Chisholm, Shirley 1924-2005
  Obituary ....................... **2006**:1
Chissano, Joaquim 1939- .............. **1987**:4
Chittister, Joan D. 1936- .............. **2002**:2
Chizen, Bruce 1955(?)- ................. **2004**:2
Cho, Margaret 1970- .................... **1995**:2
Choo, Jimmy 1957(?)- .................. **2006**:3
Chopra, Deepak 1947- .................. **1996**:3
Chouinard, Yvon 1938(?)- ............ **2002**:2
Chow, Stephen 1962- ................... **2006**:1
Chow Yun-fat 1955- ..................... **1999**:4
Chretien, Jean 1934- .................... **1990**:4
Chretien, Joseph Jacques Jean
  See Chretien, Jean
Christensen, Hayden 1981- ........... **2003**:3
Christensen, Kate 1962- ................ **2009**:4
Christie, Julie 1941- ..................... **2008**:4
Christo 1935- ............................. **1992**:3
Christopher, Warren 1925- ........... **1996**:3

Chu, Paul C.W. 1941- ........................ **1988**:2
Chung, Connie 1946- ......................... **1988**:4
Chung Ju Yung 1915-2001
    Obituary ............................ **2002**:1
Chyna 1970- ..................................... **2001**:4
Ciampi, Carlo Azeglio 1920- ......... **2004**:3
Ciccone, Madonna Louise
    See Madonna
Cisneros, Henry 1947- ..................... **1987**:2
Claiborne, Liz 1929- ......................... **1986**:3
Clancy, Tom 1947- ........................... **1998**:4
Clapp, Eric Patrick
    See Clapton, Eric
Clapton, Eric 1945- .......................... **1993**:3
Clark, J. E.
    Brief entry ......................... **1986**:1
Clark, Jim 1944- ............................... **1997**:1
Clark, John Elwood
    See Clark, J.E.
Clark, Kenneth B. 1914-2005
    Obituary ............................ **2006**:3
Clark, Marcia 1954(?)- ..................... **1995**:1
Clark, Mary Higgins 1929- ............. **2000**:4
Clark, Maxine 1949- ......................... **2009**:4
Clarke, Arthur C. 1917-2008
    Obituary ............................ **2009**:2
Clarke, Richard A. 1951(?)- ............ **2002**:2
Clarke, Stanley 1951- ...................... **1985**:4
Clarkson, Kelly 1982- ...................... **2003**:3
Clarkson, Patricia 1959- .................. **2005**:3
Clavell, James 1924(?)-1994
    Obituary ............................ **1995**:1
Clay, Andrew Dice 1958- ................ **1991**:1
Clay, Cassius Marcellus, Jr.
    See Ali, Muhammad
Cleaver, Eldridge 1935-1998
    Obituary ............................ **1998**:4
Cleese, John 1939- ........................... **1989**:2
Clemens, Roger 1962- ...................... **1991**:4
Clemente, Francesco 1952- .............. **1992**:2
Clements, George 1932- ................... **1985**:1
Cleveland, James 1932(?)-1991
    Obituary ............................ **1991**:3
Cliburn, Van 1934- ........................... **1995**:1
Clijsters, Kim 1983- ......................... **2006**:3
Clinton, Bill 1946- ........................... **1992**:1
Clinton, Hillary Rodham 1947- ..... **1993**:2
Clooney, George 1961- ..................... **1996**:4
Clooney, Rosemary 1928-2002
    Obituary ............................ **2003**:4
Close, Glenn 1947- ........................... **1988**:3
Clowes, Daniel 1961- ....................... **2007**:1
Clyburn, James 1940- ....................... **1999**:4
Cobain, Kurt
    See Nirvana
Cobain, Kurt 1967-1944
    Obituary ............................ **1994**:3
Coburn, James 1928-2002
    Obituary ............................ **2004**:1
Coca, Imogene 1908-2001
    Obituary ............................ **2002**:2
Cochran, Johnnie 1937- ................... **1996**:1
Coco, James 1929(?)-1987
    Obituary ............................ **1987**:2
Codrescu, Andreaa 1946- ................ **1997**:3
Cody, Diablo 1978- .......................... **2009**:1
Coen, Ethan
    See Coen, Joel and Ethan
Coen, Joel
    See Coen, Joel and Ethan
Coen, Joel and Ethan ...................... **1992**:1
Coetzee, J. M. 1940- ......................... **2004**:4

Coffey, Paul 1961- ........................... **1985**:4
Coffin, William Sloane, Jr. 1924- .... **1990**:3
Cohen, Ben
    See Ben & Jerry
Cohen, Bennet
    See Ben & Jerry
Cohen, William S. 1940- ................. **1998**:1
Colasanto, Nicholas 1923(?)-1985
    Obituary ............................ **1985**:2
Colbert, Claudette 1903-1996
    Obituary ............................ **1997**:1
Colbert, Stephen 1964- .................... **2007**:4
Colby, William E. 1920-1996
    Obituary ............................ **1996**:4
Coldplay .......................................... **2004**:4
Cole, Anne 1930(?)- ......................... **2007**:3
Cole, Johnetta B. 1936- ................... **1994**:3
Cole, Kenneth 1954(?)- ................... **2003**:1
Cole, Natalie 1950- .......................... **1992**:4
Coleman, Dabney 1932- ................... **1988**:3
Coleman, Sheldon, Jr. 1953- ........... **1990**:2
Coles, Robert 1929(?)- ..................... **1995**:1
Colley, Sarah Ophelia
    See Pearl, Minnie
Collier, Sophia 1956(?)- ................... **2001**:2
Collins, Albert 1932-1993
    Obituary ............................ **1994**:2
Collins, Billy 1941- .......................... **2002**:2
Collins, Cardiss 1931- ..................... **1995**:3
Collins, Eileen 1956- ....................... **1995**:3
Collins, Jackie 1941- ........................ **2004**:4
Collins, Kerry 1972- ........................ **2002**:3
Collor, Fernando
    See Collor de Mello, Fernando
Collor de Mello, Fernando 1949- .. **1992**:4
Colosio, Luis Donaldo 1950-1994 . **1994**:3
Colosio Murrieta, Luis Donaldo
    See Colosio, Luis Donaldo
Colwell, Rita Rossi 1934- ............... **1999**:3
Combs, Sean Puffy 1970- ............... **1998**:4
Comfort, Alex 1920-2000
    Obituary ............................ **2000**:4
Commager, Henry Steele 1902-1998
    Obituary ............................ **1998**:3
Como, Perry 1912-2001
    Obituary ............................ **2002**:2
Condit, Phil 1941- ........................... **2001**:3
Condon, Bill 1955- ........................... **2007**:3
Condon, Richard 1915-1996
    Obituary ............................ **1996**:4
Conigliaro, Anthony Richard
    See Conigliaro, Tony
Conigliaro, Tony 1945-1990
    Obituary ............................ **1990**:3
Connally, John 1917-1993
    Obituary ............................ **1994**:1
Connelly, Jennifer 1970- ................. **2002**:4
Connelly, Michael 1956- ................. **2007**:1
Conner, Bruce 1933-2008
    Obituary ............................ **2009**:3
Conner, Dennis 1943- ...................... **1987**:2
Connerly, Ward 1939- ..................... **2000**:2
Connery, Sean 1930- ........................ **1990**:4
Connick, Harry, Jr. 1967- ............... **1991**:1
Conrad, Pete 1930-1999
    Obituary ............................ **2000**:1
Conseil, Dominique Nils 1962(?)- . **2007**:2
Convy, Bert 1934(?)-1991
    Obituary ............................ **1992**:1
Conyers, John, Jr. 1929- .................. **1999**:1
Cook, Peter 1938-1995
    Obituary ............................ **1995**:2

Cook, Robert Brian
    See Cook, Robin
Cook, Robin 1940- ........................... **1996**:3
Cook, William
    See Tudor, Antony
Cooke, Alistair 1908-2004
    Obituary ............................ **2005**:3
Cool, Tre 1972-
    See Green Day
Coolio 1963- ..................................... **1996**:4
Cooper, Alexander 1936- ................ **1988**:4
Cooper, Anderson 1967- .................. **2006**:1
Cooper, Chris 1951- ......................... **2004**:1
Cooper, Cynthia 1999- ..................... **1999**:1
Cooper, Stephen F. 1946- ................ **2005**:4
Coors, William K.
    Brief entry ......................... **1985**:1
Copeland, Al 1944(?)- ...................... **1988**:3
Copland, Aaron 1900-1990
    Obituary ............................ **1991**:2
Copperfield, David 1957- ................. **1986**:3
Coppola, Carmine 1910-1991
    Obituary ............................ **1991**:4
Coppola, Francis Ford 1939- ......... **1989**:4
Coppola, Sofia 1971- ....................... **2004**:3
Copps, Sheila 1952- ......................... **1986**:4
Corbett, John 1962- .......................... **2004**:1
Corea, Anthony Armando
    See Corea, Chick
Corea, Chick 1941- .......................... **1986**:3
Cornum, Rhonda 1954- .................... **2006**:3
Cornwell, Patricia 1956- .................. **2003**:1
Correa, Rafael 1963- ........................ **2008**:1
Corwin, Jeff 1967- ........................... **2005**:1
Cosby, Bill 1937- .............................. **1999**:2
Cosell, Howard 1918-1995
    Obituary ............................ **1995**:4
Costas, Bob 1952- ............................ **1986**:4
Costas, Robert Quinlan
    See Costas, Bob
Costello, Elvis 1954(?)- ................... **1994**:4
Costner, Kevin 1955- ....................... **1989**:4
Cotillard, Marion 1975- ................... **2009**:1
Cotter, Audrey
    See Meadows, Audrey
Couples, Fred 1959- ......................... **1994**:4
Couric, Katherine 1957- ................... **1991**:4
Courier, Jim 1970- ........................... **1993**:2
Courtney, Erica 1957- ...................... **2009**:3
Cousteau, Jacques-Yves
    1910-1997 ......................... **1998**:2
Cousteau, Jean-Michel 1938- ......... **1988**:2
Covey, Stephen R. 1932- ................. **1994**:4
Cowell, Simon 1959- ........................ **2003**:4
Cowley, Malcolm 1898-1989
    Obituary ............................ **1989**:3
Cox, Courteney 1964- ...................... **1996**:2
Cox, Richard Joseph
    Brief entry ......................... **1985**:1
Cozza, Stephen 1985- ...................... **2001**:1
Craig, Daniel 1968- .......................... **2008**:1
Craig, James 1956- ........................... **2001**:1
Craig, Jenny
    See Craig, Sid and Jenny
Craig, Sid
    See Craig, Sid and Jenny
Craig, Sid and Jenny ...................... **1993**:4
Crais, Robert 1954(?)- ..................... **2007**:4
Cram, Donald J. 1919-2001
    Obituary ............................ **2002**:2
Crandall, Robert L. 1935- ............... **1992**:1
Craven, Wes 1939- ........................... **1997**:3

Crawford, Broderick 1911-1986
    Obituary ........................................ **1986**:3
Crawford, Cheryl 1902-1986
    Obituary ........................................ **1987**:1
Crawford, Cindy 1966- .................... **1993**:3
Crawford, Michael 1942- ............... **1994**:2
Cray, Robert 1953- .......................... **1988**:2
Cray, Seymour R. 1925-1996
    Brief entry .................................... **1986**:3
    Obituary ........................................ **1997**:2
Creamer, Paula 1986- ..................... **2006**:2
Crenna, Richard 1926-2003
    Obituary ........................................ **2004**:1
Cresson, Edith 1934- ...................... **1992**:1
Crichton, Michael 1942- ................. **1995**:3
Crick, Francis 1916-2004
    Obituary ........................................ **2005**:4
Crisp, Quentin 1908-1999
    Obituary ........................................ **2000**:3
Cronenberg, David 1943- .............. **1992**:3
Cronkite, Walter Leland 1916- ...... **1997**:3
Cronyn, Hume 1911-2003
    Obituary ........................................ **2004**:3
Crosby, David 1941- ........................ **2000**:4
Crosby, Sidney 1987- ...................... **2006**:3
Crothers, Benjamin Sherman
    See Crothers, Scatman
Crothers, Scatman 1910-1986
    Obituary ........................................ **1987**:1
Crow, Sheryl 1964- .......................... **1995**:2
Crowe, Cameron 1957- .................... **2001**:2
Crowe, Russell 1964- ....................... **2000**:4
Cruise, Tom 1962(?)- ...................... **1985**:4
Crumb, R. 1943- ............................... **1995**:4
Crump, Scott 1954(?)- ..................... **2008**:1
Cruz, Arturo 1923- .......................... **1985**:1
Cruz, Celia 1925-2003
    Obituary ........................................ **2004**:3
Cruz, Nilo 1961(?)- .......................... **2004**:4
Cruz, Penelope 1974- ...................... **2001**:4
Cruzan, Nancy 1957(?)-1990
    Obituary ........................................ **1991**:3
Crystal, Billy 1947- .......................... **1985**:3
Crystal, William
    See Crystal, Billy
Cuaron, Alfonso 1961- .................... **2008**:2
Cugat, Xavier 1900-1990
    Obituary ........................................ **1991**:2
Culkin, Macaulay 1980(?)- ............ **1991**:3
Cummings, Sam 1927- ..................... **1986**:3
Cummings, Samuel
    See Cummings, Sam
Cunningham, Merce 1919- ............. **1998**:1
Cunningham, Michael 1952- ......... **2003**:4
Cunningham, Randall 1963- ......... **1990**:1
Cunningham, Reverend William
    1930-1997
    Obituary ........................................ **1997**:4
Cuomo, Mario 1932- ....................... **1992**:2
Curran, Charles E. 1934- ............... **1989**:2
Curren, Tommy
    Brief entry .................................... **1987**:4
Curry, Ann 1956- ............................. **2001**:1
Curtis, Ben 1977- ............................. **2004**:2
Curtis, Jamie Lee 1958- .................. **1995**:1
Cusack, John 1966- .......................... **1999**:3
Cushing, Peter 1913-1994
    Obituary ........................................ **1995**:1
Cyrus, Billy Ray 1961(?)- ............... **1993**:1
Cyrus, Miley 1992- .......................... **2008**:3

D'Abruzzo, Alfonso Guiseppe Giovanni
    Roberto
    See Alda, Robert
Dafoe, Willem 1955- ........................ **1988**:1
Daft Punk 1975- ............................... **2009**:4
da Graca Meneghel, Maria
    See Xuxa
Dahl, Roald 1916-1990
    Obituary ........................................ **1991**:2
Dahmer, Jeffrey 1959-1994
    Obituary ........................................ **1995**:2
Daily, Bishop Thomas V. 1927- ...... **1990**:4
Dalai Lama 1935- ............................. **1989**:1
D'Alessio, Catherine Anne
    See D'Alessio, Kitty
D'Alessio, Kitty
    Brief entry .................................... **1987**:3
Dali, Salvador 1904-1989
    Obituary ........................................ **1989**:2
Dalton, Timothy 1946- .................... **1988**:4
Daly, Carson 1973- .......................... **2002**:4
D'Amato, Al 1937- ........................... **1996**:1
Damon, Johnny 1973- ..................... **2005**:4
Damon, Matt 1970- .......................... **1999**:1
Danes, Claire 1979- ......................... **1999**:4
Dangerfield, Rodney 1921-2004
    Obituary ........................................ **2006**:1
Daniels, Faith 1958- ........................ **1993**:3
Daniels, Jeff 1955- ............................ **1989**:4
Danticat, Edwidge 1969- ............... **2005**:4
Danza, Tony 1951- ........................... **1989**:1
D'Arby, Terence Trent 1962- .......... **1988**:4
Darden, Christopher 1957(?)- ........ **1996**:4
Darling, Erik 1933-2008
    Obituary ........................................ **2009**:4
Darwish, Mahmud 1942-2008
    Obituary ........................................ **2009**:4
Darwish, Tiffany Renee
    See Tiffany
Daschle, Tom 1947- ......................... **2002**:3
Davenport, Lindsay 1976- ............. **1999**:2
David, George 1942- ....................... **2005**:1
David, Larry 1948- ........................... **2003**:4
Davis, Angela 1944- ........................ **1998**:3
Davis, Bette 1908-1989
    Obituary ........................................ **1990**:1
Davis, Crispin 1949- ........................ **2004**:1
Davis, Eric 1962- .............................. **1987**:4
Davis, Geena 1957- .......................... **1992**:1
Davis, Miles 1926-1991
    Obituary ........................................ **1992**:2
Davis, Noel ........................................ **1990**:3
Davis, Ossie 1917-2005
    Obituary ........................................ **2006**:1
Davis, Paige 1969- ........................... **2004**:2
Davis, Patti 1952- ............................. **1995**:1
Davis, Raymond, Jr. 1914-2006
    Obituary ........................................ **2007**:3
Davis, Sammy, Jr. 1925-1990
    Obituary ........................................ **1990**:4
Davis, Terrell 1972- .......................... **1998**:2
Davison, Ian Hay 1931- .................. **1986**:1
Dawson, Rosario 1979- ................... **2007**:2
Day, Dennis 1917-1988
    Obituary ........................................ **1988**:4
Day, Pat 1953- ................................... **1995**:2
Day-Lewis, Daniel 1957- ................ **1989**:4
Dean, Howard 1948- ....................... **2005**:4
Dean, Laura 1945- ........................... **1989**:4
Dearden, John Cardinal 1907-1988
    Obituary ........................................ **1988**:4

de Arias, Margot Fonteyn
    See Fonteyn, Margot
de Arriortua, Jose Ignacio
    See Lopez de Arriortua, Jose Ignacio
DeBakey, Michael 1908-2008
    Obituary ........................................ **2009**:3
DeBartolo, Edward J., Jr. 1946- ...... **1989**:3
Deby, Idriss 1952- ............................ **2002**:2
DeCarava, Roy 1919- ....................... **1996**:3
DeCarava, Rudolph
    See DeCarava, Roy
De Cordova, Frederick 1910- ......... **1985**:2
de Cuellar, Javier Perez
    See Perez de Cuellar, Javier
Dee, Janie 1966(?)- .......................... **2001**:4
Dee, Sandra 1942-2005
    Obituary ........................................ **2006**:2
Deen, Paula 1947- ............................ **2008**:3
Dees, Morris 1936- ........................... **1992**:1
DeGeneres, Ellen .............................. **1995**:3
de Gortari, Carlos Salinas
    See Salinas, Carlos
de Homem-Christo, Guy-Manuel 1975-
    See Daft Punk
de Hoop Scheffer, Jaap 1948- ........ **2005**:1
Dekker, Desmond 1941-2006
    Obituary ........................................ **2007**:2
de Klerk, Frederick Willem
    See de Klerk, F.W.
de Klerk, F.W. 1936- ........................ **1990**:1
de Kooning, Willem 1904-1997 ..... **1994**:4
    Obituary ........................................ **1997**:3
De La Hoya, Oscar 1973- ............... **1998**:2
Delany, Dana 1956- ......................... **2008**:4
Delany, Sarah 1889-1999
    Obituary ........................................ **1999**:3
de la Renta, Oscar 1932- ................ **2005**:4
DeLay, Tom 1947- ............................ **2000**:4
Dell, Michael 1965- .......................... **1996**:2
Delors, Jacques 1925- ...................... **1990**:2
del Ponte, Carla 1947- ..................... **2001**:1
Del Toro, Benicio 1967- ................... **2001**:4
DeLuca, Fred 1947- .......................... **2003**:3
De Luca, Guerrino 1952- ................ **2007**:1
De Matteo, Drea 1973- .................... **2005**:2
DeMayo, Neda 1960(?)- .................. **2006**:2
de Mello, Fernando Collor
    See Collor de Mello, Fernando
de Mille, Agnes 1905-1993
    Obituary ........................................ **1994**:2
Deming, W. Edwards 1900-1993 ... **1992**:2
    Obituary ........................................ **1994**:2
Demme, Jonathan 1944- ................. **1992**:4
Dempsey, Patrick 1966- .................. **2006**:1
Dench, Judi 1934- ............................ **1999**:4
Deneuve, Catherine 1943- .............. **2003**:2
Deng Xiaoping 1904-1997 .............. **1995**:1
    Obituary ........................................ **1997**:3
De Niro, Robert 1943- ..................... **1999**:1
Dennehy, Brian 1938- ...................... **2002**:1
Dennis, Sandy 1937-1992
    Obituary ........................................ **1992**:4
Denver, Bob 1935-2005
    Obituary ........................................ **2006**:4
Denver, John 1943-1997
    Obituary ........................................ **1998**:1
De Palma, Brian 1940- .................... **2007**:3
Depardieu, Gerard 1948- ............... **1991**:2
de Passe, Suzanne 1946(?)- ........... **1990**:4
de Pinies, Jamie
    Brief entry .................................... **1986**:3
Depp, Johnny 1963(?)- .................... **1991**:3

Derminer, Robert
  See Tyner, Rob
Dern, Laura 1967- ........................... **1992**:3
Derrida, Jacques 1930-2005
  Obituary ........................................ **2006**:1
Dershowitz, Alan 1938(?)- .............. **1992**:1
Desormeaux, Kent 1970- ................ **1990**:2
Destiny's Child ............................... **2001**:3
de Tirtoff, Romain
  See Erte
Deutch, John 1938- .......................... **1996**:4
de Valois, Dame Ninette 1898-2001
  Obituary ........................................ **2002**:1
Devi, Phoolan 1955(?)- ................... **1986**:1
  Obituary ........................................ **2002**:3
Devine, John M. 1944- ..................... **2003**:2
DeVita, Vincent T., Jr. 1935- ........... **1987**:3
De Vito, Danny 1944- ..................... **1987**:1
DeWalt, Autry. Jr.
  See Walker, Junior
Dewhurst, Colleen 1924-1991
  Obituary ........................................ **1992**:2
Dhlakama, Afonso 1953- ................. **1993**:3
Diamond, I.A.L. 1920-1988
  Obituary ........................................ **1988**:3
Diamond, Isidore A.L.
  See Diamond, I.A.L.
Diamond, Mike
  See Beastie Boys, The
Diamond, Selma 1921(?)-1985
  Obituary ........................................ **1985**:2
Diana, Princess of Wales
  1961-1997 ...................................... **1993**:1
  Obituary ........................................ **1997**:4
Diaz, Cameron 1972- ...................... **1999**:1
DiBello, Paul
  Brief entry .................................... **1986**:4
DiCaprio, Leonardo Wilhelm
  1974- ............................................. **1997**:2
Dickerson, Nancy H. 1927-1997 .... **1998**:2
Dickey, James 1923-1997 ................ **1998**:2
Dickinson, Brian 1937- ................... **1998**:2
Dickinson, Janice 1953- .................. **2005**:2
Diddley, Bo 1928-2008
  Obituary ........................................ **2009**:3
Dido 1971- ....................................... **2004**:4
Diebenkorn, Richard 1922-1993
  Obituary ........................................ **1993**:4
Diemer, Walter E. 1904(?)-1998 ..... **1998**:2
Diesel, Vin 1967- ............................ **2004**:1
Dietrich, Marlene 1901-1992
  Obituary ........................................ **1992**:4
DiFranco, Ani 1970(?)- ................... **1997**:1
Diggs, Taye 1971- ........................... **2000**:1
Diller, Barry 1942- .......................... **1991**:1
Diller, Elizabeth and Ricardo
  Scofidio ........................................ **2004**:3
Dillon, Matt 1964- .......................... **1992**:2
DiMaggio, Joe 1914-1999
  Obituary ........................................ **1999**:3
Di Meola, Al 1954- .......................... **1986**:4
Dimitrova, Ghena 1941- .................. **1987**:1
Dinkins, David N. 1927- ................. **1990**:2
Dion, Celine 1970(?)- ...................... **1995**:3
Dirnt, Mike 1972-
  See Green Day
Disney, Lillian 1899-1997
  Obituary ........................................ **1998**:3
Disney, Roy E. 1930- ....................... **1986**:3
Dith Pran 1942-2008
  Obituary ........................................ **2009**:2

Divine 1946-1988
  Obituary ........................................ **1988**:3
Dixie Chicks ................................... **2001**:2
Djerassi, Carl 1923- ........................ **2000**:4
Djokovic, Novak 1987- ................... **2008**:4
Doctorow, E. L. 1931- ...................... **2007**:1
Doe, Samuel 1952-1990
  Obituary ........................................ **1991**:1
Doherty, Denny 1940-2007
  Obituary ........................................ **2008**:2
Doherty, Shannen 1971(?)- ............. **1994**:2
Doi, Takako
  Brief entry .................................... **1987**:4
Dolan, John Terrance
  See Dolan, Terry
Dolan, Terry 1950-1986 .................. **1985**:2
Dolan, Tom 1975- ........................... **2001**:2
Dolby, Ray Milton
  Brief entry .................................... **1986**:1
Dolce, Domenico and Stefano
  Gabbana ....................................... **2005**:4
Dole, Bob 1923- .............................. **1994**:2
Dole, Elizabeth Hanford 1936- ...... **1990**:1
Dole, Robert
  See Dole, Bob
Dolenz, George Michael
  See Dolenz, Micky
Dolenz, Micky 1945- ....................... **1986**:4
Domar, Alice 1958- ......................... **2007**:1
Domingo, Placido 1941- ................. **1993**:2
Don, Rasa
  See Arrested Development
Donahue, Tim 1950(?)- ................... **2004**:3
Donahue, Troy 1936-2001
  Obituary ........................................ **2002**:4
Dong, Pham Van 1906-2000
  Obituary ........................................ **2000**:4
Donghia, Angelo R. 1935-1985
  Obituary ........................................ **1985**:2
Donnadieu, Marguerite
  See Duras, Marguerite
Donnellan, Nanci ............................ **1995**:2
Dorati, Antal 1906-1988
  Obituary ........................................ **1989**:2
Dorris, Michael 1945-1997
  Obituary ........................................ **1997**:3
Dorsey, Thomas A. 1899-1993
  Obituary ........................................ **1993**:3
Doubleday, Nelson, Jr. 1933- ......... **1987**:1
Douglas, Buster 1960(?)- ................ **1990**:4
Douglas, James
  See Douglas, Buster
Douglas, Marjory Stoneman
  1890-1998 ...................................... **1993**:1
  Obituary ........................................ **1998**:4
Douglas, Michael 1944- .................. **1986**:2
Douglas, Mike 1925-2006
  Obituary ........................................ **2007**:4
Dove, Rita 1952- ............................. **1994**:3
Dowd, Maureen Brigid 1952- ......... **1997**:1
Downey, Bruce 1947- ...................... **2003**:1
Downey, Morton, Jr. 1932- ............. **1988**:4
Downey, Robert, Jr. 1965- ............... **2007**:1
Downey, Sean Morton, Jr.
  See Downey, Morton, Jr.
Doyle, Roddy 1958- ........................ **2008**:1
Dr. Demento 1941- ......................... **1986**:1
Dr. Dre 1965(?)- .............................. **1994**:3
Dravecky, Dave 1956- ..................... **1992**:1
Drayton, William
  See Public Enemy
Drescher, Fran 1957(?)- .................. **1995**:3

Drexler, Clyde 1962- ....................... **1992**:4
Drexler, Millard S. 1944- ................ **1990**:3
Dreyfus, Julia Louis
  See Louis-Dreyfus, Julia
Dreyfuss, Richard 1947- ................. **1996**:3
Driver, Minnie 1971- ...................... **2000**:1
Drucker, Peter F. 1909- ................... **1992**:3
Drysdale, Don 1936-1993
  Obituary ........................................ **1994**:1
Duan, Le
  See Le Duan
Duarte, Henry 1963(?)- ................... **2003**:3
Duarte, Jose Napoleon 1925-1990
  Obituary ........................................ **1990**:3
Duarte Fuentes, Jose Napoleon
  See Duarte, Jose Napoleon
Dubinin, Yuri 1930- ....................... **1987**:4
Dubinsky, Donna
  See Hawkins, Jeff and Donna
  Dubinsky
Dubrof, Jessica 1989-1996
  Obituary ........................................ **1996**:4
Dubuffet, Jean 1901-1985
  Obituary ........................................ **1985**:4
Duchovny, David 1960- .................. **1998**:3
Dudley, Jane 1912-2001
  Obituary ........................................ **2002**:4
Duff, Hilary 1987- .......................... **2004**:4
Duffy, Karen 1962- ......................... **1998**:1
Duhalde, Eduardo 1941- ................ **2003**:3
Duisenberg, Wim 1935-2005
  Obituary ........................................ **2006**:4
Dukakis, Michael 1933- .................. **1988**:3
Dukakis, Olympia 1931- ................. **1996**:4
Duke, David 1951(?)- ...................... **1990**:2
Duke, Doris 1912-1993
  Obituary ........................................ **1994**:2
Duke, James Henry, Jr.
  See Duke, Red
Duke, Red
  Brief entry .................................... **1987**:1
Dumont, Tom 1968-
  See No Doubt
Dunagan, Deanna 1940- ................. **2009**:2
Duncan, Sheena
  Brief entry .................................... **1987**:1
Duncan, Tim 1976- ......................... **2000**:1
Duncan, Todd 1903-1998
  Obituary ........................................ **1998**:3
Dunham, Carroll 1949- ................... **2003**:4
Dunham, Katherine 1909-2006
  Obituary ........................................ **2007**:2
Dunlap, Albert J. ............................. **1997**:2
Dunne, Dominick 1925- .................. **1997**:1
Dunst, Kirsten 1982- ...................... **2001**:4
Dunwoody, Ann 1953- .................... **2009**:2
Dupri, Jermaine 1972- .................... **1999**:1
Duran Duran ................................... **2005**:3
Duras, Marguerite 1914-1996
  Obituary ........................................ **1996**:3
Durocher, Leo 1905-1991
  Obituary ........................................ **1992**:2
Durrell, Gerald 1925-1995
  Obituary ........................................ **1995**:3
Dutt, Hank
  See Kronos Quartet
Duval, David 1971- ......................... **2000**:3
Duvall, Camille
  Brief entry .................................... **1988**:1
Duvall, Robert 1931- ...................... **1999**:3
Dworkin, Andrea 1946-2005
  Obituary ........................................ **2006**:2

Dykstra, Lenny 1963- .................... **1993**:4
Dylan, Bob 1941- ............................ **1998**:1
Dyson, James 1947- ....................... **2005**:4
Dzhanibekov, Vladimir 1942- ........ **1988**:1
Eagleson, Alan 1933- ...................... **1987**:4
Eagleson, Robert Alan
   See Eagleson, Alan
Earle, Sylvia 1935- .......................... **2001**:1
Earnhardt, Dale 1951-2001
   Obituary ...................................... **2001**:4
Earnhardt, Dale, Jr. 1974- .............. **2004**:4
Eastwood, Clint 1930- .................... **1993**:3
Eaton, Robert J. 1940- .................... **1994**:2
Eazy-E 1963(?)-1995
   Obituary ...................................... **1995**:3
Ebadi, Shirin 1947- ........................ **2004**:3
Ebbers, Bernie 1943- ...................... **1998**:1
Eberhart, Richard 1904-2005
   Obituary ...................................... **2006**:3
Ebersole, Christine 1953- ............... **2007**:2
Ebert, Roger 1942- .......................... **1998**:3
Ebsen, Buddy 1908-2003
   Obituary ...................................... **2004**:3
Ecevit, Bulent 1925-2006
   Obituary ...................................... **2008**:1
Eckert, Robert A. 1955(?)- ............. **2002**:3
Eckhart, Aaron 1968- ..................... **2009**:2
Ecko, Marc 1972- ............................ **2006**:3
Eckstine, Billy 1914-1993
   Obituary ...................................... **1993**:4
Edelman, Marian Wright 1939- ..... **1990**:4
Edelson-Rosenberg, Evelyn
   See Rosenberg, Evelyn
Ederle, Gertrude 1905-2003
   Obituary ...................................... **2005**:1
Edmonds, Kenneth Babyface
   See Edmonds, Kenneth Babyface
Edmonds, Kenneth Babyface
   1958(?)- ...................................... **1995**:3
Edwards, Bob 1947- ....................... **1993**:2
Edwards, Harry 1942- .................... **1989**:4
Edwards, Robert Alan
   See Edwards, Bob
Efron, Zac 1987- ............................. **2008**:2
Egan, John 1939- ............................ **1987**:2
Eggers, Dave 1970- ......................... **2001**:3
Egoyan, Atom 1960- ....................... **2000**:2
Ehrlichman, John 1925-1999
   Obituary ...................................... **1999**:3
Eilberg, Amy
   Brief entry .................................. **1985**:3
Eisenman, Peter 1932- .................... **1992**:4
Eisenstaedt, Alfred 1898-1995
   Obituary ...................................... **1996**:1
Eisner, Michael 1942- ..................... **1989**:2
Eisner, Will 1917-2005
   Obituary ...................................... **2006**:1
ElBaradei, Mohamed 1942- ........... **2006**:3
Elbaz, Alber 1961- .......................... **2008**:1
Elders, Joycelyn 1933- ................... **1994**:1
Eldridge, Roy 1911-1989
   Obituary ...................................... **1989**:3
Elfman, Jenna 1971- ....................... **1999**:4
Ellerbee, Linda 1944- ..................... **1993**:3
Elliott, Denholm 1922-1992
   Obituary ...................................... **1993**:2
Elliott, Missy 1971- ........................ **2003**:4
Ellis, David 1971- ........................... **2009**:4
Ellis, Perry 1940-1986
   Obituary ...................................... **1986**:3
Ellison, Larry 1944- ........................ **2004**:2

Ellison, Ralph 1914-1994
   Obituary ...................................... **1994**:4
Ellroy, James 1948- ........................ **2003**:4
Elway, John 1960- ........................... **1990**:3
Emin, Tracey 1963- ......................... **2009**:2
Eminem 1974- .................................. **2001**:2
Engelbreit, Mary 1952(?)- .............. **1994**:3
Engibous, Thomas J. 1953- ............ **2003**:3
Engler, John 1948- .......................... **1996**:3
Engles, Gregg L. 1957- ................... **2007**:3
Englund, Richard 1932(?)-1991
   Obituary ...................................... **1991**:3
Engstrom, Elmer W. 1901-1984
   Obituary ...................................... **1985**:2
Enkhbayar, Nambaryn 1958- ......... **2007**:1
Eno, Brian 1948- ............................. **1986**:2
Ensler, Eve 1954(?)- ....................... **2002**:4
Entwistle, John 1944-2002
   Obituary ...................................... **2003**:3
En Vogue ......................................... **1994**:1
Enya 1962(?)- ................................... **1992**:3
Ephron, Henry 1912-1992
   Obituary ...................................... **1993**:2
Ephron, Nora 1941- ........................ **1992**:3
Epps, Omar 1973- ........................... **2000**:4
Epstein, Jason 1928- ....................... **1991**:1
Epstein, Theo 1973- ........................ **2003**:4
Erdrich, Louise 1954- ..................... **2005**:3
Erickson, Arthur 1924- .................. **1989**:3
Erte 1892-1990
   Obituary ...................................... **1990**:4
Ertegun, Ahmet 1923- .................... **1986**:3
Ervin, Sam 1896-1985
   Obituary ...................................... **1985**:2
Ervin, Samuel J., Jr.
   See Ervin, Sam
Eshe, Montsho
   See Arrested Development
Esiason, Boomer 1961- ................... **1991**:1
Esiason, Norman Julius
   See Esiason, Boomer
Esquivel, Juan 1918- ...................... **1996**:2
Estefan, Gloria ............................... **1991**:4
Estes, Elliott Marantette
   See Estes, Pete
Estes, Pete 1916-1988
   Obituary ...................................... **1988**:3
Estevez, Emilio 1962- ..................... **1985**:4
Estrich, Susan 1953- ...................... **1989**:1
Etheridge, Melissa 1961(?)- ........... **1995**:4
Etzioni, Amitai 1929- ..................... **1994**:3
Evanovich, Janet 1943- .................. **2005**:2
Evans, Dale 1912-2001
   Obituary ...................................... **2001**:3
Evans, Janet 1971- .......................... **1989**:1
Evans, Joni 1942- ............................ **1991**:4
Evans, Nancy 1950- ........................ **2000**:4
Evans, Robert 1930- ....................... **2004**:1
Eve 1978- ......................................... **2004**:3
Everage, Dame Edna
   See Humphries, Barry
Everett, Rupert 1959- ..................... **2003**:1
Evers-Williams, Myrlie 1933- ........ **1995**:4
Everything But The Girl .................. **1996**:4
Ewing, Patrick 1962- ...................... **1985**:3
Eyler, John. H., Jr. 1948(?)- ........... **2001**:3
Fabio 1961(?)- .................................. **1993**:4
Fabris, Enrico 1981- ....................... **2006**:4
Factor, Francis, Jr.
   See Factor, Max
Factor, Max 1904-1996
   Obituary ...................................... **1996**:4

Fagan, Garth 1940- ......................... **2000**:1
Fahd, King of Saudi Arabia 1923(?)-2005
   Obituary ...................................... **2006**:4
Fairbanks, Douglas, Jr. 1909-2000
   Obituary ...................................... **2000**:4
Fairstein, Linda 1948(?)- ................ **1991**:1
Falco
   Brief entry .................................. **1987**:2
Falconer, Ian 1960(?)- .................... **2003**:1
Faldo, Nick 1957- ........................... **1993**:3
Falkenberg, Nanette 1951- ............. **1985**:2
Fallon, Jimmy 1974- ....................... **2003**:1
Faludi, Susan 1959- ........................ **1992**:4
Falwell, Jerry 1933-2007
   Obituary ...................................... **2008**:3
Fang Lizhi 1937- ............................. **1988**:1
Fanning, Dakota 1994- ................... **2005**:2
Fanning, Shawn 1980- .................... **2001**:1
Fano, Ugo 1912-2001
   Obituary ...................................... **2001**:4
Farley, Chris 1964-1997 .................. **1998**:2
Farmer, James 1920-1999
   Obituary ...................................... **2000**:1
Farrakhan, Louis 1933- .................. **1990**:4
Farrell, Colin 1976- ........................ **2004**:1
Farrell, Perry 1960- ........................ **1992**:2
Farrell, Suzanne 1945- ................... **1996**:3
Farrow, Mia 1945- .......................... **1998**:3
Fassa, Lynda 1963(?)- .................... **2008**:4
Fast, Howard 1914-2003
   Obituary ...................................... **2004**:2
Faubus, Orval 1910-1994
   Obituary ...................................... **1995**:2
Fauci, Anthony S. 1940- ................. **2004**:1
Faulkner, Shannon 1975- ............... **1994**:4
Faust, Drew Gilpin 1947- ............... **2008**:1
Favre, Brett Lorenzo 1969- ............ **1997**:2
Favreau, Jon 1966- ......................... **2002**:3
Fawcett, Farrah 1947- .................... **1998**:4
Federer, Roger 1981- ...................... **2004**:2
Federov, Sergei 1969- ..................... **1995**:1
Fehr, Donald 1948- ......................... **1987**:2
Feinstein, Dianne 1933- ................. **1993**:3
Fekkai, Frederic 1959(?)- ............... **2003**:2
Felber, Dean 1967(?)-
   See Hootie and the Blowfish
Feld, Eliot 1942- ............................. **1996**:1
Feld, Kenneth 1948- ....................... **1988**:2
Feldman, Fivel
   See Foster, Phil
Feldman, Sandra 1939- .................. **1987**:3
Feldshuh, Tovah 1952- ................... **2005**:3
Felix, Maria 1914-2002
   Obituary ...................................... **2003**:2
Fell, Norman 1924-1998
   Obituary ...................................... **1999**:2
Fellini, Federico 1920-1993
   Obituary ...................................... **1994**:2
Fender, Leo 1909-1991
   Obituary ...................................... **1992**:1
Fenley, Molissa 1954- ..................... **1988**:3
Fenwick, Millicent H.
   Obituary ...................................... **1993**:2
Ferguson, Craig 1962- .................... **2005**:4
Ferguson, Niall 1964- ..................... **2006**:1
Ferguson, Sarah
   See Ferguson, Sarah
Ferguson, Sarah 1959- .................... **1990**:3
Fernández, Leonel 1953- ................ **2009**:2
Fernández de Kirchner, Cristina
   1953- ........................................... **2009**:1
Fernandez, Joseph 1935- ................ **1991**:3

Ferrari, Enzo 1898-1988 ................. **1988**:4
Ferraro, Geraldine 1935- ................. **1998**:3
Ferre, Gianfranco 1944-2007
   Obituary ........................... **2008**:3
Ferrell, Trevor
   Brief entry ........................ **1985**:2
Ferrell, Will 1968- ...................... **2004**:4
Ferrer, Jose 1912-1992
   Obituary ........................... **1992**:3
Ferrera, America 1984- ................. **2006**:2
Ferretti, Alberta 1950(?)- ................. **2004**:1
Ferri, Alessandra 1963- ................. **1987**:2
Fertel, Ruth 1927- ...................... **2000**:2
Fetchit, Stepin 1892(?)-1985
   Obituary ........................... **1986**:1
Fey, Tina 1970- ......................... **2005**:3
Fforde, Jasper 1961- ................... **2006**:3
Ficker, Roberta Sue
   See Farrell, Suzanne
Fieger, Geoffrey 1950- ................. **2001**:3
Field, Patricia 1942(?)- ................. **2002**:2
Field, Sally 1946- ...................... **1995**:3
Fielder, Cecil 1963- ................... **1993**:2
Fielding, Helen 1959- ................. **2000**:4
Fields, Debbi 1956- ...................... **1987**:3
Fields, Debra Jane
   See Fields, Debbi
Fields, Evelyn J. 1949- ................. **2001**:3
Fiennes, Ralph 1962- ................... **1996**:2
Fiennes, Ranulph 1944- ................. **1990**:3
Fierstein, Harvey 1954- ................. **2004**:2
Filipovic, Zlata 1981(?)- ................. **1994**:4
Filo, David
   See Filo, David and Jerry Yang
Filo, David and Jerry Yang ........... **1998**:3
Finley, Karen 1956- ................... **1992**:4
Finnamore, Suzanne 1959- ........... **2009**:1
Finnbogadoaattir, Vigdiaas
   Brief entry ........................ **1986**:2
Finney, Albert 1936- ................... **2003**:3
Fiorina, Carleton S. 1954- ........... **2000**:1
Fireman, Paul
   Brief entry ........................ **1987**:2
Firestone, Roy 1953- ................... **1988**:2
Fischer, Bobby 1943-2008
   Obituary ........................... **2009**:1
Fischer, Joschka 1948- ................. **2005**:2
Fish, Hamilton 1888-1991
   Obituary ........................... **1991**:3
Fishburne, Laurence 1961(?)- ......... **1995**:3
Fisher, Carrie 1956- ................... **1991**:1
Fisher, Mary 1948- ................... **1994**:3
Fisher, Mel 1922(?)- ................... **1985**:4
Fisher, Melvin A.
   See Fisher, Mel
Fittipaldi, Emerson 1946- ........... **1994**:2
Fitzgerald, A. Ernest 1926- ........... **1986**:2
Fitzgerald, Arthur Ernest
   See Fitzgerald, A. Ernest
Fitzgerald, Ella 1917-1996
   Obituary ........................... **1996**:4
Fitzgerald, Patrick 1960- ............. **2006**:4
Fitzgerald, Roy
   See Hudson, Rock
Flanders, Ed 1934-1995
   Obituary ........................... **1995**:3
Flatley, Michael 1958- ................. **1997**:3
Flavor Flav 1959- ...................... **2007**:3
Fleischer, Ari 1960- ................... **2003**:1
Fleiss, Mike 1964- ...................... **2003**:4
Fleming, Art 1925(?)-1995
   Obituary ........................... **1995**:4

Fleming, Claudia 1959- ................. **2004**:1
Fleming, Renee ...................... **2001**:4
Flockhart, Calista 1964- ............. **1998**:4
Flood, Curt 1938-1997
   Obituary ........................... **1997**:2
Florio, James J. 1937- ................. **1991**:2
Flutie, Doug 1962- ...................... **1999**:2
Flynn, Ray 1939- ...................... **1989**:1
Flynn, Raymond Leo
   See Flynn, Ray
Flynt, Larry 1942- ...................... **1997**:3
Fo, Dario 1926- ......................... **1998**:1
Fodor, Eugene 1906(?)-1991
   Obituary ........................... **1991**:3
Fogelberg, Dan 1951-2007
   Obituary ........................... **2009**:1
Foley, Thomas S. 1929- ................. **1990**:1
Folkman, Judah 1933- ................. **1999**:1
Fomon, Robert M. 1925- ............. **1985**:3
Fonda, Bridget 1964- ................. **1995**:1
Fonteyn, Margot 1919-1991
   Obituary ........................... **1991**:3
Fonyo, Stephen J.
   See Fonyo, Steve
Fonyo, Steve
   Brief entry ........................ **1985**:4
Foo Fighters ........................... **2006**:2
Foote, Shelby 1916- ................... **1991**:2
Forbes, Malcolm S. 1919-1990
   Obituary ........................... **1990**:3
Forbes, Steve 1947- ................... **1996**:2
Ford, Ernest Jennings
   See Ford, Tennessee Ernie
Ford, Faith 1964- ...................... **2005**:3
Ford, Gerald R. 1913-2007
   Obituary ........................... **2008**:2
Ford, Glenn 1916-2006
   Obituary ........................... **2007**:4
Ford, Harrison 1942- ................. **1990**:2
Ford, Henry II 1917-1987
   Obituary ........................... **1988**:1
Ford, Tennessee Ernie 1919-1991
   Obituary ........................... **1992**:2
Ford, Tom 1962- ...................... **1999**:3
Ford, William Clay, Jr. 1957- ......... **1999**:1
Foreman, Dave 1947(?)- ............. **1990**:3
Foreman, George 1949- ............. **2004**:2
Forsythe, William 1949- ............. **1993**:2
Foss, Joe 1915- ......................... **1990**:3
Fosse, Bob 1927-1987
   Obituary ........................... **1988**:1
Fosse, Robert Louis
   See Fosse, Bob
Fossett, Steve 1944- ................... **2007**:2
Fossey, Dian 1932-1985
   Obituary ........................... **1986**:1
Foster, David 1950(?)- ................. **1988**:2
Foster, Jodie 1962- ................... **1989**:2
Foster, Norman 1935- ................. **1999**:4
Foster, Phil 1914-1985
   Obituary ........................... **1985**:3
Foster, Sutton 1975- ................... **2003**:2
Foster, Tabatha 1985-1988
   Obituary ........................... **1988**:3
Foster, Vincent 1945(?)-1993
   Obituary ........................... **1994**:1
Fowlkes, Cassandra Marie
   See Wilson, Cassandra
Fox, Matthew 1940- ................... **1992**:2
Fox, Matthew 1966- ................... **2006**:1
Fox, Michael J. 1961- ................. **1986**:1

Fox, Timothy James
   See Fox, Matthew
Fox, Vicente 1942- ................... **2001**:1
Fox, Vivica 1964- ...................... **1999**:1
Foxworthy, Jeff 1958- ................. **1996**:1
Foxx, Jamie 1967- ...................... **2001**:1
Foxx, Redd 1922-1991
   Obituary ........................... **1992**:2
Frahm, Herbert Ernst Karl
   See Brandt, Willy
Frame, Janet 1924-2004
   Obituary ........................... **2005**:2
France, Johnny
   Brief entry ........................ **1987**:1
Franchitti, Dario 1973- ............. **2008**:1
Francis, Philip L. 1946- ............. **2007**:4
Franciscus, James 1934-1991
   Obituary ........................... **1992**:1
Frank, Anthony M. 1931(?)- ......... **1992**:1
Frank, Barney 1940- ................... **1989**:2
Frank, Robert 1924- ................... **1995**:2
Franken, Al 1952(?)- ................... **1996**:3
Frankenheimer, John 1930-2002
   Obituary ........................... **2003**:4
Frankenthaler, Helen 1928- ......... **1990**:1
Frankfort, Lew 1946- ................. **2008**:2
Frankl, Viktor E. 1905-1997
   Obituary ........................... **1998**:1
Franklin, Aretha 1942- ............. **1998**:3
Franklin, Melvin 1942-1995
   Obituary ........................... **1995**:3
Franks, Tommy 1945- ................. **2004**:1
Franz, Dennis 1944- ................... **1995**:2
Franzen, Jonathan 1959- ............. **2002**:3
Fraser, Brendan 1967- ................. **2000**:1
Fraser, Claire M. 1955- ............. **2005**:2
Frazier, Charles 1950- ................. **2003**:2
Freedman, Rory 1971-
   See Kim Barnouin and Rory Freedman
Freeh, Louis J. 1950- ................. **1994**:2
Freeman, Cathy 1973- ................. **2001**:3
Freeman, Cliff 1941- ................... **1996**:1
Freeman, Morgan 1937- ............. **1990**:4
Freij, Elias 1920- ...................... **1986**:4
Freleng, Friz 1906(?)-1995
   Obituary ........................... **1995**:4
French, Tana 1973- ................... **2009**:3
Freston, Kathy 1965- ................. **2009**:3
Freud, Lucian 1922- ................... **2000**:4
Frieda, John 1951- ................... **2004**:1
Friedan, Betty 1921- ................. **1994**:2
Friedman, Milton 1912-2006
   Obituary ........................... **2008**:1
Friend, Patricia A. 1946- ............. **2003**:3
Frist, Bill 1952- ......................... **2003**:4
Frowick, Roy Halston
   See Halston
Frusciante, John
   See Red Hot Chili Peppers
Frye, Northrop 1912-1991
   Obituary ........................... **1991**:3
Fudge, Ann 1951- ...................... **2000**:3
Fugard, Athol 1932- ................... **1992**:3
Fugard, Harold Athol Lannigan
   See Fugard, Athol
Fuhr, Grant 1962- ...................... **1997**:3
Fujimori, Alberto 1938- ............. **1992**:4
Fulbright, J. William 1905-1995
   Obituary ........................... **1995**:3
Fulghum, Robert 1937- ............. **1996**:1
Fuller, Simon 1960- ................... **2008**:2

Funt, Allen 1914-1999
    Obituary ................... **2000**:1
Furman, Rosemary
    Brief entry ................... **1986**:4
Furse, Clara 1957- ................... **2008**:2
Furtado, Nelly 1978- ................... **2007**:2
Furyk, Jim 1970- ................... **2004**:2
Futrell, Mary Hatwood 1940- ....... **1986**:1
Futter, Ellen V. 1949- ................... **1995**:1
G, Kenny
    See Kenny G
Gabor, Eva 1921(?)-1995
    Obituary ................... **1996**:1
Gacy, John Wayne 1942-1994
    Obituary ................... **1994**:4
Gaines, William M. 1922-1992
    Obituary ................... **1993**:1
Gale, Robert Peter 1945- ................... **1986**:4
Galindo, Rudy 1969- ................... **2001**:2
Gallagher, Liam 1972(?)-
    See Oasis
Gallagher, Noel 1967(?)-
    See Oasis
Gallagher, Peter 1955- ................... **2004**:3
Galliano, John 1960- ................... **2005**:2
Gallo, Robert 1937- ................... **1991**:1
Galvin, John R. 1929- ................... **1990**:1
Galvin, Martin
    Brief entry ................... **1985**:3
Gandhi, Indira 1917-1984
    Obituary ................... **1985**:1
Gandhi, Rajiv 1944-1991
    Obituary ................... **1991**:4
Gandhi, Sonia 1947- ................... **2000**:2
Gandolfini, James 1961- ................... **2001**:3
Gandy, Kim 1954(?)- ................... **2002**:2
Ganzi, Victor 1947- ................... **2003**:3
Gao Xingjian 1940- ................... **2001**:2
Garbage ................... **2002**:3
Garbo, Greta 1905-1990
    Obituary ................... **1990**:3
Garcia, Alan 1949- ................... **2007**:4
Garcia, Amalia 1951- ................... **2005**:3
Garcia, Andy 1956- ................... **1999**:3
Garcia, Cristina 1958- ................... **1997**:4
Garcia, Jerome John
    See Garcia, Jerry
Garcia, Jerry 1942-1995 ................... **1988**:3
    Obituary ................... **1996**:1
Garcia, Joe
    Brief entry ................... **1986**:4
Garcia Marquez, Gabriel 1928- ..... **2005**:2
Gardenia, Vincent 1922-1992
    Obituary ................... **1993**:2
Gardner, Ava Lavinia 1922-1990
    Obituary ................... **1990**:2
Gardner, David and Tom ............. **2001**:4
Gardner, Randy 1957- ................... **1997**:2
Garneau, Marc 1949- ................... **1985**:1
Garner, Jennifer 1972- ................... **2003**:1
Garnett, Kevin 1976- ................... **2000**:3
Garofalo, Janeane 1964- ................... **1996**:4
Garr, Teri 1949- ................... **1988**:4
Garrison, Earling Carothers
    See Garrison, Jim
Garrison, Jim 1922-1992
    Obituary ................... **1993**:2
Garson, Greer 1903-1996
    Obituary ................... **1996**:4
Garzarelli, Elaine M. 1951- ............. **1992**:3
Gassman, Vittorio 1922-2000
    Obituary ................... **2001**:1

Gates, Bill 1955- ................... **1987**:4
Gates, Robert M. 1943- ................... **1992**:2
Gates, William H. III
    See Gates, Bill
Gather, Temelea (Montsho Eshe)
    See Arrested Development
Gathers, Hank 1967(?)-1990
    Obituary ................... **1990**:3
Gatien, Peter
    Brief entry ................... **1986**:1
Gault, Willie 1960- ................... **1991**:2
Gaultier, Jean-Paul 1952- ................... **1998**:1
Gayle, Helene 1955- ................... **2008**:2
Gbagbo, Laurent 1945- ................... **2003**:2
Gebbie, Kristine 1944(?)- ................... **1994**:2
Geffen, David 1943- ................... **1985**:3
Gehry, Frank O. 1929- ................... **1987**:1
Geisel, Theodor
    See Geisel, Theodor
Geisel, Theodor 1904-1991
    Obituary ................... **1992**:2
Geithner, Timothy F. 1961- ............. **2009**:4
Geldof, Bob 1954(?)- ................... **1985**:3
Gellar, Sarah Michelle 1977- ................... **1999**:3
Geller, Margaret Joan 1947- ................... **1998**:2
Gentine, Lou 1947- ................... **2008**:2
George, Elizabeth 1949- ................... **2003**:3
George and Lena Korres 1971- ..... **2009**:1
Gephardt, Richard 1941- ................... **1987**:3
Gerba, Charles 1945- ................... **1999**:4
Gerberding, Julie 1955- ................... **2004**:1
Gere, Richard 1949- ................... **1994**:3
Gergen, David 1942- ................... **1994**:1
Gerstner, Lou 1942- ................... **1993**:4
Gerstner, Louis Vincent, Jr.
    See Gerstner, Lou
Gertz, Alison 1966(?)-1992
    Obituary ................... **1993**:2
Gerulaitis, Vitas 1954-1994
    Obituary ................... **1995**:1
Getty, Estelle 1923-2008
    Obituary ................... **2009**:3
Getz, Stan 1927-1991
    Obituary ................... **1991**:4
Ghali, Boutros Boutros 1922- ........ **1992**:3
Ghosn, Carlos 1954- ................... **2008**:2
Giamatti, A. Bartlett 1938-1989 ..... **1988**:4
    Obituary ................... **1990**:1
Giamatti, Angelo Bartlett
    See Giamatti, A. Bartlett
Giamatti, Paul 1967- ................... **2009**:4
Giannulli, Mossimo 1963- ................... **2002**:3
Gibb, Andy 1958-1988
    Obituary ................... **1988**:3
Gibb, Barry
    See Bee Gees, The
Gibb, Maurice
    See Bee Gees, The
Gibb, Robin
    See Bee Gees, The
Gibson, Althea 1927-2003
    Obituary ................... **2004**:4
Gibson, Kirk 1957- ................... **1985**:2
Gibson, Mel 1956- ................... **1990**:1
Gibson, William Ford, III 1948- ..... **1997**:2
Gielgud, John 1904-2000
    Obituary ................... **2000**:4
Gifford, Kathie Lee 1953- ................... **1992**:2
Gift, Roland 1960(?)- ................... **1990**:2
Giguere, Jean-Sebastien 1977- ........ **2004**:2
Gilbert, Walter 1932- ................... **1988**:3

Gilford, Jack 1907-1990
    Obituary ................... **1990**:4
Gill, Vince 1957- ................... **1995**:2
Gillespie, Dizzy 1917-1993
    Obituary ................... **1993**:2
Gillespie, John Birks
    See Gillespie, Dizzy
Gillespie, Marcia 1944- ................... **1999**:4
Gillett, George 1938- ................... **1988**:1
Gilmour, Doug 1963- ................... **1994**:3
Gilruth, Robert 1913-2000
    Obituary ................... **2001**:1
Gingrich, Newt 1943- ................... **1991**:1
Ginsberg, Allen 1926-1997
    Obituary ................... **1997**:3
Ginsberg, Ian 1962(?)- ................... **2006**:4
Ginsburg, Ruth Bader 1933- ......... **1993**:4
Gioia, Dana 1950- ................... **2008**:4
Gish, Lillian 1893-1993
    Obituary ................... **1993**:4
Giuliani, Rudolph 1944- ................... **1994**:2
Glaser, Elizabeth 1947-1994
    Obituary ................... **1995**:2
Glass, David 1935- ................... **1996**:1
Glass, Ira 1959- ................... **2008**:2
Glass, Philip 1937- ................... **1991**:4
Glasser, Ira 1938- ................... **1989**:1
Glaus, Troy 1976- ................... **2003**:3
Glazman, Lev and Alina
    Roytberg ................... **2007**:4
Gleason, Herbert John
    See Gleason, Jackie
Gleason, Jackie 1916-1987
    Obituary ................... **1987**:4
Glenn, John 1921- ................... **1998**:3
Gless, Sharon 1944- ................... **1989**:3
Glover, Corey
    See Living Colour
Glover, Danny 1947- ................... **1998**:4
Glover, Savion 1973- ................... **1997**:1
Gobel, George 1920(?)-1991
    Obituary ................... **1991**:4
Gober, Robert 1954- ................... **1996**:3
Godard, Jean-Luc 1930- ................... **1998**:1
Godunov, Alexander 1949-1995
    Obituary ................... **1995**:4
Goetz, Bernhard Hugo 1947(?)- .... **1985**:3
Goff, Helen Lyndon
    See Travers, P.L.
Goizueta, Roberto 1931-1997 ........ **1996**:1
    Obituary ................... **1998**:1
Gold, Christina A. 1947- ................... **2008**:1
Gold, Thomas 1920-2004
    Obituary ................... **2005**:3
Goldberg, Gary David 1944- ........ **1989**:4
Goldberg, Leonard 1934- ................... **1988**:4
Goldberg, Whoopi 1955- ................... **1993**:3
Goldblum, Jeff 1952- ................... **1988**:1
Golden, Thelma 1965- ................... **2003**:3
Goldhaber, Fred
    Brief entry ................... **1986**:3
Goldman, William 1931- ................... **2001**:1
Goldman-Rakic, Patricia 1937- ...... **2002**:4
Goldsworthy, Andy 1956- ............. **2007**:2
Goldwater, Barry 1909-1998
    Obituary ................... **1998**:4
Gomez, Lefty 1909-1989
    Obituary ................... **1989**:3
Gong Li 1965- ................... **1998**:4
Goodall, Jane 1934- ................... **1991**:1
Gooden, Dwight 1964- ................... **1985**:2
Gooding, Cuba, Jr. 1968- ............. **1997**:3

Goodman, Benjamin David
See Goodman, Benny
Goodman, Benny 1909-1986
Obituary ........................ **1986**:3
Goodman, Drew and Myra ......... **2007**:4
Goodman, John 1952- ............... **1990**:3
Goody, Joan 1935- .................. **1990**:2
Goody, Sam 1904-1991
Obituary ........................ **1992**:1
Gorbachev, Mikhail 1931- ......... **1985**:2
Gorbachev, Raisa 1932-1999
Obituary ........................ **2000**:2
Gordeeva, Ekaterina 1972- ......... **1996**:4
Gorder, Genevieve 1974- ........... **2005**:4
Gordon, Dexter 1923-1990 ......... **1987**:1
Gordon, Gale 1906-1995
Obituary ........................ **1996**:1
Gordon, James 1941- ............... **2009**:4
Gordon, Jeff 1971- .................. **1996**:1
Gordon, Michael 1951(?)- ......... **2005**:1
Gore, Albert, Jr. 1948(?)- ......... **1993**:2
Gore, Albert, Sr. 1907-1998
Obituary ........................ **1999**:2
Gore, Mary Elizabeth
See Gore, Tipper
Gore, Tipper 1948- ................. **1985**:4
Gorelick, Kenny
See Kenny G
Goren, Charles H. 1901-1991
Obituary ........................ **1991**:4
Gorman, Leon
Brief entry ...................... **1987**:1
Gossard, Stone
See Pearl Jam
Gossett, Louis, Jr. 1936- ......... **1989**:3
Gottlieb, William 1917-2006
Obituary ........................ **2007**:2
Gould, Chester 1900-1985
Obituary ........................ **1985**:2
Gould, Gordon 1920- ............... **1987**:1
Gould, Stephen Jay 1941-2002
Obituary ........................ **2003**:3
Goulet, Robert 1933-2007
Obituary ........................ **2008**:4
Gowda, H. D. Deve 1933- ......... **1997**:1
Grace, J. Peter 1913- ............... **1990**:2
Grace, Topher 1978- ............... **2005**:4
Graden, Brian 1963- ............... **2004**:2
Graf, Steffi 1969- .................. **1987**:4
Grafton, Sue 1940- ................. **2000**:2
Graham, Bill 1931-1991 ............ **1986**:4
Obituary ........................ **1992**:2
Graham, Billy 1918- ............... **1992**:1
Graham, Donald 1945- ............. **1985**:4
Graham, Heather 1970- ............ **2000**:1
Graham, Katharine Meyer 1917- .. **1997**:3
Obituary ........................ **2002**:3
Graham, Lauren 1967- ............. **2003**:4
Graham, Martha 1894-1991
Obituary ........................ **1991**:4
Graham, Nicholas 1960(?)- ........ **1991**:4
Graham, Robert 1938- ............. **1993**:4
Grajonca, Wolfgang
See Graham, Bill
Gramm, Phil 1942- ................. **1995**:2
Grammer, Kelsey 1955(?)- ......... **1995**:1
Granato, Cammi 1971- ............. **1999**:3
Grandin, Temple 1947- ............ **2006**:1
Grange, Harold
See Grange, Red
Grange, Red 1903-1991
Obituary ........................ **1991**:3

Granholm, Jennifer 1959- ........... **2003**:3
Grant, Amy 1961(?)- ................. **1985**:4
Grant, Cary 1904-1986
Obituary ........................ **1987**:1
Grant, Charity
Brief entry ...................... **1985**:2
Grant, Hugh 1960- ................. **1995**:3
Grant, Rodney A. ................... **1992**:1
Grappelli, Stephane 1908-1997
Obituary ........................ **1998**:1
Grass, Gunter 1927- ............... **2000**:2
Graves, Michael 1934- ............. **2000**:1
Graves, Nancy 1940- ............... **1989**:3
Graves, Ron 1967- .................. **2009**:3
Gray, David 1970- .................. **2001**:4
Gray, Frizzell
See Mfume, Kweisi
Gray, Hanna 1930- ................. **1992**:4
Gray, John 1952(?)- ................. **1995**:3
Gray, Macy 1970(?)- ................ **2002**:1
Gray, Simon 1936-2008
Obituary ........................ **2009**:4
Gray, Spalding 1941-2004
Obituary ........................ **2005**:2
Grazer, Brian 1951- ................. **2006**:4
Graziano, Rocky 1922-1990
Obituary ........................ **1990**:4
Graziano, Thomas Rocco
See Graziano, Rocky
Grebenshikov, Boris 1953- ......... **1990**:1
Green, Philip 1952- ................. **2008**:2
Green, Richard R. 1936- ........... **1988**:3
Green, Tom 1972- ................... **1999**:4
Greenberg, Hank 1911-1986
Obituary ........................ **1986**:4
Greenberg, Henry Benjamin
See Greenberg, Hank
Greenberg, Robert 1940(?)- ....... **2003**:2
Green Day ........................... **1995**:4
Greene, Brian 1963- ................. **2003**:4
Greene, Graham 1904-1991
Obituary ........................ **1991**:4
Greene, Graham 1952- ............. **1997**:2
Greene, Lorne 1915-1987
Obituary ........................ **1988**:1
Greenfield, Jerry
See Ben & Jerry
Greenspan, Alan 1926- ............ **1992**:2
Greenwald, Julie 1970- ............ **2008**:1
Gregorian, Vartan 1934- ........... **1990**:3
Gregory, Cynthia 1946- ............ **1990**:2
Gregory, Dick 1932- ............... **1990**:3
Gregory, Rogan 1972- ............. **2008**:2
Gretzky, Wayne 1961- ............. **1989**:2
Grier, Pam 1949- ................... **1998**:3
Griff, Professor
See Public Enemy
Griffey, Ken Jr. 1969- .............. **1994**:1
Griffin, Merv 1925-2008
Obituary ........................ **2008**:4
Griffin, Richard
See Public Enemy
Griffith, Melanie 1957- ............. **1989**:2
Griffiths, Martha 1912-2003
Obituary ........................ **2004**:2
Grinkov, Sergei 1967-1995
Obituary ........................ **1996**:2
Grisham, John 1955- ............... **1994**:4
Groban, Josh 1981- ................. **2009**:1
Grodin, Charles 1935- ............. **1997**:3
Groening, Matt 1955(?)- ........... **1990**:4

Grohl, Dave
See Nirvana
Gromyko, Andrei 1909-1989
Obituary ........................ **1990**:2
Gross, Terry 1951- ................. **1998**:3
Grove, Andrew S. 1936- ........... **1995**:3
Grucci, Felix 1905- ................. **1987**:1
Gruden, Jon 1963- ................. **2003**:4
Grusin, Dave
Brief entry ...................... **1987**:2
Gucci, Maurizio
Brief entry ...................... **1985**:4
Guccione, Bob 1930- ............... **1986**:1
Guccione, Bob, Jr. 1956- ........... **1991**:4
Gudmundsdottir, Bjork
See Bjork
Guebuza, Armando 1943- ......... **2008**:4
Guelleh, Ismail Omar 1947- ....... **2006**:2
Guest, Christopher 1948- ......... **2004**:2
Guggenheim, Charles 1924-2002
Obituary ........................ **2003**:4
Guillem, Sylvie 1965(?)- ........... **1988**:2
Guinness, Alec 1914-2000
Obituary ........................ **2001**:1
Gul, Abdullah 1950- ............... **2009**:4
Gumbel, Bryant 1948- ............. **1990**:2
Gumbel, Greg 1946- ............... **1996**:4
Gund, Agnes 1938- ................. **1993**:2
Gunn, Hartford N., Jr. 1926-1986
Obituary ........................ **1986**:2
Guo Jingjing 1981- ................. **2009**:2
Gupta, Sanjay 1969- ............... **2009**:4
Gursky, Andreas 1955- ............ **2002**:2
Gustafsson, Greta Lovisa
See Garbo, Greta
Gutierrez, Carlos M. 1953- ........ **2001**:4
Gutmann, Amy 1949- ............. **2008**:4
Guyer, David
Brief entry ...................... **1988**:1
Gwynn, Tony 1960- ................. **1995**:1
Gyllenhaal, Jake 1980- ............ **2005**:3
Gyllenhaal, Maggie 1977- ......... **2009**:2
Haas, Robert D. 1942- ............. **1986**:4
Habash, George 1925(?)- .......... **1986**:1
Habibie, Bacharuddin Jusuf
1936- ............................ **1999**:3
Hackett, Buddy 1924-2003
Obituary ........................ **2004**:3
Hackman, Gene 1931- ............. **1989**:3
Hackney, Sheldon 1933- ........... **1995**:1
Haddon, Mark 1962- ............... **2005**:2
Hadid, Zaha 1950- ................. **2005**:3
Hagelstein, Peter
Brief entry ...................... **1986**:3
Hagen, Uta 1919-2004
Obituary ........................ **2005**:2
Haggis, Paul 1953- ................. **2006**:4
Hagler, Marvelous Marvin 1954- .. **1985**:2
Hagler, Marvin Nathaniel
See Hagler, Marvelous Marvin
Hahn, Carl H. 1926- ............... **1986**:4
Hahn, Jessica 1960- ................. **1989**:4
Hair, Jay D. 1945- .................. **1994**:3
Ha Jin 1956- ........................ **2000**:3
Hakuta, Ken
Brief entry ...................... **1986**:1
Haladjian, Rafi 1962(?)- ........... **2008**:3
Halberstam, David 1934-2007
Obituary ........................ **2008**:3
Haldeman, H. R. 1926-1993
Obituary ........................ **1994**:2
Hale, Alan 1957- ................... **1997**:3

Hale, Clara
 See Hale, Clara
Hale, Clara 1905-1992
 Obituary ........................................ **1993**:3
Hale, Victoria 1961(?)- .................... **2008**:4
Haley, Alex 1924-1992
 Obituary ........................................ **1992**:3
Hall, Anthony Michael 1968- ........ **1986**:3
Hall, Arsenio 1955- ......................... **1990**:2
Hall, Gus 1910-2000
 Obituary ........................................ **2001**:2
Hall, Michael Anthony Thomas Charles
 See Hall, Anthony Michael
Hallstrom, Lasse 1946- .................... **2002**:3
Halonen, Tarja 1943- ....................... **2006**:4
Halston 1932-1990
 Obituary ........................................ **1990**:3
Hamels, Cole 1983- .......................... **2009**:4
Hamilton, Hamish 1900-1988
 Obituary ........................................ **1988**:4
Hamilton, Laurell K. 1963- ............ **2008**:2
Hamilton, Lewis 1985- .................... **2008**:4
Hamilton, Margaret 1902-1985
 Obituary ........................................ **1985**:3
Hamilton, Scott 1958- ..................... **1998**:2
Hamm, Jon 1971- ............................. **2009**:2
Hamm, Mia 1972- ............................. **2000**:1
Hamm, Paul 1982- ............................ **2005**:1
Hammer, Armand 1898-1990
 Obituary ........................................ **1991**:3
Hammer, Jan 1948- ........................... **1987**:3
Hammer, M. C. ................................. **1991**:2
Hammond, E. Cuyler 1912-1986
 Obituary ........................................ **1987**:1
Hammond, Edward Cuyler
 See Hammond, E. Cuyler
Hammond, John 1910-1987
 Obituary ........................................ **1988**:2
Hampton, Lionel 1908-2002
 Obituary ........................................ **2003**:4
Hanauer, Chip 1954- ........................ **1986**:2
Hanauer, Lee Edward
 See Hanauer, Chip
Hancock, Herbert Jeffrey
 See Hancock, Herbie
Hancock, Herbie 1940- .................... **1985**:1
Hand, Elizabeth 1957- ..................... **2007**:2
Handford, Martin ............................. **1991**:3
Handler, Chelsea 1975- ................... **2009**:3
Handler, Daniel 1970- ..................... **2003**:3
Handler, Ruth 1916-2002
 Obituary ........................................ **2003**:3
Haney, Chris
 Brief entry ...................................... **1985**:1
Hani, Chris 1942-1993
 Obituary ........................................ **1993**:4
Hani, Martin Thembisile
 See Hani, Chris
Hanks, Tom 1956- ............................ **1989**:2
Hanna, William 1910-2001
 Obituary ........................................ **2002**:1
Hannah, Daryl 1961- ........................ **1987**:4
Hannigan, Alyson 1974- .................. **2007**:3
Hansen, Barret Eugene
 See Dr. Demento
Harbert, Ted 1955- ........................... **2007**:2
Hardaway, Anfernee 1971- ............. **1996**:2
Harden, Marcia Gay 1959- ............. **2002**:4
Hargitay, Mariska 1964- .................. **2006**:2
Haring, Keith 1958-1990
 Obituary ........................................ **1990**:3
Harker, Patrick T. 1958- .................. **2001**:2

Harkes, John 1967- .......................... **1996**:4
Harmon, Mark 1951- ....................... **1987**:1
Harmon, Thomas Dudley
 See Harmon, Tom
Harmon, Tom 1919-1990
 Obituary ........................................ **1990**:3
Harper, Stephen J. 1959- ................. **2007**:3
Harriman, Pamela 1920- .................. **1994**:4
Harriman, W. Averell 1891-1986
 Obituary ........................................ **1986**:4
Harriman, William Averell
 See Harriman, W. Averell
Harrington, David
 See Kronos Quartet
Harris, Barbara ............................... **1996**:3
Harris, Barbara 1930- ...................... **1989**:3
Harris, E. Lynn 1955- ...................... **2004**:2
Harris, Ed 1950- ............................... **2002**:2
Harris, Emmylou 1947- ................... **1991**:3
Harris, Katherine 1957- ................... **2001**:3
Harris, Michael Deane 1945- ......... **1997**:2
Harris, Patricia Roberts 1924-1985
 Obituary ........................................ **1985**:2
Harris, Richard 1930-2002
 Obituary ........................................ **2004**:1
Harris, Thomas 1940(?)- .................. **2001**:1
Harrison, George 1943-2001
 Obituary ........................................ **2003**:1
Harrison, Rex 1908-1990
 Obituary ........................................ **1990**:4
Harry, Deborah 1945- ...................... **1990**:1
Hart, Carey 1975- ............................ **2006**:4
Hart, Johnny 1931-2007
 Obituary ........................................ **2008**:2
Hart, Kitty Carlisle 1910-2007
 Obituary ........................................ **2008**:2
Hart, Mary
 Brief entry ...................................... **1988**:1
Hart, Melissa Joan 1976- ................. **2002**:1
Hart, Mickey 1944(?)- ...................... **1991**:2
Hartman, Phil 1948-1998 ................ **1996**:2
 Obituary ........................................ **1998**:4
Harvard, Beverly 1950- ................... **1995**:2
Harvey, Paul 1918- .......................... **1995**:3
Harvey, Polly Jean 1970(?)- ........... **1995**:4
Harwell, Ernie 1918- ....................... **1997**:3
Hasek, Dominik 1965- ..................... **1998**:3
Haseltine, William A. 1944- ........... **1999**:2
Hassan, Hussein Kamel
 See Kamel, Hussein
Hassenfeld, Stephen 1942- ............. **1987**:4
Hastert, Dennis 1942- ...................... **1999**:3
Hastings, Reed 1961(?)- ................... **2006**:2
Hatch, Orin G. 1934- ....................... **2000**:2
Hatch, Richard 1961- ....................... **2001**:1
Hatcher, Teri 1964- .......................... **2005**:4
Hatem, George 1910(?)-1988
 Obituary ........................................ **1989**:1
Hathaway, Anne 1982- .................... **2007**:2
Hau, Lene Vestergaard 1959- ......... **2006**:4
Havel, Vaclav 1936- ......................... **1990**:3
Hawk, Tony 1968- ............................ **2001**:4
Hawke, Ethan 1971(?)- ................... **1995**:4
Hawking, Stephen W. 1942- .......... **1990**:1
Hawkins, Jeff
 See Hawkins, Jeff and Donna
 Dubinsky
Hawkins, Jeff and Donna
 Dubinsky ...................................... **2000**:2
Hawkins, Sally 1976- ....................... **2009**:4
Hawkins, Screamin' Jay 1929-1999
 Obituary ........................................ **2000**:3

Hawn, Goldie Jeanne 1945- .......... **1997**:2
Hayakawa, Samuel Ichiye 1906-1992
 Obituary ........................................ **1992**:3
Hayek, Salma 1968- ......................... **1999**:1
Hayes, Helen 1900-1993
 Obituary ........................................ **1993**:4
Hayes, Isaac 1942- ........................... **1998**:4
Hayes, Robert M. 1952- .................. **1986**:3
Hayes, Wayne Woodrow
 See Hayes, Woody
Hayes, Woody 1913-1987
 Obituary ........................................ **1987**:2
Haysbert, Dennis 1954- ................... **2007**:1
Hayse, Bruce 1949(?)- ...................... **2004**:3
Hayworth, Rita 1918-1987
 Obituary ........................................ **1987**:3
Headroom, Max 1985- ..................... **1986**:4
Healey, Jack 1938(?)- ....................... **1990**:1
Healy, Bernadine 1944- ................... **1993**:1
Healy, Timothy S. 1923- .................. **1990**:2
Heaney, Seamus 1939- ..................... **1996**:2
Heard, James Charles
 See Heard, J.C.
Heard, J.C. 1917-1988
 Obituary ........................................ **1989**:1
Hearst, Randolph A. 1915-2000
 Obituary ........................................ **2001**:3
Heat-Moon, William Least 1939- .. **2000**:2
Hebard, Caroline 1944- ................... **1998**:2
Heche, Anne 1969- .......................... **1999**:1
Heckerling, Amy 1954- .................... **1987**:2
Heckert, Richard E.
 Brief entry ...................................... **1987**:3
Hefner, Christie 1952- ..................... **1985**:1
Hefner, Christine Ann
 See Hefner, Christie
Heid, Bill
 Brief entry ...................................... **1987**:2
Heifetz, Jascha 1901-1987
 Obituary ........................................ **1988**:2
Heigl, Katharine 1978- .................... **2008**:3
Heineken, Alfred 1923-2002
 Obituary ........................................ **2003**:1
Heinz, Henry John II
 See Heinz, H.J.
Heinz, H.J. 1908-1987
 Obituary ........................................ **1987**:2
Heinz, John 1938-1991
 Obituary ........................................ **1991**:4
Held, Al 1928-2005
 Obituary ........................................ **2006**:4
Helfgott, David 1937(?)- .................. **1997**:2
Helgenberger, Marg 1958- .............. **2002**:2
Heller, Joseph 1923-1999
 Obituary ........................................ **2000**:2
Heller, Walter 1915-1987
 Obituary ........................................ **1987**:4
Helms, Bobby 1936-1997
 Obituary ........................................ **1997**:4
Helms, Jesse 1921- ........................... **1998**:1
Helmsley, Leona 1920- .................... **1988**:1
Heloise 1951- .................................... **2001**:4
Helton, Todd 1973- .......................... **2001**:1
Hemingway, Margaux 1955-1996
 Obituary ........................................ **1997**:1
Hemming, Nikki 1967- .................... **2009**:1
Hempleman-Adams, David 1956- ... **2004**:3
Henderson, Rickey 1958- ................ **2002**:3
Henin-Hardenne, Justine 1982- .... **2004**:4
Hennessy, Jill 1969- ......................... **2003**:2
Hennessy, John L. 1952- .................. **2002**:2

Henning, Doug 1947-1999
　　Obituary .................... **2000**:3
Henry, Carl F.H. 1913-2003
　　Obituary .................... **2005**:1
Hensel, Abigail 1990-
　　See Hensel Twins
Hensel, Brittany, 1990-
　　See Hensel Twins
Hensel Twins ........................ **1996**:4
Henson, Brian 1964(?)- .................. **1992**:1
Henson, Jim 1936-1990 ................. **1989**:1
　　Obituary .................... **1990**:4
Hepburn, Audrey 1929-1993
　　Obituary .................... **1993**:2
Hepburn, Katharine 1909- ............. **1991**:2
Herbert, Don 1917-2007
　　Obituary .................... **2008**:3
Herman, Pee-wee
　　See Reubens, Paul
Hernandez, Felix 1986- ................. **2008**:2
Hernandez, Guillermo Villanueva
　　See Hernandez, Willie
Hernandez, Lazaro and Jack
　　McCollough .................... **2008**:4
Hernandez, Willie 1954- ................. **1985**:1
Hero, Peter 1942- ......................... **2001**:2
Herrera, Carolina 1939- ................. **1997**:1
Herrera, Maria Carolina Josefina
　　Pacanins y Nino Tello
　　See Herrera, Carolina
Herrera, Paloma 1975- .................. **1996**:2
Hershberger, Sally 1961(?)- ........... **2006**:4
Hershey, Barbara 1948- ................. **1989**:1
Hershiser, Orel 1958- .................... **1989**:2
Herz, Rachel 1963- ........................ **2008**:1
Herzog, Chaim 1918-1997
　　Obituary .................... **1997**:3
Herzog, Doug 1960(?)- .................. **2002**:4
Herzog, Vivian
　　See Herzog, Chaim
Hess, Rudolph 1894-1987
　　Obituary .................... **1988**:1
Hess, Walther Rudolph
　　See Hess, Rudolph
Heston, Charlton 1924- .................. **1999**:4
Hewitt, Jennifer Love 1979- .......... **1999**:2
Hewitt, Lleyton 1981- .................... **2002**:2
Hewlett, William 1913-2001
　　Obituary .................... **2001**:4
Hewson, Paul
　　See Bono
Hextall, Ron 1964- ........................ **1988**:2
Hextall, Ronald Jeffrey
　　See Hextall, Ron
Heyer, Steven J. 1952- ................... **2007**:1
Hiaasen, Carl 1953- ...................... **2007**:2
Hicks, India 1967- ........................ **2008**:2
Highsmith, Patricia 1921-1995
　　Obituary .................... **1995**:3
Hilbert, Stephen C. 1946- ............. **1997**:4
Hilfiger, Tommy 1952- ................... **1993**:3
Hill, Alfred
　　See Hill, Benny
Hill, Andrew 1931-2007
　　Obituary .................... **2008**:3
Hill, Anita 1956- .......................... **1994**:1
Hill, Benny 1925-1992
　　Obituary .................... **1992**:3
Hill, Faith 1967- .......................... **2000**:1
Hill, George Roy 1921-2002
　　Obituary .................... **2004**:1
Hill, Grant 1972- .......................... **1995**:3

Hill, J. Edward 1938- ..................... **2006**:2
Hill, Lauryn 1975- ........................ **1999**:3
Hill, Lynn 1961(?)- ....................... **1991**:2
Hillary, Edmund 1919-2008
　　Obituary .................... **2009**:1
Hillegass, Clifton Keith 1918- ........ **1989**:4
Hillery, Patrick 1923-2008
　　Obituary .................... **2009**:2
Hilliard, Harriet
　　See Nelson, Harriet
Hills, Carla 1934- ......................... **1990**:3
Hills, L. Rust 1924-2008
　　Obituary .................... **2009**:4
Hindmarch, Anya 1969- ................ **2008**:2
Hines, Gregory 1946- .................... **1992**:4
Hingis, Martina 1980- ................... **1999**:1
Hinton, Milt 1910-2000
　　Obituary .................... **2001**:3
Hirohito, Emperor of Japan 1901-1989
　　Obituary .................... **1989**:2
Hirschhorn, Joel
　　Brief entry .................... **1986**:1
Hirshberg, Gary 1954(?)- .............. **2007**:2
Hirt, Al 1922-1999
　　Obituary .................... **1999**:4
Hiss, Alger 1904-1996
　　Obituary .................... **1997**:2
Ho, David 1952- ........................... **1997**:2
Ho, Don 1930-2007
　　Obituary .................... **2008**:2
Hoch, Jan Ludwig
　　See Maxwell, Robert
Hockfield, Susan 1951- ................. **2009**:2
Hockney, David 1937- ................... **1988**:3
Hodges, Carl 1937- ....................... **2008**:1
Hoff, Syd 1912-2004
　　Obituary .................... **2005**:3
Hoffa, Jim, Jr. 1941- ..................... **1999**:2
Hoffman, Abbie 1936-1989
　　Obituary .................... **1989**:3
Hoffman, Dustin 1937- .................. **2005**:4
Hoffman, Philip Seymour 1967- ... **2006**:3
Hoffs, Susanna 1962(?)- ................ **1988**:2
Hogan, Ben 1912-1997
　　Obituary .................... **1997**:4
Hogan, Hulk 1953- ....................... **1987**:3
Holbrooke, Richard 1941(?)- ......... **1996**:2
Holden, Betsy 1955- ..................... **2003**:2
Holder, Jr., Eric H. 1951- .............. **2009**:4
Holl, Steven 1947- ........................ **2003**:1
Hollander, Joel 1956(?)- ............... **2006**:4
Holliday, Chad 1948- .................... **2006**:4
Hollinghurst, Alan 1954- .............. **2006**:1
Holmes, John C. 1945-1988
　　Obituary .................... **1988**:3
Holtz, Lou 1937- .......................... **1986**:4
Holtz, Louis Leo
　　See Holtz, Lou
Holyfield, Evander 1962- .............. **1991**:3
Houmlzel, Johann
　　See Falco
Honda, Soichiro 1906-1991
　　Obituary .................... **1986**:1
Honecker, Erich 1912-1994
　　Obituary .................... **1994**:4
Hooker, John Lee 1917- ................. **1998**:1
　　Obituary .................... **2002**:3
hooks, bell 1952- .......................... **2000**:2
Hootie and the Blowfish ............... **1995**:4
Hope, Bob 1903-2003
　　Obituary .................... **2004**:4
Hopkins, Anthony 1937- ............... **1992**:4

Horn, Mike 1966- ......................... **2009**:3
Hornby, Nick 1957- ...................... **2002**:2
Horne, Lena 1917- ........................ **1998**:4
Horner, Jack 1946- ....................... **1985**:2
Horner, John R.
　　See Horner, Jack
Hornsby, Bruce 1954(?)- ............... **1989**:3
Horovitz, Adam
　　See Beastie Boys, The
Horovitz, Adam 1968(?)- ............... **1988**:3
Horowitz, Paul 1942- .................... **1988**:2
Horowitz, Vladimir 1903-1989
　　Obituary .................... **1990**:1
Horrigan, Edward, Jr. 1929- .......... **1989**:1
Horvath, David and Sun-Min
　　Kim .................... **2008**:4
Horwich, Frances 1908-2001
　　Obituary .................... **2002**:3
Hoskins, Bob 1942- ....................... **1989**:1
Hosokawa, Morihiro 1938- ............ **1994**:1
Hosseini, Khaled 1965- ................. **2008**:3
Hou Hsiao-hsien 1947- .................. **2000**:2
Hounsfield, Godfrey 1919- ............ **1989**:2
Houseman, John 1902-1988
　　Obituary .................... **1989**:1
Housenbold, Jeffrey 1969- ............ **2009**:2
Houser, Sam 1972(?)- .................... **2004**:4
Houston, Cissy 1933- .................... **1999**:3
Houston, Whitney 1963- ............... **1986**:3
Howard, Desmond Kevin 1970- ... **1997**:2
Howard, Ron .................... **1997**:2
Howard, Trevor 1916-1988
　　Obituary .................... **1988**:2
Howell, Vernon Wayne
　　See Koresh, David
Howser, Dick 1936-1987
　　Obituary .................... **1987**:4
Howser, Richard Dalton
　　See Howser, Dick
Hoyle, Sir Fred 1915-2001
　　Obituary .................... **2002**:4
Hrabal, Bohumil 1914-1997
　　Obituary .................... **1997**:3
Hua Guofeng 1921-2008
　　Obituary .................... **2009**:4
Hubbard, Freddie 1938- ................ **1988**:4
Hubbard, Frederick Dewayne
　　See Hubbard, Freddie
Hudson, Dawn 1957- .................... **2008**:1
Hudson, Jennifer 1981- ................. **2008**:1
Hudson, Kate 1979- ...................... **2001**:2
Hudson, Rock 1925-1985
　　Obituary .................... **1985**:4
Huerta, Dolores 1930- ................... **1998**:1
Huffington, Arianna 1950- ............ **1996**:2
Huffman, Felicity 1962- ................ **2006**:2
Hughes, Cathy 1947- .................... **1999**:1
Hughes, Karen 1957- .................... **2001**:2
Hughes, Mark 1956- ..................... **1985**:3
Hughes, Robert 1938- ................... **1996**:4
Hughes, Sarah 1985- ..................... **2002**:4
Hughes, Ted 1930-1998
　　Obituary .................... **1999**:2
Hughley, D.L. 1964- ...................... **2001**:1
Huizenga, Wayne 1938(?)- ............ **1992**:1
Hu Jintao 1942- ........................... **2004**:1
Hull, Brett 1964- .......................... **1991**:4
Hull, Jane Dee 1935- .................... **1999**:2
Hullinger, Charlotte
　　Brief entry .................... **1985**:1
Hume, Basil Cardinal 1923-1999
　　Obituary .................... **2000**:1

Hume, John 1938- ............................ **1987**:1
Humphries, Barry
  See Humphries, Barry
Humphries, Barry 1934- ................. **1993**:1
Humphry, Derek 1931(?)- .............. **1992**:2
Hundt, Reed Eric 1948- ................. **1997**:2
Hunt, Helen 1963- ........................... **1994**:4
Hunter, Catfish 1946-1999
  Obituary ...................................... **2000**:1
Hunter, Evan 1926-2005
  Obituary ...................................... **2006**:4
Hunter, Holly 1958- ........................ **1989**:4
Hunter, Howard 1907- ................... **1994**:4
Hunter, Madeline 1916(?)- ............ **1991**:2
Hurley, Elizabeth ............................ **1999**:2
Hurt, William 1950- ......................... **1986**:1
Hussein, Ibn Talal
  See Hussein I, King
Hussein, Saddam 1937- ................. **1991**:1
Husseini, Faisal 1940- .................... **1998**:4
Hussein I, King 1935-1999 ............. **1997**:3
  Obituary ...................................... **1999**:3
Huston, Anjelica 1952(?)- .............. **1989**:3
Huston, John 1906-1987
  Obituary ...................................... **1988**:1
Hutchence, Michael 1960-1997
  Obituary ...................................... **1998**:1
Hutton, Timothy 1960- ................... **1986**:3
Hu Yaobang 1915-1989
  Obituary ...................................... **1989**:4
Hwang, David Henry 1957- .......... **1999**:1
Hyatt, Joel 1950- ............................. **1985**:3
Hyde, Henry 1924- .......................... **1999**:1
Hynde, Chrissie 1951- .................... **1991**:1
Hyra, Margaret
  See Ryan, Meg
Iacocca, Lee 1924- ........................... **1993**:1
Iacocca, Lido Anthony
  See Iacocca, Lee
Iannidinardo, Victor A.
  See Tanny, Vic
Ice Cube 1969- ................................. **1999**:2
Ice-T ................................................. **1992**:3
Ifill, Gwen 1955- ............................. **2002**:4
Iger, Bob 1951- ................................ **2006**:1
Iglesias, Enrique 1975- .................. **2000**:1
Ilitch, Mike 1929- ............................ **1993**:4
Ilves, Toomas Hendrik 1953- ........ **2007**:4
Iman 1955- ....................................... **2001**:3
Immelt, Jeffrey R. 1956- ................. **2001**:2
Imus, Don 1940- .............................. **1997**:1
Imus, John Donald 1940-
  See Imus, Don 1940-
Inatome, Rick 1953- ........................ **1985**:4
Indigo Girls ..................................... **1994**:4
Indurain, Miguel 1964- .................. **1994**:1
Ingersoll, Ralph II 1946- ................ **1988**:2
Inkster, Juli 1960- ........................... **2000**:2
Inman, Bobby Ray 1931- ................ **1985**:1
Iovine, Jimmy 1953- ....................... **2006**:3
Ireland, Jill 1936-1990
  Obituary ...................................... **1990**:4
Ireland, Patricia 1946(?)- ............... **1992**:2
Irons, Jack
  See Red Hot Chili Peppers
Irons, Jeremy 1948- ........................ **1991**:4
Irvin, Michael 1966- ....................... **1996**:3
Irving, John 1942- ........................... **2006**:2
Irwin, Bill ........................................ **1988**:3
Irwin, Hale 1945- ............................ **2005**:2
Irwin, James 1930-1991
  Obituary ...................................... **1992**:1

Irwin, Steve 1962- .......................... **2001**:2
Irwin, William Mills
  See Irwin, Bill
Isaacson, Portia
  Brief entry ................................. **1986**:1
Isaacson, Walter 1952- ................... **2003**:2
Isozaki, Arata 1931- ....................... **1990**:2
Israel, Melvin Allen
  See Allen, Mel
Itami, Juzo 1933-1997 .................... **1998**:2
Ito, Lance 1950(?)- .......................... **1995**:3
Ivanisevic, Goran 1971- ................. **2002**:1
Ive, Jonathan 1967- ........................ **2009**:2
Iverson, Allen 1975- ....................... **2001**:4
Ives, Burl 1909-1995
  Obituary ...................................... **1995**:4
Ivey, Artis, Jr.
  See Coolio
Ivins, Molly 1942(?)- ...................... **1993**:4
Iyengar, B.K.S. 1918- ...................... **2005**:1
Izetbegovic, Alija 1925- ................. **1996**:4
Izzard, Eddie 1963- ........................ **2008**:1
Jablonski, Nina G. 1953- ............... **2009**:3
Jackman, Hugh 1968- ..................... **2004**:4
Jackson, Alan 1958- ....................... **2003**:1
Jackson, Bo 1962- ........................... **1986**:3
Jackson, Cordell 1923- ................... **1992**:4
Jackson, Janet 1966(?)- .................. **1990**:4
Jackson, Jesse 1941- ....................... **1996**:1
Jackson, Jesse, Jr. 1965- ................. **1998**:3
Jackson, Lisa P. 1962- ..................... **2009**:4
Jackson, Michael 1958- .................. **1996**:2
Jackson, Peter 1961- ....................... **2004**:4
Jackson, Phil 1945- ......................... **1996**:3
Jackson, Philip D.
  See Jackson, Phil
Jackson, Samuel L. 1949(?)- .......... **1995**:4
Jackson, Thomas Penfield 1937- .... **2000**:2
Jackson, Vincent Edward
  See Jackson, Bo
Jacobs, Joe 1945(?)- ........................ **1994**:1
Jacobs, Marc 1963- ......................... **2002**:3
Jacobson, Nina 1965- ..................... **2009**:2
Jacques, Brian 1939- ....................... **2002**:2
Jacuzzi, Candido 1903-1986
  Obituary ...................................... **1987**:1
Jagdeo, Bharrat 1964- .................... **2008**:1
Jagger, Jade 1971- ........................... **2005**:1
Jagr, Jaromir 1972- .......................... **1995**:4
Jahn, Helmut 1940- ........................ **1987**:3
James, Etta 1938- ............................ **1995**:2
James, Jesse 1969- ........................... **2004**:4
James, LeBron 1984- ....................... **2007**:3
James, Rick 1948-2004
  Obituary ...................................... **2005**:4
Jamison, Judith 1944- .................... **1990**:3
Janklow, Morton 1930- ................... **1989**:3
Janney, Allison 1959- ..................... **2003**:3
Janzen, Daniel H. 1939- ................. **1988**:4
Jarmusch, Jim 1953- ....................... **1998**:3
Jarrett, Keith 1945- ........................ **1992**:4
Jarvik, Robert K. 1946- ................... **1985**:1
Javacheff, Christo
  See Christo
Jay, Ricky 1949(?)- .......................... **1995**:1
Jay-Z 1970- ...................................... **2006**:1
Jeanrenaud, Jean
  See Kronos Quartet
Jefferts Schori, Katharine 1954- ..... **2007**:2
Jeffords, James 1934- ...................... **2002**:2
Jeffrey, Mildred 1910-2004
  Obituary ...................................... **2005**:2

Jelinek, Elfriede 1946- .................... **2005**:3
Jemison, Mae C. 1956- ................... **1993**:1
Jen, Gish 1955- ................................ **2000**:1
Jenkins, Roy Harris 1920-2003
  Obituary ...................................... **2004**:1
Jenkins, Sally 1960(?)- ................... **1997**:2
Jennings, Peter Charles 1938- ........ **1997**:2
Jennings, Waylon 1937-2002
  Obituary ...................................... **2003**:2
Jessy Raphael, Sally
  See Raphael, Sally Jessy
Jeter, Derek 1974- ........................... **1999**:4
Jewel 1974- ...................................... **1999**:2
Jiang Quing 1914-1991
  Obituary ...................................... **1992**:1
Jiang Zemin 1926- .......................... **1996**:1
Jianying, Ye
  See Ye Jianying
Jillette, Penn
  See Penn & Teller
Jillian, Ann 1951- ........................... **1986**:4
Jindal, Bobby 1971- ........................ **2006**:1
Jobs, Steve 1955- ............................ **2000**:1
Joel, Billy 1949- ............................... **1994**:3
Joffrey, Robert 1930-1988
  Obituary ...................................... **1988**:3
Johansson, Lars-Olof
  See Cardigans, The
Johansson, Scarlett 1984- .............. **2005**:4
John, Daymond 1968- ..................... **2000**:1
John, Elton 1947- ............................ **1995**:4
John Paul II, Pope
  See John Paul II, Pope
John Paul II, Pope 1920- ................. **1995**:3
Johnson, Abigail 1961- ................... **2005**:3
Johnson, Betsey 1942- .................... **1996**:2
Johnson, Beverly 1952- .................. **2005**:2
Johnson, Caryn
  See Goldberg, Whoopi
Johnson, Diane 1934- ..................... **2004**:3
Johnson, Don 1949- ........................ **1986**:1
Johnson, Earvin Magic 1959- ........ **1988**:4
Johnson, Jack 1975- ....................... **2006**:4
Johnson, Jimmie 1975- ................... **2007**:2
Johnson, Jimmy 1943- .................... **1993**:3
Johnson, John H. 1918-2005
  Obituary ...................................... **2005**:4
Johnson, Kevin 1966(?)- ................. **1991**:1
Johnson, Keyshawn 1972- ............. **2000**:1
Johnson, Lady Bird 1912-2007
  Obituary ...................................... **2008**:4
Johnson, Larry 1969- ...................... **1993**:3
Johnson, Magic
  See Johnson, Earvin Magic
Johnson, Marguerite
  See Angelou, Maya
Johnson, Michael ............................ **2000**:1
Johnson, Philip 1906- ..................... **1989**:2
Johnson, Pierre Marc 1946- ........... **1985**:4
Johnson, Randy 1963- .................... **1996**:2
Johnson, Robert L. 1946- ............... **2000**:4
Johnson, Shawn 1992- .................... **2009**:2
Jolie, Angelina 1975- ...................... **2000**:2
Jonas Brothers ................................ **2008**:4
Jones, Arthur A. 1924(?)- ............... **1985**:3
Jones, Bill T. ..................................... **1991**:4
Jones, Cherry 1956- ........................ **1999**:3
Jones, Chuck 1912- ......................... **2001**:2
Jones, Donald (Rasa Don)
  See Arrested Development
Jones, E. Fay 1921-2004
  Obituary ...................................... **2005**:4

Jones, Edward P. 1950-  .................. **2005**:1
Jones, Etta 1928-2001
   Obituary  ...................................... **2002**:4
Jones, Gayl 1949-  ......................... **1999**:4
Jones, Jenny 1946-  ....................... **1998**:2
Jones, Jerral Wayne
   See Jones, Jerry
Jones, Jerry 1942-  ......................... **1994**:4
Jones, Marion 1975-  ..................... **1998**:4
Jones, Norah 1979-  ....................... **2004**:1
Jones, Quincy 1933-  ..................... **1990**:4
Jones, Sarah 1974(?)-  ................... **2005**:2
Jones, Taree
   See Arrested Development
Jones, Tom 1940-  .......................... **1993**:4
Jones, Tommy Lee 1947(?)-  ......... **1994**:2
Jong, Erica 1942-  .......................... **1998**:3
Jonze, Spike 1961(?)-  ................... **2000**:3
Jordan, Barbara 1936-1996
   Obituary  ...................................... **1996**:3
Jordan, Charles M. 1927-  ............. **1989**:4
Jordan, Irving King
   See Jordan, King
Jordan, James 1936(?)-1993
   Obituary  ...................................... **1994**:1
Jordan, King 1943(?)-  ................... **1990**:1
Jordan, Michael 1963-  .................. **1987**:2
Jordan, Neil 1950(?)-  .................... **1993**:3
Jordan, Vernon, Jr. 1935-  ............. **2002**:3
Jorgensen, Christine 1926-1989
   Obituary  ...................................... **1989**:4
Joseph, Wendy Evans 1955(?)-  ...... **2006**:2
Jovovich, Milla 1975-  ................... **2002**:1
Joyce, William 1957-  .................... **2006**:1
Joyner, Florence Griffith
   1959-1998  .................................. **1989**:2
   Obituary  ...................................... **1999**:1
Joyner-Kersee, Jackie 1962-  ......... **1993**:1
Juan Carlos I 1938-  ....................... **1993**:1
Juanes 1972-  .................................. **2004**:4
Judd, Ashley 1968-  ....................... **1998**:1
Judd, Wynonna
   See Wynonna
Judge, Mike
   See Judge, Mike
Judge, Mike 1963(?)-  .................... **1994**:2
Judkins, Reba
   Brief entry  ................................. **1987**:3
Julavits, Heidi 1968-  .................... **2007**:4
Julia, Raul 1940-1994
   Obituary  ...................................... **1995**:1
Juliana 1909-2004
   Obituary  ...................................... **2005**:3
July, Miranda 1974-  ...................... **2008**:2
Jumblatt, Walid 1949(?)-  .............. **1987**:4
Junck, Mary E. 1948(?)-  ............... **2003**:4
Juneau, Pierre 1922-  ..................... **1988**:3
Jung, Andrea  ................................. **2000**:2
Jurgensen, Karen 1949(?)-  ........... **2004**:3
Justin, John Jr. 1917-  .................... **1992**:2
Justiz, Manuel J. 1948-  ................. **1986**:4
Kabila, Joseph 1971-  .................... **2003**:2
Kabila, Laurent 1939-  ................... **1998**:1
   Obituary  ...................................... **2001**:3
Kaczynski, Lech 1949-  .................. **2007**:2
Kael, Pauline 1919-2001  ............... **2000**:4
   Obituary  ...................................... **2002**:4
Kagame, Paul 1957-  ...................... **2001**:4
Kahane, Meir 1932-1990
   Obituary  ...................................... **1991**:2
Kahlo, Frida 1907-1954  ................. **1991**:3

Kahn, Madeline 1942-1999
   Obituary  ...................................... **2000**:2
Kallen, Jackie 1946(?)-  ................. **1994**:1
Kamali, Norma 1945-  .................... **1989**:1
Kamel, Hussein 1954-  ................... **1996**:1
Kamen, Dean 1951(?)-  ................... **2003**:1
Kanakaredes, Melina 1967-  .......... **2007**:1
Kanal, Tony 1970-
   See No Doubt
Kandel, Eric 1929-  ........................ **2005**:2
Kanokogi, Rena
   See Kanokogi, Rusty
Kanokogi, Rusty
   Brief entry  ................................. **1987**:1
Kapor, Mitch 1950-  ....................... **1990**:3
Karadzic, Radovan 1945-  ............. **1995**:3
Karamanlis, Costas 1956-  ............. **2009**:1
Karan, Donna 1948-  ...................... **1988**:1
Karimov, Islam 1938-  ................... **2006**:3
Karmazin, Mel 1943-  .................... **2006**:1
Karsh, Yousuf 1908-2002
   Obituary  ...................................... **2003**:4
Karzai, Hamid 1955(?)-  ................ **2002**:3
Kasem, Casey 1933(?)-  ................. **1987**:1
Kasem, Kemal Amin
   See Kasem, Casey
Kashuk, Sonia 1959(?)-  ................ **2002**:4
Kaskey, Ray
   Brief entry  ................................. **1987**:2
Kaskey, Raymond John
   See Kaskey, Ray
Kasparov, Garry 1963-  .................. **1997**:4
Kassebaum, Nancy 1932-  .............. **1991**:1
Kasyanov, Mikhail 1957-  .............. **2001**:1
Katayama, Yutaka 1909-  ............... **1987**:1
Kathwari, M. Farooq 1944-  .......... **2005**:4
Katz, Alex 1927-  ........................... **1990**:3
Katz, Lillian 1927-  ........................ **1987**:4
Katzenberg, Jeffrey 1950-  ............ **1995**:3
Kaufman, Charlie 1958-  ................ **2005**:1
Kaufman, Elaine  ............................ **1989**:4
Kavner, Julie 1951-  ....................... **1992**:3
Kaye, Danny 1913-1987
   Obituary  ...................................... **1987**:2
Kaye, Nora 1920-1987
   Obituary  ...................................... **1987**:4
Kaye, Sammy 1910-1987
   Obituary  ...................................... **1987**:4
Kazan, Elia 1909-2003
   Obituary  ...................................... **2004**:4
Keating, Charles H., Jr. 1923-  ....... **1990**:4
Keaton, Diane 1946-  ..................... **1997**:1
Keaton, Michael 1951-  .................. **1989**:4
Keeler, Ruby 1910-1993
   Obituary  ...................................... **1993**:4
Keeling, Charles 1928-2005
   Obituary  ...................................... **2006**:3
Keeshan, Bob 1927-2004
   Obituary  ...................................... **2005**:2
Keitel, Harvey 1939-  ..................... **1994**:3
Keith, Brian 1921-1997
   Obituary  ...................................... **1997**:4
Keith, Louis 1935-  ........................ **1988**:2
Kekkonen, Urho 1900-1986
   Obituary  ...................................... **1986**:4
Kelleher, Herb 1931-  ..................... **1995**:1
Kellerman, Jonathan 1949-  .......... **2009**:1
Kelley, DeForest 1929-1999
   Obituary  ...................................... **2000**:1
Kelley, Virginia 1923-1994
   Obituary  ...................................... **1994**:3
Kelly, Ellsworth 1923-  ................. **1992**:1

Kelly, Gene 1912-1996
   Obituary  ...................................... **1996**:3
Kelly, Jim 1960-  ............................ **1991**:4
Kelly, Maureen 1972(?)-  ............... **2007**:3
Kelly, Patrick 1954(?)-1990
   Obituary  ...................................... **1990**:2
Kelly, R. 1968-  .............................. **1997**:3
Kelly, Robert
   See Kelly, R.
Kelly, William R. 1905-1998  ......... **1998**:2
Kemp, Jack 1935-  .......................... **1990**:4
Kemp, Jan 1949-  ........................... **1987**:2
Kemp, Shawn 1969-  ...................... **1995**:1
Kendricks, Eddie 1939-1992
   Obituary  ...................................... **1993**:2
Kennan, George 1904-2005
   Obituary  ...................................... **2006**:2
Kennedy, John F., Jr. 1960-1999  ..... **1990**:1
   Obituary  ...................................... **1999**:4
Kennedy, Rose 1890-1995
   Obituary  ...................................... **1995**:3
Kennedy, Weldon 1938-  ................ **1997**:3
Kenny G 1957(?)-  .......................... **1994**:4
Keno, Leigh and Leslie 1957(?)-  .... **2001**:2
Kent, Arthur 1954-  ........................ **1991**:4
Kent, Corita 1918-1986
   Obituary  ...................................... **1987**:1
Keough, Donald Raymond 1926-  . **1986**:1
Keplinger, Dan 1973-  .................... **2001**:1
Kerger, Paula A. 1957-  .................. **2007**:2
Kerkorian, Kirk 1917-  ................... **1996**:2
Kerr, Clark 1911-2003
   Obituary  ...................................... **2005**:1
Kerr, Cristie 1977-  ........................ **2008**:2
Kerr, Deborah 1921-2007
   Obituary  ...................................... **2008**:4
Kerr, Jean 1922-2003
   Obituary  ...................................... **2004**:1
Kerr, Walter 1913-1996
   Obituary  ...................................... **1997**:1
Kerrey, Bob 1943-  ......................... **1986**:1
Kerrey, Joseph Robert
   See Kerrey, Bob
Kerrigan, Nancy 1969-  .................. **1994**:3
Kerry, John 1943-  .......................... **2005**:2
Kesey, Ken 1935-2001
   Obituary  ...................................... **2003**:1
Kessler, David 1951-  ..................... **1992**:1
Ketcham, Hank 1920-2001
   Obituary  ...................................... **2002**:2
Kevorkian, Jack 1928(?)-  .............. **1991**:3
Keyes, Alan 1950-  ......................... **1996**:2
Keyes, Marian 1963-  ..................... **2006**:2
Keys, Alicia 1981-  ......................... **2006**:1
Khan, Taidje
   See Brynner, Yul
Khatami, Mohammed 1943-  ......... **1997**:4
Khomeini, Ayatollah Ruhollah
   1900(?)-1989
   Obituary  ...................................... **1989**:4
Kibaki, Mwai 1931-  ...................... **2003**:4
Kidd, Jason 1973-  ......................... **2003**:2
Kidd, Jemma 1974-  ....................... **2009**:1
Kidd, Michael 1915-2007
   Obituary  ...................................... **2009**:1
Kidman, Nicole 1967-  ................... **1992**:4
Kid Rock 1972-  ............................. **2001**:1
Kiedis, Anthony
   See Red Hot Chili Peppers
Kiefer, Anselm 1945-  .................... **1990**:2
Kielburger, Craig 1983-  ................ **1998**:1

Kieslowski, Krzysztof 1941-1996
 Obituary ........................................ **1996**:3
Kilborn, Craig 1964- ........................ **2003**:2
Kilby, Jack 1923- ............................. **2002**:2
Kiley, Dan 1912-2004
 Obituary ........................................ **2005**:2
Kilgore, Marcia 1968- ...................... **2006**:3
Kilmer, Val ........................................ **1991**:4
Kilpatrick, Kwame 1970- ................. **2009**:2
Kilts, James M. 1948- ....................... **2001**:3
Kim, Eugenia 1974(?)- ..................... **2006**:1
Kim Barnouin and Rory Freedman 1971-
 ...................................................... **2009**:4
Kim Dae Jung 1925- ........................ **1998**:3
Kim Il Sung 1912-1994
 Obituary ........................................ **1994**:4
Kim Jong Il 1942- ............................ **1995**:2
Kimmel, Jimmy 1967- ..................... **2009**:2
Kimsey, James V. 1940(?)- ............... **2001**:1
King, Alan 1927-2004
 Obituary ........................................ **2005**:3
King, Bernice 1963- ......................... **2000**:2
King, Coretta Scott 1927- ............... **1999**:3
King, Don 1931- .............................. **1989**:1
King, Larry 1933- ............................ **1993**:1
King, Mary-Claire 1946- ................. **1998**:3
King, Stephen 1947- ........................ **1998**:1
King Hassan II 1929-1999
 Obituary ........................................ **2000**:1
Kingsborough, Donald
 Brief entry .................................... **1986**:2
Kingsley, Patricia 1932- ................. **1990**:2
Kingsolver, Barbara 1955- .............. **2005**:1
Kinison, Sam 1954(?)-1992
 Obituary ........................................ **1993**:1
Kinney, Jeff 1971- ............................ **2009**:3
Kinsella, Sophie 1969- ..................... **2005**:2
Kinski, Klaus 1926-1991 .................. **1987**:2
 Obituary ........................................ **1992**:2
Kiraly, Karch
 Brief entry .................................... **1987**:1
Kirk, David 1956(?)- ........................ **2004**:1
Kirkpatrick, Jeane 1926-2006
 Obituary ........................................ **2008**:1
Kissinger, Henry 1923- .................... **1999**:4
Kissling, Frances 1943- ................... **1989**:2
Kistler, Darci 1964- ......................... **1993**:1
Kitaj, R. B. 1932-2007
 Obituary ........................................ **2008**:4
Kite, Tom 1949- ............................... **1990**:3
Klarsfeld, Beate 1939- ..................... **1989**:1
Klass, Perri 1958- ............................ **1993**:2
Klein, Calvin 1942- .......................... **1996**:2
Kleinpaste, Ruud 1952- ................... **2006**:2
Klemperer, Werner 1920-2000
 Obituary ........................................ **2001**:3
Klensch, Elsa .................................... **2001**:4
Klima, Petr 1964- ............................. **1987**:1
Kline, Kevin 1947- ........................... **2000**:1
Kloss, Henry E.
 Brief entry .................................... **1985**:2
Kluge, John 1914- ............................ **1991**:1
Klum, Heidi 1973- ........................... **2006**:3
Knievel, Evel 1938-2007
 Obituary ........................................ **2009**:1
Knievel, Robbie 1963- ..................... **1990**:1
Knight, Bobby 1940- ........................ **1985**:3
Knight, Jonathan
 See New Kids on the Block
Knight, Jordan
 See New Kids on the Block
Knight, Philip H. 1938- ................... **1994**:1

Knight, Robert Montgomery
 See Knight, Bobby
Knight, Ted 1923-1986
 Obituary ........................................ **1986**:4
Knight, Wayne 1956- ....................... **1997**:1
Knightley, Keira 1985- ..................... **2005**:2
Knopfler, Mark 1949- ...................... **1986**:2
Knotts, Don 1924-2006
 Obituary ........................................ **2007**:1
Knowles, John 1926-2001
 Obituary ........................................ **2003**:1
Koch, Bill 1940- ............................... **1992**:3
Koch, Jim 1949- ............................... **2004**:3
Kohl, Helmut 1930- ......................... **1994**:1
Kohnstamm, Abby 1954- ................. **2001**:1
Koizumi, Junichiro 1942- ................ **2002**:1
Kominsky, David Daniel
 See Kaye, Danny
Konigsberg, Allen
 See Allen, Woody
Konstantinov, Vladimir 1967- ........ **1997**:4
Koogle, Tim 1951- ........................... **2000**:4
Koolhaas, Rem 1944- ...................... **2001**:1
Kooning, Willem de
 See de Kooning, Willem
Koons, Jeff 1955(?)- .......................... **1991**:4
Koontz, Dean 1945- ......................... **1999**:3
Koop, C. Everett 1916- .................... **1989**:3
Kopits, Steven E.
 Brief entry .................................... **1987**:1
Koplovitz, Kay 1945- ....................... **1986**:3
Kopp, Wendy .................................... **1993**:3
Koppel, Ted 1940- ........................... **1989**:1
Korchinsky, Mike 1961- .................. **2004**:2
Kordich, Jay 1923- ........................... **1993**:2
Koresh, David 1960(?)-1993
 Obituary ........................................ **1993**:4
Korman, Harvey 1927-2008
 Obituary ........................................ **2009**:2
Kornberg, Arthur 1918(?)- .............. **1992**:1
Kors, Michael 1959- ........................ **2000**:4
Kosinski, Jerzy 1933-1991
 Obituary ........................................ **1991**:4
Kostabi, Mark 1960- ........................ **1989**:4
Kostova, Elizabeth 1964- ................ **2006**:2
Kostunica, Vojislav 1944- ............... **2001**:1
Kouchner, Bernard 1939- ................ **2005**:3
Kournikova, Anna 1981- ................. **2000**:3
Kovacevich, Dick 1943- ................... **2004**:3
Kozinski, Alex 1950- ........................ **2002**:2
Kozol, Jonathan 1936- ..................... **1992**:1
Kramer, Larry 1935- ........................ **1991**:2
Kramer, Stanley 1913-2001
 Obituary ........................................ **2002**:1
Krantz, Judith 1928- ....................... **2003**:1
Krause, Peter 1965- ......................... **2009**:2
Kravitz, Lenny 1964(?)- ................... **1991**:1
Krim, Mathilde 1926- ...................... **1989**:2
Kristiansen, Kjeld Kirk 1948(?)- .... **1988**:3
Kroc, Ray 1902-1984
 Obituary ........................................ **1985**:1
Kroc, Raymond Albert
 See Kroc, Ray
Krogner, Heinz 1941(?)- .................. **2004**:2
Krol, John 1910-1996
 Obituary ........................................ **1996**:3
Kroll, Alexander S. 1938- ............... **1989**:3
Krone, Julie 1963(?)- ....................... **1989**:2
Kronos Quartet .............................. **1993**:1
Kruk, John 1961- ............................. **1994**:4
Krupp, Fred 1954- ........................... **2008**:3
Krzyzewski, Mike 1947- ................. **1993**:2

Kubler-Ross, Elisabeth 1926-2004
 Obituary ........................................ **2005**:4
Kubrick, Stanley 1928-1999
 Obituary ........................................ **1999**:3
Kudrow, Lisa 1963(?)- ..................... **1996**:1
Kufuor, John Agyekum 1938- ........ **2005**:4
Kukoc, Toni 1968- ........................... **1995**:4
Kullman, Ellen 1956- ....................... **2009**:4
Kulp, Nancy 1921-1991
 Obituary ........................................ **1991**:3
Kuma, Kengo 1954- ......................... **2009**:1
Kunitz, Stanley J. 1905- .................. **2001**:2
Kunstler, William 1919-1995
 Obituary ........................................ **1996**:1
Kunstler, William 1920(?)- .............. **1992**:3
Kuralt, Charles 1934-1997
 Obituary ........................................ **1998**:3
Kurokawa, Kisho 1934-2007
 Obituary ........................................ **2008**:4
Kurosawa, Akira 1910-1998 ........... **1991**:1
 Obituary ........................................ **1999**:1
Kurzban, Ira 1949- .......................... **1987**:2
Kurzweil, Raymond 1948- .............. **1986**:3
Kushner, Tony 1956- ....................... **1995**:2
Kutaragi, Ken 1950- ........................ **2005**:3
Kutcher, Ashton 1978- .................... **2003**:4
Kwoh, Yik San 1946(?)- ................... **1988**:2
Kyprianou, Spyros 1932-2002
 Obituary ........................................ **2003**:2
Kyser, James King Kern
 See Kyser, Kay
Kyser, Kay 1906(?)-1985
 Obituary ........................................ **1985**:3
LaBeouf, Shia 1986- ......................... **2008**:1
Lachey, Nick and Jessica
 Simpson ....................................... **2004**:4
Lacroix, Christian 1951- .................. **2005**:2
LaDuke, Winona 1959- .................... **1995**:2
Laettner, Christian 1969- ............... **1993**:1
Lafley, A. G. 1947- ........................... **2003**:4
LaFontaine, Pat 1965- ..................... **1985**:1
Lagasse, Emeril 1959- ..................... **1998**:3
Lagerburg, Bengt
 See Cardigans, The
Lagerfeld, Karl 1938- ...................... **1999**:4
Lagos, Ricardo 1938- ...................... **2005**:3
Lahiri, Jhumpa 1967- ...................... **2001**:3
Lahti, Christine 1950- ..................... **1988**:2
Laimbeer, Bill 1957- ........................ **2004**:3
Laing, R.D. 1927-1989
 Obituary ........................................ **1990**:1
Laing, Ronald David
 See Laing, R.D.
Lake, Ricki 1968(?)- ......................... **1994**:4
Lalami, Laila ................................... **2007**:1
Lalas, Alexi 1970- ............................ **1995**:1
Lalas, Panayotis Alexander
 See Lalas, Alexi
Lalonde, Marc 1929- ....................... **1985**:1
Lam, Derek 1966- ............................ **2009**:2
Lamarr, Hedy 1913-2000
 Obituary ........................................ **2000**:3
Lamb, Wally 1950- ........................... **1999**:1
Lamborghini, Ferrucio 1916-1993
 Obituary ........................................ **1993**:3
Lamour, Dorothy 1914-1996
 Obituary ........................................ **1997**:1
L'Amour, Louis 1908-1988
 Obituary ........................................ **1988**:4
Lancaster, Burt 1913-1994
 Obituary ........................................ **1995**:1

Land, Edwin H. 1909-1991
   Obituary ............................ **1991**:3
Lander, Toni 1931-1985
   Obituary ............................ **1985**:4
Landers, Ann 1918-2002
   Obituary ............................ **2003**:3
Landon, Alf 1887-1987
   Obituary ............................ **1988**:1
Landon, Michael 1936-1991
   Obituary ............................ **1992**:1
Landrieu, Mary L. 1955- ................. **2002**:2
Landry, Tom 1924-2000
   Obituary ............................ **2000**:3
Landsbergis, Vytautas 1932- ......... **1991**:3
Lane, Burton 1912-1997
   Obituary ............................ **1997**:2
Lane, Diane 1965- .......................... **2006**:2
Lane, Joseph
   See Lane, Nathan
Lane, Nathan 1956- ....................... **1996**:4
Lane, Ronnie 1946-1997
   Obituary ............................ **1997**:4
Lang, Eugene M. 1919- .................. **1990**:3
Lang, Helmut 1956- ...................... **1999**:2
Lang, Katherine Dawn
   See Lang, K.D.
Lang, K.D. 1961- ........................... **1988**:4
Lange, Jessica 1949- ...................... **1995**:4
Lange, Liz 1967(?)- ........................ **2003**:4
Langella, Frank 1940- .................... **2008**:3
Langer, Robert 1948- ..................... **2003**:4
Langevin, James R. 1964- .............. **2001**:2
Langston, J. William
   Brief entry .......................... **1986**:2
Lanier, Jaron 1961(?)- .................... **1993**:4
Lanois, Daniel 1951- ...................... **1991**:1
Lansbury, Angela 1925- ................. **1993**:1
Lansdale, Edward G. 1908-1987
   Obituary ............................ **1987**:2
Lansing, Sherry 1944- .................... **1995**:4
Lantos, Tom 1928-2008
   Obituary ............................ **2009**:2
Lanza, Robert 1956- ...................... **2004**:3
Lanzoni, Fabio
   See Fabio
LaPaglia, Anthony 1959- ............... **2004**:4
Lapidus, Morris 1902-2001
   Obituary ............................ **2001**:4
Larbalestier, Justine 1968(?)- ......... **2008**:4
Lardner Jr., Ring 1915-2000
   Obituary ............................ **2001**:2
Larian, Isaac 1954- ........................ **2008**:1
Larroquette, John 1947- ................. **1986**:2
Larson, Jonathan 1961(?)-1996
   Obituary ............................ **1997**:2
LaSalle, Eriq 1962- ........................ **1996**:4
Lasdun, Denys 1914-2001
   Obituary ............................ **2001**:4
Lasseter, John 1957- ...................... **2007**:2
Latifah, Queen
   See Queen Latifah
Lauder, Estee 1908(?)- ................... **1992**:2
Lauper, Cyndi 1953- ...................... **1985**:1
Lauren, Ralph 1939- ...................... **1990**:1
Laurie, Hugh 1959- ....................... **2007**:2
Lavigne, Avril 1984- ...................... **2005**:2
Law, Jude 1971- ............................ **2000**:3
Lawless, Lucy 1968- ...................... **1997**:4
Lawrence, Martin 1966(?)- ............. **1993**:4
Lawrence, Ruth
   Brief entry .......................... **1986**:3
Lawson, Nigella 1960- ................... **2003**:2

Laybourne, Geraldine 1947- ......... **1997**:1
Lazarus, Charles 1923- .................. **1992**:4
Lazarus, Shelly 1947- .................... **1998**:3
Leach, Archibald Alexander
   See Grant, Cary
Leach, Penelope 1937- ................... **1992**:4
Leach, Robin 1942(?)-
   Brief entry .......................... **1985**:4
Leakey, Mary Douglas 1913-1996
   Obituary ............................ **1997**:2
Leakey, Richard 1944- ................... **1994**:2
Lear, Frances 1923- ....................... **1988**:3
Leary, Denis 1958- ........................ **1993**:3
Leary, Timothy 1920-1996
   Obituary ............................ **1996**:4
Lebed, Alexander 1950- ................. **1997**:1
LeBlanc, Matt 1967- ...................... **2005**:4
le Carre, John 1931- ...................... **2000**:1
Lederman, Leon Max 1922- ........... **1989**:4
Ledger, Heath 1979- ...................... **2006**:3
Le Duan 1908(?)-1986
   Obituary ............................ **1986**:4
Le Duc Tho
   See Le Duc Tho
Le Duc Tho 1911-1990
   Obituary ............................ **1991**:1
Lee, Ang 1954- .............................. **1996**:3
Lee, Brandon 1965(?)-1993
   Obituary ............................ **1993**:4
Lee, Chang-Rae 1965- ................... **2005**:1
Lee, Chang-Yuh
   See Lee, Henry C.
Lee, Henry C. 1938- ...................... **1997**:1
Lee, Jason 1970- ............................ **2006**:4
Lee, Martin 1938- .......................... **1998**:2
Lee, Pamela 1967(?)- ..................... **1996**:4
Lee, Peggy 1920-2002
   Obituary ............................ **2003**:1
Lee, Sandra 1966- ......................... **2008**:3
Lee, Shelton Jackson
   See Lee, Spike
Lee, Spike 1957- ............................ **1988**:4
Lee Jong-Wook 1945- .................... **2005**:1
Lee Myung-bak 1941- .................... **2009**:2
Lee Teng-hui 1923- ....................... **2000**:1
Lefebvre, Marcel 1905- .................. **1988**:4
Legend, John 1978- ....................... **2007**:1
Leguizamo, John 1965- .................. **1999**:1
Lehane, Dennis 1965- .................... **2001**:4
Leibovitz, Annie 1949- .................. **1988**:4
Leigh, Dorian 1917-2008
   Obituary ............................ **2009**:3
Leigh, Janet 1927-2004
   Obituary ............................ **2005**:4
Leigh, Jennifer Jason 1962- ........... **1995**:2
Lelyveld, Joseph S. 1937- .............. **1994**:4
Lemieux, Claude 1965- .................. **1996**:1
Lemieux, Mario 1965- .................... **1986**:4
Lemmon, Jack 1925- ...................... **1998**:4
   Obituary ............................ **2002**:3
Lemon, Ted
   Brief entry .......................... **1986**:4
LeMond, Greg 1961- ...................... **1986**:4
LeMond, Gregory James
   See LeMond, Greg
L'Engle, Madeleine 1918-2007
   Obituary ............................ **2008**:4
Lennox, Annie 1954- ...................... **1985**:4
Leno, James Douglas Muir
   See Leno, Jay
Leno, Jay 1950- ............................. **1987**:1
Leonard, Elmore 1925- .................. **1998**:4

Leonard, Ray Charles
   See Leonard, Sugar Ray
Leonard, Sugar Ray 1956- ............. **1989**:4
Leone, Sergio 1929-1989
   Obituary ............................ **1989**:4
Leopold, Luna 1915-2006
   Obituary ............................ **2007**:1
Lepore, Nanette 1964(?)- ............... **2006**:4
Lerner, Michael 1943- .................... **1994**:2
Lerner, Sandy 1955(?)- ................... **2005**:1
Leslie, Lisa 1972- .......................... **1997**:4
Lessing, Doris 1919- ...................... **2008**:4
Letterman, David 1947- ................. **1989**:3
LeVay, Simon 1943- ....................... **1992**:2
Leaavesque, Reneaa
   Obituary ............................ **1988**:1
Levi, Zachary 1980- ...................... **2009**:4
Levin, Gerald 1939- ....................... **1995**:2
Levin, Ira 1929-2007
   Obituary ............................ **2009**:1
Levine, Arnold 1939- ..................... **2002**:3
Levine, James 1943- ...................... **1992**:3
Levinger, Moshe 1935- .................. **1992**:1
Levinson, Arthur D. 1950- ............. **2008**:3
Levinson, Barry 1932- ................... **1989**:3
Levitt, Arthur 1931- ...................... **2004**:2
Levy, Burton
   See Lane, Burton
Levy, David 1938- ......................... **1987**:2
Levy, Eugene 1946- ....................... **2004**:3
Lewis, Edward B. 1918-2004
   Obituary ............................ **2005**:4
Lewis, Edward T. 1940- ................. **1999**:4
Lewis, Henry 1932-1996
   Obituary ............................ **1996**:3
Lewis, Huey 1951- ........................ **1987**:3
Lewis, John 1920-2001
   Obituary ............................ **2002**:1
Lewis, Juliette 1973- ..................... **1999**:3
Lewis, Kenneth D. 1947- ............... **2009**:2
Lewis, Lennox 1965- ..................... **2000**:2
Lewis, Loida Nicolas 1942- ............ **1998**:3
Lewis, Ray 1975- ........................... **2001**:3
Lewis, Reggie 1966(?)-1993
   Obituary ............................ **1994**:1
Lewis, Reginald F. 1942-1993 • **1988**:4
   Obituary ............................ **1993**:3
Lewis, Richard 1948(?)- ................. **1992**:1
Lewis, Shari 1934-1998 .................. **1993**:1
   Obituary ............................ **1999**:1
Lewis, Stephen 1937- ..................... **1987**:2
LeWitt, Sol 1928- .......................... **2001**:2
Lewitzky, Bella 1916-2004
   Obituary ............................ **2005**:3
Leyland, Jim 1944- ........................ **1998**:2
Lhuillier, Monique 1971(?)- ........... **2007**:4
Li, Jet 1963- .................................. **2005**:3
Liberace 1919-1987
   Obituary ............................ **1987**:2
Liberace, Wladziu Valentino
   See Liberace
Libeskind, Daniel 1946- ................. **2004**:1
Lichtenstein, Roy 1923-1997 ......... **1994**:1
   Obituary ............................ **1998**:1
Lidstrom, Nicklas 1970- ................. **2009**:1
Lieberman, Joseph 1942- ............... **2001**:1
Ligeti, Gyorgy 1923-2006
   Obituary ............................ **2007**:3
Lightner, Candy 1946- ................... **1985**:1
Liguori, Peter 1960- ....................... **2005**:2
Lilly, John C. 1915-2001
   Obituary ............................ **2002**:4

Lil Wayne 1982- .............................. **2009**:3
Lim, Phillip 1974(?)- ..................... **2008**:1
Liman, Arthur 1932- ...................... **1989**:4
Liman, Doug 1965- ......................... **2007**:1
Limbaugh, Rush .............................. **1991**:3
Lin, Maya 1960(?)- .......................... **1990**:3
Lincoln, Blanche 1960- .................. **2003**:1
Lindbergh, Anne Morrow 1906-2001
   Obituary ...................... **2001**:4
Lindbergh, Pelle 1959-1985
   Obituary ...................... **1985**:4
Lindgren, Astrid 1907-2002
   Obituary ...................... **2003**:1
Lindros, Eric 1973- ......................... **1992**:1
Lindsay, John V. 1921-2000
   Obituary ...................... **2001**:3
Lindsay-Abaire, David 1970(?)- ... **2008**:2
Lines, Ray 1960(?)- ......................... **2004**:1
Ling, Bai 1970- ................................ **2000**:3
Ling, Lisa 1973- ............................... **2004**:2
Linklater, Richard 1960- ................ **2007**:2
Linney, Laura 1964- ....................... **2009**:4
Lipinski, Tara 1982- ....................... **1998**:3
Lipkis, Andy
   Brief entry ................... **1985**:3
Lipsig, Harry H. 1901- .................... **1985**:1
Lipton, Martin 1931- ...................... **1987**:3
Lisick, Beth 1969(?)- ...................... **2006**:2
Lithgow, John 1945- ....................... **1985**:2
Little, Benilde 1959(?)- .................. **2006**:2
Little, Cleavon 1939-1992
   Obituary ...................... **1993**:2
Litzenburger, Liesel 1967(?)- ........ **2008**:1
Liu, Lucy 1968- ............................... **2000**:4
Lively, Blake 1987- .......................... **2009**:1
Lively, Penelope 1933- ................... **2007**:4
Livi, Yvo
   See Montand, Yves
Living Colour .................................. **1993**:3
Livingston, Ron 1968- .................... **2007**:2
Livingstone, Ken 1945- .................. **1988**:3
Lizhi, Fang
   See Fang Lizhi
LL Cool J 1968- ............................... **1998**:2
Lloyd Webber, Andrew 1948- ........ **1989**:1
Lobell, Jeanine 1964(?)- ................. **2002**:3
Locklear, Heather 1961- ................. **1994**:3
Lodge, Henry Cabot 1902-1985
   Obituary ...................... **1985**:1
Loewe, Frederick 1901-1988
   Obituary ...................... **1988**:2
Lofton, Kenny 1967- ....................... **1998**:1
Lofton, Ramona
   See Sapphire
Logan, Joshua 1908-1988
   Obituary ...................... **1988**:4
Lohan, Lindsay 1986- ..................... **2005**:3
Long, Nia 1970- ............................... **2001**:3
Long, Shelley 1950(?)- .................... **1985**:1
Longo, Robert 1953(?)- ................... **1990**:4
Lon Nol
   Obituary ...................... **1986**:1
Lopes, Lisa 1971-2002
   Obituary ...................... **2003**:3
Lopes, Lisa Left Eye
   See TLC
Lopez, George 1963- ....................... **2003**:4
Lopez, Ignacio
   See Lopez de Arriortua, Jose Ignacio
Lopez, Inaki
   See Lopez de Arriortua, Jose Ignacio
Lopez, Jennifer 1970- ..................... **1998**:4

Lopez, Mario 1973- ......................... **2009**:3
Lopez, Nancy 1957- ........................ **1989**:3
Lopez de Arriortua, Jose Ignacio 1941- ..
   **1993**:4
Lord, Bette Bao 1938- ..................... **1994**:1
Lord, Jack 1920-1998 ...................... **1998**:2
Lord, Winston
   Brief entry ................... **1987**:4
Lords, Traci 1968- ........................... **1995**:4
Lorenz, Konrad 1903-1989
   Obituary ...................... **1989**:3
Lott, Trent 1941- ............................. **1998**:1
Louboutin, Christian 1963- ........... **2006**:1
Louganis, Greg 1960- ..................... **1995**:3
Louis-Dreyfus, Julia 1961(?)- ........ **1994**:1
Louv, Richard 1949- ....................... **2006**:2
Love, Courtney 1964(?)- ................. **1995**:1
Love, Susan 1948- ........................... **1995**:2
Loveless, Patty 1957- ...................... **1998**:2
Lovett, Lyle 1958(?)- ....................... **1994**:1
Lovley, Derek 1954(?)- .................... **2005**:3
Lowe, Edward 1921- ....................... **1990**:2
Lowe, Rob 1964(?)- ......................... **1990**:4
Lowell, Mike 1974- .......................... **2003**:2
Lowry, Adam and Eric Ryan ........ **2008**:1
Loy, Myrna 1905-1993
   Obituary ...................... **1994**:2
Lucas, George 1944- ....................... **1999**:4
Lucci, Susan 1946(?)- ...................... **1999**:4
Luce, Clare Boothe 1903-1987
   Obituary ...................... **1988**:1
Lucid, Shannon 1943- ..................... **1997**:1
Lucke, Lewis 1951(?)- ..................... **2004**:4
Ludacris 1977- ................................. **2007**:4
Ludlum, Robert 1927-2001
   Obituary ...................... **2002**:1
Luhrmann, Baz 1962- ..................... **2002**:3
Lukas, D. Wayne 1936(?)- .............. **1986**:2
Lukas, Darrell Wayne
   See Lukas, D. Wayne
Lukashenko, Alexander 1954- ....... **2006**:4
Lum, Olivia 1961- ........................... **2009**:1
Lupino, Ida 1918(?)-1995
   Obituary ...................... **1996**:1
LuPone, Patti 1949- ........................ **2009**:2
Lutz, Robert A. 1932- ..................... **1990**:1
Lynch, David 1946- ......................... **1990**:4
Lyne, Adrian 1941- ......................... **1997**:2
Lyne, Susan 1950- ........................... **2005**:4
Lynn, Loretta 1935(?)- .................... **2001**:1
Ma, Jack 1964- ................................. **2007**:1
Ma, Pony 1971(?)- ........................... **2006**:3
Maathai, Wangari 1940- ................. **2005**:3
Mac, Bernie 1957- ........................... **2003**:1
Macapagal-Arroyo, Gloria 1947- .. **2001**:4
MacArthur, Ellen 1976- ................. **2005**:3
MacCready, Paul 1925- ................... **1986**:4
Macdonald, Julien 1973(?)- ........... **2005**:3
MacDonald, Laurie and Walter
   Parkes ......................... **2004**:1
MacDowell, Andie 1958(?)- ........... **1993**:4
MacDowell, Rosalie Anderson
   See MacDowell, Andie
MacFarlane, Seth 1973- .................. **2006**:1
Machel, Samora 1933-1986
   Obituary ...................... **1987**:1
Mack, John J. 1944- ........................ **2006**:3
Mackey, John 1953- ........................ **2008**:2
MacKinnon, Catharine 1946- ........ **1993**:2
Macmillan, Harold 1894-1986
   Obituary ...................... **1987**:2

MacMillan, Kenneth 1929-1992
   Obituary ...................... **1993**:2
Macmillan, Maurice Harold
   See Macmillan, Harold
MacMurray, Fred 1908-1991
   Obituary ...................... **1992**:2
MacNelly, Jeff 1947-2000
   Obituary ...................... **2000**:4
Macquarrie, John 1919-2007
   Obituary ...................... **2008**:3
MacRae, Gordon 1921-1986
   Obituary ...................... **1986**:2
Macy, William H. ............................ **1999**:3
Madden, Chris 1948- ....................... **2006**:1
Madden, John 1936- ........................ **1995**:1
Madden, Steve 1958- ...................... **2007**:2
Maddux, Greg 1966- ....................... **1996**:2
Madonna 1958- ................................ **1985**:2
Maglich, Bogdan C. 1928- ............. **1990**:1
Magliozzi, Ray
   See Magliozzi, Tom and Ray
Magliozzi, Tom
   See Magliozzi, Tom and Ray
Magliozzi, Tom and Ray ............... **1991**:4
Maguire, Tobey 1975- ..................... **2002**:2
Maher, Bill 1956- ............................. **1996**:2
Mahesh Yogi, Maharishi 1911(?)- .. **1991**:3
Mahfouz, Naguib 1911-2006
   Obituary ...................... **2007**:4
Mahony, Roger M. 1936- ............... **1988**:2
Maida, Adam Cardinal 1930- ........ **1998**:2
Mailer, Norman 1923- .................... **1998**:1
Maiman, Theodore 1927-2007
   Obituary ...................... **2008**:3
Majerle, Dan 1965- ......................... **1993**:4
Majid, Hussein Kamel
   See Kamel, Hussein
Major, John 1943- ........................... **1991**:2
Makeba, Miriam 1934- ................... **1989**:2
Mako 1933-2006
   Obituary ...................... **2007**:3
Malda, Rob 1976- ............................ **2007**:3
Malkovich, John 1953- ................... **1988**:2
Malle, Louis 1932-1995
   Obituary ...................... **1996**:2
Malloy, Edward Monk 1941- ......... **1989**:4
Malone, Jo 1964(?)- ......................... **2004**:3
Malone, John C. 1941- .................... **1988**:3
Malone, Karl 1963- .......................... **1990**:1
Maltby, Richard, Jr. 1937- .............. **1996**:3
Mamet, David 1947- ........................ **1998**:4
Manchin, Joe 1947- ......................... **2006**:4
Mancini, Henry 1924-1994
   Obituary ...................... **1994**:4
Mandel, Howie 1955- ...................... **1989**:1
Mandela, Nelson 1918- ................... **1990**:3
Mandela, Winnie 1934- ................... **1989**:3
Manheimer, Heidi 1963- ................ **2009**:3
Mankiller, Wilma P.
   Brief entry ................... **1986**:2
Mann, Sally 1951- ........................... **2001**:2
Manning, Eli 1981- ......................... **2008**:4
Manning, Peyton 1976- .................. **2007**:4
Mansfield, Mike 1903-2001
   Obituary ...................... **2002**:4
Mansion, Gracie
   Brief entry ................... **1986**:3
Manson, JoAnn E. 1953- ................ **2008**:3
Manson, Marilyn 1969- .................. **1999**:4
Mantegna, Joe 1947- ....................... **1992**:1
Mantle, Mickey 1931-1995
   Obituary ...................... **1996**:1

Mapplethorpe, Robert 1946-1989
  Obituary ........................ **1989**:3
Mara, Ratu Sir Kamisese 1920-2004
  Obituary ........................ **2005**:3
Maradona, Diego 1961(?)- ............ **1991**:3
Maraldo, Pamela J. 1948(?)- .......... **1993**:4
Maravich, Pete 1948-1988
  Obituary ........................ **1988**:2
Marber, Patrick 1964- ................ **2007**:4
Marceau, Marcel 1923-2007
  Obituary ........................ **2008**:4
Marchand, Nancy 1928-2000
  Obituary ........................ **2001**:1
Marchetto, Marisa Acocella
  1962(?)- .......................... **2007**:3
Marcos, Ferdinand 1917-1989
  Obituary ........................ **1990**:1
Marcus, Stanley 1905-2002
  Obituary ........................ **2003**:1
Mardin, Brice 1938- .................. **2007**:4
Margolis, Bobby 1948(?)- ............. **2007**:2
Marier, Rebecca 1974- ................ **1995**:4
Marin, Cheech 1946- .................. **2000**:1
Marineau, Philip 1946- ............... **2002**:4
Maris, Roger 1934-1985
  Obituary ........................ **1986**:1
Mark, Marky
  See Marky Mark
Mark, Mary Ellen 1940- .............. **2006**:2
Markle, C. Wilson 1938- ............. **1988**:1
Markle, Clarke Wilson
  See Markle, C. Wilson
Marky Mark 1971- ................... **1993**:3
Marley, Ziggy 1968- ................. **1990**:4
Maroon 5 ........................... **2008**:1
Marriott, J. Willard 1900-1985
  Obituary ........................ **1985**:4
Marriott, J. Willard, Jr. 1932- ........ **1985**:4
Marriott, John Willard
  See Marriott, J. Willard
Marriott, John Willard, Jr.
  See Marriott, J. Willard, Jr.
Marrow, Tracey
  See Ice-T
Marsalis, Branford 1960- ............. **1988**:3
Marsalis, Wynton 1961- .............. **1997**:4
Marsden, Brian 1937- ................ **2004**:4
Marsh, Dorothy Marie
  See West, Dottie
Marshall, Penny 1942- ............... **1991**:3
Marshall, Susan 1958- ............... **2000**:4
Marshall, Thurgood 1908-1993
  Obituary ........................ **1993**:3
Martin, Agnes 1912-2004
  Obituary ........................ **2006**:1
Martin, Alfred Manuel
  See Martin, Billy
Martin, Billy 1928-1989 .............. **1988**:4
  Obituary ........................ **1990**:2
Martin, Casey 1972- ................. **2002**:1
Martin, Dean 1917-1995
  Obituary ........................ **1996**:2
Martin, Dean Paul 1952(?)-1987
  Obituary ........................ **1987**:3
Martin, Judith 1938- ................. **2000**:3
Martin, Lynn 1939- .................. **1991**:4
Martin, Mary 1913-1990
  Obituary ........................ **1991**:2
Martin, Paul 1938- .................. **2004**:4
Martin, Ricky 1971- ................. **1999**:4
Martin, Steve 1945- ................. **1992**:2
Martinez, Bob 1934- ................. **1992**:1

Marvin, Lee 1924-1987
  Obituary ........................ **1988**:1
Mary Mary 1972- .................... **2009**:4
Masako, Crown Princess 1963- ..... **1993**:4
Mas Canosa, Jorge 1939-1997 ....... **1998**:2
Mashouf, Manny 1938(?)- ........... **2008**:1
Masina, Giulietta 1920-1994
  Obituary ........................ **1994**:3
Master P 1970- ..................... **1999**:4
Masters, William H. 1915-2001
  Obituary ........................ **2001**:4
Mastroianni, Marcello 1914-1996
  Obituary ........................ **1997**:2
Masur, Kurt 1927- .................. **1993**:4
Matadin, Vinoodh and Inez van
  Lamsweerde ...................... **2007**:4
Matalin, Mary 1953- ................ **1995**:2
Mateschitz, Dietrich 1944- .......... **2008**:1
Mathews, Dan 1965- ................ **1998**:3
Mathias, Bob 1930-2006
  Obituary ........................ **2007**:4
Mathis, Clint 1976- ................. **2003**:1
Matlin, Marlee 1965- ............... **1992**:2
Matlovich, Leonard P. 1944(?)-1988
  Obituary ........................ **1988**:4
Matsuhisa, Nobuyuki 1949- ......... **2002**:3
Matsui, Hideki 1974- ............... **2007**:4
Matthau, Walter 1920- .............. **2000**:3
Matthews, Dave 1967- .............. **1999**:3
Mattingly, Don 1961- ............... **1986**:2
Mattingly, Donald Arthur
  See Mattingly, Don
Matuszak, John 1951(?)-1989
  Obituary ........................ **1989**:4
Mauldin, Bill 1921-2003
  Obituary ........................ **2004**:2
Mauresmo, Amelie 1979- ............ **2007**:2
Max, Peter 1937- ................... **1993**:2
Maxwell, Hamish 1926- ............. **1989**:4
Maxwell, Robert 1923- .............. **1990**:1
Maxwell, Robert 1923-1991
  Obituary ........................ **1992**:2
Mayer, John 1977- .................. **2007**:4
Mayes, Frances 1940(?)- ............ **2004**:3
Ma Ying-jeou 1950- ................ **2009**:4
Maynard, Joyce 1953- .............. **1999**:4
Mbeki, Thabo 1942- ................ **1999**:4
McAuliffe, Christa 1948-1986
  Obituary ........................ **1985**:4
McAuliffe, Sharon Christa
  See McAuliffe, Christa
McCain, John S. 1936- .............. **1998**:4
McCall, Nathan 1955- .............. **1994**:4
McCall Smith, Alexander 1948- .... **2005**:2
McCarroll, Tony
  See Oasis
McCarron, Chris 1955- ............. **1995**:4
McCarthy, Carolyn 1944- ........... **1998**:4
McCarthy, Cormac 1933- ........... **2008**:1
McCarthy, Jenny 1972- ............. **1997**:4
McCartney, Bill 1940- .............. **1995**:3
McCartney, Linda 1942-1998
  Obituary ........................ **1998**:4
McCartney, Paul 1942- ............. **2002**:4
McCartney, Stella 1971- ............ **2001**:3
McCary, Michael S.
  See Boyz II Men
McCloskey, J. Michael 1934- ........ **1988**:2
McCloskey, James 1944(?)- .......... **1993**:1
McCloskey, John Michael
  See McCloskey, J. Michael

McCloy, John J. 1895-1989
  Obituary ........................ **1989**:3
McColough, C. Peter 1922- .......... **1990**:2
McConaughey, Matthew David
  1969- ............................ **1997**:1
McCourt, Frank 1930- ............... **1997**:4
McCrea, Joel 1905-1990
  Obituary ........................ **1991**:1
McCready, Mike
  See Pearl Jam
McDermott, Alice 1953- ............. **1999**:2
McDonagh, Martin 1970- ........... **2007**:3
McDonald, Camille 1953(?)- ......... **2004**:1
McDonnell, Mary 1952- ............. **2008**:2
McDonnell, Patrick 1956- ........... **2009**:4
McDonnell, Sanford N. 1922- ....... **1988**:4
McDonough, William 1951- ......... **2003**:1
McDormand, Frances 1957- ......... **1997**:3
McDougall, Ron 1942- .............. **2001**:4
McDowall, Roddy 1928-1998
  Obituary ........................ **1999**:1
McDuffie, Robert 1958- ............. **1990**:2
McElligott, Thomas J. 1943- ........ **1987**:4
McEntire, Reba 1954- ............... **1987**:3
McEwan, Ian 1948- ................. **2004**:2
McFarlane, Todd 1961- ............. **1999**:1
McFerrin, Bobby 1950- ............. **1989**:1
McGahern, John 1934-2006
  Obituary ........................ **2007**:2
McGillis, Kelly 1957- ............... **1989**:3
McGinley, Ryan 1977- .............. **2009**:3
McGinley, Ted 1958- ................ **2004**:4
McGowan, William 1927- ........... **1985**:2
McGowan, William G. 1927-1992
  Obituary ........................ **1993**:1
McGrath, Judy 1953- ............... **2006**:1
McGraw, Phil 1950- ................ **2005**:2
McGraw, Tim 1966- ................ **2000**:3
McGraw, Tug 1944-2004
  Obituary ........................ **2005**:1
McGreevey, James 1957- ............ **2005**:2
McGregor, Ewan 1971(?)- ........... **1998**:2
McGruder, Aaron 1974- ............. **2005**:4
McGuigan, Paul
  See Oasis
McGuinness, Martin 1950(?)- ........ **1985**:4
McGuire, Dorothy 1918-2001
  Obituary ........................ **2002**:4
McGwire, Mark 1963- .............. **1999**:1
McIntyre, Joseph
  See New Kids on the Block
McIntyre, Richard
  Brief entry ...................... **1986**:2
McKee, Lonette 1952(?)- ............ **1996**:1
McKellen, Ian 1939- ................ **1994**:1
McKenna, Terence ................... **1993**:3
McKinnell, Henry 1943(?)- .......... **2002**:3
McKinney, Cynthia A. 1955- ........ **1997**:1
McKinney, Stewart B. 1931-1987
  Obituary ........................ **1987**:4
McLachlan, Sarah 1968- ............ **1998**:4
McLaren, Norman 1914-1987
  Obituary ........................ **1987**:2
McLaughlin, Audrey 1936- .......... **1990**:3
McLaughlin, Betsy 1962(?)- ......... **2004**:3
McMahon, James Robert
  See McMahon, Jim
McMahon, Jim 1959- ............... **1985**:4
McMahon, Julian 1968- ............. **2006**:1
McMahon, Vince, Jr. 1945(?)- ....... **1985**:4
McManus, Declan
  See Costello, Elvis

McMillan, Terry 1951- .................... **1993**:2
McMillen, Tom 1952- ..................... **1988**:4
McMurtry, James 1962- .................. **1990**:2
McMurtry, Larry 1936- .................. **2006**:4
McNamara, Robert S. 1916- .......... **1995**:4
McNealy, Scott 1954- ..................... **1999**:4
McNerney, W. James 1949- ........... **2006**:3
McRae, Carmen 1920(?)-1994
   Obituary ........................ **1995**:2
McSally, Martha 1966(?)- .............. **2002**:4
McTaggart, David 1932(?)- ............ **1989**:4
McVeigh, Timothy 1968-2001
   Obituary ........................ **2002**:2
Meadows, Audrey 1925-1996
   Obituary ........................ **1996**:3
Medvedev, Dmitry 1965- ............... **2009**:4
Megawati Sukarnoputri 1947- ....... **2000**:1
Mehta, Zubin 1938(?)- ................... **1994**:3
Meier, Richard 1934- ..................... **2001**:4
Meisel, Steven 1954- ...................... **2002**:4
Melendez, Bill 1916-2008
   Obituary ........................ **2009**:4
Mellinger, Frederick 1924(?)-1990
   Obituary ........................ **1990**:4
Mello, Dawn 1938(?)- ..................... **1992**:2
Mellon, Paul 1907-1999
   Obituary ........................ **1999**:3
Melman, Richard
   Brief entry ...................... **1986**:1
Melton, Douglas 1954- ................... **2008**:3
Meltzer, Brad 1970- ....................... **2005**:4
Menchu, Rigoberta 1960(?)- .......... **1993**:2
Mendoza, Lydia 1916-2007
   Obituary ........................ **2009**:1
Meneghel, Maria da Graca
   See Xuxa
Mengele, Josef 1911-1979
   Obituary ........................ **1985**:2
Mengers, Sue 1938- ....................... **1985**:3
Menninger, Karl 1893-1990
   Obituary ........................ **1991**:1
Menuhin, Yehudi 1916-1999
   Obituary ........................ **1999**:3
Merchant, Ismail 1936-2005
   Obituary ........................ **2006**:3
Merchant, Natalie 1963- ................ **1996**:3
Mercier, Laura 1959(?)- ................. **2002**:2
Mercury, Freddie 1946-1991
   Obituary ........................ **1992**:2
Meredith, Burgess 1909-1997
   Obituary ........................ **1998**:1
Merkerson, S. Epatha 1952- .......... **2006**:4
Merrick, David 1912-2000
   Obituary ........................ **2000**:4
Merrill, James 1926-1995
   Obituary ........................ **1995**:3
Merritt, Justine
   Brief entry ...................... **1985**:3
Mesic, Stipe 1934- ......................... **2005**:4
Messick, Dale 1906-2005
   Obituary ........................ **2006**:2
Messier, Mark 1961- ...................... **1993**:1
Messing, Debra 1968- .................... **2004**:4
Metallica ......................................... **2004**:2
Meyer, Stephenie 1973- ................. **2009**:1
Meyers, Nancy 1949- ..................... **2006**:1
Mfume, Kweisi 1948- ..................... **1996**:3
Michael, George 1963- ................... **1989**:2
Michelangeli, Arturo Benedetti
   1920- ............................... **1988**:2
Michelman, Kate 1942- .................. **1998**:4

Michener, James A. 1907-1997
   Obituary ........................ **1998**:1
Mickelson, Phil 1970- .................... **2004**:4
Midler, Bette 1945- ........................ **1989**:4
Mikan, George 1924-2005
   Obituary ........................ **2006**:3
Mikulski, Barbara 1936- ................ **1992**:4
Milano, Alyssa 1972- ..................... **2002**:3
Milbrett, Tiffeny 1972- ................... **2001**:1
Milburn, Rodney Jr. 1950-1997 ..... **1998**:2
Millan, Cesar 1969- ....................... **2007**:4
Milland, Ray 1908(?)-1986
   Obituary ........................ **1986**:2
Millard, Barbara J.
   Brief entry ...................... **1985**:3
Millepied, Benjamin 1977(?)- ........ **2006**:4
Miller, Andre 1976- ....................... **2003**:3
Miller, Ann 1923-2004
   Obituary ........................ **2005**:2
Miller, Arthur 1915- ...................... **1999**:4
Miller, Bebe 1950- ......................... **2000**:2
Miller, Bode 1977- ......................... **2002**:4
Miller, Dennis 1953- ...................... **1992**:4
Miller, Frank 1957- ........................ **2008**:2
Miller, Merton H. 1923-2000
   Obituary ........................ **2001**:1
Miller, Nicole 1951(?)- ................... **1995**:4
Miller, Percy
   See Master P
Miller, Rand 1959(?)- ..................... **1995**:4
Miller, Reggie 1965- ...................... **1994**:4
Miller, Robyn 1966(?)-
   See Miller, Rand
Miller, Roger 1936-1992
   Obituary ........................ **1993**:2
Miller, Sue 1943- ........................... **1999**:3
Milligan, Spike 1918-2002
   Obituary ........................ **2003**:2
Mills, Malia 1966- ......................... **2003**:1
Mills, Wilbur 1909-1992
   Obituary ........................ **1992**:4
Milne, Christopher Robin 1920-1996
   Obituary ........................ **1996**:4
Milosevic, Slobodan 1941- ............ **1993**:2
Milosz, Czeslaw 1911-2004
   Obituary ........................ **2005**:4
Milstead, Harris Glenn
   See Divine
Mina, Denise 1966- ....................... **2006**:1
Minghella, Anthony 1954- ............. **2004**:3
Minner, Ruth Ann 1935- ............... **2002**:2
Minnesota Fats 1900(?)-1996
   Obituary ........................ **1996**:3
Minogue, Kylie 1968- .................... **2003**:4
Minsky, Marvin 1927- ................... **1994**:3
Mintz, Shlomo 1957- ..................... **1986**:2
Miro, Joan 1893-1983
   Obituary ........................ **1985**:1
Mirren, Helen 1945- ...................... **2005**:1
Misrach, Richard 1949- ................. **1991**:2
Mitarai, Fujio 1935- ....................... **2002**:4
Mitchell, Arthur 1934- ................... **1995**:1
Mitchell, George J. 1933- .............. **1989**:3
Mitchell, John 1913-1988
   Obituary ........................ **1989**:2
Mitchell, Joni 1943- ....................... **1991**:4
Mitchell, Joseph 1909-1996
   Obituary ........................ **1997**:1
Mitchelson, Marvin 1928- ............. **1989**:2
Mitchum, Robert 1917-1997
   Obituary ........................ **1997**:4
Mittal, Lakshmi 1950- ................... **2007**:2

Mitterrand, Francois 1916-1996
   Obituary ........................ **1996**:2
Mixon, Oscar G.
   See Walker, Junior
Miyake, Issey 1939- ....................... **1985**:2
Miyake, Kazunaru
   See Miyake, Issey
Miyazaki, Hayao 1941- .................. **2006**:2
Miyazawa, Kiichi 1919- ................. **1992**:2
Mizrahi, Isaac 1961- ...................... **1991**:1
Moakley, Joseph 1927-2001
   Obituary ........................ **2002**:2
Mobutu Sese Seko 1930-1997 ....... **1993**:4
   Obituary ........................ **1998**:1
Mobutu Sese Seko 1930-1998
   Obituary ........................ **1998**:4
Moby 1965- ..................................... **2000**:1
Modano, Mike 1970- ...................... **2008**:2
Mohajer, Dineh 1972- .................... **1997**:3
Moi, Daniel arap 1924- .................. **1993**:2
Moiseyev, Igor 1906-2007
   Obituary ........................ **2009**:1
Molina, Alfred 1953- ...................... **2005**:3
Molinari, Susan 1958- ................... **1996**:4
Molotov, Vyacheslav Mikhailovich
   1890-1986
   Obituary ........................ **1987**:1
Monaghan, Thomas S.
   See Monaghan, Tom
Monaghan, Tom 1937- .................... **1985**:1
Mondavi, Robert 1913- .................. **1989**:2
Moneo, Jose Rafael 1937- .............. **1996**:4
Monica 1980- .................................. **2004**:2
Mo'Nique 1967- ............................. **2008**:1
Monk, Art 1957- ............................. **1993**:2
Monroe, Bill 1911-1996
   Obituary ........................ **1997**:1
Monroe, Rose Will 1920-1997
   Obituary ........................ **1997**:4
Montagu, Ashley 1905-1999
   Obituary ........................ **2000**:2
Montana, Joe 1956- ....................... **1989**:2
Montand, Yves 1921-1991
   Obituary ........................ **1992**:2
Montgomery, Elizabeth 1933-1995
   Obituary ........................ **1995**:4
Montoya, Carlos 1903-1993
   Obituary ........................ **1993**:4
Moody, John 1943- ........................ **1985**:3
Moody, Rick 1961- ......................... **2002**:2
Moog, Robert 1934-2005
   Obituary ........................ **2006**:4
Moon, Warren 1956- ...................... **1991**:3
Moonves, Les 1949- ....................... **2004**:2
Moore, Ann 1950- .......................... **2009**:1
Moore, Archie 1913-1998
   Obituary ........................ **1999**:2
Moore, Clayton 1914-1999
   Obituary ........................ **2000**:3
Moore, Demi 1963(?)- .................... **1991**:4
Moore, Dudley 1935-2002
   Obituary ........................ **2003**:2
Moore, Henry 1898-1986
   Obituary ........................ **1986**:4
Moore, Julianne 1960- ................... **1998**:1
Moore, Mandy 1984- ...................... **2004**:2
Moore, Mary Tyler 1936- ............... **1996**:2
Moore, Michael 1954(?)- ................ **1990**:3
Moore, Rachel 1965- ...................... **2008**:2
Moose, Charles 1953(?)- ................ **2003**:4
Morales, Evo 1959- ........................ **2007**:2
Moreno, Arturo 1946- .................... **2005**:2

Morgan, Claire
  See Highsmith, Patricia
Morgan, Dodge 1932(?)- ................. **1987**:1
Morgan, Robin 1941- ...................... **1991**:1
Morgan, Tracy 1968- ..................... **2009**:3
Morgentaler, Henry 1923- ............. **1986**:3
Mori, Yoshiro 1937- ....................... **2000**:4
Morissette, Alanis 1974- ............... **1996**:2
Morita, Akio 1921- ......................... **1989**:4
Morita, Akio 1921-1999
  Obituary ..................................... **2000**:2
Morita, Noriyuki Pat 1932- ........... **1987**:3
Morita, Pat
  See Morita, Noriyuki Pat
Moritz, Charles 1936- .................... **1989**:3
Morris, Dick 1948- ......................... **1997**:3
Morris, Doug 1938- ....................... **2005**:1
Morris, Henry M. 1918-2006
  Obituary ..................................... **2007**:2
Morris, Kathryn 1969- ................... **2006**:4
Morris, Mark 1956- ........................ **1991**:1
Morris, Nate
  See Boyz II Men
Morris, Wanya
  See Boyz II Men
Morrison, Sterling 1942-1995
  Obituary ..................................... **1996**:1
Morrison, Toni 1931- ...................... **1998**:1
Morrison, Trudi
  Brief entry ................................. **1986**:2
Morrissey 1959- .............................. **2005**:2
Morrow, Rob 1962- ........................ **2006**:4
Morrow, Tracey
  See Ice-T
Mortensen, Viggo 1958- ................. **2003**:3
Mosbacher, Georgette 1947(?)- ...... **1994**:2
Mos Def 1973- ................................ **2005**:4
Mosley, Walter 1952- ..................... **2003**:4
Moss, Carrie-Anne 1967- ............... **2004**:3
Moss, Cynthia 1940- ...................... **1995**:2
Moss, Kate 1974- ........................... **1995**:3
Moss, Randy 1977- ......................... **1999**:3
Mother Teresa 1910-1997 ............. **1993**:1
  Obituary ..................................... **1998**:1
Motherwell, Robert 1915-1991
  Obituary ..................................... **1992**:1
Mott, William Penn, Jr. 1909- ........ **1986**:1
Mottola, Tommy 1949- ................... **2002**:1
Mourning, Alonzo 1970- ................ **1994**:2
Moyers, Bill 1934- .......................... **1991**:4
Moynihan, Daniel Patrick 1927-2003
  Obituary ..................................... **2004**:2
Mubarak, Hosni 1928- .................... **1991**:4
Mueck, Ron 1958- .......................... **2008**:3
Mugabe, Robert 1924- .................... **1988**:4
Mulcahy, Anne M. 1952- ................ **2003**:2
Muldowney, Shirley 1940- ............. **1986**:1
Mulkey-Robertson, Kim 1962- ...... **2006**:1
Mullenger, Donna Belle
  See Reed, Donna
Mullis, Kary 1944- ......................... **1995**:3
Mulroney, Brian 1939- ................... **1989**:2
Mumford, Lewis 1895-1990
  Obituary ..................................... **1990**:2
Muniz, Frankie 1985- ..................... **2001**:4
Munro, Alice 1931- ........................ **1997**:1
Murakami, Haruki 1949- ................ **2008**:3
Murakami, Takashi 1962- .............. **2004**:2
Murano, Elsa 1959- ........................ **2009**:1
Murcia, Ann Jura Nauseda
  See Jillian, Ann

Murdoch, Iris 1919-1999
  Obituary ..................................... **1999**:4
Murdoch, Keith Rupert
  See Murdoch, Rupert
Murdoch, Rupert 1931- .................. **1988**:4
Murkoff, Heidi 1958- ..................... **2009**:3
Murphy, Brittany 1977- ................. **2005**:1
Murphy, Eddie 1961- ...................... **1989**:2
Murphy, Kathleen A. ...................... **2009**:2
Murray, Arthur 1895-1991
  Obituary ..................................... **1991**:3
Murray, Bill 1950- .......................... **2002**:4
Murrieta, Luis Donaldo Colosio
  See Colosio, Luis Donaldo
Musburger, Brent 1939- ................. **1985**:1
Museveni, Yoweri 1944- ................. **2002**:1
Musharraf, Pervez 1943- ............... **2000**:2
Muskie, Edmund S. 1914-1996
  Obituary ..................................... **1996**:3
Mutter, Anne-Sophie 1963- ........... **1990**:3
Mydans, Carl 1907-2004
  Obituary ..................................... **2005**:4
Myers, Mike 1964(?)- ..................... **1992**:3
Nadal, Rafael 1986- ....................... **2009**:1
Nader, Ralph 1934- ........................ **1989**:4
Nagako, Empress Dowager 1903-2000
  Obituary ..................................... **2001**:1
Nagin, Ray 1956- ........................... **2007**:1
Nair, Mira 1957- ............................ **2007**:4
Nakszynski, Nikolaus Gunther
  See Kinski, Klaus
Nance, Jack 1943(?)-1996
  Obituary ..................................... **1997**:3
Napolitano, Janet 1957- ................. **1997**:1
Nara, Yoshitomo 1959- .................. **2006**:2
Narayan, R.K. 1906-2001
  Obituary ..................................... **2002**:2
Nardelli, Robert 1948- ................... **2008**:4
Nars, Francois 1959- ...................... **2003**:1
Nas 1973- ...................................... **2009**:2
Nasreen, Taslima
  See Nasrin, Taslima
Nasrin, Taslima 1962- .................... **1995**:1
Natori, Josie 1947- ........................ **1994**:3
Natsios, Andrew 1949- ................... **2005**:1
Nauman, Bruce 1941- ..................... **1995**:4
Navratilova, Martina 1956- ........... **1989**:1
Nazarbayev, Nursultan 1940- ........ **2006**:4
Neal, James Foster 1929- ............... **1986**:2
Nechita, Alexandra 1985- .............. **1996**:4
Neeleman, David 1959- .................. **2003**:3
Neeson, Liam 1952- ....................... **1993**:4
Ne-Yo 1982- ................................... **2009**:4
Neiman, LeRoy 1927- .................... **1993**:3
Nelson, Byron 1912-2006
  Obituary ..................................... **2007**:4
Nelson, Gaylord A. 1914-2005
  Obituary ..................................... **2006**:3
Nelson, Harriet 1909(?)-1994
  Obituary ..................................... **1995**:1
Nelson, Rick 1940-1985
  Obituary ..................................... **1986**:1
Nelson, Willie 1933- ...................... **1993**:4
Nemerov, Howard 1920-1991
  Obituary ..................................... **1992**:1
Netanyahu, Benjamin 1949- ........... **1996**:4
Neuharth, Allen H. 1924- ............... **1986**:1
Nevelson, Louise 1900-1988
  Obituary ..................................... **1988**:3
Newhouse, Samuel I., Jr. 1927- ..... **1997**:1
New Kids on the Block ................... **1991**:2
Newkirk, Ingrid 1949- ................... **1992**:3

Newman, Arnold 1918- .................. **1993**:1
Newman, Joseph 1936- .................. **1987**:1
Newman, Paul 1925- ...................... **1995**:3
Newman, Ryan 1977- ..................... **2005**:1
Newsom, Gavin 1967- .................... **2009**:3
Newton, Helmut 1920- ................... **2002**:1
Newton, Huey 1942-1989
  Obituary ..................................... **1990**:1
Newton-John, Olivia 1948- ............ **1998**:4
Ngau, Harrison ............................... **1991**:3
Ni Bhraonain, Eithne
  See Enya
Nichols, Mike 1931- ....................... **1994**:4
Nicholson, Jack 1937- .................... **1989**:2
Nickelback ..................................... **2007**:2
Nidal, Abu 1937- ........................... **1987**:1
Nielsen, Jerri 1951(?)- ................... **2001**:3
Niezabitowska, Malgorzata
  1949(?)- ..................................... **1991**:3
Nilsson, Birgit 1918-2005
  Obituary ..................................... **2007**:1
Nipon, Albert
  Brief entry ................................. **1986**:4
Niro, Laura
  See Nyro, Laura
Nirvana .......................................... **1992**:4
Nissel, Angela 1974- ...................... **2006**:4
Nixon, Bob 1954(?)- ....................... **2006**:4
Nixon, Pat 1912-1993
  Obituary ..................................... **1994**:1
Nixon, Richard 1913-1994
  Obituary ..................................... **1994**:4
No Doubt ....................................... **1997**:3
Nol, Lon
  See Lon Nol
Nolan, Christopher 1970(?)- .......... **2006**:3
Nolan, Lloyd 1902-1985
  Obituary ..................................... **1985**:4
Nolte, Nick 1941- .......................... **1992**:4
Nomo, Hideo 1968- ....................... **1996**:2
Noonan, Peggy 1950- ..................... **1990**:3
Nooyi, Indra 1955- ........................ **2004**:3
Norman, Greg 1955- ...................... **1988**:3
Norman, Gregory John
  See Norman, Greg
Norrington, Roger 1934- ................ **1989**:4
North, Alex 1910- .......................... **1986**:3
North, Oliver 1943- ....................... **1987**:4
Northam, Jeremy 1961- .................. **2003**:2
Northrop, Peggy 1954- ................... **2009**:2
Norton, Andre 1912-2005
  Obituary ..................................... **2006**:2
Norton, Edward 1969- .................... **2000**:2
Norville, Deborah 1958- ................ **1990**:3
Norwood, Brandy
  See Brandy
Notorious B.I.G. 1973(?)-1997
  Obituary ..................................... **1997**:3
Novello, Antonia 1944- .................. **1991**:2
Novoselic, Chris
  See Nirvana
Nowitzki, Dirk 1978- ..................... **2007**:2
Noyce, Robert N. 1927- ................. **1985**:4
'N Sync ........................................... **2001**:4
Nuesslein-Volhard, Christiane
  1942- ......................................... **1998**:1
Nujoma, Sam 1929- ....................... **1990**:4
Nunn, Sam 1938- ........................... **1990**:2
Nunn, Trevor 1940- ....................... **2000**:2
Nureyev, Rudolf 1938-1993
  Obituary ..................................... **1993**:2
Nussbaum, Karen 1950- ................. **1988**:3

Nye, Bill 1955- ............................... **1997**:2
Nyerere, Julius 1922(?)-1999
   Obituary ............................... **2000**:2
Nyro, Laura 1947-1997
   Obituary ............................... **1997**:3
Oasis ............................................... **1996**:3
Oates, Joyce Carol 1938- ................ **2000**:1
Obama, Barack 1961- .................... **2007**:4
Obando, Miguel 1926- .................... **1986**:4
Obasanjo, Olusegun 1937(?)- ......... **2000**:2
O'Brien, Conan 1963(?)- .............. **1994**:1
Obuchi, Keizo 1937- ...................... **1999**:2
Obuchi, Keizo 1937-2000
   Obituary ............................... **2000**:4
Ocalan, Abdullah 1948(?)- ............ **1999**:4
Ochoa, Lorena 1981- ...................... **2007**:4
O'Connor, Cardinal John 1920- ..... **1990**:3
O'Connor, Carroll 1924-2001
   Obituary ............................... **2002**:3
O'Connor, Donald 1925-2003
   Obituary ............................... **2004**:4
O'Connor, John 1920-2000
   Obituary ............................... **2000**:4
O'Connor, Sandra Day 1930- ........ **1991**:1
O'Connor, Sinead 1967- ................. **1990**:4
O'Day, Anita 1919-2006
   Obituary ............................... **2008**:1
O'Donnell, Bill
   Brief entry ............................ **1987**:4
O'Donnell, Rosie 1962- ................. **1994**:3
Oe, Kenzaburo 1935- ..................... **1997**:1
Ogilvy, David 1911-1999
   Obituary ............................... **2000**:1
O'Hara, Catherine 1954- ................ **2007**:4
Oje, Baba
   See Arrested Development
O'Keefe, Sean 1956- ...................... **2005**:2
Okoye, Christian 1961- .................. **1990**:2
Olajuwon, Akeem 1963- ................ **1985**:1
Olav, King of Norway
   See Olav, King of Norway
Olav, King of Norway 1903-1991
   Obituary ............................... **1991**:3
Oldham, Todd 1961- ...................... **1995**:4
Oldman, Gary 1958- ...................... **1998**:1
O'Leary, Hazel 1937- ..................... **1993**:4
Olin, Ken 1955(?)- .......................... **1992**:3
Olin, Lena 1956- ............................ **1991**:2
Oliver, Daniel 1939- ...................... **1988**:2
Oliver, Jamie 1975- ........................ **2002**:3
Olivier, Laurence 1907-1989
   Obituary ............................... **1989**:4
Ollila, Jorma 1950- ........................ **2003**:4
Olmos, Edward James 1947- ......... **1990**:1
Olopade, Olufunmilayo 1957(?)- .. **2006**:3
Olsen, Kenneth H. 1926- ............... **1986**:4
Olsen, Mary-Kate and Ashley
   1986- ................................... **2002**:1
Olsen, Sigrid 1953- ........................ **2007**:1
Olson, Billy 1958- .......................... **1986**:3
Olson, Johnny 1910(?)-1985
   Obituary ............................... **1985**:4
O'Malley, Susan 1962(?)- .............. **1995**:2
Onassis, Jacqueline Kennedy 1929-1994
   Obituary ............................... **1994**:4
Ondaatje, Philip Michael 1943- ..... **1997**:3
O'Neal, Shaquille 1972- ................. **1992**:1
O'Neil, Buck 1911-2006
   Obituary ............................... **2007**:4
O'Neill, Paul H. 1935- ................... **2001**:4
O'Neill, Thomas Philip, Jr.
   See O'Neill, Tip

O'Neill, Tip 1912-1994
   Obituary ............................... **1994**:3
Ono, Yoko 1933- ............................ **1989**:2
Oppenheimer, Harry 1908-2000
   Obituary ............................... **2001**:3
Orbach, Jerry 1935-2004
   Obituary ............................... **2006**:1
Orbison, Roy 1936-1988
   Obituary ............................... **1989**:2
O'Reilly, Bill 1949- ........................ **2001**:2
Orman, Suze 1951(?)- ..................... **2003**:1
Ormandy, Eugene 1899-1985
   Obituary ............................... **1985**:2
Ornish, Dean 1953- ........................ **2004**:2
Orr, Kay 1939- .............................. **1987**:4
Ortega, Daniel 1945- ...................... **2008**:2
Ortenberg, Elisabeth Claiborne
   See Claiborne, Liz
Osborne, Joan 1962- ...................... **1996**:4
Osborne, John 1929-1994
   Obituary ............................... **1995**:2
Osbournes, The ............................. **2003**:4
Osgood, Charles 1933- ................... **1996**:2
Osteen, Joel 1963- .......................... **2006**:2
O'Steen, Van
   Brief entry ............................ **1986**:3
Ostin, Mo 1927- ............................. **1996**:2
Ostroff, Dawn 1960- ...................... **2006**:4
O'Sullivan, Maureen 1911-1998
   Obituary ............................... **1998**:4
Otte, Ruth 1949- ............................ **1992**:4
OutKast ......................................... **2004**:4
Ovechkin, Alexander 1985- ........... **2009**:2
Ovitz, Michael 1946- ...................... **1990**:1
Owada, Masako
   See Masako, Crown Princess
Owen, Clive 1964- ......................... **2006**:2
Owen-Jones, Lindsay 1946(?)- ...... **2004**:2
Owens, Buck 1929-2006
   Obituary ............................... **2007**:2
Owens, Dana
   See Queen Latifah
Owens, Delia
   See Owens, Delia and Mark
Owens, Delia and Mark ................ **1993**:3
Owens, Mark
   See Owens, Delia and Mark
Oz, Mehmet 1960- ......................... **2007**:2
Paar, Jack 1918-2004
   Obituary ............................... **2005**:2
Pacelle, Wayne 1965- ..................... **2009**:4
Pacino, Al 1940- ............................ **1993**:4
Pacino, Alfredo James
   See Pacino, Al
Pack, Ellen 1963(?)- ....................... **2001**:2
Packard, David 1912-1996
   Obituary ............................... **1996**:3
Page, Geraldine 1924-1987
   Obituary ............................... **1987**:4
Pagels, Elaine 1943- ....................... **1997**:1
Paglia, Camille 1947- ..................... **1992**:3
Paige, Emmett, Jr.
   Brief entry ............................ **1986**:4
Paige, Rod 1933- ............................ **2003**:2
Paisley, Brad 1972- ........................ **2008**:3
Pak, Se Ri 1977- ............................ **1999**:4
Pakula, Alan 1928-1998
   Obituary ............................... **1999**:2
Palahniuk, Chuck 1962- ................ **2004**:1
Palance, Jack 1919-2006
   Obituary ............................... **2008**:1

Paley, William S. 1901-1990
   Obituary ............................... **1991**:2
Palin, Sarah 1964- .......................... **2009**:1
Palme, Olof 1927-1986
   Obituary ............................... **1986**:2
Palme, Sven Olof Joachim
   See Palme, Olof
Palmeiro, Rafael 1964- ................... **2005**:1
Palmer, Jim 1945- .......................... **1991**:2
Palmer, Robert 1949-2003
   Obituary ............................... **2004**:4
Palmer, Violet 1964(?)- .................. **2005**:2
Palmisano, Samuel J. 1952(?)- ....... **2003**:1
Paltrow, Gwyneth 1972- ................ **1997**:1
Pamuk, Orhan 1952- ...................... **2007**:3
Panetta, Leon 1938- ....................... **1995**:1
Panettiere, Hayden 1989- .............. **2008**:4
Panichgul, Thakoon 1974- ............. **2009**:4
Panofsky, Wolfgang 1919-2007
   Obituary ............................... **2008**:4
Pantoliano, Joe 1951- ..................... **2002**:3
Paolozzi, Eduardo 1924-2005
   Obituary ............................... **2006**:3
Papandreou, Andrea 1919-1996
   Obituary ............................... **1997**:1
Papirofsky, Yosl
   See Papp, Joseph
Papp, Joseph 1921-1991
   Obituary ............................... **1992**:2
Paquin, Anna 1982- ....................... **2009**:4
Paretsky, Sara 1947- ...................... **2002**:4
Parizeau, Jacques 1930- ................. **1995**:1
Park, Nick 1958- ............................ **1997**:3
Parker, Brant 1920-2007
   Obituary ............................... **2008**:2
Parker, Colonel Tom 1929-1997
   Obituary ............................... **1997**:2
Parker, Mary-Louise 1964- ............ **2002**:2
Parker, Sarah Jessica 1965- ........... **1999**:2
Parker, Suzy 1932-2003
   Obituary ............................... **2004**:2
Parker, Tony 1982- ........................ **2008**:1
Parker, Trey
   See Parker, Trey and Matt Stone
Parker, Trey and Matt Stone ......... **1998**:2
Parker, Willie 1980- ....................... **2009**:3
Parks, Bert 1914-1992
   Obituary ............................... **1992**:3
Parks, Gordon 1912-2006
   Obituary ............................... **2006**:2
Parks, Rosa 1913-2005
   Obituary ............................... **2007**:1
Parks, Suzan-Lori 1964- ................ **2003**:2
Parsons, David 1959- ..................... **1993**:4
Parsons, Gary 1950(?)- ................... **2006**:2
Parsons, Richard 1949- .................. **2002**:4
Parton, Dolly 1946- ....................... **1999**:4
Pascal, Amy 1958- ......................... **2003**:3
Pass, Joe 1929-1994
   Obituary ............................... **1994**:4
Passalaqua, Joseph Anthony
   See Pass, Joe
Pastorius, Jaco 1951-1987
   Obituary ............................... **1988**:1
Pastorius, John Francis Anthony
   See Pastorius, Jaco
Pastrana, Andres 1954- .................. **2002**:1
Pataki, George 1945- ...................... **1995**:2
Patchett, Ann 1963- ....................... **2003**:2
Paterno, Joe 1926- ......................... **1995**:4
Paton, Alan 1903-1988
   Obituary ............................... **1988**:3

Patrick, Danica 1982- ...................... **2003**:3
Patrick, Robert 1959- ...................... **2002**:1
Patten, Christopher 1944- .............. **1993**:3
Patterson, Richard North 1947- ..... **2001**:4
Patton, John 1947(?)- ...................... **2004**:4
Pauley, Jane 1950- .......................... **1999**:1
Pauling, Linus 1901-1994
    Obituary ...................................... **1995**:1
Paulsen, Pat 1927-1997
    Obituary ...................................... **1997**:4
Paulucci, Jeno
    Brief entry .................................. **1986**:3
Paulucci, Luigino Francesco
    See Paulucci, Jeno
Pausch, Randy 1960-2008
    Obituary ...................................... **2009**:3
Pavarotti, Luciano 1935- ................ **1997**:4
Pavin, Corey 1959- .......................... **1996**:4
Paxton, Bill 1955- ............................ **1999**:3
Payne, Alexander 1961- .................. **2005**:4
Payton, Lawrence 1938(?)-1997
    Obituary ...................................... **1997**:4
Payton, Walter 1954-1999
    Obituary ...................................... **2000**:2
Paz, Octavio 1914- .......................... **1991**:2
Pearl, Minnie 1912-1996
    Obituary ...................................... **1996**:3
Pearl Jam ........................................ **1994**:2
Peck, Gregory 1916-2003
    Obituary ...................................... **2004**:3
Peckford, Brian 1942- ...................... **1989**:1
Pedersen, William 1938(?)- ............ **1989**:4
Peebles, R. Donahue 1960- ............ **2003**:2
Peete, Calvin 1943- .......................... **1985**:4
Peete, Holly Robinson 1964- .......... **2005**:2
Pegg, Simon 1970- .......................... **2009**:1
Pei, Ieoh Ming
    See Pei, I.M.
Pei, I.M. 1917- ................................ **1990**:4
Peller, Clara 1902(?)-1987
    Obituary ...................................... **1988**:1
Pelli, Cesar 1927(?)- ........................ **1991**:4
Pelosi, Nancy 1940- ........................ **2004**:2
Peltier, Leonard 1944- .................... **1995**:1
Peluso, Michelle 1971(?)- .............. **2007**:4
Pendleton, Clarence M. 1930-1988
    Obituary ...................................... **1988**:4
Penn, Kal 1977- .............................. **2009**:1
Penn, Sean 1960- ............................ **1987**:2
Penn & Teller .................................. **1992**:1
Pennington, Ty 1965- ...................... **2005**:4
Penrose, Roger 1931- ...................... **1991**:4
Penske, Roger 1937- ........................ **1988**:3
Pep, Willie 1922-2006
    Obituary ...................................... **2008**:1
Pepper, Claude 1900-1989
    Obituary ...................................... **1989**:4
Percy, Walker 1916-1990
    Obituary ...................................... **1990**:4
Perdue, Frank 1920-2005
    Obituary ...................................... **2006**:2
Perelman, Ronald 1943- .................. **1989**:2
Peres, Shimon 1923- ........................ **1996**:3
Perez, Carlos Andre 1922- ............ **1990**:2
Perez, Rosie .................................... **1994**:2
Perez de Cuellar, Javier 1920- ....... **1991**:3
Perkins, Anthony 1932-1992
    Obituary ...................................... **1993**:2
Perkins, Carl 1932-1998 .................. **1998**:2
Perlman, Steve 1961(?)- .................. **1998**:2
Perot, H. Ross 1930- ........................ **1992**:4
Perry, Carrie Saxon 1932(?)- .......... **1989**:2

Perry, Harold A. 1917(?)-1991
    Obituary ...................................... **1992**:1
Perry, Lincoln Theodore Monroe Andrew
    See Fetchit, Stepin
Perry, Luke 1966(?)- ........................ **1992**:3
Perry, Matthew 1969- ...................... **1997**:2
Perry, Tyler 1969- ............................ **2006**:1
Perry, William 1927- ........................ **1994**:4
Perske, Betty Joan
    See Bacall, Lauren
Persson, Nina
    See Cardigans, The
Persson, Stefan 1947- ...................... **2004**:1
Perutz, Max 1914-2002
    Obituary ...................................... **2003**:2
Pesci, Joe 1943- .............................. **1992**:4
Peter, Valentine J. 1934- ................ **1988**:2
Peters, Bernadette 1948- ................ **2000**:1
Peters, Mary E. 1948- ...................... **2008**:3
Peters, Tom 1942- ............................ **1998**:1
Petersen, Donald Eugene 1926- .... **1985**:1
Peterson, Cassandra
    See Peterson, Cassandra
Peterson, Cassandra 1951- ............ **1988**:1
Peterson, David 1943- ...................... **1987**:1
Peterson, Oscar 1925-2007
    Obituary ...................................... **2009**:1
Peterson, Roger Tory 1908-1996
    Obituary ...................................... **1997**:1
Peterson, Toni Pihl
    See Lander, Toni
Petrossian, Christian
    Brief entry .................................. **1985**:3
Petty, Tom 1952- .............................. **1988**:1
Peyton, Elizabeth 1965- .................. **2007**:1
Pfeiffer, Eckhard 1941- .................. **1998**:4
Pfeiffer, Michelle 1957- .................. **1990**:2
Phair, Liz 1967- .............................. **1995**:3
Phelan, John Joseph, Jr. 1931- ....... **1985**:4
Phelps, Michael 1985- .................... **2009**:2
Phifer, Mekhi 1975- ........................ **2004**:1
Philbin, Regis 1933- ........................ **2000**:2
Philby, Harold Adrian Russell
    See Philby, Kim
Philby, Kim 1912-1988
    Obituary ...................................... **1988**:3
Phillips, John 1935-2001
    Obituary ...................................... **2002**:1
Phillips, Julia 1944- ........................ **1992**:1
Phillips, Sam 1923-2003
    Obituary ...................................... **2004**:4
Phoenix, Joaquin 1974- .................. **2000**:4
Phoenix, River 1970-1993 .............. **1990**:2
    Obituary ...................................... **1994**:2
Piano, Renzo 1937- .......................... **2009**:2
Piazza, Mike 1968- .......................... **1998**:4
Picasso, Paloma 1949- .................... **1991**:1
Pickett, Wilson 1941-2006
    Obituary ...................................... **2007**:1
Picoult, Jodi 1966- .......................... **2008**:1
Pierce, David Hyde 1959- .............. **1996**:3
Pierce, Frederick S. 1934(?)- .......... **1985**:3
Pierce, Mary 1975- .......................... **1994**:4
Pierce, Paul 1977- ............................ **2009**:2
Pilatus, Robert 1966(?)-1998
    Obituary ...................................... **1998**:3
Pilkey, Dav 1966- ............................ **2001**:1
Pincay, Laffit, Jr. 1946- .................. **1986**:3
Pinchot, Bronson 1959(?)- .............. **1987**:4
Pink 1979- ...................................... **2004**:3
Pinker, Steven A. 1954- .................. **2000**:1
Pinkett Smith, Jada 1971- .............. **1998**:3

Pinochet, Augusto 1915- ................ **1999**:2
Pipher, Mary 1948(?)- ...................... **1996**:4
Pippen, Scottie 1965- ...................... **1992**:2
Pirro, Jeanine 1951- ........................ **1998**:2
Pitt, Brad 1964- .............................. **1995**:2
Pittman, Robert W. 1953- .............. **1985**:1
Piven, Jeremy 1965- ........................ **2007**:3
Plater-Zyberk, Elizabeth 1950- ...... **2005**:2
Plato, Dana 1964-1999
    Obituary ...................................... **1999**:4
Pleasence, Donald 1919-1995
    Obituary ...................................... **1995**:3
Pleshette, Suzanne 1937-2008
    Obituary ...................................... **2009**:2
Plimpton, George 1927-2003
    Obituary ...................................... **2004**:4
Plotkin, Mark 1955(?)- .................... **1994**:3
Pocklington, Peter H. 1941- .......... **1985**:2
Poehler, Amy 1971- ........................ **2009**:1
Pogorelich, Ivo 1958- ...................... **1986**:4
Poitier, Sidney 1927- ...................... **1990**:3
Polgar, Judit 1976- .......................... **1993**:3
Politkovskaya, Anna 1958-2006
    Obituary ...................................... **2007**:4
Polke, Sigmar 1941- ........................ **1999**:4
Pollack, Sydney 1934-2008
    Obituary ...................................... **2009**:2
Pol Pot 1928-1998
    Obituary ...................................... **1998**:4
Ponce de Leon, Ernesto Zedillo
    See Zedillo, Ernesto
Ponti, Carlo 1912-2007
    Obituary ...................................... **2008**:2
Ponty, Jean-Luc 1942- .................... **1985**:4
Popcorn, Faith
    Brief entry .................................. **1988**:1
Pope, Generoso 1927-1988 ............ **1988**:4
Pople, John 1925-2004
    Obituary ...................................... **2005**:2
Porco, Carolyn 1953- ...................... **2005**:4
Porizkova, Paulina
    Brief entry .................................. **1986**:4
Porras, Arturo Jose Cruz
    See Cruz, Arturo
Porsche, Ferdinand 1909-1998
    Obituary ...................................... **1998**:4
Porter, George 1920-2002
    Obituary ...................................... **2003**:4
Porter, Sylvia 1913-1991
    Obituary ...................................... **1991**:4
Portman, John 1924- ...................... **1988**:2
Portman, Natalie 1981- .................. **2000**:3
Posen, Zac 1980- ............................ **2009**:3
Post, Peggy 1940(?)- ........................ **2001**:4
Poston, Tom 1921-2007
    Obituary ...................................... **2008**:3
Potok, Anna Maximilian
    Brief entry .................................. **1985**:2
Potok, Chaim 1929-2002
    Obituary ...................................... **2003**:4
Potter, Michael 1960(?)- .................. **2003**:3
Potts, Annie 1952- .......................... **1994**:1
Potts, Paul 1970- ............................ **2009**:1
Pough, Richard Hooper 1904- ....... **1989**:1
Pouillon, Nora 1943- ...................... **2005**:1
Povich, Maury 1939(?)- .................. **1994**:3
Powell, Colin 1937- ........................ **1990**:1
Powell, Lewis F. 1907-1998
    Obituary ...................................... **1999**:1
Power, Samantha 1970- .................. **2005**:4
Powter, Susan 1957(?)- .................. **1994**:3
Pozzi, Lucio 1935- .......................... **1990**:2

Prada, Miuccia 1950(?)- ................. **1996**:1
Pratt, Christopher 1935- ................. **1985**:3
Pratt, Jane 1963(?)- ........................... **1999**:1
Predock, Antoine 1936- .................. **1993**:2
Preminger, Otto 1906-1986
   Obituary ........................ **1986**:3
Presley, Lisa Marie 1968- ............... **2004**:3
Presley, Pricilla 1945- ..................... **2001**:1
Presser, Jackie 1926-1988
   Obituary ........................ **1988**:4
Pressler, Paul 1956(?)- ................... **2003**:4
Preston, Billy 1946-2006
   Obituary ........................ **2007**:3
Preston, Robert 1918-1987
   Obituary ........................ **1987**:3
Preaaval, Reneaa 1943- .................. **1997**:2
Prevor, Barry and Steven Shore .... **2006**:2
Price, Vincent 1911-1993
   Obituary ........................ **1994**:2
Pride, Charley 1938(?)- ................... **1998**:1
Priestly, Jason 1970(?)- ................... **1993**:2
Primakov, Yevgeny 1929- ............... **1999**:3
Prince 1958- ..................................... **1995**:3
Prince, Faith 1959(?)- ...................... **1993**:2
Princess Margaret, Countess of Snowdon
   1930-2002
   Obituary ........................ **2003**:2
Prinze, Freddie, Jr. 1976- ............... **1999**:3
Pritzker, Abram Nicholas
   See Pritzker, A.N.
Pritzker, A.N. 1896-1986
   Obituary ........................ **1986**:2
Probst, Larry 1951(?)- ..................... **2005**:1
Proctor, Barbara Gardner 1933(?)- ... **1985**:3
Profet, Margie 1958- ....................... **1994**:4
Prost, Alain 1955- ........................... **1988**:1
Proulx, E. Annie 1935- .................... **1996**:1
Prowse, Juliet 1937-1996
   Obituary ........................ **1997**:1
Prusiner, Stanley 1942- ................... **1998**:2
Pryce, Deborah 1951- ..................... **2006**:3
Pryor, Richard .................................. **1999**:3
Public Enemy ................................... **1992**:1
Puccio, Thomas P. 1944- ................ **1986**:4
Puck, Theodore 1916-2005
   Obituary ........................ **2007**:1
Puck, Wolfgang 1949- ..................... **1990**:1
Puckett, Kirby 1960-2006
   Obituary ........................ **2007**:2
Puente, Tito 1923-2000
   Obituary ........................ **2000**:4
Pujols, Albert 1980- ........................ **2005**:3
Puleston, Dennis 1905-2001
   Obituary ........................ **2002**:2
Pullman, Philip 1946- ..................... **2003**:2
Puryear, Martin 1941- ..................... **2002**:4
Putin, Vladimir 1952- ..................... **2000**:3
Puzo, Mario 1920-1999
   Obituary ........................ **2000**:1
Pynchon, Thomas 1937- ................. **1997**:4
Qaddhafi, Muammar 1942- ............ **1998**:3
Quaid, Dennis 1954- ....................... **1989**:4
Quayle, Dan 1947- .......................... **1989**:2
Quayle, James Danforth
   See Quayle, Dan
Queen Elizabeth the Queen Mother
   1900-2002
   Obituary ........................ **2003**:2
Queen Latifah 1970(?)- ................... **1992**:2
Queer Eye for the Straight Guy
   cast ................................. **2004**:3

Questrom, Allen 1940- ................... **2001**:4
Quill, Timothy E. 1949- .................. **1997**:3
Quindlen, Anna 1952- ..................... **1993**:1
Quing, Jiang
   See Jiang Quing
Quinlan, Karen Ann 1954-1985
   Obituary ........................ **1985**:2
Quinn, Anthony 1915-2001
   Obituary ........................ **2002**:2
Quinn, Jane Bryant 1939(?)- .......... **1993**:4
Quinn, Martha 1959- ....................... **1986**:4
Quivers, Robin 1953(?)- ................. **1995**:4
Ra, Sun
   See Sun Ra
Rabbitt, Eddie 1941-1998
   Obituary ........................ **1998**:4
Rabin, Leah 1928-2000
   Obituary ........................ **2001**:2
Rabin, Yitzhak 1922-1995 ............... **1993**:1
   Obituary ........................ **1996**:2
Radcliffe, Daniel 1989- ................... **2007**:4
Radecki, Thomas
   Brief entry ..................... **1986**:2
Radiohead ....................................... **2009**:3
Radner, Gilda 1946-1989
   Obituary ........................ **1989**:4
Radocy, Robert
   Brief entry ..................... **1986**:3
Raffi 1948- ....................................... **1988**:1
Rafsanjani, Ali Akbar Hashemi
   1934(?)- .......................... **1987**:3
Rafter, Patrick 1972- ....................... **2001**:1
Rahman, Sheik Omar Abdel- 1938- . **1993**
   :3
Raimi, Sam 1959- ............................ **1999**:2
Raimondi, John
   Brief entry ..................... **1987**:4
Raines, Franklin 1949- .................... **1997**:4
Rainier III, Prince of Monaco 1923-2005
   Obituary ........................ **2006**:2
Raitt, Bonnie 1949- ......................... **1990**:2
Raitt, John 1917-2005
   Obituary ........................ **2006**:2
Rajneesh, Bhagwan Shree 1931-1990
   Obituary ........................ **1990**:2
Ram, Jagjivan 1908-1986
   Obituary ........................ **1986**:4
Ramaphosa, Cyril 1953- ................. **1988**:2
Ramaphosa, Matamela Cyril
   See Ramaphosa, Cyril
Ramey, Estelle R. 1917-2006
   Obituary ........................ **2007**:4
Ramirez, Manny 1972- ................... **2005**:4
Ramo, Roberta Cooper 1942- ........ **1996**:1
Ramone, Joey 1951-2001
   Obituary ........................ **2002**:2
Ramos, Fidel 1928- ......................... **1995**:2
Rampal, Jean-Pierre 1922- ............. **1989**:2
Ramsay, Gordon 1966- ................... **2008**:2
Ramsay, Mike 1950(?)- ................... **2002**:1
Rand, A. Barry 1944- ...................... **2000**:3
Randall, Lisa 1962- ......................... **2009**:2
Randall, Tony 1920-2004
   Obituary ........................ **2005**:3
Randi, James 1928- ......................... **1990**:2
Rao, P. V. Narasimha 1921- ............ **1993**:2
Raphael, Sally Jessy 1943- ............. **1992**:4
Rapp, Carl Joseph
   See Rapp, C.J.
Rapp, C.J.
   Brief entry ..................... **1987**:3
Rascal Flatts ..................................... **2007**:1

Rashad, Phylicia 1948- ................... **1987**:3
Raskin, Jef 1943(?)- ......................... **1997**:4
Rasmussen, Anders Fogh 1953- .... **2006**:1
Rattle, Simon 1955- ........................ **1989**:4
Rauschenberg, Robert 1925- ......... **1991**:2
Ravalomanana, Marc 1950(?)- ....... **2003**:1
Raven 1985- ..................................... **2005**:1
Rawlings, Mike 1954- ..................... **2003**:1
Rawls, Lou 1933-2006
   Obituary ........................ **2007**:1
Ray, Amy
   See Indigo Girls
Ray, James Earl 1928-1998
   Obituary ........................ **1998**:4
Ray, Rachael 1968- .......................... **2007**:1
Raye, Martha 1916-1994
   Obituary ........................ **1995**:1
Raymond, Lee R. 1930- .................. **2000**:3
Reagan, Ronald 1911-2004
   Obituary ........................ **2005**:3
Reasoner, Harry 1923-1991
   Obituary ........................ **1992**:4
Redenbacher, Orville 1907-1995
   Obituary ........................ **1996**:1
Redfield, James 1952- ..................... **1995**:2
Redford, Robert 1937- .................... **1993**:2
Redgrave, Lynn 1943- ..................... **1999**:3
Redgrave, Vanessa 1937- ............... **1989**:2
Red Hot Chili Peppers .................... **1993**:1
Redig, Patrick 1948- ....................... **1985**:3
Redman, Joshua 1969- ................... **1999**:2
Redmond, Tim 1947- ...................... **2008**:1
Redstone, Sumner 1923- ................ **1994**:1
Reed, Dean 1939(?)-1986
   Obituary ........................ **1986**:3
Reed, Donna 1921-1986
   Obituary ........................ **1986**:1
Reed, Ralph 1961(?)- ...................... **1995**:1
Reed, Robert 1933(?)-1992
   Obituary ........................ **1992**:4
Reese, Della 1931- .......................... **1999**:2
Reeve, Christopher 1952- ............... **1997**:2
Reeves, Keanu 1964- ....................... **1992**:1
Reeves, Steve 1926-2000
   Obituary ........................ **2000**:4
Regan, Judith 1953- ........................ **2003**:1
Rehnquist, William H. 1924- ......... **2001**:2
Reich, Robert 1946- ........................ **1995**:4
Reichs, Kathleen J. 1948- ............... **2007**:3
Reid, Harry 1939- ........................... **2006**:1
Reid, Vernon
   See Living Colour
Reilly, Charles Nelson
   Obituary ........................ **2008**:3
Reilly, John C. 1965- ....................... **2003**:4
Reiner, Rob 1947- ........................... **1991**:2
Reiser, Paul 1957- ........................... **1995**:2
Reisman, Simon 1919- .................... **1987**:4
Reisman, Sol Simon
   See Reisman, Simon
Reisz, Karel 1926-2002
   Obituary ........................ **2004**:1
Reitman, Ivan 1946- ....................... **1986**:3
Remick, Lee 1936(?)-1991
   Obituary ........................ **1992**:1
Rendell, Ruth 1930- ........................ **2007**:2
Reno, Janet 1938- ........................... **1993**:3
Renvall, Johan
   Brief entry ..................... **1987**:4
Retton, Mary Lou 1968- ................. **1985**:2
Reuben, Gloria 1964- ...................... **1999**:4
Reubens, Paul 1952- ....................... **1987**:2

Rey, Margret E. 1906-1996
  Obituary ........................... **1997**:2
Reynolds, Paula Rosput 1956- ....... **2008**:4
Reza, Yasmina 1959(?)- ................. **1999**:2
Reznor, Trent 1965- ........................ **2000**:2
Rhea, Caroline 1964- ...................... **2004**:1
Rhodes, Zandra 1940- ................... **1986**:2
Rhys Meyers, Jonathan 1977- ........ **2007**:1
Ribicoff, Abraham 1910-1998
  Obituary ........................... **1998**:3
Ricci, Christina 1980- ..................... **1999**:1
Rice, Anne 1941- ............................ **1995**:1
Rice, Condoleezza 1954- ................ **2002**:1
Rice, Jerry 1962- ............................ **1990**:4
Rice, Peter 1967(?)- ....................... **2007**:2
Rich, Bernard
  See Rich, Buddy
Rich, Buddy 1917-1987
  Obituary ........................... **1987**:3
Rich, Charlie 1932-1995
  Obituary ........................... **1996**:1
Richard, Maurice 1921-2000
  Obituary ........................... **2000**:4
Richards, Ann 1933- ....................... **1991**:2
Richards, Keith 1943- ..................... **1993**:3
Richards, Lloyd 1919-2006
  Obituary ........................... **2007**:3
Richards, Michael 1949(?)- ............ **1993**:4
Richmond, Julius B. 1916-2008
  Obituary ........................... **2009**:4
Richter, Charles Francis 1900-1985
  Obituary ........................... **1985**:4
Richter, Gerhard 1932- ................... **1997**:2
Rickover, Hyman 1900-1986
  Obituary ........................... **1986**:4
Riddle, Nelson 1921-1985
  Obituary ........................... **1985**:4
Ridenhour, Carlton
  See Public Enemy
Ridge, Tom 1945- ........................... **2002**:2
Rifkin, Jeremy 1945- ...................... **1990**:3
Riggio, Leonard S. 1941- ............... **1999**:4
Riggs, Bobby 1918-1995
  Obituary ........................... **1996**:2
Rigopulos, Alex 1970- .................... **2009**:4
Rihanna 1988- ................................ **2008**:4
Riley, Pat 1945- .............................. **1994**:3
Riley, Richard W. 1933- ................. **1996**:3
Rimes, LeeAnn 1982- .................... **1997**:4
Riney, Hal 1932- ............................ **1989**:1
Ringgold, Faith 1930- ..................... **2000**:3
Ringwald, Molly 1968- ................... **1985**:4
Riordan, Richard 1930- .................. **1993**:4
Ripa, Kelly 1970- ........................... **2002**:2
Ripken, Cal, Jr. 1960- ..................... **1986**:2
Ripken, Cal, Sr. 1936(?)-1999
  Obituary ........................... **1999**:4
Ripken, Calvin Edwin, Jr.
  See Ripken, Cal, Jr.
Ritchie, Dennis
  See Ritchie, Dennis and Kenneth
    Thompson
Ritchie, Dennis and Kenneth
  Thompson ..................... **2000**:1
Ritchie, Guy 1968- ......................... **2001**:3
Ritter, John 1948- ........................... **2003**:4
Ritts, Herb 1954(?)- ........................ **1992**:4
Rivera, Geraldo 1943- .................... **1989**:1
Rivers, Joan 1933- .......................... **2005**:3
Rizzo, Frank 1920-1991
  Obituary ........................... **1992**:1
Rizzoli, Paola 1943(?)- ................... **2004**:3

Robards, Jason 1922-2000
  Obituary ........................... **2001**:3
Robb, Charles S. 1939- ................... **1987**:2
Robbins, Harold 1916-1997
  Obituary ........................... **1998**:1
Robbins, Jerome 1918-1998
  Obituary ........................... **1999**:1
Robbins, Tim 1959- ........................ **1993**:1
Robelo, Alfonso 1940(?)- ............... **1988**:1
Roberts, Brian L. 1959- .................. **2002**:4
Roberts, Cokie 1943- ..................... **1993**:4
Roberts, Corinne Boggs
  See Roberts, Cokie
Roberts, Doris 1930- ...................... **2003**:4
Roberts, Julia 1967- ....................... **1991**:3
Roberts, Steven K. 1952(?)- ........... **1992**:1
Roberts, Xavier 1955- .................... **1985**:3
Robertson, Marion Gordon
  See Robertson, Pat
Robertson, Pat 1930- ...................... **1988**:2
Robinson, David 1965- ................... **1990**:4
Robinson, Earl 1910(?)-1991
  Obituary ........................... **1992**:1
Robinson, Eddie 1919-2007
  Obituary ........................... **2008**:2
Robinson, Frank 1935- .................... **1990**:2
Robinson, Mary 1944- .................... **1993**:1
Robinson, Max 1939-1988
  Obituary ........................... **1989**:2
Robinson, Peter 1950- .................... **2007**:4
Robinson, Sugar Ray 1921-1989
  Obituary ........................... **1989**:3
Robinson, V. Gene 1947- ............... **2004**:4
Roche, Eamonn Kevin
  See Roche, Kevin
Roche, Kevin 1922- ........................ **1985**:1
Rock, Chris 1967(?)- ...................... **1998**:1
Rock, John
  Obituary ........................... **1985**:1
Rock, The 1972- ............................. **2001**:2
Rockwell, David 1956- ................... **2003**:3
Roddenberry, Gene 1921-1991
  Obituary ........................... **1992**:2
Roddick, Andy 1982- ...................... **2004**:3
Roddick, Anita 1943(?)- ................. **1989**:4
Rodin, Judith 1945(?)- .................... **1994**:4
Rodman, Dennis 1961- ................... **1991**:3
Rodriguez, Alex 1975- .................... **2001**:2
Rodriguez, Narciso 1961- ............... **2005**:1
Rodriguez, Robert 1968- ................ **2005**:1
Roedy, Bill 1949(?)- ....................... **2003**:2
Roemer, Buddy 1943- ..................... **1991**:4
Rogen, Seth 1982- .......................... **2009**:3
Rogers, Adrian 1931- ...................... **1987**:4
Rogers, Fred 1928- ......................... **2000**:4
Rogers, Ginger 1911(?)-1995
  Obituary ........................... **1995**:4
Rogers, Norman
  See Public Enemy
Rogers, Roy 1911-1998
  Obituary ........................... **1998**:4
Rogers, Samuel Shepard, III
  See Shepard, Sam
Rogers, William P. 1913-2001
  Obituary ........................... **2001**:4
Roh Moo-hyun 1946- ..................... **2005**:1
Roizen, Michael 1946- .................... **2007**:4
Roker, Al 1954- .............................. **2003**:1
Roker, Roxie 1929(?)-1995
  Obituary ........................... **1996**:2
Rolle, Esther 1922-1998
  Obituary ........................... **1999**:2

Rollins, Henry 1961- ...................... **2007**:3
Rollins, Howard E., Jr. 1950- ......... **1986**:1
Romano, Ray 1957- ....................... **2001**:4
Romijn, Rebecca 1972- .................. **2007**:1
Romo, Tony 1980- .......................... **2008**:3
Ronaldinho 1980- ........................... **2007**:3
Ronaldo 1976- ................................ **1999**:2
Roncal, Mally 1972- ....................... **2009**:4
Ronson, Charlotte 1977(?)- ............ **2007**:3
Rooney, Art 1901-1988
  Obituary ........................... **1989**:1
Roosevelt, Franklin D., Jr. 1914-1988
  Obituary ........................... **1989**:1
Rose, Axl 1962(?)- .......................... **1992**:1
Rose, Charlie 1943- ........................ **1994**:2
Rose, Pete 1941- ............................. **1991**:1
Rosenberg, Evelyn 1942- ............... **1988**:2
Rosenberg, Steven 1940- ................ **1989**:1
Rosendahl, Bruce R.
  Brief entry ....................... **1986**:4
Rosenfeld, Irene 1953- ................... **2008**:3
Rosenthal, Joseph 1911-2006
  Obituary ........................... **2007**:4
Rosenzweig, Ilene 1965(?)- ........... **2004**:1
Rosgen, Dave 1942(?)- ................... **2005**:2
Ros-Lehtinen, Ileana 1952- ............ **2000**:2
Ross, Herbert 1927-2001
  Obituary ........................... **2002**:4
Ross, Percy
  Brief entry ....................... **1986**:2
Ross, Steven J. 1927-1992
  Obituary ........................... **1993**:3
Rossellini, Isabella 1952- ............... **2001**:4
Rossner, Judith 1935-2005
  Obituary ........................... **2006**:4
Rosso, Renzo 1955- ....................... **2005**:2
Rosten, Leo 1908-1997
  Obituary ........................... **1997**:3
Rostropovich, Mstislav 1927-2007
  Obituary ........................... **2008**:3
Roth, Philip 1933- .......................... **1999**:1
Roth, Tim 1961- ............................. **1998**:2
Roth, William Victor, Jr. 1921-2003
  Obituary ........................... **2005**:1
Rothenberg, Susan 1945- ............... **1995**:3
Rothschild, Philippe de 1902-1988
  Obituary ........................... **1988**:2
Rothstein, Ruth ............................... **1988**:2
Rothwax, Harold 1930- .................. **1996**:3
Rourke, Mickey 1956- .................... **1988**:4
Rourke, Philip Andre
  See Rourke, Mickey
Rouse, James 1914-1996
  Obituary ........................... **1996**:4
Rove, Karl 1950- ............................ **2006**:2
Rowan, Carl 1925-2000
  Obituary ........................... **2001**:2
Rowan, Dan 1922-1987
  Obituary ........................... **1988**:1
Rowe, Jack 1944- ........................... **2005**:2
Rowland, Pleasant ......................... **1992**:3
Rowley, Coleen 1955(?)- ................ **2004**:2
Rowley, Cynthia 1958- ................... **2002**:1
Rowling, J.K. 1965- ....................... **2000**:1
Roy, Patrick 1965- ......................... **1994**:2
Roybal-Allard, Lucille 1941- .......... **1999**:4
Royko, Mike 1932-1997
  Obituary ........................... **1997**:4
Rozelle, Pete 1926-1996
  Obituary ........................... **1997**:2
Rubin, Jerry 1938-1994
  Obituary ........................... **1995**:2

Rucker, Darius 1966(?)-
    See Hootie and the Blowfish
Rudd, Kevin 1957- ......................... **2009**:1
Rudd, Paul 1969- ........................... **2009**:4
Rudner, Rita 1956- ......................... **1993**:2
Rudnick, Paul 1957(?)- ................... **1994**:3
Rudolph, Wilma 1940-1994
    Obituary ................................. **1995**:2
Ruehl, Mercedes 195(?)- ............... **1992**:4
Ruffin, David 1941-1991
    Obituary ................................. **1991**:4
Rugova, Ibrahim 1944-2006
    Obituary ................................. **2007**:1
Rumsfeld, Donald 1932- ............... **2004**:1
Runcie, Robert 1921-2000 ............. **1989**:4
    Obituary ................................. **2001**:1
Runyan, Marla 1969- ..................... **2001**:1
RuPaul 1961(?)- ............................. **1996**:1
Ruppe, Loret Miller 1936- ............ **1986**:2
Rush, Geoffrey 1951- ..................... **2002**:1
Rushdie, Salman 1947- .................. **1994**:1
Rusk, Dean 1909-1994
    Obituary ................................. **1995**:2
Russell, Keri 1976- ........................ **2000**:1
Russell, Kurt 1951- ....................... **2007**:4
Russell, Mary 1950- ...................... **2009**:2
Russell, Nipsey 1924-2005
    Obituary ................................. **2007**:1
Russert, Tim 1950-2008
    Obituary ................................. **2009**:3
Russo, Patricia 1952- ..................... **2008**:4
Russo, Rene 1954- ......................... **2000**:2
Russo, Richard 1949- ..................... **2002**:3
Rutan, Burt 1943- .......................... **1987**:2
Ryan, Meg 1962(?)- ....................... **1994**:1
Ryan, Nolan 1947- ........................ **1989**:4
Ryder, Carl
    See Public Enemy
Ryder, Winona 1971- ..................... **1991**:2
Rykiel, Sonia 1930- ....................... **2000**:3
Rylance, Mark 1960- ...................... **2009**:3
Rypien, Mark 1962- ....................... **1992**:3
Saakashvili, Mikhail 1967- ............ **2008**:4
Saatchi, Charles 1943- ................... **1987**:3
Saatchi, Maurice 1946- .................. **1995**:4
Sabatini, Gabriela
    Brief entry ............................. **1985**:4
Saberhagen, Bret 1964- ................. **1986**:1
Sabin, Albert 1906-1993
    Obituary ................................. **1993**:4
Sachs, Jeffrey D. 1954- .................. **2004**:4
Sacks, Oliver 1933- ....................... **1995**:4
Sade 1959- ..................................... **1993**:2
Sadler, Eric
    See Public Enemy
Safin, Marat 1980- ........................ **2001**:3
Safire, William 1929- ..................... **2000**:3
Sagal, Katey 1954- ......................... **2005**:2
Sagan, Carl 1934-1996
    Obituary ................................. **1997**:2
Sagansky, Jeff 1952- ...................... **1993**:2
Sainte-Marie, Buffy 1941- ............. **2000**:1
Saint Laurent, Yves 1936-2008
    Obituary ................................. **2009**:3
Sajak, Pat
    Brief entry ............................. **1985**:4
Sakharov, Andrei Dmitrievich
    1921-1989
    Obituary ................................. **1990**:2
Sakic, Joe 1969- ............................ **2002**:1
Salbi, Zainab 1969(?)- ................... **2008**:3
Saleh, Ali Abdullah 1942- ............. **2001**:3

Salerno-Sonnenberg, Nadja
    1961(?)- ................................. **1988**:4
Salgado, Sebastiao 1944- ............... **1994**:2
Saliers, Emily
    See Indigo Girls
Salinas, Carlos 1948- ..................... **1992**:1
Salinas de Gortari, Carlos
    See Salinas, Carlos
Salk, Jonas 1914-1995 ................... **1994**:4
    Obituary ................................. **1995**:4
Salonga, Lea 1971- ........................ **2003**:3
Salzman, Mark 1959- ..................... **2002**:1
Samaranch, Juan Antonio 1920- .... **1986**:2
Sammons, Mary 1946- ................... **2007**:4
Sample, Bill
    Brief entry ............................. **1986**:2
Sampras, Pete 1971- ...................... **1994**:1
Sams, Craig 1944- .......................... **2007**:3
Samuel, Sealhenry Olumide
    See Seal
Sanchez, Loretta 1960- .................. **2000**:3
Sanchez, Oscar Arias
    See Arias Sanchez, Oscar
Sanchez de Lozada, Gonzalo
    1930- ..................................... **2004**:3
Sander, Jil 1943- ........................... **1995**:2
Sanders, Barry 1968- ..................... **1992**:1
Sanders, Bernie 1941(?)- ............... **1991**:4
Sanders, Deion 1967- .................... **1992**:4
Sandler, Adam 1966- ..................... **1999**:2
Sanford, John Elroy
    See Foxx, Redd
Sanger, Steve 1946- ....................... **2002**:3
Santana, Carlos 1947- ................... **2000**:2
Santana, Johan 1979- .................... **2008**:1
Saporta, Vicki
    Brief entry ............................. **1987**:3
Sapphire 1951(?)- .......................... **1996**:4
Saralegui, Cristina 1948- ............... **1999**:2
Saramago, Jose 1922- .................... **1999**:1
Sarandon, Susan 1946- .................. **1995**:3
Sarazen, Gene 1902-1999
    Obituary ................................. **1999**:4
Sargsyan, Serzh 1954- ................... **2009**:3
Sarkis, Elias 1924-1985
    Obituary ................................. **1985**:3
Sarkisian, Cherilyn
    See Cher
Sarkozy, Nicolas 1955- .................. **2008**:4
Saro-Wiwa, Ken 1941-1995
    Obituary ................................. **1996**:2
Sarraute, Nathalie 1900-1999
    Obituary ................................. **2000**:2
Sasakawa, Ryoichi
    Brief entry ............................. **1988**:1
Satcher, David 1941- ..................... **2001**:4
Satrapi, Marjane 1969- .................. **2006**:3
Satriani, Joe 1957(?)- .................... **1989**:3
Saul, Betsy 1968- .......................... **2009**:2
Savage, Fred 1976- ........................ **1990**:1
Savalas, Telly 1924-1994
    Obituary ................................. **1994**:3
Savimbi, Jonas 1934- ..................... **1986**:2
Sawyer, Diane 1945- ...................... **1994**:4
Scalia, Antonin 1936- .................... **1988**:2
Scardino, Marjorie 1947- ............... **2002**:1
Scavullo, Francesco 1921-2004
    Obituary ................................. **2005**:1
Schaap, Dick 1934-2001
    Obituary ................................. **2003**:1
Schaefer, William Donald 1921- .... **1988**:1
Schank, Roger 1946- ...................... **1989**:2

Scheck, Barry 1949- ...................... **2000**:4
Scheider, Roy 1932-2008
    Obituary ................................. **2009**:2
Schembechler, Bo 1929(?)- ............ **1990**:3
Schembechler, Glenn Edward, Jr.
    See Schembechler, Bo
Schenk, Dale 1957(?)- ................... **2002**:2
Schiavo, Mary 1955- ...................... **1998**:2
Schilling, Curt 1966- ..................... **2002**:3
Schily, Otto
    Brief entry ............................. **1987**:4
Schirra, Wally 1923-2007
    Obituary ................................. **2008**:3
Schlesinger, John 1926-2003
    Obituary ................................. **2004**:3
Schlessinger, David
    Brief entry ............................. **1985**:2
Schlessinger, Laura 1947(?)- .......... **1996**:3
Schmelzer, Sheri 1965- .................. **2009**:4
Schmidt, Eric 1955- ...................... **2002**:4
Schmidt, Michael Jack
    See Schmidt, Mike
Schmidt, Mike 1949- ..................... **1988**:3
Schnabel, Julian 1951- .................. **1997**:1
Schneerson, Menachem Mendel
    1902-1994 .............................. **1992**:4
    Obituary ................................. **1994**:4
Schneider, Rob 1965- .................... **1997**:4
Schoenfeld, Gerald 1924- .............. **1986**:2
Scholz, Tom 1949- ........................ **1987**:2
Schott, Margaret
    See Schott, Marge
Schott, Marge 1928- ...................... **1985**:4
Schreiber, Liev 1967- .................... **2007**:2
Schrempp, Juergen 1944- .............. **2000**:2
Schroder, Gerhard 1944- ............... **1999**:2
Schroeder, Barbet 1941- ................ **1996**:1
Schroeder, William J. 1932-1986
    Obituary ................................. **1986**:4
Schulefand, Richard
    See Shawn, Dick
Schultes, Richard Evans 1915-2001
    Obituary ................................. **2002**:1
Schultz, Howard 1953- .................. **1995**:3
Schulz, Charles 1922-2000
    Obituary ................................. **2000**:3
Schulz, Charles M. 1922- .............. **1998**:1
Schumacher, Joel 1929- ................. **2004**:3
Schumacher, Michael 1969- ........... **2005**:2
Schuman, Patricia Glass 1943- ...... **1993**:2
Schwab, Charles 1937(?)- .............. **1989**:3
Schwartz, Allen 1945(?)- ............... **2008**:2
Schwartz, David 1936(?)- .............. **1988**:3
Schwarzenegger, Arnold 1947- ...... **1991**:1
Schwarzkopf, Elisabeth 1915-2006
    Obituary ................................. **2007**:3
Schwarzkopf, Norman 1934- .......... **1991**:3
Schwimmer, David 1966(?)- ........... **1996**:2
Schwinn, Edward R., Jr.
    Brief entry ............................. **1985**:4
Scorsese, Martin 1942- .................. **1989**:1
Scott, Gene
    Brief entry ............................. **1986**:1
Scott, George C. 1927-1999
    Obituary ................................. **2000**:2
Scott, George Randolph
    See Scott, Randolph
Scott, H. Lee, Jr. 1949- ................. **2008**:3
Scott, Randolph 1898(?)-1987
    Obituary ................................. **1987**:2
Scott, Ridley 1937- ....................... **2001**:1
Sculley, John 1939- ....................... **1989**:4

Seacrest, Ryan 1976- ..................... **2004**:4
Seal 1962(?)- ............................. **1994**:4
Sears, Barry 1947- ...................... **2004**:2
Sebelius, Kathleen 1948- .............. **2008**:4
Sebold, Alice 1963(?)- .................. **2005**:4
Secretariat 1970-1989
   Obituary ..................... **1990**:1
Sedaris, Amy 1961- ..................... **2009**:3
Sedaris, David 1956- .................. **2005**:3
Sedelmaier, Joe 1933- ................. **1985**:3
Sedelmaier, John Josef
   See Sedelmaier, Joe
Sedgwick, Kyra 1965- .................. **2006**:2
Segal, Shelli 1955(?)- .................. **2005**:3
Seger, Bob 1945- ........................ **1987**:1
Seger, Robert Clark
   See Seger, Bob
Segovia, Andreaas 1893-1987
   Obituary ..................... **1987**:3
Seidelman, Susan 1953(?)- ........... **1985**:4
Seidenberg, Ivan 1946- ............... **2004**:1
Seinfeld, Jerry 1954- .................. **1992**:4
Selena 1971-1995
   Obituary ..................... **1995**:4
Seles, Monica 1974(?)- ................. **1991**:3
Selig, Bud 1934- ........................ **1995**:2
Semel, Terry 1943- ..................... **2002**:2
Sendler, Irena 1910-2008
   Obituary ..................... **2009**:2
Senghor, Leopold 1906-2001
   Obituary ..................... **2003**:1
Senk, Glen 1956- ........................ **2009**:3
Senna, Ayrton 1960(?)-1994 .......... **1991**:4
   Obituary ..................... **1994**:4
Sentamu, John 1949- .................. **2006**:2
Seo, Danny 1977- ....................... **2008**:3
Serkin, Rudolf 1903-1991
   Obituary ..................... **1992**:1
Serra, Richard 1939- ................... **2009**:1
Serrano, Andres 1950- ................. **2000**:4
Serros, Michele 1967(?)- .............. **2008**:2
Sethi, Simran 1971(?)- ................. **2008**:1
Seuss, Dr.
   See Geisel, Theodor
Sevareid, Eric 1912-1992
   Obituary ..................... **1993**:1
Sevigny, Chloe 1974- .................. **2001**:4
Seyfried, Amanda 1985- .............. **2009**:3
Seymour, Jane 1951- ................... **1994**:4
Shabazz, Betty 1936-1997
   Obituary ..................... **1997**:4
Shaffer, Paul 1949- ..................... **1987**:1
Shah, Gyanendra 1947- ............... **2006**:1
Shaich, Ron 1953- ...................... **2004**:4
Shakira 1977- ............................ **2002**:3
Shakur, Tupac 1971-1996
   Obituary ..................... **1997**:1
Shalala, Donna 1941- .................. **1992**:3
Shalikashvili, John 1936- ............. **1994**:2
Shandling, Garry 1949- ............... **1995**:1
Shanley, John Patrick 1950- ......... **2006**:1
Sharapova, Maria 1987- .............. **2005**:2
Sharkey, Ray 1953-1993
   Obituary ..................... **1994**:1
Sharma, Nisha 1982(?)- ............... **2004**:2
Sharon, Ariel 1928- .................... **2001**:4
Sharpe, Sterling 1965- ................ **1994**:3
Sharpton, Al 1954- ..................... **1991**:2
Shaw, Artie 1910-2004
   Obituary ..................... **2006**:1
Shaw, Carol 1958(?)- ................... **2002**:1
Shaw, William 1934(?)- ............... **2000**:3

Shawn, Dick 1924(?)-1987
   Obituary ..................... **1987**:3
Shawn, William 1907-1992
   Obituary ..................... **1993**:3
Shcharansky, Anatoly 1948- ......... **1986**:2
Shea, Jim, Jr. 1968- .................... **2002**:4
Sheedy, Alexandra Elizabeth
   See Sheedy, Ally
Sheedy, Ally 1962- ...................... **1989**:1
Sheehan, Daniel P. 1945(?)- .......... **1989**:1
Sheen, Charlie 1965- ................... **2001**:2
Sheen, Martin 1940- ................... **2002**:1
Sheffield, Gary 1968- .................. **1998**:1
Sheindlin, Judith
   See Sheindlin, Judith
Sheindlin, Judith 1942(?)- ............ **1999**:1
Sheldon, Sidney 1917-2007
   Obituary ..................... **2008**:2
Shepard, Alan 1923-1998
   Obituary ..................... **1999**:1
Shepard, Sam 1943- .................... **1996**:4
Shepherd, Cybill 1950- ................ **1996**:3
Sherba, John
   See Kronos Quartet
Sherman, Cindy 1954- ................. **1992**:3
Sherman, Jack
   See Red Hot Chili Peppers
Sherman, Russell 1930- ............... **1987**:4
Shields, Brooke 1965- .................. **1996**:3
Shields, Carol 1935-2003
   Obituary ..................... **2004**:3
Shilts, Randy 1951-1994 ............... **1993**:4
   Obituary ..................... **1994**:3
Shimomura, Tsutomu 1965- ......... **1996**:1
Shipley, Jenny 1952- ................... **1998**:3
Shirley, Donna 1941- ................... **1999**:1
Shocked, Michelle 1963(?)- ........... **1989**:4
Shocklee, Hank
   See Public Enemy
Shocklee, Keith
   See Public Enemy
Shoemaker, Bill 1931-2003
   Obituary ..................... **2004**:4
Shore, Dinah 1917-1994
   Obituary ..................... **1994**:3
Short, Martin 1950- .................... **1986**:1
Shreve, Anita 1946(?)- ................. **2003**:4
Shriver, Lionel 1957- ................... **2008**:4
Shriver, Maria
   Brief entry ................. **1986**:2
Shue, Andrew 1964- ................... **1994**:4
Shula, Don 1930- ....................... **1992**:2
Shyamalan, M. Night 1970- .......... **2003**:2
Sidney, Ivan
   Brief entry ................. **1987**:2
Sidransky, David 1960- ............... **2002**:4
Siebert, Muriel 1932(?)- ............... **1987**:2
Sigmund, Barbara Boggs 1939-1990
   Obituary ..................... **1991**:1
Silber, Joan 1945- ...................... **2009**:4
Silber, John 1926- ...................... **1990**:1
Silva, Luiz Inacio Lula da 1945- ... **2003**:4
Silverman, Jonathan 1966- .......... **1997**:2
Silverman, Sarah 1970- ............... **2008**:1
Silvers, Phil 1912-1985
   Obituary ..................... **1985**:4
Silversmith, Philip
   See Silvers, Phil
Silverstein, Shel 1932-1999
   Obituary ..................... **1999**:4
Silverstone, Alicia 1976- .............. **1997**:4
Simmons, Adele Smith 1941- ........ **1988**:4

Simmons, Russell and Kimora
   Lee .......................... **2003**:2
Simmons, Ruth 1945- .................. **1995**:2
Simon, Lou Anna K. 1947- ........... **2005**:4
Simon, Paul 1928-2003
   Obituary ..................... **2005**:1
Simon, Paul 1942(?)- ................... **1992**:2
Simone, Nina 1933-2003
   Obituary ..................... **2004**:2
Simpson, Lorna 1960- ................. **2008**:1
Simpson, Wallis 1896-1986
   Obituary ..................... **1986**:3
Simpson-Wentz, Ashlee 1984- ...... **2009**:1
Sin, Jaime 1928-2005
   Obituary ..................... **2006**:3
Sinatra, Frank 1915-1998
   Obituary ..................... **1998**:4
Sinclair, Mary 1918- ................... **1985**:2
Singer, Bryan 1965- .................... **2007**:3
Singer, Isaac Bashevis 1904-1991
   Obituary ..................... **1992**:1
Singer, Margaret Thaler 1921-2003
   Obituary ..................... **2005**:1
Singh, Vijay 1963- ...................... **2000**:4
Singleton, John 1968- .................. **1994**:3
Sinise, Gary 1955(?)- ................... **1996**:1
Sinopoli, Giuseppe 1946- ............ **1988**:1
Sirica, John 1904-1992
   Obituary ..................... **1993**:2
Sirleaf, Ellen Johnson 1938- ......... **2007**:3
Siskel, Gene 1946-1999
   Obituary ..................... **1999**:3
Sisulu, Walter 1912-2003
   Obituary ..................... **2004**:2
Skaist-Levy, Pam and Gela
   Taylor ...................... **2005**:1
Skelton, Red 1913-1997
   Obituary ..................... **1998**:1
Skillings, Muzz
   See Living Colour
Skinner, B.F. 1904-1990
   Obituary ..................... **1991**:1
Skinner, Burrhus Frederic
   See Skinner, B.F.
Skinner, Sam 1938- .................... **1992**:3
Slater, Christian 1969- ................ **1994**:1
Slater, Rodney E. 1955- ............... **1997**:4
Slatkin, Harry 1961(?)- ................ **2006**:2
Slaton, Mary Leta Dorothy
   See Lamour, Dorothy
Slick, Grace 1939- ...................... **2001**:2
Slotnick, Barry
   Brief entry ................. **1987**:4
Slovo, Joe 1926- ........................ **1989**:2
Smale, John G. 1927- .................. **1987**:3
Smigel, Robert 1959(?)- ............... **2001**:3
Smiley, Jane 1949- ..................... **1995**:4
Smirnoff, Yakov 1951- ................. **1987**:2
Smith, Anna Deavere 1950- .......... **2002**:2
Smith, Anna Nicole 1967-2007
   Obituary ..................... **2008**:2
Smith, Anthony Terrell
   See Tone-Loc
Smith, Buffalo Bob 1917-1998
   Obituary ..................... **1999**:1
Smith, Chad
   See Red Hot Chili Peppers
Smith, Emmitt ............................ **1994**:1
Smith, Frederick W. 1944- ........... **1985**:4
Smith, Howard K. 1914-2002
   Obituary ..................... **2003**:2

Smith, Ian 1919-2007
  Obituary ..................... **2009**:1
Smith, Jack 1938- .............. **1994**:3
Smith, Jada Pinkett
  See Pinkett Smith, Jada
Smith, Jeff 1939(?)- ............ **1991**:4
Smith, Jerry 1943-1986
  Obituary ..................... **1987**:1
Smith, Jimmy 1928-2005
  Obituary ..................... **2006**:2
Smith, John Francis
  See Smith, Jack
Smith, Kate 1907(?)-1986
  Obituary ..................... **1986**:3
Smith, Kathryn Elizabeth
  See Smith, Kate
Smith, Kevin 1970- ............. **2000**:4
Smith, Lanty 1942- ............. **2009**:3
Smith, Paul 1946- .............. **2002**:4
Smith, Robert Weston
  See Wolfman Jack
Smith, Roger 1925- ............. **1990**:3
Smith, Samantha 1972-1985
  Obituary ..................... **1985**:3
Smith, Will 1968- .............. **1997**:2
Smith, Willi 1948-1987
  Obituary ..................... **1987**:3
Smith, Zadie 1975- ............. **2003**:4
Smits, Jimmy 1956- ............. **1990**:1
Smoot, George F. 1945- ......... **1993**:3
Smyth, Russell P. 1958- ........ **2009**:4
Snead, Sam 1912-2002
  Obituary ..................... **2003**:3
Snider, Daniel Dee
  See Snider, Dee
Snider, Dee 1955- .............. **1986**:1
Snider, Stacey 1961(?)- ........ **2002**:4
Snipes, Wesley 1962- ........... **1993**:1
Snoop Doggy Dogg 1972(?)- ...... **1995**:2
Snow, Hank 1914-1999
  Obituary ..................... **2000**:3
Snow, John W. 1939- ............ **2006**:2
Snow, Tony 1955-2008
  Obituary ..................... **2009**:3
Snowe, Olympia 1947- ........... **1995**:3
Snyder, Jimmy 1919-1996
  Obituary ..................... **1996**:4
Snyder, Mitch 1944(?)-1990
  Obituary ..................... **1991**:1
Snyder, Ron 1956(?)- ........... **2007**:4
Sobieski, Leelee 1982- ......... **2002**:3
Sobol, Donald J. 1924- ......... **2004**:4
Soderbergh, Steven 1963- ....... **2001**:4
Solti, Georg 1912-1997
  Obituary ..................... **1998**:1
Solzhenitsyn, Aleksandr 1918-2008
  Obituary ..................... **2009**:4
Som, Peter 1971- ............... **2009**:1
Somers, Suzanne 1946- .......... **2000**:1
Sondheim, Stephen 1930- ........ **1994**:4
Sonefeld, Jim 1965(?)-
  See Hootie and the Blowfish
Sontag, Susan 1933-2004
  Obituary ..................... **2006**:1
Soren, David
  Brief entry .................. **1986**:3
Soren, Howard David
  See Soren, David
Sorenstam, Annika 1970- ........ **2001**:1
Soriano, Alfonso 1976- ......... **2008**:1
Sorkin, Aaron 1961- ............ **2003**:2
Sorvino, Mira 1970(?)- ......... **1996**:3

Sosa, Sammy 1968- .............. **1999**:1
Sothern, Ann 1909-2001
  Obituary ..................... **2002**:1
Souter, David 1939- ............ **1991**:3
Southern, Terry 1926-1995
  Obituary ..................... **1996**:2
Sowell, Thomas 1930- ........... **1998**:3
Spacek, Sissy 1949- ............ **2003**:1
Spacey, Kevin 1959- ............ **1996**:4
Spade, David 1965- ............. **1999**:2
Spade, Kate 1962- .............. **2003**:1
Spader, James 1960- ............ **1991**:2
Spahn, Warren 1921-2003
  Obituary ..................... **2005**:1
Spears, Britney 1981- .......... **2000**:3
Spector, Phil 1940- ............ **1989**:1
Spelke, Elizabeth 1949- ........ **2003**:1
Spelling, Aaron 1923-2006
  Obituary ..................... **2007**:3
Spelling, Tori 1973- ........... **2008**:3
Spellings, Margaret 1957- ...... **2005**:4
Spergel, David 1961- ........... **2004**:1
Spheeris, Penelope 1945(?)- .... **1989**:2
Spice Girls ................... **2008**:3
Spiegelman, Art 1948- .......... **1998**:3
Spielberg, Steven 1947- ........ **1993**:4
Spillane, Mickey 1918-2006
  Obituary ..................... **2007**:3
Spitzer, Eliot 1959- ........... **2007**:2
Spock, Benjamin 1903-1998 ...... **1995**:2
  Obituary ..................... **1998**:3
Spong, John 1931- .............. **1991**:3
Spray, Ed 1941- ................ **2004**:1
Sprewell, Latrell 1970- ........ **1999**:4
Springer, Jerry 1944- .......... **1998**:4
Springfield, Dusty 1939-1999
  Obituary ..................... **1999**:3
Sprouse, Stephen 1953-2004
  Obituary ..................... **2005**:2
St. James, Lyn 1947- ........... **1993**:2
Stack, Robert 1919-2003
  Obituary ..................... **2004**:2
Stafford, Jo 1917-2008
  Obituary ..................... **2009**:3
Stahl, Lesley 1941- ............ **1997**:1
Staller, Ilona
  See Staller, Ilona
Staller, Ilona 1951- ........... **1988**:3
Stallings, George A., Jr. 1948- **1990**:1
Stallone, Sylvester 1946- ...... **1994**:2
Stamos, John 1963- ............. **2008**:1
Staples, Roebuck Pops 1915-2000
  Obituary ..................... **2001**:3
Stapleton, Maureen 1925-2006
  Obituary ..................... **2007**:2
Starck, Philippe 1949- ......... **2004**:1
Stargell, Willie 1940-2001
  Obituary ..................... **2002**:1
Starr, Kenneth 1946- ........... **1998**:3
Steel, Danielle 1947- .......... **1999**:2
Steel, Dawn 1946-1997 .......... **1990**:1
  Obituary ..................... **1998**:2
Steele, Shelby 1946- ........... **1991**:2
Stefani, Gwen 1969- ............ **2005**:4
Stefanidis, John 1937- ......... **2007**:3
Steger, Will 1945(?)- .......... **1990**:4
Steig, William 1907-2003
  Obituary ..................... **2004**:4
Steiger, Rod 1925-2002
  Obituary ..................... **2003**:4
Stein, Ben 1944- ............... **2001**:1

Stein, Julius Kerwin
  See Stein, Jule
Steinberg, Leigh 1949- ......... **1987**:3
Steinbrenner, George 1930- ..... **1991**:1
Steinem, Gloria 1934- .......... **1996**:2
Stella, Frank 1936- ............ **1996**:2
Stempel, Robert 1933- .......... **1991**:3
Stephanopoulos, George 1961- ... **1994**:3
Stephens, Arran and Ratana ..... **2008**:4
Stephney, Bill
  See Public Enemy
Steptoe, Patrick 1913-1988
  Obituary ..................... **1988**:3
Sterling, Bruce 1954- .......... **1995**:4
Stern, David 1942- ............. **1991**:4
Stern, Howard 1954- ............ **1988**:2
Stern, Isaac 1920-2001
  Obituary ..................... **2002**:4
Stevens, Anne 1949(?)- ......... **2006**:3
Stevens, Eileen 1939- .......... **1987**:3
Stevens, James
  Brief entry .................. **1988**:1
Stevenson, McLean 1929-1996
  Obituary ..................... **1996**:3
Stewart, Dave 1957- ............ **1991**:1
Stewart, Jimmy 1908-1997
  Obituary ..................... **1997**:4
Stewart, Jon 1962- ............. **2001**:2
Stewart, Julia 1955- ........... **2008**:3
Stewart, Martha 1942(?)- ....... **1992**:1
Stewart, Patrick 1940- ......... **1996**:1
Stewart, Payne 1957-1999
  Obituary ..................... **2000**:2
Stewart, Potter 1915-1985
  Obituary ..................... **1986**:1
Stewart, Rod 1945- ............. **2007**:1
Stewart, Tony 1971- ............ **2003**:4
Stiles, Julia 1981- ............ **2002**:3
Stiller, Ben 1965- ............. **1999**:1
Stine, R. L. 1943- ............. **2003**:1
Sting 1951- .................... **1991**:4
Stockman, Shawn
  See Boyz II Men
Stockton, John Houston 1962- ... **1997**:3
Stockton, Shreve 1977- ......... **2009**:4
Stofflet, Ty
  Brief entry .................. **1987**:1
Stofflet, Tyrone Earl
  See Stofflet, Ty
Stokes, Carl 1927-1996
  Obituary ..................... **1996**:4
Stoltenberg, Jens 1959- ........ **2006**:4
Stone, I.F. 1907-1989
  Obituary ..................... **1990**:1
Stone, Irving 1903-1989
  Obituary ..................... **1990**:2
Stone, Isidor Feinstein
  See Stone, I.F.
Stone, Joss 1987- .............. **2006**:2
Stone, Matt
  See Parker, Trey and Matt Stone
Stone, Oliver 1946- ............ **1990**:4
Stone, Sharon 1958- ............ **1993**:4
Stonesifer, Patty 1956- ........ **1997**:1
Stoppard, Tom 1937- ............ **1995**:4
Strait, George 1952- ........... **1998**:3
Strange, Curtis 1955- .......... **1988**:4
Strauss, Robert 1918- .......... **1991**:4
Streep, Meryl 1949- ............ **1990**:2
Street, Picabo 1971- ........... **1999**:3
Streisand, Barbra 1942- ........ **1992**:2
Stritch, Elaine 1925- .......... **2002**:4

Strobl, Fritz 1972- ......................... **2003**:3
Stroessner, Alfredo 1912-2006
  Obituary ..................................... **2007**:4
Stroh, Peter W. 1927- ..................... **1985**:2
Stroman, Susan ........................... **2000**:4
Strong, Maurice 1929- .................... **1993**:1
Strout, Elizabeth 1956- ................... **2009**:1
Strug, Kerri 1977- ......................... **1997**:3
Strummer, Joe 1952-2002
  Obituary ..................................... **2004**:1
Studi, Wes 1944(?)- ....................... **1994**:3
Styler, Trudie 1954- ....................... **2009**:1
Styne, Jule 1905-1994
  Obituary ..................................... **1995**:1
Styron, William 1925-2006
  Obituary ..................................... **2008**:1
Suarez, Xavier
  Brief entry ................................. **1986**:2
Suckling, Kierán 1964- ................... **2009**:2
Sugarland 1970- ........................... **2009**:2
Suharto 1921-2008
  Obituary ..................................... **2009**:2
Sui, Anna 1955(?)- ......................... **1995**:1
Sullivan, Andrew 1964(?)- .............. **1996**:1
Sullivan, Leon 1922-2001
  Obituary ..................................... **2002**:2
Sullivan, Louis 1933- ..................... **1990**:4
Sulzberger, Arthur O., Jr. 1951- ..... **1998**:3
Summers, Anne 1945- ..................... **1990**:2
Summitt, Pat 1952- ......................... **2004**:1
Sumner, Gordon Matthew
  See Sting
Sun Ra 1914(?)-1993
  Obituary ..................................... **1994**:1
Sununu, John 1939- ....................... **1989**:2
Susskind, David 1920-1987
  Obituary ..................................... **1987**:2
Sutherland, Kiefer 1966- ................ **2002**:4
Suu Kyi, Aung San 1945(?)- ........... **1996**:2
Suzman, Helen 1917- ..................... **1989**:3
Suzuki, Ichiro 1973- ....................... **2002**:2
Suzuki, Sin'ichi 1898-1998
  Obituary ..................................... **1998**:3
Svenigsson, Magnus
  See Cardigans, The
Svensson, Peter
  See Cardigans, The
Swaggart, Jimmy 1935- .................. **1987**:3
Swank, Hilary 1974- ....................... **2000**:3
Swanson, Mary Catherine 1944- ... **2002**:2
Swayze, John Cameron 1906-1995
  Obituary ..................................... **1996**:1
Sweeney, John J. 1934- ................... **2000**:3
Swift, Jane 1965(?)- ....................... **2002**:1
Swift, Taylor 1989- ......................... **2009**:3
Swinton, Tilda 1960- ....................... **2008**:4
Swoopes, Sheryl 1971- ................... **1998**:2
Sykes, Wanda 1964- ....................... **2007**:4
Synodinos, Emitrios George
  See Snyder, Jimmy
System of a Down ......................... **2006**:4
Szent-Gyoergyi, Albert 1893-1986
  Obituary ..................................... **1987**:2
Szot, Paulo 1969- ......................... **2009**:3
T. I. 1980- ..................................... **2008**:1
Tadic, Boris 1958- ......................... **2009**:3
Tafel, Richard 1962- ....................... **2000**:4
Tagliabue, Paul 1940- ..................... **1990**:2
Takada, Kenzo 1938- ..................... **2003**:2
Takei, Kei 1946- ........................... **1990**:2
Takeshita, Noboru 1924-2000
  Obituary ..................................... **2001**:1

Tamayo, Rufino 1899-1991
  Obituary ..................................... **1992**:1
Tambo, Oliver 1917- ....................... **1991**:3
Tan, Amy 1952- ............................. **1998**:3
Tanaka, Tomoyuki 1910-1997
  Obituary ..................................... **1997**:3
Tan Dun 1957- ............................... **2002**:1
Tandy, Jessica 1901-1994 .............. **1990**:4
  Obituary ..................................... **1995**:1
Tange, Kenzo 1913-2005
  Obituary ..................................... **2006**:2
Taniguchi, Yoshio 1937- ................ **2005**:4
Tannen, Deborah 1945- .................. **1995**:1
Tanny, Vic 1912(?)-1985
  Obituary ..................................... **1985**:3
Tarantino, Quentin 1963(?)- ........... **1995**:1
Taree, Aerle
  See Arrested Development
Tarkenian, Jerry 1930- ................... **1990**:4
Tartakovsky, Genndy 1970- ........... **2004**:4
Tartikoff, Brandon 1949-1997 ......... **1985**:2
  Obituary ..................................... **1998**:1
Tartt, Donna 1963- ......................... **2004**:3
Tautou, Audrey 1978- ..................... **2004**:2
Taylor, Elizabeth 1932- ................... **1993**:3
Taylor, Graham 1958(?)- ................. **2005**:3
Taylor, Jeff 1960- ........................... **2001**:3
Taylor, Lawrence 1959- ................... **1987**:3
Taylor, Lili 1967- ........................... **2000**:2
Taylor, Maxwell 1901-1987
  Obituary ..................................... **1987**:3
Taylor, Paul 1930- ......................... **1992**:3
Taylor, Susan L. 1946- ................... **1998**:2
Tellem, Nancy 1953(?)- ................... **2004**:4
Temperley, Alice 1975- ................... **2008**:2
Tenet, George 1953- ....................... **2000**:3
Teresa, Mother
  See Mother Teresa
Terry, Randall ............................... **1991**:4
Terzi, Zehdi Labib 1924- ................ **1985**:3
Tesh, John 1952- ........................... **1996**:3
Testaverde, Vinny 1962- ................ **1987**:2
Testino, Mario 1954- ....................... **2002**:1
Teter, Hannah 1987- ....................... **2006**:4
Thain, John 1955- ........................... **2009**:2
Thaksin Shinawatra 1949- .............. **2005**:4
Thalheimer, Richard 1948-
  Brief entry ................................. **1988**:3
Tharp, Twyla 1942- ......................... **1992**:4
Thatcher, Margaret 1925- .............. **1989**:2
Theron, Charlize 1975- ................... **2001**:4
Thiebaud, Wayne 1920- ................. **1991**:1
Tho, Le Duc
  See Le Duc Tho
Thom, Rene 1923-2002
  Obituary ..................................... **2004**:1
Thomas, Clarence 1948- ................ **1992**:2
Thomas, Danny 1914-1991
  Obituary ..................................... **1991**:3
Thomas, Dave ............................... **1986**:2
  Obituary ..................................... **2003**:1
Thomas, Debi 1967- ....................... **1987**:2
Thomas, Derrick 1967-2000
  Obituary ..................................... **2000**:3
Thomas, Edmond J. 1943(?)- ......... **2005**:1
Thomas, Frank 1968- ..................... **1994**:3
Thomas, Helen 1920- ..................... **1988**:4
Thomas, Isiah 1961- ....................... **1989**:2
Thomas, Michael Tilson 1944- ....... **1990**:3
Thomas, Michel 1911(?)- ................ **1987**:4
Thomas, R. David
  See Thomas, Dave

Thomas, Rozonda Chilli
  See TLC
Thomas, Thurman 1966- .............. **1993**:1
Thomas, Todd (Speech)
  See Arrested Development
Thomas-Graham, Pamela 1963- .... **2007**:1
Thomason, Linda Bloodworth
  See Bloodworth-Thomason, Linda
Thompson, Emma 1959- ................ **1993**:2
Thompson, Fred 1942- ................... **1998**:2
Thompson, Hunter S. 1939- ........... **1992**:1
Thompson, John 1941- ................... **1988**:3
Thompson, John W. 1949- .............. **2005**:1
Thompson, Kenneth
  See Ritchie, Dennis and Kenneth
  Thompson
Thompson, Lonnie 1948- ................ **2003**:3
Thompson, Starley
  Brief entry ................................. **1987**:3
Thomson, James 1958- ................... **2002**:3
Thorn, Tracey 1962-
  See Everything But The Girl
Thornton, Billy Bob 1956(?)- ......... **1997**:4
Thurman, Uma 1970- ..................... **1994**:2
Thurmond, Strom 1902-2003
  Obituary ..................................... **2004**:3
Tiffany 1972- ................................. **1989**:1
Tilberis, Elizabeth 1947(?)- ............ **1994**:3
Tilghman, Shirley M. 1946- ........... **2002**:1
Tillion, Germaine 1907-2008
  Obituary ..................................... **2009**:2
Tillman, Robert L. 1944(?)- ............ **2004**:1
Tillmans, Wolfgang 1968- .............. **2001**:4
Tillstrom, Burr 1917-1985
  Obituary ..................................... **1986**:1
Tilly, Jennifer 1958(?)- ................... **1997**:2
Timbaland 1971- ........................... **2007**:4
Timberlake, Justin 1981- ................ **2008**:4
Timmerman, Jacobo 1923-1999
  Obituary ..................................... **2000**:3
Tisch, Laurence A. 1923- ................ **1988**:2
Tito, Dennis 1940(?)- ..................... **2002**:1
Titov, Gherman 1935-2000
  Obituary ..................................... **2001**:3
TLC ............................................. **1996**:1
Toguri, Iva 1916-2006
  Obituary ..................................... **2007**:4
Tohe, Laura 1953- ......................... **2009**:2
Tom and Ray Magliozzi ................ **1991**:4
Tomba, Alberto 1966- ..................... **1992**:3
Tomei, Marisa 1964- ....................... **1995**:2
Tompkins, Susie
  Brief entry ................................. **1987**:2
Tone-Loc 1966- ............................. **1990**:3
Toomer, Ron 1930- ......................... **1990**:1
Toone, Bill
  Brief entry ................................. **1987**:2
Torello, Juan Antonio Samaranch
  See Samaranch, Juan Antonio
Torme, Mel 1925-1999
  Obituary ..................................... **1999**:4
Torre, Joseph Paul 1940- ................ **1997**:1
Torres, Dara 1967- ......................... **2009**:1
Torvalds, Linus 1970(?)- ................ **1999**:3
Tosh, Peter 1944-1987
  Obituary ..................................... **1988**:2
Totenberg, Nina 1944- ................... **1992**:2
Touitou, Jean 1952(?)- ................... **2008**:4
Tower, John 1926-1991
  Obituary ..................................... **1991**:4
Townsend, Kathleen Kennedy
  1951- ....................................... **2001**:3

Toyoda, Eiji 1913- ........................... **1985**:2
Trajkovski, Boris 1956-2004
   Obituary ...................................... **2005**:2
Trask, Amy 1961- ........................... **2003**:3
Traub, Marvin
   Brief entry ................................. **1987**:3
Travers, Pamela Lyndon
   See Travers, P.L.
Travers, P.L. 1899(?)-1996
   Obituary ...................................... **1996**:4
Travis, Randy 1959- ....................... **1988**:4
Travolta, John 1954- ...................... **1995**:2
Tretheway, Natasha 1966- ............. **2008**:3
Treurnicht, Andries 1921- ............. **1992**:2
Treybig, James G. 1940- ................. **1988**:3
Tribe, Laurence H. 1941- ............... **1988**:1
Trimble, David 1944- ...................... **1999**:1
Trinidad, Felix 1973- ...................... **2000**:4
Tritt, Travis 1964(?)- ...................... **1995**:1
Trotman, Alex 1933- ....................... **1995**:4
Trotter, Charlie 1960- ..................... **2000**:4
Troutt, Kenny A. 1948- ................... **1998**:1
Trudeau, Garry 1948- ..................... **1991**:2
Trudeau, Pierre 1919-2000
   Obituary ...................................... **2001**:1
Truitt, Anne 1921- .......................... **1993**:1
Trump, Donald 1946- ...................... **1989**:2
Trump, Ivana 1949- ......................... **1995**:2
Truscott-Jones, Reginald Alfred John
   See Milland, Ray
Tsongas, Paul Efthemios 1941-1997
   Obituary ...................................... **1997**:2
Tucci, Stanley 1960- ....................... **2003**:2
Tuck, Lily 1938- .............................. **2006**:1
Tucker, Chris 1973(?)- .................... **1999**:1
Tucker, Forrest 1919-1986
   Obituary ...................................... **1987**:1
Tudjman, Franjo 1922- .................... **1996**:2
Tudjman, Franjo 1922-1999
   Obituary ...................................... **2000**:2
Tudor, Antony 1908(?)-1987
   Obituary ...................................... **1987**:4
Tully, Tim 1954(?)- ......................... **2004**:3
Tune, Tommy 1939- ......................... **1994**:2
Tunick, Spencer 1967- .................... **2008**:1
Turabi, Hassan 1932(?)- ................. **1995**:4
Ture, Kwame 1941-1998
   Obituary ...................................... **1999**:2
Turk, Danilo 1952- .......................... **2009**:3
Turlington, Christy 1969(?)- .......... **2001**:4
Turner, Ike 1931-2007
   Obituary ...................................... **2009**:1
Turner, Janine 1962- ....................... **1993**:2
Turner, Kathleen 1954(?)- .............. **1985**:3
Turner, Lana 1921-1995
   Obituary ...................................... **1996**:1
Turner, Robert Edward III
   See Turner, Ted
Turner, Ted 1938- ........................... **1989**:1
Turner, Tina 1939- .......................... **2000**:3
Turturro, John 1957- ...................... **2002**:2
Tutwiler, Margaret 1950- ............... **1992**:4
Twain, Eileen
   See Twain, Shania
Twain, Shania 1965- ....................... **1996**:3
Twitty, Conway 1933-1993
   Obituary ...................................... **1994**:1
Twombley, Cy 1928(?)- ................... **1995**:1
Twombley, Edward Parker, Jr.
   See Twombley, Cy
Tyler, Anne 1941- ........................... **1995**:4
Tyler, Liv 1978- .............................. **1997**:2

Tyler, Richard 1948(?)- .................. **1995**:3
Tymoshenko, Yulia 1960- .............. **2009**:1
Tyner, Rob 1945(?)-1991
   Obituary ...................................... **1992**:2
Tyson, Don 1930- ............................ **1995**:3
Tyson, Laura D'Andrea 1947- ....... **1994**:1
Tyson, Mike 1966- .......................... **1986**:4
U2 ................................................... **2002**:4
Uchida, Mitsuko 1949(?)- .............. **1989**:3
Udall, Mo 1922-1998
   Obituary ...................................... **1999**:2
Ullman, Tracey 1961- ..................... **1988**:3
Umeki, Miyoshi 1929-2007
   Obituary ...................................... **2008**:4
Underwood, Carrie 1983- ............... **2008**:1
Ungaro, Emanuel 1933- .................. **2001**:3
Union, Gabrielle 1972- ................... **2004**:2
Unitas, Johnny 1933-2002
   Obituary ...................................... **2003**:4
Unz, Ron 1962(?)- ........................... **1999**:1
Updike, John 1932- ......................... **2001**:2
Upshaw, Dawn 1960- ...................... **1991**:2
Upshaw, Eugene, Jr.
   See Upshaw, Gene
Upshaw, Gene 1945- ....................... **1988**:1
Urban, Keith 1967- ......................... **2006**:3
Uribe, Alvaro 1952- ........................ **2003**:3
Urich, Robert 1947- ........................ **1988**:1
   Obituary ...................................... **2003**:3
Usher 1979- ..................................... **2005**:1
Ustinov, Peter 1921-2004
   Obituary ...................................... **2005**:3
Vagelos, P. Roy 1929- ..................... **1989**:4
Vajpayee, Atal Behari 1926- .......... **1998**:4
Valdes-Rodriguez, Alisa 1969- ...... **2005**:4
Valente, Benita 1934(?)- ................. **1985**:3
Valenti, Jack 1921-2007
   Obituary ...................................... **2008**:3
Valli, Giambattista 1966- ............... **2008**:3
Valvo, Carmen Marc 1954- ........... **2003**:4
Van Allen, James 1914-2006
   Obituary ...................................... **2007**:4
Van Andel, Jay 1924-2004
   Obituary ...................................... **2006**:1
Vander Zalm, Wilhelmus Nicholaas
   Theodoros Maria
   See Vander Zalm, William
Vander Zalm, William 1934- .......... **1987**:3
Vandross, Luther 1951-2005
   Obituary ...................................... **2006**:3
Van Duyn, Mona 1921- .................. **1993**:2
Van Dyken, Amy 1973- ................... **1997**:1
Van Halen, Edward 1957- .............. **1985**:2
Vanilla Ice 1967(?)- ........................ **1991**:3
van Kuijk, Andreas Cornelius 1929-1997
   See Parker, Colonel Tom
Van Sant, Gus 1952- ....................... **1992**:2
Van Slyke, Andy 1960- ................... **1992**:4
Van Winkle, Robbie
   See Vanilla Ice
Van Winkle, Robert Matthew
   See Vanilla Ice
Vardalos, Nia 1962- ........................ **2003**:4
Varnado, Cordavar
   See Snoop Doggy Dogg
Varney, Jim 1949-2000
   Brief entry ................................. **1985**:4
   Obituary ...................................... **2000**:3
Varone, Doug 1956- ........................ **2001**:2
Varvatos, John 1956(?)- .................. **2006**:2
Vasella, Daniel 1953- ...................... **2005**:3

Vaughan, Sarah 1924-1990
   Obituary ...................................... **1990**:3
Vaughan, Stevie Ray 1956(?)-1990
   Obituary ...................................... **1991**:1
Vaughn, Mo 1967- .......................... **1999**:2
Vaughn, Vince 1970- ....................... **1999**:2
Vazquez, Tabare 1940- ................... **2006**:2
Vedder, Eddie
   See Pearl Jam
Veeck, Bill 1914-1986
   Obituary ...................................... **1986**:1
Veeck, William Louis
   See Veeck, Bill
Vega, Suzanne 1959- ....................... **1988**:1
Venter, J. Craig 1946- ..................... **2001**:1
Ventura, Jesse 1951- ....................... **1999**:2
Venturi, Robert 1925- .................... **1994**:4
Verdi-Fletcher, Mary 1955- ........... **1998**:2
Verdon, Gwen 1925-2000
   Obituary ...................................... **2001**:2
Verhofstadt, Guy 1953- .................. **2006**:3
Vernon, Lillian
   See Katz, Lillian
Versace, Donatella 1955- ............... **1999**:1
Versace, Gianni 1946-1997
   Brief entry ................................. **1988**:1
   Obituary ...................................... **1998**:2
Vickrey, William S. 1914-1996
   Obituary ...................................... **1997**:2
Vidal, Gore 1925- ........................... **1996**:2
Vidov, Oleg 194- ............................. **1987**:4
Vieira, Meredith 1953- ................... **2001**:3
Villechaize, Herve 1943(?)-1993
   Obituary ...................................... **1994**:1
Villeneuve, Jacques 1971- .............. **1997**:1
Vincent, Fay 1938- .......................... **1990**:2
Vincent, Francis Thomas, Jr.
   See Vincent, Fay
Vinton, Will
   Brief entry ................................. **1988**:1
Violet, Arlene 1943- ........................ **1985**:3
Vischer, Phil 1966- ......................... **2002**:2
Vitale, Dick 1939- ........................... **1988**:4
Vitetta, Ellen S. 1942(?)- ................ **2005**:4
Vitousek, Peter 1949- ..................... **2003**:1
Vogel, Paula 1951- .......................... **1999**:2
Voight, Jon 1938- ............................ **2002**:3
Volkow, Nora 1956- ........................ **2009**:1
Vollenweider, Andreas 1953- ......... **1985**:2
Von D, Kat 1982- ............................. **2008**:3
von Furstenberg, Diane 1946- ....... **1994**:2
Von Hellermann, Sophie 1975- ...... **2006**:3
von Karajan, Herbert 1908-1989
   Obituary ...................................... **1989**:4
Vonnegut, Kurt 1922- ..................... **1998**:4
von Trapp, Maria 1905-1987
   Obituary ...................................... **1987**:3
vos Savant, Marilyn 1946- ............. **1988**:2
Vreeland, Diana 1903(?)-1989
   Obituary ...................................... **1990**:1
Wachner, Linda 1946- ..................... **1988**:3
Wadd, Johnny
   See Holmes, John C.
Waddell, Thomas F. 1937-1987
   Obituary ...................................... **1988**:2
Wade, Dwyane 1982- ...................... **2007**:1
Wagner, Catherine F. 1953- ........... **2002**:3
Wagoner, Porter 1927-2007
   Obituary ...................................... **2008**:4
Wahid, Abdurrahman 1940- .......... **2000**:3
Wahlberg, Donnie
   See New Kids on the Block

Wahlberg, Mark
  See Marky Mark
Waitt, Ted 1963(?)- ........................ **1997**:4
Waldron, Hicks B. 1923- ................ **1987**:3
Walesa, Lech 1943- ........................ **1991**:2
Walgreen, Charles III
  Brief entry ................................. **1987**:4
Walker, Alice 1944- ........................ **1999**:1
Walker, Jay 1955- .......................... **2004**:2
Walker, Junior 1942(?)-1995
  Obituary .................................... **1996**:2
Walker, Kara 1969- ........................ **1999**:2
Walker, Nancy 1922-1992
  Obituary .................................... **1992**:3
Wallace, Ben 1974- ........................ **2004**:3
Wallace, Christopher G.
  See Notorious B.I.G.
Wallace, George 1919-1998
  Obituary .................................... **1999**:1
Wallace, Irving 1916-1990
  Obituary .................................... **1991**:1
Wallis, Hal 1898(?)-1986
  Obituary .................................... **1987**:1
Wallis, Harold Brent
  See Wallis, Hal
Walls, Jeannette 1960(?)- ................ **2006**:3
Walsh, Bill 1931- .......................... **1987**:4
Walsh, William
  See Walsh, Bill
Walters, Barbara 1931- .................. **1998**:3
Walton, Sam 1918-1992 .................. **1986**:2
  Obituary .................................... **1993**:1
Wanderone, Rudolf Walter, Jr.
  See Minnesota Fats
Wang, An 1920-1990 ...................... **1986**:1
  Obituary .................................... **1990**:3
Wang, Vera 1949- .......................... **1998**:4
Wapner, Joseph A. 1919- .............. **1987**:1
Ward, Sela 1956- .......................... **2001**:3
Warden, Jack 1920-2006
  Obituary .................................... **2007**:3
Ware, Lancelot 1915-2000
  Obituary .................................... **2001**:1
Warhol, Andy 1927(?)-1987
  Obituary .................................... **1987**:2
Warhola, Andrew
  See Warhol, Andy
Wariner, Jeremy 1984- .................. **2006**:3
Warner, Kurt 1971- ........................ **2000**:3
Warren, Christopher Minor
  See Christopher, Warren
Warren, Robert Penn 1905-1989
  Obituary .................................... **1990**:1
Washington, Alonzo 1967- ............ **2000**:1
Washington, Denzel 1954- ............ **1993**:2
Washington, Grover, Jr. 1943- ........ **1989**:1
Washington, Harold 1922-1987
  Obituary .................................... **1988**:1
Wasserman, Lew 1913-2002
  Obituary .................................... **2003**:3
Wasserstein, Wendy 1950- ............ **1991**:3
Waterman, Cathy 1950(?)- ............ **2002**:2
Waters, Alice 1944- ...................... **2006**:3
Waters, John 1946- ........................ **1988**:3
Waters, Maxine 1938- .................... **1998**:4
Waterston, Sam 1940- .................... **2006**:1
Watkins, Sherron 1959- ................ **2003**:1
Watkins, Tionne T-Boz
  See TLC
Watson, Elizabeth 1949- ................ **1991**:2
Watson, Emily 1967- ...................... **2001**:1

Watt, Ben 1962-
  See Everything But The Girl
Watterson, Bill 1958(?)- ................ **1990**:3
Watterson, William B., II
  See Watterson, Bill
Wattleton, Alyce Faye
  See Wattleton, Faye
Wattleton, Faye 1943- .................... **1989**:1
Watts, J.C. 1957- .......................... **1999**:2
Watts, Naomi 1968- ...................... **2006**:1
Wayans, Damon 1960- .................. **1998**:4
Wayans, Keenen Ivory 1958(?)- ..... **1991**:1
Wayne, David 1914-1995
  Obituary .................................... **1995**:3
Wayne, Don
  See Johnson, Don
Weaver, Sigourney 1949- .............. **1988**:3
Webb, Karrie 1974- ...................... **2000**:4
Webb, Wellington E. 1941- ............ **2000**:3
Webber, Andrew Lloyd
  See Lloyd Webber, Andrew
Webber, Chris 1973- ...................... **1994**:1
Webber, Mayce Edward Christopher
  See Webber, Chris
Weber, Pete 1962- ........................ **1986**:3
Wegman, William 1942(?)- ............ **1991**:1
Weicker, Lowell P., Jr. 1931- ......... **1993**:1
Weihui, Zhou 1973- ...................... **2001**:1
Wei Jingsheng 1950- ...................... **1998**:2
Weil, Andrew 1942- ...................... **1997**:4
Weill, Sandy 1933- ........................ **1990**:4
Weill, Sanford
  See Weill, Sandy
Weinberger, Caspar 1917-2006
  Obituary .................................... **2007**:2
Weiner, Jennifer 1970- .................. **2006**:3
Weinstein, Bob
  See Weinstein, Bob and Harvey
Weinstein, Bob and Harvey .......... **2000**:4
Weinstein, Harvey
  See Weinstein, Bob and Harvey
Weintraub, Jerry 1937- .................. **1986**:1
Weir, Mike 1970- .......................... **2004**:1
Weisz, Rachel 1971- ...................... **2006**:4
Weitz, Bruce 1943- ........................ **1985**:4
Weizman, Ezer 1924-2005
  Obituary .................................... **2006**:3
Welch, Bob 1956- .......................... **1991**:3
Welch, Jack 1935- .......................... **1993**:3
Weldon, William 1948- .................. **2007**:4
Wells, David 1963- ........................ **1999**:3
Wells, Linda 1958- ........................ **2002**:3
Wells, Mary 1943-1992
  Obituary .................................... **1993**:1
Wells, Sharlene
  Brief entry ................................. **1985**:1
Wellstone, Paul 1944-2002
  Obituary .................................... **2004**:1
Welty, Eudora 1909-2001
  Obituary .................................... **2002**:3
Wences, Senor 1896-1999
  Obituary .................................... **1999**:4
Wenner, Jann 1946- ...................... **1993**:1
Werner, Ruth 1907-2000
  Obituary .................................... **2001**:1
Wescott, Seth 1976- ...................... **2006**:4
West, Cornel 1953- ........................ **1994**:2
West, Dorothy 1907- ...................... **1996**:1
West, Dottie 1932-1991
  Obituary .................................... **1992**:2
West, Kanye 1977- ........................ **2006**:1
West, Michael Lee 1953- ................ **2009**:2

Westmoreland, William C. 1914-2005
  Obituary .................................... **2006**:4
Westwood, Vivienne 1941- ............ **1998**:3
Wexler, Jerry 1917-2008
  Obituary .................................... **2009**:4
Wexler, Nancy S. 1945- ................ **1992**:3
Whaley, Suzy 1966- ...................... **2003**:4
Whedon, Joss 1964- ...................... **2006**:3
Whelan, Tensie 1960- .................... **2007**:1
Whelan, Wendy 1967(?)- ................ **1999**:3
Whipple, Fred L. 1906-2004
  Obituary .................................... **2005**:4
Whitaker, Forest 1961- .................. **1996**:2
White, Alan
  See Oasis
White, Barry 1944-2003
  Obituary .................................... **2004**:3
White, Bill 1934- .......................... **1989**:3
White, Byron 1917-2002
  Obituary .................................... **2003**:3
White, Jaleel 1976- ........................ **1992**:3
White, Julie 1961- ........................ **2008**:2
White, Reggie 1961- ...................... **1993**:4
White, Ryan 1972(?)-1990
  Obituary .................................... **1990**:3
Whitehead, Robert 1916-2002
  Obituary .................................... **2003**:3
Whitestone, Heather 1973(?)- ........ **1995**:1
White Stripes, The ........................ **2006**:1
Whiting, Susan 1956- .................... **2007**:4
Whitman, Christine Todd 1947(?)- .. **1994**
                                                           :3
Whitman, Meg 1957- ...................... **2000**:3
Whitmire, Kathryn Jean
  See Whitmire, Kathy
Whitmire, Kathy 1946- .................. **1988**:2
Whitney, Patrick 1952(?)- .............. **2006**:1
Whitson, Peggy 1960- .................... **2003**:3
Whittle, Christopher 1947- ............ **1989**:3
Wickramasinghe, Ranil 1949- ........ **2003**:2
Wiesel, Elie 1928- .......................... **1998**:1
Wiesenthal, Simon 1908-2005
  Obituary .................................... **2006**:4
Wiest, Dianne 1948- ...................... **1995**:2
Wigand, Jeffrey 1943(?)- ................ **2000**:4
Wigler, Michael
  Brief entry ................................. **1985**:1
Wilder, Billy 1906-2002
  Obituary .................................... **2003**:2
Wilder, L. Douglas 1931- .............. **1990**:3
Wilder, Lawrence Douglas
  See Wilder, L. Douglas
Wildmon, Donald 1938- ................ **1988**:4
Wiles, Andrew 1953(?)- .................. **1994**:1
Wilkens, Lenny 1937- .................... **1995**:2
Wilkinson, Tom 1948- .................... **2003**:2
William, Prince of Wales 1982- ..... **2001**:3
Williams, Anthony 1952- .............. **2000**:4
Williams, Brian 1959- .................... **2009**:4
Williams, Doug 1955- .................... **1988**:2
Williams, Douglas Lee
  See Williams, Doug
Williams, Edward Bennett 1920-1988
  Obituary .................................... **1988**:4
Williams, G. Mennen 1911-1988
  Obituary .................................... **1988**:2
Williams, Gerhard Mennen
  See Williams, G. Mennen
Williams, Hosea 1926-2000
  Obituary .................................... **2001**:2
Williams, Joe 1918-1999
  Obituary .................................... **1999**:4

Williams, Lynn 1924- ...................... **1986**:4
Williams, Pharrell 1973- ................. **2005**:3
Williams, Ricky 1977- ...................... **2000**:2
Williams, Robin 1952- ...................... **1988**:4
Williams, Serena 1981- ................... **1999**:4
Williams, Ted 1918-2002
    Obituary .................... **2003**:4
Williams, Treat 1951- ...................... **2004**:3
Williams, Vanessa L. 1963- ............ **1999**:2
Williams, Venus 1980- ...................... **1998**:2
Williams, Willie L. 1944(?)- ........... **1993**:1
Williamson, Marianne 1953(?)- ..... **1991**:4
Willis, Bruce 1955- ......................... **1986**:4
Willson, S. Brian 1942(?)- ............. **1989**:3
Wilmut, Ian 1944- ........................... **1997**:3
Wilson, August 1945- ...................... **2002**:2
Wilson, Bertha
    Brief entry ...................... **1986**:1
Wilson, Brian 1942- ......................... **1996**:1
Wilson, Carl 1946-1998 .................. **1998**:2
Wilson, Cassandra 1955- ............... **1996**:3
Wilson, Edward O. 1929- ............... **1994**:4
Wilson, Flip 1933-1998
    Obituary ...................... **1999**:2
Wilson, Gretchen 1970- ................... **2006**:3
Wilson, Jerry
    Brief entry ...................... **1986**:2
Wilson, Owen 1968- ......................... **2002**:3
Wilson, Pete 1933- ........................... **1992**:3
Wilson, Peter C. 1913-1984
    Obituary ...................... **1985**:2
Wilson, William Julius 1935- ........ **1997**:1
Wimbish, Doug
    See Living Colour
Winans, CeCe 1964- ....................... **2000**:1
Winehouse, Amy 1983- ................... **2008**:1
Winfield, Paul 1941-2004
    Obituary ...................... **2005**:2
Winfrey, Oprah 1954- ...................... **1986**:4
Winger, Debra 1955- ....................... **1994**:3
Winick, Judd 1970- ......................... **2005**:3
Winokur, Marissa Jaret 1973- ....... **2005**:1
Winslet, Kate 1975- ......................... **2002**:4
Winston, George 1949(?)- ............... **1987**:1
Winter, Paul 1939- ........................... **1990**:2
Winters, Shelley 1920-2006
    Obituary ...................... **2007**:1
Wintour, Anna 1949- ...................... **1990**:4
Wise, Robert 1914-2005
    Obituary ...................... **2006**:4
Wiseman, Len 1973- ......................... **2008**:2
Witherspoon, Reese 1976- ............. **2002**:1
Witkin, Joel-Peter 1939- ................. **1996**:1
Witt, Katarina 1966(?)- ................... **1991**:3
Witten, Edward 1951- ..................... **2006**:2
Woertz, Patricia A. 1953- ............... **2007**:3
Wolf, Naomi 1963(?)- ...................... **1994**:3
Wolf, Stephen M. 1941- ................... **1989**:3
Wolfe, Tom 1930- ............................. **1999**:2
Wolff, Tobias 1945- ......................... **2005**:1
Wolfman Jack 1938-1995
    Obituary ...................... **1996**:1
Womack, Lee Ann 1966- ................. **2002**:1
Wong, Andrea 1966- ....................... **2009**:1
Wong, B.D. 1962- ............................. **1998**:1
Woo, John 1945(?)- ........................... **1994**:2
Wood, Daniel
    See New Kids on the Block
Wood, Elijah 1981- ........................... **2002**:4
Wood, Sharon
    Brief entry ...................... **1988**:1
Woodard, Lynette 1959(?)- ............. **1986**:2

Woodcock, Leonard 1911-2001
    Obituary .................... **2001**:4
Woodruff, Robert Winship 1889-1985
    Obituary .................... **1985**:1
Woods, Donald 1933-2001
    Obituary .................... **2002**:3
Woods, James 1947- ......................... **1988**:3
Woods, Tiger 1975- ........................... **1995**:4
Woodson, Ron 1965- ....................... **1996**:4
Woodward, Thomas Jones
    See Jones, Tom
Woodwell, George S. 1928- ........... **1987**:2
Worrell, Ernest P.
    See Varney, Jim
Worth, Irene 1916-2002
    Obituary .................... **2003**:2
Worthy, James 1961- ....................... **1991**:2
Wren, John 1952(?)- ......................... **2007**:2
Wright, Eric
    See Eazy-E
Wright, Joe 1972- ............................. **2009**:1
Wright, Richard 1943-2008
    Obituary .................... **2009**:4
Wright, Steven 1955- ....................... **1986**:3
Wright, Will 1960- ........................... **2003**:4
Wrigley, William, Jr. 1964(?)- ........ **2002**:2
Wu, Harry 1937- ............................... **1996**:1
Wu Yi 1938- ....................................... **2005**:2
Wyatt, Jane 1910-2006
    Obituary .................... **2008**:1
Wyland, Robert 1956- ..................... **2009**:3
Wyle, Noah 1971- ............................. **1997**:3
Wyman, Jane 1917-2007
    Obituary .................... **2008**:4
Wynette, Tammy 1942-1998
    Obituary .................... **1998**:3
Wynn, Francis Xavier Aloysius James
    Jeremiah Keenan
    See Wynn, Keenan
Wynn, Keenan 1916-1986
    Obituary .................... **1987**:1
Wynn, Stephen A. 1942- ................. **1994**:3
Wynonna 1964- ................................. **1993**:3
Xenakis, Iannis 1922-2001
    Obituary .................... **2001**:4
Xuxa 1963(?)- ..................................... **1994**:2
Xzibit 1974- ....................................... **2005**:4
Yamaguchi, Kristi 1971- ................. **1992**:3
Yamamoto, Kenichi 1922- ............... **1989**:1
Yamasaki, Minoru 1912-1986
    Obituary .................... **1986**:2
Yang, Jerry
    See Filo, David and Jerry Yang
Yankovic, Frank 1915-1998
    Obituary .................... **1999**:2
Yankovic, Weird Al 1959- ............... **1985**:4
Yao Ming 1980- ................................. **2004**:1
Yar'Adua, Umaru 1951- ................. **2008**:3
Yard, Molly ..................................... **1991**:4
Yauch, Adam
    See Beastie Boys, The
Yeager, Chuck 1923- ....................... **1998**:1
Yeang, Ken 1948- ............................. **2008**:3
Yearwood, Trisha 1964- ................. **1999**:1
Ye Jianying 1897-1986
    Obituary .................... **1987**:1
Yeltsin, Boris 1931- ......................... **1991**:1
Yen, Samuel 1927- ........................... **1996**:4
Yeoh, Michelle 1962- ....................... **2003**:2
Yetnikoff, Walter 1933- ................... **1988**:1
Yoakam, Dwight 1956- ................... **1992**:4
Yogi, Maharishi Mahesh
    See Mahesh Yogi, Maharishi

Yokich, Stephen P. 1935- ................. **1995**:4
York, Dick 1923-1992
    Obituary .................... **1992**:4
Young, Adrian 1969-
    See No Doubt
Young, Andre
    See Dr. Dre
Young, Coleman A. 1918-1997
    Obituary .................... **1998**:1
Young, Loretta 1913-2000
    Obituary .................... **2001**:4
Young, Neil 1945- ............................. **1991**:2
Young, Robert 1907-1998
    Obituary .................... **1999**:1
Young, Steve 1961- ........................... **1995**:2
Youngblood, Johnny Ray 1948- ..... **1994**:1
Youngman, Henny 1906(?)-1998
    Obituary .................... **1998**:3
Yunus, Muhammad 1940- ............. **2007**:3
Yushchenko, Viktor 1954- ............. **2006**:1
Yzerman, Steve 1965- ..................... **1991**:2
Zagat, Tim and Nina ...................... **2004**:3
Zahn, Paula 1956(?)- ....................... **1992**:3
Zamboni, Frank J.
    Brief entry ...................... **1986**:4
Zamora, Pedro 1972-1994
    Obituary .................... **1995**:2
Zanardi, Alex 1966- ......................... **1998**:2
Zanker, Bill
    Brief entry ...................... **1987**:3
Zanker, William I.
    See Zanker, Bill
Zanuck, Lili Fini 1954- ................... **1994**:2
Zappa, Frank 1940-1993
    Obituary .................... **1994**:2
Zarnocay, Samuel
    See Kaye, Sammy
Zatopek, Emil 1922-2000
    Obituary .................... **2001**:3
Zech, Lando W.
    Brief entry ...................... **1987**:4
Zedillo, Ernesto 1951- ..................... **1995**:1
Zeffirelli, Franco 1923- ................... **1991**:3
Zellweger, Renee 1969- ................... **2001**:1
Zemeckis, Robert 1952- ................... **2002**:1
Zerhouni, Elias A. 1951- ................. **2004**:3
Zeroual, Liamine 1951- ................... **1996**:2
Zeta-Jones, Catherine 1969- .......... **1999**:4
Zetcher, Arnold B. 1940- ............... **2002**:1
Zetsche, Dieter 1953- ....................... **2002**:3
Zevon, Warren 1947-2003
    Obituary .................... **2004**:4
Zhang, Ziyi 1979- ........................... **2006**:2
Zhao Ziyang 1919- ......................... **1989**:1
Zhirinovsky, Vladimir 1946- .......... **1994**:2
Zia ul-Haq, Mohammad 1924-1988
    Obituary .................... **1988**:4
Ziff, William B., Jr. 1930- ............... **1986**:4
Zigler, Edward 1930- ....................... **1994**:1
Zinnemann, Fred 1907-1997
    Obituary .................... **1997**:3
Zinni, Anthony 1943- ..................... **2003**:1
Ziskin, Laura 1950- ......................... **2008**:2
Zito, Barry 1978- ............................. **2003**:3
Zucker, Jeff 1965(?)- ......................... **1993**:3
Zucker, Jerry 1950- ......................... **2002**:2
Zuckerberg, Mark 1984- ................. **2008**:2
Zuckerman, Mortimer 1937- ........... **1986**:3
Zwilich, Ellen 1939- ....................... **1990**:1
Zylberberg, Joel
    See Hyatt, Joel